ABORIGINAL LAW

CASES, MATERIALS, AND COMMENTARY

SECOND EDITION

SELECTED TITLES FROM PURICH PUBLISHING

Aboriginal Self-Government in Canada: Current Issues and Trends edited by John Hylton. 1994, paper, 264 pages, bibliography, index, $29.00

The Cypress Hills: The Land and Its People by Walter Hildebrandt and Brian Hubner. 1994, paper, 136 pages, maps, photographs, bibliography, index, $16.50

The Dynamics of Native Politics: The Alberta Metis Experience by Joe Sawchuk. 1998, paper, 192 pages, bibliography, index, $26.00

In Palliser's Triangle: Living in the Grasslands, 1850–1930 by Barry Potyondi. 1995, paper, 144 pages, map, photographs, bibliography, index, $18.50

Indigenous Peoples of the World: An Introduction to Their Past, Present, and Future by Brian Goehring. 1993, paper, 80 pages, maps, bibliography, index, $15.50

Justice in Aboriginal Communities: Sentencing Alternatives by Ross Gordon Green. 1998, paper, 192 pages, map, photographs, index, $27.00

Municipalities and Canadian Law: Defining the Authority of Local Governments by Felix Hoehn. 1996, paper, 400 pages, index, $39.00

Tom Three Persons: Legend of an Indian Cowboy by Hugh Dempsey. 1997, paper, map, photographs, index, $19.50

Mail orders: add $4.50 shipping and handling for the first title and $0.50 for each additional title. Canadian orders, unless exempt, must also add 7% GST (our registration 133216069) to the order.

**Purich Publishing
Box 23032, Market Mall Post Office
Saskatoon, SK, Canada, S7J 5H3
Telephone: (306) 373-5311
Facsimile: (306) 373-5315
Email: purich@sk.sympatico.ca**

**For more information on these titles, visit our web site at
www3.sk.sympatico.ca/purich.**

PURICH'S ABORIGINAL ISSUES SERIES

ABORIGINAL LAW

CASES, MATERIALS, AND COMMENTARY

■ THOMAS ISAAC, B.A., M.A., LL.B., LL.M.

SECOND EDITION

PURICH PUBLISHING

SASKATOON, SASKATCHEWAN

CANADA

All inquiries and orders regarding this publication should be addressed to:
Purich Publishing
Box 23032, Market Mall Postal Outlet
Saskatoon, SK Canada S7J 5H3
Tel: (306) 373–5315; facsimile: (306) 373–5311
www3.sk.sympatico.ca/purich

Canadian Cataloguing in Publication Data

> Isaac, Thomas F. (Thomas Francis), 1966–
>   Aboriginal law: cases, materials and commentary
>   (Purich's aboriginal issues series)
>   2nd ed.
>   Includes bibliographical references.
>   ISBN 1–895830–11–7
> 1. Native peoples - Legal status, laws, etc. - Canada.*
> 2. Native peoples - Canada - Government relations.*
> 3. Native peoples - Legal status, laws, etc. - Canada -
> Cases.* I. Title.   II. Series.
> KE7708.5.I73 1999 342.71'0872 C99–920008–9
> KF8205.A2 I7 1999

Editing, design, and layout by Page Wood Publishing Services, Saskatoon
Cover design and maps by NEXT Communications, Inc., Saskatoon
Printed in Canada by Printcrafters, Winnipeg. Printed on acid-free paper

NOTE TO READERS

In choosing case excerpts for this volume, we have tried to be as true to the original as possible. Judges in writing their judgments often emphasize certain statements or words with underlining, boldface, or italic type. For the sake of consistency, all such passages have been italicized. Where judges have divided their judgments into parts, some part numbers will be missing because less crucial portions of the judgments have been ommitted.

Readers will note that words such as "Aboriginal," "Native," and "Indigenous" have been capitalized. In recent years, many Aboriginal people have argued that such words should be capitalized when referring to specific people, in the same manner that words such as "European" and "American" are capitalized. We agree. Hence, the capitalization. However, we have tried to keep excerpts of judgments as close to the original as possible and have not altered word usage in the same.

In many instances, the transliteration of names of First Nations has varied. Therefore, readers will note some differences, in particular in excerpts from court decisions. For example, "Sto:lo" also appears as "Stolo," "Nishga" as "Nisga'a," and "Métis" as "Metis." In the latter case, throughout the book we have tried to use Métis.

TABLE OF CONTENTS

FOREWORD TO THE SECOND EDITION
BY GOO ARLOOKTOO, DEPUTY PREMIER AND MINISTER OF JUSTICE, GOVERNMENT OF THE NORTHWEST TERRITORIES, AND INUIT BENEFICIARY UNDER THE NUNAVUT LAND CLAIM

I had the pleasure of working closely with Mr. Isaac in his capacity as the senior official of the government of the Northwest Territories responsible for planning the division of the Northwest Territories and the creation of Nunavut, the homeland of the Inuit people. Mr. Iaaac has technical, practical, and personal experience dealing with a wide range of Aboriginal issues. This experience has given him the ability to break down the issues into a discussion most readers can relate to, an exercise that is much needed in the area of Aboriginal law.

Mr. Isaac's second edition to his Aboriginal law textbook is welcomed in a dynamic political and legal environment. Building on the earlier edition, the new text provides up-to-date insight into and analysis of the rapidly changing field of Aboriginal law. In particular, Mr. Isaac discusses important Supreme Court of Canada decisions such as *Delgamuukw, Van der Peet,* and *Badger* in a straightforward and easy-to-read manner.

Canada has a diverse Aboriginal population with a wide range of historical and geographic realities. As a result, there is a wide range of issues in the area of Aboriginal law. For example, in the Northwest Territories there are very few reserves and a majority of the population is Aboriginal. In the eastern Northwest Territories, we are focused on implementing the *Nunavut Land Claim Agreement* and, most importantly, on creating the Nunavut Territory on April 1, 1999. Therefore our perspective is a unique one. Mr. Isaac's book presents a balance of important issues that cover the key areas of Aboriginal law for all of Canada. This text is part of a growing compendium of information that is being developed to deepen and expand non-Aboriginal peoples' understanding of Aboriginal rights. It is in this way that Mr. Isaac's book serves all Aboriginal peoples in Canada—Indian, Métis, and Inuit.

FOREWORDS TO THE FIRST EDITION
GRAYDON NICHOLAS, PROVINCIAL COURT JUDGE
NEW BRUNSWICK, AND
MEMBER OF THE MALISEET NATION AT TOBIQUE

This publication is both timely and informative. The issues that are facing Aboriginal peoples in Canada need to be understood and appreciated. This book will help to focus on the issues by presenting relevant case law on contemporary and historical concerns. The author gives a useful explanation at the beginning of each chapter and significant insights are also to be found in the footnotes. Many teachers and students involved in courses on Aboriginal studies will be appreciative of the selection of topics and appropriate cases.

Because of the historical interplay of colonial, federal, and provincial legislation and policies, it is not easy to understand the dilemma of the legal basis for Aboriginal title, Aboriginal rights, and treaty rights. This book will help the reader to appreciate the emerging priorities of Aboriginal self-government, the important roles of Aboriginal women and Aboriginal leadership in the context of judicial decisions, and past and present issues in the ongoing struggle for the recognition and identification of Aboriginal and treaty rights.

CHIEF STRATER J. CROWFOOT, SIKSIKA NATION, TREATY 7

Mr. Isaac's compilations provide enlightened insights on the comparative interpretations that challenge issues for First Nations' self-determination. With clarity, a sensible premise is formed that reaffirms the right and need for self-government with recognition of land title and due entitlement to resource wealth.

This useful work recognizes the distinct heritage and means of First Nations' self-reliance—freedom and land. Our spirit, which formed over many generations, surviving the hardness of the land and life, is in greater peril of extinction now than ever before. In the name of "good faith," patronage not only threatens First Nations people but weakens great numbers of individuals who are shrouded in the worm-eaten blanket of lives devoid of initiative and hope, separate from the earth and numb to the spirit.

When Canada fully recognizes and accepts self-governing rights and powers, healing nations may become wiser nations and stronger for the challenges of the new century. Forget implications of national conscience, political ambition, good business, or righteous endeavour, human decency alone is long overdue.

As one among many original First Nations who founded this land, the Siksika Nation believes we have something worth remembering, honouring, restoring, and holding onto—certainly more than a spotlight for dancing and drumming before cameras. Mr. Isaac's book is a help to that end.

| Author's Note

Much has changed in three years since the first edition to this book. At that time, most of the focus was on developing a better understanding of the *Sparrow* decision. Since then, the Supreme Court of Canada has released an array of important decisions touching on the core of the meaning of Aboriginal rights and title in Canada and, more importantly, on their application. All of these decisions are reproduced, in part, in this second edition, or are referenced. They include *Delgamuukw, Van der Peet, Pamajewon, Badger, Adams, N.T.C. Smokehouse,* and *Gladstone.* Additionally, the Royal Commission on Aboriginal Peoples has concluded its work and the federal government has released its policy statement regarding the inherent right of self-government. Additionally, the *Nisga'a Final Agreement* was initialled and has constitutionally protected a right to self-government—as defined by the *Agreement.* All of this means that a new text was required to bring the book up-to-date so that it can continue to serve as a useful resource for students, Aboriginal leaders, and advisors in the area.

With all the recent case law, it has become increasingly clear that certain parameters are being established that deepen the understanding of what s. 35 and constitutional protection means for Aboriginal and treaty rights. At the same time, however, it is also becoming clear that the courts are not necessarily the best or the most efficient venue—nor should they be—to conclude some of the difficult policy issues facing Canada with respect to its relations with Aboriginal peoples. The one thing that is becoming apparent is that whatever form Aboriginal rights take, either as treaty rights or title issues or as subsistence activities, governments have been delivered an extremely clear message—change the way you have traditionally conducted your actions with respect to Aboriginal peoples and their inherent interest in their tribal lands.

Dealing with Aboriginal peoples and their interests is simply a cost of doing business in Canada. This fact is based on a number of legal, social, and moral reasons. Governments have an obligation to ensure that their mechanisms for consultation and engagement are appropriately resourced and that they are given a clear message to engage at a substantive level appropriate to the situation at hand. These issues are not merely issues for governments' "Aboriginal affairs agencies"—including the federal government's Department of Indian Affairs and Northern Development—nor are these issues simply for central agencies such as departments of justice or attorneys general. Rather, these are pan-government issues that directly affect what some refer to as "line agencies"—especially those dealing with renewable and non-renewable resources, health, education, oil and gas, corrections, justice, forestry, and fisheries.

I will not attempt to outline a single "answer" to this situation—because there is no single answer. The answers lie, in part, with governments who cannot continue to disregard the fact that Aboriginal peoples must be consulted in a substantive manner regarding activities that directly affect them. The application of the standard to be applied (and there is a great degree of flexibility in this standard) will vary from Aboriginal group to Aboriginal group, from province to province, from jurisdiction to jurisdiction. What the standard may be for the government of Prince Edward Island will undoubtedly be different from the standard to be used by the government of British Columbia.

The Supreme Court of Canada, in *Sparrow,* quoted, with approval, Professor Lyon. He writes:

> [T]he context of 1982 is surely enough to tell us that this [s. 35] is not just a codification of the case law on aboriginal rights that had accumulated by 1982. Section 35 calls for a just settlement for aboriginal peoples. It renounces the old rules of the game under which the Crown established courts of law and denied those courts the authority to question sovereign claims made by the Crown.[1]

Forcing issues through litigation, although it has established some parameters for a greater understanding of Aboriginal rights, is not the total solution. Rather, negotiated settlements, based on trust and goodwill, are ultimately the only means by which Aboriginal peoples will see their aspirations met. They are also the only means by which the uncertainty regarding the full meaning and effect of Aboriginal rights will be dealt with to the satisfaction of governments in Canada.

This revised edition continues to be a resource for the "non-expert." It is intended to give an introduction to, and an overview of, the major themes that have developed in Canadian Aboriginal law over the past two hundred years. The intent is to give readers a good understanding of the issues without overwhelming them with details. There are a number of areas where the book deliberately does not venture, notably justice issues, Aboriginal customary law, and a wide array of decisions relating to the *Indian Act* and its application. Many chapters have been fundamentally revised, notably chapters 1, 2, 3, and 7, while others have been fine-tuned and updated.

The term "Aboriginal" is used in this text to describe those persons who come within the meaning of s. 35(2) of the *Constitution Act, 1982,* namely the Indian, Inuit, and Métis peoples of Canada. When the term "Indian" is used alone, it refers to those persons identified and registered as Indians within the meaning of the federal *Indian Act.*[2] To use space efficiently and make decision citations consistent, citations in cases and introductions to chapters have been limited to one or two case reports. In most instances, multiple-decision citations have been deleted from the excerpts. Comprehensive decision citations can be found in the table of cases at the beginning of the book. Where applicable, paragraph numbers have been deleted from decision excerpts, with the exception of the recent round of Supreme Court of Canada decisions. Footnotes have either been deleted or incorporated into the text of the excerpted decisions. All the Canadian decisions include the names of the

---

1   N. Lyon, "An Essay on Constitutional Interpretation" (1988) 26 *Osgoode Hall L.J.* 95 at 100; as cited in *R.* v. *Sparrow,* [1990] 3 C.N.L.R. 160 (S.C.C.).

2   The terms "Aboriginal" and "Indian" are used for legal clarity. The author acknowledges that these terms may be offensive to some readers. For a discussion of the term "Aboriginal," see T. Isaac, "The Power of Constitutional Language: The Case Against Using 'Aboriginal Peoples' as a Referent for First Nations" (1993) 19:2 *Queen's L.J.* 415.

members of the court giving judgment and the dates of the decisions. The selected bibliographies at the end of each chapter are not meant to be all-inclusive; they identify materials that provide an introduction to the areas covered in the chapter. Additional materials are noted in the footnotes.

I wish to thank all those who provided comments on the first edition, either by letter, by review, or otherwise. In particular, I thank Zandra Wilson, of the University of Saskatchewan's Native Law Centre, for her continuing assistance and Carlon Big Snake of the Siksika Nation. I also acknowledge the superb editorial skills of Don Purich, who provided a great deal of encouragement to me as I worked on this edition. I wish to thank Mary Sue for her support to me on this project. This edition is dedicated to Zoe, Angus, and Samson.

Victoria, British Columbia
January 1999

Table of Cases

| TABLE OF AUTHORITIES

Aronson, S., "The Authority of the Crown to Make Treaties with Indians" [1993] 2 C.N.L.R. 1.

Asch, M., "Aboriginal Self-Government and the Construction of Canadian Constitutional Identity" (1992) 30:2 *Alta. L. Rev.* 465.

Asch, M., and P. Macklem, "Aboriginal Rights and Canadian Sovereignty: An Essay on *R. v. Sparrow*" (1991) 26:2 *Alta. L. Rev.* 502.

Asch, M., and N. Zlotkin, "Affirming Aboriginal Title: A New Basis for Comprehensive Claims Negotiations." In *Aboriginal and Treaty Rights in Canada,* M. Asch, ed. Vancouver: U.B.C. Press, 1997.

Ayers, N., "Aboriginal Land Rights in the Maritimes" [1984] 2 C.N.L.R. 1.

Barkwell, P., "The Medicine Chest Clause in Treaty No. 6" [1981] 4 C.N.L.R. 1.

Bartlett, R., "Provincial Jurisdiction and Resource Development on Indian Reserve Lands" [1986] *Managing Resources* 189.

———, "The Fiduciary Duty of the Crown to the Indians" (1989) 53 *Sask. L. Rev.* 301.

———. *Indian Reserves and Aboriginal Lands in Canada: A Homeland.* Saskatoon, Sask.: University of Saskatchewan Native Law Centre, 1990.

———, "The *Mabo* Decision" (1993) *Australian Property L.J.* 236.

———, "The High Court of Australia Upholds the *Federal Native Title Act* and Rejects Racist State Legislation" [1995] 2 C.N.L.R.

———, "The Fundamental Significance of *Wik* v. *State of Queensland* in the High Court of Australia" [1997] 2 C.N.L.R. 1.

Bell, Catherine, "Who are the Metis People in Section 35(1)" (1991) XXIX:2 *Alta. L. Rev.* 351.

———, "Comments on *Partners in Confederation:* A Report on Self-Government by the Royal Commission on Aboriginal Peoples" (1993) 27:2 *U.B.C. Law Rev.* 361.

———. *Alberta's Metis Settlement Legislation: An Overview of Ownership and Management of Settlement Lands.* Regina: Canadian Plains Research Center, University of Regina, 1994.

———, "*R.* v. *Badger:* One Step Forward and Two Steps Back?" (1997) 8 *Const. Forum* 21.

Berger, T. *A Long and Terrible Shadow: White Values, Native Rights in the Americas 1492–1992.* Vancouver/Toronto: Douglas & McIntyre, 1991.

Binnie, W.I.C., "The *Sparrow* Doctrine: Beginning of the End or End of the Beginning?" (1991) 15 *Queen's L.J.* 217.

Boldt, M. *Surviving As Indians: The Challenge of Self-Government.* Toronto: University of Toronto Press, 1993.

Borrows, J., "A Genealogy of Law: Inherent Sovereignty and First Nations Self-Government" (1992) 30 *Osgoode Hall L.J.* 2.

British Columbia, Ministry of Aboriginal Affairs, *In Fairness to All: Moving Towards Treaty Settlements in British Columbia.* Victoria, B.C.: Ministry of Aboriginal Affairs, 1994.

Canada, DIAND. *Outstanding Business: A Native Claims Policy.* Ottawa: DIAND, 1982.

———, House of Commons, Standing Committee on Indian Affairs and Northern Development. *Minutes of Proceedings and Evidence of the Sub-Committee on Indian Women and the Indian Act.* Issue No. 5, September 14, 1982.

————. *Living Treaties, Lasting Agreements: Report of the Task Force to Review Comprehensive Claims Policy.* Ottawa: DIAND, 1985.

————. *Comprehensive Land Claims Policy.* Ottawa: DIAND, 1987.

————, Indian and Northern Affairs. *Impacts of the 1985 Amendments to the Indian Act (Bill C–31): Summary Report.* Ottawa: DIAND, 1990.

————. *Gathering Strength—Canada's Aboriginal Action Plan.* Ottawa: Minister of Public Works and Government Services Canada, 1997.

Cardinal, H. *The Unjust Society: The Tragedy of Canada's Indians.* Edmonton: Hurtig, 1969.

Cassidy, F., and R. Bish. *Indian Government: Its Meaning In Practice.* Montreal: The Institute for Research on Public Policy, 1989.

Chartier, C., "'Indian': An Analysis of the Term as Used in Section 91(24) of the *British North America Act, 1867*" (1978–79) 43 *Sask. L. Rev.* 37.

————, "Aboriginal Self-Government and the Metis Nation." In *Aboriginal Self-Government in Canada*, J. Hylton, ed. Saskatoon, Sask.: Purich Publishing, 1994.

Chartrand, P. *Manitoba's Metis Settlement Scheme of 1870.* Saskatoon, Sask.: Native Law Centre, University of Saskatchewan, 1991.

————, "Aboriginal Rights: The Dispossession of the Metis" (1991) 29 *Osgoode Hall L.J.* 457.

————, "'Terms of Division': Problems of 'Outside-Naming' for Aboriginal People in Canada" (1991) 2:2 *Journal of Indigenous Studies* 1.

Clark, B. *Indian Title in Canada.* Toronto: Carswell, 1987.

————. *Native Liberty, Crown Sovereignty.* Montreal & Kingston: McGill-Queen's University Press, 1990.

Coates, K., ed. *Aboriginal Land Claims Agreements: A Regional Perspective.* Toronto: Copp Clark Pitman, 1997.

Consolidated Native Law Statutes, Regulations and Treaties 1994. Toronto: Carswell, 1993.

Cree-Naskapi Commission, Special Hearing on Implementation of the *Cree-Naskapi (of Quebec) Act.* Hull, Que.,: October 28–30, 1986.

Culhane, D. *The Pleasures of the Crown: Anthropology, Law and First Nations.* Burnaby, B.C.: Talon Books, 1998.

Cumming, P.A., "Canada's North and Native Rights." In *Aboriginal Peoples and the Law: Indian, Metis and Inuit Rights in Canada*, B. Morse, ed. Ottawa: Carleton University Press, 1985.

Cumming, P.A., and N.H. Mickenburg, eds. *Native Rights in Canada,* 2d ed. Toronto: General, 1972.

Doerr, A., "Building New Orders of Government—The Future of Aboriginal Self-Government" (1997) 40:2 *Can. Public Admin.* 274.

Duffy, R.Q. *The Road to Nunavut: The Progress of the Eastern Arctive Inuit Since the Second World War.* Kingston & Montreal: McGill-Queen's University Press, 1988.

Eidsvik, P., "The Aboriginal Fisheries Strategy: Legalizing an Illegal Practice" (November 1996) *Policy Options* 26

Elliot, D., "Aboriginal Title." In *Aboriginal Peoples and the Law: Indian, Metis and Inuit Rights in Canada*, B. Morse, ed. Ottawa: Carleton University Press, 1985.

————, "Baker Lake and the Concept of Aboriginal Title" (1980) 18 *Osgoode Hall L.J.* 653.

————, "In the Wake of *Sparrow*" (1991) 40 *U.N.B.L.J.* 23.

————, "Fifty Dollars of Fish: A Comment on *R. v. Van der Peet*" (1997) 35:3 *Alta L. Rev.*

Flanagan, T., "The Case Against Metis Aboriginal Rights." In *The Quest For Justice: Abo-*

riginal Peoples and Aboriginal Rights, M. Boldt *et al.,* eds. Toronto: University of Toronto Press, 1985.

Foster, H., "The Saanichton Bay Marina Case: Imperial Law, Colonial History and Competing Theories of Aboriginal Title" (1989) 23 *U.B.C. L. Rev.* 34.

———, "Aboriginal Title and the Provincial Obligation to Respect It: Is *Delgamuukw* v. *B.C.* 'Invented Law'?" (March 1998) 56 *Advocate* 221.

Frideres, J. *Native Peoples in Canada: Contemporary Conflicts,* 3rd ed. Scarborough, Ont.: Prentice-Hall, 1988.

Fumoleau, R. *As Long As This Land Shall Last: A History of Treaty 8 and Treaty 11 1870–1939.* Toronto: McClelland & Stewart, 1973.

Funston, B., and E. Meehan, eds. *Canadian Constitutional Documents Consolidated.* Toronto: Carswell, 1994.

Gaffney, R.E., G.P. Gould, and A.J. Semple. *Broken Promises: The Aboriginal Constitutional Conferences.* Fredericton, N.B.: Association of Metis and Non-Status Indians, 1984.

Gerber, G.M., "Multiple Jeopardy: A Socio-Economic Comparison of Men and Women Among the Indian, Metis and Inuit Peoples of Canada" (1990) 22:3 *Canadian Ethnic Studies* 69.

Gilbert, L. *Entitlement to Indian Status and Membership Codes in Canada.* Toronto: Carswell, 1997.

Grammond, S., "Aboriginal Treaties and Canadian Law" (1994) 20 *Queen's L.J.* 57.

Greschner, D., "Aboriginal Women, the Constitution and Criminal Justice" (1992) *U.B.C. L. Rev.* 338.

Griffiths, O.B., "Case Commentary on *Blueberry River:* Is the Crown Fiduciary Obligation in the Currents of Change?" [1996] 3 C.N.L.R. 25.

Grinde D., and B. Johansen. *Exemplar of Liberty: Native America and the Evolution of Democracy.* Los Angeles: University of California Press, 1991.

Hall, D., "A Serene Atmostphere? Treaty 1 Revisited." In *The Recognition of Aboriginal Rights,* S. Corrigan and J. Sawchuk, eds. Brandon, Man.: Bearpaw Publishing, 1996.

Hamilton, A.C. *Canada and Aboriginal Peoples: A New Partnership.* Ottawa: Public Works and Government Services Canada, 1995.

Hardy, R., "Metis Rights in the Mackenzie River District of the Northwest Territories" [1980] 1 C.N.L.R. 1.

Henderson, W., and D. Ground, "Survey of Aboriginal Land Claims" (1994) 26:1 *Ottawa L. Rev.* 187.

Hogg, P. *Constitutional Law of Canada,* 4th ed. Toronto: Carswell, 1997.

Hughes, P., "Indians and Lands Reserved for the Indians: Off Limits to the Provinces?" (1983) 21 *Osgoode Hall L.J.* 82.

Hunt, C.D., "Knowing the North: The Law and Its Institutions" [1986] 4 C.N.L.R. 1.

Indian Treaties and Surrenders Volumes 1 to 3. 1891, 1912; reprint, Saskatoon, Sask.: Fifth House, 1992, 1993.

Isaac, T., "Aboriginal Self-Government in Canada: The *Cree-Naskapi (of Quebec) Act*" (1991) 7:2 *Native Studies Review* 69.

———, "The *Constitution Act, 1982* and the Constitutionalization of Aboriginal Self-Government in Canada: The *Cree-Naskapi (of Quebec) Act*" [1991] 1 C.N.L.R. 1.

———, "The Honour of the Crown: Aboriginal Rights and the *Constitution Act, 1982*; The Significance of *R.* v. *Sparrow*" (1992) 13:1 *Policy Options/Politiques* 22.

———, "Individual Versus Collective Rights: Aboriginal People and the Significance of *Thomas* v. *Norris*" [1992] 21:3 *Man. L.J.* 618.

———, "The Nunavut Agreement-in-Principle and Section 35 of the *Constitution Act, 1982*" (1992) 21:3 *Man. L.J.* 390.

———, "The Storm Over Aboriginal Self-Government: Section 35 of the *Constitution Act, 1982* and the Redefinition of the Inherent Right of Aboriginal Self-Government" [1992] 2 C.N.L.R. 6.

———. *Pre-1868 Legislation Concerning Indians*. Saskatoon, Sask.: University of Saskatchewan Native Law Centre, 1993.

———. *An Analysis of the Aboriginal Government Provisions of the 1992 Charlottetown Accord: Self-Government in the Post-Charlottetown Era*. LL.M. Thesis, University of Saskatchewan, College of Law, 1993.

———, "The Power of Constitutional Language: The Case Against Using 'Aboriginal Peoples' As a Referent for First Nations" (1993) 19:1 *Queen's L.J.* 415.

Jamieson, K., "Sex Discrimination and the *Indian Act*." In *Arduous Journey: Canadian Indians and Decolonization,* J.R. Ponting, ed. Toronto: McClelland & Stewart, 1986.

Johnston, D., "A Theory of Crown Trust towards Aboriginal People" (1986) 30 *Ottawa L. Rev.* 307.

Kirkness, V., "Emerging Native Women" (1987–88) 2:2 *Canadian Journal of Women and the Law*, 411.

Knoll, D., "Treaty and Aboriginal Hunting Rights" [1979] 1 C.N.L.R. 1.

Kunin, R., ed. *Prospering Together: The Economic Impact of the Aboriginal Title Settlements in B.C.* Vancouver, B.C.: The Laurier Institution, 1998.

LeDressay, A., "A Brief Tax(on a me) of First Nations Taxation and Economic Development." In *Sharing the Harvest: The Road to Self-Reliance*. Ottawa: Royal Commission on Aboriginal Peoples, 1993.

Lester, G.S. *The Territorial Rights of the Inuit of the Canadian Northwest Territories: A Legal Argument*. Unpublished Ph.D. Dissertation. Toronto, York University, 1981.

Lysyk, K., "The Unique Constitutional Position of the Canadian Indian" (1967) 45 *Can. Bar Rev.* 513.

———, "The Indian Title Question in Canada: An Appraisal in the Light of *Calder*" (1973) 51 *Can. Bar Rev.* 450.

Macklem, P., "First Nations, Self-Government and the Borders of the Canadian Legal Imagination" (1991) 36 *McGill L.J.* 382.

———, "What's Law Got to Do With It? The Protection of Aboriginal Title in Canada" (Spring 1997) 35 *Osgoode Hall L.J.* 125.

Mandell, L., "Gitksan-Wet'suwet'en Land Title Action" [1988] 1 C.N.L.R. 14.

McLeod, C., "The Oral Histories of Canada's Northern People, Anglo-Canadian Evidence Law, and Canada's Fiduciary Duty to First Nations: Breaking Down the Barriers of the Past" (1992) 30 *Alta. L. Rev.* 1276.

McMurtry, W.R., and A. Pratt, "Indians and the Fiduciary Concept, Self-Government and the Constitution" [1986] 3 C.N.L.R. 19.

McNeil, K. *Indian Hunting, Trapping and Fishing Rights in the Prairie Provinces of Canada*. Saskatoon, Sask.: Native Law Centre, University of Saskatchewan, 1983.

———. *Common Law, Aboriginal Title*. Oxford: Clarendon Press, 1989.

McRae, H., G. Nettheim, and L. Beacroft. *Aboriginal Legal Issues: Cases and Materials*. Sidney, Australia: The Law Book Co., 1991.

Merritt, J., *et al. Nunavut: Political Choices and Manifest Destiny.* Ottawa: Canadian Arctic Resources Committee, 1989.

Morris, A. *The Treaties of Canada with the Indians of Manitoba and the North-West Territories.* 1880; reprint, Saskatoon, Sask.: Fifth House Publishers, 1991.

Morse, B., ed. *Aboriginal Peoples and the Law: Indian, Metis and Inuit Rights in Canada.* Ottawa: Carleton University Press, 1985.

Morse, B., "Permafrost Rights: Aboriginal Self-Government and the Supreme Court in *R.* v. *Pamajewon*" (September 1997) 42 *McGill L.J.* 1011.

Moss, W., *Practically Millionaires.* Ottawa: National Indian Brotherhood, 1981.

———, "Indigenous Self-Government in Canada and Sexual Equality under the *Indian Act:* Resolving Conflicts Between Collective and Individual Rights" (1990) 15:2 *Queen's L.J.* 281.

Nakatsuru, S., "A Constitutional Right of Indian Self-Government" (1985) 43 *U.T. Fac. L. Rev.* 72.

Native Women's Association of Canada. *Matriarchy and the Canadian Charter: A Discussion Paper.* Ottawa: Native Women's Association of Canada, c. 1991.

Newell, D. *Tangled Webs of History: Indians and the Law in Canada's Pacific Coast Fisheries.* Toronto: University of Toronto Press, 1993.

Notzke, C. *Aboriginal Peoples and Natural Resources in Canada.* North York: Captus, 1994.

Olynyk, J., "Approaches to Sorting Out Jurisdiction in a Self-Government Context" (Spring 1995) *U.T. Fac. L. Rev.* 235.

Owen, D.P., "Fiduciary Obligations and Aboriginal Peoples: Devolution in Action" [1994] 3 C.N.L.R. 1.

Paul, D. *We Were Not the Savages: A Micmac Perspective on the Collision of European and Aboriginal Civilization.* Halifax, N.S.: Nimbus, 1993.

Pentney, W., "The Rights of the Aboriginal Peoples of Canada and the *Constitution Act, 1982;* Part I: The Interpretive Prism of Section 25" (1988) 22:1 *U.B.C. L. Rev.* 21.

Price, R., ed. *The Spirit of the Alberta Indian Treaties.* Montreal: Institute for Research on Public Policy, 1980.

Purich, D. *The Metis.* Toronto: Lorimer, 1988.

———. *The Inuit and Their Land: The Story of Nunavut.* Toronto: Lorimer, 1992.

Rotman, L.I., "Provincial Fiduciary Obligations to First Nations: The Nexus Between Governmental Power and Responsibility" (1994) 32:4 *Osgoode Hall L.J.* 735.

———. *Parallel Paths: Fiduciary Doctrine and the Crown-Native Relationship in Canada.* Toronto: University of Toronto Press, 1996.

———, "Taking Aim at the Canons of Treaty Interpretation in Canadian Aboriginal Rights Jurisprudence" (1997) 46 *U.N.B.L.J.* 11.

Royal Commission on Aboriginal Peoples. *Partners in Confederation: Aboriginal Peoples, Self-Government and the Constitution.* Ottawa: RCAP, 1993.

———. *Sharing the Harvest: The Road to Self-Reliance.* Ottawa: RCAP, 1993.

———. *Report of the RCAP.* Ottawa: RCAP, 1996.

Ryder, B., "The Demise and Rise of the Classical Paradigm in Canadian Federalism: Promoting Autonomy for the Provinces and First Nations" (1991) 36 *McGill L.J.* 308.

Salembier, J.P., "Crown Fiduciary Duty, Indian Title and the Lost Treasure of I.R. 172: The Legacy of *Apsassin* v. *The Queen (Blueberry River)*" [1996] 3 C.N.L.R. 1.

Salisbury, R. *A Homeland for the Cree.* Kingston & Montreal: McGill-Queen's University Press, 1986.

Sanders, D., "The Application of Provincial Laws." In *Aboriginal Peoples and the Law: Indian, Metis and Inuit Rights in Canada*, B. Morse, ed. Ottawa: Carleton University Press, 1985.

Savino, V., and E. Schumacher, "'Whenever the Indians of the Reserve Should Desire It: An Analysis of the First Nation Treaty Right to Education" (1992) 21:3 *Man. L.J.* 476.

Schulze, D., "The Privy Council Decision Concerning George Allsopp's Petition, 1767: An Imperial Precedent on the Application of the Royal Proclamation to the Old Province of Quebec" [1995] 2 C.N.L.R. 1.

Schwarz, B. *First Principles, Second Thoughts: Aboriginal Peoples, Constitutional Reform and Canadian Statecraft.* Kingston, Ont.: Institute for Intergovernmental Relations, 1985.

Silman, J., ed. *Enough Is Enough: Aboriginal Women Speak Out.* Toronto: Women's Press, 1987.

Sinclair, A.M. *Introduction to Real Property Law*, 3d ed. Toronto: Butterworths, 1987.

Slattery, B. *The Land Rights of Indigenous Canadian Peoples as Affected by the Crown's Acquisition of their Territories.* D.Phil. Thesis, Oxford University. Saskatoon, Sask.: University of Saskatchewan Native Law Centre, 1979.

———, "The Constitutional Guarantee of Aboriginal and Treaty Rights" (1983) 8 *Queen's L.J.* 232.

———, "Understanding Aboriginal Rights" (1987) 66 *Can. Bar Rev.* 727.

———, "The Legal Basis of Aboriginal Title." In *Aboriginal Title in British Columbia: Delgamuukw v. The Queen*, F. Cassidy, ed. Lantzville, B.C.: Oolichan Books, 1992.

Smith, J.C., "The Concept of Native Title" (1974) 24 *U.T.L.J.* 1.

Treaty 7 Elders and Tribal Council. *The True Spirit and Original Intent of Treaty 7.* Kingston & Montreal: McGill-Queen's University Press, 1996.

Venne, S., ed. *Indian Acts and Amendments 1868–1975: An Indexed Collection.* Saskatoon, Sask.: University of Saskatchewan Native Law Centre, 1981.

Venne, S., "Treaty Indigenous Peoples and the Charlottetown Accord: The Message in the Breeze" [1993] 4:2 *Constitutional Forum* 43.

———, "Understanding Treaty 6: An Indigenous Perspective." In *Aboriginal and Treaty Rights in Canada*, M. Asch, ed. Vancouver: U.B.C. Press, 1997.

Weaver, S.M. *Making Canadian Indian Policy: The Hidden Agenda 1968–1970.* Toronto: University of Toronto Press, 1981.

Wildsmith, B., "Pre-Confederation Treaties." In *Aboriginal Peoples and the Law*, B. Morse, ed. Ottawa: Carleton University Press, 1985.

———. *Aboriginal Peoples and Section 25 of the Canadian Charter of Rights and Freedoms.* Saskatoon, Sask.: University of Saskatchewan Native Law Centre, 1988.

Woodward, J. *Native Law*. Toronto: Carswell, 1989.

Wright, R. *Stolen Continents: The "New World" Through Indian Eyes.* Toronto: Penguin, 1993.

Zlotkin, N. *Unfinished Business: Aboriginal Peoples and the 1983 Constitutional Conference.* Kingston, Ont.: Institute of Intergovernmental Relations, Queen's University, 1983.

———, "Judicial Recognition of Aboriginal Customary Law in Canada: Selected Marriage and Adoption Cases" [1984] 4 C.N.L.R. 1.

———, "The 1983 and 1984 Constitutional Conferences: Only the Beginning" [1984] 3 C.N.L.R. 3.

———, "Post-Confederation Treaties." In *Aboriginal Peoples and the Law*, B. Morse, ed. Ottawa: Carleton University Press, 1985.

| ABBREVIATIONS

CANADIAN LAW REPORTERS AND JOURNALS

Alta. L.R.	Alberta Law Reports	Osgoode Hall L.J.	Osgoode Hall Law Journal
A.R.	Alberta Reports		
All. E.R.	All England Law Reports	Ottawa L. Rev.	Ottawa Law Review
		Peters	Peters Reports
App. Cas.	Appeal Cases	Q.A.C.	Quebec Appeal Cases
A.P.R.	Atlantic Provinces Reports	Queen's L.J.	Queen's Law Journal
		R.F.L.	Reports of Family Law
B.C.R.	Columbia Reports		
B.C.L.R.	British Columbia Law Reports	R.J.R.Q.	Rapports Judiciaires Revisés de la Province de Québec
Can. Bar Rev.	Canadian Bar Review		
C.C.C.	Canadian Criminal Cases	R.P.R.	Real Property Reports
		S.C.R.	Supreme Court Reports
C.C.E.L.	Canadian Cases on Employment Law	U.B.C.L.J.	University of British Columbia Law Journal
C.N.L.B.	Canadian Native Law Bulletin	U.N.B.L.J.	University of New Brunswick Law Journal
C.N.L.C.	Canadian Native Law Cases		
C.N.L.R.	Canadian Native Law Reporter	U.T. Fac. L. Rev.	University of Toronto Faculty of Law Review
C.R.	Criminal Reports		
C.R.R.	Canadian Rights Reporter	U.T.L.J.	University of Toronto Law Journal
C.T.C.	Canadian Tax Cases	W.W.R.	Western Weekly Reports
D.L.R.	Dominion Law Reports		
D.T.C.	Dominion Tax Cases		
E.T.R.	Estates and Trusts Reports		
F.C.	Federal Court of Canada Reports		
L.C. Jur.	Lower Canada Jurist		
McGill L.J.	McGill Law Journal		
M.V.R.	Motor Vehicle Reports		
N.R.	National Reporter		
N.B.R.	New Brunswick Reports		
N.S.R.	Nova Scotia Reports		
O.R.	Ontario Reports		

COURTS

App. Div.	Appellate Division
(A.D.)	Appellate Division
Can. H.R.T.	Canadian Human Rights Tribunal
C.A.	Court of Appeal
Co. Ct.	County Court
Ct. J.	Court of Justice
C.Q.	Court of Quebec
C.S.P.	Cour des Sessions de la paix
Dist. Ct.	District Court
Div. Ct.	Divisional Court
Fed. Ct.	Federal Court
F.C.	Federal Court
H.C.	High Court
J.C.P.C.	Judicial Committee of the Privy Council
Prov. Ct.	Provincial Court
Q.B.	Court of Queen's Bench
S.C.	Supreme Court
S.C.C.	Supreme Court of Canada
T.C.C.	Tax Court of Canada
Terr. Ct.	Territorial Court
T.D.	Trial Division
U.S.S. Ct.	United States Supreme Court

STATUTES

C.R.C.	Consolidated Regulations of Canada
C.S.U.C.	Consolidated Statutes of Upper Canada
R.S.B.C.	Revised Statutes of British Columbia
R.S.C.	Revised Statutes of Canada
R.S.M.	Statutes of Manitoba
S.A.	Statutes of Alberta
S.B.C.	Statutes of British Columbia
S.C.	Statutes of Canada
S.Prov.C.	Statutes of the Province of Canada
S.S.	Statutes of Saskatchewan
SOR	Statutory Orders and Regulations (Canada)

JURISDICTIONS

Alta.	Alberta
B.C.	British Columbia
Man.	Manitoba
Nfld.	Newfoundland
N.B.	New Brunswick
N.S.	Nova Scotia
N.W.T.	Northwest Territories
Ont.	Ontario
P.E.I.	Edward Island
Prov. C.	Province of Canada (pre-1867)
Que.	Quebec
Sask.	Saskatchewan
U.C.	Upper Canada (pre-1867)
Y.T.	Yukon Territory

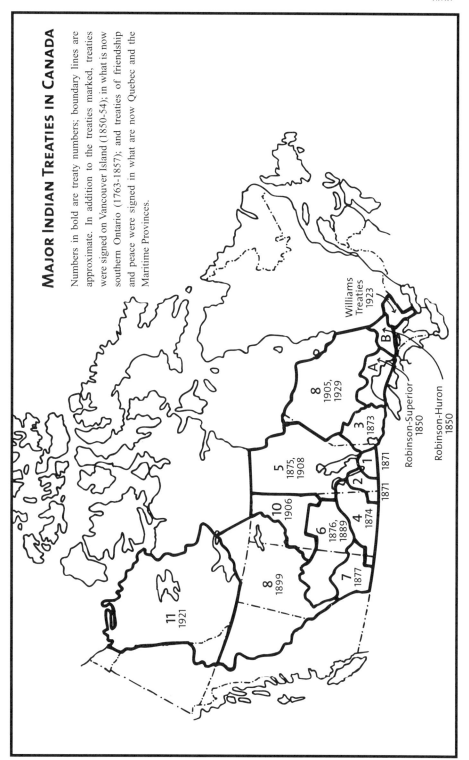

Major Indian Treaties in Canada

Numbers in bold are treaty numbers; boundary lines are approximate. In addition to the treaties marked, treaties were signed on Vancouver Island (1850-54); in what is now southern Ontario (1763-1857); and treaties of friendship and peace were signed in what are now Quebec and the Maritime Provinces.

11
1921

8
1899

10
1906

6
1876,
1889

7
1877

4
1874

5
1875,
1908

2
1871

1
1871

8
1905,
1929

3
1873

Williams
Treaties
1923

A

B

Robinson-Superior
1850

Robinson-Huron
1850

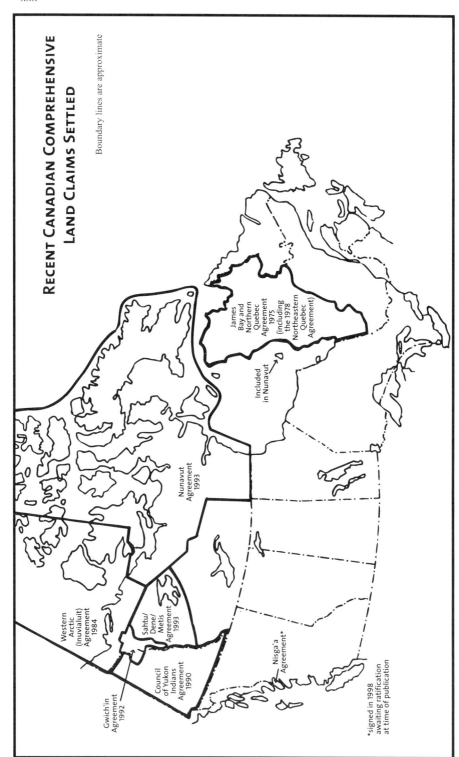

RECENT CANADIAN COMPREHENSIVE LAND CLAIMS SETTLED

Boundary lines are approximate

James Bay and Northern Quebec Agreement 1975 (including the 1978 Northeastern Quebec Agreement)

Included in Nunavut

Nunavut Agreement 1993

Western Arctic (Inuvialuit) Agreement 1984

Sahtu/ Dene/ Metis Agreement 1993

Gwich'in Agreement 1992

Council of Yukon Indians Agreement 1990

Nisga'a Agreement*

*signed in 1998 awaiting ratification at time of publication

CHAPTER 1
ABORIGINAL TITLE

■ INTRODUCTION

Throughout the history of Canada, Aboriginal peoples have sought to have their distinct rights confirmed and respected. For the most part, Aboriginal peoples have been forced to rely upon the courts to provide for a recognition of their rights and an affirmation of their interests in their tribal lands. The federal and provincial governments, indeed the judicial system, have historically not provided for a great deal of support for and implementation of Aboriginal rights. The *Constitution Act, 1982*[1] changed this by recognizing and affirming Aboriginal and treaty rights and by giving these the status of being incorporated into the supreme law of Canada.[2] Recent processes and developments, such as the British Columbia treaty process and the *Report of the Royal Commission on Aboriginal Peoples,* also seek to change this historical neglect and to deal with the rights of Aboriginal peoples in a forthcoming and clear manner.

Aboriginal rights are the legal embodiment of Aboriginal peoples' claims to their traditional lands and to the activities, customs, and traditions flowing therefrom. Although the discussion and presentation of Aboriginal law in this text is segmented into various chapters, the reality is that Aboriginal law is a rapidly developing area of Canadian law that is in many respects, and notwithstanding significant Supreme Court of Canada decisions to date, a relatively new legal discipline. As Chief Justice Lamer noted in the 1997 Supreme Court of Canada decision of *Delgamuukw* v. *British Columbia,*[3] "the content of common law Aboriginal title . . . has not been authoritatively determined by the Court."[4]

THE SOURCE AND NATURE OF ABORIGINAL TITLE

Any examination of Aboriginal law requires a discussion of the historical and legal context within which Aboriginal law is evolving. Central to this discussion is an examination of the source and nature of Aboriginal rights and Aboriginal title, which serve as the basis for a majority of the law in this area. Another important element to this discussion is the relationship between Aboriginal rights and Aboriginal title. The recent Supreme Court of Canada decision of *Delgamuukw* v. *British Columbia* has clarified this relationship and is discussed later in this chapter.

Aboriginal peoples have occupied what is now called South, Central, and North America, for thousands and thousands of years. Ronald Wright notes:

---

1   R.S.C. 1985, App. II, No. 44, being Schedule B of the *Canada Act 1982* (U.K.), 1982, c. 11.
2   See chap. 7, *Constitution Act, 1982.*
3   *Delgamuukw* v. *British Columbia,* [1998] 1 C.N.L.R. 14 (S.C.C.).
4   Ibid., para. 75.

In 1992, the West—by which I mean nations and cultures that are either European or derived from Europe's expansion of the past 500 years—celebrated the quincentenary of Columbus's first voyage from an "old" world to a "new." . . . The inhabitants of America saw it differently. Their ancestors had made the same discovery long before. . . . They had developed every kind of society: nomadic, hunting groups, settled farming communities, and dazzling civilizations with cities as large as any then on earth. By 1492 there were approximately 100 million Native Americans—a fifth, more or less, of the human race.[5]

Historically, Aboriginal peoples had their own forms of government, social organization, and economies. Aboriginal peoples presence in and occupation of North America, prior to European settlement, is the basic premise upon which the doctrine of Aboriginal rights and title has developed. As the Supreme Court of Canada decision of *R.* v. *Van der Peet*[6] confirmed:

The doctrine of Aboriginal rights exists, and is recognized and affirmed by s. 35(1), because of one simple fact: when Europeans arrived in North America, Aboriginal peoples were already here, living in communities on the land, and participating in distinctive cultures, as they had done for centuries.[7]

The Royal Commission on Aboriginal Peoples noted:

Aboriginal peoples' experience with the law of Aboriginal title has been one of promise and frustration. The law of Aboriginal rights, including rights associated with Aboriginal title, provides a bridge between Aboriginal nations and the broader Canadian community. . . . The law of Aboriginal title thus acknowledges that societies and cultures evolve and transform over time and that legal recognition of Aboriginal rights is premised on continuity, not conformity, with the past. . . . [C]urrent jurisprudence cannot . . . accomplish all that is required to protect Aboriginal lands and resources. . . . [T]he law of Aboriginal title serves as a backdrop to complex nation-to-nation negotiations concerning ownership, jurisdiction and co-management.[8]

In *R.* v. *Van der Peet*,[9] the Supreme Court of Canada clarified the relationship between Aboriginal title and rights. Although the jurisprudence surrounding Aboriginal rights has flowed from Aboriginal title litigation, Lamer C.J., for the majority, affirmed that "Aboriginal title is a subcategory of Aboriginal rights which deals solely with claims of rights to land." Thus, Aboriginal rights can exist independently of Aboriginal title.[10]

---

5   Ronald Wright, *Stolen Continents: The "New World" Through Indian Eyes* (Toronto: Penguin, 1993), 3–4; see also Thomas Berger, *A Long and Terrible Shadow* (Vancouver/Toronto: Douglas & McIntyre, 1991).

6   *R.* v. *Van der Peet,* [1996] 4 C.N.L.R. 177 (S.C.C.).

7   Ibid., para. 30.

8   Royal Commission on Aboriginal Peoples, *Report of the Royal Commission on Aboriginal Peoples,* vol. 2 (Ottawa: RCAP, 1996), 559, 561, 562.

9   *R.* v. *Van der Peet,* [1996] 4 C.N.L.R. 177 at 210, para. 74.

10 In *R.* v. *Adams,* [1996] 4 C.N.L.R. 1 at 11, para. 27, the Supreme Court noted: "To

One of the first and most significant instruments recognizing the nature and scope of Aboriginal title is the *Royal Proclamation of 1763*,[11] which was issued by King George III of Great Britain on October 7, 1763, following the British conquest of New France and its resulting cession to Great Britain in the Treaty of Paris. The *Royal Proclamation* consolidated Great Britain's dominion over North America. It recognized the rights of Indians to unceded lands in their possession and that the Indians may only cede such lands to the Crown. The *Royal Proclamation* noted that "great Frauds and Abuses have been committed in purchasing Land of the Indians" and as a result, the *Royal Proclamation* prohibited the purchasing of lands from Indians by the settlers. The Crown possesses the sole right to acquire lands from Indians. The *Royal Proclamation* also reserved lands for Indians "as their hunting grounds." Although not a constitutional document, it has the force of law in Canada and is referenced in s. 25 of the *Canadian Charter of Rights and Freedoms.*[12] Section 25 reads in part:

> The guarantee in this Charter of certain rights and freedoms shall not be construed as to abrogate or derogate from an aboriginal, treaty or other rights or freedoms . . . including . . . any rights or freedoms that have been recognized by the Royal Proclamation of October 7, 1763.

As important as the *Royal Proclamation* has been in the development of Aboriginal jurisprudence, strictly speaking, it is "an Executive Order having the force and effect of an Act of Parliament."[13]

The cession provision (only to the Crown) provided the basis, and the necessity, for the Crown to enter into treaties with Aboriginal peoples. In *R.* v. *Sparrow*[14] the Supreme Court of Canada wrote the following about the nature of the *Royal Proclamation* vis-à-vis Aboriginal title:

> It is worth recalling that while British policy towards the native population was based on respect for their right to occupy their traditional lands, a proposition to which the *Royal Proclamation of 1763* bears witness, there was from the outset never any doubt that sovereignty and legislative power, and indeed the underlying title, to such lands vested in the Crown.[15]

A major issue of contention has been the Eurocentric basis of the courts as they legitimized non-Aboriginal occupation and "ownership" of the New World. This issue is perhaps best exemplified by the discussion on extinguishment of Aboriginal title later in this chapter and by the restrictive interpretation given to the

---

understand why Aboriginal rights cannot be inexorably linked to Aboriginal title it is only necessary to recall that some Aboriginal peoples were nomadic, varying the location of their settlements with the season and changing circumstances."

11 *Royal Proclamation of 1763*, R.S.C. 1985, App. II, No. 1.

12 Part I of the *Constitution Act, 1982,* being Schedule B to the *Canada Act 1982* (U.K.), 1982, c. 11.

13 See *Calder* v. *A.-G. B.C.,* 7 C.N.L.C. 91 at 150.

14 *R.* v. *Sparrow*, [1990] 3 C.L.N.R. 160 (S.C.C.).

15 Ibid. at 177.

Royal Proclamation by the Supreme Court of Canada in *Sparrow.* There are further examples in chapters 3 and 4, where the 1930 *Natural Resources Transfer Agreements*[16] are discussed in light of the ability of the federal Crown to alter unilaterally treaties made with Indians (prior to 1982). The Supreme Court of Canada decision of *R.* v. *Delgamuukw* affirmed that Aboriginal oral history, which up to this point had an uncertain and dubious status in the legal system, is admissible as evidence in Aboriginal rights cases. This broader approach to Aboriginal legal issues will undoubtedly bring about change, perhaps significant change, as the Canadian legal system attempts to scope out and further define the rights of Aboriginal people.

Using the *Royal Proclamation* as a starting point for their discussion, the two leading American decisions of *Johnson and Graham's Lessee* v. *M'Intosh*[17] and *Worcester* v. *Georgia*[18] discuss the origins of Aboriginal title and have been frequently cited by Canadian courts, including the Supreme Court of Canada. Both decisions were written by Chief Justice Marshall and maintain that the basis for Aboriginal title is derived from the *Royal Proclamation of 1763*. Interestingly, both decisions struggle with the issue of "how" the Crown assumed sovereignty over North America and seem to conclude that either conquest or discovery forms a sound basis to limit Aboriginal title as a burden on the Crown's title.

Connolly v. *Woolrich*[19] was one of the first and few early Canadian decisions that took the same expansive approach outlined in *Worcester* v. *Georgia.* The case concerned whether the common law recognized a Cree customary marriage. Monk J. concluded that the customary marriage was recognizable at common law and therefore valid. This conclusion was based, in part, on the premise that the Indians' laws, customs, and political and legislative rights were in full force and applicable. Although the appeal court upheld the verdict, they did not affirm, to the same degree as the trial court, the degree to which Indian laws were applicable.

The Privy Council held in *St. Catherine's Milling and Lumber Co.* v. *R.* that Indians possessed a "personal and usufructory right, dependent upon the good will of the Sovereign"[20] over which they enjoyed Indian title. Aboriginal title, and Aboriginal rights as they relate to land, are recognized as being part of the law of Canada. In *R.* v. *Calder*[21] and affirmed by *R.* v. *Guerin,*[22] the Supreme Court of Canada affirmed the existence of Aboriginal title as being guaranteed by Canadian common law. The judges participating in the *Calder* decision agreed that Aboriginal title was not dependent upon legislative enactments, executive orders, or trea-

---

16   See *Constitution Act, 1930*, R.S.C., App. II, No. 26.

17   *Johnson and Graham's Lessee* v. *M'Intosh* (1823), 8 Wheaton 543 (U.S.S. Ct.).

18   *Worcester* v. *Georgia*, (1832), 31 U.S. 530 (U.S.S. Ct.).

19   *Connolly* v. *Woolrich*, 1 C.N.L.C. 70, (1867), 11 L.C. Jur. 197, 17 R.J.R.Q. 75 (Que. S.C.), Monk, J., July 9, 1867, affirmed in result in *Johnstone et al.* v. *Connolly*, 1 C.N.L.C. 151, 17 R.J.R.Q. 266 (Que. C.A.(Q.B.)).

20   *St. Catherine's Milling and Lumber Co.* v. *R.*, 2 C.N.L.C. 541 (J.C.P.C.) at 549.

21   *R.* v. *Calder*, [1973] S.C.R. 313.

22   *R.* v. *Guerin*, [1985] 1 C.N.L.R. 120.

ties, including the *Royal Proclamation of 1763* as suggested in *St. Catherine's*. Rather, Aboriginal title is a legal right derived from the Indians' traditional occupation and use of their tribal lands, thus underscoring the significance of *Calder* and explaining why it was so influential in subsequent court and government decisions.

However, in *Guerin*, the Supreme Court of Canada noted that Aboriginal title has also been interpreted to encompass a "beneficial interest" in lands.[23] *Guerin* ultimately summarizes the unique or *sui generis* nature of Aboriginal title as follows:

> Indians have a legal right to occupy and possess certain lands, the ultimate title to which is in the Crown. While their interest does not, strictly speaking, amount to beneficial ownership, neither is its nature completely exhausted by the concept of a personal right. It is true that the *sui generis* interest which the Indians have in the land is personal in the sense that it cannot be transferred to a grantee, but it is also true, . . . that the interest gives rise upon surrender to a distinctive fiduciary duty obligation on the part of the Crown to deal with the land for the benefit of the surrendering Indians. . . . The nature of the Indians' interest is therefore best characterized by its general inalienability, coupled with the fact that the Crown is under an obligation to deal with the land on the Indians' behalf when the interest is surrendered.[24]

Finally, it is important to note that the excerpt of the *Guerin* decision in this chapter also includes a discussion of the Crown's fiduciary obligations to Aboriginal peoples. *Guerin* is the leading Supreme Court of Canada decision on this matter. The fiduciary obligations of the Crown to Aboriginal people are discussed in the introduction to chapter 3.

The common law basis of Aboriginal title was affirmed by the Supreme Court of Canada in *Roberts* v. *Canada*.[25] *Roberts* also affirmed that Aboriginal title is within the jurisdiction of the Federal Court of Canada. *R.* v. *Smith*[26] held that once Aboriginal title was surrendered, the rights associated with the title also disappeared and the land became as all other Crown land and not land necessarily "reserved" for Indians as per s. 91(24) of the *Constitution Act, 1867*.[27]

Relying heavily upon Canadian jurisprudence, the High Court of Australia in 1992 recognized a form of Aboriginal title that continues, subject to being extinguished, to exist in Australia.[28] The *Mabo* decision focused on the settlement doctrine as the basis for Aboriginal rights in Australia. As such, the court affirmed that

---

23 Ibid., 135. With respect to beneficial interest, the court cites *A.G. Canada* v. *Giroux*, 4 C.N.L.C. 147 (S.C.C.); *Cardinal* v. *A.G. Alberta*, 7 C.N.L.C. 307 (S.C.C.) (Laskin J. dissenting); and *Western Int. Contractors Ltd.* v. *Sarcee Development Ltd.*, [1979] 2 C.N.L.R. 107 (Alta. C.A.).

24 Ibid., 136.

25 *Roberts* v. *Canada*, [1989] 2 C.N.L.R. 146 (S.C.C.).

26 *R.* v. *Smith*, [1983] 3 C.N.L.R. 161 (S.C.C.).

27 *Constitution Act, 1867* (U.K.), 30 & 31 Vict., c. 3 (R.S.C. 1985, App. II, No. 5).

28 *Mabo* v. *Queensland*, [1992] 5 C.N.L.R. (High Court of Australia).

the Crown retained the radical or underlying title to the lands in question and that the Aboriginal interest in the lands can only be alienated to the Crown. Similarly, the Crown can extinguish Aboriginal title so long as it demonstrates a clear and plain intention to do so.

In general, the issue of Aboriginal title is an issue for debate only in those areas where treaties have not been signed or where the issue of extinguishment of Aboriginal title is still in question. For example, a large portion of land in British Columbia and parts of the western Northwest Territories are not covered by treaty and are, therefore, open to claims based on Aboriginal title. Of course, the use and occupancy of land continue to be important issues with respect to determining whether or not Aboriginal rights exist or whether they have been extinguished. In some cases, land claims agreements have been ratified to meet the Crown's obligations to deal with outstanding claims of Aboriginal title. Among these agreements is the 1975 *James Bay and Northern Quebec Agreement,* which permitted the government of Quebec to proceed with the James Bay hydroelectric project. Land claims agreements have also been concluded in the Yukon Territory[29] and the Northwest Territories.[30] The *Nisga'a Final Agreement,* British Columbia's first modern treaty, was initialed on August 4, 1998, and, at the time of writing, was in the final stages of ratification. It is noteworthy that the "peace and friendship" treaties signed in the eighteenth century in the Maritime provinces did not extinguish Aboriginal title. Writing on the Maritime situation, Cumming and Mickenburg note:

> Since there were no treaties following the Proclamations of 1762 and 1763 directly extinguishing aboriginal rights, it seems probable that there were claims surviving which remained unextinguished by the procedure set out in the proclamation. Nevertheless, Indian title may be extinguished by means other than the negotiation of formal land cession treaties.[31]

Thus, Aboriginal title can be said to come from the historic use and occupation of certain lands, from the *Royal Proclamation of 1763,* and from the common law. It is a burden on the Crown's title.[32]

---

29   *Yukon Final Agreement* (Ottawa: DIAND, 1993).

30   For example, see *Agreement Between the Inuit of the Nunavut Settlement Area and Her Majesty The Queen in Right of Canada* (Ottawa: DIAND and Tunngavik, 1993); *Gwich'in Comprehensive Land Claim Agreement* (Ottawa: DIAND, 1992); *Sahtu Dene and Metis Comprehensive Land Claim Agreement* (Ottawa: DIAND, 1993); *The Inuvialuit Final Agreement* (Ottawa: DIAND, 1984).

31   P.A. Cumming and N.H. Mickenburg, *Native Rights in Canada,* 2d ed. (Toronto: General, 1972), 102.

32   In *Haida Nation* v. *B.C.,* [1998] 1 C.N.L.R. 98 (B.C.C.A.); leave to appeal to the S.C.C. refused May 8, 1998 (No. 26394), the British Columbia Court of Appeal considered a petition from the Haida Nation to have s. 28 of the British Columbia *Forestry Act* (R.S.B.C. 1979, c. 140, now 1996, c. 157) interpreted in a manner so as to recognize Aboriginal title as an encumbrance to be considered when issuing a tree farm licence. The Court of Appeal agreed with the Haida Nation and found that

The much-awaited December 1997 Supreme Court of Canada decision of *Delgamuukw* v. *British Columbia* is a landmark decision for its treatment of oral histories as meeting the evidentiary rules of court, for Aboriginal title generally, and for the importance of negotiated settlements in the development of Aboriginal jurisprudence.[33] While an extensive excerpt from the majority judgment is reproduced in this chapter, the following comments are offered with respect to this notable decision as it relates to Aboriginal title generally.

Writing for the majority, Lamer C.J. begins interestingly by stating that since the respondents (British Columbia) suffered some prejudice due to the fact that the appellants did not amend their pleadings to amalgamate the individual claims brought by the 51 Gitksan and Wet'suwet'en Houses into two collective claims, the court was prevented from considering the merits of the appeal. As such, he states that a new trial would be an appropriate remedy and then goes to provide other reasons a new trial would be appropriate. It is through the "other reasons" that Lamer C.J. outlines a great deal of substantive law on the issue of Aboriginal title claims.

Delgamuukw reaffirmed the Supreme Court's discussion of the rules of evidence in the *Van der Peet* decision.[34] Specifically, trial courts must consider evidentiary rules in light of the special nature of Aboriginal claims, in keeping with the *sui generis* nature of Aboriginal rights.[35] In *Van der Peet,* the Supreme Court stated that when courts adjudicate Aboriginal rights cases, they should

> approach the rules of evidence, and interpret the evidence that exists, with a consciousness of the special nature of Aboriginal claims, and of the evidentiary difficulties in proving a right which originates in times where there were no written records of the practices, customs and traditions engaged in. The courts must not undervalue the evidence presented by Aboriginal claimants simply because that evidence does not conform precisely with the evidentiary standards that would be applied in, for example, a private law torts case.[36]

The Supreme Court decision in *Delgamuukw* affirms that oral histories, rejected by the trial court judge in this case, must be considered in Aboriginal rights decisions. The laws of evidence must accommodate Aboriginal oral history and place it "on an equal footing with the types of historical evidence that courts are

---

Aboriginal title would constitute an encumbrance on Crown title, that Aboriginal title to land can include an interest in standing timber, and that the terminology "otherwise encumbered" used in the *Forestry Act* includes any such encumbrance found in Aboriginal title. Leave to appeal was refused by the Supreme Court of Canada.

33 An interesting study of the history of Aboriginal title in British Columbia, especially in the context of the *Delgamuukw* decision, can be found in D. Culhane, *The Pleasure of the Crown: Anthropology, Law and First Nations* (Burnaby, B.C.: Talon Books, 1998).

34 For example, see *R.* v. *Van der Peet,* [1996] 4 C.N.L.R. 177 (S.C.C.), paras. 42, 49, 50, and 68.

35 *Delgamuukw* v. *British Columbia,* [1998] 1 C.N.L.R. 14 (S.C.C.), para. 82.

36 *R.* v. *Van der Peet,* [1996] 4 C.N.L.R. 177 (S.C.C.), para. 68.

familiar with."[37] This decision on the admissibility of oral histories is critical and not simply a procedural matter. Given that the trial judge in *Delgamuukw* rejected the argument that the Gitksan and Wet'suwet'en people had the required extent of occupation necessary for ownership of the lands in question and given that, to a large degree, the oral history evidence as presented dealt with the historical nature of the use and occupation of the lands in question, the finding that this important evidence is now admissible and must be considered focuses a new light on the case. This broader interpretation of the admissibility of oral historical evidence will undoubtedly prove useful for all Aboriginal peoples in litigation and illustrates the broader approach to interpreting aspects of Aboriginal rights offered by the Supreme Court.

In *Delgamuukw,* Lamer C.J. also discusses the *sui generis* nature of Aboriginal title and its various dimensions: namely, that it is inalienable, that its source arises from the prior occupation of Canada by Aboriginal peoples, and that it is held communally.[38] Aboriginal title includes the right to exclusive use and occupation of the land for an array of purposes, which are not limited to Aboriginal practices, customs, and traditions that are integral to distinct Aboriginal cultures. As well, Aboriginal title imposes on the lands in question a limit that the use of the land cannot be irreconcilable with the Aboriginal occupation of the land and that it is the relationship that the Aboriginal group in question had with the land that gave rise to the Aboriginal title in the first place.[39] Aboriginal title is a right to land being claimed. Aboriginal rights are activities that must be an element of a practice, custom, or tradition integral to the distinctive culture of the Aboriginal people claiming the right.[40] Aboriginal title is a distinct variation of Aboriginal rights, which are recognized and affirmed in s. 35(1) of the *Constitution Act, 1982.*[41]

Delgamuukw affirms that Aboriginal title is a right in land. It confers the right to use land for a variety of activities, some of which are aspects of practices, customs, and traditions that are integral to the distinctive cultures of the Aboriginal peoples concerned and some of which are not. Those activities that are not aspects of practices, customs, and traditions that are integral are "parasitic to the underlying Aboriginal title."[42] Aboriginal title includes mineral rights and the right to exploit the land for oil and gas.[43] However, these rights are not absolute. They must be balanced and are limited by the special nature of the Aboriginal title to the land in question. For example, they must be balanced with the inherent limitation that the lands must not be used in a manner irreconcilable with the intent of Aboriginal title. What this means in practical terms is uncertain.[44]

---

37   *Delgamuukw* v. *British Columbia,* [1998] 1 C.N.L.R. 14 (S.C.C.), para. 87.

38   Ibid., paras. 113–15.

39   Ibid., paras. 117 and 128.

40   Ibid., para. 140; *R.* v. *Van der Peet,* [1996] 4 C.N.L.R. 177 (S.C.C.), para. 46.

41   Ibid., *Delgamuukw* v. *British Columbia,* para. 2.

42   Ibid., para. 111.

43   See also *Blueberry River Indian Band* v. *Canada,* [1996] 2 C.N.L.R. 25 (S.C.C.).

44   *Delgamuukw* v. *British Columbia,* [1998] 1 C.N.L.R. 14 (S.C.C.), para. 122.

Common law Aboriginal title is protected in its complete form by s. 35(1) of the *Constitution Act, 1982.* Aboriginal rights protected by s. 35(1) fall within a spectrum. At one end are those Aboriginal rights that are practices, customs, and traditions that are integral to the distinctive culture of the group claiming a right. However, the occupation and use of the land where the activities are occurring is not sufficient to support a claim of title to the land. Nevertheless, these activities can receive constitutional protection. In the middle of the spectrum there are activities that, out of necessity, take place on land and indeed, might be intimately related to a particular piece of land. Even though an Aboriginal group may not be able to prove title to this land, it may be able to prove a site-specific right to engage in a particular activity. Finally, at the other end of spectrum there is Aboriginal title itself.[45]

An infringement of Aboriginal title, like an infringement of Aboriginal rights generally, must be justified. In *Delgamuukw,* Lamer C.J. summarizes the law in this regard. First, the infringement of an Aboriginal right must be in pursuit of a legislative objective that is compelling and substantive. Lamer C.J. cites agricultural development, forestry, mining, hydroelectric development, economic development generally, protection of the environment and of endangered species, and infrastructure development as objectives consistent with a valid legislative objective capable of infringing Aboriginal title.[46] In *Gladstone,*[47] the Supreme Court noted that compelling and substantial objectives are those that strike at the purposes behind the recognition and affirmation of Aboriginal rights in s. 35(1). These purposes are "the recognition of the prior occupation of North America by aboriginal peoples or . . . the reconciliation of aboriginal prior occupation with the assertion of sovereignty of the Crown."[48] The list of valid legislative objectives capable of infringing Aboriginal title is so long that the meaning of *Delgamuukw* generally is questionable. The court notes that a case-by-case analysis is required in order to understand that meaning.

The second element of the test to justify an infringement of Aboriginal title is a determination if the infringement is in keeping with the Crown's fiduciary relationship with Aboriginal peoples. The nature of this relationship depends on the "legal and factual context" of each particular case.[49] While the *Sparrow* test of justification applies to Aboriginal title cases, a number of other factors peculiar to Aboriginal title are relevant, namely (1) Aboriginal title is a right to the exclusive use and occupation of land, (2) Aboriginal title provides to the holders of the title the right to choose how the land may be used, subject to the land not being used for purposes that would destroy the land for future generations of Aboriginal people, and (3) the lands to which Aboriginal title apply invariably have an economic element integral to them.

---

45   Ibid., para. 138.

46   Ibid., para. 165.

47   *R.* v. *Gladstone,* [1996] 4 C.N.L.R. 65 (S.C.C.).

48   Ibid., para. 72, as cited in *Delgamuukw,* para. 161.

49   Ibid., para. 56, as cited in *Delgamuukw,* para. 162.

Lamer C.J.'s conclusions to his majority judgment in *Delgamuukw* are reveal-
ing in that he reaffirms that litigation is not necessarily the best route to find solutions to such broad issues as how Aboriginal and non-Aboriginal peoples are to
live together in Canada. He writes:

> By ordering a new trial, I do not necessarily encourage the parties to proceed to litiga-
> tion. . . . [U]ltimately, it is through negotiated settlements, with good faith and give
> and take on all sides, reinforced by judgments of this Court, that we will achieve . . . a
> basic purpose of s. 35(1)—"the reconciliation of the pre-existence of aboriginal soci-
> eties with the sovereignty of the Crown". Let us face it, we are all here to stay.[50]

The Chief Justice's conclusion is quite telling in its purpose and is consistent with
the court's approach in those matters of a particularly political and public policy
nature.[51] Indeed, as in *Sparrow,* the court placed s. 35(1) into a much broader political and public policy realm by suggesting that it "at the least, provides a solid
constitutional base upon which subsequent negotiations can take place."[52] The importance of negotiated settlements, and the court's strong suggestion that these
guide Aboriginal-Crown relations, underscores a fundamental weakness inherent
in the law. Although the law can provide a solid basis upon which societal relations
can be based, the law cannot be used to shape fundamental aspects of society. It is
but a tool to a larger end. Recent jurisprudence from the Supreme Court attempts to
provide signposts to steer the discussions that lie ahead between Aboriginal peoples and their governments and the rest of Canadian society.

The manner by which Aboriginal title must be proven to exist is next for discussion. Issues to consider include whether Aboriginal rights and Aboriginal title
apply only to those activities that are land based. That is, are Aboriginal rights
restricted solely to the use, occupation, enjoyment, and possession of traditional
lands, or can they apply beyond the land base? Clearly, *Delgamuukw* suggests this
may be the case. Examples of issues that do not necessarily require a land base but
yet have been claimed as being Aboriginal rights are gambling and gaming, non-
application of the *Criminal Code,*[53] and the jurisdiction of Aboriginal governments
over those Aboriginal persons not living on an Aboriginal land base such as an
Indian reserve.

PROOF OF ABORIGINAL TITLE

Proving Aboriginal title is becoming more difficult for Aboriginal peoples, primarily because of the Eurocentric definitions attributed to concepts such as "title,"
"ownership," and "beneficial interest." As outlined in the 1979 decision of *Hamlet*

---

50 *Delgamuukw* v. *British Columbia,* [1998] 1 C.N.L.R. 14 (S.C.C.), para. 186.

51 See, for example, *Reference re Amendment of the Constitution of Canada* (the Patriation
Case), [1981] 1 S.C.R. 753, whereby the Supreme Court balanced constitutional convention with strict jurisprudence and recommended a more conciliatory approach to
federal-provincial relations. The result was the repatriated constitution: the *Constitution Act, 1982.*

52 *R.* v. *Sparrow,* [1990] 3 C.N.L.R. 160 at 178 (S.C.C.).

53 *Criminal Code of Canada,* R.S.C. 1985, c. C–46.

of Baker Lake v. *Minister of Indian Affairs and Northern Development*,[54] Canadian courts have adopted a four-part test to establish and prove the existence of Aboriginal title. The four principles outlined in the case, and subsequently adopted by the Supreme Court of Canada, are:

1. membership in an organized society;
2. occupation by the organized society of the specific territory over which Aboriginal title is being claimed;
3. occupation by the organized society was to the exclusion of other organized societies; and
4. that the occupation was an established fact at the time English sovereignty was asserted.

This test for proving Aboriginal title gives rise to numerous questions. How does one define "organized"? Why is "organization" a prerequisite to Aboriginal title? Why must possession be "exclusive"? Why is English sovereignty the critical date for assertion of Aboriginal title? These last two questions could be particularly important for the Métis, who may not meet the time requirement and who did not necessarily occupy their "traditional lands" to the exclusion of others—namely Indians.[55]

The *Calder* decision established that possession of lands is proof for the existence of Aboriginal title and that once established, Aboriginal title is presumed to continue until extinguished. The *Kruger*[56] decision affirmed that in establishing and dealing with the issue of Aboriginal title, each community must be looked at individually and must have its unique situation considered.

In *Delgamuukw,* Lamer C.J. laid out the criteria to make a claim for Aboriginal title.[57] These criteria are (1) prior to sovereignty, the land must have been occupied by the ancestors of the Aboriginal group claiming title, (2) continuity between existing and pre-sovereignty occupation must be demonstrated when existing occupation of the lands in question is being offered as proof of pre-sovereignty occupation, and (3) at the time of sovereignty, the occupation by the Aboriginal group must have been exclusive.[58] The exclusivity of the occupation does not mean that other Aboriginal groups were not present, but rather must take into account the context of the Aboriginal society at sovereignty. Lack of providing exclusivity, however, does not prevent the Aboriginal group from claiming, and indeed establishing, Aboriginal rights. Noticeably missing from this listing is *Baker Lake*'s reference to the need for an "organized society." This, perhaps, is an implicit recognition by the court not to judge the nature of pre-contact Aboriginal governance structures. Occupation, continuity, and exclusivity are enough to make an Aboriginal title claim. The court relied on Australia's *Mabo* decision to conclude that the

---

54 *Hamlet of Baker Lake* v. *Minister of Indian Affairs and Northern Development*, [1979] 3 C.N.L.R. 17 (F.C.T.D.).

55 In *R.* v. *McPherson*, [1992] 4 C.N.L.R. 144 at 151–54, Gregoire J. of the Manitoba Provincial Court applies a test similar to the *Baker Lake* test to Métis rights.

56 *Kruger and Manuel* v. *R.*, 9 C.N.L.C. 136 (S.C.C.).

57 *Delgamuukw* v. *British Columbia,* [1998] 1 C.N.L.R. 14 (S.C.C.), paras. 140–59.

58 Ibid., para.143.

"substantial maintenance of the connection" between the people and the land is a critical relationship when proving Aboriginal title.[59]

EXTINGUISHMENT OF ABORIGINAL TITLE

The ways by which Aboriginal title can be extinguished, other than by express means on the part of Aboriginal peoples or the federal Crown, remain unclear.[60] The excerpts in this chapter seek to identify the circumstances under which Aboriginal title can be extinguished. As the *Royal Proclamation* bears witness, Indians' interest in their lands cannot be extinguished without their "consent." Namely, Indian lands were reserved for Indians until the Indians "should be inclined to dispose of the said lands." *St. Catherine's* makes it clear that Aboriginal title is "dependent upon the goodwill of the Sovereign."[61] Steele J. of the Ontario High Court adopted this reasoning in the *Bear Island* decision when he wrote that Aboriginal title "exists solely at the pleasure of the Crown."[62] In *R. v. Howard*[63] the Supreme Court of Canada held that a treaty is one way by which the Crown can extinguish Aboriginal title.

In *Delgamuukw,* Lamer C.J., writing for the majority of the Supreme Court of Canada, considered the issue of whether or not the province of British Columbia had the power to extinguish Aboriginal rights after 1871, either by way of its own jurisdiction or by the application of s. 88 of the *Indian Act.*[64] Lamer C.J. made it clear that the federal government has had the exclusive jurisdiction to legislate with respect to "Indians and lands reserved for Indians" pursuant to s. 91(24) of the *Constitution Act, 1867* and within that authority is the exclusive power to extinguish Aboriginal title and Aboriginal rights.[65] Noteworthy is that Lamer C.J. only deals with British Columbia's authority to extinguish Aboriginal rights after 1871 when it joined Canada. The issue of whether British Columbia had the authority, as a colonial power, prior to 1871 is not explicitly considered.

ALTERNATIVES TO EXTINGUISHMENT

Traditionally, treaties have required that Indians "cede, release and surrender" (or extinguish) their rights and interests in the land to the Crown in return for specified rights and interests in a treaty. Although this has accomplished a key goal of governments in securing treaties, namely certainty over title and rights, it has been a sore point for First Nations.

In December 1994 Indian and Northern Affairs Minister Ron Irwin appointed the Honourable A.C. Hamilton as an independent fact-finder to analyze alternatives to extinguishment and other means of providing certainty through land claims

---

59   *Delgamuukw* v. *British Columbia,* [1998] 1 C.N.L.R. 14 (S.C.C.), para. 153.

60   *United States* v. *Santa Fe Pacific Railroad,* 314 U.S. 339 (1941) (U.S.S.Ct.).

61   *St. Catherine's Milling and Lumber Co.* v. *R.,* 2 C.N.L.C. 541 (J.C.P.C.) at 549.

62   *Bear Island Foundation* v. *A.-G. of Ontario,* [1985] 1 C.N.L.R. 1 at 28.

63   *R.* v. *Howard,* [1994] 3 C.N.L.R. 146.

64   *Delgamuukw* v. *British Columbia,* [1998] 1 C.N.L.R. 14 (S.C.C.), paras. 172–82.

65   Ibid., para. 173.

agreements.[66] Mr. Hamilton reported back in June 1995 with his report *Canada and Aboriginal Peoples: A New Partnership.*[67] His report provides a number of recommendations that seek to limit the need for extinguishment by way of treaty. For example, he suggests that treaties could recognize that an Aboriginal group possesses Aboriginal rights and that treaties detail, to the best extent possible, the land and resource rights associated with the land in question. A critical aspect of Mr. Hamilton's recommendations is the inclusion of "mutual assurance" clauses in new treaties, which would state that the parties to the treaty would abide by the treaty and would exercise their rights in association with the land affected according to the treaty. A dispute-resolution mechanism would also be included in the treaty.

This novel approach would keep Aboriginal rights intact and, at the same time, provide certainty to the Crown that the rights would be exercised in a particular manner. Nevertheless, this approach would require a fundamental shift with respect to the current and long-standing approach of the federal Crown, which is to extinguish Aboriginal rights when settling a treaty. The Royal Commission apparently also favours a more liberal approach to treaty making and extinguishment.[68]

The *Nisga'a Final Agreement* (initialed on August 4, 1998) deals with alternatives to extinguishment by focusing on the "certainty" the treaty provides. Thus the Nisga'a treaty is the "full and final settlement in respect of the aboriginal rights (and title)" of the Nisga'a (s. 22), the exhaustive setting out of Nisga'a s. 35 rights (s. 23), the embodiment of modifying Nisga'a Aboriginal title (ss. 24 and 25), and, finally, the Nisga'a release of British Columbia and Canada from any Aboriginal rights and title that did exist outside those rights modified in the treaty (ss. 26 and 27).[69]

With more than one hundred years of jurisprudence on Aboriginal title behind us, it is evident that there are many more questions to be answered. This is especially true in light of the fact that to ascertain the nature of Aboriginal title, the particular factual situation must be considered in depth. The Supreme Court of Canada's recent *Delgamuukw* decision has gone a long way to assist in clarifying the nature and meaning of Aboriginal title. However, although the court's decision has been helpful, it did not deal with the practical issues of what to do with Aboriginal title in a modern capitalistic society. Rather the court sent the issue back to trial, which will only delay the resolution of the issue and cost even more money and resources. The court's decisions in *Delgamuukw* and in other cases have created a body of law that is extremely complex and in many instances sends conflicting messages. Indeed, the law in this regard has become so complex that perhaps the best thing *Delgamuukw* has done is to demonstrate that the law cannot solve basic societal problems, such as the relations between two groups of peoples and their

---

66   See also M. Asch and N. Zlotkin, "Affirming Aboriginal Title: A New Basis for Comprehensive Claims Negotiations." In M. Asch, ed., *Aboriginal and Treaty Rights in Canada* (Vancouver: U.B.C. Press, 1997), 208.

67   Ottawa: Public Works and Government Services Canada, 1995.

68   See Royal Commission on Aboriginal Peoples, *Report of the Royal Commission on Aboriginal Peoples,* vol. 2 (Ottawa: RCAP, 1996), 44–47.

69   See chapter 2, pp. 130–133.

respective rights, and that negotiated settlements, based on good faith and fairness, are the only reasonable solution.

■ CASES AND MATERIALS

ABORIGINAL TITLE

1. *Royal Proclamation of 1763*, R.S.C. 1985, App. II, No. 1

The *Royal Proclamation of 1763* recognizes the right of Indians to unceded lands in their possession and evidences that such rights can only be ceded to the Crown. The *Royal Proclamation* is recognized explicitly in s. 25 of the *Canadian Charter of Rights and Freedoms* whereby the guarantee of certain rights and freedoms in the *Charter* shall not be interpreted so as to "abrogate or derogate" from Aboriginal or treaty rights including "any rights or freedoms recognized by the *Royal Proclamation of October 7, 1763*." There is also a substantial body of case law to suggest that the *Royal Proclamation* has the force of law in Canada. Yet, as important as the *Royal Proclamation* has been in the development of Aboriginal jurisprudence, strictly speaking, it is "an Executive Order having the force and effect of an Act of Parliament" (see *Calder* v. *A.G.B.C.,* 7 C.N.L.C. 91 at 150). Thus, on its face, it could be repealed by the Parliament of Canada, thereby underscoring the necessity for Aboriginal rights to have a basis in law not solely dependent upon the *Royal Proclamation,* which they do in s. 35 of the *Constitution Act, 1982.*

The following is an excerpt from the *Royal Proclamation* that deals specifically with Indian peoples.

October 7, 1763

BY THE KING, A PROCLAMATION

GEORGE R.

AND whereas it is just and reasonable, and essential to our Interest, and the security of our Colonies, that the several Nations or Tribes of Indians with whom We are connected, and who live under our protection, should not be molested or disturbed in the Possession of such Parts of Our Dominions and Territories as, not having been ceded to or purchased by Us, are reserved to them or any of them, as their Hunting Grounds—We do therefore, with the Advice of our Privy Council, declare it to be our Royal Will and Pleasure, that no Governor or Commander in Chief in any of our Colonies of Quebec, East Florida, or West Florida, do presume, upon any Pretence whatever, to grant Warrants of Survey, or pass any Patents for Lands beyond the Bounds of their respective Governments, as described in their Commissions; as also that no Governor or Commander in Chief in any of our other Colonies or Plantations in America do presume for the present, and until our further Pleasure be Known, to grant warrants of Survey, or pass Patents for any Lands beyond the Heads or Sources of any of the Rivers which fall into the Atlantic Ocean from the West and North West, or upon any Lands whatever, which, not having been ceded to or purchased by Us as aforesaid, are reserved to the said Indians, or any of them.

And We do further declare it to be Our Royal Will and Pleasure, for the present as aforesaid, to reserve under our Sovereignty, Protection, and Dominion, for the use of the said Indians, all the Lands and Territories not included within the Limits of Our Said New Governments, or within the Limits of the Territory granted to the Hudson's Bay Company, as also all the Lands and Territories lying to the Westward of the Sources of the Rivers which fall into the Sea from the West and North West as aforesaid:

And We do hereby strictly forbid, on Pain of our Displeasure, all our loving subjects from making any Purchase or Settlements whatever, or taking Possession of any of the Lands above reserved, without our especial leave and Licence for the Purpose First obtained.

And, We do further strictly enjoin and require all Persons whatever who have either wilfully or inadvertently seating themselves upon any Lands within the Countries above described, or upon any other Lands which, not having been ceded to or purchased by Us, are still reserved to the said Indians as aforesaid, forthwith to remove themselves from such Settlements.

And Whereas Great Frauds and Abuses have been committed in purchasing Lands of the Indians, to the Great Prejudice of our Interests, and to the Great Dissatisfaction of the said Indians; In Order, therefore, to prevent such Irregularities for the future, and to the End that the Indians may be convinced of our Justice and determined Resolution to remove all reasonable Cause of Discontent, We do, with the Advice of our Privy Council, strictly enjoin and require, that no private Person do presume to make any Purchase from the said Indians of any Lands reserved to the said Indians, within those parts of our Colonies where, We have thought proper to allow Settlement; but that, if at any Time any of the said Indians should be inclined to dispose of the said Lands, the same shall be Purchased only for Us, in our Name, at some public Meeting or Assembly of the said Indians, to be held for the Purpose of the Governor or Commander in Chief of our Colony respectively within which they shall lie; and in case they shall lie within the limits of any Proprietary Government, they shall be purchased only for the Use and in the name of such Proprietaries, conformable to such Directions and Instructions as We or they shall think proper to give for the Purpose; And We do, by the Advice of our Privy Council, declare and enjoin, that the Trade with the said Indians shall be free and open to all our Subjects whatever, provided that every Person who may incline to Trade with the said Indians do take out a Licence for carrying on such Trade from the Governor or Commander in Chief of any of our Colonies respectively where such Person shall reside, and also give Security to observe such Regulations as We shall at any Time think fit, by ourselves or by our Commissaries to be appointed for this Purpose, to direct and appoint for the Benefit of the said Trade:

And We do hereby authorize, enjoin, and require the Governors and Commanders in Chief of all our Colonies respectively, as well those under Our immediate Government as those under the Government and Direction of Proprietaries, to grant such Licences without Fee or Regard, taking especial care to insert therein a Condition, that such Licence shall be void, and the Security forfeited in the case the Person to whom the same is granted shall refuse or neglect to observe such Regulations as We shall think proper to prescribe as aforesaid.

And We do further expressly enjoin and require all Officers whatever, as well Military as those Employed in the Management and Direction of Indian Affairs, within the Territories reserved as aforesaid for the Use of the said Indians, to seize and apprehend all Persons whatever, who standing charged with Treason, Misprisons of Treason, Murders, or other Felonies or Misdemeanors, shall fly from Justice and take Refuge in the said Territory, and to send them under a proper Guard to the Colony where the Crime was committed of which they stand accused, in order to take their Trial for the same.

Given at our Court at St. James's the 7th Day of October, 1763, in the Third Year of our Reign.

GOD SAVE THE KING

2.   *Johnson and Graham's Lessee* v. *M'Intosh*, (1823), 8 Wheaton 543 (U.S.S. Ct.). Marshall C.J.

> This leading American decision deals with the origins and nature of Aboriginal title and has been cited with approval by many Canadian courts. The issue in the case is whether the title passed in a land grant by certain Indian chiefs was recognizable under American law. Chief Justice Marshall develops an alternative to the doctrines of conquest and settlement to support the non-Aboriginal attainment of North America. His "discovery" doctrine left the Aboriginal right to occupation intact and made this encumbrance on the land alienable only by the Crown. In the end, the judgment supports the ultimate title of the United States to the detriment of the Illinois and Piankeshaw Indian Nations.

MR. CHIEF JUSTICE MARSHALL delivered the opinion of the court:—The plaintiffs in this cause claim the land, in their declaration mentioned, under two grants, purporting to be made, the first in 1773, and the last in 1775, by the chiefs of certain Indian tribes, constituting the Illinois and the Piankeshaw nations; and the question is, whether this title can be recognized in the courts of the United States?

The facts as stated in the case agreed, show the authority of the chiefs who executed this conveyance, so far as it could be given by their own people; and likewise show that the particular tribes for whom these chiefs acted were in rightful possession of the land they sold. The inquiry, therefore, is, in a great measure, confined to the power of the Indians to give, and of private individuals to receive, a title which can be sustained in the courts of this country.

As the right of society to prescribe those rules by which property may be acquired and preserved is not, and cannot be drawn into question; as the title to lands, especially, is and must be admitted to depend entirely on the law of the nation in which they lie; it will be necessary, in pursuing this inquiry, to examine, not singly those principles of abstract justice, which the Creator of all things has impressed on the mind of his creature man, and which are admitted to regulate, in a great degree, the rights of civilized nations, whose perfect independence is acknowledged; but those principles also which our own government has adopted in the particular case, and given us as the rule for our decision.

On the discovery of this immense continent, the great nations of Europe were eager to appropriate to themselves so much of it as they could respectively acquire. Its vast extent offered an ample field to the ambition and enterprise of all; and the character and religion of its inhabitants afforded an apology for considering them as a people over whom the superior genius of Europe might claim an ascendency.

The potentates of the old world found no difficulty in convincing themselves that they made ample compensation to the inhabitants of the new, by bestowing on them civilization and Christianity, in exchange for unlimited independence. But, as they were all in pursuit of nearly the same object, it was necessary, in order to avoid conflicting settlements, and consequent war with each other, to establish a principle which all should acknowledge as the law by which the right of acquisition, which they all asserted, should be regulated as between themselves. This principle was that discovery gave title to the government by whose subjects, or by whose authority, it was made, against all other European governments, which title might be consummated by possession.

The exclusion of all other Europeans, necessarily gave to the nation making the discovery the sole right of acquiring the soil from the natives, and establishing settlements upon it. It was a right with which no Europeans could interfere. It was a right which all asserted for themselves, and to the assertion of which, by others, all assented.

Those relations which were to exist between the discoverer and the natives, were to be regulated by themselves. The rights thus acquired being exclusive, no other power could interpose between them.

In the establishment of these relations, the rights of the original inhabitants were, in no instance, entirely disregarded; but were necessarily, to a considerable extent, impaired. They were admitted to be the rightful occupants of the soil, with a legal as well as just claim to retain possession of it, and to use it according to their own discretion; but their rights to complete sovereignty, as independent nations, were necessarily diminished, and their power to dispose of the soil as their own will, to whomsoever they pleased, was denied by the original fundamental principle that discovery gave exclusive title to those who made it.

While the different nations of Europe respected the right of the natives, as occupants, they asserted the ultimate dominion to be in themselves; and claimed and exercised as a consequence of this ultimate dominion, a power to grant the soil, while yet in possession of the natives. These grants have been understood by all to convey a title to the grantees, subject only to the Indian right of occupancy.

The history of America, from its discovery to the present day, proves, we think, the universal recognition of these principles. . . .

The United States, then, have unequivocally acceded to that great and broad rule by which its civilized inhabitants now hold this country. They hold, and assert in themselves, the title by which it was acquired. They maintain, as all other have maintained, that discovery gave an exclusive right to extinguish the Indian title of occupancy, either by purchase or by conquest; and gave also a right to such a degree of sovereignty as the circumstances of the people would allow them to exercise.

The power now possessed by the government of the United States to grant lands, resided, while we were colonies, in the crown, or its grantees. The validity of the titles given by either has never been questioned in our courts. It has been exercised uniformly over territory in possession of the Indians. The existence of this power must negative the existence of any right which may conflict with, and control it. An absolute title to lands cannot exist, at the same time, in different persons, or in different governments. An absolute, must be an exclusive title, or at least a title which excludes all others not compatible with it. All our institutions recognize the absolute title of the crown, subject only to the Indian right of occupancy, and recognized the absolute title of the crown to extinguish that right. This is incompatible with an absolute and complete title in the Indians.

We will not enter into the controversy, whether agriculturists, merchants, and manufacturers, have a right, on abstract principles, to expel hunters from the territory they possess, or to contract their limits. Conquest gives a title which the courts of the conqueror cannot deny, whatever the private and speculative opinions of individuals may be, respecting the original justice of the claim which has been successfully asserted. The British government, which was then our government, and whose rights have passed to the United States, asserted a title to all the lands occupied by Indians within the chartered limits of the British colonies. It asserted also a limited sovereignty over them, and the exclusive right of extinguishing the title which occupancy gave to them. These claims have been maintained and established as far west as the river Mississippi, by the sword. The title to a vast portion of the lands we now hold, originates in them. It is not for the courts of this country to question the validity of this title, or to sustain one which is incompatible with it.

Although we do not mean to engage in the defense of those principles which Europeans have applied to Indian title, they may, we think, find some excuse, if not justification, in the character and habits of the people whose rights have been wrested from them.

The title by conquest is acquired and maintained by force. The conqueror prescribes its limits. Humanity, however, acting on public opinion, has established, as a general rule, that the conquered shall not be wantonly oppressed, and that their condition shall remain as eligible as is compatible with the objects of the conquest. Most usually they are incorporated with the victorious nation and become subjects or citizens of the government with which they are connected. The new and old members of the society mingle with each other; the distinction between them is gradually lost, and they make one people. Where this incorporation is practicable, humanity demands, and a wise policy requires, that the rights of the conquered to property should remain unimpaired; that the new subjects should be governed as equitably as the old, and that confidence in their security should gradually banish the painful sense of being separated from the ancient connections, and united by force to strangers.

When the conquest is complete, and the conquered inhabitants can be blended with the conquerors, or safely governed as a distinct people, public opinion, which not even the conqueror can disregard, imposes these restraints upon him; and he cannot neglect them without injury to his fame, and hazard to his power.

But the tribes of Indians inhabiting this country were fierce savages, whose occupation was war, and whose subsistence was drawn chiefly from the forest. To leave them in possession of their country was to leave the country a wilderness; to govern them as a distinct people was impossible, because they were as brave and high spirited as they were fierce, and were ready to repel by arms every attempt on their independence.

What was the inevitable consequences of this state of things? The Europeans were under the necessity either of abandoning the country, and relinquishing their pompous claims to it, or of enforcing those claims by the sword, and by the adoption of principles adapted to the condition of a people with whom it was impossible to mix, and who could not be governed as a distinct society, or of remaining in their neighborhood and exposing themselves and their families to the perpetual hazard of being massacred.

Frequent and bloody wars, in which the whites were not always the aggressors, unavoidably ensued. European policy, numbers and skill, prevailed. As the white population advanced, that of the Indians necessarily receded. The country in the immediate neighborhood of the agriculturalists became unfit for them. The game fled into thicker and more unbroken forests, and the Indians followed. The soil, to which the crown originally claimed title, being no longer occupied by its ancient inhabitants, was parcelled out accordingly to the will of the sovereign power, and taken possession of by persons who claimed immediately from the crown, or mediately, through its grantees or deputies.

That law which regulates, and ought to regulate in general, the relations between the conqueror and conquered, was incapable of application to a people under such circumstances. The resort to some new and different rule, better adapted to the actual state of things, was unavoidable. Every rule which can be suggested will be found to be attended with great difficulty.

However extravagant the pretension of converting the discovery of an inhabited country into conquest may appear, if the principle has been asserted in the first instance, and afterwards sustained; if a country has been acquired and held under it; if the property of the great mass of the community originates in it, it becomes the law of the land, and cannot be questioned. So, too, with respect to the concomitant principle, that the Indian inhabitants are to be considered merely as occupants, to be protected, indeed, while in peace, in the possession of their lands, but to be deemed incapable of transferring the absolute title to others. However this restriction may be opposed to natural right, and to the usages of civilized nations, yet, if it be indispensable to that system under which the country has been settled, and be adapted to the actual condition of the two people, it may, perhaps be supported by reason, and certainly cannot be rejected by courts of justice. . . .

According to the theory of the British constitution, all vacant lands are vested in the crown, as representing the nation; and the exclusive power to grant them is admitted to reside in the crown, as a branch of the royal prerogative. It has been already shown that this principle was as fully recognized in America as in the island of Great Britain. All the lands we hold were originally granted by the crown; and the establishment of a regal government has never been considered as impairing its right to grant lands within the chartered limits of such colony. In addition to the proof of this principle, furnished by the immense grants, already mentioned, of lands lying within the chartered limits of Virginia, the continuing right of the crown to grant lands lying within that colony was always admitted. A title might be obtained, either by making an entry with the surveyor of a county, in pursuance of law, or by an order of the governor-in-council, who was the deputy of the King, or by an immediate grant from the crown. In Virginia, therefore, as well as elsewhere in the British dominions, the complete title of the crown to vacant lands was acknowledged.

So far as respected the authority of the crown, no distinction was taken between vacant lands and lands occupied by the Indians. The title, subject only to the right of occupancy by the Indians, was admitted to be in the King, as was his right to grant that title. The lands, then, to which this proclamation referred, were lands which the King has a right to grant, or to reserve for the Indians.

According to the theory of the British constitution, the royal prerogative is very extensive so far as respects the political relations between Great Britain and foreign nations. The peculiar situation of the Indians, necessarily considered in some respects, as a dependent, and in some respects as a distinct people, occupying a country claimed by Great Britain, and yet too powerful and brave not to be dreaded as formidable enemies, required that means should be adopted for the preservation of peace, and that their friendship should be secured by quieting their alarms for their property. This was to be effected by restraining the encroachments of the whites; and the power to do this was never, we believe, denied, the colonies to the crown. . . .

It has never been contended that the Indian title amounted to nothing. Their right of possession has never been questioned. The claim of government extends to the complete ultimate title, charged with this right of possession, and to the exclusive power of acquiring that right. The object of the crown was to settle the sea-coast of America; and when a portion of it was settled, without violating the rights of others, by persons professing their loyalty, and soliciting the royal sanction of an act, the consequences of which were ascertained to be beneficial, it would have been as unwise as ungracious to expel them from their habitations because they had obtained the Indian title otherwise than through the agency of government. The very grant of a charter is an assertion of the title of the crown, and its words convey the same idea. The country granted is said to be "our island called Rhode Island;" and the charter contains an actual grant of the soil, as well as of the powers of government. . . .

After bestowing on this subject a degree of attention which was more required by the magnitude of the interest in litigation, and the able and elaborate arguments of the bar, than by its intrinsic difficulty, the court is decidedly of opinion that the plaintiffs do not exhibit a title which can be sustained in courts of the United States, and that there is no error in the judgment which was rendered against them in the District Court of Illinois.

Judgment affirmed with costs.

3.   *Worcester* v. *Georgia*, (1832), 31 U.S. 530 (U.S.S. Ct.). Marshall C.J.

> In this decision, the plaintiff was charged under a law of Georgia for residing in the Cherokee Nation without a licence from the governor of the state. The plaintiff claimed that he was not subject to the laws of the state because of certain treaties made between the United States and the Cherokee Nation by which the territory they then inhabited was guaranteed to them.
>
> The laws of Georgia were declared not to apply to Cherokee territory. The decision means that the Indian nations in question were independent with land rights and their own political systems and laws but were still under the protection of the Crown. The decision has been cited frequently by Canadian courts as jurisprudential evidence of Indian tribes being self-governing entities, and it underscores the existence of Indian title. This decision was cited with approval by the Supreme Court of Canada in *R. v. Sioui*, [1990] 3 C.N.L.R. 127 at 146.

MR. CHIEF JUSTICE MARSHALL delivered the opinion of the court:— . . . But power, war, conquest, give rights, which after possession, are conceded by the world; and which can never be controverted by those on whom they descend. We proceed, then, to the actual state of things, having glanced at their origin, because holding it in our recollection might shed some light on existing pretensions.

The great maritime powers of Europe discovered and visited different parts of this continent at nearly the same time. The object was too immense for any one of them to grasp the whole, and the claimants were too powerful to submit to the exclusive or unreasonable pretensions of any single potentate. To avoid bloody conflicts, which might terminate disastrously to all, it was necessary for the nations of Europe to establish some principle which all would acknowledge, and which should decide their respective rights as between themselves. This principle, suggested by the actual state of things, was, "that discovery gave title to the government by whose subjects or by whose authority it was made, against all other European governments, which title might be consummated by possession." 8 Wheaton 573.

This principle, acknowledged by all Europeans, because it was the interest of all to acknowledge it, gave to the nation making the discovery, as its inevitable consequence, the sole right of acquiring the soil and of making settlements on it. It was an exclusive principle which shut out the right of competition among those who had agreed to it; not one which could annul the previous rights of those who had not agreed to it. It regulated the right given by discovery among the European discoverers, but could not affect the rights of those already in possession, either as aboriginal occupants, or as occupants by virtue of a discovery made before the memory of man. It gave the exclusive right to purchase, but did not found that right on a denial of the right of the possessor to sell.

The relation between the Europeans and the natives was determined in each case by the particular government which asserted and could maintain this preemptive privilege in the particular place. The United States succeeded to all the claims of Great Britain, both territorial and political; but no attempt, so far as is known, has been made to enlarge them. So far as they existed merely in theory, or were in their nature only exclusive of the claims of other European nations, they still retain their original character, and remain dormant. So far as they have been practically exerted, they exist in fact, are understood by both parties, are asserted by the one, and admitted by the other. . . .

The Indian nations had always been considered as distinct, independent political communities, retaining their original natural rights, as the undisputed possessors of the soil from time immemorial, with the single exception of that imposed by irresistible power, which excluded them from intercourse with any other European potentate than the first discoverer of the coast of the particular region claimed: and this was a restriction which those European potentates imposed on themselves, as well as on the Indians. The very term "nation," so generally applied to them, means "a people distinct from others." The Constitution, by declaring treaties already made, as well as those to be made, to be the supreme law of the land, has adopted and sanctioned the previous treaties with the Indian nations, and consequently admits their rank among those powers who are capable of making treaties.

The words "treaty" and "nation" are words of our own language, selected in our diplomatic and legislative proceedings, by ourselves, having each a definite and well understood meaning. We have applied them to Indians, as we have applied them to the other nations of the earth. They are applied to all in the same sense. . . .

The Cherokee nation, then, is a distinct community, occupying its own territory, with boundaries accurately described, in which the laws of Georgia can have no force, and which the citizens of Georgia have no right to enter but with the assent of the Cherokees themselves or in conformity with treaties and with the acts of Congress. The whole intercourse between the United States and this nation is, by our Constitution and laws, vested in the government of the United States.

The act of the State of Georgia under which the plaintiff in error was prosecuted is consequently void, and the judgment a nullity. . . .

4.   *Connolly* v. *Woolrich*, 1 C.N.L.C. 70, (1867), 11 L.C. Jur. 197, 17 R.J.R.Q. 75 (Que. S.C.), Monk, J., July 9, 1867; affirmed in result in *Johnstone et al.* v. *Connolly*, 1 C.N.L.C. 151 (Que. C.A.(Q.B.))

> *Connolly* v. *Woolrich* was one of the first and few early Canadian decisions that took the same expansive approach outlined in *Worcester* v. *Georgia.* At issue was whether the common law could recognize a Cree customary marriage. Monk J. concluded that the customary marriage was recognizable at common law and therefore valid. He made his conclusion based, in part, on the premise that the Indians' laws, customs, and political and legislative rights were in full force and applicable. Although the appeal court upheld the verdict, they did not affirm, to the same degree as the trial court, the degree to which Indian laws were applicable. The excerpt below is from the trial decision.

MONK, J.— . . . [E]ven admitting, for the sake of argument, the existence prior to the Charter of Charles, of the common law of France, and that of England, at these two trading posts …yet it will be contended that the territorial rights, political organization such as it was, or the laws and usages of the Indian tribes, were abrogated - that they ceased to exist when those two European nations began to trade with the aboriginal inhabitants? In my opinion, it is beyond controversy that they did not—that so far from being abolished, they were left in full force, and were not even modified in the slightest degree in regard to the civil rights of the natives.

. . . I have no hesitation in saying that . . . the Indian political and territorial rights, laws and usages remained in full force—both at Athabaska and in the Hudson Bay region, previous to the Charter of 1670, and even after that date. . . .

The Charter did introduce the English law, but did not, at the same time, make it applicable generally or indiscriminately—it did not abrogate the Indian laws and usages. The Crown has not done so. . . .

5.   *Johnstone et al.* v. *Connolly*, 1 C.N.L.C. 151 (Que. C.A. (Q.B.)). Duval, C.J., Caron, Badgley, Loranger, and McKay, JJ., September 8, 1869

> The following brief excerpt is the appeal decision arising from *Connolly* v. *Woolrich*.

BADGLEY, J. — . . . It is plain, therefore, that neither the common nor the statutory enactments of England and Great Britain, had any footing in Rebaska, in 1803, or before or since that time. It is also true to say that the law of England could not legally be introduced or enforced as the law of even conquered countries, by the mere power of the prerogative, much less could it be so into countries which were neither ceded nor conquered. It is true that conquest gives a title which the courts of conqueror cannot deny, whatever may be the speculative opinion of individuals, respecting the original justice of the claim which has been successfully asserted. But, although this title is acquired and maintained by force, humanity, resting on public opinion, has prescribed rules and limits, by which it may be governed, and, hence it is very unusual, even in case of conquest, to do more than displace the former Sovereign, and assume dominion over the conquered country, as in the instance of this country, and its cession by France. The modern usage by nations would be violated if private property should be confiscated and private rights annulled. Therefore the relations of the people to their ancient sovereign or government are dissolved, but the relations to each other, and their customs and usages remain undisturbed.

. . . The legislative power alone can change the local law, and substitute, by its mere power, some other, but, even the legislature, would not exercise that power over countries where the local nations have been left in territorial possession, as the Crees of Rebaska. There is nothing to show that the Indian title of the Crees, in the Rebaska territory, has ever been interfered with, or set aside. . . . It is unquestionable that the law of England, common or statutory, was never introduced or established, even by implication, beyond the area of the company's territorial grant; it certainly did not control the Indians of the Cree nation, outside of that area. . . .

6. *St. Catherine's Milling and Lumber Company* v. *R.*, 2 C.N.L.C. 541 (J.C.P.C.). The Earl of Selborne, Lord Watson, Lord Hobhouse, Sir Barnes Peacock, Sir Montague E. Smith, and Sir Richard Couch, December 12, 1888

> *St. Catherine's Milling* was the first decision to discuss substantively the effects and meaning of the *Royal Proclamation of 1763*. The Judicial Committee of the Privy Council held that Aboriginal title is a burden on the Crown, even though the Crown holds the underlying or radical title to the lands. Indians have a "personal and usufructory" right of occupancy to the lands and may surrender this title only to the federal Crown. As well, the court focuses its decision on the source of Aboriginal title flowing exclusively from the *Royal Proclamation,* an argument that was later rejected in *Calder* and other Supreme Court of Canada decisions. This decision bears a resemblance to the reasoning made by the United States Supreme Court in its decision of *Johnson and Graham's Lessee* v. *M'Intosh* (1823), 8 Wheaton 543 (U.S.S. Ct.).

The judgment of their Lordships was delivered by LORD WATSON:—On the 3rd of October, 1873, a formal treaty or contract was concluded between commissioners appointed by the Government of the Dominion of Canada, on behalf of Her Majesty the Queen, of the one part, and a number of chiefs and headmen duly chosen to represent the Salteaux tribe of Ojibbeway Indians, of the other part, by which the latter, for certain considerations, released and surrendered to the Government of the Dominion, for Her Majesty and her successors, the whole right and title of the Indian inhabitants whom they represented, to a tract of country upwards of 50,000 square miles in extent. By an article of the treaty it is stipulated that, subject to such regulations as may be made by the Dominion Government, the Indians are to have right to pursue their avocations of hunting and fishing throughout the surrendered territory, with the exception of those portions of it which may, from time to time, be required or taken up for settlement, mining, lumbering, or other purposes.

Of the territory thus ceded to the Crown, an area of not less than 32,000 square miles is situated within the boundaries of the Province of Ontario; and, with respect to that area, a controversy has arisen between the Dominion and Ontario, each of them maintaining that the legal effect of extinguishing the Indian title has been to transmit to itself the entire beneficial interest of the lands, as now vested in the Crown, freed from incumbrance of any kind, save the qualified privilege of hunting and fishing mentioned in the treaty.

Acting on the assumption that the beneficial interest in these lands had passed to the Dominion Government, their Crown Timber Agent, on the 1st of May, 1883, issued to the appellants, the St. Catherine's Milling and Lumber Company, a permit to cut and carry away one million feet of lumber from a specified portion of the disputed area. The appellants having availed themselves of that licence, a writ was filed against them in the Chancery Division of the High Court of Ontario, at the instance of the Queen on the information of the Attorney-General of the Province, praying—(1) a declaration that the appellants have no rights in respect of the timber cut by them upon the lands specified in their permit; (2) an injunction restraining them from trespassing on the premises and from cutting any timber thereon; (3) an injunction against the removal of timber already cut; and (4) decree for the damage occasioned by their wrongful acts. . . .

The territory in dispute has been in Indian occupation from the date of the proclamation until 1873. During that interval of time Indian affairs have been administered successively by the Crown, by the Provincial Governments, and (since the passing of the British North America Act, 1867), by the Government of the Dominion. The policy of these administrations has been all along the same in this respect, that the Indian inhabitants have been precluded from entering into any transaction with a subject for the sale or transfer of their interest in the land, and have only been permitted to surrender their rights to the Crown by a formal contract, duly ratified in a meeting of their chiefs or head men convened for the purpose. Whilst there have been changes in the administrative authority, there has been no change since the year 1763 in the character of the interest which its Indian inhabitants had in the lands surrendered by the treaty. Their possession, such as it was, can only be ascribed to the general provisions made by the royal proclamation in favour of all Indian tribes then living under the sovereignty and protection of the British Crown. It was suggested in the course of the argument for the Dominion, that inasmuch as the proclamation recites that the territories thereby reserved for Indians had never "been ceded to or purchased by" the Crown, the entire property of the land remained with them. That inference is, however, at variance with the terms of the instrument, which shew that the tenure of the Indians was a personal and usufructuary right, dependent upon the good will of the Sovereign. The lands reserved are expressly stated to be "parts of Our dominions and territories;" and it is declared to be the will and pleasure of the sovereign that, "for the present," they shall be reserved for the use of the Indians, as their hunting grounds, under his protection and dominion. There was a great deal of learned discussion at the Bar with respect to the precise quality of the Indian right, but their lordships do not consider it necessary to express any opinion upon the point. It appears to them to be sufficient for the purposes of this case that there has been all along vested in the Crown a substantial and paramount estate, underlying the Indian title, which became a plenum dominium whenever that title was surrendered or otherwise extinguished.

By an Imperial statute passed in the year 1840 (3 & 4 Vict. c. 35), the provinces of Ontario and Quebec, then known as Upper and Lower Canada, were united under the name of the Province of Canada, and it was, inter alia, enacted that, in consideration of certain annual payments which Her Majesty had agreed to accept by way of civil list, the produce of all territorial and other revenues at the disposal of the Crown arising in either of the united Provinces should be paid into the consolidated fund of the new Province. There was no transfer to the Province of any legal estate in the Crown lands, which continued to be vested in the Sovereign; but all moneys realized by sales or in any other manner became the property of the Province. In other words, all beneficial interest in such lands within the provincial boundaries belong to the Queen, and either producing or capable of producing revenue, passed to the Province, the title still remaining in the Crown. That continued to be the right of the Province until the passing of the British North America Act, 1867. Had the Indian inhabitants of the area in question released their interest in it to the Crown at any time between 1840 and the date of that Act, it does not seem to admit of doubt, and it was not disputed by the learned counsel for the Dominion, that all revenues derived from its being taken up for settlement, mining, lumbering, and other purposes would have been the property of the Province of Canada. The case maintained for the appellants is that the Act of 1867 transferred to the Dominion all interest in Indian lands which previously belonged to the Province.

The Act of 1867, which created the Federal Government, repealed the Act of 1840, and restored the Upper and Lower Canadas to the condition of separate Provinces, under the titles of Ontario and Quebec, due provision being made (sect. 142) for the division between them of the property and assets of the United Province, with the exception of certain items specified in the fourth schedule, which are still held by them jointly. The Act also contains careful provisions for the distribution of legislative powers and of revenues and assets between the respective Provinces included in the Union, on the one hand, and the Dominion, on the other. The conflicting claims to the ceded territory maintained by the Dominion and the Province of Ontario are wholly dependent upon these statutory provisions. In construing these enactments, it must always be kept in view that, wherever public land with its incidents is described as "the property of" or as "belonging to" the Dominion or a Province, these expressions merely import that the right to its beneficial use, or to its proceeds, has been appropriated to the Dominion or the Province, as the case may be, and is subject to the control of its legislature, the land itself being vested in the Crown.

Sect. 108 enacts that the public works and undertakings enumerated in Schedule 3 shall be the property of Canada. As specified in the schedule, these consist of public undertakings which might be fairly considered to exist for the benefit of all the Provinces federally united, of lands and buildings necessary for carrying on the customs or postal service of the Dominion, or required for the purpose of national defence, and of "lands set apart for general public purposes." It is obvious that the enumeration cannot be reasonably held to include Crown lands which are reserved for Indian use. The only other clause in the Act by which a share of what previously constituted provincial revenues and assets is directly assigned to the Dominion is sect. 102. It enacts that all "duties and revenues" over which the respective legislatures of the United Provinces had and have power of appropriation, "except such portions thereof as are by this Act reserved to the respective legislatures of the Provinces, or are raised by them in accordance with the special powers conferred upon them by this Act," shall form one consolidated fund, to be appropriated for the public service of Canada. The extent to which duties and revenues arising within the limits of Ontario, and over which the legislature of the old Province of Canada possessed the power of appropriation before the passing of the Act, have been transferred to the Dominion by this clause, can only be ascertained by reference to the two exceptions which it makes in favour of the new provincial legislatures.

The second of these exceptions has really no bearing on the present case, because it comprises nothing beyond the revenues which provincial legislatures are empowered to raise by means of direct taxation for Provincial purposes, in terms of sect. 92(2). The first of them, which appears to comprehend the whole sources of revenue reserved to the provinces by sect. 109, is of material consequence. Sect. 109 provides that "all lands, mines, minerals, and royalties belonging to the several Provinces of Canada, Nova Scotia, and New Brunswick, at the union, and all sums then due or payable for such lands, mines, minerals, or royalties, shall belong to the several Provinces of Ontario, Quebec, Nova Scotia, and New Brunswick, in which the same are situate or arise, subject to any trusts existing in respect thereof, and to any interest other than that of the Province in the same." In connection with this clause it may be observed that, by sect 117, it is declared that the Provinces shall retain their respective public property not otherwise disposed of in the Act, subject to the right of Canada to assume any lands or public property required for fortifications or for the defence of the country. A different form of expression is used to define the subject-matter of the first exception, and the property which is directly appropriated to the Provinces; but it hardly admits of doubt that the interests in land, mines, minerals, and royalties, which by sect. 109 are declared to belong to the Provinces, include, if they are not identical with, the "duties and revenues" first excepted in sect. 102.

The enactments of sect. 109 are, in the opinion of their Lordships, sufficient to give to each Province, subject to the administration and control of its own Legislature, the entire beneficial interest of the Crown in all lands within its boundaries, which at the time of the union were vested in the Crown, with the exception of such lands as the Dominion acquired right to under sect. 108, or might assume for the purposes specified in sect. 117. Its legal effect is to exclude from the "duties and revenues" appropriated to the Dominion, all the ordinary territorial revenues of the

Crown arising within the Provinces. That construction of the statute was accepted by this Board in deciding *Attorney-General of Ontario* v. *Mercer* (8 App. Cas. 767), where the controversy related to land granted in fee simple to a subject before 1867, which became escheat to the Crown in the year 1871. The Lord Chancellor (Earl Selborne) in delivering judgment in that case, said (8 App. Cas. 776): "It was not disputed, in the argument for the Dominion at the bar, that all territorial revenues arising within each Province from 'lands' (in which term must be comprehended all estates in land), which at the time of the union belonged to the Crown, were reserved to the respective Provinces by sect. 109; and it was admitted that no distinction could, in that respect, be made between lands then ungranted, and lands which had previously reverted to the Crown by escheat. But it was insisted that a line was drawn at the date of the union, and that the words were not sufficient to reserve any lands afterwards escheated which at the time of the union were in private hands, and did not then belong to the Crown. Their Lordships indicated an opinion to the effect that the escheat would not, in the special circumstances of that case, have passed to the Province as "lands;" but they held that it fell within the class of rights reserved to the Provinces as "royalties" by sect. 109.

Had its Indian inhabitants been the owners in fee simple of the territory which they surrendered by the treaty of 1873, *Attorney-General of Ontario* v. *Mercer* (8 App. Cas. 767) might have been an authority for holding that the Province of Ontario could derive no benefit from the cession, in respect that the land was not vested in the Crown at the time of the union. But that was not the character of the Indian interest. The Crown has all along had a present proprietary estate in the land, upon which the Indian title was a mere burden. The ceded territory was at the time of the union, land vested in the Crown, subject to "an interest other than that of the Province in the same," within the meaning of sect. 109; and must now belong to Ontario in terms of that clause, unless its rights have been taken away by some provision of the Act of 1867 other than those already noticed.

In the course of the argument the claim of the Dominion to the ceded territory was rested upon the provisions of sect. 91(24), which in express terms confer upon the Parliament of Canada power to make laws for "Indians, and lands reserved for the Indians." It was urged that the exclusive power of legislation and administration carried with it, by necessary implication, any patrimonial interest which the Crown might have had in the reserved lands. In reply to that reasoning, counsel for Ontario referred us to a series of provincial statutes prior in date to the Act of 1867, for the purpose of shewing that the expression "Indian reserves" was used in legislative language to designate certain lands in which the Indians had, after the royal proclamation of 1763, acquired a special interest, by treaty or otherwise, and did not apply to land occupied by them in virtue of the proclamation. The argument might have deserved consideration if the expression had been adopted by the British Parliament in 1867, but it does not occur in sect. 91(24), and the words actually used are, according to their natural meaning, sufficient to include all lands reserved, upon any terms or conditions, for Indian occupation. It appears to be the plain policy of the Act that, in order to ensure uniformity of administration, all such lands, and Indian affairs generally, shall be under the legislative control of one central authority.

Their Lordships are, however, unable to assent to the argument for the Dominion founded on sect. 92 (24). There can be no a priori probability that the British Legislature, in a branch of the statute which professes to deal only with the distribution of legislative power, intended to deprive the Provinces of rights which are expressly given them in that branch of it which relates to the distribution of revenues and assets. The fact that the power of legislating for Indians, and for lands which are reserved to their use, has been entrusted to the Parliament of the Dominion is not in the least degree inconsistent with the right of the Provinces to a beneficial interest in these lands, available to them as a source of revenue whenever the estate of the Crown is disencumbered of the Indian title.

By the treaty of 1873 the Indian inhabitants ceded and released the territory in dispute, in order that it might be opened up for settlement, immigration, and such other purpose as to Her Majesty might seem fit, "to the Government of the Dominion of Canada," for the Queen and Her successors for ever. It was argued that a cession in these terms was in effect a conveyance to the Dominion Government of the whole rights of the Indians, with consent of the Crown. That is not the natural import of the language of the treaty, which purports to be from beginning to end a transaction between the Indians and the Crown; and the surrender is in substance made to the Crown. Even if its language had been more favourable to the argument of the Dominion upon this point, it is abundantly clear that the commissioners who represented Her Majesty, whilst they had full authority to accept a surrender to the Crown, had neither authority nor power to take away from Ontario the interest which had been assigned to that province by the Imperial Statute of 1867.

These considerations appear to their Lordships to be sufficient for the disposal of this appeal. The treaty leaves the Indians no right whatever to the timber growing upon the lands which they gave up, which is now fully vested in the Crown, all revenues derivable from the sale of such portions of it as are situate within the boundaries of Ontario being the property of that Province. The fact, that it still possesses exclusive power to regulate the Indians' privilege of hunting and fishing, cannot confer upon the Dominion power to dispose, by issuing permits or otherwise, of that beneficial interest in the timber which has now passed to Ontario. Seeing that the benefit of the surrender accrues to her, Ontario must, of course, relieve the Crown, and the Dominion, of all obligations involving the payment of money which were undertaken by Her Majesty, and which are said to have been in part fulfilled by the Dominion Government. There may be other questions behind, with respect to the right to determine to what extent, and at what periods, the disputed territory, over which the Indians still exercise their avocations of hunting and fishing, is to be taken up for settlement or other purposes, but none of these questions are raised for decision in the present suit.

Their Lordships will therefore humbly advise Her Majesty that the judgment of the Supreme Court of Canada ought to be affirmed, and the appeal dismissed. It appears to them that there ought to be no costs of the appeal.

7.   *Calder* v. *Attorney-General of British Columbia*, 7 C.N.L.C. 91 (S.C.C.). Martland, Judson, Ritchie, Hall, Spence, Pigeon, and Laskin JJ., January 31, 1973

Calder is one of the most influential decisions by the Supreme Court of Canada dealing with the issue of Aboriginal title. The Supreme Court's decision was divided and complex. Mr. Justice Judson wrote the decision, with Justices Ritchie and Martland concurring with him, while Mr. Justice Hall wrote a dissenting opinion, with Justices Laskin and Spence concurring with him. Mr. Justice Pigeon, holding the deciding vote on the court, refused to deal with the substantive issue in the case and held that the appeal should be dismissed on the basis of a technicality not directly related to the issue of Aboriginal title.

Although there was disagreement on whether the *Royal Proclamation of 1763* applied in the province of British Columbia, all of the judges, with the exception of Pigeon J., agreed that Aboriginal title existed at common law and continued to exist, unless validly extinguished by the Crown. The court was split on whether or not the title, which the Nisga'a claimed, was extinguished. However, because of Pigeon J.'s dismissal of the appeal on technical grounds, the Nisga'a lost their case. *Calder* affirmed that Aboriginal rights to land exist, that they are not solely dependent upon the *Royal Proclamation* for their existence but rather flow from Aboriginal peoples' traditional use and occupancy of the land, thereby rejecting the notion that the *Royal Proclamation* was the source of Aboriginal rights, as held in *St. Catherine's*. The *Calder* decision is a good example of how courts can influence governments taking action on certain matters. Not long after the *Calder* decision, the federal government, which until then had denied the existence of Aboriginal title, initiated its comprehensive land claims process to settle the issue of Aboriginal title over those tracts of land where Aboriginal title had not been ceded by treaty.

MARTLAND J., concurs with JUDSON J.

JUDSON, J.:—The appellants sue, as representatives of the Nishga Indian Tribe, for a declaration "that the aboriginal title, otherwise known as the Indian title, of the Plaintiffs . . . has never been lawfully extinguished." The action was dismissed at trial. The Court of Appeal rejected the appeal. The appellants appeal from both decisions. . . .

Any Canadian inquiry into the nature of the Indian title must begin with *R.* v. *St. Catherine's Milling & Lumber Co.* v. *The Queen* (1888), 14 App. Cas. 46. . . .

The decision throughout was that the extinction of the Indian title enured to the benefit of the Province and that it was not possible for the Dominion to preserve that title so as to oust the vested right of the Province to the land as part of the public domain of Ontario. It was held that the Crown had at all times a present proprietary estate, which title, after Confederation, was in the Province, by virtue of s. 109 of the *B.N.A. Act*. The Indian title was a mere burden upon that title which, following the cession of the lands under the treaty, was extinguished.

The reasons for judgment delivered in the Canadian Courts in the *St. Catherine's* case were strongly influenced by two early judgments delivered in the Supreme Court of the United States by Chief Justice Marshall—*Johnson and Graham's Lessee* v. *M'Intosh* (1823), 8 Wheaton 543, and *Worcester* v. *State of Georgia* (1832), 6 Peters 515. In *Johnson* v. *M'Intosh* the actual decision was that a title to lands, under grants to private individuals, made by Indian tribes or nations north-west of the river Ohio, in 1773 and 1775, could not be recognized in the Courts of the United States. In *Worcester* v. *Georgia,* the plaintiff, who was a missionary, was charged with residing among the Cherokees without a licence from the State of Georgia. His defence was that his residence was in conformity with treaties between the United States and the Cherokee nation and that the law under which he was charged was repugnant to the constitution, treaties and laws of the United States. The Supreme Court made a declaration to this effect. Both cases raised the question of aboriginal title to land. The following passage from 8 Wheaton at pp. 587–8 gives a clear summary of the views of the Chief Justice:

> The United States, then, have unequivocally acceded to that great and broad rule by which its civilized inhabitants now hold this country. They hold, and assert in themselves, the title by which it was acquired. They maintain, as all others have maintained, that discovery gave an exclusive right to extinguish the Indian title of occupancy, either by purchase or by conquest; and gave also a right to such a degree of sovereignty, as the circumstances of the people would allow them to exercise.
>
> The power now possessed by the government of the United States to grant lands, resided, while we were colonies, in the crown, or its grantees. The validity of the titles given by either has never been questioned in our Courts. It has been exercised uniformly over territory in possession of the Indians. The existence of this power must negative the existence of any right which may conflict with, and control it. An absolute title to lands cannot exist, at the same time in different persons, or in different governments. An absolute, must be an exclusive title, or at least a title which excludes all others not compatible with it. All our institutions recognise the absolute title of the crown, subject only to the Indian right of occupancy, and recognise the absolute title of the crown to extinguish that right. This is incompatible with an absolute and complete title in the Indians.

The description of the nature of Indian title in the Canadian Courts in the *St. Catherine's* case is repeated in the reasons delivered in the Privy Council. . . .

There can be no doubt that the Privy Council [in the *St. Catherine's* case] found that the *Proclamation of 1763* was the origin of the Indian title—"Their possession, such as it was, can only be ascribed to the . . . royal proclamation in favour of all Indian tribes then living under the sovereignty and protection of the British Crown."

I do not take these reasons to mean that the Proclamation was the exclusive source of Indian title. The territory in the *St. Catherine's* appeal was clearly within the geographical limits set out in the Proclamation. It is part of the appellants' case that the Proclamation does apply to the Nishga territory and that they are entitled to its protection. They also say that if it does not apply to the Nishga territory, their Indian title is still entitled to recognition by the Courts. These are two distinct questions.

I say at once that I am in complete agreement with judgments of the British Columbia Courts in this case that the Proclamation has no bearing upon the problem of Indian title in British Columbia. I base my opinion upon the very terms of the Proclamation and its definition of its geographical limits and upon the history of the discovery, settlement and establishment of what is now British Columbia.

Following the Treaty of Paris, General Murray was appointed the first Governor of Quebec. By Royal Proclamation, dated October 7, 1763 [see R.S.C. 1952, vol. VI, p. 6127], which accompanied his commission, he was directed with respect to Indians that he should "upon no account molest or disturb them in the possession of such parts of the said province as they at present occupy or possess".

The Crown created four distinct and separate Governments, styled, respectively, Quebec, East Florida, West Florida and Grenada, specific boundaries being assigned to each of them. Upon the recital that it was just and reasonable that the several nations and tribes of Indians, who lived under British protection, should not be molested or disturbed in the "Possession of such Parts of Our Dominions and Territories as, not having been ceded to or purchased by Us, are reserved to them or any of them, as their Hunting Grounds", it is declared that no Governor or Commander-in-Chief in any of the new Colonies of Quebec, East Florida or West Florida, do presume on any pretence to grant warrants of survey or pass any patents for lands beyond the bounds of their respective Governments or, "until our further Pleasure be Known," upon any lands whatever which, not having been ceded or purchased as aforesaid, are reserved to the said Indians or any of them. It was further declared "to be Our Royal Will and Pleasure, for the present as aforesaid, to reserve under our Sovereignty, Protection, and Dominion, for the use of the said Indians, all the lands and Territories not included . . . within the Limits of the Territory granted to the Hudson's Bay Company". The Proclamation also provides that no private person shall make any purchase from the Indians of lands reserved to them within those Colonies where settlement was permitted, and that all purchases must be on behalf of the Crown, in a public assembly of the Indians, by the Governor or Commander-in-Chief of the Colony in which the lands lie.

It is clear, as the British Columbia Courts have held, and whose reasons I adopt, that the Nishga bands represented by the appellants were not any of the several nations or tribes of Indians who lived under British protection and were outside the scope of the Proclamation. . . .

As to the establishment of British sovereignty in British Columbia in 1818 by a Convention of Commerce between His Majesty and the United States of America, the British Crown and the United States settled the boundary to the height of land in the Rockies, referred to in the Convention as the "Stoney Mountains". The boundary was the 49th parallel of latitude. The Convention provided for the joint occupancy of the lands to the west of that point for a term of 10 years. This Convention was extended indefinitely by a further Convention in 1827.

The area in question in this action never did come under British sovereignty until the Treaty of Oregon in 1846. This treaty extended the boundary along the 49th parallel from the point of termination, as previously laid down, to the channel separating the Continent from Vancouver Island, and thus through the Gulf Islands to Fuca's Straits. The Oregon Treaty was, in effect, a treaty of cession whereby American claims were ceded to Great Britain. There was no mention of Indian rights in any of these Conventions or the treaty.

As to establishment of the northern boundary of what became British Columbia, the Courts below relied on the evidence of Dr. Willard Ireland, Provincial Archivist, who had published a work on the evolution of the boundaries of the Province. He begins with the Imperial ukase of the Czar, dated September 16, 1821, asserting exclusive rights of trade on the Pacific coast as far south as the 51st parallel. There was opposition to this pretension immediately both from Great Britain and the United States. The United States proposed a tri-partite treaty under the terms of which no settlements should be made by Russia south of 55 degrees, by the United States north of 51 degrees or by Great Britain north of 55 degrees or south of 51 degrees. The United States was prepared, if necessary, to accept the

49th parallel as the northern limit for its settlements. This proposal was rejected by the British Government, which preferred to negotiate separately with Russia and the United States. The discussions with Russia culminated in the Convention of February 28, which laid down a line of demarcation.

It was the opinion of Dr. Ireland that although the exact interpretation of these terms became a matter of serious dispute after Russian America was purchased by the United States, this Convention, broadly speaking, established the boundary as it exists today between Canada and Alaska. In other words, it determined the northern limit of British territory on the Pacific coast.

The Colony of Vancouver Island was established by the British Crown in 1849. James Douglas was appointed Governor in 1851. The Colony of British Columbia, being the mainland of what is now the Province, was established by the British Crown in 1858 and the same James Douglas was the first Governor of the Colony with full executive powers. Douglas remained Governor of both Colonies until 1864. On November 17, 1866, the two Colonies were united as one Colony under the British Crown and under the name of British Columbia. This Colony entered Confederation on July 20, 1871, and became the Province of British Columbia and part of the Dominion of Canada.

When the Colony of British Columbia was established in 1858, there can be no doubt that the Nishga territory became part of it. The fee was in the Crown in right of the Colony until July 20, 1871, when the Colony entered Confederation, and thereafter in the Crown in light of the Province of British Columbia, except only in respect of those lands transferred to the Dominion under the Terms of Union. . . .

Although I think that it is clear that Indian title in British Columbia cannot owe its origin to the *Proclamation of 1763,* the fact is that when the settlers came, the Indians were there, organized in societies and occupying the land as their fore-fathers had done for centuries. This is what Indian title means and it does not help one in the solution of this problem to call it a "personal or usufructuary right". What they are asserting in this action is that they had a right to continue to live on their lands as their forefathers had lived and that this right has never been lawfully extinguished. There can be no question that this right was "dependent on the good-will of the Sovereign".

It was the opinion of the British Columbia Courts that this right, if it ever existed, had been lawfully extinguished, that with two societies in competition for land—the white settlers demanding orderly settlement and the Indians demanding to be let alone—the proper authorities deliberately chose to set apart reserves for Indians in various parts of the territory and open up the rest for settlements. They held that this had been done when British Columbia entered Confederation in 1871 and that the Terms of Union recognized this fact. . . .

From what I have already said, it is apparent that before 1871 there were no treaties between the Indian tribes and the Colony relating to lands on the mainland. From the material filed, it appears that on Vancouver Island there were, in all, fourteen purchases of Indian lands in the area surrounding Fort Victoria. These are the ones referred to in the correspondence between James Douglas and the Colonial Office. In 1899, Treaty 8 was negotiated and certain tribes of northeastern British Columbia were grouped with the Cree, Beaver, Chipewyan, Alberta and

Northwest Territories' tribes, and included in the treaty. The area covered by this treaty is vast—both in the Northwest Territories and northeastern British Columbia. There can be no doubt that by this treaty the Indians surrendered their rights in both areas. . . .

In my opinion, in the present case, the sovereign authority elected to exercise complete dominion over the lands in question, adverse to any right of occupancy which the Nishga Tribe might have had, when, by legislation, it opened up such lands for settlement, subject to the reserves of land set aside for Indian occupation.

We were not referred to any cases subsequent to *Tee-Hit-Ton* on the problem of compensation for claims arising out of original Indian title. The last word on the subject from the Supreme Court of the United States is, therefore, that there is no right to compensation for such claims in the absence of a statutory direction to pay. An *Indian Claims Commission Act* was, in fact, passed by Congress in 1946. I note the concluding paragraph in the reasons for judgment in *Tee-Hit-Ton* (1955) 348 U.S. 272 at pp. 290–1. In my opinion, it has equal application to the appeal now before us:

> In the light of the history of Indian relations in this Nation, no other course would meet the problem of the growth of the United States except to make congressional contributions for Indian lands rather than to subject the Government to an obligation to pay the value when taken with interest to the date of payment. Our conclusion does not uphold harshness as against tenderness toward the Indians, but it leaves with Congress, where it belongs, the policy of Indian gratuities for the termination of Indian occupancy of Government-owned land rather than making compensation for its value a rigid constitutional principle.

For the foregoing reasons I have reached the conclusion that this action fails and that the appeal should be dismissed.

There is the further point raised by the respondent that the Court did not have jurisdiction to make the declaratory order requested because the granting of a fiat under the *Crown Procedure Act,* R.S.B.C. 1960, c. 89, was a necessary prerequisite to bringing the action and it had not been obtained. While it is not necessary, in view of my conclusion as to the disposition of this appeal, to determine this point, I am in agreement with the reasons of my brother Pigeon dealing with it.

I would dismiss the appeal and would make no order as to costs.

RITCHIE, J., concurs with JUDSON, J.

HALL, J. (dissenting):—This appeal raises issues of vital importance to the Indians of northern British Columbia and, in particular, to those of the Nishga tribe. The Nishga tribe has persevered for almost a century in asserting an interest in the lands which their ancestors occupied since time immemorial. The Nishgas were never conquered nor did they at any time enter into a treaty or deed of surrender as many other Indian tribes did throughout Canada and in southern British Columbia. The Crown has never granted the lands in issue in this action other than a few small parcels later referred to prior to the commencement of the action. . . .

The assessment and interpretation of the historical documents and enactments tendered in evidence must be approached in the light of present-day research and knowledge disregarding ancient concepts formulated when understanding of the customs and culture of our original people was rudimentary and incomplete and when they were thought to be wholly without cohesion, laws or culture, in effect a subhuman species. This concept of the original inhabitants of America led Chief Justice Marshall in his otherwise enlightened judgment in *Johnson and Graham's Lessee* v. *M'Intosh* (1823), 8 Wheaton 543, which is the outstanding judicial pronouncement on the subject of Indian rights to say [8 Wheaton 590], "But the tribes of Indians inhabiting this country were fierce savages, whose occupation was war . . .". We now know that assessment was ill-founded. The Indians did in fact at times engage in some tribal wars but war was not their vocation and it can be said that their preoccupation with war pales into insignificance when compared to the religious and dynastic wars of "civilized" Europe of the 16th and 17th centuries. Chief Justice Marshall was, of course, speaking with the knowledge available to him in 1823. Chief Justice Davey in the judgment under appeal [13 D.L.R. (3d) 64,74 W.W.R. 481], with all the historical research and material available since 1823 and notwithstanding the evidence in the record which Gould, J. [8 D.L.R. (3d) 59, 71 W.W.R. 81], found was given "with total integrity", said of the Indians of the mainland of British Columbia [p. 66]:

> . . . they were undoubtedly at the time of settlement a very primitive people with few of the institutions of civilized society, and none at all of our notions of private property.

In so saying this in 1970, he was assessing the Indian culture of 1858 by the same standards that the Europeans applied to the Indians of North America two or more centuries before. . . .

In enumerating the *indicia* of ownership, the trial Judge overlooked that possession is of itself proof of ownership. *Prima facie,* therefore, the Nishgas are the owners of the lands that have been in their possession from time immemorial and, therefore the burden of establishing that their right has been extinguished rests squarely on the respondent.

What emerges from the foregoing evidence is the following: the Nishgas in fact are, and were from time immemorial a distinctive cultural entity with concepts of ownership indigenous to their culture and capable of articulation under the common law having, in the words of Dr. Duff, "developed their culture to higher peaks in many respects than in any other part of the continent north of Mexico". A remarkable confirmation of this statement comes from Captain Cook who, in 1778, at Cape Newenham claimed the land for Great Britain. He reported having gone ashore and entered one of the native houses which he said was 150 ft. in length, 24 to 30 ft. wide and 7 to 8 ft. high and that "there were no native buildings to compare with these north of Mexico". The report continues that Cook's officers were full of admiration for the skill and patience required to erect these buildings which called for a considerable knowledge of engineering.

While the Nishga claim had not heretofore been litigated, there is a wealth of jurisprudence affirming common law recognition of aboriginal rights to possession and enjoyment of lands of aborigines precisely analogous to the Nishga situation here. . . .

The dominant and recurring proposition stated by Chief Justice Marshall in *Johnson* v. *M'Intosh* is that on discovery or on conquest the aborigines of newly-found lands were conceded to be the rightful occupants of the soil with a legal as well as a just claim to retain possession of it and to use it according to their own discretion, but their rights to complete sovereigny as independent nations were necessarily diminished and their power to dispose of the soil on their own will to whomsoever they pleased was denied by the original fundamental principle that discovery or conquest gave exclusive title to those who made it. . . .

The view that the Indians had a legal as well as a just claim to the territory they occupied was confirmed as recently as 1946 by the Supreme Court of the United States in the case of *United States* v. *Alcea Band of Tillamooks et al.* (1946), 329 U.S. 40. In that case it was held that the Indian claims legislation of 1935 did not confer any substantive rights on the Indians, that is, it did not convert a moral claim for taking their land without their consent and without compensation into a legal claim, because they already had a valid legal claim, and there was no necessity to create one. The statute simply removed the necessity that previously existed for the Indians to obtain the consent of the Government of the United States to sue for an alleged wrongful taking. The judgment is based squarely on the recognition by the Court of "original Indian title" founded on their previous possession of the land. It was held that "the Indians have a cause of action for compensation arising out of an involuntary taking of lands held by original Indian title". Vinson, C.J., said at pp. 45–8:

> The language of the 1935 Act is specific, and its consequences are clear. By this Act Congress neither admitted or denied liability. The Act removes the impediments of sovereign immunity and lapse of time and provides for judicial determination of the designated claims. No new right or cause of action is created. A merely moral claim is not made a legal one. . . .
>
> It has long been held that by virtue of discovery the title to lands occupied by Indian tribes vested in the sovereign. This title was deemed subject to a right of occupancy in favour of Indian tribes, because of their original and previous possession. It is with the content of this right of occupancy, this original Indian title, that we are concerned here.
>
> As against any but the sovereign, original Indian title was accorded the protection of complete ownership; but it was vulnerable to affirmative action by the sovereign, which possessed exclusive power to extinguish the right of occupancy at will. Termination of the right by sovereign action was complete and left the land free and clear of Indian claims. Third parties could not question the justness or fairness of the methods used to extinguish the right of occupancy. Nor could the Indians themselves prevent a taking of tribal lands or forestall a termination of their title. However, it is now for the first time asked whether the Indians have a cause of action for compensation arising out of an involuntary taking of lands held by original Indian title. . . .
>
> A contrary decision would ignore the plain import of traditional methods of extinguishing original Indian title. The early acquisition of Indian lands, in the main, progressed by a process of negotiation and treaty. The first treaties reveal the striking deference paid to Indian claims, as the analysis in *Worcester* v. *Georgia,* supra, clearly details. It was usual policy not to coerce the surrender of lands without consent and without compensation. *The great drive to open western lands in the 19th Century, however productive of sharp dealing, did not wholly subvert the settled practice of*

negotiated extinguishment of original Indian title. In 1896, this Court noted that ". . . nearly every tribe and band of Indians within the territorial limits of the United States was under some treaty relations with the Government." Marks v. *United States,* 161 U.S. 297, 302 (1896). Something more than sovereign grace prompted the obvious regard given to original Indian title.

(Emphasis added.) The same considerations applied in Canada. Treaties were made with the Indians of the Canadian West covering enormous tracts of land. See Kerr's *Historical Atlas of Canada* (1961), p. 57 (map 81). These treaties were a recognition of Indian title. . . .

In *Re Southern Rhodesia*, (1919) A.C. 211, Lord Summer said at pp. 233–4:

. . . The estimation of the rights of aboriginal tribes is always inherently difficult. Some tribes are so low in the scale of social organization that their usage and conceptions of rights and duties are not to be reconciled with the institutions or the legal ideas of civilized society. Such a gulf cannot be bridged. It would be idle to impute to such people some shadow of the rights known to our law and then to transmute it into the substance of transferable rights of property as we know them. In the present case it would make each and every person by a fictional inheritance a landed proprietor "richer than all his tribe." *On the other hand, there are indigenous peoples whose legal conceptions, though differently developed, are hardly less precise than our own. When once they have been studied and understood they are no less enforceable than rights arising under English law.*

(Emphasis added.)

Chief Justice Marshall in his judgment in *Johnson* v. *M'Intosh* referred to the English case of *Campbell* v. *Hall* (1774), 1 Cowp. 204, 98 E.R. 1045. This case was an important and decisive one which has been regarded as authoritative throughout the Commonwealth and the United States. It involved the rights and status of residents of the Island of Grenada which had recently been taken by British arms in open war with France. The judgment was given by Lord Mansfield. In his reasons he said at pp. 208–9:

A great deal has been said, and many authorities cited relative to propositions, in which both sides seem to be perfectly agreed; and which, indeed are too clear to be controverted. The stating some of those propositions which we think quite clear, will lead us to see with greater perspicuity, what is the question upon the first point, and upon what hinge it turns. I will state the propositions at large, and the first is this:

A country conquered by the British arms becomes a dominion of the King in the right of his Crown; and, therefore, necessarily subject to the Legislature, and Parliament of Great Britain.

The 2d is, that the conquered inhabitants once received under the King's protection, become subjects, and are to be universally considered in that light, not as enemies or aliens.

The 3d, that the articles of capitulation upon which the country is surrendered and the articles of peace by which it is ceded, are sacred and inviolable according to their true intent and meaning.

The 4th, that the law and legislative government of every dominion, equally affects all persons and all property within the limits thereof; and is the rule of decision for all questions which arise there. Whoever purchases, lives, or sues there, puts himself under the law of the place. An Englishman in Ireland, Minorca, the Isle of Man, or the plantations, has no privilege distinct from the natives.

The 5th, that the laws of a conquered country continue in force, until they are altered by the conqueror: the absurd exception as to pagans, mentioned in Calvin's case [(1608), 7 Co. Rep. 1a, Moore (R.B.) 790 sub nom. Case del Union, del Realm D'Escose, ove Angleterre, 72 E.R. 908], shews the universality and antiquity of the maxim. For that distinction could not exist before the Christian era; and in all probability arose from the mad enthusiasm of the Crusades. In the present case the capitulation expressly provides and agrees, that they shall continue to be governed by their own laws, until His Majesty's further pleasure be known.

The 6th, and last proposition is, that if the King (and when I say the King, I always mean the King without the concurrence of Parliament,) has a power to alter the old and to introduce new laws in a conquered country, this legislation being subordinate, that is, subordinate to his own authority in Parliament, he cannot make any new change contrary to fundamental principles: he cannot exempt an inhabitant from that particular dominion; as for instance, from the laws of trade, or from the power of Parliament or give him privileges exclusive of his other subjects; and so in many other instances which might be put.

A fortiori the same principles, particularly Nos. 5 and 6, must apply to lands which become subject to British sovereignty by discovery or by declaration. . . .

Paralleling and supporting the claim of the Nishgas that they have a certain right or title to the lands in question is the guarantee of Indian rights contained in the *Proclamation of 1763.* This Proclamation was an Executive Order having the force and effect of an Act of Parliament and was described by Gwynne, J., in *St. Catherine's Milling* case at (1887), 13 S.C.R. 577 at 652 as the "Indian Bill of Rights"; see also *Campbell* v. *Hall.* Its force as a statute is analogous to the status of Magna Carta which has always been considered to be the law throughout the Empire. It was a law which followed the flag as England assumed jurisdiction over newly-discovered or acquired lands or territories. It follows, therefore, that the *Colonial Laws Validity Act,* 1865 (U.K.), c. 63, applied to make the Proclamation the law of British Columbia. That it was regarded as being the law of England is clear from the fact that when it was deemed advisable to amend it the amendment was affected by an Act of Parliament, namely the *Quebec Act* of 1774 [1774 (U.K.) (14 Geo. III), c. 83].

In respect of this Proclamation, it can be said that when other exploring nations were showing a ruthless disregard of native rights England adopted a remarkably enlightened attitude towards the Indians of North America. The Proclamation must be regarded as a fundamental document upon which any just determination of original rights rests. Its effect was discussed by Idington, J., in this Court in *Province of Ontario* v. *Dominion of Canada* (1909), 42 S.C.R. 1 at pp. 103–4 [affd [1910] A.C. 637], as follows:

> A line of *policy* begotten of prudence, humanity and justice adopted by the British Crown to be observed in all future dealings with the Indians in respect of such rights as they might suppose themselves to possess was outlined in the *Royal Proclamation of 1763* erecting, after the Treaty of Paris in that year, amongst others, a separate

government for Quebec, ceded by that treaty to the British Crown.

That policy adhered to thenceforward, by those responsible for the honour of the Crown led to many treaties whereby Indians agreed to surrender such rights as they were supposed to have in areas respectively specified in such treaties.

In these surrendering treaties there generally were reserves provided for Indians making such surrenders to enter into or be confined to for purposes of residence.

The history of this mode of dealing is very fully outlined in the judgment of the learned Chancellor Boyd in the case of *The Queen* v. *St. Catherine's Milling Co.,* 10 O.R. 196 (affirmed 13 O.A.R. 148].

[Italics added.]

The question of the Proclamation's applicability to the Nishgas is, accordingly, relevant in this appeal. The point has been before provincial Courts in Canada on a number of occasions but never specifically dealt with by this Court.

It is necessary, therefore, to face the issue as one of first impression and to decide it with due regard to the historical record and the principles of the common law. . . .

The wording of the Proclamation itself seems quite clear that it was intended to include the lands west of the Rocky Mountains. The relevant paragraph reads [p. 6130]:

And We do further declare it to be Our Royal Will and Pleasure, for the present as aforesaid, to reserve under our Sovereignty, Protection, and Dominion, for the use of the said Indians, all the Lands and Territories not included within the Limits of Our Said Three New Governments, or within the Limits of the Territory granted to the Hudson's Bay Company, as also all the Lands and Territories lying to the Westward of the Sources of the Rivers which fall into the Sea from the West and North West as aforesaid;

The only territories not included were: (1) Those within the limits of the three new Governments; and (2) within the limits of the territory granted to the Hudson's Bay Company. The concluding sentence of the paragraph just quoted, "as also all the Lands and Territories lying to the Westward of the Sources of the Rivers which fall into the Sea from the West and North West as aforesaid; shows clearly that the framers of the paragraph were well aware that there was territory to the west of the sources of the rivers which ran from the west and north-west. . . .

This important question remains: were the rights either at common law or under the Proclamation extinguished? Tysoe, J.A., said in this regard at p. 95 [13 D.L.R. (3d) 59] of his reasons: "It is true, as the appellants have submitted, *that nowhere can one find express words extinguishing Indian title. . .*" (emphasis added).

The parties here agree that if extinguishment was accomplished, it must have occurred between 1858 and when British Columbia joined Confederation in 1871. The respondent relies on what was done by Governor Douglas and by his successor, Frederick Seymour, who became Governor in 1864. . . .

The appellants rely on the presumption that the British Crown intended to respect native rights; therefore, when the Nishga people came under British sovereignty (and that is subject to what I said about sovereignty over part of the lands not being determined until 1903) they were entitled to assert, as a legal right, their Indian title. It being a legal right, it could not thereafter be extinguished except by surrender to the Crown or by competent legislative authority, and then only by specific legislation. There was no surrender by the Nishgas and neither the Colony of British Columbia nor the Province, after Confederation, enacted legislation specifically purporting to extinguish the Indian title nor did Parliament at Ottawa. . . .

It would, accordingly, appear to be beyond question that the onus of proving that the Sovereign intended to extinguish the Indian title lies on the respondent and that intention must be "clear and plain". There is no such proof in the case at bar; no legislation to that effect.

The Court of Appeal also erred in holding that there "is no Indian Title capable of judicial interpretation . . . unless it has previously been recognized either by the Legislature or the Executive Branch of Government" [see 13 D.L.R. (3d) 59 at 70]. Relying on *Cook et al.* v. *Sprigg,* [1899] A.C. 572, and other cases, the Court of Appeal erroneously applied what is called the Act of State Doctrine. This doctrine denies a remedy to the citizens of an acquired territory for invasion of their rights which may occur during the change of sovereignty. English Courts have held that a municipal Court has no jurisdiction to review the manner in which the Sovereign acquires new territory. The Act of State is the activity of the Sovereign by which he acquires the property. Professor D. P. O'Connell in his work *International Law,* 2nd ed. (1970), at p. 378 says:

> This doctrine, which was affirmed in several cases arising out of the acquisition of territory in Africa and India, has been misinterpreted to the effect that the substantive rights themselves have not survived the change. In fact English courts have gone out of their way to repudiate the construction, and it is clear that the Act of State doctrine is no more than a procedural bar to municipal law action, and as such is irrelevant to the question whether in international law change of sovereignty affects acquired rights.

The Act of State doctrine has no application in the present appeal for the following reasons: (a) It has never been invoked in claims dependent on aboriginal title. An examination of its rationale indicates that it would be quite inappropriate for the Courts to extend the doctrine to such cases: (b) It is based on the premise that an Act of State is an exercise of the Sovereign power which a municipal Court has no power to review: see *Salaman* v. *Secretary of State in Council of India,* [1906] 1 K.B. 613 at pp. 639–40; *Cook* v. *Sprigg,* supra, at p. 578. . . .

Once it is apparent that the Act of State doctrine has no application, the whole argument of the respondent that there must be some form of "recognition" of aboriginal rights falls to the ground.

On the question of extinguishment, the respondent relies on what was done by Governors Douglas and Seymour and the Council of British Columbia. The appellants, as I have previously mentioned, say that if either Douglas or Seymour or the Council of the Colony of British Columbia did purport to extinguish the Nishga title that any such attempt was beyond the powers of either the Governors or of the Council and that what, if anything, was attempted in this respect was *ultra vires.* . . .

If in any of the Proclamations or actions of Douglas, Seymour or of the Council of the Colony of British Columbia there are elements which the respondent says extinguish by implication the Indian title, then it is obvious from the Commission of the Governor and from the Instructions under which the Governor was required to observe and neither the Commission nor the Instructions contain any power or authorization to extinguish the Indian title, then it follows logically that if any attempt was made to extinguish the title it was beyond the power of the Governor or of the Council to do so and, therefore, *ultra vires*. . . .

Having reviewed the evidence and cases in considerable detail and having decided that if the Nishgas ever had any right or title that it had been extinguished, Tysoe J.A., was inexorably driven to the conclusion which he stated as follows [13 D.L.R. (3d) 59 at 94]:

> As a result of these pieces of legislation the Indians of the Colony of British Columbia *became in law trespassers* on and liable to actions of ejectment from lands in the Colony other than those set aside as reserves for the use of Indians.

(Emphasis added.) Any reasoning that would lead to such a conclusion must necessarily be fallacious. The idea is self-destructive. If trespassers, the Indians are liable to prosecution as such, a proposition which reason itself repudiates. . . .

Blackburn, J., after an extensive review of the facts and historical records involving some 50 pages, held as follows [*Milirrpum et al.* v. *Nabalco Pty. Ltd.* (1971), 17 F.L.R. 141 at 198]:

> This question of fact has been for me by far the most difficult of all the difficult questions of fact in the case. I can, in the last resort, do no more than express that degree of conviction which all the evidence has left upon my mind, and it is this: that I am not persuaded that the plaintiffs' contention is more probably correct than incorrect. In other words, I am not satisfied, on the balance of probabilities, that the plaintiffs' predecessors had in 1788 the same links to the same areas of land as those which the plaintiffs now claim.

That finding necessarily disposed of the claim being made. However, the learned Justice proceeded with a very comprehensive review of much of the case law regarding the rights of aborigines and the questions of the recognition and extinguishment of aboriginal title. It is obvious that all of the observations contained in his judgment following the finding of fact above set out were *obiter dicta*. In his review he dealt with the trial and appeal judgments in this case and said [*Milirrpum et al.* v. *Nabalco Pty. Ltd.* (1971), 17 F.L.R. 141 at 223]:

> I consider, with respect, that Calder's case, though it is not binding on this Court, is weighty authority for these propositions:
>
> 1. In a settled colony there is no principle of communal native title except such as can be shown by prerogative or legislative act, or a course of dealing.
>
> 2. In a settled colony a legislative and executive policy of treating the land of the colony as open to grant by the Crown, together with the establishment of native reserves, operates as an extinguishment of aboriginal title, if that ever existed.

It will be seen that he fell into the same errors as did Gould J., and the Court of Appeal. The essence of his concurrence with the Court of Appeal judgment lies in his acceptance of the proposition that after conquest or discovery the native peoples have no rights at all except those subsequently granted or recognized by the conqueror or discoverer. That proposition is wholly wrong as the mass of authorities previously cited, including *Johnson* v. *M'Intosh* and *Campbell* v. *Hall,* establishes. . . .

I would, therefore, allow the appeal with costs throughout and declare that the appellants' right to possession of the lands delineated in ex. 2 with the exceptions before mentioned and their right to enjoy the fruits of the soil, of the forest, and of the rivers and streams within the boundaries of said lands have not been extinguished by the Province of British Columbia or by its predecessor, the Colony of British Columbia, or by the Governors of that Colony.

SPENCE, J., concurs with HALL, J.

PIGEON, J.:— . . . I have to hold that the preliminary objection that the declaration prayed for, being a claim of title against the Crown in the right of the Province of British Columbia, the Court has no jurisdiction to make it in the absence of a fiat of the Lieutenant-Governor of that Province. I am deeply conscious of the hardship involved in holding that the access to the Court for the determination of the plaintiffs' claim is barred by sovereign immunity from suit without a fiat. However, I would point out that in the United States, claims in respect of the taking of lands outside of reserves and not covered by any treaty were not held justiciable until legislative provisions had removed the obstacle created by the doctrine of immunity. In Canada, immunity from suit has been removed by legislation at the federal level and in most Provinces. However, this has not yet been done in British Columbia.

I would therefore dismiss the appeal and make no order as to costs. . . .

LASKIN, J., concurs with HALL, J. . . .

Appeal dismissed.

8. *R. v. Guerin*, [1985] 1 C.N.L.R. 120 (S.C.C.). Laskin C.J.C. (took no part in the judgment), Dickson, Beetz, Chouinard, Lamer, Estey, Wilson, Ritchie, and McIntyre JJ., November 1, 1984

Guerin deals with the claim of the Musqueam Indian Band of British Columbia that the federal government breached its trust and fiduciary obligations to the band regarding the leasing of band lands to a golf club. The Supreme Court of Canada provides its single most important decision to date on the fiduciary relationship between the Crown and Aboriginal peoples. By discussing and affirming the fiduciary relationship between Aboriginal peoples and the Crown, *Guerin* set the stage for an ongoing references by the courts to the fiduciary rights of Aboriginal peoples. The legal understanding of this fiduciary relationship is still developing (see chapter 3). As well, the decision provides further illumination of the court's understanding of the nature and scope of Aboriginal title, particularly by affirming the recognition of Aboriginal title in the *Calder* decision. A brief excerpt from Estey J.'s reasons are included to point out his preference for defining the Crown-Aboriginal relationship as one of agency as opposed to a trust.

DICKSON J. (BEETZ, CHOUINARD and LAMER JJ. concurring):— . . . Before adverting to the facts, reference should be made to several of the relevant sections of the *Indian Act*, R.S.C. 1952, c. 149 [now R.S.C. 1970, c. I–6], as amended. Section 18(1) provides in part that reserves shall be held by Her Majesty for the use of the respective Indian bands for which they were set apart. Generally, lands in a reserve shall not be sold, alienated, leased or otherwise disposed of until they have been surrendered to Her Majesty by the band for whose use and benefit in common the reserve was set apart (s. 37). A surrender may be absolute or qualified, conditional or unconditional (s. 38(2)). To be valid, a surrender must be made to Her Majesty, assented to by a majority of the electors of the band, and accepted by the Governor in Council (s. 39(l) [re-en. 1956, c. 40, s. 11]).

The gist of the present action is a claim that the federal Crown was in breach of its trust obligations in respect of the leasing of approximately 162 acres of reserve land to the Shaughnessy Heights Golf Club of Vancouver. The band alleged that a number of the terms and conditions of the lease were different from those disclosed to them before the surrender vote and that some of the lease terms were not disclosed to them at all. The band also claimed failure on the part of the federal crown to exercise the requisite degree of care and management as a trustee. . . .

The issue of the Crown's liability was dealt with in the courts below on the basis of the existence or non-existence of a trust. In dealing with the different consequences of a "true" trust, as opposed to a "political" trust, Le Dain J. noted that the Crown could be liable only if it were subject to an "equitable obligation enforceable in a court of law". I have some doubt as to the cogency of the terminology of "higher" and "lower" trusts, but I do agree that the existence of an equitable obligation is the sine qua non for liability. Such an obligation is not, however, limited to relationships which can be strictly defined as "trusts". As will presently appear, it is my view that the Crown's obligations vis-à-vis the Indians cannot be defined as a trust. That does not, however, mean that the Crown owes no enforceable duty to the Indians in the way in which it deals with Indian land.

In my view, the nature of Indian title and the framework of the statutory scheme established for disposing of Indian land places upon the Crown an equitable obligation, enforceable by the courts, to deal with the land for the benefit of the Indians. This obligation does not amount to a trust in the private law sense. It is rather a fiduciary duty. If, however, the Crown breaches this fiduciary duty it will be liable to the Indians in the same way and to the same extent as if such a trust were in effect.

The fiduciary relationship between the Crown and the Indians has its roots in the concept of aboriginal, native or Indian title. The fact that Indian bands have a certain interest in lands does not, however, in itself give rise to a fiduciary relationship between the Indians and the Crown. The conclusion that the Crown is a fiduciary depends upon the further proposition that the Indian interest in the land is inalienable except upon surrender to the Crown.

An Indian band is prohibited from directly transferring its interest to a third party. Any sale or lease of land can only be carried out after a surrender has taken place, with the Crown then acting on the band's behalf. The Crown first took this responsibility upon itself in the *Royal Proclamation of 1763* [see R.S.C. 1970, App. II]. It is still recognized in the surrender provisions of the *Indian Act*. The surrender requirement, and the responsibility it entails, are the source of a distinct fiduciary obligation owed by the Crown to the Indians. In order to explore the character of this obligation, however, it is first necessary to consider the basis of aboriginal title and the nature of the interest in land which it represents. . . .

It does not matter, in my opinion, that the present case is concerned with the interest of an Indian band in a reserve rather than with unrecognized aboriginal title in traditional tribal lands. The Indian interest in the land is the same in both cases: see *A.-G. Que.* v. *A.-G. Can.*, [1921] 1 A.C. 401 at 410–11, 56 D.L.R. 373 (P.C.) (the *"Star Chrome"* case). It is worth noting, however, that the reserve in question here was created out of the ancient tribal territory of the Musqueam band by the unilateral action of the colony of British Columbia, prior to Confederation.

(b) *The Nature of Indian Title*

In the *St. Catherine's Milling* case, (1888), 14 App. Cas. 46 at 54, the Privy Council held that the Indians had a "personal and usufructuary right" in the lands which they had traditionally occupied. Lord Watson said that "there has been all along vested in the Crown a substantial and paramount estate, underlying the Indian title, which became a plenum dominium whenever that title was surrendered or otherwise extinguished" (supra, at p. 55). He reiterated this idea, stating that the Crown "has all along had a present proprietary estate in the land, upon which the Indian title was a mere burden" (at p. 58). This view of aboriginal title was affirmed by the Privy Council in the *Star Chrome* case, sub nom. *A.-G. Que.* v. *A.-G. Can.,* [1921] 1 A.C. 401. In *Amodu Tijani* v. *Southern Nigeria (Secretary),* [1921] 2 A.C. 399, Viscount Haldane, adverting to the *St. Catherine's Milling* and *Star Chrome* decisions, explained the concept of a usufructuary right as "a mere qualification of or burden on the radical or final title of the Sovereign" (p. 403). He described the title of the Sovereign as a pure legal estate, but one which could be qualified by a right of "beneficial user" that did not necessarily take the form of an estate in land. Indian title in Canada was said to be one illustration "of the necessity for getting rid of the assumption that the ownership of land naturally breaks itself up into estates, conceived as creatures of inherent legal principle" [p. 403]. Marshall C.J. took a similar view in *Johnson* v. *M'Intosh*, 21 U.S. (8 Wheaton) 543, saying, "All our institutions recognize the absolute title of the Crown, subject only to the Indian right of occupancy" (p. 588).

It should be noted that the Privy Council's emphasis on the personal nature of aboriginal title stemmed in part from constitutional arrangements peculiar to Canada. The Indian territory at issue in *St. Catherine's Milling* was land which in 1867 had been vested in the Crown subject to the interest of the Indians. The Indians' interest was an "Interest other than that of the Province", within the meaning of s. 109 of the *Constitution Act, 1867*. Section 109 provides:

> 109. All Lands, Mines, Minerals, and Royalties belonging to the several Provinces of Canada, Nova Scotia, and New Brunswick at the Union, and all Sums then due or payable for such Lands, Mines, Minerals, or Royalties, shall belong to the several Provinces of Ontario, Quebec, Nova Scotia, and New Brunswick in which the same are situate or arise subject to any Trusts existing in respect thereof, and to any Interest other than that of the Province in the same.

When the land in question in *St. Catherine's Milling* was subsequently disencumbered of the native title upon its surrender to the federal government by the Indian occupants in 1873, the entire beneficial interest in the land was held to have passed, because of the personal and usufructuary nature of the Indians' right, to the province of Ontario under s. 109 rather than to Canada. The same constitutional issue arose recently in this court in *Can.* v. *Smith*, [1983] 1 S.C.R. 554, 147 D.L.R. (3d) 237 (sub nom. *R.* v. *Smith*), [1983] 3 C.N.L.R. 161, 47 N.R. 132, in which the court held that the Indian right in a reserve, being personal, could not be transferred to a grantee, whether an individual or the Crown. Upon surrender the right disappeared "in the process of release".

No such constitutional problem arises in the present case, since in 1938 the title to all Indian reserves in British Columbia was transferred by the provincial government to the Crown in right of Canada.

It is true that in contexts other than the constitutional the characterization of Indian title as "a personal and usufructuary right" has sometimes been questioned. In *Calder*, [1973] S.C.R. 313, for example, Judson J. intimated at p. 328 that this characterization was not helpful in determining the nature of Indian title. In *A.G. Can.* v. *Giroux* (1916), 53 S.C.R. 172, 30 D.L.R. 123, Duff J., speaking for himself and Anglin J., distinguished *St. Catherine's Milling* on the ground that the statutory provisions in accordance with which the reserve in question in *Giroux* had been created conferred beneficial ownership on the Indian band which occupied the reserve. In *Cardinal* v. *A.G. Alta.*, [1974] S.C.R. 695, [1973] 6 W.W.R. 205, 13 C.C.C. (2d) 1, 40 D.L.R. (3d) 553, Laskin J., dissenting on another point, accepted the possibility that Indians may have a beneficial interest in a reserve. The Alberta Court of Appeal in *Western Int. Contractors Ltd.* v. *Sarcee Dev. Ltd.*, [1979] 3 W.W.R. 631, 98 D.L.R. (3d) 424, [1979] 2 C.N.L.R. 107 (sub nom. *Western Indust. Contractors Ltd.* v. *Sarcee Dev. Ltd.*), 15 A.R. 309, accepted the proposition that an Indian band does indeed have a beneficial interest in its reserve. In the present case this was the view as well of Le Dain J. in the Federal Court of Appeal. See also the judgment of Kellock J. in *Miller* v. *R.*, [1950] S.C.R. 168, [1950] 1 D.L.R. 513, in which he seems implicitly to adopt a similar position. None of these judgments mentioned the *Star Chrome* case, however, in which the Indian interest in land specifically set aside as a reserve was held to be the same as the "personal and usufructuary right" which was discussed in *St. Catherine's Milling*.

It appears to me that there is no real conflict between the cases which characterize Indian title as a beneficial interest of some sort, and those which characterize it a personal, usufructuary right. Any apparent inconsistency derives from the fact that in describing what constitutes a unique interest in land the courts have almost inevitably found themselves applying a somewhat inappropriate terminology drawn from general property law. There is a core of truth in the way that each of the two lines of authority has described native title, but an appearance of conflict has nonetheless arisen because in neither case is the categorization quite accurate.

Indians have a legal right to occupy and possess certain lands, the ultimate title to which is in the Crown. While their interest does not, strictly speaking, amount to beneficial ownership, neither is its nature completely exhausted by the concept of a personal right. It is true that the *sui generis* interest which the Indians have in the land is personal in the sense that it cannot be transferred to a grantee, but it is also true, as will presently appear, that the interest gives rise upon surrender to a distinctive fiduciary obligation on the part of the Crown to deal with the land for the benefit of the surrendering Indians. These two aspects of Indian title go together, since the Crown's original purpose in declaring the Indians' interest to be inalienable otherwise than to the Crown was to facilitate the Crown's ability to represent the Indians in dealings with third parties. The nature of the Indians' interest is therefore best characterized by its general inalienability, coupled with the fact that the Crown is under an obligation to deal with the land on the Indians' behalf when the interest is surrendered. Any description of Indian title which goes beyond these two features is both unnecessary and potentially misleading.

(c) *The Crown's Fiduciary Obligation*
The concept of fiduciary obligation originated long ago in the notion of breach of confidence, one of the original heads of jurisdiction in Chancery. In the present appeal its relevance is based on the requirement of a "surrender" before Indian land can be alienated.

The *Royal Proclamation of 1763* provided that no private person could purchase from the Indians any lands that the Proclamation had reserved to them, and provided further that all purchases had to be by and in the name of the Crown, in a public assembly of the Indians held by the governor or commander-in-chief of the colony in which the lands in question lay. As Lord Watson pointed out in *St. Catherine's Milling*, supra, at p. 54, this policy with respect to the sale or transfer of the Indians' interest in land has been continuously maintained by the British Crown, by the governments of the colonies when they became responsible for the administration of Indian affairs, and, after 1867, by the federal government of Canada. Successive federal statutes, predecessors to the present *Indian Act*, have all provided for the general inalienability of Indian reserve land except upon surrender to the Crown, the relevant provisions in the present Act being ss. 37–41.

The purpose of this surrender requirement is clearly to interpose the Crown between the Indians and prospective purchasers or lessees of their land, so as to prevent the Indians from being exploited. This is made clear in the Royal Proclamation itself, which prefaces the provision making the Crown an intermediary with a declaration that [at p. 128] "great Frauds and Abuses have been committed in purchasing Lands of the Indians, to the great Prejudice of our Interests, and to the great Dissatisfaction of the said Indians . . .". Through the confirmation in the *Indian Act* of the historic responsibility which the Crown has undertaken, to act on behalf of the Indians so as to protect their interests in transactions with third parties, Parliament has conferred upon the Crown a discretion to decide for itself where the Indians' best interests really lie. This is the effect of s. 18(1) of the Act.

This discretion on the part of the Crown, far from ousting, as the Crown contends, the jurisdiction of the courts to regulate the relationship between the Crown and the Indians, has the effect of transforming the Crown's obligation into a fiduciary one. Professor Ernest J. Weinrib maintains in his article "The Fiduciary Obligation" (1975), 25 U.T.L.J. 1, at p. 7, that "the hallmark of a fiduciary relation is that the relative legal positions are such that one party is at the mercy of the other's discretion". Earlier, at p. 4, he puts the point in the following way:

> [Where there is a fiduciary obligation] there is a relation in which the principal's interests can be affected by, and are therefore dependent on, the manner in which the fiduciary uses the discretion which has been delegated to him. The fiduciary obligation is the law's blunt tool for the control of this discretion.

I make no comment upon whether this description is broad enough to embrace all fiduciary obligations. I do agree, however, that where by statute, agreement, or perhaps by unilateral undertaking, one party has an obligation to act for the benefit of another, and that obligation carries with it a discretionary power, the party thus empowered becomes a fiduciary. Equity will then supervise the relationship by holding him to the fiduciary's strict standard of conduct.

It is sometimes said that the nature of fiduciary relationships is both established and exhausted by the standard categories of agent, trustee, partner, director, and the like. I do not agree. It is the nature of the relationship, not the specific category of actor involved that gives rise to the fiduciary duty. The categories of fiduciary, like those of negligence, should not be considered closed: see, e.g., *Laskin* v. *Bache & Co.*, [1972] 1 O.R. 465, 23 D.L.R. (3d) 385 at 392 (C.A.); *Goldex Mines Ltd.* v. *Revill*; *Probe Mines Ltd.* v. *Goldex Mines Ltd.* (1974), 7 O.R. (2d) 216, 54 D.L.R. (3d) 672 at 224 (C.A.).

It should be noted that fiduciary duties generally arise only with regard to obligations originating in a private law context. Public law duties, the performance of which requires the exercise of discretion, do not typically give rise to a fiduciary relationship. As the "political trust" cases indicate, the Crown is not normally viewed as a fiduciary in the exercise of its legislative or administrative function. The mere fact, however, that it is the Crown which is obligated to act on the Indians' behalf does not of itself remove the Crown's obligation from the scope of the fiduciary principle. As was pointed out earlier, the Indians' interest in land is an independent legal interest. It is not a creation of either the legislative or executive branches of government. The Crown's obligation to the Indians with respect to that interest is therefore not a public law duty. While it is not a private law duty in the strict sense either, it is nonetheless in the nature of a private law duty. Therefore, in this *sui generis* relationship, it is not improper to regard the Crown as a fiduciary.

Section 18(1) of the *Indian Act* confers upon the Crown a broad discretion in dealing with surrendered land. In the present case, the document of surrender, set out in part earlier in these reasons, by which the Musqueam band surrendered the land at issue, confirms this discretion in the clause conveying the land to the Crown "in trust to lease . . . upon such terms as the Government of Canada may deem most conducive to our Welfare and that of our people." When, as here, an Indian band surrenders its interest to the Crown, a fiduciary obligation takes hold to regulate the manner in which the Crown exercises its discretion in dealing with the land on the Indians' behalf.

I agree with Le Dain J. that before surrender the Crown does not hold the land in trust for the Indians. I also agree that the Crown's obligation does not somehow crystallize into a trust, express or implied, at the time of surrender. The law of trusts is a highly developed, specialized branch of the law. An express trust requires a settlor, a beneficiary, a trust corpus, words of settlement, certainty of object and certainty of obligation. Not all of these elements are present here. Indeed, there is not even a trust corpus. As the *Smith* decision, supra, makes clear, upon unconditional surrender the Indians' right in the land disappears. No property interest is transferred which could constitute the trust res, so that even if the other indicia of an express or implied trust could be made out, the basic requirement of a settlement of property has not been met. Accordingly, although the nature of Indian title coupled with the discretion vested in the Crown are sufficient to give rise to a fiduciary obligation, neither an express nor an implied trust arises upon surrender.

Nor does surrender give rise to a constructive trust. As was said by this court in *Pettkus* v. *Becker*, [1980] 2 S.C.R. 834 at 847, "The principle of unjust enrichment lies at the heart of the constructive trust". . . . Any similarity between a constructive trust and the Crown's fiduciary obligation to the Indians is limited to the fact that both arise by operation of law; the former is an essentially restitutionary remedy, while the latter is not. In the present case, for example, the Crown has in no way been enriched by the surrender transaction, whether unjustly or otherwise, but the fact that this is so cannot alter either the existence or the nature of the obligation which the Crown owes.

The Crown's fiduciary obligation to the Indians is therefore not a trust. To say as much is not to deny that the obligation is trust-like in character. As would be the case with a trust, the Crown must hold surrendered land for the use and benefit of the surrendering band. The obligation is thus subject to principles very similar to those which govern the law of trusts concerning, for example, the measure of damages for breach. The fiduciary relationship between the Crown and the Indians also bears a certain resemblance to agency, since the obligation can be characterized as a duty to act on behalf of the Indian bands who have surrendered lands, by negotiating for the sale or lease of the land to third parties. But just as the Crown is not a trustee for the Indians, neither is it their agent; not only does the Crown's authority to act on the band's behalf lack a basis in contract, but the band is not a party to the ultimate sale or lease, as it would be if it were the Crown's principal. I repeat, the fiduciary obligation which is owed to the Indians by the Crown is *sui generis*. Given the unique character both of the Indians' interest in land and of their historical relationship with the Crown, the fact that this is so should occasion no surprise.

The discretion which is the hallmark of any fiduciary relationship is capable of being considerably narrowed in a particular case. This is as true of the Crown's discretion vis-à-vis the Indians as it is of the discretion of trustees, agents, and other traditional categories of fiduciary. The *Indian Act* makes specific provision for such narrowing in ss. 18(1) and 38(2). A fiduciary obligation will not, of course, be eliminated by the imposition of conditions that have the effect of restricting the fiduciary's discretion. A failure to adhere to the imposed conditions will simply itself be a prima facie breach of the obligation. In the present case both the surrender and the Order-in-Council accepting the surrender referred to the Crown leasing the land on the band's behalf. Prior to the surrender the band had also been given to understand that a lease was to be entered into with the Shaughnessy Heights Golf Club upon certain terms, but this understanding was not incorporated into the surrender document itself. The effect of these so-called oral terms will be considered in the next section.

(d) *Breach of the Fiduciary Obligation*

The trial judge found that the Crown's agents promised the band to lease the land in question on certain specified terms and then, after surrender, obtained a lease on different terms. The lease obtained was much less valuable. As already mentioned, the surrender document did not make reference to the "oral" terms. I would not wish to say that those terms had nonetheless somehow been incorporated as conditions into the surrender. They were not formally assented to by a majority of the electors of the band, nor were they accepted by the Governor in Council, as required by s. 39(l)(b) and (c). I agree with Le Dain J. that there is no merit in the appellants' submission that for purposes of s. 39 a surrender can be considered independently of its terms. This makes no more sense than would a claim that a contract can have an existence which in no way depends on the terms and conditions that comprise it.

Nonetheless, the Crown, in my view, was not empowered by the surrender document to ignore the oral terms which the band understood would be embodied in the lease. The oral representations form the backdrop against which the Crown's conduct in discharging its fiduciary obligation must be measured. They inform and confine the field of discretion within which the Crown was free to act. After the Crown's agents had induced the band to surrender its land on the understanding that the land would be leased on certain terms, it would be unconscionable to permit the Crown simply to ignore those terms. When the promised lease proved impossible to obtain, the Crown, instead of proceeding to lease the land on different, unfavourable terms, should have returned to the band to explain what had occurred and seek the band's counsel on how to proceed. The existence of such unconscionability is the key to a conclusion that the Crown breached its fiduciary duty. Equity will not countenance unconscionable behaviour in a fiduciary, whose duty is that of utmost loyalty to his principal.

While the existence of the fiduciary obligation which the Crown owes to the Indians is dependent on the nature of the surrender process, the standard of conduct which the obligation imports is both more general and more exacting than the terms of any particular surrender. In the present case the relevant aspect of the required standard of conduct is defined by a principle analogous to that which underlies the doctrine of promissory or equitable estoppel. The Crown cannot promise the band that it will obtain a lease of the latter's land on certain stated terms, thereby inducing the band to alter its legal position by surrendering the land, and then simply ignore that promise to the band's detriment: see, e.g., *Central London Property Trust Ltd.* v. *High Trees House Ltd.*, [1947] 1 K.B. 130; *Robertson* v. *Min. of Pensions*, [1949] 1 K.B. 227 (C.A.).

In obtaining without consultation a much less valuable lease than that promised, the Crown breached the fiduciary obligation it owed the band. It must make good the loss suffered in consequence. . . .

I would therefore allow the appeal, set aside the judgment in the Federal Court of Appeal and reinstate without variation the trial judge's award, with costs to the present appellants in all courts.

ESTEY J. (concurring in the result): . . . The *Indian Act*, R.S.C. 1952, c. 149 [now R.S.C. 1970, c. I–6], as amended, the Constitution, the pre-Confederation laws of the colonies in British North America, and the *Royal Proclamation of 1763* [see R.S.C. 1970, App. II] all reflect a strong sense of awareness of the community interest in protecting the rights of the native population in those lands to which they had a longstanding connection. One common feature in all these enactments is reflected in the present-day provision in the *Indian Act*, s. 37, which requires anyone interested in acquiring ownership or some lesser interest in lands set aside for native populations, from a willing grantor, to do so through the appropriate level of government, now the federal government. This section has already been set out by my colleagues. In the elaborate provisions in the *Indian Act*, there are many alternative ways of protecting the interests of the Indians and of reflecting the community interest in that protection. The statute and the cases make provision for a surrender of the Indian interest in Indian lands as defined in the Act. And cases such as *St. Catherine's* indicate the extent to which the Indian band must go in order to sever entirely the connection of the native population from the lands in question. This type of surrender would be better described as a release, in the modern lexicon.

Unfortunately, the statute employs the word "surrender" in another connotation. In order to deal with what has been found to be the personal interest of the Indian population in Indian lands, the Act requires the band to "surrender" the land to the Crown in the right of Canada in order to effect the proposed alternate use of the land for the benefit of the Indians. The Act, in short, does not require the Indian to limit his interest in Indian lands to present and continuous occupation. The band may vicariously occupy the lands, or part of such lands, through the medium of a lease or licence. The marketing of the personal interest is not only permitted by the statute, but the machinery is provided for the proper exploitation of this interest by the Indians, subject always to compliance with the statute: vide *St. Ann's Island Shooting Fishing Club Ltd.* v. *R.*, [1950] S.C.R. 211. The step to be taken by the Indian band in seeking to avail itself of the benefits of their right of possession in this manner is, unhappily, also referred to in the statute and in the cases as a "surrender" of the lands and their interest therein to the Crown. This is not a release in the sense of that term in the general law. Indeed, it is quite the opposite. It is a retention of interest and the exploitation of that interest in the manner and to the extent permitted by statute law. The Crown becomes the appointed agent of the Indians to develop and exploit, under the direction of the Indians and for their benefit, the usufructuary interest as described in *St. Catherine's*. . . .

The fact that the agent is prescribed by statute in no way detracts in law from the legal capacity of the agent to act as such. The further consideration that the principal (the Indian band as holder of the personal interest in the land) is constrained by statute to act through the agency of the Crown, in no way reduces the rights of the instructing principal to call upon the agent to account for the performance of the mandate. The measure of damages applied by the learned trial judge is in no way affected by ascribing the resultant rights in the plaintiff to a breach of agency. Indeed, it is consonant with the purpose of the statutory agency as prescribed by Parliament, now and historically, that the agent (the Crown), in all its actions, shall serve only the interests of the native population whose rights alone are the subject of the protective measures of the statute. If anything, the principal in this relationship is more secure in his rights than in the absence of a statutorily prescribed agency. The principal is restricted in the selection of the agent, but the agent is nowhere protected in the statute from the consequences in law of a breach of that agency.

For these reasons, I would, with great respect to all who hold a contrary view, hesitate to resort to the more technical and far-reaching doctrines of the law of trusts and the concomitant law attaching to the fiduciary. The result is the same but, in my respectful view, the future application of the Act and the common law to native rights is much simpler under the doctrines of the law of agency.

I therefore share with my colleagues the conclusion that this appeal should be allowed with costs.

WILSON J. (concurring in the result) (RITCHIE and MCINTYRE JJ. concurring):
. . .

9.   *Roberts* v. *Canada*, [1989] 2 C.N.L.R. 146 (S.C.C.) [*sub nom. Wewayakum Indian Band* v. *Canada*]. **Dickson C.J., Beetz, Lamer, Wilson, and Le Dain (took no part in the judgment) JJ., March 9, 1989**

> *Roberts* is significant because it confirms the jurisdiction of the Federal Court of Canada to adjudicate cases concerning Aboriginal rights and title. More importantly, this decision also affirms that Aboriginal title is part of the federal common law and that issues respecting the fiduciary obligations of the Crown are automatically raised upon the advancement of an Aboriginal title claim.

WILSON J. (DICKSON C.J., BEETZ and LAMER JJ. concurring):—The issue in this appeal is whether the Federal Court of Canada has jurisdiction to hear the trespass action brought by the respondent Indian band against the appellant Indian band. . . .

The essential requirements to support a finding of jurisdiction in the Federal Court have been set out and expanded upon by this Court on a number of occasions. In *ITO-International Terminal Operators Ltd.* v. *Miida Electronics Inc.*, [1986] 1 S.C.R. 752, McIntyre J., speaking for the majority and drawing primarily upon this Court's judgments in *Quebec North Shore Paper Co.* v. *Canadian Pacific Ltd.*, [1977] 2 S.C.R. 1054, and in *McNamara Construction (Western) Ltd.* v. *The Queen*, [1977] 2 S.C.R. 654, summarized the test to be applied in assessing whether the Federal Court is properly seized of a matter at p. 766:

> 1. There must be a statutory grant of jurisdiction by the federal Parliament.
> 2. There must be an existing body of federal law which is essential to the disposition of the case and which nourishes the statutory grant of jurisdiction.
> 3. The law on which the case is based must be "a law of Canada" as the phrase is used in s. 101 of the *Constitution Act, 1867.*

This test is well established as the one to be applied in every case where the jurisdiction of the Federal Court is in issue. . . .

My conclusion that s. 17(3)(c) of the *Federal Court Act* confers jurisdiction on the Federal Court to deal with the issues in this case is, of course, premised on the constitutionality of the section. In *Dywidag Systems International Canada Ltd.* v. *Zutphen Brothers Construction Ltd.* (1987), 76 N.S.R. (2d) 398, the Nova Scotia Court of Appeal held that the exclusive jurisdiction of the Federal Court with respect to claims against the federal Crown, as a result of which the federal Crown can sue the subject in the provincial superior courts but the subject cannot sue the Crown in these courts, infringes the guarantee of equality before the law contained in s. 15 of the *Canadian Charter of Rights and Freedoms.* . . .

Having found that the first element in the *ITO* test is satisfied, i.e., that there is a statutory grant of jurisdiction to the Federal Court, I turn now to the two remaining elements. The second element is that there be an existing body of federal law essential to the disposition of the case which nourishes the statutory grant of jurisdiction. The Federal Court of Appeal found that body of federal law in a combination of the law concerning aboriginal title and the provisions of the *Indian Act.* Hugessen J. concluded that the aboriginal title must be in either the Plaintiff or Defendant Band and is essential to the disposition of the appeal. He noted that while the *Indian Act* did not create the right to possession of reserve lands, the provisions of that Act which deal with that right would be essential elements in the disposition of the case on the merits. He further found that it was beyond question that both the *Indian Act* and the law of aboriginal title are "Laws of Canada" within the meaning of s. 101 of the *Constitution Act, 1867*, thus satisfying the third and final component of the *ITO* test.

In this Court the Plaintiff Band conceded that its claim was not based upon aboriginal title, but contended that such title would be relevant to the determination of the right to occupation of the reserve. While I do not disagree with Hugessen J.'s conclusion that both the law of aboriginal title and the provisions of the *Indian Act* are relevant in the present case, I do not believe that this is adequate to satisfy the third requirement of the test for Federal Court jurisdiction, namely that the claim itself be "based" upon "a law of Canada" within the meaning of s. 101 of the *Constitution Act, 1867.*

The right to the use and occupancy of reserve lands flows from the *sui generis* nature of Indian title. However, where the issue in the case is which of two claimant Bands has the right to use and occupy a particular reserve, we have to go to other sources for an answer. One of these sources is the executive act which originally established the Indian reserve and allotted it either through the Ashdown Green report or the McKenna-McBride Commission Report to one or other of the claimant Bands. Other sources we must look at are the provisions of the *Indian Act* which, while not constitutive of the obligations owed to the Indians by the Crown, codify the pre-existing duties of the Crown toward the Indians. Still another source is the common law relating to aboriginal title which underlies the fiduciary nature of the Crown's obligations. It is interesting to note that Hugessen J. relied on s. 91(24) of the *Constitution Act, 1867* and on *Derrickson* v. *Derrickson*, [1986] 1 S.C.R. 285, [1986] 2 C.N.L.R. 45, for his statement that "it cannot be seriously argued that the law of aboriginal title is today anything other than existing federal law." The reference is to the conclusion of Chouinard J., writing for the Court in *Derrickson* on the question whether provincial family law legislation dealing with family assets could apply to land on an Indian reserve. Chouinard J. stated at p. 296 [p. 55 C.N.L.R.]:

> The right to possession of lands on an Indian reserve is manifestly of the very essence of the federal exclusive legislative power under s. 91(24) of the *Constitution Act, 1867*. It follows that provincial legislation cannot apply to the right of possession of Indian reserve lands.

While I do not question the soundness of Chouinard J.'s conclusion that provincial legislation cannot apply to Indian lands because of the exclusive federal legislative power in relation to "Indians, and Lands reserved for Indians" under s. 91(24) of the *Constitution Act, 1867*, it does not, in my view, address the issue before us which is: is the law of aboriginal title a "law of Canada" within the meaning of s. 101? I turn to Laskin C.J. in *McNamara Construction* and *Quebec North Shore* for guidance.

In these two cases Laskin C.J. made it abundantly clear that federal legislative competence over a subject matter is not enough to satisfy the third branch of the test for Federal Court jurisdiction. He stated at pp. 658–59 of *McNamara*:

> In *Quebec North Shore Paper Company* v. *Canadian Pacific Limited* (a decision which came after the judgments of the Federal Court of Appeal in the present appeals), this Court held that the quoted provisions of s. 101, make it a prerequisite to the exercise of jurisdiction by the Federal Court that there be existing and applicable federal law which can be invoked to support any proceedings before it. It is not enough that the Parliament of Canada have legislative jurisdiction in respect of some matter which is the subject of litigation in the Federal Court. As this Court indicated in the *Quebec North Shore Paper Company* case, judicial jurisdiction contemplated by s. 101 is not co-extensive with federal legislative jurisdiction. It follows that the mere fact that Parliament has exclusive legislative authority in relation to "the public debt and prop-erty" under s. 91(1A) of the *British North America Act* and in relation to "the establish-ment, maintenance and management of penitentiaries" under s. 91(28), and that the subject matter of the construction contract may fall within either or both of these grants of power, is not enough to support a grant of jurisdiction to the Federal Court to entertain the claim for damages made in these cases.

He further stated at p. 659:

> In the *Quebec North Shore Paper Company* case, this Court observed, referring to this provision, that the Crown in right of Canada in seeking to bring persons in the Ex-chequer Court as defendants must have founded its action *on some existing federal law, whether statute or regulation or common law.*
>
> What must be decided in the present appeals, therefore, is not whether the Crown's action is in respect of matters that are within federal legislative jurisdiction but *whether it is founded on existing federal law.* [Emphasis added.]

Commenting on *Quebec North Shore* and *McNamara Construction*, Professor Evans observes, Evans, J., "Federal Jurisdiction: A Lamentable Situation" (1981) 59 *Can. Bar Rev.* 124 at 125:

> The thrust of *Quebec North Shore* and *McNamara Construction* was to deny, in gen-eral terms, the existence of a body of federal common law that was co-extensive with the unexercised constitutional legislative competence of Parliament over matters as-signed to it. *Thus a law will normally only be a law of Canada for the purpose of section 101 of the British North America Act if it is enacted by or under federal legis-lation.* [Emphasis added.]

If Professor Evans is saying in the above-quoted paragraph that only federal *legislation* can meet the description of a "law of Canada" within the meaning of s. 101, I think he must be wrong since Laskin C.J. clearly includes "common law" as existing federal law inasmuch as he says that the cause of action must be founded "on some existing federal law, whether statute or regulation or common law." Pro-fessor Evans may be right that *Quebec North Shore* and *McNamara Construction* deny the existence of a federal body of common law co-extensive with the federal legislature's unexercised legislative jurisdiction over the subject matters assigned to it. However, I think that the existence of "federal common law" in some areas is expressly recognized by Laskin C.J. and the question for us, therefore, is whether the law of aboriginal title is federal common law.

I believe that it is. In *Calder* v. *Attorney-General of British Columbia*, [1973] S.C.R. 313, this Court recognized aboriginal title as a legal right derived from the Indians' historic occupation and possession of their tribal lands. As Dickson J. (as he then was) pointed out in *Guerin*, supra, aboriginal title pre-dated colonization by the British and survived British claims of sovereignty. The Indians' right of occupation and possession continued as a "burden on the radical or final title of the Sovereign": *per* Viscount Haldane in *Amodu Tijani* v. *Southern Nigeria (Secretary)*, [1921] 2 A.C. 399 (P.C.), at p. 403. While, as was made clear in *Guerin*, s. 18(1) of the *Indian Act* did not create the unique relationship between the Crown and the Indians, it certainly incorporated it into federal law by affirming that "reserves are held by Her Majesty for the use and benefit of the respective bands for which they were set apart."

I would conclude therefore that "laws of Canada," are exclusively required for the disposition of this appeal, namely the relevant provisions of the *Indian Act*, the act of the federal executive pursuant to the *Indian Act* in setting aside the reserve in issue for the use and occupancy of one or other of the two claimant Bands, and the common law of aboriginal title which underlies the fiduciary obligations of the Crown to both Bands. The remaining two elements of the test set out in *ITO*, supra are accordingly satisfied.

For the foregoing reasons I would dismiss the appeal with costs.

10. *Mabo* v. *Queensland*, [1992] 5 C.N.L.R. 1 High Court of Australia. Mason C.J., Brennan, Deane, Dawson, Toohey, Gaudron, and McHugh JJ., June 3, 1992

This High Court of Australia decision (the Australian equivalent of the Supreme Court of Canada) involved a claim by the Murray Islanders, members of the Meriam people, that they, since time immemorial, occupied and enjoyed the Murray Islands and had their own forms of social and political organization. Although the Islanders recognized the sovereignty of the Crown, they sought a declaration affirming that this sovereignty was subject to their Aboriginal rights based on their local custom, their traditional Aboriginal title, and their actual possession, use, and enjoyment of the Islands. Even though, as an Australian decision, *Mabo,* strictly speaking, carries little judicial authority in Canada, Lamer C.J. noted in *R. v. Van der Peet* that *Mabo* was "persuasive" in the Canadian context (see para. 38). *Mabo* is relevant in understanding the similarities and differences between Canada and Australia in their approaches to dealing with Aboriginal rights' issues. This decision affirms the existence of Aboriginal title in Australia. The following excerpt is from the judgments of Mason C.J. and McHugh J. and from Brennan J. writing for the majority. Readers interested in additional material from Australia are encouraged to examine McRae, Nettheim, and Beacroft's *Aboriginal Legal Issues: Cases and Materials* and a number of articles by R. Bartlett noted in the bibliography to this chapter.

MASON C.J. and McHUGH J.:—We agree with the reasons for judgment of Brennan J. and with the declaration which he proposes.

In the result, six members of the Court (Dawson J. dissenting) are in agreement that the common law of this country recognizes a form or Native title which, in the cases where it has not been extinguished, reflects the entitlement of the Indigenous inhabitants, in accordance with their laws or customs, to their traditional lands and that, subject to the effect of some particular Crown leases, the land entitlement of the Murray Islanders in accordance with their laws or customs is preserved, as Native title, under the law of Queensland. The main difference between those members of the Court who constitute the majority is that, subject to the operation of the *Racial Discrimination Act 1975* (Cth), neither of us nor Brennan J. agrees with the conclusion to be drawn from the judgments of Deane, Toohey and Gaudron JJ. that, at least in the absence of clear and unambiguous statutory provision to the contrary, extinguishment of Native title by the Crown by inconsistent grant is wrongful and gives rise to a claim for compensatory damages. We note that the judgment of Dawson J. supports the conclusion of Brennan J. and ourselves on that aspect of the case since his Honour considers that Native title, where it exists, is a form of permissive occupancy at the will of the Crown. . . .

BRENNAN J.: . . .

The Theory of Universal and Absolute Crown Ownership

It may be assumed that on 1 August 1879 the Meriam people knew nothing of the events in Westminster and in Brisbane that effected the annexation of the Murray Islands and their incorporation into Queensland and that, had the Meriam people been told of the Proclamation made in Brisbane on 21 July 1879, they would not have appreciated its significance. The legal consequences of these events are in issue in this case. Oversimplified, the chief question in this case is whether these transactions had the effect on 1 August 1879 of vesting in the Crown absolute ownership of, legal possession of and exclusive power to confer title to, all land in the Murray Islands. The defendant submits that that was the legal consequence of the Letters Patent and of the events which brought them into effect. If that submission be right, the Queen took the land occupied by the Meriam people on 1 August 1879 without their knowing of the expropriation; they were no longer entitled without the consent of the Crown to continue to occupy the land they had occupied for centuries past. . . .

On analysis, the defendant's argument is that, when the territory of a settled colony became part of the Crown's dominions, the law of England so far as applicable to colonial conditions became the law of the colony and, by that law, the Crown acquired the absolute beneficial ownership of all land in the territory so that the colony became the Crown's demesne and no right or interest in any land in the territory could thereafter be possessed by any other person unless granted by the Crown. Perhaps the clearest statement of these propositions is to be found in *Attorney-General* v. *Brown*, (1847), 1 Legge 312, at p. 316, when the Supreme Court of New South Wales rejected a challenge to the Crown's title to the possession of the land in the colony. Stephen C.J. stated the law to be,

that the waste lands of this Colony are, and ever have been, from the time of its first settlement in 1788, in the Crown; that they are, and ever have been, from that date (in point of legal intendment), without office found, in the Sovereign's possession; and that, as his or her property, they have been and may now be effectually granted to subjects of the Crown. . . .

The proposition that, when the Crown assumed sovereignty over an Australian colony, it became the universal and absolute beneficial owner of all the land therein, invites critical examination. If the conclusion at which Stephen C.J. arrived in *Attorney-General* v. *Brown* be right, the interests of Indigenous inhabitants in colonial land were extinguished so soon as British subjects settled in a colony, though the Indigenous inhabitants had neither ceded their lands to the Crown nor suffered them to be taken as the spoils of conquest. According to the cases, the common law itself took from Indigenous inhabitants any right to occupy their traditional land, exposed them to deprivation of the religious, cultural and economic sustenance which the land provides, vested the land effectively in the control of the Imperial authorities without any right to compensation and made the Indigenous inhabitants intruders in their own homes and mendicants for a place to live. Judged by any civilized standard, such a law is unjust and its claim to be part of the common law to be applied in contemporary Australia must be questioned. This Court must now determine whether, by the common law of this country, the rights and interests of the Meriam people of today are to be determined on the footing that their ancestors lost their traditional rights and interests in the land of the Murray Islands on 1 August 1879. . . .

However, recognition by our common law of the rights and interests in land of the Indigenous inhabitants of a settled colony would be precluded if the recognition were to fracture a skeletal principle of our legal system. The proposition that the Crown became the beneficial owner of all colonial land on first settlement has been supported by more than a disregard of Indigenous rights and interests. It is necessary to consider these other reasons for past disregard of Indigenous rights and interests and then to return to a consideration of the question whether and in what way our contemporary common law recognizes such rights and interests in land.

Crown Title to Colonies and Crown Ownership of Colonial Land Distinguished
In the trilogy of cases cited earlier in this judgment, supra, pp. 23–25: *Attorney-General* v. *Brown; Randwick Corporation* v. *Rutledge;* the *Seas and Submerged Lands Case*, it was said that colonial land became a royal demesne—that is, that the Crown became the absolute beneficial owner in possession of all colonial land— on first settlement, the event which conferred sovereignty on the Imperial Crown. Curiously, in *Williams* v. *Attorney-General for New South Wales*, (1913), 16 C.L.R. 404, at p. 439, Isaacs J. said it was unquestionable that,

> when Governor Phillip received his first Commission from King George III. on 12th October 1786, the whole of the lands of Australia were already in law the *property* of the King of England.

With respect to Isaacs J., that proposition is wholly unsupported. Roberts-Wray comments, *Commonwealth and Colonial Law*, op. cit., p. 631, that the proposition is "startling and, indeed, incredible". We need not be concerned with the date on which sovereignty over the Australian colonies was acquired by the Crown but we are concerned with the proposition that on, and by reason of, the acquisition of sovereignty, the Crown acquired all colonial land as a royal demesne.

There is a distinction between the Crown's title to a colony and the Crown's ownership of land in the colony, as Roberts-Wray points out, *Commonwealth and Colonial Law*, op. cit., p. 625:

> If a country is part of Her Majesty's dominions, the sovereignty vested in her is of two kinds. The first is the power of government. The second is title to the country . . .
>
> This ownership of the country is radically different from ownership of the land: the former can belong only to a sovereign, the latter to anyone. Title to land is not, *per se*, relevant to the constitutional status of a country; land may have become vested in the Queen, equally in a Protectorate or in a Colony, by conveyance or under statute . . .
>
> The distinction between these two conceptions has, however, become blurred by the doctrine that the acquisition of sovereignty over a Colony, whether by settlement, cession or conquest, or even of jurisdiction in territory which remains outside the British dominions, imports Crown rights in, or in relation to, the land itself. . . .

It was only by fastening on the notion that a settled colony was *terra nullius* that it was possible to predicate of the Crown the acquisition of ownership of land in a colony already occupied by Indigenous inhabitants. It was only on the hypothesis that there was nobody in occupation that it could be said that the Crown was the owner because there was on other. If that hypothesis be rejected, the notion that sovereignty carried ownership in its wake must be rejected too. Though the rejection of the notion of *terra nullius* clears away the fictional impediment to the recognition of Indigenous rights and interests in colonial land, it would be impossible for the common law to recognize such rights and interests if the basic doctrines of the common law are inconsistent with their recognition.

A basic doctrine of the land is the doctrine of tenure, to which Stephen C.J. referred in *Attorney-General* v. *Brown*, and it is a doctrine which could not be overturned without fracturing the skeleton which gives our land law its shape and consistency. . . .

The Nature and Incidents of Native Title

Native title has its origin in and is given its content by the traditional laws acknowledged by and the traditional customs observed by the Indigenous inhabitants of a territory. The nature and incidents of Native title must be ascertained as a matter of fact by reference to those laws and customs. The ascertainment may present a problem of considerable difficulty, as Moynihan J. perceived in the present case. It is a problem that did not arise in the case of a settled colony so long as the fictions were maintained that customary rights could not be reconciled "with the institutions or the legal ideas of civilized society," In *re Southern Rhodesia*, [1919] A.C., at p. 233, that there was no law before the arrival of the British colonists in a settled colony and that there was no sovereign law-maker in the territory of a settled colony before sovereignty was acquired by the Crown. These fictions denied the possibility of a Native title recognized by our laws. But once it is acknowledged that an inhabited territory which became a settled colony was no more a legal desert than it was "desert uninhabited" in fact, it is necessary to ascertain by evidence the nature and incidents of Native title. Though these are matters of fact, some general propositions about Native title can be stated without reference to evidence.

First, unless there are pre-existing laws of a territory over which the Crown acquires sovereignty which provide for the alienation of interests in land to strangers, the rights and interests which constitute a Native title can be possessed only by the Indigenous inhabitants and their descendants. Native title, through recognized by the common law, is not an institution of the common law and is not alienable by the common law. Its alienability is dependent on the laws from which it is derived. If alienation of a right or interest in land is a mere matter of the custom observed by the Indigenous inhabitants, not provided for by law enforced by a sovereign power, there is no machinery which can enforce the rights of the alienee. The common law cannot enforce as a proprietary interest the rights of a putative alienee whose title is not created either under a law which was enforceable against the putative alienor at the time of the alienation and thereafter until the change of sovereignty or under the common law. And, subject to an important qualification, the only title dependent on custom which the common law will recognize is one which is consistent with the common law. . . . At that stage in its development, the common law was too rigid to admit recognition of a Native title based on other laws or customs, but that rigidity has been relaxed, at lease since the decision of the Privy Council in *Amodu Tijani*. The general principle that the common law will recognize a customary title only if it be consistent with the common law is subject to an exception in favour of traditional Native title.

Of course, since European settlement of Australia, many clans or groups of Indigenous people have been physically separated from their traditional land and have lost their connection with it. But that is not the universal position. It is clearly not the position of the Meriam people. Where a clan or group has continued to acknowledge the laws and (so far as practicable) to observe the customs based on the traditions of that clan or group, whereby their traditional connection with the land has been substantially maintained, the traditional community title of that clan or group can be said to remain in existence. The common law can, by reference to the traditional laws and customs of an Indigenous people, identify and protect the Native rights and interests to which they give rise. However, when the tide of history has washed away any real acknowledgment of traditional law and any real observance of traditional customs, the foundation of Native title has disappeared. A Native title which has ceased with the abandoning of laws and customs based on tradition cannot be revived for contemporary recognition. Australian law can protect the interests of members of an Indigenous clan or group, whether communally or individually, only in conformity with the traditional laws and customs of the people to whom the clan or group belongs and only where members of the clan or group acknowledge those laws and observe those customs (so far as it is practicable to do so). Once traditional Native title expires, the Crown's radical title expands to a full beneficial title, for then there is no other proprietor than the Crown.

It follows that a right or interest possessed as a Native title cannot be acquired from an Indigenous people by one who, not being a member of the Indigenous people, does not acknowledge their laws and observe their customs; nor can such a right or interest be acquired by a clan, group or member of the Indigenous people unless the acquisition is consistent with the laws and customs of that people. Such right or interest can be acquired outside those laws and customs only by the Crown. This result has been reached in other jurisdictions, though for different reason: see *Reg.* v. *Symond* (1847), N.Z.P.C.C., at p. 390; *Johnson* v. *M'Intosh* (1823), 8 Wheaton, at p. 586 (21 U.S., at p. 259); *St. Catherine's Milling & Lumber Co.* v. *The Queen* (1887), 13 S.C.R. 577, at p. 599. Once the Crown acquires sovereignty and the common law becomes the law of the territory, the Crown's sovereignty over all land in the territory carries the capacity to accept a surrender of Native title. The Native title may be surrendered on purchase or surrendered voluntarily, whereupon the Crown's radical title is expanded to absolute ownership, a plenum dominium, for there is then no *other* owner, *St. Catherine's Milling and Lumber Co.* v. *The Queen* (1888), 14 App. Cas., at p. 55. If Native title were surrendered to the Crown in expectation of a grant of a tenure to the Indigenous title holders, there may be a fiduciary duty on the Crown to exercise its discretionary power to grant a tenure in land so as to satisfy the expectation, see *Guerin* v. *The Queen* (1984), 13 D.L.R. (4th) 321, at pp. 334, 339, 342–43, 356–57, 360–61 [[1985] 1 C.N.L.R. 120 at 131, 136, 138–39, 151–52, 155–56], but it is unnecessary to consider the existence or extent of such a fiduciary duty in this case. Here, the fact that strangers were not allowed to settle on the Murray Islands and, even after annexation in 1879, strangers who were living on the islands were deported. The Meriam people asserted an exclusive right to occupy the Murray Islands and, as a community, held a proprietary interest in the Islands. They have maintained their identity as a people and they observe customs which are traditional based. There was a possible alienation of some kind of interest in 2 acres to the London Missionary society prior to annexation but it is unnecessary to consider whether that land was alienated by Meriam law or whether the alienation was sanctioned by custom alone. As we shall see, Native title to that land was lost to the Meriam people in any event on the grant of a lease by the Crown in 1882 or by its subsequent renewal.

Secondly, Native title, being recognized by the common law (though not as a common law tenure), may be protected by such legal or equitable remedies as are appropriate to the particular rights and interests established by the evidence, whether proprietary or personal and usufructuary in nature and whether possessed by a community, a group or an individual. The incidents of a particular Native title relating to inheritance, the transmission or acquisition of rights and interest on death or marriage, the transfer of rights and interests in land and the grouping of persons to possess rights and interests in land are matters to be determined by the laws and customs of the Indigenous inhabitants, provided those laws and customs are not so repugnant to natural justice, equity and good conscience that judicial sanctions under the new regime must be withheld: *Idewu Inasa* v. *Oshodi*, [1934] A.D. 99, at p. 105. Of course in time the laws and customs of any people will change and the rights and interests of the members of the people among themselves will change too. But so long as the people remain as an identifiable community, the members of whom are identified by one another as members of that community living under its laws and customs, the communal Native title survives to be enjoyed by the members according to the rights and interests to which they are respectively entitled under the traditional based laws and customs, as currently acknowledged and observed. Here, the Meriam people have maintained their own identity and their own customs. The Murray Islands clearly remain their home country. Their land disputes have been dealt with over the years by the Island Court in accordance with the customs of the Meriam people.

Thirdly, where an Indigenous people (including a clan or group), as a community are in possession or are entitled to possession of land under a proprietary Native title, their possession may be protected or their entitlement to possession may be enforced by a representative action brought on behalf of the people or by a subgroup or individual who sues to protect or enforce rights or interests which are dependent on the communal Native title. Those rights and interests are, so to speak, carved out of the communal Native title. A subgroup or individual asserting a Native title dependent on a communal Native title has sufficient interest to sue to enforce or protect the communal title, *Australian Conservation Foundation* v. *The Commonwealth* (1980), 146 C.L.R. 493, at pp. 530–31, 537–39, 547–48; *Onus* v. *Alcoa of Australia Ltd.* (1981), 149 C.L.R. 27, at pp. 35–36, 41–42, 46, 51, 62, 74–75. A communal Native title enures for the benefit of the community as a whole and for the sub-groups and individuals within it who have particular rights and interests in the community's lands. . . .

Whatever be the precision of Meriam laws and customs with respect to land, there is abundant evidence that land was traditionally occupied by individuals or family groups and that contemporary rights and interests are capable of being established with sufficient precision to attract declaratory or other relief. Although the findings made by Moynihan J. do not permit a confident conclusion that, in 1879, there were parcels of land in the Murray Islands owned allodially by individual or groups, the absence of such a finding is not critical to the final resolution of this case. . . . [B]y applying the rule that the communal proprietary interests of the Indigenous inhabitants survive the Crown's acquisition of sovereignty, it is possible to determine, according to the laws and customs of the Meriam people, contests among members of the Meriam people relating to rights and interests in particular parcels of land. . . .

The Extinguishing of Native Title
Sovereignty carries the power to create and to extinguish private rights and interests in land within the Sovereign's territory, *Joint Tribal Council of the Passamaquoddy Tribe* v. *Morton* (1975) 528 Fed. 2d 370, at p. 376, n. 6. It follows that, on a change of sovereignty, rights and interests in land that may have been indefeasible under the old regime become liable to extinction by exercise of the new sovereign power. The sovereign power may or may not be exercised with solicitude for the welfare of Indigenous inhabitants but, in the case of common law countries, the courts cannot review the merits, as distinct from the legality, of the exercise of sovereign power, *United States* v. *Santa Fe Pacific Railroad Company* (1941) 314 U.S. 339, at p. 347; *Tee-Hit-Ton Indians* v. *United States* (1954) 348 U.S. 272, at pp. 281–85. However, under a constitutional law of this country, the legality (and hence the validity) of an exercise of a sovereign power depends on the authority vested in the organ of government purporting to exercise its municipal constitutional law determines the scope of authority to exercise a sovereign

power over matters governed by municipal law, including rights and interests in land. . . .

. . . [T]he exercise of a power to extinguish Native title must reveal a clear and plain intention to do so, whether the action by taken by the Legislature or by the Executive. This requirement, which flows from the seriousness of the consequences to Indigenous inhabitants of extinguishing their traditional rights and interests in land, has been repeatedly emphasized by courts dealing with the extinguishing of the Native title of Indian bands in North America. It is unnecessary for our purposes to consider the several juristic foundations—proclamation, policy, treaty or occupation—on which Native title has been rested in Canada and the United States but reference to the leading cases in each jurisdiction reveals that, whatever the juristic foundation assigned by those courts might be, Native title is not extinguished unless there be a clear and plain intention to do so. . . .

A clear and plain intention to extinguish Native title is not revealed by a law which merely regulates the enjoyment of Native title, *R.* v. *Sparrow*, [1990] 1 S.C.R., at p. 1097; 70 D.L.R. (4th), at p. 400 [[1990] 3 C.N.L.R. 160 at 173], or which creates a regime of control that is consistent with the continued enjoyment of Native title, *United States* v. *Santa Fe Pacific Railroad Co.* (1941), 314 U.S., at pp. 353–54. A fortiori, a law which reserves or authorizes the reservation of land from sale for the purpose of permitting Indigenous inhabitants and their descendants to enjoy their Native title works no extinguishment.

The Crown did not purport to extinguish Native title to the Murray Islands when they were annexed in 1879. In 1882, in purported exercise of powers conferred by the *Crown Lands Alienation Act* of 1876 (Qld), the Murray Islands were reserved from sale. The 1882 instrument of reservation has not been traced, and it is arguable that the 1876 Act did not apply to land in the Murray Islands for the Murray Islands were not part of Queensland when the Act was passed. That Act was repealed by the *Crown Lands Act* 1884(Qld), which took its place. In 1912, a proclamation was made pursuant to s. 180 of the *Land Act 1910* which "permanently reserved and set apart" the Murray Islands "for use of the Aboriginal Inhabitants of the State". Section 180(1) of the *Land Act* 1910 empowered the Governor in Council to reserve any Crown land from sale or lease "which, in the opinion of the Governor in Council, is or may be required for public purposes". "Public purposes" included "Aboriginal reserves," s. 4. . . .

Native title was not extinguished by the creation of reserves nor by the mere appointment of "trustees" to control a reserve where no grant of title was made. To reserve land from sale is to protect Native title from being extinguished by alienation under a power of sale. To appoint trustees to control a reserve does not confer on the trustees a power to interfere with the rights and interests in land possessed by Indigenous inhabitants under a Native title. Nor is Native title impaired by a declaration that land is reserved not merely for use by the Indigenous inhabitants of the land but "for use of Aboriginal Inhabitants of the State" generally, assuming that that term relates to all Indigenous inhabitants of the State whether having any connection with the particular reserve or not: see *Corporation of the Director of Aboriginal and Islanders Advancement* v. *Peinkinna* (1978), 52 A.L.J.R. 286. If the creation of a reserve of land for Aboriginal Inhabitants of the State who have no other rights or interest in that land confers a right to use that land, the right of user is necessarily subordinate to the right of user consisting in legal rights and interests conferred by Native title. Of course, a Native title which confers a mere usufruct may leave room for other persons to use the land either contemporaneously or from time to time. . . .

A Crown grant which vests in the grantee an interest in land which is inconsistent with the continued right to enjoy a Native title in respect of the same land necessarily extinguishes the Native title. The extinguishing of Native title does not depend on the actual intention of the Governor in Council (who may not have adverted to the rights and interests of the Indigenous inhabitants or their descendants), but on the effect which the grant has on the right to enjoy the Native title. If a lease be granted, the lessee acquires possession and the Crown acquires the reversion expectant on the expiry of the term. The Crowns title is thus expanded from the mere radical title and, on the expiry of the term, becomes a plenum dominium. Where the Crown grants land in trust or reserves and dedicates land for a public purpose, the question whether the Crown has revealed a clear and plain intention to extinguish Native title will sometimes be a question of fact, sometimes a question of law and sometimes a mixed question of fact and law. Thus, if a reservation is made for a public purpose other than for the benefit of the Indigenous inhabitants, a right to continued enjoyment of Native title may be consistent with the specified purpose—at least for a time—and Native title will not be extinguished. But if the land is used and occupied for the public purpose and the manner of occupation is inconsistent with the continued enjoyment of Native title, Native title will be extinguished. A reservation of land for future use as a school, a courthouse or a public office will not by itself extinguish Native title: construction of the building, however, would be inconsistent with the continued enjoyment of Native title which would thereby be extinguished. But where the Crown has not granted interests in land or reserved and dedicated land inconsistently with the right to continued enjoyment of Native title by the Indigenous inhabitants, Native title survives and is legally enforceable.

As the governments of the Australian Colonies and, latterly, the governments of the Commonwealth, States and Territories have alienated or appropriated to their own purposes most of the land in this country during the last 200 years, the Australian Aboriginal peoples have been substantially dispossessed of their traditional lands. They were dispossessed by the Crown's exercise of its sovereign powers to grant land to whom it chose and to appropriate to itself the beneficial ownership of parcels of land for the Crown's purposes. Aboriginal rights and interests were not stripped away by operation of the common law on first settlement by British colonists, but by the exercise of a sovereign authority over land exercised recurrently by governments. To treat the dispossession of the Australian Aborigines as the working out of the Crown's acquisition of ownership of all land on first settlement is contrary to history. Aborigines were dispossessed of their land parcel by parcel, to make way for expanding colonial settlement. Their dispossession underwrote the development of the nation. But, if this be the consequence in law of colonial settlement, is there any occasion now to overturn the cases which held the Crown to have become the absolute beneficial owner of land when British colonists first settled here? Does it make any difference whether Native title failed to survive British colonization or was subsequently extinguished by government action? In this case, the difference is critical: except for certain transactions next to be mentioned, nothing has been done to extinguish Native title in the Murray Islands. There, the Crown has alienated only part of the land and has not acquired for itself the beneficial ownership of any substantial area. And there may be other areas of Australia where Native title has not been extinguished and where an Aboriginal people, maintaining their identity and their customs, are entitled to enjoy their Native title. Even if there be no such areas, it is appropriate to identify the events which resulted in the dispossession of the Indigenous inhabitants of Australia, in order to dispel the misconception that it is the common law rather than the action of governments which made many of the Indigenous people of this country trespassers on their own land.

After this lengthy examination of the problem, it is desirable to state in summary form what I hold to be the common law of Australia with reference to land titles:

1. The Crown's acquisition of sovereignty over the several parts of Australia cannot be challenged in an Australian municipal court.
2. On acquisition of sovereignty over a particular part of Australia, the Crown acquired a radical title to the land in that part.
3. Native title to land survived the Crown's acquisition of sovereignty and radical title. The rights and privileges conferred by Native title were unaffected by the Crown's acquisition of radical title but the acquisition of sovereignty exposed Native title to extinguishment by a valid exercise of sovereign power inconsistent with the continued right to enjoy Native title.
4. Where the Crown has validly alienated land by granting an interest that is wholly or partially inconsistent with a continuing right to enjoy Native title, Native title is extinguished to the extent of the inconsistency. This Native title has been extinguished by grants of estates of freehold or of leases but not necessarily by the grant of lesser interests (e.g., authorities to prospect for minerals).
5. Where the Crown has validly and effectively appropriated land to itself and the appropriation is wholly or partially inconsistent with a continuing right to enjoy Native title, Native title is extinguished to the extent of the inconsistency. Thus Native title has been extinguished to parcels of the waste lands of the Crown that have been validly appropriated for use (whether by dedication, setting aside, reservation or other valid means) and used for roads, railways, post offices and other permanent public works which preclude the continuing concurrent enjoyment of Native title. Native title continues where the waste lands of the Crown have not been so appropriated or used or where the appropriation and use is consistent with the continuing concurrent enjoyment of Native title over the land. (e.g. land set aside as a national park).
6. Native title to particular land (whether classified by the common law as proprietary, usufructuary or otherwise), its incidents and the persons entitled thereto are ascertained according to the laws and customs of the Indigenous people who, by those laws and customs, have a connection with the land. It is immaterial that the laws and customs have undergone some change since the Crown acquired sovereignty provided the general nature of the connection between the Indigenous people and the land remains. Membership of the Indigenous

people depends on biological descent from the Indigenous people and on mutual recognition of a particular person's membership by that person and by the elders or other persons enjoying traditional authority among those people.

7. Native title to an area of land which a clan or group is entitled to enjoy under the laws and customs of an Indigenous people is extinguished if the clan or group, by ceasing to acknowledge those laws, and (so far as practicable) observe those customs, loses its connection with the land or on the death of the last of the members of the group or clan.

8. Native title over any parcel of land can be surrendered to the Crown voluntarily by all those clans or groups who, by the traditional laws and customs of the Indigenous people, have a relevant connection with the land but the rights and privileges conferred by Native title are otherwise inalienable to persons who are not members of the Indigenous people to whom alienation is permitted by the traditional laws and customs.

9. If Native title to any parcel of the waste lands of the Crown is extinguished, the Crown becomes the absolute beneficial owner.

These propositions leave for resolution by the general law the question of the validity of any purported exercise by the Crown of the power to alienate or to appropriate to itself waste lands of the Crown. In Queensland, these powers are and at all material times have been exercisable by the Executive Government subject, in the case of the power of alienation, to the statutes of the State in force from time to time. The power of alienation and the power of appropriation vested in the Crown in right of a State are also subject to the valid laws of the commonwealth, including the *Racial Discrimination Act*. Where a power has purportedly been exercised as a prerogative power, the validity of the exercise depends on the scope of the prerogative and the authority of the purported repository in the particular case.

It remains to apply these principles to the Murray Islands and the Meriam people. . . .

The declaration is founded on the decision in *Mabo* v. *Queensland,* (1988), 166 C.L.R. 186, in which it was held that the Queensland Coast Islands Act 1985 (Qld) which purported to extinguish the plaintiffs' Native title, was nullified by operation of s. 10 of the *Racial Discrimination Act*. The plaintiffs now seek to deny the power of the Governor in Council to grant a deed of grant in trust because, if effective, the alienation of the Murray Islands to a trustee—albeit the trustee would be the Island Council constituted under the *Community Service: (Torres Strait) Act*—would extinguish Native title including the Native title claimed by the individual plaintiffs. Under the relevant provisions of the *Land Act*, the Island council as trustee would have power to lease land inconsistently with Native title.

There are two reasons why the declaration sought by the plaintiffs should be refused. First, there is no evidence that the Governor in Council intends to grant a deed of grant in trust in respect of land in the Murray Islands and the Solicitor-General denied that there were "the slightest indications" that the Governor in Council would do so. Secondly, s. 10 of the *Racial Discrimination Act* may not have an effect on the granting of a deed of grant in trust similar to the effect which s. 10 had upon the *Queensland Coast Islands Declaratory Act 1985*. It will not have a nullifying effect if the action taken under the relevant State laws constitutes a special measure falling within s. 8(1) of the *Racial Discrimination Act* and thereby es-

capes the operation of s. 10, *Gerhardy* v. *Brown* (1985), 159 C.L.R. 70. Whether the granting of a deed of grant in trust would constitute a special measure is a question which cannot be answered without an examination of all the relevant circumstances; it involves findings of fact. In the absence of findings which determine whether a deed of grant in trust would constitute a special measure, no declaration that the granting of such a deed would be "unlawful" can be made. There is no need to determine whether s. 9 of the *Racial Discrimination Act* is inconsistent with the relevant provisions of the *Land Act* 1962, for there is nothing to show that those provisions will be used to affect interests which the plaintiffs seek to protect.
. . .

The plaintiffs seek declarations that the Meriam people are entitled to the Murray Islands,

(a) as owners
(b) as possessors
(c) as occupiers, or
(d) as persons entitled to use and enjoy the said islands;

that,

the Murray Islands are not and never have been "Crown Lands" within the meaning of the *Land Act* 1962 (Qld) (as amended) and prior Crown lands legislation

and that the State of Queensland is not entitled to extinguish the title of the Meriam people.

As the Crown holds the radical title to the Murray Islands and as Native title is not a title created by grant nor is it a common law tenure, it may be confusing to describe the title of the Meriam people as conferring "ownership", a term which connotes an estate in fee simple or at least an estate of freehold. Nevertheless, it is right to say that their Native title is effective as against the State of Queensland and as against the whole world unless the State, in valid exercise of its legislative or executive power, extinguishes the title. It is also right to say that the Murray Islands are not Crown land because the land has been either "reserved for or dedicated to public purposes" or is "subject to . . . lease". However, that does not deny that the Governor in Council may, by appropriate exercise of his statutory powers, extinguish Native title. The Native title has already been extinguished over land which has been leased pursuant to power conferred by the *Land Act* in force at the time of the granting or renewal of the lease. Accordingly, title to the land leased to the Trustees of the Australian Board of Missions has been extinguished and title to Dauar and Waier may have been extinguished. It may be that areas on Mer have been validly appropriated for use for administrative purposes the use of which is inconsistent with the continued enjoyment of the rights and interests of Meriam people in those areas pursuant to Meriam law or custom and, in that event, Native title has been extinguished over those areas. None of these areas can be included in the declaration.

I would therefore make a declaration in the following terms:
Declare—
1.   that the land in the Murray Islands is not Crown land within the meaning of that term in s. 5 of the *Land Act* 1962–1988 (Qld);

2. that the Meriam people are entitled as against the whole world to possession, occupation, use and enjoyment of the island of Mer except for that parcel of land leased to the Trustees of the Australian Board of Missions and those parcels of land (if any) which have been validly appropriated for use for administrative purposes the use of which is inconsistent with the continued enjoyment of the rights and privileges of Meriam people under Native title;

3. that the title of the Meriam people is subject to the power of the Parliament of Queensland and the power of the Government in Council of Queensland to extinguish that title by valid exercise of their respective powers, provided any exercise of those powers in not inconsistent with the laws of the Commonwealth.

11. *Delgamuukw* v. *British Columbia*, [1998] 1 C.N.L.R. 14 (S.C.C.). Lamer C.J., and LaForest, L'Heureux-Dubé, Sopinka (took no part in judgment), Cory, McLachlin, and Major, JJ., December 11, 1997

In *Delgamuukw* v. *B.C.*, the Gitksan and Wet'suwet'en peoples of northwestern British Columbia sought a declaration from the court affirming their ownership, jurisdiction, and Aboriginal rights over a large portion of British Columbian territory. This case is particularly significant because most of British Columbia is without treaties. Although the Court of Appeal overturned the earlier, and more conservative, British Columbia Supreme Court decision of McEachern J. and recognized unextinguished non-exclusive Aboriginal rights of the Gitksan and Wet'suwet'en, the court's judgment did not provide a substantive basis for a right of ownership and jurisdiction over the lands. An excerpt from the Court of Appeal's Lambert J. is included in chapter 8 on self-government. In his dissent to the majority judgment, Lambert J. describes an existing right of "self-regulation."

In December 1997 the Supreme Court of Canada released its much awaited *Delgamuukw* decision. The issues raised in the appeal were vast and included such technical issues as whether the pleadings prevented the court from examining Aboriginal title and self-government claims and to what degree, if any, the court could interfere with findings of fact made by the trial judge. The appeal also considered weightier issues such as the inherent meaning of Aboriginal title and the means by which it may be extinguished, the right of self-government, and whether British Columbia possessed the power to extinguish Aboriginal rights after 1871. This decision is significant not only because it legitimizes Aboriginal oral history as being acceptable evidence to prove Aboriginal title and rights, but also because of its detailed discussion and analysis of Aboriginal title generally. Readers are encouraged to note the Chief Justice's closing paragraph whereby he qualifies the remedy of a new trial by encouraging the parties to negotiate a settlement in the spirit of the *Sparrow* decision and stresses the importance of the Crown fulfilling its moral if not legal duty to enter into good faith negotiations. The following excerpt is from the majority judgment written by Lamer C.J.

LAMER, C.J. (CORY, MCLACHLIN and MAJOR JJ. concurring):

1 This appeal is the latest in a series of cases in which it has fallen to this Court to interpret and apply the guarantee of existing Aboriginal rights found in s. 35(1)

of the *Constitution Act, 1982*. Although that line of decisions, commencing with *R. v. Sparrow*, [1990] 1 S.C.R. 1075, proceeding through the *Van der Peet* trilogy (*R. v. Van der Peet*, [1996] 2 S.C.R. 507, *R. v. N. T. C. Smokehouse Ltd.*, [1996] 2 S.C.R. 672, and *R. v. Gladstone*, [1996] 2 S.C.R. 723), and ending in *R. v. Pamajewon*, [1996] 2 S.C.R. 821, *R. v. Adams*, [1996] 3 S.C.R. 101, and *R. v. Côté*, [1996] 3 S.C.R. 139, have laid down the jurisprudential framework for s. 35(1), this appeal raises a set of interrelated and novel questions which revolve around a single issue—the nature and scope of the constitutional protection afforded by s. 35(1) to common law Aboriginal title.

2   In *Adams*, and in the companion decision in *Côté*, I considered and rejected the proposition that claims to Aboriginal rights must also be grounded in an underlying claim to Aboriginal title. But I held, nevertheless, that Aboriginal title was a distinct species of Aboriginal right that was recognized and affirmed by s. 35(1). Since Aboriginal title was not being claimed in those earlier appeals, it was unnecessary to say more. This appeal demands, however, that the Court now explore and elucidate the implications of the constitutionalization of Aboriginal title. The first is the specific content of Aboriginal title, a question which this Court has not yet definitively addressed, either at common law or under s. 35(1). The second is the related question of the test for the proof of title, which, whatever its content, is a right in land, and its relationship to the definition of the Aboriginal rights recognized and affirmed by s. 35(1) in *Van der Peet* in terms of activities. The third is whether Aboriginal title, as a right in land, mandates a modified approach to the test of justification first laid down in *Sparrow* and elaborated upon in *Gladstone.*

3   In addition to the relationship between Aboriginal title and s. 35(1), this appeal also raises an important practical problem relevant to the proof of Aboriginal title which is endemic to Aboriginal rights litigation generally—the treatment of the oral histories of Canada's Aboriginal peoples by the courts. In *Van der Peet*, I held that the common law rules of evidence should be adapted to take into account the *sui generis* nature of Aboriginal rights. In this appeal, the Court must address what specific form those modifications must take.

4   Finally, given the existence of Aboriginal title in British Columbia, this Court must address, on cross-appeal, the question of whether the province of British Columbia, from the time it joined Confederation in 1871, until the entrenchment of s. 35(1) in 1982, had jurisdiction to extinguish the rights of Aboriginal peoples, including Aboriginal title, in that province. Moreover, if the province was without this jurisdiction, a further question arises—whether provincial laws of general application that would otherwise be inapplicable to Indians and Indian lands could nevertheless extinguish Aboriginal rights through the operation of s. 88 of the *Indian Act*, R.S.C., 1985, c. I-5. . . .

A.   Do the pleadings preclude the Court from entertaining claims for Aboriginal title and self-government?

73   In their pleadings, the appellants, 51 Chiefs representing most of the houses of the Gitksan and Wet'suwet'en nations, originally advanced 51 individual claims

on their own behalf and on behalf of their houses for "ownership" and "jurisdiction" over 133 distinct territories which together comprise 58,000 square kilometres of northwestern British Columbia. On appeal, that original claim was altered in two different ways. First, the claims for ownership and jurisdiction have been replaced with claims for Aboriginal title and self-government, respectively. Second, the individual claims by each house have been amalgamated into two communal claims, one advanced on behalf of each nation. However, there were no formal amendments to the pleadings to this effect, and the respondents accordingly argue that claims which are central to this appeal are not properly before the Court. Furthermore, the respondents argue that they have suffered prejudice as a result because they might have conducted the defence quite differently had they known the case to meet.

74   I reject the respondents' submission with respect to the substitution of Aboriginal titleland self-government for the original claims of ownership and jurisdiction. Although it is true that the pleadings were not formally amended, the trial judge, at p. 158, did allow a de facto amendment to permit "a claim for Aboriginal rights other than ownership and jurisdiction". Had the respondents been concerned about the prejudice arising from this ruling, they could have appealed accordingly. However, they did not, and, as a result, the decision of the trial judge on this point must stand. . . .

76   However, no such amendment was made with respect to the amalgamation of the individual claims brought by the 51 Gitksan and Wet'suwet'en Houses into two collective claims, one by each nation, for Aboriginal title and self-government. Given the absence of an amendment to the pleadings, I must reluctantly conclude that the respondents suffered some prejudice. The appellants argue that the respondents did not experience prejudice since the collective and individual claims are related to the extent that the territory claimed by each nation is merely the sum of the individual claims of each house; the external boundaries of the collective claims therefore represent the outer boundaries of the outer territories. Although that argument carries considerable weight, it does not address the basic point that the collective claims were simply not in issue at trial. To frame the case in a different manner on appeal would retroactively deny the respondents the opportunity to know the appellants' case.

77   This defect in the pleadings prevents the Court from considering the merits of this appeal. However, given the importance of this case and the fact that much of the evidence of individual territorial holdings is extremely relevant to the collective claims now advanced by each of the appellants, the correct remedy for the defect in [i]pleadings is a new trial, where, to quote the trial judge at p. 368, "[i]t will be for the parties to consider whether any amendment is required in order to make the pleadings conform with the evidence". Moreover, as I will now explain, there are other reasons why a new trial should be ordered.

B.   What is the ability of this Court to interfere with the factual findings made by the trial judge?

(1) General principles

78 I recently reviewed the principles governing the appellate review of findings of fact in *Van der Peet, supra.* As a general rule, this Court has been extremely reluctant to interfere with the findings of fact made at trial, especially when those findings of fact are based on an assessment of the testimony and credibility of witnesses. Unless there is a "palpable and overriding error", appellate courts should not substitute their own findings of fact for those of the trial judge. The leading statement of this principle can be found in *Stein* v. *The Ship "Kathy K"*, [1976] 2 S.C.R. 802, *per* Ritchie J., at p. 808:

> These authorities are not to be taken as meaning that the findings of fact made at trial are immutable, but rather that they are not to be reversed unless it can be established that the learned trial judge made some palpable and overriding error which affected his assessment of the facts. While the Court of Appeal is seized with the duty of re-examining the evidence in order to be satisfied that no such error occurred, it is not, in my view, a part of its function to substitute its assessment of the balance of probability for the findings of the judge who presided at the trial.

The same deference must be accorded to the trial judge's assessment of the credibility of expert witnesses: see *N.V. Bocimar S.A.* v. *Century Insurance Co.* of Canada, [1987] 1 S.C.R. 1247.

79 The policy reason underlying this rule is protection of "[t]he autonomy and integrity of the trial process" (*Schwartz* v. *Canada,* [1996] 1 S.C.R. 254, at p. 278), which recognizes that the trier of fact, who is in direct contact with the mass of the evidence, is in the best position to make findings of fact, particularly those which turn on credibility. Moreover, *Van der Peet* clarified that deference was owed to findings of fact even when the trial judge misapprehended the law which was applied to those facts, a problem which can arise in quickly evolving areas of law such as the jurisprudence surrounding s. 35(1).

80 I recently held, in *Van der Peet,* that these general principles apply to cases litigated under s. 35(1). On the other hand, while accepting the general principle of non-interference, this Court has also identified specific situations in which an appeal court can interfere with a finding of fact made at trial. For example, appellate intervention is warranted "where the courts below have misapprehended or overlooked material evidence": see *Chartier* v. *Attorney General of Quebec,* [1979] 2 S.C.R. 474, at p. 493. In cases involving the determination of Aboriginal rights, appellate intervention is also warranted by the failure of a trial court to appreciate the evidentiary difficulties inherent in adjudicating Aboriginal claims when, first, applying the rules of evidence and, second, interpreting the evidence before it. As I said in *Van der Peet,* at para. 68:

> In determining whether an aboriginal claimant has produced evidence sufficient to demonstrate that her activity is an aspect of a practice, custom or tradition integral to a distinctive aboriginal culture, *a court should approach the rules of evidence, and interpret the evidence that exists,* with a consciousness of the special nature of aboriginal claims, and of the evidentiary difficulties in proving a right which originates in times where there were no written records of the practices, customs and traditions

engaged in. *The courts must not undervalue the evidence presented by aboriginal claimants simply because that evidence does not conform precisely with the evidentiary standards that would be applied in, for example, a private law torts case.* [Emphasis added.]

81   The justification for this special approach can be found in the nature of Aboriginal rights themselves. I explained in *Van der Peet* that those rights are aimed at the reconciliation of the prior occupation of North America by distinctive Aboriginal societies with the assertion of Crown sovereignty over Canadian territory. They attempt to achieve that reconciliation by "their bridging of Aboriginal and non-Aboriginal cultures" (at para. 42). Accordingly, "a court must take into account the perspective of the aboriginal people claiming the right . . . while at the same time taking into account the perspective of the common law" such that "[t]rue reconciliation will, equally, place weight on each" (at paras. 49 and 50).

82   In other words, although the doctrine of Aboriginal rights is a common law doctrine, Aboriginal rights are truly *sui generis,* and demand a unique approach to the treatment of evidence which accords due weight to the perspective of Aboriginal peoples. However, that accommodation must be done in a manner which does not strain "the Canadian legal and constitutional structure" (at para. 49). Both the principles laid down in *Van der Peet*—first, that trial courts must approach the rules of evidence in light of the evidentiary difficulties inherent in adjudicating Aboriginal claims, and second, that trial courts must interpret that evidence in the same spirit—must be understood against this background.

83   A concrete application of the first principle can be found in *Van der Peet* itself, where I addressed the difficulties inherent in demonstrating a continuity between current Aboriginal activities and the pre-contact practices, customs and traditions of Aboriginal societies. As I reiterate below, the requirement for continuity is one component of the definition of Aboriginal rights (although, as I explain below, in the case of title, the issue is continuity from sovereignty, not contact). However, given that many Aboriginal societies did not keep written records at the time of contact or sovereignty, it would be exceedingly difficult for them to produce (at para. 62) "conclusive evidence from pre-contact times about the practices, customs and traditions of their community". Accordingly, I held that (at para. 62):

The evidence relied upon by the applicant and the courts may relate to aboriginal practices, customs and traditions *post-contact;* it simply needs to be directed at demonstrating which aspects of the aboriginal community and society have their origins *pre-contact.* [Emphasis added.]

The same considerations apply when the time from which title is determined is sovereignty.

84   This appeal requires us to apply not only the first principle in *Van der Peet* but the second principle as well, and adapt the laws of evidence so that the Aboriginal perspective on their practices, customs and traditions and on their relationship with

the land, are given due weight by the courts. In practical terms, this requires the courts to come to terms with the oral histories of Aboriginal societies, which, for many Aboriginal nations, are the only record of their past. Given that the Aboriginal rights recognized and affirmed by s. 35(1) are defined by reference to pre-contact practices or, as I will develop below, in the case of title, pre-sovereignty occupation, those histories play a crucial role in the litigation of Aboriginal rights. . . .

Oral accounts of the past include a good deal of subjective experience. They are not simply a detached recounting of factual events but, rather, are "facts enmeshed in the stories of a lifetime". They are also likely to be rooted in particular locations, making reference to particular families and communities, This contributes to a sense that there are many histories, each characterized in part by how a people see themselves, how they define their identity in relation to their environment, and how they express their uniqueness as a people. . . .

87   Notwithstanding the challenges created by the use of oral histories as proof of historical facts, the laws of evidence must be adapted in order that this type of evidence can be accommodated and placed on an equal footing with the types of historical evidence that courts are familiar with, which largely consists of historical documents. This is a long-standing practice in the interpretation of treaties between the Crown and Aboriginal peoples: *Sioui, supra,* at p. 1068; *R.* v. *Taylor* (1981), 62 C.C.C. (2d) 227, at p. 232. To quote Dickson C.J., given that most Aboriginal societies "did not keep written records", the failure to do so would "impose an impossible burden of proof" on Aboriginal peoples, and "render nugatory" any rights that they have (*Simon* v. *The Queen,* [1985] 1 2 S.C.R. 387, at p. 408). This process must be undertaken on a case-by-case basis. I will take this approach in my analysis of the trial judge's findings of fact. . . .

(2) Application of General Principles . . .
89   The general principle of appellate non-interference applies with particular force in this appeal. The trial was lengthy and very complex. There were 318 days of testimony. There were a large number of witnesses, lay and expert. The volume of evidence is enormous. . . .

90   It is not open to the appellants to challenge the trial judge's findings of fact merely because they disagree with them. I fear that a significant number of the appellants' objections fall into this category. Those objections are too numerous to list in their entirety. The bulk of these objections, at best, relate to alleged instances of misapprehension or oversight of material evidence by the trial judge. However, the respondents have established that, in most situations, there was some contradictory evidence that supported the trial judge's conclusion. The question, ultimately, was one of weight, and the appellants have failed to demonstrate that the trial judge erred in this respect. . . .

92   . . . [T]he appellants have alleged that the trial judge made a number of serious errors relating to the treatment of the oral histories of the appellants. Those oral

histories were expressed in three different forms: (i) the adaawk of the Gitksan, and the kungax of the Wet'suwet'en; (ii) the personal recollections of members of the appellant nations, and (iii) the territorial affidavits filed by the heads of the individual houses within each nation. The trial judge ruled on both the admissibility of, and the weight to be given to, these various forms of oral history without the benefit of my reasons in *Van der Peet,* as will become evident in the discussion that follows. . . .

93   The adaawk and kungax of the Gitksan and Wet'suwet'en nations, respectively, are oral histories of a special kind. They were described by the trial judge, at p. 164, as a "sacred 'official' litany, or history, or recital of the most important laws, history, traditions and traditional territory of a House". The content of these special oral histories includes its physical representation totem poles, crests and blankets. The importance of the adaawk and kungax is underlined by the fact that they are "repeated, performed and authenticated at important feasts". . . .

94   It is apparent that the adaawk and kungax are of integral importance to the distinctive cultures of the appellant nations. . . .

97   Although he had earlier recognized, when making his ruling on admissibility, that it was impossible to make an easy distinction between the mythological and "real" aspects of these oral histories, he discounted the adaawk and kungax because they were not "literally true", confounded "what is fact and what is belief", "included some material which might be classified as mythology", and projected a "romantic view" of the history of the Appellants. He also cast doubt on the authenticity of these special oral histories (at p. 181) because, *inter alia,* "the verifying group is so small that they cannot safely be regarded as expressing the reputation of even the Indian community, let alone the larger community whose opportunity to dispute territorial claims would be essential to weight". Finally, he questioned (at p. 181) the utility of the adaawk and kungax to demonstrate use and occupation because they were "seriously lacking in detail about the specific lands to which they are said to relate".

98   Although he framed his ruling on weight in terms of the specific oral histories before him, in my respectful opinion, the trial judge in reality based his decision on some general concerns with the use of oral histories as evidence in Aboriginal rights cases. In summary, the trial judge gave no independent weight to these special oral histories because they did not accurately convey historical truth, because knowledge about those oral histories was confined to the communities whose histories they were and because those oral histories were insufficiently detailed. However, as I mentioned earlier, these are features, to a greater or lesser extent, of all oral histories, not just the adaawk and kungax. The implication of the trial judge's reasoning is that oral histories should never be given any independent weight and are only useful as confirmatory evidence in Aboriginal rights litigation. I fear that if this reasoning were followed, the oral histories of Aboriginal peoples would be consistently and systematically undervalued by the Canadian legal system, in con-

tradiction of the express instruction to the contrary in *Van der Peet* that trial courts interpret the evidence of Aboriginal peoples in light of the difficulties inherent in adjudicating Aboriginal claims.

(c)   Recollections of Aboriginal life

99   The trial judge also erred when he discounted the "recollections of Aboriginal life" offered by various members of the appellant nations. I take that term to be a reference to testimony about personal and family history that is not part of an adaawk or a kungax. That evidence consisted of the personal knowledge of the witnesses and declarations of witnesses' ancestors as to land use. This history had been adduced by the appellants in order to establish the requisite degree of use and occupation to make out a claim to ownership and, for the same reason as the adaawk and kungax, is material to the proof of Aboriginal title. . . .

101   In my opinion, the trial judge expected too much of the oral history of the appellants, as expressed in the recollections of Aboriginal life of members of the appellant nations. He expected that evidence to provide definitive and precise evidence of pre-contact Aboriginal activities on the territory in question. However, as I held in *Van der Peet,* this will be almost an impossible burden to meet. Rather, if oral history cannot conclusively establish pre-sovereignty (after this decision) occupation of land, it may still be relevant to demonstrate that current occupation has its origins prior to sovereignty. This is exactly what the appellants sought to do.

(d)   Territorial affidavits

102   Finally, the trial judge also erred in his treatment of the territorial affidavits filed by the appellant chiefs. Those affidavits were declarations of the territorial holdings of each of the Gitksan and Wet'suwet'en houses and, at trial, were introduced for the purposes of establishing each House's ownership of its specific territory. Before this Court, the appellants tried to amalgamate these individual claims into collective claims on behalf of each nation and the relevance of the affidavits changed accordingly. I have already held that it is not open to the appellants to alter fundamentally the nature of their claim in this way on appeal. Nevertheless, the treatment of the affidavits is important because they will be relevant at a new trial to the existence and nature of the land tenure system within each nation and, therefore material to the proof of title.

103   The affidavits rely heavily on the declarations of deceased persons of use or ownership of the lands, which are a form of oral history. But those declarations are a kind of hearsay and the appellants therefore argued that the affidavits should be admitted through the reputation exception to the hearsay rule. Although he recognized, at p. 438, that the territorial affidavits were "the best evidence [the appellants] could adduce on the question of internal boundaries", the trial judge held that this exception did not apply and refused to admit the declarations contained in the affidavits.

104   I am concerned by the specific reasons the trial judge gave for refusing to apply the reputation exception. He questioned the degree to which the declarations

amounted to a reputation because they were largely confined to the appellants' communities. The trial judge asserted that neighbouring Aboriginal groups whose territorial claims conflicted with those of the appellants, as well as non-Aboriginals who potentially possessed a legal interest in the claimed territory, were unaware of the content of the alleged reputation at all. Furthermore, the trial judge reasoned that since the subject-matter of the affidavits was disputed, its reliability was doubtful. Finally, the trial judge questioned, at p. 441, the "independence and objectivity" of the information contained in the affidavits, because the appellants and their ancestors (at p. 440) "have been actively discussing land claims for many years".

105 Although he regretted this finding, the trial judge felt bound to apply the rules of evidence because it did not appear to him (at p. 442) "that the Supreme Court of Canada has decided that the ordinary rules of evidence do not apply to this kind of case". The trial judge arrived at this conclusion, however, without the benefit of *Van der Peet,* where I held that the ordinary rules of evidence must be approached and adapted in light of the evidentiary difficulties inherent in adjudicating Aboriginal claims.

106 Many of the reasons relied on by the trial judge for excluding the evidence contained in the territorial affidavits are problematic because they run against this fundamental principle. The requirement that a reputation be known in the general community, for example, ignores the fact that oral histories, as noted by the Royal Commission on Aboriginal Peoples, generally relate to particular locations, and refer to particular families and communities and may, as a result, be unknown outside of that community, even to other Aboriginal nations. Excluding the territorial affidavits because the claims to which they relate are disputed does not acknowledge that claims to Aboriginal rights, and Aboriginal title in particular, are almost always disputed and contested. Indeed, if those claims were uncontroversial, there would be no need to bring them to the courts for resolution. Casting doubt on the reliability of the territorial affidavits because land claims had been actively discussed for many years also fails to take account of the special context surrounding Aboriginal claims, in two ways. First, those claims have been discussed for so long because of British Columbia's persistent refusal to acknowledge the existence of Aboriginal title in that province until relatively recently, largely as a direct result of the decision of this Court in *Calder, supra.* It would be perverse, to say the least, to use the refusal of the province to acknowledge the rights of its Aboriginal inhabitants as a reason for excluding evidence which may prove the existence of those rights. Second, this rationale for exclusion places Aboriginal claimants whose societies record their past through oral history in a grave dilemma. In order for the oral history of a community to amount to a form of reputation, and to be admissible in court, it must remain alive through the discussions of members of that community; those discussions are the very basis of that reputation. But if those histories are discussed too much, and too close to the date of litigation, they may be discounted as being suspect, and may be held to be inadmissible. The net effect may be that a society with such an oral tradition would never be able to establish a historical claim through the use of oral history in court.

(e) Conclusion

107   The trial judge's treatment of the various kinds of oral histories did not satisfy the principles I laid down in *Van der Peet*. These errors are particularly worrisome because oral histories were of critical importance to the appellants' case. They used those histories in an attempt to establish their occupation and use of the disputed territory, an essential requirement for Aboriginal title. The trial judge, after refusing to admit, or giving no independent weight to these oral histories, reached the conclusion that the appellants had not demonstrated the requisite degree of occupation for "ownership". Had the trial judge assessed the oral histories correctly, his conclusions on these issues of fact might have been very different.

108   In the circumstances, the factual findings cannot stand. However, given the enormous complexity of the factual issues at hand, it would be impossible for the Court to do justice to the parties by sifting through the record itself and making new factual findings. A new trial is warranted, at which the evidence may be considered in light of the principles laid down in *Van der Peet* and elaborated upon here. In applying these principles, the new trial judge might well share some or all of the findings of fact of McEachern C.J.

C.   What is the content of Aboriginal title, how is it protected by s. 35(1), and what is required for its proof?

109   The parties disagree over whether the appellants have established Aboriginal title to the disputed area. However, since those factual issues require a new trial, we cannot resolve that dispute in this appeal. But factual issues aside, the parties also have a more fundamental disagreement over the content of Aboriginal title itself, and its reception into the Constitution by s. 35(1). In order to give guidance to the judge at the new trial, it is to this issue that I will now turn.

110   I set out these opposing positions by way of illustration and introduction because I believe that all of the parties have characterized the content of Aboriginal title incorrectly. The appellants argue that Aboriginal title is tantamount to an inalienable fee simple, which confers on Aboriginal peoples the rights to use those lands as they choose and which has been constitutionalized by s. 35(1). The respondents offer two alternative formulations: first, that Aboriginal title is no more than a bundle of rights to engage in activities which are themselves Aboriginal rights recognized and affirmed by s. 35(1), and that the *Constitution Act, 1982,* merely constitutionalizes those individual rights, not the bundle itself, because the latter has no independent content; and second, that Aboriginal title, at most, encompasses the right to exclusive use and occupation of land in order to engage in those activities which are Aboriginal rights themselves, and that s. 35(1) constitutionalizes this notion of exclusivity.

111   The content of Aboriginal title, in fact, lies somewhere in between these positions. Aboriginal title is a right in land and, as such, is more than the right to engage in specific activities which may be themselves Aboriginal rights. Rather, it confers the right to use land for a variety of activities, not all of which need be aspects of practices, customs and traditions which are integral to the distinctive cultures of Aboriginal societies. Those activities do not constitute the right *per se;*

rather, they are parasitic on the underlying title. However, that range of uses is subject to the limitation that they must not be irreconcilable with the nature of the attachment to the land which forms the basis of the particular group's Aboriginal title. This inherent limit, to be explained more fully below, flows from the definition of Aboriginal title as a *sui generis* interest in land, and is one way in which Aboriginal title is distinct from a fee simple.

(2) Aboriginal Title at Common Law

(a) General features

112 The starting point of the Canadian jurisprudence on Aboriginal title is the Privy Council's decision in *St. Catherine's Milling and Lumber Co.* v. *The Queen* (1888), 14 A.C. 46, which described Aboriginal title as a "personal and usufructuary right" (at p. 54). The subsequent jurisprudence has attempted to grapple with this definition, and has in the process demonstrated that the Privy Council's choice of terminology is not particularly helpful to explain the various dimensions of Aboriginal title. What the Privy Council sought to capture is that Aboriginal title is a *sui generis* interest in land. Aboriginal title has been described as *sui generis* in order to distinguish it from "normal" proprietary interests, such as fee simple. However, as I will now develop, it is also *sui generis* in the sense that its characteristics cannot be completely explained by reference either to the common law rules of real property or to the rules of property found in Aboriginal legal systems. As with other Aboriginal rights, it must be understood by reference to both common law and Aboriginal perspectives.

113 The idea that Aboriginal title is *sui generis* is the unifying principle underlying the various dimensions of that title. One dimension is its *inalienability.* Lands held pursuant to Aboriginal title cannot be transferred, sold or surrendered to anyone other than the Crown and, as a result, is inalienable to third parties. This Court has taken pains to clarify that Aboriginal title is only "personal" in this sense, and does not mean that Aboriginal title is a non-proprietary interest which amounts to no more than a licence to use and occupy the land and cannot compete on an equal footing with other proprietary interests: see *Canadian Pacific Ltd.* v. *Paul,* [1988] 2 S.C.R. 654, at p. 677.

114 Another dimension of Aboriginal title is its *source.* It had originally been thought that the source of Aboriginal title in Canada was the Royal Proclamation, 1763: see *St. Catharines Milling.* However, it is now clear that although Aboriginal title was recognized by the Proclamation, it arises from the prior occupation of Canada by Aboriginal peoples. That prior occupation, however, is relevant in two different ways, both of which illustrate the *sui generis* nature of Aboriginal title. The first is the physical fact of occupation, which derives from the common law principle that occupation is proof of possession in law: see Kent McNeil, *Common Law Aboriginal Title* (1989), at p. 7. Thus, in *Guerin, supra,* Dickson J. described Aboriginal title, at p. 376, as a "legal right derived from the Indians' historic occupation and possession of their tribal lands". What makes Aboriginal title *sui generis* is that it arises from possession before the assertion of British sovereignty, whereas normal estates, like fee simple, arise afterward: see Kent McNeil, "The Meaning of

Aboriginal Title", in Michael Asch, ed., *Aboriginal and Treaty Rights in Canada* (1997), 135, at p. 144. This idea has been further developed in *Roberts* v. *Canada,* [1989] 1 S.C.R. 322, where this Court unanimously held at p. 340 that "aboriginal title pre-dated colonization by the British and survived British claims to sovereignty" (also see *Guerin, supra,* at p. 378). What this suggests is a second source for Aboriginal title—the relationship between common law and pre-existing systems of Aboriginal law.

115   A further dimension of Aboriginal title is the fact that it is held *communally.* Aboriginal title cannot be held by individual Aboriginal persons; it is a collective right to land held by all members of an Aboriginal nation. Decisions with respect to that land are also made by that community. This is another feature of Aboriginal title which is *sui generis* and distinguishes it from normal property interests.

(b)   The content of Aboriginal title

116   Although cases involving Aboriginal title have come before this Court and Privy Council before, there has never been a definitive statement from either court on the *content* of Aboriginal title. In *St. Catharines Milling,* the Privy Council, as I have mentioned, described the Aboriginal title as a "personal and usufructuary interest", but declined to explain what that meant because it was not "necessary to express any opinion on the point" (at p. 55). Similarly, in *Calder, Guerin,* and *Paul,* the issues were the extinguishment of, the fiduciary duty arising from the surrender of, and statutory easements over land held pursuant to, Aboriginal title, respectively; the content of title was not at issue and was not directly addressed.

117   Although the courts have been less than forthcoming, I have arrived at the conclusion that the content of Aboriginal title can be summarized by two propositions: first, that Aboriginal title encompasses the right to exclusive use and occupation of the land held pursuant to that title for a variety of purposes, which need not be aspects of those Aboriginal practices, customs and traditions which are integral to distinctive Aboriginal cultures; and second, that those protected uses must not be irreconcilable with the nature of the group's attachment to that land. For the sake of clarity, I will discuss each of these propositions separately.

Aboriginal title encompasses the right to use the land held pursuant to that title for a variety of purposes, which need not be aspects of those Aboriginal practices, cultures and traditions which are integral to *distinctive Aboriginal cultures.*

118   The respondents argue that Aboriginal title merely encompasses the right to engage in activities which are aspects of Aboriginal practices, customs and traditions which are integral to distinctive Aboriginal cultures of the Aboriginal group claiming the right and, at most, adds the notion of exclusivity; i.e., the exclusive right to use the land for those purposes. However, the uses to which lands held pursuant to Aboriginal title can be put are not restricted in this way. This conclusion emerges from three sources: (i) the Canadian jurisprudence on Aboriginal title, (ii) the relationship between reserve lands and lands held pursuant to Aboriginal title, and (iii) the *Indian Oil and Gas Act,* R.S.C., 1985, c. I-7. As well, although this is not legally determinative, it is supported by the critical literature. In

particular, I have profited greatly from Professor McNeil's article, "The Meaning of Aboriginal Title", *supra.*

(i) Canadian jurisprudence on Aboriginal title

119 Despite the fact that the jurisprudence on Aboriginal title is somewhat under-developed, it is clear that the uses to which lands held pursuant to Aboriginal title can be put is not restricted to the practices, customs and traditions of Aboriginal peoples integral to distinctive Aboriginal cultures. In *Guerin,* for example, Dickson J. described Aboriginal title as "an interest in land" which encompassed "a legal right to occupy and possess certain lands" (at p. 382). The "right to occupy and possess" is framed in broad terms and, significantly, is not qualified by reference to traditional and customary uses of those lands. Any doubt that the right to occupancy and possession encompasses a broad variety of uses of land was put to rest in *Paul,* where the Court went even further and stated that Aboriginal title was "more than the right to enjoyment and occupancy" (at p. 688). Once again, there is no reference to Aboriginal practices, customs and traditions as a qualifier on that right. Moreover, I take the reference to "more" as emphasis of the broad notion of use and possession.

(ii) Reserve land

120 Another source of support for the conclusion that the uses to which lands held under Aboriginal title can be put are not restricted to those grounded in practices, customs and traditions integral to distinctive Aboriginal cultures can be found in *Guerin,* where Dickson J. stated at p. 379 that the same legal principles governed the Aboriginal interest in reserve lands and lands held pursuant to Aboriginal title:

> It does not matter, in my opinion, that the present case is concerned with the interest of an Indian Band in a reserve rather than with unrecognized aboriginal title in traditional tribal lands. *The Indian interest in the lands is the same in both cases.* [Emphasis added.]

121 The nature of the Indian interest in reserve land is very broad, and can be found in s. 18 of the *Indian Act, . . .* The principal provision is s. 18(1), which states that reserve lands are held "for the use and benefit" of the bands which occupy them; those uses and benefits, on the face of the *Indian Act,* do not appear to be restricted to practices, customs and traditions integral to distinctive Aboriginal cultures. The breadth of those uses is reinforced by s. 18(2), which states that reserve lands may be used "for any other purpose for the general welfare of the band". The general welfare of the band has not been defined in terms of Aboriginal practices, customs and traditions, nor in terms of those activities which have their origin pre-contact; it is a concept, by definition, which incorporates a reference to the present-day needs of Aboriginal communities. On the basis of *Guerin,* lands held pursuant to Aboriginal title, like reserve lands, are also capable of being used for a broad variety of purposes.

(iii) Indian Oil and Gas Act

122 The third source for the proposition that the content of Aboriginal title is not restricted to practices, customs and traditions which are integral to distinctive Abo-

riginal cultures is the *Indian Oil and Gas Act.* The overall purpose of the statute is to provide for the exploration of oil and gas on reserve lands through their surrender to the Crown. The statute presumes that the Aboriginal interest in reserve land includes mineral rights, a point which this Court unanimously accepted with respect to the *Indian Act* in *Blueberry River Indian Band* v. *Canada* (Department of Indian Affairs and Northern Development), [1995] 4 S.C.R. 344. On the basis of *Guerin,* Aboriginal title also encompass mineral rights, and lands held pursuant to Aboriginal title should be capable of exploitation in the same way, which is certainly not a traditional use for those lands. This conclusion is reinforced by s. 6(2) of the Act, which provides:

> 6. . . . (2) Nothing in this Act shall be deemed to abrogate the rights of Indian people or preclude them from negotiating for oil and gas benefits in those areas in which land claims have not been settled. . . .

The areas referred to in s. 6(2), at the very least, must encompass lands held pursuant to Aboriginal title, since those lands by definition have not been surrendered under land claims agreements. The presumption underlying s. 6(2) is that Aboriginal title permits the development of oil and gas reserves. . . .

124 In conclusion, the content of Aboriginal title is not restricted to those uses which are elements of a practice, custom or tradition integral to the distinctive culture of the Aboriginal group claiming the right. However, nor does Aboriginal title amount to a form of inalienable fee simple, as I will now explain.

(c) Inherent limit: Lands held pursuant to Aboriginal title cannot be used in a manner that is irreconcilable with the nature of the attachment to the land which forms the basis of the group's claim to Aboriginal title

125 The content of Aboriginal title contains an inherent limit that lands held pursuant to title cannot be used in a manner that is irreconcilable with the nature of the claimants' attachment to those lands. This limit on the content of Aboriginal title is a manifestation of the principle that underlies the various dimensions of that special interest in land—it is a *sui generis* interest that is distinct from "normal" proprietary interests, most notably fee simple.

126 I arrive at this conclusion by reference to the other dimensions of Aboriginal title which are *sui generis* as well. I first consider the source of Aboriginal title. As I discussed earlier, Aboriginal title arises from the prior occupation of Canada by Aboriginal peoples. That prior occupation is relevant in two different ways: first, because of the physical fact of occupation, and second, because Aboriginal title originates in part from pre-existing systems of Aboriginal law. However, the law of Aboriginal title does not only seek to determine the historic rights of Aboriginal peoples to land; it also seeks to afford legal protection to prior occupation in the present-day. Implicit in the protection of historic patterns of occupation is a recognition of the importance of the continuity of the relationship of an Aboriginal community to its land over time.

127 I develop this point below with respect to the test for Aboriginal title. The

relevance of the continuity of the relationship of an Aboriginal community with its land here is that it applies not only to the past, but to the future as well. That relationship should not be prevented from continuing into the future. As a result, uses of the lands that would threaten that future relationship are, by their very nature, excluded from the content of Aboriginal title.

128 Accordingly, in my view, lands subject to Aboriginal title cannot be put to such uses as may be irreconcilable with the nature of the occupation of that land and the relationship that the particular group has had with the land which together have given rise to Aboriginal title in the first place. As discussed below, one of the critical elements in the determination of whether a particular Aboriginal group has Aboriginal title to certain lands is the matter of the occupancy of those lands. Occupancy is determined by reference to the activities that have taken place on the land and the uses to which the land has been put by the particular group. If lands are so occupied, there will exist a special bond between the group and the land in question such that the land will be part of the definition of the group's distinctive culture. It seems to me that these elements of Aboriginal title create an inherent limitation on the uses to which the land, over which such title exists, may be put. For example, if occupation is established with reference to the use of the land as a hunting ground, then the group that successfully claims Aboriginal title to that land may not use it in such a fashion as to destroy its value for such a use (e.g., by strip mining it). Similarly, if a group claims a special bond with the land because of its ceremonial or cultural significance, it may not use the land in such a way as to destroy that relationship (e.g., by developing it in such a way that the bond is destroyed, perhaps by turning it into a parking lot.)

129 It is for this reason also that lands held by virtue of Aboriginal title may not be alienated. Alienation would bring to an end the entitlement of the Aboriginal people to occupy the land and would terminate their relationship with it. I have suggested above that the inalienability of Aboriginal lands is, at least in part, a function of the common law principle that settlers in colonies must derive their title from Crown grant and, therefore, cannot acquire title through purchase from Aboriginal inhabitants. It is also, again only in part, a function of a general policy "to ensure that Indians are not dispossessed of their entitlements": see *Mitchell* v. *Peguis Indian Band*, [1990] 2 S.C.R. 85, at p. 133. What the inalienability of lands held pursuant to Aboriginal title suggests is that those lands are more than just a fungible commodity. The relationship between an Aboriginal community and the lands over which it has Aboriginal title has an important non-economic component. The land has an inherent and unique value in itself, which is enjoyed by the community with Aboriginal title to it. The community cannot put the land to uses which would destroy that value.

130 I am cognizant that the *sui generis* nature of Aboriginal title precludes the application of "traditional real property rules" to elucidate the content of that title (*St. Mary's Indian Band* v. *Cranbrook (City)*, [1997] 2 S.C.R. 657, at para. 14). Nevertheless, a useful analogy can be drawn between the limit on Aboriginal title and the concept of equitable waste at common law. Under that doctrine, persons

who hold a life estate in real property cannot commit "wanton or extravagant acts of destruction" (E.H. Burn, *Cheshire and Burn's Modern Law of Real Property* (14th ed. 1988), at p. 264) or "ruin the property" (Robert E. Megarry and H.W.R. Wade, *The Law of Real Property*, 4th ed. (1975) at p. 105). This description of the limits imposed by the doctrine of equitable waste capture the kind of limit I have in mind here.

131   Finally, what I have just said regarding the importance of the continuity of the relationship between an Aboriginal community and its land, and the non-economic or inherent value of that land, should not be taken to detract from the possibility of surrender to the Crown in exchange for valuable consideration. On the contrary, the idea of surrender reinforces the conclusion that Aboriginal title is limited in the way I have described. If Aboriginal peoples wish to use their lands in a way that Aboriginal title does not permit, then they must surrender those lands and convert them into non-title lands to do so.

132   The foregoing amounts to a general limitation on the use of lands held by virtue of Aboriginal title. It arises from the particular physical and cultural relationship that a group may have with the land and is defined by the source of Aboriginal title over it. This is not, I must emphasize, a limitation that restricts the use of the land to those activities that have traditionally been carried out on it. That would amount to a legal straitjacket on Aboriginal peoples who have a legitimate legal claim to the land. The approach I have outlined above allows for a full range of uses of the land, subject only to an overarching limit, defined by the special nature of the Aboriginal title in that land.

(d) Aboriginal title under s. 35(1) of the Constitution Act, 1982

133   Aboriginal title at common law is protected in its full form by s. 35(1). This conclusion flows from the express language of s. 35(1) itself, which states in full: "[t]he *existing* aboriginal and treaty rights of the aboriginal peoples of Canada are hereby recognized and affirmed" (emphasis added). On a plain reading of the provision, s. 35(1) did not create aboriginal rights; rather, it accorded constitutional status to those rights which were "existing" in 1982. The provision, at the very least, constitutionalized those rights which Aboriginal peoples possessed at common law, since those rights existed at the time s. 35(1) came into force. Since Aboriginal title was a common law right whose existence was recognized well before 1982 (e.g., *Calder, supra*), s. 35(1) has constitutionalized it in its full form.

134   I expressed this understanding of the relationship between common law Aboriginal rights, including Aboriginal title, and the Aboriginal rights protected by s. 35(1) in Van der Peet. While explaining the purposes behind s. 35(1), I stated that "it must be remembered that s. 35(1) did not create the legal doctrine of Aboriginal rights; Aboriginal rights existed and were recognized under the common law" (at para. 28). Through the enactment of s. 35(1), "a pre-existing legal doctrine was elevated to constitutional status" (at para. 29), or in other words, s. 35(1) had achieved "the constitutionalization of those rights" (at para. 29). . . .

136   I hasten to add that the constitutionalization of common law Aboriginal rights by s. 35(1) does not mean that those rights exhaust the content of s. 35(1). As I said in *Côté, supra,* at para. 52:

> [s]ection 35(1) would fail to achieve its noble purpose of preserving the integral and defining features of distinctive aboriginal societies if it only protected those defining features which were fortunate enough to have received the legal recognition and approval of European colonizers.

I relied on this proposition in *Côté* to defeat the argument that the possible absence of Aboriginal rights under French colonial law was a bar to the existence of Aboriginal rights under s. 35(1) within the historic boundaries of New France. But it also follows that the existence of a particular Aboriginal right at common law is not a *sine qua non* for the proof of an Aboriginal right that is recognized and affirmed by s. 35(1). Indeed, none of the decisions of this Court handed down under s. 35(1) in which the existence of an Aboriginal right has been demonstrated has relied on the existence of that right at common law. The existence of an Aboriginal right at common law is therefore sufficient, but not necessary, for the recognition and affirmation of that right by s. 35(1).

137   The acknowledgment that s. 35(1) has accorded constitutional status to common law Aboriginal title raises a further question—the relationship of Aboriginal title to the "aboriginal rights" protected by s. 35(1). I addressed that question in *Adams, supra,* where the Court had been presented with two radically different conceptions of this relationship. The first conceived of Aboriginal rights as being "inherently based in aboriginal title to the land" (at para. 25), or as fragments of a broader claim to Aboriginal title. By implication, Aboriginal rights must rest either in a claim to title or the unextinguished remnants of title. Taken to its logical extreme, this suggests that Aboriginal title is merely the sum of a set of individual Aboriginal rights, and that it therefore has no independent content. However, I rejected this position for another—that Aboriginal title is "simply one manifestation of a broader-based conception of aboriginal rights" (at para. 25). Thus, although Aboriginal title is a species of Aboriginal right recognized and affirmed by s. 35(1), it is distinct from other Aboriginal rights because it arises where the connection of a group with a piece of land "was of a central significance to their distinctive culture" (at para. 26).

138   The picture which emerges from *Adams* is that the Aboriginal rights which are recognized and affirmed by s. 35(1) fall along a spectrum with respect to their degree of connection with the land. At the one end, there are those Aboriginal rights which are practices, customs and traditions that are integral to the distinctive Aboriginal culture of the group claiming the right. However, the "occupation and use of the land" where the activity is taking place is not "sufficient to support a claim of title to the land" (at para. 26). Nevertheless, those activities receive constitutional protection. In the middle, there are activities which, out of necessity, take place on land and indeed, might be intimately related to a particular piece of land. Although an Aboriginal group may not be able to demonstrate title to the land, it may nevertheless have a site-specific right to engage in a particular activity. I

put the point this way in *Adams,* at para. 30:

> Even where an aboriginal right exists on a tract of land to which the aboriginal people in question do not have title, that right may well be site specific, with the result that it can be exercised only upon that specific tract of land. For example, *if an aboriginal people demonstrates that hunting on a specific tract of land was an integral part of their distinctive culture then, even if the right exists apart from title to that tract of land, the aboriginal right to hunt is nonetheless defined as, and limited to, the right to hunt on the specific tract of land.* [Emphasis added.]

At the other end of the spectrum, there is Aboriginal title itself. As *Adams* makes clear, Aboriginal title confers more than the right to engage in site-specific activities which are aspects of the practices, customs and traditions of distinctive Aboriginal cultures. Site-specific rights can be made out even if title cannot. What Aboriginal title confers is the right to the land itself.

139 Because Aboriginal rights can vary with respect to their degree of connection with the land, some Aboriginal groups may be unable to make out a claim to title, but will nevertheless possess Aboriginal rights that are recognized and affirmed by s. 35(1), including site-specific rights to engage in particular activities. As I explained in *Adams,* this may occur in the case of nomadic peoples who varied "the location of their settlements with the season and changing circumstances" (at para. 27). The fact that Aboriginal peoples were non-sedentary, however (at para. 27) does not alter the fact that nomadic peoples survived through reliance on the land prior to contact with Europeans and, further, that many of the practices, customs and traditions of nomadic peoples that took place on the land were integral to their distinctive cultures.

(e)   Proof of Aboriginal title

(i)   Introduction

140 In addition to differing in the degree of connection with the land, Aboriginal title differs from other Aboriginal rights in another way. To date, the Court has defined Aboriginal rights in terms of activities. As I said in *Van der Peet* (at para. 46):

> in order to be an aboriginal right an activity must be an element of a practice, custom or tradition integral to the distinctive culture of the aboriginal group claiming the right. [Emphasis added.]

Aboriginal title, however, is a right to the land itself. Subject to the limits I have laid down above, that land may be used for a variety of activities, none of which need be individually protected as Aboriginal rights under s. 35(1). Those activities are parasitic on the underlying title.

141 This difference between Aboriginal rights to engage in particular activities and Aboriginal title requires that the test I laid down in *Van der Peet* be adapted accordingly. I anticipated this possibility in *Van der Peet* itself, where I stated that (at para. 74):

Aboriginal rights arise from the prior occupation of land, but they also arise from the prior social organization and distinctive cultures of aboriginal peoples on that land. In considering whether a claim to an aboriginal right has been made out, courts must look at both the relationship of an aboriginal claimant to the land *and* [emphasis in original] at the practices, customs and traditions arising from the claimant's distinctive culture and society. Courts must not focus so entirely on the relationship of aboriginal peoples with the land that they lose sight of the other factors relevant to the identification and definition of aboriginal rights. [Emphasis added.]

Since the purpose of s. 35(1) is to reconcile the prior presence of Aboriginal peoples in North America with the assertion of Crown sovereignty, it is clear from this statement that s. 35(1) must recognize and affirm both aspects of that prior presence—first, the occupation of land, and second, the prior social organization and distinctive cultures of Aboriginal peoples on that land. To date the jurisprudence under s. 35(1) has given more emphasis to the second aspect. To a great extent, this has been a function of the types of cases which have come before this Court under s. 35(1)—prosecutions for regulatory offences that, by their very nature, proscribe discrete types of activity.

142   The adaptation of the test laid down in *Van der Peet* to suit claims to title must be understood as the recognition of the first aspect of that prior presence. However, as will now become apparent, the tests for the identification of Aboriginal rights to engage in particular activities and for the identification of Aboriginal title share broad similarities. The major distinctions are first, under the test for Aboriginal title, the requirement that the land be integral to the distinctive culture of the claimants is subsumed by the requirement of occupancy, and second, whereas the time for the identification of Aboriginal rights is the time of first contact, the time for the identification of Aboriginal title is the time at which the Crown asserted sovereignty over the land.

(ii)   The test for the proof of Aboriginal title

143   In order to make out a claim for Aboriginal title, the Aboriginal group asserting title must satisfy the following criteria: (i) the land must have been occupied prior to sovereignty, (ii) if present occupation is relied on as proof of occupation pre-sovereignty, there must be a continuity between present and pre-sovereignty occupation, and (iii) at sovereignty, that occupation must have been exclusive.

The land must have been occupied prior to sovereignty

144   In order to establish a claim to Aboriginal title, the Aboriginal group asserting the claim must establish that it occupied the lands in question at the time at *which the Crown asserted sovereignty over the land subject to the title.* The relevant time period for the establishment of title is, therefore, different than for the establishment of Aboriginal rights to engage in specific activities. In *Van der Peet,* I held, at para. 60 that "[t]he time period that a court should consider in identifying whether the right claimed meets the standard of being integral to the aboriginal community claiming the right is the period prior to contact. . . ." This arises from the fact that in defining the central and distinctive attributes of pre-existing Aboriginal socie-

ties it is necessary to look to a time prior to the arrival of Europeans. Practices, customs or traditions that arose solely as a response to European influences do not meet the standard for recognition as Aboriginal rights.

145 On the other hand, in the context of Aboriginal title, sovereignty is the appropriate time period to consider for several reasons. First, from a theoretical standpoint, Aboriginal title arises out of prior occupation of the land by Aboriginal peoples and out of the relationship between the common law and pre-existing systems of Aboriginal law. Aboriginal title is a burden on the Crown's underlying title. However, the Crown did not gain this title until it asserted sovereignty over the land in question. Because it does not make sense to speak of a burden on the underlying title before that title existed, Aboriginal title crystallized at the time sovereignty was asserted. Second, Aboriginal title does not raise the problem of distinguishing between distinctive, integral Aboriginal practices, customs and traditions and those influenced or introduced by European contact. Under common law, the act of occupation or possession is sufficient to ground Aboriginal title and it is not necessary to prove that the land was a distinctive or integral part of the Aboriginal society before the arrival of Europeans. Finally, from a practical standpoint, it appears that the date of sovereignty is more certain than the date of first contact. It is often very difficult to determine the precise moment that each Aboriginal group had first contact with European culture. I note that this is the approach has support in the academic literature: Brian Slattery, "Understanding Aboriginal Rights", *supra,* at p. 742; Kent McNeil, *Common Law Aboriginal Title, supra,* at p. 196. For these reasons, I conclude that Aboriginals must establish occupation of the land from the date of the assertion of sovereignty in order to sustain a claim for Aboriginal title. McEachern C.J. found, at pp. 233–34, and the parties did not dispute on appeal, that British sovereignty over British Columbia was conclusively established by the Oregon Boundary Treaty of 1846. This is not to say that circumstances subsequent to sovereignty may never be relevant to title or compensation; this might be the case, for example, where native bands have been dispossessed of traditional lands after sovereignty.

146 There was a consensus among the parties on appeal that proof of historic occupation was required to make out a claim to Aboriginal title. However, the parties disagreed on how that occupancy could be proved. The respondents assert that in order to establish Aboriginal title, the occupation must be the physical occupation of the land in question. The appellant Gitksan nation argue, by contrast, that Aboriginal title may be established, at least in part, by reference to Aboriginal law.

147 This debate over the proof of occupancy reflects two divergent views of the source of Aboriginal title. The respondents argue, in essence, that Aboriginal title arises from the physical reality at the time of sovereignty, whereas the Gitksan effectively take the position that Aboriginal title arises from and should reflect the pattern of land holdings under Aboriginal law. However, as I have explained above, the source of Aboriginal title appears to be grounded both in the common law and in the Aboriginal perspective on land; the latter includes, but is not limited to, their systems of law. It follows that both should be taken into account in establishing the

proof of occupancy. Indeed, there is precedent for doing so. In *Baker Lake, supra,* Mahoney J. held that to prove Aboriginal title, the claimants needed both to demonstrate their "physical presence on the land they occupied" (at p. 561) and the existence "among [that group of] . . . a recognition of the claimed rights . . . by the regime that prevailed before" (at p. 559).

148 This approach to the proof of occupancy at common law is also mandated in the context of s. 35(1) by *Van der Peet.* In that decision, as I stated above, I held at para. 50 that the reconciliation of the prior occupation of North America by Aboriginal peoples with the assertion of Crown sovereignty required that account be taken of the "aboriginal perspective while at the same time taking into account the perspective of the common law" and that "[t]rue reconciliation will, equally, place weight on each". I also held that the Aboriginal perspective on the occupation of their lands can be gleaned, in part, but not exclusively, from their traditional laws, because those laws were elements of the practices, customs and traditions of Aboriginal peoples: at para. 41. As a result, if, at the time of sovereignty, an Aboriginal society had laws in relation to land, those laws would be relevant to establishing the occupation of lands which are the subject of a claim for Aboriginal title. Relevant laws might include, but are not limited to, a land tenure system or laws governing land use.

149 However, the Aboriginal perspective must be taken into account alongside the perspective of the common law. Professor McNeil has convincingly argued that at common law, the fact of physical occupation is proof of possession at law, which in turn will ground title to the land: *Common Law Aboriginal Title, supra,* at p. 73; also see Cheshire and Burn, *Modern Law of Real Property, supra,* at p. 28; and Megarry and Wade, *The Law of Real Property, supra,* at p. 1006. Physical occupation may be established in a variety of ways, ranging from the construction of dwellings through cultivation and enclosure of fields to regular use of definite tracts of land for hunting, fishing or otherwise exploiting its resources: see McNeil, *Common Law Aboriginal Title, supra,* at pp. 201–202. In considering whether occupation sufficient to ground title is established, "one must take into account the group's size, manner of life, material resources, and technological abilities, and the character of the lands claimed": Brian Slattery, "Understanding Aboriginal Rights", at p. 758.

150 In *Van der Peet,* I drew a distinction between those practices, customs and traditions of Aboriginal peoples which were "an aspect of, or took place in" the society of the Aboriginal group asserting the claim and those which were "a central and significant part of the society's culture" (at para. 55). The latter stood apart because they "made the culture of that society distinctive . . . it was one of the things which truly made the society what it was" (at para. 55). The same requirement operates in the determination of the proof of Aboriginal title. As I said in *Adams,* a claim to title is made out when a group can demonstrate "that their connection with the piece of land . . . was of central significance to their distinctive culture" (at para. 26).

151 Although this remains a crucial part of the test for Aboriginal rights, given the occupancy requirement in the test for Aboriginal title, I cannot imagine a situation where this requirement would actually serve to limit or preclude a title claim. The requirement exists for rights short of title because it is necessary to distinguish between those practices which were central to the culture of claimants and those which were more incidental. However, in the case of title, it would seem clear that any land that was occupied pre-sovereignty, and which the parties have maintained a substantial connection with since then, is sufficiently important to be of central significance to the culture of the claimants. As a result, I do not think it is necessary to include explicitly this element as part of the test for Aboriginal title.

If present occupation is relied on as proof of occupation pre-sovereignty, *there must be a continuity between present and pre-sovereignty occupation.*

152 In *Van der Peet,* I explained that it is the pre-contact practices, customs and traditions of Aboriginal peoples which are recognized and affirmed as Aboriginal rights by s. 35(1). But I also acknowledged it would be "next to impossible" (at para. 62) for an Aboriginal group to provide conclusive evidence of its pre-contact practices, customs and traditions. What would suffice instead was evidence of post-contact practices, which was "directed at demonstrating which aspects of the Aboriginal community and society have their origins pre-contact" (at para. 62). The same concern, and the same solution, arises with respect to the proof of occupation in claims for Aboriginal title, although there is a difference in the time for determination of title. Conclusive evidence of pre-sovereignty occupation may be difficult to come by. Instead, an Aboriginal community may provide evidence of present occupation as proof of pre-sovereignty occupation in support of a claim to Aboriginal title. What is required, in addition, is a continuity between present and pre-sovereignty occupation, because the relevant time for the determination of Aboriginal title is at the time before sovereignty.

153 Needless to say, there is no need to establish "an unbroken chain of continuity" (*Van der Peet,* at para. 65) between present and prior occupation. The occupation and use of lands may have been disrupted for a time, perhaps as a result of the unwillingness of European colonizers to recognize Aboriginal title. To impose the requirement of continuity too strictly would risk "undermining the very purposes of s. 35(1) by perpetuating the historical injustice suffered by Aboriginal peoples at the hands of colonizers who failed to respect" Aboriginal rights to land (*Côté, supra* at para. 53). In *Mabo, supra,* the High Court of Australia set down the requirement that there must be "substantial maintenance of the connection" between the people and the land. In my view, this test should be equally applicable to proof of title in Canada.

154 I should also note that there is a strong possibility that the precise nature of occupation will have changed between the time of sovereignty and the present. I would like to make it clear that the fact that the nature of occupation has changed would not ordinarily preclude a claim for Aboriginal title, as long as a substantial connection between the people and the land is maintained. The only limitation on this principle might be the internal limits on uses which land that is subject to

Aboriginal title may be put, i.e., uses which are inconsistent with continued use by future generations of Aboriginals.

At sovereignty, occupation must have been exclusive

155 Finally, at sovereignty, occupation must have been exclusive. The requirement for exclusivity flows from the definition of Aboriginal title itself, because I have defined Aboriginal title in terms of the right to exclusive use and occupation of land. Exclusivity, as an aspect of Aboriginal title, vests in the Aboriginal community which holds the ability to exclude others from the lands held pursuant to that title. The proof of title must, in this respect, mirror the content of the right. Were it possible to prove title without demonstrating exclusive occupation, the result would be absurd, because it would be possible for more than one Aboriginal nation to have Aboriginal title over the same piece of land, and then for all of them to attempt to assert the right to exclusive use and occupation over it.

156 As with the proof of occupation, proof of exclusivity must rely on both the perspective of the common law and the Aboriginal perspective, placing equal weight on each. At common law, a premium is placed on the factual reality of occupation, as encountered by the Europeans. However, as the common law concept of possession must be sensitive to the realities of Aboriginal society, so must the concept of exclusivity. Exclusivity is a common law principle derived from the notion of fee simple ownership and should be imported into the concept of Aboriginal title with caution. As such, the test required to establish exclusive occupation must take into account the context of the Aboriginal society at the time of sovereignty. For example, it is important to note that exclusive occupation can be demonstrated even if other Aboriginal groups were present, or frequented the claimed lands. Under those circumstances, exclusivity would be demonstrated by "the intention and capacity to retain exclusive control" (McNeil, *Common Law Aboriginal Title, supra,* at p. 204). Thus, an act of trespass, if isolated, would not undermine a general finding of exclusivity, if Aboriginal groups intended to and attempted to enforce their exclusive occupation. Moreover, as Professor McNeil suggests, the presence of other Aboriginal groups might actually reinforce a finding of exclusivity. For example, "[w]here others were allowed access upon request, the very fact that permission was asked for and given would be further evidence of the group's exclusive control" (at p. 204).

157 A consideration of the Aboriginal perspective may also lead to the conclusion that trespass by other Aboriginal groups does not undermine, and that presence of those groups by permission may reinforce, the exclusive occupation of the Aboriginal group asserting title. For example, the Aboriginal group asserting the claim to Aboriginal title may have trespass laws which are proof of exclusive occupation, such that the presence of trespassers does not count as evidence against exclusivity. As well, Aboriginal laws under which permission may be granted to other Aboriginal groups to use or reside even temporarily on land would reinforce the finding of exclusive occupation. Indeed, if that permission were the subject of treaties between the Aboriginal nations in question, those treaties would also form part of the Aboriginal perspective.

158 In their submissions, the appellants pressed the point that requiring proof of exclusive occupation might preclude a finding of joint title, which is shared between two or more Aboriginal nations. The possibility of joint title has been recognized by American courts: *United States* v. *Sante Fe Pacific Railroad Co.,* 314 U.S. 339 (1941). I would suggest that the requirement of exclusive occupancy and the possibility of joint title could be reconciled by recognizing that joint title could arise from shared exclusivity. The meaning of shared exclusivity is well-known to the common law. Exclusive possession is the right to exclude others. Shared exclusive possession is the right to exclude others except those with whom possession is shared. There clearly may be cases in which two Aboriginal nations lived on a particular piece of land and recognized each other's entitlement to that land but nobody else's. However, since no claim to joint title has been asserted here, I leave it to another day to work out all the complexities and implications of joint title, as well as any limits that another band's title may have on the way in which one band uses its title lands.

159 I should also reiterate that if Aboriginals can show that they occupied a particular piece of land, but did not do so exclusively, it will always be possible to establish Aboriginal rights short of title. These rights will likely be intimately tied to the land and may permit a number of possible uses. However, unlike title, they are not a right to the land itself. Rather, as I have suggested, they are a right to do certain things in connection with that land. If, for example, it were established that the lands near those subject to a title claim were used for hunting by a number of bands, those shared lands would not be subject to a claim for Aboriginal title, as they lack the crucial element of exclusivity. However, they may be subject to site-specific Aboriginal rights by all of the bands who used it. This does not entitle anyone to the land itself, but it may entitle all of the bands who hunted on the land to hunting rights. Hence, in addition to shared title, it will be possible to have shared, non-exclusive, site-specific rights. In my opinion, this accords with the general principle that the common law should develop to recognize Aboriginal rights (and title, when necessary) as they were recognized by either *de facto* practice or by the Aboriginal system of governance. It also allows sufficient flexibility to deal with this highly complex and rapidly evolving area of the law.

(f)   Infringements of Aboriginal title: the test of justification . . .

160 The Aboriginal rights recognized and affirmed by s. 35(1), including Aboriginal title, are not absolute. Those rights may be infringed, both by the federal (e.g., *Sparrow*) and provincial (e.g., *Côté*) governments. However, s. 35(1) requires that those infringements satisfy the test of justification. In this section, I will review the Court's nascent jurisprudence on justification and explain how that test will apply in the context of infringements of Aboriginal title.

(ii)   General principles

161 The test of justification has two parts, which I shall consider in turn. First, the infringement of the Aboriginal right must be in furtherance of a legislative objective that is compelling and substantial. I explained in *Gladstone* that compelling and substantial objectives were those which were directed at either one of the pur-

poses underlying the recognition and affirmation of Aboriginal rights by s. 35(1), which are (at para. 72):

> the recognition of the prior occupation of North America by aboriginal peoples or . . . the reconciliation of aboriginal prior occupation with the assertion of the sovereignty of the Crown.

I noted that the latter purpose will often "be most relevant" (at para. 72) at the stage of justification. I think it important to repeat why (at para. 73) that is so:

> Because . . . distinctive Aboriginal societies exist within, and are part of, a broader social, political and economic community, over which the Crown is sovereign, there are circumstances in which, in order to pursue objectives of compelling and substantial importance to that community as a whole (taking into account the fact that Aboriginal societies are part of that community), some limitation of those rights will be justifiable. *Aboriginal rights are a necessary part of the reconciliation of Aboriginal societies with the broader political community of which they are part; limits placed on those rights are, where the objectives furthered by those limits are of sufficient importance to the broader community as a whole, equally a necessary part of that reconciliation.* [Emphasis added; "equally" emphasized in original.]

The conservation of fisheries, which was accepted as a compelling and substantial objective in *Sparrow,* furthers both of these purposes, because it simultaneously recognizes that fishing is integral to many Aboriginal cultures, and also seeks to reconcile Aboriginal societies with the broader community by ensuring that there are fish enough for all. But legitimate government objectives also include "the pursuit of economic and regional fairness" and "the recognition of the historical reliance upon, and participation in, the fishery by non-aboriginal groups" (para. 75). By contrast, measures enacted for relatively unimportant reasons, such as sports fishing without a significant economic component (*Adams, supra*) would fail this aspect of the test of justification.

162 The second part of the test of justification requires an assessment of whether the infringement is consistent with the special fiduciary relationship between the Crown and Aboriginal peoples. What has become clear is that the requirements of the fiduciary duty are a function of the "legal and factual context" of each appeal (*Gladstone, supra,* at para. 56). *Sparrow* and *Gladstone,* for example, interpreted and applied the fiduciary duty in terms of the idea of priority. The theory underlying that principle is that the fiduciary relationship between the Crown and Aboriginal peoples demands that Aboriginal interests be placed first. However, the fiduciary duty does not demand that Aboriginal rights always be given priority. As was said in *Sparrow, supra,* at pp. 1114–15:

> The nature of the constitutional protection afforded by s. 35(1) *in this context* demands that there be a link between the question of justification and the allocation of priorities in the fishery. [Emphasis added.]

Other contexts permit, and may even require, that the fiduciary duty be articulated in other ways (at p. 1119):

Within the analysis of justification, there are further questions to be addressed, depending on the circumstances of the inquiry. These include the questions of whether there has been as little infringement as possible in order to effect the desired result; whether, in a situation of expropriation, fair compensation is available; and, whether the aboriginal group in question has been consulted with respect to the conservation measures being implemented.

Sparrow did not explain when the different articulations of the fiduciary duty should be used. Below, I suggest that the choice between them will in large part be a function of the nature of the Aboriginal right at issue.

163 In addition to variation in the *form* which the fiduciary duty takes, there will also be variation in degree of scrutiny required by the fiduciary duty of the infringing measure or action. The degree of scrutiny is a function of the nature of the Aboriginal right at issue. The distinction between *Sparrow* and *Gladstone,* for example, turned on whether the right amounted to the exclusive use of a resource, which in turn was a function of whether the right had an internal limit. In *Sparrow,* the right was internally limited, because it was a right to fish for food, ceremonial and social purposes, and as a result would only amount to an exclusive right to use the fishery in exceptional circumstances. Accordingly, the requirement of priority was applied strictly to mean that (at p. 1116) "any allocation of priorities after valid conservation measures have been implemented must give top priority to Indian food fishing".

164 In *Gladstone,* by contrast, the right to sell fish commercially was only limited by supply and demand. Had the test for justification been applied in a strict form in *Gladstone,* the Aboriginal right would have amounted to an exclusive right exploit the fishery on a commercial basis. This was not the intention of *Sparrow,* and I accordingly modified the test for justification, by altering the idea of priority in the following way (at para. 62):

> ... the doctrine of priority requires that the government demonstrate that, in allocating the resource, it has taken account of the existence of aboriginal rights and allocated the resource in a manner respectful of the fact that those rights have priority over the exploitation of the fishery by other users. This right is at once both procedural and substantive; at the stage of justification the government must demonstrate both that the process by which it allocated the resource and the actual allocation of the resource which results from that process reflect the prior interest of aboriginal rights holders in the fishery.

After *Gladstone,* in the context of commercial activity, the priority of Aboriginal rights is constitutionally satisfied if the government had taken those rights into account and has allocated a resource "in a manner respectful" (at para. 62) of that priority. A court must be satisfied that "the government has taken into account the existence and importance of [Aboriginal] rights" (at para. 63) which it determines by asking the following questions (at para. 64):

> Questions relevant to the determination of whether the government has granted priority to aboriginal rights holders are . . . questions such as whether the government has

accommodated the exercise of the aboriginal right to participate in the fishery (through reduced licence fees, for example), whether the government's objectives in enacting a particular regulatory scheme reflect the need to take into account the priority of aboriginal rights holders, the extent of the participation in the fishery of aboriginal rights holders relative to their percentage of the population, how the government has accommodated different aboriginal rights in a particular fishery (food versus commercial rights, for example), how important the fishery is to the economic and material well-being of the band in question, and the criteria taken into account by the government in, for example, allocating commercial licences amongst different users.

(iii) Justification and Aboriginal title

165 The general principles governing justification laid down in *Sparrow,* and embellished by *Gladstone,* operate with respect to infringements of Aboriginal title. In the wake of *Gladstone,* the range of legislative objectives that can justify the infringement of Aboriginal title is fairly broad. Most of these objectives can be traced to the *reconciliation* of the prior occupation of North America by Aboriginal peoples with the assertion of Crown sovereignty, which entails the recognition that "distinctive aboriginal societies exist within, and are a part of, a broader social, political and economic community" (at para. 73). In my opinion, the development of agriculture, forestry, mining, and hydroelectric power, the general economic development of the interior of British Columbia, protection of the environment or endangered species, the building of infrastructure and the settlement of foreign populations to support those aims, are the kinds of objectives that are consistent with this purpose and, in principle, can justify the infringement of Aboriginal title. Whether a particular measure or government act can be explained by reference to one of those objectives, however, is ultimately a question of fact that will have to be examined on a case-by-case basis.

166 The manner in which the fiduciary duty operates with respect to the second stage of the justification test—both with respect to the standard of scrutiny and the particular form that the fiduciary duty will take—will be a function of the nature of Aboriginal title. Three aspects of Aboriginal title are relevant here. First, Aboriginal title encompasses the right to exclusive use and occupation of land; second, Aboriginal title encompasses the right to choose to what uses land can be put, subject to the ultimate limit that those uses cannot destroy the ability of the land to sustain future generations of Aboriginal peoples; and third, that lands held pursuant to Aboriginal title have an inescapable *economic component.*

167 The exclusive nature of Aboriginal title is relevant to the degree of scrutiny of the infringing measure or action. For example, if the Crown's fiduciary duty requires that Aboriginal title be given priority, then it is the altered approach to priority that I laid down in *Gladstone* which should apply. What is required is that the government demonstrate (at para. 62) "both that the process by which it allocated the resource and the actual allocation of the resource which results from that process reflect the prior interest" of the holders of Aboriginal title in the land. By analogy with *Gladstone,* this might entail, for example, that governments accommo-

date the participation of Aboriginal peoples in the development of the resources of British Columbia, that the conferral of fee simples for agriculture, and of leases and licences for forestry and mining reflect the prior occupation of Aboriginal title lands, that economic barriers to Aboriginal uses of their lands (e.g., licensing fees) be somewhat reduced. This list is illustrative and not exhaustive. This is an issue that may involve an assessment of the various interests at stake in the resources in question. No doubt, there will be difficulties in determining the precise value of the Aboriginal interest in the land and any grants, leases or licences given for its exploitation. These difficult economic considerations obviously cannot be solved here.

168   Moreover, the other aspects of Aboriginal title suggest that the fiduciary duty may be articulated in a manner different than the idea of priority. This point becomes clear from a comparison between Aboriginal title and the Aboriginal right to fish for food in *Sparrow*. First, Aboriginal title encompasses within it a right to choose to what ends a piece of land can be put. The Aboriginal right to fish for food, by contrast, does not contain within it the same discretionary component. This aspect of Aboriginal title suggests that the fiduciary relationship between the Crown and Aboriginal peoples may be satisfied by the involvement of Aboriginal peoples in decisions taken with respect to their lands. There is always a duty of consultation. Whether the Aboriginal group has been consulted is relevant to determining whether the infringement of Aboriginal title is justified, in the same way that the Crown's failure to consult an Aboriginal group with respect to the terms by which reserve land is leased may breach its fiduciary duty at common law: *Guerin*. The nature and scope of the duty of consultation will vary with the circumstances. In occasional cases, when the breach is less serious or relatively minor, it will be no more than a duty to discuss important decisions that will be taken with respect to lands held pursuant to Aboriginal title. Of course, even in these rare cases when the minimum acceptable standard is consultation, this consultation must be in good faith, and with the intention of substantially addressing the concerns of the Aboriginal peoples whose lands are at issue. In most cases, it will be significantly deeper than mere consultation. Some cases may even require the full consent of an Aboriginal nation, particularly when provinces enact hunting and fishing regulations in relation to Aboriginal lands.

169   Second, Aboriginal title, unlike the Aboriginal right to fish for food, has an inescapably economic aspect, particularly when one takes into account the modern uses to which lands held pursuant to Aboriginal title can be put. The economic aspect of Aboriginal title suggests that compensation is relevant to the question of justification as well, a possibility suggested in *Sparrow* and which I repeated in *Gladstone*. Indeed, compensation for breaches of fiduciary duty are a well-established part of the landscape of Aboriginal rights: *Guerin*. In keeping with the duty of honour and good faith on the Crown, fair compensation will ordinarily be required when Aboriginal title is infringed. The amount of compensation payable will vary with the nature of the particular Aboriginal title affected and with the nature and severity of the infringement and the extent to which Aboriginal interests were accommodated. Since the issue of damages was severed from the

principal action, we received no submissions on the appropriate legal principles that would be relevant to determining the appropriate level of compensation of infringements of Aboriginal title. In the circumstances, it is best that we leave those difficult questions to another day.

D. Has a claim to self-government been made out by the appellants?

170 . . . The errors of fact made by the trial judge, and the resultant need for a new trial, make it impossible for this Court to determine whether the claim to self-government has been made out. . . .

E. Did the province have the power to extinguish Aboriginal rights after 1871, either under its own jurisdiction or through the operation of s. 88 of the Indian Act? . . .

172 For Aboriginal rights to be recognized and affirmed by s. 35(1), they must have existed in 1982. Rights which were extinguished by the sovereign before that time are not revived by the provision. In a federal system such as Canada's, the need to determine whether Aboriginal rights have been extinguished raises the question of which level of government has jurisdiction to do so. In the context of this appeal, that general question becomes three specific ones. First, there is the question whether the province of British Columbia, from the time it joined Confederation in 1871, until the entrenchment of s. 35(1) in 1982, had the jurisdiction to extinguish the rights of Aboriginal peoples, including Aboriginal title, in that province. Second, if the province was without such jurisdiction, another question arises —whether provincial laws which were not in pith and substance aimed at the extinguishment of Aboriginal rights could have done so nevertheless if they were laws of general application. The third and final question is whether a provincial law, which could otherwise not extinguish Aboriginal rights, be given that effect through referential incorporation by s. 88 of the *Indian Act.*

(2) Primary Jurisdiction

173 Since 1871, the exclusive power to legislate in relation to "Indians, and Lands reserved for Indians" has been vested with the federal government by virtue of s. 91(24) of the *Constitution Act, 1867.* That head of jurisdiction, in my opinion, encompasses within it the exclusive power to extinguish Aboriginal rights, including Aboriginal title.

"Lands reserved for the Indians"

174 I consider the second part of this provision first, which confers jurisdiction to the federal government over "Lands reserved for the Indians". The debate between the parties centred on whether that part of s. 91(24) confers jurisdiction to legislate with respect to Aboriginal title. The province's principal submission is that "Lands reserved for the Indians" are lands which have been specifically set aside or designated for Indian occupation, such as reserves. However, I must reject that submission, because it flies in the face of the judgment of the Privy Council in *St. Catherine's Milling.* One of the issues in that appeal was the federal jurisdiction to accept the surrender of lands held pursuant to Aboriginal title. It was argued that

the federal government, at most, had jurisdiction over "Indian Reserves". Lord Watson, speaking for the Privy Council, rejected this argument, stating that had the intention been to restrict s. 91(24) in this way, specific language to this effect would have been used. He accordingly held that (at p. 59):

> . . . the words actually used are, according to their natural meaning, sufficient to in-clude all lands reserved, upon any terms or conditions, for Indian occupation.

Lord Watson's reference to "all lands" encompasses not only reserve lands, but lands held pursuant to Aboriginal title as well. Section 91(24), in other words, carries with it the jurisdiction to legislate in relation to Aboriginal title. It follows, by implication, that it also confers the jurisdiction to extinguish that title.

175 The province responds by pointing to the fact that underlying title to lands held pursuant to Aboriginal title vested with the provincial Crown pursuant to s. 109 of the *Constitution Act, 1867*. In its submission, this right of ownership carried with it the right to grant fee simples which, by implication, extinguish Aboriginal title, and so by negative implication excludes Aboriginal title from the scope of s. 91(24). The difficulty with the province's submission is that it fails to take account of the language of s. 109, which states in part that:

> 109. All Lands, Mines, Minerals and Royalties belonging to the several Provinces of Canada . . . at the Union . . . shall belong to the several Provinces . . . subject to any Trusts existing in respect thereof, and to any Interest other than that of the Province in the same.

Although that provision vests underlying title in provincial Crowns, it qualifies provincial ownership by making it subject to the "any Interest other than that of the Province in the same". In *St. Catherine's Milling,* the Privy Council held that Abo-riginal title was such an interest, and rejected the argument that provincial owner-ship operated as a limit on federal jurisdiction. The net effect of that decision, therefore, was to separate the ownership of lands held pursuant to Aboriginal title from jurisdiction over those lands. Thus, although on surrender of Aboriginal title the province would take absolute title, jurisdiction to accept surrenders lies with the federal government. The same can be said of extinguishment—although on extinguishment of Aboriginal title, the province would take complete title to the land, the jurisdiction to extinguish lies with the federal government.

176 I conclude with two remarks. First, even if the point were not settled, I would have come to same conclusion. The judges in the court below noted that separating federal jurisdiction over Indians from jurisdiction over their lands would have a most unfortunate result—the government vested with primary constitutional re-sponsibility for securing the welfare of Canada's Aboriginal peoples would find itself unable to safeguard one of the most central of native interests—their interest in their lands. Second, although the submissions of the parties and my analysis have focused on the question of jurisdiction over Aboriginal title, in my opinion, the same reasoning applies to jurisdiction over any Aboriginal right which relates to land. As I explained earlier, *Adams* clearly establishes that Aboriginal rights may be tied to land but nevertheless fall short of title. Those relationships with the

land, however, may be equally fundamental to Aboriginal peoples and, for the same reason that jurisdiction over Aboriginal title must vest with the federal government, so too must the power to legislate in relation to other Aboriginal rights in relation to land.

"Indians"

177 The extent of federal jurisdiction over Indians has not been definitively addressed by this Court. We have not needed to do so because the vires of federal legislation with respect to Indians, under the division of powers, has never been at issue. The cases which have come before the Court under s. 91(24) have implicated the question of jurisdiction over Indians from the other direction—whether provincial laws which on their face apply to Indians intrude on federal jurisdiction and are inapplicable to Indians to the extent of that intrusion. As I explain below, the Court has held that s. 91(24) protects a "core" of Indianness from provincial intrusion, through the doctrine of interjurisdictional immunity.

178 It follows, at the very least, that this core falls within the scope of federal jurisdiction over Indians. That core, for reasons I will develop, encompasses Aboriginal rights, including the rights that are recognized and affirmed by s. 35(1). Laws which purport to extinguish those rights therefore touch the core of Indianness which lies at the heart of s. 91(24), and are beyond the legislative competence of the provinces to enact. The core of Indianness encompasses the whole range of Aboriginal rights that are protected by s. 35(1). Those rights include rights in relation to land; that part of the core derives from s. 91(24)'s reference to "Lands reserved for the Indians". But those rights also encompass practices, customs and traditions which are not tied to land as well; that part of the core can be traced to federal jurisdiction over "Indians". Provincial governments are prevented from legislating in relation to both types of Aboriginal rights.

(3) Provincial Laws of General Application

179 The vesting of exclusive jurisdiction with the federal government over Indians and Indian lands under s. 91(24), operates to preclude provincial laws in relation to those matters. Thus, provincial laws which single out Indians for special treatment are *ultra vires,* because they are in relation to Indians and therefore invade federal jurisdiction: see *R.* v. *Sutherland,* [1980] 2 S.C.R. 451. However, it is a well established principle that (*Four B Manufacturing Ltd., supra,* at p. 1048):

> The conferring upon Parliament of exclusive legislative competence to make laws relating to certain classes of persons does not mean that the totality of these persons' rights and duties comes under primary federal competence to the exclusion of provincial laws of general application.

In other words, notwithstanding s. 91(24), provincial laws of general application apply *proprio vigore* to Indians and Indian lands. Thus, this Court has held that provincial labour relations legislation (*Four B*) and motor vehicle laws (*R.* v. *Francis,* [1988] 1 S.C.R. 1025), which purport to apply to all persons in the province, also apply to Indians living on reserves.

180 What must be answered, however, is whether the same principle allows provincial laws of general application to extinguish Aboriginal rights. I have come to the conclusion that a provincial law of general application could not have this effect, for two reasons. First, a law of general application cannot, by definition, meet the standard which has been set by this Court for the extinguishment of Aboriginal rights without being *ultra vires* the province. That standard was laid down in *Sparrow, supra,* at p. 1099, as one of "clear and plain" intent. In that decision, the Court drew a distinction between laws which extinguished Aboriginal rights, and those which merely regulated them. Although the latter types of laws may have been "necessarily inconsistent" with the continued exercise of Aboriginal rights, they could not extinguish those rights. While the requirement of clear and plain intent does not, perhaps, require that the Crown "use language which refers expressly to its extinguishment of aboriginal rights" (*Gladstone, supra,* at para. 34), the standard is still quite high. My concern is that the only laws with the sufficiently clear and plain intention to extinguish Aboriginal rights would be laws in relation to Indians and Indian lands. As a result, a provincial law could never, *proprio vigore,* extinguish Aboriginal rights, because the intention to do so would take the law outside provincial jurisdiction.

181 Second, as I mentioned earlier, s. 91(24) protects a core of federal jurisdiction even from provincial laws of general application, through the operation of the doctrine of interjurisdictional immunity. That core has been described as matters touching on "Indianness" or the "core of Indianness" (*Dick , supra,* at pp. 326 and 315; also see *Four B, supra,* at p. 1047 and *Francis, supra,* at pp. 1028–29). The core of Indianness at the heart of s. 91(24) has been defined in both negative and positive terms. Negatively, it has been held to not include labour relations (*Four B*) and the driving of motor vehicles (*Francis*). The only positive formulation of Indianness was offered in *Dick.* Speaking for the Court, Beetz J. assumed, but did not decide, that a provincial hunting law did not apply *proprio vigore* to the members of an Indian band to hunt and because those activities were "at the centre of what they do and who they are" (*supra,* at p. 320). But in *Van der Peet,* I described and defined the Aboriginal rights that are recognized and affirmed by s. 35(1) in a similar fashion, as protecting the occupation of land and the activities which are integral to the distinctive Aboriginal culture of the group claiming the right. It follows that Aboriginal rights are part of the core of Indianness at the heart of s. 91(24). Prior to 1982, as a result, they could not be extinguished by provincial laws of general application.

(4) Section 88 of the Indian Act

182 Provincial laws which would otherwise not apply to Indians *proprio vigore,* however, are allowed to do so by s. 88 of the *Indian Act,* which incorporates by reference provincial laws of general application . . . in Professor Hogg's words, . . . s. 88 does not "invigorate" provincial laws which are invalid because they are in relation to Indians and Indian lands (*Constitutional Law of Canada* (3rd ed. 1992), at p. 676; . . . What this means is that s. 88 extends the effect of provincial laws of general application which cannot apply to Indians and Indian lands because they touch on the Indianness at the core of s. 91(24). For example, a provincial law

which regulated hunting may very well touch on this core. Although such a law would not apply to Aboriginal people *proprio vigore,* it would still apply through s. 88 of the *Indian Act,* being a law of general application. Such laws are enacted to conserve game and for the safety of all. . . .

I see nothing in the language of the provision [s. 88] which even suggests the intention to extinguish Aboriginal rights. Indeed, the explicit reference to treaty rights in s. 88 suggests that the provision was clearly not intended to undermine Aboriginal rights.

VI. Conclusion and Disposition

184 For the reasons I have given above, I would allow the appeal in part, and dismiss the cross-appeal. Reluctantly, I would also order a new trial.

185 I conclude with two observations. The first is that many Aboriginal nations with territorial claims that overlap with those of the appellants did not intervene in this appeal, and do not appear to have done so at trial. This is unfortunate, because determinations of Aboriginal title for the Gitksan and Wet'suwet'en will undoubtedly affect their claims as well. This is particularly so because Aboriginal title encompasses an *exclusive* right to the use and occupation of land, i.e., to the *exclusion* of both non-Aboriginals and members of other Aboriginal nations. It may, therefore, be advisable if those Aboriginal nations intervened in any new litigation.

186 Finally, this litigation has been both long and expensive, not only in economic but in human terms as well. By ordering a new trial, I do not necessarily encourage the parties to proceed to litigation and to settle their dispute through the courts. As was said in *Sparrow,* at p. 1105, s. 35(1) "provides a solid constitutional base upon which subsequent negotiations can take place". Those negotiations should also include other Aboriginal nations which have a stake in the territory claimed. Moreover, the Crown is under a moral, if not a legal, duty to enter into and conduct those negotiations in good faith. Ultimately, it is through negotiated settlements, with good faith and give and take on all sides, reinforced by the judgments of this Court, that we will achieve what I stated in *Van der Peet, supra,* at para. 31, to be a basic purpose of s. 35(1)—"the reconciliation of the pre-existence of Aboriginal societies with the sovereignty of the Crown". Let us face it, we are all here to stay. . . .

PROOF OF ABORIGINAL TITLE

12. *Hamlet of Baker Lake* v. *Minister of Indian Affairs and Northern Development,* [1979] 3 C.N.L.R. 17 (F.C.T.D.). Mahoney J., November 15, 1979

> This decision is the result of the Inuit of Baker Lake, Northwest Territories, seeking a declaration that they possessed Aboriginal title to a large portion of land and an injunction against mining companies from interfering with their claimed right to harvest caribou. *Baker Lake* sets out the test to prove the existence of Aboriginal title and has been adopted by the Supreme Court of Canada. The decision has been criticized

for being too restrictive in its successful application and for being Eurocentric in nature. The Supreme Court of Canada, both in *R. v. Van der Peet,* [1996] 4 C.N.L.R. 177, and *Delgamuukw* v. *British Columbia,* has maintained the general approach outlined in *Baker Lake,* except that there seems to be less reliance on the need for an "organized society." Rather, the test has been broadened so as to allow courts to look at the entire context surrounding a particular Aboriginal group, particularly emphasizing the need for continuity of presence by the Aboriginal group.

MAHONEY, J.:—

. . . The plaintiffs assert an existing aboriginal title over an undefined portion of the Northwest Territories of Canada including approximately 78,000 square kilometers around the community of Baker Lake. That specified area is hereafter called the "Baker Lake Area". . . .

The relief sought by the plaintiffs, in summary, is:

(a) an order restraining the government Defendants from issuing land use permits, prospecting permits, granting mining leases and recording mining claims which would allow mining activities in the Baker Lake Area;

(b) an order restraining the Defendant mining companies from carrying on such activities there;

(c) a declaration that the lands comprising the Baker Lake Area are "subject to the aboriginal right and title of the Inuit residing in or near that area to hunt or fish thereon";

(d) a declaration that the lands comprising the Baker Lake Area are neither "territorial lands" nor "public lands" as defined respectively in the *Territorial Lands Act* and the *Public Lands Grants Act,* R.S.C. 1970, c. P–29, nor subject to the *Canada Mining Regulations;*

(e) a declaration that, until such time as the terms of the Imperial Order in Council, R.S.C. 1970, App. I, No. 9, which admitted Rupert's Land into Canada are fulfilled by Canada, Canada lacks legislative jurisdiction to abrogate Inuit aboriginal rights in the Baker Lake Area;

(f) as an alternative to (e), a declaration that, until such aboriginal rights are *expressly* abrogated by Parliament, no one is entitled to deal with the Baker Lake Area in a manner inconsistent with Inuit aboriginal rights, notwithstanding other statutory authority;

(g) a declaration that the Inuit resident in the Baker Lake Area have "rights previously acquired" and are "holders of surface rights" within the meaning of the mining laws with respect to the Baker Lake Area;

(h) costs. . . .

THE SOURCE OF INUIT ABORIGINAL TITLE

While the *Royal Proclamation of 1763*, various statutes and almost all the decided cases refer to Indians and do not mention Inuit or Eskimos, the term "Indians", in Canadian constitutional law, includes the Inuit: *Re Eskimos*, [1939] 2 D.L.R. 417, [1939] S.C.R. 104 sub nom. *Reference as to whether "Indians" in 91(24) of the B.N.A. Act, 1867, includes Eskimo inhabitants of Quebec.* In the absence of their exclusion from that term, either expressly or by compelling inference, decisions relevant to the aboriginal rights of Indians in Canada apply to the Inuit. In light of the *Sigeareak* decision, [1966] S.C.R. 645, the Royal Proclamation must be dismissed as a source of aboriginal title in Rupert's Land. However, the Proclamation is not the only source of aboriginal title in Canada.

In *Calder et al.* v. *A.-G. B.C.* (1973), 34 D.L.R. (3d) 145, [1973] S.C.R. 313, the six members of the Supreme Court who found it necessary to consider the substantive issues, which dealt with territory outside the geographic limits of the Proclamation, all held that an aboriginal title recognized at common law had existed. Judson, J., with Martland and Ritchie, JJ., concurring, put it, at p. 156 D.L.R., p. 328 S.C.R., as follows:

> Although I think that it is clear that Indian title in British Columbia cannot owe its origin to the Proclamation of 1763, the fact is that when the settlers came, the Indians were there, *organized in societies* and occupying the land as their forefathers had done for centuries. This is what Indian title means and it does not help one in the solution of this problem to call it a "personal or usufructuary right". What they are asserting in this action is that they had a right to continue to live on their lands as their forefathers had lived and that this right has never been lawfully extinguished. There can be no question that this right was "dependent on the goodwill of the Sovereign".

The emphasis is mine. In the result, he held that "Indian title" to have been extinguished. The dissenting judgment, which held the aboriginal title, with certain exceptions, not to have been extinguished, was delivered by Hall, J., with Spence and Laskin, JJ., concurring. Pigeon, J., disposed of the matter exclusively on the procedural ground that the plaintiffs had not obtained the required *fiat* to sue the Crown in right of British Columbia, a conclusion concurred in by Judson, Martland and Ritchie, JJ. While it appears that the judgment of Pigeon, J., embodies the *ratio decidendi* of the Supreme Court, the clear agreement of the other six judges on the point is solid authority for the general proposition that the law of Canada recognizes the existence of an aboriginal title independent of the Royal Proclamation or any other prerogative Act or legislation. It arises at common law. Its recognition by the Supreme Court of Canada may well be based upon an acceptance of the reasoning of Chief Justice Marshall in *Worcester* v. *State of Georgia* (1832), 6 Peters 515 at p. 542, a decision referred to in both their judgments by Judson and Hall, JJ.:

> America, separated from Europe by a wide ocean, was inhabited by a distinct people, divided into separate nations, independent of each other and of the rest of the world, *having institutions of their own, and governing themselves by their own laws.* It is difficult to comprehend the proposition, that the inhabitants of either quarter of the globe could have rightful original claims of dominion over the inhabitants of the other, or over the lands they occupied; or that the discovery of either by the other should give the discoverer rights in the country discovered, which annulled the pre-existing rights of its ancient possessors.

The emphasis was included in the passage when it was quoted by Mr. Justice Hall at p. 195 D.L.R., p. 383 S.C.R. . . .

PROOF OF ABORIGINAL TITLE

The elements which the plaintiffs must prove to establish an aboriginal title cognizable at common law are:

1.   That they and their ancestors were members of an organized society.
2.   That the organized society occupied the specific territory over which they assert the aboriginal title.
3.   That the occupation was to the exclusion of other organized societies.
4.   That the occupation was an established fact at the time sovereignty was asserted by England.

Decisions supporting these propositions include those of the Supreme Court of Canada in *Kruger and Manuel* v. *The Queen* (1977), 75 D.L.R. (3d) 434, [1978] S.C.R. 104, and the *Calder* case and those of the United States Supreme Court in *Johnson and Graham's Lessee* v. *M'Intosh* (1823), 8 Wheaton 543; *Worcester* v. *Georgia*, supra; and *United States* v. *Santa Fe Pacific R. Co.* (1941), 314 U.S. 339.

Proof that the plaintiffs and their ancestors were members of an organized society is required by the authorities. In quoting Mr. Justice Judson's *Calder* judgment, I emphasized the phrase "organized in societies" and I repeated the emphasis Mr. Justice Hall had included in quoting the passage from *Worcester* v. *Georgia*: "having institutions of their own, and governing themselves by their own laws". The *rationale* of the requirement is to be found in the following *dicta* of the Privy Council in *Re Southern Rhodesia* [1919] A.C. 211 at pp. 233–4:

> The estimation of the rights of aboriginal tribes is always inherently difficult. Some tribes are so low in the scale of social organization that their usages and conceptions of rights and duties are not to be reconciled with the institutions or the legal ideas of civilized society. Such a gulf cannot be bridged. It would be idle to impute to such people some shadow of the rights known to our law and then to transmute it into the substance of transferable rights of property as we know them. In the present case it would make each and every person by a fictional inheritance a landed proprietor "richer than all his tribe". On the other hand, there are indigenous peoples whose legal conceptions, though differently developed, are hardly less precise than our own. When once they have been studied and understood they are no less enforceable than rights arising under English law. Between the two there is a wide tract of much ethnological interest, but the position of the natives of Southern Rhodesia within it is very uncertain; clearly they approximate rather to the lower than to the higher limit.

Their Lordships did not find it necessary to pursue the question further since they found that the aboriginal rights, if any, that might once have existed had been expressly extinguished by the Crown.

It is apparent that the relative sophistication of the organization of any society will be a function of the needs of its members, the demands they make of it. While the existence of an organized society is a prerequisite to the existence of an aboriginal title, there appears no valid reason to demand proof of the existence of a society more elaborately structured than is necessary to demonstrate that there existed among the aborigines a recognition of the claimed rights, sufficiently defined to permit their recognition by the common law upon its advent in the territory. The thrust of all the authorities is not that the common law necessarily deprives aborigines of their enjoyment of the land in any particular but, rather, that it can give effect only to those incidents of that enjoyment that were, themselves, given effect by the regime that prevailed before: *Amodu Tijani* v. *Secretary, Southern Nigeria*, [1921] 2 A.C. 399.

The fact is that the aboriginal Inuit had an organized society. It was not a society with very elaborate institutions but it was a society organized to exploit the resources available on the barrens and essential to sustain human life there. That was about all they could do: hunt and fish and survive. The aboriginal title asserted here encompasses only the right to hunt and fish as their ancestors did.

The organized society of the Caribou Eskimos, such as it was, and it was sufficient to serve them, did not change significantly from well before England's assertion of sovereignty over the barren lands until their settlement. For the most part, the ancestors of the individual plaintiffs were members of that society; many of them were themselves members of it. That their society has materially changed in recent years is of no relevance.

The specificity of the territory over which aboriginal title has heretofore been claimed in the reported cases appears not to have been a disputed issue of fact. In the *Calder* case, supra, the subject territory was agreed between the parties. In the *Kruger* case, the Court did not find it necessary to deal with the questions of aboriginal title and extinguishment and disposed of the appeal on other grounds to which I will return. It did, however, give a clear signal as to what its approach would be in the future. Mr. Justice Dickson, for the Court, at p. 108 S.C.R., said:

> ...Claims to aboriginal title are woven with history, legend, politics and moral obligations. If the claim of any Band in respect of any particular land is to be decided as a justiciable issue and not a political issue, it should be so considered on the facts pertinent to that Band and to that land, and not on any global basis...

There were obviously great differences between the aboriginal societies of the Indians and the Inuit and decisions expressed in the context of Indian societies must be applied to the Inuit with those differences in mind. The absence of political structures like tribes was an inevitable consequence of the *modus vivendi* dictated by the Inuit's physical environment. Similarly the Inuit appear to have occupied the barren lands without competition except in the vicinity of the tree line. That, too, was a function of their physical environment. The pressures of other peoples, except from the fringes of the boreal forest, were non-existent and, thus, the Inuit were not confined in their occupation of the barrens in the same way Indian tribes may have confined each other elsewhere on the continent. Furthermore, the exigences of survival dictated the sparse, but wide ranging, nature of their occupation. . . .

The nature, extent or degree of the aborigines' physical presence on the land they occupied, required by the law as an essential element of their aboriginal title is to be determined in each case by a subjective test. To the extent human beings were capable of surviving on the barren lands, the Inuit were there; to the extent the barrens lent themselves to human occupation, the Inuit occupied them.

The occupation of the territory must have been to the exclusion of other organized societies. In the *Santa Fe* case, *supra*, at p. 345, Mr. Justice Douglas, giving the opinion of the court, held:

Occupancy necessary to establish aboriginal possession is a question of fact to be determined as any other question of fact. If it were established as a fact that the lands in question were, or were included in, the ancestral home of the Walapais in the sense that they constituted definable territory occupied exclusively by the Walapais (as distinguished from lands wandered over by many tribes), then the Walapais had "Indian title" which, unless extinguished, survived the railroad grant of 1866. . . .

On the evidence, I cannot find that the entire Baker Lake Area was exclusively occupied by the Inuit on the advent of English sovereignty. The archaeological and historical evidence leads to the conclusion that probably, at that date, the boundary between Inuit and Indian land traversed the southwesterly portion of the Baker Lake Area. I have concluded, admittedly on the basis of very meagre evidence and recognizing a large element of arbitrariness as necessary to a definition of the boundary of exclusive Inuit occupation, that the territory to the south and west of a line drawn from the east end of Aberdeen Lake to the confluence of the Kazan and Kunyak Rivers was not Inuit territory. . . .

In the result, I find, on a balance of probabilities on the evidence before me, that, at the time England asserted sovereignty over the barren lands west of Hudson Bay, the Inuit were the exclusive occupants of the portion of barren lands extending from the vicinity of Baker Lake north and east toward the Arctic and Hudson Bay to the boundaries of the Baker Lake R.C.M.P. detachment area as they were in 1954 including, specifically, that portion of the detachment area lying north and east of a line drawn from its boundary downstream along the Thelon River to its outlet from Aberdeen Lake, thence southeasterly to the confluence of the Kazan and Kunwak Rivers and thence upstream along the Kazan to the boundary of the area. An aboriginal title to that territory, carrying with it the right freely to move about and hunt and fish over it, vested at common law in the Inuit.

EXTINGUISHMENT BEFORE 1870

The Defendants say that the Inuit's aboriginal title in Rupert's Land was extinguished by the Royal Charter of May 2, 1670, granting Rupert's Land to the Hudson's Bay Company or, if not by that, by the admission of Rupert's Land to Canada in 1870. The limits of Rupert's Land are not in issue here nor does anything turn on the formal name of the grantee which will simply be referred to as "the company".

The Royal Charter granted the company "the sole Trade and Commerce of" Rupert's Land. It constituted Rupert's Land "one of our Plantacions or Colonyes in America" and went on:

. . . and further WEE DOE by these presentes for us our heires and successors make create and constitute the said Governor and Company for the tyme being and theire successors the true and absolute Lordes and Proprietors of the same Territory lymittes and places aforesaid And of all other the premisses SAVING ALWAYS the faith Allegiance and Soveraigne Dominion due to us our heires and successors for the same TO HAVE HOLD possesse and enjoy the said Territory lymittes and places and all and singular other the premisses hereby granted as aforesaid with theire and every of their Rightes Members Jurisdiccions Prerogatives Royaltyes and Appurtenances whatsoever to them the said Govenor and Company and theire Successors for ever TO BEE HOLDEN of us our heires and successors as of our Mannor of East Greenwich in our

County of Kent in free and common Soccage and not in Capite or by Knightes Service YEILDING AND PAYING yearly to us our heires and Successors for the same two Elkes and two Black beavers whensoever and as often as Wee our heires and successors shall happen to enter into the said Countryes Territoryes and Regions hereby granted. . . .

It seems to me that the grant of title to the company was intended solely to define its ownership of the land in relation to the Crown, not to extinguish the aboriginal title. That conclusion is consistent with what had already happened in other North American colonies where, unlike Rupert's Land, settlement had made necessary the extinguishment of aboriginal title. It is consistent with the policy of the company itself, expressed as early as 1683, with respect to lands required for trading posts. It is consistent with what the company in fact did, through its surrogate Lord Selkirk, the only time it was required to make provision for a settlement. It is consistent with what the Canadian Government has done since the admission of Rupert's Land to Canada.

The coexistence of an aboriginal title with the estate of the ordinary private land holder is readily recognized as an absurdity. The communal right of aborigines to occupy it cannot be reconciled with the right of a private owner to peaceful enjoyment of his land. However, its coexistence with the radical title of the Crown to land is characteristic of aboriginal title and the company, in its ownership of Rupert's Land, aside from its trading Posts, was very much in the Position of the Crown. Its occupation of the territory in issue was, at most, notional.

I therefore find that the Royal Charter of May 2, 1670, did not extinguish aboriginal title in Rupert's Land. Nothing in the 1690 Act of Parliament that confirmed the Charter had any bearing on this question (2 W. & M., c. 23). Likewise, I find nothing in the Imperial Order in Council (R.S.C. 1970, App. II, No. 9) of June 23, 1870, whereby Rupert's Land was admitted to Canada that had any effect on aboriginal title. . . .

The aboriginal title, vested at common law in the Inuit, had not been extinguished prior to the admission of Rupert's Land to Canada. That title was not extinguished by or in the process of admission. It subsisted when Rupert's Land became part of Canada.

EXTINGUISHMENT SINCE 1870

The Inuit's aboriginal title has not been extinguished by surrender. Since the admission of Rupert's Land to Canada, it has been within the legislative competence of the Parliament of Canada to extinguish it. Parliament has not enacted legislation expressly extinguishing that title.

The Plaintiffs argue that any such extinguishment must be effected expressly. They find support for that proposition in the judgment of Mr. Justice Hall in the *Calder* case. The Defendants argue that extinguishment may be the necessary result of legislation even though the intention is not expressed. They find support for their position in the judgment of Mr. Justice Judson in the *Calder* case.

At page 402, Mr. Justice Hall, referring to the "Indian title" in issue, said:

It being a legal right, it could not thereafter be extinguished except by surrender to the Crown or by competent legislative authority, *and then only by specific legislation.*

The emphasis is mine. After citing a number of authorities, he concluded his discussion of the particular point, at p. 210 D.L.R., p. 404 S.C.R., as follows:

> It would, accordingly, appear to be beyond question that the onus of proving that the Sovereign intended to extinguish the Indian title lies on the respondent and that *the intention must be "clear and plain"*.

Again, the emphasis is mine. If I understand the plaintiffs well, they argue that, to extinguish aboriginal title, legislation must state expressly that such extinguishment is its object.

I have perused the authorities cited by Mr. Justice Hall and the one upon which he appears to have relied for the qualification embraced in the phrases I have emphasized is the following passage from the opinion of Davis, J., for the United States Court of Claims, in *Lipan Apache Tribe* v. *United States* (1967), 180 Ct. Cl. 487 at p. 492:

> The correct inquiry is, not whether the Republic of Texas accorded or granted the Indians any rights, but whether that sovereign extinguished their pre-existing occupancy rights. Extinguishment can take several forms; it can be effected "by treaty, by the sword, by purchase, by the exercise of complete dominion adverse to the right of occupancy, or otherwise . . .". *United States* v. *Santa Fe Pac. R.R.*, supra, 314 U.S at 347. While the selection of a means is a governmental prerogative, the actual act (or acts) of extinguishment must be plain and unambiguous. *In the absence of a "clear and plain indication" in the public records that the sovereign "intended to extinguish all of the [claimants] rights" in their property, Indian title continues. Id.* at 353.

The emphasis was added by Mr. Justice Hall. . . .

I cannot accept the Plaintiffs' argument that Parliament's intention to extinguish an aboriginal title must be set forth explicitly in the pertinent legislation. I do not agree that Mr. Justice Hall went that far. Once a statute has been validly enacted, it must be given effect. If its necessary effect is to abridge or entirely abrogate a common law right, then that is the effect that the Courts must give it. That is as true of an aboriginal title as of any other common law right. Section 1(a) of the *Canadian Bill of Rights* does not make the aboriginal title in issue here an exception to the general rule. . . .

To say that the necessary result of legislation is adverse to any right of aboriginal occupancy is tantamount to saying that the legislator has expressed a clear and plain intention to extinguish that right of occupancy. Justices Hall and Judson were, I think, in agreement on the law, if not its application in the particular circumstances.

I now turn to the legislation said to have effected the extinguishment of the aboriginal title in issue. All apply to the District of Keewatin. No real doubt as to the validity of any has been suggested, or suggests itself, to me. . . .

Extinguishment of the Inuit's aboriginal title is not a necessary result of legislation enacted since 1870. The aboriginal title in issue has not been extinguished.

THE MINING LAWS

No real doubt as to the validity of the mining laws has been raised in my mind. I do not, therefore, intend to recite them, except to the extent necessary to deal with the questions of whether, by virtue of their aboriginal title, the Inuit have "rights previously acquired" within the meaning of s-s. 29(11) of the *Canada Mining Regulations* and are "holders of surface rights" within the meaning of s. 8 of the *Territorial Lands Act.*

With the exception of a number of parcels in the hamlet itself, I am entirely satisfied that the entire territory in issue remains "territorial lands" within the meaning of the *Territorial Lands Act* and "public lands" within the meaning of the *Public Lands Grants Act.* They are subject to the *Canada Mining Regulations.* To the extent that their aboriginal rights are diminished by those laws, the Inuit may or may not be entitled to compensation. That is not sought in this action. There can, however, be no doubt as to the effect of competent legislation and that, to the extent it does diminish the rights comprised in a aboriginal title, it prevails. . . .

CONCLUSION

The plaintiffs are entitled to a declaration that the lands comprised in District E2, the Baker Lake R.C.M.P. detachment area in 1954, excluding that portion, which has previously been more particularly described, lying south and west of the Thelon and Kazan Rivers, are subject to the aboriginal right and title of the Inuit to hunt and fish thereon. The action will otherwise be dismissed. . . .

EXTINGUISHMENT OF ABORIGINAL TITLE

13. *St. Catherine's Milling and Lumber Company* v. *R.* (1887), 2 C.N.L.C. 441. This S.C.C. decision was affirmed by the J.C.P.C. at (1888), 14 A.C. 46, 2 C.N.L.C. 541

STRONG J.:— . . . It thus appears, that in the United States a traditional policy, derived from colonial times, relative to the Indians and their lands has ripened into well established rules of law, and that the result is that the lands in the possession of the Indians are, until surrendered, treated as their rightful though inalienable property, so far as the possession and enjoyment are concerned; in other words, that the *dominium utile* is recognized as belonging to or reserved for the Indians, though the *dominium directum* is considered to be in the United States. Then, if this is so as regards Indian lands in the United States, which have been preserved to the Indians by the constant observance of a particular rule of policy acknowledged by the United States courts to have been originally enforced by the crown of Great Britain, how is it possible to suppose that the law can, or rather could have been, at the date of confederation, in a state any less favorable to the Indians whose lands were situated within the dominion of the British crown, the original author of this beneficient doctrine so carefully adhered to in the United States from the days of the colonial governments? Therefore, when we consider that with reference to Canada the uniform practice has always been to recognize the Indian title as one which could only be dealt with by surrender to the crown, I maintain that if there had been an entire absence of any written legislative act ordaining this rule as an express positive law, we ought, just as the United States courts have done, to hold that it nevertheless existed as a rule of the unwritten common law, which the courts were bound to enforce as such, and consequently, that the 24th sub-section of section 91, as well as the 109th section and the 5th sub-section of section 92 of the *British North America Act,* must all be read and construed upon the assumption that these territorial rights of the Indians were strictly legal rights which had to be taken into account and dealt with in that distribution of property and proprietary rights made upon confederation between the federal and provincial governments. . . .

14. *Attorney-General of Ontario* v. *Bear Island Foundation et al.,* [1985] 1 C.N.L.R. 1. (Ont. S.C.). Steele J., December 11, 1984

> In *A.-G. Ontario* v. *Bear Island Foundation,* Steele J. of the Ontario Supreme Court held that Aboriginal title exists solely at the pleasure of the Crown and that extinguishment of Aboriginal rights, as affirmed by the Supreme Court of Canada, may take place by treaty even though the treaty itself may be flawed in that not all of the affected Indian tribes or bands were signatories. The case concerns an action brought by the attorney-general of Ontario against the Bear Island Foundation, representing the Temagami Band, after the Foundation registered cautions on unceded land north of Lake Nipissing, Ontario. The band claimed Aboriginal rights over the area in question while the Crown was seeking a declaration that it had clear title to the land. The Supreme Court of Canada affirmed the Ontario Court of Appeal decision that the Robinson-Huron Treaty of 1850 extinguished the Temagami's Aboriginal rights over the area.

STEELE J.:— . . . In *Calder* v. *A.-G. B.C.,* [1973] S.C.R. 313, it was held by Judson J. that, though the British Columbia government had not made land surveys of the area, nevertheless, it had made alienations in the area inconsistent with the existence of an aboriginal title. Hall J., when dissenting in *Calder,* appears to have stated at p. 402 that Indian title may only be extinguished by surrender to the Crown or by competent legislative authority, and then only by "specific legislation", and that the intention to extinguish must be "clear and plain". He did not go so far as to say that there must be legislation stating that its express intent is to extinguish aboriginal title. I have reviewed the decision of Mahoney J, in *Hamlet of Baker Lake* v. *Min. of Indian Affairs and Northern Dev.,* [1980] 1 F.C. 518, [1979] 3 C.N.L.R. 17. I agree with him that there is no Canadian statute that requires that legislative extinguishment of aboriginal rights (as opposed to extinguishment of rights in reserves established under the *Indian Act*) be effected in a particular way. I also agree with him when he said, at p. 568 [p. 55 C.N.L.R.]:

> Once a statute has been validly enacted, it must be given effect. If its necessary effect is to abridge or entirely abrogate a common law right, then that is the effect that the Courts must give it. That is as true of an aboriginal title as of any other common law right.

and also his statement at p. 569 [p. 56 C.N.L.R.]:

> *To say that the necessary result of legislation is adverse to any right of aboriginal occupancy is tantamount to saying that the legislator has expressed a clear and plain intention to extinguish that right of occupancy. Justices Hall and Judson were, I think, in agreement on the law,* if not its application in the particular circumstances. (Emphasis added)

In the *Baker Lake* case, notwithstanding that it was found that there was no intention to open up the lands in question for settlement, it was held that, where there had been grants of interest in the lands by the crown pursuant to legislation, these grants prevailed over the aboriginal title of the plaintiffs. In our case, there is a clear intent by the Crown to open the lands for settlement.

The opening up of land to settlement pursuant to such legislation (or even in the absence of legislation) is sufficient to extinguish aboriginal rights. . . .

I disagree with the defendants' contention that the *Constitution Act, 1982* protects the aboriginal and treaty rights of the aboriginal peoples of Canada as these rights existed in 1763. This totally ignores the wording of section 35(1) which provides: "The *existing* aboriginal and treaty rights of the aboriginal peoples of Canada are hereby recognized and affirmed." (Emphasis added). It is only those rights that still survived at the time of proclamation of the *Constitution Act, 1982* that are protected, and no others (see *R.* v. *Eninew* [1984] 2 C.N.L.R. 126).

Section 25 of the *Constitution Act, 1982* provides that no guarantee of rights and freedoms set out in the Charter shall be construed so as to abrogate or derogate from any aboriginal, treaty or other rights that pertain to the aboriginal peoples of Canada, including any rights or freedoms that have been recognized by the Royal Proclamation and any rights or freedoms that may have been acquired by way of land claims settlements. Obviously, this section means that the rights and freedoms given generally to the people of Canada shall not be construed so as to override aboriginal rights. It has nothing to do with the question of what aboriginal and treaty rights are protected by the *Constitution Act, 1982*, that question being specifically dealt with in section 35. I cannot interpret section 25 to be a limitation upon what was dealt with in section 35. The Parliaments of the United Kingdom and Canada knew full well that many aboriginal rights that existed in 1763 had been interfered with over the centuries by the statutes and actions of the United Kingdom, Canada and Ontario. If the Parliaments had intended to reverse all of those encroachments and reinstate aboriginal rights to the state they were in when enjoyed in 1763, the Parliaments would have clearly said so, rather than inserting the word "existing" in the *Constitution Act, 1982*. The reference in section 25 cannot, by inference, move the clock back over 200 years, nor was it intended so to do.

Section 52 of the *Constitution Act, 1982* provides that it is the supreme law of Canada, and that any law that is inconsistent with the Constitution, to the extent of the inconsistency, shall be of no force or effect. There is no evidence in the present case as to new facts or altered facts that have occurred since the coming into force of the *Constitution Act, 1982*, nor of any legislation enacted either by Canada or Ontario since that date. Therefore, it is not necessary to express my opinion as to the effect of the *Constitution Act, 1982* on the Crown's right of extinguishment after 1982.

It is not necessary for me to comment on section 92A of the *Constitution Act, 1867* [am. by *Constitution Act, 1982* s. 50], which section deals with the exclusive authority of the province over natural resources because there is no evidence of any legislation or dealings having taken place since the commencement of the action which would fall under that head, and also because this action was commenced prior to the passage of the *Constitution Act, 1982*. . . .

I will now deal with the Robinson-Huron Treaty, the existence, validity and effects (re extinguishment of aboriginal rights) of which must be proved on a balance of probabilities by the Crown.

A treaty is not a conveyance of title because title is already in the Crown. A treaty is merely a simple acknowledgement that may be formal or informal in nature. . . .

With respect to the Robinson-Huron Treaty, I find that there was an intention on the part of the government to take a surrender from the Indians of all lands in Upper Canada south of the Height of Land, which would include the major portion of the Temagami Land Claim Area. . . .

Throughout the period of 1883 to the date of trial, Canada has consistently taken the position that the Temagami Indians did not sign the treaty and that their Indian title has not been extinguished, while Ontario consistently has taken the position that the Temagami Indians were party to the treaty and that their title has been extinguished. Ontario's actions over the years confirm its position. At trial, Canada, though represented only with respect to the constitutional issue, has through its counsel now taken the position that the Indians have adhered to the treaty and are bound by it. Canada's previous position is somewhat suspect because, if the Indians were not party to the treaty, why were they admitted to the Robinson-Huron pay list in 1883, and why has Canada consistently argued for a reserve for the Indians? I note that, with one minor exception, Canada has always agreed that the Land Claim Area falls within the territorial limits of the Robinson-Huron Treaty, and I find that it does. . . .

Assuming the existence of valid aboriginal title, the onus rests on the Crown to prove extinguishment of aboriginal title. . . .

All of the legislation in the *Indian Acts* of 1859, 1868, 1876 and 1880 was repealed by the *Indian Act*, R.S.C. 1886, c. 43 which, itself, had a saving provision with respect to any transaction, matter or thing anterior to the repeal. Sections 7 and 8 of the 1886 statute specifically dealt with some anterior matters by spelling out in detail what was to continue and remain in force. Clearly, the saving provisions were to apply to specific matters and not to the general law. Therefore, all prior general saving provisions were repealed and the defendants can claim no rights thereunder.

To conclude, in my opinion, by passing legislation with respect to surveys and issuing patents which fostered settlement and development of the Land Claim Area, development which has severely interfered with the hunting and fishing rights of the Indians thereon, the Crown, and in particular Ontario, has indicated an intention to exercise complete dominion over the Land Claim Area. The result has been that the defendants' aboriginal right to use or occupy or possess the lands, as did their forefathers, has been extinguished. The legislation also clearly shows that it was the intention and understanding of the Province of Canada, and later Ontario, that the Robinson-Huron Treaty covered all the lands in that part of Ontario, including the Land Claim Area south of the Height of Land. . . .

A.   *The Competence of the Province of Canada to Extinguish Aboriginal Rights*
. . . It was within the competence of the Crown, acting upon the advice of the colonial legislature, to take away aboriginal rights if it so wished. The *Union Act, 1840*, supra, provided that the Governor of Canada could assent to all Acts unless

he expressly reserved them for the Imperial Crown, and that the Imperial Crown could disallow any legislation that referred to its prerogative, within two years of the enactment of the colonial legislation. In the present case, there is no evidence of any disallowance of any of the statutes in question, and those that were reserved were approved. Therefore, those Acts enacted by the Province of Canada from 1840 to 1867 were valid. In addition, the *Union Act, 1840* also provided that, where any Act affected the Royal prerogative with respect to the granting of waste lands, such Act was to be sent and placed before the United Kingdom Parliament for thirty days prior to the Crown giving any consent. In 1854, the clause in the *Union Act, 1840* that required tabling before the United Kingdom Parliament was repealed, and a provision enacted that read that no prior Act should be deemed to be invalid because the tabling requirement had not been complied with. It is therefore my opinion that, as of 1840, the Crown, acting upon the advice of the provincial legislature, had full power to grant unceded lands if it so desired. Other than the Royal Proclamation, there was no legislation prior to 1868 that affected the Crown in Canada's right to grant unceded Indian lands.

. . . As a result of the *Union Act, 1840*, and the *Territorial Revenue Act* of 1847, there was authority for the Governor (i.e. the Crown), with the advice of the colonial legislature, to enter into treaties. The Imperial Crown had the right to review or repudiate acts of the colonial legislature, including treaties entered into, but there is no evidence that was done in the present case. I find that the Governor, Lord Elgin, did not exceed his authority when he approved the signing of the Robinson-Huron Treaty of 1850.

Prior to Confederation in 1867, the Crown in the Right of the Province of Canada had full power, by legislation, administrative acts and treaties, to unilaterally revoke Indian rights.

B. *The Competence of Ontario to Extinguish Aboriginal Rights . . .*
The only limitation on Ontario's power to extinguish aboriginal rights is that the Ontario legislation must fall under a head of general provincial legislative power and competence and not purport specifically to extinguish aboriginal rights.

As to Canada's legislative jurisdiction to preserve or extinguish aboriginal rights on unceded Proclamation lands, the Privy Council in the *St. Catherine's Milling* case made no adverse comment concerning Canadian administration of these lands up to 1873, held that section 91(24) included unceded Proclamation lands, and stated, *R. v. St. Catherine's Milling* (1888), 14 App. Cas. 46 at p. 59:

> It appears to be the plain policy of the Act that, in order to ensure uniformity of administration, all such lands, and Indian affairs generally, shall be under the legislative control of one central authority.

I therefore conclude that, after Confederation, Canada had the specific power to legislate in respect of aboriginal rights on unceded Proclamation lands. In the case at bar, there is no inconsistent federal and provincial legislation affecting the Land Claim Area. Laws are presumed constitutionally valid unless the contrary is proved. (See Hogg, *Constitutional Law of Canada*, (1977), at 88.) . . .

Therefore, after cession, the Proclamation lands ceased to be "Lands reserved for the Indians", and became Ontario public lands. Hence, I conclude that Ontario, since Confederation, has had the right to enact general legislation which can, in effect, extinguish aboriginal rights on ceded Proclamation lands. The only limitation on Ontario's power to extinguish aboriginal rights is that the legislation must fall under a head of general provincial legislative power and competence. For example, Ontario could enact legislation under section 92(5) or (13) (see *Ont. Mining Co. Ltd. et al.* v. *Seybold,* [1903] A.C. 73 (J.C.P.C.); *A.-G. Can.* v. *A.-G. Ont., Que., N.S.* (the *Fisheries* case), [1898] A.C. 700; and *Reference re Saskatchewan Natural Resources,* [1931] S.C.R. 263). Absent an area of legislative competence, Ontario could not purport to specifically extinguish aboriginal rights because they are personal and usufructuary and Ontario has no legislative competence over "Indians".

All my conclusions are, of course, subject to the *Constitution Act, 1982.*

Therefore, in the case at bar, whether or not the defendants were party to the Robinson-Huron Treaty in 1850 or adhered to it in 1883, Ontario had the legislative competence to enact otherwise valid, general legislation which, in effect, extinguished the defendants' aboriginal rights. . . .

15. *Attorney-General of Ontario* v. *Bear Island Foundation,* **[1991] 3 C.N.L.R. 79 (S.C.C.). Lamer C.J., La Forest, Gonthier, McLachlin, and Stevenson JJ., August 15, 1991**

> This decision affirms the earlier decision made by Steele J. on whether or not the Aboriginal title in question had been extinguished. See summary and comments on this decision on page 106.

PER CURIAM:— . . . Steele J. ([1985] 1 C.N.L.R. 1) found that the appellants had no aboriginal right to the land, and that even if such a right had existed, it had been extinguished by the Robinson-Huron Treaty of 1850, to which the Temagami Band was originally a party or to which it had subsequently adhered. These findings were essentially factual, and were drawn from the mass of historical documentary evidence adduced over the course of 130 days of trial. Steele J. also dismissed the counterclaim. . . .

An appeal to the Ontario Court of Appeal ([1989] 2 C.N.L.R. 73) was dismissed. On the assumption that an aboriginal right existed, the court held that right had been extinguished either by the Robinson-Huron Treaty or by the subsequent adherence to that treaty by the Indians, or because the treaty constituted a unilateral extinguishment by the sovereign.

This case, it must be underlined, raises for the most part essentially factual issues on which the courts below were in agreement. On such issues, the rule is that an appellate court should not reverse the trial judge in the absence of palpable and overriding error which affected his or her assessment of the facts: *Stein* v. *The Ship "Kathy K",* [1976] 2 S.C.R. 802; *Century Insurance Co.* v. *N.V. Bocimar S.A.,* [1987] 1 S.C.R. 1247; *Beaudoin-Daigneault* v. *Richard,* [1984]1 S.C.R. 2. The rule is all the stronger in the face of concurrent findings of both courts below. We have undertaken a detailed examination of the facts on this basis. We do not take issue with the numerous specific findings of fact in the court below, and it is, therefore, not necessary to recapitulate them here.

It does not necessarily follow, however, that we agree with all the legal findings based on those facts. In particular, we find that on the facts found by the trial judge the Indians exercised sufficient occupation of the lands in question throughout the relevant period to establish an Aboriginal right; . . .

It is unnecessary, however, to examine the specific nature of the aboriginal right because, in our view, whatever may have been the situation upon the signing of the Robinson-Huron Treaty, that right was in any event surrendered by arrangements subsequent to that treaty by which the Indians adhered to the treaty in exchange for treaty annuities and a reserve. It is conceded that the Crown has failed to comply with some of its obligations under this agreement, and thereby breached its fiduciary obligations to the Indians. These matters currently form the subject of negotiations between the parties. It does not alter the fact, however, that the aboriginal right has been extinguished.

For these reasons, the appeal is dismissed.

16. *R.* v. *Sparrow*, [1990] 3 C.N.L.R. 160 (S.C.C.). Dickson C.J., Lamer, Wilson, La Forest, L'Heureux-Dubé, McIntyre (took no part in the judgment), Sopinka JJ., May 31, 1990

Per DICKSON C.J. and LA FOREST J.:— . . . The word "existing" makes it clear that the rights to which s. 35(1) applies are those that were in existence when the *Constitution Act, 1982* came into effect. This means that extinguished rights are not revived by the *Constitution Act, 1982.* A number of courts have taken the position that "existing" means being in actuality in 1982: . . .

As noted by Blair J.A., academic commentary lends support to the conclusion that "existing" means "unextinguished" rather than exercisable at a certain time in history. Professor Slattery, "Understanding Aboriginal Rights" (1987), 66 *Can. Bar Rev.* 726, at pp. 781–82, has observed the following about reading regulations into the rights:

> This approach reads into the Constitution the myriad of regulations affecting the exercise of aboriginal rights, regulations that differed considerably from place to place across the country. It does not permit differentiation between regulations of long-term significance and those enacted to deal with temporary conditions, or between reasonable and unreasonable restrictions. Moreover, it might require that a constitutional amendment be enacted to implement regulations more stringent than those in existence on 17 April 1982. This solution seems unsatisfactory. . . .

It is this progressive restriction and detailed regulation of the fisheries which, respondent's counsel maintained, have had the effect of extinguishing any aboriginal right to fish. The extinguishment need not be express, he argued, but may take place where the sovereign authority is exercised in a manner "necessarily inconsistent" with the continued enjoyment of aboriginal rights. For this proposition, he particularly relied on *St. Catherine's Milling and Lumber Co.* v. *The Queen* (1888), 14 App. Cas. 46 (P.C.); *Calder* v. *Attorney-General of British Columbia*, [1973] S.C.R. 313; *Baker Lake (Hamlet)* v. *Minister of Indian Affairs and Northern Development*, [1979] 3 C.N.L.R. 17, (F.C.T.D.); and *Attorney-General of Ontario* v. *Bear Island Foundation*, supra. The consent to its extinguishment before the *Con-*

stitution Act, 1982 was not required; the intent of the sovereign could be effected not only by statute but by valid regulations. Here, in his view, the regulations had entirely displaced any aboriginal right. There is, he submitted, a fundamental inconsistency between the communal right to fish embodied in the aboriginal right, and fishing under a special licence or permit issued to individual Indians (as was the case until 1977) in the discretion of the Minister and subject to terms and conditions which, if breached, may result in cancellation of the licence. The *Fisheries Act* and its regulations were, he argued, intended to constitute a complete Code inconsistent with the continued existence of an aboriginal right.

At bottom, the respondent's argument confuses regulation with extinguishment. That the right is controlled in great detail by the regulations does not mean that the right is thereby extinguished. The distinction to be drawn was carefully explained, in the context of federalism, in the first fisheries case, *Attorney-General for Canada* v. *Attorney-General for Ontario*, [1898] A.C. 700. There, the Privy Council had to deal with the interrelationship between, on the one hand, provincial property, which by s. 109 of the *Constitution Act, 1867* is vested in the provinces (and so falls to be regulated *qua* property exclusively by the provinces) and, on the other hand, the federal power to legislate respecting the fisheries thereon under s. 91(12) of that Act. The Privy Council said the following in relation to the federal regulation (at pp. 712–13):

> . . . the power to legislate in relation to fisheries does necessarily to a certain extent enable the Legislature so empowered to affect proprietary rights. An enactment, for example, prescribing the times of the year during which fishing is to be allowed, or the instruments which may be employed for the purpose (which it was admitted the Dominion Legislature was empowered to pass) might very seriously touch the exercise of proprietary rights, and the extent, character, and scope of such legislation is left entirely to the Dominion Legislature. The suggestion that the power might be abused so as to amount to a practical confiscation of property does not warrant the imposition by the Courts of any limit upon the absolute power of legislation conferred. The supreme legislative power in relation to any subject-matter is always capable of abuse, but it is not to be assumed that it will be improperly used; if it is, the only remedy is an appeal to those by whom the Legislature is elected.

In the context of aboriginal rights, it could be argued that, before 1982, an aboriginal right was automatically extinguished to the extent that it was inconsistent with a statute. As Mahoney J. stated in *Baker Lake*, supra, at p. 568 [p. 55 C.N.L.R.]:

> Once a statute has been validly enacted, it must be given effect. If its necessary effect is to abridge or entirely abrogate a common law right, then that is the effect that the courts must give it. That is as true of an aboriginal title as of any other common law right.

See also *Attorney-General of Ontario* v. *Bear Island Foundation*, supra, at pp. 439–40 [pp. 80–81 C.N.L.R.]. That in Judson J.'s view was what had occurred in *Calder*, supra, where, as he saw it, a series of statutes evinced a unity of intention to exercise a sovereignty inconsistent with any conflicting interest, including aboriginal title. But Hall J. in that case stated (at p. 404) that "the onus of proving that the Sovereign intended to extinguish the Indian title lies on the respondent and *that intention must be 'clear and plain'* " (emphasis added). The test of extinguishment to be adopted, in our opinion, is that the Sovereign's intention must be clear and plain if it is to extinguish an aboriginal right.

There is nothing in the *Fisheries Act* or its detailed regulations that demonstrates a clear and plain intention to extinguish the Indian aboriginal right to fish. The fact that express provision permitting the Indians to fish for food may have applied to all Indians and that for an extended period permits were discretionary and issued on an individual rather than a communal basis in no way shows a clear intention to extinguish. These permits were simply a manner of controlling the fisheries, not defining underlying rights.

We would conclude then that the Crown has failed to discharge its burden of proving extinguishment. In our opinion, the Court of Appeal made no mistake in holding that the Indians have an existing aboriginal right to fish in the area where Mr. Sparrow was fishing at the time of the charge. This approach is consistent with ensuring that an aboriginal right should not be defined by incorporating the ways in which it has been regulated in the past. . . .

■ SELECTED BIBLIOGRAPHY

Ayers, N., "Aboriginal Land Rights in the Maritimes" [1984] 2 C.N.L.R. 1.

Bartlett, R., "The Fiduciary Duty of the Crown to the Indians" (1989) 53 *Sask. L. Rev.* 301.

——, "The High Court of Australia Upholds the Federal Native Title Act and Rejects Racist State Legislation" [1995] 2 C.N.L.R. 47.

——, "The Fundamental Significance of *Wik* v. *State of Queensland* in the High Court of Australia" [1997] 2 C.N.L.R. 1.

——, "The *Mabo* Decision" (1993) 1 *Australian Property Law Journal* 236.

Clark, B. *Indian Title in Canada.* Toronto: Carswell, 1987.

Culhane, D. *The Pleasure of the Crown: Anthropology, Law and First Nations.* Burnaby, B.C.: Talon Books, 1998.

Cumming, P.A., and N.H. Mickenburg, eds. *Native Rights in Canada,* 2d ed. Toronto: General, 1972.

Elliot, D., "Aboriginal Title." In *Aboriginal Peoples and the Law: Indian, Metis and Inuit Rights in Canada,* B. Morse, ed. Ottawa: Carleton University Press, 1985.

——, "Baker Lake and the Concept of Aboriginal Title" 18 *Osgoode Hall L.J.* 653.

Foster, H., "The Saanichton Bay Marina Case: Imperial Law, Colonial History and Competing Theories of Aboriginal Title" (1989) 23 *U.B.C. L. Rev.* 34.

——, "Aboriginal Title and the Provincial Obligation to Respect It: Is *Delgamuukw* v. *B.C.* 'Invented Law'?" (March 1998) 56 *Advocate* 221.

Hurley, J., "The Crown's Fiduciary Duty and Indian Title: *Guerin* v. *The Queen*" (1985) 30 *McGill L.J.* 559.

Lysyk, K., "The Indian Title Question in Canada: An Appraisal in the Light of *Calder*" (1973) 51 *Can. Bar Rev.* 450.

Macklem, P., "What's Law Got to Do With It? The Protection of Aboriginal Title in Canada" (Spring 1997) 35 *Osgoode Hall L.J.* 125.

Mandell, L., "Gitksan-Wet'suwet'en Land Title Action" [1988] 1 C.N.L.R. 14.

McLeod, C., "The Oral Histories of Canada's Northern People, Anglo-Canadian Evidence

Law, and Canada's Fiduciary Duty to First Nations: Breaking Down the Barriers of the Past" (1992) 30 *Alta. L. Rev.* 1276.

McMurtry, W.R., and A. Pratt, "Indians and the Fiduciary Concept, Self-Government and the Constitution" [1986] 3 C.N.L.R. 19.

McNeil, K. *Common Law, Aboriginal Title.* Oxford: Clarendon Press, 1989.

———, "The Meaning of Aboriginal Title." In *Aboriginal and Treaty Rights in Canada,* M. Asch, ed. Vancouver: U.B.C. Press, 1997, at 134.

McRae, H., G. Nettheim, and L. Beacroft. *Aboriginal Legal Issues: Cases and Studies.* Sidney, Australia: The Law Book Co. Ltd., 1991.

Owen, D. P., "Fiduciary Obligations and Aboriginal Peoples: Devolution in Action" [1994] 3 C.N.L.R. 1.

Royal Commission on Aboriginal Peoples, *Report of the Royal Commission on Aboriginal Peoples,* vol. 2. Ottawa: RCAP, 1996, at 44–47 and 559–89.

Schulze, D., "The Privy Council Decision Concerning George Allsopp's Petition, 1767: An Imperial Precedent on the Application of the Royal Proclamation to the Old Province of Quebec" [1995] 2 C.N.L.R. 1.

Slattery, B. *The Land Rights of Indigenous Canadian Peoples as Affected by the Crown's Acquisition of their Territories.* D.Phil. Thesis, Oxford University. Saskatoon, Sask.: University of Saskatchewan Native Law Centre, 1979.

———, "Understanding Aboriginal Rights" (1987) 66 *Can. Bar Rev.* 727.

———, "The Legal Basis of Aboriginal Title." In *Aboriginal Title in British Columbia: Delgamuukw v. The Queen,* F. Cassidy, ed. Lantzville, B.C.: Oolichan Books, 1992.

Smith, J.C., "The Concept of Native Title" (1974) 24 *U.T.L.J.* 1.

CHAPTER 2
TREATY RIGHTS

■ INTRODUCTION

Chapter 1 illustrated that Aboriginal title and Aboriginal rights are not dependent upon any legislative enactment or constitutional document. Rather they inhere in the reality that Aboriginal peoples occupied North America prior to European contact and this occupation was in societies with distinctive cultures and political systems. Aboriginal rights and title arise from the historic use and occupation of Aboriginal peoples in what is now known as Canada. Treaty rights are negotiated rights set out in treaties between Indian peoples and the Crown. Treaties, and their modern equivalents—land claims agreements—are the formal mechanisms detailing Crown–First Nations relationships. Although in some cases, unilateral declarations by the Crown[1] have been interpreted as being treaties. In some cases, there is evidence which suggests that the Crown did not negotiate in good faith and that the Indians did not fully comprehend the Crown's intent behind signing treaties.[2] Through many of the treaties, the Crown acknowledged that Indian peoples possessed some interest or title in the land. Aboriginal and treaty rights have been constitutionally recognized and affirmed in s. 35(1) of the *Constitution Act, 1982,*[3] which states that the "existing aboriginal and treaty rights of the aboriginal peoples of Canada are hereby recognized and affirmed." Federal and provincial governments have an interest in seeing modern treaties negotiated because they clarify the nature of the Indian burden on the Crown's title.

With the Supreme Court's *Delgamuukw*[4] decision adding to the growing body of Supreme Court level jurisprudence on Aboriginal rights, there is a feeling that with each decision come two conflicting aspects. First, each decision has attempted to clarify and scope-out the nature of Aboriginal rights and title. Second, with each clarification, the developing body of law is becoming increasingly complex and ironically, at the same time, vague. With all of the decisions to date, some very lengthy, there remains a great deal of uncertainty regarding what the precise nature of Aboriginal rights and title are. Nowhere is this more true than in British Columbia,

---

1   See, for example, *R. v. Sioui,* [1990] 3 C.N.L.R. 127 (S.C.C.) (page 156 in this chapter), wherein the Supreme Court of Canada held that a brief document signed only by the governor of Quebec in 1760 outlining certain rights for the Huron Indians constituted a treaty.

2   See, for example, R. Fumoleau, *As Long As This Land Shall Last: A History of Treaty 8 and Treaty 11* (Toronto: McClelland & Stewart, 1973); also see D. Hall, " 'A Serene Atmosphere'? Treaty 1 Revisited" in S. Corrigan and J. Sawchuk, eds., *The Recognition of Aboriginal Rights* (Brandon, Man.: Bearpaw Publishing, 1996).

3   *Constitution Act, 1982,* being Sched. B of the *Canada Act 1982* (U.K.), 1982, c. 11.

4   *Delgamuukw* v. *B.C.,* [1998] 1 C.N.L.R. 14 (S.C.C.).

where almost the entire province is involved in outstanding Aboriginal title claims and under treaty negotiation. Thus, with this ironic increased lack of clarity in the law, coupled with the increased expectations being placed on the legal system to address Aboriginal claims and issues, negotiated treaties and agreements stand out as being the best means of addressing Aboriginal issues generally.

The earliest treaties made between Indians and settlers were the peace and friendship treaties in eastern North America in the seventeenth and eighteenth centuries. These treaties were primarily concerned with guaranteeing certain hunting and fishing rights to Indians in return for peaceful relationships and military alliances with the settlers. Unlike the later treaties, they did not require land cession by the Indians. In *R. v. Simon,*[5] the Supreme Court of Canada affirmed that peace and friendship treaties are valid treaties, even though they did not cede land.

The legal distinction between pre- and post-confederation treaties is nominal. Treaties made with the British Crown, before Confederation, are held to be treaties with the Canadian Crown after Confederation. Essentially, there was a transfer of responsibility from one crown to another.[6]

As settlement moved west, so did the treaty-making process. For example, in 1850 the Robinson Treaties (Lake Huron and Lake Superior) were signed, and between 1871 and 1921 the numbered treaties were signed (11 in total).[7] The numbered treaties cover most of the land in northwestern Ontario and the prairie provinces. The Douglas Treaties and part of Treaty No. 8 extend into British Columbia. Treaty No. 11 and part of Treaty No. 8 apply to the Northwest Territories. In 1973, the Supreme Court of Canada's *Calder* decision[8] affirmed Aboriginal rights in Canadian law and had the effect of the Canadian federal government changing its policy of "non-affirmation" of Aboriginal rights to one of recognizing that the Aboriginal interest in unceded lands needed to be resolved. In response, the federal government developed its modern treaty-making policy of negotiating land claims agreements. The modern treaty process is discussed later in this chapter.

Whereas governments and the Canadian legal system have tended to view Indian treaties from a positivist, literal view, many Indian peoples see the treaties as being much more. For example, Harold Cardinal writes:

> To the Indians of Canada, the treaties represent an Indian Magna Carta. The treaties are important to us, because we entered into these negotiations with faith, with hope for a better life with honour. . . . The treaties were the way in which the white people legitimized in the eyes of the world their presence in our country. It was an attempt to settle the terms of occupancy on a just basis, legally and morally to extinguish the legitimate claims of our people to title to the lands in our country.[9]

---

5   *R. v. Simon*, [1986] 1 C.N.L.R. 153.

6   *R. v. Secretary of State*, [1981] 4 C.N.L.R. 86.

7   A collection of the texts of many treaties can be found in *Consolidated Native Law Statutes, Regulations and Treaties 1994* (Toronto: Carswell, 1993).

8   *Calder* v. *A.-G. B.C.,* [1973] S.C.R. 313.

9   Harold Cardinal, *The Unjust Society: The Tragedy of Canada's Indians* (Edmonton: Hurtig, 1969), 28–29.

Each treaty is unique or *sui generis*.[10] However, their validity is dependent upon a number of factors. Relying primarily on *R.* v. *Sioui*[11] and *R.* v. *Simon*,[12] Professor Hogg provides a succinct summary of the characteristics of a valid Indian treaty:

> 1. Parties: The parties to the treaty must be the Crown, on the one side, and an aboriginal nation, on the other side.
>
> 2. Agency: The signatories to the treaty must have the authority to bind their principals, namely, the Crown and the aboriginal nation.
>
> 3. Intention to create legal relations: The parties must intend to create legally binding obligations.
>
> 4. Consideration: The obligations must be assumed by both sides, so that the agreement is a bargain.
>
> 5. Formality: there must be "a certain measure of solemnity."[13]

Section 88 of the *Indian Act* spells out the relationship between treaty rights and provincial legislation. It reads in part:

> 88. *Subject to the terms of any treaty* . . . all laws of general application from time to time in force in any province are applicable to and in respect of Indians in the province, . . . [emphasis added][14]

This federal legislative provision ensures that provincial legislatures do not stray into federal jurisdiction (with respect to Indians), ensures that there is no legislative vacuum for Indians, and ensures that provincial laws of general application are subject to the terms of any treaty.[15] With treaty rights being constitutionally protected under s. 35 of the *Constitution Act, 1982,* thereby ensuring their supremacy over provincial laws that cannot be justified, this particular aspect of s. 88, as it relates to treaty rights, is not as critical to treaty rights' protection.

In *R.* v. *Francis*, the Supreme Court of Canada held that the term "treaty" in s. 88 does not include international treaties, like the Jay Treaty (a 1794 treaty between Great Britain and the U.S.A. proposing a duty exemption for Indians who crossed what is now the U.S./Canada border), but rather refers only to treaties made with Indians.[16] Although they are not international treaties and not formally

---

10 See *R.* v. *Simon,* [1985] 2 S.C.R. 387 at 404, and *R.* v. *Sioui,* [1990] 1 S.C.R. 1025 at 1043.

11 *R.* v. *Sioui,* [1990] 3 C.N.L.R. 127 (S.C.C.).

12 *R.* v. *Simon,* [1986] 1 C.N.L.R. 153 (S.C.C.).

13 Peter Hogg, *Constitutional Law of Canada*, 4th ed. (Toronto: Carswell, 1997), 27.6(c); p. 691.

14 *Indian Act*, R.S.C. 1985, c. I–5.

15 See *R.* v. *White and Bob*, 6 C.N.L.C. 684 (S.C.C.); *R.* v. *Simon* and *R.* v. *Sioui.*

16 *R.* v. *Francis*, 5 C.N.L.C. 170 (S.C.C.). For a critique of *Francis*, see K. Lysyk, "The Unique Constitutional Position of the Canadian Indian" (1967) 45 *Can. Bar Rev.* 513 at 527–28. The Ontario Court of Appeal held in *R.* v. *Vincent*, [1993] 2 C.N.L.R. 165; leave to appeal to S.C.C. dismissed, [1993] 4 C.N.L.R. vi; that the Jay Treaty was not a treaty for the purposes of s. 35(1) of the *Constitution Act, 1982.*

implemented in Canadian law, except to the extent that they are mentioned in s. 88, Indian treaties are nevertheless enforceable (both before and after 1982).[17] The Jay Treaty is not a treaty for the purposes of s. 35(1), but it can serve as a useful historical document to illustrate the treatment of Aboriginal peoples when the treaty was signed.[18]

In *R.* v. *Sikyea,*[19] the Northwest Territories Court of Appeal dealt with the issue of whether or not Treaty No. 11 hunting rights were excluded from the application of the federal *Migratory Birds Convention Act.*[20] The Court of Appeal, affirmed by the Supreme Court of Canada, held that the *Migratory Birds Convention Act* applied to Indians notwithstanding their hunting rights guaranteed by Treaty No. 11.[21] *Sikyea* demonstrates that prior to the enactment of s. 35 of the *Constitution Act, 1982,* whereby treaty rights are recognized and affirmed and therefore constitutionally protected, they could be altered and modified by federal statute.

In *R.* v. *White and Bob,*[22] the Supreme Court of Canada affirmed that provincial game laws could be superseded by treaty provisions, however vague, by virtue of s. 88 of the *Indian Act. White and Bob* affirmed the legal status of Indian treaties in Canadian law and emphasized the importance of the honour of the Crown. It also illustrated the origins of a broad and liberal approach to treaty interpretation and to the rules governing whether or not a document is, in fact, a treaty.

The 1981 Ontario Court of Appeal decision of *R.* v. *Taylor and Williams*[23] was significant because it brought together a number of critical factors to be considered in interpreting treaties. The case dealt with a treaty signed in 1818. The court held that although fishing and hunting were not guaranteed by the written terms of the treaty, the minutes from the negotiation of the treaty revealed that these rights were discussed. These oral portions of the treaty are as much part of the treaty as the written portions. The court stated that the history and oral traditions of the tribes concerned were important to consider. Treaties should be interpreted in a manner that upholds the honour of the Crown and avoids the appearance of "sharp dealings," resolves any ambiguity in favour of the Indians, and considers the parties' understanding of the terms of the treaty when it was signed.

In 1973, the Northwest Territories Supreme Court held in *Re Paulette*[24] that Aboriginal rights, such as those contained in Treaty Nos. 8 and 11, constitute an

---

17 See *R.* v. *Wesley,* 5 C.N.L.C. 540 (Alta. C.A.); *R.* v. *Prince,* 6 C.N.L.C. 543 (S.C.C.).In *R.* v. *Agawa,* [1988] 3 C.N.L.R. 73, the Ontario Court of Appeal held that Indian treaties are not like international treaties and that they are *sui generis* and are not self-executing. They acquire the force of law in Canada when they are protected by a statute or by the Constitution.

18 *Mitchell* v. *M.N.R.,* [1997] 4 C.N.L.R. 103 (F.C.T.D.).

19 *R.* v. *Sikyea,* 6 C.N.L.C. 583 (N.W.T.C.A.), aff'd by 6 C.N.L.C. 597 (S.C.C.).

20 *Migratory Birds Convention Act,* R.S.C. 1985, c. M–7.

21 The Supreme Court of Canada affirmed this result in both *R.* v. *George,* [1966] S.C.R. 267 and *Daniels* v. *White,* [1968] S.C.R. 517.

22 *R.* v. *White and Bob,* 6 C.N.L.C. 684 (S.C.C.).

23 *R.* v. *Taylor and Williams,* [1981] 3 C.N.L.R. 114 (Ont. C.A.).

24 *Re Paulette,* 9 C.N.L.C. 307 (N.W.T.S.C.).

interest in land and that the *Royal Proclamation of 1763* did not create Aboriginal rights but rather confirmed their existence.

In the 1990 decision of *R. v. Horseman*,[25] the Supreme Court of Canada affirmed that the onus to prove the extinguishment of a treaty right rests with the Crown and that ambiguities in treaties must be resolved in favour of the Indians. As well, prior to the enactment of the *Constitution Act, 1982*, the federal government had the exclusive authority to modify treaty rights.[26] This is evidenced by the *Constitution Act, 1930*[27] (*Natural Resources Transfer Agreement*), where the federal government unilaterally "merged and consolidated" Treaty No. 8 rights to hunt. This agreement not only dealt with hunting rights, but also recognized that the federal government may need provincial land in order to fulfil its legal obligations to provide land to Indians under the treaties. Prior to the *Constitution Act, 1982*, treaty rights could be unilaterally extinguished by the federal government. This explains the significance of the s. 35(1) affirmation and recognition of treaty rights and existing land claims agreements being considered as "treaties" for the purposes of s. 35(1) (s. 35(3)). Section 25 of the *Canadian Charter of Rights and Freedoms*[28] ensures that treaty rights cannot be abrogated or derogated by rights and freedoms guaranteed in the *Charter*.

The Nova Scotia Court of Appeal has held that specific references in treaties cannot necessarily be used to establish a general right. In *R. v. Marshall*,[29] the issue was whether or not a Micmaq Indian charged with illegally selling fish could use the Treaties of 1760–61 to affirm a treaty right to trade generally. The passage of the treaty relied upon reads: "And I do further engage that we will not traffick, barter or Exchange any Commodities in any manner but with such persons or the managers of such Truck houses as shall be appointed or established by His Majesty's Governor." The court determined that although the Micmaq were authorized and required to trade goods exclusively at truck houses, this, by itself, does not constitute a right. It was a means to control the Micmaq by the British to ensure peace and to prevent trade with British enemies.

Like Aboriginal rights (see chapter 7 on the *Constitution Act, 1982*), treaty rights are not absolute. They are subject to reasonable regulation and statutory limitations.[30] This was particularly true before 1982. The pre-1982 Supreme Court of Canada decision of *R. v. Sikyea*[31] provides a clear example of the vulnerability of Indian treaties before the enactment of s. 35 of the *Constitution Act, 1982* whereby

---

25   *R. v. Horseman*, [1990] 3 C.N.L.R. 95 (S.C.C.).

26   Ibid.

27   *Constitution Act, 1930*, R.S.C. 1985, App. II, No. 26.

28   Part I of the *Constitution Act, 1982*, being Schedule B to the *Canada Act 1982* (U.K.), 1982, c. 11.

29   *R. v. Marshall*, [1997] 3 C.N.L.R. 209 (N.S.C.A.).

30   See, for example, *R. v. Machatis*, [1991] 1 C.N.L.R. 154 (Alta. Q.B.); *R. v. McGillivary*, [1990] 1 C.N.L.R. 124 (Sask. Q.B.) (hunting rights qualified and conditional); Treaty No. 8 hunting rights subject to valid conservation laws, *R. v. Horseman*, [1990] 3 C.N.L.R. 95 (S.C.C.).

31   *R. v. Sikyea*, 6 C.N.L.C. 597.

treaty rights were constitutionally "recognized and affirmed."

In *Sikyea*, the court held that the *Migratory Birds Convention Act*[32] applied to Indians notwithstanding that their hunting rights were guaranteed by Treaty No. 11. The Supreme Court affirmed this result in both *R.* v. *George*[33] and *Daniels* v. *White*.[34] At the same time, however, treaty rights have been interpreted by the courts to also be *sui generis* or unique.[35]

The unfairness of some treaty negotiations has not gone unnoticed by the courts.[36] In *R.* v. *Battisse*,[37] Justice Bernstein wrote that where the terms of a treaty seem unfair or where the bargaining power of one party greatly outweighs that of the other:

> [T]he courts must not assume that His Majesty's Commissioners were attempting to trick or fool the Indians into signing an agreement under false pretences. . . . [A]mbiguity should be resolved in favour of the Indian.[38]

The courts must show flexibility when determining the legal nature of documents recording transactions with Indians.[39] In *R.* v. *Simon*, the Supreme Court of Canada held that Indian treaties must be liberally construed and uncertainties resolved in favour of the Indians.[40] *Simon* also made clear that like Aboriginal title, Indian treaties are *sui generis* and are not created or terminated based on the rules governing international law.[41] In the earlier Supreme Court decision of *Nowegijick* v. *R.*,[42] Dickson J. stated:

> It seems to me, however, that treaties and statutes relating to Indians should be liberally construed and doubtful expressions resolved in favour of the Indian. . . . In *Jones* v. *Meehan*, 175 U.S. 1, it was held that "Indian treaties must be construed, not according to the technical meaning of their words, but in the sense in which they would naturally be understood by the Indians."[43]

---

32 *Migratory Birds Convention Act*, R.S.C. 1985, c. M–7.

33 *R.* v. *George*, 6 C.N.L.C. 360.

34 *Daniels* v. *White*, 6 C.N.L.C. 199.

35 *R.* v. *Simon*, [1986] 1 C.N.L.R. 153 at 169 (S.C.C.), and *R.* v. *Sioui*, [1990] 3 C.N.L.R. 127 at 139 (S.C.C.).

36 See also Harold Cardinal, *The Unjust Society: The Tragedy of Canada's Indians* (Edmonton: Hurtig, 1969), 28–29.

37 *R.* v. *Battisse*, 9 C.N.L.C. 429 (Ont. Dist. Ct.); see also *Re Paulette et al. and Registrar of Titles (No.2)*, 9 C.N.L.C. 288 and 307.

38 Ibid., *R.* v. *Battisse*, at 437.

39 *R.* v. *Sioui*, [1990] 3 C.N.L.R. 127 at 133 (S.C.C.).

40 *R.* v. *Simon*, [1986] 1 C.N.L.R. 153, note 22 at 167 (S.C.C.); *R.* v. *Horseman*, [1990] 3 C.N.L.R. 95 (S.C.C.); *R.* v. *Sioui*, [1990] 3 C.N.L.R. 127 (S.C.C.); *Claxton* v. *Saanichton Marina Ltd.*, [1989] 3 C.N.L.R. 46 (B.C.C.A.); *R.* v. *White and Bob*, 6 C.N.L.C. 684 (S.C.C.).

41 Ibid., *R.* v. *Simon*, at 165–66.

42 *Nowegijick* v. *R.*, [1983] 2 C.N.L.R. 89 (S.C.C.).

43 Ibid., at 94.

This broad approach to treaty interpretation is further illustrated by the 1981 Ontario Court of Appeal decision of *R.* v. *Taylor*.[44] The court held that a member of a Treaty No. 20 (1818) First Nation had the right to hunt for bullfrogs. The minutes of the treaty's negotiations provided evidence that the rivers within the territory concerned were open to all and that the First Nations had "an equal right to fish and hunt on them." The court held that this included the right to hunt bullfrogs. The Supreme Court of Canada's *Horse* decision stands for the proposition that extrinsic evidence, such as minutes of negotiation meetings, cannot be used as an aid in interpreting a treaty in the absence of ambiguity or where the result would be to alter the terms of the written agreement.[45]

Treaty rights must be interpreted in an evolutionary manner.[46] For example, in *Simon*, the Supreme Court dealt with the phrase "it is agreed that the said Tribe of Indians shall not be hindered from, but have free liberty of hunting and Fishing as usual." The phrase "as usual" is described by Dickson C.J. as follows:

> I do not read the phrase "as usual" as referring to the types of weapons to be used by the Micmac and limiting them to those used in 1752. Any such construction would place upon the ability of the Micmac to hunt an unnecessary and artificial constraint out of keeping with the principle that Indian treaties should be liberally construed. Indeed, the inclusion of the phrase "as usual" appears to reflect a concern that the right to hunt be interpreted in a flexible way that is sensitive to the evolution of changes in normal hunting practices.[47]

Another example of the expansive interpretation given to treaty rights concerns whether the rights of hunting or fishing under treaties include commercial hunting[48] and fishing[49] rights. The British Columbia Court of Appeal summarized the principles applicable to treaty interpretation in *Claxton* v. *Saanichton Marina Ltd.*:[50]

> 1. The treaty should be given a fair, large and liberal construction in favour of the Indians;
> 2. Treaties must be construed, not according to the technical meaning of their words but in the sense that they would naturally be understood by the Indians;
> 3. As the honour of the Crown is always involved, no appearance of "sharp dealing" should be sanctioned;
> 4. Any ambiguity in wording should be interpreted as against the drafters and

---

44   *R.* v. *Taylor*, [1981] 3 C.N.L.R. 114 (Ont. C.A.).

45   *R.* v. *Horse,* [1988] 2 C.N.L.R. 112 at 124 (S.C.C.).

46   For example, see *R.* v. *Ireland*, [1991] 2 C.N.L.R. 120 (Ont. Ct. J. (Gen. Div.)); *R.* v. *Norn*, [1991] 3 C.N.L.R. 135 (Alta. Prov. Ct.).

47   *R.* v. *Simon*, [1986] 1 C.N.L.R. 153 at 167.

48   See, for example, *R.* v. *Potts*, [1992] 1 C.N.L.R. 142 (Alta. Prov. Ct.); *R.* v. *Littlewolf*, [1992] 3 C.N.L.R. 83 (Alta. Prov. Ct.).

49   *R.* v. *Jackson*, [1992] 4 C.N.L.R. 121 (Ont. Prov. Ct.).

50   *Claxton* v. *Saanichton Marina Ltd.*, [1989] 3 C.N.L.R. 46 at 50 (B.C.C.A.).

should not be interpreted to the prejudice of the Indians if another construction is reasonably possible; and

  5. Evidence of conduct or otherwise as to how the parties understood the treaty is of assistance in giving it content.

The interpretive regime within which treaty rights are to be analyzed has been made much clearer with the 1996 Supreme Court of Canada decision of *R.* v. *Badger.*[51] The decision concerns Treaty No. 8 and whether registered Indians possess the right to hunt on privately owned land within the treaty's territory, whether treaty hunting rights were extinguished or modified by the *Natural Resources Transfer Agreement* (1930) *(NRTA),* and the degree to which legislation requiring hunting licences applies to registered Indians. Although the court held that the treaty right to hunt for food was not extinguished by the *NRTA,* the right was limited geographically by using the concept of "visible incompatible land use." This concept requires a case-by-case analysis and means that if privately owned land is occupied or put to a visible use, Indians do not have a right to access. If the land is unoccupied and not being put to visible use, Indians will have a right to access, pursuant to Treaty No. 8. The court held that in this case, the requirement of licences is a *prima facie* infringement of treaty rights that must be justified. A new trial was ordered for one of the appellants (to deal with the issue of justification), while the other two appellants' claims were dismissed because they were hunting on occupied land.

  Badger is also significant because it provides a useful summary of the principles of interpretation to be used when adjudicating treaty rights' cases.[52] These principles are:

1. A treaty represents an exchange of solemn promises between the Crown and Indian nations and the nature of this agreement is sacred.

2. The honour of the Crown is always at stake when dealing with Indian people, and it is always to be assumed that the Crown intends to fulfill its promises. The integrity of the Crown must be maintained when interpreting statutes or treaties that affect Aboriginal and treaty rights. The appearance of "sharp dealing" is not sanctioned.

3. When interpreting a treaty or document, any ambiguities or doubtful expressions in the wording must be resolved in favour of the Indians. Any limitations that restrict Indian treaty rights must be narrowly construed.

4. The onus of proving the extinguishment of a treaty right lies with the Crown. Strict proof of the extinguishment is required, as is a clear and plain intention to do so.

  Badger also affirmed that the *Sparrow* justificatory analysis (used to determine whether government infringement of s. 35(1) rights may be justified) is to be

---

51 *R.* v. *Badger,* [1996] 2 C.N.L.R. 77 (S.C.C.). The *Badger* analysis was recently applied in the Alberta Court of Appeal decision of *R.* v. *Gladue,* [1996] 1 C.N.L.R. 153; also see L. Rotman, "Taking Aim at the Canons of Treaty Interpretation in Canadian Aboriginal Rights Jurisprudence" (1997) 46 *U.N.B.L.J.* 11.

52 Ibid., *Badger,* para. 41.

applied in cases concerning treaty rights.[53] Cory J. notes:

> . . . justification of provincial regulations enacted pursuant to the NRTA should meet the same test for justification set out in *Sparrow*. The reason for this is obvious. The effect of s. 12 of the NRTA is to place the provincial government in exactly the same position which the federal Crown formerly occupied. Thus the provincial government has the same duty not to infringe unjustifiably the hunting right provided by Treaty 8 as modified by the NRTA. Paragraph 12 of the NRTA provides that the province may make laws for a conservation purpose, subject to the Indian right to hunt and fish for food. Accordingly, there is a need for a means to assess which conservation laws will if they infringe that right, nevertheless be justifiable. The *Sparrow* analysis provides a reasonable, flexible and current method of assessing conservation regulations and enactments.[54]

Badger applies the principle of co-existence on Crown lands, developed in *Sioui,* to private lands, thereby underscoring the significance of the decision. *Badger* also uses oral history as a basis for interpreting treaty rights and stresses the importance of such history in understanding the context surrounding the signing of a treaty.[55]

A 1998 New Brunswick Court of Queen's Bench decision[56] affirmed that, based on a number of eighteenth-century treaties (for example, *The Dummer Proclamation* of December 15, 1725) affecting the Micmaq and Maliseet Indians of eastern Canada, the trees on Crown land belong to the Indians. Obviously the impact of this decision in a province where logging is so prevalent is significant. Turnbull J. refers to the Indians' interest in the trees as one of "ownership." He writes:

> I believe there are several ways one could describe the status of rights in Crown land. A legally correct way would be to consider Crown lands as reserved for Indians. Not exclusively, but their rights to them are protected by treaty. The trees on Crown land are Indian trees. Not exclusively, but their rights are protected by treaty. The Crown has jurisdiction and dominion over all land. Undoubtedly the Legislature and Parliament can enact laws which affect Indian treaty rights in New Brunswick. Governments must accept that Dummer's Treaty was understood to protect Indian land and recognize the Indians' primacy when enacting legislation if it intends to enact laws affecting treaty rights. At the present time Indians have the right to cut trees on all Crown land. If this provision in the *Crown Lands and Forests Act* (supra) had met the

---

53 The *Sparrow* analysis was also applied by the British Columbia Court of Appeal in *R. v. Little,* [1996] 2 C.N.L.R. 136 (B.C.C.A.), when it examined whether or not the Douglas Treaty (1854) protected fishing rights. The court held that the B.C. fisheries regulations did not infringe on the Indian fishing rights as little possible and that the Indian food fishing requirements were not given priority over the commercial and sport fisheries.

54 *R. v. Badger,* [1996] 2 C.N.L.R. 77 (S.C.C.), para. 96.

55 Ibid., para. 45.

56 *R. v. Paul,* [1998] 1 C.N.L.R. 209 (N.B.Q.B.), rev'd by [1998] 3 C.N.L.R. 221 (N.B.C.A.).

guidelines set out in *R.* v. *Sparrow* [1990] 1 S.C.R. 1075 the law would apply to Mr. Paul. Such a license to Stone Consolidated Inc. would in my opinion be considered an exclusive license. My rationale is that the Act is not applicable to the Indians of New Brunswick. Considerable argument was advanced before me that one must slash a maple tree to first determine if it is bird's eye. This is indeed deplorable, but an owner is legally entitled to do so.[57]

The New Brunswick Court of Appeal allowed an appeal by the Crown on the basis that the defendant did not produce sufficient evidence to demonstrate possession of an Aboriginal right to harvest and sell timber. The Court of Appeal decision underscores the burden on Aboriginal peoples to produce evidence to claim a right.

The liberal approach to treaty interpretation appearing in *Paul*'s Queen Bench decision also appears in a recent Saskatchewan Court of Appeal decision. Treaty No. 6 guarantees hunting for food at all seasons, and treaty Indians may cut trees and construct permanent dwellings in provincial parks since the use of a dwelling (like a cabin) is reasonably incidental to the act of hunting for food. Limitations on building in provincial parks is not justifiable.[58]

TREATY LAND ENTITLEMENT

In some instances there are outstanding claims under existing treaties which remain to be fulfilled. An example of the treaty land obligation being fulfilled is the September 22, 1992, *Saskatchewan Treaty Land Entitlement Framework Agreement* between the governments of Saskatchewan and Canada and the chiefs of 22 treaty land entitlement bands in Saskatchewan. This agreement is the fulfillment of the province's obligation to provide land to the federal government and is the fulfillment of the federal government's obligation to treaty Indian peoples for land to satisfy the terms of the treaties signed in Saskatchewan. The agreement provides approximately $450 million over 12 years to bands to purchase land and mineral rights. The bands are entitled to purchase a maximum of 1.67 million acres of land as "reserve" land.

In the Northwest Territories, Canada and the Treaty No. 8 Dene First Nations initialed the *N.W.T. Treaty 8 Treaty Entitlement Negotiations Protocol Agreement* in November 1994. Its purpose is to initiate negotiations between the two parties for a formal treaty entitlement settlement. Alberta has seven settled treaty land entitlement claims, with another 16 either in negotiations or being reviewed by Canada. Manitoba has 31 bands with outstanding treaty land entitlement claims. To date, four of these claims have been settled.

Specific claims by Indians against the federal government relate to "the administration of land and other Indian assets and to the fulfillment of Indian treaties."[59] Treaty land entitlement, along with a breach of an obligation under the *Indian Act* or other statutes, a breach of an obligation arising from government

---

57   Ibid., para. 71.

58   *R.* v. *Sundown,* [1997] 4 C.N.L.R. 241 (Sask. C.A.).

59   *Outstanding Business: A Native Claims Policy* (Ottawa: DIAND, 1982), 19.

administration of Indian funds or assets, or an illegal disposition of land, are all examples of specific claims. Non-compensation for reserve lands taken or damaged by the federal government, and fraud in connection with the disposition or acquisition of reserve lands by employees or agents of the federal government, may also give rise to a specific claim.[60]

MODERN TREATIES AND LAND CLAIMS AGREEMENTS[61]

Treaties are not ancient processes that are relegated to history. Treaties have constitutional recognition and affirmation in s. 35 and form part of the supreme law of Canada. As well, modern forms of treaties have developed—namely land claims agreements—to settle outstanding Aboriginal title and rights claims. Section 35(3) of the *Constitution Act, 1982* provides that land claims agreements are to be included within the legal meaning of the "treaty rights" that are recognized and affirmed by s. 35(1). Section 35(3) reads:

> (3) For greater certainty, in subsection (1) "treaty rights" includes rights that now exist by way of land claims agreements or maybe so acquired.

The federal government's willingness to negotiate comprehensive claims[62] was the result of a number of judicial decisions made in the mid-1970s. The most notable was the Supreme Court of Canada's *Calder*[63] decision, with its split decision on the existence of Aboriginal title. It set the stage for the federal government's recognition that comprehensive claims must be dealt with. As in so many other instances in Canadian history, the courts have been the most successful modus for Aboriginal peoples to secure their rights. Not only is the *Calder* case an example of this, but an injunction[64] at the time the James Bay project was being proposed led to the *James Bay and Northern Quebec Agreement*. As Lamer C.J. noted in the Supreme Court of Canada decision of *R. v. Delgamuukw*, ultimately it will be through negotiated settlements that Aboriginal rights will be fully realized.[65]

The most recent version of the federal government's policy on land claims can be found in its *Comprehensive Land Claims Policy*.[66] Its objectives are summarized as follows:

> The purpose of settlement agreements is to provide certainty and clarity to ownership

---

60   Ibid., 20.

61   See map on page *xxx*.

62   For a good discussion of the history of the development of the comprehensive land claims policy, readers should refer to the Royal Commission on Aboriginal Peoples, *Report of the Royal Commission on Aboriginal Peoples*, vol. 2 (Ottawa: RCAP, 1996), 527–57.

63   *Calder* v. *A.-G. B.C.*, 7 C.N.L.C. 91 (S.C.C.).

64   See *Gros-Louis* v. *La Société de Développement de la Baie James*, [1974–1975] 8 C.N.L.C. 188.

65   *Delgamuukw* v. *British Columbia*, [1998] 1 C.N.L.R. 14 (S.C.C.), para. 186.

66   *Comprehensive Land Claims Policy* (Ottawa: DIAND, 1987); see also *Living Treaties: Lasting Agreements: Report of the Task Force to Review Comprehensive Claims Policy* (Ottawa: DIAND, 1985).

and use of land and resources in those areas of Canada where aboriginal title has not been dealt with by treaty or superseded by law. . . . [T]he claimant group will receive defined rights, compensation and other benefits in exchange for relinquishing rights relating to the title claimed over all or part of the land in question.[67]

The first modern land claims agreement[68] was the 1975 *James Bay and Northern Quebec Agreement.*[69] Signed by the Cree, Inuit, and subsequently the Naskapi Indians,[70] the *James Bay Agreement* allowed for the development of the James Bay hydroelectric project in northern Quebec. In return for ceding most of their land, the Cree, Inuit, and subsequently the Naskapi, received certain rights related to the regulation of their lands, environment, and governance. The rights to governance are outlined in the *Cree-Naskapi (of Quebec) Act.*[71] Its implementation has been a matter of much discussion over the past two decades.[72]

There are four settled land claims in the Northwest Territories (NWT). The *Inuvialuit Final Agreement*[73] was signed on June 5, 1984, and included approximately 2,500 Inuvialuit beneficiaries who live in the northwestern region of the NWT (namely the communities of Inuvik, Aklavik, Sachs Harbour, Tuktoyaktuk, Paulatuk, and Holman). The claim includes title to 91,000 square kilometres (including 11,000 square kilometres of subsurface mineral rights) of land and a cash compensation package of more than $169 million payable over 14 years. The total Inuvialuit settlement area exceeds 310,000 square kilometres. The Inuvialuit also received preferential and exclusive hunting and harvesting rights in the settlement area.

The Inuvialuit are presently negotiating a self-government agreement in partnership with the Gwich'in (see below). The federal government and the government of the NWT are also at the table. Although they do not have a specific entitlement to negotiate self-government pursuant to their claim, the Inuvialuit have relied on s. 4(3) of their claim agreement to support their right to engage in self-government negotiations with Canada and the government of the NWT. Section 4(3) reads:

---

67   *Comprehensive Land Claims Policy* (Ottawa: DIAND, 1987), 9.

68   See K. Coates, ed., *Aboriginal Land Claims Agreements: A Regional Perspective* (Toronto: Copp Clark Pitman, 1997).

69   Québec: Editeur official du Québec, 1976; affirmed in legislation by the *James Bay and Northern Quebec Native Claims Settlement Act,* S.C. 1976–77, c. 32; with corresponding provincial legislation, *James Bay Agreement,* S.Q. 1976, c. 32; see *Cree Regional Authority* v. *Robinson,* [1991] 3 C.N.L.R. 82 (F.C.A.).

70   The Naskapi signed a similar agreement in 1978, the *Northeastern Quebec Agreement.*

71   S.C. 1984, c. 46; see T. Isaac, "Aboriginal Self-Government in Canada: *Cree-Naskapi (of Quebec) Act*" (1991) 7:2 *Native Studies Review* 69.

72   See, for example, W. Moss, *Practically Millionaires* (Ottawa: National Indian Brotherhood, 1981) and R. Salisbury, *A Homeland for the Cree* (Montreal: McGill-Queen's University Press, 1986).

73   Enacted by *Western Arctic (Inuvialuit) Claims Settlement Act,* S.C. 1984, c. 24, as am. by S.C. 1988, c. 16.

Canada agrees that where restructuring of the public institutions of government is considered for the Western Arctic Region, the Inuvialuit shall not be treated any less favourably than any other native groups or native people with respect to the governmental powers and authority conferred on them.

The Inuvialuit and Gwich'in are negotiating self-government, including their inherent right of self-government, within the context of regional public government. What will result from these negotiations is unclear. What is clear is that any resulting agreement will be unique as it will couple the aspirations of Aboriginal peoples and their inherent right of self-government with the need to operate, for purposes of efficiency and practicality, within the context of public government in a unified territorial government regime for the western Arctic.

On April 22, 1992, the Gwich'in Dene and Métis, Canada, and the NWT signed the *Gwich'in Final Agreement*.[74] With approximately 2,200 beneficiaries, the Gwich'in claim included a $75-million compensation package (1990 dollars) payable over 15 years and gave the Gwich'in a share of resource royalties in the western Arctic. They also received a 15-year subsidy on property taxes on certain Gwich'in municipal lands, title to more than 22,000 square kilometres (including 6,158 square kilometres of subsurface mineral rights) of land and an exclusive license to conduct commercial wildlife activities on Gwich'in lands and preferential rights in the settlement area. Finally, all of the parties agreed in the claim to pursue self-government negotiations with the Gwich'in. The Gwich'in, along with the Inuvialuit, are engaged in self-government negotiations with the federal and NWT governments.

The *Sahtu Dene and Métis Land Claim Agreement* was signed on September 6, 1993,[75] and affected approximately 2,000 beneficiaries. It is similar to the Gwich'in agreement. Like the Gwich'in, the Sahtu Dene and Métis received a $75-million compensation package (1990 dollars) payable over 15 years and a share of resource royalties in the western Arctic. They received title to more than 41,000 square kilometres (including 1,813 square kilometres of subsurface mineral rights) of land. Like the Gwich'in, the Sahtu can enter into self-government negotiations with the federal and NWT governments. One of the five Sahtu communities has initiated community-based self-government discussions with the federal government and the government of the NWT.

The Dogrib of the lower Mackenzie Valley, NWT, are in a unique situation. Whereas most groups in Canada, with the exception of the Nisga'a in British Columbia, have negotiated their land claims and self-government arrangements at different times, the Dogribs are negotiating self-government and their land claim concurrently with the federal government and NWT governments. The Dogribs, Gwich'in, and Sahtu are signatories to Treaty No. 11.

The Treaty No. 8 Indians, primarily on the eastern and southern shores of Great Slave Lake, are discussing a treaty land entitlement agreement with the federal and NWT governments. Treaty land entitlement is a process by which an Aboriginal

---

74 Enacted by the *Gwich'in Land Claim Settlement Act,* S.C. 1992, c. 53.
75 Enacted by the *Sahtu Dene and Métis Land Claim Settlement Act,* S.C. 1994, c. 27.

group acquires the full amount of land to which it is entitled but never received as a result of signing a treaty, in this case Treaty No. 8.

The Deh Cho Indians, who are signatories to Treaty No. 11, live primarily on the southern shores of Great Slave Lake. They presently have a self-government proposal before the federal government for review. The Métis of the southern part of Great Slave Lake signed a framework agreement in 1996 and are currently negotiating lands, resources, programs, and services with the federal government and the government of the NWT.

The creation of Nunavut, in the eastern half of Canada's North, is the result of the May 23, 1993, *Nunavut Land Claims Agreement* (*Nunavut Agreement*)[76] between the governments of Canada and the NWT and the Inuit represented by the Tunngavik Federation of Nunavut, now Nunavut Tunngavik Inc. The notion of dividing the NWT into two territories is not new. It was discussed in the early 1950s but did not gain momentum until the mid-1970s. At this time, the Aboriginal groups in the western NWT, namely the Inuvialuit, the Dene, and the Métis, put proposals forward for Aboriginal governments in the western NWT. The Inuvialuit wanted a strong regional type of government, while the Dene and Métis wanted their own territory: Denendeh. The Inuit put forward their proposal for the eastern NWT: the creation of Nunavut.

The May 1993 *Nunavut Land Claims Agreement,* signed between Canada, the NWT, and the Tunngavik Federation of Nunavut (now Nunavut Tunngavik Inc.), affects more than 17,000 Inuit living in the eastern Arctic and calls for the transfer of approximately 350,000 square kilometres (including 36,000 square kilometres of subsurface mineral rights) of land to the Inuit. The total settlement area is almost 2 million square kilometres, with a total cash compensation, to be paid over 14 years, of more than $1 billion dollars. It is the largest land claim in Canadian history and on April 1, 1999, a new third territory in Canada was created—Nunavut.

Article 4 of the *Nunavut Agreement* provides that Canada will recommend to Parliament legislation to establish a new Nunavut Territory with its own legislative assembly and public government separate from the existing government of the Northwest Territories. In June 1993 the *Nunavut Act*[77] was proclaimed. In many ways it is a modern version of the *Northwest Territories Act.*[78]

Article 4 of the *Nunavut Agreement* also requires Canada, the NWT, and the Inuit to negotiate a political accord to deal with the establishment of Nunavut. On October 30, 1992, the *Nunavut Political Accord* was formally signed by the Inuit, Canada, and the NWT. It will remain in effect until three months after the establishment of Nunavut. The accord contains some basic principles to guide the division of the NWT and the creation of Nunavut, including:

1. April 1, 1999 as the date for division;
2. the boundaries of Nunavut;
3. the *Nunavut Act* to provide the legislative authority for the transfer of administration and control to the Nunavut government;

---

76   Enacted by the *Nunavut Land Claim Agreement Act,* S.C. 1993, c. 29.

77   *Nunavut Act,* S.C. 1993, c. 28.

78   *Northwest Territories Act,* R.S.C. 1985, c. N–27.

4. the mandate for the Nunavut Implementation Commission;
5. recognition that financial stability is critical to both territories (Nunavut and the remainder of the NWT); and
6. Canada's commitment to fund "reasonable incremental costs" arising from the creation and operation of the Nunavut government.

A December 1995 plebiscite in Nunavut indicated that Iqaluit, the largest community in the eastern Arctic, was the preferred location of the capital city. The federal government subsequently confirmed Iqaluit as the capital of Nunavut.

Although the Inuit form the majority of residents in Nunavut and the creation of Nunavut is a direct result of the land claims agreement, Nunavut is not, strictly speaking, self-government for the Inuit in the traditional sense. Nunavut is a public government, albeit one that will have a majority Inuit representation. In the western NWT, the self-government discussions have focused on exclusive Aboriginal government arrangements, similar to those in existence in southern Canada (for example, reserve-style governments), and on meshed public-Aboriginal government systems.

Land claims negotiations between the Labrador Inuit Association, the federal government, and the Newfoundland government have been ongoing since 1989. Also in Newfoundland and with the same parties as the Inuit, the Innu Nation is negotiating a land claims and self-government package.

In 1993 the *Yukon Final Agreement* was signed between Canada, the Yukon Territory, and the Council for Yukon Indians. The *Yukon Final Agreement* serves as the basis for the parties to negotiate individual First Nations final agreements with regard to settlement of outstanding claims. Section 2.2.1 of the agreement states: "Settlement Agreements shall be land claims agreements within the meaning of section 35 of the *Constitution Act, 1982.*" Presently, six out of 14 Yukon First Nations have completed and signed claims agreements and self-government agreements. Although the claims agreements are "treaties" within the meaning of s. 35, the self-government agreements are not. When all of the final agreements are finalized, the Yukon First Nations will receive approximately 16,000 square miles of land (10,000 square miles of which include surface and subsurface rights and 6000 square miles in fee simple), along with approximately $240 million in compensation.

Since British Columbia is almost entirely without treaties[79] or land claims agreements, a new process has begun to enter into treaties with First Nations in British Columbia. On September 21, 1992, the British Columbia First Nations Summit and the Governments of British Columbia and Canada signed the *British Columbia Treaty Commission Agreement,* which is designed to oversee the treaty negotiation process and to monitor the progress of the negotiations. At the time of writing, there were more than 50 First Nations involved in this process, representing about two-thirds of the almost 200 bands in British Columbia. Important to note is that British Columbia's treaty process includes not only a land and compensation pack-

---

79 The exceptions are the pre-Confederation Douglas Treaties (covering less that 360 square miles) and a small portion of Treaty No. 8.

age, like historical land claims agreements, but also governance provisions.[80]

On August 4, 1998, the governments of Canada and British Columbia, along with the Nisga'a Tribal Council, initialed the *Nisga'a Final Agreement*—the first modern treaty in British Columbia. Over 20 years in the making, since the 1973 Supreme Court of Canada decision in *Calder*, the *Nisga'a Agreement* marks a significant turn in Aboriginal relations in British Columbia. Although not formally ratified at the time of writing, the Nisga'a treaty represents the full and final settlement between the Nisga'a and the governments of Canada and British Columbia regarding Nisga'a Aboriginal rights and title.

The agreement is a "lands claims agreement" and a "treaty" within the meaning of s. 35(3) and ensures that the *Canadian Charter of Rights and Freedoms* will apply to Nisga'a government. The former Nisga'a Indian reserves (56 in total, including four villages) will no longer be governed by the *Indian Act* but rather by the agreement. A total of 1,992 square kilometres of land in the lower Nass River area will be owned by the Nisga'a (population of approximately 5,500), of which approximately 62 square kilometres consists of former Nisga'a Indian reserve land.

The *Final Agreement* provides for the Nisga'a to own the forest resources, and to develop their own regulations and standards to govern forest practices on their lands, with provincial standards being a minimum requirement. The Nisga'a will hold their land in fee simple and have agreed to allow public access to these lands for non-commercial and recreational purposes, including hunting, fishing, and public transportation corridors. With respect to fishing, the Nisga'a are guaranteed an allocation of salmon returning to Canadian waters that must consider conservation and equitable distribution. Canada and British Columbia continue to manage the fisheries as they relate to the Nisga'a. In return for their undefined Aboriginal rights to hunt, the Nisga'a receive, under the treaty, a portion of the total allowable harvest for wildlife such as moose and grizzly bear in the Nass Wildlife Area. The Nisga'a remain subject to provincial laws governing conservation, public health, and safety. The Nass Wildlife Area provides for a mechanism for an increased Nisga'a role in the management of the area.

The treaty affirms that the Nisga'a have the right to self-government and the authority to make law as provided for in the *Final Agreement* (see chapter 8, "Self-Government," where an excerpt from the Nisga'a government chapter is provided). There will be a central Nisga'a Lisims government, along with four Nisga'a village governments. The Nisga'a will also have a constitution that will set out the necessary rules and procedures related to a functioning democratic government. Non-Nisga'a residents on Nisga'a lands are provided with the right to participate in Nisga'a public institutions that directly affect them, such as a school board or a health board, and with the right to be consulted regarding decisions that directly affect them. In general, the Nisga'a governance model is a combination of municipal-style governmental authorities, authorities currently provided for in the *Indian Act,* and some new powers not normally held by the former two; for example,

---

80   For a discussion of the economic importance of concluding treaties in B.C., see R. Kunin, ed., *Prospering Together: The Economic Impact of the Aboriginal Title Settlements in B.C.* (Vancouver, B.C.: The Laurier Institution, 1998).

environmental assessment, wills and estates, and post-secondary education.

The treaty also allows the Nisga'a to provide full policing services on Nisga'a lands, with provincial standards continuing to apply for police training, conduct, and qualifications. A Nisga'a court can also be established pursuant to the treaty to deal, with Nisga'a laws on Nisga'a lands. The cash component of the treaty provides for the Nisga'a to receive $190 million to be paid out over 15 years. Additionally, the Nisga'a receive $11.5 million to purchase commercial fishing vessels and licences. The treaty calls for five-year fiscal financing agreements to be negotiated between Canada, British Columbia, and the Nisga'a regarding the funding of public services and programs on Nisga'a lands. A central principle for these agreements will be that the level of public programs and services provided on Nisga'a lands will be at a level generally comparable to those delivered by other local and regional governments in northwestern British Columbia. Noteworthy is that the *Indian Act*'s s. 87 income tax exemption for reserve-based income will be phased out over a twelve-year period.

Although the *Final Agreement* is initialed, it must be ratified by all three parties before coming into force. Among other requirements, the Nisga'a must have a referendum among its members and receive a simple majority of eligible voters for the *Final Agreement* to be ratified. It did so in November 1998. Canada requires that the *Final Agreement* be signed by a federal minister authorized by the governor in council and that settlement legislation be enacted by the Parliament of Canada. British Columbia has the same requirements as Canada, except that it is the lieutenant governor in council and the provincial legislature respectively that are the authorities in question.

An outstanding national issue that may have finally been settled by the Nisga'a treaty is the issue of the "cede, release and surrender" language found in most older treaties. The purpose of this language was to ensure that the treaty replaced any outstanding Aboriginal rights and that the First Nations involved ceded, released, and surrendered any interests in the land to the Crown. First Nations have found this language particularly distasteful and have sought better, more sensitive language. At the same time, public governments at the treaty table have been concerned that without such strong language, the certainty and finality that they seek to resolve as a result of treaties cannot be achieved. The Nisga'a treaty appears to have solved this problem. Sections 23 to 27 of chapter 2 seek to describe the nature of the rights in the *Final Agreement* in such a manner that it is clear that all the Aboriginal and treaty rights of the Nisga'a are contained therein. Section 22 reads:

> This Agreement constitutes the full and final settlement in respect of the aboriginal rights, including aboriginal title, in Canada of the Nisga'a Nation.

Section 26 reads:

> If, despite this Agreement and the settlement legislation, the Nisga'a Nation has an aboriginal right, including aboriginal title, in Canada, that is other than, or different in attributes or geographical extent from, the Nisga'a section 35 rights as set out in this Agreement, the Nisga'a Nations releases that aboriginal right to Canada to the extent that the aboriginal right is other than, or different in attributes or geographical extent from, the Nisga'a section 35 rights as set out in this Agreement.

The Nisga'a *Final Agreement* is a significant agreement for the Nisga'a and for the people of British Columbia. It is to be hoped that it is the start to a segment of British Columbia's history that will see many more agreements reached between the Aboriginal peoples of British Columbia and the government of British Columbia and Canada.

The *Delgamuukw* decision has caused a great degree of confusion and flux in British Columbia both for governments and for the First Nations. Effectively recognizing that Aboriginal title exists in parts of British Columbia and affirming that there is a burden on the Crown's title to the land, *Delgamuukw* has increased substantially the expectations of First Nations in British Columbia and has put both the federal and provincial governments in the difficult situation of trying to ratchet forward what they are prepared to live with. Regardless, treaty-making is a vital step for British Columbia to move forward into the 21st century in that treaties will not only provide certainty and scope to Aboriginal interests in the province, but they will also offer a degree of political and economic stability to a province that is largely dependent upon the resource sector.

SECTION 35(3) AND LAND CLAIMS AGREEMENTS

The precise meaning of s. 35(3) has not been determined. On its face, however, it is clear that rights contained in land claims agreements enjoy constitutional protection.[81] That being the case, it could also be assumed that pursuant to s. 52 of the *Constitution Act, 1982,*[82] any law (federal, provincial, or territorial) that is inconsistent with rights contained in a land claims agreement is of no force or effect. Even though the effect of this constitutional protection may have significant consequences over vast tracts of land in Canada, to date little commentary, academic or judicial, is available.[83]

Equally unclear, and perhaps more significant, is what is deemed to be a "right" within a land claims agreement. Put another way, what precisely is constitutionally protected in a land claims agreement? If past jurisprudence is any guide, the term "right" probably does not need to be present in every provision in order for it to be considered a "right" for the purposes of s. 35(1). In *Cree School Board* v. *Canada,*[84]

---

81   See *Cree Regional Authority* v. *Robinson,* [1991] 4 C.N.L.R. 84 at 102 (F.C.T.D.).

82   Section 52(1) reads: "The Constitution of Canada is the supreme law of Canada, and any law which is inconsistent with the provisions of the Constitution is, to the extent of the inconsistency, of no force or effect."

83   See T. Isaac, "The *Constitution Act, 1982* and the Constitutionalization of Aboriginal Self-Government in Canada: *Cree-Naskapi (of Quebec) Act,*" [1991] 1 C.N.L.R. 1. In this piece the author argues that s. 35 implicitly recognizes and constitutionally protects self-government, to the extent that self-governing provisions are contained in land claims agreements for the purposes of s. 35(3). Further, legislation flowing as a direct result of the constitutionalized agreement, such as the *Cree-Naskapi Act,* may have some quasi-constitutional status at law. See also *Eastmain Band* v. *Gilpin* and *Waskaganish Band* v. *Blackned;* excerpts for both may be found in chap. 8 on self-government.

84   *Cree School Board* v. *Canada,* [1998] 3 C.N.L.R. 24 (Que. Sup. Ct.), 50, 51, 57 and 58.

Croteau S.C.J. held that the Cree school board created under the *James Bay and Northern Quebec Agreement* enjoys constitutional status.

The Federal Court of Appeal in *Eastman Band* v. *Canada*[85] held that although the principle of interpreting treaties "liberally" applies to modern treaties, the principle of doubtful expressions being construed in favour of the Indians does not apply. Decar J.A. writes:

> We must be careful, in construing a document as modern as the 1975 [James Bay] Agreement, that we do not blindly follow the principles laid down by the Supreme Court in analyzing treaties entered into in an earlier era. The principle that ambiguities must be construed in favour of the Aboriginals rests, in the case of historic treaties, on the unique vulnerability of the Aboriginal parties, who were not educated and were compelled to negotiate with parties who had a superior bargaining position, ... When it is modern treaties that are at stake, the Aboriginal party must now, too, be bound by the informed commitment that it is now in a position to make. No serious and lasting political compromise can be entered into in an atmosphere of distrust and uncertainty.[86]

To date, the Supreme Court of Canada has not made any such distinction between "historic" treaties and "modern" treaties. It is perhaps safe to assume that although the precise degree to which all of the interpretive principles surrounding treaties apply to land claims agreements is uncertain, the rights contained in land claims agreements and modern treaties are constitutionally protected. Although they will undoubtedly play a significant role in the governance of major portions of Canada's land mass, the understanding of the effect of these agreements on land management and governance is limited. The Federal Court, Trial Division, recently held that the federal Crown has a positive duty to consult Aboriginal peoples regarding the creation of a national park in an area under land claims agreement negotiations.[87]

Another interesting decision that affects the understanding of s. 35(3) and the potential weight of constitutionalized land claims agreements is *Nunavut Tunngavik Inc. (N.T.I.)* v. *Canada (Minister of Fisheries and Oceans)*.[88] N.T.I. applied to have a decision made by the minister of Fisheries and Oceans dealing with turbot quotas affecting an area within the boundaries of the area set aside in the *Nunavut Land Claims Agreement.* N.T.I. maintained that the minister failed to consider the advice of the land claim's Nunavut Wildlife Management Board (NWMB). The court granted the application, stating that the *Nunavut Land Claims Agreement* requires shared decision-making regarding those areas within the mandate of the NWMB. The minister's authority is not absolute and the minister is obligated to consider the advice of the NWMB. Consideration requires that the relationship between the minister and the NWMB be mandatory, close, cooperative, and highly respectful. The *Nunavut Agreement* is a solemn arrangement and the agreement must be given full force and effect.

---

85 *Eastman Band* v. *Canada,* [1993] 3 C.N.L.R. 55 (F.C.A.).

86 Ibid., 61 and 64.

87 *Nunavik Inuit* v. *Min. of Canadian Heritage,* [1998] 4 C.N.L.R. 68 (F.C.T.D.).

88 *Nunavut Tunngavik Inc.* v. *Canada,* [1997] 4 C.N.L.R. 193 (F.C.T.D.).

The future course of modern treaties as a mechanism for implementing Aboriginal self-government has yet to be determined. Certainly, the British Columbia process will most likely set the agenda for modern comprehensive treaty negotiations. Federal, provincial, and territorial governments are more than likely going to continue the "treaty-making" approach to settling land claims, treaty entitlement, and claims to self-government (as is the case with the treaty process in British Columbia).

The 1992 Charlottetown Accord,[89] proposed extensive changes to existing constitutional provisions affecting Aboriginal peoples. The Accord recognized the inherent right of self-government and proposed that the inherent right be interpreted in a manner consistent with the recognition of Aboriginal governments constituting one of three orders of government in Canada. Treaty rights were guaranteed an interpretation that would be "just, broad and liberal" and that would consider the "spirit, intent and the context" of treaty negotiations. Self-government agreements would have the force of law and would create treaty rights within the meaning of s. 35. Although the Accord was rejected in a national referendum, it remains a relevant document in that it details the possibilities for a broader approach to constitutionally entrenching treaty rights.

Treaties represent negotiation, and negotiation is a fundamental tool that all governments in Canada see as the most useful and practical means to recognize and implement self-government, and settle the outstanding Aboriginal burden on Crown title. However, the reason negotiations and "treaties" are the preferred *modus operandi* for governments has more to do with practical self-interest and self-preservation than with principles related to the maintenance of, and respect for, Aboriginal rights. Time and time again, governments have "moved" on Aboriginal issues as a result of legal actions initiated by Aboriginal peoples. Negotiation is an alternative to court-induced action.

■ CASES AND MATERIALS

1. ***R.* v. *Sikyea*, 6 C.N.L.C. 583 (N.W.T.C.A.). Smith C.J.A., Johnson, Kane, McDermid JJ., and Parker J., January 24, 1964**

> This decision provides a clear example of the vulnerability of Indian treaties before the enactment of s. 35 of the *Constitution Act, 1982,* whereby treaty rights were constitutionally "recognized and affirmed." In *Sikyea*, 6 C.N.L.C. 597, the Supreme Court of Canada affirmed the Northwest Territories' Court of Appeal decision and held that the *Migratory Birds Convention Act*, R.S.C. 1985, c. M–7, applied to Indians notwithstanding their hunting rights guaranteed by Treaty No. 11. The Supreme Court affirmed this result in both *R.* v. *George*, [1966] S.C.R. 267, and *Daniels* v. *White*, [1968] S.C.R. 517. Prior to 1982, federal legislation could prevail over treaty rights. After

---

89   See chapter 8; also see T. Isaac, "An Analysis of the Aboriginal Government Provisions of the 1992 Charlottetown Accord: Self-Government in the Post-Charlottetown Era" (LL.M. Thesis, University of Saskatchewan College of Law, 1993), and S. Venne, "Treaty Indigenous Peoples and the Charlottetown Accord: The Message in the Breeze" [1993] 4:2 *Constitutional Forum* 43.

1982, s. 35(1) of the *Constitution Act, 1982* afforded treaty rights constitutional status. The following is a portion of the Court of Appeal decision.

JOHNSON J.A.:—The respondent in this case was convicted by a magistrate at Yellowknife upon a charge of unlawfully killing a migratory bird in an area described in Sched. A of the *Migratory Bird Regulations* at a time not during an open season for that bird in the area, in violation of sec. 5(1)(a) of the *Migratory Bird Regulations*. . . . The respondent appealed to Sissons, J. and, after a trial *de novo,* (1962–63) 40 W.W.R. 494, that judge set aside the conviction, acquitted the respondent and ordered the return of the gun and the duck to the respondent. From that decision the crown appeals. . . .

The right of Indians to hunt and fish for food on unoccupied crown lands has always been recognized in Canada—in the early days as incident of their "ownership" of the land, and later by the treaties by which the Indians gave up their ownership right in these lands. McGillivray J.A. in *Rex* v. *Wesley* [1932] 2 W.W.R. 337, discussed quite fully the origin, history and nature of the right of Indians both in the lands and under the treaties by which these were surrendered and it is unnecessary to repeat what he has said. It is sufficient to say that these rights had their origin in the *Royal Proclamation* that followed the Treaty of Paris in 1763. By that proclamation it was declared that the Indians "should not be molested or disturbed in the possession of such parts of Our Dominions and Territories as, not having been ceded to or purchased by Us are reserved to them or any of them as their hunting grounds."

The Indians inhabiting Hudson Bay Company lands were excluded from the benefit of the proclamation, and it is doubtful, to say the least, if the Indians of at least the western part of the Northwest Territories could claim any rights under the proclamation, for these lands at the time were *terra incognita* and lay to the north and not "to the westward of the sources of the river which fall into the sea from the west or northwest," (from the 1763 proclamation describing the area to which the proclamation applied). That fact is not important because the government of Canada has treated all Indians across Canada, including those living on lands claimed by the Hudson Bay Company, as having an interest in the lands that required a treaty to effect its surrender.

Two of the earliest treaties (called the "Robinson Treaties" in the book *The Treaties of Canada with the Indians of Manitoba the Northwest Territories and Kee-Wa-Tin* by the Hon. Alexander Morris, P.C.) entered into in 1850 contained the following:

> And the said William Benjamin Robinson of the first part, on behalf of Her Majesty and the Government of this Province, hereby promises and agrees . . . to allow the said Chiefs and their tribes the full and free privilege to hunt over the territory now ceded by them, and to fish in the waters thereof as they have heretofore been in the habit of doing, saving and excepting only such portions of the said territory as may from time to time be sold or leased to individuals, or companies of individuals and occupied by them with the consent of the Provincial Government.

In the North-West Angle Treaty of 1873, a clause that became the model for all subsequent treaties appears. By 1877, seven treaties had been signed by which the Indians surrendered most of the arable and grazing lands from the Great Lakes to the mountains. In 1899, by treaty No. 8, the Indians surrendered the Peace River and Northern Alberta area. It was not until 1921 that the Indian rights in that part of the Northwest Territories that includes Yellowknife were surrendered by Treaty 11. As part of the consideration for surrendering their interest in the lands covered by the treaty, the Indians received the following covenant:

> And His Majesty the King hereby agrees with the said Indians that they shall have the right to pursue their usual vocations of hunting, trapping and fishing throughout the tract surrendered as heretofore described, subject to such regulations as may from time to time be made by the Government of the Country acting under the authority of His Majesty, and saving and excepting such tracts as may be required or taken up from time to time for settlement, mining, lumbering, trading or other purposes.

This substantially the same covenant as appears in all of the other treaties that I have been able to examine. . . .

These Indians, as well as all others, would have been surprised indeed if, in the face of such assurances, the clause in their treaty which purported to continue their rights to hunt and fish could be used to restrict their right to shoot game birds to one and one-half months each year. I agree with the view of McGillivray, J.A., in *R. v. Wesley*, [1932] 4 D.L.R. 774 at 789, where he says:

> It is true that Government regulations in respect of hunting are contemplated in the treaty but considering that treaty in its proper setting I do not think that any of the makers of it could by any stretch of the imagination be deemed to have contemplated a day when the Indians would be deprived of an unfettered right to hunt game of all kinds for food on unoccupied Crown land. . . .

I have quoted s. 5(1) of the regulations which says that ". . . no person shall . . . kill . . . a migratory bird at any time except during an open season. . . ." It is difficult to see how this language admits of any exceptions. When, however, we find that reference in the both the Convention and in the regulations to what kind of birds an Indian an Eskimo may "take" at any time for food, it is impossible for me to say that the hunting rights of the Indians as to these migratory birds have not been abrogated, abridged or infringed upon.

It is, I think, clear that the rights given to the Indians by their treaties as they apply to migratory birds have been taken away by this Act and its regulations. How are we to explain this apparent breach of faith on the part of the government, for I cannot think it can be described in any other terms? This cannot be described as a minor or insignificant curtailment of these treaty rights, for game birds have always been a most plentiful, a most reliable and a readily obtainable food in large areas of Canada. I cannot believe that the government of Canada realized that in implementing the Convention, they were at the same time breaching the treaties that they had made with the Indians. It is much more likely that these obligations under the treaties were overlooked—a case of the left hand having forgotten what the right hand had done. The subsequent history of the government's dealing with the Indians would seem to bear this out. When the treaty we are concerned with here was signed in 1921, only five years after the enactment of *The Migratory Birds Convention Act*, we find the commissioners,who negotiated the treaty reporting:

The Indians seemed afraid, for one thing, that their liberty to hunt, trap and fish would be taken away or curtailed, but were assured by me that this would not be the case, and the Government will expect them to support themselves in their own way, and, in fact, that more twine for nets and more ammunition were given under the terms of this treaty than under any of the preceding ones, this went a long way to calm their fears. I also pointed out that any game laws made were to their advantage, and, whether they took treaty or not, they were subject to the laws of the Dominion.

[A]nd there is nothing in this report which would indicate that the Indians were told that their right to shoot migratory birds had already been taken away from them. I have referred to Art. 12 of the agreement between the government of Canada and the province of Alberta signed in 1930 by which that province was required to assure to the Indians the right of

hunting, trapping and fishing game and fish for food at all seasons of the year on all unoccupied Crown lands. . . .

The amendment to the *BNA Act, 1930*, that confirmed this agreement, declared that it should

have the force of law notwithstanding anything in the British North America Act . . . or any Act of the Parliament of Canada. . . .

It is of some importance that while the Indians in the Northwest Territories continued to shoot ducks at all seasons for food, it is only recently that any attempt has been made to enforce the Act.

I can come to no other conclusion than that the Indians, notwithstanding the rights given to them by their treaties, are prohibited by this Act and its Regulations from shooting migratory birds out of season. Unless one or other of the matters mentioned in the learned trial Judge's reasons for judgment or raised by the respondent's counsel at the hearing of the appeal is a defence to the charge, the appeal must be allowed and the conviction sustained. . . .

We were invited by counsel for the respondent to apply to the *Migratory Birds Convention* those rules which have been laid down for the interpretation of treaties in international law and we have been referred to many authorities on how these treaties should be interpreted. We are not, however, concerned with interpreting the Convention but only the legislation by which it is implemented. To that statute the ordinary rules of interpretation are applicable and the authorities referred to have no application.

The appeal must be allowed and the conviction imposed by the Magistrate affirmed. In coming to this conclusion, I regret that I cannot share the satisfaction that was expressed by McGillivary J.A. in *R. v. Wesley*, supra, when he was writing his judgment dismissing the appeal in that case (at p. 790):

It is satisfactory to be able to come to this conclusion and not to have to decide that 'the Queen's promises' have not been fulfilled. It is satisfactory to think that legislators have not so enacted but that the Indians may still be "convinced of our justice and determined resolution to remove all reasonable cause of discontent".

Appeal allowed.

2. *Re Paulette et al. and Registrar of Titles (No.2)*, 9 C.N.L.C. 307 (N.W.T.S.C.). Morrow J., September 6, 1973

In *Re Paulette*, Morrow J. of the Northwest Territories Supreme Court held that Aboriginal rights constitute an interest in land and the *Royal Proclamation of 1763* did not create Aboriginal rights but rather confirmed their existence. As well, Morrow J. doubted whether Treaties 8 and 11 extinguished Aboriginal title to the land in question. Morrow J. writes:

> Unless therefore the negotiation of Treaty 8 and Treaty 11 legally terminated or extinguished the Indian land rights or aboriginal rights; it would appear that there was a clear constitutional obligation to protect the legal rights of the indigenous people in the area covered by the proposed caveat, and a clear recognition of such rights. 42 D.L.R. (3d) 8 at 30.

This liberal approach to treaty interpretation and this positive treatment of oral history as evidence were forerunners for what was to come from the Supreme Court of Canada. Note that this decision was overruled on technical grounds.

MORROW J:—On 3rd April 1973 this matter came before me as a result of a Reference under s. 154(1)(b) of the Land Titles Act, R.S.C. 1970, c. L–4. The Reference resulted from a purported caveat being presented for registration under s. 132 of the Act which claimed an interest in an area comprising some 400,000 square miles of land located in the western portion of the Northwest Territories. The caveat was based on a claim for aboriginal rights and was signed by 16 Indian chiefs representing the various Indian bands resident in the area covered by the lands referred to in the caveat.

The caveat document follows the form provided for in the Act. The pertinent portion of the caveat is as follows:

CAVEAT

TO THE REGISTRAR, Land Titles Office, Yellowknife, Northwest Territories,

TAKE NOTICE that we Chief Francois Paulette (Fort Smith) . . . [there follow the names of the remaining 15 chiefs] . . . being residents of the Northwest Territories and members of the Indian bands in the Northwest Territories by virtue of Aboriginal Rights in all land in that tract of land in the Northwest Territories within the limits of the land described in Treaties 8 and 11 of 1899 and 1921, respectively, with adhesions of 1900 and 1922, between Her Most Gracious Majesty Queen Victoria and His Most Gracious Majesty King George V, respectively, and the Indian inhabitants of the land described in the said Treaties; which said tract of land may be more particularly described as land included within the following limits: [Then follows a metes and bounds description covering the lands shown on a map, copy of which was attached to the document.] but, SAVING, AND EXCEPTING THERE FROM all lands for which a Certificate of Title in Fee Simple has been issued: FORBID the registration of any transfer affecting such land or the granting of a certificate of title thereto except subject to the claim set forth. . . .

While it may not be pertinent to this judgment, I would like to observe that I found this part of the case most interesting and intriguing. I think almost every member of the Court party felt that for a short moment the pages of history were being turned back and we were privileged to relive the treaty-negotiating days in the actual setting. The interest shown by today's inhabitants in each settlement helped to recreate some of the atmosphere. These witnesses, for the most part very old men and women, one of them 101 years old, were dignified and showed that they were and had been persons of strong character and leaders in their respective communities. . . .

There is no doubt in my mind that their testimony was the truth and represented their best memory of what to them at the time must have been an important event. It is fortunate indeed that their stories are now preserved. . . .

Those Indians who had either taken part in the treaty negotiations or who had been present while the negotiations were under way and heard parts or all of the conversation, seemed to be in general agreement that their leaders were concerned about what they were giving up, if anything, in exchange for the treaty money, i.e., they were suspicious of something for nothing; that up to the time of treaty the concept of chief was unknown to them, only that of leader, but the Government man was the one who introduced them to the concept of chief when he placed the medal over the Indian's head after he had signed for his people; that they understood that by signing the treaty they would get a grubstake, money, and the promised protection of the Government from the expected intrusion of white settlers. It is clear also that the Indians for the most part did not understand English and certainly there is no evidence of any of the signatories to the treaties understanding English. Some signatures purport to be what one would call a signature, some are in syllabic form, but most are by mark in the form of an "X". The similarity of the "X"'s is suggestive that perhaps the Government party did not even take care to have each Indian make his own "X". Most witnesses were firm in their recollection that land was not to be surrendered, reserves were not mentioned, and the main concern and chief thrust of the discussions centred around the fear of losing their hunting and fishing rights, the Government officials always reassuring them with variations of the phrase that so long as the sun shall rise in the east and set in the west, and the rivers shall flow, their free right to hunt and fish would not be interfered with.

It seems also that very little, if any, reference to a map was made at any of the settlements. In several cases, also, it is apparent that fairly large segments of the Indian community were not present on the occasion of the first treaty, and that the recognized leaders of the respective bands were not always there either. . . .

On the evidence before me I have no difficulty finding as fact that the area embraced by the caveat has been used and occupied by an indigenous people, Athapascan-speaking Indians from time immemorial, that this land has been occupied by distinct groups of these same Indians, organized in societies and using the land as their forefathers had done for centuries, and that those persons who signed the caveat are chiefs representing the present-day descendants of these distinct Indian groups.

3. *An indigenous population have a legal title to land if they were in occupation of that land prior to colonial entry into the area. . . .*

From these authorities I conclude that there are certain well-established characteristics of Indian legal title if the Indians or aborigines were in occupation of the land prior to colonial entry. These are:

1. Possessory right—right to use and exploit the land.
2. It is a communal right.
3. There is a Crown interest underlying this title—it being an estate held of the Crown.
4. It is inalienable—it cannot be transferred but can only be terminated by reversion to the Crown.

I am satisfied on my view of the facts that the indigenous people who have been occupying the area covered by the proposed caveat come fully within these criteria and that, in the terms of the language of Hall J. in the *Calder* case may, therefore be "*prima facie* the owners of the lands".

4. *The land rights of the caveators have been confirmed or recognized by the Royal Proclamation of 1763, the Imperial Order in Council of 1870 transferring the Northwestern Territory to Canada, the early Dominion Lands Act and by the Government actions relating to Treaty 8 and Treaty 11*

Once it is established, as concluded under heading 3 above, that the Indians may be owners of their lands, it is perhaps unnecessary to examine as to whether this prima facie ownership has enjoyed acceptance from the various levels of Government down through the years. None the less, such an examination may he reassuring, especially when the question of whether such ownership has been extinguished or not has to be looked into as well. . . .

Unless, therefore, the negotiations of Treaty No. 8 and Treaty No. 11 legally terminated or extinguished the Indian land rights or aboriginal rights, it would appear that there was a clear constitutional obligation to protect the legal rights of the indigenous people in the area covered by the proposed caveat, and a clear recognition of such rights.

5. *Treaty No. 8 and Treaty No. 11 could not legally terminate Indian land rights. The Indian people did not understand or agree to the terms appearing in the written version of the treaties; only the mutually understood promises relating to wild life, annuities, relief and friendship became legally effective commitments.*

Treaty No. 8 contains several recitals of particular significance to the issues under the present heading: . . .

> AND WHEREAS, the said commissioners have proceeded to negotiate a treaty with the Cree, Beaver, Chipewyan, and other Indians, inhabiting the district herinafter defined and described, and the same has been agreed upon and concluded by the respective bands at the dates mentioned hereinafter, the said Indians DO HEREBY CEDE, RELEASE, SURRENDER AND YIELD UP to the Government of the Dominion of Canada, for Her Majesty the Queen and Her Successors for ever, all their rights, titles and privileges whatsoever, to the lands included within the following limits. . . .
>
> And Her Majesty the Queen HEREBY AGREES with the said Indians that they shall have the right to pursue their usual vocations of hunting, trapping and fishing throughout

the tract surrendered as heretofore described, subject to such regulations as may from time to time be made by the Government of the Country, acting under the authority of Her Majesty, and saving and excepting such tracts as may be required or taken up from time to time for settlement, mining, lumbering, trading or other purposes.

It is not necessary to repeat the equivalent paragraphs contained in Treaty No. 11. It is to be observed that this treaty, which covered all that part of the caveat area not covered by Treaty No. 8, by far the larger part, contained language almost identical in wording.

Treaty No. 8 was negotiated by a Commission made up of three, Treaty No. 11 by a Commission of one.

In the light of the evidence which was adduced during the present hearing it is perhaps of interest to quote H.A. Conroy, the Treaty No. 11 Commissioner, where in his report to his Deputy Superintendent General, Department of Indian Affairs, he said, "They were very apt in asking questions, and here, as in all the other posts where the treaty was signed, the questions asked and the difficulties encountered were much the same. The Indians seemed afraid, for one thing, that their liberty to hunt, trap and fish would be taken away or curtailed, but were assured by me that this would not be the case."

While the important phrase in respect of surrender of the land is in each case camouflaged to some extent by being included in one of the preambles, none the less the clear intention would seem to be to obtain from the Indians "all their rights, titles and privileges whatsoever, to the lands". The actual words are: "the said Indians DO HEREBY CEDE. RELEASE, SURRENDER AND YIELD UP". Read in conjunction with "all their rights, titles and privileges" it is about as complete and all-embracing language as can be imagined. If one was to stop there, of course, the Indians were left nothing.

It seems to me that there are two possible qualifications:

1. That really all the Government did was confirm its paramount title and, by assuring the Indians that "their liberty to hunt, trap and fish" was not to be taken away or curtailed, was in effect a form of declaration by the Government of continuing aboriginal rights in the Indians.

In the present proceedings, I do not have to go so far as to decide whether this is the case or not. In my role as "inquirer" under the *Land Titles Act,* as I see it, I merely have to ascertain if there is some chance of success by the caveators in this respect.

I am satisfied here that the caveators have an arguable case under this heading and have at least the possibility of persuading the Federal Court, or whichever other court may be called upon to rule, that the two treaties are not effective instruments to terminate their aboriginal rights for the above reason. In other words, the Federal Government sought these treaties to reassure their dominant title only.

2. That, unlike perhaps the previous treaties, the manner of negotiation, the "ultimatum" effect of the discussions between the parties in the Northwest Territories was such as to make it possible for the caveators to succeed in persuading a court exercising the final say on these matters that there was either a failure in the meeting of the minds or that the treaties were mere "peace" treaties and did not effectively terminate Indian title—certainly to the extent that

it covered what is normally referred to as surface rights—the use of the land for hunting, trapping and fishing.

Under this subheading it is necessary to examine the evidence in somewhat closer detail than has been done heretofore in this judgment.

Throughout the hearings before me there was a common thread in the testimony —that the Indians were repeatedly assured they were not to be deprived of their hunting, fishing and trapping rights. To me, hearing the witnesses at first hand as I did, many of whom were there at the signing, some of them having been directly involved in the treaty-making, it is almost unbelievable that the Government party could have ever returned from their efforts with any impression but that they had given an assurance in perpetuity to the Indians in the Territories that their traditional use of the lands was not affected.

Ted Trindle, present at the signing of Treaty No. 11 at Fort Simpson, said:

> Well, they talked about land and the Indians were scared that by taking treaty they would lose all of their rights but the Indians were told not, but if they were taking treaty they would get protection. They were told it was not to get the land but they would still be free to hunt and roam as usual, no interference.

At Fort Wrigley, Phillip Moses remembers that the Commissioner said, "Nothing would be changed, everything would be the same as way back, and everything would be the same in the future." . . .

The comments of Mr Harris in his report in 1925 for the Simpson Agency lend some credence to the anxiety. He reports:

> I believe it to be my duty to inform you that I know that certain promises were made these Indians at the first Treaty which in my opinion never should have been made. The Indians at Fort Simpson did not wish to accept the Treaty at first, and I think the wisest course would have been to let them alone till they asked for it themselves, though I do not in any way wish to criticise the action of my superiors in the Department.

Confirmation of haste and perhaps irregularities is easy to find from the suggestion put forth during the hearing that at Fort Simpson, when the Indians led by Old Norwegian (their recognized spokesman) refused to sign and left, the treaty party then appointed Antoine as chief and treaty was signed. Again there is the testimony of Chief Yendo, who is shown as having signed for Fort Wrigley, but who has no memory of having signed and swears that he cannot read or write.

The impracticability of expecting the indigenous peoples with whom the treaties were concerned here to be able to sustain themselves on the area of land each was to receive when reserves came to be allocated and set aside offers one more reason to suspect the bona fides of the negotiations. Perhaps the extreme southwestern area might permit a bare subsistence living to be grubbed from the soil, but most of the area embraced by the treaties is as already described—rock, lake and tundra—with hunting, trapping and fishing offering the only viable method of maintaining life.

In examining agreements such as treaties where, as in the present case, one side, the Indians, were in such an inferior bargaining position, it is perhaps well to remember the cautionary words of Matthews. J. in *Choctaw Nation* v. *U.S.* (1886), 119 U.S. 1 at 28, where he said:

> The recognized relation between the parties to this controversy, therefore, is that between a superior and an inferior, whereby the latter is placed under the care and control of the former, and which, while it authorizes the adoption on the part of the United States of such policy as their own public interests may dictate, recognizes, on the other hand, such an interpretation of their acts and promises as justice and reason demand in all cases where power is exerted by the strong over those to whom they owe care and protection. The parties are not on an equal footing, and that inequality is to be made good by the superior justice which looks only to the substance of the right, without regard to technical rules framed under a system of municipal jurisprudence, formulating the rights and obligations of private persons, equally subject to the same laws.

Justice Hall, in *Calder et al.* v. *A.-G. B.C.*, [1973] 34 D.L.R. (3d) 145 at 210 in discussing onus, states:

> It would, accordingly, appear to be beyond question that the onus of proving that the Sovereign intended to extinguish the Indian title lies on the respondent and that intention must be "clear and plain". There is no such proof in the case at bar; no legislation to that effect.

With the above principle in mind I conclude under this heading that there is enough doubt as to whether the full aboriginal title had been extinguished, certainly in the minds of the Indians, to justify the caveators attempting to protect the Indian position until a final adjudication can be obtained.

6. *The caveators have a legal title and interest in the lands described in the caveat, which title and interest can be protected by the filing of the caveat in the Land Titles Registry of the Northwest Territories . . .*
   1. I am satisfied that those who signed the caveat are present-day descendants of those distinct Indian groups who, organized in societies and using the land as their forefathers had done for centuries, have since time immemorial used the land embraced by the caveat as theirs.
   2. I am satisfied that those same indigenous people as mentioned in (1) above are *prima facie* owners of the lands covered by the caveat—that they have what are known as aboriginal rights.
   3. That there exists a clear constitutional obligation on the part of the Canadian Government to protect the legal rights of the indigenous peoples in the area covered by the caveat.
   4. That notwithstanding the language of the two treaties, there is sufficient doubt on the facts that aboriginal title was extinguished that such claim for title should he permitted to be put forward by the caveators.
   5. That the above purported claim for aboriginal rights constitutes an interest in land which can be protected by caveat under the *Land Titles Act*.
   6. That the provisions of the *Land Titles Act* permit the filing or registering of a caveat such as is presented here even in the case of unpatented land. . . .

3.   *R. v. White and Bob,* 6 C.N.L.C. 629 (B.C.C.A.). Davey, Sheppard, Norris, Lord, and Sullivan, JJ.A., December 15, 1964

This decision illustrates the origins of the Supreme Court of Canada's adoption of the broad and liberal approach to treaty interpretation and to the rules governing whether or not a document is, in fact, a treaty. This decision affirmed that provincial game laws could be superseded by treaty provisions, however vague, by virtue of s. 88 of the *Indian Act,* which provides that provincial laws of general application apply to Indians "subject to the terms of any treaty." The Supreme Court of Canada, 6 C.N.L.C. 684, dismissed an appeal from the Court of Appeal, stating: "[T]he majority of the Court of Appeal were right in their conclusions that the document, . . . was a 'treaty' within the meaning of that term as used in s. 87 of the *Indian Act.*"

DAVEY, J.A.:—The Crown appeals from the respondents' acquittal by Swencisky, Co. Ct. J., on their appeal to him from their summary conviction by L. Beevor-Potts, Esq., P.M., of having game, namely, the carcasses of six deer, in their possession during the closed season without having a valid and subsisting permit under the *Game Act,* contrary to the provisions of that Act. The *Game Act* is an Act of the Provincial legislature, R.S.B.C. 1960, c. 160. . . .

It is common ground that ex. 8 must be taken to include the following clause appearing in all other transfers of Vancouver Island Indian land, which, for reasons that need not be mentioned, does not appear in this instrument:

The condition of, or understanding of this sale, is this, that our village sites and enclosed fields, are to be kept for our own use, for the use of our children, and for those who may follow after us, and the lands shall be properly surveyed hereafter; it is understood however, that the land itself with these small exceptions, becomes the entire property of the white people forever, it is also understood that we are at liberty to hunt over the unoccupied land, and to carry on our fisheries as formerly.

The Crown does not deny that the respondents are entitled to exercise and enjoy whatever rights or privileges there may be under ex. 8 until they have been effectively extinguished. It does contend that ex. 8 conferred no hunting rights, and if it did, that these rights have been extinguished by s. 87 of the *Indian Act,* R.S.C. 1952, c. 149, first enacted in 1951, which the Crown says extends in effect the general provisions of the *Game Act* to Indians.

Section 87 reads as follows:

87.   Subject to the terms of any treaty and any other Act of the Parliament of Canada, all laws of general application from time to time in force in any province are applicable to and in respect of Indians in the province, except to the extent that such laws are inconsistent with this Act or any order, rule, regulation or by-law made thereunder, and except to the extent that such laws make provision for any matter for which provision is made by or under this Act. . . .

It is unnecessary to venture any extended definition of the word "Treaty" in this context but it can be safely said that it does not mean an "executive act establishing relationships between what are recognized as two or more independent states acting in sovereign capacities. . .", per Rand, J., in *Francis* v. *The Queen*, 3

D.L.R. (2d) 641 at p. 647. It is also clear in my opinion that the word is not used in its widest sense as including agreements between individuals dealing with their private and personal affairs. Its meaning lies between those extremes. Counsel for the Crown submits on the authority of Kellock, J., in *Francis* v. *The Queen*, supra, at p. 652 D.L.R., that the word means only those Treaties referred to in other sections of the Act, *i.e.*, ss. 11(b), 15(l)(b), 18(1), 71, 89(1)(b), and 112(4) [repealed 1960–61, c. 9, s. 1]. Taking the learned Judge's remarks in their context, I do not understand him to mean that s. 87 refers only to those Treaties, but that it means Treaties of that type, as opposed to solemn conventions between states, such an the Jay Treaty, which was relied upon by Francis in that case.

In considering whether ex. 8 is a Treaty within the meaning of s. 87, regard ought to be paid to the history of our country: its original occupation and settlement; the fact that the Hudson's Bay Co. was the proprietor, and to use a feudal term contained in its charters, the Lord of the lands in the Northwest Territories and Vancouver Island; and, the part that company played in the settlement and development of this country. In the Charter granting Vancouver Island to the Hudson's Bay Co., it was charged with the settlement and colonization of that Island. That was clearly part of the Imperial policy to head off American settlement of and claims to the territory. In that sense the Hudson's Bay Co. was an instrument of Imperial policy. It was also the long standing policy of the Imperial government and of the Hudson's Bay Co. that the Crown or the company should buy from the Indians their land for settlement by white colonists. In pursuance of that policy many agreements, some very formal, others informal, were made with various bands and tribes of Indians for the purchase of their lands. These agreements frequently conferred upon the grantors hunting rights over the unoccupied lands so sold. Considering the relationship between the Crown and the Hudson's Bay Co. in the colonization of this country, and the Imperial and corporate policies reflected in those agreements, I cannot regard ex. 8 as a mere agreement for the sale of land made between a private vendor and a private purchaser. In view of the notoriety of these facts, I entertain no doubt that Parliament intended the word "Treaty" in s. 87 to include all such agreements, and to except their provisions from the operative part of the section. That being so, s. 87 does not extend the general provisions of the *Game Act* to the respondents in the exercise of their hunting rights under ex. 8 over the lands in question. . . .

Sections 8 [rep. & sub 1961, c. 21, s. 3] and 15 [rep. & sub. 1961, c. 21, s. 6] of the *Game Act* specifically exempt Indians from the operation of certain provisions of the Act, and from that I think it clear that the other provisions are intended to be of general application and to include Indians. If these general sections are sufficiently clear to show an intention to abrogate or qualify the contractual rights of hunting notoriously reserved to Indians by agreements such as ex. 8, they would, in my opinion, fail in that purpose because that would be legislation in relation to Indians that falls within Parliament's exclusive legislative authority under s. 91(24) of the *B.N.A. Act*, and also because that would conflict with s. 87 of the *Indian Act* passed under that authority. Legislation that abrogates or abridges the hunting rights reserved to Indians under the treaties and agreements by which they sold their ancient territories to the Crown and to the Hudson's Bay Company for white settlement is, in my respectful opinion, legislation in relation to Indians because it deals with rights peculiar to them. Lord Watson's judgment in *St. Catherine's Milling & Lumber Co.* v. *The Queen* (1888), 58 L.J.P.C. 54, if any authority is needed, makes that clear. At p. 60 he observed that the plain policy of the *B.N.A. Act* is to vest legislative control over Indian affairs generally in one central authority. On the same page he spoke of Parliament's exclusive power to regulate the Indians' privilege of hunting and fishing. In my opinion, their peculiar rights of hunting and fishing over their ancient hunting grounds arising under agreements by which they collectively sold their ancient lands are Indian affairs over which Parliament has exclusive legislative authority, and only Parliament can derogate from those rights.

In the result, the right of the respondents to hunt over the lands in question reserved to them by ex. 8 are preserved by s. 87, and remain unimpaired by the *Game Act*, and it follows that the respondents were rightfully in possession of the carcasses. It becomes unnecessary to consider other aspects of a far-reaching argument addressed to us by the respondents' counsel.

I would dismiss the appeal. . . .

NORRIS, J.A.: . . .

As to whether or not the document Exhibit 8 is a Treaty within Section 87 of the Indian Act:

On this branch of this appeal as has been stated, I agree with the conclusions of my brother Davey and substantially with his reasons. What I have to say following is by way of detail and in extension of those reasons. The question is, in my respectful opinion, to be resolved not by the application of rigid rules of construction without regard to the circumstances, existing when the document was completed nor by the tests of modern day draftsmanship. In determining what the intention of Parliament was at the time of the enactment of s. 87 of the *Indian Act*, Parliament is to be taken to have had in mind the common understanding of the parties to the document at the time it was executed. In the section "Treaty" is not a word of art and in my respectful opinion, it embraces all such engagements made by persons in authority as may be brought within the term "the word of the white man" the sanctity of which was, at the time of British exploration and settlement, the most important means of obtaining the good-will and co-operation of the native tribes and ensuring that the colonists would be protected from death and destruction. On such assurance the Indians relied. In view of the argument before us, it is necessary to point out that on numerous occasions in modern days, rights under what were entered into with Indians as solemn engagements, although completed with what would now be considered informality, have been whittled away on the excuse that they do not comply with present day formal requirements and with rules of interpretation applicable to transactions between people who must be taken in the light of advanced civilization to be of equal status. Reliance on instances where this has been done is merely to compound injustice without real justification at law. The transaction in question here was a transaction between, on the one hand, the strong representative of a proprietary company under the Crown and representing the Crown, who had gained the respect of the Indians by his integrity and the strength of his personality and was thus able to bring about the completion of the agreement, and, on the other hand, uneducated savages. The nature of the transaction itself was consistent with the informality of frontier days in this Province and such as the necessities of the occasion and the customs and illiteracy of the Indians demanded. The transaction in itself was a primitive one—a surrender of land in exchange for blankets to be divided between the Indian signatories according to arrangements between them—with a reservation of aboriginal rights, the document being executed by the Indians by the affixing of their marks. The unusual (by the standards of legal draftsmen) nature and form of the document considered in the light of the circumstances on Vancouver Island in 1854 does not detract from it as being a "Treaty". . . .

In determining the question as to whether ex. 8 is a "Treaty" within the meaning of s. 87 of the *Indian Act* of Canada the golden rule of construction is to be applied, *viz.*, that the grammatical and ordinary sense of the word is to be adhered to unless that would lead to some absurdity or some repugnance or inconsistency with the rest of the statute in which case the grammatical and ordinary sense of the word may be modified so as to avoid that absurdity, repugnance and inconsistency, but no further: *Becke* v. *Smith* (1836), 2 M. & W. 191 at p. 195, 150 E.R. 724; *Miller v. Salomons* (1852), 7. Ex. 475 at p. 546, 155 E.R. 1036. The Shorter Oxford dictionary, p. 2238, gives as a meaning of "treat", "To deal or carry on negotiations (*with* another) with a view to settling terms; to bargain, negotiate", and of "treaty", "A settlement arrived at by treating or negotiation; an agreement, covenant, compact, contract". In ex. 4, the instructions to Douglas under which ex. 8 was completed, words in the sense of the dictionary meaning quoted were used. The application of that meaning does not lead to any absurdity, repugnance or inconsistency, and indeed, in the light of the history and circumstances it is difficult to conceive of a term which would be more appropriate to describe the engagement entered into.

In *Francis* v. *The Queen*, 3 D.L.R. (2d) 641 (S.C.C.), Kellock, J., at p. 652 D.L.R. excluded the more formal meaning of the word "Treaty" as it is used in respect of international treaties. My brother Davey has, in my respectful opinion, effectively disposed of the argument that Kellock, J., meant that s. 87 applied only to those Treaties referred to in other sections of the *Indian Act* and I would merely add that in my opinion the word as used in the section should, for the reasons already stated herein, be given its widest meaning in favour of the Indians. See also s. 15 of the *Interpretation Act*, R.S.C. 1952, c. 158 and *Worcester* v. *State of Georgia* (1832), 8 Law Ed. 512 at p. 579: "The language used in treaties with the Indians should never be construed to their prejudice." . . .

In my opinion, therefore, the document (ex. 8) is a Treaty within the meaning of s. 87 of the *Indian Act*. As has already been indicated, the right could only be extinguished by Federal legislation as was done with respect to the shooting of migratory birds by the *Migratory Birds Convention Act* referred to in *Sikyea v. The Queen*, 50 D.L.R. (2d) 80 (S.C.C.). That Judgment upheld the Judgment of the Manitoba Court of Appeal (Johnson. J.A., per curiam), 43 D.L.R. (2d) 150. With respect I agree with what the last-mentioned learned Judge said at p. 158 D.L.R. as follows:

> I cannot believe that the Government of Canada realized that in implementing the
> Convention they were at the same time breaching the treaties that they had made with

the Indians. It is much more likely that these obligations under the treaties were over-looked—a case of the left hand having forgotten what the right hand had done. The subsequent history of the Government's dealing with the Indians would seem to bear this out.

To summarize, it is my opinion:

1.   That aboriginal rights existed in favour of Indians from time immemorial.

2.   That upon the British attaining sovereignty over British Columbia and in particular Vancouver Island, the British Crown held a substantial and paramount estate—a proprietory estate in the territory, the tenure of the Indians being a personal and usufructuary right (the aboriginal right) dependent on the goodwill of the Sovereign.

3.   That the right of the Indian respondents to hunt and fish on unoccupied lands was such a right.

4.   That the *Royal Proclamation of 1763* confirming such Indian rights applied to the territories claimed by the British with the exception mentioned in the *Proclamation* and applied in particular to Vancouver Island by virtue of the claim of Sir Francis Drake in 1579 and subsequent British claims to the Island.

5.   That Vancouver Island was not within the exceptions mentioned in the *Proclamation* as it was not Hudson's Bay Co.'s land in 1763 and therefore the Indians' right of hunting and fishing on unoccupied land applied to Vancouver Island.

6.   That before *Confederation* these rights had been recognized by British and Colonial Governments.

7.   That before *Confederation* these rights could only be extinguished by surrender to the British Crown and after *Confederation* by surrender to the Dominion Government which alone has the power to regulate the exercise of these rights.

8.   That after *Confederation* these rights had been recognized by the Dominion and Provincial Governments.

9.   That the said rights have never been surrendered or extinguished.

10. That the document ex. 8 is a Treaty within the meaning of s. 87 of the *Indian Act* by virtue of the *Royal Proclamation of 1763* as confirming aboriginal rights or *per se* because of its very nature and the circumstances of its completion by the Hudson's Bay Co. as a delegate of the British Crown and James Douglas having the power to execute it either as the authorized representative of the delegate of the Crown—the Hudson's Bay Co.—or as Governor of Vancouver Island.

11. That the sections of the *Game Act* of British Columbia under which the prosecution has been launched do not apply to the two respondents as native Indians hunting for food on unoccupied land. . . .

4.   *R.* v. *Francis*, 5 C.N.L.C. 170 (S.C.C.). Kerwin C.J.C., Taschereau, Rand, Kellock, Cartwright, Fauteux, and Abbott JJ., June 11, 1956

This decision affirms the distinction in Canadian law between the ratification of an international treaty (a treaty between nation-states) and its implementation. In order for an international treaty to become part of Canadian law, it must be expressly incorporated into Canadian law. In this case, the Jay Treaty, although properly ratified, was never formally integrated into Canadian law and therefore was not available for Indians to use as the basis for certain border rights. As a result, the term "treaty" in s. 88 of the *Indian Act* is limited to Indian treaties and does not include international treaties.

KERWIN, C.J.C.:—This is an appeal against a decision of the Exchequer Court [[1955] 4 D.L.R. 760] dismissing the petition of right of the suppliant (an Indian resident in a reserve in Canada) and the question is whether three articles, a washing machine, a refrigerator and an oil heater, brought by him into Canada from the United States of America are subject to duties of customs and sales tax under the relevant statues of Canada. None was paid and in fact the articles were not brought into this country at a port of entry; they were subsequently placed under customs detention or seizure and in order to obtain their release, the appellant, under protest, paid the sum demanded by the Crown. The petition of right claims the return of this money and a declaration that no duties or taxes were payable by the appellant with respect to the goods. . . .

The Jay Treaty was not a treaty of peace and it is clear that in Canada such rights and privileges as are here advanced of subjects of a contracting party to a treaty are enforceable by the Courts only where the treaty has been implemented or sanctioned by legislation. This is an adaptation of the language of Lamont J., speaking for himself and Cannon J. in *Re Arrow River and Tributaries Slide & Boom Co.*, [1932], 2 D.L.R. 250, S.C.R 495, and is justified by a continuous line of authority in England. Although it may be necessary in connection with other matters to consider in the future the judgment of the Judicial Committee in the *Labour Conventions Case [Reference re Weekly Rest in Industrial Undertakings Act, etc.]*, [1932], 1 D.L.R. 673, so far as the point under discussion is concerned it is there put in the same sense by Lord Atkin. It has been held that no rights under a treaty of cession can be enforced in the Courts except in so far as they have been incorporated in municipal law: *Vajesingji Joravarsingji* v. *Secretary of State for India* (1924), L.R. 51 Ind. App. 357; *Hoani Te Heuheu Tukino* v. *Aotea District Maori Land Board*, [1941] A.C. 308. The case of *Sutton* v. *Sutton* (1830), 39 E.R. 255, relied upon by the Appellant, dealt with the construction of another provision of the Jay Treaty and of the statute of 37 Geo. III., c. 97, which was passed for the purpose of carrying certain terms of the Treaty into execution. This is not a case where vested rights of property are concerned and it is unnecessary to consider the question whether the terms of the Jay Treaty were abrogated by the war of 1812.

I agree with Cameron J. that cl. (b) of s. 86(1) of the *Indian Act* does not apply, because customs duties are not taxes upon personal property of an Indian situated on a Reserve but are imposed upon the importation of goods into Canada. I also agree that, so far as the refrigerator and the oil heater are concerned, s. 49 of c. 25 of the 1949 [2nd Sess.] statutes is a complete bar. That is *An Act to amend the Income Tax Act and the Income War Tax Act*. While it is true that in s. 48 there are references to residents in Newfoundland and in ss. 49 and 50 to Newfoundland, most of the sections deal with income tax throughout all of Canada. The words are clear that no one is entitled to any deduction, exemption or immunity from, or any privilege in respect of any duty or tax imposed by an Act of the Parliament of Canada; and the *Customs Act*, R.S.C. 1952, c. 58, certainly provides for a duty on all the goods brought into the country by the appellant. Counsel for the appellant points to the words "notwithstanding any other law heretofore enacted" and argues that the rights upon which the appellant bases his claim under the Jay Treaty do not arise under any enactment. For the reasons already given, I cannot agree that any relevant rights of the appellant within that Treaty are judiciable in the Courts of this country.

The appeal should be dismissed with costs.

TASCHEREAU J. concurs with KERWIN C.J.C.

RAND J.:—.... A peace treaty in its primary and legitimate meaning is a treaty concluding a war, "an agreement"—in the words of Sir William Scott in *The "Eliza Ann"* (1813), 1 Dods. 244 at p. 249—"to waive all discussion concerning the respective rights of the parties, and to bury in oblivion all the original causes of the war". The Treaty of Paris, 1783, was of that nature; it recognized the independence of the United States, fixed boundaries, secured the property of former and continuing subjects and citizens in both countries against prosecution and against confiscation of their Property, provided for the withdrawal of British troops from the lands of and border points in the United States and for other matters not germane here.

The question of the Indians, however, was left untouched, and during the years that followed they presented both Governments with problems of reconciliation. Generally speaking, the tribes in the east between New York state and the Ohio river, and in particular those belonging to the confederation known as the Six Nations had tended to support the British, and the bitterness then aroused continued after the peace. No clear political conception had been formulated of the relationship of the Indians either to the old or the new Government especially in respect of rights in the lands over which the natives had formerly roamed at will; and their protest was that the British had purported to transfer to the United States, a title which they did not possess. As a measure of mitigation, the British conceived the idea of setting apart a neutral zone between the two countries for Indian settlement, but this did not, apparently, develop to the point of definite proposal. In addition to this, charges and countercharges were made by both countries of failure to carry out the terms of the treaty in such matters as the return of slaves, the confiscation of properties, the prosecution of individuals and the withdrawal of British troops from fortified border points. These, with the events developing in Europe and the need of both for the restoration of trade, induced a common desire to remove these frictions, which eventuated in the Treaty of 1794 (*Jay's Treaty, A Study in Commerce and Diplomacy,* Bemis, pp. 109 *et seq.*).

Assuming then, a broader authority under the prerogative in negotiating a peace treaty, neither the causes nor the purposes of the Treaty of 1794 bring it within that category.

A treaty is primarily an executive act establishing relationships between what are recognized as two or more independent states acting in sovereign capacities; but as will be seen, its implementation may call for both legislative and judicial action. Speaking generally, provisions that give recognition to incidents of sovereignty or deal with matters in exclusively sovereign aspects, do not require legislative confirmation: for example, the recognition of independence, the establishments of boundaries and, in a treaty of peace, the transfer of sovereignty over property, are deemed executed and the treaty becomes the muniment or evidence of the political or proprietary title. Stipulations for future social or commercial relations assume a state of peace: when peace is broken by war, by reason of the impossibility of their exercise, they are deemed to be abrogated as upon a failure of the condition on which they depend. But provisions may expressly or impliedly break in upon these general considerations; the terms may contemplate continuance or suspension during a state of war. The interpretation is according to the rules that govern that of instruments generally; from the entire circumstantial background, the nature of the matters dealt with and the objects in view, we gather the intention of the parties as expressed in the language used. When such matters touch individuals, the judicial organ must act but a result that brought about non-concurrence between the judicial and the executive branches, say as to abrogation, and apart from any question of an international adjudication, would, to say the least, be undesirable. . . .

Similarly in 86(1), property "situated on a reserve" is unequivocal and does not mean property entering this country or passing an international boundary. On the argument made, the exemption would be limited to situations in which that boundary bounded also the Reserve and would be a special indulgence to the small fraction of Indians living on such a Reserve, a consequence itself appears to me to be a sufficient answer.

The appeal must therefore be dismissed and with costs if demanded.

KELLOCK J.: . . . I think it is quite clear that "treaty" in this section does not extend to an international treaty such as the Jay Treaty but only to treaties with Indians which are mentioned throughout the statute.

In my opinion the provisions of the *Indian Act* constitute a code governing the rights and privileges of Indians, and except to the extent that immunity from general legislation such as the *Customs Act* or the *Customs Tariff Act* is to be found in the *Indian Act*, the terms of such general legislation apply to Indians equally with other citizens of Canada.

I would dismiss the appeal with costs.

CARTWRIGHT J. concurs with RAND J.

FAUTEUX J. concurs with KERWIN C.J.C.

ABBOTT J. concurs with KELLOCK J.

5. **R. v. *Simon*, [1986] 1 C.N.L.R. 153 (S.C.C.). Dickson C.J., Beetz, Estey, McIntyre, Chouinard, Wilson, and Le Dain JJ., November 21, 1985**

In *Simon,* the Supreme Court of Canada recognized a treaty of peace and friendship (1752) even though the cession of land by Indians was not involved. Thus, a surrender of rights is not required to make a valid treaty. The court did not, however, deal with whether or not a breach of the peace or friendship (for example, starting war) voided or invalidated a treaty. This matter remains unanswered. This decision emphasized that treaties are *sui generis* or unique in their nature and must be interpreted in a manner that is evolutionary and not static in nature. *Simon* affirms that provincial laws are subject to treaties by way of s. 88 of the *Indian Act* and that before 1982, the federal Parliament, under s. 91(24) of the *Constitution Act, 1867*, had authority to derogate from rights recognized by a treaty. Overall, *Simon* is significant because of its application of a liberal approach to interpreting treaty rights. The court clarified this approach further in the *Sioui* decision.

DICKSON C.J.:—This case raises the important question of the interplay between the treaty rights of native peoples and provincial legislation. The right to hunt, which remains important to the livelihood and way of life of the Micmac people, has come into conflict with game preservation legislation in effect in the province of Nova Scotia. The main question before this Court is whether, pursuant to a Treaty of 1752 between the British Crown and the Micmac, and to s. 88 of the *Indian Act*, R.S.C. 1970, c. I–6, the appellant, James Matthew Simon, enjoys hunting rights which preclude his prosecution for offences under the *Lands and Forests Act*, R.S.N.S. 1967, c. 163. . . .

Was the Treaty of 1752 Validly Created by Competent Parties?
The respondent raised the issue of the capacity of the parties for two reasons which are stated at p. 8 of the factum:

> The issue of capacity is raised for the purpose of illustrating that the Treaty of 1752 was of a lesser status than an International Treaty and therefore is more easily terminated. The issue is also raised to give the document an historical legal context as this issue has been raised in previous cases.

The question of whether the Treaty of 1752 constitutes an international-type treaty is only relevant to the respondent's argument regarding the appropriate legal tests for the termination of the treaty. I will address this issue, therefore, in relation to the question of whether the Treaty of 1752 was terminated by hostilities between the British and the Micmac in 1753. . . .

The treaty was entered into for the benefit of both the British Crown and the Micmac people, to maintain peace and order as well as to recognize and confirm the existing hunting and fishing rights of the Micmac. In my opinion, both the Governor and the Micmac entered into the treaty with the intention of creating mutually binding obligations which would be solemnly respected. It also provided a mechanism for dispute resolution. The Micmac Chief and the three other Micmac signatories, as delegates of the Micmac people, would have possessed full capacity to enter into a binding treaty on behalf of the Micmac. Governor Hopson was the delegate and legal representative of His Majesty the King. It is fair to assume that the Micmac would have believed that Governor Hopson, acting on behalf of His Majesty the King, had the necessary authority to enter into a valid treaty with them. I would hold that the Treaty of 1752 was validly created by competent parties.

Does the Treaty Contain a Right to Hunt and What is the Nature and Scope of this Right?
Article 4 of the Treaty of 1752 states, "it is agreed that the said Tribe of Indians shall not be hindered from, but have free liberty of hunting and Fishing as usual . . .".

What is the nature and scope of the "liberty of hunting and Fishing" contained in the treaty? . . .

The fact that the right to hunt already existed at the time the Treaty was entered into by virtue of the Micmac's general aboriginal right to hunt does not negate or minimize the significance of the protection of hunting rights expressly included in the treaty.

Such an interpretation accords with the generally accepted view that Indian treaties should be given a fair, large and liberal construction in favour of the Indians. This principle of interpretation was most recently affirmed by this Court in *Nowegijick* v. *The Queen*, [1983] 1 S.C.R. 29, [1983] 2 C.N.L.R. 89. I had occasion to say the following at p. 36 [p. 94 C.N.L.R.]:

> It is legal lore that, to be valid, exemptions to tax laws should be clearly expressed. It seems to me, however, that treaties and statutes relating to Indians should be liberally construed and doubtful expressions resolved in favour of the Indians. . . . In *Jones* v. *Meehan*, 175 U.S. 1, it was held that "Indian treaties must be construed not according to the technical meaning of their words, but in the sense that they would naturally be understood by the Indians."

Having determined that the treaty embodies a right to hunt, it is necessary to consider the respondent's contention that the right to hunt is limited to hunting for purposes and by methods usual in 1752 because of the inclusion of the modifier "as usual" after the right to hunt.

First of all, I do not read the phrase "as usual" as referring to the types of weapons to be used by the Micmac and limiting them to those used in 1752. Any such construction would place upon the ability of the Micmac to hunt an unnecessary and artificial constraint out of keeping with the principle that Indian treaties should be liberally construed. Indeed, the inclusion of the phrase "as usual" appears to reflect a concern that the right to hunt be interpreted in a flexible way that is sensitive to the evolution of changes in normal hunting practices. The phrase thereby ensures that the treaty will be an effective source of protection of hunting rights.

Secondly, the respondent maintained that "as usual" should be interpreted to limit the treaty protection to hunting for non-commercial purposes. It is difficult to see the basis for this argument in the absence of evidence regarding the purpose for which the appellant was hunting. In any event, article 4 of the treaty appears to contemplate hunting for commercial purposes when it refers to the construction of a truck house as a place of exchange and mentions the liberty of the Micmac to bring game to sale: see *R.* v. *Paul*, [1981] 2 C.N.L.R. 83 (N.B.C.A), at p. 563, per Ryan J.A., dissenting in part. . . .

In my opinion, it is implicit in the right granted under article 4 of the Treaty of 1752 that the appellant has the right to possess a gun and ammunition in a safe manner in order to be able to exercise the right to hunt. Accordingly, I conclude that the appellant was exercising his right to hunt under the treaty. . . .

It seems clear that, at a minimum, the treaty recognizes *some* hunting rights in Nova Scotia on the Shubenacadie Reserve and that any Micmac Indian who enjoys those rights has an incidental right to transport a gun and ammunition to places where he could legally exercise them. In this vein, it is worth noting that both parties agree that the highway on which the appellant was stopped "is adjacent to the Shubenacadie Indian Reserve" and "passes through or by a forest, wood, or other resource frequented by moose or deer".

The respondent tries to meet the apparent right of the appellant to transport a gun and ammunition by asserting that the treaty hunting rights have been extinguished. In order to succeed on this argument it is absolutely essential, it seems to me, that the respondent lead evidence as to where the appellant hunted or intended to hunt and what use has been or is currently made of those lands. It is impossible for this Court to consider the doctrine of extinguishment 'in the air'; the respondent must anchor that argument in the bedrock of specific lands. That has not happened in this case. In the absence of evidence as to where the hunting occurred or was intended to occur, and the use of the lands in question, it would be impossible to determine whether the appellant's treaty hunting rights have been extinguished. Moreover, it is unnecessary for this Court to determine whether those rights have been extinguished because, at the very least, these rights extended to the adjacent Shubenacadie reserve. I do not wish to be taken as expressing any view on whether, as a matter of law, treaty rights may be extinguished. . . .

The appellant, Simon, as a member of the Shubenacadie Indian Brook Band of Micmac Indians, residing in Eastern Nova Scotia, the area covered by the Treaty of 1752, can therefore raise the treaty in his defense. . . .

Is the Treaty a "Treaty" Within the Meaning of s. 88 of the Indian Act?
Section 88 of the *Indian Act* stipulates that, "Subject to the terms of any treaty. . . , all laws of general application from time to time in force in any province are applicable to and in respect of Indians in the province . . .". . . .

In my view, Parliament intended to include within the operation of s. 88 all agreements concluded by the Crown with the Indians that would otherwise be enforceable treaties, whether land was ceded or not. None of the Maritime treaties of the eighteenth century cedes land. To find that s. 88 applies only to land cession treaties would be to limit severely its scope and run contrary to the principle that Indian treaties and statutes relating to Indians should be liberally construed and uncertainties resolved in favour of the Indians.

Finally, it should be noted that several cases have considered the Treaty of 1752 to be a valid "treaty" within the meaning of s. 88 of the *Indian Act* (for example, *R.* v. *Paul*, supra; and *R.* v. *Atwin and Sacobie*, [1981] 2 C.N.L.R. 99 (N.B. Prov. Ct.). The Treaty was an exchange of solemn promises between the Micmacs and the King's representative entered into to achieve and guarantee peace. It is an enforceable obligation between the Indians and the white man and, as such, falls within the meaning of the word "treaty" in s. 88 of the *Indian Act*.

Do The Hunting Rights Contained in the Treaty Exempt the Appellant from Prosecution under s. 150(1) of the Lands and Forests Act?
As a result of my conclusion that the appellant was validly exercising his right to hunt under the Treaty of 1752 and the fact he has admitted that his conduct otherwise constitutes an offence under the *Lands and Forests Act*, it must now be determined what the result is when a treaty right comes into conflict with provincial

legislation. This question is governed by s. 88 of the *Indian Act*, which, it will be recalled, states that "Subject to the terms of any treaty, all laws of general application . . . in force in the province are applicable to . . . Indians". . . .

Under s. 88 of the *Indian Act*, when the terms of a treaty come into conflict with federal legislation, the latter prevails, subject to whatever may be the effect of s. 35 of the *Constitution Act, 1982*. It has been held to be within the exclusive power of Parliament under s. 91(24) of the *Constitution Act, 1867*, to derogate from rights recognized in a treaty agreement made with the Indians. See *R.* v. *Sikyea* (1964), 43 D.L.R. (2d) 150, *R.* v. *George*, supra, *R.* v. *Cooper*, supra; *R.* v. *White and Bob*, supra, at p. 618.

Here, however, we are dealing with provincial legislation. The effect of s. 88 of the *Indian Act* is to exempt the Indians from provincial legislation which restricts or contravenes the terms of any treaty. In *Frank* v. *The Queen*, [1978] 1 S.C.R. 95, the Court held, at p. 99:

> The effect of this section is to make applicable to Indians except as stated, all laws of general application from time to time in force in any province, including provincial game laws, but subject to the terms of any treaty and subject also to any other Act of the Parliament of Canada.

Similarly, in *Kruger* v. *The Queen*, [1978] 1 S.C.R. 104, the Court held, at pp. 111–12:

> However abundant the right of Indians to hunt and to fish, there can be no doubt that such right is subject to regulation and curtailment by the appropriate legislative authority. Section 88 of the *Indian Act* appears to be plain in purpose and effect. In the absence of treaty protection or statutory protection, Indians are brought within provincial regulatory legislation.

and at pp. 114–15 the Court held in reference to Indian treaties and s. 88:

> The terms of the treaty are paramount; in the absence of a treaty, provincial laws of general application apply.

Therefore, the question here is whether s. 150(1) of the *Lands and Forests Act*, a provincial enactment of general application in Nova Scotia, restricts or contravenes the right to hunt in article 4 of the Treaty of 1752. If so, the treaty right to hunt prevails and the appellant is exempt from the operation of the provincial game legislation at issue. . . .

In my opinion, s. 150 of the *Lands and Forests Act* of Nova Scotia restricts the appellant's right to hunt under the treaty. The section clearly places seasonal limitations and licensing requirements, for the purposes of wildlife conservation, on the right to possess a rifle and ammunition for the purposes of hunting. The restrictions imposed in this case conflict, therefore, with the appellant's right to possess a firearm and ammunition in order to exercise this free liberty to hunt over the lands covered by the treaty. As noted, it is clear that under s. 88 of the *Indian Act* provincial legislation cannot restrict native treaty rights. If conflict arises, the terms of the treaty prevail. Therefore, by virtue of s. 88 of the *Indian Act*, the clear terms of article 4 of the treaty must prevail over s. 150(1) of the provincial *Lands and Forests Act*.

Several cases have particular relevance. These also deal with charges similar to those in the present case where Indians were accused of unlawful possession of certain objects without the permit required under provincial legislation. In each case, the accused Indians raised their treaty rights in defence and it was held that they should be acquitted because they were not bound by the terms of the provincial statutes: See *R. v. White and Bob*, supra; *R. v. Paul*, supra; *R. v. Atwin and Sacobie*, supra; *R. v. Paul and Polchies*, supra; *R. v. Batisse* (1978), 84 D.L.R. (3d) 377 (Dist. Ct.); *R. v. Taylor and Williams*, [1981] 3 C.N.L.R. 114 (Ont. C.A.); *R. v. Moses* (1969), 13 D.L.R. (3d) 50 (Ont. Dist. Ct.); *R. v. Penasse and McLeod* (1971), 8 C.C.C. (2d) 569 (Ont. Prov. Ct.); *Cheeco v. R.*, [1981] 3 C.N.L.R. 45 (Ont. Dist. Ct.).

I conclude that the appellant has a valid treaty right to hunt under the Treaty of 1752 which, by virtue of s. 88 of the *Indian Act*, cannot be restricted by provincial legislation. It follows, therefore, that the appellant's possession of a rifle and ammunition in a safe manner, referable to his treaty right to hunt, cannot be restricted by s. 150(1) of the *Lands and Forests Act*.

I would accordingly quash the convictions and enter verdicts of acquittal on both charges. . . .

To summarize:

1. The Treaty of 1752 was validly created by competent parties.
2. The treaty contains a right to hunt which covers the activities engaged in by the appellant.
3. The treaty was not terminated by subsequent hostilities in 1753. Nor has it been demonstrated that the right to hunt protected by the treaty has been extinguished.
4. The appellant is a Micmac Indian covered by the treaty.
5. The Treaty of 1752 is a "treaty" within the meaning of s. 88 of the *Indian Act*.
6. By virtue of s. 88 of the *Indian Act*, the appellant is exempt from prosecution under s. 150(1) of the *Lands and Forests Act*.
7. In light of these conclusions, it is not necessary to answer the constitutional question raised in this appeal.

I would, therefore, allow the appeal, quash the convictions of the appellant and enter verdicts of acquittal on both charges.

6. *R. v. Sioui*, [1990] 3 C.N.L.R. 127 (S.C.C.). Dickson C.J., Lamer, Wilson, La Forest, L'Heureux-Dubé, Sopinka, Gonthier, Cory, and McLachlin JJ., May 24, 1990

As with *Simon*, in *Sioui* the Supreme Court of Canada held that treaty rights are *sui generis* in nature and that they demand a liberal, generous interpretive approach in favour of the Indian peoples concerned. The court held that s. 88 of the *Indian Act* affirmed the validity of the treaty in question to exempt the Huron Indians from the application of the provincial park regulations. Perhaps more important is that this decision illustrates the recognition afforded by the court that Indian nations were regarded by the Europeans as "independent nations" capable of making treaties. Treaty rights are in addition to rights recognized by the *Royal Proclamation of 1763* and other like instruments. Treaty rights are not extinguished merely because they have not been utilized or invoked for a long period of time. The court used a wide array of evidence to come to the conclusion that the document purported to be a treaty was a treaty for the purposes of s. 88 and constitutional protection. The document affirmed as a "treaty" was very brief and signed only by the governor of Quebec in 1760. The document was a declaration to confirm that the chief of the Huron people had come to make peace, that the Huron people were under his protection, and that they could practice their religions and customs and were at liberty to trade with the English. The occupancy by the Huron people of the territory in Jacques-Cartier Park, in exercise of their treaty rights, did not seriously compromise the objectives of the Crown.

LAMER J.:— . . . The four respondents were convicted by the Court of Sessions of the Peace of cutting down trees, camping and making fires in places not designated in Jacques-Cartier park contrary to ss. 9 and 37 of the *Regulation respecting the Parc de la Jacques-Cartier* (Order in Council 3108–81 of November 11, 1981, (1981) 113 *O.G.* II, 3518), adopted pursuant to the *Parks Act*, R.S.Q. 1977, c. P–9. . . .

The respondents are Indians within the meaning of the *Indian Act*, R.S.C., 1985, c. I–5 (formerly R.S.C. 1970, c. I–6), and are members of the Huron Band on the Lorette Indian reserve. They admit that they committed the acts with which they were charged in Jacques-Cartier park, which is located outside the boundaries of the Lorette reserve. However, they alleged that they were practising certain ancestral customs and religious rites which are the subject of a treaty between the Hurons and the British, a treaty which brings s. 88 of the *Indian Act* into play and exempts them from compliance with the regulations. . . .

The appellants are asking this Court to dispose of the appeal solely on the basis of the document of September 5, 1760 and s. 88 of the *Indian Act*. The following constitutional questions were stated by the Chief Justice:

> 1. Does the following document, signed by General Murray on 5 September 1760, constitute a treaty within the meaning of s. 88 of the *Indian Act* (R.S.C. 1970, c. I–6)?
>
>> THESE are to certify that the CHIEF of the HURON tribe of Indians having come to me in the name of His Nation, to submit to His BRITANNICK MAJESTY, and make Peace, has been received under my Protection, with his whole Tribe; and henceforth no English Officer or party is to molest, or interrupt them in returning to their Settlement at LORRETTE; and they are received upon the same terms with the Canadians, being allowed the free Exercise of their Religion, their Customs, and Liberty of trading with the English:—recommending it to the Officers commanding the Posts, to treat them kindly.
>> Given under my hand at Longueil, this 5th day of September, 1760.
>> By the Genl's Command,
>> JA. MURRAY
>> JOHN COSNAN,
>> Adjut. Genl.
>
> 2. If the answer to question 1 is in the affirmative, was the "treaty" still operative on 29 May 1982, at the time when the alleged offence were committed?
> 3. If the answers to questions 1 and 2 are in the affirmative, are the terms of the

document of such a nature as to make ss. 9 and 37 of the *Regulation respecting the Parc de la Jacques-Cartier* (Order in Council 3108–81, *Gazette officielle du Québec*, Part II, November 25, 1981, pp. 3518 *et seq.*) made under the *Parks Act* (R.S.Q., c. P–9) unenforceable in respect of the respondents? . . .

Our courts and those of our neighbours to the south have already considered what distinguishes a treaty with the Indians from other agreements affecting them. The task is not an easy one. In *Simon* v. *The Queen*, [1985] 2 S.C.R. 387, [1986] 1 C.N.L.R. 153 this Court adopted the comment of Norris J.A. in *R.* v. *White and Bob* (1964), 52 W.W.R. 193, 50 D.L.R. (2d) 613 (B.C.C.A.) (affirmed in the Supreme Court (1965), 52 D.L.R. (2d) 481), that the courts should show flexibility in determining the legal nature of a document recording a transaction with the Indians. In particular, they must take into account the historical context and perception each party might have as to the nature of the undertaking contained in the document under consideration. To the question of whether the document at issue in *White and Bob* was a treaty within the meaning of the *Indian Act*, Norris J.A. replied (at pp. 648–49 D.L.R.):

> The question is, in my respectful opinion, to be resolved not by the application of rigid rules of construction without regard to the circumstances existing when the document was completed nor by the tests of modern day draftsmanship. In determining what the intention of Parliament was at the time of the enactment of s. 87 [now s. 88] of the *Indian Act*, Parliament is to be taken to have had in mind the common understanding of the parties to the document at the time it was executed.

As the Chief Justice said in *Simon*, supra, treaties and statutes relating to Indians should be liberally construed and uncertainties resolved in favour of the Indians (at 410) [p. 174 C.N.L.R.]. In our quest for the legal nature of the document of September 5, 1760, therefore, we should adopt a broad and generous interpretation of what constitutes a treaty.

In my opinion, this liberal and generous attitude, heedful of historical fact, should also guide us in examining the preliminary question of the capacity to sign a treaty, as illustrated by *Simon* and *White and Bob*.

Finally, once a valid treaty is found to exist, that treaty must in turn be given a just, broad and liberal construction. This principle, for which there is ample precedent, was recently reaffirmed in *Simon*. The factors underlying this rule were eloquently stated in *Jones* v. *Meehan*, 175 U.S. 1 (1899), a judgment of the United States Supreme Court, and are I think just as relevant to questions involving the existence of a treaty and the capacity of the parties as they are to the interpretations of a treaty (at pp. 10–11):

> In construing any treaty between the United States and an Indian tribe, it must always . . . be borne in mind that the negotiations for the treaty are conducted, on the part of the United States, an enlightened and powerful nation, by representatives skilled in diplomacy, masters of a written language, understanding the modes and forms of creating the various technical estates known to their law, and assisted by an interpreter employed by themselves; that the treaty is drawn up by them and in their own language; that the Indians, on the other hand, are a weak and dependent people, who have

no written language and are wholly unfamiliar with all the forms of legal expression, and whose only knowledge of the terms in which the treaty is framed is that imparted to them by the interpreter employed by the United States; and that the treaty must therefore be construed, not according to the technical meaning of its words to learned lawyers, but in the sense in which they would naturally be understood by the Indians.

The Indian people are today much better versed in the art of negotiation with public authorities than they were when the United States Supreme Court handed down its decision in *Jones.* As the document in question was signed over a hundred years before that decision, these considerations argue all the more strongly for the courts to adopt a generous and liberal approach. . . .

C. *Legal nature of the document of September 5, 1760*
1. *Constituent elements of a treaty*
In *Simon* this Court noted that a treaty with the Indians is unique, that it is an agreement *sui generis* which is neither created nor terminated according to the rules of international law. In that case the accused had relied on an agreement concluded in 1752 between Governor Hopson and the Micmac Chief Cope, and the Crown disputed that this was a treaty. The following are two extracts illustrating the reasons relied on by the Chief Justice in concluding that a treaty had been concluded between the Micmacs and the British Crown (at pp. 401 and 410) [at pp. 166 and 174 C.N.L.R.]:

> In my opinion, both the Governor and the Micmac entered into the Treaty with the intention of creating mutually binding obligations which would be solemnly respected. It also provided a mechanism for dispute resolution.
> . . . The Treaty was an exchange [of] solemn promises between the Micmacs and the King's representative entered into to achieve and guarantee peace. It is an enforceable obligation between the Indians and the white man and, as such, falls within the meaning of the word "treaty" in s. 88 of the *Indian Act.*

From these extracts it is clear that what characterizes a treaty is the intention to create obligations, the presence of mutually binding obligations and a certain measure of solemnity. . . .

The decision of the Ontario Court of Appeal in *R.* v. *Taylor and Williams,* [1981] 3 C.N.L.R. 114, also provides valuable assistance by listing a series of factors which are relevant to analysis of the historical background. In that case the Court had to interpret a treaty, and not determine the legal nature of a document, but the factors mentioned may be just as useful in determining the existence of a treaty as in interpreting it. In particular, they assist in determining the intent of the parties to enter into a treaty. Among these factors are:
1. continuous exercise of a right in the past and at present,
2. the reasons why the Crown made a commitment,
3. the situation prevailing at the time the document was signed,
4. evidence of relations of mutual respect and esteem between the negotiators, and
5. the subsequent conduct of the parties. . . .
While the analysis thus far seems to suggest that the document of September 5

is not a treaty, the presence of a clause guaranteeing the free exercise of religion, customs and trade with the English cannot but raise serious doubts about this proposition. It seems extremely strange to me that a document which is supposedly only a temporary, unilateral and informal safe conduct should contain a clause guaranteeing rights of such importance. As Bisson J.A. noted in the Court of Appeal judgment, there would have been no necessity to mention the free exercise of religion and customs in a document the effects of which were only to last for a few days. Such a guarantee would definitely have been more natural in a treaty where "the word of the white man" is given. . . .

As this Court recently noted in *R*. v. *Horse*, [1988] 1 S.C.R. 187 at 201, [1988] 2 C.N.L.R. 112 at 124, extrinsic evidence is not to be used as an aid to interpreting a treaty in the absence of ambiguity or where the result would be to alter its terms by adding words to or subtracting words from the written agreement. This rule also applies in determining the legal nature of a document relating to the Indians. However, a more flexible approach is necessary as the question of the existence of a treaty within the meaning of s. 88 of *Indian Act* is generally closely bound up with the circumstances existing when the document was prepared (*White and Bob*, supra, at pp. 648–49, and *Simon*, supra, at pp. 409–10 [p. 173–74 C.N.L.R.]). In any case, the wording alone will not suffice to determine the legal nature of the document before the Court. On the one hand, we have before us a document the form of which and some of whose subject-matter suggest that it is not a treaty, and on the other, we find it to contain protection of fundamental rights which supports the opposite conclusion. The ambiguity arising from this document thus means that the Court must look at extrinsic evidence to determine it legal nature. . . .

[W]e can conclude from the historical documents that both Great Britain and France felt that the Indian nations had sufficient independence and played a large enough role in North America for it to be good policy to maintain relations with them very close to those maintained between sovereign nations.

The mother countries did everything in their power to secure the alliance of each Indian nation and to encourage nations allied with the enemy to change sides. When these efforts met with success, they were incorporated in treaties of alliance or neutrality. This clearly indicates that the Indian nations were regarded in their relations with the European nations which occupied North America as independent nations. The papers of Sir William Johnson (*The Papers of Sir William Johnson*, 14 vol.), who was in charge of Indian affairs in British North America, demonstrate the recognition by Great Britain that nation-to-nation relations had to be conducted with the North American Indians. As an example, I cite an extract from a speech by Sir Johnson at the Onondaga Conference held in April 1748, attended by the Five nations:

> Brethern of the five Nations I will begin upon a thing of a long standing, our first *Brothership*. My Reason for it is, I think: there are several among you who seem to forget it; It may seem strange to you how I a *Foreigner* should know this, But I tell you I found out some of the old Writings of our Forefathers which was thought to have been lost and in this old valuable Record I find, that our first *Friendship* Commenced at the Arrival of the first great Canoe or Vessel at Albany . . . [Emphasis added.]
> (*The Papers of Sir William Johnson*, vol. 1, 1921, at p. 157)

As the Chief Justice of the United States Supreme Court said in 1832 in *Worcester* v. *State of Georgia*, 31 U.S. (6 Pet.) 515 (1832), at pp. 548–49, about British policy towards the Indians in the mid-eighteenth century:

> Such was the policy of Great Britain towards the Indian nations inhabiting the territory from which she excluded all other Europeans; such her claims, and such her practical exposition of the charters she had granted: *she considered them as nations capable of maintaining the relations of peace and war: of governing themselves, under her protection: and she made treaties with them, the obligation of which she acknowledged.* [Emphasis added.]

Further, both the French and the English recognized the critical importance of alliances with the Indians, or at least their neutrality, in determining the outcome of the war between them and the security of the North American colonies.

Following the crushing defeats of the English by the French in 1755, the English realized that control of North America could not be acquired without the co-operation of the Indians. Accordingly, from then on they made efforts to ally themselves with as many Indian nations as possible. The French, who had long realized the strategic role of the Indians in the success of any war effort, also did everything they could to secure their alliance or maintain alliances already established (Jack Stagg, *Anglo-Indian Relations in North America to 1763* (1981); "Mr. Nelson's Memorial about the State of the Northern Colonies in America," September 24, 1696, reproduced in O'Callaghan ed., *Documents relative to the Colonial History of New York* (1856), vol. VII, at p. 206; "Letter from Sir William Johnson to William Pitt," October 24, 1760, in *The Papers of Sir William Johnson*, vol. III, 1921 at pp. 269 et seq.; "Mémoire de Bougainville sur l'artillerie du Canada," January 11, 1759, in *Rapport de l'archiviste de la Province de Québec pour* 1923–1924 (1924), at p. 58; *Journal du Marquis de Montcalm durant ses campagnes en Canada de 1756 (1759* (1895), at p. 428).

England also wished to secure the friendship of the Indian nations by treating them with generosity and respect for fear that the safety and development of the colonies and their inhabitants would be compromised by Indians with feelings of hostility. One of the extracts from Knox's work which I cited above reports that the Canadians and the French soldiers who surrendered asked to be protected from Indians on the way back to their parishes. Another passage from Knox, also cited above, relates that the Canadians were terrified at the idea of seeing Sir William Johnson's Indians coming among them. This proves that in the minds of the local population the Indians represented a real and disturbing threat. The fact that England was also aware of the danger the colonies and their inhabitants might run if the Indians withdrew their co-operation is echoed in the following documents: "Letter from Sir William Johnson to the lords of Trade," November 13, 1763, reproduced in O'Callaghan ed., *op. cit.*, at pp. 574, 579 and 580; "Letter from Sir William Johnson to William Pitt," October 24, 1760, in *The Papers of Sir William Johnson*, vol. III at pp. 270 and 274; Ratelle, *Contexte historique de la localisation des Attikameks et des Montagnais de 1760 (nos jours* (1987); "Letter from Amherst to Sir William Johnson," August 30,1760, in *The Papers of Sir William Johnson*, vol. X, 1951, at p. 177; "Instructions from George H to Amherst," September 18,

1758, National Archives of Canada (MG 18 L 4 File 0 20/8); C. Colden, *The History of the Five Indian Nations of Canada* (1747), at p. 180; Stagg, op. cit., at pp. 166–67; and by analogy Murray, *Journal of the Siege of Quebec*, supra, entry of December 31, 1759, at pp. 15–16.

This "generous" policy which the British chose to adopt also found expression in other areas. The British Crown recognized that the Indians had certain ownership rights over their land, it sought to establish trade with them which would rise above the level of exploitation and give them a fair return. It also allowed them autonomy in their internal affairs, intervening in this area as little as possible.

Whatever the similarities between a document recording the laying down of arms by French soldiers or Canadians and the document at issue, the analogy does not go so far as to preclude the conclusion that the document was nonetheless a treaty.

Such a document could not be regarded as a treaty so far as the French and the Canadians were concerned because under international law they had no authority to sign such a document: they were governed by a European nation which alone was able to represent them in dealings with other European nations for the signature of treaties affecting them. The colonial powers recognized that the Indians had the capacity to sign treaties directly with the European nations occupying North American territory. The *sui generis* situation in which the Indians were placed had forced the European mother countries to acknowledge that they had sufficient autonomy for the valid creation of solemn agreements which were called "treaties," regardless of the strict meaning given to that word then and now by international law. The question of the competence of the Hurons and of the French or the Canadians is essential to the question of whether a treaty exists. The question of capacity has to be examined from a fundamentally different viewpoint and in accordance with different principles for each of these groups. Thus, I reject the argument that the legal nature of the document at issue must necessarily be interpreted in the same way as the capitulations of the French and the Canadians. The historical context which I have briefly reviewed even supports the proposition that both the British and the Hurons could have intended to enter into a treaty on September 5, 1760. I rely, in particular, on Great Britain's stated wish to form alliances with as many Indians as possible and on the demoralizing effect for the French, the Canadians and their allies which would result from the loss of this long-standing Indian ally whose allegiance to the French cause had until then been very seldom shaken.

. . .

Lastly, the Court was asked to consider the subsequent conduct of the parties as extrinsic evidence of their intent to enter into a treaty. I do not think this is necessary,since the general historical context of the time and the events closely surrounding the document at issue have persuaded me that the document of September 5, 1760 is a treaty within the meaning of s. 88 of the *Indian Act*. The fact that the document has allegedly not been used in the courts or other institutions of our society does not establish that it is not a treaty. Non-use may very well be explained by observance of the rights contained in the document or mere oversight. Moreover, the subsequent conduct which is most indicative of the parties' intent is undoubtedly that which most closely followed the conclusion of the document. Eleven days after it was concluded, at the conference to which I have just referred, the parties gave a clear indication that they had intended to conclude a treaty.

I am therefore of the view that the document of September 5, 1760 is a treaty within the meaning of s. 88 of the *Indian Act*. At this point, the appellant raises two arguments against its application to the present case. First, he argues that the treaty has been extinguished. In the event that it has not been, he argues that the treaty is not such as to render ss. 9 and 37 of the *Regulation respecting the Parc de la Jacques-Cartier* inoperative. Let us first consider whether on May 29,1982, the date on which the respondents engaged in the activities which are the subject of the charges, the treaty still had any legal effects. . . .

Neither the documents nor the legislative and administrative history to which the appellant referred the Court contain any express statement that the treaty of September 5, 1760 has been extinguished. Even assuming that a treaty can be extinguished implicitly, a point on which I express no opinion here, the appellant was not able in my view to meet the criterion stated in *Simon* regarding the quality of evidence that would be required in any case to support a conclusion that the treaty had been extinguished. That case clearly established that the onus is on the party arguing that the treaty has terminated to show the circumstances and events indicating it has been extinguished. This burden can only be discharged by strict proof, as the Chief Justice said at pp. 405–6 [p. 170 C.N.L.R.]:

> Given the serious and far-reaching consequences of a finding that a treaty right has been extinguished, it seems appropriate to demand strict proof of the fact of extinguishment in each case where the issue arises.

The appellant did not submit any persuasive evidence of extinguishment of the treaty. He argues, first, that the treaty had become obsolete because the *Act of Capitulation of Montreal* replaced all other acts of capitulation, thereby extinguishing them. This argument is based on article 50 of the *Act of Capitulation,* which reads as follows:

> The present capitulation shall be inviolably executed in all its articles, and bona fide, on both sides, notwithstanding any infraction, and any other pretence, with regard to the *preceding capitulations*, and without making use of reprisals. [Emphasis added.]

As I have concluded that this is a peace treaty and not a capitulation, art. 50 has no application in this case, so far as extinguishment of the treaty of September 5 is concerned. That article was designed to ensure that the signatories would comply with the *Act of Capitulation,* in spite of the existence of reasons for retaliation which the parties might have had as the result of breaches of an earlier act of capitulation. Article 50 can only apply to preceding acts signed on behalf of France, such as the *Act of Capitulation of Québec* in late 1759. I see nothing here to support the conclusion that this article was also intended to extinguish a treaty between an Indian nation and the British.

The appellant also cites art. 40 of the *Act of Capitulation of Montreal,* which provides that:

> *The Savages or Indian allies* of his most Christian Majesty, shall be maintained in the

Lands they inhabit, if they chuse to remain there; they shall not be molested on any pretence whatsoever, for having carried arms, and served his most Christian Majesty.They shall have, as well as the French, liberty of religion, and shall keep their missionaries. [Emphasis added]

France could not have claimed to represent the Hurons at the time the *Act of Capitulation* was made, since the latter had abandoned their alliance with the French some days before. As they were no longer allies of the French, this article does not apply to them. In my opinion, the article can only be interpreted as a condition on which the French agreed to capitulate. Though the Indian allies of the French were its beneficiaries, it was fundamentally an agreement between the French and the British which in no way prevented independent agreements between the British and the Indian nations, whether allies of the French or of the British, being concluded or continuing to exist. Further, I think it is clear that the purpose of art. 40 was to assure the Indians of certain rights, not to extinguish existing rights.

It would be contrary to the general principles of law for an agreement concluded between the English and the French to extinguish a treaty concluded between the English and the Hurons. It must be remembered that a treaty is a solemn agreement between the Crown and the Indians, an agreement the nature of which is sacred: *Simon*, supra, at p. 410 [p. 173–74 C.N.L.R.], and *White and Bob*, supra, at p. 649. The very definition of a treaty thus makes it impossible to avoid the conclusion that a treaty cannot be extinguished without the consent of the Indians concerned. Since the Hurons had the capacity to enter into a treaty with the British, therefore, they must be the only ones who could give the necessary consent to its extinguishment.

The same reasoning applies to the appellant's argument that the Treaty of Paris of February 10, 1763 between France and England terminated the treaty of September 5, 1760 between the Hurons and the English. England and France could not validly agree to extinguish a treaty between the Hurons and the English, nor could France claim to represent the Hurons regarding the extinguishment of a treaty the Hurons had themselves concluded with the British Crown.

The appellant then argued that it follows that the Royal Proclamation of October 7, 1763 extinguished the rights arising out of the treaty of September 5, 1760, because it did not confirm them. I cannot accept such a proposition: the silence of the Royal Proclamation regarding the treaty at issue cannot be interpreted as extinguishing it. The purpose of the Proclamation was first and foremost to organize, geographically and politically, the territory of the new American colonies, namely Quebec, East Florida, West Florida and Grenada, and to distribute their possession and use. It also granted certain important rights to the native peoples and was regarded by many as a kind of charter of rights for the Indians: *White and Bob*, supra, at p. 636; *Calder* v. *Attorney-General of British Columbia*, [1973] S.C.R 313 at 395, (Hall J., dissenting); *R.* v. *Secretary of State for Foreign and Commonwealth Affairs*, [1982] 2 All E.R 118 at 124–25, [1981] 4 C.N.L.R. 86 at 91 (C.A.) (Lord Denning). The very wording of the Royal Proclamation clearly shows that its objective, so far as the Indians were concerned, was to provide a solution to the problems created by the greed which hitherto some of the English had all too often demonstrated in buying up Indian land at low prices. The situation was causing dangerous trouble among the Indians and the Royal Proclamation was meant to remedy this:

And whereas it is just and reasonable, and essential to our Interest, and the Security of our Colonies, that the several Nations or Tribes of Indians with whom We are connected, and who live under our Protection, should not be molested or disturbed in the Possession of such Parts of Our Dominions and Territories as, not having been ceded to or purchased by Us, are reserved to them, or any of them, as their Hunting Grounds.—— We do therefore, with the Advice of our Privy Council, declare it to be our Royal Will and Pleasure, that no Governor or Commander in Chief in any of our Colonies of Quebec, East Florida or West Florida, do presume, upon any Pretence whatever to grant, Warrant of Survey or pass any Patents for Lands beyond the Bounds of their respective Governments, as described in their Commissions. . . .

And We do further declare it to be our Royal Will and Pleasure for the present as aforesaid, to reserve under our Sovereignty, Protection, and Dominion, for the use of the said Indians, all the lands and Territories not included within the Limits of Our said Three new Governments, or within the Limits of the Territory granted to the Hudson's Bay Company, as also all the Lands and Territories lying to the Westward of the Sources of the Rivers which fall into the Sea from the West and North West as aforesaid.

I see nothing in these passages which can be interpreted as an intention on the part of the British Crown to extinguish the treaty of September 5. The Proclamation confers rights on the Indians without necessarily thereby extinguishing any other right conferred on them by the British Crown under a treaty.

Legislative and administrative history also provides no basis for concluding that the treaty was extinguished. In 1853, 9,600 acres of land located outside the territory at issue were ceded to the Hurons by the Government of Lower Canada. These lands were within the boundaries of the lands frequented by the Hurons when the treaty of September 5 was concluded. In 1903 the Hurons again ceded these 9,600 acres, without reserving the rights that had been granted to them under the treaty of September 5. The Attorney General of Quebec considers that by making this cession without reservation, the Hurons indicated beyond all doubt that this document was not a source of rights so far as they were concerned. This argument cannot stand. Assuming that the 9,600 acres ceded were initially the subject of the treaty, the absence of any reservation in the deed ceding this territory clearly cannot be interpreted as a waiver of the benefits of the treaty in the territory which was not the subject of the cession, whatever the effect of the absence of such a reservation may be with respect to the territory ceded.

The appellant further argues that by adopting the *Act to establish the Laurentides National Park*, S.Q. 1895, 58 Vict., c. 22, and by making the territory in question a park, the Quebec legislator clearly expressed his intention to prohibit the carrying on of certain activities in this territory, whether or not such activities are protected by an Indian's treaty.

Section 88 of the *Indian Act* is designed specifically to protect the Indians from provincial legislation that might attempt to deprive them of rights protected by a treaty. A legislated change in the use of the territory thus does not extinguish rights otherwise protected by treaty. If the treaty gives the Hurons the right to carry on their customs and religion in the territory of Jacques-Cartier park, the existence of a provincial statute and subordinate legislation will not ordinarily affect that right.

Finally, the appellant argues that non-use of the treaty over a long period of time may extinguish its effect. He cites no authority for this. I do not think that this argument carries much weight: a solemn agreement cannot lose its validity merely because it has not been invoked to, which in any case is disputed by the respondents, who maintain that it was relied on in a seigneurial claim in 1824. Such a proposition would mean that a treaty could be extinguished merely because it had not been relied on in litigation, which is untenable.

In view of the liberal and generous approach that must be adopted towards Indians rights and the evidence in the record, I cannot conclude that the treaty of September 5 no longer had any legal effect on May 29, 1982.

The question that arises at this point is as to whether the treaty is capable of rendering ss. 9 and 37 of the Regulations inoperative. To answer this it will now be necessary to consider the territorial scope of the rights guaranteed by the treaty, since the appellant recognizes that the activities with which the respondents are charged are customary or religious in nature. . . .

Accordingly, I conclude that in view of the absence of any express mention of the territorial scope of the treaty, it has to be assumed that the parties to the treaty of September 5 intended to reconcile the Hurons' need to protect the exercise of their customs and the desire of the British conquerors to expand. Protecting the exercise of the customs in all parts of the territory frequented when it is not incompatible with its occupancy is in my opinion the most reasonable way of reconciling the competing interests. This, is my view, is the definition of the common intent of the parties which best reflects the actual intent of the Hurons and of Murray on September 5, 1760. Defining the common intent of the parties on the question of territory in this way makes it possible to give full effect to the spirit of conciliation, while respecting the practical requirements of the British. This gave the English the necessary flexibility to be able to respond in due course to the increasing need to use Canada's resources, in the event that Canada remained under British sovereignty. The Hurons, for their part, were protecting their customs wherever their exercise would not be prejudicial to the use to which the territory concerned would be put. The Hurons could not reasonably expect that the use would forever remain what it was in 1760. Before the treaty was signed, they had carried on their customs in accordance with restrictions already imposed by an occupancy incompatible with such exercise. The Hurons were only asking to be permitted to continue to carry on their customs on the lands frequented to the extent that those customs did not interfere with enjoyment of the lands by their occupier. I readily accept that the Hurons were probably not aware of the legal consequences, and in particular of the right to occupy to the exclusion of others, which the main European legal systems attached to the concept of private ownership. Nonetheless I cannot believe that the Hurons ever believed that the treaty gave them the right to cut down trees in the garden of a house as part of their right to carry on their customs.

Jacques-Cartier park falls into the category of land occupied by the Crown, since the province has set it aside for a specific use. What is important is not so much that the province has legislated with respect to this territory but that it is using it, is in fact occupying the space. As occupancy has been established, the question is whether the type of occupancy to which the park is subject is incompatible with the exercise of the activities with which the respondents were charged, as these undoubtedly constitute religious customs or rites. Since, in view of the situation in 1760, we must assume some limitation on the exercise of rights protected by the treaty, it is up to the Crown to prove that its occupancy of the territory cannot be accommodated to reasonable exercise of the Hurons' rights.

The Crown presented evidence on such compatibility but that evidence did not persuade me that exercise of the rites and customs at issue here is incompatible with the occupancy. . . .

For the exercise of rites and customs to be incompatible with the occupancy of the park by the Crown, it must not only be contrary to the purpose underlying that occupancy, it must prevent the realization of that purpose. First, we are dealing with Crown lands, lands which are held for the benefit of the community. Exclusive use is not an essential aspect of public ownership. Second, I do not think that the activities described seriously compromise the Crown's objectives in occupying the park. Neither the representative nature of the natural region where the park is located nor the exceptional nature of this natural site are threatened by the collecting of a few plants, the setting up of a tent using a few branches picked up in the area or the making of a fire according to the rules dictated by caution to avoid fires. These activities also present no obstacle to cross-country recreation. I therefore conclude that it has not been established that occupancy of the territory of Jacques-Cartier park is incompatible with the exercise of Huron rites and customs with which the respondents are charged. . . .

For all these reasons, I would dismiss the appeal with costs.

I would dispose of the constitutional questions stated by the Chief Justice as follows:

1. Does the following document, signed by General Murray on 5 September 1760, constitute a treaty within the meaning of s. 88 of the *Indian Act* (R.S.C. 1970, c. 1–6)? . . .
   Answer: Yes.

2. If the answer to question 1 is in the affirmative, was the "treaty" still operative on 29 May 1982, at the time when the alleged offences were committed?
   Answer: Yes.

3. If the answer to questions 1 and 2 are in the affirmative, are the terms of the document of such a nature as to make ss. 9 and 37 of the *Regulation respecting the Parc de la Jacques-Cartier* (Order in Council 3108–81, *Gazette officielle du Québec*, Part II, November 25, 1981, pp. 3518 et seq.) made under the *Parks Act* (R.S.Q., c. P–9) unenforceable in respect of the respondents?
   Answer: Yes.

7. **R. v. *Horseman*, [1990] 3 C.N.L.R. 95 (S.C.C.). Dickson C.J., Lamer, Wilson, La Forest, L'Heureux-Dubé, Gonthier, and Cory JJ., May 3, 1990**

Horseman affirmed that the onus of proving extinguishment (implicit or explicit) of a treaty right rests with the Crown and that ambiguities in treaties must be resolved in favour of the Indians. Although the hunting rights protected by Treaty No. 8 included hunting for commercial purposes, these rights are not absolute. Rather they are to be exercised subject to such laws as are necessary to protect wildlife. The federal government had the unilateral authority to modify and restrict treaty hunting rights to food hunting only, as it did when it passed the *Natural Resources Transfer Agreements (NRTA)*. Thus, although the commercial right to hunt had existed under Treaty No. 8, it was extinguished by the Alberta NRTA, *1930*, S.C. 1930, c. 3. Wilson J.'s dissent is also included in the excerpt. Note she concludes that provincial regulations apply to Treaty No. 8 only to the extent that Treaty No. 8 Indians are engaged in commercial sport or hunting. Treaty No. 8 hunting rights, she states, were not extinguished by the Alberta NRTA.

CORY J. (LAMER, LA FOREST and GONTHIER JJ., concurring):—At issue on this appeal is whether the provisions of s. 42 and s. 1(s) of the *Wildlife Act,* R.S.A. 1980, c. W–9, apply to the appellant, whose forebears were members of one of the Indian bands party to Treaty 8 signed in 1899 which guaranteed substantive hunting rights to certain Indian people. . . .

The sole defence raised on behalf of Horseman was that the *Wildlife Act* did not apply to him and that he was within his Treaty 8 rights when he sold the bear hide. Nothing is to turn on the killing of the bear in self-defence. Nor is it argued that Horseman was induced into a mistake of the law by the words of an official of the government. Rather, it is the appellant's position that he can, at any time, on Crown lands or on lands to which Indians have access, kill a grizzly bear for food. Further, it is said that he can sell the hide of any grizzly bear he kills in order to buy food. . . .

APPLICABLE LEGISLATION
Treaty 8, 1899:

> And Her Majesty the Queen HEREBY AGREES with the said Indians that they shall have right to pursue their usual vocations of hunting, trapping and fishing throughout the tract surrendered as heretofore described, subject to such regulations as may from time to time be made by the Government of the country, acting under the authority of Her Majesty, and saving and excepting such tracts as may be required or taken up from time to time for settlement, mining, lumbering, trading or other purpose.

Constitution Act, 1930

> 1. The agreements set out in the Schedule to this Act are hereby confirmed and shall have the force of law notwithstanding anything in the Constitution Act, 1867, or any Act amending the same, or any Act of the Parliament of Canada, or in any Order in Council or terms or conditions of union made or approved under any such Act as aforesaid.

Natural Resources Transfer Agreement, 1930 (Alberta):

> 12. In Order to secure to the Indians of the Province the continuance of the supply of game and fish for their support and subsistence, Canada agrees that the laws respecting game in force in the Province from time to time shall apply to the Indians within the boundaries thereof, provided, however, that the said Indians shall have the right, which the Province hereby assures to them, of hunting, trapping, and fishing game and fish

for food at all seasons of the year on all unoccupied Crown lands and on any other lands to which the said Indians may have a right of access.

Wildlife Act, R.S.A. 1980, c. W–9:

42. No person shall traffic in any wildlife except as is expressly permitted by this Act or by the regulations.

1(s) "traffic" means any single act of selling, offering for sale, buying, bartering, soliciting or trading; . . .

I am in complete agreement with the finding of the trial judge that the original treaty right clearly included hunting for purposes of commerce. The next question that must be resolved is whether or not that right was in any way limited or affected by the Transfer Agreement of 1930.

THE EFFECT OF THE 1930 TRANSFER AGREEMENT
At the outset two established principles must be borne in mind. First, the onus of proving either express or implicit extinguishment lies upon the Crown. See *Simon* v. *The Queen*, [1985] 2 S.C.R. 387, [1986] 1 C.N.L.R. 153; *Calder* v. *Attorney-General of British Columbia*, [1973] S.C.R. 313. Secondly, any ambiguities in the wording of the treaty or document must be resolved in favour of the native people. This was expressed by Dickson J., as he then was, speaking for the Court in *Nowegijick* v. *The Queen*, [1983] 1 S C.R. 29 at 36, [1983] 2 C.N.L.R. 89 at 94, in these words:

. . . treaties and statutes relating to Indians should be liberally construed and doubtful expressions resolved in favour of the Indians. . . .

[P]ara. 12 of the 1930 Transfer Agreement was carefully considered and interpreted by Chief Justice Dickson in the three recent cases of *Frank* v. *The Queen*, [1978] 1 S.C.R. 95; *R.* v. *Sutherland*, [1980] 2 S.C.R. 451; and *Moosehunter* v. *The Queen*, [1981] 1 S.C.R. 282. These cases dealt with the analogous problems arising from the Transfer Agreements with Manitoba and Saskatchewan which were worded in precisely the same way as the Transfer Agreement with Alberta under consideration in this case. These reasons constitute the carefully considered recent opinion of this Court. They are just as persuasive today as they were when they were released. Nothing in the appellant's submission would lead me to vary in any way the reasons so well and clearly expressed in those cases.

It is also clear that the Transfer Agreements were meant to modify the division of powers originally set out in the *Constitution Act, 1867* (formerly the *British North America Act, 1867*). Section 1 of the *Constitution Act, 1930* is unambiguous in this regard. "The agreements. . . shall have the force of law notwithstanding anything in the Constitution Act, 1867. . . "

In addition, there was in fact a *quid pro quo* granted by the Crown for the reduction in the hunting right. Although the Agreement did take away the right to hunt commercially, the nature of the right to hunt for food was substantially enlarged. The geographical areas in which the Indian people could hunt was widely extended. Further, the means employed by them in hunting for their food was placed beyond the reach of provincial governments. For example, they may hunt deer with night lights and with dogs, methods which are or may be prohibited for others. Nor are the Indians subject to seasonal limitations as are all other hunters. That is to say, they can hunt ducks and geese in the spring as well as the fall, just as they may hunt deer at any time of the year. Indians are not limited with regard to the type of game they may kill. That is to say, while others may be restricted as to the species or sex of the game they may kill, the Indians may kill for food both does and bucks; cock pheasants and hen pheasants; drakes and hen ducks. It can be seen that the *quid pro quo* was substantial. Both the area of hunting and the way in which the hunting could be conducted was extended and removed from the jurisdiction of provincial governments.

The true effect of para. 12 of the Agreement was recognized by Laskin J., as he then was, in *Cardinal* v. *A.-G. Alta.,* [1974] S.C.R. 695 at p. 722, where he wrote:

> [Section 12] is concerned rather with Indians as such, and with guaranteeing to them a continuing right to hunt, trap and fish for food regardless of provincial game laws which would otherwise confine Indians in parts of the Province that are under provincial administration. *Although inelegantly expressed s. 12 does not expand Provincial legislative power but contracts it.* Indians are to have the right to take game and fish for food from all unoccupied Crown lands (these would certainly not include Reserves) and from all other lands to which they may have a right of access. There is hence, by virtue of the sanction of the *British North America Act, 1930*, a limitation upon provincial authority regardless of whether or not Parliament legislates. [Emphasis added.]

This effect of para. 12 of the Agreement was also recognized by Dickson J., as he then was, in *Myran* v. *The Queen*, [1976] 2 S.C.R. 137 at 141:

> I think it is clear from *Prince and Myron* that an Indian of the Province is free to hunt or trap game in such numbers, at such times of the year, by such means or methods and with such contrivances, as he may wish, provided he is doing so in order to obtain food for his own use and on unoccupied Crown lands or other lands to which he may have a right of access.

It is thus apparent that although the Transfer Agreement modified the treaty rights as to hunting, there was a very real *quid pro quo* which extended the native rights to hunt for food. In addition, although it might well be politically and morally unacceptable in today's climate to take such a step as that set out in the 1930 Agreement without consultation with and concurrence of the native peoples affected, nonetheless the power of the federal government to unilaterally make such a modification is unquestioned and has not been challenged in this case.

Further, it must be remembered that Treaty 8 itself did not grant an unfettered right to hunt. That right was to be exercised "subject to such regulations as may from time to time be made by the Government of the country." This provision is clearly in line with the original position of the Commissioners who were bargaining with the Indians. The Commissioners specifically observed that the right of the Indians to hunt, trap and fish as they always had done would continue with the proviso that these rights would have to be exercised subject to such laws as were necessary to protect the fish and fur bearing animals on which the Indians depended for their sustenance and livelihood. . . .

In summary, the hunting rights granted by the 1899 Treaty were not unlimited. Rather they were subject to governmental regulation. The 1930 Agreement widened the hunting territory and the means by which the Indians could hunt for food thus providing a real *quid pro quo* for the reduction in the right to hunt for purposes of commerce granted by the Treaty of 1899. The right of the federal government to act unilaterally in that manner is unquestioned. I therefore conclude that the 1930 Transfer Agreement did alter the nature of the hunting rights originally guaranteed by Treaty 8.

SECTION 42 OF THE WILDLIFE ACT

At the outset it must be recognized that the *Wildlife Act* is a provincial law of general application affecting Indians not *qua* Indians but rather as inhabitants of the province. It follows that the Act can be applicable to Indians pursuant to the provisions of s. 88 of the *Indian Act* so long as it does not conflict with a treaty right. It has been seen that the Treaty 8 hunting rights have been limited by the provisions of the 1930 Transfer Agreement to the right to hunt for food, that is to say, for sustenance for the individual Indian or the Indian's family. In the case at bar the sale of the bear hide was part of a "multi-stage process" whereby the product was sold to obtain funds for purposes which might include purchasing food for nourishment. The courts below correctly found that the sale of the bear hide constituted a hunting activity that had ceased to be that of hunting "for food" but rather was an act of commerce. As a result it was no longer a right protected by Treaty 8, as amended by the 1930 Transfer Agreement. Thus the application of s. 42 to Indians who are hunting for commercial purposes is not precluded by s. 88 of the *Indian Act*.

The fact that a grizzly bear was killed by the appellant in self-defence must engender admiration and sympathy, but it is unfortunately not relevant to a consideration of whether there has been a breach of s. 42 of the *Wildlife Act*. Obviously if it were permissible to traffic in hides of grizzly bears that were killed in self-defence, then the numbers of bears slain in self-defence could be expected to increase dramatically. Unfortunate as it may be in this case, the prohibition against trafficking in bear hides without a licence cannot admit of any exceptions.

Neither, regrettably, can it be relevant to the breach of the s. 42 that the appellant in fact obtained a grizzly bear hunting permit after he was in the possession of a bear hide. The granting of a permit does not bring a hunter any guarantee of success but only an opportunity to legitimately slay a bear. The evidence presented at trial indicated that the limitations placed upon obtaining a licence and the limited chance of success in a bear hunt resulted in the success rate of between 2 and 4 per cent of the licence holder. This must be an important factor in the management of the bear population. Wildlife administrators must be able to rely on the success ratio and proceed on the assumption that those applying for a permit have not already shot a bear. The success ratio will determine the number of licenses issued in any year. The whole management scheme which is essential to the survival of the grizzly bear would be undermined if a licence were granted to an applicant who had already completed a successful hunt.

As well, s. 42 of the *Wildlife Act* is consistent with the very spirit of Treaty 8 which specified that the right to hunt would still be subject to government regulations. The evidence indicates that there remain only 575 grizzly bears on provincial lands. This population cannot sustain a mortality rate higher than 11 per cent per annum if it is even to maintain its present numbers. The statistics indicate that the population will decline if death resulting from natural causes, legal hunting and poaching (and indications are that levels of poaching match legal takings) reached a total of more than 60 bears in a year. The grizzly bear requires a large range and is particularly sensitive to encroachment on its habitat. This magnificent animal is in a truly precarious position. All Canadians and particularly Indians who have a rich and admirable history and tradition of respect for and harmony with all forms of life, will applaud and support regulations which encourage the bears' survival. Trafficking in bear hides, other than pursuant to the provisions of the *Wildlife Act*, threatens the very existence of the grizzly bear. The bear may snarl defiance and even occasionally launch a desperate attack upon man, but until such time as it masters the operation of firearms, it cannot triumph and must rely on man for protection and indeed for survival. That protection is provided by the *Wildlife Act*, but if it is to succeed it must be strictly enforced.

Section 42 of the *Wildlife Act* is valid legislation enacted by the government with jurisdiction in the field. It reflects a bona fide concern for the preservation of a species. It is a law of general application which does not infringe upon the Treaty 8 hunting rights of Indians as limited by the 1930 Transfer Agreement.

DISPOSITION

In the result, I would dismiss the appeal. The constitutional question posed should be answered as follows:

Question:

Between February 1, 1984 and May 30,1984, was section 42 of the Wildlife Act, R.S.A. 1980, c. W–9, constitutionally applicable to Treaty 8 Indians in virtue of the hunting rights granted to them under the said Treaty? In particular, were the hunting rights granted by Treaty 8 of 1899 extinguished, reduced or modified by paragraph 12 of the Alberta Natural Resources Transfer Agreement, as confirmed by the *Constitution Act, 1930*?

Answer

The answer to both queries framed in the Question should be in the affirmative.

The *Wildlife Act* applied to the appellant and Horseman is guilty of violating s. 42 of the Act. Nonetheless he did not seek out the bear and shot it only in self-defence. The trial judge found that he acted in good faith when he obtained the license to hunt bear. He was in financial difficulties when he sold the hear hide in an isolated transaction. He has provided the means whereby the application of the *Wildlife Act* to Indians was explored. If it were not for statutory requirement of a minimum fine, in the unique circumstances of the case, I would vary the sentence by waiving the payment of the minimum fine. Nevertheless, in light of the circumstances of the case, and the time that has elapsed, I would order a stay of proceedings. There should be no order as to costs.

WILSON J., dissenting (DICKSON C.J. and L'HEUREUX-DUBÉ J., concurring): I have had the advantage of reading the reasons of my colleague Justice Cory and must respectfully disagree with his conclusion that the appellant's conduct is caught by s. 42 of the *Wildlife Act*, R.S.A. 1980, c. W–9.

While my colleague has reviewed the facts of this appeal and the decisions of the lower courts, I believe it is important to emphasize that all parties were agreed and the trial judge so found that Mr. Horseman was legitimately engaged in hunting moose for his own use in the Treaty 8 area when he killed the bear in self-defence. Mr. Horseman did not kill the bear with a view to selling its hide although he was eventually driven to do so a year later in order to feed himself and his family. The sale of the bear hide was an isolated act and not part of any planned commercial activity. None of this is in dispute.

The narrow question before us in this appeal then is whether the isolated sale for food of a bear hide obtained by the appellant fortuitously as the result of an act of self-defence is something that the government of Alberta is entitled to penalize under the *Wildlife Act*. In my view, the answer to this question requires a careful examination of the terms of Treaty 8 and the wording of para. 12, of the Natural Resources Transfer Agreement, 1930 (Alberta) (the "Transfer Agreement"). . . .

The interpretive principles developed in *Nowegijick,* [1983] 1 S.C.R. 29, [1983] 2 C.N.L.R. 89, and *Simon,* [1985] 2 S.C.R. 387, [1986] 1 C.N.L.R. 153, recognize that Indian treaties are *sui generis* (per Dickson C.J. at p. 404 [p. 169 C.N.L.R.] of *Simon*, supra). These treaties were the product of negotiation between very different cultures and the language used in them probably does not reflect, and should not be expected to reflect, with total accuracy each party's understanding of their effect at the time they were entered into. This is why the courts must be especially sensitive to the broader historical context in which such treaties were negotiated. They must be prepared to look at that historical context in order to ensure that they reach a proper understanding of the meaning that particular treaties held for their signatories at the time.

But the interpretive principles set out in *Nowegijick* and *Simon* were developed not only to deal with the unique nature of Indian treaties but also to address a problem identified by Norris J.A. in *R. v. White and Bob* (1964), 50 D.L.R. (2d) 613 at 649 (B.C.C.A.) (aff'd [1965] S.C.R. vi, 52 D.L.R. (2d) 481):

> In view of the argument before us, it is necessary to point out that on numerous occasions in modern days, rights under what were entered into with Indians as solemn engagements, although completed with what would now be considered informality, have been whittled away on the excuse that they do not comply with present day formal requirements and with rules of interpretation applicable to transactions between people who must be taken in the light of advanced civilization to be of equal status.

In other words, to put it simply, Indian treaties must be given the effect the signatories obviously intended them to have at the time they were entered into even if they do not comply with today's formal requirements. Nor should they be undermined by the application of the interpretive rules we apply today to contracts entered into by parties of equal bargaining power.

In my view, the interpretive principles set out in *Nowegijick* and *Simon* are fundamentally sound and have considerable significance for this appeal. Any assessment of the impact of the Transfer Agreement on the rights that Treaty 8 Indians were assured in the treaty would continue to be protected cannot ignore the fact that Treaty 8 embodied a "solemn engagement." Accordingly, when interpreting the Transfer Agreement between the federal and provincial governments we must keep in mind the solemn commitment made to the Treaty 8 Indians by the federal government in 1899. We should not readily assume that the federal government intended to renege on the commitment it had made. Rather we should give it an interpretation, if this is possible on the language, which will implement and be fully consistent with that commitment. It is appropriate, therefore, to begin the analysis of the issues in this appeal with a review of the nature of the "solemn engagement" embodied in Treaty 8. . . .

In my view, it is in light of this historical context, one which did not, from the Indians' perspective, allow for simple distinctions between hunting for domestic use and hunting for commercial purposes and which involved a solemn engagement that Indians would continue to have unlimited access to wildlife, that one must understand the provision in Treaty 8 that reads:

> And Her Majesty the Queen HEREBY AGREES with the said Indians that they shall have *the right to pursue their usual vocations of hunting, trapping and fishing* throughout the tract surrendered as heretofore described, *subject to such regulations as may from time to time be made by the Government of the country*, acting under the authority of Her Majesty, and saving and excepting such tracts as may be required or taken up from time to time for settlement, mining, lumbering, trading or other purposes. [Emphasis added.]

If we are to remain faithful to the interpretive principles set out in *Nowegijick* and *Simon*, then we must not only be careful to understand that the language of Treaty 8 embodied a solemn engagement to Indians in the Treaty 8 area that their livelihood would be respected, but we must also recognize that in referring to potential "regulations" with respect to hunting, trapping and fishing the government of Canada was promising that such regulations would always be designed so as to ensure that the Indians' way of life would continue to be respected. To read Treaty 8 as an agreement that was to enable the government of Canada to regulate hunting, fishing and trapping in any manner that it saw fit, regardless of the impact of the regulations on the "usual vocations" of Treaty 8 Indians, is not credible in light of oral and archival evidence that includes a Commissioners' report stating that a solemn assurance was made that only such laws "as were in the interest of the Indians and were found necessary in Order to protect the fish and fur-bearing animals would be made."

In other words, while the treaty was obviously intended to enable the government of Canada to pass regulations with respect to hunting, fishing and trapping, it becomes clear when one places the treaty in its historical context that the government of Canada committed itself to regulate hunting in a manner that would respect the lifestyle of the Indians and the way in which they had traditionally pursued their livelihood. Because any regulations concerning hunting and fishing were to be "in the interest" of the Indians, and because the Indians were promised that they would he free to hunt, fish and trap "after the treaty as they would be if they never entered into it," such regulations had to be designed to preserve an environment in which the Indians could continue to hunt, fish and trap as they had always done.

NATURAL RESOURCES TRANSFER AGREEMENT

When the province of Alberta was created in 1905 its government did not receive the power to control natural resources in the province. Control over natural resources in Alberta remained in the hands of the federal government until 1930 when Canada and Alberta entered into the Transfer Agreement which placed Alberta on the same footing as the other provinces. Mindful of the government of Canada's responsibilities under a series of numbered treaties with Indians, the parties to the Transfer Agreement inserted a paragraph dealing with the Indians' treaty rights to hunt, fish and trap. Paragraph 12 of the Transfer Agreement stated:

> *In order to secure to the Indians of the Province the continuance of the supply of game and fish for their support and subsistence,* Canada agrees that the laws respecting game in force in the Province from time to time shall apply to the Indians within the boundaries thereof, provided, however, that *the said Indians shall have the right, which the Province hereby assures to them, of hunting, trapping, and fishing game and fish for food* at all seasons of the year on all unoccupied Crown lands and on any other lands to which the said Indians may have a right of access. [Emphasis added.] . . .

The proposition that para. 12 of the Transfer Agreement was formulated with a view to protecting Treaty 8 rights and that it is therefore quite proper to look at Treaty 8 in order to understand the meaning of para. 12 of the Transfer Agreement has been emphasized on a number of occasions. For example, in *R.* v. *Smith*, [1935] 3 D.L.R. 703 at 705–6, Turgeon J.A. (Mackenzie J.A. concurring) stated:

> As I have said, it is proper to consult this treaty in order to glean from it whatever may throw some light on the meaning to be given to the words in question. *I would even say that we should endeavour, within the bounds of propriety, to give such meaning to these words as would establish the intention of the Crown and the Legislature to maintain the rights accorded to the Indians by the treaty.* [Emphasis added]

Similarly, in *R.* v. *Strongquill* (1953), 8 W.W.R. (N.S.) 247, (Sask. C.A.) (a case relied upon by this Court in *Frank* v. *The Queen*, [1978] 1 S.C.R. 95 at 100) McNiven J.A. stated at p. 269 [W.W.R.]:

> I have already said that whatever rights with respect to hunting were granted to the Indians by the said treaty were merged in par. 12 of the Natural Resources Agreement, supra. *I have only referred to the treaty for such assistance as its terms may give in interpreting the language used in par. 12 for we must attribute to parliament an intention to fulfil its terms.* It is also a cardinal rule of interpretation that words used in a statute are to be given their common ordinary and generally accepted meaning. *Statutes are to be given a liberal construction so that effect may be given to each Act and every*

part thereof according to its spirit, true intent and meaning. [Emphasis added.]

The view expressed in *Smith* and in *Strongquill* to the effect that one should assume that Parliament intended to live up to its obligations under treaties with the Indians was subsequently approved by this Court in *Prince and Myron* v. *The Queen*, [1964] S.C.R. 81. Hall J. (for the Court) adopted the following passage from *R.* v. *Wesley*, [1932] 2 W.W.R. 337 in which McGillivray J.A. had commented at p. 344:

> I think the intention was that in hunting for sport or for commerce the Indian like the white man should be subject to laws which make for the preservation of game but, in hunting wild animals for the food necessary to his life, the Indian should be placed in a very different position from the white man who, generally speaking, does not hunt for food *and was by the proviso to Sec. 12 reassured of the continued enjoyment of a right which he has enjoyed from time immemorial.* [Emphasis added.]

More recently, in *Frank* v. *The Queen*, supra, this Court reiterated that para. 12 was in part designed to ensure that the rights embodied in Treaty 8 were respected. Dickson J. stated at p. 100:

> It would appear the overall purpose of para. 12 of the Natural Resources Transfer Agreement was to effect a merger and consolidation of the treaty rights theretofore enjoyed by the Indians *but of equal importance was the desire to re-state and reassure to the treaty Indians the continued enjoyment of the right to hunt and fish for food.* See *R.* v. *Wesley*: *R.* v. *Smith*: *R.* v. *Strongquill.* [Emphasis added.]

In my view, the decisions in *Smith* and *Wesley*, cases that were decided shortly after the Transfer Agreement came into force, as well as later decisions in cases like *Strongquill* and *Frank*, make clear that, to the extent that it is possible, one should view para. 12 of the Transfer Agreement as an attempt to respect the solemn engagement embodied in Treaty 8, not as an attempt to abrogate or derogate from that treaty. While it is clear that para. 12 of the Transfer Agreement adjusted the areas within which Treaty 8 Indians would thereafter be able to engage in their traditional way of life, given the oral and archival evidence with respect to the negotiation of Treaty 8 and the pivotal nature of the guarantee concerning hunting, fishing and trapping, one should be extremely hesitant about accepting the proposition that para. 12 of the Transfer Agreement was also designed to place serious and invidious restrictions on the range of hunting, fishing and trapping related activities that Treaty 8 Indians could continue to engage in. In so saying I am fully aware that this Court has stated on previous occasions that it is not in a position to question an unambiguous decision on the part of the federal government to modify its treaty obligations: *Sikyea* v. *The Queen*, [1964] S.C.R. 642; *R.* v. *George*, [1966] S.C.R. 267; and *Moosehunter* v. *The Queen*, [1981] 1 S.C.R. 282 at 293, [1981] 1 C.N.L.R. 61 at 68. We must, however, be satisfied that the federal government did make an "unambiguous decision" to renege on its Treaty 8 obligations when it signed the 1930 Transfer Agreement. . . .

In *Moosehunter* v. *The Queen*, supra, a case that involved a treaty Indian who had killed deer in Manitoba, Dickson J. did have occasion to consider the nature of the dividing line created by the term "for food" in somewhat more detail. He observed at p. 285 [pp. 62–63 C.N.L.R.]:

> The reasons or purpose underlying paragraph 12 was to secure to the Indians a supply of game and fish *for their support and subsistence* and clearly to permit hunting, trapping and fishing for food at all seasons of the year on all unoccupied Crown lands and lands to which the Indians had access. The Agreement had the effect of merging and consolidating the treaty rights of the Indians in the area and restricting the power of the province to regulate the Indians' right to hunt for food. *The right of Indians to hunt for sport or commercially could be regulated by provincial game laws but the right to hunt for food could not.* [Emphasis added.]

In my view, the distinction that Dickson J. drew in *Moosehunter* between hunting for "support and subsistence," and hunting for "sport or commercially" is far more consistent with the spirit of Treaty 8 and with the proposition that one should not assume that the legislature intended to abrogate or derogate from Treaty 8 hunting rights than the respondent's submission that in using the term "for food" the legislature intended to restrict Treaty 8 hunting rights to hunting for direct consumption of the product of the hunt. And if we are to give para. 12 the "broad and liberal" construction called for in *Sutherland*, a construction that reflects the principle enunciated in *Nowegijick* and *Simon* that statutes relating to Indians must be given a "fair, large and liberal construction," then we should be prepared to accept that the range of activity encompassed by the term "for food" extends to hunting for "support and subsistence" i.e. hunting not only for direct consumption but also hunting in order to exchange the product of the hunt for other items as was their wont, as opposed to purely commercial or sport hunting.

And, indeed, when one thinks of it this makes excellent sense. The whole emphasis of Treaty 8 was on the preservation of the Indian's traditional way of life. But this surely did not mean that the Indians were to be forever consigned to a diet of meat and fish and were to have no opportunity to share in the advances of modern civilization over the next one hundred years. Of course, the Indians' hunting and fishing rights were to be preserved and protected; the Indians could not have survived otherwise. But this cannot mean that in 1990 they are to be precluded from selling their meat and fish to buy other items necessary for their sustenance and the sustenance of their children. Provided the purpose of their hunting is either to consume the meat or to exchange or sell it in order to support themselves and their families, I fail to see why this is precluded by any common sense interpretation of the words "for food". It will, of course, be a question of fact in each case whether a sale is made for purposes of sustenance or for purely commercial profit.

If we are to be sensitive to Professor Ray's observation that the distinction between hunting for commerce and domestic hunting is not one that can readily be imposed on the Indian hunting practices protected by Treaty 8, and if we are to approach para. 12 as a proviso that was intended to respect the guarantees enshrined in Treaty 8 (which I think we must do if at all possible), then para. 12 must be construed as a provision conferring on the province of Alberta the power to regulate sport hunting and hunting for purely commercial purposes rather than as a provision that was to enable the province to place serious and invidious restrictions on the Indians' right to hunt for "support and subsistence" in the broader sense.

When the phrase "for food" is read in this way para. 12 of the Transfer Agreement remains faithful to the Treaty 8 Commissioners' solemn engagement that the government of Canada would only enact "such laws as to hunting as were in the interest of the Indians and were found necessary in order to protect the fish and fur-bearing animals. ... ." and that Treaty 8 Indians "would be free to hunt and fish after the treaty as they would be if they never entered into it" While Treaty 8 Indians and the government of Canada may not have foreseen in 1899 that limits would one day have to be placed on the extent to which people could engage in commercial and sport hunting, such restrictions are obviously necessary today in order to preserve particular species. Provided such restrictions on commercial and sport hunting are imposed in order to preserve species that might otherwise be endangered, the government would appear to be acting in the interests of the Indians in maintaining the well-being of the environment that is the pre-condition to their ability to pursue their traditional way of life. Such restrictions are entirely consistent with the spirit and language of Treaty 8. What is not consistent with the spirit and language of Treaty 8 is to restrict the ability of the Indians to hunt for "support and subsistence" unless this restriction also is required for the preservation of species threatened with extinction.

In summary, it seems to me that the term hunting "for food" was designed to draw a distinction between traditional hunting practices that the Indians were to be free to pursue and sport hunting or hunting for purely commercial purposes. And if we are to avoid paying mere lip-service to the interpretive principles set out in *Nowegijick* and *Simon*, principles that require us to resolve ambiguities with respect to the language of statutes like the Transfer Agreement in favour of the Indians, then any uncertainties regarding the nature of the boundary between purely commercial or sport hunting and the Indians' traditional hunting practices must be resolved by favouring an interpretation of para. 12 of the Transfer Agreement that gives the province of Alberta the power to regulate commercial and sport hunting but that leaves traditional Indian hunting practices untouched.

My colleague, Cory J., takes a different view. He concludes that para. 12 of the Transfer Agreement was designed to "cut down the scope of Indian hunting rights" and that there was a "*quid pro quo*" granted to the Indians by the Crown for the reduction in hunting rights. Describing this "*quid pro quo*," Cory J. suggests that the "area of hunting and the way in which the hunting could, he conducted was extended and removed from the jurisdiction of provincial governments. " But in my view the historical evidence suggests both that the Indians had been guaranteed the right to hunt for their support and subsistence in the manner that they wished some four decades before the Transfer Agreement was ratified and that it is doubtful whether the provinces were ever in a legitimate constitutional position to regulate that form of hunting prior to the Transfer Agreement. As a result, I have difficulty in accepting my colleague's conclusion that the Transfer Agreement involved some sort of expansion of these hunting rights. Moreover, it seems to me somewhat disingenuous to attempt to justify any unilateral "cutting down of hunting rights" by the use of terminology connoting a reciprocal process in which contracting parties engage in a mutual exchange of promises. Be that as it may, I see no evidence at all that the federal government intended to renege in any way from the solemn engagement embodied in Treaty 8. . . .

I would allow the appeal, set aside the order of the Court of Appeal, and restore the acquittal. I would answer the constitutional question as follows:

Question:

Between February 1, 1984 and May 30, 1984, was section 42 of the *Wildlife Act,* R.S.A. 1980, c. W–9, constitutionally applicable to Treaty 8 Indians in virtue of the hunting rights granted to them under the said Treaty? In particular, were the hunting rights granted by Treaty 8 of 1899 extinguished, reduced or modified by paragraph 12 of the Alberta Natural Resources Transfer Agreement, as confirmed by the *Constitution Act, 1930*?

Answer:

Section 42 of the *Wildlife Act* was applicable to Treaty 8 Indians only to the extent that they were engaged in commercial or sport hunting. The Treaty 8 hunting rights were neither extinguished nor reduced by paragraph 12 of the Alberta Natural Resources Transfer Agreement. The territorial limits within which they could be exercised were, however, modified by paragraph 12.

8. *R.* v. *Badger,* [1996] 2 C.N.L.R. 77 (S.C.C.). Lamer C.J., La Forest, L'Heureux-Dubé, Sopinka, Gonthier, Cory, and Iacobucci JJ., April 3, 1996

> *Badger* is significant in that it represents the culmination of the Supreme Court's deliberations on treaty rights generally and clarifies the nature and status of treaty rights in Canadian law. The decision is concerned with Treaty No. 8 and whether registered Indians possess the right to hunt on privately owned land within the treaty's territory, whether treaty hunting rights were extinguished or modified by the *Natural Resources Transfer Agreement (1930)* (NRTA), and the degree to which legislation requiring hunting licences applies to registered Indians. Although the court held that the treaty right to hunt for food was not extinguished by the NRTA, the right was limited geographically by using the concept of "visible incompatible land use." Although requiring a case-by-case application, this concept means that if privately owned land is occupied or put to a visible use, Indians do not have a right to access. Likewise, if the land is unoccupied and not being put to visible use, Indians will have a right to access the land, pursuant to Treaty No. 8.
>
> The court held that in this case, the requirement of licences is a *prima facie* infringement of treaty rights that must be justified. A new trial was ordered for one of the appellants (to deal with the issue of justification), while the other two appellants' claims were dismissed because they were hunting on occupied land. At paragraph 41, Cory J. provides a useful summary of the principles of interpretation to be used when adjudicating treaty rights' cases. Finally, it should be noted that *Badger* affirms that the *Sparrow* justificatory analysis (used to determine whether government infringement of s. 35(1) rights may be justified) is to be applied in cases concerning treaty rights.

1   SOPINKA J. (LAMER C.J. concurring)—I have had the benefit of reading the reasons for judgment prepared in this appeal by my colleague, Justice Cory, and I am in agreement with his disposition of the appeal and with his reasons with the exception of his exposition of the relationship between Treaty No. 8, the *Natural*

Resources Transfer Agreement, 1930 (*Constitution Act, 1930,* Schedule 2) (*NRTA*), and s. 35 of the *Constitution Act, 1982.*

2   In my view, the rights of Indians to hunt for food provided in Treaty No. 8 were merged in the *NRTA* which is the sole source of those rights. While I agree that the impugned provision of the *Wildlife Act,* S.A. 1984, c. W–9.1, infringes the constitutional right of Indians to hunt for food, I disagree that this constitutional right is one covered by s. 35(1) of the *Constitution Act, 1982.* I agree, however, that the constitutional right to hunt for food must be balanced against the right of the province to pass laws for the purpose of conservation and that this balancing may be carried out on the basis of the principles set out in *R.* v. *Sparrow,* [1990] 1 S.C.R. 1075.

3   There is no disagreement that the *NRTA*:
(a) duplicated the right of Indians to hunt for food which was contained in Treaty No. 8;
(b) widely extended the geographical area to include the whole of the province rather than being limited to the tract of land surrendered;
(c) shifted responsibility for passing game laws from the federal government to the provinces;
(d) eliminated the right to hunt for commercial purposes;
(e) is a constitutional document and the Treaty is not, although the Treaty receives constitutional protection by virtue of s. 35(1) of the *Constitution Act, 1982.*

4   In these circumstances, I am of the view that it was clearly the intention of the framers to merge the rights in the Treaty in the *NRTA*. To characterize the *NRTA* as modifying the Treaty is to treat it as an amending document to the Treaty. This clearly was not the intent of the *NRTA*. In enlarging the area in which hunting for food was permitted to extend to the whole of the province, it could not be suggested that the *NRTA* extended the Treaty to all of the province. Rather, the right to hunt for food was extended by the *NRTA* to the whole of the province, including the area covered by the Treaty. An Indian hunting on land outside the Treaty lands could not claim to be covered by the Treaty. If the *NRTA* merely modified the Treaty, an Indian hunting on Treaty lands could claim the right under the Treaty while an Indian hunting in other parts of the province could claim only under the *NRTA*. This would invite bifurcation of the rights of Indians hunting for food in the province.

5   Similarly, the provisions which transferred to the province the power to pass gaming laws for the purpose of conservation could not have been intended simply to amend the Treaty. As an amendment to the Treaty, this provision would have no constitutional force and could not alter the constitutionally entrenched division of powers. It might be suggested that the *NRTA* both amended the Treaty and, as an independent constitutional document, amended the Constitution. If this were the intent, it is difficult to understand why all the terms of the Treaty relating to the right to hunt for food were replicated in *NRTA*. It must have been the intention to merge these rights in the *NRTA* so that they could be balanced with the power of the

provinces to legislate for conservation purposes. In order to achieve a reasonable balance between them, it was important that they both appear in one document having constitutional status.

6   I can suggest no reason why the framers of the *NRTA* would have wanted to maintain any aspects of the Treaty except as an interpretative tool. They surely did not do so in order to allow these rights to be recognized under s. 35(1) of the *Constitution Act, 1982* which appears to be the sole present justification for preserving the Treaty. However, even that justification loses any force when considered in light of the fact that the *NRTA* is itself a constitutional document and recognition under s. 35(1) is unnecessary for the protection of these important Indian rights.

7   From the foregoing, I conclude that it was the intention of the framers of para. 12 of the *NRTA* to effectuate a merger and consolidation of the Treaty rights. This was the view of Dickson J. (as he then was), speaking for the Court, in *Frank* v. *The Queen,* [1978] 1 S.C.R. 95, at p. 100:

> It would appear that the overall purpose of para. 12 of the Natural Resources Transfer Agreement was to effect a merger and consolidation of the treaty rights theretofore enjoyed by the Indians but of equal importance was the desire to re-state and reassure to the treaty Indians the continued enjoyment of the right to hunt and fish for food.

As pointed out, these rights were restated in the *NRTA* and their preservation was assured by being placed in a constitutional instrument.

8   If this was the intention, and I conclude that it was, then the proper characterization of the relationship between the *NRTA* and the Treaty rights is that the sole source for a claim involving the right to hunt for food is the *NRTA*. The Treaty rights have been subsumed in a document of a higher order. The Treaty may be relied on for the purpose of assisting in the interpretation of the *NRTA*, but it has no other legal significance.

9   The fact that the source of the appellants' rights to hunt and fish for sustenance is found within the provisions of the *NRTA* does not alter the analysis that has previously been employed in the interpretation of treaty rights. The key interpretative principles which apply to treaties are first, that any ambiguity in the treaty will be resolved in favour of the Indians and, second, that treaties should be interpreted in a manner that maintains the integrity of the Crown, particularly the Crown's fiduciary obligation toward aboriginal peoples. These principles apply equally to the rights protected by the *NRTA*; the principles arise out of the nature of the relationship between the Crown and aboriginal peoples with the result that, whatever the document in which that relationship has been articulated, the principles should apply to the interpretation of that document. I find support for this reasoning in the prior decisions of this Court concerning the interpretation of the *NRTA*. In *R.* v. *Sutherland,* [1980] 2 S.C.R. 451, for example, this Court specifically stated, at p. 461, that the *NRTA* should be given a "broad and liberal construction", and, at

p. 464, that any ambiguity should be "interpreted so as to resolve any doubts in favour of the Indians". Moreover, this position is compatible with the concept that the *NRTA* constitutes a merger and consolidation of treaty rights, and with the view that it was through the enactment of the *NRTA* that the "federal government attempted to fulfil their treaty obligations" (see *Moosehunter* v. *The Queen,* [1981] 1 S.C.R. 282, at p. 293).

Validity of the provisions of the Wildlife Act

10   In light of my conclusion that the right of Indian persons to hunt for food is constitutional in nature, the issue remaining for determination is whether the provisions of the *Wildlife Act* under which the appellants were convicted are constitutionally permissible. On the bare wording of para. 12 of the *NRTA*, it appears as though such an issue could never arise. The *NRTA* grants legislative power over "gaming" *subject to* the Indians' right to hunt for food, apparently suggesting that the province has no jurisdiction to legislate in relation to those rights. This interpretation arises out of the mandatory language used in para. 12, wherein the legislative power is granted to the province, but qualified by the statement that the power exists "*provided, however,* that the said Indians shall have the right. . . ."

11   The reasoning in *R.* v. *Horseman,* [1990] 1 S.C.R. 901, informs us that such a formalistic interpretation of the language of the *NRTA* is incorrect. At the time the treaties that preceded the *NRTA* were signed, there was already in place legislation enacted for conservation purposes which affected the Indians' rights. Indeed, there existed total bans on the hunting of certain species. As a result, at the time the treaties were signed and, even more so, at the time that the *NRTA* was agreed to by the provinces and the federal government, it would have been clearly understood that the rights of Indians pursuant to either document would be subject to governmental regulation for conservation purposes. The rights protected by the *NRTA* thus cannot be viewed as being constitutional rights of an absolute nature for which governmental regulation is prohibited.

12   How, then, is the governmental regulation permitted by the *NRTA*, and the extent of the protection of the appellants' rights in the face of such regulation, to be assessed? Cory J. has taken the position that the standard against which the validity of the *Wildlife Act* is to be assessed is s. 35(1) of the *Constitution Act, 1982,* and the test set out in *Sparrow, supra.* I am unable to agree with my colleague on this point. Section 35(1) was intended to provide constitutional protection for aboriginal rights and treaty rights that did not enjoy such protection. It cannot have been intended to be redundant and provide constitutional protection for rights that already enjoyed constitutional protection. Moreover, para. 12 of the *NRTA* is a constitutional provision and, as such, s. 35(1) has no direct application to it. Infringements of constitutional rights cannot be remedied by the application of a different constitutional provision. As Estey J. stated in *Reference Re Bill 30, An Act to Amend the Education Act* (Ont.), [1987] 1 S.C.R. 1148, at p. 1207, the *Canadian Charter of Rights and Freedoms* "cannot be interpreted as rendering unconstitutional distinctions that are expressly permitted by the *Constitution Act, 1867*". That case

concerned the application of s. 15 of the *Charter* to s. 93 of the *Constitution Act, 1867*. Although the case is not directly on point with the issues arising in this appeal, in my view, Estey J.'s comment provides support for the position that constitutional provisions enacted later in time are not to be read as impliedly amending the earlier enacted provisions. (See Peter W. Hogg, *Constitutional Law of Canada* (3rd ed. 1992), at p. 1183.) Nor are later provisions of the constitution applicable in terms of the interpretation of earlier provisions. On that reasoning, s. 35(1) is inapplicable to the provision of the NRTA that protects the right of aboriginal persons to hunt for food.

13   That is not to say, however, that the principles underlying the interpretation of s. 35(1) have no relevance to the determination of whether a particular legislative enactment has an acceptable purpose and whether it constitutes an acceptable limitation on the rights granted by the NRTA. There is no method provided in the NRTA whereby government measures that may impinge upon the rights the same document grants to Indians can be scrutinized. It is clear, however, that the NRTA does require a balancing of rights. The right of the province to legislate with respect to conservation must be balanced against the right granted to the Indians to hunt for food. Thus, it falls to the Court to develop a test through which this task can be accomplished. In *Sparrow,* this Court developed principles for balancing the constitutionally protected right to fish for food against the federal government's power to pass laws for conservation. Although the *Sparrow* test was developed in the context of s. 35(1), the basic thrust of the test, to protect aboriginal rights but also to permit governments to legislate for legitimate purposes where the legislation is a justifiable infringement on those protected rights, applies equally well to the regulatory authority granted to the provinces under para. 12 of the NRTA as to federal power to legislate in respect of Indians.

14   In this way, the *Sparrow* test is applied to the NRTA by analogy, with the result that the Court will have a means by which to ensure that the rights in the NRTA are protected, but that provincial governments are also provided with some flexibility in terms of their ability to affect those rights for the purpose of legislating in relation to conservation. As Cory J. points out, the criteria set out in *Sparrow* do not purport to be exhaustive and are to be applied flexibly. In applying them in this context, it is important to bear in mind that what is being justified is the exercise of a power granted to the provinces, which power is made subject to the right to hunt for food. Both are contained in a constitutional document. The application of the *Sparrow* criteria should be consonant with the intention of the framers as to the reconciliation of these competing provisions.

15   I agree with Cory J. that, in the absence of evidence with respect to justification, there must be a new trial and I would dispose of the appeal as suggested by him.

16   The constitutional question and answers are as follows:

> If Treaty 8 confirmed to the Indians of the Treaty 8 Territory the right to hunt throughout the tract surrendered, does the right continue to exist or was it extinguished and

replaced by para. 12 of the *Natural Resources Transfer Agreement, 1930* (*Constitution Act, 1930*, 20–21 George V, c. 26 (U.K.)), and if the right continues to exist, could that right be exercised on the lands in question and, if so, was the right impermissibly infringed upon by s. 26(1) or s. 27(1) of the *Wildlife Act*, S.A. 1984, c. W–9.1, given Treaty 8 and s. 35(1) of the *Constitution Act, 1982*?

17   The right to hunt for food referred to in Treaty No. 8 was merged in the NRTA which is the sole source of the right.

18   Sections 26(1) and 27(1) of the *Wildlife Act* did not infringe the constitutional rights of Mr. Badger or Mr. Kiyawasew to hunt for food.

19   Mr. Ominayak was exercising his constitutional right to hunt for food. Section 26(1) of the *Wildlife Act* is a *prima facie* infringement of his right to hunt for food under NRTA and is invalid unless justified.

20   CORY J. (LA FOREST, L'HEUREUX-DUBÉ, GONTHIER, and IACOBUCCI JJ. concurring):—Three questions must be answered on this appeal. First, do Indians who have status under Treaty No. 8 have the right to hunt for food on privately owned land which lies within the territory surrendered under that Treaty? Secondly, have the hunting rights set out in Treaty No. 8 been extinguished or modified as a result of the provisions of para. 12 of the *Natural Resources Transfer Agreement, 1930* (*Constitution Act, 1930*, Schedule 2)? Thirdly, to what extent, if any, do s. 26(1) and s. 27(1) of the *Wildlife Act*, S.A. 1984, c. W–9.1, apply to the appellants? . . .

21   Each of the three appellants was charged with an offence under the *Wildlife Act.* Their trials and appeals have proceeded together.

22   . . . All three appellants, Cree Indians with status under Treaty No. 8, were hunting for food upon lands falling within the tracts surrendered to Canada by the Treaty.

23   The lands in question were all privately owned. . . .

Relevant Treaty and Statutory Provisions

24   The relevant part of Treaty No. 8, made 21 June 1899, provides:

> And Her Majesty the Queen hereby agrees with the said Indians that they shall have right to pursue their usual vocations of hunting, trapping and fishing throughout the tract surrendered as heretofore described, subject to such regulations as may from time to time be made by the Government of the country, acting under the authority of Her Majesty, and saving and excepting such tracts as may be required or taken up from time to time for settlement, mining, lumbering, trading or other purposes. . . .

32   The *Constitution Act, 1930*, s. 1 provides:

1. The agreements set out in the Schedule to this Act are hereby confirmed and shall have the force of law notwithstanding anything in the Constitution Act, 1867, or any Act amending the same, or any Act of the Parliament of Canada, or in any Order in Council or terms or conditions of union made or approved under any such Act as aforesaid.

33   The *Natural Resources Transfer Agreement, 1930* is the Schedule referred to in s. 1. Paragraph 12 of the NRTA provides:

12. In order to secure to the Indians of the Province the continuance of the supply of game and fish for their support and subsistence, Canada agrees that the laws respecting game in force in the Province from time to time shall apply to the Indians within the boundaries thereof, provided, however, that the said Indians shall have the right, which the Province hereby assures to them, of hunting, trapping and fishing game and fish for food at all seasons of the year on all unoccupied Crown lands and on any other lands to which the said Indians may have a right of access. . . .

35   Sections 26(1) and 27(1) of the *Wildlife Act* provide:

26(1) A person shall not hunt wildlife unless he holds a licence authorizing him, or is authorized by or under a licence, to hunt wildlife of that kind. 27(1) A person shall not hunt wildlife outside an open season or if there is no open season for that wildlife.

Constitutional Question

36   The constitutional question stated by this Court on May 2, 1994 is as follows:

If Treaty 8 confirmed to the Indians of the Treaty 8 Territory the right to hunt throughout the tract surrendered, does the right continue to exist or was it extinguished and replaced by para. 12 of the *Natural Resources Transfer Agreement, 1930 (Constitution Act, 1930,* 20–21 George V, c. 26 (U.K.)), and if the right continues to exist, could that right be exercised on the lands in question and, if so, was the right impermissibly infringed upon by s. 26(1) or s. 27(1) of the *Wildlife Act,* S.A. 1984, c. W–9.1, given Treaty 8 and s. 35(1) of the *Constitution Act, 1982?*

Analysis

37   On this appeal, the extent of the existing right to hunt for food possessed by Indians who are members of bands which were parties to Treaty No. 8 must be determined. The analysis should proceed through three stages. First, it is necessary to decide what effect para. 12 of the NRTA had upon the rights enunciated in Treaty No. 8. After resolving which instrument sets out the right to hunt for food, it is necessary to examine the limitations which are inherent in that right. It must be remembered that, even by the terms of Treaty No. 8, the Indians' right to hunt for food was circumscribed by both geographical limitations and by specific forms of government regulation. Second, consideration must then be given to the question of whether the existing right to hunt for food can be exercised on privately owned land. Third, it is necessary to determine whether the impugned sections of the

provincial *Wildlife Act* come within the specific types of regulation which have, since 1899, limited and defined the scope of the right to hunt for food. If they do, those sections do not infringe upon an existing treaty right and will be constitutional. If not, the sections may constitute an infringement of the Treaty rights guaranteed by Treaty No. 8, as modified by the NRTA. In this case the impugned provisions should be considered in accordance with the principles set out in *R.* v. *Sparrow,* [1990] 1 S.C.R. 1075, to determine whether they constitute a *prima facie* infringement of the Treaty rights as modified, and if so, whether the infringement can be justified. . . .

The Existing Right to Hunt for Food . . .

39   Treaty No. 8 is one of eleven numbered treaties concluded between the federal government and various Indian bands between 1871 and 1923. Their objective was to facilitate the settlement of the West. Treaty No. 8, made on June 21, 1899, involved the surrender of vast tracts of land in what is now northern Alberta, northeastern British Columbia, northwestern Saskatchewan and part of the Northwest Territories. In exchange for the land, the Crown made a number of commitments, for example, to provide the bands with reserves, education, annuities, farm equipment, ammunition, and relief in times of famine or pestilence. However, it is clear that for the Indians the guarantee that hunting, fishing and trapping rights would continue was the essential element which led to their signing the treaties. The report of the Commissioners who negotiated Treaty No. 8 on behalf of the government underscored the importance to the Indians of the right to hunt, fish and trap. The Commissioners wrote:

> There was expressed at every point the fear that the making of the treaty would be followed by the curtailment of the hunting and fishing privileges. . . .
>
> We pointed out . . . that the same means of earning a livelihood would continue after the treaty as existed before it, and that the Indians would be expected to make use of them. . . .
>
> Our chief difficulty was the apprehension that the hunting and fishing privileges were to be curtailed. The provision in the treaty under which ammunition and twine is to be furnished went far in the direction of quieting the fears of the Indians, for they admitted that it would be unreasonable to furnish the means of hunting and fishing if laws were to be enacted which would make hunting and fishing so restricted as to render it impossible to make a livelihood by such pursuits. But over and above the provision, *we had to solemnly assure them that only such laws as to hunting and fishing as were in the interest of the Indians and were found necessary in order to protect the fish and fur-bearing animals would be made, and that they would be as free to hunt and fish after the treaty as they would be if they never entered into it.* [Emphasis added.]

40   Treaty No. 8, then, guaranteed that the Indians "shall have the right to pursue their usual vocations of hunting, trapping and fishing". The Treaty, however, im-

posed two limitations on the right to hunt. First, there was a geographic limitation. The right to hunt could be exercised "throughout the tract surrendered . . . saving and excepting such tracts as may be required or taken up from time to time for settlement, mining, lumbering, trading or other purposes". Second, the right could be limited by government regulations passed for conservation purposes.

Impact of Paragraph 12 of the NRTA

Principles of Interpretation

41   At the outset, it may be helpful to once again set out some of the applicable principles of interpretation. First, it must be remembered that a treaty represents an exchange of solemn promises between the Crown and the various Indian nations. It is an agreement whose nature is sacred. See *R.* v. *Sioui,* [1990] 1 S.C.R. 1025, at p. 1063; *Simon* v. *The Queen,* [1985] 2 S.C.R. 387, at p. 401. Second, the honour of the Crown is always at stake in its dealing with Indian people. Interpretations of treaties and statutory provisions which have an impact upon treaty or aboriginal rights must be approached in a manner which maintains the integrity of the Crown. It is always assumed that the Crown intends to fulfil its promises. No appearance of "sharp dealing" will be sanctioned. See *Sparrow, supra,* at pp. 1107–8 and 1114; *R.* v. *Taylor* (1981), 34 O.R. (2d) 360 (Ont. C.A.), at p. 367. Third, any ambiguities or doubtful expressions in the wording of the treaty or document must be resolved in favour of the Indians. A corollary to this principle is that any limitations which restrict the rights of Indians under treaties must be narrowly construed. See *Nowegijick* v. *The Queen,* [1983] 1 S.C.R. 29, at p. 36; *Simon, supra,* at p. 402; *Sioui, supra,* at p. 1035; and *Mitchell* v. *Peguis Indian Band,* [1990] 2 S.C.R. 85, at pp. 142–43. Fourth, the onus of proving that a treaty or aboriginal right has been extinguished lies upon the Crown. There must be "strict proof of the fact of extinguishment" and evidence of a clear and plain intention on the part of the government to extinguish treaty rights. See *Simon, supra,* at p. 406; *Sioui, supra,* at p. 1061; *Calder* v. *Attorney-General of British Columbia,* [1973] S.C.R. 313, at p. 404.

42   These principles of interpretation must now be applied to this case.

Interpreting the NRTA

43   The issue at this stage is whether the NRTA extinguished and replaced the Treaty No. 8 right to hunt for food. It is my conclusion that it did not.

44   For ease of reference, para. 12 of the NRTA provides:

> 12. In order to secure to the Indians of the Province the continuance of the supply of game and fish for their support and subsistence, Canada agrees that the laws respecting game in force in the Province from time to time shall apply to the Indians within the boundaries thereof, provided, however, that the said Indians shall have the right, which the Province hereby assures to them, of hunting, trapping and fishing game and fish for food at all seasons of the year on all unoccupied Crown lands and on any other lands to which the said Indians may have a right of access.

45   It has been held that the NRTA had the clear intention of both limiting and expanding the treaty right to hunt. In *Frank* v. *The Queen,* [1978] 1 S.C.R. 95, consideration was given to the differences between Treaty No. 6 (which, for this purpose, has a hunting rights clause similar to that in Treaty No. 8) and para. 12 of the NRTA. Dickson J., as he then was, held at p. 100:

> The essential differences, for present purposes, between the Treaty and the Agreement are (i) under the former the hunting rights were at large while under the latter the right is limited to hunting for food and (ii) under the former the rights were limited to about one-third of the Province of Alberta, while under the latter they extend to the entire province.

And at p. 101, he stated:

> The Appellate Division . . . held that para. 12 of the Natural Resources Transfer Agreements of Alberta and Saskatchewan did two things: (i) it enlarged the areas in which Alberta and Saskatchewan Indians could respectively hunt and fish for food; (ii) it limited their rights to hunt and fish otherwise than for food by making those rights subject to provincial game laws. I would agree that such is the effect of para. 12.

To the same effect, see *R.* v. *Wesley,* [1932] 2 W.W.R. 337 (Alta. S.C. App. Div.), at p. 344, as adopted in *Prince* v. *The Queen,* [1964] S.C.R. 81, at p. 84.

46   This Court most recently considered the effect the NRTA had upon treaty rights in *Horseman, supra.* There, it was held that para. 12 of the NRTA evidenced a clear intention to extinguish the treaty protection of the right to hunt *commercially.* However, it was emphasized that the right to hunt *for food* continued to be protected and had in fact been expanded by the NRTA. At page 933, this appears:

> Although the Agreement did take away the right to hunt commercially, *the nature of the right to hunt for food was substantially enlarged. The geographical areas in which the Indian people could hunt was widely extended. Further, the means employed by them in hunting for their food was placed beyond the reach of provincial governments.* For example, they may hunt deer with night lights and with dogs, methods which are or may be prohibited for others. *Nor are the Indians subject to seasonal limitations as are all other hunters.* That is to say, they can hunt ducks and geese in the spring as well as the fall, just as they may hunt deer at any time of the year. *Indians are not limited with regard to the type of game they may kill.* That is to say, while others may be restricted as to the species or sex of the game they may kill, the Indians may kill for food both does and bucks; cock pheasants and hen pheasants; drakes and hen ducks. [Emphasis added.]

See also *Cardinal* v. *Attorney General of Alberta,* [1974] S.C.R. 695, at p. 722; and *Myran* v. *The Queen,* [1976] 2 S.C.R. 137, at p. 141. I might add that *Horseman, supra,* is a recent decision which should be accepted as resolving the issues which it considered. The decisions of this Court confirm that para. 12 of the NRTA did, to the extent that its intent is clear, modify and alter the right to hunt for food provided in Treaty No. 8.

47   Pursuant to s. 1 of the *Constitution Act, 1930,* there can be no doubt that para. 12 of the *NRTA* is binding law. It is the legal instrument which currently sets out and governs the Indian right to hunt. However, the existence of the *NRTA* has not deprived Treaty No. 8 of legal significance. Treaties are sacred promises and the Crown's honour requires the Court to assume that the Crown intended to fulfil its promises. Treaty rights can only be amended where it is clear that effect was intended. It is helpful to recall that Dickson J. in *Frank, supra,* observed at p. 100 that, while the *NRTA* had partially amended the scope of the Treaty hunting right, *"of equal importance* was the desire to re-state and reassure to the treaty Indians the continued enjoyment of the right to hunt and fish for food" (emphasis added). I believe that these words support my conclusion that the Treaty No. 8 right to hunt has only been altered or modified by the *NRTA to the extent that* the *NRTA* evinces a clear intention to effect such a modification. This position has been repeatedly confirmed in the decisions referred to earlier. Unless there is a direct conflict between the *NRTA* and a treaty, the *NRTA* will not have modified the treaty rights. Therefore, the *NRTA* language which outlines the right to hunt for food must be read in light of the fact that this aspect of the treaty right continues in force and effect.

48   Like Treaty No. 8, the *NRTA* circumscribes the right to hunt for food with respect to both the geographical area within which this right may be exercised as well as the regulations which may properly be imposed by the government. The geographical limitations must now be considered.

Geographical Limitations on the Right to Hunt for Food

49   Under the *NRTA,* Indians may exercise a right to hunt for food "on all unoccupied Crown lands and on any other lands to which the said Indians may have a right of access". In the present appeals, the hunting occurred on lands which had been included in the 1899 surrender but were now privately owned. Therefore, it must be determined whether these privately owned lands were "other lands" to which the Indians had a "right of access" under the Treaty.

50   At this stage, three preliminary points should be made. First, the "right of access" in the *NRTA* does not refer to a general right of access but, rather, it is limited to a right of access *for the purposes of hunting: R.* v. *Mousseau,* [1980] 2 S.C.R. 89, at p. 97; *R.* v. *Sutherland,* [1980] 2 S.C.R. 451, at p. 459. For example, everyone can travel on public highways, but this general right of access cannot be read as conferring upon Indians a right to hunt on public highways.

51   Second, because the various treaties affected by the *NRTA* contain different wording, the extent of the treaty right to hunt on privately owned land may well differ from one treaty to another. While some treaties contain express provisions with respect to hunting on private land, others, such as Treaty No. 8, do not. Under Treaty No. 8, the right to hunt for food could be exercised "throughout the tract surrendered" to the Crown "saving and excepting such tracts as may be required or taken up from time to time for settlement, mining, lumbering, trading or other

purposes." Accordingly, if the privately owned land is not "required or taken up" in the manner described in Treaty No. 8, it will be land to which the Indians had a right of access to hunt for food.

52   Third, the applicable interpretative principles must be borne in mind. Treaties and statutes relating to Indians should be liberally construed and any uncertainties, ambiguities or doubtful expressions should be resolved in favour of the Indians. In addition, when considering a treaty, a court must take into account the context in which the treaties were negotiated, concluded and committed to writing. The treaties, as written documents, recorded an agreement that had already been reached orally and they did not always record the full extent of the oral agreement: see Alexander Morris, *The Treaties of Canada with the Indians of Manitoba and the North-West Territories* (1880), at pp. 338–42; *Sioui, supra,* at p. 1068; *Report of the Aboriginal Justice Inquiry of Manitoba* (1991); Jean Friesen, *Grant me Wherewith to Make my Living* (1985). The treaties were drafted in English by representatives of the Canadian government who, it should be assumed, were familiar with common law doctrines. Yet, the treaties were not translated in written form into the languages (here Cree and Dene) of the various Indian nations who were signatories. Even if they had been, it is unlikely that the Indians, who had a history of communicating only orally, would have understood them any differently. As a result, it is well settled that the words in the treaty must not be interpreted in their strict technical sense nor subjected to rigid modern rules of construction. Rather, they must be interpreted in the sense that they would naturally have been understood by the Indians at the time of the signing. This applies, as well, to those words in a treaty which impose a limitation on the right which has been granted. See *Nowegijick, supra,* at p. 36; *Sioui, supra,* at pp. 1035–36 and 1044; *Sparrow, supra,* at p. 1107; and *Mitchell, supra,* where La Forest J. noted the significant difference that exists between the interpretation of treaties and statutes which pertain to Indians.

53   The evidence led at trial indicated that in 1899 the Treaty No. 8 Indians would have understood that land had been "required or taken up" when it was being put to a use which was incompatible with the exercise of the right to hunt. Historian John Foster gave expert evidence in this case. His testimony indicated that, in 1899, Treaty No. 8 Indians would not have understood the concept of private and exclusive property ownership separate from actual land use. They understood land to be required or taken up for settlement when buildings or fences were erected, land was put into crops, or farm or domestic animals were present. Enduring church missions would also be understood to constitute settlement. These physical signs shaped the Indians' understanding of settlement because they were the manifestations of exclusionary land use which the Indians had witnessed as new settlers moved into the West. The Indians' experience with the Hudson's Bay Company was also relevant. Although that company had title to vast tracts of land, the Indians were not excluded from and in fact continued hunting on these lands. In the course of their trading, the Hudson's Bay Company and the Northwest Company had set up numerous posts that were subsequently abandoned. The presence of abandoned buildings, then, would not necessarily signify to the Indians that land was taken up in a way which precluded hunting on them. Yet, it is dangerous to

pursue this line of thinking too far. The abandonment of land may be temporary. Owners may return to reoccupy the land, to undertake maintenance, to inspect it or simply to enjoy it. How "unoccupied" the land was at the relevant time will have to be explored on a case-by-case basis.

54   An interpretation of the Treaty properly founded upon the Indians' understanding of its terms leads to the conclusion that the geographical limitation on the existing hunting right should be based upon a concept of visible, incompatible land use. This approach is consistent with the oral promises made to the Indians at the time the Treaty was signed, with the oral history of the Treaty No. 8 Indians, with earlier case law and with the provisions of the Alberta *Wildlife Act* itself.

55   The Indian people made their agreements orally and recorded their history orally. Thus, the verbal promises made on behalf of the federal government at the times the treaties were concluded are of great significance in their interpretation. Treaty No. 8 was initially concluded with the Indians at Lesser Slave Lake. The Commissioners then travelled to many other bands in the region and sought their adhesion to the Treaty. Oral promises were made with the Lesser Slave Lake band and with the other Treaty signatories and these promises have been recorded in the Treaty Commissioners' Reports and in contemporary affidavits and diaries of interpreters and other government officials who participated in the negotiations. See in particular: Richard Daniel, "The Spirit and Terms of Treaty Eight", in Richard Price, ed., *The Spirit of the Alberta Indian Treaties* (1979), at pp. 47–100; and René Fumoleau, O.M.I., *As Long as this Land Shall Last: A History of Treaty 8 and Treaty 11, 1870–1939* (1973), at pp. 73–100. The Indians' primary fear was that the treaty would curtail their ability to pursue their livelihood as hunters, trappers and fishers. Commissioner David Laird, as cited in Daniel, "The Spirit and Terms of Treaty Eight", at p. 76, told the Lesser Slave Lake Indians in 1899:

> Indians have been told that if they make a treaty they will not be allowed to hunt and fish as they do now. This is not true. *Indians who take treaty will be just as free to hunt and fish all over as they now are.*
>
> *In return for this the Government expects that the Indians will not interfere with or molest any miner, traveller or settler.* [Emphasis added.]

Since the Treaty No. 8 lands were not well suited to agriculture, the government expected little settlement in the area. The Commissioners, cited in Daniel, at p. 81, indicated that "it is safe to say that so long as the fur-bearing animals remain, the great bulk of the Indians will continue to hunt and to trap". The promise that this livelihood would not be affected was repeated to all the bands who signed the Treaty. Although it was expected that some white prospectors might stake claims in the north, this was not expected to have an impact on the Indians' hunting rights. For example, one commissioner, cited in René Fumoleau, O.M.I., *As Long as this Land Shall Last,* at p. 90, stated:

> We are just making peace between Whites and Indians—for them to treat each other well. And we do not want to change your hunting. If Whites should prospect, stake claims, that will not harm anyone.

56   Commissioner Laird told the Indians that the promises made to them were to be similar to those made with other Indians who had agreed to a treaty. Accordingly, it is significant that the earlier promises also contemplated a limited interference with Indians' hunting and fishing practices. See, for example, Alexander Morris, *The Treaties of Canada with the Indians of Manitoba and the North-West Territories, supra.* In negotiating Treaty No. 1, the Lieutenant Governor of Manitoba, A. G. Archibald, made the following statement to the Indians, at p. 29:

> When you have made your treaty you will still be free to hunt over much of the land included in the treaty. Much of it is rocky and unfit for cultivation, much of it that is wooded is beyond the places where the white man will require to go, at all events for some time to come. *Till these lands are needed for use you will be free to hunt over them, and make all the use of them which you have made in the past. But when lands are needed to be tilled or occupied, you must not go on them any more. There will still be plenty of land that is neither tilled nor occupied where you can go and roam and hunt as you have always done,* and, if you wish to farm, you will go to your own reserve where you will find a place ready for you to live on and cultivate. [Emphasis added.]

With respect to Treaty No. 4, Lt. Gov. Morris made the following statement to the Indians, at p. 96:

> We have come through the country for many days and we have seen hills and but little wood and in many places little water, and it may be a long time before there are many white men settled upon this land, and you will have the right of hunting and fishing just as you have now *until the land is actually taken up.* [Emphasis added.]

With respect to Treaty No. 6, Lt. Gov. Morris stated at p. 218:

> You want to be at liberty to hunt as before. I told you we did not want to take that means of living from you, you have it the same as before, only this, *if a man, whether Indian or Half-breed, had a good field of grain, you would not destroy it with your hunt.* [Emphasis added.]

57   The oral history of the Treaty No. 8 Indians reveals a similar understanding of the treaty promises. Dan McLean, an elder from the Sturgeon Lake Indian Reserve, gave evidence in this trial. He indicated that the understanding of the treaty promise was that Indians were allowed to hunt anytime for food to feed their families. They could hunt on unoccupied Crown land and on abandoned land. If there was no fence on the land, they could hunt, but if there was a fence, they could not hunt there. This testimony is consistent with the oral histories presented by other Treaty No. 8 elders whose stories have been recorded by historians. The Indians understood that land would be taken up for homesteads, farming, prospecting and mining and that they would not be able to hunt in these areas or to shoot at the settlers' farm animals or buildings. No doubt the Indians believed that most of the Treaty No. 8 land would remain unoccupied and so would be available to them for hunting, fishing and trapping. See *The Spirit of the Alberta Indian Treaties, supra,* at pp. 92–100.

58　Accordingly, the oral promises made by the Crown's representatives and the Indians' own oral history indicate that it was understood that land would be taken up and occupied in a way which precluded hunting when it was put to a visible use that was incompatible with hunting. Turning to the case law, it is clear that the courts have also accepted this interpretation and have concluded that whether or not land has been taken up or occupied is a question of fact that must be resolved on a case-by-case basis.

59　Most of the cases which have considered the geographical limitations on the right to hunt have been concerned with situations where the hunting took place on Crown land. In those cases, it was held that Crown lands were only "occupied" or "taken up" when they were actually put to an active use which was incompatible with hunting. For example, *R.* v. *Smith,* [1935] 2 W.W.R. 433 (Sask. C.A.), considered whether Indians had a right to hunt for food on a game preserve located on Crown land. There, in my view, it was correctly observed at p. 436 that "it is proper to consult th[e] treaty in order to glean from it whatever may throw some light on the meaning to be given to the words" in the NRTA. It was sensibly held at p. 437 that the Indians did not have a right of access to hunt on the game preserve because to do so would be incompatible with the fundamental purpose of establishing a preserve: "a game preserve would be one in name only if the Indians, or any other class of people, were entitled to shoot in it". See also *R.* v. *Mirasty,* [1942] 1 W.W.R. 343 (Police Ct.), in which Crown land was taken up for a forest and game preserve; and *Mousseau, supra,* in which Crown land was taken up for a public road. However, the courts have recognized an existing treaty right to hunt on Crown land taken up as a forest because hunting for food is not incompatible with that particular land use: *R.* v. *Strongquill,* [1953] 8 W.W.R. (N.S.) 247 (Sask. C.A.). Finally, where limited hunting by non-Indians is permitted on Crown land taken up as a wildlife management area or a fur conservation area, the courts have held that Indians continue to have an unlimited right of access for the purposes of hunting for food: *Strongquill, supra,* at pp. 267 and 271; *Sutherland, supra,* at pp. 460 and 464-65; and *Moosehunter* v. *The Queen,* [1981] 1 S.C.R. 282, at p. 292.

60　A second but shorter line of cases has considered whether Indians have a treaty right of access to hunt on privately owned lands. While various factual situations have been considered, the courts have not settled the question as to whether the Treaty No. 8 right to hunt for food extends to privately owned land which is not put to visible use. . . .

62　In *Horse, supra,* the accused persons were hunting on privately owned land without the owner's permission. This Court stated repeatedly that Treaty No. 6 did not afford the accused a right of access to hunt on "*occupied* private lands" (see pp. 198, 204 and 209–10). In *Horse, supra,* the private lands were not posted, but they were sown to hay and grain and, thus, were visibly and actively used for farming. In light of these facts, there was no need to consider what was encompassed by the term "occupied private land". The use of the land was so readily apparent that it clearly fell within the category of occupied land. Similarly, in

Mousseau, supra, at p. 97, this Court indicated that Indians had a right to hunt on: (a) all unoccupied Crown lands; (b) any occupied Crown land to which they had a right of access by statute, common law or otherwise; and (c) "any *occupied private lands* to which the Indians have a right of access by custom, usage, or consent of the owner or occupier, for the purpose of hunting, trapping, or fishing". However, that case involved hunting on a public highway which was clearly occupied Crown land. Although *Mousseau, supra,* summarized this Court's position on that point, the question of hunting on *unoccupied* private land was neither then, nor previously, before the Court. As a result, in both *Horse, supra,* and *Mousseau, supra,* the question of whether the Treaty protected a right of access to *unoccupied* private lands—private lands which had not been taken up for settlement or other purposes—was left unresolved.

63   One case which has specifically considered the treaty right to hunt on *unoccupied* private land is *R.* v. *Bartleman* (1984), 55 B.C.L.R. 78 (B.C.C.A.). There, the accused was charged with using ammunition which was prohibited under the provincial *Wildlife Act.* He had been hunting on uncultivated bush land. No livestock or buildings were present, no fence surrounded the land, and no signs had been posted. He claimed that, on the basis of his Treaty hunting right, the provincial legislation did not apply to him. His hunting rights were set out in the 1852 North Saanich Indian Treaty (quoted in *Bartleman,* at p. 87) which provided that the Indians "are at liberty to hunt over the unoccupied lands, and to carry on our fisheries as formerly". The B.C. Court of Appeal held that it was necessary to interpret the right on the basis of what the Indians would have understood in 1852 by the words of the Treaty. It held that the Treaty right to hunt could be exercised where to do so would not interfere with the actual use being made of the privately owned land. At page 97 this was written:

> . . . the hunting must take place on land that is unoccupied in the sense that the particular form of hunting that is being undertaken does not interfere with the actual use and enjoyment of the land by the owner or occupier.

64   The Court of Appeal found that hunting was not incompatible with the minimal level of use to which the land was being put.

65   The "visible, incompatible use" approach, which focuses upon the use being made of the land, is appropriate and correct. Although it requires that the particular land use be considered in each case, this standard is neither unduly vague nor unworkable.

66   In summary, then, the geographical limitation on the right to hunt for food is derived from the terms of the particular treaty if they have not been modified or altered by the provisions of para. 12 of the NRTA. In this case, the geographical limitation on the right to hunt for food provided by Treaty No. 8 has not been modified by para. 12 of the NRTA. Where lands are privately owned, it must be determined on a case-by-case basis whether they are "other lands" to which Indi-

ans had a "right of access" under the Treaty. If the lands are occupied, that is, put to visible use which is incompatible with hunting, Indians will not have a right of access. Conversely, if privately owned land is unoccupied and not put to visible use, Indians, pursuant to Treaty No. 8, will have a right of access in order to hunt for food. The facts presented in each of these appeals must now be considered.

67   The first is Mr. Badger. He was hunting on land covered with second growth willow and scrub. Although there were no fences or signs posted on the land, a farm house was located only one quarter of a mile from the place the moose was killed. The residence did not appear to have been abandoned. Second, Mr. Kiyawasew was hunting on a snow-covered field. Although there was no fence, there were run-down barns nearby and signs were posted on the land. Most importantly, the evidence indicated that in the fall, a crop had been harvested from the field. In the situations presented in both cases, it seems clear that the land was visibly being used. Since the appellants did not have a right of access to these particular tracts of land, their treaty right to hunt for food did not extend to hunting there. As a result, the limitations on hunting set out in the *Wildlife Act* did not infringe upon their existing right and were properly applied to these two appellants. The appeals of Mr. Badger and Mr. Kiyawasew must, therefore, be dismissed.

68   However, Mr. Ominayak's appeal presents a different situation. He was hunting on uncleared muskeg. No fences or signs were present. Nor were there any buildings located near the site of the kill. Although it was privately owned, it is apparent that this land was not being put to any visible use which would be incompatible with the Indian right to hunt for food. Accordingly, the geographical limitations upon the Treaty right to hunt for food did not preclude Mr. Ominayak from hunting upon this parcel of land. This, however, does not dispose of his appeal. It remains to be seen whether the existing right to hunt was in any other manner circumscribed by a form of government regulation which is permitted under the Treaty.

Permissible Regulatory Limitations on the Right to Hunt for Food
69   Pursuant to the provisions of s. 88 of the *Indian Act,* provincial laws of general application will apply to Indians. This is so except where they conflict with aboriginal or treaty rights, in which case the latter must prevail: *Kruger* v. *The Queen,* [1978] 1 S.C.R. 104, at pp. 114–15; *Simon, supra,* at pp. 411–14; *Sparrow, supra,* at p. 1109. In any event, the regulation of Indian hunting rights would ordinarily come within the jurisdiction of the Federal government and not the Province. However, the issue does not arise in this case since we are dealing with the right to hunt provided by Treaty No. 8 as modified by the NRTA. Both the Treaty and the NRTA specifically provided that the right would be subject to regulation pertaining to conservation.

70   Treaty No. 8 provided that the right to hunt would be "subject to such regulations as may from time to time be made by the Government of the country". In the West, a wide range of legislation aimed at conserving game had been enacted by

the government beginning as early as the 1880s. Acts and regulations pertaining to conservation measures continued to be passed throughout the entire period during which the numbered treaties were concluded. In *Horseman, supra,* the aim and intent of the regulations was recognized. At page 935, I noted:

> Before the turn of the century the federal game laws of the Unorganized Territories provided for a total ban on hunting certain species (bison and musk oxen) in order to preserve both the species and the supply of game for Indians in the future. See *The Unorganized Territories' Game Preservation Act, 1894,* S.C. 1894, c. 31, ss. 2, 4 to 8 and 26. Even then the advances in firearms and the more efficient techniques of hunting and trapping, coupled with the habitat loss and the over-exploitation of game, (undoubtedly by Europeans more than by Indians), had made it essential to impose conservation measures to preserve species and to provide for hunting for future generations. Moreover, beginning in 1890, provision was made in the federal *Indian Act* for the Superintendent General to make the game laws of Manitoba and the Unorganized Territories applicable to Indians. See *An Act further to amend "The Indian Act" chapter forty-three of the Revised Statutes,* S.C. 1890, c. 29, s. 10. A similar provision was in force in 1930. See *Indian Act,* R.S.C. 1927, c. 98, s. 69.

In light of the existence of these conservation laws prior to signing the Treaty, the Indians would have understood that, by the terms of the Treaty, the government would be permitted to pass regulations with respect to conservation. This concept was explicitly incorporated into the NRTA in a modified form providing for Provincial regulatory authority in the field of conservation. Paragraph 12 of the NRTA begins by stating its purpose:

> 12. In order to secure to the Indians of the Province the continuance of the supply of game and fish for their support and subsistence, Canada agrees that the *laws respecting game in force in the Province from time to time shall apply to the Indians.* . . . [Emphasis added.]

It follows that by the terms of both the Treaty and the NRTA, provincial game laws would be applicable to Indians so long as they were aimed at conserving the supply of game. However, the provincial government's regulatory authority under the Treaty and the NRTA did not extend beyond the realm of conservation. It is the constitutional provisions of para. 12 of the NRTA authorizing provincial regulations which make it unnecessary to consider s. 88 of the *Indian Act* and the general application of provincial regulations to Indians.

71   The licensing provisions contained in the *Wildlife Act* are in part, but not wholly, directed towards questions of conservation. At first blush, then, they may seem to form part of the permissible government regulation which can establish the boundaries of the existing right to hunt for food. However, the partial concern with conservation does not automatically lead to the conclusion that s. 26(1) is permissible regulation. It must still be determined whether the manner in which the licensing scheme is administered conflicts with the hunting right provided under Treaty No. 8 as modified by the NRTA.

72   This analysis should take into account the wording of the Treaty and the NRTA. I believe this to be appropriate since the object will be to determine first whether there has been a *prima facie* infringement of the Treaty No. 8 right to hunt as modified by the NRTA and secondly if there is such an infringement whether it can be justified. In essence, we are dealing with a modified treaty right. This, I believe, follows from the principle referred to earlier that treaty rights should only be considered to be modified if a clear intention to do so has been manifested, in this case, by the NRTA. Further, the solemn promises made in the treaty should be altered or modified as little as possible. The NRTA clearly intended to modify the right to hunt. It did so by eliminating the right to hunt commercially and by preserving and extending the right to hunt for food. The Treaty right thus modified pertains to the right to hunt for food which prior to the Treaty was an aboriginal right.

73   For reasons that I will amplify later, it seems logical and appropriate to apply the recently formulated *Sparrow* test in these circumstances. I would add that it can properly be inferred that the concept of reasonableness forms an integral part of the *Sparrow* test. It follows that this concept should be taken into account in the consideration of the justification of an infringement. As a general rule the criteria set out in *Sparrow, supra,* should be applied. However, the reasons in *Sparrow, supra,* make it clear that the suggested criteria are neither exclusive nor exhaustive. It follows that additional criteria may be helpful and applicable in the particular situation presented.

Conflict Between the Wildlife Act and Rights Under Treaty No. 8

74   It has been recognized that aboriginal and treaty rights are not absolute. The reasons in *Sparrow, supra,* made it clear that aboriginal rights may be overridden if the government is able to justify the infringement.

75   In *Sparrow, supra,* certain criteria were set out pertaining to justification at pp. 1111 and following. While that case dealt with the infringement of aboriginal rights, I am of the view that these criteria should, in most cases, apply equally to the infringement of treaty rights.

76   There is no doubt that aboriginal and treaty rights differ in both origin and structure. Aboriginal rights flow from the customs and traditions of the native peoples. To paraphrase the words of Judson J. in *Calder, supra,* at p. 328, they embody the right of native people to continue living as their forefathers lived. Treaty rights, on the other hand, are those contained in official agreements between the Crown and the native peoples. Treaties are analogous to contracts, albeit of a very solemn and special, public nature. They create enforceable obligations based on the mutual consent of the parties. It follows that the scope of treaty rights will be determined by their wording, which must be interpreted in accordance with the principles enunciated by this Court.

77   This said, there are also significant aspects of similarity between aboriginal and treaty rights. Although treaty rights are the result of mutual agreement, they,

like aboriginal rights, may be unilaterally abridged. See *Horseman, supra,* at p. 936; *R.* v. *Sikyea,* [1964] 2 C.C.C. 325 (N.W.T.C.A.), at p. 330, aff'd [1964] S.C.R. 642; and *Moosehunter, supra,* at p. 293. It follows that limitations on treaty rights, like breaches of aboriginal rights, should be justified.

78   In addition, both aboriginal and treaty rights possess in common a unique, *sui generis* nature. See *Guerin* v. *The Queen,* [1984] 2 S.C.R. 335, at p. 382; *Simon, supra,* at p. 404. In each case, the honour of the Crown is engaged through its relationship with the native people. As Dickson C.J. and La Forest J. stated at p. 1110 in *Sparrow, supra:*

> By giving aboriginal rights constitutional status and priority, Parliament and the prov-inces have sanctioned challenges to social and economic policy objectives embodied in legislation to the extent that aboriginal rights are affected. Implicit in this constitu-tional scheme is the obligation of the legislature to satisfy the test of justification. *The way in which a legislative objective is to be attained must uphold the honour of the Crown and must be in keeping with the unique contemporary relationship, grounded in history and policy, between the Crown and Canada's aboriginal peoples. The ex-tent of legislative or regulatory impact on an existing aboriginal right may be scruti-nized so as to ensure recognition and affirmation.* [Emphasis added.]

79   The wording of s. 35(1) of the *Constitution Act, 1982* supports a common approach to infringements of aboriginal and treaty rights. It provides that "[t]he existing aboriginal and treaty rights of the aboriginal peoples of Canada are hereby recognized and affirmed". In *Sparrow, supra,* Dickson C.J. and La Forest J. ap-peared to acknowledge the need for justification in the treaty context. They said this at pp. 1118–19 in relation to *R.* v. *Eninew* (1984), 12 C.C.C. (3d) 365 (Sask. C.A.), a case which considered the effect of the *Migratory Birds Convention Act* on rights guaranteed under Treaty No. 10:

> As we have pointed out, management and conservation of resources is indeed an im-portant and valid legislative objective. Yet, the fact that the objective is of a "reason-able" nature cannot suffice as constitutional recognition and affirmation of aboriginal rights. *Rather, the regulations enforced pursuant to a conservation or management objective may be scrutinized according to the justificatory standard outlined above.* [Emphasis added.]

80   This standard of scrutiny requires that the Crown demonstrate that the legisla-tion in question advances important general public objectives in such a manner that it ought to prevail. In *R.* v. *Agawa* (1988), 65 O.R. (2d) 505 (C.A.), at p. 524, Blair J.A. recognized the need for a balanced approach to limitations on treaty rights, stating:

> . . . Indian treaty rights are like all other rights recognized by our legal system. The exercise of rights by an individual or group is limited by the rights of others. Rights do not exist in a vacuum and the exercise of any right involves a balancing with the interests and values involved in the rights of others. This is recognized in s. 1 of the

Canadian Charter of Rights and Freedoms which provides that limitation of Charter rights must be justified as reasonable in a free and democratic society.

81   Dickson C.J. and La Forest J. arrived at a similar conclusion in *Sparrow, supra,* at pp. 1108–9.

82   In summary, it is clear that a statute or regulation which constitutes a *prima facie* infringement of aboriginal rights must be justified. In my view, it is equally if not more important to justify *prima facie* infringements of treaty rights. The rights granted to Indians by treaties usually form an integral part of the consideration for the surrender of their lands. For example, it is clear that the maintenance of as much of their hunting rights as possible was of paramount concern to the Indians who signed Treaty No. 8. This was, in effect, an aboriginal right recognized in a somewhat limited form by the treaty and later modified by the NRTA. To the Indians, it was an essential element of this solemn agreement.

83   It will be remembered that the NRTA modified the Treaty right to hunt. It did so by eliminating the right to hunt commercially but enlarged the geographical areas in which the Indian people might hunt in all seasons. The area was to include all unoccupied Crown land in the province together with any other lands to which the Indians may have a right of access. Lastly, the province was authorized to make laws for conservation. Specifically:

> 12. In order to secure to the Indians of the Province the continuance of the supply of game and fish for their support and subsistence, Canada agrees that the laws respecting game in force in the Province from time to time shall apply to the Indians within the boundaries thereof, provided, however, that the said Indians shall have the right, which the Province hereby assures to them, of hunting, trapping and fishing game and fish for food at all seasons of the year on all unoccupied Crown lands and on any other lands to which the said Indians may have a right of access.

84   The NRTA only modifies the Treaty No. 8 right. Treaty No. 8 represents a solemn promise of the Crown. For the reasons set out earlier, it can only be modified or altered to the extent that the NRTA clearly intended to modify or alter those rights. The Federal government, as it was empowered to do, unilaterally enacted the NRTA. It is unlikely that it would proceed in that manner today. The manner in which the NRTA was unilaterally enacted strengthens the conclusion that the right to hunt which it provides should be construed in light of the provisions of Treaty No. 8.

85   It follows that any *prima facie* infringement of the rights guaranteed under Treaty No. 8 or the NRTA must be justified. How should the infringement of a treaty right be justified? Obviously, the challenged limitation must be considered within the context of the treaty itself. Yet, the recognized principles to be considered and applied in justification should generally be those set out in *Sparrow, supra.* There may well be other factors that should influence the result. The *Sparrow* decision itself recognized that it was not setting a complete catalogue of factors. Neverthe-

less, these factors may serve as a rough guide when considering the infringement of treaty rights.

Prima Facie Infringement of the Treaty Right to hunt as modified by the NRTA
86   The licensing provisions of the *Wildlife Act* address two objectives: public safety and conservation. These objectives, in and of themselves, are not unconstitutional. However, it is evident from the wording of the Act and its regulations that the manner in which the licensing scheme is set up results in a *prima facie* infringement of the Treaty No. 8 right to hunt as modified by the NRTA. The statutory scheme establishes a two-step licensing process. The public safety component is the first one that is engaged.

87   Under s.15(1)(c) of the *Wildlife Act*, the Lieutenant Governor in Council may pass regulations which "specify training and testing qualifications required for the obtaining and holding of a licence or permit". . . .

88   Standing on its own, the requirement that all hunters take gun safety courses and pass hunting competency tests makes eminently good sense. This protects the safety of everyone who hunts, including Indians. It has been held on a number of occasions that aboriginal or treaty rights must be exercised with due concern for public safety. *Myran, supra,* dealt with two Indians charged with hunting without due regard for the safety of others, contrary to the provisions of the *Manitoba Wildlife Act.* The accused argued that they were immune from the Act on the basis of their right to hunt for food guaranteed under the *Manitoba Natural Resources Act* (parallel to the NRTA). Dickson J. (as he then was) for the Court found at pp. 141–42 that:

> I think it is clear from *Prince and Myron* that an Indian of the Province is free to hunt or trap game in such numbers, at such times of the year, by such means or methods and with such contrivances, as he may wish, provided he is doing so in order to obtain food for his own use and on unoccupied Crown lands or other lands to which he may have a right of access. *But that is not to say that he has the right to hunt dangerously and without regard for the safety of other persons in the vicinity.* [Emphasis added.]

He went on at p. 142 to state that:

> In *my opinion there is no irreconcilable conflict or inconsistency in principle between the right to hunt for food assured under para. 13 of the Memorandum of Agreement approved under The Manitoba Natural Resources Act and the requirement of s. 10(1) of The Wildlife Act that such right be exercised in a manner so as not to endanger the lives of others.* The first is concerned with conservation of game to secure a continuing supply of food for the Indians of the Province and protect the right of the Indians to hunt for food at all seasons of the year; the second is concerned with risk of death or serious injury omnipresent when hunters fail to have due regard for the presence of others in the vicinity. [Emphasis added.]

89   That decision was subsequently affirmed by this Court in *Sutherland, supra,*

and *Moosehunter, supra.* See to the same effect *R.* v. *Napoleon,* [1986] 1 C.N.L.R. 86 (B.C.C.A.) and *R.* v. *Fox,* [1994] 3 C.N.L.R. 132 (Ont. C.A.). Accordingly, it can be seen that reasonable regulations aimed at ensuring safety do not infringe aboriginal or treaty rights to hunt for food. Similarly these regulations do not infringe the hunting rights guaranteed by Treaty No. 8 as modified by the NRTA.

90   While the general safety component of the licensing provisions may not constitute a *prima facie* infringement, the conservation component appears to present just such an infringement. Provincial regulations for conservation purposes are authorized pursuant to the provisions of the NRTA. However, the routine imposition upon Indians of the specific limitations that appear on the face of the hunting licence may not be permissible if they erode an important aspect of the Indian hunting rights. This Court has held on numerous occasions that there can be no limitation on the method, timing and extent of Indian hunting under a Treaty. I would add that a Treaty as amended by the NRTA should be considered in the same manner. *Horseman, supra,* clearly indicated that such restrictions conflicted with the treaty right. Moreover, in *Simon, supra,* this appears at p. 413:

> The section clearly places seasonal limitations and licensing requirements, for the purposes of wildlife conservation, on the right to possess a rifle and ammunition for the purposes of hunting. The restrictions imposed in this case conflict, therefore, with the appellant's right to possess a firearm and ammunition in order to exercise his free liberty to hunt over the lands covered by the Treaty. As noted, it is clear that under s. 88 of the Indian Act provincial legislation cannot restrict native treaty rights. If conflict arises, the terms of the treaty prevail.

91   The *Simon* case dealt with Provincial regulations which the government attempted to justify under s. 88 of the *Indian Act.* By contrast, in this case, para. 12 of the NRTA specifically provides that the provincial government may make regulations for conservation purposes, which affect the Treaty rights to hunt. Accordingly, Provincial regulations pertaining to conservation will be valid so long as they are not clearly unreasonable in their application to aboriginal people.

92   Under the present licensing scheme, an Indian who has successfully passed the approved gun safety and hunting competency courses would not be able to exercise the right to hunt without being in breach of the conservation restrictions imposed with respect to the hunting method, the kind and numbers of game, the season and the permissible hunting area, all of which appear on the face of the licence. Moreover, while the Minister may determine how many licences will be made available and what class of licence these will be, no provisions currently exist for "hunting for food" licences.

93   At present, only sport and commercial hunting are licensed. It is true that the regulations do provide for a subsistence hunting licence. See Alta. Reg. 50/87, s. 25; Alta. Reg. 95/87, s. 7. However, its provisions are so minimal and so restricted that it could never be considered a licence to hunt for food as that term is

used in Treaty No. 8 and as it is understood by the Indians. Accordingly, there is no provision for a licence which does not contain the facial restrictions set out earlier. Finally, there is no provision which would guarantee to Indians preferential access to the limited number of licences, nor is there a provision that would exempt them from the licence fee. As a result, Indians, like all other Albertans, would have to apply for a hunting licence from the same limited pool of licences. Further, if they were fortunate enough to be issued a licence, they would have to pay a licensing fee, effectively paying for the privilege of exercising a treaty right. This is clearly in conflict with both the Treaty and *NRTA* provisions.

94   The present licensing system denies to holders of treaty rights as modified by the *NRTA* the very means of exercising those rights. Limitations of this nature are in direct conflict with the treaty right. Therefore, it must be concluded that s. 26(1) of the *Wildlife Act* conflicts with the hunting right set out in Treaty No. 8 as modified by the *NRTA*.

95   Accordingly, it is my conclusion that the appellant, Mr. Ominayak, has established the existence of a *prima facie* breach of his treaty right. It now falls to the government to justify that infringement.

Justification

96   In my view justification of provincial regulations enacted pursuant to the *NRTA* should meet the same test for justification of treaty rights that was set out in *Sparrow*. The reason for this is obvious. The effect of para. 12 of the *NRTA* is to place the Provincial government in exactly the same position which the Federal Crown formerly occupied. Thus the Provincial government has the same duty not to infringe unjustifiably the hunting right provided by Treaty No. 8 as modified by the *NRTA*. Paragraph 12 of the *NRTA* provides that the province may make laws for a conservation purpose, subject to the Indian right to hunt and fish for food. Accordingly, there is a need for a means to assess which conservation laws will if they infringe that right, nevertheless be justifiable. The *Sparrow* analysis provides a reasonable, flexible and current method of assessing conservation regulations and enactments.

97   In *Sparrow*, at p. 1113, it was held that in considering whether an infringement of aboriginal or treaty rights could be justified, the following questions should be addressed sequentially:

> First, is there *a valid legislative objective?* Here the court would inquire into whether the objective of Parliament in authorizing the department to enact regulations regarding fisheries is valid. The objective of the department in setting out the particular regulations would also be scrutinized. [Emphasis added.]

At page 1114, the next step was set out in this way:

> If a valid legislative objective is found, the analysis proceeds to the second part of the justification issue. Here, we refer back to the guiding interpretive principle derived from *Taylor and Williams* and *Guerin, supra*. That is, the honour of the Crown is at stake in dealings with aboriginal peoples. The special trust relationship and the re-

sponsibility of the government vis-à-vis aboriginals must be the first consideration in determining whether the legislation or action in question can be justified. [Emphasis added.]

Finally, at p.1119, it was noted that further questions might also arise depending on the circumstances of the inquiry:

These include the questions of whether there has been *as little infringement as possible* in order to effect the desired result; whether, *in a situation of expropriation, fair compensation* is available; and, whether the aboriginal group in question has been *consulted with respect to the conservation measures being implemented.* The aboriginal peoples, with their history of conservation-consciousness and interdependence with natural resources, would surely be expected, at the least, to be informed regarding the determination of an appropriate scheme for the regulation of the fisheries.

We would *not wish to set out an exhaustive list of the factors to be considered in the assessment of justification.* Suffice it to say that recognition and affirmation requires sensitivity to and respect for the rights of aboriginal peoples on behalf of the government, courts and indeed all Canadians. [Emphasis added.]

98   In the present case, the government has not led any evidence with respect to justification. In the absence of such evidence, it is not open to this Court to supply its own justification. Section 26(1) of the *Wildlife Act* constitutes a *prima facie* infringement of the appellant Mr. Ominayak's treaty right to hunt. Yet, the issue of conservation is of such importance that a new trial must be ordered so that the question of justification may be addressed. . . .

99   The constitutional question posed before this Court was:

If Treaty 8 confirmed to the Indians of the Treaty 8 Territory the right to hunt throughout the tract surrendered, does the right continue to exist or was it extinguished and replaced by para. 12 of the *Natural Resources Transfer Agreement, 1930 (Constitution Act, 1930,* 20–21 George V, c. 26 (U.K.)), and if the right continues to exist, could that right be exercised on the lands in question and, if so, was the right impermissibly infringed upon by s. 26(1) or s. 27(1) of the *Wildlife Act,* S.A. 1984, c. W–9.1, given Treaty 8 and s. 35(1) of the *Constitution Act, 1982?*

100   It is evident from these reasons that the constitutional question should be answered as follows. The hunting rights confirmed by Treaty No. 8 were modified by para. 12 of the NRTA to the extent indicated in these reasons. Paragraph 12 of the NRTA provided for a continuing right to hunt for food on unoccupied land.

101   Mr. Badger and Mr. Kiyawasew were hunting on occupied land to which they had no right of access under Treaty No. 8 or the NRTA. Accordingly, ss. 26(1) and 27(1) of the *Wildlife Act* do not infringe their constitutional right to hunt for food.

102   However, Mr. Ominayak was exercising his constitutional right on land which was unoccupied for the purposes of this case. Section 26(1) of the *Wildlife Act*

constitutes a *prima facie* infringement of his Treaty right to hunt for food. As a result of their conclusions, the issue of justification was not considered by the courts below. Therefore, in his case, a new trial must be ordered so that the issue of justification may be addressed. . . .

103 The appeals of Mr. Badger and Mr. Kiyawasew are dismissed.

104 The appeal of Mr. Ominayak is allowed and a new trial directed so that the issue of the justification of the infringement created by s. 26(1) of the *Wildlife Act* and any regulations passed pursuant to that section may be addressed.

9.   Robinson Treaty (Lake Superior)

> The following is an excerpt for the 1850 Robinson Treaty (Lake Superior). See *A.G. Ontario v. Bear Island Foundation* in chapter 1, at pages 106 and 110, whereby the Supreme Court of Canada affirmed that the Robinson Treaty (Huron) extinguished the Aboriginal rights of the Temagami Indians.

ROBINSON TREATY (LAKE SUPERIOR)
With the Ojibewa Indians of Lake Superior conveying certain lands to the Crown

THIS AGREEMENT made and entered into on the seventh day of September, in the year of Our Lord one thousand eight hundred and fifty, at Sault Ste. Marie, in the Province of Canada between the Honourable WILLIAM BENJAMIN ROBINSON, *of the one part on behalf of* HER MAJESTY THE QUEEN, *and* JOSEPH PEANDECHAT, JOHN IUINWAY, MISHE-MUCKQUA, TOTOMENCIE, Chiefs, *and* JACOB WARPELA, AHMUTCHIWA GABOU, MICHEL SHELAGESHICK, MANITSHAINSE, *and* CHIGINANS, *principal men of the* OJIBEWA *Indians inhabiting the Northern Shore of Lake Superior, in the said Province of Canada, from Batchewana Bay to Pigeon River, at the western extremity of said Lake, and inland throughout that extent to the height of land which separates the territory covered by the charter of the Honourable the Hudson's Bay Company front the said tract, and also the Islands in the said Lake within the boundaries of the British possessions therein, of the other part, witnesseth:*

THAT for and in consideration of the sum of two thousand pounds of good and lawful money of Upper Canada, to them in hand paid, and for the further perpetual annuity of five hundred pounds, the same to be paid and delivered to the said Chiefs and their Tribes at, convenient season of each summer, not later than the first day of August at the Honorable the Hudson's Bay Company's Posts of Michipicoton and Fort William, they the said chiefs and principal men do freely, fully and voluntarily surrender, cede, grant and convey unto Her Majesty, Her heirs and successors forever, all their right, title and interest in the whole of the territory above described, save and except the reservations set forth in the schedule hereunto annexed, which reservations shall be held and occupied by the said Chiefs and their Tribes in common, for the purpose of residence and cultivation,—and should the said Chiefs and their respective Tribes at any time desire to dispose of any mineral or other valuable productions upon the said reservations, the same will be at their request sold by order of the Superintendent General of the Indian Department for the time being, for their sole use and benefit, and to the best advantage.

And the said William Benjamin Robinson of the first part, on behalf of Her Majesty and the Government of this province, hereby promises and agrees to make the payments as before mentioned; and further to allow the said chiefs and their tribes the full and free privilege to hunt over the territory now ceded by them, and to fish in the waters thereof as they have heretofore been in the habit of doing, saving and excepting only such portions of the said territory as may from time to time be sold or leased to individuals, or companies of individuals, and occupied by them with the consent of the provincial Government. The parties of the second part further promise and agree that they will not sell, lease, or otherwise dispose of any portion of their reservations without the consent of the Superintendent General of Indian Affairs being first had and obtained; nor will they at any time hinder or prevent persons from exploring or searching for mineral or other valuable productions in any part of the territory hereby ceded to Her Majesty as before mentioned. The parties of the second part also agree that in case the Government of this province should before the date of this agreement have sold, or bargained to sell, any mining locations or other property on the portions of the territory hereby reserve for their use and benefit, then and in that case such sale, or promise of sale, shall be forfeited, if the parties interested desire it, by the Government, and the amount accuring therefrom shall be paid to the tribe to whom the reservation belongs. The said William Benjamin Robinson on behalf of Her Majesty, who desires to deal liberally and justly with all Her subjects, further promises and agrees that in case the territory hereby ceded by the parties of the second part shall at any future period produce an amount which will enable the Government of this Province without incurring loss to increase the annuity hereby secured to them, then, and in that case, the same shall be augmented from time to time, provided that the amount paid to each individual shall not exceed the sum of one pound provincial currency in any one year, or such further sum as Her Majesty may be graciously pleased to order; and provided further that the number of Indians entitled to the benefit of this Treaty shall amount to two thirds of their present numbers (which is twelve hundred and forty) to entitle them to claim the full benefit thereof, and should their numbers at any future period not amount to two thirds of twelve hundred and forty, the annuity shall be diminished in proportion to their actual numbers.

Schedule of Reservations made by the above named and subscribing Chiefs and principal men. . . .

10. Treaty No. 6

Signed in 1876, Treaty No. 6 covers the mid-portions of Saskatchewan and Alberta. Notable in Treaty No. 6 is its reference to a medicine chest being kept in each house and its potential use as a right to medical care; see P. Barkwell, "The Medicine Chest Clause in Treaty No. 6," [1981] 4 C.N.L.R. 1; also see S. Venne, "Understanding Treaty 6: An Indigenous Perspective," in M. Asch, ed., *Aboriginal and Treaty Rights in Canada,* (Vancouver: U.B.C. Press, 1997) at 173.

Between Her Majesty the Queen and the Plains and Wood Cree Indians and
other tribes of Indians at Fort Carlton, Fort Pitt and Battle River.
ARTICLES OF A TREATY made and concluded near Carlton on the 23rd day of August, and on the 28th day of said month, respectively, and near Fort Pitt on the 9th
day of September, in the year of Our Lord one thousand eight hundred and sev-
enty-six, between Her Most Gracious Majesty the Queen of Great Britain and Ireland, by Her Commissioners, the Honourable Alexander Morris, Lieutenant-Governor of the Province of Manitoba and the North-West Territories, and the Honourable James McKay, and the Honourable William Joseph Christie, of the one
part, and the Plain and Wood Cree Tribes of Indians, and the other Tribes of Indians, inhabitants of the country within the limits hereinafter defined and described,
by their Chiefs, chosen and named as hereinafter mentioned, of the other part.

Whereas the Indians inhabiting the said country have, pursuant to an appoint-
ment made by the said commissioners, been convened at meetings at Fort Carlton,
Fort Pitt and Battle River, to deliberate upon certain matters of interest to Her Most
Gracious Majesty, of the one part, and the said Indians of the other;

And whereas the said Indians have been notified and informed by Her Majesty's said Commissioners that it is the desire of Her Majesty to open up for settlement, immigration and such other purposes as to Her Majesty may seem meet, a
tract of country, bounded and described as hereinafter mentioned, and to obtain the
consent thereto of Her Indian subjects inhabiting the said tract, and to make a
treaty and arrange with them, so that there may be peace and good will between
them and Her Majesty, and that they may know and be assured of what allowance
they are to count upon and receive from Her Majesty's bounty and benevolence;

And whereas the Indians of the said tract, duly convened in council as aforesaid, and being requested by Her Majesty's Commissioners to name certain Chiefs
and head men, who should be authorized, on their behalf, to conduct such negotiations and sign any treaty to be founded thereon, and to become responsible to Her
Majesty for their faithful performance by their respective bands of such obligations as shall be assumed by them, the said Indians have thereupon named for that
purpose, that is to say, representing:—the Indians who make the treaty at Carlton,
the several Chiefs and Councillors who have subscribed hereto, and representing
the Indians who make the treaty at Fort Pitt, the several Chiefs and Councillors
who have subscribed hereto;

And thereupon, in open council, the different bands having presented their
Chiefs to the said Commissioners as the Chiefs and head men, for the purposes
aforesaid, of the respective bands of Indians inhabiting the said district hereinafter
described;

And whereas, the said Commissioners then and there received and acknowledged the persons so represented, as Chiefs and head men, for the purposes aforesaid, of the respective bands of Indians inhabiting the said district hereinafter described;

And whereas the said Commissioners have proceeded to negotiate a treaty
with the said Indians, and the same has been finally agreed upon and concluded as
follows, that is to say:

The Plain and Wood Cree Tribes of Indians, and all other the Indians inhabiting the district hereinafter described and defined, do hereby cede, release, surrender and yield up to the Government of the Dominion of Canada for Her Majesty the Queen and Her successors forever, all their rights, titles and privileges whatsoever, to the lands included within the following limits, that is to say:

Commencing at the mouth of the river emptying into the north-west angle of Cumberland Lake, thence westerly up the said river to its source, thence on a straight line in a westerly direction to the head of Green Lake, thence northerly to the elbow in the Beaver River, thence down the said river northerly to a point twenty miles from the said elbow; thence in westerly direction, keeping on a line generally parallel with the said Beaver River (above the elbow), and about twenty miles distance therefrom, to the source of the said river; thence northerly to the north-easterly point of the south shore of Red Deer Lake, continuing westerly along the said shore to the western limit thereof and thence due west to the Athabaska River, thence up the said river, against the stream, to the Jasper House, in the Rocky Mountains; thence on a course south-easterly, following the easterly range of the Mountains, to the source of the main branch of the Red Deer River; thence down the said river, with the stream, to the junction therewith of the outlet of the river, being the outlet of the Buffalo Lake; thence due east twenty miles; thence on a straight line south-eastwardly to the mouth of the said Red Deer River on the south branch of the Saskatchewan River; thence eastwardly and northwardly, following on the boundaries of the tracts conceded by the several Treaties numbered Four and Five, to the place of beginning;

And also all their rights, titles and privileges whatsoever, to all other lands, wherever situated, in the North-West Territories, or in any other Province or portion of Her Majesty's Dominions, situated and being within the Dominion of Canada.

The tract comprised within the lines above described, embracing an area of 121,000 square miles, be the same more or less;

To have and to hold the same to Her Majesty the Queen and Her successors forever;

And Her Majesty the Queen hereby agrees and undertakes to lay aside reserves for farming lands, due respect being had to lands at present cultivated by the said Indians, and other reserves for the benefit of the said Indians, to be administered and dealt with for them by Her Majesty's Government of the Dominion of Canada, provided all such reserves shall not exceed in all one square mile for each family of five, or in that proportion for larger or smaller families, in manner following, that is to say:—

That the Chief Superintendent of Indian Affairs shall depute and send a suitable person to determine and set apart the reserves for each band, after consulting with the Indians thereof as to the locality which may be found to be most suitable for them;

Provided, however, that Her Majesty reserves the right to deal with any settlers within the bounds of any lands reserved for any band as She shall deem fit, and also that the aforesaid reserves of lands or any interest therein, maybe sold or otherwise disposed of by Her Majesty's Government for the use and benefit of the said Indians entitled thereto, with their consent first had and obtained; and with a view to show the satisfaction of Her Majesty with the behaviour and good conduct of Her Indians, She hereby, through Her Commissioners, makes them a present of twelve dollars for each man, woman and child belonging to the bands here represented, in extinguishment of all claims heretofore preferred;

And further, Her Majesty agrees to maintain schools for instruction in such reserves hereby made, as to Her Government of the Dominion of Canada may seem advisable, whenever the Indians of the reserve shall desire it;

Her Majesty further agrees with Her said Indians that within the boundary of Indian reserves, until otherwise determined by Her Government of the Dominion of Canada, no intoxicating liquor shall be allowed to be introduced or sold, and all laws now in force or hereafter to be enacted to preserve Her Indian subjects inhabiting the reserves or living elsewhere within Her North-West Territories from the evil influence of the use of intoxicating liquors, shall be strictly enforced;

Her Majesty further agrees with Her said Indians that they, the said Indians, shall have right to pursue their avocations of hunting and fishing throughout the tract surrendered as hereinbefore described, subject to such regulations as may from time to time be made by Her Government of Her Dominion of Canada, and saving and excepting such tracts as may from time to time be required or taken up for settlement, mining, lumbering or other purposes by Her said Government of the Dominion of Canada, or by any of the subjects thereof, duly authorized therefor, by the said Government;

It is further agreed between Her Majesty and Her said Indians, that such sections of the reserves above indicated as may at any time be required for public works or buildings of what nature soever, may he appropriated for that purpose by Her Majesty's Government of the Dominion of Canada, due compensation being made for the value of any improvements thereon;

And further, that Her Majesty's Commissioners shall, as soon as possible after the execution of this treaty, cause to be taken, an accurate census of all the Indians inhabiting the tract above described, distributing them in families, and shall in every year ensuing the date hereof, at some period in each year, to be duly notified to the Indians, and at a place or places to be appointed for that purpose within the territory ceded, pay to each Indian person the sum of $5 per head yearly;

It is further agreed between Her Majesty and the said Indians, that the sum of $1500.00 per annum, shall be yearly and every year expended by Her Majesty in the purchase of ammunition and twine for nets for the use of the said Indians, in manner following, that is to say:—In the reasonable discretion as regards the distribution thereof, among the Indians inhabiting the several reserves, or otherwise included herein, of Her Majesty's Indian Agent having the supervision of this treaty;

It is further agreed between Her Majesty and the said Indians that the following articles shall be supplied to any band of the said Indians who are now cultivating the soil, or who shall hereafter commence to cultivate the land, that is to say:— Four hoes for every family actually cultivating, also two spades per family as aforesaid; one plough for every three families as aforesaid, one harrow for every three families as aforesaid; two scythes, and one whetstone and two hay forks and two reaping-hooks for every family as aforesaid; and also two axes, and also one crosscut saw, and also one hand-saw, one pit-saw, the necessary files, one grindstone and one auger for each band; and also for each Chief for the use of his band, one chest of ordinary carpenter's tools; also for each band enough of wheat, barley, potatoes and oats to plant the land actually broken up for cultivation by such band; also for each band, four oxen, one bull and six cows, also one boar and two sows, and one handmill when any band shall raise sufficient grain therefor; all the aforesaid articles to be given *once for all* for the encouragement of the practice of agriculture among the Indians;

It is further agreed between Her Majesty and the said Indians, that each Chief, duly recognized as such, shall receive an annual salary of $25 per annum; and each subordinate officer, not exceeding four for each band, shall receive $15 per annum; and each such Chief and subordinate officer as aforesaid, shall also receive, once every three years, a suitable suit of clothing, and each Chief shall receive, in recognition of the closing of the treaty, a suitable flag and medal, and also, as soon as convenient, one horse, harness and waggon;

That in the event hereafter of the Indians comprised within this treaty being overtaken by any pestilence, or by a general famine, the Queen, on being satisfied and certified thereof by Her Indian Agent or Agents, will grant to the Indians assistance of such character and to such extent as Her Chief Superintendent of Indian Affairs shall deem necessary and sufficient to relieve the Indians from the calamity that shall have befallen them;

That during the next three years, after two or more of the reserves hereby agreed to be set apart to the Indians, shall have been agreed upon and surveyed, there shall be granted to the Indians included under the Chiefs adhering to the treaty at Carlton, each spring, the sum of $1000 to be expended for them by Her Majesty's Indian Agents, in the purchase of provisions for the use of such of the band as are actually settled on the reserves and are engaged in cultivating the soil, to assist them in such cultivation;

That a medicine chest shall be kept at the house of each Indian Agent for the use and benefit of the Indians, at the direction of such Agent;

That with regard to the Indians included under the Chiefs adhering to the treaty at Fort Pitt, and to those under Chiefs within the treaty limits who may hereafter give their adhesion hereto (exclusively, however, of the Indians of the Carlton region) there shall, during three years, after two or more reserves shall have been agreed upon and surveyed, be distributed each spring among the bands cultivating the soil on such reserves, by Her Majesty's Chief Indian Agent for this treaty in his discretion, a sum not exceeding $1000, in the purchase of provisions for the use of such members of the band as are actually settled on the reserves and engaged in the cultivation of the soil, to assist and encourage them in such cultivation;

That in lieu of waggons, if they desire it, and declare their option to that effect, there shall be given to each of the Chiefs adhering hereto, at Fort Pitt or elsewhere hereafter (exclusively of those in the Carlton district) in recognition of this treaty, as soon as the same can be conveniently transported, two carts, with iron bushings and tires;

And the undersigned Chiefs on their own behalf, and on behalf of all other Indians inhabiting the tract within ceded, do hereby solemnly promise and engage to strictly observe this treaty, and also to conduct and behave themselves as good and loyal subjects of Her Majesty the Queen;

They promise and engage that they will in all respects obey and abide by the law, and they will maintain peace and good order between each other, and also between themselves and other tribes of Indians, and between themselves and others of Her Majesty's subjects, whether Indians or whites, now inhabiting or hereafter to inhabit any part of the said ceded tracts, and that they will not molest the person or property of any inhabitant of such ceded tracts, or the property of Her Majesty the Queen, or interfere with or trouble any person passing or travelling through the said tracts or any part thereof; and that they will aid and assist the officers of Her Majesty in bringing to justice and punishment any Indian offending against the stipulations of this treaty or infringing the laws in force in the country so ceded.

IN WITNESS WHEREOF, Her Majesty's said Commissioners and the said Indian Chiefs have hereunto subscribed and set their hands, at or near Fort Carlton, on the day and year aforesaid, and near Fort Pitt on the day above aforesaid.

Signed by the Chiefs within named in the presence of the following witnesses, the same having been first read and explained by Peter Erasmus, Peter Ballendine and the Rev. John McKay. . . .

11. Treaty of 1760 (see *R.* v. *Sioui*, p. 156)

This is the text of the treaty at issue in the 1990 Supreme Court of Canada's *Sioui* decision. Note that it is very brief and is a unilateral declaration by the Governor of Quebec. The Huron Indians did not sign this document but it is, neverthless, a treaty recognized under Canadian law.

These are to certify that the chief of the Huron Tribe of Indians, having come to me in the name of His Nation, to submit to His Britannick Majesty, and make Peace, has been received under my protection, with his whole Tribe; and henceforth no English Officer or party is to molest, or interrupt them in returning to their settlement at Lorette; and they are received upon the same terms with the Canadians, being allowed the free Exercise of their Religion, their Customs, and Liberty of trading with the English:—recommending it to the Officers commanding the Posts, to treat them kindly.

Given under my hand at Longueil, this 5th day of September, 1760.

By the Genl's Command,

John Cosnan,

Adjut. Genl.

Ja. Murray. . . .

12. Report of the Commissioners for Treaty No. 8, September 22, 1899 (Ottawa: Queen's Printer, 1966)

WINNIPEG, MANITOBA, 22nd September, 1899.

The Honourable

CLIFFORD SIFTON,

Superintendent General of Indian Affairs,

Ottawa.

SIR,—We have the honour to transmit herewith the treaty which, under the Commission issued to us on the 5th day of April last, we have made with the Indians of the provisional district of Athabasca and parts of the country adjacent thereto, as described in the treaty and shown on the map attached. . . .

We met the Indians on the 20th, and on the 21st the treaty was signed.

As the discussions at the different points followed on much the same lines, we shall confine ourselves to a general statement of their import. There was a marked absence of the old Indian style of oratory. Only among the Wood Crees were any formal speeches made, and these were brief. The Beaver Indians are taciturn. The Chipewyans confined themselves to asking questions and making brief arguments. They appeared to be more adept at cross-examination than at speech-making, and the Chief at Fort Chipewyan displayed considerable keenness of intellect and much practical sense in pressing the claims of his band. They all wanted as liberal, if not more liberal, terms than were granted to the Indians of the plains. Some expected to be fed by the Government after the making of treaty, and all asked for assistance in seasons of distress and urged that the old and indigent who were no longer able to hunt and trap and were consequently often in distress should be cared for by the Government. They requested that medicines be furnished. At Vermilion, Chipewyan and Smith's Landing, an earnest appeal was made for the services of a medical man. There was expressed at every point the fear that the making of the treaty would be followed by the curtailment of the hunting and fishing privileges, and many were impressed with the notion that the treaty would lead to taxation and enforced military service. They seemed desirous of securing educational advantages for their children, but stipulated that in the matter of schools there should be no interference with their religious beliefs.

We pointed out that the Government could not undertake to maintain Indians in idleness; that the same means of earning a livelihood would continue after treaty as existed before it, and that the Indians would be expected to make use of them. We told them that the Government was always ready to give relief in cases of actual destitution, and that in seasons of distress they would without any special stipulation in the treaty receive such assistance as it was usual to give in order to prevent starvation among Indians in any part of Canada; and we stated that the attention of the Government would be called to the need of some special provision being made for assisting the old and indigent who were unable to work and [were] dependent on charity for the means of sustaining life. We promised that supplies of medicines would be put in the charge of persons selected by the Government at different points, and would be distributed free to those of the Indians who might require them. We explained that it would be preactically impossible for the Government to arrange for regular medical attendance upon Indians so widely scattered over such an extensive territory. We assured them, however, that the Government would always be ready to avail itself of any opportunity of affording medical service just as it provided that the physician attached to the Commission should give free attendance to all Indians whom he might find in need of treatment as he passed through the country.

Our chief difficulty was the apprehension that the hunting and fishing privileges were to be curtailed. The provision in the treaty under which ammunition and twine is to be furnished went far in the direction of quieting the fears of the Indians, for they admitted that it would be unreasonable to furnish the means of hunting and fishing if laws were to be enacted which would make hunting and fishing so restricted as to render it impossible to make a livelihood by such pursuits. But over and above the provision, we had to solemnly assure them that only such laws as to hunting and fishing as were in the interest of the Indians and were found necessary in order to protect the fish and fur-bearing animals would be made, and that they would be as free to hunt and fish after the treaty as they would be if they never entered into it.

We assured them that the treaty would not lead to any forced interference with their mode of life, that it did not open the way to the imposition of any tax, and that there was no fear of enforced military service. We showed them that, whether treaty was made or not, they were subject to the law, bound to obey it, and liable to punishment for any infringements of it. We pointed out that the law was designed for the protection of all, and must be respected by all the inhabitants of the country, irrespective of colour or origin; and that, in requiring them to live at peace with white men who came into the country, and not to molest them in person or in property, it only required them to do what white men were required to do as to the Indians.

As to education, the Indians were assured that there was no need of any special stipulation, as it was the policy of the Government to provide in every part of the country, as far as circumstances would permit, for the education of Indian children, and that the law, which was as strong as a treaty, provided for non-interference with the religion of the Indians in schools maintained or assisted by the Government. . . .

In addition to the annuity, which we found it necessary to fix at the figures of Treaty Six, which covers adjacent territory, the treaty stipulates that assistance in the form of seed and implements and cattle will be given to those of the Indians who may take to farming, in the way of cattle and mowers to those who may devote themselves to cattle-raising, and that ammunition and twine will be given to those who continue to fish and hunt. The assistance in farming and ranching is only to be given when the Indians actually take to these pursuits, and it is not likely that for many years there will be a call for any considerable expenditure under these heads. The only Indians of the territory ceded who are likely to take to cattle-raising are those about Lesser Slave Lake and along the Peace River, where there is quite an extent of ranching country; and although there are stretches of cultivable land in those parts of the country, it is not probable that the Indians will, while present conditions obtain, engage in farming further than the raising of roots in a small way, as is now done to some extent. In the main, the demand will be for ammunition and twine, as the great majority of the Indians will continue to hunt and fish for a livelihood. It does not appear likely that the conditions of the country on either side of the Athabasca and Slave Rivers or about Athabasca Lake will be so changed as to affect hunting or trapping, and it is safe to say that so long as the fur-bearing animals remain, the great bulk of the Indians will continue to hunt and to trap.

The Indians are given the option of taking reserves or land in severalty. As the extent of the country treated for made it impossible to define reserves or holdings, and as the Indians were not prepared to make selections, we confined ourselves to an undertaking to have reserves and holdings set apart in the future, and the Indians were satisfied with the promise that this would be done when required. There is no immediate necessity for the general laying out of reserves or the allotting of land. It will be quite time enough to do this as advancing settlement makes necessary the surveying of the land. Indeed, the Indians were generally averse to being placed on reserves. It would have been impossible to have made a treaty if we had not assured them that there was no intention of confining them to reserves. We had to very clearly explain to them that the provision for reserves and allotments of land were made for their protection, and to secure to them in perpetuity a fair portion of the land ceded, in the event of settlement advancing. . . .

The Indians with whom we treated differ in many respects from the Indians of the organized territories. They indulge in neither paint nor feathers, and never clothe themselves in blankets. Their dress is of the ordinary style and many of them are well clothed. In the summer they live in teepees, but many of them have log houses in which they live in winter. The Cree language is the chief language of trade, and some of the Beavers and Chipewyans speak it in addition to their own tongues. All the Indians we met were with rare exceptions professing Christians, and showed evidences of the work which missionaries have carried on among them for many years. A few of them have had their children avail themselves of the advantages afforded by boarding schools established at different missions. None of the tribes appear to have any very definite organization. They are held together mainly by the language bond. The chiefs and headmen are simply the most efficient hunters and trappers. They are not law-makers and leaders in the sense that the chiefs and headmen of the plains and of old Canada were. The tribes have no very distinctive characteristics, and as far as we could learn no traditions of any import. The Wood Crees are an off-shoot of the Crees of the South. The Beaver Indians bear some resemblance to the Indians west of the mountains. The Chipewyans are physically the superior tribe. The Beavers have apparently suffered most from scrofula and phthisis, and there are marks of these diseases more or less among all the tribes.

Although in manners and dress the Indians of the North are much further advanced in civilization than other Indians were when treaties were made with them, they stand as much in need of the protection afforded by the law to aborigines as do any other Indians of the country, and are as fit subjects for the paternal care of the Government. . . .

We desire to express our high appreciation of the valuable and most willing service rendered by Inspector Snyder and the corps of police under him, and at the same time to testify to the efficient manner in which the members of our staff performed their several duties. The presence of a medical man was much appreciated by the Indians, and Dr. West, the physician to the Commission, was most assiduous in attending to the great number of Indians who sought his services. We would add that the Very Reverend Father Lacombe, who was attached to the Commission, zealously assisted us in treating with the Crees.

The actual number of Indians paid was:—

7 Chiefs at $32 .... $ 224 00
23 Headmean at $22 .... 506 00
2,187 Indians at $12 .... 26,974 00
$26,974 00

A detailed statement of the Indians treated with and of the money paid is appended.

We have the honour to be, sir,

Your obedient servants,

DAVID LAIRD,

J. H. ROSS,

J. A. J. MCKENNA.

Indian Treaty Commissioners.

■ SELECTED BIBLIOGRAPHY

Aronson, S., "The Authority of the Crown to Make Treaties with Indians" [1993] 2 C.N.L.R. 1.

Barkwell, P., "The Medicine Chest Clause in Treaty No. 6" [1981] 4 C.N.L.R. 1.

Bell, C., "*R.* v. *Badger:* One Step Forward and Two Steps Back?" (1997) 8 *Const. Forum* 21.

Canada, DIAND. *Living Treaties, Lasting Agreements: Report of the Task Force to Review Comprehensive Claims Policy.* Ottawa: DIAND, 1985.

Cardinal, H. *The Unjust Society: The Tragedy of Canada's Indians.* Edmonton: Hurtig, 1969.

Coates, K., ed. *Aboriginal Land Claims Agreements: A Regional Perspective.* Toronto, Copp Clark Pitman, 1997.

Fumoleau, R. *As Long As This Land Shall Last: A History of Treaty 8 and Treaty 11 1870– 1939.* Toronto: McClelland and Stewart, 1973.

Grammond, S., "Aboriginal Treaties and Canadian Law" (1994) 20 *Queen's L.J.* 57.

Green, L.C., "Legal Significance of Treaties Affecting Canada's Indians" (1972) 1 *Anglo-American L. Rev.* 119.

Henderson W., and D. Ground, "Survey of Aboriginal Land Claims" (1994) 26:1 *Ottawa L. Rev.* 187.

Indian Treaties and Surrenders Volumes 1 to 3. 1891, 1912; reprint, Saskatoon, Sask.: Fifth House, 1992, 1993.

Knoll, D., "Treaty and Aboriginal Hunting Rights" [1979] 1 C.N.L.R. 1.

Lysyk, K., "The Unique Constitutional Position of the Canadian Indian" (1967) 45 *Can. Bar Rev.* 513.

Morris, A. *The Treaties of Canada with the Indians of Manitoba and the North-West Territories.* 1880; reprint, Saskatoon, Sask.: Fifth House, 1991.

Paul, D. *We Were Not the Savages: A Micmac Perspective on the Collision of European and Aboriginal Civilization.* Halifax: Nimbus, 1993.

Price, R., ed. *The Spirit of the Alberta Indian Treaties.* Montreal: Institute for Research on Public Policy, 1980.

Rotman, L., "Taking Aim at the Canons of Treaty Interpretation in Canadian Aboriginal Rights Jurisprudence" (1997) 46 *U.N.B.L.J.* 11.

Savino, V., and E. Schumacher, "'Whenever the Indians of the Reserve Should Desire It: An Analysis of the First Nation Treaty Right to Education" [1992] 21:3 *Man. L.J.* 476.

Treaty 7 Elders and Tribal Council. *The True Spirit and Original Intent of Treaty 7.* Montreal & Kingston: McGill-Queen's University Press, 1996.

Venne, S., "Understanding Treaty 6: An Indigenous Perspective." In *Aboriginal and Treaty Rights in Canada,* M. Asch, ed. Vancouver: U.B.C. Press, 1997, at 173.

Wildsmith, B., "Pre-Confederation Treaties." In *Aboriginal Peoples and the Law,* B. Morse, ed. Ottawa: Carleton University Press, 1985.

Woodward, J., Chapter XXI, pp. 403–16. In *Native Law.* Toronto: Carswell, 1989.

Zlotkin, N., "Post-Confederation Treaties." In *Aboriginal Peoples and the Law,* B. Morse, ed. Ottawa: Carleton University Press, 1985.

CHAPTER 3
FEDERAL-PROVINCIAL-TERRITORIAL LEGISLATIVE AUTHORITY

■ INTRODUCTION

FEDERAL AUTHORITY

Section 91(24) of the *Constitution Act, 1867*[1] assigns exclusive legislative authority to the federal Parliament over "Indians, and Lands reserved for the Indians." Beginning in 1868 and culminating with the present *Indian Act*,[2] Parliament has exercised exclusive legislative jurisdiction by enacting legislation dealing specifically with Indians and lands reserved for them, including the *Indian Oil and Gas Act*.[3] Regulations such as the *Indian Mining Regulations*,[4] the *Indian Oil and Gas Regulations*,[5] and the *Indian Timber Regulations*,[6] among others,[7] complete the statutes and regulatory regime exercised by Parliament regarding Indians.

First enacted in the late 1800s and amended over the years,[8] the modern *Indian Act* attempts to govern almost every aspect of Indian life and government on and off reserve. The act contains various rights, privileges, and restrictions and establishes the reserve system. Reserves can be created under the act and are lands that are set aside for the use and benefit of Indians. Certain rights are attached to reserve land, such as the tax exemption for property situated on a reserve.[9] In addi-

---

1 *Constitution Act, 1867*, 30 & 31 Vict., c. 3 (U.K.), (R.S.C. 1985, App. II, No. 5).
2 *Indian Act*, R.S.C. 1985, c. I–5.
3 *Indian Oil and Gas Act*, R.S.C. 1985, c. I–7.
4 *Indian Mining Regulations*, C.R.C. 1978, c. 956.
5 *Indian Oil and Gas Regulations*, C.R.C. 1978, c. 963.
6 *Indian Timber Regulations*, C.R.C. 1978, c. 961.
7 Other regulations enacted under the *Indian Act* include Disposal of Forfeited Goods and Chattels Regulations, C.R.C. 1978, c. 948; Indian Band Council Borrowing Regulations, C.R.C. 1978, c. 949; Indian Band Council Procedure Regulations, C.R.C. 1978, c. 950; Indian Band Election Regulations, C.R.C. 1978, c. 952; Indian Band Revenue Moneys Regulations, C.R.C. 1978, c. 953; Indian Estates Regulations, C.R.C. 1978, c. 954; Indian Reserve Traffic Regulations, C.R.C. 1978, c. 959; Indian Reserve Waste Disposal Regulations, C.R.C. 1978, c. 960; and Indian Bands Council Method of Election Regulations, SOR/90–46.
8 See S. Venne, ed., *Indian Acts and Amendments 1868–1975: An Indexed Collection* (Saskatoon: University of Saskatchewan Native Law Centre, 1981), *The Indian Act and Amendments 1970–1993: An Indexed Collection* (Saskatoon: University of Saskatchewan Native Law Centre, 1993), and T. Isaac, *Pre-1868 Legislation Concerning Indians* (Saskatoon: University of Saskatchewan Native Law Centre, 1993).
9 *Indian Act*, R.S.C. 1985, c. I–5, s. 87.

tion, property owned by an Indian and situated on a reserve cannot be seized by a non-Indian.[10] Although this protects Indian property from seizure, it also makes it difficult for Indians to obtain loans because their on-reserve property, including all reserve lands, cannot be used as collateral. Many self-government discussions currently under way or concluded seek to limit, to a great degree, the applicability of the *Indian Act* governance regime.

On December 12, 1996, Bill C-79, the *Indian Act Optional Modification Act,* was introduced into the House of Commons. The intention behind the bill was to allow First Nations the option of adopting a set of modifications that would give more control to the band governments and less control to the federal minister of Indian Affairs and Northern Development and federal officials. The proposed amendments would have eliminated the requirement for ministerial authority to approve the allotment and transfer of reserve lands among members, the sale of artifacts, the disposal of agricultural products, and the operation of farms on reserves. To simplify the process of approval in other matters, the minister, and not the governor in council, would have had the authority to grant management and control of reserve lands and the authority to control, manage, and expend revenue moneys to First Nations governments. Although this switch to increased ministerial authority under the proposed act could have shortened the time for bureaucratic approval, it would also have increased the minister's discretionary authority without providing a systemic check on this authority within the federal government. Some noteworthy proposals included lengthening the term of office for chief and councillors under the *Indian Act* electoral system (as opposed to the customary system) to three years from two years.[11] This initiative died primarily because First Nations and the federal government could not agree on the nature of the amendments. Obviously, this cannot be the end of attempts to amend the *Indian Act,* since the act remains in critical need of repair.

On January 7, 1998, the federal minister of Indian Affairs and federal Interlocutor for Métis and Non-Status Indians[12] released the federal government's response to the Royal Commission on Aboriginal Peoples, a report entitled *Gathering Strength—Canada's Aboriginal Action Plan.* The action plan includes a $350-million fund to support community-based healing as a mechanism to deal with the aftermath of abuse in the residential school system, as a commitment to further develop Aboriginal governance options, including capacity building and the creation of a body to assist Aboriginal groups to negotiate and implement self-government, as a means to develop a new fiscal relationship with Aboriginal peoples, and

---

10 Ibid., s. 89.

11 This would have been particularly helpful for governance on reserve since, under the existing system of two-year terms, a chief and council does not have enough time to implement their mandate.

12 Note that the Department of Indian Affairs and Northern Development does not have responsibility for Métis and non-status Indians. The federal government maintains that it does not have jurisdictional authority over Métis and non-status Indians, thereby limiting the federal government's fiduciary and fiscal responsibilities for these people.

as a platform for the development of a strong Aboriginal human resource and economic base. Notable was the federal government's inclusion of a "Statement of Reconciliation" in the action plan. Along with acknowledging the federal government's role in the residential school system and the death of Métis leader Louis Riel, the statement affirms that the "Government of Canada . . . formally expresses to all Aboriginal people in Canada our profound regret for past actions of the federal government which have contributed to these difficult pages in the history of our relationship together."[13]

Federal legislation that infringes a right recognized and affirmed by s. 35 of the *Constitution Act, 1982*[14] can be declared by a court to be of no force or effect. The precise limitations that s. 35 places on federal legislation, and perhaps federal jurisdiction with regard to self-government, remain unclear. In *R.* v. *Sparrow*, the Supreme Court of Canada stated that "rights that are recognized and affirmed are not absolute."[15] Federal legislative powers continue to exist, including the power to legislate on matters relating to "Indians, and Lands reserved for the Indians" under s. 91(24).[16] Ministerial discretionary authority came into question in the Supreme Court decision of *R.* v. *Adams*.[17] The issue in *Adams* concerned a Mohawk Indian who was charged with fishing without a licence. The minister possessed authority, however, to issue a special licence to permit the catching of fish for food. The licence requirement was held to be an infringement of Aboriginal rights that could not be justified. The court also noted that

> the regulatory scheme subjects the exercise of the appellant's Aboriginal rights to a pure act of Ministerial discretion, and sets out no criteria regarding how that discretion is to be exercised. . . . [T]he scheme both imposes undue hardship on the appellant and interferes with his preferred means of exercising his rights.[18]

In the 1996 Supreme Court of Canada decision of *R.* v. *Van der Peet,* Lamer C.J., writing for the majority, notes that the Crown's sovereignty must be reconciled with the fact that Aboriginal peoples were here before European settlement. The rights within s. 35 must be "directed towards the reconciliation of the pre-existence of Aboriginal societies with the sovereignty of the Crown."[19] Notwithstanding the need for reconciliation between the two realities, the court has affirmed, time and time again, the exclusive authority of the federal government to legislate with respect to Indians. In *Delgamuukw* v. *B.C.,* Lamer C.J. writes,

> [T]he exclusive power to legislate in relation to "Indians, and lands reserved for the Indians" has been vested with the federal government by virtue of s. 91(24). . . . That

---

13   Canada, DIAND, *Gathering Strength—Canada's Aboriginal Action Plan* (Ottawa: Minister of Public Works and Government Services Canada, 1997), 4–5.

14   *Constitution Act, 1982*, R.S.C. 1985, App. II, No. 44.

15   *R.* v. *Sparrow*, [1990] 3 C.N.L.R. 160 at 181.

16   Ibid.

17   *R.* v. *Adams,* [1996] 4 C.N.L.R. 1 (S.C.C.).

18   Ibid., para. 52.

19   *R.* v. *Van der Peet,* [1996] 4 C.N.L.R. 177 at 193, para. 31.

head of jurisdiction . . . encompasses within it the exclusive power to extinguish Aboriginal rights, including Aboriginal title.[20]

JURISDICTION REGARDING "ABORIGINAL PEOPLES"

"Aboriginal peoples" is not only a term commonly used to define the Indian, Métis, and Inuit peoples of Canada, but is also the term used in the *Constitution Act, 1982* in s. 25 of the *Canadian Charter of Rights and Freedoms* and in s. 35. Section 35(2) defines Aboriginal peoples as being the "Indian, Inuit and Métis peoples of Canada." Approximately 2.8 percent[21] of the population of Canada, or more than 1 million people, identify themselves as being of Aboriginal origin. However, "Aboriginal origin" does not denote the vast cultural differences that exist not only between Métis, Inuit, and Indian peoples, but also between groups and tribes within these groups. As well, although the term "Aboriginal peoples" has a legal definition within the context of the Constitution, by itself, the term does not encompass all the legal categories affecting Aboriginal peoples.[22]

Of the almost 800,000 people who identify as being of "Aboriginal origin, approximately 462,000 are registered Indians under the *Indian Act.* About 550,000 identify as being "North American Indian," with 210,000 as "Métis," and 41,000 as "Inuit." Section 91(24) of the *Constitution Act, 1867* states that Indians (including the Inuit)[23] and their lands are within the jurisdiction of the federal Parliament. The status of the Métis and non-registered Indians under s. 91(24) remains undetermined, although the federal government strongly maintains that it does not have exclusive jurisdictional responsibility for the Métis and that the Métis are a provincial responsibility. The *Indian Act* distinguishes who is, and who is not, an Indian for the purposes of the act.

In defining who is, and who is not, an Indian for the purposes of the *Indian Act,* the act provides that an Indian is a person who is registered as an Indian pursuant to the act, or who may be entitled to such registration.[24] Generally speaking, courts have held that corporations wholly owned by Indians are not "Indians" for the purposes of the act.[25] The act also establishes a register to list those who qualify

---

20 *Delgamuukw* v. *British Columbia,* [1998] 1 C.N.L.R. 14 (S.C.C.), para. 173.

21 Canada, Statistics Canada, *1996 Census of Canada: 1996 Aboriginal Peoples Survey.*

22 See T. Isaac, "The Power of Constitutional Language: The Case Against Using 'Aboriginal Peoples' As a Referent for First Nations" (1993) 19:1 *Queen's L.J.* 415; C. Chartier, "'Indian': An Analysis of the Term Used in Section 91(24) of the British North America Act, 1867" (1978–79) 43 *Sask. L. Rev.* 37; and P. Chartrand, "'Terms of Division': Problems of 'Outside-Naming' for Aboriginal People in Canada" (1991) 2:2 *Journal of Indigenous Stud.* 1.

23 See *Re Eskimos,* [1939] S.C.R. 104, and p. 341 of chap. 5.

24 *Indian Act,* R.S.C. 1985, c. I–5, s. 2(1).

25 See *Four B. Manufacturing Ltd.* v. *U.G.W.,* [1979] 4 C.N.L.R. 21 (S.C.C.); *Re Stony Plain Indian Reserve No. 135,* [1982] 1 C.N.L.R. 133 (Alta. C.A.); *Kinookimaw Beach Assn.* v. *R.,* [1979] 4 C.N.L.R. 101 (Sask. C.A.); and *Western Industrial Contractors Ltd.* v. *Sarcee Development Ltd.,* [1979] 2 C.N.L.R. 107 (Alta. C.A.).

as "Indians" for the purposes of the act.[26]

On April 17, 1985, the so-called Bill C-31 amendments to the *Indian Act* came into force. These amendments sought to update and modernize the membership and registration provisions of the *Indian Act.* Prior to Bill C-31, the act ensured that Indian status was passed on through the male line, allowed for no or little First Nations involvement in determining and managing membership and registration, and notably discriminated against women on the basis of their sex. In the latter case, registered Indian women who married non-Indian men lost their status and thus their right to live on reserve, among other benefits. Conversely, registered Indian men who married non-Indian women retained their status and additionally passed status along to their new wives (who became "Indians"). Although the new membership regime has sought to clarify and modernize the older membership and status provisions, and indeed has done so to a great extent, it is amazingly complex and has not cleared up the issue of who has a right to "reside" on reserve lands. For a more detailed discussion of this issue, see the introduction to chapter 9, "Aboriginal Women."

There is also a distinction between treaty and non-treaty Indians. Treaty Indians are those Indians who can trace their ancestry to people who signed treaties in Canada, whereas non-treaty Indians have no such claim. To confuse matters even more, one can be a treaty Indian and yet not be registered under the *Indian Act.* This means that although a person may be entitled to rights under a treaty, he or she may not be entitled to rights as an Indian under the *Indian Act.* For example, at the national level, the Assembly of First Nations represents registered (or status) Indian interests, while the Congress of Aboriginal Peoples represents the interests of non-registered Indians, some urban Indians, and some Métis. The Métis National Council represents national Métis interests, while the Inuit Tapirisat of Canada represents the interests of the Inuit nationally. Another group that is critical are those Aboriginal peoples who are beneficiaries under land claims agreements. Land claims agreements, like the *James Bay and Northern Quebec Agreement* (1975) and the *Inuvialuit Final Agreement* (1984), generally provide lands, cash, and some governance-type authorities to settle outstanding claims by the Aboriginal groups against the Crown.

The definition of Métis generally recognizes two groups. First, the Métis are those peoples who were known as the Métis and whose origin can be traced back to the Red River (Manitoba) in the early 1800s. Second, the Métis are a group of people of mixed Indian and non-Indian ancestry who are not directly connected to the Métis of the Red River but who nevertheless consider themselves to be Métis.[27] Those people who are of mixed Indian and non-Indian ancestry sometimes also refer to themselves as "Aboriginal" or "native."

The only Métis-specific legislation is found in Alberta where eight Metis settlements are governed by specific provincial legislation.[28] Inuit are not governed

---

26   *Indian Act,* R.S.C. 1985, c. I–5, s. 5.

27   See the discussion of Métis in chap. 5.

28   See *Métis Settlements Land Protection Act,* S.A. 1990, c. M–14.8 and *Métis Settlements Act,* S.A. 1990, c. M–14.3.

by the *Indian Act* nor by any other national legislation. Their primary means of government in the Northwest Territories is through the public government of the Northwest Territories. In 1999, the Northwest Territories will be divided to create two new territories. The eastern territory is Nunavut and has a public government. The Inuit form approximately 85 percent of the population of Nunavut. The Inuit of northern Quebec are covered by the *James Bay and Northern Quebec Agreement.*

PROVINCIAL AUTHORITY

The basic rule is that provincial laws apply to Indians and lands reserved for Indians.[29] For example, in *R.* v. *Francis,*[30] the Supreme Court of Canada held that provincial traffic laws apply to Indians driving vehicles on Indian reserves.

Although the basic rule is that provincial laws apply to Indians, this rule is subject to a number of conditions. First, provincial legislation must not "single out" Indians and lands reserved for Indians because in so doing it would infringe upon an area of exclusive federal jurisdiction.[31] Second, provincial laws must not affect "an integral part of primary federal jurisdiction over Indians and lands reserved for the Indians."[32] Third, the provinces of Alberta, Saskatchewan, and Manitoba are subject to the 1930 *Natural Resources Transfer Agreements,*[33] which provide that provincial laws cannot deprive Indians of their right to take game and fish for food.[34] Fourth, if a provincial law of general application is inconsistent with a federal law in its application to Indians or to lands reserved for Indians, then the doctrine of federal paramountcy applies. Finally, a provincial law, like a federal law, may be declared by a court to be of no force or effect if it infringes an existing Aboriginal or treaty right protected by s. 35 of the *Constitution Act, 1982.* Section 35 is discussed in detail in chapter 7.[35]

Section 88 of the *Indian Act* incorporates by reference provincial laws of general application. Section 88 reads:

> Subject to the terms of any treaty and any other Act of the Parliament of Canada, all laws of general application . . . in force in any province are applicable to . . . Indians in

---

29 P. Hughes, "Indians and Lands Reserved for the Indians: Off Limits to the Provinces?" (1983) 21 *Osgoode Hall L.J.* 82.

30 *R.* v. *Francis*, [1988] 4 C.N.L.R. 98 (S.C.C.).

31 *R.* v. *Sutherland*, [1980] 3 C.N.L.R. 71; *Dick* v. *R.*, [1985] 4 C.N.L.R. 55; and *Leighton* v. *B.C.*, [1989] 3 C.N.L.R. 136 (B.C.C.A.).

32 *Four B Manufacturing* v. *UGW*, [1979] 4 C.N.L.R. 21 at 25 (S.C.C.).

33 *Constitution Act, 1930*, R.S.C. 1985, App. II, No. 8.

34 See, for example, *R.* v. *Horseman*, [1990] 3 C.N.L.R. 95 (S.C.C.).

35 In *R.* v. *Perry,* [1996] 2 C.N.L.R. 67 (Ont. Gen. Div.), the court held that Ontario's distinction between status and non-status Indians in its *Interim Enforcement Policy* violated s. 15 (equality provisions) of the *Charter* and was *ultra vires* the province because of the federal government's jurisdiction in s. 91(24). The court read-up the policy to provide that where the terms "status" or "non-status" are used, the term "Aboriginal" is to be used in its place.

the province, except to the extent that such laws are inconsistent with this Act or any order, rule, regulation or by-law made thereunder. . . .

Although Indians are subject to provincial laws of general application, the Supreme Court of Canada has held that the laws to which Indians are subject must be "general" in nature and cannot relate exclusively or directly to Indians. In *Kruger* v. *R.*,[36] Dickson J. stated:

> [There are] two indicia by which to discern whether or not a provincial enactment is a law of general application. . . . If the Act does not extend uniformly throughout the territory, the inquiry is at an end. . . . If the law does extend uniformly throughout the jurisdiction, the intention and effects of the enactment need to be considered. The law must not be in relation to one class of citizens in object and purpose. . . . There are few laws which have a uniform impact. The line is crossed, however, when an enactment, though in relation to another matter, by its effect impairs the status or capacity of a particular group.

Since the *Kruger* decision, the Supreme Court of Canada has expanded its interpretation of "laws of general application." Provincial legislation can impair the status and capacity of an Indian without necessarily singling out an Indian. This was the decision of *R.* v. *Dick*.[37] The Supreme Court of Canada held that although the British Columbia *Wildlife Act*[38] prevented year-round hunting and therefore affected the accused Indian, who wished to hunt to maintain or follow a traditional way of life, the act, nevertheless, did not single out Indians specifically and therefore, was *intra vires* the province. In *R.* v. *Dick*[39] the Supreme Court of Canada held that provincial laws of general application that did not affect the status or capacity of Indians, or did not affect "Indianness," could apply *ex proprio vigore* (of their own force). This interpretation of s. 88 has been reaffirmed by the Supreme Court in *Derrickson* v. *Derrickson*[40] and *R.* v. *Francis*.[41]

On the issue of whether provincial laws of general application apply to the use of reserve lands, the Alberta Court of Appeal stated the following in *Re Stony Plains Indian Reserve No. 135*:[42]

> We accept, the general proposition that provincial legislation relating to the use of reserved lands is inapplicable to lands that are found to be reserved for Indians.

Re Stony Plains affirms that once land is surrendered and title is transferred in fee simple, the land is no longer a reserve within the meaning of the *Indian Act* and is no longer land "reserved for the Indians" for the purposes of s. 91(24) of the

---

36   *Kruger and Manuel* v. *R.*, 9 C.N.L.C. 624 at 628 (S.C.C.).
37   *R.* v. *Dick*, [1985] 4 C.N.L.R. 55 (S.C.C.). See also, *Derrickson* v. *Derrickson*, [1986] 2 C.N.L.R. 45 (S.C.C.).
38   *Wildlife Act*, R.S.B.C. 1979, c. 433, ss. 3 & 8.
39   *R.* v. *Dick*, [1985] 4 C.N.L.R. 55 (S.C.C.).
40   *Derrickson* v. *Derrickson*, [1986] 2 C.N.L.R. 45 (S.C.C.).
41   *R.* v. *Francis*, [1988] 4 C.N.L.R. 98 (S.C.C.).
42   *Re Stony Plain Indian Reserve No.135*, [1982] 1 C.N.L.R. 133 at 151 (Alta. C.A.).

Constitution Act, 1867. Thus, the land is subject to provincial legislative jurisdiction. However, when the fee simple title to the surrendered land is held by the grantee in trust for the benefit of the Indian band and its members, no band interest is ceded and the land therefore remains a reserve. If the terms of a surrender provide that the Crown in right of Canada retains title to the surrendered land, then the Indian band affected retains landlord rights, including the right of reversion. The court in *Re Stony Plains* also noted that a corporation cannot be an Indian for the purposes of either the *Indian Act* or s. 91(24). Finally, the court held that where provincial legislation affects the use, enjoyment of, and interests in reserve lands, provincial legislation is inapplicable to those lands. If lands are surrendered for leasing purposes, the reversion is held by the Indians and provincial legislation limiting reversion will not be applicable. Surrendered land remains land "reserved for the Indians" and therefore remains as a federal responsibility for its control and management.

The 1997 Supreme Court of Canada decision of *R. v. Delgamuukw* reaffirms the nature of applying provincial laws of general application to Indians. Laws of general application that do not affect the "Indianness" apply by way of their own force. Laws that do affect "Indianness" must depend on s. 88 of the *Indian Act*, which referentially incorporates provincial legislation into federal law.[43] Furthermore, s. 91(24) of the *Constitution Act, 1867* contains the exclusive right of the federal Parliament to extinguish Aboriginal rights and title.[44] The right to extinguish Aboriginal rights and title is not held by the provinces.[45]

Unlike the other provinces, Manitoba, Saskatchewan, and Alberta did not initially own their public lands and natural resources as provided for in ss. 109 and 117 of the *Constitution Act, 1867*.[46] The federal Crown retained ownership of Crown lands and natural resources in the prairie provinces to facilitate federal policies with respect to immigration, land settlement, and railways. In 1929 and 1930, the Dominion government signed *Natural Resources Agreements* with the three prairie provinces to give them ownership of natural resources and Crown lands. These agreements were given constitutional effect by the *Constitution Act, 1930*.

The *1930 Natural Resources Transfer Agreements*[47] (*NRTA* or *Constitution Act, 1930*) also present a limitation on the applicability of provincial legislation to Indians.[48] In the Alberta (para. 12), Saskatchewan (para. 12), and Manitoba (para. 13)

---

43   *Delgamuukw* v. *British Columbia,* [1998] 1 C.N.L.R. 14 (S.C.C.), para. 37.

44   *Constitution Act, 1867,* 30 & 31 Vict., c. 3 (U.K.), (R.S.C. 1985, App. II, No. 5), para. 173.

45   *Delgamuukw* v. *British Columbia,* [1998] 1 C.N.L.R. 14 (S.C.C.), paras. 180 and 183.

46   The Crown in right of Canada retains ownership of most public lands and their natural resources in the NWT/Nunavut and the Yukon Territory.

47   Numerous amendments have been made to the Natural Resources Transfer Agreements. A listing of these amendments can be found in B. Funston and E. Meehan, eds., *Canadian Constitutional Documents Consolidated* (Toronto: Carswell, 1994), 297.

48   Cory J. for a majority of the Supreme Court of Canada in *R. v. Horseman,* [1990] 3 C.N.L.R. 95 at 104–05 cited with approval Laskin J.'s dissenting judgment in *Cardinal* v.

agreements, the following clause is found:

> In order to secure to the Indians of the Province the continuance of the supply of game
> and fish for their support and subsistence, Canada agrees that the laws respecting
> game in force in the Province from time to time shall apply to the Indians within the
> boundaries thereof, provided, however, that the said Indians shall have the right, which
> the Province hereby assures to them of hunting, trapping and fishing game for food at
> all seasons of the year on all unoccupied Crown lands and on any other lands to which
> the said Indians may have a right of access.

In *R.* v. *Horse*,[49] the Supreme Court of Canada held that para. 12 of the Saskatchewan *NRTA* must be given a broad and liberal interpretation and resolve any ambiguity in the phrase "right of access" in favour of the Indians. However, notwithstanding this interpretation, the Indian right to take game and fish for food is limited to the lands specified. In the *Horse* decision, the Indians had no right of access to the private lands in question. *R.* v. *Horseman* gave a broader interpretation to the Alberta *NRTA*. The Supreme Court of Canada held in *Horseman*[50] that the Indian commercial right to hunt guaranteed by Treaty No. 8 in 1899 was "merged and consolidated" by para. 12 of the Alberta *NRTA* and that the Indians' hunting rights were now limited to those specified by the *NRTA*.

Paragraph 12 provides that Canada and Saskatchewan recognize that Indians have special hunting, fishing, and trapping rights and that the Indians are dependent on game and fish for food. It should be noted that para. 12 applies only to provincial legislation. Federal legislation respecting migratory birds, inland fisheries, and the sea coast continue to apply, subject to s. 35.

The primary purpose of para. 12 was first stated by Mr. Justice McGillivray of the Alberta Supreme Court, Appellate Division, in the 1932 decision of *R.* v. *Wesley*:[51]

> It seems to me that the language of sec. 12 is unambiguous and the intention of Parliament to be gathered therefrom clearly is to assure to the Indians a supply of game in the future for their support and subsistence by requiring them to comply with the game laws of the province, subject however to the express and dominant proviso that care for the future is not to deprive them of the right to satisfy their present need for food by

---

A.G. of Alberta, [1974] S.C.R. 695 at 722 on the true effect of para. 12 of the *NRTA*. The cited portion of Laskin J.'s dissent reads, in part: "[Section 12] is concerned rather with Indians as such, and with guaranteeing to them a continuing right to hunt, trap and fish for food regardless of provincial game laws which would otherwise confine Indians in parts of the Province that are under provincial administration. *Although inelegantly expressed s.12 does not expand provincial legislative power but contracts it.* . . .There is hence, by virtue of the sanction of the *British North America Act, 1930*, a limitation upon provincial authority regardless of whether or not Parliament legislates. [Emphasis added.]"

49   *R.* v. *Horse*, [1988] 2 C.N.L.R. 112 (S.C.C.).
50   *R.* v. *Horseman*, [1990] 3 C.N.L.R. 95 (S.C.C.).
51   *R.* v. *Wesley*, 5 C.N.L.C. 540 at 547 (Alta. S.C.).

hunting and trapping game, using the word "game" in its broadest sense, at all seasons on unoccupied Crown lands or other lands to which they may have a right of access.

This statement was adopted by the Supreme Court of Canada in its unanimous 1980 decision of *R. v. Sutherland.*[52] Therefore, Indians are guaranteed the right to take game and fish "for food" at all seasons of the year on the lands specified and provincial laws to the contrary are inapplicable to Indians. The words "for food" represent a notable restriction on the hunting and fishing rights conferred by the NRTA. Those Indians who by treaty may have had a right to fish and hunt for commercial purposes had their rights restricted by para. 12 of the NRTA. Thus, the Indian's treaty rights were limited to the extent specified by the agreement and had been partially extinguished by the agreement. Of course, since the NRTA applies only to the prairie provinces, the extent to which it applies to Treaty No. 8 territory in the Northwest Territories is questionable.

Paragraph 12 of Saskatchewan's NRTA "merges and consolidates" Treaty No. 6 hunting rights.[53] Section 35 of the *Constitution Act, 1982* neither expands nor constricts rights that were affected by para. 12. In *R. v. McIntyre*[54] the Saskatchewan Court of Appeal has held that para. 12 of the NRTA "merges and consolidates" Treaty No. 10 hunting rights. Section 35 of the *Constitution Act, 1982* neither expands nor contracts existing rights identified as being contained in para. 12.[55] The Court of Appeal affirmed that Saskatchewan has the authority to create game preserves (established in *R. v. Strongquill*[56] and confirmed by the Supreme Court of Canada in *R. v. Sutherland*[57]). The court also noted that Saskatchewan has the right to establish road corridor game preserves since the province was established for *bona fide* reasons.[58]

The Alberta Court of Queen's Bench in *R. v. Alexson*[59] held that leased grazing land was not "unoccupied Crown land" or "other lands" within para. 12. Thus, treaty Indians must obtain the permission of leaseholders before hunting on leased lands. In the Supreme Court of Canada decision of *R. v. Horse,*[60] the court determined that para. 12 must be given a "broad and liberal construction" and any ambiguity in the phrase "right of access" must be resolved in favour of Indians.

In summary, provincial laws apply to Indians and lands reserved for Indians, subject to a number of important qualifiers. Provincial laws cannot legislate Indians exclusively, rather they must legislate under the guise of laws of general application (to the population as a whole). Provincial laws cannot affect the "status or

52   *R. v. Sutherland,* [1980] 3 C.N.L.R. 71 at 78 (S.C.C.).

53   *R. v. Moosehunter,* [1981] 1 C.N.L.R. 61 (S.C.C.); *R. v. Horse,* [1984] 4 C.N.L.R. 99 at 106 (Sask. C.A.); *R. v. Bird,* [1992] 1 C.N.L.R. 119 (Sask. Prov. Ct.).

54   *R. v. McIntyre,* [1992] 3 C.N.L.R. 113 (Sask. C.A.).

55   See *R. v. Badger,* [1996] 2 C.N.L.R. 77 (S.C.C.).

56   *R. v. Strongquil,* 5 C.N.L.C. 567 (Sask. C.A.).

57   *R. v. Sutherland,* [1980] 3 C.N.L.R. 71 (S.C.C.).

58   *R. v. Wolverine,* [1989] 3 C.N.L.R. 181 (Sask. C.A.).

59   *R. v. Alexson,* [1990] 4 C.N.L.R. 28 (Alta. Q.B.).

60   *R. v. Horse,* [1988] 2 C.N.L.R. 112 (S.C.C.).

capacity" of Indians as Indians.[61] Provincial laws cannot encroach upon the federal jurisdiction over Indians as provided for in s. 91(24) of the *Constitution Act, 1867,* or any other federal act for that matter. The three prairie provinces within the jurisdiction of the NRTAs cannot deny Indians their hunting and fishing rights protected and recognized thereunder. Finally provincial laws are subject, of course, to s. 35— Aboriginal and treaty rights.

TERRITORIAL AUTHORITY

Unlike the provinces, the Yukon Territory and the Northwest Territories are creatures of the federal Parliament and, as such, do not possess independent sovereign status akin to the provincial legislatures and the federal Parliament. The federal statutes establishing the Northwest Territories and Nunavut (not in force until April 1, 1999) can still be amended by Parliament. Both the *Northwest Territories Act*[62] and the *Yukon Act*[63] allow for the respective commissioners in council (lieutenant governors) of each territory and the governor in council to enact ordinances (legislation) and make regulations dealing specifically with Indian and Inuit people in a narrow range of matters.

April 1, 1999, marks Canada's first major jurisdictional realignment since Newfoundland joined Confederation in 1949 with the creation of Nunavut—Canada's third territory.[64] The creation of Nunavut is the direct result of the Nunavut Land Claims Agreement and the federal government's obligation therein to put before Parliament legislation creating the new territory (which it did in 1993 in the *Nunavut Act,* S.C. 1993, c. 28). The creation of Nunavut, which has a public government, is unique in that it results from a land claims agreement with the Inuit and will be heavily influenced by the Inuit (in that they represent approximately 85 percent of the population). While there will be a great deal of commentary and analysis on the nature and form of this new northern government as it evolves, questions regarding the role of the Inuit majority, *as Aboriginal peoples,* and the degree to which the new territory is welcomed into Confederation by the other two territories and more particularly the provinces will be noteworthy.

Section 18 of the *Northwest Territories Act* and s. 19 of the *Yukon Act*[65] provide that the territorial legislatures may make laws regarding the preservation of game in the territories and that such laws are applicable to and in respect of Indian and Inuit peoples. However, such laws cannot restrict or prohibit Indians or Inuit from hunting for food on unoccupied Crown land unless the game has been declared by the governor in council as game that is in danger of becoming extinct.

---

61   See *R.* v. *Kruger,* [1978] 1 S.C.R. 104 at 110.

62   *Northwest Territories Act,* R.S.C. 1985, c. N–27.

63   *Yukon Act,* R.S.C. 1985, c. Y–2.

64   See chap. 2, p. 128 for more discussion.

65   Section 19 has been substantially amended by the *Yukon First Nations Land Claims Settlement Act,* S.C. 1994, c. 34, s. 20, and that amendment will come into force on the first day on which the final agreements of all First Nations are given effect. (See s. 19 of the *Yukon Act,* provided at p. 287 of this chapter.)

Section 22(2) of the *Northwest Territories Act* provides that "all laws of general application in force in the Territories are, except where otherwise provided, applicable to the Inuit in the Territories." The purpose of this section is unclear since the territorial governments are delegated forms of government receiving their authority to govern from the federal Parliament (which has jurisdiction over the Inuit under s. 91(24)). In *Re Noah Estate*,[66] Sissons J. stated that the purpose of then s. 17(2) (now s. 22(2))[67]

> . . . was to make legislation of the Territorial Council of the Northwest Territories in relation to the preservation of game into federal legislation relating to Indians and Eskimos and of general application [and] . . . to authorize the abrogation, abridgement or infringement of the hunting rights of the Eskimos and other rights of the Eskimos by the Territorial Government.[68]

Laws of general application in the Northwest Territories are not absolute. They are subject to federal legislative authority, s. 35 protecting Aboriginal and treaty rights, and land claims agreements (which are constitutionalized under s. 35(3)). Territorial common law has been interpreted as including some Inuit customary law. For example, in *Re Katies Adoption Petition*,[69] Sissons J. held that customary Inuit adoptions were in accordance with the laws of the Northwest Territories. In *Re Deborah*,[70] the Northwest Territories Court of Appeal stated that the territorial legislation regarding adoptions was never intended to restrict the applicability of Inuit customary law.[71]

Sections 48–51 of the *Yukon Act* and ss. 45–48 of the *Northwest Territories Act* authorize the federal minister to enter into agreements with Indian and Inuit peoples for the herding, control, management, administration, sale, slaughter, and protection of reindeer in the territories.

In *Bruce* v. *Yukon Territory (Commissioner)*,[72] Lilles J. of the Yukon Territory Supreme Court held that the terms "band community" and "band council," which were specifically mentioned in a territorial law, were merely descriptive terms of a geographical area and not necessarily restricted to Indians. The terms were used to reflect the social and political reality of the geographical area and were not used in the constitutional sense. This decision reflects the unique nature of government in the North, where most communities are mixed Indian/non-Indian.

---

66 *Re Noah Estate*, 6 C.N.L.C. 120 at 138–39, (1961), 36 W.W.R. 577, 32 D.L.R. (2d) 185 (N.W.T. Terr. Ct.).

67 *Northwest Territories Act*, R.S.C. 1952, c.331, s. 17(2) as am. by S.C. 1960 c. 20, s. 2.

68 *Re Noah Estate*, 6 C.N.L.C. 120 at 138.

69 *Re Katies Adoption Petition*, 6 C.N.L.C. 1 (N.W.T. Terr. Ct.).

70 *Re Deborah*, 7 C.N.L.C. 475 (N.W.T.C.A.).

71 For further discussion, see N. Zlotkin, "Judicial Recognition of Aboriginal Customary Law in Canada: Selected Marriage and Adoption Cases" [1984] 4 C.N.L.R. 1.

72 *Bruce* v. *Yukon Territory (Commissioner)*, [1994] 3 C.N.L.R. 25 (Y.T.S.C.).

THE FIDUCIARY RELATIONSHIP

The relationship between Aboriginal peoples and the Crown has been character-ized as a fiduciary relationship.[73] This special relationship with the Crown arises from numerous sources, including the historical, political, legal, and socio-eco-nomic relationship the federal Crown has had with Aboriginal peoples, the *Royal Proclamation of 1763*,[74] the treaties, and various pieces of legislation and instru-ments.

The fiduciary responsibility can be divided into three categories. The first is the type of fiduciary relationship noted in the *Guerin*[75] decision, where the Crown must act in the best interests of Indian peoples when dealing with Indian property and lands. The second type of fiduciary relationship is outlined in the *Sparrow*[76] decision. This aspect of the fiduciary relationship requires governments (federal, provincial, and territorial) to meet the justificatory test in *Sparrow* in order to al-low legislation to infringe Aboriginal or treaty rights. The third type of fiduciary relationship is less well defined. It relates to the "special trust-like" relationship between the Crown and Aboriginal peoples and may be linked to fiscal responsi-bilities, political responsibilities, and jurisdictional exclusivity (namely under s. 91(24)).

The provincial and territorial governments argue that this latter fiduciary rela-tionship, which includes obligations, is within the sole purview of the federal Crown. This relationship is evidenced by s. 91(24) and the treaties. Although the provinces and territories may have responsibilities, they argue essentially that they are not of the "fiduciary" nature. This issue is primarily driven by fiscal concerns. The prov-inces and territories argue that Aboriginal peoples are primarily the financial re-sponsibility of the federal government and not of the provincial and territorial gov-ernments. This issue remains unsettled legally and is the basis for an ongoing po-litical and bureaucratic debate between federal, provincial, and territorial govern-ments.

Although most of the litigation to date relating to the fiduciary obligations of the Crown relate to the federal Crown, some litigation has dealt specifically with the provincial Crowns[77] and has implied a fiduciary obligation on the provincial

---

73 For a general discussion of fiduciary obligations, see, for example, *Frame* v. *Smith*, [1987] 2 S.C.R. 99; *Lac Minerals Ltd.* v. *International Corona Resources Ltd.*, [1989] 2 S.C.R. 574; and *Canson Enterprises Ltd.* v. *Boughton and Co.*, [1991] 3 S.C.R. 543.

74 *Royal Proclamation of 1763*, R.S.C. 1985, App. II, No. 1. Indians are referred to in the *Royal Proclamation*, and in many of the treaties, as being "under the protection" of the Crown.

75 An excerpt of *R.* v. *Guerin*, [1985] 1 C.N.L.R. 120 (S.C.C.) is provided in chap. 1 at 41.

76 An excerpt of *R.* v. *Sparrow*, [1990] 3 C.N.L.R. 160 (S.C.C.) is provided in chap. 7 at 405.

77 See L.I. Rotman, "Provincial Fiduciary Obligations to First Nations: The Nexus Be-tween Governmental Power and Responsibility" (1994) 32:4 *Osgoode Hall L.J.* 735.

Crown.[78] Regardless, to date no overt distinction between the federal and provincial Crowns vis-à-vis a general fiduciary obligations has been made by the Supreme Court of Canada. Such a distinction is unlikely based on the Supreme Court's judgments to date. Although there may be specific fiduciary duties to which the federal Crown is accountable because of its unique relationship to Indians under s. 91(24) to which a provincial Crown would not be held, the general fiduciary obligations outlined in *Sparrow* and *Guerin* most likely apply to the provinces as well. It is simply a matter of fair dealing with a group of peoples who have special rights and a special history in Canada.

The Crown's fiduciary obligation to Aboriginal peoples represents a burden on the ability of the Crown to conduct its business. The constitutionalization of Aboriginal and treaty rights in s. 35 of the *Constitution Act, 1982* makes this particularly true. Brian Slattery writes:

> The Crown has a general fiduciary duty toward native people to protect them in the enjoyment of their aboriginal rights and in particular in the possession and use of their lands.[79]

This general fiduciary duty[80] supports the specific fiduciary duty of the Crown in the handling of surrendered (and possibly unsurrendered) Indian lands. The leading decision in this regard is *R.* v. *Guerin*.[81] In October 1957, the Musqueam Indian Band of British Columbia surrendered 162 acres of reserve land situated in the City of Vancouver to the federal Crown pursuant to ss. 37–41 of the *Indian Act*.[82]

---

78 For example, in *R.* v. *Smith*, [1983] 1 S.C.R. 554, Estey J., for the majority, was considering a band's release of its interests in land and how such a release could give rise to differences between the parties to the release. Estey J. quotes with approval Street, J. from *Ontario Mining Co. Ltd.* v. *Seybold*, [1901] 32 O.R. 301 at 565 (Ont. Div. Ct.): "The surrender was undoubtedly burdened with the obligation imposed by the treaty to select and lay aside special portions of the tract . . . for the special use and benefit of the Indians. The Provincial Government could not without plain disregard of justice take advantage of the surrender and refuse to perform the condition attached to it." See also *Cree Regional Authority* v. *Robinson*, [1991] 4 C.N.L.R. 84 at 106, (F.C.T.D.) and *Ontario (A.G.)* v. *Bear Island Foundation*, [1991] 3 C.N.L.R. 79 at 80 (S.C.C.). In *Bear Island*, the court noted that the "Crown has failed to comply with some of its obligations . . . and thereby breached its fiduciary obligations to the Indians." What is interesting in *Bear Island* is that the federal Crown was not the subject of the litigation, rather it was the provincial Crown of Ontario.

79 Brian Slattery, "Understanding Aboriginal Rights" (1987) 66 *Can. Bar Rev.* 727 at 753.

80 In *Kruger* v. *R.*, [1985] 3 C.N.L.R. 15 at 98, Heald J. stated: "[T]he Governor in Council is not able to default in its fiduciary relationship to the Indians on the basis of other priorities and other considerations."

81 *R.* v. *Guerin*, [1985] 1 C.N.L.R. 120 (S.C.C.). For commentary, see John Hurley, "The Crown's Fiduciary Duty and Indian Title: *Guerin* v. *The Queen*" (1985) 30 *McGill L.J.* 559.

82 *Indian Act*, R.S.C. 1952, c. 149; now R.S.C. 1985, c. I–5.

The surrender enabled the band to secure a lease with a golf club. The terms and conditions of the lease were not part of the surrender but, rather, were discussed between federal officials and the band at band meetings. The Crown executed the lease on terms that were not as favourable as the terms originally agreed upon orally. The Crown did not receive the band's permission to change the terms of the lease, nor did it provide a copy of the lease to the band until 1970. The band instituted a suit against the Crown for breach of trust.

The Supreme Court of Canada's judgment consists of three opinions (eight judges took part in the decision, but some simply concurred with the judgment of other judges). Seven of the eight judges held that the Crown has a fiduciary duty respecting Indians lands. Dickson J. wrote, for the majority:

> [T]he nature of Indian title and the framework of the statutory scheme established for disposing of Indian land places upon the Crown an equitable obligation, enforceable by the courts, to deal with the land for the benefit of the Indians. This obligation does not amount to a trust in the private law sense. It is rather a fiduciary duty. If, however, the Crown breaches this fiduciary duty it will be liable to the Indians in the same way and to the same extent as if such a trust were in effect.[83]

Dickson J. held that Indian title comes from two sources: Indians' historical occupation and possession of their lands and the *Royal Proclamation* of October 7, 1763. Aboriginal title is *sui generis*, that is, unique to Aboriginal peoples. Dickson J. wrote:

> Indians have a legal right to occupy and possess certain lands, the ultimate title to which is in the Crown. While their interest does not, strictly speaking, amount to beneficial ownership, neither is its nature completely exhausted by the concept of a personal right. It is true that the *sui generis* interest which the Indians have in the land is personal in the sense that it cannot be transferred to a grantee, but it is also true, as will presently appear, that the interest gives rise upon surrender to a distinctive fiduciary obligation on the part of the Crown to deal with the land for the benefit of the surrendering Indians. . . . The nature of the Indians' interest is therefore best characterized by its general inalienability, coupled with that fact that the Crown is under an obligation to deal with the land on the Indians' behalf when the interest is surrendered. Any description of Indian title which goes beyond these two features is both unnecessary and potentially misleading.[84]

Dickson J.'s statement on the nature of Aboriginal title is restrictive from the point of view of Aboriginal authority over their historic or traditional lands. Dickson J.'s interpretation of Aboriginal title is flexible to the extent that it is *sui generis* in nature. However, this flexibility also means uncertainty for Aboriginal peoples attempting to define the full extent of their rights. The nature of the Aboriginal interest in unsurrendered land (including reserve land) is left open for consideration. This is supported by Richard Bartlett's observation that

---

83   *R. v. Guerin*, [1985] 1 C.N.L.R. 120 at 131 (S.C.C.).
84   Ibid., 136.

[I]n 1988, in *Canadian Pacific* v. *Paul*, the Court [Supreme Court of Canada] reviewed *Guerin obiter* and declared, in what must be regarded as deliberately general language: "In *Guerin* this Court recognized that the Crown has a fiduciary obligation to the Indians with respect to the lands it holds for them." It seems that the Court has already moved to discount the distinction between surrendered and unsurrendered reserve lands.[85]

In *Sparrow*, Dickson C.J.C. noted that

[T]he Government has the responsibility to act in a fiduciary capacity with respect to aboriginal peoples. The relationship between the Government and aboriginals is trust-like, rather than adversarial, and contemporary recognition and affirmation of aboriginal rights must be defined in light of this historic relationship.[86]

The *Sparrow* statement on the fiduciary relationship is significant in that it signifies a burden on the ability of federal, provincial, and territorial governments to exercise authority.

In another decision dealing with surrendered land, the Federal Court of Appeal held that when land is taken by surrender under the threat of expropriation and the use for which the land was taken, even if it is to be used for government purposes, is not known, there is an obligation of the fiduciary (the Crown) to ensure that the land will revert back to the band once it is no longer needed. Otherwise, the Crown must find some other mechanism that provides the least possible impairment of the band's rights.[87]

In *Blueberry River Indian Band* v. *R.*,[88] the Supreme Court of Canada found that the federal government breached its fiduciary duties to the band resulting from the surrender of two parcels of reserve land and related mineral rights. The court found that the Department of Indian Affairs and Northern Development (DIAND) failed to exercise its statutory power, which, in this case, would have mitigated the band's loss. As a trustee of the band's land, DIAND was under a fiduciary obligation to deal with the band in the "best interests" of the band. Finally, the band was entitled to receive compensation based on what a reasonable price would have been for the land. This is opposed to placing an obligation on DIAND to secure the best possible price for the land.

In *Quebec (A.G.)* v. *Canada (National Energy Board)*,[89] the Supreme Court of

---

85 Richard Bartlett, *Indian Reserves and Aboriginal Lands in Canada* (Saskatoon, Sask.: Native Law Centre, 1990), 204; citing *Canadian Pacific* v. *Paul*, [1989] 1 C.N.L.R. 47 at 60 (S.C.C.).

86 *R.* v. *Sparrow*, [1990] 3 C.N.L.R. 160 at 180.

87 *Semiahmoo Indian Band* v. *Canada*, [1998] 1 C.N.L.R. 250 (F.C.A).

88 *Blueberry River Indian Band* v. *R.*, [1996] 2 C.N.L.R. 25 (S.C.C.); See also J.P. Salembier, "Crown Fiduciary Duty, Indian Title and the Lost Treasure of I.R. 172: The Legacy of *Apsassin* v. *The Queen (Blueberry River)*", [1996] 3 C.N.L.R. 1 and O.B. Griffiths, "Case Comment on *Blueberry River:* Is the Crown Fiduciary Obligation in the Currents of Change?" [1996] 3 C.N.L.R. 25.

89 *Quebec (A.G.)* v. *Canada (National Energy Board)*, [1994] 3 C.N.L.R. 49 (S.C.C.).

Canada considered a decision of the National Energy Board regarding the granting of a licence to Hydro-Quebec to sell electricity to the United States. The Grand Council of the Crees (of Quebec), among others, claimed that the National Energy Board owed them, as Aboriginal peoples, a fiduciary duty in making their decision. The Supreme Court held that the board, as a quasi-judicial body, was exempt from a fiduciary responsibility to the Aboriginal peoples concerned. The court also characterized the nature of the fiduciary duty to Aboriginal peoples as one that required the "utmost good faith" by government.

Delgamuukw further expands the understanding of the fiduciary relationship between the Crown and Aboriginal peoples. Within the justification test required to justify an infringement of an Aboriginal right by a government,[90] is a requirement to assess whether the infringement is consistent with the special fiduciary relationship between the Crown and Aboriginal peoples. The requirements of the fiduciary duty are dependent on the "legal and factual context" of each case.[91] As Lamer C.J. pointed out in *Delgamuukw,* although the notion of "priority" is a principle that may be applied to the fiduciary duty, such as it was in both Supreme Court decisions of *Sparrow* and *Gladstone,* the fiduciary duty does not require that "priority" be given to Aboriginal rights in every case. Finally, the extent of scrutiny demanded by the Crown's fiduciary duty is dependent upon the nature of the Aboriginal right in question and on the particular factual context within which the claim is being made.[92]

■ CASES AND MATERIALS

FEDERAL AUTHORITY

1.   *Constitution Act, 1867,* **30 and 31 Vict. c. 3 (U.K.) R.S.C. 1985, App. II, No. 5**

VI. DISTRIBUTION OF LEGISLATIVE POWERS
Powers of the Parliament
    91.   It shall be lawful for the Queen, by and with the Advice and Consent of the Senate and House of Commons, to make laws for the Peace, Order, and good Government of Canada, in relation to all Matters not coming within the Classes of Subjects by this Act assigned exclusively to the Legislatures of the Provinces; and for greater Certainty, but not so as to restrict the Generality of the foregoing Terms of this Section, it is hereby declared that (notwithstanding anything in this Act) the exclusive Legislative Authority of the parliament of Canada extends to all Matters coming within the Classes of Subjects next herein-after enumerated; that is to say,—
. . .

---

90   See the *Sparrow* test in chap. 7 at 396.
91   See *R.* v. *Gladstone,* [1993] 4 C.N.L.R. 75 (B.C.C.A.), para. 56.
92   *Delgamuukw* v. *British Columbia,* [1998] 1 C.N.L.R. 14 (S.C.C.), paras. 162 and 163.

24.   Indians, and Lands reserved for the Indians.

2.   Selected provisions of the *Indian Act*, R.S.C. 1985, c. I–5

RESERVES . . .

18.(1) Subject to this Act, reserves are held by Her Majesty for the use and benefit of the respective bands for which they were set apart; and subject to this Act and to the terms of any treaty or surrender, the Governor in Council may determine whether any purpose for which lands in a reserve are used or are to be used is for the use and benefit of the band.

(2) The Minister may authorize the use of lands in a reserve for the purpose of Indian schools, the administration of Indian affairs, Indian burial grounds, Indian health projects or, with the consent of the council of the band, for any other purpose for the general welfare of the band, and may take any lands in a reserve required for such purposes, but where an individual Indian, immediately prior to such taking, was entitled to the possession of such lands, compensation for such use shall be paid to the Indian, in such amount as may be agreed between the Indian and the Minister, or, failing agreement, as may be determined in such manner as the Minister may direct. R.S. 1970, c. I–6. s. 18. . . .

SURRENDERS AND DESIGNATIONS . . .

37.(1) Lands in a reserve shall not be sold nor title to them conveyed until they have been absolutely surrendered to Her Majesty pursuant to subsection 38(1) by the band for whose use and benefit in common the reserve was set apart.

(2) Except where this Act otherwise provides, lands in a reserve shall not be leased nor an interest in them granted until they have been surrendered to Her Majesty pursuant to subsection 38(2) by the band for whose use and benefit in common the reserve was set apart. R.S. 1970, c. I–6, s. 37; R.S.C. 1985 (4th Supp.), c. 17, s. 2. . . .

38.(1) A band may absolutely surrender to Her Majesty, conditionally or unconditionally, all of the rights and interests of the band and its members in all or part of a reserve.

(2) A band may, conditionally or unconditionally, designate by way of a surrender to Her Majesty that is not absolute, any right or interest of the band and its members in all or part of a reserve, for the purpose of its being leased or a right or interest therein being granted. R.S. 1970, c. I–6, s. 38; R.S. 1985 (4th Supp.), c. 17, s. 2. . . .

39.(1) An absolute surrender or designation is void unless
    (a) it is made to Her Majesty;
    (b) it is assented to by a majority of the electors of the band
        (i) at a general meeting of the band called by the council of the band
        (ii) at a special meeting of the band called by the Minister for the purpose of considering a proposed absolute surrender or designation, or
        (iii) by a referendum as provided in the regulations; and

(c) it is accepted by the Governor in Council.

(2) Where a majority of the electors of a band did not vote at a meeting or referendum called pursuant to subsection (1), the Minister may, if the proposed absolute surrender or designation was assented to by a majority of the electors who did vote, call another meeting by giving thirty days notice thereof or another referendum as provided in the regulations.

(3) Where a meeting is called pursuant to subsection (2) and the proposed absolute surrender or designation is assented to at the meeting or referendum by a majority of the electors voting, the surrender or designation shall be deemed, for the purposes of this section, to have been assented to by a majority of the electors of the band.

(4) The Minister may, at the request of the council of the band or whenever he considers it advisable, order that a vote at any meeting under this section shall be by secret ballot.

(5) Every meeting under this section shall be held in the presence of the superintendent or some other officer of the Department designated by the Minister. R.S. 1970, c. I–6, s. 39; R.S.C. 1985 (4th Supp.), c. 17, s. 3.

40.   A proposed absolute surrender or designation that is assented to by the band in accordance with section 39 shall be certified on oath by the superintendent or other officer who attended the meeting and by the chief or a member of the council of the band and then submitted to the Governor in Council for acceptance or refusal. R.S. 1970, c. I– 6, s. 40; R.S.C. 1985 (4th Supp.), c.17, s. 4. . . .

41.   An absolute surrender or designation shall be deemed to confer all rights that are necessary to enable Her Majesty to carry out the terms of the surrender or designation. R.S. 1970, c. I–6, s. 4l; R.S. 1985 (4th Supp.), c. 17, s. 4. . . .

57.   The Governor in Council may make regulations
    (a) authorizing the Minister to grant licences to cut timber on surrendered lands, or, with the consent of the council of the band, on reserve lands;
    (b) imposing terms, conditions and restrictions with respect to the exercise of rights conferred by licences granted under paragraph (a);
    (c) providing for the disposition of surrendered mines and minerals underlying lands in a reserve;
    (d) prescribing the penalty not exceeding one hundred dollars or imprisonment for a term of three months, or both, that may be imposed on summary conviction for violation of any regulation made under this section; and
    (e) providing for the seizure and forfeiture of any timber or minerals taken in violation of any regulation made under this section. R.S. 1970, c. I–6, s. 57. . . .

60.(1) The Governor in Council may at the request of a band grant to the band the right to exercise such control and management over lands in the reserve occupied by the band as the Governor in Council considers desirable.

(2) The Governor in Council may at any time withdraw from a band a right conferred upon the band under subsection (1). R.S. 1970, c. 1–6, s. 60.

MANAGEMENT OF INDIAN MONEYS

61.(1) Indian moneys shall be expended only for the benefit of the Indians or bands for whose use and benefit in common the moneys are received or held, and subject to this Act and to the terms of any treaty or surrender, the Governor in Council may determine whether any purpose for which Indian moneys are used or are to be used is for the use and benefit of the band.

(2) Interest upon Indian moneys held in the Consolidated Revenue Fund shall be allowed at a rate to be fixed from time to time by the Governor in Council. R.S. 1970, c. I–6, s. 61.

TREATY MONEY

72. Moneys that are payable to Indians or to Indian bands under a treaty between Her Majesty and the band and for the payment of which the Government of Canada is responsible, may be paid out of the Consolidated Revenue Fund. R.S. 1970, c. I–6. s. 72.

REGULATIONS

73.(1) The Governor in Council may make regulations

(a) for the protection and preservation of fur-bearing animals, fish and other game on reserves;

(b) for the destruction of noxious weeds and prevention of the spreading or prevalence of insects, pests or diseases that may destroy or injure vegetation on Indian reserves;

(c) for the control of the speed, operation and parking of vehicles on roads within reserves;

(d) for the taxation, control and destruction of dogs and for the protection of sheep on reserves;

(e) for the operation, supervision and control of pool rooms, dance halls and other places of amusement on reserves;

(f) to prevent, mitigate and control the spread of diseases on reserves, whether or not the diseases are infectious or communicable;

(g) to provide medical treatment and health services for Indians;

(h) to provide compulsory hospitalization and treatment for infectious disease among Indians;

(i) to provide for the inspection of premises on reserves and the destruction, alteration or renovation thereof;

(j) to prevent overcrowding of premises on reserves used as dwellings;

(k) to provide for sanitary conditions in private premises on reserves as well as in public places on reserves;

(l) for the construction and maintenance of boundary fences; and

(m) for empowering and authorizing the council of a band to borrow money for band projects or housing purposes and providing for the making of loans out of moneys so borrowed to members of the band for housing purposes.

(2) The Governor in Council may prescribe the penalty, not exceeding a

fine of one thousand dollars or imprisonment for a term not exceeding three months, or both, that may be imposed on summary conviction for violation of a regulation made under subsection (1).

(3) The Governor in Council may make orders and regulations to carry out the purposes and provisions of this Act. R.S. 1970, c. I–6, s. 73.

* * *

ss. 81–83, see chapter 8, page 526.

s. 88, see this chapter, page 256.

ss. 83, 87, 89, 90, see chapter 6, page 363.

3.   *R. v. Jim* (1915), 4 C.N.L.C. 328 (B.C.S.C.). Hunter C.J.B.C., April 27, 1915

> *R. v. Jim* is an early British Columbia Supreme Court decision which held that provincial legislative authority ended at the boundary to an Indian reserve, thus promoting the notion that Indian reserves were "federal enclaves" outside provincial jurisdiction. This decision has since been overturned by the Supreme Court (for example, see the next decision: *R. v. Cardinal*).

HUNTER, C.J.B.C.:—In my opinion, this conviction must be quashed. The facts are not in dispute, the central fact being that the defendant charged with an infraction of the Game Protection Act was an Indian who killed a two year old buck upon a reserve upon which he was entitled to live, and was using the meat for his household use. The question at once arises as to whether the Indian is within the scope of the prohibitions of the Provincial Game Protection Act. In my opinion, he is not. By the *British North America Act*, 1867, that is to say, by subsection (24) of section 91, Indians and lands reserved for the Indians are reserved for the exclusive jurisdiction of the Dominion Parliament. The Dominion Parliament has enacted a lengthy Act known as the *Indian Act*. Many provisions are there to be found in connection with the management of Indians upon their reserve; in fact, by section 51 it is expressly enacted "that all Indian lands . . . shall be managed, leased and sold as the Governor in Council directs." Now, I cannot conceive it possible how any wider term can be used than the word "management" in connection with the Indians as to what shall or shall not be done upon an Indian reserve. I would say that the word "management" would, at all events, include the question of regulation and prohibition in connection with fishing and hunting upon the reserves. Then, also, special provisions have been made in connection with the subject of shooting and fishing. We find in another section that special provision has been made with regard to the subject of game in certain reserves in certain other Provinces. Undoubtedly if there was jurisdiction in the Dominion Parliament to make that regulation, there certainly would be, in my opinion, jurisdiction to make similar regulations with regard to reserves in British Columbia, and possibly, as Mr. Taylor suggests, it has not done so out of respect to the early treaties with the Indians in the Province. Then laws regarding the question of bringing in intoxicants on the reserves have been passed, as I understand no question has ever been raised as to the right of the Dominion Parliament to pass those laws, and one would say that if the matter of bringing intoxicants on to reserves was within the purview of the Dominion

Parliament, that the question of what should be done with the game and fish within the reserves would *a fortiori* fall within their jurisdiction.

Moreover, I think that the question is in reality concluded by the case of *Madden* v. *Nelson and Fort Sheppard Ry. Co.* (1897), 5 B.C. 541; (1899), A.C. 626; 68 L.J., P.C. 148. It was there contended that because the Dominion did not choose to enact certain legislation regarding the fencing of railways which the Provincial legislature thought was desirable, that the Legislature could, in the absence of such legislation on the part of the Dominion, temporarily, at all events, pass such laws under its power over civic rights. It was held that it would be impossible to maintain the authority of the Dominion Parliament if the Legislature was to be permitted to enter into the former's field of legislation.

I am unable to distinguish this case in principle from that case. Obviously the proper course for the local authorities is not to attempt to pass legislation affecting the hunting by Indians on their reserves or to apply general legislation regarding game to such Indians, but if necessary to apply to the proper law making authority and make any representations that they may see fit.

Conviction quashed.

4. *Cardinal* v. *Attorney-General of Alberta*, 7 C.N.L.C. 307 (S.C.C.). Fauteux C.J.C., Abbott, Martland, Judson, Ritchie, Hall, Spence, Pigeon, and Laskin JJ., June 29, 1973

> *Cardinal* rejected outright the enclave theory, which provided that Indian reserves were federal enclaves from which all provincial laws were excluded in application. This position was later reaffirmed by the Supreme Court of Canada in *Four B Mfg. Ltd.* v. *United Garment Wkrs.* (1980), 102 D.L.R. (3d) 385 at 398–99 (S.C.C.). *Cardinal* affirmed that para. 12 of the *Alberta Natural Resources Transfer Agreement* made the provisions of the Alberta *Wildlife Act* applicable to all Indians in all areas of Alberta, including Indian reserves.

FAUTEUX, C.J.C., and ABBOTT, J., concurs with MARTLAND, J.

MARTLAND, J.:—On December 8, 1970, the appellant, a treaty Indian, at his home on an Indian reserve, in the Province of Alberta, sold a piece of moose meat to a non-Indian. He was charged with a breach of s. 37 of the *Wildlife Act*, R.S.A. 1970, c. 391, which provides:

> 37. No person shall traffic in any big game or any game bird except as is expressly permitted by this Act or by the regulations. . . .

An agreement was made between the Government of Canada and the Government of Alberta, dated December 14, 1929, hereinafter referred to as "the Agreement", for the transfer by the former to the latter of the interest of the Crown in all Crown lands, mines and minerals within the Province of Alberta, and the provisions of the *Alberta Act*, 1905 (Can.), c. 3, were modified as in the Agreement set out.

Paragraphs 10 to 12 inclusive appear in the Agreement under the heading "Indian Reserves", and it is paras. 10 and 12 which are of importance in considering this appeal. They provide as follows [schedule to *Alberta Natural Resources Act*, 1930 (Alta.), c. 21, and 1930 (Can.), c. 3]

10.   All lands included in Indian reserves within the province, including those selected and surveyed but not yet confirmed, as well as those confirmed, shall continue to be vested in the Crown and administered by the Government of Canada for the purposes of Canada, and the Province will from time to time, upon the request of the Superintendent General of Indian Affairs, set aside, out of the unoccupied Crown land hereby transferred to its administration, such further areas as the said Superintendent General may, in agreement with the appropriate Minister of the Province, select as necessary to enable Canada to fulfil its obligations under the treaties with the Indians of the Province, and such areas shall thereafter be administered by Canada in the same way in all respects as if they had never passed to the Province under the provisions hereof.

12.   In order to secure to the Indians of the Province the continuance of the supply of game and fish for their support and subsistence, Canada agrees that the laws respecting game in force in the Province from time to time shall apply to the Indians within the boundaries thereof, provided however, that the said Indians shall have the right, which the Province hereby assures to them, of hunting, trapping and fishing game and fish for food at all seasons of the year on all unoccupied Crown lands and on any other lands to which the said Indians may have a right of access.

This Agreement was approved by the Parliament of Canada and the legislature of the Province of Alberta and, thereafter, it and also agreements between the Government of Canada and the Provinces of Manitoba, Saskatchewan and British Columbia were confirmed by the *British North America Act*, 1930 (U.K.), c. 26. Section 1 of that Act provided:

1. The agreements set out in the Schedule to this Act are hereby confirmed and shall have the force of law notwithstanding anything in the *British North America Act, 1867*, or any Act amending the same, or any Act of the Parliament of Canada, or in any Order in Council or terms or conditions of union made or approved under any such Act as aforesaid.

Paragraphs 10 and 12 of the Agreement were, therefore, given the force of law, notwithstanding anything in the *British North America Act, 1867*. The question in issue on this appeal is as to whether s. 12 was effective so as to make the provisions of the *Wildlife Act* applicable to the appellant, a treaty Indian, in respect of an act which occurred on an Indian reserve in the Province of Alberta.

The submission of the appellant is that the Parliament of Canada has exclusive legislative authority to legislate to control the administration of Indian reserves and that provincial laws cannot apply on such a reserve unless referentially introduced through federal legislation. It is contended that the phrase "on all unoccupied Crown lands and on any other lands to which the said Indians may have a right of access" does not include Indian reserve lands and that the only laws to which Indians are subject, while on a reserve, are the laws of Canada. Paragraph 12, it is said, can only have application to Indians in Alberta outside the Indian reserves.

In support of this proposition the case of *R.* v. *Wesley* (1932), 58 C.C.C. 269, [1932] 4 D.L.R. 774, is cited. This is a judgment of the Alberta Appellate Division. In my opinion it is not of assistance in determining the issue in the present appeal.

The accused, an Indian, was charged with breaches of the *Game Act* of Alberta in respect of his hunting activities on unoccupied Crown land. The deer which he had killed was used for food. The issue was as to the scope of the protection provided to him by para. 12 of the Agreement with respect to hunting for food. The Crown contended that the right to hunt "game" did not include animals the killing of which was totally prohibited by the *Game Act*. It was also urged that when the right to hunt was given "at all seasons of the year" this only conferred the right to hunt out of season, but that such hunting was still subject to the limits imposed by the *Game Act*. These submissions were rejected.

The Court's conclusions are stated in the judgment of McGillivray, J.A., at p. 276 C.C.C., p. 781 D.L.R.:

> If the effect of the proviso is merely to give to the Indians the extra privilege of shooting for food "out of season" and they are otherwise subject to the game laws of the Province, it follows that in any year they may be limited in the number of animals of a given kind that they may kill even though that number is not sufficient for their support and subsistence and even though no other kind of game is available to them. I cannot think that the language of the section supports the view that this was the intention of the law makers. I think the intention was that in hunting for sport or for commerce the Indian like the white man should be subject to laws which make for the preservation of game but in hunting wild animals for the food necessary to his life, the Indian should be placed in a very different position from the white man who generally speaking does not hunt for food and was by the proviso to s. 12 reassured of the continued enjoyment of a right which he has enjoyed from time immemorial.

This passage was quoted with approval in this Court in *Prince and Myron* v. *The Queen*, [1964] 3 C.C.C. 2 at p. 5, in which the issue was as to the meaning of the word "hunt" in s. 72(1) of the *Game and Fisheries Act*, R.S.M. 1954, c. 94, which had been enacted in implementation of para. 13 of the Manitoba Natural Resources Agreement, which is the same as para. 12 of the Agreement. It was admitted that the appellants were Indians, hunting for food, on land to which they had the right of access. It was held that they were not subject to restriction as to the method of hunting. The same principle was applied, recently, by the Manitoba Court of Appeal in *R.* v. *McPherson*, [1971] 2 W.W.R. 640. . . .

The present appeal thus raises issues as to the application of para. 12 which have not been considered previously.

As indicated earlier, the appellant starts from the proposition that, prior to the making of the Agreement, Indian reserves were enclaves which were withdrawn from the application of provincial legislation, save by way of reference by virtue of federal legislation. On this premise it is contended that para. 12 should not be construed so as to make provincial game legislation applicable within Indian reserves.

I am not prepared to accept this initial premise. Section 91(24) of the *British North America Act, 1867*, gave exclusive legislative authority to the Canadian Parliament in respect of Indians and over lands reserved for the Indians. Section 92 gave to each Province, in such Province, exclusive legislative power over the subjects therein defined. It is well established, as illustrated in *Union Colliery Co. of*

B.C. v. *Bryden*, [1899] A.C. 580, that a Province cannot legislate in relation to a subject-matter exclusively assigned to the federal Parliament by s. 91. But it is also well established that provincial legislation enacted under a heading of s. 92 does not necessarily become invalid because it affects something which is subject to federal legislation. A vivid illustration of this is to be found in the Privy Council decision a few years after the *Union Colliery* case in *Cunningham et al.* v. *Tomey Homma*, [1903] A.C. 151, which sustained provincial legislation, pursuant to s. 92(1), which prohibited Japanese, whether naturalized or not, from voting in provincial elections in British Columbia.

A provincial Legislature could not enact legislation in relation to Indians, or in relation to Indian reserves, but this is far from saying that the effect of s. 91(24) of the *British North America Act, 1867*, was to create enclaves within a Province within the boundaries of which provincial legislation could have no application. In my opinion, the test as to the application of provincial legislation within a reserve is the same as with respect to its application within the Province and that is that it must be within the authority of s. 92 and must not be in relation to a subject-matter assigned exclusively to the Canadian Parliament under s. 91. Two of those subjects are Indians and Indian reserves, but if provincial legislation within the limits of s. 92 is not construed as being legislation in relation to those classes of subjects (or any other subject under s. 91) it is applicable anywhere in the Province, including Indian reserves, even though Indians or Indian reserves might be affected by it. My point is that s. 91(24) enumerates classes of subjects over which the federal Parliament has the exclusive power to legislate, but it does not purport to define areas within a Province within which the power of a Province to enact legislation, otherwise within its powers, is to be excluded.

There have been a number of cases in provincial Courts in which para. 12 of the Agreement, or its equivalent in the Manitoba and Saskatchewan Agreements, was not applicable, which have considered the question of the application of provincial laws to Indians, and their application within Indian reserves. Counsel for the appellant cites *R.* v. *Jim* (1915), 26 C.C.C. 236, 22 B.C.R. 106. In this case Hunter, C.J.B.C., held that a charge of hunting deer, without a licence issued pursuant to the British Columbia *Game Protection Act*, would not lie against an Indian hunting on an Indian reserve. The ground of the decision was that the *Indian Act*, enacted pursuant to s. 91(24) of the *British North America Act, 1867*, had provided that all Indian lands should be managed as the Governor in Council directs and that management included the regulation of hunting on a reserve.

R. v. *Rodgers* (1923), 40 C.C.C. 51, [1923] 3 D.L.R. 414, is a decision of the Manitoba Court of Appeal, to the like effect, involving the trapping of mink on an Indian reserve without a provincial licence.

In *R.* v. *Morley* (1931), 58 C.C.C. 166, [1932] 4 D.L.R. 483, the British Columbia Court of Appeal held that a provincial game law applied to a non-Indian on a charge of killing a pheasant during the closed season on an Indian reserve.

In *District of Surrey* v. *Peace Arch Enterprises Ltd.* (1970), 74 W.W.R. 380, the situation was different. It involved lands in an Indian reserve which had been "surrendered" in trust to the federal Crown for the purpose of leasing. The issue was as to whether the lands were subject, in their use by the lessees, who were non-

Indians, to certain municipal by-laws and to Regulations under the provincial *Health Act*. The Court found that the lands in question were still "lands reserved for the Indians" and, that being so, only the federal Parliament could legislate as to the use to which they might be put. The *Morley* case is not mentioned in the judgment and I presume that this was so because the cases were not considered as parallel. Once it was determined that the lands remained lands reserved for the Indians, provincial legislation relating to their use was not applicable. The game law considered in the Morley case governed the conduct of persons hunting game in British Columbia and was held to apply in all parts of the Province.

The Quebec Court of Sessions of the Peace, in *R. v. Gros-Louis* (1943), 81 C.C.C. 167, convicted an Indian merchant who resided and operated a retail store on an Indian reserve, of an offence under the *Quebec Retail Sales Tax Act* in respect of a sale of goods on the reserve to a non-Indian. The Court suggested, however, that, when selling to a non-Indian, he did an action which theoretically caused him to go outside the reserve.

The Ontario Court of Appeal held in *R. v. Hill*, (1907), 15 O.L.R. 406, that an unenfranchised treaty Indian, resident on a reserve, was subject to the provisions of the *Ontario Medical Act* when he practised medicine for hire, but not upon the reserve. That Court also held, in *R. v. Martin*, (1917), 29 C.C.C. 189, 39 D.L.R. 635, that an Indian, not on a reserve, could be convicted of an offence under the *Ontario Temperance Act*.

Riddell, J., at pp. 192–3 C.C.C., pp. 638–9 D.L.R., applied the language of the decision of the Privy Council in *C.P.R. Co.* v. *Corporation of the Parish of Notre Dame de Bonsecours*, [1899] A.C. 367 at pp. 372–3, *mutatis mutandis*, in the case before him. The passages in the *Canadian Pacific Railway* case are as follows:

> The *British North America Act*, whilst it gives the legislative control of the Indian defendant *qua* Indian to the Parliament of the Dominion, does not declare that the defendant shall cease to be a denizen of the Province in which he may be, or that he shall, in other respects, be exempted from the jurisdiction of the provincial legislatures . . . It therefore appears . . . that any attempt by the Legislature of Ontario to regulate by enactments his conduct *qua* Indian would be in excess of its powers. If, on the other hand, the enactment had no reference to the conduct of the defendant *qua* Indian, but provided generally that no one was to sell, etc., liquors, then the enactment would . . . be a piece of legislation competent to the Legislature. . .

Riddell, J., then went on to say: "In other words, no statute of the Provincial Legislature dealing with Indians or their lands as such would be valid and effective; but there is no reason why general legislation may not affect them."

In none of these cases is it decided that a provincial game law, of general application, would not affect an Indian outside a reserve. Legislation of this kind does not relate to Indians, *qua* Indians, and the passage above quoted would, in my opinion, be applicable to such legislation. The *Jim* case and the *Rodgers* case held that such legislation did not apply to an Indian on an Indian reserve. The *Morley* case is inconsistent with the idea that no provincial legislation can apply within an Indian reserve, save by reference in a federal statute.

I now turn to a consideration of the effect of para. 12 of the Agreement.

It has been noted that this paragraph along with paras. 10 and 11, appears under the heading "Indian Reserves". It begins with the words:

> In order to secure to the Indians of the Province the continuance of the supply of game and fish for their support and subsistence, Canada agrees that the laws respecting game in force in the Province from time to time shall apply to the Indians within the boundaries thereof . . .

The opening words of the paragraph define its purpose. It is to secure to the Indians of the Province a continuing supply of game and fish for their support and subsistence. It is to achieve that purpose that Indians within the boundaries of the Province are to conform to provincial game laws, subject, always, to their right to hunt and fish for food. This being the purpose of the paragraph, it could not have been intended that the controls which would apply to Indians in relation to hunting and fishing for purposes other than for their own food, should apply only to Indians not on reserves.

Furthermore, if the paragraph were to be so restricted in its scope, it would accomplish nothing towards its purpose. Cases decided before the Agreement, such as *R.* v. *Martin*, supra, had held that general legislation by a Province, not relating to Indians, *qua* Indians, would apply to them. On their facts, these cases dealt with Indians outside reserves. The point is that the provisions of para. 12 were not required to make provincial game laws apply to Indians off the reserve.

In my opinion, the meaning of para. 12 is that Canada, clothed as it was with legislative jurisdiction over "Indians, and Lands reserved for the Indians", in order to achieve the purpose of the section, agreed to the imposition of provincial controls over hunting and fishing, which, previously, the Province might not have had power to impose. By its express wording, it provides that the game laws of the Province shall apply "to the Indians within the boundaries thereof". To me this must contemplate their application to all Indians within the Province, without restriction as to where, within the Province, they might be.

This view is supported by an examination of the state of the law, in Alberta, at the time the Agreement was made. At that time, s. 69 of the *Indian Act*, R.S.C. 1927, c. 98, provided as follows:

> 69. The Superintendent General may, from time to time, by public notice, declare that, on and after a day therein named, the laws respecting game in force in the province of Manitoba, Saskatchewan or Alberta, or the Territories, or respecting such game as is specified in such notice, shall apply to Indians within the said province or Territories, as the case may be, or to Indians in such parts thereof as to him seems expedient.

The Superintendent General was thus empowered to declare that Alberta laws respecting game should apply to "Indians within the said province" or "in such parts thereof as to him seems expedient". Being a provision of the *Indian Act*, the section must have contemplated the possible exercise of the power with respect to Indians on reserves when it spoke of "Indians within the said province".

When para. 12 was drafted, it stated its general purpose and then went on to provide that the game laws of the Province should apply "to Indians within the boundaries thereof". This is practically the same as the words "Indians within the said province" in s. 69, and, in my opinion, it was intended to have the same meaning and application.

Section 69 ceased to have any effect in Alberta, Saskatchewan and Manitoba after the enactment of the *British North America Act, 1930*, which gave the agreements therein mentioned the force of law, notwithstanding anything in the *British North America Act, 1867*, or any amendments to it, or any Act of the Parliament of Canada. Section 69 disappeared from the *Indian Act* enacted in 1951 (Can.), c. 29, which then introduced s. 87 (now s. 88) to which reference will be made later, and which provided:

> 87. Subject to the terms of any treaty and any other Act of the Parliament of Canada, all laws of general application from time to time in force in any province are applicable to and in respect of Indians in the province, except to the extent that such laws are inconsistent with this Act or any order, rule, regulation or by-law made thereunder, and except to the extent that such laws make provision for any matter for which provision is made by or under this Act.

The appellant places emphasis on the words in the proviso to para. 12 of the Agreement "on any other lands to which the said Indians may have a right of access". The contention is that para. 10 provided for continuance of the vesting of title in Indian reserves in the federal Crown, as well as for the creation of additional reserves, and that, in these lands, the Indians who reside thereon have an interest considerably greater than a mere "right of access". The use of that phrase, it is submitted, is inconsistent with any reference to reserve lands, and therefore, as the proviso, by the terms used, does not apply to Indian reserves, the section, as a whole, must be taken not to have application to them.

I am unable to agree that the broad terms used in the first portion of para. 12 can be limited, inferentially, in this way. In my view, having made all Indians within the boundaries of the Province, in their own interest, subject to provincial game laws, the proviso, by which the Province assured the defined rights of hunting and fishing for food, was drawn in broad terms. The proviso assures the right to hunt and fish for food on Indian reserves, because there can be no doubt that, whatever additional rights Indian residents on a reserve may have, they certainly have the right of access to it. This view was expressed by the Saskatchewan Court of Appeal in the *Smith* case to which reference has already been made.

For these reasons, I am of the opinion that para. 12 of the Agreement made the provisions of the *Wildlife Act* applicable to all Indians, including those on reserves, and governed their activities throughout the Province, including reserves. By virtue of s. 1 of the *British North America Act, 1930*, it has the force of law, notwithstanding anything contained in the *British North America Act, 1867*, any amendment thereto, or any federal statute.

Having reached this conclusion, it is not necessary, in the circumstances of this case, to determine the meaning and effect of s. 88 (formerly s. 87) of the *Indian Act*, R.S.C. 1970, c. I–6.

I would dismiss the appeal.

JUDSON and RITCHIE, JJ., concur with MARTLAND, J.

HALL and SPENCE, JJ., concur with LASKIN, J.

PIGEON, J., concurs with MARTLAND, J.
LASKIN, J. (dissenting) . . .

Appeal dismissed.

5.   *Re Eskimos*, 5 C.N.L.C. 123 (S.C.C.). April 5, 1939

The decision of Re Eskimos affirms that the term "Indians" in s. 91(24) of the *Constitution Act, 1867* applies to the Inuit as well, thereby bringing the Inuit within federal legislative authority. Excerpts from this decision can be found in chapter 5, p. 341.

6.   *Re Stony Plains Indian Reserve No. 135*, [1982] 1 C.N.L.R. 133 (Alta. C.A.). Clement, Prowse, Laycraft, Kerans, and Stevenson JJ.A., November 19, 1981

This decision affirms the proposition that once land is surrendered and title is transferred in fee simple it is no longer a reserve within the meaning of the *Indian Act* and is no longer land "reserved for the Indians" for the purposes of s. 91(24) of the *Constitution Act, 1867.* Thus, the land is subject to provincial legislative jurisdiction. However, when the fee simple title to the surrendered land is held by the grantee in trust for the benefit of the Indian band and its members, no band interest is ceded, and the land therefore remains a reserve. If the terms of a surrender include that the Crown in right of Canada retains title to the surrendered land, then the Indian band affected retains landlord rights, including the right of reversion. The court also noted that a corporation cannot be an Indian for the purposes of either the *Indian Act* or s. 91(24). Finally, the court held that where provincial legislation affects the use and enjoyment of, and interests in, reserve land, provincial legislation is inapplicable to that land. If land is surrendered for leasing purposes, the reversion is held by the Indians and provincial legislation limiting reversion will not be applicable. Surrendered land remains land "reserved for the Indians" and therefore its control and management remains a federal responsibility.

PER CURIAM:—Pursuant to the *Constitutional Questions Act*, R.S.A. 1970, c. 63 [now the *Judicature Act*, R.S.A. 1980, c. J–1], the Lieutenant-Governor in Council referred a series of questions to us. . . . The two orders in council are App. 1 [App. 1 omitted]. The questions have in view proposals to surrender certain reserve lands in order to permit urban development to take place on the lands. The primary concern is the extent to which provincial law will apply to the lands after the surrender. . . .

The "surrendered lands", of some 1,960 acres in extent, adjoin the corporate boundaries of the city of Edmonton. The band proposes to construct an urban development which could ultimately house up to 25,000 people. The development anticipates production of substantial income for the band. . . .

In 1972 the band surrendered these lands to Her Majesty the Queen in right of Canada for a term of 60 years "in trust to lease the same for the period hereinbefore stated to such person or persons, for such term and upon such terms as the Government of Canada may deem most conducive to our welfare and that of our people".

. . .

... [T]he band incorporated Enoch Land Developments Ltd. as a private company. . . . This step was followed by a trust deed between the band as owners and six of its members as trustees, which, having recited the beneficial ownership by the band of the share capital of the company and of its assets, and that the trustees hold the shares at the request of the owners, provided:

1. The Trustees hereby declare that they shall hold the said shares upon trust for the Owners absolutely;

2. The Trustees further declare that, as directors of the said Company they shall not cause the said shares to be transferred or encumbered to any persons or corporations other than the Owners;

3. THE POWER OF DISCHARGING the Trustees who are the signatories of this Deed or appointing new Trustees is vested solely in the Owners.

In November 1976 Her Majesty, with the consent of the band council, leased the surrendered land to Enoch Land Developments Ltd. for a term of 55 years, but excepting and reserving to Her Majesty all mines and minerals and subject to prior rights granted by Her Majesty to Northwestern Utilities Ltd. . . .

Uncertainties were then felt as to the jurisdiction over urban development of the surrendered land, and in September 1979 the band council resolved:

1. That, if on the basis of legal advice it is decided that an absolute surrender into a trust or company is necessary to permit urban development on the surrendered lands, the Council shall support the submission of such a surrender to the Band Members.

Pursuant to supplemental resolutions, three forms of surrender to Her Majesty in right of Canada were prepared for consideration. One, proposal A, was absolute in its terms, free of any trusts or conditions. The second, proposal B, would surrender the land to Her Majesty, to have and to hold forever "IN TRUST TO FORTHWITH TRANSFER THE SAME to a company" the description of which fits Enoch Land Developments Ltd. The phrase "to have and to hold forever" merely emphasizes the absolute nature of the surrender. The third, proposal C, would surrender the land to Her Majesty in trust to transfer the same to such a company but subject to these conditions:

1. THAT the Company pay the sum of Fifty Million ($50,000,000.00) Dollars in consideration, which monies shall be credited to the funds of the Enoch Band of Indians.

2. THAT the lands are held by the Company in trust, in perpetuity for the benefit of the members of the Enoch Band of Indians.

3. THAT the Company, or others, shall develop and lease for a period fixed in years portions of the land to any person or persons be they Indian or non-Indian. . . .

By the disposition made by the last condition, the rents reserved are "Indian moneys" within the definition in s. 2(l) of the *Indian Act*, R.S.C. 1970, c. I–6.

In 1971 Sarcee Developments Ltd. had been incorporated pursuant to the *Companies Act* of Alberta, and it is said that the corporation is wholly owned and controlled by members of the Sarcee Band. In September 1974 Her Majesty granted a lease of the "surrendered" land to Sarcee Developments Ltd. for a term of 75 years with the provision that at the end of the term "the land and all improvements will immediately revert to Her Majesty The Queen in Right of Canada for the use and benefit of the Sarcee Band" subject to a right of removal of buildings or structures by the lessee within a limited time. Here again the provisions of the lease are extensive and appear to be in furtherance of the purpose of the surrender. Sarcee Developments Ltd. has undertaken development in stages of the leased land based on subdivision. Development has been implemented in one area, and pursuant to the head lease, subleases have been granted of lots for a term just short of the term of the head lease. There are approximately 100 non-Indian families living as subtenants in this area. By the subleases Sarcee Developments Ltd. covenanted to provide utilities and other services to the tenants, who in turn covenanted as to the use to be made of the subdemises. Many of the tenants have mortgaged their leasehold estates, as provided by the head lease and the subleases, for example, to Central Mortgage and Housing Corporation, in respect of which the Minister of Indian Affairs and Northern Development and Sarcee Developments Ltd. have given the mortgagees undertakings which are not of interest here. To date neither the government of Canada nor the government of Alberta has assumed jurisdiction in respect of municipal, educational or other local matters. It can readily be seen that the concern of the Sarcee Band is immediate and urgent. . . .

The questions are:

1. Do the surrendered lands cease to be 'Lands reserved for the Indians' within the meaning of s. 91(24) of the *B.N.A. Act, 1867,* as amended and do all the laws of Alberta, and in particular *The Dower Act* [R.S.A. 1970, c. 114; now R.S.A. 1980, c. D–38], *The Expropriation Act* [1974 (Alta.), c. 27; now R.S.A. 1980, c. E–16], *The Municipal Taxation Act* [R.S.A. 1970, c. 251; now R.S.A. c. M–31] and *The Planning Act, 1977* [(Alta.), c. 89; now R.S.A 1980, c. P–9), apply to the surrendered lands if, either at the absolute discretion of Her Majesty in right of Canada or as required by the terms of the surrender, the fee simple in the surrendered lands are granted to any of the following:

    (a) an individual who is not an Indian within the meaning of section 91(24) of the *British North America Act, 1867*, as amended;

    (b) an individual who is an Indian within the meaning of section 91(24) of the *British North America Act, 1867*, as amended;

    (c) the Enoch Band or members of the Band;

    (d) a corporation in which all shares are owned by the Enoch Band or members of the Band;

    (e) a corporation in which a majority of the shares are owned by the Enoch Band or members of the Band;

    (f) a corporation in which a minority of the shares are owned by the Enoch Band or members of the Band;

    (g) a corporation in which none of the shares are owned by the Enoch Band or members of the Band;

    (h) a corporation referred to in clauses (e) to (g) that holds the land in trust for Indians or for Indians and non-Indians or a group of persons consisting of Indians and non-Indians, notwithstanding that the land or a portion of the land may be subsequently leased to Indians or non-Indians, or both, resulting in a benefit to the Enoch Band or the members of the Band?

2.   Do the surrendered lands cease to be 'Lands reserved for the Indians' within the meaning of section 91(24) of the *British North America Act, 1867,* as amended, and do all the laws of Alberta, and in particular *The Dower Act, The Expropriation Act, The Land Titles Act* [R.S.A. 1970, c. 198; now R.S.A. 1980, c. L–5], *The Municipal Government Act* [R.S A. 1970, c. 246; now R.S.A. 1980, c. M–26], *The Municipal Election Act* [R.S.A. 1970, c. 245; now R.S.A. 1980, c. M–25], *The Municipal Taxation Act* and *The Planning Act, 1977,* apply to the surrendered lands if, either at the absolute discretion of Her Majesty in right of Canada or as required by the terms of the surrender, the fee simple in the surrendered lands is held in trust, in perpetuity, by any of the following for the benefit of the Enoch Band and the members of the Band:

(a) an individual who is not an Indian within the meaning of section 91(24) of the *British North America Act, 1867*, as amended;

(b) an individual who is an Indian within the meaning of section 91(24) of the *British North America Act, 1867*, as amended;

(c) the Enoch Band or members of the Band;

(d) a corporation in which all shares are owned by the Enoch Band or members of the Band;

(e) a corporation in which a majority of the shares are owned by the Enoch Band or members of the Band;

(f) a corporation in which a minority of the shares are owned by the Enoch Band or members of the Band;

(g) a corporation in which none of the shares are owned by the Enoch Band or members of the Band?

2.1   Do the surrendered lands cease to be 'lands reserved for the Indians' within the meaning of section 91(24) of the *British North America Act, 1867,* as amended, and so all the laws of Alberta . . . apply to the surrendered lands if, as required by the terms of the surrender, Her Majesty in right of Canada retains legal title to the surrendered lands and leases the surrendered lands in perpetuity, or for a term of years, to any of the entities referred to in section 2(a) to (g)?

3.   Is a corporation that has its registered office on an Indian reserve, in which all the shareholders are registered Indians residing on an Indian reserve and are members of an Indian band, an Indian within the meaning of section 91(24) of the *British North America Act, 1867,* as amended, or the *Indian Act* (Canada) as amended?

4.   Is a corporation that has its registered office on an Indian reserve or off an Indian reserve, in which some of the shareholders are non-Indians or are registered Indians residing on an Indian reserve and members of an Indian Band, an Indian within the meaning of section 91(24) of the *British North America Act, 1867,* as amended or the *Indian Act* (Canada), as amended?

5.   Can the agreement entered into between the Government of Canada and the Government of Alberta on the [*sic*] December 14, 1929, confirmed by the *British North America Act, 1930* [(20 & 21 Geo. 5), c. 26 (also R.S.C. 1970, App. II, No. 25)], be varied pursuant to section 24 of that agreement to provide that all the laws of Alberta . . . apply to

(a) Indian reserves or portion of Indian reserves,

(b) lands surrendered pursuant to sections 38 and 39 of the *Indian Act*

(Canada), whether conditional, unconditional or qualified,

(c) lands surrendered pursuant to sections 38 and 39 of the *Indian Act* (Canada) that are subject of an absolute surrender in perpetuity,

(d) lands surrendered pursuant to sections 38 and 39 of the *Indian Act* (Canada), if the legal title remains vested in Her Majesty in right of Canada, or

(e) lands surrendered pursuant to sections 38 and 39 of the *Indian Act* (Canada) in respect of which a fee simple maybe issued to the individuals, corporations or band referred to in section 2(a) to (g)?

THE NATURE OF A RESERVE

It will be helpful to an analysis of the problems presented to consider the nature of a "reserve". We note that we are asked to consider the characterization of the surrendered lands having regard to s. 91(24) of the *B.N.A. Act, 1867*. It was, however, common ground before us in argument that the status of the land is to be determined in accordance with the provisions of the *Indian Act*. The Stony Plain Reserve is not, of course, a pre-Confederation reserve, nor was it created pursuant to a pre-Confederation treaty.

Section 91(24) of the *B.N.A. Act* assigned to the Parliament of Canada exclusive legislative authority over "Indians, and land reserved for the Indians". This reference is primarily concerned with the second of the two grants of jurisdiction, that is, the exclusive legislative jurisdiction with respect to "land reserved for the Indians".

Although the respective rights of the province, the government of Canada and Indian bands in connection with "land reserved for the Indians" have not been fully defined by the courts, they have been considered in a number of cases, notably: *St. Catherine's Milling & Lbr. Co.* v. *R.* (1888), 14 App. Cas. 46 (P.C.) ("*St. Catherine's* case"); *Ont. Mining Co.* v. *Seybold*, [1903] A.C. 73 (P.C.) ("*Seybold* case"); and *A.G. Que.* v. *A.G. Can.*, [1921] 1 A.C. 401, 56 D.L.R. 373 (P.C.) ("*Star Chrome* case"). . . .

Hence, prior to 1924 the law relating to land reserved for the Indians in the provinces referred to in s. 109 of the *B.N.A. Act* may be summarized as follows. The underlying legal title to land in an Indian reserve is vested in the Crown in right of the province, subject to the interest of the Indians; once that interest is surrendered, the estate of the Crown is disencumbered of the Indian title, so that the land becomes indistinguishable from other Crown lands in the province; the federal government possesses a legislative and administrative right in respect of "land reserved for the Indians", and not any proprietary interest therein.

In 1924 the government of Canada and the province of Ontario entered into an agreement, *An Act for the settlement of certain questions between the Governments of Canada and Ontario respecting Indian Reserve Lands*, 1924 (Can.), c. 48, which empowered the federal government to deal with land surrendered by the Indians. Section 1 stated that portions of Indian reserves "may, upon their surrender for the purpose by the said band or bands, be sold, leased or otherwise disposed of by letters patent under the Great Seal of Canada, or otherwise under the direction of the Government of Canada". In effect, the agreement provided that land reserved to the Indians that would have otherwise reverted to the province upon surrender could be dealt with by the government of Canada pursuant to the terms of the agreement.

As Alberta did not become a province until 1905, the underlying title to the land set apart for the Enoch Band under Treaty 6 (1876) was in the Crown in the right of the government of Canada. Hence, in the province of Alberta, the Indian interest in land reserved for the Indians would upon surrender revert to the government of Canada unless such a result has been altered by the Natural Resources Transfer Agreement confirmed by the *B.N.A. Act, 1930*, hereinafter referred to as the "transfer agreement".

In our view, this question has been resolved by the opening lines of s. 1 of that agreement:

> 1. *In order that the Province may be in the same position as the original Provinces of Confederation are in virtue of section one hundred and nine of the British North America Act, 1867*, the interest of the Crown in all Crown lands, mines, minerals (precious and base) and royalties derived therefrom within the Province, and all sums due or payable for such lands, mines, minerals or royalties, shall, from and after the coming into force of this agreement and subject as therein otherwise provided, belong to the Province, subject to any trusts existing in respect thereof. (Emphasis is ours.)

Here we find a clearly expressed intention to transfer to the province of Alberta "the interest of the Crown in all Crown lands". In our view, the interest transferred included the right of reversion which arises on surrender by a band of "land reserved for the Indians". The underlying title to the Indian lands was thereby transferred to the province in order to place Alberta in the same position as the provinces referred to in s. 109 of the *B.N.A. Act* which entered Confederation in 1867. We are not here referring to "land reserved for the Indians" but rather the underlying title to such lands.

The interest of the Indians and the authority of the government of Canada in relation to "land reserved for the Indians" is dealt with specifically in s. 10 of the agreement. That section provides that the transfer of the Crown's interest to the province under s. 1 does not abrogate the Indian interest in reserve lands nor the federal government's right to administer such lands. Section 10 reads as follows:

> 10. All lands included in Indian reserve within the Province, including those selected and surveyed but not yet confirmed, as well as those confirmed, shall continue to be vested in the Crown and administered by the Government of Canada for the purposes of Canada, and the Province will from time to time, upon the request of the Superintendent General of Indian Affairs, set aside, out of the unoccupied Crown lands hereby transferred to its administration, such further areas as the said Superintendent General may, in agreement with the appropriate Minister of the Province, select as necessary to enable Canada to fulfill its obligations under the treaties with the Indians of the Province, and such areas shall thereafter be administered by Canada in the same way in all respects as if they had never passed to the Province under the provisions hereof. . . .

In essence, ss. 1 and 10 of the transfer agreement placed Alberta in the same position as the original parties to Confederation. Consequently, s. 109 of the *B.N.A.*

Act applied to it in the same manner as it did to such other provinces.

Having transferred the underlying title to the province, an agreement similar to the agreement between the province of Ontario and the government of Canada was required to permit the government of Canada to deal with "land reserved for the Indians" upon surrender by the Indians of their interest in it. This was accomplished by s. 11 of the transfer agreement. . . .

A critical question is when the surrendered lands are freed from any Indian burden or interest. Under the *Indian Act*, the lands, when surrendered, would not come within the definition of a "reserve" if not "set apart for the use and benefit" of a band or Indians.

The surrendered lands will, however, still be subject to the control and management of the responsible minister in accordance with the *Indian Act*, s. 53(1):
. . .

The question of when the burden of the Indian interest on Crown lands is lost depends, in our view, upon the interpretation of the legislation governing the creation of the reserve, in this case the *Indian Act*. That appears to us to be true at least insofar as we are considering post-Confederation reserves established pursuant to federal legislation. We recognize that reserve allocations are frequently made in fulfilment of treaty obligations, and some argument might be made based on the provision of the treaty rendering the lands perpetual reserve lands. That is not this case. *Prima facie* Parliament, in exercising its legislative power under s. 91(24), is empowered to define the extent of a reservation and the way in which the burden created by the establishment of the reservation is discharged.

There are three recent authorities dealing with this aspect to which our attention has been directed: *R.* v. *Smith*, [1981] 1 F.C. 346, 113 D.L.R.(3d) 522, (C.A.), under appeal to the Supreme Court of Canada; *Surrey* v. *Peace Arch Enterprises Ltd.* (1970), 74 W.W.R. 380 (B.C.C.A.); and the decision of this court in *Western Int. Contractors Ltd.* v. *Sarcee Dev. Ltd.*, [1979] 3 W.W.R. 631, (sub nom. *Western Indust. Contractors Ltd.* v. *Sarcee Dev. Ltd.*) 98 D.L.R. (3d) 424.

In the *Peace Arch* case, supra, the reserve lands were surrendered in trust to lease. The land was leased to a developer, and the question was whether or not the by-laws of a municipality relating to zoning, specifications for buildings, water services and sewers and requirements under the *Health Act*, R.S.B.C. 1960, c. 170 [now R.S.B.C. 1979, c. 161] were applicable. The developers claimed immunity. The court held that, while the land might not meet the definition of a "reserve" in the *Indian Act*, it still met the definition of "lands reserved for Indians" within s. 91(24) of the *B.N.A. Act*. The court concluded that, as the Indians maintained a reversionary interest, the land remained under the exclusive legislative jurisdiction of Parliament and provincial legislation could not apply to the use. We confess to having some difficulty with the expressed conclusion. Section 91(24) of the *B.N.A. Act* gives authority to Parliament to legislate in respect of Indians and land reserved for Indians. That grant would also be interpreted to carry administrative authority over the lands. We do not, however, consider that the legislative grant provided in the *B.N.A. Act* is restrictive, and could not construe it as implying that lands once reserved are indelibly characterized as reserved, with an irremovable burden. That would be contrary to the pre-Confederation understanding of a reserve. It is capable of surrender. Moreover, it cannot be said that in every case it would be in the best interests of the native population that Indian lands be inalienable. The lands might be put to better account. Insofar as the *Peace Arch* decision recognized that provincial legislation relating to use could be inapplicable as inconsistent with the reversionary interest, we express no disagreement.

In *Smith*, supra, the lands were pre-Confederation reserves. They were surrendered to permit sale to squatters, but no sales were made. The question was whether or not a possessor could set up the statute of limitation and it was held it could not. In the course of a thorough and exhaustive judgment the court reviewed the nature of reserved land and discussed the status of surrendered lands. It was held that land surrendered for sale was no longer reserve land within s. 31 of the *Indian Act* but was still subject to the control and management of Canada under s. 91(24) of the *B.N.A. Act*.

In *Sarcee*, supra, there was a surrender for purposes of lease, and the question was whether or not a builders' lien could be claimed in respect of improvements to the resulting leasehold. The court held that there was not an absolute surrender, and that the lien could be enforced only in respect of the lessee's interest, and even then subject to the overriding terms of the lease itself.

It is clear from these authorities that an absolute surrender followed by a disposition of the reserved lands frees the land from the Indian burden. It follows from them that if the band retains the reversion the burden remains, at least insofar as the reversionary interest is concerned. The status of the leasehold thus created may be the subject of some debate, but on the wording of the questions before us it does not arise to be decided. . . .

THE APPLICABILITY OF PROVINCIAL LAW

It is to be observed that, while there is reference to some specific statutes in the questions, the question reads "Do *all* the laws of Alberta" apply to "*the* surrendered lands?" The questions are directed to the lands, and we are not concerned with the fact that legislation in relation to Indians may apply to Indians on the surrendered lands, just as they would to Indians generally, a principle applied by s. 88 of the *Indian Act* itself.

The named provincial statutes were not discussed in detail in argument; they were referred to generally in relation to their application, or difficulties arising out of their application, in the various contingencies of surrender, actual or hypothetical, with which this reference is concerned. In consequence, it can only be said that this opinion is limited to provincial statutes of general operation that affect the use and enjoyment of land, or an interest therein. . . .

We accept the general proposition that provincial legislation relating to use of reserve lands is inapplicable to lands that are found to be reserved for Indians: *Cardinal* v. *A.G. Alta.*, [1974] S.C.R. 695, 40 D.L.R. 553 at 561. Moreover, if land is surrendered for the purpose of a leasing, the reversion still remains reserved for Indians, and any provincial law impairing the full enjoyment of the reversion will be inapplicable. Finally, even if surrendered lands no longer remain part of a reserve as defined by the *Indian Act*, they remain, until finally disposed of, "lands reserved for the Indians" within the meaning of s. 91(24) and, as such, within federal legislative and administrative jurisdiction. This proposition comes from the *Smith* decision, supra, at p. 563. The federal government has continuing responsibility for the control and management of such land until its final disposition. Again, provincial law would have to be tested as to whether or not its purported exercise impaired the federal power derived from s. 91(24) and enshrined in s. 53(1) of the *Indian Act*.

THE ANSWERS

We preface these answers with some cautions.

Firstly, provincial laws of general application may apply to Indians whether on a reserve or not; the questions are primarily directed to the use and enjoyment of land. Secondly, we were asked about the application of "all" provincial laws, and argument was not specifically directed to particular statutes. It is perfectly clear that some provincial statutes will apply to Indians on reserves, as was illustrated in *Four B Mfg. Ltd.* v. *United Garment Wkrs. of Amer.* (1979), 30 N.R. 421 (S.C.C.). Finally, we are concerned with existing legislation, both federal and provincial. It is conceivable, for example, that amendments to the *Indian Act* might impair the validity of some conclusions.

Question 1

Once land is surrendered and granted in fee simple to a grantee, it ceases to be a "reserve" within the definition of the *Indian Act*, and it seems to us that such a conclusion would be fully justified apart from express statutory provisions. There was general agreement among counsel representing all parties that the lands would cease to be "lands reserved for the Indians" if a fee simple were granted to any of the persons or entities referred to in Q.1(a), (b), (d), (e) or (f). That conclusion with respect to lands in Ontario was reached in *A.G. Can.* v. *Giroux* (1916), 53 S.C.R. 172. A surrender which permits or requires a grant in fee simple necessarily imports an absolute surrender of all the rights and interests of the band. The grant imposes no qualifications or conditions on the grantee. There is no reversion of interest to the band. Such a grant would be registrable under the *Land Titles Act*, and legal title would issue to the grantee. The legal title would no longer be vested in Her Majesty; nor does a simple grant in fee simple bear any implication that the land conveyed continues to be set aside for the use and benefit of a band. The natural assumption is to the contrary. There can be no doubt that, when such a grant is made to a non-Indian, the surrendered land is no longer part of a reserve and is subject to the general laws of Alberta.

What the question raises, then, are ethnic considerations, namely, the right of an Indian or of a band and its members, personally or by incorporation, to own land in fee simple outside an established reserve and use it with the same freedom as accorded to other citizens of different racial origins. In short, does the use of the word "Indian" in s. 91(24) of the *B.N.A. Act* make him, or a corporation of which he is a member, impermeable in any event to such general provincial laws as are in contemplation?

In our opinion, the narrow ethnic point in these two categories of this question is decided in principle by *R.* v. *Sutherland*, supra. The law creates no impediment to an Indian to acquire and hold land alone or with others in his own right and for his own purposes, independent of reserves, as may any other Canadian. Land so acquired, whether from Her Majesty or otherwise, does not fall within the definition of a "reserve", and the general laws of Alberta would apply to it.

In answering Q.1(c), we note that our answer is restricted to the question precisely as it is put. A grant to the band or members of the band does not carry any implication of a continuing interest in the band or its members. Such a grant does not imply that the land will be kept by the grantees, let alone that it will be held for the use and benefit of the band or its members. Were such an implication present, it could open up other arguments, for example, that the effect of the grant was to engage the operation of s. 36 and create a new reserve. . . .

Whether the question is considered under s. 91(24) of the *B.N.A. Act* or under the *Indian Act*, the status of a corporation as a legal entity which exists independently of the character or status of its shareholders is recognized in law. It follows that the status of any or all of its shareholders, or the presence of a registered office on or off a reservation, has no bearing on the status accorded it at law. A suggestion was made in argument that the *Indian Act* could be amended in such a way as to give a corporation a special "Indian" status. We do not intend this opinion to be taken as considering the constitutionality of such an amendment.

For the purposes of both the *Indian Act* and the *B.N.A. Act*, neither an Indian nor a band is created by the process of incorporation.

Category (h) is subject to the same considerations, but it adds a further stipulation which, for the assistance intended for the protagonists, must be discussed:

> (h)   a corporation referred to in clauses (e) to (g) that holds the land in trust for Indians or for Indians and non-Indians or a group of persons consisting of Indians and non-Indians.

The addition is that the corporation, whatever the ethnic mix of its shareholders, holds the surrendered land on undefined trusts. It is apparent that it is not intended that the trusts be for the use and benefit of the band, as a trust so defined is part of Q.2. The interests of an Indian or a non-Indian, or a group of them, are by no means necessarily coincidental with the interests of "the band for whose use in common the reserve was set apart", to employ the phrase used in s. 37. A grant on such a trust does not come within s. 36 of the Act. Beyond that, on the assumption that such grant in fee simple was required by the terms of this surrender, then the disposition of the land to the grantee, impressed with the trust, whatever its terms may be, ends the obligations of Her Majesty to the band in respect of the surrendered land. By the grant, the obligation of Her Majesty's minister under s. 53(l) has been fulfilled, and Her Majesty has divested herself from the duties, responsibilities and powers imposed and given by the Act. We take it that the grant has the effect of making the grantee the trustee, and so the trust must be administered and enforced at law outside the operation of the Act, since the land is not within the operation of s. 36 and is no longer a reserve. In the result, this added stipulation cannot affect the answer to Q.1 that the surrendered lands cease to be lands reserved for the Indians and that the laws of Alberta apply to it.

Question 2

The second question varies and expands para. (h) of the first question. All hypotheses remain the same, except that the trust is for the benefit of the band and its members in perpetuity. We take it that what is intended is a trust for their use and benefit, as the phrase is used in various sections of the Act. It must be determined whether this additional hypothesis affects the conclusions we have reached on Q.1.

The hypothesis requires some analysis, and we will assume first that the terms of the surrender require that the land be granted in fee simple to one or other of the categorized grantees with such a trust imposed on it. Thus, the band has not ceded an iota of these benefits and usufructs appurtenant to a reserve; it has been at specific pains to state its retention of them. The change in title of the land from Her Majesty to the grantee cannot affect the scope and operation of the trust. There are no other details, information or circumstances given, and we are left with no alternative to the conclusion that the land falls within s. 36 and remains a reserve for the purposes of the Act.

In our view, if such a grant were made, it would come within s. 36, and the *Indian Act* would apply.

Question 2.1

We do not think that the ethnic considerations are of juridical significance. What is vital is that the legal title is retained by Her Majesty, and the disposition is of only a leasehold interest, in perpetuity or for a term of years. The matter for decision is whether a surrender for this purpose amounts to a surrender of the use and benefit for the band of the surrendered land, so that it is no longer "land reserved for the Indians" and so is removed from the definition of a "reserve". For this purpose, ss. 37 and 38 of the Act must be construed and given their proper effect in the context of the whole, particularly s. 53(1). . . .

In our view, s. 38 of the Act must be construed and applied in the light of the duties imposed on the minister by s. 53(1). A surrender for the purposes of granting a lease is a conditional or qualified surrender of such rights and interests of the band in the surrendered land as may be necessary for the efficacy of the lease according to its terms, but the rights and interests of the band therein have not been wholly surrendered by such a condition. They have not been finally disposed of. In place of personal use and occupation, the band chooses to obtain benefit for itself on the terms of a lease. It retains as to this the rights of a landlord through the agency of the minister, including the right of reversion of its interest. The rents reserved are "Indian moneys", in which the band has a direct interest in their collection and benefit. All of the band's interests are enforceable on its behalf only by the minister under s. 53(1), which contemplates just such a lease. We do not think that a conditional surrender of an interest by a band pursuant to s. 38 is intended to abrogate the powers and duties of the minister which may arise out of the operation of the subsequent section, which has directly in view that the qualification or condition of the surrender may require his continuing attention. If this is so, we do not see how it can be said that the interest of the band in lands so conditionally surrendered has been terminated so effectively that the land ceases to be "lands reserved for the Indians" during the term of the lease. The constitutionality of s. 38 was not in issue before us.

We do not think that a lease in perpetuity would bring about a different result. The band still retains its interests as beneficial landlord, and the terms of the lease would still have to be enforced, with the possibility of early termination and reversion. . . .

We conclude that the answer to Q.2.1 must be "No".

Question 3
We do not think that the site of the registered office has any juridical significance. It is subject to change. For the reasons given in connection with Q.l, this question is to be answered "No".

Question 4
Having concluded that Q.3 is to be answered "No", Q.4 is similarly answered. . . .

Q.5   We respectfully decline to answer in the absence of the proposed amendment.

7.   **Note from Appeal Committee of the House of Lords: [1982] 3 C.N.L.R. 195.** *Re The Queen* v. *The Secretary of State for Foreign and Commonwealth Affairs, ex parte the Indian Association of Alberta, Union of New Brunswick Indians, Union of Nova Scotian Indians,* **[1981] 4 C.N.L.R. 86 (C.A.) U.K. Lord Diplock, Lord Fraser of Tullybelron, Lord Russell of Killowen, Lord Scarman and Lord Bridge of Harwich, March 11, 1982**

> This appeal dealt with a suit brought by a number of Canadian Indian associations to the courts of the United Kingdom in order to have obligations undertaken by the Crown enforced. Both the Court of Appeal and the House of Lords affirmed that no residual responsibility for Canada's Indians is held by the Crown in right of the United Kingdom. Rather, the Crown in right of Canada holds these responsibilities and it is thus a matter for Canadian, not English, courts.

LORD DIPLOCK (for the Court):—Their Lordships do not grant leave to appeal in this case. They wish to make it clear that their refusal of leave is not based on any technical or procedural grounds, although it is not to be taken as their view that there is jurisdiction to entertain an application for judicial review in such a case as this. Their refusal of leave is because in their opinion, for the accumulated reasons given in the judgments of the Court of Appeal, it simply is not arguable that any obligations of the Crown in respect of the Indian peoples of Canada are still the responsibility of Her Majesty's government in the United Kingdom. They are the responsibility of Her Majesty's government in Canada, and it is the Canadian courts and not the English courts that alone have jurisdiction to determine what those obligations are.

PROVINCIAL AUTHORITY

8.   **Section 88, *Indian Act*, R.S.C. 1985, c. I–5**

LEGAL RIGHTS . . .

88. Subject to the terms of any treaty and any other Act of the Parliament of Canada, all laws of general application from time to time in force in any province are applicable to and in respect of Indians in the province, except to the extent that such laws are inconsistent with this Act or any order, rule, regulation or by-law, made thereunder, and except to the extent that such laws make provision for any matter for which provision is made by or under the Act. R.S. 1970, c. I–6, s. 88.

9.   ***Kruger and Manuel v. R.*, 9 C.N.L.C. 624 (S.C.C.). Laskin C.J.C., Martland, Judson, Ritchie, Spence, Pigeon, Dickson, Beetz, and de Grandpré JJ., May 31, 1977**

> This decision dealt with s. 88 of the *Indian Act* and held that laws of general application are those laws that apply uniformly throughout a jurisdiction and are not in relation to one class of citizens, namely Indians. This interpretation of s. 88 has since been expanded by the Supreme Court in the decision of *R. v. Dick* provided later in this chapter. *Kruger* also stated that when examining the issue of Aboriginal title, each community must be dealt with individually, with each case relying on its particular factual situation.

DICKSON, J.:—These appeals raise the question whether provincial game laws apply to non-treaty Indians hunting off a reserve on unoccupied Crown land. They fall to be decided upon a statement of agreed facts. The appellants, Jacob Kruger and Robert Manuel, are Indians living in British Columbia and are members of the Penticton Indian Band. Between September 5, and September 8, 1973, during the closed season for hunting, while hunting for food near Penticton, they killed four deer. The acts of hunting took place upon unoccupied Crown land which was and is the traditional hunting ground of the Penticton Indian Band. The accused did not have permits issued under the *Wildlife Act,* 1966 (B.C.), c. 55, authorizing them to hunt and kill deer for food during the closed season. Such permits were readily obtainable by local native Indians and both appellants had obtained permits in the past. . . .

It is contended on behalf of the appellants that the British Columbia Court of Appeal erred in three respects, namely:

1. In ruling that the *Wildlife Act,* 1966 (B.C.), c. 55, was a law of general application within the meaning of the phrase in s. 88 of the *Indian Act.*

2. In ruling, in effect that s. 88 of the *Indian Act* constituted a federal incorporation by reference of certain provincial laws rather than a statement of the general principles relating to the application of provincial laws to Indians.

3. In ruling, in effect, that aboriginal hunting rights could be expropriated without compensation and without explicit federal legislation.

The third point can be disposed of shortly. The British Columbia Court of

Appeal was not asked to decide, nor did it decide, as I read its judgment, whether aboriginal hunting rights were or could be expropriated without compensation. It is argued that absence of compensation supports the proposition that there has been no loss or regulation of rights. That does not follow. Most legislation imposing negative prohibitions affects previously enjoyed rights in ways not deemed compensatory. The *Wildlife Act* illustrates the point. It is aimed at wildlife management and to that end it regulates the time, place, and manner of hunting game. It is not directed to the acquisition of property.

Before considering the two other grounds of appeal, I should say that the important constitutional issue as to the nature of aboriginal title, if any, in respect of lands in British Columbia, the further question as to whether it had been extinguished, and the force of the Royal Proclamation of 1763—issues discussed in *Calder et al.* v. *A.-G. B.C.* (1973), 34 D.L.R (3d) 145, [1973] S.C.R 313,—will not be determined in the present appeal. They were not directly placed in issue by the appellants and a sound rule to follow is that questions of title should only be decided when title is directly in issue. Interested parties should be afforded an opportunity to adduce evidence in detail bearing upon the resolution of the particular dispute. Claims to aboriginal title are woven with history, legend, politics and moral obligations. If the claim of any Band in respect of any particular land is to be decided as a justiciable issue and not a political issue, it should be so considered on the facts pertinent to that Band and to that land, and not on any global basis. Counsel were advised during argument, and indeed seemed to concede, that the issue raised in the present appeal could be resolved without determining the broader questions I have mentioned. . . .

Argument was addressed to the Court that the *Wildlife Act* affects Indian people in a manner quite different than it affects non-Indian people and for that reason cannot be considered as a law of general application within the meaning of the *Indian Act*, s. 88. The first thing to notice in this respect is the precise terms of s. 88 itself. It subjects Indians to "all laws of general application from time to time *in force in any province*". There formerly existed a doubt as to whether s. 88 was restricted to provincially enacted laws but that question has been settled in the affirmative by this Court in *R.* v. *George,* supra. Mr. Justice Martland gave this interpretation to the relevant phrase in s. 88, at p. 151 C.C.C., p. 398 D.L.R. p. 281 S.C.R.:

> *In my view the expression refers only to those rules of law in a Province which are provincial in scope*, and would include provincial legislation and any laws which were made a part of the law of a Province, as for example in the Provinces of Alberta and Saskatchewan, the laws of England as they existed on July 15, 1870.
>
> This section was not intended to be a declaration of the paramountcy of treaties over Federal legislation. The reference to treaties was incorporated in a section *the purpose of which was to make provincial laws applicable to Indians, so as to preclude any interference with rights under treaties resulting from the impact of provincial legislation.*

The emphasis throughout is mine.

There are two *indicia* by which to discern whether or not a provincial enactment is a law of general application. It is necessary to look first to the territorial reach of the Act. If the Act does not extend uniformly throughout the territory, the inquiry is at an end and the question is answered in the negative. If the law does extend uniformly throughout the jurisdiction the intention and effects of the enactment need to be considered. The law must not be "in relation to" one class of citizens in object and purpose. But the fact that a law may have graver consequence to one person than to another does not, on that account alone, make the law other than one of general application. There are few laws which have a uniform impact. The line is crossed, however, when an enactment, though in relation to another matter, by its effect, impairs the status or capacity of a particular group. The analogy may be made to a law which in its effect paralyzes the status and capacities of a federal company: see *Great West Saddlery Co. Ltd.* v. *The King*, [1921] 2 A.C. 91. Such an act is no "law of general application": see also *Cunningham* v. *Tomey Homma*, [1903] A.C. 151.

Apply these criteria to the case at bar. There is no doubt that the *Wildlife Act* has a uniform territorial operation. Similarly, it is clear that in object and purpose the Act is not aimed at Indians. Section 4 of the *Wildlife Act* which the accused were charged commences: "No person shall" and so, on its face, applies to all persons. Subsections (1), (2) and (3) [of s. 4] of the *Wildlife Act* impose licensing requirements on those wishing to hunt, trap or fish. Subsection (4) states that s-ss. (1) (2) and (3) do not apply to an Indian residing in the Province. From this, it is clear that the other sections are intended to apply to Indians, as well as all other persons within the Province. Provincial game laws, which have as their object the conservation and management of provincial wildlife resources, have been held by this Court not to relate to Indians *qua* Indians: *Cardinal* v. *A.-G. Alta.* (1973), 13 C.C.C. (2d) 1 at p. 9, 40 D.L.R. (3d) 553 at p. 562, [1974] S.C.R. 695 at p. 706; *R.* v. *George,* supra. It was long ago decided that provincial laws may affect Indians, in so far as the Act was not in relation to them.

> In other words, no statute of the Provincial Legislature dealing with Indians or their lands as such would be valid and effective, but there is no reason why general legislation may not affect them.

These words of Riddell, J., in *R.* v. *Martin* (1917), 29 C.C.C. 189 at p. 193, 39 D.L.R. 635 at p. 639, were cited with approval in this Court by Martland, J., in *Cardinal* v. *A.-G. Alta.,* supra, at p. 9 C.C.C., p. 553 D.L.R., p. 706 S.C.R. Mr. Justice Martland continued at p. 10 C.C.C., p. 562 D.L.R. p. 707 S.C.R: "The point is that the provisions of para. 12 [of the Alberta Natural Resources Transfer Agreement] were not required to make Provincial game laws apply to Indians off the reserve."

The Chief Justice of this Court, then Laskin, J., wrote in dissent in *Cardinal*, but on the point of concern in the present inquiry, namely, the applicability of provincial game laws to Indians off reserves, his views seem to accord with those of Mr. Justice Martland. After referring to the exclusion of reserves from provincial control, he had this to say, p. 20 C.C.C., p. 572 D.L.R., p. 722 S.C.R.:

> They do not return to that control under para. 12 in respect of the application of provincial game laws. That paragraph deals with a situation unrelated to Indian reserves.

It is concerned rather with Indians as such, and with guaranteeing to them a continuing right to hunt, trap and fish for food regardless of *provincial game laws which would otherwise confine Indians in parts of the Province that are under Provincial administration.* Although inelegantly expressed, para. 12 does not expand provincial legislative power but contracts it.

However abundant the right of Indians to hunt and to fish, there can be no doubt that such right is subject to regulation and curtailment by the appropriate legislative authority. Section 88 of the *Indian Act* appears to be plain in purpose and effect. In the absence of treaty protection or statutory protection Indians are brought within provincial regulatory legislation.

Game conservation laws have as their policy the maintenance of wildlife resources. It might be argued that without some conservation measures the ability of Indians or others to hunt for food would become a moot issue in consequence of the destruction of the resource. The presumption is for the validity of a legislative enactment and in this case the presumption has to mean that in the absence of evidence to the contrary the measures taken by the British Columbia Legislature were taken to maintain an effective resource in the Province for its citizens and not to oppose the interests of conservationists and Indians in such a way as to favour the claims of the former. If, of course, it can be shown in future litigation that the province has acted in such a way as to oppose conservation and Indian claims to the detriment of the latter—to "preserve moose before Indians" in the words of Gordon, J.A., in *R. ex rel. Clinton* v. *Strongquill* (1953), 105 C.C.C. 262, [1953] 2 D.L.R. 264, 8 W.W.R. (N.S.) 247—it might very well be concluded that the effect of the legislation is to cross the line demarking laws of general application from other enactments. It would have to be shown that the policy of such an Act was to impair the status and capacities of Indians. Were that so, s. 88 would not operate to make the Act applicable to Indians. But that has not been done here and in the absence of clear evidence the Court cannot so presume.

The judgment of this Court in *R.* v. *White and Bob* (1965), 52 D.L.R. (2d) 481n, [1965] S.C.R. vi affirming 50 D.L.R. (2d) 613, 52 W.W.R. 193, is of no assistance to appellants in the present case. In *White and Bob* the accused were charged with having game in their possession during the closed season without having a valid and subsisting permit under the *Game Act*, R.S.B.C. 1960, c. 160. The accused raised the defence that an agreement between their ancestors, members of the Saalequun tribe and Governor Douglas, dated December 23, 1854 gave them the right to hunt for food over the land in question and, alternatively, that as native Indians they possessed the aboriginal right to hunt for food over unoccupied land lying within their ancient tribal hunting grounds. The position of the Crown was that the agreement in question conferred no hunting rights and, if it did, these rights were extinguished by s. 87 (now s. 88) of the *Indian Act*, which the Crown said extended the provisions of the *Game Act* (the forerunner of the *Wildlife Act*) to Indians. Mr. Justice Davey (with whom Mr. Justice Sullivan concurred) was of the opinion that Parliament intended the word "treaty" in s. 87 to include agreements such as the one in question and to except their provisions from the operative part of the section. He held that, that being so, s. 87 did not extend the general provisions of the *Game Act* to the respondents in the exercise of their hunting rights under the agreement over the lands in question. The following passage of his judgment is important, p. 618 D.L.R., p. 198 W.W.R.:

> Sections 8 [rep. & sub. 1961, c. 21. s. 3] and 15 [rep. & sub. 1961, c. 21, s.6] of the *Game Act* specifically exempt Indians from the operation of certain provisions if the Act, and from what *I think it clear that the other provisions are intended to be of general application and to include* Indians. If these general sections are sufficiently clear to show an intention to abrogate or qualify the contractual rights of hunting notoriously reserved to Indians by agreements such as ex. 8, they would, in my opinion, fail in that purpose because that would be legislation in relation to Indians that falls within Parliament's exclusive legislative authority under s. 91(24) of the *B.N.A. Act*, and also because that would conflict with s. 87 of the *Indian Act* passed under that authority.

[Emphasis added.] He concluded, p. 619 D.L.R. p. 199 W.W.R.:

> In the result, the right of the respondents to hunt over the lands in question reserved to them by ex. 8 are preserved by s. 87, and remain unimpaired by the *Game Act*, and it follows that the respondents were rightfully in possession of the carcasses. It becomes unnecessary to consider other aspects of a far-reaching argument addressed to us by respondents' counsel.

Mr. Justice Sheppard (with whom Mr. Justice Lord concurred) dissented. He considered that the agreement was not a treaty and was therefore not within the opening words of s. 87. He said that the section of the *Game Act* in question was within the legislative jurisdiction of the Province and was applicable to Indians not on their reserve. Mr. Justice Norris wrote separate reasons in which he agreed, substantially for the reasons given by Mr. Justice Davey, that the agreement was a treaty within the meaning of s. 87 of the *Indian Act*. He then dealt at length with the matter of aboriginal rights in general and the applicability of the Royal Proclamation of 1763.

As I read the judgments in the Court of Appeal for British Columbia four of the five Judges accepted that the section of the *Game Act* under which the accused were charged would apply to the accused unless the agreement of 1854 could be said to be a treaty within the opening words of s. 87 of the *Indian Act*. When the case reached this Court, the only question decided was whether or not the agreement constituted such a treaty. At the conclusion of argument for the appellant the Court rendered the following oral judgment [p. 481 D.L.R.]:

> Mr. Berger, Mr. Manders and Mr. Christie. We do not find it necessary to hear you. We are all of the opinion that the majority in the Court of Appeal were right in their conclusion that the document, Exhibit 8, was a 'treaty' within the meaning of that term as used in s. 87 of the *Indian Act* [R.S.C. 1952, c. 149]. We therefore think that in the circumstances of the case, the operation of s. 25 of the *Game Act* [R.S.B.C. 1960, c. 160] was excluded by reason of the existence of that treaty.
>
> The appeal is accordingly dismissed with costs throughout.

The operation of s. 25 of the *Game Act* was excluded because the agreement was a "treaty".

It has been urged in argument that Indians having historic hunting rights which they have not surrendered should not be placed in a more invidious position than those who entered into treaties, the terms of which preserved those rights. However receptive one may be to such an argument on compassionate grounds, the plain fact is that s. 88 of the *Indian Act*, enacted by the Parliament of Canada, provides that "subject to the terms of any treaty" all laws of general application from time to time in force in any Province are applicable to and in respect of Indians in the Province, except as stated. The terms of the treaty are paramount; in the absence of a treaty provincial laws of general application apply. . . .

There is in the legal literature a juridicial controversy respecting whether s. 88 referentially incorporates provincial laws of general application or whether such laws apply to Indians *ex proprio vigore*. The issue was considered by this Court in *Natural Parents* v. *Superintendent of Child Welfare et al.* (1975), 60 D.L.R. (3d) 148, [1976] 2 S.C.R. 751. The question in that appeal concerned the validity of an adoption order made in respect of a male Indian child in favour of a non-Indian couple. The Chief Justice (Judson, Spence and Dickson, JJ., concurring, de Grandpré J., concurring in the result) rejected the submission that the *Adoption Act*, R.S.B.C. 1960, c. 4, applied *ex proprio vigore* to the adoption of Indian children and, treating the *Adoption Act* as referentially incorporated, considered whether and to what extent that Act was inconsistent with the *Indian Act*. Mr. Justice Martland (with whom Pigeon, J., concurred) was of the opinion that the ambit of authority conferred on the Parliament of Canada by s. 91(24) to legislate on the subject of "Indians and Lands reserved for the Indians" was not such that Parliament alone could enact legislation which might affect Indians: it was not such that Indians were totally exempted from the application of provincial laws. After referring to the *Cardinal* case, Mr. Justice Martland said, p. 163 D.L.R.:

> The extent to which provincial legislation could apply to Indians was stated to be that the legislation must be within the authority of s. 92 of the *British North America Act, 1867* and that the legislation must not be enacted in relation to Indians. Such legislation, generally applicable throughout the Province, could affect Indians.

Mr. Justice Ritchie, considering s. 88, said, p. 170 D.L.R.:

> In my view, when the Parliament of Canada passed the *Indian Act* it was concerned with the preservation of the special status of Indians and with their rights to Indian lands, but it was made plain by s. 88 that Indians were to be governed by the laws of their Province of residence except to the extent that such laws are inconsistent with the *Indian Act* or relate to any matter for which provision is made under the Act.

Mr. Justice Beetz did not find it necessary to express an opinion on the purview of s. 88 of the *Indian Act*. In the result four members of the Court, less than a majority, adopted the position that the section is a referential incorporation of provincial legislation which takes effect under the section as federal legislation.

On either view of this issue present appellants must fail. If the provisions of the *Wildlife Act* are referentially incorporated by s. 88 of the *Indian Act*, appellants, in order to succeed, would have the burden of demonstrating inconsistency or duplication with the *Indian Act* or any order, Rule, Regulation or by-law made thereunder.

That burden has not been discharged and, having regard to the terms of the Wildlife Act, manifestly could not have been discharged. Accordingly, such provisions take effect as federal legislation in accordance with their terms. Assuming, without deciding, that the theory of aboriginal title as elaborated by Hall, J., in *Calder et al.* v. *A.-G. B.C.* (1973), 34 D.L.R. (3d) 145, [1973] S.C.R. 313, is available in respect of present appellants it has been conclusively decided that such title, as any other, is subject to Regulations imposed by validly enacted federal laws: *Noll Derriksan* v. *The Queen* (a recent decision of this Court not yet reported). That was also the result in *R.* v. *George*, [1966] S.C.R. 267; *Daniels* v. *The Queen*, [1968] S.C.R. 517, and *Sikyea* v. *The Queen*, [1964] S.C.R. 642. The latter two cases are instructive as the hunting rights there stood on stronger ground in that they were protected, in the case of *Sikyea*, by treaty, and in *Daniels'* case by the Manitoba Natural Resources Agreement. In neither case did the protection prevail against the federal *Migratory Birds Convention Act*, R.S.C. 1952, c. 179.

If s. 88 does not referentially incorporate the *Wildlife Act*, the only question at issue is whether the Act is a law of general application. Since that proposition has not been here negatived, the enactment would apply to Indians *ex proprio vigore*. It is, therefore, immaterial to the present appeals whether s. 88 takes effect by way of referential incorporation or not. In either case, these appeals must fail.

I would dismiss the appeals.

Appeals dismissed.

10. *Paul Band* v. *R.*, [1984] 1 C.N.L.R. 87 (Alta. C.A.). McDermid, Haddad, and Belzil JJ.A., December 30, 1983

Jurisdiction over labour relations is shared by the federal and provincial governments. Issues relating to labour relations, in this case the activities of special constables, formed a central component of the band council's normal operations. This decision affirms that the *Canada Labour Code* applies to employees of a band council and supersedes the application of provincial laws in this area. *Paul Band* also provides that band councils are created by, and derive their authority from, the *Indian Act*.

BELZIL J.A.:—The appellant, Paul Band, is a legally constituted band under the *Indian Act*, R.S.C. 1970, c. I–6. It was charged under the *Alberta Labour Act*, 1973, S.A. 1973, c. 33 [later R.S.A. 1980, c. L–l; repealed by *Employment Standards Act*, R.S.A, 1980 (Supp.), c. E–10.1, s. 121; *Labour Relations Act*, R.S.A. 1980 (Supp.), c. L–1.1, s. 182], for failing to pay to two employees wages earned by them while employed by the band as special constables on the Paul Band Wabamun Indian Reserve No. 133.

The band was convicted in summary conviction proceedings in provincial court [[1982] 4 C.N.L.R. 120]: it was fined, and judgments were awarded against it for the wages due. The conviction and judgments were sustained on appeal to the Court of Queen's Bench. . . .

The principal issue raised in this appeal is whether the *Alberta Labour Act* applies to the labour relations of the "band" and its special constables. It is on this constitutional issue that the intervenants appeared, and that the main submissions were made before us, and it is therefore on this issue that I propose to determine this appeal. The subsidiary issue is whether the appellant band, *qua* band, was an *"employer"* within the definition of that term in the *Alberta Labour Act, 1973*. This subsidiary issue evaporates with my conclusion on the main issue. The trial judge (wrongly in my view) treated the band as a corporate body managed by the band council, and therefore liable for the acts of the council. In considering the main issue, I will treat the band council as the employer.

The two employees, who were not members of the band, were hired by the band council for the purpose of limited law enforcement on the Reserve. Upon application by the band council they received an appointment under s. 38 of the *Police Act, 1973*, S.A. 1973, c. 44 [now the *Police Act*, R.S.A. 1980, c. P–12], as special constables authorized to enforce certain provincial statutes, . . . as well as the provisions of ss. 30, 94 and 97 of the *Indian Act*, R.S.C. 1970, c. I–6.

The question whether or not the province has authority to appoint special constables to enforce its laws on Indian reserves is not in issue in this appeal. The fact is that they were hired, worked at their employment and they earned wages to which will be entitled irrespective of the constitutional validity of their appointment. . . .

The general rule to be applied in determining jurisdictional competence over labour relations is stated by Ritchie J. in *Letter Carriers' Union of Canada* v. *Can. Union of Postal Workers*, [1975] 1 S.C.R. 178 at 181:

> It has been accepted, at least since the case of *Toronto Electric Commissioners* v. *Snider et al.*, that, generally speaking, legislation respecting employer and employee relationships relates to property and civil rights and is therefore within the exclusive jurisdiction of the provincial legislature, but under the *Industrial Relations and Disputes Investigation Act*, 1948 (Can.), c. 54, which was the precursor of the present *Canada Labour Code*, and the decision of this Court in the Reference relating to the validity and application of that statute, it has been established that it is not within the competency of a provincial legislature to legislate concerning industrial relations of persons employed in a *work, business or undertaking coming within the exclusive jurisdiction of the Parliament of Canada*. (Emphasis added)

And by Beetz J. in *Four B Manufacturing* v. *United Garment Workers of America*, [1980] S.C.R. 1031, [1979] 4 C.N.L.R. 21 at p. 1045 [pp. 23–4 C.N.L.R.]:

> In my view the established principles relevant to this issue can be summarized very briefly. With respect to labour relations, exclusive provincial legislative competence is the rule, exclusive federal competence is the exception. The exception comprises, in the main, labour relations in undertakings, services and businesses which, having regard to the functional test of the nature of their operations and their normal activities, can be characterized as federal undertakings, services or businesses. . . .
>
> The functional test is a particular method of applying a more general rule namely that exclusive federal jurisdiction over labour relations arises only if it can be shown that *such jurisdiction forms an integral part of primary federal jurisdiction over some other federal object: the Stevedoring case*. (Emphasis added)

In *Canada Labour Relations Board, Public Alliance of Canada* v. *City of Yellowknife*, 76 D.L.R. (3d) 85 (S.C.C.), Pigeon J. said at p. 87:

Section 109 deals with employees of the Government of Canada or a corporation established to perform any function or duty on its behalf. It is important to note that the criterion for the application of Part V *to all other employees* is whether they are employed upon or in connection with the operation of any "federal work, undertaking or business".

And at p. 90:

In considering this question, one has to bear in mind that *it is well settled that jurisdiction over labour matters depends* on legislative authority over the operation, not over the person of the employer. (Emphasis added)

Employees are thus to be classified for jurisdictional purposes not by reference to their particular activities in their employment but by reference to the character, or nature, of the operation of the *employer* in which they are employed, and to the legislative authority over that operation. The ultimate test is legislative authority over the operation. . . .

In the *Letter Carriers'* case, Ritchie J. said at p. 188:

As 90 per cent of the activities of M & B Enterprises Ltd. was confined to work for the Post Office, it is obvious that this work composed *the main and principal part of its business and the Labour Relations Board* of Saskatchewan cannot, in my opinion, acquire jurisdiction to entertain an application for certification of a bargaining representative on behalf of a unit composed of all truck driver employees of such a company other than supervisors, *simply because two or three drivers in the unit were occasionally engaged in casual employment driving trucks for the transportation of furniture for others than the Post Office.* (Emphasis added)

In *Letter Carriers'*, the Supreme Court of Canada overruled the Court of Appeal of Saskatchewan because that Court of Appeal had decided that employees could not meet the test prescribed by Mr. Justice Estey in the *Stevedores* case [*Reference Re Industrial Relations and Disputes Investigation Act*, [1955] S.C.R. 529] unless they were *exclusively* employed upon or in connection with the operation of a federal work.

In *Four B Manufacturing*, Beetz J. in arriving at the conclusion that the operation of the employer was not a federal concern said at p. 1046 [p. 24 C.N.L.R.]:

There is nothing about the business or operation of *Four B* which might allow it to be considered as a federal business: the sewing of uppers on sport shoes is an ordinary industrial activity which clearly comes under provincial legislative authority for the purposes of labour relations.

When considering *Four B Manufacturing*, it is important to keep in mind that the employer whose operation was classified as provincial was a private corporation separate from the band council, although its shareholders and employees were band members and its operations were carried on exclusively on the reserve.

The words "operation", "activity", "business" "undertaking" used interchangeably in the foregoing authorities do not necessarily embrace the entire activities of the employer. There are cases where a particular operation of an employer does not form an integral part of the main operation of that employer and in that situation the particular operation will be characterized for jurisdictional purposes in labour relations separately from the main operation, and the functional test to determine legislative authority will be applied to it is as a separate entity. In the *Empress Hotel* case [*C.P.R.* v. *A.-G. of B.C.*], [1950] A.C. 122, it was held that the hotel operated by the Canadian Pacific Railway Company was a business separate from the main railway system operated by that company and that while the railway system was clearly under federal labour jurisdiction, the Hotel was under provincial jurisdiction. The company was authorized by its constituent Act to build and operate hotels. The Privy Council said at p. 143:

> A company may be authorized to carry on, and may in fact carry on, more than one undertaking. Because a company is a railway company it does not follow that all its works must be railway works or that all its activities must be related to its railway undertaking.

That is not the situation here. In enforcing provincial laws on the reserve, the band council was carrying out one of a number of powers entrusted to it by s. 81 of the *Indian Act* (infra), namely, the regulation of traffic, and the observance of law and order. This was an integral part of the normal operation assigned to the band council by s. 81 of the *Indian Act*. . . .

In determining the nature of the operation of the band council, the trial judge was required to look "*at the normal or habitual activities*" of the council "*as a going concern*": [per Beetz J. in *Montcalm*] and at the legislative authority over that operation [per Pigeon J. in *City of Yellowknife*].

The only operations or activities that a band council is empowered to carry on are those authorized by Parliament under the *Indian Act*, and in particular by s. 81:
. . .

Band councils are created under the *Indian Act* and derive their authority to operate *qua band councils* exclusively from that Act. In the exercise of their powers they are concerned with the administration of band affairs on their respective reserves whether under direct authority of Parliament or as administrative arms of the Minister. They have no other source of power. Band councils are thus within the exclusive legislative jurisdiction and control of the Parliament of Canada over "Indians, and Lands reserved for Indians" assigned to it by s. 91(24) of the *Constitution Act, 1867* and such councils are thus immune to provincial legislation. In *Commission du Salaire Minimum* v. *Bell Telephone Co.*, [1966] S.C.R. 767, Martland J. for the court said at p. 772:

> In my opinion, regulation of the field of employer and employee relationships in an undertaking such as that of the respondent's, as in the case of the regulation of rates which they charge to their customers, is a "matter" coming within the class of subject defined in s. 92(10)(a) and, that being so, is within the exclusive legislative jurisdiction of the Parliament of Canada. Consequently, any provincial legislation in that field, while valid in respect of employers not within exclusive federal legislative jurisdiction, cannot apply to employers who are within that exclusive control.

There can accordingly be no doubt that the normal operations or activities of the Paul Band Council were those which it was carrying on under authority of the

Indian Act and thus constituted a federal undertaking or business. That the special constables in question may have been enforcing provincial statutes on the reserve is irrelevant.

The court was urged to adopt the reasoning of the Court of Appeal of Saskatchewan in *Whitebear Band Council* v. *Carpenters Provincial Council of Sask.,* [1982] 3 W.W.R. 554, [1982] 3 C.N.L.R. 181 (Sask. C.A.). In that case, the operation of the band council under review arose under an agreement between the council and the Department of Indian and Northern Affairs whereby the council agreed to manage a capital spending program of house construction, etc., on the reserve funded by the Department. While I do not disagree with that decision, I have not relied on it because different considerations may apply. . . .

The appeal is accordingly allowed, the convictions quashed, and the judgments awarded are set aside. . . .

11. *R.* v. *Dick*, [1985] 4 C.N.L.R. 55 (S.C.C.). Dickson C.J., Beetz, Estey, McIntyre, and Chouinard JJ., October 31, 1985

> This decision was definitive in establishing a new interpretation of s. 88 of the *Indian Act* and, in general, the application of provincial laws to Indians. The general proposition that provincial laws apply to Indians remains, and s. 88 deals only with those laws that affect Indians "as Indians." Thus, provincial laws that affect Indians as Indians or that affect the status and capacities of Indians and that are not ordinarily applicable to them are incorporated by reference into federal law by s. 88. This decision has been subsequently affirmed by the Supreme Court in *Derrickson* v. *Derrickson*, [1986] 1 S.C.R. 285, and *R.* v. *Francis*, [1988] 1 S.C.R. 1025.

BEETZ J.:—. . . Appellant and respondent appear to agree in substance as to the issues raised by this appeal, save one. But they express them differently and I find it preferable to rephrase them as follows:

1. Is the practice of year-round foraging for food so central to the Indian way of life of the Alkali Lake Shuswap that it cannot be restricted by ss. 3(1) and 8(1) of the *Wildlife Act,* R..S. B.C. 1979, c .433 [rep. by S. B.C. 1982, c. 57, s. 123] without impairment of their status and capacity as Indians, and invasion of the federal field under para. 91(24) of the *Constitution Act, 1867*?

2. If the answer to the first question is in the affirmative and, consequently, the *Wildlife Act* cannot apply *ex proprio vigore* to the appellant, then is this Act a law of general application referentially incorporated into federal law by s. 88 of the *Indian Act,* R.S.C. 1970, c. I–6, which provides:

> 88. Subject to the terms of any treaty and any other Act of the Parliament of Canada, all laws of general application from time to time in force in any Province are applicable to and in respect of Indians in the province, except to the extent that such laws are inconsistent with this Act or any order, rule, regulation or by-law made thereunder, and except to the extent that such laws make provision for any matter for which provision is made by or under this Act.

3. Does this appeal raise a question of law alone for the purpose of s. 114 of the *Offence Act,* R.S.B.C. 1979, c. 305?

The third issue was raised only by respondent.

In addition, a constitutional question was stated by the Chief Justice:

Are ss. 3(1)(c) and 8(1) of the *Wildlife Act*, R.S.B.C. 1979, c .433, constitutionally inapplicable in the circumstances of this case on the ground that the restriction imposed by such sections affects the appellant *qua* Indian and therefore may only be enacted by the Parliament of Canada pursuant to s. 9l(24) of the *Constitution Act, 1867*? . . .

Another issue had been raised by appellant in the Court of Appeal, namely whether the County Court Judge had erred in holding that the manner of administration of the *Wildlife Act* by provincial officials,—somewhat misleadingly referred to as the policy of the Act—had not significantly changed since the judgment of this Court in *Kruger and Manuel* v. *R.* [1978] 1 S.C.R. 104, [1977] 4 W.W.R. 300, 75 D.L.R. (3d) 434, 15 N.R. 495, 34 C.C.C. (2d) 377. But the Court of Appeal, following *R.* v. *Haines* (1981), 34 B.C.L.R. 148, [1981] 6 W.W.R. 664, [1982] 2 C.N.L.R. 135, unanimously held that this issue was not a "ground that involved a question of law alone". While appellant referred in his factum to the policy of the provincial government not to issue sustenance permits for out of season hunting by Indians who regularly depend on hunting for their food, I did not understand him to press this matter in this Court as a distinct issue. . . .

Appellant's main submission which was apparently presented in the Court of Appeal as an alternative argument, is that the *Wildlife Act* strikes at the core of Indianness, that the question stated in the first issue should accordingly be answered in the affirmative and the *Wildlife Act*, while valid legislation, should be read down so as not to apply to Appellant in the circumstances of the case at bar. . . .

The reasons of Lambert J.A., dissenting, are quite elaborate. For the greater part, they expound the similarities and differences between the case at bar and *Kruger and Manuel* and his understanding of the tests adopted in the latter case to determine whether a law is one of general application, a matter to which I will return in dealing with the second issue. But he used the same tests to answer the question stated in the first issue, namely whether the application of the *Wildlife Act* to appellant would regulate him *qua* Indian. Here is what he wrote in *R.* v. *Dick*, 3 C.C.C. (3d) 481 at p. 492 (B.C.C.A.), [1983] 2 C.N.L.R. 134 at pp. 144–45:

. . . it seems to me that the same tests as are applied to determine whether the application of a provincial law to a particular group of Indians in a particular activity is the application of a law of general application, should also be applied to determine whether the application of provincial law to a particular group of Indians in a particular activity is the legislation in relation to Indians in their Indianness. . . .

And, before concluding at p. 495 [p. 147 C.N.L.R.] Lambert J.A. wrote:

Indeed, I would add that if the facts in this case do not place the killing of the deer within the central core of Indianness, if there is one, or within the boundary that outlines the status and capacities of the Alkali Lake Band, then it is difficult to imagine other facts that would do so.

In *Cardinal* v. *Attorney General of Alberta*, [1974] S.C.R. 695 at p. 706, it had already been held, apart from any evidence, that provincial game laws do not relate to Indians *qua* Indians. In the case at bar, there was considerable evidence capable of supporting the conclusions of Lambert J.A. to the effect that the *Wildlife Act* did impair the Indianness of the Alkali Lake Band, as well as the opposite conclusions of the courts below.

I am prepared to assume, without deciding, that Lambert J A. was right on this point and that appellant's submission on the first issue is well taken. . . .

On the basis of this assumption and subject to the question of referential incorporation which will be dealt with in the next chapter, it follows that the *Wildlife Act* could not apply to the appellant ex proprio vigore, and, in order to preserve its constitutionality, it would be necessary to read it down to prevent its applying to appellant in the circumstances of this case. . . .

In holding that the tests adopted by this Court in *Kruger and Manuel* to determine whether a law is one of general application are the same tests which should be applied to determine whether the application of the *Wildlife Act* to appellant would regulate him in his Indianness, Lambert J. A. fell into error, in my respectful opinion. And this error resulted from a misapprehension of what was decided in *Kruger and Manuel* as to the nature of a law of general application.

The tests which Lambert J.A. applied in reviewing the evidence in his above quoted reasons are perfectly suitable to determine whether the application of the *Wildlife Act* to the appellant would have the effect of regulating him *qua* Indian, with the consequential necessity of a reading down if it did; but, apart from legislative intent and colourability, they have nothing to do with the question whether the *Wildlife Act* is a law of general application. On the contrary, it is precisely because the *Wildlife Act* is a law of general application that it would have to be read down were it not for s. 88 of the *Indian Act*. If the special impact of the *Wildlife Act* on Indians had been the very result contemplated by the legislature and pursued by it as a matter of policy, the Act could not be read down because it would be in relation to Indians and clearly ultra vires. . . .

Lambert J.A. then emphasized the importance of the effect of the legislation as opposed to its purpose. At p. 489 [p. 142 C.N.L.R.] *R.* v. *Dick,* 3 C.C.C. (3d) 481 (B.C.C.A.), [1983] 2 C.N.L.R. 134, of his reasons he wrote:

> . . . evidence about the motives of individual members of the Legislature or even about the more abstract "intention of the legislature" or "legislative purpose of the enactment" is not relevant. What is relevant is evidence about the effect of the legislation. In fact, evidence about its "application".

With all due deference, it seems to me that the correct view is the reverse one and that what Dickson J., as he then was, referred to in *Kruger and Manuel* when he mentioned laws which had crossed the line of general application were laws which, either overtly or colourably, single out Indians for special treatment and impair their status as Indians. Effect and intent are both relevant. Effect can evidence intent. But in order to determine whether a law is not one of general application, the intent, purpose or policy of the legislation can certainly not be ignored: they form an essential ingredient of a law which discriminates between various classes of persons as opposed to a law of general application. This in my view is what Dickson J. meant when in the above quoted passage, he wrote:

It would have to be shown that the policy of such an Act was to impair the status and capacities of Indians.

I am reinforced in this view by the fact that at p. 113 S.C.R., Dickson J. quoted with approval the following passage of Davey J.A. in *R.* v. *White and Bob* (1965), 52 W.W.R. 193, at p. 198:

> Secs. 8 and 15 of the *Game Act* specifically exempt Indians from the operation of certain provisions of the Act, and from that I think it clear that the other provisions are intended to be of general application and to include Indians. If these general sections are sufficiently clear to show an intention to abrogate or qualify the contractual rights of hunting notoriously reserved to Indians by agreements such as Ex. 8, they would, in my opinion, fail in that purpose because that would be legislation in relation to Indians that falls within parliament's exclusive legislative authority under sec. 91(24) of the *B.N.A. Act, 1867*, 30 & 31 Vict., ch. 3 and also because that would conflict with sect. 87 of the *Indian Act* passed under that authority. . . .

It has already been held in *Kruger and Manuel* that on its face, and in form, the *Wildlife Act* is a law of general application. In the previous chapter, I have assumed that its application to appellant would have the effect of regulating the latter *qua* Indian. However, it has not been demonstrated, in my view, that this particular impact has been intended by the provincial legislator. While it is assumed that the *Wildlife Act* impairs the status or capacity of appellant, it has not been established that the legislative policy of the *Wildlife Act* singles out Indians for special treatment or discriminates against them in any way.

I accordingly conclude that the *Wildlife Act* is a law of general application within the meaning of s. 88 of the *Indian Act*.

It remains to decide whether the *Wildlife Act* has been referentially incorporated to federal laws by s. 88 of the *Indian Act*.

In *Kruger and Manuel*, Dickson J. wrote at p. 115:

> There is in the legal literature a juridical controversy respecting whether s. 88 referentially incorporates provincial laws of general application or whether such laws apply to Indians *ex proprio vigore*. The issue was considered by this Court in *Natural Parents* v. *Superintendent of Child Welfare*, [1976] 2 S.C.R. 751.

This controversy has so far remained unresolved in this Court.

I believe that a distinction should be drawn between two categories of provincial laws. There are, on the one hand, provincial laws which can be applied to Indians without touching their Indianness, like traffic legislation; there are on the other hand, provincial laws which cannot apply to Indians without regulating them *qua* Indians.

Laws of the first category, in my opinion, continue to apply to Indians *ex proprio vigore* as they always did before the enactment of s. 88 in 1951, then numbered s. 87—Statutes of Canada, 1951 c. 29, s. 87—and quite apart from s. 88— *Vide Rex* v. *Hill* (1980), 15 O.L.R. 406 where an Indian was convicted of unlawful practice of medicine contrary to a provincial medical act, and *Rex* v. *Martin* (1917– 18), 41 O.L.R. 79 where an Indian was convicted of unlawful possession of intoxicating liquor, contrary to a provincial temperance act.

I have come to the view that it is to the laws of the second category that s. 88 refers. I agree with what Laskin C.J. wrote in the *Natural Parents* case at p. 763:

> When s. 88 refers to "all laws of general application from time to time in force in any province" it cannot be assumed to have legislated a nullity but, rather, to have in mind provincial legislation which, per se, would not apply to Indians under the *Indian Act* unless given force by federal reference.
>
> I am fully aware of the contention that it is enough to give force to the several opening provisions of s. 88, which, respectively, make the "provincial" reference subject to the terms of any treaty and any other federal Act and subject also to inconsistency with the *Indian Act* and orders, rules, regulations or by-laws thereunder. That contention would have it that s. 88 is otherwise declaratory. On this view, however, it is wholly declaratory save perhaps in its reference to "the terms of any treaty", a strange reason, in my view, to explain all the other provisions of s. 88. I think too that the concluding words of s. 88, "except to the extent that such laws make provision for any matter for which provision is made by or under this Act" indicate clearly that Parliament is indeed effecting incorporation by reference.

I also adopt the suggestion expressed by Professor Lysyk, as he then was in "The Unique Constitutional Position of the Canadian Indian" (1967) 45 *Can. Bar Rev.* 513 at p. 552:

> Provincial laws of general application will extend to Indians whether on or off reserves. It has been suggested that the constitution permits this result without the assistance of section 87 of the *Indian Act,* and that the only significant result of that section is, by expressly embracing *all* laws of general application (subject to the exceptions stated in the section), to contemplate extension of particular laws which otherwise might have been held to be so intimately bound up with the essential capacities and rights inherent in Indian status as to have otherwise required a conclusion that the provincial legislation amounted to an inadmissible encroachment upon section 91(24) of the *British North America Act.*

The word "all" in s. 88 is telling but, as was noticed by the late Chief Justice, the concluding words of s. 88 are practically decisive: it would not be open to Parliament in my view to make the *Indian Act* paramount over provincial laws simply because the *Indian Act* occupied the field. Operational conflict would be required to this end. But Parliament could validly provide for any type of paramountcy of the *Indian Act* over other provisions which it alone could enact, referentially or otherwise. It is true that the paramountcy doctrine may not have been as precise in 1951 as it has become, at a later date, but it is desirable to adopt a construction of s. 88 which accords with established constitutional principles. . . .

I accordingly conclude that, in view of s. 88 of the *Indian Act*, the *Wildlife Act* applied to appellant even if, as I have assumed, it has the effect of regulating him *qua* Indian. . . .

I would answer the constitutional question as follows:

> Ss. 3(1) and 8(1) of the *Wildlife Act*, R.S.B.C. 1979 c. 433, being laws of general application in the Province of British Columbia, are applicable to the Appellant either

by referential incorporation under s. 88 of the *Indian Act*, R.S.C. 1970 c. I–6, or of their own force. . . .

I would dismiss the appeal and make no order as to costs.

12. *Derrickson* v. *Derrickson*, [1986] 2 C.N.L.R. 45 (S.C.C.). Dickson C.J.C., Beetz, McIntyre, Chouinard, Lamer, Le Dain, and La Forest JJ., March 27, 1986

Derrickson affirms the Supreme Court of Canada's interpretation of s. 88 of the *Indian Act* in *R. v. Dick* (see p. 266). The provincial laws of general application to which s. 88 refers are those laws that could not apply to Indians without regulating them "as Indians." Provincial laws are applicable to Indians subject to the exceptions in s. 88. Provincial laws of general application under s. 88 are applicable to Indians by referential incorporation in the *Indian Act*. Title to reserve lands can rest with either the federal or provincial Crowns.

CHOUINARD J.:—The constitutional question stated in this appeal is as follows:

Whether the provisions of Part 3 of the *Family Relations Act*, R.S.B.C. 1979, c. 121, dealing with the division of family assets, are constitutionally applicable to lands in a reserve held by an Indian, in view of the *Indian Act*, R.S.C. 1970, c. I–6?

The factual background is summarized by Hinkson J.A., who wrote the unanimous judgment of the Court of appeal of British Columbia, [1984] 2 W.W.R. 754, at p. 755 [[1984] 3 C.N.L.R. 58, at pp. 58–59]:

The appellant wife and the respondent husband are members of the Westbank Indian Band. Each of them holds certificates of possession issued to them pursuant to the provisions of the *Indian Act*, R.S.C. 1970, c. I–6.

The wife brought a petition for divorce and for other relief including a division of family assets pursuant to the provisions of the *Family Relations Act*, R.S.B.C. 1979, c. 121.

At trial, the trial Judge raised with counsel the question of whether the provisions of the *Family Relations Act* applied to lands allotted to the spouses by the Westbank Indian Band and for which they held certificates of possession issued pursuant to s. 20 of the *Indian Act*.

The wife sought a declaration pursuant to Pt. 3 of the *Family Relations Act* that she was entitled to an undivided one-half interest in the properties for which her husband held certificates of possession. The husband resisted that claim for relief on the basis that if the lands in question were family assets as defined in the *Family Relations Act*, then that Act had no application to the lands because they were Indian lands. . . .

1. Are the Provisions of the Family Relations Act Applicable of Their Own Force to Lands Reserved for the Indians?

Subsection 91(24) of the *Constitution Act, 1867* confers exclusive legislative authority on the Parliament of Canada in "all Matters" coming within the subject "Indians, and Lands reserved for the Indians".

Title to reserve lands is vested in the Crown, federal or provincial. So long as they remain such, reserve lands are administered by the federal government and Parliament has exclusive legislative authority over them. The *Indian Act* enacted under that authority, provides in subs. 18(1):

> 18.(1) Subject to this Act, reserves are held by Her Majesty for the use and benefit of the respective bands for which they were set apart; and subject to this Act and to the terms of any treaty or surrender, the Governor in Council may determine whether any purpose for which lands in a reserve are used or are to be used is for the use and benefit of the band.

The purpose of the above subsection is to ensure that lands reserved for Indians are and remain used for the use and benefit of the band.

Under s. 20 already cited, possession of lands in a reserve is allotted to individual members of the band by the band council with the approval of the Minister of Indian Affairs and Northern Development who issues a Certificate of Possession.

By virtue of s. 24 cited above, a member of the band may transfer his right to possession only to the band or to another member of the band but no such transfer is effective until it is approved by the Minister. . . .

The appellant argues that the pith and substance of the *Family Relations Act* is the division of matrimonial property, not the use of Indian lands. She further argues that it in no way encroaches on the exclusive federal jurisdiction as to the use of Indian lands. She is supported in these views by the Attorney General of British Columbia and the Attorney General of Ontario.

With respect I do not accept the latter proposition where Indian lands are involved.

The various orders that can be made under subs. 52(2) deal inter alia with ownership, right of possession, transfer of title, partition or sale of property, severance of joint tenancy.

K.M. Lysyk, "Constitutional Developments Relating to Indians and Indian Lands: an Overview" in *Special Lectures of the Law Society of Upper Canada*, 1978, writes at p. 227, footnote 49:

> . . . As to what is embraced within provincial "land law" in this sense, Laskin, C.J. observed in *Morgan v. Attorney General for Prince Edward Island*, [1976] 2 S.C.R. 349 at 357, that: "The power of a provincial legislature to regulate the way in which land in the province may be held, how it may be transferred , how it may be used (and this, whether the land be privately owned or be land held by the Crown in right of the province) is not contested." By analogy, presumably the matters contained within exclusive federal authority over Indian reserve lands include regulation of the manner of land-holding, disposition of interests in reserve lands and how reserve lands may be used (e.g., zoning regulations). . . .

I cannot but agree with the Attorney General of Canada who writes in his factum:

> In essence, Part 3 of the *Family Relations Act* is legislation which regulates who may

own or possess land or other property. Its true nature and character is to regulate the right to the beneficial use of property and its revenues and the disposition thereof.

I also agree with the following submission of the Attorney General of Canada:

To paraphrase the *ratio* of the Court below: if one is declared to be entitled to an interest in a Certificate of Possession issued pursuant to section 20 of the *Indian Act* then one has a right to possess the lands to which the Certificate applies and hence the right to use those lands. . . .

The right to possession of lands on an Indian reserve is manifestly of the very essence of the federal exclusive legislative power under subs. 91(24) of the *Constitution Act, 1867*. It follows that provincial legislation cannot apply to the right of possession of Indian reserve lands.

When otherwise valid provincial legislation, given the generality of its terms, extends beyond the matter over which the legislature has jurisdiction and over a matter of federal exclusive jurisdiction, it must, in order to preserve its constitutionality, be read down and given the limited meaning which will confine it within the limits of the provincial jurisdiction.

It follows that the provisions of the *Family Relations Act* dealing with the right of ownership and possession of immovable property, while valid in respect of other immovable property, cannot apply to lands on an Indian reserve.

2. Is the Family Relations Act Referentially Incorporated in the Indian Act by the Application of s. 88 of the Latter Act?

With respect to Indians, valid provincial legislation of general application which would normally have to be read down in order to preserve its constitutionality, may be made applicable to Indians by referential incorporation in the *Indian Act* through the operation of s. 88 of the Act, subject to the exceptions stated in the section. . . .

It is now settled that the provincial laws of general application to which s. 88 refers are those laws which could not apply to Indians without regulating them *qua* Indians. It is also settled that those laws that are made applicable to Indians by the operation of s. 88 are not applicable to them *ex proprio vigore* but are so made applicable by referential incorporation in the *Indian Act*. See *Dick* v. *The Queen*, [1985] 2 S.C.R. 309, [1985] 4 C.N.L.R. 55.

In that case it was held that the *Wildlife Act*, R.S.B.C. 1979, c. 433, is a law of general application and that it applies to a non-treaty Indian either by its own force or, assuming the *Wildlife Act* has the effect of regulating him *qua* Indian, by referential incorporation under s. 88 of the *Indian Act*.

It is far from settled however that s. 88 contemplates referential incorporation with respect to lands reserved for the Indians.

It follows that the provisions of the *Family Relations Act* at issue will be found not to be referentially incorporated in the *Indian Act* if s. 88 does not apply to lands reserved for the Indians.

If it were found that s. 88 does apply to Indian lands, the provisions of the *Family Relations Act* would still not be referentially incorporated if they fall within one of the exceptions provided for in that section. Hence the two following questions.

(a)   Does s. 88 of the Indian Act Apply to Lands Reserved for the Indians? . . .
I have already determined that the impugned provisions of the *Family Relations Act* are not applicable of their own force to lands reserved for the Indians. They could be made applicable only if s. 88 applies to reserve lands and then only if the provisions of the *Family Relations Act* do not fall within one of the exceptions provided for in that section.

The submission that s. 88 does not apply to lands reserved for Indians is quite simple. It is to the effect that not one but two subject matters are the object of subs. 91(24) of the *Constitution Act, 1867*, namely: "Indians" and "Lands reserved for the Indians" Since only Indians are mentioned in s. 88, that section would not apply to lands reserved for the Indians. . . .

Be that as it may, it is not essential for the resolution of this case to determine the issue if we find, as I think we must, that even assuming that s. 88 applies to lands reserved for the Indians the impugned provisions of the *Family Relations Act* are not referentially incorporated in the *Indian Act* since they are excluded by the application of federal paramountcy set out in the section.

*(b)   Do the Provisions of the Family Relations Act fall within one of the
        Exceptions in s. 88?*
In P.W. Hogg, *Constitutional Law of Canada*, 2nd ed., (Toronto: Carswell Co., 1985), it is stated at pp. 561 and 562:

> The importance of s. 88 lies in its definition of the laws that do *not* apply to Indians. The section is explicitly "subject to the terms of any treaty", which means that any conflict between a treaty made with the Indians and a provincial law of general application has to be resolved in favour of the treaty provision, thus reversing the normal rule for such conflicts.
>
> The section is also subject to "any other act of the Parliament of Canada", so that any conflict between a federal statute and a provincial law has to be resolved in favour of the federal statute. A provincial law is also inapplicable where it is "inconsistent with this Act or any order, rule, regulation or by-law made thereunder". These two parts of the section seem to be intended to make clear that the paramountcy doctrine applies to provincial laws, notwithstanding their adoption by a federal statute. However, the closing language of the section goes on to provide that the provincial laws are applicable "except to the extent that such laws make provision for any matter for which provision is made by or under this Act". This language in its context seems to contemplate that a provincial law which makes provision for any matter for which provision is made by (or under) the *Indian Act* must yield to the provisions of the *Indian Act*. The doctrine of paramountcy, on the other hand, at least as it has been interpreted recently, applies only where there is an express contradiction between a federal and a provincial law. It does not apply where the federal and provincial laws, while not in direct conflict, are merely occupying the same field, or in other words making provision for the same matters. It seems probable therefore that the closing words of s. 88 go further than the paramountcy doctrine and will render inapplicable to Indians some provincial laws which would have been applicable under general law.

As to the paramountcy doctrine the test now most often referred to is that set out in *Multiple Access Ltd* v. *McCutcheon et al.* [1982] 2 S.C.R. 161, 138 D.L.R. (3d) 1, 44 N.R. 181, where Dickson J., as he then was, wrote, for the majority, at p. 191 [S.C.R.]:

> In principle, there would seem to be no good reasons to speak of paramountcy and preclusion except where there is actual conflict in operation as where one enactment says "yes" and the other says "no"; "the same citizens are being told to do inconsistent things"; "compliance with one is defiance of the other".

That test is contemplated by s. 88 where it is said that laws of general application are applicable to Indians "except to the extent that such laws are inconsistent with this Act or any order, rule, regulation or by-law made thereunder, . . .".

Applying that test the Court of Appeal found an "actual conflict" Hinkson J.A. wrote for the court, at p. 760 [p. 63 C.N.L.R.]:

> In the present case, in my opinion, applying the test in the *Multiple Access* case, there is an actual conflict between the provisions of the *Indian Act* and the *Family Relations Act*. Implicit in the submissions of counsel for the wife and counsel for the Attorney General of British Columbia is an acknowledgement that there is such a conflict. On the one hand the provisions of s. 20 of the *Indian Act* do not permit an Indian who is lawfully in possession of lands in a reserve to transfer the right to possession until such transfer is approved by the Minister. On the other hand under the *Family Relations Act*, the court is empowered in dealing with the land which is a family asset, to declare the ownership or right of possession to such property, to order the title to a specified property be transferred to a spouse or order partition or sale of such property. If the court exercised the powers granted to it by the *Family Relations Act* in favour of a spouse, it would result in a conflict with respect to Indian reserve lands as between the order made by the court and the right of the Minister to approve a transfer of the right to possession of such lands. It is for this reason that the court is urged to make a conditional order.
>
> When this problem is considered in the light of the approach enunciated in the *Multiple Access* case it is apparent that there is a conflict between the *Indian Act* and the *Family Relations Act* and that in those circumstances the provisions of the *Family Relations Act* dealing with real property cannot extend to Indian reserve lands. It can have no application.

I agree. With respect, in my view, the impugned provisions of the *Family Relations Act* do conflict with the *Indian Act*.

Section 18 of the *Indian Act* provides that reserves are held by Her Majesty for the use and benefit of the bands.

Section 20 provides that the possession by an individual Indian can only come through allotment by the council together with the approval of the Minister.

Section 24 permits transfer only to the band or to another member of the band and only with the consent of the Minister.

Section 25 requires an Indian who leaves the reserve to transfer to another member.

Section 28 prohibits any arrangement or occupation save to another member.

Section 29 provides that reserve lands are not subject to seizure under legal process.

Section 37 exempts reserve lands from execution, prohibits sale or lease except by surrender to Her Majesty.

Sections 42 to 47 control testamentary succession.

Sections 48 to 50 control distribution of property on intestacy.

Section 53 provides that the Minister may lease, for the benefit of any Indian, upon his application for that purpose, the land of which he is lawfully in possession without the land being surrendered.

Section 81 provides that, if so authorized by the Governor in Council, under s. 60, the council of a band may make by-laws for inter alia (i) the survey and allotment of reserve lands among the members of the band and the establishment of a register of Certificates of Possession and Certificates of Occupation.

Section 89 prohibits mortgages except to another Indian.

Provisions such as are made in s. 52 of the *Family Relations Act* for orders dealing with ownership, right of possession, transfer of title, partition or sale of property, severance of joint tenancy are, in my view, in "actual conflict" with the above provisions of the *Indian Act*.

Were the provisions of both Acts to be applied at once as was sought in this case, the husband by virtue of his Certificate of the Possession issued by the Minister following an allotment by the band council would be entitled to the sole possession of the land while the wife by virtue of an order of the court would be entitled to a half interest in the Certificate of Possession and the rights flowing therefrom.

In my respectful view to make the order conditional on the approval of the Minister would not change the situation. I accept the following submission of the Attorney General of Canada:

> . . . since Part 3 of the *Family Relations Act* dealing with the division of family assets is constitutionally inapplicable to the lands in question, the Supreme Court of British Columbia lacks jurisdiction to make an order pursuant to such legislation relating to said lands, whether expressed to be conditional on the approval of the Minister of Indian Affairs and Northern Developments or not.

In the result, even assuming that s. 88 of the *Indian Act* applies to lands reserved for the Indians, the provisions of the *Family Relations Act* would, in my opinion, fall within that exception of s. 88 and would not be applicable to lands reserved for the Indians.

In reaching this conclusion I am not unmindful of the ensuing consequences for the spouses, arising out of the laws in question, according as real property is located on a reserve or not. In this respect I borrow the following sentence, albeit in a different context, from P.W. Hogg, *op. cit.*, at p. 554:

> Whether such laws are wise or unwise is of course a much-controverted question, but it is not relevant to their constitutional validity. . . .

I would answer the constitutional question as follows:

Question

Whether the provisions of Part 3 of the *Family Relations Act*, R.S.B.C. 1979, c. 121, dealing with the division of family assets, are constitutionally applicable to lands in a reserve held by an Indian, in view of the *Indian Act*, R.S.C. 1910, c. I–6?

Answer

No.

I would dismiss the appeal. . . .

13. *R. v. Francis*, [1988] 4 C.N.L.R. 98 (S.C.C.). Dickson C.J., Beetz, McIntyre, Lamer, Wilson, Le Dain, La Forest, and L'Heureux-Dubé JJ. (Estey J. took no part in the judgment), May 26, 1988

> *Francis* held that provincial motor vehicle legislation applies on Indian reserves in the absence of conflicting federal legislation. The incorporation by reference in s. 6 of the *Indian Reserve Traffic Regulations*, C.R.C. 1978, c. 959, of provincial laws and regulations relating to motor vehicles does not prevent the provincial law from applying in its own right. Federal and provincial laws that duplicate one another can exist together.

LA FOREST J.:—This is an appeal from a decision of the Court of Appeal for New Brunswick [[1986] 3 C.N.L.R. 112] in which it upheld the conviction of the appellant under s. 167(b) of the *Motor Vehicle Act*, R.S.N.B. 1973, c. M–17, for failing while driving a motor vehicle to yield the right-of-way when entering a highway from a driveway. Since the incident occurred on an Indian reserve, the appellant argues that he could only be charged and convicted under s. 6 of the *Indian Reserve Traffic Regulations*, C.R.C. 1978, c. 959. That provision was enacted pursuant to s. 73(1)(c) of the *Indian Act*, R.S.C. 1970, c. I–6, which empowers the Governor in Council to make regulations for the control of the speed, operation and parking of vehicles on roads within reserves. Section 6 of the regulations reads as follows:

> 6. The driver of any vehicle shall comply with all laws and regulations relating to motor vehicles, which are in force from time to time in the province in which the Indian reserve is situated, except such laws or regulations as are inconsistent with these Regulations.

On June 18, 1985, Chief Justice Dickson set the following constitutional questions to be determined on this appeal:

> 1. Is section 167(b) of the *Motor Vehicle Act*, R.S.N.B. 1973, c. M–17 constitutionally applicable to the regulation and control of the operation of motor vehicles on an Indian Reserve?
>
> 2. If so, is s. 167(b) of the *Motor Vehicle Act*, R.S.N.B. 1973, c. M–17 in conflict with the *Indian Reserve Traffic Regulations*, C.R.C. 1978, c. 959 passed pursuant to the *Indian Act*, R.S.C. 1970, c. I–6 and therefore inoperative to the extent of the conflict?
> . . .

I shall begin by saying that, in the absence of conflicting federal legislation, provincial motor vehicle laws of general application apply *ex proprio vigore* on Indian reserves. To hold otherwise would amount to resuscitating the "enclave" theory which was rejected by a majority of this Court in *Cardinal* v. *Attorney General of Alberta*, [1974] S.C.R. 695; see also *Four B Manufacturing Ltd.* v.

United Garment Workers of America, [1980] 1 S.C.R. 1031, [1979] 4 C.N.L.R. 21. In *Kruger* v. *The Queen*, [1978] 1 S.C.R. 104, (1977) 4 W.W.R. 300, 75 D.L.R. (3d) 434, this Court held that general provincial legislation relating to hunting applies on reserves, a matter which is obviously far more closely related to the Indian way of life than driving motor vehicles. Indeed Beetz J., speaking for the Court in *Dick* v. *The Queen*, [1985] 2 S.C.R. 309 at 326, [1985] 4 C.N.L.R. 55 at 71 expressly stated that provincial traffic legislation applies to Indians without touching their Indianness.

The question remaining then is whether, under the doctrine of paramountcy, the provincial law is inoperative because it is inconsistent with the *Indian Reserve Traffic Regulations*; see *Multiple Access Ltd.* v. *McCutcheon*, [1982] 2 S.C.R. 161. Section 6 of the regulations is the main area of contention, but before going further, it should be noted that in the courts below, the appellant contended that s. 5 deals expressly with driving at intersections. That section provides that "a person in charge of any vehicle . . . shall keep the vehicle in such control when approaching a[n]. . . intersection . . . as will enable him to prevent a collision with, or damage to, all other persons and vehicles". Here the appellant had collided with another vehicle on the highway. However, the courts below found, rightly in my opinion, no inconsistency between s. 5 of the regulations and s. 167(b) of the *Motor Vehicle Act*, and the appellant did not appeal this finding.

The Court of Appeal disposed of any alleged conflict between s. 6 of the regulations and s. 167(b) of the *Motor Vehicle Act* by holding that s. 6 did not incorporate the latter provision by reference but was merely of a declaratory nature, being intended simply to define "the obligation of obedience that Indians and non-Indians alike owe to provincial legislation while on reserves": following *R.* v. *Twoyoungmen*, [1979] 5 W.W.R. 712 at 721, [1979] 3 C.N.L.R. 85 at 93 (Alta.C.A.); see also *R.* v. *Maloney* (1982), 51 N.S.R. (2d) 441 at 445 [1983] 2 C.N.L.R. 148 at 150 (N.S.C.A.), and *R.* v. *Charlie and Joe*, [1985] 4 W.W.R. 472, [1985] 4 C.N.L.R. 143 (B.C.C.A.). This view, as counsel for the Attorney General for Alberta noted, may be buttressed by the fact that s. 6 is expressed in such a way as to be capable of being read as extending beyond the matters mentioned in the empowering provision. Section 73(1)(c) of the *Indian Act* provides for the enactment of regulations respecting the "speed, operation and parking of vehicles"; s. 6 refers to "all laws and regulations relating to motor vehicles".

The foregoing argument, however, is by no means determinative. Section 6 must be construed in terms of its empowering statute. One may also wonder why the federal government would engage in the idle exercise of simply enjoining people to comply with provincial laws; see *Dick* v. *The Queen*, supra. The reason for the enactment of s. 6 and similar federal regulations in related fields, for example national parks, appears to be that at the time of their original enactment, the prevailing judicial view of the extent to which the provinces could enact legislation affecting federal public property and Indian lands was more limited than it is today. Because of this and the then prevalent wider view of federal paramountcy, it was natural to think it was necessary to enact such measures with a view to incorporating or adopting provincial laws. It is also possible that the federal government wanted to have the option of having traffic rules on Indian reserves enforced by either federal or provincial officials. These considerations have led me to the view that s. 6 incorporates by reference or adopts provincial traffic regulations as federal laws. Several other courts have arrived at the same conclusion; see *R.* v. *Johns* (1962), 133 C.C.C. 43 (Sask. C.A.), and *R.* v. *Isaac* (1973), 14 C.C.C. (2d) 374 (Ont. C.A.).

In considering the interpretation of s. 6, counsel made reference, as had the courts below, to s. 88 of the *Indian Act*, which bears some resemblance to s. 6 of the regulations in issue here. Section 88 provides that all provincial laws of general application are applicable to Indians. Counsel on all sides rightly conceded that this provision had no direct bearing on this case. In *Dick* v. *The Queen*, supra this Court held that s. 88 served to incorporate only those provincial laws that did not extend to Indians *ex proprio vigore*. In particular, Beetz J. expressly referred to traffic regulations as laws that applied to Indian reserves *ex proprio vigore* and as such not falling within the types of provincial laws extended to Indians by s. 88. Obviously, the reasoning in *Dick* does not apply to s. 6 since it is directly aimed at traffic regulations on Indian reserves.

The fact that a provincial law may be incorporated by reference as a federal law does not prevent the provincial law from operating in its own right. Since the *Multiple Access* case, supra, it is clear that federal and provincial laws that merely duplicate one another but do not conflict can exist side by side. A person may be charged with violating the provincial statute or the federal regulation; see *R.* v. *Chiasson* (1982), 39 N.B.R. (2d) 631, aff'd [1984] 1 S.C.R. 266. To the extent that cases like *R.* v. *Kenny* (1982), 20 Sask. R. 361, [1983] 1 C.N.L.R. 78 (Q.B.), aff'd (1983), 36 Sask. R. 280, [1983] 2 C.N.L.R. 196 (C.A.), conflict with this, they must be deemed to be overruled.

The mere fact that the federal government has adopted the provincial traffic laws does not, in my view, display a sufficient intent that it wished to cover the field exclusively. As Professor Laskin, later Chief Justice, observed in "Occupying the Field; Paramountcy in Penal Legislation" (1963), 41 *Can. Bar. Rev.* 234 at 263, "It may be the better part of wisdom . . . to require the federal Parliament to speak clearly if it seeks, as it constitutionally can demand, paramountcy for its policies"; applied in *R.* v. *Chiasson*, supra, at p. 641. Nor does the fact that there is a separate penalty for breach of the federal regulations clearly establish such an intention. That argument, I may say, can only have weight if *R.* v. *Johns*, supra, is correct in holding that only the provincial regulations and not the penalties for their infraction are imported into the federal regulations. It is possible however, that the penalty section (s. 9) was intended to be confined to provisions other than the provincial laws, which carry their own penalty. That issue was not really addressed in argument and I need not pronounce on it. For, assuming that s. 9 applies to provincial laws incorporated by s. 6, it must be remembered that s. 6 incorporates laws throughout Canada which, though similar in many respects, carry different penalties from province to province. The federal authorities appear to have preferred to have a single penalty applicable to Indian reserves throughout Canada when they enforce the provincial laws adopted in the regulations.

I would dismiss the appeal and answer the first constitutional question in the affirmative and the second in the negative.

NATURAL RESOURCES TRANSFER AGREEMENTS

14. *Constitution Act, 1930* (formerly the *British North America Act*, 1930, 20–21 George V, c. 26 (U.K.)

An Act to confirm and give effect to certain agreements entered into between the Government of the Dominion of Canada and the Governments of the Provinces of Manitoba, British Columbia, Alberta and Saskatchewan respectively. . . .

(3) SASKATCHEWAN
Memorandum of Agreement . . .
Transfer of Public Lands Generally

1.   In order that the Province may be in the same position as the original Provinces of Confederation are in virtue of section one hundred and nine of the *British North America Act*, 1867, the interest of the Crown in all Crown lands, mines, minerals (precious and base) and royalties derived therefrom within the Province, and all sums due or payable for such lands, mines, minerals or royalties, shall from and after the coming into force of this agreement and subject as therein otherwise provided, belong to the province subject to any trusts existing in respect thereof, and to any interest other than that of the Crown in the same, and the said lands, mines, minerals and royalties shall be administered by the Province for the purposes thereof, subject, until the Legislature of the Province otherwise provides, to the provisions of any Act of the Parliament of Canada relating to such administration; and payment received by Canada in respect of any such lands, mines, minerals or royalties before the coming into force of this agreement shall continue to belong to Canada whether paid in advance or otherwise, it being the intention that, except as herein otherwise specially provided, Canada shall not be liable to account to the Province for any payment made in respect of any of the said lands, mines, minerals, or royalties before the coming into force of this agreement, and that the Province shall not be liable to account to Canada for any such payment made thereafter.

2.   The Province will carry out in accordance with the terms thereof every contract to purchase or lease any Crown lands, mines or minerals and every other arrangement whereby any person has become entitled to any interest therein as against the Crown, and further agrees not to affect or alter any term of any such contract to purchase, lease or other arrangement by legislation or otherwise, except either with the consent of all the parties thereto other than Canada or in so far as any legislation may apply generally to all similar agreements relating to lands, mines or minerals in the Province or to interests therein, irrespective of who may be the parties thereto. . . .

Indian Reserves

10.   All lands included in Indian reserves within the Province, including those selected and surveyed but not yet confirmed, as well as those confirmed, shall continue to be vested in the Crown and administered by the Government of Canada for the purposes of Canada, and the Province will from time to time, upon the

request of the Superintendent General of Indian Affairs, set aside, out of the unoccupied Crown lands hereby transferred to its administration, such further areas as the said Superintendent General may, in agreement with the appropriate Minister of the Province, select as necessary to enable Canada to fulfil it obligations under the treaties with the Indians of the Province, and such areas shall thereafter be administered by Canada in the same way in all respects as if they had never passed to the Province under the provisions hereof.

15. *R.* v. *Horse*, [1988] 2 C.N.L.R. 112 (S.C.C.). Beetz, Estey, McIntyre, Lamer, Wilson, Le Dain, and L'Heureux-Dubé JJ., January 28, 1988

> This leading decision on the applicability of the *Natural Resources Transfer Agreement* (NRTA) to the treaty rights of Indians held that s. 35(1) of the *Constitution Act, 1982* does not provide an absolute guarantee of rights and therefore remains subject to para. 12 of the NRTA and that s. 35(1) has no effect on the application of provincial game laws to treaty Indians under the NRTA.

ESTEY J.:— . . . Each of the appellants was charged with an offence under s. 37 of the Saskatchewan *Wildlife Act*, S.S. 1979, c. W–13.1, which prohibits the use of a spotlight for the purpose of hunting any wildlife. . . .

Each of the appellants was convicted at Provincial Court by Seniuk Prov. Ct. J. . . . An appeal to the Saskatchewan Queen's Bench was allowed and the convictions were set aside by Dielschneider J. . . . The Crown appealed this judgment and the Saskatchewan Court of Appeal restored the convictions. . . .

To succeed the appellants must demonstrate a right in law to hunt on these privately owned lands and to do notwithstanding the regulation of hunting under the provincial statute.

The right of access to the land in issue for the purpose of hunting is alleged to derive from the *Wildlife Act* itself, or from the provisions of Treaty No. 6, or from custom and usage. If such a right exists in law then the appellants claim immunity from prosecution by means of provisions of the Natural Resources Transfer Agreement, as confirmed by the *Constitution Act, 1930* (U.K.), 20 & 21 Geo. 5, c. 26 (reprinted in R.S.C. 1970, App. II, No. 25), or under the *Indian Act*, R.S.C. 1970, c. I–6, s. 88. They also rely on s. 35(1) of the *Constitution Act, 1982*.

In my view, the appellants were properly convicted under s. 37 of the *Wildlife Act* and the appeal must be dismissed.

1. *The Natural Resources Transfer Agreement*

In 1929 and 1930 agreements were entered into between each of the provinces of Alberta, Manitoba and Saskatchewan and the Canadian government for the primary purpose of effecting a transfer of control of natural resources and Crown lands from the Dominion government to the Prairie provinces. They were confirmed by legislation enacted in each of the provinces, and by the Parliament of Canada. The United Kingdom Parliament, by enacting the *Constitution Act, 1930*, gave these agreements the force of law.

Paragraph 12 of the Saskatchewan agreement, with which we are here concerned, provides:

12.   In order to secure to the Indians of the Province the continuance of the supply of game and fish for their support and subsistence, Canada agrees that the laws respecting game in force in the Province from time to time shall apply to the Indians within the boundaries thereof, provided, however, that the said Indians shall have the right, which the Province hereby assures to them of hunting, trapping and fishing game and fish for food at all seasons of the year *on all unoccupied Crown lands and on any other lands to which the said Indians may have a right of access.* [emphasis added]

This appeal concerns the category "other lands" which on the facts here, means privately owned lands. . . .

(a)   *Statutory Rights*

The appellants claim that s. 38 of the *Wildlife Act* creates a statutory right of access to private lands. They also contend that the Act contemplates that private lands will be used for hunting by reason of the fact that reference is made to an owner giving consent to hunting on his or her land. Section 38 provides in part:

38.(1) Where there are legible signs, of a size specified in the regulations, promi- nently placed along the boundaries of any land so as to provide reasonable notice bearing the words "No Trespassing", "No Hunting", "No Shooting" or words or symbols to like effect, no person shall hunt any wildlife within the boundaries of such land except with the consent of the owner or occupant.

(2)   Subject to this Act and the regulations,where there are legible signs of the size specified in the regulations prominently placed along the boundaries of any land so as to provide reasonable notice of instructions concerning the method of hunting or the use of vehicles connected with hunting, no person shall hunt any wildlife on such land except in accordance with the posted instructions.

(6)   Nothing in this section limits or affects any rights or remedies of an owner or occupier of land for trespass at common law, and, where he has not erected or placed signs along the boundaries of his land in accordance with subsection (1) or (2), that fact alone is not to be deemed to imply consent by him to entry upon his land or to imply a right of access to his land for the purpose of hunting.

These provincial provisions came before the court in *Prince and Myron* v. *The Queen,* [1964] S.C.R. 81, with reference to similar legislation in the province of Manitoba. The Manitoba legislation prescribed a notice procedure whereby land could be protected from hunting. The notice requirement stemmed from the fol- lowing provision in the Manitoba legislation:

76.(1) No person shall hunt any bird or any animal mentioned in this Part if it is upon or over any land with regard to which notice has been given under this Part, without having obtained the consent of the owner or lawful occupant thereof.

From this provision the Manitoba Court of Appeal concluded that in the ab- sence of signs posted as prescribed Indians had a right of access to occupied private land for the purpose of hunting. (See *R.* v. *Prince* (1962), 40 W.W.R. 234)

This court in *Myron* v. *The Queen,* supra, and later in *McKinney* v. *The Queen,* [1980] 1 S.C.R. 401, [1981] 2 C.N.L.R. 113 took occasion to "reserve" the Mani- toba court's conclusion in *Prince,* supra, with reference to right of access to private lands. In commenting upon the earlier Manitoba Court of Appeal decision in *Prince*, supra, Dickson J. (as he then was) in *Myron*, supra, stated (p. 145):

> I would have grave doubt that this can be the law. Section 40 of *The Wildlife Act* [of Manitoba) does not deal with interests in property. It is intended, I would have thought, to create a separate offence under the provincial statute in respect of posted lands and not to confer entry rights in respect of unposted lands. . . . With great respect, in my opinion the majority of the Manitoba Court of Appeal in *Prince and Myron* v. *The Queen* may have erred in their view of the import of s. 76 of *The Game and Fisheries Act*, the antecedent of s. 40, in failing to appreciate the importance of s. 76(4) reading: 76.(4) Nothing in this section limits or affects the remedy at common law of any such owner or occupant for trespass.

Dickson J., in dealing with substantially the same legislation as that now before the court in this appeal, then concluded (p. 146):

> . . . that in Manitoba at the present time hunters enter private property with no greater rights than other trespassers; that they have no right of access except with the owner's permission; and, lacking permission, are subject to civil action for trespass and prosecution. . . .

It is noted that the foregoing extracts from the *Myron* judgment, supra, were not necessary in resolving these issues arising in that appeal. These comments came before this court in *McKinney* v. *The Queen*, supra, where Chief Justice Laskin stated (at p. 401) [p. 113 C.N.L.R.]:

> We adopt as a correct statement of the law what was said *obiter* by Dickson J. in *Myron, Meeches et al.* v. *The Queen*, at p. 145. We agree with the Manitoba Court of Appeal that *R.* v. *Prince* was wrongly decided.

The opposite result to that reached in this court in the combination of *Myron* and *McKinney*, supra, was reached by the Saskatchewan Court of Appeal in *R.* v. *Tobacco*, [1981] 1 W.W.R. 545, 4 Sask. R. 380, [1980] 3 C.N.L.R. 81. That case, however, was predicated upon the then Saskatchewan *Wildlife Act* which did not include the above-mentioned provision in the Manitoba *Wildlife Act* dealing with the rights of an owner at common law or by statute for trespass in respect of his land. As can be seen from the excerpts from the present Saskatchewan statute, supra, subs, (6) of s. 38 contains a provision preserving the rights of an owner or occupant at common law for trespass and accordingly the *Tobacco* case is of no application here.

Additionally, the appellants seek to establish a statutory right of access by reason of the *Wildlife Act* as the result of judicial decisions in this court in *R.* v. *Sutherland*, [1980] 2 S.C.R. 451, [1980] 3 C.N.L.R. 71, and *Moosehunter* v. *The Queen*, [1981] 1 S.C.R. 282, [1981] 1 C.N.L.R. 61. In *Sutherland* the right to hunt accorded to the public generally by the province was limited to enumerated animals. The court concluded that once any hunting was allowed to the general public, Indians under paragraph 13 of the Manitoba agreement enjoyed unlimited hunting rights. *Moosehunter*, supra was to the same effect. It should be noted that in those two cases the court was not dealing with privately owned land but with Crown lands in respect of which the Crown in the right of the province has granted to all persons a limited right to hunt. In *Sutherland*, supra, the court stated through Dickson J., as he then was, at p. 459 [p. 76 C.N.L.R.]:

> It is arguable that where the Crown has validly occupied lands, there is *prima facie* no right of access, as is the case with land occupied by private owners, save and except that right of access the Crown confers on the public and/or Indians, as occupant of the land. In the Management Area the Crown has granted public access to hunt, but *on certain terms*. The province cannot deny access to Indians while granting it to the public, but the province can deny access for purposes of hunting which binds Indians and non-Indians alike.

It is a long jump to move from the concept of "a limited right to hunt" to unlimited hunting by Indians on private land by reason of the right of the owner of the private land in general law to grant or withhold access to anybody for any purpose. The mere capacity in the owner to grant right of access for hunting to friends or licensees or invitees is not a limited right of hunting in the sense that Indians therefore, without consent, can proceed upon the land for the purpose of hunting.

The appellants have not, by either submission or approach, succeeded in establishing that the *Wildlife Act* accords to them a statutory right of access for the purpose of hunting on private lands.

(b) *Custom or Usage*

Admitting, only for the purpose of examining the rights of appellants, that Indians and/or others may by custom or usage acquire a right of access to lands for hunting, there is no evidence or material adduced in these proceedings which demonstrate the existence of any such right by custom or usage arising in the appellants. In my view this renders this appeal a wholly unsatisfactory basis upon which to determine the argument of access based on custom. I agree with the view expressed by Vancise J.A. in the Saskatchewan Court of Appeal below where he stated [pp. 105–106 C.N.L.R.]:

> In this case the respondent sought to argue issues such as custom and usage, implied consent, right of access to surrendered lands under the treaties and access for the purpose of pursuing the avocation of hunting and fishing on which there was no evidence before the court. If the parties wish to argue these matters on an agreed statement of facts the statement should contain sufficient factual information and underpinning to allow a full and complete arguing of the issues and evidence should be called to establish factual underpinning.

In view of the total absence of the necessary evidence it cannot be determined whether the appellants have a right of access based on custom or usage.

2. *Treaty No. 6*

The appellants argue that the terms of the treaty give them a right to hunt for food on private land. If such a right exists under the treaty then they contend that it is protected by both paragraphs 2 and 12 of the Natural Resources Transfer Agreement. Paragraph 2 reads:

2. The Province will carry out in accordance with the terms thereof every contract to purchase or lease any Crown lands, mines or minerals and every other arrangement whereby any person has become entitled to any interest therein as against the Crown, and further agrees not to affect or alter any term of any such contract to purchase, lease or other arrangement by legislation or otherwise, except either with the consent of all the parties thereto other than Canada or in so far as any legislation may apply generally to all similar agreements relating to lands, mines or minerals in the Province or to interests therein, irrespective of who may be the parties thereto.

They also invoke s. 35(1) of the *Constitution Act, 1982* which provides:

35.(1) The existing aboriginal and treaty rights of the aboriginal peoples of Canada are hereby recognized and affirmed.

Finally, s. 88 of the *Indian Act* is invoked to protect treaty rights from application of the *Wildlife Act.* . . .

The operative provision of Treaty No. 6 is as follows:

Her Majesty further agrees with her said Indians that they, the said Indians, shall have right to pursue their avocations of hunting and fishing throughout the tract surrendered as hereinbefore described, subject to such regulations as may from time to time be made by her Government of her Dominion of Canada, and *saving and excepting such tracts as may from time to time be required or taken up for settlement*, mining, lumbering or other purposes by her said Government of the Dominion of Canada, or by any of the subjects thereof, duly authorized therefor, by the said Government . . . [emphasis added]

The comparable provision in Treaty No. 7 was considered in *R.* v. *Little Bear* (1958), 25 W.W.R. 580 (Alta. Dist. Ct.) (affirmed (1958), 26 W.W.R. 335 (Alta. C.A.)). On the facts in that case the accused Indian had consent from the private owner of the lands to hunt and thus he came under the protection of paragraph 12 in the Alberta Natural Resources Transfer Agreement.

The trial judge in *Little Bear*, supra, also considered whether Treaty No. 7 gave the accused a right of access to privately owned land. The judge considered the hunting rights proviso in the treaty which is in all material respects the same as the clause at issue here in Treaty No. 6 , supra. At page 583 this ground of argument is rejected by Turcotte D.C.J.

It is clear that, without more, the treaty of 1877 did not give Little Bear the right to kill a deer on the Wellman land, because the Wellsan land "had been taken up for settlement by one of Her Majesty's subjects duly authorized thereof by the said Government."

It is evident that the clause relating to hunting rights in Treaty No. 6 should be given the same interpretation as the court in *Little Bear*, supra, gave to the comparable clause in Treaty No. 7. . . .

In summary then the terms of the treaty are clear and unambiguous: the right to hunt preserved in Treaty No. 6 did not extend to land occupied by private owners. When the passages from the negotiations sought to be introduced by the appellants are viewed in the context of the various treaties covered in the Morris text it becomes clear that while the Indians were entitled to continue their mode of life by hunting, the preservation of that right did not include the grant of access to lands privately owned and occupied by settlers. Settlement of these lands was the goal of the government along with the intention of including, where possible, the nomadic Indian population at least to the extent that some of them would turn to agriculture with government assistance as their principal source of sustenance and survival. The extraneous material which properly should be examined when ambiguity in the treaty is encountered, in any case supports and does not contradict the unambiguous terms of the treaty. . . .

I would note in closing that the appellants, in their factum, presented an argument that s. 38(6) of the *Wildlife Act*, as amended by the *Wildlife Amendment Act*, 1982, S.S. 1982–83, c. 20, s. 7, is inoperative by virtue of s. 88 of the *Indian Act*, supra. The submission must be rejected for two reasons. Firstly, it cannot be said that the amendment of s. 38 (6) affects the appellants' status as treaty Indians because, for the reasons given above, the treaty did not give to the appellants a right of access to the lands in question. Secondly, the appellants have not demonstrated, in my view, that the purpose or the effect of the amendment is to deprive them, as Indians , of the right of access. The decisions of this court in *Dick* v. *The Queen*, [1985] 2 S.C.R. 309, 23 D.L.R. (4th) 33, [1985] 4 C.N.L.R, 55, and *Kruger* v. *The Queen*, [1978] 1 S.C.R. 104, 75 D.L.R (3d) 434, are determinative of this argument in my opinion.

For the reasons given above I do not believe that the appellants have established that they had a right of access to occupied private lands on any of the grounds put forward. Having failed on this point, the appellants are not immune from the provisions of the *Wildlife Act* and thus they were properly convicted of the offences for which they were found guilty at trial. I would dismiss this appeal and restore the orders of the trial Judge with respect to conviction and sentence.

YUKON AND THE NORTHWEST TERRITORIES

16. *Northwest Territories Act*, R.S.C. 1985, c. N–27

GOVERNMENT
Legislative Powers of Commissioner in Council . . .
GAME ORDINANCES

18.(1) Notwithstanding section 17 but subject to subsection (3), the Commissioner in Council may make ordinances for the government of the Territories in relation to the preservation of game in the Territories that are applicable to and in respect of Indians and Inuit.

(2) Any ordinances made by the Commissioner in Council in relation to the preservation of game in the Territories, unless the contrary intention appears therein, are applicable to and in respect of Indians and Inuit.

(3) Nothing in subsections (1) and (2) shall be construed as authorizing the Commissioner in Council to make ordinances restricting or prohibiting Indians or Inuit from hunting for food, on unoccupied Crown lands, game other than game declared by the Governor in Council to be game in danger of becoming extinct. . . .

Laws Applicable to the Territories

22.(2) All laws of general application in force in the Territories are, except where otherwise provided, applicable to and in respect of Inuit in the Territories. . . .

Reindeer

45. The Governor in Council may make regulations

(a) authorizing the Minister to enter into agreements with Indians or Inuit, or persons with Indian or Inuit blood living the life of an Indian or Inuk, for the herding of reindeer that are the property of Her Majesty, which agreements, if deemed advisable by the Minister, shall include provisions for the transfer of such portions of the herds as may be therein specified to the herders on satisfactory completion of the agreements;

(b) for the control, management, administration and protection of reindeer in the Territories, whether they are the property of Her Majesty or otherwise;

(c) for the sale of reindeer and the slaughter or other disposal of surplus reindeer and the carcasses thereof; and

(d) controlling or prohibiting the transfer or shipment by any means of reindeer or their carcasses or parts thereof, whether they are the property of Her Majesty or otherwise, from any place in the Territories to any other place within or outside the Territories.

17. *Yukon Act*, R.S.C. 1985, c. Y–2

GOVERNMENT

Legislative Powers of Commissioner in Council . . .

GAME ORDINANCES

19.(1) Notwithstanding section 18 but subject to subsection (3), the Commissioner in Council may make ordinances for the government of the Territory, in relation to the preservation of game in the Territory, that are applicable to and in respect of Indians and Inuit.

(2) Any ordinances made by the Commissioner in Council in relation to the preservation of game in the Territory, unless the contrary intention appears therein, are applicable to and in respect of Indians and Inuit.

(3) Nothing in subsections (1) and (2) shall be construed as authorizing the Commissioner in Council to make ordinances restricting or prohibiting Indians or Inuit from hunting for food, on unoccupied Crown lands, game other than game declared by the Governor in Council to be game in danger of becoming extinct. . . .

Laws Applicable to Territory

23.(2) All laws of general application in force in the Territory are, except where otherwise provided, applicable to and in respect of Inuit in the Territory. . . .

Reindeer

48. The Governor in Council may make regulations

(a) authorizing the Minister to enter into agreements with Indians or Inuit, or persons with Indian or Inuit blood living the life of an Indian or Inuk, for the herding of reindeer that are the property of Her Majesty, which agreements, if deemed advisable by the Minister, shall include provisions for the transfer of such portions of the herds as may be therein specified to the herders on satisfactory completion of the agreements;

(b) for the control, management, administration and protection of reindeer in the Territory, whether they are the property of Her Majesty or otherwise;

(c) for the sale of reindeer and the slaughter or other disposal of surplus reindeer and the carcasses thereof, and

(d) controlling or prohibiting the transfer or shipment by any means of reindeer or their carcasses or parts thereof, whether they are the property of Her Majesty or otherwise, from any place in the Territory to any other place within or outside the Territory.

Section 19 has been amended as follows by s. 20 of the *Yukon First Nations Land Claims Settlement Act,* S.C. 1994, c. 34. Section 20 of that act provides that the amended ss. 19(1), (2), and (4) of the *Yukon Act* come into force on the first day on which the final agreements of all First Nations are given effect.

20(1) Subsection 19(1) of the *Yukon Act* is replaced by the following:

19(1) Notwithstanding section 18, the Commissioner in Council may make ordinances for the government of the Territory, in relation to the preservation of game in the Territory, that are applicable to and in respect of Indians and Inuit.

(2) Subsection 19(3) of the Act is repealed.

(3) Section 19 of the Act is amended by adding the following after subsection (3):

(4) After a first nation's final agreement within the meaning of the *Yukon First Nations Land Claims Settlement Act,* is given effect by or under that Act, subsection (3) does not apply in respect of

(a) hunting by persons eligible to be enrolled under the agreement; or

(b) hunting by any person in the first nation's traditional territory as identified in the agreement.

(4) Subsection 19(4) of the Act, as enacted by subsection (3), is repealed.

18. *Bruce* v. *Yukon Territory (Commissioner)*, [1994] 3 C.N.L.R. 25 (Y.T. Terr. Ct.). Lilles C.J.T.C., August 3, 1993

This decision affirmed that the terms "band community" and "band council" could be used as simply descriptive terms of a geographical area and not necessarily terms that touched upon "Indianness." The terms were used to reflect the social and political reality of the geographical area and were not used in the constitutional sense. Thus, s. 88 of the *Indian Act* was inapplicable and the law in question was validly enacted by the Commissioner in Executive Council of the Yukon Territory.

LILLES C.J.T.C.:— . . .The *Liquor Act* was amended in 1991 by the addition of s. 105.1 to allow the Commissioner in Executive Council to make regulations for the establishment of a system for the prohibition of liquor in the band community of Old Crow if a majority of votes cast in a plebiscite by adults residing in the band community was in favour of such a system. A plebiscite was held in July of 1991, and a majority of the votes favoured the system. As a result of the vote, and under the regulation making authority given him by virtue of s. 105.l, the Commissioner in Executive Council enacted the *Old Crow Liquor Prohibition Regulations* which prohibited the possession, consumption, sale, purchase or transportation of liquor anywhere in, or on the area immediately contiguous to Old Crow. The plebiscite provided that all residents of Old Crow could vote.

Each of the defendants has been charged with an offence contrary to s. 2 of the *Old Crow Liquor Prohibition Regulations* and challenges the constitutional validity of these Regulations. . . .

The defence position is that s. 105.1 of the *Liquor Act*, R.S.Y. 1986, c. 105 as amended by S.Y. 1989/90, c. 37 and the *Old Crow Liquor Prohibition Regulations*, O.I.C. 1991/227 are ultra vires the Commissioner in Executive Council and of no force or effect.

The basis for the argument is that:

(a)   The *Yukon Act,* R.S.C. 1985, c. Y–2, does not authorize the Commissioner in Council to enact laws applicable to Indians, except in respect to paragraph 17(m) of the *Yukon Act* "the preservation of game in the territory";

(b)   That it is only section 88 of the *Indian Act* which subjects Yukon Indians to territorial laws of general application;

(c)   That section 105.1 of the *Liquor Act* and the *Old Crow Liquor Regulations* are not laws of general application within the meaning of s. 88 of the *Indian Act.*

The defence also contends that if the legislation is within the legislative authority of the Commissioner in Executive Council it is contrary to ss. 7 and 15 of the Charter of Rights and Freedoms. . . .

Unlike the provinces of Canada which look primarily to s. 92 of the *Constitution Act, 1867*, for the source of their legislative authority, the Yukon Territory obtained its extensive powers of self-government by way of direct federal delegation. . . .

Section 105 of the *Liquor Act* provided a mechanism for regulating alcohol consumption in public places, but only in Yukon municipalities and hamlets. There was no mechanism for other communities to make a request to the Commissioner in Executive Council for similar restrictions. This explains the 1988 amendment which defined "band community" and extended to these communities the right to apply for similar restrictions to public drinking. The purpose was to extend certain rights available to larger communities to other smaller communities. The "band community" definition was chosen, apparently, because it accurately described a number of these small Yukon communities, as being a geographical area occupied primarily by members of an Indian band.

In this sense, "band community" is a descriptive term. It defines a geographical area. While it includes a population of persons who are members of an Indian band, it is not restricted to Indians. It is evident that the *Indian Act* definition of

"Indian band" was used as a matter of drafting convenience only.

The *Liquor Act* was further amended in 1989–90 c. 37 to permit the making of regulations,which establish a system of alcohol prohibition in the band community of Old Crow. Subsequent events point to this amendment being made at the request of elected officials from that community. Provision was also made for a plebiscite of all the people in the community to determine the support for such a prohibition. That plebiscite was not restricted to Indians. It consisted of a secret ballot of all adult persons who lived in Old Crow at the time. As the vote favoured prohibition by a simple majority, the *Old Crow Prohibition Regulations*, O.I.C. 1991/227 was promulgated, and is now the subject matter of this constitutional challenge. . . .

By s. 85.1 of the *Indian Act* a band council may make by-laws relating to intoxication, and sale or possession of intoxicants on a reserve. It appears that such a by-law would be ineffective in small Yukon communities whose inhabitants are not exclusively Native and where there are no large reserves encompassing both the community and the area contiguous to it. Under these circumstances, it was necessary to resort to the *Territorial Liquor Act* in order to put into effect a program for effective prohibition.

Moreover, it is now generally accepted that provincial liquor legislation is generally applicable to Indians, both on and off reserves, except where ousted by a band by-law under s. 85.1, Jack Woodward, *Native Law* (Carswell, 1989) at p. 27. No such by-law has been brought to my attention. . . .

I am satisfied that the Old Crow Liquor Regulations fall squarely within the legislative powers of the Commissioner in Executive Council as defined in s. 17 of the *Yukon Act*. More specifically, this regulation is authorized by the following powers therein enumerated, namely: property and civil rights in the Territory; intoxicants; and generally, all matters of a merely local or private nature. The subject matter deals exclusively with intoxicants within the Territory. While the legislation incidently impacts or affects Indians who live within the defined geographic area, its pith and substance is intoxicants. Indians have not been singled out for special treatment, although the majority of persons affected are Indian due to their chosen place of residence. (Even if Indians were singled out, the regulation's dominant feature is not "Indians" *qua* Indians; . . . The purpose and effect of the law is to regulate intoxicants within the Territory.

I am further satisfied that the references to "band community" and "band council" are descriptive, in the sense that these definitions accurately reflect the composition of the community and the form of local governance. These definitions do not reveal an intention to legislate with regard to "Indians" in the constitutional sense.

Is The Commissioner in Executive Council Authorized to Enact Laws With Respect to Indians Beyond What is Specifically Set Out in S. 17(M) of the Yukon Act? . . .

Section 23(2) of the *Yukon Act* is necessary because s. 4(1) specifically excludes Inuit from the operation and application of the *Indian Act*. As a result, s. 88 of the *Indian Act*, which provides that provincial laws of general application apply to Indians, does not apply to Inuit. As there is no legislation comparable to the *Indian Act* applicable to Inuit, I infer that it was convenient and necessary to insert s. 23(2) in the *Yukon Act*, in order to extend to Inuit peoples similar privileges and to impose on Inuit the same obligations that apply to Indians.

The purpose of s. 19 of the *Yukon Act* is to specifically preserve the Aboriginal right of Indians and Inuit to hunt on unoccupied Crown land, while permitting the Commissioner in Executive Council to make laws for the preservation of game on occupied lands, which laws would apply to Indians and Inuit. This is not a law of general application, and it would not otherwise fall within the scope of s. 23 of the *Yukon Act* or within s. 88 of the *Indian Act*. For that reason, it was necessary to set it out as a separate section of the *Yukon Act*, making specific reference to Indians and Inuit.

I have concluded that the *Yukon Act* does authorize the Commissioner in Executive Council to enact laws within its legislative authority applicable to Indians. Those laws which can apply to Indians without touching upon their "Indianness", continue to apply quite apart from s. 88 of the *Indian Act*. Laws of general application which touch on their Indianness, such as laws relating to hunting, fishing and trapping, apply by virtue of s. 88 of the *Indian Act* [*Dick* v. *The Queen* (1985), 22 C.C.C. 129 [[1985] 2 S.C.R. 309, [1985] 4 C.N.L.R. 55, [1986] 1 W.W.R. 1, 23 D.L.R. (4th) 33, 69 B.C.L.R. 184, 62 N.R. 1]. In this regard, the Territory is no different from a province. Therefore, I do not accept the defence contention that it is only s. 88 of the *Indian Act* which subjects Yukon Indians to territorial laws.

Are S. 105.1 of the Liquor Act and the Old Crow Liquor Regulations Laws of General Application Within the Meaning of S. 88 of the Indian Act?
Mr. Justice Beetz, in *Dick* v. *The Queen,* supra, reinterpreted the court's earlier decision in *Kruger and Manuel* v. *The Queen* (1977), 75 D.L.R. (3d) 434 (S.C.C.) stating [p. 71 C.N.L.R.]:

> I believe that a distinction should be drawn between two categories of provincial laws. There are, on the one hand, provincial laws which can be applied to Indians without touching their Indianness, like traffic legislation; there are on the other hand, provincial laws which cannot apply to Indians without regulating them *qua* Indians.
>
> Laws of the first category, in my opinion, continue to apply to Indians ex proprio vigore as they always did before the enactment of s. 88 in 1951 . . . vide *R.* v. *Hill* (1907), 15 O.L.R. 406, where an Indian was convicted of unlawful practice of medicine contrary to a provincial medical act, and *R.* v. *Martin* (1917), C.C.C. 189 . . . where an Indian was convicted of unlawful possession of intoxicating liquor, contrary to a provincial temperance act.
>
> I have come to the view that it is to the laws of the second category that s. 88 refers. I agree with Laskin C.J.C., who wrote in *Natural Parents* v. *Superintendent of Child Welfare et al.* . . .
>
> > When s. 88 refers to "all laws of general application from time to time in force in any province" it cannot he assumed to have legislated a nullity but, rather, to have in mind provincial legislation which, per se would not apply to Indians under the *Indian Act* unless given force by federal reference.

The *Dick* decision has been explained by Professor Hogg as follows [Hogg, supra, at 676, para. 27.3(b)]:

In *Dick* v. *The Queen* (1985), the Court changed its mind about the scope of s. 88. Beetz J., for the Court held that s. 88 did apply to provincial laws that affected Indianness by impairing the status or capacity of Indians. These were the only laws to which s. 88 needed to apply, because these were the laws that could not apply to Indians of their own force. Indeed, Beetz J. held these were the only laws to which s. 88 applied. Those provincial laws that can be applied to Indians without touching their Indianness, like traffic legislation", applied to Indians of their own force. Section 88 was not needed to make those laws applicable to Indians, and s. 88 should be interpreted as not extending to those laws.

The *Dick* interpretation of "laws of general application" in s. 88 has been reaffirmed in later cases, and seems to be firmly established. It means that s. 88 is not merely declaratory of the existing constitutional position. On the contrary, s. 88 expands the body of provincial law that is applicable to Indians. Provincial laws affecting Indianness, which do not apply to Indians of their own force, are made applicable by s. 88. Provincial laws not affecting Indianness, which do apply to Indians of their own force, are not caught by s. 88.

Based on the above, I agree "with the Crown submission that unless the impugned legislation and regulations affect or touch on the defendant's Indianness, s. 88 of the *Indian Act* does not come into play. It is not necessary to determine whether the law is a "law of general application", only whether it is a validly enacted Territorial law. The *Liquor Act* will apply to Indians by virtue of its own force unless that Act cannot apply to Indians without affecting their "Indianness". In the latter case, the legislation will still apply to Indians by virtue of s. 88 of the *Indian Act*, provided that the legislation meets the test of general applicability.

I also agree with the Crown that the *Liquor Act* and the *Old Crow Liquor Prohibition Regulations* can be applied to Indians without touching their Indianness. Indeed, there is no evidence before the Court that the restrictions on the right to consume, sell, purchase or possess liquor in Old Crow impair the status and capacity of the accused as Indians. There is no evidence from which I can infer that such possession, sale, consumption or purchase is central to the traditional way of life of the band members of Old Crow. Section 105 makes reference to the applicability of regulations to the "band community" of Old Crow and not to the "band members" of Old Crow. It applies to all those within the area within one hundred kilometres of the Old Crow Community Centre regardless of whether they are Indian or non-Indian, resident or non-resident. Because the *Liquor Act* and the *Old Crow Liquor Regulations* can be applied to Indians without touching their Indianness, it is not a law of the "second category" as described by Justice Beetz and it is therefore unnecessary to address the issue as to whether it is a law of general application to which s. 88 refers.

In the result, I have concluded that the impugned legislation falls within the legislative authority of the Territory as defined by the *Yukon Act*, that it does not impact on the defendants' Indianness, and that it is valid without resort to s. 88 of the *Indian Act*. . . .

THE FIDUCIARY RELATIONSHIP

19. *R. v. Guerin,* [1985] 1 C.N.L.R. 120 (S.C.C.). November 1, 1984

In *Guerin,* the Supreme Court of Canada discussed the nature of the federal fiduciary responsibility and trustlike relationship with Indian peoples. An excerpt of this decision can be found in chapter 1.

20. *Blueberry River Indian Band* v. *Canada,* [1996] 2 C.N.L.R. 25 (S.C.C.). La Forest, L'Heureux-Dubé, Sopinka, Gonthier, Cory, McLachlin, and Major JJ., December 14, 1995

This decision concerns an Indian band that surrendered reserve land to the Crown for lease and subsequently for lease "or" sale. The Department of Indian Affairs and Northern Development (DIAND) inadvertently transferred the valuable mineral rights with the reserve land, against a standing policy of not doing so previously. DIAND did not correct the oversight, even though it had the statutory authority to do so. The court held that DIAND and the Crown breached their fiduciary duty to the band. Finally, McLachlin J. found that DIAND was responsible only for getting a reasonable price for the land at issue and not necessarily for getting the best price possible. The following excerpts are from Gonthier and McLachlin respectively. Note that McLachlin J. held that the first surrender prevented the sale or transfer of the mineral rights. This is contrary to Gonthier, who held that the second transfer altered the terms of the first.

GONTHIER J. (LA FOREST, L'HEUREUX-DUBÉ, SOPINKA, JJ.)—6 . . . principles of common law property are not helpful in the context of this case. Since Indian title in reserves is *sui generis,* it would be most unfortunate if the technical land transfer requirements embodied in the common law were to frustrate the intention of the parties, and in particular the Band, in relation to their dealings with I.R. 172. For this reason, the legal character of the 1945 surrender, and its impact on the 1940 surrender, should be determined by reference to the intention of the Band. Unless some statutory bar exists (which, as noted above, is not the case here), then the Band members' intention should be given legal effect.

7   An intention-based approach offers a significant advantage, in my view. As McLachlin J. observes, the law treats aboriginal peoples as autonomous actors with respect to the acquisition and surrender of their lands, and for this reason, their decisions must be respected and honoured. It is therefore preferable to rely on the understanding and intention of the Band members in 1945, as opposed to concluding that regardless of their intention, good fortune in the guise of technical land transfer rules and procedures rendered the 1945 surrender of mineral rights null and void. In a case such as this one, a more technical approach operates to the benefit of the aboriginal peoples. However, one can well imagine situations where that same approach would be detrimental, frustrating the well-considered plans of the aboriginals. In my view, when determining the legal effect of dealings between aboriginal peoples and the Crown relating to reserve lands, the *sui generis* nature

of aboriginal title requires courts to go beyond the usual restrictions imposed by the common law, in order to give effect to the true purpose of the dealings.

8   While McLachlin J. dedicates a considerable portion of her reasons to an analysis of the Band's intention, the fact remains that under her approach, the Band's intention in 1945 is irrelevant. Even if McLachlin J. were to agree with my conclusion that the Band intended to surrender the mineral rights as part of the 1945 agreement, she would be forced to the conclusion that the mineral rights were not part of the 1945 surrender because of her findings in relation to the 1927 Act, the operation of *nemo dat quod non habet,* and the administrative procedures adopted by the DIA for surrender revocation. Although McLachlin J. and I might disagree on the Band's intention in this case, since I prefer to rely on the factual findings of the trial judge, I think that in principle an intention-based approach is preferable to my colleague's more technical reasoning. . . .

> 1. That the plaintiffs had known for some considerable time that an absolute surrender of I.R.172 was being contemplated;
>
> . . .
>
> 6. That Mr. Grew [the local Indian agent] fully explained to the Indians the consequences of a surrender;
>
> 7. That, although they would not have understood and probably would have been incapable of understanding the precise nature of the legal interest they were surrendering, *they did in fact understand that by the surrender they were giving up forever all rights to I.R. 172,* in return for the money which would be deposited to their credit once the reserve was sold and with their being furnished with alternate sites near their trapping lines to be purchased from the proceeds;   [Emphasis added.]
>
> ([1988] 3 F.C. 20, at pp. 66–67.) . . .

12   Although the "revocation-resurrender" description offered by Stone J.A. is one plausible construction of the 1945 agreement, I think that the true nature of the 1945 dealings can best be characterized as a *variation of a trust in Indian land.* In 1940, the Band transferred the mineral rights in I.R. 172 to the Crown in trust, requiring the Crown to lease those rights for the benefit of the Band. The 1945 agreement was also framed as a trust, in which the Band surrendered all of its rights over I.R. 172 to the Crown "to sell or lease". The 1945 agreement subsumed the 1940 agreement, and expanded upon it in two ways: first, while the 1940 surrender concerned mineral rights only, the 1945 surrender covered all rights in I.R. 172, including both mineral rights and surface rights; and second, while the 1940 surrender constituted a trust for "lease", the 1945 surrender gave the Crown, as trustee, the discretion "to sell or lease". This two-pronged variation of the 1940 trust agreement afforded the Crown considerably greater power to act as a fiduciary on behalf of the Band. Of course, under the terms of the trust, and because of

the Crown's fiduciary role in the dealings, the DIA was required to exercise its enlarged powers in the best interests of the Band.

13   I should add that my reasons should not be interpreted to equate a trust in Indian land with a common law trust. I am well aware that this issue was not resolved in *Guerin* v. *The Queen,* [1984] 2 S.C.R. 335, and I do not wish to pronounce upon it in this case. However, this Court did recognize in *Guerin* that "trust-like" obligations and principles would be relevant to the analysis of a surrender of Indian lands. In this case, both the 1940 and 1945 surrenders were framed as trusts, and the parties therefore intended to create a trust-like relationship. Thus, for lack of a better label, I think that it is appropriate to refer to these surrenders as trusts in Indian land.

14   I should also add that I would be reluctant to give effect to this surrender variation if I thought that the Band's understanding of its terms had been inadequate, or if the conduct of the Crown had somehow tainted the dealings in a manner which made it unsafe to rely on the Band's understanding and intention. However, neither of these situations arises here. As the trial judge found, the consequences of the 1945 surrender were fully explained to the Indians by the local agent of the DIA during the negotiations. There was also substantial compliance with the technical surrender requirements embodied in s. 51 of the 1927 *Indian Act,* and as McLachlin J. concludes, the evidence amply demonstrates the valid assent of the Band members to the 1945 agreement. Moreover, by the terms of the surrender instrument, the DIA was required to act in the best interests of the Band in dealing with the mineral rights. In fact, the DIA was under a fiduciary duty to put the Band's interests first. I therefore see nothing during the negotiations prior to the 1945 surrender, or in the terms of the surrender instrument, which would make it inappropriate to give effect to the Band's intention to surrender all their rights in I.R. 172 to the Crown in trust "to sell or lease". In fact, the guiding principle that the decisions of aboriginal peoples should be honoured and respected leads me to the opposite conclusion.

15   I therefore conclude that under the 1945 agreement, both the surface rights and the mineral rights in I.R. 172 were surrendered to the Crown in trust "to sell or lease" . . .

17   In my view, it is critical to the outcome of this case that the 1945 agreement was a surrender in trust, to sell or lease. The terms of the trust agreement provided the DIA with the discretion to sell or lease, and since the DIA was under a fiduciary duty *vis-à-vis* the Band, it was required to exercise this discretion in the Band's best interests. Of equal importance is the fact that the 1945 surrender gave the DIA a virtual *carte blanche* to determine the terms upon which I.R. 172 would be sold or leased. The only limitation was that these terms had to be "conducive" to the "welfare" of the Band. Because of the scope of the discretion granted to the DIA, it would have been open to the DIA to sell the surface rights in I.R. 172 to the Director, *The Veterans' Land Act* ("DVLA"), while continuing to lease the mineral rights

for the benefit of the Band, as per the 1940 surrender agreement.

18   Why this option was not chosen is a mystery. As my colleague McLachlin J. observes, the DIA had a long-standing policy, pre-dating the 1945 surrender, to reserve out mineral rights for the benefit of the aboriginal peoples when surrendered Indian lands were sold off. This policy was adopted precisely because reserving mineral rights was thought to be "conducive to the welfare" of aboriginal peoples in all cases. The existence and rationale of this policy (the wisdom of which, though obvious, is evidenced by the facts of this case) justifies the conclusion that the DIA was under a fiduciary duty to reserve, for the benefit of the Beaver Band, the mineral rights in I.R. 172 when it sold the surface rights to the DVLA in March 1948. In other words, the DIA should have continued to lease the mineral rights for the benefit of the Band as it had been doing since 1940. Its failure to do so can only be explained as "inadvertence".

19   The DIA's failure to continue the leasing arrangement could be excused if the Department had received a clear mandate from the Band to sell the mineral rights. As I stated above, the Band's intention leads me to the conclusion that both the surface and mineral rights in I.R. 172 were included in the 1945 surrender. However, the 1945 surrender was "to sell or lease". At no time during the negotiations leading to the 1945 agreement was the sale of the mineral rights discussed specifically. The authorization given encompassed leasing as well as selling. There was therefore no clear authorization from the Band which justified the dia in departing from its long-standing policy of reserving mineral rights for the benefit of the aboriginals when surface rights were sold. This underscores the critical distinction between the Band's intention to include the mineral rights in the 1945 surrender, and an intention of the Band that the mineral rights must be sold and not leased by the Crown. Given these circumstances, the dia was under a fiduciary duty to continue the leasing arrangement which had been established in the 1940 surrender. It was a violation of the fiduciary duty to sell the mineral rights to the DVLA in 1948.

IV. Limitation of Actions

20   I agree with McLachlin J. that the breach of fiduciary duty committed by the DIA is not limited to the date when the mineral rights in I.R. 172 were sold to the DVLA. The DIA was under a duty to act in the best interests of the Beaver Band in all of its dealings with the mineral rights in I.R. 172, and as I noted above, this gave rise to a specific duty to lease those mineral rights for the benefit of the Band according to the terms of the 1945 agreement. So long as the DIA had the power, whether under the terms of the surrender instrument, or under the *Indian Act,* to reserve the mineral rights through a leasing arrangement, the DIA was under a fiduciary duty to exercise this power. Thus, like McLachlin J., I think that s. 64 of the Act is very significant, since it gave the DIA the power to revoke an erroneous sale or lease of Indian lands. Because the mineral rights in I.R. 172 were sold inadvertently, s. 64 provided the DIA with the power to reacquire the reserve lands, and thus afforded the DIA a "second chance" to effect a lease of the mineral rights.

21   In her reasons, McLachlin J. amply demonstrates that between July 15, 1949 and August 9, 1949, the DIA became aware of two facts: (1) the mineral rights in I.R. 172 were potentially of considerable value; and (2) the mineral rights had been sold to the DVLA in 1948. It should also be recalled that the DIA had a long-standing policy of reserving mineral rights for the benefit of aboriginal peoples when selling Indian lands. Given these circumstances, it is rather astonishing that no action was taken by the DIA to determine how the mineral rights could have been sold to the DVLA. Little effort would have been required to detect the error which had occurred.

22   As a fiduciary, the DIA was required to act with reasonable diligence. In my view, a reasonable person in the DIA's position would have realized by August 9, 1949 that an error had occurred, and would have exercised the s. 64 power to correct the error, reacquire the mineral rights, and effect a leasing arrangement for the benefit of the Band. That this was not done was a clear breach of the DIA's fiduciary duty to deal with I.R. 172 according to the best interests of the Band.

23   Thus, I conclude that the appellants may recover any losses stemming from transfers by the DVLA after August 9, 1949 as such losses fall within the 30-year limitation period imposed by the British Columbia *Limitation Act,* and are not barred by any other provision of that Act as explained in the reasons of McLachlin J. . . .

MCLACHLIN J. (CORY and MAJOR JJ.)— . . .

35   My view is that the *Indian Act*'s provisions for surrender of band reserves strikes a balance between the two extremes of autonomy and protection. The band's consent was required to surrender its reserve. Without that consent the reserve could not be sold. But the Crown, through the Governor in Council, was also required to consent to the surrender. The purpose of the requirement of Crown consent was not to substitute the Crown's decision for that of the band, but to prevent exploitation. As Dickson J. characterized it in *Guerin* (at p. 383):

> The purpose of this surrender requirement is clearly to interpose the Crownbetween the Indians and prospective purchasers or lessees of their land, so asto prevent the Indians from being exploited.

It follows that under the *Indian Act,* the Band had the right to decide whether to surrender the reserve, and its decision was to be respected. At the same time, if the Band's decision was foolish or improvident—a decision that constituted exploitation—the Crown could refuse to consent. In short, the Crown's obligation was limited to preventing exploitative bargains.

36   Subject to the issue of the value of the reserve and the matter of mineral rights, which I deal with later, the evidence does not support the view that the surrender of the Fort St. John reserve was foolish, improvident or amounted to exploitation. In fact, viewed from the perspective of the Band at the time, it made good sense. The measure of control which the Act permitted the Band to exercise over the surrender

of the reserve negates the contention that absent exploitation, the Act imposed a fiduciary obligation on the Crown with respect to the surrender of the reserve.

(b)   Whether the Circumstances of the Case Gave Rise to a Fiduciary Duty on the Crown with Respect to the Surrender

37   If the *Indian Act* did not impose a duty on the Crown to block the surrender of the reserve, the further question arises of whether on the particular facts of this case a fiduciary relationship was superimposed on the regime for alienation of Indian lands contemplated by the *Indian Act.*

38   Generally speaking, a fiduciary obligation arises where one person possesses unilateral power or discretion on a matter affecting a second "peculiarly vulnerable" person: see *Frame* v. *Smith,* [1987] 2 S.C.R. 99 . . . ; *Norberg* v. *Wynrib,* [1992] 2 S.C.R. 226; and *Hodgkinson* v. *Simms,* [1994] 3 S.C.R. 377. The vulnerable party is in the power of the party possessing the power or discretion, who is in turn obligated to exercise that power or discretion solely for the benefit of the vulnerable party. A person cedes (or more often finds himself in the situation where someone else has ceded for him) his power over a matter to another person. The person who has ceded power *trusts* the person to whom power is ceded to exercise the power with loyalty and care. This is the notion at the heart of the fiduciary obligation. . . .

43   The true object of ss. 51(3) and 51(4) of the *Indian Act* was to ensure that the surrender was validly assented to by the Band. The evidence, including the voter's list, in the possession of the DIA amply established valid assent. Moreover, to read the provisions as mandatory would work serious inconvenience, not only where the surrender is later challenged, but in any case where the provision was not fulfilled, as the Band would have to go through the process again of holding a meeting, assenting to the surrender, and then certifying the assent. I therefore agree with the conclusion of the courts below that the "shall" in the provisions should not be considered mandatory. Failure to comply with s. 51 of the *Indian Act* therefore does not defeat the surrender.

(d)   Conclusions on Pre-surrender Duty and Breach

44   I conclude that the Bands have not established that the Crown wrongly failed to prevent the surrender of the Fort St. John reserve in 1945.

(2)   Post-surrender Duties and Breaches Regarding Surface Rights

45   The 1945 surrender conveyed the Band's lands to the Crown "in trust to sell or lease the same to such person or persons, and upon such terms as the Government of the Dominion of Canada may *deem most conducive to our Welfare and that of our people*" (emphasis added). The Crown concedes that this surrender imposed a fiduciary duty on the Crown with respect to the subsequent sale or lease of the lands: *Guerin, supra.* The only issue is whether the Crown breached that duty when in 1948 it sold the lands to the DVLA for $70,000.

46 The duty imposed upon the Crown by the terms of surrender (converted to a statutory duty by s. 54 of the Act) was broad. It extended not only to the monetary aspects of the transaction, but to whether the arrangement would be conducive to the welfare of the Indians in the broader sense. The Bands argue that the Crown breached this duty by: (a) failing to consider leasing rather than selling the land; (b) selling the land under value; and (c) not restoring the reserve to the Band after surrender in view of its impoverished situation. . . .

55 This evidence does not appear to support the trial judge's conclusion that the Crown was in breach of its fiduciary obligation to sell the land at a fair value. In finding a breach despite this evidence, the trial judge misconstrued the effect of the onus on the Crown. The Crown adduced evidence showing that the sale price lay within a range established by the appraisals. This raised a *prima facie* case that the sale price was reasonable. The onus then shifted to the Bands to show it was unreasonable. The Bands did not adduce such evidence. On this state of the record, a presumption of breach of the Crown's fiduciary duty to exact a fair price cannot be based on a failure to discharge the onus upon it. I note that the trial judge made no finding as to the true value of the property, nor any finding that it was significantly greater than $70,000, deferring this to the stage of assessment of damages.

56 I conclude that the trial judge erred in concluding that the Crown breached its fiduciary duty to the Band by selling the land for $70,000. . . .

66 . . . Prior to 1940, the Band held a right in both the surface rights and the mineral rights of the reserve. The Band surrendered the mineral rights in the reserve to the Crown in 1940. The effect of this was to remove the mineral rights from the reserve. When the Band surrendered its interest in the Fort St. John reserve to the Crown in 1945, it could transfer only those rights in the reserve which it still possessed: *nemo dat quod non habet*—a person cannot give what he does not possess. The 1945 surrender could not therefore have included surrender of the Band's reserve rights over the minerals. Rather, it involved only the surrender of those rights which still belonged to the Band to surrender, namely the surface rights. The minerals remained in the Crown and the Crown remained bound by the terms of the 1940 surrender, even after the 1945 surrender of the Indian's remaining interest in the lands. . . .

80 Before leaving my conclusion that the 1940 surrender of mineral rights precluded the resurrender of the mineral rights in 1945, I must deal with the comments of Gonthier J. with respect to it. Gonthier J. suggests that this argument is academic. In his view, the result in this case should not depend on "technical" interpretations of the *Indian Act* and rules of property transfer, but only on the intention of the Band in 1945. If the Band intended to transfer the mineral rights in 1945, then the mineral rights should be deemed to be transferred, in his view.

81 With respect, I cannot agree. My reasons are two. First, neither the 1940 transfer and the obligations the Crown incurred under it, nor the provisions of the

Indian Act can be swept aside by some vague intention five years later. Second, the alleged intention, in my view, is not established.

82   If intention were all that mattered, there would be no purpose to the detailed provisions of the *Indian Act* and regulations under it regarding surrender, nor any substance to the fiduciary duty which the Crown assumed with respect to the Band's mineral rights when it accepted their surrender in 1940. It is not disputed that the property of Indians, like the property of any other person, must be dealt with according to law. The stark facts are that the Band conveyed the mineral rights in I.R. 172 to the Crown in 1940, on the trust that the Crown would lease those mineral rights for their benefit. With respect, I find it neither academic nor technical to suggest, that the 1940 surrender removed the mineral rights from I.R. 172, with the result that they could not pass when what remained of the Band's rights in I.R. 172 was surrendered in 1945.

83   The basic purpose of the surrender provisions of the *Indian Act* is to ensure that the intention of Indian bands with respect to their interest in their reserves be honoured. One must wonder why, if the Band intended to alter the terms of the 1940 conditional surrender to make an absolute surrender, it did not avail itself of the provisions of the *Indian Act* for the proper legal expression of that intention? One may also ask why, if it was the intention of the Band to surrender the mineral rights for purposes of sale in 1945, mineral rights were never discussed in the negotiations leading to the 1945 surrender?

84   Even assuming that an intention to transfer the mineral rights in 1945 could somehow sweep aside these problems, finding such an intention in 1945 is difficult. My colleague Gonthier J. asserts that the trial judge found as a fact that the Band intended to give up all rights in I.R. 172 forever in 1945. With respect, the trial judge's findings fall short of this. . . .

86   It follows that the finding of the trial judge that the Band intended to give up all rights in I.R. 172 forever is a legal finding based on his reading of the wording of the 1945 surrender rather than a finding of fact based on the evidence presented at trial. In fact the only witness whose oral testimony with respect to the 1945 surrender was accepted by the trial judge testified: "No mention of mineral rights were made at the meeting" (p. 201 F.T.R.). Likewise, the notes of the Indian agent in Fort St. John, Galibois, indicate that no mention was made of mineral rights. At page 184 F.T.R., the trial judge states that "from and including the surrender in 1945 . . . mineral rights were never mentioned or considered either one way or the other". What the evidence does establish is that the Band was promised replacement reserves at the 1945 surrender meeting. It also establishes that the replacement reserves purchased for the Band did *not* include mineral rights.

87   While the reasons of my colleague Gonthier J. claim to reflect the intention of the Band, the only evidence on the record of an intention to vary the terms under which the Crown held the mineral rights is that they were not mentioned either at

the meeting at which assent was given to the 1945 surrender nor in the 1945 surrender document. With respect, this constitutes a weak evidentiary basis on which to establish an intention which would have the effect of revoking or varying an explicit surrender on different terms to which full and informed consent was given. In fact, later in his reasons, my colleague accepts that in 1945 the Crown did not receive a clear mandate from the Band to sell the mineral rights.

88   In my opinion, we should not overturn a deliberately executed and statutorily authorized surrender on the basis of no evidence. In determining something as nebulous as intention over 40 years later one must look to all available sources. Here the written source is silent where one would have expected clear wording to revoke the previous surrender and the oral testimony establishes that the issue was never even discussed. This cannot be evidence of intention and the Band should be entitled to the protection of the *Indian Act* and the common law which prevent the Crown from unilaterally changing the terms under which it held the property as fiduciary without obtaining the informed consent of the Band. In the words of Gonthier J., the DIA never received a clear mandate from the Band to sell the mineral rights. How then, one may ask, can one conclude that the Band intended that the mineral rights be surrendered for purposes of sale?

89   My colleague, Gonthier J. asserts that the 1945 surrender specifically included the mineral rights. He reaches this conclusion by importing the definition of "reserve" from the 1927 *Indian Act* into the 1945 surrender agreement. He notes that the statutory definition in s. 2(j) includes "minerals" and therefore that minerals were included in the 1945 surrender. With respect, this assertion conveniently overlooks the requirement in s. 2(j) that a reserve includes only that which "has not been surrendered to the Crown". Given the legitimacy of the 1940 surrender with respect to the mineral rights, which my colleague accepts, it would be more accurate to say that applying the statutory definition of "reserve" to the 1945 surrender would specifically *exclude* minerals from that surrender.

90   It should be remembered that this is not a case where an Indian band is arguing that the Crown's failure to follow the proper administrative procedures has thwarted its true intentions. Rather, this is a case where the Crown, as fiduciary, has acted in a manner not authorized by the original surrender under which it became the fiduciary of the property. If the Crown wished to gain a broader discretion with respect to the property that it held in a "trust-like" manner there were certain steps it was required to follow. These steps included informing the Band specifically of the Crown's intention to alter the terms on which it held the mineral rights and following its own administrative procedures by revoking the 1940 surrender by order in council to allow for a new surrender in accordance with the *Indian Act.* Neither of these steps were taken here.

91   Gonthier J. suggests that the 1945 dealings may best be "characterized as a variation of a trust in Indian land" (para. 12), a concept of trust which we are told is not to be equated with a common law trust. Whatever the legal characteristics of

the proposed "trust in Indian land", it is difficult to see how it advances the case. The difficulties of applying trust principles directly to the *sui generis* Indian interest in their reserves point to the fact that it is better to stay within the protective confines of the *Indian Act.* The 1927 *Indian Act* contains provisions which regulate in some detail the manner in which Indians may surrender their reserves or interests in their reserves to the Crown. The formal surrender requirements contained in the *Indian Act* serve to protect the Indians' interest by requiring that free and informed consent is given by a band to the precise manner in which the Crown handles property which it holds on behalf of the Band. The Act also recognizes the Indians as autonomous actors capable of making decisions concerning their interest in reserve property and ensures that the true intent of an Indian Band is respected by the Crown. No matter how appealing it may appear, this Court should be wary of discarding carefully drafted protections created under validly enacted legislation in favour of an *ad hoc* approach based on novel analogies to other areas of the law.

92   I conclude that the 1940 surrender of the mineral rights was a valid surrender of a portion of the reserve which converted that portion into "Indian lands". By the definition of the Act, a reserve cannot include what has already been surrendered. It follows that the 1945 surrender of the reserve could not include the mineral rights as a matter of law and according to the wording and the statutory scheme of the *Indian Act.* I conclude that the 1945 surrender had no effect on the mineral rights. The Crown continued to hold them in trust for the Band on terms that they be leased for the welfare of the Band. . . .

95   There exist two grounds for arguing that transfer of the minerals to the DVLA in 1948 constituted a breach of fiduciary duty by the Crown. The first argument is that the transfer breached the 1940 surrender of the minerals, which restricted the DIA to *leasing* them for the benefit of the Band. A fiduciary is at very least bound to adhere to the terms of the instrument which bestows his powers and creates the trust.

96   In any event, even if one were to accept for the sake of the argument that the 1945 surrender revoked the 1940 surrender of mineral rights, the 1945 surrender still imposed an obligation on the Crown to lease or sell *in the best interests of the Band.* This would leave for consideration the argument that the Crown breached its fiduciary obligations by transferring the mineral rights to the DVLA in 1948, because transfer rather than reservation for future leasing was contrary to the best interests of the Indians.

97   The trial judge rejected this argument on the ground that it was not foreseeable in 1948 that the mineral rights could have any value (at p. 49 F.C.):

> I find that, taking into account the fiduciary relationship then existing between Her Majesty the Queen and the plaintiffs, none of her officers, servants or agents, exercising due care, consideration and attention in the discharge of those fiduciary duties, could reasonably be expected to have anticipated at any time during 1948 or previ-

ously that there would be any real value attached to potential mineral rights under I.R. 172 or that there would be any reasonably foreseeable advantage in retaining them. . . .

105 I conclude that the 1940 surrender of the mineral rights imposed a fiduciary duty to the Band with respect to the mineral rights under the terms of the 1940 surrender, and that the DIA breached this duty by conveying the mineral rights to the DVLA. . . .

114 It follows that the DIA had the power to revoke the inadvertent, erroneous grant of the mineral rights to the DVLA up to the time they were transferred to veterans. The remaining questions are whether the DIA was under a duty to use this power to revoke the transfer, and how this affects the timing of a breach of fiduciary duty.

115 In my view, the DIA was under a duty to use this power to rectify errors prejudicing the interests of the Indians as part of its ongoing fiduciary duty to the Indians. The fiduciary duty associated with the administration of Indian lands may have terminated with the sale of the lands in 1948. However, an ongoing fiduciary duty to act to correct error in the best interests of the Indians may be inferred from the exceptional nature of s. 64. That section gave the DIA the power to revoke erroneous grants of land, even as against *bona fide* purchasers. It is not unreasonable to infer that the enactors of the legislation intended the DIA to use that power in the best interests of the Indians. If s. 64 above is not enough to establish a fiduciary obligation to correct the error, it would certainly appear to do so, when read in the context of jurisprudence on fiduciary obligations. Where a party is granted power over another's interests, and where the other party is correspondingly deprived of power over them, or is "vulnerable", then the party possessing the power is under a fiduciary obligation to exercise it in the best interests of the other: *Frame* v. *Smith, supra, per* Wilson J.; and *Hodgkinson* v. *Simms, supra.* Section 64 gave to DIA power to correct the error that had wrongly conveyed the Band's minerals to the DVLA. The Band itself had no such power; it was vulnerable. In these circumstances, a fiduciary duty to correct the error lies.

116 The DIA's duty was the usual duty of a fiduciary to act with reasonable diligence with respect to the Indians' interest. Reasonable diligence required that the DIA move to correct the erroneous transfer when it came into possession of facts suggesting error and the potential value of the minerals that it had erroneously transferred. . . .

118 I conclude that the Crown, having first breached its fiduciary duty to the Indians by transferring the minerals to the DVLA, committed a second breach by failing to correct the error on August 9, 1949 when it learned of the error's existence and the potential value of the mineral rights.

119 This action was filed on September 18, 1978. Any losses stemming from transfers after August 9, 1949, are therefore still permissible under the s. 8 general

limitation. As of this date, 6.75 sections of the 31 transferred to the DVLA remained in the hands of the DVLA. Had the DIA discharged its duty to the Indians, the mineral title would have been returned to them. Instead, mineral title was passed on to the veterans, and in the case of 2.5 sections, directly conveyed to oil companies to the credit of the Consolidated Revenue Fund. . . .

123 The appeal is allowed with costs . . . and the cross-appeal is allowed without costs. The judgments below are set aside. The appellants are entitled to damages against the Crown for breach of fiduciary duty with respect to such mineral rights in Indian Reserve 172. . . . The action is remitted to the Federal Court, Trial Division, for assessment of damages accordingly.

21. *Quebec (A.G.)* v. *Canada (National Energy Board)*, [1994] 3 C.N.L.R. 49 (S.C.C.) (*sub nom. Grand Council of the Crees* v. *Canada*). Lamer C.J., La Forest, L'Heureux-Dubé, Sopinka, Gonthier, Cory, McLachlin, Iacobucci, and Major JJ., February 24, 1994

> This decision concerned a decision of the National Energy Board regarding the granting of a licence to Hydro-Quebec to sell electricity to the United States. The Grand Council of the Crees (of Quebec), among others, claimed that the National Energy Board owed them, as Aboriginal peoples, a fiduciary duty in making their decision. The Supreme Court held that the board, as a quasi-judicial body, was exempt from a fiduciary responsibility to the Aboriginal peoples concerned. The court also characterized the nature of the fiduciary duty to Aboriginal peoples as one which required the "utmost good faith" by government.

IACOBUCCI J. — . . . The appellants claim that, by virtue of their status as aboriginal peoples, the Board owes them a fiduciary duty extending to the decision-making process used in considering applications for export licences. The appellants' argument is that the fiduciary duty owed to aboriginal peoples by the Crown, as recognized by this Court in *R.* v. *Sparrow, supra,* extends to the Board, as an agent of government and creation of Parliament, in the exercise of its delegated powers. The duty applies whenever the decision made pursuant to a federal regulatory process is likely to affect aboriginal rights.

The appellants characterize the scope of this duty as twofold. They argue that it includes the duty to ensure the full and fair participation of the appellants in the hearing process, as well as the duty to take into account their best interests when making decisions. The appellants argue that such an obligation imports with it rights that go beyond those created by the dictates of natural justice, and that in this case, at a minimum, the Board should have required disclosure to the appellants of all information necessary to the making of their case against the applications. The respondents to this appeal, on the other hand, dispute both the existence of a duty, and, if it does exist, that the Board failed to meet it.

It is now well settled that there is a fiduciary relationship between the federal Crown and the aboriginal peoples of Canada: *Guerin* v. *The Queen,* [1984] 2 S.C.R. 335. Nonetheless, it must be remembered that not every aspect of the relationship between fiduciary and beneficiary takes the form of a fiduciary obligation: *Lac*

Minerals Ltd. v. *International Corona Resources Ltd.,* [1989] 2 S.C.R. 574. The nature of the relationship between the parties defines the scope, and the limits, of the duties that will be imposed. The courts must be careful not to compromise the independence of quasi-judicial tribunals and decision-making agencies by imposing upon them fiduciary obligations which require that their decisions be made in accordance with a fiduciary duty.

Counsel for the appellants conceded in oral argument that it could not be said that such a duty should apply to the courts, as a creation of government, in the exercise of their judicial function. In my view, the considerations which apply in evaluating whether such an obligation is impressed on the process by which the Board decides whether to grant a licence for export differ little from those applying to the courts. The function of the Board in this regard is quasi-judicial: *Committee for Justice and Liberty* v. *National Energy Board,* [1978] 1 S.C.R. 369, at p. 385. While this characterization may not carry with it all the procedural and other requirements identical to those applicable to a court, it is inherently inconsistent with the imposition of a relationship of utmost good faith between the Board and a party appearing before it.

It is for this reason that I do not find helpful the authorities cited to me by the appellants as indicative of this evolving trend: *Gitludahl* v. *Minister of Forests,* B.C.S.C., August 13, 1992, Vancouver A922935, unreported, and *Dick* v. *The Queen,* F.C.T.D., June 3, 1992, Ottawa T-951-89, unreported. Those cases were concerned, respectively, with the decision-making of the Minister of Forests, and the conduct of the Crown when adverse in interest to aboriginal peoples in litigation. The considerations which may animate the application of a fiduciary duty in these contexts are far different from those raised in the context of a licence application before an independent decision-making body operating at arm's length from government.

Therefore, I conclude that the fiduciary relationship between the Crown and the appellants does not impose a duty on the Board to make its decisions in the best interests of the appellants, or to change its hearing process so as to impose superadded requirements of disclosure. When the duty is defined in this manner, such tribunals no more owe this sort of fiduciary duty than do the courts. Consequently, no such duty existed in relation to the decision-making function of the Board.

Moreover, even if this Court were to assume that the Board, in conducting its review, should have taken into account the existence of the fiduciary relationship between the Crown and the appellants, I am satisfied that, for the reasons set out above relating to the procedure followed by the Board, its actions in this case would have met the requirements of such a duty. There is no indication that the appellants were given anything less than the fullest opportunity to be heard. They had access to all the evidence that was before the Board, were able to make submissions and argument in reply, and were entitled to cross-examine the witnesses called by the respondent Hydro-Québec. This argument must therefore fail for the same reasons as the arguments relating to the nature of the review conducted by the Board. . . .

This Court, in *R.* v. *Sparrow, supra,* recognized the interrelationship between the recognition and affirmation of aboriginal rights constitutionally enshrined in s. 35(1) of the *Constitution Act, 1982,* and the fiduciary relationship which has historically existed between the Crown and aboriginal peoples. It is this relationship that indicates that the exercise of sovereign power may be limited or restrained when it amounts to an unjustifiable interference with aboriginal rights. In this appeal, the appellants argue that the decision of the Board to grant the licences will have a negative impact on their aboriginal rights, and that the Board was therefore required to meet the test of justification as set out in *Sparrow.*

It is obvious that the Board must exercise its decision-making function, including the interpretation and application of its governing legislation, in accordance with the dictates of the Constitution, including s. 35(1) of the *Constitution Act, 1982.* Therefore, it must first be determined whether this particular decision of the Board, made pursuant to s. 119.08(1) of the *National Energy Board Act,* could have the effect of interfering with the existing aboriginal rights of the appellants so as to amount to a *prima facie* infringement of s. 35(1).

The respondents in this appeal argue that it cannot. They assert that, with the signing by the appellants of the James Bay and Northern Quebec Agreement, incorporated in the *James Bay and Northern Quebec Native Claims Settlement Act,* S.C. 1976-77, c. 32 ("*the James Bay Act*"), the appellants ceded and renounced all aboriginal rights except as set out in the Agreement. Since the act of granting a licence neither requires nor permits the construction of the new production facilities which the appellants claim will interfere with their rights, and since the Agreement itself provides for a participatory review process to authorize the construction of such facilities, Hydro-Québec and the Attorney General of Quebec argue that no *prima facie* infringement results from the decision of the Board.

The evaluation of these competing arguments requires an examination and interpretation of the Agreement as embodied in the James Bay Act. The appellants, however, requested that this question be determined without reference to the Agreement or to the Act, since its interpretation and application form the subject of other legal proceedings involving the parties to this appeal. The appellants accordingly placed no reliance on this document in their assertion of a breach of aboriginal rights.

In my view, it is not possible to evaluate realistically the impact of the decision of the Board on the rights of the appellants without reference to the *James Bay Act.* The respondents assert that the rights of the appellants are limited to those set out in this document. The validity of this assertion cannot be tested without construing the provisions of the Agreement.

Moreover, even assuming that the decision of the Board is one that has, *prima facie,* an impact on the aboriginal rights of the appellants, and that the appellants are correct in arguing that, for the Board to justify its interference, it must, at a minimum, conduct a rigorous, thorough, and proper cost-benefit review, I find, for the reasons expressed above, that the review carried out in this case was not wanting in this respect. . . .

■ SELECTED BIBLIOGRAPHY

Bartlett, R. *Indian Reserves and Aboriginal Lands in Canada: A Homeland.* Saskatoon, Sask.: Native Law Centre, University of Saskatchewan, 1990.

———, "Provincial Jurisdiction and Resource Development on Indian Reserve Lands" [1986] *Managing Resources* 189.

Griffiths, O.B., "Case Commentary on *Blueberry River:* Is the Crown Fiduciary Obligation in the Currents of Change?" [1996] 3 C.N.L.R. 25.

Hughes, P., "Indians and Lands Reserved for the Indians: Off-limit to the Provinces" (1983) 21 *Osgoode Hall L.J.* 82.

Hurley, J., "The Crown's Fiduciary Duty and Indian Title: *Guerin* v. *The Queen*" (1985) 30 *McGill L.J.* 559.

Isaac T. *Pre-1868 Legislation Concerning Indians.* Saskatoon, Sask.: University of Saskatchewan Native Law Centre, 1993.

Johnston, D., "A Theory of Crown Trust Towards Aboriginal People" (1986) 30 *Ottawa L. Rev.* 307.

Notzke, C. *Aboriginal Peoples and Natural Resources in Canada.* Toronto: Captus University Publications, 1994.

Rotman, L.I., "Provincial Fiduciary Obligations to First Nations: The Nexus Between Governmental Power and Responsibility" [1994] 32:4 *Osgoode Hall L.J.* 735.

———. *Parallel Paths: Fiduciary Doctrine and the Crown-Native Relationship in Canada* (Toronto: University of Toronto Press, 1996).

Ryder, B., "The Demise and Rise of the Classical Paradigm in Canadian Federalism: Promoting Autonomy for the Provinces and First Nations" (1991) 36 *McGill L.J.* 308.

Salembier, J.P., "Crown Fiduciary Duty, Indian Title and the Lost Treasure of I.R. 172: The Legacy of *Apsassin* v. *The Queen (Blueberry River)*" [1996] 3 C.N.L.R. 1.

Sanders, D., "The Application of Provincial Laws." In *Aboriginal Peoples and the Law: Indian, Metis and Inuit Rights in Canada,* B. Morse, ed. Ottawa: Carleton University Press, 1985.

Slattery, B., "Understanding Aboriginal Rights" [1987] 66 *Can. Bar Rev.* 727.

Venne, S., ed. *Indian Acts and Amendments 1868–1975: An Indexed Collection.* Saskatoon, Sask.: Native Law Centre, University of Saskatchewan, 1981.

Weaver, S.M. *Making Canadian Indian Policy: The Hidden Agenda 1968–1970.* Toronto: University of Toronto Press, 1981.

CHAPTER 4
HUNTING, FISHING, AND TRAPPING RIGHTS

■ INTRODUCTION

Hunting, fishing, and trapping rights are derived from the historical use and occupation of Canada by Aboriginal peoples. The existence of these rights is not dependent upon the existence of Aboriginal title, as confirmed by the Supreme Court of Canada in its 1997 decision of *Delgamuukw* v. *B.C.*[1] Aboriginal hunting, fishing, and trapping rights are also provided for in many of the treaties and in the *Natural Resources Transfer Agreements.*[2] Finally, s. 35, which recognizes and affirms Aboriginal and treaty rights, also includes among these rights those related to hunting, fishing, and trapping. Many of the cases discussed in this book concern, and indeed a great deal of the development of Aboriginal law has been derived from, Aboriginal hunting, fishing, and trapping rights conflicting with federal, provincial, and territorial legislation. This chapter does not include any case excerpts. Many of the significant cases discussed in this chapter can be found in other parts of the book. The intent of this chapter to is provide readers with an introduction to this subject matter and to provide brief highlights of the most significant cases in this area.

ABORIGINAL RIGHTS

Existing hunting, fishing, and trapping rights are constitutionally protected in s. 35(1) of the *Constitution Act, 1982*[3] and, as such, prevail over federal, provincial, and territorial legislation unless that legislation is justifiable. Section 35(1) reads:

> The existing aboriginal and treaty rights of the aboriginal peoples of Canada are hereby recognized and affirmed.

The leading decision on interpreting the meaning of s. 35(1) is the 1990 Supreme Court of Canada decision of *R.* v. *Sparrow.*[4] *Sparrow* dealt with whether or not a gill-net length restriction violated the Aboriginal right to fish for food. In its decision, the court outlined the analysis to be used when determining whether or not an Aboriginal right takes precedence over federal or provincial legislation. The court outlined a justificatory analysis to determine whether or not such legislation can be

---

1   *Delgamuukw* v. *British Columbia,* [1998] 1 C.N.L.R. 14 (S.C.C.).
2   *Constitution Act, 1930,* R.S.C. 1985, App. II, No. 26.
3   *Constitution Act, 1982,* being Sched. B of the *Canada Act 1982* (U.K.), 1982, c.11.
4   *R.* v. *Sparrow,* [1990] 3 C.N.L.R. 160 (S.C.C.).

justified if it infringes upon an Aboriginal right. An important point arising from *Sparrow* is that only rights existing as of April 17, 1982, when the *Constitution Act, 1982* came into effect, are protected by s. 35(1). If an Aboriginal right was extinguished prior to 1982, it does not receive the constitutional protection afforded by s. 35. For a more thorough discussion of *Sparrow* and the effect of s. 35, see the introduction to chapter 7 and the text of the *Sparrow* decision at p. 405.

The British Columbia Court of Appeal decision of *R. v. Jack*[5] provides a good example of the *Sparrow* test being applied. Mr. Jack, who possessed an Aboriginal right to fish for food and for ceremonial purposes, was fishing with others who were assisting him in preparation for a traditional family ceremony. The fishing occurred at a time not authorized by the *Fisheries Act*[6] and without a licence. The Court of Appeal overturned the trial court's conviction of Mr. Jack. The closure of the particular location where Mr. Jack was fishing was an infringement of his Aboriginal right to fish and was not justified. The federal Department of Fisheries and Oceans (DFO) did not give priority to Mr. Jack's rights, even though sport fishing was permitted in an area nearby. As well, the consultations between DFO and the band were insufficient, and DFO did not infringe Mr. Jack's rights to as little degree as possible. The court was critical of DFO imposing allocations with little contact with the Aboriginal peoples affected.

In *R. v. Adams,*[7] the Supreme Court determined that Aboriginal title claims fall within the ambit of Aboriginal rights generally. However, Aboriginal title is not necessary to prove the existence of an Aboriginal right. An Aboriginal group must demonstrate that a particular activity, custom, or tradition was integral to the distinctive culture of that group, even though their use and occupation of the land may not have been sufficient to support a claim of Aboriginal title. In *Adams,* the issue concerned fishing rights, and the court held that the Aboriginal right to fish was not dependent upon Aboriginal title to the area where the fishing occurred.

In *R. v. Gladstone,*[8] the court found that the Heiltsuk people of British Columbia possessed an Aboriginal right, protected under s. 35(1), to trade in herring spawn on kelp because this activity was a central and significant feature of their society. Noteworthy is that this activity, best described as commercial in nature, existed amongst the Heiltsuk prior to European contact. Because of the commercial nature of this right, after the conservation objectives have been achieved over the resource, the government is not obligated to give the Heiltsuk a priority right to fish, as was the case in *Sparrow* when dealing with fishing for food rights. Rather, the government must allocate the resource in a way that is respectful of the fact that

---

5   *R. v. Jack,* [1996] 2 C.N.L.R. 113 (B.C.C.A.); see also *R. v. Samson,* [1996] 2 C.N.L.R. 184, (B.C.C.A.), and *R. v. Little,* [1996] 2 C.N.L.R. 136 (B.C.C.A.). For a critical discussion of the Aboriginal Fisheries Strategy in B.C., see P. Eidsvik, "The Aboriginal Fisheries Strategy: Legalizing an Illegal Practice" November 1996 *Policy Options* 26.

6   *Fisheries Act,* R.S.C. 1985, c. F–14.

7   *R. v. Adams,* [1996] 4 C.N.L.R. 1 (S.C.C.).

8   *R. v. Gladstone,* [1996] 4 C.N.L.R. 65 (S.C.C.).

the Aboriginal rights have priority over other interests in the fishery.[9] Issues to be considered by government when allocating a resource in this manner include the extent of the participation by Aboriginal peoples in the fishery relative to their percentage of the population generally affected, how the government has accommodated different Aboriginal rights in a particular fishery (for example, food versus commercial), how important the fishery is to the economic well-being of the First Nation or Aboriginal group, and what other factors the government considered when allocating commercial licences in the area in question. The court notes that these factors are not an exhaustive list.[10]

Fishing licences as a rule do not constitute a *prima facie* infringement of the Aboriginal right to fish. Regardless, the government is still required to provide justification for conditions in a licence that infringe an Aboriginal right to fish.[11] In *R. v. Van der Peet,*[12] the Supreme Court discussed the criteria by which an activity is deemed to be an Aboriginal right. To be an Aboriginal right, an activity must be an element of a practice, custom, or tradition that is integral to the distinctive culture of the Aboriginal peoples claiming the right. Although, the practice, custom, or tradition must have existed prior to European contact, evolution of the activity into a modern form will not preclude it from protection as an Aboriginal right so long as continuity with precontact practices, customs, and traditions can be demonstrated. The activity, as illustrated by *Smokehouse,*[13] cannot be incidental to another practice, custom, or tradition. It must be integral to the distinctive culture, on its own, to receive protection. In *Van der Peet,* the appellant failed to demonstrate that the exchange of fish for money or other goods was an integral part of the distinctive Stolo culture that existed prior to contact. Thus, the charge of selling fish under an Indian food fish licence of the *British Columbia Fishery (General) Regulations* (s. 27(5)) remained in force.

The Supreme Court applied the *Van der Peet* analysis in *R. v. N.T.C. Smokehouse Ltd.*[14] The issue in *Smokehouse* was whether the exchange of fish at potlatches and at other traditional ceremonies constituted a right to engage in the commercial selling of fish. The court held, based on the evidence, that the exchange of fish at these ceremonies was incidental to the ceremonies and did not possess any significance independently. Thus, the exchange of fish was not an "integral" part of the Aboriginal group's distinctive culture.

The *Royal Proclamation of 1763* has been held to recognize the rights of Indians to fish for their own consumption and for limited commercial purposes.[15] The Manitoba Queen's Bench decision of *R. v. Muswagon*[16] affirmed that the Métis

---

9   Ibid., paras. 61 and 62.

10   Ibid., para. 64.

11   *R. v. Nikal,* [1996] 3 C.N.L.R. 178 (S.C.C.).

12   *R. v. Van der Peet,* [1996] 4 C.N.L.R. 177 (S.C.C.).

13   *R. v. N.T.C. Smokehouse Ltd.,* [1996] 4 C.N.L.R. 130 (S.C.C.).

14   Ibid.

15   See *R. v. Jackson,* [1992] 4 C.N.L.R. 121 (Ont. Prov. Div.).

16   *R. v. Muswagon,* [1992] 4 C.N.L.R. 159 (Man. Q.B.).

living in Manitoba have numerous Aboriginal rights, which may include the right to hunt and fish for food at all seasons.

The Manitoba Court of Queen's Bench decision of *R.* v. *McPherson*[17] dealt with an appeal by a Métis convicted for hunting moose out of season. The court held that there was an existing Métis right to hunt for moose for subsistence purposes within the meaning of s. 35(1). Provincial legislation, in this case the Manitoba *Wildlife Act*,[18] must be read down (that is to say, interpreted in a manner so that it is not held to be completely invalid but rather invalid only to the extent absolutely necessary) when it conflicts with existing Aboriginal rights.

TREATY RIGHTS

Treaty rights to hunt are protected by s. 35(1), and the *Migratory Birds Convention Act*[19] cannot infringe these rights. In *R.* v. *Flett*[20] the Manitoba Court of Queen's Bench, and in *R.* v. *Arcand*[21] the Alberta Court of Queen's Bench, dealt with Indians hunting migratory birds out of season contrary to the act. Both courts held that s. 35(1) provided a defence to contravening the act. By being constitutionalized under s. 35, treaty rights take on a stronger authoritative stature. An Ontario District Court has held that trapping by Treaty No. 9 Indians cannot be regulated by provincial legislation.[22]

However, the Saskatchewan Court of Appeal took a different turn in *R.* v. *Eninew,*[23] whereby the *Migratory Birds Convention Act* was held to be valid, notwithstanding s. 35(1). Being a 1984 decision, *Eninew* predated the 1990 *Sparrow* decision. Important to note, however, is that *Eninew* dealt with a specific treaty provision that contemplated government regulation.

In *R.* v. *Agawa*[24] the Ontario Court of Appeal held that the existing treaty right to fish in the Robinson-Huron Treaty was not absolute and was subject to "reasonable" regulation. The requirement of a gill-net licence under the *Ontario Fisheries Regulations*[25] was deemed to be for conservation purposes and, as such, was a reasonable limitation on the right. Treaty No. 3 establishes an Aboriginal right to fish that is recognized and affirmed by s. 35(1).[26]

Treaty rights must be exercised in a safe manner.[27] Night hunting is not a safe

---

17 *R.* v. *McPherson*, [1994] 2 C.N.L.R. 137 (Man. Q.B.); see also *R.* v. *Chevrier*, [1989] 1 C.N.L.R. 128 (Ont. Dist. Ct.).

18 *Wildlife Act*, R.S.M. 1987, c. W–130.

19 *Migratory Birds Convention Act*, R.S.C. 1985, c. M–7.

20 *R.* v. *Flett*, [1989] 4 C.N.L.R. 128 (Man. Q.B.).

21 *R.* v. *Arcand*, [1989] 2 C.N.L.R. 110 (Alta. Q.B.).

22 *Cheechoo* v. *R.*, [1981] 3 C.N.L.R. 45 (Ont. Dist. Ct.).

23 *R.* v. *Eninew*, [1984] 2 C.N.L.R. 126 (Sask. C.A.).

24 *R.* v. *Agawa*, [1988] 3 C.N.L.R. 73 (Ont. C.A.).

25 *Ontario Fisheries Regulations*, C.R.C. 1978, c. 849, s. 12(1).

26 *R.* v. *Bombay*, [1993] 1 C.N.L.R. 92 (Ont. C.A.).

27 See *R.* v. *Napoleon*, [1986] 1 C.N.L.R. 86 (B.C.C.A.); *R.* v. *Bigstone*, [1981] 3 C.N.L.R. 103 (Sask. C.A.) and *R.* v. *Kytwayhat*, [1984] 4 C.N.L.R. 107 (Sask. C.A.).

practice and the Treaty of 1725 provides affords no excuse for the practice.[28] The Northwest Territories Territorial Court decision of *R. v. Noel*[29] puts an interesting twist on the issue of public safety and the exercise of Aboriginal rights. There, the accused Aboriginal person was charged for discharging a firearm within a no-shooting zone that ran along a well-used road outside Yellowknife. The primary purpose of the no-shooting zone was for public safety. Regardless, Halifax J. held that the regulation was unenforceable against the Aboriginal person because the government did not give proper consideration to less intrusive alternatives, nor were the consultations as exhaustive as possible. This case raises the issue of process over substance. Although consultation may not have been adequate and should have been addressed, the decision does not adequately discuss how the very apparent issue of public safety in this case is to be resolved in the interim.

Although many Indian treaties affirmed hunting and fishing rights, some actually extinguished such rights. In *R. v. Howard*[30] the Supreme Court of Canada held that a 1923 treaty signed with the Hiawatha Indians surrendered any Aboriginal rights to hunt and fish within the affected area.

In addition to the actual terms of a treaty, the minutes of meetings at which negotiations took place and the events leading up to the signing of a treaty have been interpreted to convey rights. For example, in *R. v. Taylor*[31] the Ontario Court of Appeal found that although the written terms of an 1818 treaty did not contain a guarantee of hunting and fishing rights, the minutes of the council meeting between the deputy superintendent of Indian Affairs and the chiefs of the six tribes who were parties to the treaty reveal that hunting and fishing rights on Crown lands in areas covered by the treaty were retained by the tribes. It is important to note that treaty Indians can exercise their particular treaty hunting, fishing, and trapping rights only within the area covered by their treaty.[32]

In *R. v. Badger,*[33] the Supreme Court affirmed that Treaty No. 8 guaranteed Indian hunting rights subject to two limitations. First, there is a limitation with respect to geography. That is, the right could be exercised throughout the tract surrendered excepts for those tracts required or taken for the purposes of settlement, mining, lumbering, trading, or other purposes. Second, the right could be limited by government regulations regarding conservation measures. Paragraph 12 of the *Natural Resources Transfer Agreement* (*Constitution Act, 1930*) (*NRTA*) is the legal instrument that governed the Indian right to hunt. Unless there is a direct conflict between the *NRTA* and Treaty No. 8, the *NRTA* does not modify treaty rights. Paragraph 12 of the *NRTA* specifically mentions a right to hunt for food. It should be understood as extinguishing the right to hunt commercially and as pro-

28 *R. v. McCoy*, [1994] 2 C.N.L.R. 129 (N.B.C.A.); see also *R. v. Prince*, [1964] S.C.R. 81, which held that night hunting was an acceptable method of hunting under para. 12 of the *NRTA*.

29 *R. v. Noel*, [1995] 4 C.N.L.R. 78 (N.W.T.T.C.).

30 *R. v. Howard*, [1994] 3 C.N.L.R. 146 (S.C.C.).

31 *R. v. Taylor*, [1981] 3 C.N.L.R. 114 (Ont. C.A.).

32 See *R. v. Wesley*, 8 C.N.L.C. 572 (Ont. Dist. Ct.).

33 *R. v. Badger,* [1996] 2 C.N.L.R. 77 (S.C.C.).

tecting and expanding the Treaty No. 8 right. Paragraph 12, on its face, did not extinguish or replace the Treaty No. 8 right. Finally, with respect to access, the court found that if lands are occupied and being put to a visible use that is incompatible with hunting, Indians will not have a right to access. However, if privately owned unoccupied land is not being put to a visible use, then Indians, pursuant to Treaty No. 8, will have a right of access to hunt for food.

NATURAL RESOURCES TRANSFER AGREEMENTS

All three of the *Natural Resources Transfer Agreements* (*NRTA*) contain the following paragraph (para. 12, Alberta and Saskatchewan; para. 13, Manitoba):

> In order to secure to the Indians of the Province the continuance of the supply of game and fish for their support and subsistence, Canada agrees that the laws respecting game in force in the Province from time to time shall apply to the Indians within the boundaries thereof, provided, however, that the said Indians shall have the right, which the Province hereby assures to them, of hunting, trapping and fishing game and fish for food at all seasons of the year on all unoccupied Crown lands and on any other lands to which the said Indians may have a right of access.

A primary purpose of para. 12 was to ensure that Indians had an ample supply of game for their subsistence (a) by requiring Indians to be subject to provincial gaming laws and (b) by guaranteeing them the right to hunt and trap game for food during all seasons on unoccupied Crown lands and other lands to which they had a right of access.[34]

Indians are guaranteed the right to take game and fish "for food" at all seasons of the year on the lands specified, and provincial laws to the contrary are inapplicable to Indians. The words "for food" represent a notable restriction on the hunting and fishing rights conferred by the *NRTA*. Those Indians who by treaty may have had a right to fish and hunt for commercial purposes had their rights restricted by para. 12 of the *NRTA*. In *R.* v. *Horseman*[35] the Supreme Court of Canada held that an Alberta Indian's treaty right to hunt commercially had been "merged and consolidated" in para. 12 of the Alberta *NRTA* (same as Saskatchewan). Thus, the Indian's treaty rights were limited to the extent specified by the agreement and had been partially extinguished by the agreement.

In *R.* v. *Badger*,[36] the Supreme Court of Canada affirmed that the Treaty No. 8 right to hunt did not apply on lands that are settled, that are being mined, that are being used for lumber, or that are being used for other purposes. Additionally, this right, it is still subject to justifiable regulation. The *NRTA* further modified the treaty right by limiting it to a right to hunt for food, by extending its scope to all the

---

34 *R.* v. *Wesley*, 5 C.N.L.C. 540 at 547 (Alta. C.A.); affirmed by *R.* v. *Sutherland*, [1980] 3 C.N.L.R. 71 at 78 (S.C.C.).

35 *R.* v. *Horseman* [1990] 3 C.N.L.R. 95 (S.C.C.).

36 *R.* v. *Badger*, [1996] 2 C.N.L.R. 77 (S.C.C.). At the time of writing, this case had been heard by the S.C.C. but no judgment had been rendered.

prairie provinces (not just the boundaries of Treaty No. 8) and limiting its application to all "unoccupied" Crown lands and other lands to which affected Indians may have a right of access.

Saskatchewan's NRTA "merges and consolidates" Treaty No. 6 hunting rights.[37] Section 35 of the *Constitution Act, 1982* has no effect on the application of provincial laws to treaty Indians under para. 12. In *R. v. McIntyre*,[38] the Saskatchewan Court of Appeal held that para. 12 "merges and consolidates" Treaty 10 hunting rights. Section 35 of the *Constitution Act, 1982* neither expands nor contracts existing rights identified as being contained in para. 12. The court also affirmed that the province has the authority to create game preserves,[39] including road corridor game preserves, since they were established for *bona fide* reasons.[40]

The Alberta Court of Queen's Bench in *R. v. Alexson*[41] held that leased grazing land was not "unoccupied Crown land" or "other lands" within the meaning of para. 12. Thus, treaty Indians must obtain permission of leaseholders before hunting. In the Supreme Court of Canada decision of *R. v. Horse*,[42] it was held that para. 12 must be given a "broad and liberal construction" and any ambiguity in the phrase "right of way" must be resolved in favour of Indians.

Treaty No. 6 included the right to hunt on unoccupied provincial land for personal use and a right to hunt commercially. However, this right was extinguished by the merger and consolidation of rights in the 1930 Alberta NRTA and thus was not protected as an existing right under s. 35(1). Hence, Treaty No. 6 Indians hunting on unoccupied provincial lands are subject to the Alberta *Wildlife Act*.[43]

The term "hunting" in para. 12 of the Saskatchewan NRTA means "hunting" only and does not include trapping. Hunting, trapping, and fishing are distinct terms and one term cannot replace the other in meaning.[44] The Supreme Court of Canada dealt with the meaning of the phrase "for food" in para. 12 of the NRTA in its 1990 decision of *R. v. Horseman*.[45] Paragraph 12 merges and consolidates treaty hunting rights. The hunting rights recognized by Treaty No. 8 included commercial hunting rights but were subsequently limited and altered by the NRTA. Under the NRTA, there was a limitation set on the nature of the hunting right (that it is to say, it could not be for commercial purposes) and the territory the right included and the means by which Indians could hunt for food were expanded. There is no question that

---

37 *R. v. Bird*, [1992] 1 C.N.L.R. 119 (Sask. Prov. Ct.).

38 *R. v. McIntyre*, [1992] 3 C.N.L.R. 113 (Sask. C.A.).

30 See *R. v. Strongquill*, 5 C.N.L.C. 567 (Sask. C.A.) and confirmed by *R. v. Sutherland*, [1980] 3 C.N.L.R. 71 (S.C.C.).

40 *R. v. Wolverine*, [1989] 3 C.N.L.R. 181 (Sask. C.A.).

41 *R. v. Alexson*, [1990] 4 C.N.L.R. 28 (Alta. Q.B.).

42 *R. v. Horse*, [1988] 2 C.N.L.R. 112 (S.C.C.).

43 *Wildlife Act*, S.A., 1984, c.W-9.1; see *R. v. Littlewolf; R. v. Potts*, [1992] 3 C.N.L.R. 100 (Alta. Q.B.).

44 *R. v. Wolverine*, [1989] 3 C.N.L.R. 181 (Sask. C.A.); R. v. Brertton, [1998] 3 C.N.L.R. 122 (Alta. Q.B.)..

45 *R. v. Horseman*, [1990] 3 C.N.L.R. 95 (S.C.C.).

prior to 1982 the federal government had the power to modify treaty rights. The right to hunt is subject to measures that ensure conservation of the resource. The right to hunt for food cannot be regulated by provincial legislation on its own accord. However, s. 88 of the *Indian Act* provides that, subject to treaty rights, provincial laws of general application apply to Indians.

The challenge for governments is to balance federal, provincial, and territorial regulatory regimes with the requirements of the *Sparrow, Van der Peet,* and *Delgamuukw* decisions for the protection of Aboriginal hunting, trapping, and fishing rights. In particular, governments will have to come to terms with the threshold of where government regulation is justifiable and those instances where it becomes too intrusive to be legitimized. Key to the obligations and responsibilities of governments is to ensure that proper consultation has been given to those areas where they may be a conflict with Aboriginal usage and rights. As the population increases and the scarcity of resources becomes more apparent, the importance of understanding the scope and nature of Aboriginal hunting, fishing, and trapping rights increases.

■ SELECTED BIBLIOGRAPHY

Eidsvik, P., "The Aboriginal Fisheries Strategy: Legalizing an Illegal Practice" (November 1996) *Policy Options* 26.

McNeil, K. *Indian Hunting, Trapping and Fishing Rights in the Prairie Provinces of Canada.* Saskatoon, Sask.: Native Law Centre, University of Saskatchewan, 1983.

Newell, D. *Tangled Webs of History: Indians and the Law in Canada's Pacific Coast Fisheries.* Toronto: University of Toronto Press, 1993.

Notzke, C. *Aboriginal Peoples and Natural Resources in Canada.* North York: Captus Press, 1994.

Woodward, J., "Hunting, Fishing, Trapping and Gathering." In *Native Law.* Toronto: Carswell, 1989.

CHAPTER 5
THE MÉTIS AND INUIT

■ INTRODUCTION

The development of Aboriginal legal jurisprudence has focused on Indians or First Nations peoples. Although the basis for Aboriginal law rests on principles involving First Nations, much of Aboriginal law is equally applicable to the Métis and Inuit. Relatively, there have been some litigation and judicial decisions relating to the Métis and almost none with respect to the Inuit. With this in mind, this chapter's purpose is to provide an introduction to some of the unique features of Aboriginal law as it relates to both the Inuit and Métis.

THE MÉTIS

Who Are the Métis?

The 1991 census revealed that approximately 135,000 people in Canada identify as being solely Métis. There is no single definition of who is, and who is not, a Métis.[1] Historically, Métis people were those people who were part Indian and lived a distinct Aboriginal lifestyle. The Alberta *Metis Settlements Act*[2] defines Métis as meaning "a person of aboriginal ancestry who identifies with Métis history and culture." Alberta has enacted additional legislation dealing with its eight Métis Settlements,[3] including an amendment to the *Alberta Act*.[4] An excerpt from this act, along with the constitutional amendment, are included in this chapter.

Donald Purich provides three different usages for the term "Métis." Métis can be used to refer to all Aboriginal peoples who are not registered Indians and are not Inuit, to all mixed-blood persons, and to all those persons who can trace their ancestry to the historic Métis of the Red River (early 1800s).[5] The last two groups of Purich's listing are most accurate. This is further confirmed by Catherine Bell, who identifies five broad groups in which the term "Métis" applies:

1. anyone of mixed Indian/non-Indian blood who is not a status Indian;
2. a person who identifies as Metis and is accepted by a successor community of the Metis Nation;
3. a person who identifies as Metis and is accepted by a self-identifying

---

1   See P. Chartrand, "Aboriginal Rights: The Dispossession of the Metis" (1991) 29 *Osgoode Hall L.J.* 457.

2   *Metis Settlements Act*, S.A. 1990, c. M–14.3, s. 1.

3   *Metis Settlements Land Protection Act*, S.A. 1990, c. M–14.8, and *Metis Settlements Accord Implementation Act*, S.A. 1990, c. M–14.5.

4   *Alberta Act*, S.C. 1905, c. 3; *Constitution of Alberta Amendment Act, 1990*, S.A. 1990, c. C–22.2.

5   D. Purich, *The Metis* (Toronto: Lorimer, 1988), 9–11.

Metis community;

4.   persons who took, or were entitled to take, half-breed grants under the *Manitoba Act* or *Dominion Lands Act*, and their descendants; [footnote deleted] and

5.   descendants of persons excluded from the *Indian Act* regime by virtue of a way of life criterion.[6]

James Frideres outlines the dilemma of identifying the Métis:

> The Métis are a unique people in Canadian society. Originally they grew out of the symbiotic relationship that existed between Natives and the European immigrants to the New World. Yet it was the later government implementation of a complex set of social and political acts that ultimately determined their status as a separate ethnic group.[7]

The Supreme Court of Canada has not yet determined whether the Métis are included within the meaning of "Indians" in s. 91(24).[8] Section 35(2) of the *Constitution Act, 1982* defines the Aboriginal peoples of Canada as including the Métis peoples, in addition to the Indian and Inuit peoples. Aside from this explicit constitutional definition, there are few legal documents, including legislation and cases, that assist in understanding who the Métis people are, and what rights they possess. At the federal level, Métis affairs are not dealt with by the Department of Indian Affairs and Northern Development but rather by the Privy Council Office. The Métis also have a separate cabinet voice; namely the federal interlocutor for Métis and Non-Status Indians. The heart of this separation with the federal government deals with legislative, and ultimately, financial responsibility. The federal government has consistently maintained that the Métis, although one of the Aboriginal peoples of Canada, are not within its exclusive legislative jurisdiction held under s. 91(24) of the *Constitution Act, 1867*. The federal government maintains that the Métis are primarily a provincial responsibility. Métis people are represented nationally by the Métis National Council, with corresponding provincial and territorial political organizations. The national Congress of Aboriginal Peoples also claims to represent Métis people.

The Honourable A.C. Hamilton in his report to the federal minister of Indian Affairs on alternatives to extinguishment[9] provides an interesting aside with respect to the Métis. Hamilton focuses on the need for the federal government, in one form or another, to deal squarely with the issue of Métis people and their rights. He writes in part:

---

6   C. Bell, "Who are the Metis People in Section 35(2)?" (1991) XXIX:2 *Alta. L. Rev.* 351 at 374.

7   J. Frideres, *Native Peoples in Canada: Contemporary Conflicts*, 3rd ed. (Scarborough, Ont.: Prentice-Hall, 1988), 295.

8   In *R.* v. *Blais,* [1998] 4 C.N.L.R. 103 (Man. Q.B.), the court held that Métis are not included in the reference to "Indians" in s. 91(24) of the *Constitution Act, 1867.*

9   Hon. A.C. Hamilton, *Canada and Aboriginal Peoples: A New Partnership* (Ottawa: Minister of Public Works and Government Services Canada, 1995).

I do not wish to enter into the debate as to who qualifies to be a Métis. It is obvious however that there are certainly Métis in Canada, and that due to their constitutional recognition, they have rights as Aboriginal peoples.

. . . The federal government has given some recognition to Métis rights by agreeing that they be involved in comprehensive claims negotiations in the Northwest Territories where some have signed treaties in conjunction with the Dene. The federal government is also providing funding to the Labrador Métis Association to research its claim. . . .

In any event, a determination should be made as to whether the federal government's Comprehensive Land Claims Policy is available to deal with these Aboriginal people or whether some other approach may be necessary.[10]

Métis Government in Alberta

Alberta is the only province to enact legislation dealing specifically with Métis local government and a land base (including 1.25 million acres of settlement land). Proclaimed into force on November 1, 1990, the *Alberta Metis Settlements Act*[11] provides a system of local government and, combined with other legislation, a land base for the Métis Settlements. It establishes Settlement Corporations and the General Council as legal entities. The Settlement Councils deal with matters relating to local government and the needs of each community, whereas the General Council deals with issues that affect the Settlements collectively. The legislation was developed cooperatively between the Alberta government and the Alberta Federation of Metis Settlements. The *Constitution of Alberta Amendment Act*[12] provides for certainty of tenure to the lands in question and has the effect of ensuring that the Métis legislation has some permanency within the provincial system.

Métis Rights

The *Manitoba Act 1870*[13] conferred certain rights to the "half-breeds" who have come to be known as the Métis. These rights are codified in s. 31 of the *Manitoba Act, 1870*. The *Dominion Lands Act*[14] provided that the delegated powers of the Governor in Council included satisfying

> any claims existing in connection with the extinguishment of the Indian title, preferred by half-breeds resident in the North-West Territories outside of the limits of Manitoba.

Both of these enactments recognize, to some extent, that the Métis had an interest in land.[15]

---

10   Ibid., 32–34.
11   *Metis Settlements Act*, S.A. 1990, c. M–14.3.
12   *Constitution of Alberta Amendment Act*, S.A. 1990, c. C–22.2.
13   *Manitoba Act*, R.S.C. 1985, App. II, No. 8.
14   *Dominion Lands Act*, S.C. 1879, c. 31, s. 125(e) [re-enacted S.C. 1883, c. 17, s. 81].
15   See D.N. Sprague, "Metis Land Claims," in *Aboriginal Land Claims in Canada: A Regional Perspective*, K. Coates, ed. (Toronto: Copp Clark Pitman, 1997).

In 1874, the half-breeds of Rainy River signed an adhesion to Treaty No. 3 (1873). The adhesion to the treaty states that the half-breeds surrender "all claim, right, title or interest which they, by virtue of their Indian blood, have or possess." In return, they received reserve lands, in addition to annuities and other items.

In *Manitoba Metis Federation Inc.* v. *Canada*,[16] the Manitoba Court of Appeal dealt with an application by the federal government to have the statement of claim of the Manitoba Metis Federation struck because there was no cause of action. The Manitoba Metis Federation and individual Métis sought a declaration that various federal and provincial statutes and orders-in-council enacted during the 1870s and 1880s were unconstitutional because they had the effect of depriving the Métis of land to which they were entitled under the *Manitoba Act, 1870*. In deciding the procedural issue, both the Manitoba Court of Appeal and the Supreme Court of Canada provided some substantive statements about the nature of Métis title and rights.

A majority of the Court of Appeal agreed with the federal attorney-general and held that the impugned legislation did not negatively affect Métis rights. Section 31 of the *Manitoba Act* did not create a communal interest in the land for Métis, but rather individual rights. Thus, the Manitoba Metis Federation did not have a cause of action. O'Sullivan J.A. dissented and held that s. 35 of the *Constitution Act, 1982* recognizes and affirms Métis rights. The Manitoba Metis Federation, and the individual Métis, were in a good position to enforce these rights. Finally, O'Sullivan stated that the *Manitoba Act, 1870* was not merely a statute, it represented a treaty negotiated between the Crown and the Métis people.

The Supreme Court of Canada unanimously disagreed with the Manitoba Court of Appeal decision and held that the Métis application for a declaration did not have a "plain and obvious" conclusion or outcome that was "beyond doubt." The issue of whether or not certain pieces of legislation violated Métis rights recognized by the *Manitoba Act, 1870* is a justiciable issue. (An issue that can be brought before the courts.)[17]

In *R.* v. *Muswagon*,[18] Jewers J. of the Manitoba Court of Appeal stated:

> Aboriginals and Metis living in Manitoba may very well have inherent rights to hunt and fish for food in all seasons; many, if not all, treaty Indians certainly have that right under the various Indian treaties applicable in this province.

In *R.* v. *McPherson*,[19] Schulman J. of the Manitoba Court of Queen's Bench affirmed that where provincial laws of general application have been found inapplicable to Aboriginal peoples because these laws conflict with treaty rights or federal legislation in relation to Indians, the legislation should be read down so as not to apply to such Aboriginal peoples. Schulman J. affirmed Gregoire J.'s decision of the Manitoba Provincial Court, which held that the two Métis persons charged

16   *Manitoba Metis Federation Inc.* v. *A.-G. Canada* (*sub nom. Dumont* v. *A.-G. Canada*), [1988] 3 C.N.L.R. 39 (Man. C.A.).

17   *Manitoba Metis Federation Inc.* v. *A.-G. Canada*, [1990] 2 C.N.L.R. 19 (S.C.C.).

18   *R.* v. *Muswagon*, [1992] 4 C.N.L.R. 159 at 163 (Man. Q.B.).

19   *R.* v. *McPherson*, [1994] 2 C.N.L.R. 137 (Man. Q.B.).

under the *Wildlife Act*[20] for hunting moose out of season possessed hunting rights protected by s. 35(1) of the *Constitution Act, 1982* and that these rights could be limited for conservation purposes pursuant to the justificatory analysis found in the Supreme Court of Canada's 1990 decision of *R. v. Sparrow*. (See chapter 7.) The *Sparrow* test was not upheld in this instance due to both a lack of consultation with the Métis and a lack of priority for Métis hunting rights.[21]

In *R. v. Morin*,[22] the Saskatchewan Court of Queen's Bench considered a trial court judgment that affirmed that the Métis of northwest Saskatchewan had an Aboriginal right to fish within a specified area, that this right had not been extinguished by the taking of scrip, and that the requirements of the *Saskatchewan Fishery Regulations* for obtaining a fishing licence were unjustified infringements of the Métis right to fish. The Queen's Bench decision upheld the majority of the trial judgment but restricted it to a finding that the Métis had established their right to fish for food. The trial judgment[23] held that the Métis and Indians of northwest Saskatchewan are two "similarly situated" groups of people who were not being similarly treated. Métis were required to purchase their fishing licences, whereas Indians could obtain them for no charge.

In *R. v. Grumbo*,[24] the Saskatchewan Court of Appeal considered whether a Métis person convicted of illegal possession of wildlife was an "Indian" for the purposes para. 12 of the *Natural Resources Transfer Agreement* (*NRTA*) and thereby possessed certain rights to hunt. Although the Court of Appeal did not resolve the issue, they did dismiss the possibility. Instead, the court stated that some fundamental questions needed to be answered, including whether the Métis people are an Aboriginal people distinct from Indians and, if they are, whether they possess a form of Aboriginal title or a right to hunt in Saskatchewan and whether this right was affected by the *NRTA*.

In *R. v. Van der Peet*,[25] Lamer C.J., for the majority, made a number of comments regarding the Métis, even though the case itself had nothing to do with Métis rights. Lamer C.J. writes:

> Although s. 35 includes the Metis within its definition of "aboriginal peoples of Canada", and thus seems to link their claims to those of other Aboriginal peoples under the general heading of "aboriginal rights", the history of the Metis, and the reasons underlying their inclusion in the protection given by s. 35, are quite distinct from those of other Aboriginal peoples in Canada. As such, the manner in which the

---

20 *Wildlife Act*, R.S.M. 1987, c. W130, s. 26.

21 Also see *R. v. Ferguson*, [1994] 1 C.N.L.R. 117 (Alta. Q.B.), which held that a Métis person could be considered an "Indian" for the purposes of para. 12 of the *NRTA*, and *R. v. Chevrier*, [1989] 1 C.N.L.R. 128 (Ont. Dist. Ct.), which held that a "mixed blood" person could exercise treaty hunting rights even though s/he was not entitled to be registered as an "Indian" under the *Indian Act*.

22 *R. v. Morin*, [1998] 1 C.N.L.R. 182 (Sask.Q.B.).

23 [1996] 3 C.N.L.R. 157 (Sask. Prov. Ct.).

24 *R. v. Grumbo*, [1998] 3 C.N.L.R. 172 at 184 (Sask. C.A.).

25 *R. v. Van der Peet*, [1996] 4 C.N.L.R. 177 at 207, para. 67 (S.C.C.).

Aboriginal rights of other Aboriginal peoples are defined is not necessarily determinative of the manner in which the Aboriginal rights of the Metis are defined.[26]

Considering that this is perhaps one of the most substantive statements to date from the Supreme Court regarding the rights of Métis people, it leaves many questions unanswered. Most notably, if Métis rights are to be understood differently, does that mean that they are to be understood in a way that will make them less authoritative than other Aboriginal rights? This statement by Lamer C.J. has undoubtedly raised concerns for those advocating an expansive approach to interpreting Aboriginal rights vis-à-vis the Métis people of Canada.

THE INUIT

Who Are the Inuit?

Thirty-two thousand people were identified as being solely Inuit in the 1991 Canadian census. The Inuit come within the legislative authority of the federal Parliament pursuant to s. 91(24) of the *Constitution Act, 1867*. Although the responsibility of the federal Department of Indian Affairs and Northern Development, and unlike Indians registered under the *Indian Act*, the Inuit are not governed by specific federal legislation. Section 4(1) of the *Indian Act* provides: "A reference in this Act to an Indian does not include any person of the race of aborigines commonly referred to as Inuit." Section 35(2) of the *Constitution Act, 1982* includes the Inuit as one of the Aboriginal peoples of Canada, along with the Métis and Indian peoples. In *Re Eskimos*[27] the Supreme Court of Canada unanimously decided that the term "Indians" in s. 91(24) of the *Constitution Act, 1867* included the Inuit, thereby bringing the Inuit within the legislative authority of the federal Parliament.

Inuit Land Claims

In May 1993 the *Nunavut Land Claims Agreement*[28] was signed between Canada (the Northwest Territories [NWT] being part of the federal team) and the Tungavik Federation of Nunavut (TFN) (on behalf of the Inuit of the Nunavut settlement area and now known as Nunavut Tunngavik Inc.). The *Nunavut Agreement* settles the Inuit's comprehensive claim over a large portion of the central NWT and the eastern Arctic. Their claim covered more than 2 million square kilometres.[29]

The TFN claim was initially submitted to the federal government by the Inuit Tapirisat of Canada (ITC) (representing the Inuit nationally) in February 1976. The claim was amended and resubmitted to the federal government in December 1977. The Inuit proposals for a new territory (Nunavut) made little progress during 1978 and 1979. By 1980, negotiations resumed on the understanding that the issue of a

---

26   Ibid., para. 67.

27   *Re Eskimos*, 5 C.N.L.C. 123 (S.C.C.).

28   *Nunavut Land Claims Agreement* (Ottawa: DIAND, 1993).

29   For an historical perspective, see R.Q. Duffy, *The Road to Nunavut: The Progress of the Eastern Arctic Inuit Since the Second World War* (Kingston & Montreal: McGill-Queen's University Press, 1988).

new territory would be negotiated outside of the comprehensive claims frame-work. The ITC was replaced by the TFN as the negotiating vehicle for the Inuit in 1982. Although a number of sub-agreements were in place by 1986, it was not until April 30, 1990, that the agreement-in-principle was signed at Igloolik, NWT.

The agreement provides that the Inuit receive title to approximately 350,000 square kilometres of land, including 36,300 square kilometres of land over which they have mineral rights. The Inuit receive $580 million to be paid over 14 years to the beneficiaries of the agreement. A Nunavut Wildlife Management Board with equal public and Inuit representation is to be created. As well, three national parks are proposed for the area affected. The Inuit are guaranteed equal representation on a number of administrative boards responsible for land management, environ-mental and socio-economic reviews, wildlife management, and water use. Finally, the agreement ensures that the federal government will recommend legislation to Parliament to create a Nunavut Territory, in addition to the Yukon and the NWT.

The *Nunavut Agreement* is like other land claims agreements, in that the Inuit agree to

> [c]ede, release and surrender to Her Majesty in Right of Canada, all their aboriginal claims, rights, title and interests, if any, in and to lands and waters anywhere within Canada and adjacent offshore areas within the sovereignty or jurisdiction of Canada.

In addition, the Inuit agree not to assert any legal action against Canada based on Aboriginal rights, claims, title, or interests.

In 1999, the Nunavut Territory comes into existence. By dividing the NWT in two, the *Nunavut Agreement* has generated a great amount of political and admin-istrative work for the Inuit and their leadership, as well as for the government of the NWT. The NWT is currently dealing with numerous land claims, specific claims, self-government negotiations, and the inevitability of the creation of the Nunavut Territory. This massive change in the political, economic, and administrative real-ity of the NWT will have major effects on the majority Aboriginal population in Nunavut and on their claims and various negotiations.

An interesting decision that affects the understanding of s. 35(3) and the po-tential weight of constitutionalized land claims agreements is *Nunavut Tunngavik Inc.(N.T.I.)* v. *Canada (Minister of Fisheries and Oceans).*[30] N.T.I. applied to have a decision made by the minister of Fisheries and Oceans dealing with turbot quotas affecting an area within the area set aside in the boundaries of the *Nunavut Agree-ment.* N.T.I. maintained that the minister failed to consider the advice of the *Agree-ment*'s Nunavut Wildlife Management Board (NWMB). The court granted the ap-plication, stating that the *Agreement* requires shared decision-making regarding those areas within the mandate of the NWMB. The minister's authority is not abso-lute, and the minister is obligated to consider the advice of the NWMB. Considera-tion requires that the relationship between the minister and the NWMB be manda-tory, close, cooperative, and highly respectful. The *Nunavut Agreement* is a sol-emn arrangement and the agreement must be given full force and effect.

---

30   *Nunavut Tunngavik Inc.(N.T.I.)* v. *Canada (Minister of Fisheries and Oceans),* [1997]
     4 C.N.L.R. 193 (F.C.T.D.).

■ CASES AND MATERIALS

THE MÉTIS

1. *Manitoba Act, 1870*, ss. 30–32, R.S.C. 1985, App. II, No. 8, and *Constitution Act, 1982*, s. 35(2)

30. All ungranted or waste lands in the Province shall be, from and after the date of the said transfer, vested in the Crown, and administered by the Government of Canada for the purposes of the Dominion, subject to, and except and so far as the same may be affected by, the conditions and stipulations contained in the agreement for the surrender of Rupert's Land by the Hudson's Bay Company to Her Majesty.

31. And whereas, it is expedient, towards the extinguishment of the Indian Title to the lands in the Province, to appropriate a portion of such ungranted lands, to the extent of one million four hundred thousand acres thereof, for the benefit of the families of the half-breed residents, it is hereby enacted, that, under regulations to be from time to time made by the Governor General in Council, the Lieutenant-Governor shall select such lots or tracts in such parts of the Province as he may deem expedient, to the extent aforesaid, and divide the same among the children of the half-breed heads of families residing in the Province at the time of the said transfer to Canada, and the same shall be granted to the said children respectively, in such mode and on such conditions as to settlement and otherwise, as the Governor General in Council may from time to time determine. . . .

32. For the quieting of titles, and assuring to the settlers in the province the peaceable possession of the lands now held by them, it is enacted as follows:
   1. All grants of land in freehold made by the Hudson's Bay Company up to the eighth day of March, in the year 1869, shall, if required by the owner, be confirmed by grant from the Crown.
   2. All grants of estates less than freehold in land made by the Hudson's Bay Company up to the eighth day of March aforesaid, shall, if required by the owner, be converted into an estate in free-hold by grant from the Crown.
   3. All titles by occupancy with the sanction and under the license and authority of the Hudson's Bay Company up to the eighth day of March aforesaid, of land in that part of the Province in which the Indian Title has been extinguished, shall, if required by the owner, be converted into an estate in freehold by grant from the Crown.
   4. All persons in peaceable possession of tracts of land at the time of the transfer to Canada, in those parts of the Province in which the Indian Title has not been extinguished, shall have the right of pre-emption of the same, on such terms and conditions as may be determined by the Governor in Council.
   5. The Lieutenant-Governor is hereby authorized, under regulations to be made from time to time by the Governor General in Council, to make all such provisions for ascertaining and adjusting, on fair and

equitable terms, the rights of Common, and rights of cutting Hay held and enjoyed by the settlers in the Province, and for the commutation of the same by grants of land from the Crown.

Constitution Act, 1982, s. 35(2) . . .

(2) In this Act, "aboriginal peoples of Canada" includes the Indian, Inuit and Métis peoples of Canada.

2.   *Manitoba Metis Federation Inc.* v. *Attorney-General of Canada (sub nom. Dumont* v. *A.-G. Canada),* [1988] 3 C.N.L.R. 39 (Man. C.A.). O'Sullivan, Huband, Philp, Twaddle, and Lyon JJ.A., June 17, 1988

> This decision concerns an application by the federal government to have the state-ment of claim of the Manitoba Metis Federation struck because there was no cause of action. The Manitoba Metis Federation and individual Métis sought a declaration that various federal and provincial statutes and orders-in-council enacted during the 1870s and 1880s were unconstitutional because they had the effect of depriving the Métis of land to which they were entitled under the *Manitoba Act, 1870.*
>
> A majority of the Court of Appeal agreed with the federal attorney-general and held that the impugned legislation did not negatively affect Métis rights. Section 31 of the *Manitoba Act* did not create a communal interest in the land for Métis, but rather individual rights. Thus, the Manitoba Metis Federation did not have a cause of action. O'Sullivan J.A. dissented and held that s. 35 of the *Constitution Act, 1982* recognizes and affirms Métis rights. The Manitoba Metis Federation, and the individual Métis, were in a good position to enforce these rights. Finally, O'Sullivan stated that the *Manitoba Act, 1870* was not merely a statute, it represented a treaty negotiated be-tween the Crown and the Métis people.

TWADDLE J.A.:—The plaintiffs challenge the constitutional validity of several pieces of federal legislation enacted between 1871 and 1886. They say the legislation was unconstitutional because it altered provisions of the *Manitoba Act,* S.C. 1870, c. 3, contrary to the prohibition against such alteration contained in the *Constitution Act, 1871* (U.K. c. 28). The Attorney General of Canada seeks to abort the chal-lenge on the ground, amongst others, that the validity of the impugned legislation is a matter of academic interest only.

The learned judge in Motions Court, who dismissed the Attorney General's application to strike out the claim, understood the plaintiffs' claim to be that the allegedly invalid legislation had deprived the plaintiffs' forebears of a community of interest in land which, but for the legislation, would have been inherited by the plaintiffs as the descendants of those to whom the community of interest was given. Based on this understanding of the plaintiffs' case, the learned judge dismissed the application to strike out the claim. It is from the order dismissing his application that the Attorney General of Canada now appeals. . . .

Doubts having been expressed as to the authority of the Parliament of Canada to establish the Province of Manitoba, the United Kingdom Parliament enacted the *Constitution Act, 1871,* which retroactively validated the *Manitoba Act.* Section 6 of the *Constitution Act, 1871* provided:

6. Except as provided by the third section of this Act, it shall not be competent for the Parliament of Canada to alter the provisions of the last-mentioned Act of the said Parliament in so far as it relates to the Province of Manitoba, or of any other Act hereafter establishing new Provinces in the said Dominion, subject always to the right of the Legislature of the Province of Manitoba to alter from time to time the provisions of any law respecting the qualification of electors and members of the Legislative Assembly and to make laws respecting elections in the said Province.

Subsequent legislation enacted by the Parliament of Canada and by the Governor General in Council regulated the allocation of land to half-breed children and the making of claims to land under s. 32 of the *Manitoba Act*. The plaintiffs allege that the subsequent legislation went beyond mere regulation. They say that it altered or embellished the original statutory provisions. They also say that this alteration or embellishment was contrary to the provisions of s. 6 of the *Constitution Act, 1871*.

I must say that, when I read the impugned legislation, I do not find provisions which can readily be regarded as alterations to the original enactment. Indeed, one of the impugned statutes actually conferred additional rights on individual half-breeds (S.C. 1874, c. 20). I do not find it necessary, however, to decide this appeal on the basis that the plaintiffs do not have a reasonable cause of action. It is my view that this appeal can be decided on the question of whether the issue which the plaintiffs wish to raise is justifiable.

Before turning to that question, let me make it clear that, for the purpose of this appeal, I assume the truth of all allegations of fact contained in the statement of claim. Those allegations include the allegation that all half-breeds of 1870 were "Métis"; that the Métis of 1870 were a distinct people; and that all their descendants are included within the undefined group of persons constitutionally recognized today as "the Métis people." These allegations which I assume as true also include the allegation that some half-breeds of 1870 did not receive, or were deprived of, constitutionally entrenched rights and the allegation that their loss of those rights was a result of the impugned legislation. . . .

It is, in any event, impossible to construe s. 31 of the *Manitoba Act* as conferring on half-breed children generally a community of interest in the 1,400,000 acres appropriated for the benefit of the families of half-breed residents. The section makes it quite clear that the land was to he divided "among the children of the half-breed heads of families residing in the Province" and "granted to the said children respectively." . . .

The *Constitution Act, 1982* recognized the Métis as an aboriginal people. The enactment also recognized the existing aboriginal rights of the Métis, whatever they were. The proclamation of 1984 recognized the future rights which the Métis might acquire by way of a land claims agreement. The federal government has expressed a willingness to negotiate a settlement of the claim. Once it has been settled, the rights which the agreement confers on the Métis will be part of the Constitution of Canada Until then, the federal government is obliged to do no more than negotiate with the Métis in good faith.

The legal basis of the land claim is a matter of great uncertainty. Unlike the Nishga Indian Tribe in *Calder* v. *Attorney-General of British Columbia*, [1973]

S.C.R. 313, 34 D.L.R. (3d) 145, the Métis people did not occupy a clearly defined area of land and only on one side of their families can they show descent from persons who inhabited the land from time immemorial. Even if they had aboriginal rights prior to July 15, 1870, these rights may have been extinguished by the *Manitoba Act* or its subsequent validation. The issue of extinguishment divided the Supreme Court of Canada in the *Calder* case. It cannot be assumed that it will be resolved in favour of the Métis.

The federal government will be influenced in its negotiations with the Métis by many considerations. As well as by the Métis claim to legal rights, the federal government will be influenced by social and political considerations and by the historical circumstances which have resulted in the Métis being an aboriginal people without a land base. Those historical circumstances include the effects of the impugned legislation on the land holdings of individual Métis. The federal government will be able to consider those effects regardless of the legislation's constitutional validity. . . .

For these reasons, I am of the opinion that the appeal should be allowed, the order made in Motions Court set aside and an order made striking out the plaintiffs' claim against the Attorney General of Canada. . . .

O'SULLIVAN J.A.: (dissenting) . . . The problem confronting us is how can the rights of the Métis people as a people be asserted. Must they turn to international bodies or to the conscience of humanity to obtain redress for their grievances as a people, or is it possible for us at the request of their representatives, to recognize their people claims as justiciable?

Whatever may have been the case prior to 1982, I think it is indisputable that the Canadian Constitution recognizes the existence of aboriginal peoples of Canada and that the Métis are an aboriginal people. Section 35 of the *Constitution Act, 1982* reads as follows:

> 35.(1) The existing aboriginal and treaty rights of the aboriginal peoples of Canada are hereby recognized and affirmed.
>
> (2) In this Act, "aboriginal peoples of Canada" includes the Indian, Inuit and Métis peoples of Canada.
>
> (3) For greater certainty, in subsection (1) "treaty rights" includes rights that now exist by way of land claims agreements or may be so acquired. . . .

I know there is a school of thought that says that the framers of the Constitution were of the view that the Métis people as such had no rights and that a cruel deception was practised on them and on the Queen whose duty it is to respect the treaties and understandings that she has entered into with her Métis people. But I do not subscribe to this school of thought.

In my opinion, it is impossible in our jurisprudence to have rights without a remedy and the rights of the Métis people must be capable of being asserted by somebody. If not by the present plaintiffs, then by whom?

It must be noted that the existence of the Métis people is asserted in the Constitution as of the present, not simply as of the past. Each individual plaintiff can, I think, prove indisputably his membership in the Métis nation. Their genealogical records are unparalleled in modern societies. See Sprague and Frye, *The Geneal-*

ogy of the First Métis Nation (1983). In any event, the question of their membership in this nation should not be called into question at the preliminary stage of a motion to strike out.

I may say in parenthesis that I find it most extraordinary that as I understand it the federal government should be funding a lawsuit which the government's Attorney General is simultaneously attempting to kill at birth.

One of the difficulties in enforcing the rights of native peoples is that they are difficult to define in common-law terms. Even the question of membership in a people may provide perplexing issues. But that a half-breed people existed as a people in the western plains of British North America in 1869 can hardly be doubted by those familiar with the history of this country. The half-breeds formed the overwhelming majority of the population of the Red River colony and had achieved such a degree of self-awareness as a people that with the acquiescence of Donald A. Smith and under the chairmanship of Judge Black they were able to form a provisional government which maintained law and order for many months in 1870. This provisional government may not have been recognized by some of the Canadian settlers in Ruperts' land, but it was recognized by the British government which entered into negotiations with delegates appointed by the convention that sanctioned and elected the provisional government.

The *Manitoba Act* sanctioned by Imperial legislation, is not only a statute; it embodies a treaty which was entered into between the delegates of the Red River settlement and the Imperial authority. Although some historians have suggested that concessions made to the Métis were "granted" by Macdonald, the truth is that the negotiations proceeded in the presence of Imperial delegates. . . .

It has been accepted by everyone that the aboriginal rights could not be lost save by the consent of those who enjoyed them. If the Métis people did not give up their aboriginal rights by agreeing to accept the provisions of the *Manitoba Act* in lieu thereof, then the aboriginal rights of this people must still subsist.

But when they state the rights given to them under the *Manitoba Act* were given to them as a people and not simply as individuals, they are met with incomprehension.

As I understand the claim of the plaintiffs they say that the rights which the Métis were led to expect they had as a result of their agreement to give up their aboriginal titles were never honoured and they are seeking in a variety of ways to assert their grievances as a result.

One of the things which stands in the way of their claim is that the federal and provincial legislatures and governments have passed a series of statutes and regulations which were designed to have the effect, and did have the effect, of rendering nugatory the scheme which the Métis representatives had negotiated.

That scheme envisioned the developing of tracts of land en bloc to the extent of 1,400,000 acres in Manitoba. The people say they expected to have the land surveyed and allotted in such a way as to enable the half-breeds to continue their way of life which was not to live in isolated square sections, but in communities with community resources, with provision not only for individual cultivation but also for common pasturage and hunting. This point of view was put clearly enough in the negotiations by one of the delegates, Msgr. Ritchot, in the following words as set out in his diary for May 2, 1870:

> We continued to claim 1,500,000 acres and we agreed on the mode of distribution as
> follows: the land will be chosen throughout the province by each lot and in several
> different lots and in various places, if it is judged to be proper by the local legislature
> which ought itself to distribute these parcels of lands to heads of families in proportion
> to the number of children existing at the time of the distribution; that these lands
> should then be distributed among the children by their parents or guardians, always
> under the supervision of the above-mentioned local legislature which could pass laws
> to ensure the continuance of these lands in the Métis families. [W.L. Morton, *Manitoba:
> The Birth of a Province*]

The governments knew well how to allot land in such a way as to enable a
community to live as such. They were able to accommodate the Mennonites by the
eastern reserve and the western reserve and they were able to accommodate the
French-Canadians on Pembina mountain. There, settlers were not given land at
random; land was allotted only to persons who shared common values.

Many of the Métis themselves proved how possible it was to allot land in
accordance with their customs by themselves setting up settlements on the banks
of the Saskatchewan after it became clear to them that the government's understanding of the "treaty" they made was different from theirs. As to these settlements,
reference may be made to Beal and Macleod, *Prairie Fire* (Toronto 1984).

The plaintiffs want court declarations nullifyng the laws which, according to
them, amended and changed the *Manitoba Act* in an unconstitutional way. . . .

Since constitutional facts can only be ascertained by a process quite foreign to
the ordinary trial procedures, it may be that justice with regard to minorities can
only be attained by the creation of constitutional courts or by developing within
the existing court system a special process for dealing with constitutional facts. A
time-honoured method of dealing with the kind of claim now before us is the Royal
Commission and that may be at the present time the best way to deal with the claim
of the Métis.

Nevertheless, I think it is important to accept that the claims asserted by the
plaintiffs in the present action are justiciable and not merely political. The plaintiffs have status to assert their claims in the Court of Queen's Bench. I am sure the
judge assigned to try the case will have a difficult time and will have to be able to
adapt the process of the court to suit the nature of the case. But, in the end, in my
opinion it is in the development of law to deal with claims of "peoples" that lies the
best hope of achieving justice and harmony in a world full of minority groups.

3.   *Dumont v. Attorney-General of Canada (sub nom. Manitoba Metis Fed. v.
     A.-G. Canada)*, [1990] 2 C.N.L.R. 19 (S.C.C.). Dickson C.J.C., Wilson, La
     Forest, Sopinka, Gonthier, Cory, and McLachlin JJ., March 2, 1990

> The Supreme Court of Canada unanimously overturned the Manitoba Court of Appeal
> decision and held that the Métis application for a declaration did not have a "plain and
> obvious" conclusion or outcome that was "beyond doubt." The issue of whether or
> not certain pieces of legislation violated Métis rights recognized by the *Manitoba Act,
> 1870* is a justiciable issue.

DICKSON C.J.C. (orally):—We are all of the view that this appeal succeeds. The judgment of the Court will be delivered by Mme. Justice Wilson.

WILSON J. (orally):—The members of the Court are all of the view that the test laid down in *Attorney General of Canada* v. *Inuit Tapirisat*, [1980] 2 S.C.R. 735 for striking out a statement of claim is not met in this case. It cannot be said that the outcome of the case is "plain and obvious" or "beyond doubt".

Issues as to the proper interpretation of the relevant provisions of the *Manitoba Act* of 1870 and the *Constitution Act* of 1871 and the effect of the impugned ancillary legislation upon them would appear to be better determined at trial where a proper factual base can be laid.

The Court is of the view also that the subject matter of the dispute, inasmuch as it involves the constitutionality of legislation ancillary to the *Manitoba Act*, is justiciable in the courts and that declaratory relief may be granted in the discretion of the court in aid of extra-judicial claims in an appropriate case.

We see no reason, therefore, why the action should not proceed to trial. The appeal is accordingly allowed and the order of the Court of Appeal striking out the appellants' claim against the Attorney General of Canada is set aside.

4. *R.* v. *McPherson*, [1994] 2 C.N.L.R. 137 (Man. Q.B.). Schulman J., January 19, 1994

McPherson is important in that it states that where provincial laws of general application have been found inapplicable to Aboriginal peoples because these laws conflict with treaty rights or with federal legislation in relation to Indians, the legislation should be read down so as not to apply to such Aboriginal peoples. The Provincial Court, affirmed by the Court of Queen's Bench, held that the two charged Métis persons possessed hunting rights protected by s. 35(1) of the *Constitution Act, 1982*, and that these rights could be limited for conservation purposes pursuant to the *Sparrow* justificatory analysis. (See chapter 7.) The *Sparrow* standard of justification was not met in this instance due to both a lack of consultation with the Métis and a lack of priority for Métis hunting rights.

SCHULMAN J.:—These applications are summary conviction appeals. The Crown appealed, and the defence cross-appealed, against the decision made by the Honourable Judge Gregoire on charges that Mr. McPherson and Mr. Christie, on or about the 6th day of January 1990, at or near Wanless, in Manitoba, did unlawfully kill a wild animal during the period of the year prohibited or not permitted, contrary to s. 26 of the *Wildlife Act*, C.C.S.M., c. W130.

The trial of these charges took place over four days between February 20, 1992 and July 3, 1992. At the conclusion of the trial, Gregoire P.C.J. reserved decision. At the trial, Crown counsel sought a conviction; defence counsel sought an acquittal.

On September 4, 1992, the learned Provincial Court Judge made the following findings ([1992] 4 C.N.L.R. 144):

(a) The respondents relied to a significant extent upon their hunting, fishing and gathering skills for their survival and to supplement the income which they earned.

(b)   The respondents were the progeny of ancestors who also relied on these skills and the hunt for their subsistence.

(c)   The respondents were acknowledged Métis.

(d)   The respondents had Aboriginal hunting rights.

(e)   The hunting rights of the respondents had not been extinguished.

(f)   The Regulations passed pursuant to s. 26 of the *Wildlife Act* under which the Respondents were charged, were an infringement of the hunting rights of the respondents.

(g)   The Crown had not justified its infringement of the hunting rights of the respondent.

Based on these findings, the learned Provincial Court Judge convicted Mr. McPherson and Mr. Christie. He also made the following orders:

(a)   declaring that the provisions of the regulations under the *Wildlife Act* establishing open and closed hunting seasons under which Mr. McPherson and Mr. Christie were charged are of no force and effect;

(b)   suspending the declaration of invalidity until August 1, 1994; and

(c)   directing the Crown, in the interim, to enact new regulations which would provide for the registration of those Métis who rely on subsistence hunting as a way of life, and permit such Métis to harvest the number of moose which would be reasonably required to feed their families, in priority over non-Aboriginal hunters.

He disposed of the charges by imposing conditional discharges for a period of three months on the condition that Mr. McPherson and Mr. Christie assist the proper officers of the Crown in establishing the register of Metis who rely upon subsistence hunting as a way of life.

Although the order directing the Crown to enact new regulations was not made expressly, it is the clear implication from:

•   the declaration of invalidity

•   the suspension of the declaration

•   the statement made at p. 34 [1992] 4 C.N.L.R. 144 (Prov. Ct.) [p. 156 C.N.L.R.] of the reasons, "To assist in determining its trust relationship, the province of Manitoba is entitled to direction from court as to which persons of Metis ancestry have, in fact, an Aboriginal right to hunt."

•   the statement at p. 44, "Because of the nature of what the crown has to do . . . As well, they'll have to draft comprehensive regulations to ascertain which Métis are close to the land . . ."

•   the condition of the discharge imposed on Mr. McPherson and Mr. Christie, and

•   the statement at p. 50, ". . . you're now partially responsible for part of the solution that I have ordered."

The Crown appealed against the declaration of invalidity and the orders made. Mr. McPherson and Mr. Christie cross-appealed against their convictions and sentences. . . .

2.   It appears that the learned Provincial Court Judge adopted the view that he could only affirm the hunting rights of Mr. McPherson and Mr. Christie by finding that the regulations in question are invalid. It is arguable that the preferable

course would have been to hold that the *Wildlife Act* and regulations simply do not apply to Mr. McPherson and Mr. Christie, and this is the approach which has been adopted in cases where provincial laws of general application are found to be inapplicable to Aboriginals because they conflict with treaty rights or the federal legislation in relation to Indians. See, for example, *Derrickson* v. *Derrickson*, [1986] 1 S.C.R. 285, at 296 [1986] 2 C.N.L.R. 45 at 55–56; *Simon* v. *The Queen*, [1985] 2 S.C.R. 387 [1986] 1 C.N.L.R.; *R.* v. *Sioui*, [1990] 1 S.C.R. 1025 [1990] 3 C.N.L.R. 127. . . .

> 3.   It is arguable that the direction to create a registry for Metis persons under the *Wildlife Act* is unconstitutional in light of the provisions of s. 91(24) of the *Constitution Act, 1867*, and the decision of the Supreme Court of Canada in *Reference as to whether "Indians" in s. 91(24) of B.N.A. Act includes Eskimos and inhabitants of the Province of Quebec*, [1939] S.C.R. 104.

> 4.   There was a better solution to the problem which the Provincial Court Judge found to exist. A better solution would involve the implementation of a co-management agreement. By that phrase I understood him to mean that the most satisfactory solution to the problem could best be achieved by negotiation of a solution by the federal government, the provincial government and representatives of the Metis community. . . .

In my view, the above-mentioned submissions are substantial, and if submissions had been made to Gregoire P.C.J. he might have reached a different conclusion than he did as to the appropriate remedy to be given in the circumstances of this case. Because these appeals were argued as part of a joint submission, I would prefer not to make a final decision on the issues raised in paragraphs 1, 3 and 4. It would be preferable, before giving a decision as to such important matters, that argument be heard from counsel whose clients are adverse in interest on the various points.

I have reached the conclusion, however, that these appeals should be allowed on the following bases: . . .

> 2.   I am certain, after reading the reasons for judgment of the learned Provincial Court Judge, that had he not felt that he could create a broad solution to the problem which was presented to him, he would have acquitted Mr. McPherson and Mr. Christie. Following his discussion of the *Schacter* case, he gave consideration to the constitutional concepts of reading in a remedy, or in the alternative, to invalidating the statute in question. He also considered and gave effect to the doctrine of suspending the invalidity of a statute. In his reasons, however, he did not expressly give consideration to the possibility of reading down the *Wildlife Act* so as to confine its operation to the limits of provincial jurisdiction. I accept the submission of Crown counsel that there is substantial authority to support a finding that, where provincial laws of general application have been found to be inapplicable to Aboriginal persons because they conflict with treaty rights or federal legislation in relation to Indians, the legislation should be read down so as not to apply to such Aboriginal persons. As Chouinard J. stated in the *Derrickson* case at p. 296 [S.C.R.; p. 55 C.N.L.R.]:

> > When otherwise valid provincial legislation, given the generality of its terms, extends beyond the matter over which the legislature has jurisdiction and over a matter of

federal exclusive jurisdiction, it must, in order to preserve its constitutionality, be read down and given the limited meaning which will confine it within the limits of the provincial jurisdiction.

It follows that the provisions of the *Family Relations Act* dealing with the right of ownership and possession of immovable property, while valid in respect of other immovable property, cannot apply to lands on an Indian reserve.

I assume that the learned Provincial Court Judge was aware of the doctrine and chose a different solution to the problem in the hope that he could provide a broader solution than is required for the purpose of this case. In doing so, I find that he erred and that he ought to have followed the well-carved remedy provided for in the *Derrickson* case. In my opinion, the regulations passed pursuant to s. 26 of the *Wildlife Act* should be interpreted in such a way that they do not apply to Mr. McPherson and Mr. Christie. In my view, it is as appropriate to read down these regulations in order to preserve the Aboriginal right which exists in this case as it was to read down the *Family Relations Act*, R.S.B.C. 1979, c. 121, in order to preserve the Aboriginal right in the *Derrickson* case.

At the conclusion of oral argument I advised the parties that I had been persuaded to make the following orders:
1.   I allowed the appeal and cross-appeal;
2.   I acquitted Mr. Mcpherson and Mr. Christie of the charge;
3.   I set aside the orders made by the learned Provincial Court Judge referred to on p. 2 [p. 138 supra] of these reasons.

I stated that I would provide reasons for my decision, and I have attempted to provide them herewith.

5.   *Delgamuukw* v. *British Columbia*, [1993] 5 C.N.L.R., (B.C.C.A.). Taggart, Lambert, Hutcheon, Macfarlane, and Wallace JJ.A., June 25, 1993

MACFARLANE J.A. (TAGGART J.A., concurring):— . . . I have one more observation with respect to the consideration of a time depth component in determining the existence of Aboriginal rights.

It has been said that the inclusion of the Métis in s. 35 of the *Constitution Act, 1982* as one of the categories of persons benefitting from Aboriginal rights guarantees must exclude any time depth consideration when proving Aboriginal rights. But the Métis, although sharing a common constitutional basis for the protection of their rights, are unique. Certainly, they have a unique history and a different cultural makeup which sets them apart from other Aboriginal groups. Their traditional ties to the land and each other are different. The Métis distinction is advanced with pride by the Métis people and should not be treated dismissively.

The requirement that the plaintiffs' practices had to be traditional before qualifying for the protection of the common law as Aboriginal rights may involve a time consideration which has no parallel in the determination of the Aboriginal rights of the Métis.

I should add that the application of the federal jurisdiction in s. 91(24) to the Métis people may well also involve special considerations. At least, the manner in which this jurisdiction applies to the Métis remains a question to be decided in future cases. . . .

6.   *Constitution of Alberta Amendment Act,* 1990, S.A. c. C–22.2

WHEREAS the Metis were present when the Province of Alberta was established and they and the land set aside for their use form a unique part of the history and culture of the Province; and

WHEREAS it is desired that the Metis should continue to have a land base to provide for the preservation and enhancement of Metis culture and identity and to enable the Metis to attain self-governance under the laws of Alberta and, to that end, Her Majesty in right of Alberta is granting title to land to the Metis Settlements General Council; and

WHEREAS Her Majesty in right of Alberta has proposed the land so granted be protected by the Constitution of Canada, but until that happens it is proper that the land be protected by the constitution of the Province; and

WHEREAS section 45 of the *Constitution Act, 1982* empowers the legislature of a province, subject to section 41 of that Act, to amend the constitution of the province; and

WHEREAS nothing in this Act, the *Metis Settlements Land Protection Act,* the *Metis Settlements Accord Implementation Act* or the *Metis Settlements Act* is to be construed so as to abrogate or derogate from any aboriginal rights referred to in section 35 of the *Constitution Act, 1982;*

NOW THEREFORE HER MAJESTY, by and with the advice and consent of the Legislative Assembly of Alberta, enacts as follows:

Constitution amended
1   The constitution of Alberta is amended by this Act.

Definition
2   In this Act, "Metis settlement land" means land held in fee simple by the Metis Settlements General Council under letters patent from Her Majesty in right of Alberta.

Expropriation
3   The fee simple estate in Metis settlement land, or any interest in it less than fee simple, may not be acquired through expropriation by Her Majesty in right of Alberta or any person, but an interest less than fee simple may be acquired in that land in a manner permitted by the *Metis Settlements Land Protection Act.*

Exemption from seizure
4   The fee simple estate in Metis settlement land is exempt from seizure and sale under court order, writ of execution or any other process whether judicial or extra-judicial.

Restriction on Legislative Assembly

5   The Legislative Assembly may not pass any Bill that would

(a) amend or repeal the *Metis Settlements Land Protection Act,*

(b) alter or revoke letters patent granting Metis settlement land to the Metis Settlements General Council, or

(c) dissolve the Metis Settlements General Council or result in its being composed of persons who are not settlement members, without the agreement of the Metis Settlements General Council.

Application of laws

6   Nothing in this Act shall be construed as limiting

(a) the application of the laws of Alberta to, or

(b) the jurisdiction of the Legislature to enact laws in and for Alberta applicable to, the Metis settlement land and any activities on or in respect of that land, except to the extent necessary to give effect to this Act.

Power to affect Act

7   A Bill that would amend or repeal this Act may be passed by the Legislative Assembly of Alberta only after a plebiscite of settlement members under the Election Act where a majority of the members of each settlement vote in favour of the subject-matter of the Bill.

Repeal

8   Notwithstanding section 7, this Act may be repealed by the Legislature after the Metis settlement land is protected by the Constitution of Canada.

Coming into force

9   This Act comes into force on Proclamation.

7.   *Metis Settlements Act,* c. M–14.3

Proclaimed on November 1, 1990, the *Metis Settlements Act* is part of a package of Alberta legislation that seeks to provide a governance and land tenure regime for some Métis in Alberta. It is the only such example of legislation relating exclusively to the Métis, on this scale, in Canada.

METIS SETTLEMENTS ACT . . .

(2) Each settlement consists of the persons who are settlement members of that settlement. . . .

3(1) Subject to this Act, a settlement has the rights, powers and privileges of a natural person.

(2) A settlement council may carry out the following activities only if it is permitted to do so under subsection (3):

(a) engage in commercial activities,

(b) make investments other than those described in Schedule 2,

(c) lend money,

(d) borrow money,

(e) guarantee the repayment of a loan by a lender to someone other than the settlement, or

(f) guarantee the payment of interest on a loan by a lender to someone other than the settlement.

(3) A settlement council may do some or all of the activities described in subsection (2) if

(a) a regulation passed under section 239 or 240 approves the activity, or

(b) the activity is

> (i) authorized by a General Council Policy, and
>
> (ii) permitted by a settlement by-law. . .

8(1)Each settlement has a settlement council composed of 5 councillors.

(2) A settlement council is a continuing body. . . . .

10(1) At the organizational meeting of a settlement council after an annual election, the councillors must elect a settlement chairman from among themselves. . . . .

12(1) An annual election must be held for each settlement council.

Election procedure
13(1) Councillors must be elected to a settlement council in accordance with the *Local Authorities Election Act* and this Act.

(2) If there is inconsistency between this Act and the *Local Authorities Election Act,* this Act prevails.

(3) If the *Local Authorities Election Act* or this Act cannot be applied to an election under this Act, the Minister may make regulations governing the matter.

Eligibility to vote
14 No person is eligible to vote at an annual election or by-election unless that person

(a) is a settlement member,

(b) has resided in the settlement area for the 12 months immediately preceding election day, or any lesser period prescribed in a settlement by-law, and

(c) has his or her principal residence in the settlement area on election day. . . .

50(1) Except where the context otherwise requires, the by-law making authority of a settlement council is confined to the geographic area of the settlement. . . .

51 A settlement council may make by-laws respecting

(a) the matters set out in Schedule 1;
(b) the matters described or referred to elsewhere in this Act and in other enactments. . . .

63(1) A settlement council may state the maximum penalty that can be imposed by a court if a by-law made under this Act or any other enactment is contravened.

(2) The maximum penalty may be included in a general penalty by-law or in the by-law in respect of which the penalty is to apply.

(3) The penalties that can be included in by-laws are:
(a) a fine not exceeding $2500;
(b) a minimum and maximum fine applicable to first, 2nd or subsequent offences, but the maximum fine for each offence must not exceed $2500;
(c) imprisonment for any period up to 6 months if a fine is not paid.

(4) In addition to any other fine or penalty that a court may impose under this Act or any other enactment or any by-law made under this Act or any other enactment, the court may
(a) when a conviction is for non-payment of money payable to a settlement, also order payment of that sum of money, and
(b) when a conviction is for the failure or refusal of a person to comply with a by-law, order that the person comply with the by-law. . . .

72(1) A by-law or resolution that is inconsistent with this Act or any other enactment is of no effect to the extent of the inconsistency, unless it is a by-law or resolution to implement a General Council Policy on hunting, trapping, fishing or gathering.

(2) A by-law or resolution that is inconsistent with a General Council Policy is of no effect to the extent of the inconsistency.

Regulations
73 The Minister may, in accordance with section 240, make regulations
(a) respecting an administrative and employment policy to be followed by the settlement council and its employees;
(b) respecting payments to be made to councillors, settlement employees and representatives of a settlement. . . .

74(1) A person may apply to a settlement council for membership in a settlement only if
(a) the applicant is a Metis and at least 18 years old, and
(b) the applicant
    (i) has previously been a settlement member or a member of a settlement association under the former Act, or
    (ii) has lived in Alberta for the 5 years immediately preceding the date of application. . . .

75(1) An Indian registered under the *Indian Act* (Canada) or a person who is registered as an Inuk for the purposes of a land claims settlement is not eligible to apply for membership or to be recorded as a settlement member unless subsection (2) applies.

(2) An Indian registered under the *Indian Act* (Canada) or a person who is registered as an Inuk for the purposes of a land claims settlement may be approved as a settlement member if
(a) the person was registered as an Indian or an Inuk when less than 18 years old,
(b) the person lived a substantial part of his or her childhood in the settlement area,
(c) one or both parents of the person are, or at their death were, members of the settlement, and
(d) the person has been approved for membership by a settlement by-law specifically authorizing the admission of that individual as a member of the settlement.

(3) If a person who is registered as an Indian under the *Indian Act* (Canada) is able to apply to have his or her name removed from registration, subsection (2) ceases to be available as a way to apply for or to become a settlement member. . . .

76   Every application for membership in a settlement must be sent to the settlement office and must be accompanied by
(a) a statutory declaration that
     (i) the applicant has Canadian aboriginal ancestry, describing the facts on which the declaration is based, and
     (ii) the applicant identifies with Métis history and culture;
(b) one or more of the following:
     (i) genealogical records as evidence that the applicant has aboriginal ancestry;
     (ii) a statutory declaration of at least 2 Métis who are recognized as Métis elders that the applicant has aboriginal ancestry, describing the facts on which the declaration is made;
     (iii) such other evidence satisfactory to the settlement council that the applicant has aboriginal ancestry; . . .

214(1) The Metis Settlements General Council is established as a corporation.

(2) The General Council consists of the councillors of all the settlement councils and the officers of the General Council. . . .

239(1) A regulation to be made in accordance with this section may be made, amended or repealed only if the General Council requests the Minister to make the regulation.

(2) The Minister may make, amend or repeal a regulation without a request under subsection (1) if the regulation, amendment or repeal is required to protect the public interest.

(3) Before making, amending or repealing a regulation under subsection (1) or (2), the Minister must

(a) provide the General Council with notice in writing and a copy of the proposed regulation, and

(b) give due consideration to written suggestions about the regulation that are received from the General Council within 45 days of the notice. . . .

240(1) A regulation to be made in accordance with this section may be made, amended or repealed only if the General Council or a settlement council requests the Minister to make the regulation.

(2) The Minister may make, amend or repeal a regulation without a request under subsection (1) if the regulation, amendment or repeal is required to protect the public interest. . . .

SCHEDULE 1
BY-LAWS

By-law Making Authority of Settlement Councils
General governance
1   A settlement council may make by-laws for the general governance of the settlement area. . . .

2   A settlement council may make by-laws for the internal management of the settlement, including. . . .

3   A settlement council may make by-laws
(a) describing the circumstances when a settlement member who is on an authorized leave of absence is not considered to be a resident of the settlement area;
(b) respecting the establishment of holidays in a settlement area;
(c) describing the persons who have a right to live on patented land in addition to those described in section 92;
(d) respecting those matters that may, by this or any other enactment, be subject to a settlement by-law.

Health, safety and welfare
4   A settlement council may make by-laws to promote the health, safety and welfare of the residents of the settlement area.

Public order and safety
5   A settlement council may make by-laws respecting public order and safety, including by-laws
(a) prohibiting or regulating the discharge of firearms as defined in section 84(1) of the *Criminal Code* (Canada);
(b) prohibiting or regulating activities or conduct offensive to or not in the public interest as determined by the council;

(c) establishing curfews for children who are not accompanied by a parent or appropriate guardian and providing for penalties in respect of parents or guardians whose children contravene the by-law.

Fire protection

6   A settlement council may make by-laws to prevent and extinguish fires, preserve life and property and protect persons from injury or destruction by fire, including. . . .

Nuisances and pests

7   A settlement council may make by-laws

(a) prohibiting unsightly or untidy land or buildings or anything on land that is unsightly or untidy;
(b) prohibiting or regulating noise generally or during specified periods throughout or in designated areas of the settlement area;
(c) requiring or providing for the removal or burning of trees or shrubs that may interfere with settlement works or utilities;
(d) regulating or controlling activities for the purpose of eliminating or mitigating animal or insect pests and diseases.

Animals

8   A settlement council may make by-laws

(a) preventing the leading, riding and driving of cattle or horses in any public place;
(b) prohibiting or regulating the running at large of dogs and other animals. . . .
(c) regulating the keeping by any person of poultry or wild or domestic animals;
(d) prohibiting the keeping by any person of poultry or wild or domestic animals in any specified part or parts of the settlement area when, in the opinion of the council, that keeping is likely to cause a nuisance;
(e) preventing cruelty to animals.

Airports

9   A settlement council, subject to any Act of the Parliament of Canada, may make by-laws establishing, controlling, operating or maintaining an airport, aerodrome or seaplane base.

Posters and advertising

10   A settlement council may make by-laws (a) prohibiting or regulating the posting or exhibition of pictures, posters or other material; ....

Refuse disposal

11(1) A settlement council may make by-laws

(a) defining "refuse" for the purpose of this section and the by-laws;
(b) prohibiting or regulating the placement or depositing of refuse;
(c) regulating the activities or use of waste disposal sites established by the settlement council;

(d) establishing and regulating a system for the collection and disposal of refuse.
     . . .

Public health

12   A settlement council may make by-laws

(a) respecting the health of the residents of the settlement area and against the spread of diseases;

(b) regulating and controlling the use of wells, springs and other sources of water for the settlement area and preventing the contamination of it or of any water in the settlement area;

(c) compelling the removal of dirt, filth or refuse or any other obstruction from public rights of way or private roads by the person depositing it and providing for its removal at the expense of that person if he or she fails to remove it;

(d) compelling the removal from any place within the settlement area of anything considered dangerous to the health or lives of the inhabitants.

Parks and recreation

13   A settlement council may make by-laws respecting the regulating of activities and equipment in

(a) parks or recreation areas;

(b) trailer courts or mobile home parks;

(c) campgrounds;

(d) exhibition or rodeo grounds.

Control of business

14(1) A settlement council may make by-laws to control and regulate businesses, industries and activities carried on in the settlement area, including . . .

Sewerage system fees

16(1) A settlement council may by by-law impose a service charge payable by all persons occupying property connected to the sewerage system of the settlement. . . .

17   A settlement council may by by-law impose special levies for the purposes of providing recreation and community services and facilities to residents, and may provide for the charging of admissions or the raising of funds as the council may decide.

Planning, land use and development by-laws

18   A settlement council may make by-laws

(a) establishing a general plan for land use and development in a settlement area;

(b) prohibiting or regulating and controlling the use and development of land and buildings in the settlement area;

(c) authorizing the settlement council, or a person designated by it, to prohibit the development or use of land or buildings if there are inadequate arrangements for access to, and for utilities and other services to, the land or buildings.

By-laws under a General Council Policy

19   If there is a General Council Policy in effect, a settlement council may, in accordance with that Policy, make by-laws

(a) prohibiting persons who are not settlement members from hunting, trapping, gathering or fishing in the settlement area;

(b) prescribing the terms and conditions under which a person or class of person is permitted to occupy, hunt, trap, gather or fish in the settlement area;

(c) prescribing the manner in which and the terms and conditions subject to which a settlement member may acquire
(i) the right to trap, hunt or gather in the settlement area;
(ii) the right to fish in a marsh, pond, lake, stream or creek in the settlement area and the circumstances under which that right may be suspended, limited or revoked;

(d) as to the use by settlement members of a part of the land allocated for occupation by a settlement council in respect of which no person has the exclusive right of occupation;

(e) respecting the cutting of timber on all or part of the settlement area, . . .

THE INUIT

8.   *Indian Act*, R.S.C. 1985, c. I–5 s. 4(1)

4.(1) A reference in this Act to an Indian does not include any person of the race of aborigines commonly referred to as Inuit. . . .

9.   *Re Eskimos,* [1939] 5 C.N.L.C. 123. Duff C.J.C., Cannon, Crocket, Davis, Kerwin, and Hudson JJ., April 5, 1939

In *Re Eskimos* the Supreme Court of Canada unanimously decided that the term "Indians" in s. 91(24) of the *Constitution Act, 1867* included the Inuit. As a result, the Inuit are within the legislative authority of the federal Parliament.

SIR LYMAN P. DUFF C.J.C.:—The reference with which we are concerned arises out of a controversy between the Dominion and the Province of Quebec touching the question whether the Eskimo inhabitants of that Province are "Indians" within the contemplation of head no. 24 of s. 91 of the *B.N.A. Act* which is in these words, "Indians and Lands Reserved for Indians"; and under the reference we are to pronounce upon that question. Among the inhabitants of the three Provinces, Nova Scotia, New Brunswick and Canada that, by the immediate operation of the *B.N.A. Act* became subject to the constitutional enactments of that statute there were few, if any, Eskimo. But the *B.N.A. Act* contemplated the eventual admission into the Union of other parts of British North America as is explicitly declared in the preamble and for which provision is made by s. 146 thereof.

The Eskimo population of Quebec, with which we are now concerned, inhabits (in the northern part of the Province) a territory that in 1867 formed part of

Rupert's Land; and the question we have to determine is whether these Eskimo, whose ancestors were aborigines of Rupert's Land in 1867 and at the time of its annexation to Canada, are Indians in the sense mentioned.

In 1867 the Eskimo population of what is now Canada, then between four and five thousand in number, occupied, as at the present time, the northern littoral of the continent from Alaska to, and including part of, the Labrador coast within the territories under the control of the Hudson's Bay Co., that is to say, in Rupert's Land and the North-Western Territory which, under the authority given by s. 146 of the *B.N.A. Act* were acquired by Canada in 1871. In addition to these Eskimo in Rupert's Land and the North-Western Territory, there were some hundreds of them on that part of the coast of Labrador (east of Hudson Strait) which formed part of, and was subject to the Government of, Newfoundland. The *B.N.A. Act* is a statute dealing with British North America, and, in determining the meaning of the word "Indians" in the statute, we have to consider the meaning of that term as applied to the inhabitants of British North America. In 1867 more than half of the Indian population of British North America were within the boundaries of Rupert's Land and the North-Western Territory; and of the Eskimo population nearly 90% were within those boundaries. It is, therefore, important to consult the reliable sources of information as to the usage of the term "Indian" in relation to the Eskimo in those territories. Fortunately, there is evidence of the most authoritative character furnished by the Hudson's Bay Co. itself.

It will be recalled that the Hudson's Bay Co., besides being a trading company, possessed considerable powers of government and administration. Some years before the passing of the *B.N.A. Act* complaints having been made as to the manner in which these responsibilities had been discharged, a committee of the House of Commons in 1856 and 1857 investigated the affairs of the company. Among the matters which naturally engaged the attention of the Committee was the company's relations with and conduct towards the aborigines; and for the information of the Committee a census was prepared and produced before it by the officers of the company showing the Indian populations under its rule throughout the whole of the North American continent. This census was accompanied by a map showing the "location" of the various tribes and was included in the Report of the Committee; and was made an appendix to the Committee's Report which was printed and published by the order of the House of Commons. It is indisputable that in the census and in the map the "Esquimaux" fall under the general designation "Indians" and that, indeed, in these documents, "Indians" is used as synonymous with "aborigines." The map bears this description, "An Aboriginal Map of North America denoting the boundaries and locations of various Indian Tribes." Among these "Indian Tribes" the Eskimo are shown inhabiting the northern littoral of the continent from Labrador to Russian America. In the margin of the map are tables. Two are of great significance. The first of these is headed "Statement of the Indian Tribes of the Hudson's Bay Territories." The tribes "East of the Rocky Mountains" are given as "Blackfeet and Sioux groups comprising eight tribes, Algonquins comprising twelve tribes" and "Esquimaux."

The second is headed "Indian Nations once dwelling East of the Mississippi." The list is as follows:

Algonquin	Uchee (extinct)	Kolooch
Dahcotah or Sioux	Natches (extinct)	Athabascan
Huron Iroquois	Mobilian	Sioux
Catawba (extinct)	Esquimaux	Iroquois
Cherokee		

The census concludes with a summary which is in these words: The Indian Races shown in detail in the foregoing census may be classified as follows:

Thickwood Indians on the east side of the Rocky Mountains	35,000
The Plain Tribes (Blackfeet, etc.)	25,000
The Esquimaux	4,000
Indians settled in Canada	3,000
Indian in British Oregon and on the North West Coast	80,000
Total Indians	147,000
Whites and half-breeds in Hudson's Bay Territory	11,000
Souls	158,000

. . . The *B.N.A. Act* came into force on July 1, 1867, and, in December of that year, a joint address to Her Majesty was voted by the Senate and House of Commons of Canada praying that authority might be granted to the Parliament of Canada to legislate for the future welfare and good government of these regions and expressing the willingness of Parliament to assume the duties and obligations of government and legislation as regards those territories. In the Resolution of the Senate expressing the willingness of that body to concur in the joint address is this paragraph: "Resolved that upon the transference of the Territories in question to the Canadian Government, it will be the duty of the Government to make adequate provisions for the protection of the Indian Tribes, whose interest and well being are involved in the transfer."

By Order-in-Council of June 23, 1870, it was ordered that from and after July 15, 1870, the North-West Territory and Rupert's Land should be admitted into, and become part of, the Dominion of Canada and that, from that date, the Parliament of Canada should have full power and authority to legislate for the future welfare and good government of the territory. As regards Rupert's Land, such authority had already been conferred upon the Parliament of Canada by s. 5 of the Rupert's Land Act of 1868.

The vast territories which by these transactions became part of the Dominion of Canada and were brought under the jurisdiction of the Parliament of Canada were inhabited largely, indeed almost entirely, by aborigines. It appears to me to be a consideration of great weight in determining the meaning of the word "Indians" in the *B.N.A. Act* that, as we have seen, the Eskimo were recognized as an Indian tribe by the officials of the Hudson's Bay Co. which, in 1867, as already observed, exercised powers of government and administration over this great tract; and that, moreover, this employment of the term "Indians" is evidenced in a most unequivocal way by documents prepared by those officials and produced before the Select Committee of the House of Commons which were included in the Report of that Committee which, again, as already mentioned, was printed and published by the order of the House. It is quite clear from the material before us that this Report was the principal source of information as regards the aborigines in those territories until some years after Confederation.

I turn now to the Eskimo inhabiting the coast of Labrador beyond the confines of the Hudson's Bay territories and within the boundaries and under the Government of Newfoundland. As regards these, the evidence appears to be conclusive that, for a period beginning about 1760 and extending down to a time subsequent to the passing of the *B.N.A. Act*, they were by governors, commanders-in-chief of the fleet and other naval officers, ecclesiastics, missionaries and traders who came into contact with them, known and classified as Indians.

First of the official documents. In 1762, General Murray, then Governor of Quebec, who afterwards became first Governor of Canada, in an official report of the state of the Government of Quebec deals under the sixth heading with "Indian nations residing within the government." He introduces the discussion with this sentence: "In order to discuss this point more clearly I shall first take notice of the Savages on the North shore of the River St. Lawrence from the Ocean upwards, and then of such as inhabit the South side of the same River, as far as the present limits of the Government extend on either side of it."

In the first and second paragraphs he deals with the "Savages" on the North Shore and he says: "The first to be met with on this are the Esquimaux." In the second paragraph he deals with the Montagnais who inhabited a "vast tract" of country from Labrador to the Saguenay.

It is clear that here the Eskimo are classified under the generic term Indian. They are called "Savages," it is true, but so are the Montagnais and so also the Hurons settled at Jeune Lorette. It is useful to note that he speaks in the first paragraph of the Esquimaux as "the wildest and most untamable of any" and mentions that they are "emphatically styled by the other Nations, Savages."

Then there are two reports to His Majesty by the Lords of Trade. The first, dated June 8,1763, discusses the trade carried on by the French on the coast of Labrador. It is said that they carried on "an extensive trade with the Esquimaux Indians in Oyl, Furs, & ca. [*sic*] (in which they allowed Your Majesty's Subjects no Share)."

In the second, dated April 16, 1765, in dealing with complaints on the part of the Court of France respecting the French fishery on the coast of Newfoundland and in the Gulf of St. Lawrence, their observations on these complaints are based upon information furnished by Commodore Palliser who had been entrusted with the superintendency of the Newfoundland fishery and the Government of the island. In this report, this sentence occurs: "The sixth and last head of complaint contained in the French Ambassador's letter is, that a captain of a certain French vessel was forbid by your Majesty's Governor from having commerce with the Esquimaux Indians"; and upon that it is observed that the Governor "is to be commended for having forbid the subjects of France to trade or treat with these Indians." "These Indians" are spoken of as inhabitants ". . .who are under the protection of and dependent upon your Majesty."

Then there is a series of proclamations by successive Governors and Commanders-in-Chief in Newfoundland, the first of which was that of Sir Hugh Palliser of July 1,1764. The proclamation recites, ". . . Advantages would arise to His Majesty's Trading Subjects if a Friendly Intercourse could be Established with the

Esquimaux Indians, Inhabiting the Coast of Labrador. . ." and that the Government "has taken measures for bringing about a friendly communication between the said Indians and His Majesty's subjects." All His Majesty's subjects are strictly enjoined "to treat them in the most civil and friendly manner."

The next is a proclamation by the same governor dated April 8, 1765, which recites the desirability of "friendly intercourse with the Indians on the Coast of Labrador" and that "attempts hitherto made for that purpose have proved ineffectual, especially with the Esquimaux in the Northern Ports without the Straits of Belle Isle" and strictly enjoins and requires "all his Majesty's subjects who meet with any of the said Indians to treat them in a most civil and friendly manner."

On April 10, 1772, Governor Shuldham in a Proclamation of that date requires all His Majesty's subjects coming upon the coast of Labrador to act towards the Esquimaux Indians in a manner agreeable to the Proclamation issued at St. John's the 8th day of July 1769 respecting the savages inhabiting the coast of Labrador." In this Proclamation it should be noted that "Esquimaux savages" and "Esquimaux Indians" are used as convertible expressions.

In 1774, the boundaries of Quebec were extended, and the northeastern coast of Labrador and the Eskimo population therein came under the jurisdiction of the governor of Quebec and remained so until 1809. Nevertheless, the Governor and Commander-in-Chief of Newfoundland, who at the date was Admiral Edwards, acting under the authority of that Order in Council of March 9, 1774, took measures to protect the missionaries of the Unitas Fratrum and their settlements on the coast of Labrador from molestation or disturbance and, on May 14, 1779, Admiral Edwards issued a Proclamation requiring "all his Majesty's subjects coming upon the Coast of Labrador to act towards the Esquimaux Indians justly, humanely and agreeably to these laws, by which His Majesty's subjects are bound." Here again it is to be observed that the word "savages" and "Indians" are used as equivalents.

A further Proclamation by Admiral Edwards on January 30, 1781, employs the same phrases, the Eskimo being described as "Esquimaux savages" and as "Esquimaux Indians."

On May 15, 1774, Governor Campbell, as Governor and Commander-in-chief, issued a Proclamation in terms identical with that of 1781.

On December 3, 1821, a Proclamation was issued by Governor Hamilton as Governor and Commander-in-Chief of Newfoundland (now again including the Labrador coast) relating to a "fourth settlement" by the Moravian missionaries requiring all His Majesty's subjects "to act towards the missionaries and the Esquimaux Indians justly and humanely."

There are other official documents. In a report in 1798 by Captain Crofton, addressed to Admiral Waldegrave, Governor and Commander-in-Chief of Newfoundland, the phrase "Esquimaux Indians" occurs several times and the Eskimo are plainly treated as coming under the designation "Indians." A report to Lord Dorchester, Governor and Commander-in-Chief of Quebec, Nova Scotia, New Brunswick and their dependencies, in 1788, upon an application by George Cartwright for a grant of land at Touktoke Bay on the coast of Labrador by a special Committee of the Council appointed to consider the same refers to the applicant's exertions in "securing friendly intercourse with the Esquimaux Indians and his success in bringing about a friendly intercourse between that nation and the Mountaineers."

Evidence as to subsequent official usage is adduced in a letter of 1824 from the Advocate General of Canada to the Assistant Civil Secretary on some matter of a criminal prosecution in which "Esquimaux Indians" are concerned; and in a report of 1869 by Judge Pinsent of the Court of Labrador to the Governor of Newfoundland in which this sentence occurs: "In this number about 300 Indians and half-breeds of the Esquimaux and Mountaineer races are included." . . .

Nor do I think that the fact that British policy in relation to the Indians, as evidenced in the Instructions to Sir Guy Carleton and the Royal Proclamation of 1763, did not contemplate the Eskimo (along with many other tribes and nations of British North American aborigines) as within the scope of that policy is either conclusive or very useful in determining the question before us. For that purpose, for construing the term "Indians" in the *B.N.A. Act* in order to ascertain the scope of the provisions of that Act defining the powers of the Parliament of Canada, the Report of the Select Committee of the House of Commons in 1857 and the documents relating to the Labrador Eskimo are, in my opinion, far more trust-worthy guides.

Nor can I agree that the context (in head no. 24) has the effect of restricting the term "Indians." If "Indians" standing alone in its application to British North America denotes the aborigines, then the fact that there were aborigines for whom lands had not been reserved seems to afford no good reason for limiting the scope of the term "Indians" itself.

For these reasons I think the question referred to us should be answered in the affirmative. . . .

10. *Agreement Between the Inuit of the Nunavut Settlement Area and Her Majesty the Queen in Right of Canada.* **May 25, 1993**

1.1.1   In the Agreement, except where otherwise expressly provided in the Agreement or indicated by the context: . . .
"Designated Inuit Organization" (DIO) means
(a) the Tungavik, or
(b) in respect of a function under the Agreement, any of the Organizations that has been designated under Section 39.1.3 as responsible for that function; . . .

PART 2: STATUS AS A LAND CLAIMS AGREEMENT
2.2.1   The Agreement shall be a land claims agreement within the meaning of Section 35 of the *Constitution Act, 1982*. . . .

PART 7: CERTAINTY
2.7.1   In consideration of the rights and benefits provided to Inuit by the Agreement, Inuit hereby:
(a) cede, release and surrender to Her Majesty The Queen in Right of Canada, all their aboriginal claims, rights, title and interests, if any, in and to lands and waters anywhere within Canada and adjacent

offshore areas within the sovereignty or jurisdiction of Canada; and

(b) agree, on their behalf, and on behalf of their heirs, descendants and successors not to assert any cause of action, action for a declaration, claim or demand of whatever kind or nature which they ever had, now have or may hereafter have against Her Majesty The Queen in Right of Canada or any province, the government of any territory or any person based on any aboriginal claims, rights, title or interests in and to lands and waters described in Sub-section (a).

2.7.2   Nothing in the Agreement constitutes an admission of denial by Canada that Inuit have any aboriginal claims, rights title or interests in and to lands and waters as described in Sub-section 2.7.1(a) outside the Nunavut Settlement Area.

2.7.3   Nothing in the Agreement shall:

(a) be construed so as to deny that Inuit are an aboriginal people of Canada, or, subject to Section 2.7.1, affect their ability to participate in or benefit from any existing or future constitutional rights for aboriginal people which may be applicable to them;

(b) affect the ability of Inuit to participate in and benefit from government programs for Inuit or aboriginal people generally as the case may be; benefits received under such programs shall be determined by general criteria for such programs established from time to time; or

(c) affect the rights of Inuit as Canadian citizens and they shall continue to be entitled to all the rights and benefits of all other citizens applicable to them from time to time. . . .

PART 12: APPLICATION OF LAWS

All Laws to Apply

2.12.1   Subject to Sections 2.12.2 and 2.12.3, all federal territorial and local government laws shall apply to Inuit and Inuit Owned Lands.

Agreement to Prevail

2.12.2   Where there is any inconsistency or conflict between any federal, territorial and local government laws, and the Agreement, the Agreement shall prevail to the extent of the inconsistency or conflict.

NUNAVUT POLITICAL DEVELOPMENT

PART 1:   GENERAL

4.1.1.   The Government of Canada will recommend to Parliament, as a government measure, legislation to establish, within a defined time period, a new Nunavut Territory, with its own Legislative Assembly and public government, separate from the Government of the remainder of the Northwest Territories.

4.1.2.   Therefore, Canada and the Territorial Government and Tungavik Federation of Nunavut shall negotiate a political accord to deal with the establishment of Nunavut. The political accord shall establish a precise date for recommending to Parliament legislation necessary to establish the

Nunavut Territory and the Nunavut Government, and a transitional process. It is the intention of the Parties that the date shall coincide with recommending ratification legislation to parliament unless Tungavik Federation of Nunavut agrees otherwise. The political accord shall also provide for the types of power of the Nunavut Government, certain principles relating to the financing of the Nunavut Government, and the time limits for the coming into existence and operation of the Nunavut Territorial Government. The political accord shall be finalized before the Inuit ratification vote. It is the intention of the Parties to complete the Political Accord by no later than April 1, 1992.

4.1.3.   Neither the said political accord nor any legislation enacted pursuant to the political accord shall accompany or form part of this Agreement or any legislation ratifying this Agreement. Neither the said political accord nor anything in the legislation enacted pursuant to the political accord is intended to be a land claims agreement or treaty right within the meaning of Section 35 of the *Constitution Act, 1982. . . .*

WILDLIFE . . .

Principles

5.1.2   This Article recognizes and reflects the following principles:

(a) Inuit are traditional and current users of wildlife;

(b) the legal rights of Inuit to harvest wildlife flow from their traditional and current use;

(c) The Inuit population is steadily increasing;

(d) a long-term, healthy, renewal resource economy is both viable and desirable;

(e) there is a need for an effective system of wildlife management that complements Inuit harvesting rights and priorities, and recognizes Inuit systems of wildlife management that contribute to the conservation of wildlife and protection of wildlife habitat;

(f) there is a need for systems of wildlife management and land management that provide optimum protection to the renewable resource economy;

(g) the wildlife management system and the exercise of Inuit harvesting rights are governed by and subject to the principles of conservation;

(h) there is a need for an effective role for Inuit in all aspects of wildlife management, including research; and

(i) Government retains the ultimate responsibility for wildlife management.

Objectives

5.1.3   This Article seeks to achieve the following objectives:

(a) the creation of a system of harvesting rights, priorities and privileges that

(i) reflects the traditional current levels, patterns and character of Inuit harvesting,

(ii) subject to availability, as determined by the application of the principles of conservation, and taking into account the likely and actual increase in the population of Inuit, confers on Inuit rights to harvest wildlife sufficient to meet their basic needs, as adjusted as circumstances warrant,

    (iii) gives DIOs priority in establishing and operating economic ventures with respect to harvesting, including sports and other commercial ventures,

    (iv) provides for harvesting privileges and allows for continued access by persons other than Inuit, particularly long-term residents, and

    (v) avoids unnecessary interference in the exercise of the rights, priorities and privileges to harvest;

(b) the creation of a wildlife management system that

    (i) is governed by, and implements, principles of conservation,

    (ii) fully acknowledges and reflects the primary role of Inuit in wildlife harvesting,

    (iii) serves and promotes the long-term economic, social and cultural interests of Inuit harvesters,

    (iv) as far as practical, integrates the management of all species of wildlife,

    (v) invites public participation and promotes public confidence, particularly amongst Inuit, and

    (vi) enables and empowers the NWMB to make wildlife management decisions pertaining thereto.

Conservation

5.1.4 The principles of conservation will be interpreted and applied giving full regard to the principles and objectives outlined in Section 5.1.2 and 5.1.3 and the rights and obligations set out in this Article.

5.1.5 The principles of conservation are:

(a) the maintenance of the natural balance of ecological systems within the Nunavut Settlement Area;

(b) the protection of wildlife habitat;

(c) the maintenance of vital, healthy, wildlife populations capable of sustaining harvesting needs as defined in this Article; and

(d) the restoration and revitalization of depleted populations of wildlife and wildlife habitat.

General

5.1.6 The Government of Canada and Inuit recognize that there is a need for an effective role for Inuit in all aspects of wildlife management.

Application

5.1.7 For greater certainty, none of the rights in this Article apply in respect of wildlife harvested outside the Nunavut Settlement Area. . . .

TITLE TO INUIT OWNED LANDS . . .

PART 2: FORM OF TITLE

19.2.1 Inuit Owned Lands shall be held in either of the following forms:

(a) fee simple including the mines and minerals that may be found to exist within, upon or under such lands; or

(b) fee simple saving and excepting the mines and minerals that may be found to exist within, upon or under such lands, together with the right to work the same, but including the right to all specified substances. . . .

19.2.7   Notwithstanding anything in Section 19.2.5, Government has the right, subject to the Agreement, to protect and manage water and land covered by water, and to use water in connection with such right, throughout the Nunavut Settlement Area for public purposes, including:

(a) management and research in respect of wildlife, and aquatic habitat;

(b) protection and management of navigation and transportation, establishment of navigation aid devices, and dredging of navigable water bodies;

(c) protection of water resources from contamination and degradation; and

(d) flood control and fire fighting.

PART 3:   VESTING OF INUIT OWNED LANDS UPON RATIFICATION

19.3.1   Upon ratification of the Agreement, the Inuit Owned Lands totalling an area at least equal to the amounts specified in Schedules 19-2 to 19-7 and shown on the maps titled *Inuit Owned Lands, Ownership Map*, in the series No.s. 1 to 237 shall vest in the DIO in the form indicated on those maps and in accordance with the descriptions on those maps. . . .

19.3.4   The registrar shall record the fact of the vesting of title in the DIO of the Inuit Owned Lands referred to in Section 19.3.1 as soon as possible after the date of ratification of the Agreement.

PART 4:   FUTURE INUIT OWNED LANDS

19.4.1   Government shall grant to the DIO, as Inuit Owned Lands in the form referred to in Sub-section 19.2.1(b), the lands described in an item of Part I or II of Schedule 19-8:

(a) in the case of Part I of the Schedule, six months after

(i) the DIO provides Government with a letter obtained from the lessee referred to in that item stating that the lessee consents to its lease being located on Inuit Owned Lands, or

(ii) the lease referred to in that item terminates,

whichever event first occurs, on the condition the consent is given or the lease terminates within two years of the date of ratification of the Agreement; and

(b) in the case of Part II of the Schedule, when Government declares the lands to be surplus to its needs and the DIO pays Government their fair market value.

19.4.2   The lands described in an item of Part III of Schedule 19-8 shall vest in the DIO as Inuit Owned Lands in the form referred to in Sub-section 19.2.1(b) on the date or event specified in that item.

PART 5:   FUTURE INUIT OWNED LANDS STATUS

19.5.1   Any portion of the lands in Pangnirtung described in an item of Schedule 19-9 shall become Inuit Owned Lands in the form referred to in Sub-section 19.2.1(b) when the DIO acquires the fee simple interest to that portion at no cost to Government. . . .

PART 1:   INUIT WATER RIGHTS . . .

PART 2:   RIGHTS OF INUIT

20.2.1   In this Article, any rights vested in a DIO are vested in trust for the use and benefit of Inuit.

20.2.2   Subject to the Agreement and any exception identified in the property descriptions of Inuit Owned Lands, the DIO shall have the exclusive right to the use of water on, in, or flowing through Inuit Owned Lands.

20.2.3   Nothwithstanding Section 20.2.2, any use of water on, in, or flowing through Inuit Owned Lands must comply with the terms of Article 13.

20.2.4   Subject to Section 20.5.1, the DIO shall have the right to have water flow through Inuit Owned Lands substantially unaffected in quality and quantity and flow. . . .

PART 4:   PROJECTS OUTSIDE THE NUNAVUT SETTLEMENT AREA . . .

REAL PROPERTY TAXATION

PART 1:   DEFINITIONS

22.1.1   In this Article:

"real property taxation" means any tax, levy, charge or other assessment against lands imposed for local government services or improvements including for schools and water;

"personal property" means chattels real and personal, including all choses in action and choses in possession.

PART 2:   GENERAL

22.2.1   Subject to this Article and the Agreement, no federal, territorial, provincial or municipal charge, levy or tax of any kind whatsoever shall be assessable or payable on the value or assessed value of Inuit Owned Lands and, without limiting the generality of the foregoing, no capital, wealth, realty, school, water or business tax shall be assessable or payable on the value or assessed value of Inuit Owned Lands.

22.2.2   Subject to Section 22.2.5, Inuit Owned Lands within municipal boundaries that,

(a) have improvements, or

(b) do not have improvements, and lie within a planned and approved subdivision and are available for development,

shall be subject to real property taxation under laws of general application.

22.2.3   Subject to Section 22.2.5, Inuit Owned Lands outside municipalities on which improvements have been made shall be subject to real property taxation under laws of general application. Notwithstanding, where an improvement has been constructed, and an area of land for that improvement has not been demised, the assessor may assign an area no greater than four times the total ground area of the improvements. . . .

22.2.5   Inuit Owned Lands shall not be subject to charge, pledge, mortgage, attachment, levy, seizure, distress or execution in respect of real property taxation for purposes of collection of tax arrears. The taxation authority may, however, execute upon all personal property of the DIO, or the Nunavut Trust, by way of seizure and sale or attachment, for purposes of collection of tax arrears.

22.2.6   Nothing in this Article, or in laws of general application, shall preclude a DIO and a municipal corporation from entering into a fee-for-services agreement to govern the supply of local government services to Inuit Owned Lands.

22.2.7   No federal, territorial, provincial or municipal charge, levy or tax shall be payable in respect of the vesting in a DIO of lands pursuant to Section 19.3.1. . . .

NATURAL RESOURCE DEVELOPMENT

PART 1: PETROLEUM
         Opening of Lands for Petroleum Exploration

27.1.1   Prior to opening any lands in the Nunavut Settlement Area for petroleum exploration, Government shall notify the DIO and provide an opportunity for it to present and to discuss its views with Government regarding the terms and conditions to be attached to such rights.
          Exercise of Petroleum Rights

27.1.2   Prior to the initial exercise of rights in respect of exploration, development or production of petroleum on Crown lands in the Nunavut Settlement Area, and in order to prepare a benefits plan for the approval of the appropriate regulatory authority, the proponent shall consult the DIO, and Government shall consult the DIO, in respect to those matters listed in Schedule 27-1. . . .

SCHEDULE 27–1
MATTERS CONSIDERED APPROPRIATE FOR CONSULTATION
(Section 27.1.2, 27.2.1)

1. Inuit training.
2. Inuit hiring.
3. Employment rotation.
4. Labour relations.
5. Business opportunities for Inuit.
6. Housing, accommodation and recreation on project site.
7. Safety, health and hygiene.
8. Language of workplace.
9. Identification, protection and conservation of archaeological sites and specimens.

10. Research and development.
11. Inuit access to facilities constructed for the project such as airfields and roads.
12. Particularly important Inuit environmental concerns and disruption of wildlife.
13. Outpost camps.
14. Information flow, including liaison between Inuit and proponent regarding project management and Inuit participation and concerns.
15. Co-ordination with other developments.
16. Any other matters that the Parties consider to be relevant to the needs of the project and Inuit. . . .

ENROLMENT

PART 1: PRINCIPLES AND OBJECTIVES

35.1.1　This Article:
 (a) recognizes that Inuit are best able to define who is an Inuk for the purposes of this Agreement;
 (b) guarantees that the Inuit of the Nunavut Settlement Area will be recognized according to their own understanding of themselves, and that Inuit shall determine who is an Inuk for the purposes of this Agreement, and entitled to be enroled under the Agreement;
 (c) establishes a process that is just and equitable for determining who is an Inuk for the purposes of this Agreement, and entitled to be enroled under the Agreement.

PART 2: INUIT ENROLMENT LIST

35.2.1　A DIO shall establish and maintain a list of Inuit (Inuit Enrolment List), and enrol thereon the names of all persons who are entitled to be enroled in accordance with this Article.

35.2.2　A person who is enroled on the Inuit Enrolment List shall be entitled to benefit from the Agreement so long as he or she is alive and his or her name is enroled thereon.

PART 3: ENROLMENT REQUIREMENTS

35.3.1　Subject to Section 35.3.3. to 35.3.5, a person who
 (a) is alive,
 (b) is a Canadian citizen,
 (c) is an Inuk as determined in accordance with Inuit customs and usages,
 (d) identifies himself or herself as an Inuk, and
 (e) is associated with
  (i) a community in the Nunavut Settlement Area, or
  (ii) the Nunavut Settlement Area,
is entitled to have his or her name enroled on the Inuit Enrolment List.

35.3.2　For the purpose of Sub-section 35.3.1(d), the guardian of a person who in consequence of legal disability is unable to identify himself or herself as an Inuk may identify that person as an Inuk.

35.3.3   No persons shall be enroled under the Agreement and any other Canadian aboriginal land claims agreement at the same time.

35.3.4   A person who is entitled may transfer into the Agreement so long as that person gives up, for the duration of such transfer, the ability to benefit from or participate in a Canadian aboriginal land claims agreement out of which that person is transferring. The DIO shall determine the date upon which this provision comes into force with respect to beneficiaries or participants of any other Canadian aboriginal land claims agreements.

35.3.5   No person shall be under a legal obligation to apply for enrolment under the Agreement.

35.3.6   Any person enroled under the Agreement, may from time to time, decide to discontinue enrolment and, upon that person's written directions to that effect that person's name shall be removed from the Inuit Enrolment List. . . .

OTHER ABORIGINAL PEOPLES

PART 1: GENERAL

40.1.1   Nothing in the Agreement shall be construed to affect, recognize or provide any rights under Section 35 of the *Constitution Act, 1982*, for any aboriginal peoples other than Inuit.

40.1.2   For greater certainty, and without limiting Section 40.1.1, nothing in the Agreement, or in any legislation ratifying or implementing its terms, shall:

(a) constitute a cession, release, surrender or other qualification or limitation of any aboriginal or treaty rights under the *Constitution Act, 1982* for any aboriginal peoples other than Inuit; or

(b) be interpreted as to abrogate or derogate from or otherwise conflict or be inconsistent with, any aboriginal or treaty rights under the *Constitution Act, 1982* for any aboriginal peoples other than Inuit.

40.1.3   Nothing in the Agreement shall limit the negotiation of agreements between Inuit and any other aboriginal peoples respecting overlapping interests or claims, except that the provisions of such agreements shall not be binding on Government or any person other than Inuit and those aboriginal peoples without the consent of Government. . . .

■ SELECTED BIBLIOGRAPHY

Bell, C. *Alberta's Metis Settlement Legislation: An Overview of Ownership and Management of Settlement Lands*. Regina, Sask.: Canadian Plains Research Center, University of Regina, 1994.

————, "Who are the Metis People in Section 35(2)?" (1991) XXIX:2 *Alta. L. Rev.* 351.

Chartier, C., "'Indian': An Analysis of the Term as used in Section 91(24) of the *British North America Act, 1867*" (1978–79) 43 *Sask. L. Rev.* 37.

————, "Aboriginal Self-Government and the Metis Nation." In *Aboriginal Self-Government in Canada*, J. Hylton, ed. Saskatoon, Sask.: Purich Publishing, 1994.

Chartrand, P. *Manitoba's Metis Settlement Scheme of 1870*. Saskatoon, Sask.: Native Law Centre, University of Saskatchewan, 1991.

————, "Aboriginal Rights: The Dispossession of the Metis" (1991) 29 *Osgoode Hall L.J.* 457.

Cumming, P., "Canada's North and Native Rights." In *Aboriginal Peoples and the Law: Indian, Metis and Inuit Rights in Canada*, B. Morse, ed. Ottawa: Carleton University Press, 1985.

Flanagan, T., "The Case Against Metis Aboriginal Rights." In *The Quest For Justice: Aboriginal Peoples and Aboriginal Rights*, M. Boldt *et al.,* eds. Toronto: University of Toronto Press, 1985.

Frideres, J., "The Metis." In *Native Peoples in Canada: Contemporary Conflicts,* 3rd ed. Scarborough, Ont.: Prentice-Hall, 1988.

Hardy, R. ,"Metis Rights in the Mackenzie River District of the Northwest Territories" [1980] 1 C.N.L.R. 1.

Hunt, C.D., "Knowing the North: The Law and its Institutions" [1986] 4 C.N.L.R. 1.

Isaac, T., "The Nunavut Agreement-in-Principle and Section 35 of the *Constitution Act, 1982*" (1992) 21:3 *Man. L. J.* 390.

Lester, G.S., "The Territorial Rights of the Inuit of the Canadian Northwest Territories: A Legal Argument." Unpublished Ph.D. dissertation, Toronto: York University, 1981.

Merritt, J., *et al. Nunavut: Political Choices and Manifest Destiny.* Ottawa: Canadian Arctic Resources Committee, 1989.

Purich, D. *The Inuit and Their Land: The Story of Nunavut.* Toronto: Lorimer, 1992.

————. *The Metis.* Toronto: Lorimer, 1988.

Sprague, D.N., "Metis Land Claims." In *Aboriginal Land Claims in Canada: A Regional Perspective,* K. Coates, ed. Toronto: Copp Clark Pitman, 1997.

CHAPTER 6
TAXATION

■ INTRODUCTION

The issue of taxation and Indians, both the ability of Indians to tax and to be taxed, focuses on the legal distinction of Indians living and working on reserve from the rest of Canadian society. The present *Indian Act* tax exemption illustrates this distinction by allowing Indians resident on reserves, in some instances, to be exempt from income and consumptive taxes. Additionally, the pressures from Aboriginal governments generally to possess the authority to tax on their lands is increasing and, in many cases, is a cornerstone to Aboriginal economic development and self-government.[1] The Indian tax exemption was codified in Canadian law before Confederation. Legislation of Upper Canada in 1850 and 1859 provided for Indians to be exempt from taxation.[2] These tax exemptions are now codified in the *Indian Act*[3] in s. 87. These exemptions do not apply to the Métis, the Inuit, or to other Aboriginal peoples not registered as "Indians" under the *Indian Act.*

Currently, governments in Canada recognize only the statute-based Indian personal property tax exemption found in s. 87 of the federal *Indian Act.* Section 87 exempts Indians from taxation of (a) the interest of an Indian or a band in reserve lands or surrendered lands and (b) the personal property of an Indian or a band situated on a reserve. Under the federal *Income Tax Act,*[4] Indians are required to file tax returns even though they may be exempt from paying any tax.[5]

One of the most litigious and contentious issues regarding the *Indian Act* tax exemption is the meaning of "property situated on reserve." The 1983 Supreme Court of Canada decision of *R. v. Nowegijick*[6] held that employment income was a simple debt and the *situs* of the employer was the determining factor in whether or not the property was exempt. Thus, in order for an Indian's property to be tax exempt, the *situs* of the employer had to be "on reserve," as provided for by the *Indian Act,* even if the work itself was done off-reserve.

---

1 A wide array of bylaws enacted by First Nations under s. 83 can be found in *First Nations Gazette,* 1998, vol. 2, No. 1.

2 *An Act for the protection of the Indians in Upper Canada from imposition, and the property occupied or enjoyed by them from trespass and injury,* S. Prov. C., 1850, c. 74, s. IV, and *An Act to prevent trespasses to Public and Indian Lands,* C.S.U.C. 1859, c. 81, s. 23; as found in T. Isaac, *Pre-1868 Legislation Concerning Indians* (Saskatoon, Sask.: University of Saskatchewan Native Law Centre, 1993).

3 *Indian Act,* R.S.C. 1985, c. I–5, ss. 87 & 89.

4. *Income Tax Act,* R.S.C. 1985, c. 1 (5th Supp.).

5 See *R. v. Point* (No. 2) (1957), 22 W.W.R. 527, 119 C.C.C. 117 (B.C.C.A.).

6 *R. v. Nowegijick,* [1983] 2 C.N.L.R. 89 (S.C.C.).

The 1992 Supreme Court of Canada decision of *R.* v. *Williams*[7] held that the mere *situs* of the employer or source of income was not sufficient. Rather, in order to determine the *situs* of intangible personal property, courts must consider various "connecting factors" that bind the property to one location or another. The Supreme Court noted three important factors to be considered:

a.   the purpose of the exemption,
b.   the character of the property, and
c.   the incidence of taxation on that property.

This test is more flexible and less predictable than the 1983 Supreme Court test in determining whether or not the tax exemption applies to income. The location of the employer (head office) is simply one of a number of factors used to determine the *situs* of the work performed.

On February 16, 1993, Revenue Canada released an interpretation of *Williams*. The following is a summary of that interpretation:

a.   Although *Williams* dealt specifically with unemployment insurance benefits, it applies to all other forms of income. All applicable connecting factors must be examined to determine whether or not income is tax exempt.

b.   An employer situated on a reserve is not enough, by itself, to warrant tax exemption. The primary factor of connecting income to the reserve is where the duties are performed. The location of the employer will continue to be a factor, but other factors must also be considered.

c.   The exemption applies to (i) employment income for duties performed entirely on a reserve, (ii) employment income for duties performed entirely off-reserve but where the employer and the Indian reside on-reserve, (iii) employment income for duties, most of which, are performed on-reserve and either the employer or the Indian resides on-reserve, (iv) unemployment, pension or retiring benefits received in relation to exempt employment income, and (v) exemption shall be pro-rated where duties are performed on and off a reserve.

A detailed set of guidelines regarding the *Indian Act* tax exemption and employment income was released in June 1994 and is provided later in this chapter. *Williams* has redefined the exemption, which was deemed to apply where a head office could simply be located on reserve while the substantive business of the employer was off-reserve, with all affected parties living off-reserve. Now, a connection must be made between the *situs* of the employment income and the performance of the duties related to the income in order for the exemption to apply. *Williams* has not yet been applied to business income, but will, no doubt, affect it.

Williams was applied by the Tax Court of Canada in *Recalma* v. *Canada*.[8] The court considered whether investment income earned by investments purchased at an on-reserve bank branch was income exempt from income tax pursuant to s. 87 of the *Indian Act*. In applying *Williams,* the court noted that the investment income was the personal property of registered Indians and applied the following connecting elements in order to determine the *situs* of the investment income:

---

7   *R.* v. *Williams*, [1992] 3 C.N.L.R. 181 (S.C.C.).
8   *Recalma* v. *Canada*, [1997] 4 C.N.L.R. 272 (T.C.C.), aff'd by [1998] 3 C.N.L.R. 279 (Fed. C.A.).

1. the residence of the registered Indians;
2. the origin and location of the capital used to buy the securities;
3. the location of the bank branch where the securities were bought;
4. the location where the investment was used;
5. the location of the investment instruments;
6. the location where the investment income payment was made; and
7. the nature of the securities, including the residence of the issuer, the location of the issuer's income-generating activity from which the investment was made, and the location of the issuer's property in the event of a default that could result in a potential seizure.

After examining these factors, the court determined that all of the transactions inclined with the investment instruments occurred off-reserve. The only action that took place on reserve was the actual purchase. The investment income was held to be located off-reserve and therefore subject to income tax.

Section 87 prevents the taxation of personal property situated on reserve. The term "situated" in s. 87 includes the ownership, occupation, possession, and use of property. The paramount location of property is established by examining the pattern of use and safekeeping regarding the property. If the paramount location is on reserve, then the property is tax exempt even with respect to its off-reserve use.[9] The "paramount location test" was applied in the New Brunswick Court of Appeal decision of *Union of New Brunswick Indians* v. *New Brunswick.*[10] The issue in this case was whether personal property purchased off-reserve by an Indian or a band, but intended for ownership, consumption, or use on a reserve, fell within the meaning of s. 87(1) of the *Indian Act*'s "situated on reserve" and therefore was not subject to New Brunswick's Social Services and Education Tax (a sales tax). The paramount location test requires that a good's primary location must be determined according to its normal pattern of use and safekeeping. The court held that the purchase of goods destined for use and consumption on a reserve by an Indian or a band are not subject to the provincial sales tax. Delivery to the reserve is unnecessary for the application of s. 87.[11] The Supreme Court of Canada overturned the Court of Appeal's decision. The Supreme Court noted that the tax, when imposed on a retail sale, is a sales tax and not a consumption tax. The "paramount location test" cannot be applied to sales taxes on tangible goods because the only relevant factor is the place of sale. The intended place of consumption (that is to say, on-reserve) is of no relevance.

Corporations wholly owned by Indian band councils may be exempt from paying tax on income earned anywhere if they are deemed to be municipalities within the meaning of s. 149(1)(d) of the *Income Tax Act,*[12] which provides that

---

9   *Leighton* v. *B.C.*, [1989] 3 C.N.L.R. 136 (B.C.C.A.). Cited with approval by La Forest J. in *Mitchell* v. *Peguis Indian Band*, [1990] 3 C.N.L.R. 46 at 58 (S.C.C.).

10 *Union of New Brunswick Indians* v. *New Brunswick*, [1997] 1 C.N.L.R. 213 (N.B.C.A.), rev'd by [1998] 3 C.N.L.R. 295 (S.C.C.).

11 For another example of the paramount location test, see *Petro-Canada Inc.* v. *Fort Nelson Indian Band*, [1993] 1 C.N.L.R. 72 (B.C.S.C.).

12 *Income Tax Act*, S.C. 1970–71–72, c. 63.

municipalities are tax exempt.[13] This, of course, has nothing to do with the *Indian Act* and everything to do with whether or not the band is a "municipality" for the purposes of the *Income Tax Act.* The benefit, however, is the same.

Electricity[14] delivered to a reserve and motor vehicles[15] purchased on a reserve are personal property within the meaning of s. 87 and are therefore exempt from taxation. The phrase "situated on reserve" means situated at the time of delivery. Also, as noted in the 1997 New Brunswick Court of Appeal decision of *Union of New Brunswick Indians* v. *New Brunswick,*[16] "situated on reserve" means goods destined for consumption on reserve.

Neither the *Indian Act*'s s. 87 exemption nor the Jay Treaty (a 1794 treaty between Great Britain and the United States proposing a duty exemption for Indians who crossed what is now the United States/Canada border) have been accepted by the courts as establishing an exemption from customs or excise taxes. Customs duties apply as soon as goods cross the border. The Jay Treaty was never enacted in Canada by domestic legislation, and therefore is not in force.[17] However, in the 1997 Federal Court of Canada decision of *Mitchell* v. *Min. of Nat. Rev.,*[18] it was held that the Jay Treaty can be a useful piece of evidence in demonstrating Aboriginal rights, even though the treaty itself did not confer rights. The court held that the Mohawks of Akwesasne have an existing Aboriginal right, protected by s. 35, to pass back and forth between Canada and the United States freely. This right includes the right to bring goods from the United States into Canada for personal and community use, including such associated trade with other First Nations, without having to pay duty on those goods. This right does not include the right to bring into Canada any form of firearms, restricted drugs, alcohol, plants, et cetera, nor the right to prevent the application of the search and declaration procedures used by Canada Customs. Thus, the relevant provisions of the *Customs Act*[19] are of no force or effect as they affect the Mohawks of Akwesasne.

Indians living off-reserve are liable to pay hospitalization tax imposed by a provincial government in the absence of any agreement by the federal government that it will bear the costs of paying such a tax.[20] On-reserve purchases made by registered Indians are exempt from provincial sales tax even though the goods purchased may be used off-reserve.[21] On-reserve, for-profit corporations owned by registered Indians must pay provincial health and education taxes on purchases made on- and off-reserve. In *Kinookimaw Beach Ass.* v. *Saskatchewan*[22] the

---

13   *Otineka Development Corp. Ltd.* v. *Canada*, [1994] 2 C.N.L.R. 83 (T.C.C.). Revenue
      Canada did not appeal this decision.
14   *R.* v. *Brown*, [1979] 3 C.N.L.R. 67 (B.C.C.A.).
15   *Danes* v. *B.C.*; *Watts* v. *B.C.*, [1985] 2 C.N.L.R. 18 (B.C.C.A.).
16   *Union of New Brunswick Indians* v. *New Brunswick*, [1997] 1 C.N.L.R. 213 (N.B.C.A.).
17   *R.* v. *Francis*, 5 C.N.L.C. 170 (S.C.C.).
18   *Mitchell* v. *Min. of Nat. Rev.,* [1997] 4 C.N.L.R. 103 (F.C.T.D.).
19   *Customs Act*, R.S.C. 1985, c. 1 (2nd Supp.).
20   See *R.* v. *Johnston*, 6 C.N.L.C. 447 (Sask. C.A.); and *R.* v. *Swimmer*, 6 C.N.L.C. 621
      (Sask. C.A.).
21   *Danes* v. *B.C.*; *Watts* v. *B.C.*, [1985] 2 C.N.L.R. 18 (B.C.C.A.).
22   *Kinookimaw Beach Ass.* v. *Saskatchewan*, [1979] 4 C.N.L.R. 101 (Sask. C.A.).

Saskatchewan Court of Appeal refused to allow the personal tax exemption to be applied to corporate entities, regardless of whether or not they were owned by registered Indians.

Pursuant to *G.S.T. Technical Information Bulletin, B–039* (January 4, 1991), the federal Goods and Services Tax is not payable on on-reserve purchases of goods by registered Indians and bands, on on-reserve purchases of services by registered Indians where the benefit is realized primarily on reserve, or for off-reserve purchases of goods delivered to a reserve and purchased by registered Indians.

Some Indian groups have argued that they possess treaty and Aboriginal rights that exempt them from taxation.[23] Two Saskatchewan Court of Appeal decisions— *R.* v. *Johnston*[24] and *R.* v. *Swimmer*[25]—offer a restrictive interpretation of such a treaty right. However, the Supreme Court of Canada in *Nowegijick, Simon,*[26] *Sparrow,*[27] and *Mitchell* has put forward a broad interpretive framework to Aboriginal rights, which might include an Aboriginal right to be tax exempt. This conclusion, however, seems unlikely. There appears to be little specific judicial support for the proposition that there is a general Aboriginal right to tax exemption.[28]

The Supreme Court of Canada in its 1990 decision of *Mitchell* v. *Peguis Indian Band*[29] held that the purpose of the *Indian Act* provisions relating to property and tax exemption was not to remedy the economically disadvantaged position of Indians but rather to protect their interest in reserve lands from seizure:

> One must guard against ascribing an overly broad purpose to ss. 87 and 89. These provisions are not intended to confer privileges on Indians in respect of any property they may acquire and possess, wherever situated. Rather, their purpose is simply to insulate the property interests of Indians in their reserve lands from the intrusions and interference of the larger society so as to ensure that Indians are not dispossessed of their entitlement.[30]

Section 90(1) of the *Indian Act* provides that personal property purchased by the Crown with Indian moneys (as defined by the *Indian Act*) or moneys appropriated by Parliament for the use and benefit of Indians or bands or moneys provided to Indians or bands under a treaty or agreement between a band and the Crown are

---

23   In the *Report of Commissioners for Treaty No. 8* (September 22, 1899), the Hon. Clifford Sifton wrote: "We assured them [the Indians] that the treaty would not lead to any forced interference with their mode of life, that it did not open the way to the imposition of any tax" (Ottawa: DIAND, 1966), 6.

24   *Danes* v. *B.C.*; *Watts* v. *B.C.*, [1985] 2 C.N.L.R. 18 (B.C.C.A.).

25   Ibid.

26   *R.* v. *Simon*, [1986] 1 C.N.L.R. 153 (S.C.C.).

27   *R.* v. *Sparrow*, [1990] 3 C.N.L.R. 160 (S.C.C.).

28   For example, *R.* v. *Johnson*, [1994] 1 C.N.L.R. 129 (N.S.C.A.), noted that nothing in the Treaty of 1752 exempts Indians from paying tobacco taxes. *R.* v. *Poitras*, [1994] 3 C.N.L.R. 157 (Sask. Q.B.), held that Treaty No. 4 does not exempt Indians from paying tobacco taxes.

29   *Mitchell* v. *Peguis Indian Band*, [1990] 3 C.N.L.R. 46 (S.C.C.).

30   Ibid. at 58.

deemed to be situated on reserve. The Crown need not purchase property directly in order for s. 90 to apply. Band purchases made with moneys provided by loans from the Crown fall within the parameters of s. 90.[31]

In *Mitchell*, "Her Majesty" in s. 90(1) of the *Indian Act* was held to be limited to the federal Crown and, as such, the exemptions and privileges in ss. 87 and 89 will apply solely in respect of property that the federal Crown gives to Indians. Thus, s. 90(1) does not apply to purely private commercial transactions unless that property is situated on-reserve. La Forest J. (with Sopinka and Gonthier JJ.) noted:

> The historical record that so clearly reveals a cogent rationale for protecting the personal property that enures to Indians by operation of treaty obligations regardless of situs, is silent as to any reason why personal property that Indians bands acquire from the provincial Crowns should receive the same extraordinary level of protection. . . . I would, therefore, limit application of the term "Her Majesty" as used in s. 90(1)(b) to the federal Crown.[32]

In his dissent, Dickson C.J. held that "Her Majesty" referred to both the federal and the provincial Crowns.

Mitchell also stands for the proposition that a liberal construction should be given to legislation affecting Indians and that any doubts as to the meaning of legislation should be resolved in favour of the Indians.

Some Indians bands have entered into agreements with the provinces and territories whereby consumptive goods, such as tobacco and gasoline, are sold tax-free to First Nations retailers based on an approximate amount of the volume of these products sold to registered Indians. The remaining portion of the volume sold to First Nations retailers is sold with the provincial/territorial taxes applied.

In other instances, First Nations retailers purchase consumptive goods that include all applicable provincial/territorial taxes. These goods are then sold to registered Indians "tax-free," and the First Nations retailers apply for a refund of the original tax paid.

These so-called refund and quota systems have been held to be *intra vires* provincial authority. For example, in *Tseshaht Band* v. *British Columbia*,[33] the British Columbia Court of Appeal held that the provincial refund and quota system to regulate the sale of tobacco and gasoline products was *intra vires*. Notwithstanding this decision, the law regarding the extent and application of provincial and territorial taxation regimes on consumptive goods to registered Indians remains unclear.[34]

Section 83 of the *Indian Act* empowers an Indian band to impose taxation for local purposes of land or interests in land. In *Matsqui Indian Band* v. *Canadian Pacific Ltd.*[35] the Supreme Court of Canada dealt with a First Nation that imposed

---

31   *Kingsclear Indian Band* v. *J.E. Brooks & Ass. Ltd.*, [1992] 2 C.N.L.R. 46 (N.B.C.A.).

32   *Mitchell* v. *Peguis Indian Band*, [1990] 3 C.N.L.R. 46 at 62–64 (S.C.C.).

33   *Tseshaht Band* v. *British Columbia*, [1992] 4 C.N.L.R. 171 (B.C.C.A.); leave to appeal granted [1993] 2 C.N.L.R. vi (S.C.C.), disc'd [1995] 3 C.N.L.R. iv.

34   See, for example, *Bomberry* v. *Ontario*, [1989] 3 C.N.L.R. 27 (Ont. Div. Ct.).

35   *Matsqui Indian Band* v. *Canadian Pacific Ltd.*, [1995] 2 C.N.L.R. 92 (S.C.C.).

a tax on Canadian Pacific Ltd. pursuant to its bylaw made under s. 83. The bylaw provided that an appeal of the assessment could be made to a tribunal constituted under the bylaw. Canadian Pacific Ltd. went for a judicial review of the assessment in the Federal Court, thereby avoiding the tribunal. The Supreme Court held that the right of appeal to the Federal Court for judicial review stands notwithstanding that a purpose behind the s. 83 is to promote Aboriginal self-government and control over taxation. Lamer C.J., for the majority, wrote:

> Moreover, while I agree that the larger context of Aboriginal self-government informs the determination of whether the statutory appeal procedures established by the appellants constitute an adequate alternative remedy for the respondents, I cannot agree with Sopinka J.'s conclusion that this context is relevant to the question of whether the bands' tribunals give rise to a reasonable apprehension of bias at an institutional level. In my view, principles of natural justice apply to the bands' tribunals as they would apply to any tribunal performing similar functions. The fact that the tribunals have been constituted within the context of a federal policy promoting Aboriginal self-government does not, in itself, dilute natural justice. The Indian Taxation Advisory Board, which intervened before this Court on behalf of the appellant bands, has itself determined that appeal tribunals constituted under s. 83(3) of the *Indian Act* must comply with the principles of natural justice. I would cite the following excerpt from the Board's Introduction to Real Property Taxation on Reserve (1990), at p. 23, a manual designed to assist Aboriginal bands in establishing their taxation tribunals:

>> Subsection 83(3) of the *Indian Act* requires taxation by-laws to provide "an appeal procedure in respect of assessments made for the purposes of taxation". A statutory right of appeal is fundamental to any tax assessment process for two reasons. First, the nature of the assessment process is such that an assessment decision is made only on the strength of an assessor's judgment, without any prior hearing providing input from the party assessed. Second, a fundamental rule of the common law relating to administrative procedures, like assessments, is that everyone has a right to a hearing where matters are involved affecting that person's liberty or property rights. This rule is derived from the principles of natural justice, which are fundamental principles of administrative law that basically ensure (i) a person's right to a hearing and (ii) that the person is heard by an impartial tribunal. . . .

>> The *Indian Act* does not detail the types of appeal processes that councils should establish in their taxation by-laws. However, whatever appeal mechanisms are put in place they will have to adhere to the principles of natural justice, since, as mentioned above, the appeal is in effect a subsequent hearing. . . .

> With respect, I do not believe that either *Nowegijick* v. *The Queen,* [1983] 1 S.C.R. 29, or *Mitchell* v. *Peguis Indian Band,* [1990] 2 S.C.R. 85, the cases cited by Sopinka J., support the view that the policy of Aboriginal self-government is relevant to a determination of whether the appellant Band's taxation tribunals comply with the principles of natural justice.[36]

---

36   Ibid., para. 74.

Lands surrendered absolutely (subject to a condition subsequent, which is a right not connected to an interest in the land) do not become "designated lands" as defined by the *Indian Act*. As such, these lands do not become part of reserve lands and therefore may be subject to municipal taxes. These lands do not fall within the authority of Indian bands to levy taxes pursuant to s. 83 of the *Indian Act*.[37]

The authority of Indian bands and other Aboriginal governments to impose taxes is a cornerstone to the development of a substantive form of self-government. Of course, with taxation comes the responsibility of providing essential and basic community services. The *Nisga'a Final Agreement*[38] provides that the Nisga'a Central Government may make laws with respect of direct taxation of Nisga'a citizens on Nisga'a lands for Nisga'a government purposes. The *Final Agreement* also provides that s. 87 of the *Indian Act* will no longer apply to Nisga'a citizens after a 12-year period—the first such example of phasing out the *Indian Act* exemption.

In the *Teslin Tlingit Council Final Agreement*[39] (flowing from the *Yukon Umbrella Agreement*), s. 87 of the *Indian Act* no longer applies to an interest in reserve or surrendered land in the Yukon Territory, or to personal property situated on-reserve in and out of the Yukon Territory to any Indian (covered by the agreement), Yukon First Nation, or band. The provision (s. 20.6) took effect on February 14, 1998.

■ CASES AND MATERIALS

1. Sections 83, 87, 89, 90, *Indian Act*, R.S.C. 1985, c. I–5

83.(1) Without prejudice to the powers conferred by section 81, the council of a band may, subject to the approval of the Minister, make by-laws for any or all of the following purposes, namely,

    (a) subject to subsections (2) and (3), taxation for local purposes of land, or interests in land, in the reserve, including rights to occupy, possess or use land in the reserve;

    (a.1)the licensing of businesses, callings, trades and occupations; . . .

    (f) the raising of money from band members to support band projects; and

    (g) with respect to any matter arising out of or ancillary to the exercise of powers under this section.

(2) An expenditure made out of moneys raised pursuant to subsection (1) must be so made under the authority of a by-law of the council of the band.

(3) A by-law made under paragraph (1)(a) must provide an appeal procedure in respect of assessments made for the purposes of taxation under that paragraph.

---

37 *St. Mary's Indian Band* v. *Cranbrook,* [1996] 2 C.N.L.R. 222 (B.C.C.A.).

38 Signed August 4, 1998, between Canada, British Columbia, and the Nisga'a, see c. 16, s. 1.

39 *Teslin Tlingit Council Final Agreement* (Ottawa: DIAND, 1993).

(4) The Minister may approve the whole or a part only of a by-law made under subsection (1). . . .

87.(1) . . . Notwithstanding any other Act of Parliament or any Act of the legislature of a province, but subject to section 83, the following property is exempt from taxation, namely,

      (a) the interest of an Indian or a band in reserve lands or surrendered lands; and

      (b) the personal property of an Indian or band situated on a reserve.

(2) No Indian or band is subject to taxation in respect of the ownership, occupation, possession or use of any property mentioned in paragraph (1)(a) or (b) or is otherwise subject to taxation in respect of any such property.

(3) No succession duty, inheritance tax or estate duty is payable on the death of any Indian in respect of any property mentioned in paragraphs (1)(a) or (b) or the succession thereto if the property passes to an Indian, nor shall any such property be taken into account in determining the duty payable under the *Dominion Succession Duty Act,* being chapter 89 of the Revised Statutes of Canada, 1952, or the tax payable under the *Estate Tax Act,* on or in respect of other property passing to an Indian. . . .

89.(l) . . . Subject to this Act, the real and personal property of an Indian or a band situated on a reserve is not subject to charge, pledge, mortgage, attachment, levy, seizure, distress or execution in favour or at the instance of any person other than an Indian or a band.

(1.1) . . . Notwithstanding subsection (l), a leasehold interest in designated lands is subject to charge, pledge, mortgage, attachment, levy, seizure, distress and execution.

(2) . . . A person who sells to a band or a member of a band a chattel under an agreement whereby the right of property or right of possession thereto remains wholly or in part in the seller, may exercise his rights under the agreement notwithstanding that the chattel is situated on a reserve. R.S. 1985, c. 17 (4th Supp.), s. 12.

90.(l) . . . For the purposes of sections 87 and 89, personal property that was

      (a) purchased by Her Majesty with Indian moneys or moneys appropriated by Parliament for the use and benefit of Indians or bands, or

      (b) given to Indians or to a band under a treaty or agreement between a band and Her Majesty, shall be deemed always to be situated on a reserve.

(2) Every transaction purporting to pass title to any property that is by this section deemed to be situated on a reserve. or any interest in such property, is void unless the transaction is entered into with the consent of the Minister or is entered into between members of a band or between the band and a member thereof.

(3) Every person who enters into any transaction that is void by virtue of subsection (2) is guilty of an offence, and every person who, without the written consent of the Minister, destroys personal property that is by this section deemed to be situated on a reserve, is guilty of an offence.

2. *R.* v. *Brown,* [1979] 3 C.N.L.R. 67 (B.C.C.A.). Bull, Craig, and Taggart JJ., December 4, 1979

Electricity is personal property within the meaning of s. 87 and, therefore, exempt from taxation. The phrase "situated on reserve" means situated at the time of delivery. Taxation of Indians and their property situated on reserve is a matter of federal jurisdiction.

BULL, J:—This appeal is from a judgment dismissing an action brought by the appellant Lillian Brown against the respondents for a declaration, with consequential relief, that social services tax purportedly imposed and collected under the *Social Services Tax Act,* 1960 R.S.B.C., Ch. 361, as amended (the "Tax Act") on the purchase price of electricity sold and delivered to her, an Indian, at her home on an Indian reserve, was unlawful. The appellant sued on her own behalf and on behalf of other Indians in like position. . . .

It was common ground and conceded by all parties, rightly in my view, that (i) the *Tax Act* was *intra vires* the legislature of the Province of British Columbia coming completely within provincial competence under section 92 of the *British North America Act, 1867* (the "B.N.A. Act") and (ii) it was a statute of general application in the Province. *In limine,* it is to be noted no question arose that the provincial legislature was not entitled, if it so saw fit, as it did, to include electricity as personal property for the purposes of the levy of the tax. But it is plain that inclusion does not make electricity "personal property" as those words are used in section 87 of the federal statute, the *Indian Act.* There is no definition of "personal property" in the *Indian Act* or the *Interpretation Act of Canada.* Hence, as the statutory inclusion of electricity as personal property in the *Tax Act* has no application to personal property referred to in section 87, it is necessary to ascertain whether the words "personal property" used in section 87 are to be construed to include electricity. The resolution of this question is assisted by considering whether electricity is personal property at common law. . . .

I therefore reject the respondent's submissions that electricity is not personal property and agree with the view of the trial Judge that it is, and should in this day and age be treated as such. I am not prepared to hold that *Low* v. *Blease,* holding as it did that electricity was not property that was subject to theft, is an authority that electricity cannot be personal property in other contexts.

. . . The question to be answered was whether electricity is "personal property" within the meaning of section 87 of the *Indian Act.* The learned trial Judge held it is not because properly construed the words "personal property" do not include intangible property which is other than a chose in action and which is not capable of being subject to succession. The Judge concluded this because of the explicit references in the latter part of the section to succession, inheritance and estate taxes. He therefore decided that electricity is not personal property included in the exemption from taxation under section 87. . . .

Accordingly, I find the trial Judge erred in concluding for the reasons he outlined, that electricity was not included in the words "personal property" in section 87(b).

But the respondents submitted two other grounds upon which the trial Judge's finding that electricity was not covered by the exemption could, and should, be supported.

The first was that the exemption by its terms covered the Indian's personal property when it was "situated on a reserve". It was argued that electricity by its very nature was not and could not be so situated. It was said that electricity has no "situs". . . .

As to the suggestion that the word "situated" as used in section 87 means that there must be some degree of permanence to the occurrence of electricity on the reservation, my opinion is that the word "situated" is not used in that sense but rather in the sense of "located". I therefore consider that the electricity was clearly delivered to and situated on the reserve. . . .

[I]t seems to me plain that the *Tax Act*, although perfectly valid as provincial legislation and of uniform application applying in its general terms to the personal property of Indians situated on a reserve, is to that extent prevented from having application by the express Federal exemption, but only if that Federal legislation has paramount authority by being "strictly" within the ambit or sphere of legislation expressly provided for in section 91(24) of the *B.N.A. Act*, that is, "Indians, and Lands reserved for the Indians". . . .

In my opinion the decision of the Manitoba Court of Appeal in *Canard* v. *Attorney-General of Canada* (1972) 30 D.L.R. (3d) 9 (reversed on other grounds) sub nom. *The Attorney-General of Canada and William Barker Rees* v. *Flora Canard and The National Indian Brotherhood and the Manitoba Indian Brotherhood* [1976] 1 S.C.R. 170 contained reasoning which received at least the tacit approval of the Supreme Court of Canada and which I find compelling. The case dealt with sections 42 to 44 of the *Indian Act* giving the appropriate Minister jurisdiction in matters and causes testamentary of a deceased Indian and providing (*inter alia*) for the appointment by the Minister of an administrator of an Indian's estate when ordinarily resident on a reserve. The two issues involved were the constitutional validity of those sections of the *Indian Act* and whether they were affected and rendered inoperative by the *Canadian Bill of Rights* (1970 R.S.C., App. III). We are not concerned with the second issue. Dickson, J.A., (as he then was) had this to say with respect to the first issue, the constitutional question, at p. 16:

> Section 91, para. 24, of the *B.N.A. Act,* 1867, conferred exclusive legislative authority on the Parliament of Canada in "all Matters" coming within the subject "Indians and lands reserved for the Indians", This "enables the Dominion to legislate fully and exclusively, upon matters falling strictly within the subject 'Indians'", *per* Duff J., as he then was, in *Re Water Powers' Reference,* [1929] 2 481 at p. 485, [1929] S.C.R. 200.
>
> It has been held that the Parliament of Canada has exclusive right to legislate regarding Indians, not only as regards administration but also judicially: *Delorimier* v. *Cross* (1937), 62 Que. K.B.
>
> *In Laskin on Canadian* Constitutional *Law*, 3rd ed. (1966), p. 550, it is said:
>
> > There is no doubt but that Parliament alone has authority to regulate the lives and affairs of Indians on a reservation and, indeed, to control the administration of a

reservation, provincial laws are inapplicable on a reservation (save as they may be referentially introduced through federal legislation): see *Rex* v. *Jim* (1915), 26 B.C.R. 106, 26 Can.C.C. 2336, *Rex v Rodgers*, [1923] 3 D.L.R. 414 [1923] 2 W.W.R. 353; *Warman* v. *Francis* (1958), 20 D.L.R.(2d) 627, 43 M.P.R. 197, *The Indian Act*, R.S.C. 1942, c. 149, as amended.

I do not think it can fairly be doubted that s. 42 *et seq.* of the *Indian Act* are strictly within the subject of Indians. The "subject of Indians" embraces everything reasonably having to do with Indians, not excluding the disposition of their effects.

Section 42 *et seq.* constitute a comprehensive testamentary code in respect of Indians. It was plainly the intention of Parliament, in enacting those sections that provincial legislation on the subject of wills, devolution of estates and surrogate procedures applicable to others would not apply to Indians or to the administration of their estates unless the Minister so directed.

As s. 42 *et seq.* come within s. 91, para.24 of the *B.N.A. Act, 1867*, it is of no consequence that they incidentally affect property and civil rights within the Province. In *Re Fisheries Act, 1914; A.-G. Can.* v. *A.-G. B.C.,* [1930] 1 D.L.R. 194 at p. 196, [1930] A.C. 111, [1929] 3 W.W.R. 449, the Privy Council stated that so long as it strictly relates to subjects of legislation expressly enumerated in s. 91 the legislation of Parliament is of paramount authority, even though it trenches upon matters assigned to the provincial Legislatures by s. 92.

With respect, I consider those remarks sound, and I adopt and apply them to the situation here. In the Supreme Court of Canada the constitutional issue was not pressed, although discussed by most of the Judges to a limited extent. There, the issue was principally the second one with respect to the *Canadian Bill of Rights*. However, a careful reading of the five judgments delivered satisfies me from the comments made by most of the Judges with reference to the opinion of Dickson, J.A. on the constitutional question, that his conclusions above, with which I agree, were not only accepted but approved.

If matters testamentary referred to in *Canard,* supra, were validly included in Federal legislation in the *Indian Act* notwithstanding that the subject matter would normally be within general provincial competency and legislation, I cannot but find that even more adhesive to the power to deal or, "to do", with Indians given by section 91(24) of the *B.N.A. Act* are provisions exempting them (while living on a reserve) from the incidents of taxation including properly enacted provincial tax legislation applying generally to all persons in the Province. In my view, such an exemption from taxation should be considered, having regard to the exclusive nature of Parliament's competency given by the *B.N.A. Act* and the obvious purpose thereof to provide for the protection, welfare and guidance of Indians, to be almost essential legislation.

It follows that I am unable to accede to the respondents' submissions that the exemption from taxation on, or in respect of, personal property of an Indian situated on a reserve as provided in section 87(2) of the *Indian Act*, is *ultra vires*. In my view the section, validly enacted, has in effect ousted that part of the *Tax Act* levying the Social Services Tax on the electricity sold to the appellant, and section 87(2) of the *Indian Act* overrides.

Hence, the appellants' suit should not have been dismissed. I would allow the appeal accordingly, set aside the judgment below and, as requested by the appellant, order that the question, set out above, posed at the trial and upon which the trial was held, be answered in the negative.

3.   *R. v. Nowegijick*, [1983] 2 C.N.L.R. 89 (S.C.C.). Ritchie, Dickson, Beetz, Estey, McIntyre, Chouinard, and Lamer JJ., January 25, 1983

> *Nowegijick* affirms the proposition that statutes affecting Indians should be liberally construed and that doubtful expressions should be resolved in favour of Indians. Regarding the s. 87 taxation exemption, *Nowegijick* held that income was personal property and therefore exempt from taxation under s. 87 if the corporation or its head office is situated on reserve and the Indian lives on the reserve. Since the wages would be payable on reserve, the *situs* of the income earned was deemed to be situated "on reserve" and therefore exempt from taxation. The *Williams* decision limits the broadness of *Nowegijick*.

DICKSON J.:—The question is whether the appellant, Gene A. Nowegijick, a registered Indian can claim by virtue of the *Indian Act*, R.S.C. 1970, c. I–6, an exemption from income tax for the 1975 taxation year. . . .

Mr. Nowegijick is an Indian within the meaning of the *Indian Act* and a member of the Gull Bay (Ontario) Indian Band. During the 1975 taxation year Mr. Nowegijick was an employee of the Gull Bay Development Corporation, a company without share capital, having its head office and administrative offices on the Gull Bay Reserve. All the directors, members and employees of the Corporation live on the Reserve and are registered Indians.

During 1975 the Corporation in the course of its business conducted a logging operation 10 miles from the Gull Bay Reserve. Mr. Nowegijick was employed as a logger and remunerated on a piece-work basis. He was paid bi-weekly by cheque at the head office of the Corporation on the Reserve.

During 1975, Mr. Nowegijick maintained his permanent dwelling on the Gull Bay Reserve. Each morning he would leave the Reserve to work on the logging operations, and return to the Reserve at the end of the working day. . . .

The short but difficult question to be determined is whether the tax sought to be imposed under the *Income Tax Act*, S.C. 1970–71–72, c. 63 upon the income of Mr. Nowegijick can be said to be "in respect of" "any" personal property situated upon a reserve. . . .

CONSTRUCTION OF SECTION 87 OF THE *INDIAN ACT*

Indians are citizens and, in affairs of life not governed by treaties or the *Indian Act*, they are subject to all of the responsibilities including payment of taxes, of other Canadian citizens.

It is legal lore that, to be valid, exemptions to tax laws should be clearly expressed. It seems to me, however, that treaties and statutes relating to Indians should be liberally construed and doubtful expressions resolved in favour of the Indian. If the statute contains language which can reasonably be construed to confer tax exemption that construction, in my view, is to be favoured over a more technical construction which might be available to deny exemption. In *Jones* v. *Meehan*, 175 U.S. l, it was held that "Indian treaties must be construed, not according to the technical meaning of their words, but in the sense in which they would naturally be understood by the Indians".

There is little in the cases to assist in the construction of s. 87 of the *Indian Act*. In *R.* v. *The National Indian Brotherhood* (1978), 78 D.T.C. 6488 [[1978] C.N.L.B. (No. 4) 107] the question was as to situs, an issue which does not arise in the present case. The appeal related to the failure of the National Indian Brotherhood to deduct and pay over to the Receiver General for Canada the amount which the defendant was required by the *Income Tax Act* and regulations to deduct from the salaries of its Indian employees. The salaries in question were paid to the employees in Ottawa by cheque drawn on an Ottawa bank. Thurlow A.C.J. said at p. 6491 [pp. 113–4 C.N.L.R.]:

> I have already indicated that it is my view that the exemption provided for by subsection 87 does not extend beyond the ordinary meaning of the words and expressions used in it. There is no legal basis, notwithstanding the history of the exemption, and the special position of Indians in Canadian society, for extending it by reference to any notional extension of reserves or of what may be considered as being done on reserves. The issue, as I see it, assuming that the taxation imposed by the *Income Tax Act* is taxation of individuals in respect of property and that a salary or a right to salary is property, is whether the salary which the individual Indian received or to which he was entitled was "personal property" of the Indian "situated on a reserve". . . .

A tax on income is in reality a tax on property itself. If income can be said to be property I cannot think that taxable income is any less so. Taxable income is by definition, s. 2(2) of the *Income Tax Act,* "his income for the year minus the deductions permitted by Division C." Although the Crown in paragraph l4 of its factum recognizes that "salaries" and "wages" can be classified as "personal property" it submits that the basis of taxation is a person's "taxable" income and that such taxable income is not "personal property" but rather a "concept", that results from a number of operations. This is too fine a distinction for my liking. If wages are personal property it seems to me difficult to say that a person taxed "in respect of" wages is not being taxed in respect of personal property. It is true that certain calculations are needed in order to determine the quantum of tax but I do not think this in any way invalidates the basic proposition.

The words "in respect of" are, in my opinion, words of the widest possible scope. They import such meanings as "in relation to", "with reference to" or "in connection with". The phrase "in respect of" is probably the widest of any expression intended to convey some connection between two related subject matters.

Crown counsel submits that the effect of s. 87 of the *Indian Act* is to exempt what can properly be classified as "direct taxation on property" and the judgment of Jackett C.J. in *Minister of National Revenue* v. *Iroquois of Caughnawaga (Caughnawaga Indian Band)*, [1977] 2 F.C. 269 [[1977] C.N.L.B. (No. l) 15] is cited. The question in that case was whether the employer's share of unemployment insurance premiums was payable in respect of persons employed by an Indian band at a hospital operated by the band on a reserve. It was argued that the premiums were "taxation" on "property" within s. 87 of the *Indian Act.* Chief Justice Jackett held that even if the imposition by statute on an employer of liability to contribute to the cost of a scheme of unemployment insurance were "taxation" it would not, in the view of the Chief Justice, be taxation on "property' within the ambit of s. 87. The Chief Justice continued at p. 271:

> From one point of view, all taxation is directly or indirectly taxation on property; from another point of view, all taxation is directly or indirectly taxation on persons. It is my view, however, that when section 87 exempts "personal property of an Indian or band situated on a reserve" from "taxation", its effect is to exempt what can properly be classified as direct taxation on property. The courts have had to develop jurisprudence as to when taxation is taxation on property and when it is taxation on persons for the purposes of section 92(2) of *The British North America Act, 1867*, and there would seem to be no reason why such jurisprudence should not be applied to the interpretation of section 87 of the *Indian Act*. See, for example, with reference to section 92(2), *Provincial Treasurer of Alberta* v. *Kerr*, [1933] A.C. 710. . . .

With respect, I do not agree with Chief Justice Jackett that the effect of s. 87 of the *Indian Act* is only to exempt what can properly be classified as direct taxation on property. Section 87 provides that "the personal property of an Indian . . . on a reserve" is exempt from taxation; but it also provides that "no Indian . . . is . . . subject to taxation in respect of any such property". The earlier words certainly exempt certain property from taxation; but the latter words also exempt certain persons from taxation in respect of such property. As I read it, s. 87 creates an exemption for both persons and property. It does not matter then that the taxation of employment income may be characterized as a tax on persons, as opposed to a tax on property.

We must, I think, in these cases, have regard to substance and the plain and ordinary meaning of the language used, rather than to forensic dialectics. I do not think we should give any refined construction to the section. A person exempt from taxation in respect of any of his personal property would have difficulty in understanding why he should pay tax in respect of his wages. And I do not think it is a sufficient answer to say that the conceptualization of the *Income Tax Act* renders it so.

I conclude by saying that nothing in these reasons should be taken as implying that no Indian shall ever pay tax of any kind. Counsel for the appellant and counsel for the intervenants do not take that position. Nor do I. We are concerned here with personal property situated on a reserve and only with property situated on a reserve.

I would allow the appeal, set aside the judgment of the Federal Court of Appeal and reinstate the judgment in the Trial Division of that Court. . . .

4. *Mitchell* v. *Peguis Indian Band*, [1990] 3 C.N.L.R. 46 (S.C.C.). Dickson C.J., Lamer, Wilson, La Forest, L'Heureux-Dubé, Sopinka, and Gonthier JJ., June 21, 1990

La Forest, with the majority of the court concurring, held that "Her Majesty" in s. 90(1) of the *Indian Act* is limited to the federal Crown and as such, the exemptions and privileges in ss. 87 and 89 will apply solely in respect of property that the federal Crown gives to Indians. Thus, s. 90(1) does not apply to purely private commercial transactions unless that property is situated on a reserve. Dickson C.J. held that "Her Majesty" includes both the federal and provincial Crowns. *Mitchell* also stands for the proposition that a liberal construction should be given to legislation affecting Indians and that any doubts as to the meaning of legislation should be resolved in favour of the Indians.

LA FOREST J. (SOPINKA and GONTHIER JJ., concurring):—I have had the advantage of reading the reasons of the Chief Justice. I agree with his proposed disposition of this case, but I do so for quite different reasons. With respect, I am unable to agree with his approach and, in particular, with his adoption of the trial judge's interpretation of s. 90(1)(b) of the *Indian Act*, R.S.C. 1970, c. I-6 [now R.S.C. 1985, c. I-5].

The Chief Justice has summarized the facts and the judicial history and I need not repeat them. In broad terms, the issue to be determined involves funds in the hands of the Government of Manitoba which it agreed to pay to the respondent Indians in settlement of a claim for the return of taxes paid by the Indians to Manitoba Hydro in respect of sales of electricity on reserves. The question is whether those funds may be garnisheed by the appellants who are suing the Indians for fees for representing the Indians in negotiating the settlement.

Both the trial judge [reported [1983] 4 C.N.L.R. 50, [1983] 5 W.W.R. 117] and the Court of Appeal [reported [1985] 2 C.N.L.R. 90, [1986] 2 W.W.R 477] held the funds were not subject to garnishment. These decisions, as the Chief Justice has noted, were based on the interpretation given by those courts to s. 90(1)(b) of the *Indian Act*. In my respectful view, this interpretation not only goes beyond the clear terms and purposes of the Act, but flies in the face of the historical record and has serious implications for Indian policy that are harmful both for government and native people. . . .

As is clear from the comments of the Chief Justice in *Guerin* v. *The Queen*, [1984] 2 S.C.R, 335 at 383, [1985] 1 C.N.L.R. 120 at 136, these legislative restraints on the alienability of Indian lands are but the continuation of a policy that has shaped the dealings between the Indians and the European settlers since the time of the *Royal Proclamation of 1763*. The historical record leaves no doubt that native peoples acknowledged the ultimate sovereignty of the British Crown, and agreed to cede their traditional homelands on the understanding that the Crown would thereafter protect them in the possession and use of such lands as were reserved for their use; see the comments of Professor Slattery in his article "Understanding Aboriginal Rights" (1987), 66 *Can. Bar Rev.* 727 at 753. The sections of the *Indian Act* relating to the inalienability of Indian lands seek to give effect to this protection by interposing the Crown between the Indians and the market forces which, if left unchecked, had the potential to erode Indian ownership of these reserve lands. This Court, in its recent decision of *Canadian Pacific Ltd* v. *Paul*, [1988] 2 S.C.R. 654, [1989] 1 C.N.L.R. 47, alluded to this point when it noted, at p. 677 [pp. 59–60 C.N.L.R.], that the feature of inalienability was adopted as a protective measure for the Indian population lest it be persuaded into improvident transactions.

I take it to be obvious that the protections afforded against taxation and attachment by ss. 87 and 89 of the *Indian Act* go hand-in-hand with these restraints on the alienability of land. I noted above that the Crown, as part of the consideration for the cession of Indian lands, often committed itself to giving goods and services to the natives concerned. Taking but one example, by terms of the "numbered treaties" concluded between the Indians of the prairie regions and part of the Northwest Territories, the Crown undertook to provide Indians with assistance in such matters as education, medicine and agriculture, and to furnish supplies which Indians could use in the pursuit of their traditional vocations of hunting, fishing, and trapping. The exemptions from taxation and distraint have historically protected the ability of Indians to benefit from this property in two ways. First, they guard against the possibility that one branch of government, through the imposition of taxes, could erode the full measure of the benefits given by that branch of government entrusted with the supervision of Indian affairs. Secondly, the protection against attachment ensures that the enforcement of civil judgments by non-natives will not be allowed to hinder Indians in the untrammelled enjoyment of such advantages as they had retained or might acquire pursuant to the fulfillment by the Crown of its treaty obligations. In effect, these sections shield Indians from the imposition of the civil liabilities that could lead, albeit through an indirect route, to the alienation of the Indian land base through the medium of foreclosure sales and the like; see Brennan J.'s discussion of the purpose served by Indian tax immunities in the American context in *Bryan* v. *Itasca County*, 426 U.S. 373(1976), at p. 391.

In summary, the historical record makes it clear that ss. 87 and 89 of the Indian Act, the sections to which the deeming provision of s. 90 applies, constitute part of a legislative "package" which bears the impress of an obligation to native peoples which the Crown has recognized at least since the signing of the Royal Proclamation of 1763. From that time on, the Crown has always acknowledged that it is honour-bound to shield Indians from any efforts by non-natives to dispossess Indians of the property which they hold *qua* Indians, i.e., their land base and the chattels on that land base.

It is also important to underscore the corollary to the conclusion I have just drawn. The fact that the modern-day legislation, like its historical counterparts, is so careful to underline that exemptions from taxation and distraint apply only in respect of personal property situated on reserves demonstrates that the purpose of the legislation is not to remedy the economically disadvantaged position of Indians by ensuring that Indians may acquire, hold, and deal with property in the commercial mainstream on different terms than their fellow citizens. An examination of the decisions bearing on these sections confirms that Indians who acquire and deal in property outside lands reserved for their use, deal with it on the same basis as all other Canadians. . . .

In support of my view that Indians will have perceived that their treaty benefits were given unconditionally, I would point to the following extract from the report of the Treaty Commissioners in respect of Treaty No. 8. The passage is eloquent testimony to the fact that native peoples feared that the imposition of taxes would seriously interfere with their ability to maintain a traditional way of life on the lands reserved for their use, and, additionally, leaves no doubt that

Indians were promised that their entitlements would be exempt from taxation:

> There was expressed at every point the fear that the making of the Treaty would be followed by the curtailment of the hunting and fishing privileges, and many were impressed with the notion that the Treaty would lead to taxation and enforced military service.
>
> We assured them that the Treaty would not lead to any forced interference with their mode of life, that it did not open the way to the imposition of any tax, and that there was no fear of enforced military service. [Treaty No. 8, 1899 (Queen's Printer, Ottawa), as quoted in R. Bartlett, *Indians and Taxation in Canada,* 2d ed. (Saskatoon, Sask.: University of Saskatchewan Native Law Centre, 1987), p. 5]

In summary, I conclude that an interpretation of s. 90(1)(b), which sees its purpose as limited to preventing non-natives from hampering Indians from benefitting in full from the personal property promised Indians in treaties and ancillary agreements, is perfectly consistent with the tenor of the obligations that the Crown has always assumed vis-à-vis the protection of native property.

Section 90(1)(b) as including the Provincial Crowns

I turn next to the second of the two alternative readings of "Her Majesty" in s. 90(1)(b). If this term is meant to include the provincial Crowns, the exemptions and privileges of ss. 87 and 89 will apply to a much wider range of personal property. In effect, it would follow inexorably that the notional *situs* of s. 90(1)(b) will extend these protections to any and all personal property that could enure to Indians through the whole range of agreements that might be concluded between an Indian band and Her Majesty in right of a province.

As I see it, if one is to reject the interpretation advanced above, that s. 90(1)(b) refers solely to property which enures to Indians from the federal Crown through operation of the treaties and ancillary agreements, there is no basis in logic for the further assumption that some, but not all agreements, between Indian bands and provincial Crowns would be contemplated by the provision. Section 90(1)(b) does not qualify the term "agreement," and if one interprets "Her Majesty" as including the provincial Crown, it must follow as a matter of due course that s. 90(1)(b) takes in all agreements that could be concluded between an Indian band and a provincial Crown.

It follows inexorably that if an Indian band, pursuant to a purely commercial agreement with a provincial Crown, acquires personal property, that property will be exempt from taxation and distraint, regardless of its *situs*. Moreover, the protections of ss. 87 and 89 would apply in respect of any subsequent dealings by the Indian band respecting that property, even if those dealings were confined to ordinary commercial matters. This would have broad ramifications, and I cannot accept the notion that Parliament, in fulfilling its constitutional responsibility over Indian affairs, intended that the protective envelope of ss. 87 and 89 should apply on such a broad scale.

My conclusion rests on the fact that such a result cannot be reconciled with the scope of the protections that the Crown has traditionally extended to the property of natives. As I stated earlier, a review of the obligations that the Crown has assumed in this area shows that it has done no more than seek to shield the property of Indians that has an immediate and discernible nexus to the occupancy of reserve lands from interference at the hands of non-natives. The legislation has always distinguished between property situated on reserves and property Indians hold outside reserves. There is simply no evidence that the Crown has ever taken the position that it must protect property simply because that property is held by an Indian as opposed to a non-native. . . .

There can be no doubt, on a reading of s. 90(1)(b), that it would not apply to any personal property that an Indian band might acquire in connection with an ordinary commercial agreement with a private concern. Property of that nature will only be protected once it can be established that it is situated on a reserve. Accordingly, any dealings in the commercial mainstream in property acquired in this manner will fall to be regulated by the laws of general application. Indians will enjoy no exemptions from taxation in respect of this property, and will be free to deal with it in the same manner as any other citizen. In addition, provided the property is not situated on reserve lands, third parties will be free to issue execution on this property. I think it would be truly paradoxical if it were to be otherwise. As the Chief Justice has pointed out in *Nowegijick* v. *The Queen*, [1983] 1 S.C.R. 29 at 36, [1983] 2 C.N.L.R. 89 at 93–94:

> Indians are citizens and, in affairs of life not governed by treaties or the *Indian Act*, they are subject to all of the responsibilities, including payment of taxes, of other Canadian citizens.

But, in my respectful view, the implications flowing from the interpretation the trial judge advanced of s. 90(1)(b) go counter to this statement, for as I have pointed out earlier, as a logical consequence of that interpretation, any time Indians acquired personal property in an agreement with a provincial Crown, even one of a purely commercial character, the exemptions and protections of ss. 87 and 89 would apply in respect of that particular asset, regardless of *situs*. . . .

I conclude that the statutory notional *situs* of s. 90(1)(b) is meant to extend solely to personal property which enures to Indians through the discharge by "Her Majesty" of her treaty or ancillary obligations. Pursuant to s. 91(24) of the *Constitution Act, 1867*, it is of course "Her Majesty" in right of Canada who bears the sole responsibility for conferring any such property on Indians, and I would, therefore, limit application of the term "Her Majesty" as used in s. 90(1)(b) to the federal Crown. . . .

Moreover, I would question the conclusion that interpreting "Her Majesty" as including the provincial Crowns in the context of s. 90(1)(b) is tantamount to resolving the ambiguity of the meaning of this term in favour of the Indians. Section 87 and 89, as I have shown above, have been crafted so as to place obstacles in the way of non-natives who would presume to dispossess Indians of personal property that is situated on reserves. But when Indians deal in the general marketplace, the protections conferred by these sections have the potential to become powerful impediments to their engaging successfully in commercial matters. Access to credit is the lifeblood of commerce, and I find it very difficult to accept that Indians would see any advantage, when seeking credit, in being precluded from putting forth in pledge property they may acquire from provincial Crowns. Indians, I would have thought, would much prefer to have free rein to conduct their affairs as all other fellow citizens when dealing in the commercial mainstream.

To elaborate, if Indians are to be unable to pledge or mortgage such personal property as they acquire in agreements with provincial Crowns, businessmen will have a strong incentive to avoid dealings with Indians. This is simply because the fact that Indians will be liable to be distrained in respect of some classes of property, and not in respect of others, will introduce a level of complexity in business dealings with Indians that is not present in other transactions. I think it safe to say that businessmen place a great premium on certainty in their commercial dealings, and that, accordingly, the greatest possible incentive to do business with Indians would be the knowledge that business may be conducted with them on exactly the same basis as with any other person. Any special considerations, extraordinary protections or exemptions that Indians bring with them to the marketplace introduce complications and would seem guaranteed to frighten off potential business partners.

In summary, while I of course endorse the applicability of the canons of interpretation laid down in *Nowegijick*, it is my respectful view that the interpretation proposed in this particular instance takes one beyond the confines of the fair, large and liberal, and can, in fact, be seen to involve the resolution of a supposed ambiguity in a manner most unfavourable to Indian interests. . . .

I would dismiss the appeal with costs throughout.

WILSON J. (LAMER and L'HEUREUX-DUBÉ JJ., concurring): . . .

DICKSON C.J.: . . .

THE APPLICABLE INTERPRETIVE PRINCIPLES

I should say at the outset that I find the reasons and reasoning of Morse J. persuasive. In particular, he was correct in resorting to the principle enunciated by this Court in *Nowegijick* v. *The Queen,* [1983] 1 S.C.R. 29 at 36, [1983] 2 C.N.L.R. 89 at 94, when he found it necessary to resolve interpretive difficulties. In *Nowegijick* the Court had the following to say:

> It is legal lore that, to be valid, exemptions to tax laws should be clearly expressed. It seems to me, however, that treaties and statutes relating to Indians should be liberally construed and doubtful expressions resolved in favour of the Indians. If the statute contains language which can reasonably be construed to confer tax exemption that construction, in my view, is to be favoured over a more technical construction which might be available to deny exemption. In *Jones* v. *Meehan*, 175 U.S. 1 (1899), it was held that Indian treaties "must . . . be construed, not according to the technical meaning of [their] words . . . but in the sense in which they would naturally be understood by the Indians."

Two elements of liberal interpretation can be found in this passage: (1)ambiguities in the interpretation of treaties and statutes relating to Indians are to be resolved in favour of the Indians, and (2) aboriginal understandings of words and corresponding legal concepts in Indian treaties are to be preferred over more legalistic and technical constructions. In some cases, the two elements are indistinguishable, but in other cases the interpreter will only be able to perceive that there is an ambiguity by first invoking the second element.

The appellants maintain that the *Nowegijick* principle should not govern the present appeal. Rather, it is asserted that the normal principle that derogations from the civil rights of a creditor should be strictly construed, is applicable. The appellants attempt to distinguish *Nowegijick* in part by saying that the case was concerned with trying to resolve a conflict between the State and an Indian, in which case it was appropriate to resolve any ambiguity against the author of the doubt. The appellants are in effect arguing that *Nowegijick* is not applicable when it is a private citizen or other civil party, and not the State (the author of the doubt or ambiguity) who will lose out if the Act is interpreted in favour of aboriginal litigants.

I cannot accept that the comments in *Nowegijick* were implicitly limited in this way. The *Nowegijick* principles must be understood in the context of this Court's sensitivity to the historical and continuing status of aboriginal peoples in Canadian society. The above-quoted statement is clearly concerned with interpreting a statute or treaty with respect to the persons who are its *subjects*—Indians—not with interpreting a statute in favour of Indians simply because it is the State that is the other interested party. It is Canadian society at large which bears the historical burden of the current situation of native peoples and, as a result, the liberal interpretive approach applies to any statute relating to Indians, even if the relationship thereby affected is a private one. Underlying *Nowegijick* is an appreciation of societal responsibility, and a concern with remedying disadvantage, if only in the somewhat marginal context of treaty and statutory interpretation.

In oral argument, the appellants also sought to distinguish *Nowegijick* on the basis that the case dealt only with laws touching upon the particular status or qualities of Indians, thus providing a policy basis for the interpretive principle. *Nowegijick* dealt with tax exemptions under s. 87 of the Act, while this case deals with exemptions from garnishment ("attachment") under s. 89. Both provisions reflect the policy of the Act that Indians should be protected from the operation of laws which otherwise might allow Indians to be dispossessed of their property. In *Nowegijick*, the Court was concerned with whether a provincial law was applicable to Indians as a law of general application (s. 88, *Indian Act*). The only limitation to the principle articulated in *Nowegijick* was that the treaties or statutes must relat[e] to Indians" for the liberal interpretive principle to apply. The *Indian Act* is the quintessential Act relating to Indians and the interpretation of any provision in it is, therefore, subject to the *Nowegijick* principle.

I would finally note that the appellants' argument to the effect that as against a private party the Court should not create privileges where Parliament has not explicitly done so, even if accepted, would not avail them in this case. Section 89(1) provides that a non-Indian cannot attach personal property of an Indian in certain circumstances. It clearly contemplates that Indians will be favoured vis-à-vis non-Indians. Therefore, it would be inconsistent with *Nowegijick* to interpret s. 90, which extends s. 89's protection, in a restrictive manner. . . .

The Main Issue—The Meaning of "Her Majesty" . . .

The divisibility of the Crown in the sense just noted does not determine the interpretation to be given,to the words "Her Majesty." Even if the Court of Appeal had been correct as a matter of constitutional law regarding indivisibility of the Crown, this would not necessarily have determined the correct statutory interpretation of "Her Majesty" in s. 90(1)(b): see, for example, *Nickel Rim Mines Ltd.* v. *Attorney General for Ontario,* [1967] S.C.R. 672, 63 D.L.R. (2d) 668 in which Spence J. (in Chambers) interpreted "Her Majesty" in s. 105 of the *Supreme Court Act*, R.S.C. 1952, c. 259, as including both the federal and provincial Crowns despite his constitutional premise that "[t]here is only one Crown although there are two separate statutory purses" (at p. 674). Instead, Morse J.'s approach commends itself in all material respects (at pp. 127–28 W.W.R.) [p. 59 C.N.L.R.]:

> In the *Interpretation Act* of Canada (s. 28) it is provided that "'Her Majesty,' 'His Majesty,' 'the Queen,' 'the King' or 'the Crown' means the Sovereign of the United Kingdom, Canada, and Her other Realms and Territories, and Head of the Commonwealth." In *A.G. Que.* v. *Nipissing Ry. Co.*, [1926] A.C. 715 . . . , it was held by the Privy Council that s. 189 of the *Railway Act*, 1919 (Can.), c. 68, which empowered any railway company, with the consent of the Governor General, to take Crown lands for the use of the railway, applied to provincial Crown lands as well as to Dominion Crown lands. It was also held that the enactment was constitutionally valid by reason of the exclusive power to legislate in respect of interprovincial railways reserved to the Dominion Parliament by ss. 91(29) and 92(10) of the *B.N.A. Act, 1867* (now the *Constitution Act, 1867*).
>
> Giving a liberal construction to the words "Her Majesty" and resolving any doubt in favour of the defendants, I think that the words include Her Majesty in right of the Province of Manitoba.

In my view, the trial judge adopted the correct approach. "Her Majesty" can refer to the province; the question is whether it *does* so refer. . . .

Nowegijick directs the courts to resolve any "doubtful expression" in favour of the Indian where more than one reasonable interpretation is available. There is no doubt in my mind that it is fully in keeping with *Nipissing* and *Nickel Rim Mines* to turn to the *Nowegijick* principle in this case, given the ambiguity that exists. In each of those cases, it was found necessary to resort to some further argument beyond the text itself in order to determine the issue. In light of *Nipissing* and *Nickel Rim Mines*, I would turn, to *Nowegijick* for the resolution of the ambiguity here and would accordingly choose an interpretation that favours the Indians. I would, therefore, find that "Her Majesty" includes the provincial Crown.

This interpretation is also supported by the second aspect of the *Nowegijick* principle, namely that aboriginal understanding of words and corresponding legal concepts in Indian treaties are to be preferred over more legalistic and technical constructions. This concern with aboriginal perspective, albeit in a different context, led a majority of this Court in *Guerin* v. *The Queen,* [1984] 2 S.C.R. 335, [1985] 1 C.N.L.R. 120, to speak of the Indian interest in land as a *sui generis* interest, the nature of which cannot be totally captured by a lexicon derived from European legal systems.

While this appeal does not involve the interpretation of a treaty, I find it helpful to consider the aboriginal perspective in illustrating the ambiguity of "Her Majesty" in s. 90(1)(b). *Nowegijick* dictates taking a generous liberal approach to interpretation. In my opinion, reference to the notion of "aboriginal understanding," which respects the unique culture and history of Canada's aboriginal peoples, is an appropriate part of that approach. In the context of this appeal, the aboriginal understanding of "the Crown" or "Her Majesty" is rooted in pre-Confederation realities. The recent case of *Guerin* took as its fundamental premise the unique character both of the Indians' interest in land and of *the historical relationship with the Crown."* (at p. 387 S.C.R. [p. 139 C.N.L.R.] emphasis added.) That relationship began with pre-Confederation contact between the historic occupiers of North American lands (the aboriginal peoples) and the European colonizers (since 1763, "the Crown"), and it is this relationship between aboriginal peoples and the Crown that grounds the distinctive fiduciary obligation on the Crown. On its facts, *Guerin* only dealt with the obligation of the *federal* Crown arising upon surrender of land by Indians and it is true that, since 1867, the Crown's role has been played, as a matter of the federal division of powers, by Her Majesty in right of Canada, with the *Indian Act* representing a confirmation of the Crown's historic responsibility for the welfare and interests of these peoples. However, the Indians' relationship with the Crown or sovereign has never depended on the particular representatives of the Crown involved. From the aboriginal perspective, any federal-provincial divisions that the Crown has imposed on itself are internal to itself and do not alter the basic structure of Sovereign-Indian relations. This is not to suggest that aboriginal peoples are outside the sovereignty of the Crown, nor does it call into question the divisions of jurisdiction in relation to aboriginal peoples in federal Canada.

One can over-emphasize the extent to which aboriginal peoples are affected only by the decisions and actions of the federal Crown. Part and parcel of the division of powers is the incidental effects doctrine according to which a law in relation to a matter within the competence of one level of government may validity affect a matter within the competence of the other; as recently stated in *Alberta Government Telephones* v. *Canada (Canadian Radio-television and Telecommunications Commission),* [1989] 2 S.C.R. 225 at p. 275, "Canadian federalism has evolved in a way which tolerates overlapping federal and provincial legislation in many respects. . . ." As long as Indians are not affected *qua* Indians, a provincial law may affect Indians, and significantly so in terms of everyday life. Section 88 of the *Indian Act* greatly increases the extent to which the provinces can affect Indians by acknowledging the validity of laws of general application, unless they are supplanted by treaties or federal law. This fluidity of responsibility across lines of jurisdiction accords well with the fact that the newly entrenched s. 35 of the *Constitution Act, 1982,* applies to all levels of government in Canada.

I conclude, therefore, that "Her Majesty" in s. 90(1)(b) of the *Indian Act* is to be interpreted as referring to both the federal and provincial Crowns. . . .

Conclusion

I find that the Court of Appeal was correct in the disposition of this case and the trial judge was correct in his reasoning and interpretation of the elements of s. 90(1)(b).

"Her Majesty" in s. 90(1)(b) of the *Indian Act* refers to both the federal and provincial Crowns. Therefore, the moneys in question are protected from garnishment by virtue of s. 89(l) of the Act. The scope of this protection is defined according to the terms of the Act. General commercial transactions involving Indians are not meant to be limited by this interpretation. In this case, the substance of the appellants' claim has, of course, not been determined, and it is clearly open to the appellants to continue legal action. In the circumstances, however, the appellants are prevented from garnishing moneys owed to the respondents by the provincial Crown.

I would dismiss the appeal with costs in this Court and both courts below.

5. **R. v. *Williams*, [1992] 3 C.N.L.R. 181 (S.C.C.). La Forest, L'Heureux-Dubé, Sopinka, Gonthier, Cory, McLachlin, and Stevenson JJ., April 16, 1992**

> R. v. *Williams* held that the mere *situs* of the employer or source of income was not sufficient to determine if the income was taxable. Rather, to determine the *situs* of intangible personal property requires a court to consider various "connecting factors" that bind the property to one location or another. The Supreme Court noted three important factors to be considered:
>
> a. the purpose of the exemption,
> b. the character of the property, and
> c. the incidence of taxation on that property.
>
> This test is a more flexible and less predictable form of determining whether or not the tax exemption applies to income. The location of the employer (head office) is simply one of a number of factors used to determine the *situs* of the work performed. Other factors include the residence of the employee, the place where the work is performed, and the place where the wages are paid.

GONTHIER J.:—At issue in this case is the *situs* of unemployment insurance benefits received by an Indian for the purpose of the exemption from taxation provided by s. 87 of the *Indian Act*, R.S.C. 1970, c. I–6 (now R.S.C. 1985. c. I–5).

1. FACTS AND PROCEDURAL HISTORY

The appellant received a notice of assessment by the Minister of National Revenue which included in his income, for the taxation year 1984, certain unemployment insurance benefits. The appellant contested the assessment. His objection was overruled by the Minister of National Revenue. The appellant appealed to the Federal Court, Trial Division: [1989] 2 F.C. 318, 24 F.T.R. 169, [1989] 1 C.N.L.R. 184, 24 C.C.E.L. 119, 89 D.T.C. 5032, [1989] 1 C.T.C. 117. The appeal proceeded on the basis of an agreed statement of facts.

At all material times, the appellant was a member of the Penticton Indian Band and resided on the Penticton Indian Reserve No. 1. In 1984 he received regular unemployment insurance benefits for which he qualified because of his former employment with a logging company situated on the reserve, and his employment by the band in a "NEED Project" on the reserve. In both cases, the work was performed on the reserve, the employer was located on the reserve, and the appellant was paid on the reserve. During his employment, contributions to the unemployment insurance scheme were paid both by the appellant and his employers.

All of the regular unemployment insurance benefits were paid by federal government cheques mailed from the Canada Employment and Immigration Commission's regional computer centre in Vancouver. (While the instruments of payment may not technically have been cheques, this is of no consequence in this appeal.) . . .

3. FRAMING THE ISSUES

In order to decide the basis upon which a situs is to be assigned to the unemployment insurance benefits in this case, it is necessary to explore the purposes of the exemption from taxation in s. 87 of the *Indian Act,* the nature of the benefits in question, and the manner in which the incidence of taxation falls upon the benefits to be taxed.

A. *The Nature and Purpose of the Exemption from Taxation*

The question of the purpose of ss. 87, 89 and 90 has been thoroughly addressed by La Forest J. in the case of *Mitchell* v. *Peguis Indian Band,* [1990] 2 S.C.R. 85, [1990] 3 C.N.L.R. 46, [1990] 5 W.W.R. 97,71 D.L.R. (4th) 193. La Forest J. expressed the view that the purpose of these sections was to preserve the entitlements of Indians to their reserve lands and to ensure that the use of their property on their reserve lands was not eroded by the ability of governments to tax or creditors to seize. The corollary of this conclusion was that the purpose of the sections was not to confer a general economic benefit upon the Indians . . .

La Forest J. also noted that the protection from seizure is a mixed blessing, in that it removes the assets of an Indian on a reserve from the ordinary stream of commercial dealings (at pp. 146–47 [S.C.R., p. 66 C.N.L.R.]).

Therefore, under the *Indian Act*, an Indian has a choice with regard to his personal property. The Indian may situate this property on the reserve, in which case it is within the protected area and free from seizure and taxation, or the Indian may situate this property off the reserve, in which case it is outside the protected area, and more fully available for ordinary commercial purposes in society. Whether the Indian wishes to remain within the protected reserve system or integrate more fully into the larger commercial world is a choice left to the Indian.

The purpose of the *situs* test in s. 87 is to determine whether the Indian holds the property in question as part of the entitlement of an Indian *qua* Indian on the reserve. Where it is necessary to decide amongst various methods of fixing the location of the relevant property, such a method must be selected having regard to this purpose.

B. *Nature of Benefit and the Incidence of Taxation*

Section 56 of the *Income Tax Act* is the section which taxes income from unemployment insurance benefits. That section specifies that unemployment insurance benefits which are "received by the taxpayer in the year" are to be included in computing the income of a taxpayer. The parties have approached this question on the basis that what is being taxed is a debt owing from the Crown to the taxpayer on account of unemployment insurance which the taxpayer has qualified for. This is not precisely true, since the liability for taxation arises not when the debt (if that is what it is) arises, but rather when it is paid, and the money is received by the taxpayer. However, it is true that the taxation does not attach to the money in the hands of the taxpayer, but instead to the receipt by the taxpayer of the money. Thus the incidence of taxation in the case of unemployment insurance benefits is on the taxpayer in respect of the transaction, that is, the receipt of the benefit.

This Court's decision in *Nowegijick* v. *The Queen*, [1983] 1 S.C.R. 29, [1983] 2 C.N.L.R. 89, 144 D.L.R. (3d) 193, [1983] C.T.C. 20, 83 D.T.C. 5042, 46 N.R. 41, stands for the proposition that the receipt of salary income is personal property for the purpose of the exemption from taxation provided by the *Indian Act*. I can see no difference between salary income and income from unemployment insurance benefits in this regard, therefore I hold that the receipt of income from unemployment insurance benefits is also personal property for the purposes of the *Indian Act*.

Nowegijick also stands for the proposition that the inclusion of personal property in the calculation of a taxpayers income gives rise to a tax in respect of that personal property within the meaning of the *Indian* Act, despite the fact that the tax is on the person rather than on the property directly.

Therefore, most of the requirements of s. 87 of the *Indian Act* have clearly been met in this case. The receipt of unemployment insurance benefits is personal property. That property is owned by an Indian. The Indian is being taxed in respect of that property, since it is being included in his income for the purpose of income taxation. The remaining question is whether the property in question is situated on a reserve.

Since it is the receipt of the benefit that is taxed, the simplest argument would be that the situs of the receipt of the benefit is where it is received, which would generally be the residence of the taxpayer. However, the *Income Tax Act* qualifies "received" by "in the year." This suggests that the notion of "receipt" in the *Income Tax Act* has more to do with when the income is received, rather than where. Thus, aside from the fact that the incidence of taxation falls upon the transaction itself, rather than the money in the hands of the employer or the taxpayer, little ought to be made of the notion of receipt in this context.

C. *Comments on the "Residence of the Debtor" Test*

The factor identified in previous cases as being of primary importance to determine the *situs* of this kind of property is the residence of the debtor, that is, the person paying the income. This was clearly stated by Thurlow A.C.J. in *The Queen* v. *National Indian Brotherhood*, [1979] 1 F.C. 103 at p. 109, 92 D.L.R. (3d) 333, [1978] C.T.C. 680, 78 D.T.C. 6488:

> A chose in action such as the right to a salary in fact has no situs. But where for some purpose the law has found it necessary to attribute a situs, in the absence of anything in the contract or elsewhere to indicate the contrary, the situs of a simple contract debt has been held to be the residence or place where the debtor is found. See Cheshire, *Private International Law*, seventh edition, pp. 420 *et seq*.

This conclusion was cited with approval by this Court in *Nowegijick* v. *The Queen*, supra, at p. 34 [S.C.R., p. 92 C.N.L.R.]:

> The Crown conceded in argument, correctly in my view, that the situs of the salary which Mr. Nowegijick received was sited on the reserve because it was there that the

residence or place of the debtor, the Gull Bay Development Corporation, was to be found and it was there that the wages were payable. See Cheshire and North, *Private International Law* (10th ed., 1979) at pp. 536 *et seg.* and also the judgment of Thurlow A.C.J. in *R.* v. *National Indian Brotherhood*, [1979] 1 F.C. 103 particularly at pp. 109 *et seq.*

The only justification given in these cases for locating the *situs* of a debt at the residence of the debtor is that this is the rule applied in the conflict of laws. The rationale for this rule in the conflict of laws is that it is at the residence of the debtor that the debt may normally be enforced. Cheshire and North, *Private International Law* (11th ed. 1987), quote Atkin L.J. to this effect in *New York Life Insurance Co.* v. *Public Trustee*, [1924] 2 Ch. 101 (C.A.), at p. 119:

> . . . the reason why the residence of the debtor was adopted as that which determined where the debt was situate was because it was in that place where the debtor was that the creditor could, in fact, enforce payment of the debt.

Dicey and Morris adopt the same explanation in *The Conflict of Laws* (11th ed. 1987), vol. 2, at p. 908, as does Castel in *Canadian Conflict of Laws* (2nd ed. 1986), at p.401. This may be reasonable for the general purposes of conflicts of laws. However, one must inquire as to its utility for the purposes underlying the exemption from taxation in the *Indian Act. . . .*

In resolving this question, it is readily apparent that to simply adopt general conflicts principles in the present context would be entirely out of keeping with the scheme and purposes of the *Indian Act* and *Income Tax Act*. The purposes of the conflict of laws have little or nothing in common with the purposes underlying the *Indian Act*. It is simply not apparent how the place where a debt may normally be enforced has any relevance to the question whether to tax the receipt of the payment of that debt would amount to the erosion of the entitlements of an Indian *qua* Indian on a reserve. The test for *situs* under the *Indian Act* must be constructed according to its purposes, not the purposes of the conflict of laws. Therefore, the position that the residence of the debtor exclusively determines the *situs* of benefits such as those paid in this case must be closely reexamined in light of the purposes of the *Indian Act*. It may be that the residence of the debtor remains an important factor, or even the exclusive one. However, this conclusion cannot be directly drawn from an analysis of how the conflict of laws deals with such an issue.

4.   THE PROPER TEST

Because the transaction by which a taxpayer receives unemployment insurance benefits is not a physical object, the method by which one might fix its *situs* is not immediately apparent. In one sense, the difficulty is that the transaction has no *situs*. However, in another sense, the problem is that it has too many. There is the *situs* of the debtor, the *situs* of the creditor, the *situs* where the payment is made, the *situs* of the employment which created the qualification for the receipt of income, the *situs* where the payment will be used, and no doubt others. The task is then to identify which of these locations is the relevant one, or which combination of these factors controls the location of the transaction.

The appellant suggests that in deciding the *situs* of the receipt of income, a court ought to balance all of the relevant "connecting factors" on a case by case basis. Such an approach would have the advantage of flexibility, but it would have to be applied carefully in order to avoid several potential pitfalls. It is desirable, when construing exemptions from taxation, to develop criteria which are predictable in their application, so that the taxpayers involved may plan their affairs appropriately. This is also important as the same criteria govern an exemption from seizure.

Furthermore, it would be dangerous to balance connecting factors in an abstract manner, divorced from the purpose of the exemption under the *Indian Act*. A connecting factor is only relevant in so much as it identifies the location of the property in question for the purposes of the *Indian Act*. In particular categories of cases, therefore, one connecting factor may have much more weight than another. It would be easy in balancing connecting factors on a case by case basis to lose sight of this.

However, an overly rigid test which identified one or two factors as having controlling force has its own potential pitfalls. Such a test would be open to manipulation and abuse, and in focusing on too few factors could miss the purposes of the exemption in the *Indian Act* as easily as a test which indiscriminately focuses on too many.

The approach which best reflects these concerns is one which analyzes the matter in terms of categories of property and types of taxation. For instance, connecting factors may have different relevance with regard to unemployment insurance benefits than in respect of employment income, or pension benefits. The first step is to identify the various connecting factors which are potentially relevant. These factors should then be analyzed to determine what weight they should be given in identifying the location of the property, in light of three considerations: (1) the purpose of the exemption under the *Indian Act;* (2) the type of property in question; and (3) the nature of the taxation of that property. The question with regard to each connecting factor is therefore what weight should be given that factor in answering the question whether to tax that form of property in that manner would amount to the erosion of the entitlement of the Indian *qua* Indian on a reserve.

This approach preserves the flexibility of the case by case approach, but within a framework which properly identifies the weight which is to be placed on various connecting factors. Of course, the weight to be given various connecting factors cannot be determined precisely. However, this approach has the advantage that it preserves the ability to deal appropriately with future cases which present considerations not previously apparent.

A. *The Test for the Situs of the Unemployment Insurance Benefits*

Unemployment insurance benefits are income replacement insurance, paid when a person is out of work under certain qualifying conditions. While one often refers to unemployment insurance "benefits," the scheme is based on employer and employee premiums. These premiums are themselves tax-deductible for both the employer and employee.

There are a number of potentially relevant connecting factors in determining the location of the receipt of unemployment insurance benefits. The following have been suggested: the residence of the debtor, the residence of the person receiving the benefits, the place the benefits are paid, and the location of the employment income which gave rise to the qualification for the benefits. One's attention is naturally first drawn to the traditional test, that of the residence of the debtor. The debtor in this case is the federal Crown, through the Canada Employment and Immigration Commission. The Commission argues that the residence of the debtor in this case is Ottawa, referring to s. 11 of the *Employment and Immigration Department* and *Commission Act,* S.C. 1976–77, c. 54 (now R.S.C. 1985, c. E–5, s. 17), which mandates that the head office of the Commission be located in the National Capital Region.

There are, however, conceptual difficulties in establishing the *situs* of a Crown agency in any particular place within Canada. For most purposes, it is unnecessary to establish the *situs* of the Crown. The conflict of laws is interested in *situs* to determine jurisdictional and choice of law questions. With regard to the Crown, no such questions arise, since the Crown is present throughout Canada and may be sued anywhere in Canada. Unemployment insurance benefits are also available anywhere in Canada, to any Canadian who qualifies for them. Therefore, the purposes behind fixing the *situs* of an ordinary person do not apply to the Crown, and in particular do not apply to the Canada Employment and Immigration Commission in respect of the receipt of unemployment insurance benefits.

This does not necessarily mean that the physical location of the Crown is irrelevant to the purposes underlying the exemption from taxation provided by the *Indian Act.* However, it does suggest that the significance of the Crown being the source of the payments at issue in this case may lie more in the special nature of the public policy behind the payments, rather than the Crown's *situs*, assuming it can be fixed. Therefore, the residence of the debtor is a connecting factor of limited weight in the context of unemployment insurance benefits. For similar reasons, the place where the benefits are paid is of limited importance in this context. . . .

The general scheme of taxation with regard to unemployment insurance premiums and benefits bears further examination in this regard. As noted above, unemployment insurance is premium based. The intent of the scheme is that the premiums received will, overall, largely equal the benefits paid out. This is not to say that the scheme is completely self-financing. However, it is more accurate to characterize an unemployment insurance benefit as something paid for through the premiums of employed persons than to characterize it as a benefit granted by the government out of its general revenues.

This becomes important in analyzing the tax implications of the unemployment insurance benefit scheme. The treatment of premiums and benefits for the purposes of taxation is that the premiums paid by employed persons are deductible from their taxable income, whereas the benefits paid to unemployed persons must be included in their taxable income. By allowing premiums to be deducted from taxable income, and mandating that benefits be included in taxable income, the effect of the unemployment insurance scheme on general tax revenue is minimized. The tax revenues lost by the government due to the deductibility of premiums are offset by the revenues gained by the taxation of the benefits. This is not to say that the unemployment insurance scheme has no effect on taxation revenues, since premiums may not precisely equal benefits overall, and the effect of different rates of taxation cannot be ignored. However, it is clear that the scheme established by Parliament was intended, in principle, to minimize the tax implications of unemployment insurance.

Since unemployment insurance benefits are based on premiums arising out of previous employment, not general tax revenue, the connection between the previous employment and the benefits is a strong one. The manner in which unemployment insurance benefits are treated for the purposes of taxation further strengthens this connection, as there is a symmetry of treatment in the taxation of premiums and benefits, since premiums are tax-deductible and benefits are taxed, thereby minimizing the influence of the unemployment insurance scheme on general tax revenues.

The location of the qualifying employment income is therefore an important factor in establishing whether the taxation of subsequent benefits would erode the entitlements of an Indian *qua* Indian on the reserve. For in the case of an Indian whose qualifying employment income was on the reserve, the symmetry in the tax implications of premiums and benefits breaks down. For such an Indian, the original employment income was tax-exempt. The taxation paid on the subsequent benefits therefore does more than merely offset the tax saved by virtue of the premiums. Instead, it is an erosion of the entitlements created by the Indian's employment on the reserve.

Furthermore, since the duration and extent of the benefits are tied to the terms of employment during a specified period, it is the location of the qualifying employment income during that period that is relevant.

Having regard to the importance of the location of the qualifying employment income as a factor in identifying the location of the unemployment insurance benefits, the remaining factor of the residence of the recipient of the benefits at the time of their receipt is only potentially significant if it points to a location different from that of the qualifying employment.

B. *The Situs of the Appellant's Unemployment Insurance Benefits*
In the present case, the residence of the appellant when he received the benefits was on the reserve.

It has been assumed by the parties that the previous employment of the appellant which gave rise to the qualification for unemployment insurance benefits was also located on the reserve, since the two employers in question were located on the reserve. This question must be reexamined in light of our determination that this conclusion cannot safely be drawn from the principles of the conflict of laws.

However, this would not be an appropriate case in which to develop a test for the *situs* of the receipt of employment income. All the potential connecting factors with respect to the qualifying employment of the appellant point to the reserve. The employer was located on the reserve, the work was performed on the reserve, the appellant resided on the reserve, and he was paid on the reserve. A test for the *situs* of employment income could therefore only be developed in an abstract vacuum in this case, since there is no real controversy of relevant factors pulling in opposite directions. The same would be true of any consideration of the weight, if any, to be given to the residence of the appellant upon receipt of the benefits as this was also on the reserve.

Furthermore, as can be seen from our discussion of the test for the *situs* of unemployment insurance benefits, the creation of a test for the location of intangible property under the *Indian Act* is a complex endeavour. In the context of unemployment insurance we were able to focus on certain features of the scheme and its taxation implications in order to establish one factor as having particular importance. It is not clear whether this would be possible in the context of employment income, or what features of employment income and its taxation should be examined to that end.

. . . [T]he employment of the appellant by which he qualified for unemployment insurance benefits was clearly located on the reserve, no matter what the proper test for the *situs* of employment income is determined to be. Because the qualifying employment was located on the reserve, so too were the benefits subsequently received. The question of the relevance of the residence of the recipient of the benefits at the time of receipt does not arise in this case since it was also on the reserve. . . .

Determining the *situs* of intangible personal property requires a court to evaluate various connecting factors which tie the property to one location or another. In the context of the exemption from taxation in the *Indian Act,* there are three important considerations: the purpose of the exemption; the character of the property in question; and the incidence of taxation upon that property. Given the purpose of the exemption, the ultimate question is to what extent each factor is relevant in determining whether to tax the particular kind of property in a particular manner would erode the entitlement of an Indian *qua* Indian to personal property on the reserve.

With regard to the unemployment insurance benefits received by the appellant, a particularly important factor is the location of the employment which gave rise to the qualification for the benefits. In this case, the location of the qualifying employment was on the reserve, therefore the benefits received by the appellant were also located on the reserve. The question of the relevance of the residence of the recipient of the benefits at the time of receipt does not arise in this case.

The appeal is therefore allowed and the cross-appeal dismissed, with costs throughout. The matter is referred back to the Minister of National Revenue to be reassessed on the basis that all of the unemployment benefits in question are exempt from taxation.

6. *Indian Act* Exemption for Employment Income: Guidelines. Revenue Canada, June 1994

In most cases to date, these guidelines appear to be an accurate reflection of the law.

GUIDELINE 1
When at least 90% of the duties of an employment are performed on a reserve, all of the income of an Indian from that employment will usually be exempt from income tax. . . .

PRORATION RULE
When less than 90% of the duties of an employment are performed on a reserve
and the employment income is not exempted by another guideline, the exemption
is to be prorated. The exemption will apply to the portion of the income related to
the duties performed on the reserve. . . .

GUIDELINE 2
When:
• The employer is resident on a reserve; and
• The Indian lives on a reserve;
  all of the income of an Indian from an employment will usually be exempt
  from income tax. . . .

GUIDELINE 3
When:
• More than 50% of the duties of an employment are performed on a reserve;
  and
• The employer is resident on a reserve, or the Indian lives on a reserve;
  all of the income of an Indian from an employment will usually be exempt
  from income tax. . . .

GUIDELINE 4
When:
• The employer is resident on a reserve; and
• The employer is:
    • an Indian band which has a reserve, or a tribal council represent-
      ing one or more Indian bands which have reserves, or
    • an Indian organization controlled by one or more such bands or
      tribal councils, if the organization is dedicated exclusively to the
      social, cultural, educational, or economic development of Indians
      who for the most part live on reserves; and
  the duties of the employment are in connection with the employer's non-commercial activities carried on exclusively for the benefit of Indians who for the
  most part live on reserves;
  all of the income of an Indian from an employment will usually be exempt
  from income tax. . . .

Employment Related Income
The receipt of unemployment insurance benefits, retiring allowances, Canada Pension Plan payments, Quebec Pension Plan payments, registered pension plan benefits or wage loss replacement plan benefits will usually be exempt from income
tax when received as a result of employment income that was exempt from tax. If
a portion of the employment income was exempt, then a similar portion of these
amounts will be exempt. . . .

Meaning of Terms Used

"*Employer is resident on a reserve*" means that the reserve is the place where the central management and control over the employer organization is actually located. . . .

7.   GST Technical Information Bulletin B–039

September 1992

GST ADMINISTRATIVE POLICY

APPLICATION OF GST TO INDIANS . . .

INTRODUCTION

This bulletin summarizes the policy concerning the treatment of Indian purchases under the Goods and Services Tax (GST). . . .

The treatment of Indian purchases under the GST is consistent with the *Indian Act* under which personal property of an Indian or an Indian band situated on a reserve and their interests in reserves or designated lands are not subject to tax.

The policy is as follows:

- GST does not apply to on-reserve purchases of goods by Indians and Indian bands, or to off-reserve purchases of goods delivered to the reserve by vendors or their agents.
- GST does not apply to services purchased on-reserve by Indians, such as small engine repairs, where the benefit is realized primarily on-reserve.
- GST does not apply to services such as legal or accounting services,when purchased by an Indian band for band management activities, or in connection with real property located on-reserve.
- Unincorporated Indian-owned businesses may purchase on the same tax-free basis as Indian individuals since they qualify for the exemption under section 87 of the *Indian Act*. Like other businesses, they may claim input tax credits for purchases on which they pay the GST, for example, on off-reserve purchases.
- Incorporated Indian-owned businesses are treated the same as other businesses. The GST will be paid on their purchases and input tax credits claimed subject to the provisions of the legislation.
- Band-empowered entities situated on-reserve may purchase the same tax-free basis as an Indian band.
- To qualify for the 50 per cent GST rebate to non-profit organizations, band funding of Indian non-profit organizations will be considered equivalent to government funding.

These guidelines are without prejudice to any aboriginal or treaty rights which may exist. . . .

PURCHASES BY INDIANS, INDIAN BANDS

AND BAND EMPOWERED ENTITIES

Property

On Reserve

Indians, Indian bands, or unincorporated band-empowered entities may acquire property on reserve without paying the GST, provided they have the appropriate documentation to show the vendor.

Acquisitions of property on reserve by non-Indians will be subject to the normal GST rules.

Normally, corporations are considered to be separate legal persons from either an Indian or an Indian band and would not be eligible for relief from the GST. However, the tax will not apply to incorporated band-empowered entities purchasing for their band management activities.

Off Reserve

Indians, Indian bands and unincorporated band-empowered entities, as well as incorporated band-empowered entities purchasing for their band management activities, may acquire property off reserve without paying the GST, provided
- they have the appropriate documentation to show the vendor; and
- the property is delivered to a reserve by the vendor or the vendor's agent.

However, if the purchaser uses his or her own vehicle to transport the property to the reserve, the acquisition is subject to the normal GST rules.

Note: There is an exception for remote stores. For information, refer to page 12.

Importations

Importations by Indians, Indian bands or band-empowered entities are subject to the normal import rules, that is, they are taxable at seven per cent unless they are specifically zero-rated. GST on imported goods is collected by Canada Customs under the authority of the *Customs Act* at the time of importation.

Importations of goods are subject to the GST regardless of whether the goods have been delivered to a reserve by the vendor's agent or by Canada Post.

Services

Individual Indians

Purchases of services on reserve by an Indian where the benefit is primarily realized on reserve (e.g., small engine repairs) are not subject to the GST.

The following guidelines are used for determining whether the benefit of a service is primarily realized on reserve.
- Services for property. If a service is performed totally on reserve and the property is situated on reserve, the benefit is considered to be primarily realized on reserve.
- Services for individuals. If the service is performed totally on reserve for an Indian who is on reserve at the time the service is performed, e.g. a haircut given on the reserve, benefit is considered to be primarily realized on reserve.
- Transportation services. Only where both the origin and the destination are on the same reserve is the benefit of these services considered to be primarily realized on reserve, for example, a taxi service operating within the boundaries of a reserve.

Individual Indians must pay the seven per cent GST on all taxable services purchased off reserve unless the services are purchased for real property interests on reserve.

Services are subject to the normal GST rules when they are provided to non-Indians on reserve.

Indian Bands and Band-Empowered Entities

Services acquired on or off reserve by an Indian band, or band empowered entity, for management activities or for real property on reserve, are not subject to GST. However, the GST applies to services acquired for commercial activities of the Indian band or band-empowered entity.

Exception: Indian bands and band-empowered entities will pay the GST on off-reserve purchases of transportation, short-term accommodation, meals and entertainment. However, the band or the band-empowered entity may file a rebate claim to recover the GST paid on these purchases when these services are purchased for management activities or for real property located on reserve. . . .

DELIVERY

If the store from which property has been acquired is not located on a reserve, then the property must be delivered to a reserve for the purchase to be relieved from the GST.

The property must be delivered by either the vendor or an agent of the vendor.

If these conditions or the provisions for remote stores described on page 12 are not met, the normal GST rules apply.

Vendor

Where property is delivered to the reserve in the vendor's own vehicle, the vendor must maintain proof that delivery was made to the reserve. This will be indicated on the invoice of the vendor and the vendor's internal records, e.g., mileage log, dispatch records. Such proof must be maintained in addition to the proof of Indian status or certification by an Indian band or band empowered entity.

Normal GST rules will apply where an Indian, Indian band or band- empowered entity who is the purchaser takes possession of the property off a reserve and delivers the property to a reserve in his or her own vehicle.

Vendor's Agent

Where the property is delivered by the vendor's agent to a reserve, the vendor must maintain:

* proof of Indian status or certification by the band or band-empowered entity; and
* proof of delivery being made to the reserve (e.g., a waybill, postal receipt showing a reserve address, etc.).

An agent of the vendor includes an individual or company under contract to the vendor for making deliveries (e.g., postal services, trains, boats, couriers, etc.). The vendor would normally bear all the risks of the agent during the course of the delivery as if these risks were the vendor's own, unless specifically covered in the agency agreement.

A carrier who is under contract with the recipient is not regarded as the agent of the vendor. In addition, undertakings by purchasers of property to deliver the property to themselves as agents of the vendor are not acceptable to the Department.

SALES BY INDIANS, INDIAN BANDS
AND BAND-EMPOWERED ENTITIES

Businesses owned by Indians, Indian bands or band-empowered entities whose annual taxable sales of property and services are more than $30,000, are required to register for the GST. Like other businesses, once registered, they are required to collect and remit the GST to Revenue Canada, Customs and Excise.

Businesses, whether owned by Indians or non-Indians, selling property or services to Indians must include their taxable sales to Indians in their calculation of annual revenue to determine whether they must register for the GST. Sales of property and services taxable at seven per cent are in effect zero-rated when sold to Indians, Indian bands or band-empowered entities under conditions in which the GST is not payable.

Incorporated businesses owned by Indians or Indian bands must pay the GST on their purchases of taxable goods and services, except for those incorporated band-empowered entities acquiring supplies for use in band management activities. If such entities are registered for the GST, they must collect the tax on their sales of property and services (unless the sales are made to Indians, or Indian bands under conditions in which the GST is not payable) and claim input tax credits for the GST paid on purchases made in carrying out their businesses.

Sole proprietorships and partnerships owned by Indians receive the same treatment on purchases as individual Indians. If they are registered for the GST, they must collect the GST on their sales of taxable property and services (unless they are made to Indians and Indian bands under the conditions in which the GST is not payable) and can recover any GST they do pay on their business purchases by claiming input tax credits.

In the case of purchases made by partnerships, tax relief is available for purchases made in either the purchaser's own name or the partnership name. However, all conditions for the partner to receive tax relief on the acquisition of a supply must be met, i.e., property must be acquired on reserve or delivered to the reserve and the proper documentation must be maintained.

Where a partnership has both Indian and non-Indian participants, relief from GST only applies to purchases made by an Indian partner or partners. GST will apply where a non-Indian partner acquires a supply for the partnership and retains the supply for personal use. . . .

■ SELECTED BIBLIOGRAPHY

Bartlett, R. *Indians and Taxation in Canada*, 3rd ed. Saskatoon, Sask.: University of Saskatchewan Native Law Centre, 1992.

Dockstator, M., "The Nowegijick Case: Implications for Indian Tax Planning" [1985] 4 C.N.L.R. 1.

LeDressay, A. ,"A Brief Tax(on a me) of First Nations Taxation and Economic Development." In *Sharing the Harvest: The Road to Self-Reliance,* Royal Commission on Aboriginal Peoples. Ottawa: RCAP, 1993.

Morry, H., "Taxation of Aboriginals in Canada" (1992) 21:3 *Man. L.J.* 426.

CHAPTER 7
ABORIGINAL RIGHTS AND THE CONSTITUTION ACT, 1982

■ INTRODUCTION

As outlined in chapters 1, 2, and 3, prior to 1982, courts were reluctant to provide any substantive recognition to Aboriginal and treaty rights. They were even more reluctant to determine what remedy was available should Aboriginal rights exist. Although the 1973 *Calder*[1] decision was a watershed in that the court formally recognized the existence of Aboriginal title, it was not until the explicit constitutional protection of Aboriginal and treaty rights in 1982 that the legal status of these rights became much clearer. On April 17, 1982, the *Constitution Act, 1982*[2] was proclaimed into force and thus began a new era in Canadian constitutional development. Not only did the new *Constitution Act* contain a charter of rights and freedoms and a domestic constitutional amending formula, it also constitutionally entrenched existing Aboriginal and treaty rights. In March 1983, the *Constitution Act, 1982* was revisited by the First Ministers and Aboriginal representatives, resulting in amendments to ss. 25 and 35 and providing for additional constitutional conferences to be held on Aboriginal issues. No further amendments to ss. 25 and 34 have been made since 1983.[3]

The effect of constitutionally entrenching Aboriginal and treaty rights has been profound. The courts and academic commentary have focused on the scope and nature of the constitutionally protected rights. What remains to be seen is the effect these rights will have on the Canadian polity in general. Specifically, do the collective rights contained in s. 35 include a right to self-government? If so, to whom does it belong and to what extent may it be exercised? To what degree must governments consult with Aboriginal peoples regarding governmental decisions that either directly, or indirectly, impact upon them?

---

1   *Calder* v. *A.-G. of British Columbia,* 7 C.N.L.C. 91, [1973] S.C.R. 313.
2   *Constitution Act, 1982,* Sched. B of the *Canada Act 1982* (U.K.), 1982, c. 11 as am. by the *Constitution Amendment Proclamation 1983*, R.S.C. 1985, App. II, No. 46, adding ss. 35(3) and 35(4).
3   For additional information, see R.E. Gaffney, G.P. Gould, and A.J. Semple, *Broken Promises: The Aboriginal Constitutional Conferences* (Fredericton, N.B.: N.B. Association of Metis and Non-Status Indians, 1984); N. Zlotkin, *Unfinished Business: Aboriginal Peoples and the 1983 Constitutional Conference* (Kingston, Ont.: Institute of Intergovernmental Relations, Queen's University, 1983); and N. Zlotkin, "The 1983 and 1984 Constitutional Conferences: Only the Beginning" [1984] 3 C.N.L.R. 3.

SECTION 25, CANADIAN CHARTER OF RIGHTS AND FREEDOMS

Section 25 of the *Canadian Charter of Rights and Freedoms*[4] protects existing Aboriginal, treaty, and other rights of the Aboriginal peoples of Canada from being abrogated or derogated by *Charter* rights. Section 25 attempts to strike a balance between the protection of individual rights in the *Charter* with those rights held by Aboriginal peoples collectively. Section 25 reads:

> The guarantee in this Charter of certain rights and freedoms shall not be construed so as to abrogate or derogate from any aboriginal, treaty or other rights or freedoms that pertain to the aboriginal peoples of Canada including (a) any rights or freedoms that have been recognized by the Royal Proclamation of October 7, 1763; and (b) any rights or freedoms that now exist by way of land claims agreements or may be so acquired.

Bruce Wildsmith describes s. 25 in the following manner:

> Section 25 is not a mere canon of interpretation whose force is spent once it is determined that the rights and freedoms in the Charter cannot "be construed so as [not] to abrogate or derogate" from the rights referred to in section 25. Neither does section 25 create substantive rights or in any way enhance or entrench the position of aboriginal peoples. Its purpose and effect are to maintain the special position of Canada's aboriginal peoples unimpaired by the Charter.[5]

Of the few cases dealing with s. 25, two decisions are substantive in their analysis. First, in *Steinhauer* v. *R.*[6] the Alberta Court of Queen's Bench held that s. 25 acts as "a shield and does not add to aboriginal rights."[7] Second, the New Brunswick Court of Appeal in *Augustine and Augustine* v. *R.; Barlow* v. *R.*[8] cited with approval the following statement from Hogg's second edition of his *Constitutional Law of Canada*:[9]

> [Section 25] does not create any new rights, or even fortify existing rights. It is simply a saving provision, included to make clear that the Charter is not to be construed as

---

4   *Canadian Charter of Rights and Freedoms*, Part I of the *Constitution Act, 1982* [enacted by the *Canada Act 1982* (U.K.), 1982, c. 11, Sched. B] as am. by the *Constitution Amendment Proclamation, 1983*, R.S.C. 1985, App. II, No. 46 [am. ss. 25(b) and add. 35(3), 35(4), 35.1 and 37.1 and 54.1].

5   B. Wildsmith, *Aboriginal Peoples and Section 25 of the Canadian Charter of Rights and Freedoms* (Saskatoon, Sask.: University of Saskatchewan Native Law Centre, 1988), 2.

6   *Steinhauer* v. *R.*, [1985] 3 C.N.L.R. 187 (Alta. Q.B.); see also *Shubenacadie Indian Band* v. *Can. Human Rights Commission*, [1998] 2 C.N.L.R. 212 (F.C.T.D.).

7   Ibid., 191.

8   *Augustine and Augustine* v. *R.; Barlow* v. *R.*, [1987] 1 C.N.L.R. 20 at 44 (N.B.C.A.).

9   Peter Hogg, *Constitutional Law of Canada*, 2d ed. (Toronto: Carswell, 1985); Professor Hogg has retained this statement in his 3rd ed. (1992), 27.9, p. 694, and altered it slightly in his 4th ed. (1997) 27.9, pp. 700–01.

derogating from "any aboriginal, treaty or other rights or freedoms that pertain to the aboriginal peoples of Canada". In the absence of s. 25, it would perhaps have been arguable that rights attaching to groups defined by race were invalidated by s. 15 (the equality clause) of the Charter.

In *Batchewana Indian Band* v. *Canada*[10] the Federal Court of Appeal, in dealing with the residency requirements for voting rights in band elections under s. 77(1) of the *Indian Act,* affirmed that s. 25 acts as a shield that protects Aboriginal, treaty, and other rights from being adversely affected by *Charter* rights. The court held that the right to exclude off-reserve people from voting in band council elections is not one of the "other rights and freedoms" to which s. 25 refers.

Section 25 assists in understanding the scope of Aboriginal rights by limiting the extent to which Aboriginal rights may be infringed upon by the *Charter*. The protection afforded to Aboriginal rights by s. 25 may be particularly important to traditional forms of Aboriginal government that do not necessarily fall into the current western understanding of "democratic." Some traditional forms of Aboriginal government rely on hereditary chiefs or government based upon consensus; they do not necessarily rely upon democratic elections for legitimacy.

SECTION 35, CONSTITUTION ACT, 1982

Section 35 of the *Constitution Act, 1982* reads:

> (1) The existing aboriginal and treaty rights of the aboriginal peoples of Canada are hereby recognized and affirmed.
>
> (2) In this Act, "aboriginal peoples of Canada" includes the Indian, Inuit and Metis peoples of Canada.
>
> (3) For greater certainty, in subsection (1) "treaty rights" includes rights that now exist by way of land claims agreements or may be so acquired.
>
> (4) Notwithstanding any other provision of this Act, the aboriginal and treaty rights referred to in subsection (1) are guaranteed equally to male and female persons.

At present, s. 35(1) is the only provision in the Canadian Constitution that recognizes and affirms Aboriginal and treaty rights. It provides constitutional protection for "existing aboriginal and treaty rights." By virtue of s. 52[11] of the *Constitution Act, 1982*, s. 35 is part of the supreme law of Canada, thereby superseding federal, provincial, and territorial legislation inconsistent with its provisions. Professor Hogg describes the effect of s. 52 in the following manner:

> By virtue of s. 52(1), the Constitution of Canada is superior to all other laws in force in Canada, whatever their origin; federal statutes, provincial statutes, pre-confederation statutes, received statutes, imperial statutes and common law; all of these laws

---

10   *Batchewana Indian Band* v. *Canada,* [1997] 3 C.N.L.R. 21 at 32 (F.C.A.); *sub nom. Corbiere* v. *Canada.*

11   Section 52(1) reads: "(1) The Constitution of Canada is the supreme law of Canada, and any law that is inconsistent with the provisions of the Constitution is, to the extent of the inconsistency, of no force or effect."

must yield to inconsistent provisions of the Constitution of Canada. Section 52(1) provides an explicit basis for judicial review of legislation in Canada, for, whenever a court finds that a law is inconsistent with the Constitution of Canada, the court must hold that law to be invalid ("of no force or effect").[12]

The effect of Aboriginal and treaty rights being "constitutionalized" is profound. They have become part of the supreme law of Canada and have made the legislative authority of the federal, provincial, and territorial governments subject to their fair treatment. Aboriginal rights are not created by s. 35(1). As Brian Slattery points out, these rights are held by Aboriginal peoples

> by reason of the fact that aboriginal peoples were once independent, self-governing entities in possession of most of the lands now making up Canada.[13]

With s. 35 being added to the Constitution in 1982, the nature of Aboriginal rights in Canadian law has taken a new and expanded focus. There has been much academic commentary on s. 35(1), particularly before the landmark 1990 Supreme Court of Canada decision of *R. v. Sparrow*.[14] Prior to *Sparrow,* a number of questions regarding the basic content and meaning of s. 35 prevailed.[15] A brief discussion of *Sparrow* will shed some light on this important subsection.

The facts of *Sparrow* are as follows. Ronald Sparrow, a member of the Musqueam Indian Band of British Columbia, was charged and convicted at trial under s. 61(1) of the *Fisheries Act*[16] for fishing with a drift net that was longer than that permitted under the band's food fishing licence. Sparrow admitted that the facts constituted an offence but defended his action on the basis that he was exercising an existing Aboriginal right to fish and that the drift net length restriction was inconsistent with s. 35(1) of the *Constitution Act, 1982* and was, therefore, invalid.

The Supreme Court held that "existing" means the rights that were in existence when the *Constitution Act, 1982* came into effect on April 17, 1982. The court also stated that "existing" means unextinguished[17] and that "existing aboriginal rights" require an interpretation that is flexible so as "to permit their [aboriginal rights] evolution over time."[18] The court adopted the language of Professor Slattery in noting that "existing" means that rights are "affirmed in a contemporary form rather than in their primeval simplicity and vigour."[19]

---

12   Peter Hogg, *Constitutional Law of Canada,* 4th ed. (Toronto: Carswell, 1997), 3.4, p. 53.

13   Brian Slattery, "The Constitutional Guarantee of Aboriginal and Treaty Rights" (1983) 8 *Queen's L.J.* 232 at 242.

14   *R. v. Sparrow*, [1990] 3 C.N.L.R. 160 (S.C.C.).

15   For example, see the excerpt in this chapter of *R. v. Eninew; R. v. Bear,* [1984] 2 C.N.L.R. 126 (Sask. C.A.).

16   *Fisheries Act*, R.S.C. 1970, c. F–14, ss. 34, 61(1), now R.S.C. 1985, c. F–14, ss. 43, 79.

17   *R. v. Sparrow*, [1990] 3 C.N.L.R. 160 at 170 (S.C.C.).

18   Ibid., 171.

19   Brian Slattery, "Understanding Aboriginal Rights" (1988) 66 *Can. Bar Rev.* 782, as cited in *R. v. Sparrow*, ibid., 171.

On the issue of Crown sovereignty and legislative power and Aboriginal title, the court wrote:

> [T]here was from the outset never any doubt that sovereignty and legislative power, and indeed the underlying title, to such lands vested in the Crown.[20]

The court noted that the interpretation of "recognized and affirmed" is derived from "general principles of constitutional interpretation"[21] and that s. 35 shall be interpreted in a "purposive way." That is, it shall be given a "generous, liberal interpretation."[22] The court then cited its earlier decision of *R.* v. *Nowegijick,*[23] wherein it stated:

> [T]reaties and statutes relating to Indians should be liberally construed and doubtful expressions resolved in favour of the Indians.[24]

The court continued by providing a justificatory test to determine whether federal or provincial legislation can override an existing Aboriginal or treaty right. The *Sparrow* test is as follows:

- Is there a right?
- The next issue is whether the legislation has the effect of interfering with an existing Aboriginal right. If so, it is a *prima facie* infringement?
- In order to determine whether rights interfered with equal a *prima facie* infringement, three questions are posed.
  1. Is the limitation unreasonable?
  2. Does the regulation impose undue hardship?
  3. Does the regulation deny to the holders of the right their preferred means of exercising that right?

  The burden of proving a *prima facie* infringement is with the individual or group that is challenging the legislation.
- Once an infringement has been determined, the analysis then moves to the issue of justification. The justificatory analysis is sub-divided into two components. First, is there a valid legislative objective and second, can the legislative infringement be justified considering the honour of the Crown and the Crown's special trust relationship with Aboriginal peoples? On the issue of a valid legislative objective, the court held that such matters as conservation and resource management were valid objectives. However, arguments based on general terms such as the "public interest" were not valid. The court held that the "public interest" was "so vague as to provide no meaningful guidance and so broad as to be unworkable."
- Once a valid legislative objective is found, the analysis moves to interpreting the legislation in question with regard to the special status of Aboriginal rights in Canada and the trust relationship between the Crown and Aboriginal peoples.

---

20   Ibid. *Sparrow,* 177.
21   Ibid., 178.
22   Ibid., 179.
23   *R.* v. *Nowegijick,* [1983] 2 C.N.L.R. 89 (S.C.C.).
24   *R.* v. *Sparrow,* [1990] 3 C.N.L.R. 160 at 179 (S.C.C.).

• In addition, the Supreme Court held that the following questions may be posed within the justificatory analysis depending on the facts of the case. For example, has there been as little infringement as possible in order to achieve the desired result? In the case of expropriation, has fair compensation been made available? Has the Aboriginal group in question been consulted with regard to the conservation measures being employed?

Although s. 35 is not part of the *Charter* and its s. 1 limitation clause,[25] the justificatory analysis in *Sparrow* is similar to that of the *Charter*'s s. 1 analysis as outlined in *R.* v. *Oakes*.[26] In order for a *Charter* right to be limited by s. 1, two criteria must be met. First, the legislation in question must be of sufficient importance to warrant an override of a constitutional right. Second, the limitations imposed must be reasonably and demonstrably justified using a three-part proportionality test:

1. The measures must be designed to achieve the desired objective.
2. The measures must impair rights as little as possible.
3. The proportionality between the effects of the measures and the objectives desired must be of sufficient importance.[27]

Sparrow's "valid legislative objective" test is similar to the "sufficient importance" requirement in *Oakes*. The *Oakes* proportionality test mirrors aspects of the *Sparrow* justificatory analysis in that *Sparrow* asks if the limitation is unreasonable, does it impose undue hardship, and does it deny to the holder of the right his or her preferred means of exercising that right?

Delgamuukw v. *British Columbia*[28] also lays out a justifactory test concerning when and how Aboriginal title may be infringed and affirms that the *Sparrow* justifactory principles also operate with respect to Aboriginal title. Lamer C.J., for the court, notes that Aboriginal title is not absolute and must be balanced with the fact that Aboriginal societies are part of the broader Canadian social, economic, and political environment. To this end, activities that support economic development generally, among other things, may be justified when examined on a case-by-case basis. The court also strengthens the argument that compensation may be payable to a First Nation when its Aboriginal title has been breached.[29]

Because the *Sparrow* justification analysis is outside of the *Charter,* it can develop unhindered by the *Charter*'s s. 1 jurisprudence. This is not to suggest that the s. 1 jurisprudence will not have some effect on further judicial interpretation of *Sparrow*. The justificatory analysis in *Sparrow*, with its weaknesses, is necessary

---

25 Section 1 of the *Charter* reads: "The *Canadian Charter of Rights and Freedoms* guarantees the rights and freedoms set out in it subject only to such reasonable limits prescribed by law as can be demonstrably justified in a free and democratic society." See para. 71 of *R.* v. *Van der Peet*, [1996] 4 C.N.L.R. 177 (S.C.C.).

26 *R.* v. *Oakes*, 26 D.L.R. (4th) 200 (S.C.C.). The *Oakes* test has since been expanded and modified by numerous Supreme Court of Canada decisions.

27 Ibid., 227.

28 *Delgamuukw* v. *British Columbia*, [1998] 1 C.N.L.R. 14 (S.C.C.).

29 See commentary on *Delgamuukw* in chap. 1; also see ibid., paras. 165–69.

to keep in check the federal, provincial, and territorial governments' legislative authority.[30]

The British Columbia Court of Appeal decision of *R.* v. *Alphonse*[31] applied the *Sparrow* justificatory analysis to the British Columbia *Wildlife Act* and determined that it is a law of general application within the meaning of s. 88 of the *Indian Act* and that its requirement of shooting deer within the open season was not justifiable.

In *Thomas* v. *Norris,*[32] Hood J. of the British Columbia Supreme Court considered whether an Aboriginal right (spirit dancing) could include the right of a group of Aboriginal peoples to assault, batter, and imprison an individual against her or his will. The defendants, who were found guilty, argued that the collective rights of Aboriginal peoples under s. 35 override the rights of an individual who is a member of the First Nation exercising the right. Hood J. decided that s. 35 was not applicable in this case. In the opinion of Hood J., if spirit dancing was assumed to be an Aboriginal right that was practised prior to the assertion of British sovereignty and the introduction of English law, there are aspects of the right that were "contrary to English common law."[33] Thus, the use of force, assault, battery, and wrongful imprisonment would not have survived the introduction of English law.

> If spirit dancing generally was in existence in April of 1982 when the *Constitution Act*, 1982, came into force, the impugned aspects of it, to which I have referred, had been expressly extinguished. . . . It has never been the law of this Province that any person, or group of persons, Indians or non-Indians, had the right to subject another person to assault, battery or false imprisonment, and violate that person's original rights, with impunity. . . . The assumed aboriginal right, . . . is not absolute and the Supreme Court of Canada reaffirmed this in *Sparrow*. Like most freedoms or rights it is, and must be, limited by laws, both civil and criminal, which protect those who may be injured by the exercise of that practise.[34]

Since *Sparrow, R.* v. *Van der Peet*[35] has clarified further the nature of rights protected by s. 35. The case affirms that Aboriginal title is but a sub-category of the broader concept of Aboriginal rights. Lamer C.J. writes:

> Aboriginal rights and Aboriginal title are related concepts; Aboriginal title is a sub-category of Aboriginal rights which deals solely with claims of rights to land.[36]

The decision also confirms that Aboriginal rights are derived from the historical

---

30   See the 1996 British Columbia Court of Appeal decisions of *R.* v. *Samson,* [1996] 2 C.N.L.R. 184 (B.C.C.A.), and *R.* v. *Jack,* [1996] 2 C.N.L.R. 113 (B.C.C.A.), wherein the primary issue dealt with the application of the *Sparrow* justificatory analysis. In both cases, government failed to meet the burden imposed by *Sparrow.*

31   *R.* v. *Alphonse,* [1993] 4 C.N.L.R. 19 (B.C.C.A.).

32   *Thomas* v. *Norris,* [1992] 2 C.N.L.R. 139 (B.C.S.C.).

33   Ibid., 160.

34   Ibid.

35   *R.* v. *Van der Peet,* [1996] 4 C.N.L.R. 177 (S.C.C.); aee commentary by D.W. Elliot, "Fifty Dollars of Fish: A Comment of *R.* v. *Van der Peet*" (1997), 35:3 *Alta. Law Rev.*

36   Ibid., *Van der Peet,* para. 74.

reality that Aboriginal peoples were in Canada first, prior to European contact. The doctrine of Aboriginal rights exists, and is recognized and affirmed by s. 35(1), because of one simple fact: when Europeans arrived in North America, Aboriginal peoples were already here, living in communities on the land, and participating in distinctive cultures, as they had done for centuries.[37]

In *Van der Peet,* Lamer C.J., for the majority, outlines the test for identifying Aboriginal rights in s. 35(1). The court notes that any test aimed at identifying Aboriginal rights must be directed at the practices, traditions, and customs central to the Aboriginal peoples concerned, prior to their contact with Europeans. In order to be an Aboriginal right protected by s. 35(1), an activity must be an "element of a practice, custom or tradition integral to the distinctive culture of the Aboriginal group claiming the right."[38] The court outlined ten factors to be considered in determining whether or not an activity is "integral to a distinctive culture." They are as follows:

1.   The Aboriginal perspective must be taken into account, keeping in mind that, at the same time, the right being claimed must be put forward in a manner "cognizable to the Canadian and legal constitutional structure."[39]

2.   The Aboriginal claim should be characterized precisely. In doing so, consideration should be given to the nature of the action done pursuant to the claimed Aboriginal right; the nature of government regulation or limitation on the activity; and the Aboriginal traditions, customs, or practices being relied upon to establish the right.[40]

3.   The practice, custom, or tradition being relied upon must be significantly central to the Aboriginal society in question. With respect to this factor, Lamer C.J. states that in order for an activity to be significantly central it should be a "defining feature of the culture in question."[41]

4.   The period of time in which a court should look to establish whether or not an activity is protected as an Aboriginal right is that period prior to European contact. Those existing practices, customs, or traditions that can be shown to have their origin in pre-contact Aboriginal societies will be eligible for protection as Aboriginal rights, subject to the other factors.[42] It is this continuity with pre-contact times that is critical. As Lamer, C.J. writes:

Where an Aboriginal community can demonstrate that a particular practice, custom or tradition is integral to its distinctive culture today, and that this practice, custom or tradition has continuity with the practices, customs and traditions of pre-contact times, that community will have demonstrated that the practice, custom or tradition is an Aboriginal right for the purposes of s. 35(1).[43]

---

37   Ibid., para. 30.
38   Ibid., para. 46.
39   Ibid., para. 49.
40   Ibid., para. 53.
41   Ibid., para. 60.
42   Ibid., para. 62.
43   Ibid., para. 63.

5. The evidentiary demands of proving an Aboriginal right must be considered in the broader perspective of the special nature of Aboriginal rights in Canadian law and the evidentiary difficulties inherent in proving Aboriginal rights prior to European contact.

6. Aboriginal rights must be dealt with on a case-by-case basis and a general approach to Aboriginal rights is not appropriate.

7. The practice, custom, or tradition being claimed as an Aboriginal right must exist independently and cannot be incidental to another practice, custom, or tradition. An incidental or secondary practice, custom, or tradition does not qualify for protection as an Aboriginal right.

8. The custom, practice, or tradition must be "distinctive," but not necessarily "distinct." "Distinct" implies unique, whereas "distinctive" implies an activity that is a "distinguishing characteristic."[44]

9. European influence on Aboriginal culture is relevant only where it can be shown that the practice, custom, or tradition is integral only because of such influence.

10. Courts must consider both the relationship of Aboriginal peoples to the land and the Aboriginal peoples' distinctive cultures and societies.[45]

Perhaps the most striking feature of the *Van der Peet* test is that it appears that a right can be proven without it necessarily being linked to a particular piece of land. This is, perhaps, the reason that the court emphasized that Aboriginal title comes from Aboriginal rights and not vice versa. Thus, whereas in the past, the link to land has been a critical feature and a necessary component to proving Aboriginal rights, the focus now appears to be what Aboriginal societies did in the past. McLachlin J., in her dissent, summarizes the issue succinctly:

> [A]nything which can be said to be part of the aboriginal culture would qualify as an aboriginal right protected by the *Constitution Act, 1982.* This would confer constitutional protection on a multitude of activities, ranging from the trivial to the vital.[46]

Delgamuukw[47] further exemplifies this point wherein the Supreme Court further stresses that Aboriginal rights are not dependent on the use and occupation of land or on Aboriginal title.[48]

In *R. v. Gladstone,*[49] the Supreme Court found that the Heiltsuk people of British Columbia possessed an Aboriginal right, protected under s. 35(1), to trade in herring spawn on kelp because this activity was a central and significant feature of their society. Noteworthy is that this activity, best described as commercial in nature, existed amongst the Heiltsuk prior to European contact. Because of the commercial nature of this right, after the conservation objectives have been achieved

---

44   Ibid., para. 71.

45   Ibid., para. 74.

46   Ibid., para. 256.

47   *Delgamuukw* v. *British Columbia,* [1998] 1 C.N.L.R. 14, (S.C.C.).

48   Ibid., paras. 137–38.

49   *R.* v. *Gladstone,* [1996] 4 C.N.L.R. 65 (S.C.C.).

over the resource, the government is not obligated to give the Heiltsuk a priority right to fishery, as was the case in *Sparrow* when dealing with fishing for food rights. Rather, the government must allocate the resource in a way that is respectful of the fact that the Aboriginal rights have priority over other interests in the fishery.[50] Issues to be considered by government when allocating a resource in this manner include the extent of the participation by Aboriginal peoples in the fishery relative to their percentage of the population generally affected, how the government has accommodated different Aboriginal rights in a particular fishery (for example, food versus commercial), how important the fishery is to the economic well-being of the band, and what other factors the government considered when allocating commercial licences in the area in question. The court notes that these factors are not an exhaustive list.[51] However, what *Gladstone* demonstrates is that with all of the judicial reasoning given to s. 35(1) in recent years, there remains a fundamental vagueness (in this case with respect to the test for being a "priority") that is dependent on a case-by-case reasoning.

In *R. v. Adams,*[52] the Supreme Court of Canada applied the *Van der Peet* test to a situation where a Mohawk Indian was charged with fishing without a licence in Quebec. The court held that the licence requirement infringed the appellant's Aboriginal right to fish for food, and that the regulatory scheme was dependent upon ministerial discretion that had no criteria attached to its application. Using the *Van der Peet* criteria, the court determined that although the Mohawks' claim to occupancy over the area was weak, their claim with respect to their use of the lands and waters in question, that is their distinct practices in the area, was strong. Thus, although a link to land may be critical to support Aboriginal rights, a link to a particular piece of land is not necessary.

In *R. v. Côté,*[53] the Supreme Court again considered the *Van der Peet* criteria. This Quebec case dealt with Algonquin Indians who had entered a controlled harvest zone by way of a vehicle without paying the required fee and then had fished within that zone without a valid licence. *Côté* affirmed that although French law did not explicitly recognize the existence of a unique Aboriginal interest in the land, it also did not explicitly state that such an interest did not exist. Thus, the French Crown may not have assumed full title over the lands occupied by Aboriginal peoples because they dealt with the Aboriginal peoples as sovereign nations and in light of the nature of French settlement in New France. As in *Adams,* the court had difficulty with the vastness of the minister's discretionary authority to issue a licence. The requirement of a licence, in light of the undisciplined nature of the minister's discretionary authority, infringed, in an unjustifiable manner, the appellant's Aboriginal right to fish for food. The imposition of a fee to enter the controlled zone using a vehicle, although a condition on the exercise of the right, did not amount to an infringement. The fee was not revenue-generating in nature

---

50   Ibid., paras. 61 and 62.
51   Ibid., para. 64.
52   *R. v. Adams,* [1996] 4 C.N.L.R. 1 (S.C.C.).
53   *R. v. Coté,* [1996] 4 C.N.L.R. 26 (S.C.C.).

but rather was used to improve transportation within the land in question.

Both *Adams* and *Côté* underscore that governments have to ensure that the use of ministerial discretionary authority is clearly articulated and justified. The courts have not said that discretionary authority *per se* is unacceptable when dealing with Aboriginal rights. Rather, the courts have focused on those provisions that grant a great degree of authority with few or no criteria by which the authority is to be carried out. In a nutshell, governments must be prepared to explain their decisions and how they reached them. This is simply a cost of doing business in areas where Aboriginal rights and title exist.

The Supreme Court also applied the *Van der Peet* analysis in *R.* v. *N.T.C. Smokehouse Ltd.*[54] The issue in *Smokehouse* was whether the exchange of fish at potlatches and at other traditional ceremonies constituted a right to engage in the commercial selling of fish. The court held, based on the evidence, that the exchange of fish at these ceremonies was incidental to the ceremonies and did not possess any significance independently. Thus, the exchange of fish was not an "integral" part of the Aboriginal group's distinctive culture.

Section 35(3) provides that rights included in land claims agreements (see the introduction to chapter 2) are "treaty rights" for the purposes of s. 35(1). The effect of this provision is noteworthy because it transforms the rights in land claims agreements from being merely contractual or legislative in nature to being part of the supreme law of Canada and thus potentially able to supersede federal, provincial, or territorial legislation.[55] More problematic, however, is that it remains unclear what is a "right" protected under a land claims agreement or modern treaty, such as the Nisga'a treaty in British Columbia. Put another way, are only those provisions labeled as "rights" protected by s. 35(1) or are other provisions protected as well? Lower court decisions suggest most elements of the agreements receive constitutional protection.

Ironically, with all of the Supreme Court judgments on s. 35 to date, the law with respect to Aboriginal rights is getting more confused rather than more settled. Prior to *Sparrow*, there was great debate as to what s. 35 meant. Immediately following *Sparrow*, although questions remained, there was a degree of comfort in knowing that s. 35 meant "something." Since then, the courts have attempted to expand and better articulate the precise meaning of s. 35 by applying broad tests, including the notable *Van der Peet* test. These tests, combined with wide-reaching decisions such as *Delgamuukw*, have underscored the reality that the courts are not the best means of solving the issues that exist between Aboriginal peoples and governments in Canada. Although some of the key litigation to date has admirably set up the parameters for discussion (that is to say, *Calder, Sparrow, Van der Peet,* and *Delgamuukw*), all the judgments point out that the only way the "issue" of Aboriginal rights is going to be dealt with in a substantive and long-lasting manner is if governments fundamentally change the way they do business with respect to

---

54   *R.* v. *N.T.C. Smokehouse Ltd.*, [1996] 4 C.N.L.R. 130 (S.C.C.).

55   For discussion, see the introduction to chapter 2 and Thomas Isaac, "The *Constitution Act, 1982* and the Constitutionalization of Aboriginal Self-Government in Canada: The *Cree-Naskapi (of Quebec) Act*" [1991] 1 C.N.L.R. 1.

consultation and respecting Aboriginal rights. Better relationships, negotiated settlements, and understanding and respect are required to solve the problem, not increased litigation. Having said this, it is recognized that the most significant movements with respect to negotiations have occurred at the conclusion or threat of litigation by Aboriginal peoples (the *James Bay Agreement* being, perhaps, the most notable example). Section 35 will continue to be the cornerstone for the advancement of Aboriginal and treaty rights in Canada. Of particular interest will be the extent to which s. 35 can be used as a basis for a right of self-government; for commercial hunting, fishing, and trapping rights; and as a basis for maintaining the federal and provincial fiduciary responsibility.

■ CASES AND MATERIALS

1. *Constitution Act, 1982,* **Schedule B of the** *Canada Act 1982* **(U.K.), 1982, c. 11**

PART II
RIGHTS OF THE ABORIGINAL PEOPLES OF CANADA

35.(l)   The existing aboriginal and treaty rights of the aboriginal peoples of Canada are hereby recognized and affirmed.

(2)   In this Act, "aboriginal peoples of Canada" includes the Indian, Inuit and Métis peoples of Canada.

(3)   For greater certainty, in subsection (l) "treaty rights" includes rights that now exist by way of land claims agreements or may be so acquired.

(4)   Notwithstanding any other provision of this Act, the aboriginal and treaty rights referred to in subsection (l) are guaranteed equally to male and female persons.

35.1   The government of Canada and the provincial governments are committed to the principle that, before any amendment is made to Class 24 of section 91 of the "Constitution Act, 1867", to section 25 of this Act or to this Part,

(a)   a constitutional conference that includes in its agenda an item relating to the proposed amendment, composed of the Prime Minister of Canada and the first ministers of the provinces, will be convened by the Prime Minister of Canada; and

(b)   the Prime Minister of Canada will invite representatives of the aboriginal peoples of Canada to participate in the discussions on that item.

PART IV
CONSTITUTIONAL CONFERENCE

37.(l)   A constitutional conference composed of the Prime Minister of Canada and the first ministers of the provinces shall be convened by the Prime Minister of Canada within one year after this Part comes into force.

(2)   The conference convened under subsection (l) shall have included in its agenda an item respecting constitutional matters that directly affect the aboriginal peoples of Canada, including the identification and definition of the rights of

those peoples to be included in the Constitution of Canada, and the Prime Minister of Canada shall invite representatives of those peoples to participate in the discussions on that item.

(3) The Prime Minister of Canada shall invite elected representatives of the governments of the Yukon Territory and the Northwest Territories to participate in the discussions on any item on the agenda of the conference convened under subsection (1) that, in the opinion of the Prime Minister, directly affects the Yukon Territory and the Northwest Territories.

PART IV.I
CONSTITUTIONAL CONFERENCES

37.1(l) In addition to the conference convened in March 1983, at least two constitutional conferences composed of the Prime Minister of Canada and the first ministers of the provinces shall be convened by the Prime Minister of Canada, the first within three years after April 17,1982 and the second within five years after that date.

(2) Each conference convened under subsection (l) shall have included in its agenda constitutional matters that directly affect the aboriginal peoples of Canada, and the Prime Minister of Canada shall invite representatives of those peoples to participate in the discussions on those matters.

(3) The Prime Minister of Canada shall invite elected representatives of the governments of the Yukon Territory and the Northwest Territories to participate in the discussions on any item on the agenda of a conference convened under subsection (l) that, in the opinion of the Prime Minister, directly affects the Yukon Territory and the Northwest Territories.

(4) Nothing in this Section shall be construed so as to derogate from subsection 35(l). . . .

52.(1) The Constitution of Canada is the supreme law of Canada, and any law that is inconsistent with the provisions of the Constitution is, to the extent of the inconsistency, of no force or effect. . .

SECTION 35

2. *R. v. Eninew; R. v. Bear,* **[1984] 2 C.N.L.R. 126 (Sask. C.A.) Hall, Tallis, and Cameron JJ.A., April 26, 1984**

> *Eninew and Bear* interprets s. 35 to limit rights that existed as of April 17, 1982. Rights extinguished before 1982 are not re-instituted but rather, remain extinguished. Section 35(1) does not limit the ability of governments to regulate. In this pre-*Sparrow* decision, the Saskatchewan Court of Appeal held that the *Migratory Birds Convention Act* is not affected by s. 35(1). In the *Sparrow* decision, the Supreme Court of Canada rejected the view that s. 35(1) does not restrict the ability of governments to regulate and held governments to the onus of justifying legislation that infringes s. 35(1) rights.

HALL J.A.:—As these appeals involve the same issue they were heard together and treated as one. The appellant Eninew was charged that on or about the 29th day of April, 1982 at the Pelican Narrows District did unlawfully hunt migratory game birds out of season contrary to section 5(4) of the Migratory Birds Regulations made pursuant to the *Migratory Birds Convention Act,* R.S. c. 179, s. 1. (*sic*) [now R.S.C. 1970, c. M–12].

It was admitted that the appellant Eninew was at all times material an Indian within the meaning of the *Indian Act,* R.S.C. 1970, c. I–6, a member of the Peter Ballantyne Band residing at Deschambault Lake, Saskatchewan and as such was entitled to the benefits of any and all treaty rights contained in Treaty #10.

A similar admission was made in regard to the appellant Bear. The only difference was that Bear was entitled to treaty rights under Treaty #6.

The appellants contend that they are not subject to the *Migratory Birds Convention Act* and the regulations passed thereunder because of section 35 of the *Constitution Act, 1982.*

In my opinion it makes no difference to the outcome whether the reasons followed in the trial Courts are adopted or whether, as the appellant contends, section 35(1) of the *Constitution Act* recognizes and affirms the treaty rights as originally set out in the respective treaties. The rights so given were not unqualified or unconditional. In each case the right to pursue the avocation of hunting was subject to such regulations as may from time to time be made by the Government of Canada. Regulations made under the *Migratory Birds Convention Act* are the type of regulations which are contemplated in Treaties #6 and #10. The purpose of the *Migratory Birds Convention Act* is to conserve and preserve migratory birds including mallard ducks. That purpose is of benefit to the appellants. Indeed it was said that the Indians in general, and the appellants in particular, are concerned with and practise conservation. They would not hunt ducks during the summer nesting season. They would be affected by the regulations only during the "spring fly-in." They would accept as reasonable regulations such as those aimed at preserving the existence of the whooping crane. It follows that the treaty rights can be limited by such regulations as are reasonable. The *Migratory Birds Convention Act*, and the regulations made pursuant to it, based as they are on international convention, are reasonable, desirable limitations on the rights granted. That, in effect, is what was held in *R.* v. *Sikyea* and the other cases above noted.

The result is that the enactment of section 35(1) of the *Constitution Act* does not exempt the appellants in this case from the operation of the *Migratory Birds Convention Act.*

The appeals are therefore dismissed.

3. ***R.* v. *Sparrow*, [1990] 3 C.N.L.R. 160 (S.C.C.). Dickson C.J., Lamer, Wilson, La Forest, L'Heureux-Dubé, McIntyre (took no part in the judgement), Sopinka JJ., May 31, 1990**

Ronald Sparrow, a member of the Musqueam First Nation, was fishing in traditional waters. He was charged with fishing with a drift net longer than that permitted by his band's licence issued pursuant to the federal *Fisheries Act.* Sparrow defended his action by arguing that he had an existing Aboriginal right to fish and that the net-length restriction infringed his right and thus was inapplicable to him.

In clearly one of the most important decisions to date on s. 35, the Supreme Court of Canada held that s. 35 constitutionalized existing Aboriginal and treaty rights as they existed in 1982 when the *Constitution Act, 1982* came into effect. The court provides an interesting discussion of the nature of existing Aboriginal and treaty rights and what is meant by "recognition and affirmation" in s. 35. The court also discusses the fiduciary relationship between the federal Crown and Aboriginal peoples. Finally, the court provides a justification analysis to be used to determine whether federal, provincial, or territorial legislation can be justified, even though it may infringe an Aboriginal or treaty right. *Sparrow,* combined with *Van der Peet* and *Delgammukw,* now forms the substantive basis of Supreme Court of Canada decisions dealing with s. 35. The selected bibliography at the end of this chapter provides citations of a number of academic commentaries on the *Sparrow* decision.

DICKSON C.J. and LA FOREST J.:—This appeal requires this Court to explore for the first time the scope of s. 35(1) of the *Constitution Act, 1982,* and to indicate its strength as a promise to the aboriginal peoples of Canada. Section 35(1) is found in Part II of that Act, entitled "Rights of the Aboriginal Peoples of Canada," and provides as follows:

> 35.(1) The existing aboriginal and treaty rights of the aboriginal peoples of Canada are hereby recognized and affirmed.

The context of this appeal is the alleged violation of the terms of the Musqueam food fishing licence which are dictated by the *Fisheries Act*, R.S.C. 1970, c. F–14 (R.S.C. 1985, c. F–14), and the regulations under that Act. The issue is whether Parliament's power to regulate fishing is now limited by s. 35(1) of the *Constitution Act, 1982*, and, more specifically, whether the net length restriction in the licence is inconsistent with that provision.

FACTS

The appellant, a member of the Musqueam Indian Band, was charged under s. 61(1) of the *Fisheries Act* of the offence of fishing with a drift net longer than that permitted by the terms of the Band's Indian food fishing licence. The fishing which gave rise to the charge took place on May 25, 1984 in Canoe Passage which is part of the area subject to the Band's licence. The licence, which had been issued for a one-year period beginning March 31, 1984, set out a number of restrictions including one that drift nets were to be limited to 25 fathoms in length. The appellant was caught with a net which was 45 fathoms in length. He has throughout admitted the facts alleged to constitute the offence, but has defended the charge on the basis that he was exercising an existing aboriginal right to fish and that the net length restriction contained in the Band's licence is inconsistent with s. 35(1) of the *Constitution Act, 1982* and therefore invalid. . . .

Leave to appeal to this Court was then sought and granted. On November 24, 1987, the following constitutional question was stated:

> Is the net length restriction contained in the Musqueam Indian Band Indian Food Fishing Licence dated March 30, 1984, issued pursuant to the *British Columbia Fishery (General) Regulations* and the *Fisheries Act,* R.S.C. 1970, c. F–14, inconsistent with s. 35(1) of the *Constitution Act, 1982?*

The appellant appealed on the ground that the Court of Appeal erred (1) in holding that s. 35(1) of the *Constitution Act, 1982* protects the aboriginal right only when exercised for food purposes and permits restrictive regulation of such rights whenever "reasonably justified as being necessary for the proper management and conservation of the resource or in the public interest," and (2) in failing to find the net length restriction in the Band's food fish licence was inconsistent with s. 35(1) of the *Constitution Act, 1982*.

The respondent Crown cross-appealed on the ground that the Court of Appeal erred in holding that the aboriginal right had not been extinguished before April 17, 1982, the date of commencement of the *Constitution Act, 1982,* and in particular in holding that, as a matter of fact and law, the appellant possessed the aboriginal right to fish for food. In the alternative, the respondent alleged, the Court of Appeal erred in its conclusions respecting the scope of the aboriginal right to fish for food and the extent to which it may be regulated, more particularly in holding that the aboriginal right included the right to take fish for the ceremonial purposes and societal needs of the Band and that the Band enjoyed a constitutionally protected priority over the rights of other people engaged in fishing. Section 35(1), the respondent maintained, did not invalidate legislation passed for the purpose of conservation and resource management, public health and safety and other overriding public interests such as the reasonable needs of other user groups. Finally, it maintained that the conviction ought not to have been set aside or a new trial directed because the appellant failed to establish a *prima facie* case that the reduction in the length of the net had unreasonably interfered with his right by preventing him from meeting his food fish requirements. According to the respondent, the Court of Appeal had erred in shifting the burden of proof to the Crown on the issue before the appellant had established a *prima facie* case. . . .

THE REGULATORY SCHEME

The *Fisheries Act*, s. 34, confers on the Governor in Council broad powers to make regulations respecting the fisheries, . . .

Contravention of the Act and the regulations is made an offence under s. 61(1) under which the appellant was charged.

Acting under its regulation-making powers, the Governor in Council enacted the *British Columbia Fishery (General) Regulations*, SOR/84–248. Under these Regulations (s. 4), everyone is, *inter alia*, prohibited from fishing without a licence, and then only in areas and at the times and in the manner authorized by the Act or regulations. That provision also prohibits buying, selling, trading or bartering fish other than those lawfully caught under the authority of a commercial fishing licence. . . .

The Regulations make provision for issuing licences to Indians or a band "for the sole purpose of obtaining food for that Indian and his family and for the band," and no one other than an Indian is permitted to be in possession of fish caught pursuant to such a licence. Subsection 27(1) and (4) of the Regulations read:

> 27.(1) In this section "Indian food fish licence" means a licence issued by the Minister to an Indian or a band for the sole purpose of obtaining food for that Indian and his family or for the band. . . .

(4) No person other than an Indian shall have in his possession fish caught under the authority of an Indian food fish licence.

As in the case of other licences issued under the Act, such licences may, by s. 12 of the Regulations, be subjected to restrictions regarding the species and quantity of fish that may be taken, the places and times when they may be taken, the manner in which they are to be marked and, most important here, the type of gear and equipment that may be used . . . .

Pursuant to these powers, the Musqueam Indian Band, on March 31, 1984, was issued an Indian food fishing licence as it had since 1978 "to fish for salmon for food for themselves and their family" in areas which included the place where the offence charged occurred, the waters of Ladner Reach and Canoe Passage therein described. The licence contained time restrictions as well as the type of gear to be used, notably "One Drift net twenty-five (25) fathoms in length."

The appellant was found fishing in the waters described using a drift net in excess of 25 fathoms. He did not contest this, arguing instead that he had committed no offence because he was acting in the exercise of an existing aboriginal right which was recognized and affirmed by s. 35(1) of the *Constitution Act, 1982.*

ANALYSIS

We will address first the meaning of "existing" aboriginal rights and the content and scope of the Musqueam right to fish. We will then turn to the meaning of "recognized and affirmed," and the impact of s. 35(1) on the regulatory power of Parliament.

"Existing"

The word "existing" makes it clear that the rights to which s. 35(1) applies are those that were in existence when the *Constitution Act, 1982* came into effect. This means that extinguished rights are not revived by the *Constitution Act, 1982.* A number of courts have taken the position that "existing" means being in actuality in 1982: *R.* v. *Eninew* (1983), [1984] 2 C.N.L.R. 122 at 124 . . . (Sask. Q.B.), affd. [1984] 2 C.N.L.R. 126 . . . (Sask. C.A.). See also *Attorney-General for Ontario* v. *Bear Island Foundation* (1984), [1985] 1 C.N.L.R. 1 . . . (H.C.); *R.* v. *Hare and Debassige*, [1985] 3 C.N.L.R. 139 . . . (Ont. C.A.); Re *Steinhauer* v. *The Queen*, [1985] 3 C.N.L.R. 187 (Alta. Q.B.); *Martin* v. *The Queen,* (1985), 65 N.B.R. (2d) 21, 167 A.P.R. 21 (N.B.Q.B.); *R* v. *Agawa*, [1988] 3 C.N.L.R. 73. . . .

Further, an existing aboriginal right cannot be read so as to incorporate the specific manner in which it was regulated before 1982. The notion of freezing existing rights would incorporate into the Constitution a crazy patchwork of regulations. Blair J.A. in *Agawa,* supra had this to say about the matter, at p. 214 [p. 87 C.N.L.R.]:

> Some academic commentators have raised a further problem which cannot be ignored. The Ontario Fishery Regulations contain detailed rules which vary for different regions in the province. Among other things, the Regulations specify seasons and methods of fishing, species of fish which can be caught and catch limits. Similar detailed provisions apply under the comparable fisheries Regulations in force in other prov-

inces. These detailed provisions might be constitutionalized if it were decided that the existing treaty rights referred to in s. 35(1) were those remaining after regulation at the time of the proclamation of the *Constitution Act, 1982.*

As noted by Blair J.A., academic commentary lends support to the conclusion that "existing" means "unextinguished" rather than exercisable at a certain time in history. Professor Slattery, "Understanding Aboriginal Rights" (1987), 66 *Can. Bar Rev.* 726, at pp. 781–82, has observed the following about reading regulations into the rights:

> This approach reads into the Constitution the myriad of regulations affecting the exercise of aboriginal rights, regulations that differed considerably from place to place across the country. It does not permit differentiation between regulations of long-term significance and those enacted to deal with temporary conditions, or between reasonable and unreasonable restrictions. Moreover, it might require that a constitutional amendment be enacted to implement regulations more stringent than those in existence on 17 April 1982. This solution seems unsatisfactory. . . .

The arbitrariness of such an approach can be seen if one considers the recent history of the federal regulation in the context of the present case and the fishing industry. If the *Constitution Act, 1982* had been enacted a few years earlier, any right held by the Musqueam Band, on this approach, would have been constitutionally subjected to the restrictive regime of personal licences that had existed since 1917. Under that regime, the Musqueam catch had by 1969 become minor or non-existent. In 1978 a system of band licences was introduced on an experimental basis which permitted the Musqueam to fish with a 75 fathom net for a greater number of days than other people. Under this regime, from 1977 to 1984, the number of Band members who fished for food increased from 19 persons using 15 boats, to 64 persons using 38 boats, while 10 other members of the Band fished under commercial licences. Before this regime, the Band's food fish requirement had basically been provided by Band members who were licensed for commercial fishing. Since the regime introduced in 1978 was in force in 1982, then, under this approach, the scope and content of an aboriginal right to fish would be determined by the details of the Band's 1978 licence.

The unsuitability of the approach can also be seen from another perspective. Ninety-one other tribes of Indians, comprising over 20,000 people (compared with 540 Musqueam on the reserve and 100 others off the reserve) obtain their food fish from the Fraser River. Some or all of these bands may have an aboriginal right to fish there. A constitutional patchwork quilt would be created if the constitutional right of these bands were to be determined by the specific regime available to each of those bands in 1982.

Far from being defined according to the regulatory scheme in place in 1982, the phrase "existing aboriginal rights" must be interpreted flexibly so as to permit their evolution over time. To use Professor Slattery's expression, in "Understanding Aboriginal Rights", supra, at p. 782, the word "existing" suggests that those rights are "affirmed in a contemporary form rather than in their primeval simplicity and vigour." Clearly, then, an approach to the constitutional guarantee embodied in s. 35(1) which would incorporate "frozen rights" must be rejected.

The Aboriginal Right

We turn now to the aboriginal right at stake in this appeal. The Musqueam Indian Reserve is located on the north shore of the Fraser River close to the mouth of that river and within the limits of the City of Vancouver. There has been a Musqueam village there for hundreds of years. This appeal does not directly concern the reserve or the adjacent waters, but arises out of the Band's right to fish in another area of the Fraser River known as Canoe Passage in the South Arm of the river, some 16 kilometres (about 10 miles) from the reserve. The reserve and those waters are separated by the Vancouver International Airport and the Municipality of Richmond.

The evidence reveals that the Musqueam have lived in the area as an organized society long before the coming of European settlers, and that the taking of salmon was an integral part of their lives and remains so to this day. Much of the evidence of an aboriginal right to fish was given by Dr. Suttles, an anthropologist, supported by that of Mr. Grant, the Band administrator. The Court of Appeal thus summarized Dr. Suttles' evidence, *R.* v. *Sparrow,* 9 B.C.L.R. (2d) 300, [1987] 1 C.N.L.R. 145 (B.C.C.A.) at pp. 307–308 [pp. 151–52 C.N.L.R.]:

> Dr. Suttles was qualified as having particular qualifications in respect of the ethnography of the Coast Salish Indian people of which the Musqueams were one of several tribes. He thought that the Musqueam had lived in their historic territory, which includes the Fraser River estuary, for at least 1,500 years. That historic territory extended from the north shore of Burrard Inlet to the south shore of the main channel of the Fraser River including the waters of the three channels by which that river reaches the ocean. As part of the Salish people, the Musqueam were part of a regional social network covering a much larger area but, as a tribe, were themselves an organized social group with their own name, territory and resources. Between the tribes there was a flow of people, wealth and food. No tribe was wholly self-sufficient or occupied its territory to the complete exclusion of others.

Dr. Suttles described the special position occupied by the salmon fishery in that society. The salmon was not only an important source of food but played an important part in the system of beliefs of the Salish people, and in their ceremonies. The salmon were held to be a race of beings that had, in "myth times," established a bond with human beings requiring the salmon to come each year to give their bodies to the humans who, in turn, treated them with respect shown by performance of the proper ritual. Towards the salmon, as toward other creatures, there was an attitude of caution and respect which resulted in effective conservation of the various species.

While the trial for a violation of penal prohibition may not be the most appropriate setting in which to determine the existence of an aboriginal right, and the evidence was not extensive, the correctness of the finding of fact of the trial judge "that Mr. Sparrow was fishing in ancient tribal territory where his ancestors had fished from time immemorial in that part of the mouth of the Fraser River for salmon" is supported by the evidence and was not contested. The existence of the right, the Court of Appeal tells us, "was not the subject of serious dispute." It is not surprising, then, that, taken with other circumstances, that court should find that "the judgment appealed from was wrong in . . . failing to hold that Sparrow at the relevant time was exercising an existing aboriginal right."

In this Court, however, the respondent contested the Court of Appeal's finding, contending that the evidence was insufficient to discharge the appellant's burden of proof upon the issue. It is true that for the period from 1867 and 1961 the evidence is scanty. But the evidence was not disputed or contradicted in the courts below and there is evidence of sufficient continuity of the right to support the Court of Appeal's finding, and we would not disturb it.

What the Crown really insisted on, both in this Court and the courts below, was that the Musqueam Band's aboriginal right to fish had been extinguished by regulations under the *Fisheries Act.* . . .

See also *Attorney-General of Ontario* v. *Bear Island Foundation*, supra, at pp. 439–40 [pp. 80–81 C.N.L.R.]. That in Judson J.'s view was what had occurred in *Calder*, supra, where, as he saw it, a series of statutes evinced a unity of intention to exercise a sovereignty inconsistent with any conflicting interest, including aboriginal title. But Hall J. in that case stated (at p. 404) that "the onus of proving that the Sovereign intended to extinguish the Indian title lies on the respondent and *that intention must be 'clear and plain'* " (emphasis added). The test of extinguishment to be adopted, in our opinion, is that the Sovereign's intention must be clear and plain if it is to extinguish an aboriginal right.

There is nothing in the *Fisheries Act* or its detailed regulations that demonstrates a clear and plain intention to extinguish the Indian aboriginal right to fish. The fact that express provision permitting the Indians to fish for food may have applied to all Indians and that for an extended period permits were discretionary and issued on an individual rather than a communal basis in no way shows a clear intention to extinguish. These permits were simply a manner of controlling the fisheries, not defining underlying rights.

We would conclude then that the Crown has failed to discharge its burden of proving extinguishment. In our opinion, the Court of Appeal made no mistake in holding that the Indians have an existing aboriginal right to fish in the area where Mr. Sparrow was fishing at the time of the charge. This approach is consistent with ensuring that an aboriginal right should not be defined by incorporating the ways in which it has been regulated in the past.

The scope of the existing Musqueam right to fish must now be delineated. The anthropological evidence relied on to establish the existence of the right suggests that, for the Musqueam, the salmon fishery has always constituted an integral part of their distinctive culture. Its significant role involved not only consumption for subsistence purposes, but also consumption of salmon on ceremonial and social occasions. The Musqueam have always fished for reasons connected to their cultural and physical survival. As we stated earlier, the right to do so may be exercised in a contemporary manner. . . .

Government regulations governing the exercise of the Musqueam right to fish, as described above, have only recognized the right to fish *for food* for over a hundred years. This may have reflected the existing position. However, historical policy on the part of the Crown is not only incapable of extinguishing the existing aboriginal right without clear intention, but is also incapable of, in itself, delineating that right. The nature of government regulations cannot be determinative of the content and scope of an existing aboriginal right. Government policy *can* however, regulate the exercise of that right, but such regulation must be in keeping with s. 35(1).

In the courts below, the case at bar was not presented on the footing of an aboriginal right to fish for commercial or livelihood purposes. Rather, the focus was and continues to be on the validity of a net length restriction affecting the appellant's *food fishing licence.* We therefore adopt the Court of Appeal's characterization of the right for the purpose of this appeal, and confine our reasons to the meaning of the constitutional recognition and affirmation of the existing aboriginal right to fish for food and social and ceremonial purposes.

"Recognized and Affirmed"
We now turn to the impact of s. 35(1) of the *Constitution Act, 1982* on the regulatory power of Parliament and on the outcome of this appeal specifically. . . .

It is worth recalling that while British policy towards the native population was based on respect for their right to occupy their traditional lands, a proposition to which the *Royal Proclamation of 1763* bears witness, there was from the outset never any doubt that sovereignty and legislative power, and indeed the underlying title, to such lands vested in the Crown: see *Johnson* v. *M'Intosh* (1823), 8 Wheaton 543 (U.S.S.C.); see also the Royal Proclamation itself (R.S.C. 1985, App. II, No. 1, pp. 4–6); *Calder,* supra, *per* Judson J. at p. 328, Hall J. at pp. 383, 403. And there can be no doubt that over the years the rights of the Indians were often honoured in the breach (for one instance in a recent case in this Court, see *Canadian Pacific Ltd* v. *Paul,* [1988] 2 S.C.R. 654, [1989] 1 C.N.L.R. 47). As MacDonald J. stated in *Pasco* v. *Canadian National Railway Co.,* [1986] 1 C.N.L.R. 35 at 37, 69 B.C.L.R. 76 (B.C.S.C.): "We cannot recount with much pride the treatment accorded to the native people of this country."

For many years, the rights of the Indians to their aboriginal lands—certainly as *legal* rights—were virtually ignored. The leading cases defining Indian rights in the early part of the century were directed at claims supported by the Royal Proclamation or other legal instruments and even these cases were essentially concerned with settling legislative jurisdiction or the rights of commercial enterprises. For fifty years after the publication of Clement's *The Law of the Canadian Constitution* (3rd ed. 1916), there was a virtual absence of discussion of any kind of Indian rights to land even in academic literature. By the late 1960s, aboriginal claims were not even recognized by the federal government as having any legal status. Thus the *Statement of the Government of Canada on Indian Policy* 1969, although well meaning, contained the assertion (at p. 11) that "aboriginal claims to land . . . are so general and undefined that it is not realistic to think of them as specific claims capable of remedy except through a policy and program that will end injustice to the Indians as members of the Canadian community." In the same general period, the James Bay development by Quebec Hydro was originally initiated without regard to the right of the Indians who lived there, even though these were expressly protected by a constitutional instrument; see the *Quebec Boundary Extension Act, 1912,* S.C. 1912, c. 45. It took a number of judicial decisions and notably the *Calder* case in this Court (1973) to prompt a reassessment of the position being taken by government.

In the light of its reassessment of Indian claims following *Calder*, the federal government on August 8, 1973 issued "a statement of policy" regarding Indian lands. By it, it sought to "signify the Government's *recognition and acceptance* of its continuing responsibility under the British North America Act for Indians and lands reserved for Indians," which it regarded "as an historic evolution dating back to the *Royal Proclamation of 1763*, which, whatever differences there may be about its judicial interpretation, stands as a basic declaration of the Indian people's interests in land in this country." [Emphasis added.] See *Statement made by the Honourable Jean Chrétien, Minister of Indian Affairs and Northern Development on Claims of Indian and Inuit People,* August 8, 1973. The remarks about these lands were intended "as an expression of acknowledged responsibility." But the statement went on to express, for the first time, the government's willingness to negotiate regarding claims of aboriginal title, specifically in British Columbia, Northern Quebec, and the Territories, and this without regard to formal supporting document. "The Government," it stated, "is now ready to negotiate with authorized representatives of these native peoples on the basis that where their traditional interest in the lands concerned can be established, an agreed form of compensation or benefit will be provided to native peoples in return for their interest."

It is obvious from its terms that the approach taken towards aboriginal claims in the 1973 statement constituted an expression of a policy, rather than a legal position; see also Canada, Department of Indian Affairs and Northern Development, *In All Fairness*: *A Native Claims Policy—Comprehensive Claims* (1981), pp. 11–12; Slattery, "Understanding Aboriginal Rights" (1987), 66 *Can. Bar. Rev.* 726 at 730. As recently as *Guerin* v. *The Queen,* [1984] 2 S.C.R. 335, [1985] 1 C.N.L.R. 120 . . . , the federal government argued in this Court that any federal obligation was of a political character.

It is clear, then, that s. 35(1) of the *Constitution Act, 1982*, represents the culmination of a long and difficult struggle in both the political forum and the courts for the constitutional recognition of aboriginal rights. The strong representations of native associations and other groups concerned with the welfare of Canada's aboriginal people made the adoption of s. 35(1) possible and it is important to note that the provision applies to the Indians, the Inuit and the Métis. Section 35(1), at the least, provides a solid constitutional base upon which subsequent negotiations can take place. It also affords aboriginal peoples constitutional protection against provincial legislative power. We are, of course, aware that this would, in any event, flow from the *Guerin* case, supra, but for a proper understanding of the situation, it is essential to remember that the *Guerin* case was decided after the commencement of the *Constitution Act, 1982*. In addition to its effect on aboriginal rights, s. 35(1) clarified other issues regarding the enforcement of treaty rights (see Sanders, "Pre-existing Rights: The Aboriginal Peoples of Canada," in Beaudoin and Ratushny, eds., *The Canadian Charter of Rights and Freedoms*, 2nd ed., esp. at p. 730).

In our opinion, the significance of s. 35(1) extends beyond these fundamental effects. Professor Lyon in "An Essay on Constitutional Interpretation" (1988), 26 *Osgoode Hall L.J.* 95, says the following about s. 35(1), at p. 100:

. . . the context of 1982 is surely enough to tell us that this is not just a codification of the case law on aboriginal rights that had accumulated by 1982. Section 35 calls for a just settlement for aboriginal peoples. It renounces the old rules of the game under which the Crown established courts of law and denied those courts the authority to question sovereign claims made by the Crown.

The approach to be taken with respect to interpreting the meaning of s. 35(1) is derived from general principles of constitutional interpretation, principles relating to aboriginal rights, and the purposes behind the constitutional provision itself. Here, we will sketch the framework for an interpretation of "recognized and affirmed" that, in our opinion, gives appropriate weight to the constitutional nature of these words.

In *Reference re Manitoba Language Rights*, [1985] 1 S.C.R. 721, this Court said the following about the perspective to be adopted when interpreting a constitution, at p. 745:

> The Constitution of a country is a statement of the will of the people to be governed in accordance with certain principles held as fundamental and certain prescriptions restrictive of the powers of the legislature and government. It is, as s. 52 of the *Constitution Act, 1982* declares, the "supreme law" of the nation, unalterable by the normal legislative process, and unsuffering of laws inconsistent with it. The duty of the judiciary is to interpret and apply the laws of Canada and each of the provinces, and it is thus our duty to ensure that the constitutional law prevails.

The nature of s. 35(1) itself suggests that it be construed in a purposive way. When the purposes of the affirmation of aboriginal rights are considered, it is clear that a generous, liberal interpretation of the words in the constitutional provision is demanded. When the Court of Appeal below was confronted with the submission that s. 35 has no effect on aboriginal or treaty rights and that it is merely a preamble to the parts of the *Constitution Act, 1982*, which deal with aboriginal rights, it said the following at p. 322 [p. 168 C.N.L.R.]:

> This submission gives no meaning to s. 35. If accepted, it would result in denying its clear statement that existing rights are hereby recognized and affirmed, and would turn that into a mere promise to recognize and affirm those rights sometime in the future. . . . To so construe s. 35(1) would be to ignore its language and the principle that the Constitution should be interpreted in a liberal and remedial way. We cannot accept that that principle applies less strongly to aboriginal rights than to the rights guaranteed by the Charter particularly having regard to the history and to the approach to interpreting treaties and statutes relating to Indians required by such cases as *Nowegijick* v. *R.* [1983] 1 S.C.R. 29. . . .

In *Nowegijick* v. *The Queen*, [1983] 1 S.C.R. 29 at 36, [1983] 2 C.N.L.R. 89 at 94 . . . , the following principle that should govern the interpretation of Indian treaties and statutes was set out:

> . . . treaties and statutes relating to Indians should be liberally construed and doubtful expression resolved in favour of the Indians.

In *R* v. *Agawa*, supra, Blair J.A. stated that the above principle should apply to the interpretation of s. 35(1). He added the following principle to be equally applied, at pp. 215–16 [p. 89 C.N.L.R.]:

> The second principle was enunciated by the late Associate Chief Justice MacKinnon in *R* v. *Taylor and Williams* (1981), 34 O.R. (2d) 360, [1981] 3 C.N.L.R. 114. He emphasized the importance of Indian history and traditions as well as the perceived effect of a treaty at the time of its execution. He also cautioned against determining Indian rights "in a vacuum." The honour of the Crown is involved in the interpretation of Indian treaties and, as a consequence, fairness to the Indians is a governing consideration. He said at p. 367 [p. 123 C.N.L.R.]:
>
> > The principles to be applied to the interpretation of Indian treaties have been much canvassed over the years. In approaching the terms of a treaty quite apart from the other considerations already noted, the honour of the Crown is always involved and no appearance of 'sharp dealing' should be sanctioned.
>
> This view is reflected in recent judicial decisions which have emphasized the responsibility of Government to protect the rights of Indians arising from the special trust relationship created by history, treaties and legislation: see *Guerin* v. *The Queen*, [1984] 2 S.C.R. 335; 13 D.L.R. (4th) 321, [1985] 1 C.N.L.R. 120.

In *Guerin*, supra, the Musqueam Band surrendered reserve lands to the Crown for lease to a golf club. The terms obtained by the Crown were much less favourable than those approved by the Band at the surrender meeting. This Court found that the Crown owed a fiduciary obligation to the Indians with respect to the lands. The *sui generis* nature of Indian title, and the historic powers and responsibility assumed by the Crown constituted the source of such a fiduciary obligation. In our opinion, *Guerin*, together with *R.* v. *Taylor and Williams* (1981), 34 O.R. (2d) 360, [1981] 3 C.N.L.R. 114, ground a general guiding principle for s. 35(1). That is, the Government has the responsibility to act in a fiduciary capacity with respect to aboriginal peoples. The relationship between the Government and aboriginals is trust-like, rather than adversarial, and contemporary recognition and affirmation of aboriginal rights must be defined in light of this historic relationship.

We agree with both the British Columbia Court of Appeal below and the Ontario Court of Appeal that the principles outlined above, derived from *Nowegijick*, *Taylor and Williams* and *Guerin*, should guide the interpretation of s. 35(1). As commentators have noted, s. 35(1) is a solemn commitment that must be given meaningful content (Lyon, supra; William Pentney, "The Rights of the Aboriginal Peoples of Canada in the *Constitution Act, 1982,* Part II, Section 35:The Substantive Guarantee" (1987) 22 *U.B.C. L. Rev.* 207; Schwartz, "Unstarted Business: Two Approaches to Defining s. 35—'What's in the Box?' and 'What Kind of Box?'," Ch. XXIV, in *First Principles, Second Thoughts* (Montreal: Institute for Research on Public Policy, 1986); Slattery, supra; and Slattery, "The Hidden Constitution: Aboriginal Rights in Canada" (1984), 32 *Am. J. of Comp. Law* 361).

In response to the appellant's submission that s. 35(1) rights are more securely protected than the rights guaranteed by the Charter, it is true that s. 35(1) is not subject to s. 1 of the Charter. In our opinion, this does not mean that any law or regulation affecting aboriginal rights will automatically be of no force or effect by the operation of s. 52 of the *Constitution Act, 1982.* Legislation that affects the exercise of aboriginal rights will nonetheless be valid, if it meets the test for justifying an interference with a right recognized and affirmed under s. 35(1).

There is no explicit language in the provision that authorizes this Court or any court to assess the legitimacy of any government legislation that restricts aboriginal rights. Yet, we find that the words "recognition and affirmation" incorporate the fiduciary relationship referred to earlier and so import some restraint on the exercise of sovereign power. Rights that are recognized and affirmed are not absolute. Federal legislative powers continue, including, of course, the right to legislate with respect to Indians pursuant to s. 91(24) of the *Constitution Act, 1867.* These powers must, however, now be read together with s. 35(1). In other words, federal power must be reconciled with federal duty and the best way to achieve that reconciliation is to demand the justification of any government regulation that infringes upon or denies aboriginal rights. Such scrutiny is in keeping with the liberal interpretive principle enunciated in *Nowegijick,* supra and the concept of holding the Crown to a high standard of honourable dealing with respect to the aboriginal peoples of Canada as suggested by *Guerin* v. *The Queen,* supra.

We refer to Professor Slattery's "Understanding Aboriginal Rights," supra, with respect to the task of envisioning a s. 35(1) justificatory process. Professor Slattery, at p. 782, points out that a justificatory process is required as a compromise between a "patchwork" characterization of aboriginal rights whereby past regulations would be read into a definition of the rights, and a characterization that would guarantee aboriginal rights in their original form unrestricted by subsequent regulation. We agree with him that these two extreme positions must be rejected in favour of a justificatory scheme.

Section 35(1) suggests that while regulation affecting aboriginal rights is not precluded, such regulation must be enacted according to a valid objective. Our history has shown, unfortunately all too well, that Canada's aboriginal peoples are justified in worrying about government objectives that may be superficially neutral but which constitute *de facto* threats to the existence of aboriginal rights and interests. By giving aboriginal rights constitutional status and priority, Parliament and the provinces have sanctioned challenges to social and economic policy objectives embodied in legislation to the extent that aboriginal rights are affected. Implicit in this constitutional scheme is the obligation of the legislature to satisfy the test of justification. The way in which a legislative objective is to be attained must uphold the honour of the Crown and must be in keeping with the unique contemporary relationship, grounded in history and policy, between the Crown and Canada's aboriginal peoples. The extent of legislative or regulatory impact on an existing aboriginal right may be scrutinized so as to ensure recognition and affirmation.

The constitutional recognition afforded by the provision therefore gives a measure of control over government conduct and a strong check on legislative power. While it does not promise immunity from government regulation in a society that, in the twentieth century, is increasingly more complex, interdependent and sophisticated, and where exhaustible resources need protection and management, it does hold the Crown to a substantive promise. The government is required to bear the burden of justifying any legislation that has some negative effect on any aboriginal right protected under s. 35(1).

In these reasons, we will outline the appropriate analysis under s. 35(1) in the context of a regulation made pursuant to the *Fisheries Act*. We wish to emphasize the importance of context and a case-by-case approach to s. 35(1). Given the generality of the text of the constitutional provision, and especially in light of the complexities of aboriginal history, society and rights, the contours of a justificatory standard must be defined in the specific factual context of each case.

Section 35(1) and the Regulation of the Fisheries
Taking the above framework as guidance, we propose to set out the test for *prima facie* interference with an existing aboriginal right and for the justification of such an interference. With respect to the question of the regulation of the fisheries, the existence of s. 35(1) of the *Constitution Act, 1982*, renders the authority of *R.* v. *Derricksan*, [1976] 2 S.C.R. V, inapplicable. In that case, Laskin C.J., for this Court, found that there was nothing to prevent the *Fisheries Act* and the Regulations from subjecting the alleged aboriginal right to fish in a particular area to the controls thereby imposed. As the Court of Appeal in the case at bar noted, the *Derricksan* line of cases established that, before April 17, 1982, the aboriginal right to fish was subject to regulation by legislation and subject to extinguishment. The new constitutional status of that right enshrined in s. 35(1) suggests that a different approach must be taken in deciding whether regulation of the fisheries might be out of keeping with constitutional protection.

The first question to be asked is whether the legislation in question has the effect of interfering with an existing aboriginal right. If it does have such an effect, it represents a *prima facie* infringement of s. 35(1). Parliament is not expected to act in a manner contrary to the rights and interests of aboriginals, and, indeed, may be barred from doing so by the second stage of s. 35(1) analysis. The inquiry with respect to interference begins with a reference to the characteristics or incidents of the right at stake. Our earlier observations regarding the scope of the aboriginal right to fish are relevant here. Fishing rights are not traditional property rights. They are rights held by a collective and are in keeping with the culture and existence of that group. Courts must be careful, then, to avoid the application of traditional common law concepts of property as they develop their understanding of what the reasons for judgment in *Guerin*, supra, at p. 382 [p. 136 C.N.L.R.], referred to as the "*sui generis*" nature of aboriginal rights. (See also Little Bear, "A Concept of Native Title," [1982] 5 *Can. Legal Aid Bul.* 99.)

While it is impossible to give an easy definition of fishing rights, it is possible, and, indeed, crucial, to be sensitive to the aboriginal perspective itself on the meaning of the rights at stake. For example, it would be artificial to try to create a hard distinction between the right to fish and the particular manner in which that right is exercised.

To determine whether the fishing rights have been interfered with such as to constitute a *prima facie* infringement of s. 35(1), certain questions must be asked. First, is the limitation unreasonable? Second, does the regulation impose undue hardship? Third, does the regulation deny to the holders of the right their preferred means of exercising that right? The onus of proving a *prima facie* infringement lies on the individual or group challenging the legislation. In relation to the facts of this appeal, the regulation would be found to be a *prima facie* interference if it were found to be an adverse restriction on the Musqueam exercise of their right to fish for food. We wish to note here that the issue does not merely require looking at whether the fish catch has been reduced below that needed for the reasonable food and ceremonial needs of the Musqueam Indians. Rather the test involves asking whether either the purpose or the effect of the restriction on net length unnecessarily infringes the interests protected by the fishing right. If, for example, the Musqueam were forced to spend undue time and money per fish caught or if the net length reduction resulted in a hardship to the Musqueam in catching fish, then the first branch of the s. 35(1) analysis would be met.

If a *prima facie* interference is found, the analysis moves to the issue of justification. This is the test that addresses the question of what constitutes legitimate regulation of a constitutional aboriginal right. The justification analysis would proceed as follows. First, is there a valid legislative objective? Here the court would inquire into whether the objective of Parliament in authorizing the department to enact regulations regarding fisheries is valid. The objective of the department in setting out the particular regulations would also be scrutinized. An objective aimed at preserving s. 35(1) rights by conserving and managing a natural resource, for example, would be valid. Also valid would be objectives purporting to prevent the exercise of s. 35(1) rights that would cause harm to the general populace or to aboriginal peoples themselves, or other objectives found to be compelling and substantial.

The Court of Appeal below held, at p. 331 [p. 178 C.N.L.R.] that regulations could be valid if reasonably justified as "necessary for the proper management and conservation of the resource *or in the public interest*" (emphasis added). We find the "public interest" justification to be so vague as to provide no meaningful guidance and so broad as to be unworkable as a test for the justification of a limitation on constitutional rights.

The justification of conservation and resource management, on the other hand, is surely uncontroversial. In *Kruger* v. *The Queen*, [1978] 1 S.C.R. 104, [1977] 4 W.W.R. 300, the applicability of the B.C. *Wildlife Act*, S.B.C. 1966, c. 55, to the appellant members of the Penticton Indian Band was considered by this Court. In discussing that Act, the following was said about the objective of conservation (at p.112):

> Game conservation laws have as their policy the maintenance of wildlife resources. It might be argued that without some conservation measures the ability of Indians or others to hunt for food would become a moot issue in consequence of the destruction of the resource. The presumption is for the validity of a legislative enactment and in this case the presumption has to mean that in the absence of evidence to the contrary the measures taken by the British Columbia Legislature were taken to maintain an effective resource in the Province for its citizens and not to oppose the interests of conservationists and Indians in such a way as to favour the claims of the former.

While the "presumption" of validity is now outdated in view of the constitutional status of the aboriginal rights at stake, it is clear that the value of conservation purposes for government legislation and action has long been recognized. Further, the conservation and management of our resources is consistent with aboriginal beliefs and practices, and, indeed, with the enhancement of aboriginal rights.

If a valid legislative objective is found, the analysis proceeds to the second part of the justification issue. Here, we refer back to the guiding interpretive principle derived from *Taylor and Williams* and *Guerin*, supra. That is, the honour of the Crown is at stake in dealings with aboriginal peoples. The special trust relationship and the responsibility of the government vis-à-vis aboriginals must be the first consideration in determining whether the legislation or action in question can be justified.

The problem that arises in assessing the legislation in light of its objective and the responsibility of the Crown is that the pursuit of conservation in a heavily used modern fishery inevitably blurs with the efficient allocation and management of this scarce and valued resource. The nature of the constitutional protection afforded by s. 35(1) in this context demands that there be a link between the question of justification and the allocation of priorities in the fishery. The constitutional recognition and affirmation of aboriginal rights may give rise to conflict with the interests of others given the limited nature of the resource. There is a clear need for guidelines that will resolve the allocational problems that arise regarding the fisheries. We refer to the reasons of Dickson J. in *Jack* v. *The Queen*, [1980] 1 S.C.R. 294, [1979] 2 C.N.L.R. 25, for such guidelines.

In *Jack*, the appellants' defence to a charge of fishing for salmon in certain rivers during a prohibited period was based on the alleged constitutional incapacity of Parliament to legislate such as to deny the Indians their right to fish for food. They argued that Art. 13 of the *British Columbia Terms of Union* imposed a constitutional limitation on the federal power to regulate. While we recognize that the finding that such a limitation had been imposed was not adopted by the majority of this Court, we point out that this case concerns a different constitutional promise that asks this Court to give a meaningful interpretation to recognition and affirmation. That task requires equally meaningful guidelines responsive to the constitutional priority accorded aboriginal rights. We therefore repeat the following passage from *Jack*, at p. 313 [p. 41 C.N.L.R.]:

> Conservation is a valid legislative concern. The appellants concede as much. Their concern is in the allocation of the resource after reasonable and necessary conservation measures have been recognized and given effect to. They do not claim the right to pursue the last living salmon until it is caught. Their position, as I understand it, is one which would give effect to an order of priorities of this nature: (i) conservation; (ii) Indian fishing; (iii) non-Indian commercial fishing; or (iv) non-Indian sports fishing; the burden of conservation measures should not fall primarily upon the Indian fishery.
>
> I agree with the general tenor of this argument. . . . With respect to whatever salmon are to be caught, then priority ought to be given to the Indian fishermen, subject to the practical difficulties occasioned by international waters and the movement of the fish themselves. But any limitation upon Indian fishing that is established for a valid conservation purpose overrides the protection afforded the Indian fishery by art. 13, just as such conservation measures override other taking of fish.

The constitutional nature of the Musqueam food fishing rights means that any allocation of priorities after valid conservation measures have been implemented must give top priority to Indian food fishing. If the objective pertained to conservation, the conservation plan would be scrutinized to assess priorities. While the detailed allocation of maritime resources is a task that must be left to those having expertise in the area, the Indians' food requirements must be met first when that allocation is established. The significance of giving the aboriginal right to fish for food top priority can be described as follows. If, in a given year, conservation needs required a reduction in the number of fish to be caught such that the number equalled the number required for food by the Indians, then all the fish available after conservation would go to the Indians according to the constitutional nature of their fishing right. If, more realistically, there were still fish after the Indian food requirements were met, then the brunt of conservation measures would be borne by the practices of sport fishing and commercial fishing.

The decision of the Nova Scotia Court of Appeal in *Denny, Paul and Sylliboy* v. *The Queen,* unreported rendered March 5, 1990 [now reported [1990] 2 C.N.L.R. 115] addresses the constitutionality of the Nova Scotia Micmac Indians' right to fish in the waters of Indian Brook and the Afton River, and does so in a way that accords with our understanding of the constitutional nature of aboriginal rights and the link between allocation and justification required for government regulation of the exercise of the rights. Clarke C.J.N.S., for a unanimous court, found that the Nova Scotia *Fishery Regulations* enacted pursuant to the federal *Fisheries Act* were in part inconsistent with the constitutional rights of the appellant Micmac Indians. Section 35(1) of the *Constitution Act, 1982,* provided the appellants with the right to a top priority allocation of any surplus of the fisheries resource which might exist after the needs of conservation had been taken into account. With respect to the issue of the Indians' priority to a food fishery, Clarke C.J.N.S. noted that the official policy of the federal government recognizes that priority. He added the following, at pp. 22–23 [p. 131 C.N.L.R.]:

> I have no hesitation in concluding that factual as well as legislative and policy recognition must be given to the existence of an Indian food fishery in the waters of Indian Brook, adjacent to the Eskasoni Reserve, and the waters of the Afton River after the needs of conservation have been taken into account. . .

To afford user groups such as sports fishermen (anglers) a priority to fish over the legitimate food needs of the appellants and their families is simply not appropriate action on the part of the federal government. It is inconsistent with the fact that the appellants have for many years, and continue to possess an aboriginal right to fish for food. The appellants have, to employ the words of their counsel, a "right to share in the available resource." This constitutional entitlement is second only to conservation measures that may be undertaken by federal legislation.

Further, Clarke C.J.N.S. found that s. 35(1) provided the constitutional recognition of the aboriginal priority with respect to the fishery, and that the regulations, in failing to guarantee that priority, were in violation of the constitutional provision. He said the following, at p. 25 [p. 133 C.N.L.R.]:

> Though it is crucial to appreciate that the rights afforded to the appellants by s. 35(1) are not absolute, the impugned regulatory scheme fails to recognize that this section provides the appellants with a priority of allocation and access to any surplus of the

fisheries resource once the needs of conservation have been taken into account. Section 35(1), as applied to these appeals, provides the appellants with an entitlement to fish in the waters in issue to satisfy their food needs, where a surplus exists. To the extent that the regulatory scheme fails to recognize this, it is inconsistent with the Constitution. Section 52 mandates a finding that such regulations are of no force and effect.

In light of this approach, the argument that the cases of *R. v. Hare and Debassige*, supra, and *R. v. Eninew, R. v. Bear,* supra, stand for the proposition that s. 35(1) provides no basis for restricting the power to regulate must be rejected, as was done by the Court of Appeal below. In *Hare and Debassige*, which addressed the issue of whether the *Ontario Fishery Regulations*, C.R.C. 1978, c. 849, applied to members of an Indian band entitled to the benefit of the Manitoulin Island Treaty which granted certain rights with respect to taking fish, Thorson J.A. emphasized the need for priority to be given to measures directed to the management and conservation of fish stocks with the following observation (at p. 17) [p. 156 C.N.L.R.]:

> Since 1867 and subject to the limitations thereon imposed by the Constitution, which of course now includes s. 35 of the *Constitution Act, 1982*, the constitutional authority and responsibility to make laws in relation to the fisheries has rested with Parliament. Central to Parliament's responsibility has been, and continues to be, the need to provide for the proper management and conservation of our fish stocks, and the need to ensure that they are not depleted or imperilled by deleterious practices or methods of fishing.
>
> The prohibitions found in ss. 12 and 20 of the Ontario regulations clearly serve this purpose. Accordingly it need not be ignored by our courts that while these prohibitions place limits on the rights of all persons, they are there to serve the larger interest which all persons share in the proper management and conservation of these important resources.

In *Eninew*, Hall J.A. found, at p. 368 [p. 129 C.N.L.R.] that "the treaty rights can be limited by such regulations as are reasonable." As we have pointed out, management and conservation of resources is indeed an important and valid legislative objective. Yet, the fact that the objective is of a "reasonable" nature cannot suffice as constitutional recognition and affirmation of aboriginal rights. Rather, the regulations enforced pursuant to a conservation or management objective may be scrutinized according to the justificatory standard outlined above.

We acknowledge the fact that the justificatory standard to be met may place a heavy burden on the Crown. However, government policy with respect to the British Columbia fishery, regardless of s. 35(1), already dictates that, in allocating the right to take fish, Indian food fishing is to be given priority over the interests of other user groups. The constitutional entitlement embodied in s. 35(1) requires the Crown to ensure that its regulations are in keeping with that allocation of priority. The objective of this requirement is not to undermine Parliament's ability and responsibility with respect to creating and administering overall conservation and management plans regarding the salmon fishery. The objective is rather to guarantee that those plans treat aboriginal peoples in a way ensuring that their rights are taken seriously.

Within the analysis of justification, there are further questions to be addressed, depending on the circumstances of the inquiry. These include the questions of whether there has been as little infringement as possible in order to effect the desired result; whether, in a situation of expropriation, fair compensation is available; and, whether the aboriginal group in question has been consulted with respect to the conservation measures being implemented. The aboriginal peoples, with their history of conservation-consciousness and interdependence with natural resources, would surely be expected, at the least, to be informed regarding the determination of an appropriate scheme for the regulation of the fisheries.

We would not wish to set out an exhaustive list of the factors to be considered in the assessment of justification. Suffice it to say that recognition and affirmation requires sensitivity to and respect for the rights of aboriginal peoples on behalf of the government, courts and indeed all Canadians.

APPLICATION TO THIS CASE—IS THE NET LENGTH RESTRICTION VALID?
The Court of Appeal below found that there was not sufficient evidence in this case to proceed with an analysis of s. 35(1) with respect to the right to fish for food. In reviewing the competing expert evidence, and recognizing that fish stock management is an uncertain science, it decided that the issues at stake in this appeal were not well adopted to being resolved at the appellate court level. . . .

In conclusion, we would dismiss the appeal and the cross-appeal and affirm the Court of Appeal's setting aside of the conviction. We would accordingly affirm the order for a new trial on the questions of infringement and whether any infringement is nonetheless consistent with s. 35(1), in accordance with the interpretation set out here.

For the reasons given above, the constitutional question must be answered as follows:

Question
Is the net length restriction contained in the Musqueam Indian Band Indian Food Fishing Licence dated March 30, 1984, issued pursuant to the *British Columbia Fishery (General) Regulations* and the *Fisheries Act*, R.S.C. 1970, c. F–14, inconsistent with s. 35(1) of the *Constitution Act, 1982?*

Answer
This question will have to be sent back to trial to be answered according to the analysis set out in these reasons.

4.   *R. v. Alphonse*, [1993] 4 C.N.L.R. 19 (B.C.C.A.). Taggart, Lambert, Hutcheon, Macfarlane, and Wallace JJ.A., June 25, 1993

> In *Alphonse*, the court held that the British Columbia *Wildlife Act* is a law of general application within the meaning of s. 88 of the *Indian Act* and that the *Wildlife Act* is referentially incorporated into federal law vis-à-vis s. 88. *Alphonse* also stands for the proposition that s. 88 is not inconsistent with s. 35(1) of the *Constitution Act, 1982*. The following excerpt, from the majority judgment, provides an example of the *Sparrow* justificatory analysis being utilized. The court held that s. 27(1)(c) of the *Wildlife Act*

violated the accused's s. 35(1) Aboriginal rights and was not justifiable.

Lambert J. (concurring with the result) held that s. 27(1)(c) was not a law of general application within the meaning of s. 88 of the *Indian Act.* Lambert J. found that since s. 27(1)(c) applies only to status Indians (because of s. 88 of the *Indian Act*) and non-Indians, and does not apply to non-status Indians and Métis, it cannot be a law of general application because it singles out individuals because of their "Indianness."

MACFARLANE J.A. (TAGGART, HUTCHEON and WALLACE JJ.A. concurring):— . . . This appeal concerns Aboriginal hunting rights, and whether the provisions of the *Wildlife Act*, S.B.C. 1982, c. 57 are inconsistent with the provisions of s. 35(1) of the *Constitution Act, 1982.*

The appellant, a Shuswap Indian, was acquitted of charges laid under the *Wildlife Act*. He was charged in Count 1 with a violation of s. 27(1)(c) for hunting at a time not within the open season, and, in Count 2, with the violation of 2.34(2) of the Act for having dead wildlife in his possession, without having a license or permit. He was acquitted on both charges by His Honour, Judge Barnett, of the Provincial Court of British Columbia (the "trial judge"). That decision is reported at [1988] 3 C.N.L.R. 92. . . .

The appellant, William Alphonse, is a Shuswap Indian and a member of the Williams Lake Band. He resides on the Sugar Cane Reserve near Williams Lake. On April 3, 1985, the appellant shot and killed a male mule deer. He did so at a place within the traditional hunting grounds of the Shuswap people on a date during the closed season. He had no permit to hunt. He shot the deer on private land registered in the name of Onward Cattle Co. Ltd.

The trial judge made these findings of fact, at pp. 94–95 of his reasons:

1. The Shuswap people have a history as an organized society going back long before the coming of the white man.

2. The hunting of deer was an integral part of the life of the Shuswap people and continues to be so to this day.

3. Deer have both cultural and material importance to the Shuswap people who have traditionally regarded them with great respect which resulted in effective conservation of the species.

4. Mr. Alphonse's hunting of the deer in this case was done with proper regard for the traditions of the Shuswap people and within the traditional territory of the Shuswap people.

5. Mr. Alphonse killed a deer on land which was Crown granted by the Province of British Columbia in 1890 or 1896, and remains privately owned.

6. The land where the deer was killed was not fenced, posted, built upon, cultivated, or occupied by livestock. Mr. Alphonse did not know the land was privately owned and there was nothing which should have made that fact apparent to him.

7. Mr. Alphonse was not concerned to know if he was hunting on privately or publicly owned lands. He believes that his right to hunt deer in the traditional territory of the Shuswap people cannot be restricted by laws enacted in the legislature of the Province of British Columbia.

8. Mr. Alphonse killed the deer within an area which has been designated as MU 5–2 by the Fish and Wildlife Branch. The deer populations within this area are stable

and healthy. During the open season the previous fall, licensed hunters killed about 1,175 deer within MU 5–2. Conservation officers assume that the actual kill in any given year will be about double the number they consider to be legally killed.

9. There are official policies which allow regional managers within the Fish and Wildlife Branch to grant special permission to persons to hunt deer during the closed season. The permits granted are known as sustenance permits.

10. Mr. Alphonse never considered applying for a sustenance permit.

No contrary findings were made in the County Court. . . .

(c) *Whether s. 27(1)(c) of the Wildlife Act is inconsistent with s. 35(1) of the Constitution Act, 1982?*

Section 27(1)(c) of the *Wildlife Act* provides:

27(1) A person commits an offence where he hunts, takes, traps, wounds or kills wildlife.

(c) at a time not within the open season,

Section 35(1) of the *Constitution Act, 1982* provides:

35(1) The existing Aboriginal and treaty rights of the Aboriginal peoples of Canada are hereby recognized and affirmed.

In *R. v. Sparrow* the Supreme Court of Canada explored for the first time the scope of s. 35(1). At p. 178 C.N.L.R. the Court said:

Section 35(1), at the least, provides a solid constitutional base upon which subsequent negotiations can take place. It also affords Aboriginal peoples constitutional protection against provincial legislative power.

The analysis required by *Sparrow* with respect to the application of s. 35(1) is revealed by these passages: at p. 182 C.N.L.R.:

The first question to be asked is whether the legislation in question has the effect of interfering with an existing aboriginal right. If it does have such an effect, it represents a *prima facie* infringement of s. 35(1). Parliament is not expected to act in a manner contrary to the rights and interests of aboriginals, and, indeed, may be barred from doing so by the second stage of s. 35(1) analysis. The inquiry with respect to interference begins with a reference to the characteristics or incidents of the right at stake.

at p. 182 C.N.L.R.:

While it is impossible to give an easy definition of fishing rights, it is possible, and, indeed, crucial, to be sensitive to the aboriginal perspective itself on the meaning of the rights at stake . . .

To determine whether the fishing rights have been interfered with such as to constitute a *prima facie* infringement of s. 35(1), certain questions must be asked. First, is the limitation unreasonable? Secondly, does the regulation impose undue hardship? Thirdly, does the regulation deny to the holders of the right their preferred means of exercising that right? The onus of proving a *prima facie* infringement lies on the individual or group challenging the legislation.

at p. 183 C.N.L.R.:

If a *prima facie* interference is found, the analysis moves to the issue of justification. This is the test that addresses the question of what constitutes legitimate regulation of a constitutional Aboriginal right. The justification analysis would proceed as follows. First, is there a valid legislative objective? Here the court would inquire into whether the objective of Parliament in authorizing the department to enact regulations regarding fisheries is valid. The objective of the department in setting out the particular regulations would also be scrutinized. An objective aimed at preserving s. 35(1) rights by conserving and managing a natural resource, for example, would be valid. Also valid would be objectives purporting to prevent the exercise of s. 35(1) rights that would cause harm to the general populace or to Aboriginal peoples themselves, or other objectives found to be compelling and substantial.

The Court of Appeal below held, at p. 96, that regulations could be valid if reasonably justified as "necessary for the proper management and conservation of the resource *or in the public interest*" (Emphasis added). We find the "public interest" justification to be so vague as to provide no meaningful guidance and so broad as to be unworkable as a test for the justification of a limitation on constitutional rights.

The justification of conservation and resource management, on the other hand, is surely uncontroversial.

at pp. 183–84 C.N.L.R.:

If a valid legislative objective is found, the analysis proceeds to the second part of the justification issue. Here, we refer back to the guiding interpretive principle derived from *Taylor* and *Williams* and *Guerin,* supra. That is, the honour of the Crown is at stake in dealings with aboriginal peoples. The special trust relationship and the responsibility of the government vis-à-vis aboriginals must be the first consideration in determining whether the legislation or action in question can be justified.

The problem that arises in assessing the legislation in light of its objective and the responsibility of the Crown is that the pursuit of conservation in a heavily used modern fishery inevitably blurs with the efficient allocation and management of this scarce and valued resource. The nature of the constitutional protection afforded by s. 35(1) in this context demands that there be a link between the question of justification and the allocation of priorities in the fishery. The constitutional recognition and affirmation of aboriginal rights may give rise to conflict with the interests of others given the limited nature of the resource. There is a clear need for guidelines that will resolve the allocational problems that arise regarding the fisheries. We refer to the reasons of Dickson J. . . . in *Jack v. the Queen,* supra, for such guidelines.

at p. 184 C.N.L.R.:

We therefore repeat the following passage from *Jack,* at p. 313:

Conservation is a valid legislative concern. The appellants concede as much. Their concern is in the allocation of the resource after reasonable and necessary conservation measures have been recognized and given effect to. They do not claim the right to pursue the last living salmon until it is caught. Their position, as I understand it, is one which would give effect to an order of priorities of this nature: (i) conservation; (ii) Indian fishing; (iii) non-Indian commercial fishing; or (iv) non-Indian sports fishing; the burden of conservation measures should not fall primarily upon the Indian fishery.

I agree with the general tenor of this argument . . . With respect to whatever salmon are to be caught, then priority ought to be given to the Indian fishermen, subject to the practical difficulties occasioned by international waters and the movement of the fish themselves. But any limitation upon Indian fishing that is established for a valid con-servation purpose overrides the protection afforded the Indian fishery by art. 13, just as such conservation measures override other taking of fish . . .

While the detailed allocation of maritime resources is a task that must be left to those having expertise in the areas, the Indians' food requirements must be met first when that allocation is established.

at p. 186–87 C.N.L.R.:

We acknowledge the fact that the justificatory standard to be met may place a heavy burden on the Crown . . . The constitutional entitlement embodied in s. 35(1) requires the Crown to ensure that its regulations are in keeping with that allocation of priority. The objective of this requirement is not to undermine Parliament's ability and respon-sibility with respect to creating and administering over-all conservation and manage-ment plans regarding the salmon fishery. The objective is rather to guarantee that those plans treat aboriginal peoples in a way ensuring that their rights are taken seri-ously.

Within the analysis of justification, there are further questions to be addressed, depending on the circumstances of the inquiry. These include the questions of whether there has been as little infringement as possible in order to effect the desired result; whether, in a situation of expropriation, fair compensation is available, and whether the aboriginal group in question has been consulted with respect to the conservation measures being implemented. The aboriginal peoples, with their history of conserva-tion-consciousness and interdependence with natural resources, would surely be ex-pected, at the least, to be informed regarding the determination of an appropriate scheme for the regulation of the fisheries.

We would not wish to set out an exhaustive list of the factors to be considered in the assessment of justification. Suffice it to say that recognition and affirmation re-quires sensitivity to and respect for the rights of aboriginal peoples on behalf of the government, courts and indeed all Canadians.

The Province asserts that it should not be assumed that the same tests apply to fishing as to hunting.

The County Court judge said there is no distinction in this case between the right to fish and the right to hunt (p. 126). In *R. v. Kruger,* [1978] 1 S.C.R. 104, hunting and fishing rights were treated alike. (p. 111) In my view, the *Sparrow* analysis is equally applicable to fishing, hunting, or to any other Aboriginal right, except perhaps when it comes to a detailed allocation of resources. At that stage the task of scrutinizing a conservation plan to assess priorities "must be left to those having expertise in the area". (*Sparrow,* p. 1116 [S.C.R.; p. 184 C.N.L.R.]). Competing interests have to be balanced. The claims of the Aboriginal peoples must be taken seriously. Consultation is necessary. The plan may differ depending upon the resource in question, the steps which must be taken to conserve it, and other factors. *Sparrow* does not set out an exhaustive list of those factors (p. 187 C.N.L.R.]). They may vary from case to case and from resource to resource.

The first step in the *Sparrow* analysis is to ask whether the legislation in question has the effect of interfering with an existing Aboriginal right. In this case both judges below held that the Aboriginal rights of Mr. Alphonse had been infringed. But the Province submits that the evidence does not support a finding that Mr. Alphonse was exercising an Aboriginal right because the traditional preference of the Shuswap people was to hunt in the Fall, to hunt when food was needed, and not to kill deer of the species which Mr. Alphonse shot. The Province asserts that, therefore, the first step in the *Sparrow* analysis was not established.

But the findings of the trial judge, listed earlier, were supported by the County Court judge and, in my view, were ones which a judge, properly instructed, could reasonably have made: *R. v. Yebes*, [1987] 2 S.C.R. 168 at 185–86, [1987] 6 W.W.R. 97, 17 B.C.L.R. (2d) 1.

The appellant makes this submission with respect to prima facie infringement, in paras. 14–15 of his factum:

> 14. It is respectfully submitted that, having regard to those findings of fact, an application of the foregoing principles justifies the conclusion that s. 27(1)(c)of the *Wildlife Act* constitutes a *prima facie* infringement of s. 35(1):
> > (a) The closed season, coupled with the low bag limits, prevents subsistence hunters from obtaining sufficient venison for their food needs.
> > (b) The closed season prevents the Indian practice of hunting game for food throughout the year.
> > (c) The closed season and bag limits impact negatively upon the traditional practice whereby the Indian subsistence hunter shares the bounty of his hunt with members of his extended families and band elders.
> > (d) The subsistence permit policy does nothing to alleviate against the prima facie infringement of s. 35. Indeed, as the Provincial Court Judge ruled, it adds insult to infringement.
>
> 15. Sensitivity to the aboriginal perspective is especially important in this analysis. That perspective should inform the Court's assessment of the "undueness" of hardship caused by s. 27(1)(c), and of its "unreasonableness". In this regard, useful reference may be made to the testimony of the Indian witnesses quoted by Barnett, P.C.J., at pp. 22–25 of his Reasons for Judgment. These witnesses make clear that, for them, far more is involved than just a source of protein, their way of life and distinctive cultural identity is at stake. In the words of Chief Alice Abbey:
> > [I]t's our gift, it's a nourishment for us, a total nourishment.

I think the judges below were correct in proceeding on the basis that the provisions of the *Wildlife Act* interfered with the Aboriginal rights of Mr. Alphonse.

The Country Court judge reached his conclusion that s. 27(1)(c)of the *Wildlife Act* did not contravene s. 35(1) without having the advantage of the analysis by the Supreme Court of Canada in *Sparrow*. Thus the appropriate legal tests were not applied in this case.

Instead the County Court judge had regard to the public interest test prescribed by the Court of Appeal, which was later rejected by the Supreme Court of Canada. Although a conservation test was applied, it did not have regard to the factors mentioned and the analysis provided by the Supreme Court of Canada judgment in *Sparrow*. Accordingly I think the appeal must be allowed.

The province submits there should be a new trial so the Crown may have an opportunity to adduce evidence on the questions raised by *Sparrow.*

In my opinion this is not a case where it would be appropriate to grant a new trial. Instead, I would allow the appeal and acquit the appellant on the basis that he has established a *prima facie* infringement of his Aboriginal rights. That infringement has not been justified by the Crown. This conclusion should come as no surprise to the Province, which suggested earlier that such a course be followed. The appeal went ahead, however, because the appellant wished to fully argue his case before this Court.

Whether, in another case, the Crown can justify the closed season provision in the *Wildlife Act* is another matter. But the Crown will have to demonstrate, amongst other things, that it is justified in giving no priority in the *Wildlife Act* or its regulations to the Indians despite the fact that they have an unextinguished Aboriginal right to hunt.

PART V
SUMMARY

1.   Mr. Alphonse was exercising an unextinguished Aboriginal right when he shot a deer on unoccupied, unfenced, uncultivated private land, which was not "enclosed land" as defined by the *Trespass Act.*

2.   The *Wildlife Act* is a law of general application within the meaning of s. 88 of the *Indian Act*, and is referentially incorporated as federal law pursuant to s. 88.

3.   Section 88 is not inconsistent with s. 35(1) of the *Constitution Act, 1982.*

4.   Section 27(1)(c) of the *Wildlife Act* constitutes a prima facie infringement of Aboriginal rights which has not been justified on the evidence before the court and this it is inconsistent with s. 35(1) of the *Constitution Act, 1982.* Accordingly, applying s. 52(1) of the *Constitution Act, 1982*, s. 27(1)(c) is of no force or effect with respect to Aboriginal persons.

I would allow the appeal against conviction and sentence, and would acquit the appellant. . . .

5.   *R. v. Van der Peet,* **[1996] 4 C.N.L.R. 177 (S.C.C.). Lamer C.J., La Forest, L'Heureux-Dubé, Sopinka, Gonthier, Cory, McLachlin, Iacobucci, and Major JJ., August 21, 1996**

Since the 1990 *Sparrow* decision, no one case stands out to the extent that *Van der Peet* does with respect to its profound influence and effect on Aboriginal rights' jurisprudence. *Van der Peet* is one of a string of significant decisions made by the Supreme Court of Canada in 1996 dealing with Aboriginal rights and title issues. It provides the detail relating to the nature and content of Aboriginal title that, until now, had not been sufficiently discussed by the Supreme Court. Indeed, *Van der Peet* formed a substantial base upon which the Supreme Court decided the landmark decision of

Delgamuukw (provided in chapter 1). The case concerned an Aboriginal person charged under the *British Columbia Fishery (General) Regulations*, which prohibited the sale or barter of fish caught under the authority of an Indian food fish licence. Ultimately, the court decided that the Aboriginal person charged (Mrs. Van der Peet) did not demonstrate that the exchange of fish for money or other goods was an integral part of the distinctive Sto:lo culture that existed prior to European contact. The Supreme Court held that in assessing an Aboriginal rights claim, a court must outline the nature of the right being claimed so as to determine whether the claim meets the test of being integral to the distinctive culture of the Aboriginal group claiming the right. In order to be integral, a practice, custom, or tradition must be of a central significance to the Aboriginal group concerned and must have existed prior to contact with non-Aboriginal society. The court also noted that Aboriginal rights may evolve and do not need to remain static in order to be afforded protection under s. 35(1). The following excerpt is from the majority decision of Lamer C.J. and deals with the court's discussion of the relationship between Aboriginal rights and Aboriginal title.

LAMER C.J. (LA FOREST, SOPINKA, GONTHIER, CORY, IACOBUCCI and MAJOR JJ. concurring):—

INTRODUCTION

1.   This appeal, along with the companion appeals in *R.* v. *N.T.C. Smokehouse Ltd.,* [1996] 2 S.C.R. 672, and *R.* v. *Gladstone,* [1996] 2 S.C.R. 723, raises the issue left unresolved by this Court in its judgment in *R.* v. *Sparrow,* [1990] 1 S.C.R. 1075: How are the Aboriginal rights recognized and affirmed by s. 35(1) of the *Constitution Act, 1982* to be defined?

2.   In *Sparrow,* Dickson C.J. and La Forest J., writing for a unanimous Court, outlined the framework for analyzing s. 35(1) claims. First, a court must determine whether an applicant has demonstrated that he or she was acting pursuant to an Aboriginal right. Second, a court must determine whether that right has been extinguished. Third, a court must determine whether that right has been infringed. Finally, a court must determine whether the infringement is justified. In *Sparrow,* however, it was not seriously disputed that the Musqueam had an Aboriginal right to fish for food, with the result that it was unnecessary for the Court to answer the question of how the rights recognized and affirmed by s. 35(1) are to be defined. It is this question and, in particular, the question of whether s. 35(1) recognizes and affirms the right of the Sto:lo to sell fish, which must now be answered by this Court.

3.   In order to define the scope of Aboriginal rights, it will be necessary first to articulate the purposes which underpin s. 35(1), specifically the reasons underlying its recognition and affirmation of the unique constitutional status of Aboriginal peoples in Canada. Until it is understood why Aboriginal rights exist, and are constitutionally protected, no definition of those rights is possible. As Dickson J. (as he then was) said in *R.* v. *Big M Drug Mart Ltd.,* [1985] 1 S.C.R. 295, at p. 344, a constitutional provision must be understood "in the light of the interests it was meant to protect". This principle, articulated in relation to the rights protected by

the *Canadian Charter of Rights and Freedoms,* applies equally to the interpretation of s. 35(1). . . .

5.   The appellant Dorothy Van der Peet was charged under s. 61(1) of the *Fisheries Act,* R.S.C. 1970, c. F–14, with the offence of selling fish caught under the authority of an Indian food fish licence, contrary to s. 27(5) of the *British Columbia Fishery (General) Regulations,* SOR/84-248. At the time at which the appellant was charged s. 27(5) read:

> 27. . . .
>
> (5) No person shall sell, barter or offer to sell or barter any fish caught under the authority of an Indian food fish licence. . . .

13.   Leave to appeal to this Court was granted on March 10, 1994. The following constitutional question was stated:

> Is s. 27(5) of the *British Columbia Fishery (General) Regulations,* SOR/84-248, as it read on September 11, 1987, of no force or effect with respect to the appellant in the circumstances of these proceedings, in virtue of s. 52 of the *Constitution Act, 1982,* by reason of the Aboriginal rights within the meaning of s. 35 of the *Constitution Act, 1982,* invoked by the appellant? . . .

16.   In her factum the appellant argued that the majority of the Court of Appeal erred because it defined the rights in s. 35(1) in a fashion which "converted a Right into a Relic"; such an approach, the appellant argued, is inconsistent with the fact that the Aboriginal rights recognized and affirmed by s. 35(1) are rights and not simply Aboriginal practices. The appellant acknowledged that Aboriginal rights are based in Aboriginal societies and cultures, but argued that the majority of the Court of Appeal erred because it defined Aboriginal rights through the identification of pre-contact activities instead of as pre-existing legal rights.

17.   While the appellant is correct to suggest that the mere existence of an activity in a particular Aboriginal community prior to contact with Europeans is not, in itself, sufficient foundation for the definition of Aboriginal rights, the position she would have this Court adopt takes s. 35(1) too far from that which the provision is intended to protect. Section 35(1), it is true, recognizes and affirms existing Aboriginal *rights,* but it must not be forgotten that the rights it recognizes and affirms are *Aboriginal.*

18.   In the liberal enlightenment view, reflected in the American Bill of Rights and, more indirectly, in the *Charter,* rights are held by all people in society because each person is entitled to dignity and respect. Rights are general and universal; they are the way in which the "inherent dignity" of each individual in society is respected: *R. v. Oakes,* [1986] 1 S.C.R. 103, at p. 136; *R. v. Big M Drug Mart Ltd., supra,* at p. 336.

19.   *Aboriginal* rights cannot, however, be defined on the basis of the philosophi-
cal precepts of the liberal enlightenment. Although equal in importance and significance to the rights enshrined in the *Charter,* Aboriginal rights must be viewed
differently from *Charter* rights because they are rights held only by Aboriginal
members of Canadian society. They arise from the fact that Aboriginal people are
Aboriginal. As academic commentators have noted, Aboriginal rights "inhere in
the very meaning of Aboriginality", Michael Asch and Patrick Macklem, "Aboriginal Rights and Canadian Sovereignty: An Essay on *R.* v. *Sparrow*" (1991), 29
Alta. L. Rev. 498, at p. 502; they are the rights held by "Indians *qua* Indians", Brian
Slattery, "Understanding Aboriginal Rights" (1987), 66 *Can. Bar Rev.* 727, at p.
776.

20.   The task of this Court is to define Aboriginal rights in a manner which recognizes that Aboriginal rights are *rights* but which does so without losing sight of the
fact that they are rights held by Aboriginal people because they are *Aboriginal.*
The Court must neither lose sight of the generalized constitutional status of what s.
35(1) protects, nor can it ignore the necessary specificity which comes from granting special constitutional protection to one part of Canadian society. The Court
must define the scope of s. 35(1) in a way which captures both the Aboriginal and
the rights in Aboriginal rights.

21   The way to accomplish this task is, as was noted at the outset, through a
purposive approach to s. 35(1). It is through identifying the interests that s. 35(1)
was intended to protect that the dual nature of Aboriginal rights will be comprehended. In *Hunter* v. *Southam Inc.,* [1984] 2 S.C.R. 145, Dickson J. explained the
rationale for a purposive approach to constitutional documents. Courts should take
a purposive approach to the Constitution because constitutions are, by their very
nature, documents aimed at a country's future as well as its present; the Constitution must be interpreted in a manner which renders it "capable of growth and development over time to meet new social, political and historical realities often
unimagined by its framers": *Hunter, supra,* at p. 155. A purposive approach to s.
35(1), besides ensuring that the provision is not viewed as static and only relevant
to current circumstances, will ensure that the recognition and affirmation it offers
are consistent with the fact that what it is recognizing and affirming are "rights".
Further, because it requires the court to analyze a given constitutional provision
"in the light of the interests it was meant to protect"(*Big M Drug Mart Ltd., supra,*
at p. 344), a purposive approach to s. 35(1) will ensure that that which is found to
fall within the provision is related to the provision's intended focus: Aboriginal
people and their rights in relation to Canadian society as a whole.

22.   In *Sparrow, supra,* Dickson C.J. and La Forest J. held at p. 1106 that it was
through a purposive analysis that s. 35(1) must be understood:

> The approach to be taken with respect to interpreting the meaning of s. 35(1) is de-
> rived from general principles of constitutional interpretation, principles relating to
> Aboriginal rights, and *the purposes behind the constitutional provision itself.* [Em-
> phasis added.]

In that case, however, the Court did not have the opportunity to articulate the purposes behind s. 35(1) as they relate to the scope of the rights the provision is intended to protect. Such analysis is now required to be undertaken.

General Principles Applicable to Legal Disputes Between Aboriginal Peoples and the Crown

23.   Before turning to a purposive analysis of s. 35(1), however, it should be noted that such analysis must take place in light of the general principles which apply to the legal relationship between the Crown and Aboriginal peoples. In *Sparrow, supra,* this Court held at p. 1106 that s. 35(1) should be given a generous and liberal interpretation in favour of Aboriginal peoples:

> When the purposes of the affirmation of Aboriginal rights are considered, *it is clear that a generous, liberal interpretation of the words in the constitutional provision is demanded.* [Emphasis added.]

24.   This interpretive principle, articulated first in the context of treaty rights—*Simon* v. *The Queen,* [1985] 2 S.C.R. 387, at p. 402; *Nowegijick* v. *The Queen,* [1983] 1 S.C.R. 29, at p. 36; *R.* v. *Horseman,* [1990] 1 S.C.R. 901, at p. 907; *R.* v. *Sioui,* [1990] 1 S.C.R. 1025, at p. 1066—arises from the nature of the relationship between the Crown and Aboriginal peoples. The Crown has a fiduciary obligation to Aboriginal peoples with the result that in dealings between the government and Aboriginals the honour of the Crown is at stake. Because of this fiduciary relationship, and its implication of the honour of the Crown, treaties, s. 35(1), and other statutory and constitutional provisions protecting the interests of Aboriginal peoples, must be given a generous and liberal interpretation: *R.* v. *George,* [1966] S.C.R. 267, at p. 279. This general principle must inform the Court's analysis of the purposes underlying s. 35(1), and of that provision's definition and scope.

25.   The fiduciary relationship of the Crown and Aboriginal peoples also means that where there is any doubt or ambiguity with regards to what falls within the scope and definition of s. 35(1), such doubt or ambiguity must be resolved in favour of Aboriginal peoples. In *R.* v. *Sutherland,* [1980] 2 S.C.R. 451, at p. 464, Dickson J. held that paragraph 13 of the Memorandum of Agreement between Manitoba and Canada, a constitutional document, should be interpreted so as to resolve any doubts in favour of the Indians, the beneficiaries of the rights assured by the paragraph. This interpretive principle applies equally to s. 35(1) of the *Constitution Act, 1982* and should, again, inform the Court's purposive analysis of that provision.

Purposive Analysis of Section 35(1) . . .

27.   When the court identifies a constitutional provision's purposes, or the interests the provision is intended to protect, what it is doing in essence is explaining the rationale of the provision; it is articulating the reasons underlying the protection that the provision gives. With regards to s. 35(1), then, what the court must do is explain the rationale and foundation of the recognition and affirmation of the

special rights of Aboriginal peoples; it must identify the basis for the special status that Aboriginal peoples have within Canadian society as a whole.

28.   In identifying the basis for the recognition and affirmation of Aboriginal rights it must be remembered that s. 35(1) did not create the legal doctrine of Aboriginal rights; Aboriginal rights existed and were recognized under the common law: *Calder* v. *Attorney-General of British Columbia,* [1973] S.C.R. 313. At common law Aboriginal rights did not, of course, have constitutional status, with the result that Parliament could, at any time, extinguish or regulate those rights: *Kruger* v. *The Queen,* [1978] 1 S.C.R. 104, at p. 112; *R.* v. *Derriksan* (1976), 71 D.L.R. (3d) 159 (S.C.C.), [1976] 2 S.C.R. v; it is this which distinguishes the Aboriginal rights recognized and affirmed in s. 35(1) from the Aboriginal rights protected by the common law. Subsequent to s. 35(1) Aboriginal rights cannot be extinguished and can only be regulated or infringed consistent with the justificatory test laid out by this Court in Sparrow, *supra.*

29.   The fact that Aboriginal rights pre-date the enactment of s. 35(1) could lead to the suggestion that the purposive analysis of s. 35(1) should be limited to an analysis of why a pre-existing legal doctrine was elevated to constitutional status. This suggestion must be resisted. The pre-existence of Aboriginal rights is relevant to the analysis of s. 35(1) because it indicates that Aboriginal rights have a stature and existence prior to the constitutionalization of those rights and sheds light on the reasons for protecting those rights; however, the interests protected by s. 35(1) must be identified through an explanation of the basis for the legal doctrine of Aboriginal rights, not through an explanation of why that legal doctrine now has constitutional status.

30.   In my view, the doctrine of Aboriginal rights exists, and is recognized and affirmed by s. 35(1), because of one simple fact: when Europeans arrived in North America, Aboriginal peoples *were already here,* living in communities on the land, and participating in distinctive cultures, as they had done for centuries. It is this fact, and this fact above all others, which separates Aboriginal peoples from all other minority groups in Canadian society and which mandates their special legal, and now constitutional, status.

31.   More specifically, what s. 35(1) does is provide the constitutional framework through which the fact that Aboriginals lived on the land in distinctive societies, with their own practices, traditions and cultures, is acknowledged and reconciled with the sovereignty of the Crown. The substantive rights which fall within the provision must be defined in light of this purpose; the Aboriginal rights recognized and affirmed by s. 35(1) must be directed towards the reconciliation of the pre-existence of Aboriginal societies with the sovereignty of the Crown.

32.   That the purpose of s. 35(1) lies in its recognition of the prior occupation of North America by Aboriginal peoples is suggested by the French version of the text. For the English "existing Aboriginal and treaty rights" the French text reads

"*[l]es droits existants—ancestraux ou issus de traités*". The term "*ancestral*", which *Le Petit Robert 1* (1990) dictionary defines as "*[q]ui a appartenu aux ancêtres, qu'on tient des ancêtres*", suggests that the rights recognized and affirmed by s. 35(1) must be temporally rooted in the historical presence—the ancestry—of Aboriginal peoples in North America.

33.   This approach to s. 35(1) is also supported by the prior jurisprudence of this Court. In *Calder, supra,* the Court refused an application by the Nishga for a declaration that their Aboriginal title had not been extinguished. There was no majority in the Court as to the basis for this decision; however, in the judgments of both Judson J. and Hall J. (each speaking for himself and two others) the existence of Aboriginal title was recognized. Hall J. based the Nishga's Aboriginal title in the fact that the land to which they were claiming title had "been in their possession from time immemorial" (*Calder, supra,* at p. 375). Judson J. explained the origins of the Nishga's Aboriginal title as follows, at p. 328:

> Although I think that it is clear that Indian title in British Columbia cannot owe its origin to the Proclamation of 1763, *the fact is that when the settlers came, the Indians were there, organized in societies and occupying the land as their forefathers had done for centuries. This is what Indian title means* and it does not help one in the solution of this problem to call it a "personal or usufructuary right". What they are asserting in this action is that they had a right to continue to live on their lands as their forefathers had lived and that this right has never been lawfully extinguished. [Emphasis added.]

The position of Judson and Hall JJ. on the basis for Aboriginal title is applicable to the Aboriginal rights recognized and affirmed by s. 35(1). Aboriginal title is the aspect of Aboriginal rights related specifically to Aboriginal claims to land; it is the way in which the common law recognizes Aboriginal land rights. As such, the explanation of the basis of Aboriginal title in *Calder, supra,* can be applied equally to the Aboriginal rights recognized and affirmed by s. 35(1). Both Aboriginal title and Aboriginal rights arise from the existence of distinctive Aboriginal communities occupying "the land as their forefathers had done for centuries" (p. 328).

34.   The basis of Aboriginal title articulated in *Calder, supra,* was affirmed in *Guerin* v. *The Queen,* [1984] 2 S.C.R. 335. The decision in *Guerin* turned on the question of the nature and extent of the Crown's fiduciary obligation to Aboriginal peoples; because, however, Dickson J. based that fiduciary relationship, at p. 376, in the "concept of Aboriginal, native or Indian title", he had occasion to consider the question of the existence of Aboriginal title. In holding that such title existed, he relied, at p. 376, on *Calder, supra,* for the proposition that "Aboriginal title as a legal right *derived from the Indians' historic occupation and possession of their tribal lands*". [Emphasis added.]

35.   The view of Aboriginal rights as based in the prior occupation of North America by distinctive Aboriginal societies, finds support in the early American decisions of Marshall C.J. Although the constitutional structure of the United States

is different from that of Canada, and its Aboriginal law has developed in unique directions, I agree with Professor Slattery both when he describes the Marshall decisions as providing "structure and coherence to an untidy and diffuse body of customary law based on official practice" and when he asserts that these decisions are "as relevant to Canada as they are to the United States"—"Understanding Aboriginal Rights", *supra,* at p. 739. I would add to Professor Slattery's comments only the observation that the fact that Aboriginal law in the United States is significantly different from Canadian Aboriginal law means that the relevance of these cases arises from their articulation of general principles, rather than their specific legal holdings.

36.   In *Johnson* v. *M'Intosh,* 21 U.S. (8 Wheat.) 543 (1823), the first of the Marshall decisions on Aboriginal title, the Supreme Court held that Indian land could only be alienated by the U.S. government, not by the Indians themselves. In the course of his decision (written for the court), Marshall C.J. outlined the history of the exploration of North America by the countries of Europe and the relationship between this exploration and Aboriginal title. In his view, Aboriginal title is the right of Aboriginal people to land arising from the intersection of their pre-existing occupation of the land with the assertion of sovereignty over that land by various European nations. The substance and nature of Aboriginal rights to land are determined by this intersection (at pp. 572–74):

> On the discovery of this immense continent, the great nations of Europe were eager to appropriate to themselves so much of it as they could respectively acquire. Its vast extent offered an ample field to the ambition and enterprise of all; and the character and religion of its inhabitants afforded an apology for considering them as a people over whom the superior genius of Europe might claim an ascendency. The potentates of the old world found no difficulty in convincing themselves that they made ample compensation to the inhabitants of the new, by bestowing on them civilization and Christianity, in exchange for unlimited independence. But, as they were all in pursuit of nearly the same object, it was necessary, in order to avoid conflicting settlements, and consequent war with each other, to establish a principle, which all should acknowledge as the law by which the right of acquisition, which they all asserted, should be regulated as between themselves. This principle was, that discovery gave title to the government by whose subjects, or by whose authority, it was made, against all other European governments, which title might be consummated by possession.
>
> The exclusion of all other Europeans, necessarily gave to the nation making the discovery the sole right of acquiring the soil from the natives, and establishing settlements upon it. It was a right with which no Europeans could interfere. It was a right which all asserted for themselves, and to the assertion of which, by others, all assented.
>
> Those relations which were to exist between the discoverer and the natives, were to be regulated by themselves. The rights thus acquired being exclusive, no other power could interpose between them.
>
> *In the establishment of these relations, the rights of the original inhabitants were, in no instance, entirely disregarded; but were necessarily, to a considerable extent, impaired. They were admitted to be the rightful occupants of the soil, with a legal as*

well as just claim to retain possession of it, and to use it according to their own discretion; but their rights to complete sovereignty, as independent nations, were necessarily diminished, and their power to dispose of the soil at their own will, to whomsoever they pleased, was denied by the original fundamental principle, that discovery gave exclusive title to those who made it.

While the different nations of Europe respected the right of the natives, as occupants, they asserted the ultimate dominion to be in themselves; and claimed and exercised, as a consequence of this ultimate dominion, a power to grant the soil, while yet in possession of the natives. These grants have been understood by all, to convey a title to the grantees, subject only to the Indian right of occupancy. [Emphasis added.]

It is, similarly, the reconciliation of pre-existing Aboriginal claims to the territory that now constitutes Canada, with the assertion of British sovereignty over that territory, to which the recognition and affirmation of Aboriginal rights in s. 35(1) is directed.

37.   In *Worcester* v. *Georgia,* 31 U.S. (6 Pet.) 515 (1832) the U.S. Supreme Court invalidated the conviction under a Georgia statute of a non-Cherokee man for the offence of living on the territory of the Cherokee Nation. The court held that the law under which he was convicted was *ultra vires* the State of Georgia. In so doing the court considered the nature and basis of the Cherokee claims to the land and to governance over that land. Again, it based its judgment on its analysis of the origins of those claims which, it held, lay in the relationship between the pre-existing rights of the "ancient possessors" of North America and the assertion of sovereignty by European nations (at pp. 542–43 and 559):

America, separated from Europe by a wide ocean, was inhabited by a distinct people, divided into separate nations, independent of each other and of the rest of the world, having institutions of their own, and governing themselves by their own laws. It is difficult to comprehend the proposition, that the inhabitants of either quarter of the globe could have rightful original claims of dominion over the inhabitants of the other, or over the lands they occupied; or that the discovery of either by the other should give the discoverer rights in the country discovered, which annulled the pre-existing rights of its ancient possessors.

After lying concealed for a series of ages, the enterprise of Europe, guided by nautical science, conducted some of her adventurous sons into this western world. They found it in possession of a people who had made small progress in agriculture or manufactures, and whose general employment was war, hunting, and fishing.

Did these adventurers, by sailing along the coast, and occasionally landing on it, acquire for the several governments to whom they belonged, or by whom they were commissioned, a rightful property in the soil, from the Atlantic to the Pacific; or rightful dominion over the numerous people who occupied it? Or has nature, or the great Creator of all things, conferred these rights over hunters and fishermen, on agriculturists and manufacturers?

But power, war, conquest, give rights, which, after possession, are conceded by the world; and which can never be controverted by those on whom they descend. We proceed, then, to the actual state of things, having glanced at their origin; because holding it in our recollection might shed some light on existing pretensions. . . .

The Indian nations had always been considered as distinct, independent political communities, retaining their original natural rights, as the undisputed possessors of the soil, from time immemorial, with the single exception of that imposed by irresistible power, which excluded them from intercourse with any other European potentate than the first discoverer of the coast of the particular region claimed. [Emphasis added.]

Marshall C.J.'s essential insight that the claims of the Cherokee must be analyzed in light of their pre-existing occupation and use of the land—their "undisputed" possession of the soil "from time immemorial"—is as relevant for the identification of the interests s. 35(1) was intended to protect as it was for the adjudication of *Worcester*'s claim.

38.   The High Court of Australia has also considered the question of the basis and nature of Aboriginal rights. Like that of the United States, Australia's Aboriginal law differs in significant respects from that of Canada. In particular, in Australia the courts have not as yet determined whether Aboriginal fishing rights exist, although such rights are recognized by statute: *Halsbury's Laws of Australia* (1991), vol. 1, paras. 5–2250, 5–2255, 5–2260 and 5–2265. Despite these relevant differences, the analysis of the basis of Aboriginal title in the landmark decision of the High Court in *Mabo* v. *Queensland [No. 2]* (1992), 175 C.L.R. 1, is persuasive in the Canadian context.

39.   The *Mabo* judgment resolved the dispute between the Meriam people and the Crown regarding who had title to the Murray Islands. The islands had been annexed to Queensland in 1879 but were reserved for the native inhabitants (the Meriam) in 1882. The Crown argued that this annexation was sufficient to vest absolute ownership of the lands in the Crown. The High Court disagreed, holding that while the annexation did vest radical title in the Crown, it was insufficient to eliminate a claim for native title; the court held at pp. 50–51 that native title can exist as a burden on the radical title of the Crown: "there is no reason why land within the Crown's territory should not continue to be subject to native title. It is only the fallacy of equating sovereignty and beneficial ownership of land that gives rise to the notion that native title is extinguished by the acquisition of sovereignty".

40.   From this premise, Brennan J., writing for a majority of the Court, went on at p. 58 to consider the nature and basis of Aboriginal title:

Native title has its origin in and is given its content by the traditional laws acknowledged by and the traditional customs observed by the indigenous inhabitants of a territory. The nature and incidents of native title must be ascertained as a matter of fact by reference to those laws and customs. The ascertainment may present a problem of considerable difficulty, as Moynihan J. perceived in the present case. It is a problem that did not arise in the case of a settled colony so long as the fictions were maintained that customary rights could not be reconciled "with the institutions or the legal ideas of civilized society", *In re Southern Rhodesia*, [1919] A.C., at p. 233, that there was no law before the arrival of the British colonists in a settled colony and that there was no sovereign law-maker in the territory of a settled colony before sovereignty was acquired by the Crown. These fictions denied the possibility of a native title recognized by our laws. But once it is acknowledged that an inhabited territory which became a settled colony was no more a legal desert than it was "desert uninhabited" in fact, it is necessary to ascertain by evidence the nature and incidents of native title. [Emphasis added.]

This position is the same as that being adopted here. "Traditional laws" and "traditional customs" are those things passed down, and arising, from the pre-existing culture and customs of Aboriginal peoples. The very meaning of the word "tradition"—that which is "handed down [from ancestors] to posterity", *The Concise Oxford Dictionary* (9th ed. 1995),—implies these origins for the customs and laws that the Australian High Court in *Mabo* is asserting to be relevant for the determination of the existence of Aboriginal title. To base Aboriginal title in traditional laws and customs, as was done in *Mabo,* is, therefore, to base that title in the pre-existing societies of Aboriginal peoples. This is the same basis as that asserted here for aboriginal rights. . . .

42.   . . .

The challenge of defining aboriginal rights stems from the fact that they are rights peculiar to the meeting of two vastly dissimilar legal cultures; consequently there will always be a question about which legal culture is to provide the vantage point from which rights are to be defined. . . . a morally and politically defensible conception of aboriginal rights will incorporate both legal perspectives. [Emphasis added.]

Similarly, Professor Slattery has suggested that the law of Aboriginal rights is "neither English nor Aboriginal in origin: it is a form of intersocietal law that evolved from long-standing practices linking the various communities" (Brian Slattery, "The Legal Basis of Aboriginal Title", in Frank Cassidy, ed., *Aboriginal Title in British Columbia: Delgamuukw* v. *The Queen* (1992), at pp. 120–21) and that such rights concern "the status of native peoples living under the Crown's protection, and the position of their lands, customary laws, and political institutions" ("Understanding Aboriginal Rights", *supra,* at p. 737).

43.   The Canadian, American and Australian jurisprudence thus supports the basic proposition put forward at the beginning of this section: the Aboriginal rights recognized and affirmed by s. 35(1) are best understood as, first, the means by which the Constitution recognizes the fact that prior to the arrival of Europeans in North America the land was already occupied by distinctive Aboriginal societies, and as, second, the means by which that prior occupation is reconciled with the assertion of Crown sovereignty over Canadian territory. The content of Aboriginal rights must be directed at fulfilling both of these purposes; the next section of the judgment, as well as that which follows it, will attempt to accomplish this task.

The Test for Identifying Aboriginal Rights in Section 35(1)
44.   In order to fulfil the purpose underlying s. 35(1)—i.e., the protection and reconciliation of the interests which arise from the fact that prior to the arrival of

Europeans in North America Aboriginal peoples lived on the land in distinctive societies, with their own practices, customs and traditions—the test for identifying the Aboriginal rights recognized and affirmed by s. 35(1) must be directed at identifying the crucial elements of those pre-existing distinctive societies. It must, in other words, aim at identifying the practices, traditions and customs central to the Aboriginal societies that existed in North America prior to contact with the Europeans.

45.   In *Sparrow, supra,* this Court did not have to address the scope of the Aboriginal rights protected by s. 35(1); however, in their judgment at p. 1099 Dickson C.J. and La Forest J. identified the Musqueam right to fish for food in the fact that:

> The anthropological evidence relied on to establish the existence of the right suggests that, for the Musqueam, the salmon fishery has always constituted *an integral part of their distinctive culture.* Its significant role involved not only consumption for subsistence purposes, but also consumption of salmon on ceremonial and social occasions. The Musqueam have always fished for reasons connected to their cultural and physical survival. [Emphasis added.]

The suggestion of this passage is that participation in the salmon fishery is an Aboriginal right because it is an "integral part" of the "distinctive culture" of the Musqueam. This suggestion is consistent with the position just adopted; identifying those practices, customs and traditions that are integral to distinctive Aboriginal cultures will serve to identify the crucial elements of the distinctive Aboriginal societies that occupied North America prior to the arrival of Europeans.

46.   In light of the suggestion of *Sparrow, supra,* and the purposes underlying s. 35(1), the following test should be used to identify whether an applicant has established an Aboriginal right protected by s. 35(1): in order to be an Aboriginal right an activity must be an element of a practice, custom or tradition integral to the distinctive culture of the Aboriginal group claiming the right.

47.   I would note that this test is, in large part, consistent with that adopted by the judges of the British Columbia Court of Appeal. Although the various judges disagreed on such crucial questions as how the right should be framed, the relevant time at which the Aboriginal culture should be examined and the role of European influences in limiting the scope of the right, all of the judges agreed that Aboriginal rights must be identified through the practices, customs and traditions of Aboriginal cultures. Macfarlane J.A. held at para. 20 that Aboriginal rights exist where "the right had been exercised . . . for a sufficient length of time to become *integral to the aboriginal society*" (emphasis added); Wallace J.A. held at para. 78 that Aboriginal rights are those practices "traditional and *integral to the native society*" (emphasis added); Lambert J.A. held at para. 131 that Aboriginal rights are those "custom[s], tradition[s], or practice[s] . . . which formed *an integral part of the distinctive culture of the aboriginal people in question*" (emphasis added). While, as will become apparent, I do not adopt entirely the position of any of the judges at the Court of Appeal, their shared position that Aboriginal rights lie in those prac-

tices, customs and traditions that are integral is consistent with the test I have articulated here.

Factors to be Considered in Application of the Integral to a Distinctive Culture Test
48.   The test just laid out—that Aboriginal rights lie in the practices, customs and traditions integral to the distinctive cultures of Aboriginal peoples—requires further elaboration with regards to the nature of the inquiry a court faced with an Aboriginal rights claim must undertake. I will now undertake such an elaboration, concentrating on such questions as the time period relevant to the court's inquiry, the correct approach to the evidence presented, the specificity necessary to the court's inquiry, the relationship between Aboriginal rights and the rights of Aboriginal people as Canadian citizens, and the standard that must be met in order for a practice, custom or tradition to be said to be "integral".

Courts must take into account the perspective of Aboriginal peoples themselves
49.   In assessing a claim for the existence of an Aboriginal right, a court must take into account the perspective of the Aboriginal people claiming the right. In *Sparrow, supra,* Dickson C.J. and La Forest J. held, at p. 1112, that it is "crucial to be sensitive to the Aboriginal perspective itself on the meaning of the rights at stake". It must also be recognized, however, that that perspective must be framed in terms cognizable to the Canadian legal and constitutional structure. As has already been noted, one of the fundamental purposes of s. 35(1) is the reconciliation of the pre-existence of distinctive Aboriginal societies with the assertion of Crown sovereignty. Courts adjudicating Aboriginal rights claims must, therefore, be sensitive to the Aboriginal perspective, but they must also be aware that Aboriginal rights exist within the general legal system of Canada. To quote again Walters, at p. 413: "a morally and politically defensible conception of Aboriginal rights will incorporate both [Aboriginal and non-Aboriginal] legal perspectives". The definition of an Aboriginal right must, if it is truly to reconcile the prior occupation of Canadian territory by Aboriginal peoples with the assertion of Crown sovereignty over that territory, take into account the Aboriginal perspective, yet do so in terms which are cognizable to the non-Aboriginal legal system.

50. It is possible, of course, that the Court could be said to be "reconciling" the prior occupation of Canada by Aboriginal peoples with Crown sovereignty through either a narrow or broad conception of Aboriginal rights; the notion of "reconciliation" does not, in the abstract, mandate a particular content for Aboriginal rights. However, the only fair and just reconciliation is, as Walters suggests, one which takes into account the Aboriginal perspective while at the same time taking into account the perspective of the common law. True reconciliation will, equally, place weight on each.

Courts must identify precisely the nature of the claim being made in determining whether an Aboriginal claimant has demonstrated the existence of an Aboriginal right

51.   Related to this is the fact that in assessing a claim to an Aboriginal right a court must first identify the nature of the right being claimed; in order to determine whether a claim meets the test of being integral to the distinctive culture of the Aboriginal group claiming the right, the court must first correctly determine what it is that is being claimed. The correct characterization of the appellant's claim is of importance because whether or not the evidence supports the appellant's claim will depend, in significant part, on what, exactly, that evidence is being called to support.

52.   I would note here by way of illustration that, in my view, both the majority and the dissenting judges in the Court of Appeal erred with respect to this aspect of the inquiry. The majority held that the appellant's claim was that the practice of selling fish "on a commercial basis" constituted an Aboriginal right and, in part, rejected her claim on the basis that the evidence did not support the existence of such a right. With respect, this characterization of the appellant's claim is in error; the appellant's claim was that the practice of selling fish was an Aboriginal right, not that selling fish "on a commercial basis" was. It was, however, equally incorrect to adopt, as Lambert J.A. did, a "social" test for the identification of the practice, tradition or custom constituting the Aboriginal right. The social test casts the Aboriginal right in terms that are too broad and in a manner which distracts the court from what should be its main focus—the nature of the Aboriginal community's practices, customs or traditions themselves. The nature of an applicant's claim must be delineated in terms of the particular practice, custom or tradition under which it is claimed; the significance of the practice, custom or tradition to the Aboriginal community is a factor to be considered in determining whether the practice, custom or tradition is integral to the distinctive culture, but the significance of a practice, custom or tradition cannot, itself, constitute an Aboriginal right.

53.   To characterize an applicant's claim correctly, a court should consider such factors as the nature of the action which the applicant is claiming was done pursuant to an Aboriginal right, the nature of the governmental regulation, statute or action being impugned, and the practice, custom or tradition being relied upon to establish the right. In this case, therefore, the Court will consider the actions which led to the appellant's being charged, the fishery regulation under which she was charged and the practices, customs and traditions she invokes in support of her claim.

54.   It should be acknowledged that a characterization of the nature of the appellant's claim from the actions which led to her being charged must be undertaken with some caution. In order to inform the court's analysis the activities must be considered at a general rather than at a specific level. Moreover, the court must bear in mind that the activities may be the exercise in a modern form of a practice, custom or tradition that existed prior to contact, and should vary its characterization of the claim accordingly.

In order to be integral a practice, custom or tradition must be of central significance to the Aboriginal society in question

55.   To satisfy the integral to a distinctive culture test the Aboriginal claimant must do more than demonstrate that a practice, custom or tradition was an aspect of, or took place in, the Aboriginal society of which he or she is a part. The claimant must demonstrate that the practice, custom or tradition was a central and significant part of the society's distinctive culture. He or she must demonstrate, in other words, that the practice, custom or tradition was one of the things which made the culture of the society distinctive—that it was one of the things that truly *made the society what it was.*

56.   This aspect of the integral to a distinctive culture test arises from fact that Aboriginal rights have their basis in the prior occupation of Canada by distinctive Aboriginal societies. To recognize and affirm the prior occupation of Canada by distinctive Aboriginal societies it is *to what makes those societies distinctive* that the court must look in identifying Aboriginal rights. The court cannot look at those aspects of the Aboriginal society that are true of every human society (e.g., eating to survive), nor can it look at those aspects of the Aboriginal society that are only incidental or occasional to that society; the court must look instead to the defining and central attributes of the Aboriginal society in question. It is only by focusing on the aspects of the Aboriginal society that make that society distinctive that the definition of Aboriginal rights will accomplish the purpose underlying s. 35(1).

57.   Moreover, the Aboriginal rights protected by s. 35(1) have been said to have the purpose of reconciling pre-existing Aboriginal societies with the assertion of Crown sovereignty over Canada. To reconcile Aboriginal societies with Crown sovereignty it is necessary to identify the distinctive features of those societies; it is precisely those distinctive features which need to be acknowledged and reconciled with the sovereignty of the Crown.

58.   As was noted earlier, Lambert J.A. erred when he used the significance of a practice, custom or tradition as a means of identifying what the practice, custom or tradition is; however, he was correct to recognize that the significance of the practice, custom or tradition is important. The significance of the practice, custom or tradition does not serve to identify the nature of a claim of acting pursuant to an Aboriginal right; however, it is a key aspect of the court's inquiry into whether a practice, custom or tradition has been shown to be an integral part of the distinctive culture of an Aboriginal community. The significance of the practice, custom or tradition will inform a court as to whether or not that practice, custom or tradition can be said to be truly integral to the distinctive culture in question.

59.   A practical way of thinking about this problem is to ask whether, without this practice, custom or tradition, the culture in question would be fundamentally altered or other than what it is. One must ask, to put the question affirmatively, whether or not a practice, custom or tradition is a defining feature of the culture in question.

The practices, customs and traditions which constitute Aboriginal rights are those which have continuity with the practices, customs and traditions that existed prior to contact

60.   The time period that a court should consider in identifying whether the right claimed meets the standard of being integral to the Aboriginal community claiming the right is the period prior to contact between Aboriginal and European societies. Because it is the fact that distinctive Aboriginal societies lived on the land prior to the arrival of Europeans that underlies the Aboriginal rights protected by s. 35(1), it is to that pre-contact period that the courts must look in identifying Aboriginal rights.

61.   The fact that the doctrine of Aboriginal rights functions to reconcile the existence of pre-existing Aboriginal societies with the sovereignty of the Crown does not alter this position. Although it is the sovereignty of the Crown that the pre-existing Aboriginal societies are being reconciled with, it is to those pre-existing societies that the court must look in defining Aboriginal rights. It is not the fact that Aboriginal societies existed prior to Crown sovereignty that is relevant; it is the fact that they existed *prior to the arrival of Europeans in North America.* As such, the relevant time period is the period prior to the arrival of Europeans, not the period prior to the assertion of sovereignty by the Crown.

62.   That this is the relevant time should not suggest, however, that the Aboriginal group claiming the right must accomplish the next to impossible task of producing conclusive evidence from pre-contact times about the practices, customs and traditions of their community. It would be entirely contrary to the spirit and intent of s. 35(1) to define Aboriginal rights in such a fashion so as to preclude in practice any successful claim for the existence of such a right. The evidence relied upon by the applicant and the courts may relate to Aboriginal practices, customs and traditions post-contact; it simply needs to be directed at demonstrating which aspects of the Aboriginal community and society have their origins pre-contact. It is those practices, customs and traditions that can be rooted in the pre-contact societies of the Aboriginal community in question that will constitute Aboriginal rights.

63.   I would note in relation to this point the position adopted by Brennan J. in *Mabo, supra,* where he holds, at p. 60, that in order for an Aboriginal group to succeed in its claim for Aboriginal title it must demonstrate that the connection with the land in its customs and laws has continued to the present day:

> . . . when the tide of history has washed away any real acknowledgment of traditional law and any real observance of traditional customs, the foundation of native title has disappeared. A native title which has ceased with the abandoning of laws and customs based on tradition cannot be revived for contemporary recognition.

The relevance of this observation for identifying the rights in s. 35(1) lies not in its assertion of the effect of the disappearance of a practice, custom or tradition on an Aboriginal claim (I take no position on that matter), but rather in its suggestion of the importance of considering the continuity in the practices, customs and traditions of Aboriginal communities in assessing claims to Aboriginal rights. It is precisely those present practices, customs and traditions which can be identified as having continuity with the practices, customs and traditions that existed prior to contact that will be the basis for the identification and definition of Aboriginal rights under s. 35(1). Where an Aboriginal community can demonstrate that a particular practice, custom or tradition is integral to its distinctive culture today, and that this practice, custom or tradition has continuity with the practices, customs and traditions of pre-contact times, that community will have demonstrated that the practice, custom or tradition is an Aboriginal right for the purposes of s. 35(1).

64.   The concept of continuity is also the primary means through which the definition and identification of Aboriginal rights will be consistent with the admonition in *Sparrow, supra,* at p. 1093, that the phrase "existing Aboriginal rights" must be interpreted flexibly so as to permit their evolution over time". The concept of continuity is, in other words, the means by which a "frozen rights" approach to s. 35(1) will be avoided. Because the practices, customs and traditions protected by s. 35(1) are ones that exist today, subject only to the requirement that they be demonstrated to have continuity with the practices, customs and traditions which existed pre-contact, the definition of Aboriginal rights will be one that, on its own terms, prevents those rights from being frozen in pre-contact times. The evolution of practices, customs and traditions into modern forms will not, provided that continuity with pre-contact practices, customs and traditions is demonstrated, prevent their protection as Aboriginal rights.

65.   I would note that the concept of continuity does not require Aboriginal groups to provide evidence of an unbroken chain of continuity between their current practices, customs and traditions, and those which existed prior to contact. It may be that for a period of time an Aboriginal group, for some reason, ceased to engage in a practice, custom or tradition which existed prior to contact, but then resumed the practice, custom or tradition at a later date. Such an interruption will not preclude the establishment of an Aboriginal right. Trial judges should adopt the same flexibility regarding the establishment of continuity that, as is discussed, *infra,* they are to adopt with regards to the evidence presented to establish the prior-to-contact practices, customs and traditions of the Aboriginal group making the claim to an Aboriginal right.

66.   Further, I would note that basing the identification of Aboriginal rights in the period prior to contact is not inconsistent with the fact that s. 35(2) of the *Constitution Act, 1982* includes within the definition of "aboriginal peoples of Canada" the Métis people of Canada.

67.   Although s. 35 includes the Métis within its definition of Aboriginal peoples of Canada, and thus seems to link their claims to those of other Aboriginal peoples under the general heading of Aboriginal rights, the history of the Métis, and the reasons underlying their inclusion in the protection given by s. 35, are quite distinct from those of other Aboriginal peoples in Canada. As such, the manner in

which the Aboriginal rights of other Aboriginal peoples are defined is not necessarily determinative of the manner in which the Aboriginal rights of the Métis are
defined. At the time when this Court is presented with a Métis claim under s. 35 it
will then, with the benefit of the arguments of counsel, a factual context and a
specific Métis claim, be able to explore the question of the purposes underlying s. 35's protection of the Aboriginal rights of Métis people, and answer the
question of the kinds of claims which fall within s. 35(1)'s scope when the claimants are Métis. The fact that, for other Aboriginal peoples, the protection granted
by s. 35 goes to the practices, customs and traditions of Aboriginal peoples prior to
contact, is not necessarily relevant to the answer which will be given to that question. It may, or it may not, be the case that the claims of the Métis are determined
on the basis of the pre-contact practices, customs and traditions of their Aboriginal
ancestors; whether that is so must await determination in a case in which the issue
arises.

*Courts must approach the rules of evidence in light of the evidentiary difficulties
inherent in adjudicating Aboriginal claims*
68.   In determining whether an Aboriginal claimant has produced evidence sufficient to demonstrate that her activity is an aspect of a practice, custom or tradition
integral to a distinctive Aboriginal culture, a court should approach the rules of
evidence, and interpret the evidence that exists, with a consciousness of the special
nature of Aboriginal claims, and of the evidentiary difficulties in proving a right
which originates in times where there were no written records of the practices,
customs and traditions engaged in. The courts must not undervalue the evidence
presented by Aboriginal claimants simply because that evidence does not conform
precisely with the evidentiary standards that would be applied in, for example, a
private law torts case.

*Claims to Aboriginal rights must be adjudicated on a specific rather than
general basis*
69.   Courts considering a claim to the existence of an Aboriginal right must focus
specifically on the practices, customs and traditions of the particular Aboriginal
group claiming the right. In the case of *Kruger, supra,* this Court rejected the notion that claims to Aboriginal rights could be determined on a general basis. This
position is correct; the existence of an Aboriginal right will depend entirely on the
practices, customs and traditions of the *particular Aboriginal community claiming
the right.* As has already been suggested, Aboriginal rights are constitutional rights,
but that does not negate the central fact that the interests Aboriginal rights are
intended to protect relate to the specific history of the group claiming the right.
Aboriginal rights are not general and universal; their scope and content must be
determined on a case-by-case basis. The fact that one group of Aboriginal people
has an Aboriginal right to do a particular thing will not be, without something
more, sufficient to demonstrate that another Aboriginal community has the same
Aboriginal right. The existence of the right will be specific to each Aboriginal
community.

For a practice, custom or tradition to constitute an Aboriginal right it must be of independent significance to the Aboriginal culture in which it exists

70.   In identifying those practices, customs and traditions that constitute the Aboriginal rights recognized and affirmed by s. 35(1), a court must ensure that the practice, custom or tradition relied upon in a particular case is independently significant to the Aboriginal community claiming the right. The practice, custom or tradition cannot exist simply as an incident to another practice, custom or tradition but must rather be itself of integral significance to the Aboriginal society. Where two customs exist, but one is merely incidental to the other, the custom which is integral to the Aboriginal community in question will qualify as an Aboriginal right, but the custom that is merely incidental will not. Incidental practices, customs and traditions cannot qualify as Aboriginal rights through a process of piggybacking on integral practices, customs and traditions.

The integral to a distinctive culture test requires that a practice, custom or tradition be distinctive; it does not require that that practice, custom or tradition be distinct

71.   The standard which a practice, custom or tradition must meet in order to be recognized as an Aboriginal right is not that it be distinct to the Aboriginal culture in question; the Aboriginal claimants must simply demonstrate that the practice, custom or tradition is *distinctive*. A tradition or custom that is *distinct* is one that is unique—different in kind or quality; unlike" (*Concise Oxford Dictionary, supra*). A culture with a distinct tradition must claim that in having such a tradition it is different from other cultures; a claim of distinctness is, by its very nature, a claim relative to other cultures or traditions. By contrast, a culture that claims that a practice, custom or tradition is *distinctive*—"distinguishing, characteristic"—makes a claim that is not relative; the claim is rather one about the culture's own practices, customs or traditions considered apart from the practices, customs or traditions of any other culture. It is a claim that this tradition or custom makes the culture *what it is,* not that the practice, custom or tradition is different from the practices, customs or traditions of another culture. The person or community claiming the existence of an Aboriginal right protected by s. 35(1) need only show that the particular practice, custom or tradition which it is claiming to be an Aboriginal right is distinctive, not that it is distinct.

72.   That the standard an Aboriginal community must meet is distinctiveness, not distinctness, arises from the recognition in *Sparrow, supra,* of an Aboriginal right to fish for food. Certainly no Aboriginal group in Canada could claim that its culture is "distinct" or unique in fishing for food; fishing for food is something done by many different cultures and societies around the world. What the Musqueam claimed in *Sparrow, supra,* was rather that it was fishing for food which, in part, made Musqueam culture what it is; fishing for food was characteristic of Musqueam culture and, therefore, a distinctive part of that culture. Since it was so it constituted an Aboriginal right under s. 35(1).

The influence of European culture will only be relevant to the inquiry if it is demonstrated that the practice, custom or tradition is only integral because of that influence

73.   The fact that Europeans in North America engaged in the same practices, customs or traditions as those under which an Aboriginal right is claimed will only be relevant to the Aboriginal claim if the practice, custom or tradition in question can only be said to exist because of the influence of European culture. If the practice, custom or tradition was an integral part of the Aboriginal community's culture prior to contact with Europeans, the fact that that practice, custom or tradition continued after the arrival of Europeans, and adapted in response to their arrival, is not relevant to determination of the claim; European arrival and influence cannot be used to deprive an Aboriginal group of an otherwise valid claim to an Aboriginal right. On the other hand, where the practice, custom or tradition arose solely as a response to European influences then that practice, custom or tradition will not meet the standard for recognition of an Aboriginal right.

Courts must take into account both the relationship of Aboriginal peoples to the land and the distinctive societies and cultures of Aboriginal peoples

74.   As was noted in the discussion of the purposes of s. 35(1), Aboriginal rights and Aboriginal title are related concepts; Aboriginal title is a sub-category of Aboriginal rights which deals solely with claims of rights to land. The relationship between Aboriginal title and Aboriginal rights must not, however, confuse the analysis of what constitutes an Aboriginal right. Aboriginal rights arise from the prior occupation of land, but they also arise from the prior social organization and distinctive cultures of Aboriginal peoples on that land. In considering whether a claim to an Aboriginal right has been made out, courts must look at both the relationship of an Aboriginal claimant to the land *and* at the practices, customs and traditions arising from the claimant's distinctive culture and society. Courts must not focus so entirely on the relationship of Aboriginal peoples with the land that they lose sight of the other factors relevant to the identification and definition of Aboriginal rights.

75.   With these factors in mind I will now turn to the particular claim made by the appellant in this case to have been acting pursuant to an Aboriginal right.

Application of the Integral to a Distinctive Culture Test to the Appellant's Claim

76. The first step in the application of the integral to a distinctive culture test requires the court to identify the precise nature of the appellant's claim to have been exercising an Aboriginal right. In this case the most accurate characterization of the appellant's position is that she is claiming *an Aboriginal right to exchange fish for money or for other goods.* She is claiming, in other words, that the practices, customs and traditions of the Sto:lo include as an integral part the exchange of fish for money or other goods.

77.   That this is the nature of the appellant's claim can be seen through both the specific acts which led to her being charged and through the regulation under which

she was charged. Mrs. Van der Peet sold 10 salmon for $50. Such a sale, especially given the absence of evidence that the appellant had sold salmon on other occasions or on a regular basis, cannot be said to constitute a sale on a "commercial" or market basis. These actions are instead best characterized in the simple terms of an exchange of fish for money. It follows from this that the Aboriginal right pursuant to which the appellant is arguing that her actions were taken is, like the actions themselves, best characterized as an Aboriginal right to exchange fish for money or other goods.

78.   Moreover, the regulations under which the appellant was charged prohibit *all* sale or trade of fish caught pursuant to an Indian food fish licence. As such, to argue that those regulations implicate the appellant's Aboriginal right requires no more of her than that she demonstrate an Aboriginal right to the exchange of fish for money (sale) or other goods (trade). She does not need to demonstrate an Aboriginal right to sell fish commercially.

79.   The appellant herself characterizes her claim as based on a right "to sufficient fish to provide for a moderate livelihood". In so doing the appellant relies on the "social" test adopted by Lambert J.A. at the British Columbia Court of Appeal. As has already been noted, however, a claim to an Aboriginal right cannot be based on the significance of an Aboriginal practice, custom or tradition to the Aboriginal community in question. The definition of Aboriginal rights is determined through the process of determining whether a particular practice, custom or tradition is integral to the distinctive culture of the Aboriginal group. The *significance* of the practice, custom or tradition is relevant to the determination of whether that practice, custom or tradition is integral, but cannot itself constitute the claim to an Aboriginal right. As such, the appellant's claim cannot be characterized as based on an assertion that the Sto:lo's use of the fishery, and the practices, customs and traditions surrounding that use, had the significance of providing the Sto:lo with a moderate livelihood. It must instead be based on the actual practices, customs and traditions related to the fishery, here the custom of exchanging fish for money or other goods.

80.   Having thus identified the nature of the appellant's claim, I turn to the fundamental question of the integral to a distinctive culture test: Was the practice of exchanging fish for money or other goods an integral part of the specific distinctive culture of the Sto:lo prior to contact with Europeans? In answering this question it is necessary to consider the evidence presented at trial, and the findings of fact made by the trial judge, to determine whether the evidence and findings support the appellant's claim that the sale or trade of fish is an integral part of the distinctive culture of the Sto:lo.

81.   It is a well-settled principle of law that when an appellate court reviews the decision of a trial judge that court must give considerable deference to the trial judge's findings of fact, particularly where those findings of fact are based on the trial judge's assessment of the testimony and credibility of witnesses. In *Stein* v.

The Ship "Kathy K", [1976] 2 S.C.R. 802, Ritchie J., speaking for the Court, held at p. 808 that absent a "palpable and overriding error" affecting the trial judge's assessment of the facts, an appellate court should not substitute its own findings of fact for those of the trial judge:

> These authorities are not to be taken as meaning that the findings of fact made at trial are immutable, but rather that they are not to be reversed unless it can be established that the learned trial judge made some palpable and overriding error which affected his assessment of the facts. While the Court of Appeal is seized with the duty of re-examining the evidence in order to be satisfied that no such error occurred, it is not, in my view, a part of its function to substitute its assessment of the balance of probability for the findings of the judge who presided at the trial.

This principle has also been followed in more recent decisions of this Court: *Beaudoin-Daigneault* v. *Richard,* [1984] 1 S.C.R. 2, at pp. 8–9; *Laurentide Motels Ltd.* v. *Beauport (City),* [1989] 1 S.C.R. 705, at p. 794; *Hodgkinson* v. *Simms,* [1994] 3 S.C.R. 377, at p. 426. In the recently released decision of *Schwartz* v. *Canada,* [1996] 1 S.C.R. 254, La Forest J. made the following observation at para. 32, with which I agree, regarding appellate court deference to findings of fact:

> Unlimited intervention by appellate courts would greatly increase the number and the length of appeals generally. Substantial resources are allocated to trial courts to go through the process of assessing facts. The autonomy and integrity of the trial process must be preserved by exercising deference towards the trial courts' findings of fact . . . This explains why the rule applies not only when the credibility of witnesses is at issue, although in such a case it may be more strictly applied, but also to all conclusions of fact made by the trial judge. . . .

I would also note that the principle of appellate court deference has been held to apply equally to findings of fact made on the basis of the trial judge's assessment of the credibility of the testimony of expert witnesses, *N.V. Bocimar S.A.* v. *Century Insurance Co. of Canada,* [1987] 1 S.C.R. 1247, at pp. 1249-50.

82.   In the case at bar, Scarlett Prov. Ct. J., the trial judge, made findings of fact based on the testimony and evidence before him, and then proceeded to make a determination as to whether those findings of fact supported the appellant's claim to the existence of an Aboriginal right. The second stage of Scarlett Prov. Ct. J.'s analysis—his determination of the scope of the appellant's Aboriginal rights on the basis of the facts as he found them—is a determination of a question of law which, as such, mandates no deference from this Court. The first stage of Scarlett Prov. Ct. J.'s analysis, however—the findings of fact from which that legal inference was drawn—do mandate such deference and should not be overturned unless made on the basis of a "palpable and overriding error". This is particularly the case given that those findings of fact were made on the basis of Scarlett Prov. Ct. J.'s assessment of the credibility and testimony of the various witnesses appearing before him.

83.   In adjudicating this case Scarlett Prov. Ct. J. obviously did not have the ben-

efit of direction from this Court as to how the rights recognized and affirmed by s. 35(1) are to be defined, with the result that his legal analysis of the evidence was not entirely correct; however, that Scarlett Prov. Ct. J. was not entirely correct in his legal analysis of the facts as he found them *does not mean that he made a clear and palpable error in reviewing the evidence and making those findings of fact.* Indeed, a review of the transcript and exhibits submitted to this Court demonstrate that Scarlett Prov. Ct. J. conducted a thorough and compelling review of the evidence before him and committed no clear and palpable error which would justify this Court, or any other appellate court, in substituting its findings of fact for his. Moreover, I would note that the appellant, while disagreeing with Scarlett Prov. Ct. J.'s legal analysis of the facts, made no arguments suggesting that in making findings of fact from the evidence before him Scarlett Prov. Ct. J. committed a palpable and overriding error.

84.   Scarlett Prov. Ct. J. carefully considered all of the testimony presented by the various witnesses with regards to the nature of Sto:lo society and came to the following conclusions at p. 160:

> Clearly, the Sto:lo fish for food and ceremonial purposes. Evidence presented did not establish a regularized market system in the exchange of fish. Such fish as were exchanged through individual trade, gift, or barter were fish surplus from time to time. Natives did not fish to supply a market, there being no regularized trading system, nor were they able to preserve and store fish for extended periods of time. A market as such for salmon was not present but created by European traders, primarily the Hudson's Bay Company. At Fort Langley the Sto:lo were able to catch and deliver fresh salmon to the traders where it was salted and exported. This use was clearly different in nature and quantity from Aboriginal activity. Trade in dried salmon with the fort was clearly dependent upon Sto:lo first satisfying their own requirements for food and ceremony.
>
> This court was not satisfied upon the evidence that Aboriginal trade in salmon took place in any regularized or market sense. Oral evidence demonstrated that trade was incidental to fishing for food purposes. Anthropological and archaeological evidence was in conflict. This Court accepts the evidence of Dr. Stryd and John Dewhurst [sic] in preference to Dr. Daly and therefore, accepts that the Sto:lo were a band culture as opposed to tribal. While bands were guided by siem or prominent families, no regularized trade in salmon existed in Aboriginal times. Such trade as took place was either for ceremonial purposes or opportunistic exchanges taking place on a casual basis. Such trade as did take place was incidental only. Evidence led by the Crown that the Sto:lo had no access to salt for food preservation is accepted.
>
> Exchange of fish was subject to local conditions of availability, transportation and preservation. It was the establishment by the Hudson's Bay Company at the fort at Langley that created the market and trade in fresh salmon. Trade in dried salmon in Aboriginal times was, as stated, minimal and opportunistic.

I would add to Scarlett Prov. Ct. J.'s summation of his findings only the observation, which does not contradict any of his specific findings, that the testimony of the experts appearing before him indicated that such limited exchanges of salmon as took place in Sto:lo society were primarily linked to the kinship and family relationships on which Sto:lo society was based. For example, under cross-examination Dr. Daly described trade as occurring through the "idiom" of maintaining family relationships:

> The medium or the idiom of much trade was the idiom of kinship, of providing hospitality, giving gifts, reciprocating in gifts. . . .

Similarly, Mr. Dewhirst testified that the exchange of goods was related to the maintenance of family and kinship relations.

85.   The facts as found by Scarlett Prov. Ct. J. do not support the appellant's claim that the exchange of salmon for money or other goods was an integral part of the distinctive culture of the Sto:lo. As has already been noted, in order to be recognized as an Aboriginal right, an activity must be of central significance to the culture in question—it must be something which makes that culture what it is. The findings of fact made by Scarlett Prov. Ct. J. suggest that the exchange of salmon for money or other goods, while certainly taking place in Sto:lo society prior to contact, was not a significant, integral or defining feature of that society.

86.   First, Scarlett Prov. Ct. J. found that, prior to contact, exchanges of fish were only "incidental" to fishing for food purposes. As was noted above, to constitute an Aboriginal right, a custom must itself be integral to the distinctive culture of the Aboriginal community in question; it cannot be simply incidental to an integral custom. Thus, while the evidence clearly demonstrated that fishing for food and ceremonial purposes was a significant and defining feature of the Sto:lo culture, this is not sufficient, absent a demonstration that the exchange of salmon was itself a significant and defining feature of Sto:lo society, to demonstrate that the exchange of salmon is an integral part of Sto:lo culture.

87.   For similar reasons, the evidence linking the exchange of salmon to the maintenance of kinship and family relations does not support the appellant's claim to the existence of an Aboriginal right. Exchange of salmon as part of the interaction of kin and family is not of an independent significance sufficient to ground a claim for an Aboriginal right to the exchange of fish for money or other goods.

88.   Second, Scarlett Prov. Ct. J. found that there was no "regularized trading system" amongst the Sto:lo prior to contact. The inference drawn from this fact by Scarlett Prov. Ct. J., and by Macfarlane J.A. at the British Columbia Court of Appeal, was that the absence of a market means that the appellant could not be said to have been acting pursuant to an Aboriginal right because it suggests that there is no Aboriginal right to fish commercially. This inference is incorrect because, as has already been suggested, the appellant in this case has only claimed a right to exchange fish for money or other goods, not a right to sell fish in the commercial marketplace; the significance of the absence of regularized trading systems amongst the Sto:lo arises instead from the fact that it indicates that the exchange of salmon was not widespread in Sto:lo society. Given that the exchange of salmon was not

widespread it cannot be said that, prior to contact, Sto:lo culture was defined by trade in salmon; trade or exchange of salmon took place, but the absence of a market demonstrates that this exchange did not take place on a basis widespread enough to suggest that the exchange was a defining feature of Sto:lo society.

89.   Third, the trade engaged in between the Sto:lo and the Hudson's Bay Company, while certainly of significance to the Sto:lo society of the time, was found by the trial judge to be qualitatively different from that which was typical of the Sto:lo culture prior to contact. As such, it does not provide an evidentiary basis for holding that the exchange of salmon was an integral part of Sto:lo culture. As was emphasized in listing the criteria to be considered in applying the "integral to" test, the time relevant for the identification of Aboriginal rights is prior to contact with European societies. Unless a post-contact practice, custom or tradition can be shown to have continuity with pre-contact practices, customs or traditions, it will not be held to be an Aboriginal right. The trade of salmon between the Sto:lo and the Hudson's Bay Company does not have the necessary continuity with Sto:lo culture pre-contact to support a claim to an Aboriginal right to trade salmon. Further, the exchange of salmon between the Sto:lo and the Hudson's Bay Company can be seen as central or significant to the Sto:lo primarily as a result of European influences; activities which become central or significant because of the influence of European culture cannot be said to be Aboriginal rights.

90.   Finally, Scarlett Prov. Ct. J. found that the Sto:lo were at a band level of social organization rather than at a tribal level. As noted by the various experts, one of the central distinctions between a band society and a tribal society relates to specialization and division of labour. In a tribal society there tends to be specialization of labour—for example, specialization in the gathering and trade of fish—whereas in a band society division of labour tends to occur only on the basis of gender or age. The absence of specialization in the exploitation of the fishery is suggestive, in the same way that the absence of regularized trade or a market is suggestive, that the exchange of fish was not a central part of Sto:lo culture. I would note here as well Scarlett Prov. Ct. J.'s finding that the Sto:lo did not have the means for preserving fish for extended periods of time, something which is also suggestive that the exchange or trade of fish was not central to the Sto:lo way of life.

91.   For these reasons, then, I would conclude that the appellant has failed to demonstrate that the exchange of fish for money or other goods was an integral part of the distinctive Sto:lo society which existed prior to contact. The exchange of fish took place, but was not a central, significant or defining feature of Sto:lo society. The appellant has thus failed to demonstrate that the exchange of salmon for money or other goods by the Sto:lo is an Aboriginal right recognized and affirmed under s. 35(1) of the *Constitution Act, 1982.*

The Sparrow Test
92.   Since the appellant has failed to demonstrate that the exchange of fish was an

Aboriginal right of the Sto:lo, it is unnecessary to consider the tests for extinguishment, infringement and justification laid out by this Court in *Sparrow, supra.*

VI. DISPOSITION

93.　Having concluded that the Aboriginal rights of the Sto:lo do not include the right to exchange fish for money or other goods, I would dismiss the appeal and affirm the decision of the Court of Appeal restoring the trial judge's conviction of the appellant for violating s. 61(1) of the *Fisheries Act.* There will be no order as to costs.

94.　For the reasons given above, the constitutional question must be answered as follows:

Question
Is s. 27(5) of the *British Columbia Fishery (General) Regulations,* SOR/84-248, as it read on September 11, 1987, of no force or effect with respect to the appellant in the circumstances of these proceedings, in virtue of s. 52 of the *Constitution Act, 1982,* by reason of the Aboriginal rights within the meaning of s. 35 of the *Constitution Act, 1982,* invoked by the appellant?

Answer
No.
L'HEUREUX-DUBÉ J. (dissenting) . . .
MCLACHLIN J. (dissenting) . . .

6.　***R. v. Gladstone*, [1996] 4 C.N.L.R. 65 (S.C.C.). Lamer C.J., La Forest, L'Heureux-Dubé, Sopinka, Gonthier, Cory, McLachlin, Iacobucci, and Major JJ., August 21, 1996**

> In *R. v. Gladstone* the Supreme Court reexamined the issue of justifying infringements on Aboriginal rights and the justification test as set out in *Sparrow*. In *Gladstone* the Supreme Court again dealt with an infringement of fishing regulations and the selling of fish. Members of the Heiltsuk Band argued that they possessed an Aboriginal right to sell the fish they caught. The court held that the Heiltsuk possess an Aboriginal right to exchange and trade commercially in herring spawn on kelp because such trade is integral to their community and is based in their pre-European contact customs, traditions, and practices. This right was not extinguished by British Columbia because it failed to demonstrate a clear and plain intention to do so. Aboriginal rights are not absolute but rather may be limited based on the doctrine of priority, which gives priority to the need for conservation and Aboriginal rights over the rights of other users. In order to demonstrate the priority of conservation, the government must demonstrate that in distributing the resource, it has done so in a manner that considers, and is respectful of, the Aboriginal rights affected. Priority is a matter that must be dealt with on a case-by-case basis. After conservation goals are met, regional economic equity and the historical significance of non-Aboriginal participation in the fishery are examples of the type of objectives that can satisfy the *Sparrow* justification requirement.

LAMER C.J. (SOPINKA, GONTHIER, CORY, IACOBUCCI and MAJOR JJ. concurring):
— . . .

1.   Donald and William Gladstone, the appellants, are members of the Heiltsuk Band. The appellants were charged under s. 61(1) of the *Fisheries Act,* R.S.C. 1970, c. F–14, with the offences of offering to sell herring spawn on kelp caught under the authority of an Indian food fish licence, contrary to s. 27(5) of the *British Columbia Fishery (General) Regulations,* SOR/84-248 and of attempting to sell herring spawn on kelp not caught under the authority of a Category J herring spawn on kelp licence, contrary to s. 20(3) of the *Pacific Herring Fishery Regulations,* SOR/84-324. Only the charges arising under s. 20(3) of the *Pacific Herring Fishery Regulations* are still at issue in this appeal. . . .

17.   . . . . The appellants appealed on the basis that the courts below were in error in holding that the actions of the appellants were sufficient to constitute an attempt to sell in law. The appellants also appealed on the basis that, given that the evidence presented at trial demonstrated the extent and significance of Heiltsuk trading activities, the Court of Appeal erred in holding that the appellants do not have an Aboriginal right to trade and sell herring spawn on kelp. The appellants argued further that because the regulations constituted a total ban on the sale of any herring spawn on kelp, the Court of Appeal erred in not finding a *prima facie* infringement of the appellants' Aboriginal rights. Finally, the appellants argued that the Crown did not adduce sufficient evidence to support its assertion that the regulations fulfilled a conservation objectiveand that the Crown had failed to fulfil its fiduciary obligation to the Heiltsuk Band, with the result that the Court of Appeal erred in finding that any infringement which did exist was justified. . . .

18.   Before turning to the heart of the appellants' case—the argument that their convictions constitute an unjustifiable infringement of the Aboriginal rights recognized and affirmed by s. 35(1)—it is necessary to dispose of their argument that the facts do not demonstrate an "attempt to sell" as required by s. 20(3) of the *Pacific Herring Fishery Regulations.* The basis of the appellants' position is that because the Crown only provided evidence to show that the appellants asked Mr. Hirose if he was "interested" in herring spawn on kelp, without providing any evidence that the appellants had discussed the quantity, quality, price or delivery date of the herring spawn on kelp with Mr. Hirose, the Crown only demonstrated that the appellants had engaged in preparation for an attempt to sell; the Crown did not demonstrate that the appellants had actually attempted to sell herring spawn on kelp to Mr. Hirose.

19.   This argument is without merit. In *R.* v. *Deutsch,* [1986] 2 S.C.R. 2, Le Dain J., writing for a unanimous Court on this issue, discussed the distinction between an attempt and mere preparation at pp. 22–23:

> It has been frequently observed that no satisfactory general criterion has been, or can be, formulated for drawing the line between preparation and attempt, and that the application of this distinction to the facts of a particular case must be left to common sense judgment. . . . Despite academic appeals for greater clarity and certainty in this

area of the law I find myself in essential agreement with this conclusion.

In my opinion the distinction between preparation and attempt is essentially a qualitative one, involving the relationship between the nature and quality of the act in question and the nature of the complete offence, although consideration must necessarily be given, in making that qualitative distinction, to the relative proximity of the act in question to what would have been the completed offence, in terms of time, location and acts under the control of the accused remaining to be accomplished.

In this case the facts as found by the trial judge clearly demonstrate that the appellants attempted to sell herring spawn on kelp to Mr. Hirose. The appellants arranged for the shipment of the herring spawn on kelp to Vancouver, they took a sample of the herring spawn on kelp to Mr. Hirose's store and they specifically asked Mr. Hirose if he was "interested" in herring spawn on kelp. The appellants' actions have sufficient proximity to the acts necessary to complete the offence of selling herring spawn on kelp to move those actions beyond mere preparation to an actual attempt. I would note here that the appellants have not disputed the facts as found by the trial judge and that the courts below were unanimous in finding that the actions of the appellant were sufficient to amount to an attempt to sell.

Section 35(1) of the Constitution Act, 1982
20.   In *Sparrow, supra,* Dickson C.J. and La Forest J., writing for a unanimous court, held that an analysis of a claim under s. 35(1) has four steps: first, the court must determine whether an applicant has demonstrated that he or she was acting pursuant to an Aboriginal right; second, a court must determine whether that right was extinguished prior to the enactment of s. 35(1) of the *Constitution Act, 1982;* third, a court must determine whether that right has been infringed; finally, a court must determine whether that infringement was justified.

21.   This judgment will undertake the analysis required for the four steps of the *Sparrow* framework, taking into account the elaboration of that framework in the cases of *R. v. Van der Peet,* [1996] 2 S.C.R. 507, *R. v. N.T.C. Smokehouse Ltd.,* [1996] 2 S.C.R. 672, and *R. v. Nikal,* [1996] 1 S.C.R. 1013, all of which were heard contemporaneously with this appeal. I will also undertake to clarify the *Sparrow* framework as is required in order to apply that framework to the different circumstances of this appeal.

Definition
22.   This appeal, like those heard contemporaneously in *N.T.C. Smokehouse* and *Van der Peet,* requires the Court to consider the scope of the Aboriginal rights recognized and affirmed by s. 35(1) of the *Constitution Act, 1982.* In this case it must be determined whether the appellants Donald and William Gladstone can, on the basis of the test laid out in *Van der Peet,* claim to have been acting pursuant to an Aboriginal right when they attempted to sell herring spawn on kelp to Seaborn Enterprises. In *Van der Peet* the Court held, at para. 46, that to be recognized as an Aboriginal right an activity must be "an element of a practice, custom or tradition integral to the distinctive culture of the Aboriginal group claiming the right". Thus, the appellants in this case must demonstrate that their attempt to sell herring spawn

on kelp was an element of a practice, custom, or tradition integral to the distinctive culture of the Heiltsuk Band.

23. The first step in applying the *Van der Peet* test is the determination of the precise nature of the claim being made, taking into account such factors as the nature of the action said to have been taken pursuant to an Aboriginal right, the government regulation argued to infringe the right, and the practice, custom or tradition relied upon to establish the right. At this stage of the analysis the Court is, in essence, determining what the appellants will have to demonstrate to be an Aboriginal right in order for the activities they were engaged in to be encompassed by s. 35(1). There is no point in the appellants' being shown to have an Aboriginal right unless that Aboriginal right includes the actual activity they were engaged in; this stage of the *Van der Peet* analysis ensures that the Court's inquiry is tailored to the actual activity of the appellants.

24.   This case, like *N.T.C. Smokehouse,* potentially creates problems at the characterization stage. The actions of the appellants, like the actions of the members of the Sheshaht and Opetchesaht bands in *N.T.C. Smokehouse,* appear to be best characterized as the commercial exploitation of herring spawn on kelp. By contrast, the regulations under which the appellants were charged, like the regulations at issue in *N.T.C. Smokehouse,* prohibit all sale or trade in herring spawn on kelp without a Category J licence, appear, therefore, to be best characterized as aimed at the exchange of herring spawn on kelp for money or other goods, regardless of whether the extent or scale of that sale or trade could reasonably be characterized as commercial in nature. The means to resolve this difficulty in characterization, as was the case in *N.T.C. Smokehouse,* is by addressing both possible characterizations of the appellants' claim. This judgment will thus consider first, whether the appellants can demonstrate that the Heiltsuk Band has an Aboriginal right to exchange herring spawn on kelp for money or other goods and will then go on to consider, second, whether the appellants have demonstrated the further Aboriginal right of the Heiltsuk Band to sell herring spawn on kelp to the commercial market.

25.   The second step in the *Van der Peet* test requires the Court to determine whether the practice, custom or tradition claimed to be an Aboriginal right was, prior to contact with Europeans, an integral part of the distinctive Aboriginal society of the particular Aboriginal people in question. The Court must thus, as has just been noted, determine in this case whether the exchange of herring spawn on kelp for money or other goods, and/or the sale or trade of herring spawn on kelp in the commercial marketplace, were, prior to contact, defining features of the distinctive culture of the Heiltsuk.

26.   The facts as found by the trial judge, and the evidence on which he relied, support the appellants' claim that exchange of herring spawn on kelp for money or other goods was a central, significant and defining feature of the culture of the Heiltsuk prior to contact. Moreover, those facts support the appellants' further claim that the exchange of herring spawn on kelp on a scale best characterized as com-

mercial was an integral part of the distinctive culture of the Heiltsuk. In his reasons Lemiski Prov. Ct. J. summarized his findings of fact as follows:

> It cannot be disputed that hundreds of years ago, the Heiltsuk Indians regularly harvested herring spawn on kelp as a food source. The historical/anthropological records readily bear this out.
>
> *I am also satisfied that this Band engaged in inter-tribal trading and barter of herring spawn on kelp.* The exhibited Journal of Alexander McKenzie [sic] dated 1793 refers to this trade and the defence lead [sic] evidence of several other references to such trade.
>
> The Crown conceded that there may have been some incidental local trade but questions its extent and importance. *The very fact that early explorers and visitors to the Bella Bella region noted this trading has to enhance its significance.* All the various descriptions of this trading activity are in accord with common sense expectations. Obviously one would not expect to see balance sheets and statistics in so primitive a time and setting. [Emphasis added.]

27.   There was extensive evidence presented at trial to support Lemiski Prov. Ct. J.'s findings. . . .

28.   In *Van der Peet,* at para. 61, this Court held that a claimant to an Aboriginal right need not provide direct evidence of pre-contact activities to support his or her claim, but need only provide evidence which is "directed at demonstrating which aspects of the Aboriginal community and society have their origins pre-contact. It is those practices, customs and traditions that can be rooted in the pre-contact societies of the Aboriginal community in question that will constitute Aboriginal rights". In *Van der Peet* this was described as the requirement of "continuity"—the requirement that a practice, custom or tradition which is integral to the Aboriginal community now be shown to have continuity with the practices, customs or traditions which existed prior to contact. The evidence presented in this case, accepted by the trial judge and summarized above, is precisely the type of evidence which satisfies this requirement. The appellants have provided clear evidence from which it can be inferred that, prior to contact, Heiltsuk society was, in significant part, based on such trade. The Heiltsuk were, both before and after contact, traders of herring spawn on kelp. Moreover, while to describe this activity as "commercial" prior to contact would be inaccurate given the link between the notion of commerce and the introduction of European culture, the extent and scope of the trading activities of the Heiltsuk support the claim that, for the purposes of s. 35(1) analysis, the Heiltsuk have demonstrated an Aboriginal right to sell herring spawn on kelp to an extent best described as commercial. The evidence of Dr. Lane, and the diary of Dr. Tolmie, point to trade of herring spawn on kelp in "tons". While this evidence relates to trade post-contact, the diary of Alexander Mackenzie provides the link with pre-contact times; in essence, the sum of the evidence supports the claim of the appellants that commercial trade in herring spawn on kelp was an integral part of the distinctive culture of the Heiltsuk prior to contact.

29.   I would note that the significant difference between the situation of the appellants in this case, and the appellants in *Van der Peet* and *N.T.C. Smokehouse,* lies in the fact that for the Heiltsuk Band trading in herring spawn on kelp was not an activity taking place as an incident to the social and ceremonial activities of the community; rather, trading in herring spawn on kelp was, in itself, a central and significant feature of Heiltsuk society. In *Van der Peet* and *N.T.C. Smokehouse* the findings of fact at trial suggested that whatever trade in fish had taken place prior to contact was purely incidental to the social and ceremonial activities of the Aboriginal societies making the claim; here the evidence suggests that trade in herring spawn on kelp was not an incidental activity for the Heiltsuk but was rather a central and defining feature of Heiltsuk society.

Extinguishment, Infringement and Justification
30.   The appellants have demonstrated that they were acting pursuant to an Aboriginal right to trade herring spawn on kelp on a commercial basis. I will therefore turn to the other three stages of the *Sparrow* analysis, that is, to the questions of whether the right under which the appellants were acting has been extinguished, whether that right was infringed by the actions of the government and, finally, whether that infringement was justified.

Extinguishment
31.   The test for determining when an Aboriginal right has been extinguished was laid out by this Court in *Sparrow.* Relying on the judgment of Hall J. in *Calder* v. *Attorney-General of British Columbia,* [1973] S.C.R. 313, the Court in *Sparrow* held at p. 1099 that "[t]he test of extinguishment to be adopted, in our opinion, is that the Sovereign's intention must be clear and plain if it is to extinguish an Aboriginal right". Further, the Court held that the mere fact that a right had, in the past, been regulated by the government, and its exercise subject to various terms and conditions, was not sufficient to extinguish the right. The argument that it did so (*Sparrow,* at p. 1097)

> confuses regulation with extinguishment. That the right is controlled in great detail by the regulations does not mean that the right is thereby extinguished.

The regulations relied on by the Crown in that case were, the Court held at p. 1099 . . . , "simply a manner of controlling the fisheries, not defining underlying rights".

32.   The reasoning used to reject the Crown's argument in *Sparrow* applies equally to the Crown's argument in this case. To understand why this is so it will be necessary to review the legislation relied upon by the Crown in its argument that the Heiltsuk's right to harvest herring spawn on kelp on a commercial basis was extinguished prior to 1982.

33.   There are two types of legislative action relied upon by the Crown: the provisions of the *Fisheries Act* which, prior to 1955, prohibited the destruction of the "fry of food fishes", and the provisions of the fisheries regulations relating directly to the herring spawn fishery. The former are exemplified by s. 39 of the *Fisheries*

Act of 1927 which stated that "The fry of food fishes shall not be at any time destroyed"; identical provisions existed in the 1932 and 1952 *Fisheries Acts.* The latter first appeared in 1955. In 1955 the 1954 *British Columbia Fishery Regulations* were amended by SOR/55-260, s. 3, by the addition of a new s. 21A:

21A. No person shall take or collect by any means herring, eggs from herring spawning areas, and no person shall buy, sell, barter, process or traffic in herring eggs so taken; but an Indian may at any time take or collect herring eggs from spawning areas for use as food by Indians and their families but for no other purpose.

Similar prohibitions on the harvest and sale of herring spawn continued until 1974 (SOR/74-50, s. 9). At that time the section was amended so that the provision read

21A (1) Subject to subsection (2), no person shall, except by written permission of the Regional Director, by any means take or collect herring eggs from herring spawning areas, or buy, sell, barter, process or traffic in herring eggs so taken.

(2) An Indian may at any time take or collect herring eggs from herring spawning areas for use as food for himself and his family (SOR/72-417, s. 7).

This regulatory scheme remained in place until 1980 when the provision (which had been transferred to s. 17 of the *Pacific Herring Fishery Regulations,* C.R.C., c. 825) was amended by SOR/80-876, s. 8 to read

17. No person shall

(a) take or collect herring roe except under authority of a licence issued pursuant to the Pacific Fishery Registration and Licensing Regulations; or

(b) possess herring roe unless it was so taken or collected.

According to the submissions of the Crown, no further modifications to this regulatory scheme took place prior to the enactment of the *Constitution Act, 1982.*

34.   None of these regulations, when viewed individually or as a whole, can be said to express a clear and plain intention to extinguish the Aboriginal rights of the Heiltsuk Band. While to extinguish an Aboriginal right the Crown does not, perhaps, have to use language which refers expressly to its extinguishment of Aboriginal rights, it must demonstrate more than that, in the past, the exercise of an Aboriginal right has been subject to a regulatory scheme. In this instance, the regulations and legislation regulating the herring spawn on kelp fishery prior to 1982 do not demonstrate any consistent intention on the part of the Crown. At various times prior to 1982 Aboriginal peoples have been entirely prohibited from harvesting herring spawn on kelp, allowed to harvest herring spawn on kelp for food only, allowed to harvest herring spawn on kelp for sale with the written permission of the regional director and allowed to take herring roe pursuant to a licence granted under the *Pacific Fishery Registration and Licensing Regulations.* Such a varying regulatory scheme cannot be said to express a clear and plain intention to eliminate the Aboriginal rights of the appellants and of the Heiltsuk Band. As in *Sparrow,* the Crown has only demonstrated that it controlled the fisheries, not that it has acted so as to delineate the extent of Aboriginal rights.

35.   The Crown also argued, however, that even if the regulations do not extinguish the appellants' Aboriginal rights, their rights were extinguished by the enactment of Order in Council, P.C. 2539, of September 11, 1917. Regulation 2539 reads as follows:

> *Whereas it is represented that since time immemorial, it has been the practice of the Indians of British Columbia to catch salmon by means of spears and otherwise after they have reached the upper non-tidal portions of the rivers;*
>
> *And whereas while after commercial fishing began it became eminently desirable that all salmon that succeeded in reaching the upper waters should be allowed to go on to their spawning beds unmolested, in view of the great importance the Indians attached to their practice of catching salmon they have been permitted to do so for their own food purposes only,* and to this end subsection 2 of section 8 of the Special Fishery Regulations for British Columbia provides as follows: —
>
>> 2. Indians may, at any time, with the permission of the Chief Inspector of Fisheries, catch fish to be used as food for themselves and their families, but for no other purpose; but no Indian shall spear, trap or pen fish on their spawning grounds, or in any place leased or set apart for the natural or artificial propagation of fish, or in any other place otherwise specially reserved.
>
> And whereas notwithstanding this concession, great difficulty is being experienced in preventing the Indians from catching salmon in such waters for commercial purposes and recently, an Indian was convicted before a local magistrate for a violation of the above quoted regulation, the evidence being that he had been found fishing and subsequently selling fish. The case was appealed and the decision of the magistrate reversed, it being held that there was no proof that the fish caught by the Indian were those sold by him;
>
> And whereas it is further represented that it is practically impossible for the Fishery Officers to keep fish that may be caught by the Indians in non-tidal waters, ostensibly for their own food purposes, under observation from the time they are caught until they are finally disposed of in one way or another;
>
> And whereas the Department of the Naval Service is informed that the Indians have concluded that this regulation is ineffective, and this season arrangements are being made by them to carry on fishing for commercial purposes in an extensive way;
>
> And whereas it is considered to be in the public interest that this should be prevented and the Minister of the Naval Service, after consultation with the Department of Justice on the subject, recommends that action as follows be taken;
>
> Therefore His Excellency the Governor General in Council, under the authority of section 45 of the Fisheries Act, 4-5 George V, Chapter 8, is pleased to order and it is hereby ordered as follows:—
>
> Subsection 2 of section 8 of the Special Fishery Regulations for the Province of British Columbia, adopted by Order in Council of the 9th February, 1915, is hereby rescinded, and the following is hereby enacted and substituted in lieu thereof:—
>
>> 2. An Indian may, at any time, with the permission of the Chief Inspector of Fisheries, catch fish to be used as food for himself and his family, but for no other purpose. The Chief Inspector of Fisheries shall have the power in any such permit

(a) to limit or fix the area of the waters in which such fish may be caught; (b) to limit or fix the means by which, or the manner in which such fish may be caught, and (c) to limit or fix the time in which such permission shall be operative. An Indian shall not fish for or catch fish pursuant to the said permit except in the waters by the means or in the manner and within the timelimit expressed in the said permit, and any fish caught pursuant to any such permit shall not be sold or otherwise disposed of and a violation of the provisions of the said permit shall be deemed to be a violation of these regulations. . . .

[Emphasis added]

 The language of the Regulation suggests that the government had two purposes in enacting the amendment to the existing scheme: first, the government wished to ensure that conservation goals were met so that salmon reached their "spawning grounds"; second, the government wished to pursue those goals in a manner which would ensure that the special protection granted to the Indian food fishery would continue. The government attempted to meet these goals by making it clear that no special protection was being granted to the Indian commercial fishery and that, instead, the Indian commercial fishery would be subject to the general regulatory system governing commercial fishing in the province.

36.   Under the *Sparrow* test for extinguishment, this Regulation cannot be said to have extinguished the Aboriginal right to fish commercially held by the appellants in this case. The government's purpose was to ensure that conservation goals were met, and that the Indian food fishery's special protection would continue; its purpose was not to eliminate Aboriginal rights to fish commercially. It is true that through the enactment of this regulation the government placed Aboriginal rights to fish commercially under the general regulatory scheme applicable to commercial fishing, and therefore did not grant the Aboriginal commercial fishery special protection of the kind given to Aboriginal food fishing; however, the failure to recognize an Aboriginal right, and the failure to grant special protection to it, do not constitute the clearand plain intention necessary to extinguish the right.

37.   That the government did not in fact have this intention becomes clear when one looks at the general regulatory scheme of which this Regulation is one part. First, Aboriginal people were not prohibited, and have never been prohibited since the scheme was introduced in 1908, from obtaining licences to fish commercially under the regulatory scheme applicable to commercial fishing. Second, and more importantly, *the government has, at various times, given preferences to Aboriginal commercial fishing.* For example, the government has provided for greatly reduced licensing fees for Aboriginal fishers and has attempted to encourage Aboriginal participation in the commercial fishery. I would note the statistics cited by the interveners the British Columbia Fisheries Survival Coalition and British Columbia Wildlife Federation to the effect that, in 1929, of the 13,860 commercial salmon licences issued 3,632 were held by Aboriginal people and that, during and after World War II, there was a "substantial fleet of Indian-owned and operated seine boats, as well as gill-netters and trollers". The interveners assert that, today,

Aboriginal participation in the commercial fishery is at a considerably higher percentage than the percentage of Aboriginal people in the population as a whole. Such substantial encouragement of the Aboriginal commercial fishery is not, in my view, consistent with the assertion that through enacting a Regulation aimed at ensuring conservation of the fishery in a manner which continues the special protection given to the Aboriginal food fishery, the government had the clear and plain intention to extinguish the Aboriginal rights to fish commercially held by some Aboriginal peoples in the province.

38.   Finally, I would note that the Regulation is of an entirely different nature than the document relied on for a finding of extinguishment in *R.* v. *Horseman,* [1990] 1 S.C.R. 901, at p. 933, (per Cory J.) and *R.* v. *Badger,* [1996] 1 S.C.R. 771, at para. 46 (per Cory J.). Section 12 of the *Natural Resources Transfer Agreement* (*NRTA*), the provision at issue in those cases, is a provision in a constitutional document, the enactment of which provides for a permanent settlement of the legal rights of the Aboriginal groups to whom it applies. The Regulation, by contrast, was merely a statutory document dealing with an immediate conservation concern and was subject to amendment through nothing more elaborate than the normal legislative process. The *NRTA* was aimed at achieving a permanent clarification of the province's legislative jurisdiction and of the legal rights of Aboriginal peoples within the province; the Regulation was aimed at dealing with the immediate problems caused by the fact that an insufficient number of salmon were reaching their spawning grounds. The intention of the government in enacting the Regulation must, as a consequence, be viewed quite differently from its intention in enacting the *NRTA*, with the result that while the *NRTA* can be seen as evincing the necessary clear and plain intention to extinguish Aboriginal rights to hunt commercially in the province to which it applies, the Regulation cannot be seen as evincing the necessary clear and plain intention to extinguish Aboriginal rights to fish commercially in British Columbia.

Infringement

39.   *Sparrow* also lays out the test for determining whether or not the government has infringed the Aboriginal rights of the appellants (at pp. 1111–12):

> The first question to be asked is whether the legislation in question has the effect of interfering with an existing aboriginal right. If it does have such an effect, it represents a *prima facie* infringement of s. 35(1). Parliament is not expected to act in a manner contrary to the rights and interests of aboriginals, and, indeed, may be barred from doing so by the second stage of s. 35(1) analysis. . . .
>
>   To determine whether the fishing rights have been interfered with such as to constitute a *prima facie* infringement of s. 35(1) certain questions must be asked. First, is the limitation unreasonable? Second, does the regulation impose undue hardship? Third, does the regulation deny to the holders of the right their preferred means of exercising that right? The onus of proving a *prima facie* infringement lies on the individual or group challenging the legislation.

The test as laid out in *Sparrow* is determined to a certain extent by the factual context in which it was articulated; the Court must take into account variations in the factual context of the appeal which affect the application of the test.

40.   At the infringement stage, the primary distinction between the factual context of *Sparrow,* and the context of this appeal, is that the regulation impugned in *Sparrow*—a net length restriction—was challenged independently of the broader fisheries management scheme of which it was a part. In this case, while the appellants' constitutional challenge is focused on a single regulation—s. 20(3) of the *Pacific Herring Fishery Regulations*—the scope of the challenge is much broader than the terms of s. 20(3). The appellants' arguments on the points of infringement and justification effectively impugn the entire approach taken by the Crown to the management of the herring spawn on kelp fishery.

41.   The fact that the appellants' challenge to the legislation is broader than that of the appellant in *Sparrow* arises from the difference in the nature of the regulation being challenged. Restrictions on net length have an impact on an individual's ability to exercise his or her Aboriginal rights, and raise conservation issues, which can be subject to constitutional scrutiny independent of the broader regulatory scheme of which they are a part. The Category J licence requirement, on the other hand, cannot be scrutinized for the purposes of either infringement or justification without considering the entire regulatory scheme of which it is a part. The requirement that those engaged in the commercial fishery have licences is, as will be discussed in more detail below, simply a constituent part of a larger regulatory scheme setting the amount of herring that can be caught, the amount of herring allotted to the herring spawn on kelp fishery and the allocation of herring spawn on kelp amongst different users of the resource. All the aspects of this regulatory scheme potentially infringe the rights of the appellants in this case; to consider s. 20(3) apart from this broader regulatory scheme for the herring fishery would distort the Court's inquiry.

42.   The significance of this difference for the *Sparrow* test is that the questions asked by this Court in *Sparrow* must, in this case, be applied not simply to s. 20(3) but also to the other aspects of the regulatory scheme of which s. 20(3) is one part. In order to do this it will be necessary to consider, in some detail, the regulatory scheme being challenged by the appellants in this case. Before doing so, however, I have one further comment with regards to the test for infringement laid out by this Court in *Sparrow*.

43.   The *Sparrow* test for infringement might seem, at first glance, to be internally contradictory. On the one hand, the test states that the appellants need simply show that there has been a *prima facie* interference with their rights in order to demonstrate that those rights have been infringed, suggesting thereby that any meaningful diminution of the appellants' rights will constitute an infringement for the purpose of this analysis. On the other hand, the questions the test directs courts to answer in determining whether an infringement has taken place incorporate ideas such as unreasonableness and "undue" hardship, ideas which suggest that some-

thing more than meaningful diminution is required to demonstrate infringement. This internal contradiction is, however, more apparent than real. The questions asked by the Court in *Sparrow* do not define the concept of *prima facie* infringement; they only point to factors which will indicate that such an infringement has taken place. Simply because one of those questions is answered in the negative will not prohibit a finding by a court that a *prima facie* infringement has taken place; it will just be one factor for a court to consider in its determination of whether there has been a *prima facie* infringement.

44.   I now turn to the regulatory scheme challenged by the appellants in this case. I will consider this scheme both as it exists now and in terms of its historical development. The reason for this is that some aspects of the scheme challenged by the appellants go back to the introduction of the commercial herring spawn on kelp fishery in the early 1970s; as such, in order to scrutinize those aspects it is necessary to consider the regulation of the herring fishery from its inception.

45.   The commercial herring spawn on kelp and herring roe fisheries, in the form in which they exist today, developed in British Columbia in the early 1970s. Prior to that time herring was exploited primarily for the purpose of reducing the fish to oil. The shift in the use of the herring fishery resulted from a confluence of factors; in particular, extensive overfishing had radically depleted the herring stock (in 1965 the reduction fishery was shut down indefinitely) in response to which the Department of Fisheries and Oceans shifted from a policy of taking the maximum sustainable yield of the herring stock each year to a policy of exploiting the herring fishery so as to maximize the economic and social benefits derived from that fishery for the people of Canada. As part of this policy shift the Department of Fisheries and Oceans encouraged the growth of a commercial herring spawn on kelp fishery. Because herring spawn on kelp is eaten as part of the traditional celebration of the new year in Japan, an export market for this product existed; the herring industry and the Department of Fisheries and Oceans believed that this market could be exploited lucratively.

46.   From the time of the Department of Fisheries and Oceans' policy shift in the early 1970s, until 1982, the Department regulated the herring stock through the measurement of spawn escapement (the calculation of the number of eggs spawned in a given year). In 1982, this means for measuring and controlling the herring stock was modified; at that time the Department adopted a policy of estimating the size of the herring stock in each year and of setting the allowable catch at 20% of that stock. The 1982 stock measurement and allotment policy has been subject to only one amendment since its adoption: in 1988 the Department of Fisheries and Oceans qualified the constant harvest rate of 20% so as to allow for minimum spawn escapement.

47.   It should be noted that the measurement of the herring stock is a problem of considerable difficulty. As the defence expert, Dr. Gary Vigers, noted

    . . . in the real situation, fisheries management is full of uncertainty—from the inability to identify primary governing forces at each stage of recruitment, to subjective (but unintentional) sampling bias of fisheries officers observations . . . , to extrapolation of assessments to entire populations. Each level of measurement has intrinsic errors which may be amplified at the next level of evaluation. . . .

In my opinion, two major uncertainty factors that may defy quantification and are totally unaccounted for in the current methods of stock assessment are the predicted recruitment of eggs to larval populations, and the predicted recruitment of larval populations to juvenile populations. Examples abound to illustrate that hatching success of eggs is highly variable and affected by almost every physical factor conceivable in the nearshore environment. . . .

48. The 20% allotted herring catch is distributed by the Department to the various herring fisheries, with the herring roe fishery (where the eggs are extracted from the female fish prior to spawning) bearing the brunt of variations in the herring stock. The Department sets the herring spawn on kelp fishery at a constant level of 2,275 tons; other non-roe herring fisheries are, similarly, set at constant levels. The herring roe fishery, on the other hand, varies depending on the levels of the herring stock. The rationale for this allotment policy is that the herring roe fishery is agreed to be more destructive to the herring stock than the herring spawn on kelp and other herring fisheries; it is felt by the Department that, as such, the herring roe fishery should be the fishery most responsive to fluctuations in the herring stock. The only year in which there was a significant drop in the herring stock was 1986. The decrease in the stock in that year resulted in the closure of the herring roe fishery; the amount of herring allotted to the herring spawn on kelp fishery was also reduced.

49. Commercial herring spawn on kelp licences were first issued in 1975. At that time, applicants "were told that priority would be given to applicants who have previous experience in catching and live holding herring and to residents of remote coastal communities" (Department of Fisheries report, "1975 Herring Spawn on Kelp Fishery"). In a 1985 briefing note prepared by the Department of Fisheries and Oceans, the Department stated that the initial issuance of licences in 1975 evaluated applicants "considering the individual's previous experience and knowledge of herring, area of residence and citizenship status and/or membership in Native Indian Band. Thirteen permits were issued, each allowing 6 tons of production". . . .

51. To summarize, the government's scheme for regulating the herring spawn on kelp fishery can be divided into four constituent parts: (1) the government determines the amount of the herring stock that will be harvested in a given year; (2) the government allots the herring stock to the different herring fisheries (herring roe, herring spawn on kelp and other herring fisheries); (3) the government allots the herring spawn on kelp fishery to various user groups (commercial users and the Indian food fishery); and, (4) the government allots the commercial herring spawn on kelp licences.

52.   Because each of these constituent parts has a different objective, and each involves a different pattern of government action, at the stage of justification it will be necessary to consider them separately; however, at the infringement stage the government scheme can be considered as a whole. The reason for this is that at the infringement stage it is the cumulative effect on the appellants' rights from the operation of the regulatory scheme that the court is concerned with. The cumulative effect of the regulatory scheme on the appellants' rights is, simply, that the total amount of herring spawn on kelp that can be harvested by the Heiltsuk Band for commercial purposes is limited. Thus, in order to demonstrate that there has been a *prima facie* infringement of their rights, the appellants must simply demonstrate that limiting the amount of herring spawn on kelp that they can harvest for commercial purposes constitutes, on the basis of the test laid out in *Sparrow,* a *prima facie* interference with their Aboriginal rights.

53.   In light of the questions posed by this Court in *Sparrow,* it seems clear that the appellants have discharged their burden of demonstrating a *prima facie* interference with their Aboriginal rights. Prior to the arrival of Europeans in North America, the Heiltsuk could harvest herring spawn on kelp to the extent they themselves desired, subject only to such limitations as were imposed by any difficulties in transportation, preservation and resource availability, as well as those limitations that they thought advisable to impose for the purposes of conservation; subsequent to the enactment of the regulatory scheme described above the Heiltsuk can harvest herring spawn on kelp for commercial purposes only to the limited extent allowed by the government. To use the language of Cory J. in *R.* v. *Nikal, supra,* at para. 104, the government's regulatory scheme "clearly impinge[s]" upon the rights of the appellant and, as such, must be held to constitute a *prima facie* infringement of those rights.

Justification

54.   In *Sparrow,* Dickson C.J. and La Forest J. articulated a two-part test for determining whether government actions infringing Aboriginal rights can be justified. First, the government must demonstrate that it was acting pursuant to a valid legislative objective (at p. 1113): . . . Second, the government must demonstrate that its actions are consistent with the fiduciary duty of the government towards Aboriginal peoples. This means, Dickson C.J. and La Forest J. held, that the government must demonstrate that it has given the Aboriginal fishery priority in a manner consistent with this Court's decision in *Jack* v. *The Queen,* [1980] 1 S.C.R. 294, at p. 313, where Dickson J. (as he then was) held that the correct order of priority in the fisheries is "(i) conservation; (ii) Indian fishing; (iii) non-Indian commercial fishing; or (iv) non-Indian sports fishing". . . .

55.   Dickson C.J. and La Forest J. also held at p. 1119 that the Crown's fiduciary duty to Aboriginal peoples would require the Court to ask, at the justification stage, such further questions as:

> . . . whether there has been as little infringement as possible in order to effect the desired result; whether, in a situation of expropriation, fair compensation is available;

and, whether the aboriginal group in question has been consulted with respect to the conservation measures being implemented. . . .

We would not wish to set out an exhaustive list of the factors to be considered in the assessment of justification. Suffice it to say that recognition and affirmation requires sensitivity to and respect for the rights of aboriginal peoples on behalf of the government, courts and indeed all Canadians.

56.   As was noted with regards to the question of infringement, the framework for analysing Aboriginal rights laid out in *Sparrow* depends to a considerable extent on the legal and factual context of that appeal. In this case, where, particularly at the stage of justification, the context varies significantly from that in *Sparrow*, it will be necessary to revisit the *Sparrow* test and to adapt the justification test it lays out in order to apply that test to the circumstances of this appeal.

57.   Two points of variation are of particular significance. First, the right recognized and affirmed in this case—to sell herring spawn on kelp commercially—differs significantly from the right recognized and affirmed in *Sparrow*—the right to fish for food, social and ceremonial purposes. That difference lies in the fact that the right at issue in *Sparrow* has an inherent limitation which the right recognized and affirmed in this appeal lacks. The food, social and ceremonial needs for fish of any given band of Aboriginal people are internally limited—at a certain point the band will have sufficient fish to meet these needs. The commercial sale of the herring spawn on kelp, on the other hand, has no such internal limitation; the only limits on the Heiltsuk's need for herring spawn on kelp for commercial sale are the external constraints of the demand of the market and the availability of the resource. This is particularly so in this case where the evidence supports a right to exchange fish on a genuinely commercial basis; the evidence in this case does not justify limiting the right to harvest herring spawn on kelp on a commercial basis to, for example, the sale of herring spawn on kelp for the purposes of obtaining a "moderate livelihood". Even Lambert J.A., who used the moderate livelihood standard in dissent in the *R.* v. *Van der Peet* (1993), 80 B.C.L.R. (2d) 75, and *R.* v. *N.T.C. Smokehouse Ltd.* (1993), 80 B.C.L.R. (2d) 158, did not so confine the rights of the appellants in this case, defining their right at para. 79 as the right to "harvest herring spawn deposited on kelp . . . for the purposes of trade in quantities measured in tons, subject only to the need for conservation of the resource". I do not necessarily endorse this characterization; however, it supports the basic point that the Aboriginal right in this case is, unlike the right at issue in *Sparrow*, without internal limitation.

58.   The significance of this difference for the *Sparrow* test relates to the position taken in that case that, subject to the limits of conservation, Aboriginal rights holders must be given priority in the fishery. In a situation where the Aboriginal right is internally limited, so that it is clear when that right has been satisfied and other users can be allowed to participate in the fishery, the notion of priority, as articulated in *Sparrow*, makes sense. In that situation it is understandable that in an *exceptional* year, when conservation concerns are severe, it will be possible for

Aboriginal rights holders to be alone allowed to participate in the fishery, while in more ordinary years other users will be allowed to participate in the fishery after the Aboriginal rights to fish for food, social and ceremonial purposes have been met.

59.   Where the Aboriginal right has no internal limitation, however, what is described in *Sparrow* as an exceptional situation becomes the ordinary: in the circumstance where the Aboriginal right has no internal limitation, the notion of priority, as articulated in *Sparrow,* would mean that where an Aboriginal right is recognized and affirmed that right would become an exclusive one. Because the right to sell herring spawn on kelp to the commercial market can never be said to be satisfied while the resource is still available and the market is not sated, to give priority to that right in the manner suggested in *Sparrow* would be to give the right-holder exclusivity over any person not having an Aboriginal right to participate in the herring spawn on kelp fishery.

60.   In my view, such a result was not the intention of *Sparrow.* The only circumstance contemplated by *Sparrow* was where the Aboriginal right was internally limited; the judgment simply does not consider how the priority standard should be applied in circumstances where the right has no such internal limitation. That this is the case can be seen by a consideration of the judgment of *Jack, supra,* which was relied upon by Dickson C.J. and La Forest J. in their articulation of the notion of priority. While *Jack* undoubtedly stands for the proposition for which it was cited, it is interesting to note that in that case, Dickson J. specifically distinguished at p. 313 between food and commercial fishing:

> [The appellants'] position, as I understand it, is one which would give effect to an order of priorities of this nature: (i) conservation; (ii) Indian fishing; (iii) non-Indian commercial fishing; or (iv) non-Indian sports fishing; the burden of conservation measures should not fall primarily upon the Indian fishery.
>
>   I agree with the general tenor of this argument. Article 13 calls for distinct protection of the Indian fishery, in that pre-Confederation policy gave the Indians a priority in the fishery. *That priority is at its strongest when we speak of Indian fishing for food purposes, but somewhat weaker when we come to local commercial purposes.* [Emphasis added.]

In *Sparrow* it was obviously not necessary for Dickson C.J. and La Forest J. to address the distinction suggested by Dickson J. (as he then was) in *Jack;* that such a distinction exists suggests, however, that *Sparrow* should not be seen as the final word on the question of priority, at least where the Aboriginal right in question does not have the internal limitation which the right actually at issue in *Sparrow* did.

61.   The basic insight of *Sparrow*—that Aboriginal rights holders have priority in the fishery—is a valid and important one; however, the articulation in that case of what priority means, and its suggestion that it can mean exclusivity under certain limited circumstances, must be refined to take into account the varying cir-

cumstances which arise when the Aboriginal right in question has no internal limitations.

62.   Where the Aboriginal right is one that has no internal limitation then the doctrine of priority does not require that, after conservation goals have been met, the government allocate the fishery so that those holding an Aboriginal right to exploit that fishery on a commercial basis are given an exclusive right to do so. Instead, the doctrine of priority requires that the government demonstrate that, in allocating the resource, it has taken account of the existence of Aboriginal rights and allocated the resource in a manner respectful of the fact that those rights have priority over the exploitation of the fishery by other users. This right is at once both procedural and substantive; at the stage of justification the government must demonstrate both that the process by which it allocated the resource and the actual allocation of the resource which results from that process reflect the prior interest of Aboriginal rights holders in the fishery.

63.   The content of this priority—something less than exclusivity but which nonetheless gives priority to the Aboriginal right—must remain somewhat vague pending consideration of the government's actions in specific cases. Just as the doctrine of minimal impairment under s. 1 of the *Canadian Charter of Rights and Freedoms* has not been read as meaning that the courts will impose a standard "least drastic means" requirement on the government in all cases, but has rather been interpreted as requiring the courts to scrutinize government action for reasonableness on a case-by-case basis (see, for example, *Irwin Toy Ltd.* v. *Quebec (Attorney General),* [1989] 1 S.C.R. 927, at pp. 993–94; *Stoffman* v. *Vancouver General Hospital,* [1990] 3 S.C.R. 483, at pp. 526–27, *McKinney* v. *University of Guelph,* [1990] 3 S.C.R. 229, at pp. 285–86, *R.* v. *Butler,* [1992] 1 S.C.R. 452, at pp. 504–5), priority under *Sparrow*'s justification test cannot be assessed against a precise standard but must rather be assessed in each case to determine whether the government has acted in a fashion which reflects that it has truly taken into account the existence of Aboriginal rights. Under the minimal impairment branch of the *Oakes* test (*R.* v. *Oakes,* [1986] 1 S.C.R. 103), where the government is balancing the interests of competing groups, the court does not scrutinize the government's actions so as to determine whether the government took the least rights-impairing action possible; instead the court considers the reasonableness of the government's actions, taking into account the need to assess "conflicting scientific evidence and differing justified demands on scarce resources" *(Irwin Toy, supra,* at p. 993). Similarly, under *Sparrow*'s priority doctrine, where the Aboriginal right to be given priority is one without internal limitation, courts should assess the government's actions not to see whether the government has given exclusivity to that right (the least drastic means) but rather to determine whether the government has taken into account the existence and importance of such rights.

64.   That no blanket requirement is imposed under the priority doctrine should not suggest, however, that no guidance is possible in this area, or that the government's actions will not be subject to scrutiny. Questions relevant to the determination

of whether the government has granted priority to Aboriginal rights holders are those enumerated in *Sparrow* relating to consultation and compensation, as well as questions such as whether the government has accommodated the exercise of the Aboriginal right to participate in the fishery (through reduced licence fees, for example), whether the government's objectives in enacting a particular regulatory scheme reflect the need to take into account the priority of Aboriginal rights holders, the extent of the participation in the fishery of Aboriginal rights holders relative to their percentage of the population, how the government has accommodated different Aboriginal rights in a particular fishery (food *versus* commercial rights, for example), how important the fishery is to the economic and material well-being of the band in question, and the criteria taken into account by the government in, for example, allocating commercial licences amongst different users. These questions, like those in *Sparrow,* do not represent an exhaustive list of the factors that may be given priority to Aboriginal rights holders; they give some indication, however, of what such an inquiry should look like.

65.   Before turning to the second relevant difference between this case and *Sparrow,* I would note one or two points in favour of the interpretation of priority just adopted. As was emphasized in this Court's decision in *Van der Peet,* Aboriginal rights are highly fact specific—the existence of an Aboriginal right is determined through consideration of the particular distinctive culture, and hence of the specific practices, customs and traditions, of the Aboriginal group claiming the right. The rights recognized and affirmed by s. 35(1) are not rights held uniformly by all Aboriginal peoples in Canada; the nature and existence of Aboriginal rights vary in accordance with the variety of Aboriginal cultures and traditions which exist in this country. As a result, governments must not only make decisions about how to allocate fish between Aboriginal rights holders and those who do not enjoy such rights, but must also make decisions as to how to allocate fish both between different groups of Aboriginal rights holders and between different Aboriginal rights. The government must, for example, make decisions as to how to allocate fish between those Aboriginal peoples with the Aboriginal right to fish for food, social and ceremonial purposes, and those Aboriginal peoples who have Aboriginal rights to sell fish commercially; it must also decide, where more than one Aboriginal group has a right to sell fish commercially, how much fish each group will have access to.

66.   The existence of such difficult questions of resource allocation supports the position that, where a right has no adequate internal limitations, the notion of exclusivity of priority must be rejected. Certainly the holders of such Aboriginal rights must be given priority, along with all others holding Aboriginal rights to the use of a particular resource; however, the potential existence of other Aboriginal rights holders with an equal claim to priority in the exploitation of the resource, suggests that there must be some external limitation placed on the exercise of those Aboriginal rights which lack internal limitation. Unless the possibility of such a limitation is recognized, it is difficult to see how the government will be able to make decisions of resource allocation amongst the various parties holding prioritized

rights to participate in the fishery. And while this does not lead automatically to the conclusion that, as between Aboriginal rights holders and those who do not hold such rights, the notion of exclusivity must be rejected, it does point to some of the difficulties inherent in the recognition of such a concept in the context of this and similar cases.

67.   It should also be noted that the Aboriginal rights recognized and affirmed by s. 35(1) exist within a legal context in which, since the time of the Magna Carta, there has been a common law right to fish in tidal waters that can only be abrogated by the enactment of competent legislation:

> . . . the subjects of the Crown are entitled as of right not only to navigate but to fish in the high seas and tidal waters alike. . . .
>
> [I]t has been unquestioned law that since Magna Charta [sic] no new exclusive fishery could be created by Royal grant in tidal waters, and that no public right of fishing in such waters, then existing, can be taken away without competent legislation. [*Attorney-General of British Columbia* v. *Attorney General of Canada,* [1914] A.C. 153 (J.C.P.C.), at pp. 169–70, *per* Viscount Haldane.]

While the elevation of common law Aboriginal rights to constitutional status obviously has an impact on the public's common law rights to fish in tidal waters, it was surely not intended that, by the enactment of s. 35(1), those common law rights would be extinguished in cases where an Aboriginal right to harvest fish commercially existed. As was contemplated by *Sparrow,* in the occasional years where conservation concerns drastically limit the availability of fish, satisfying Aboriginal rights to fish for food, social and ceremonial purposes may involve, in that year, abrogating the common law right of public access to the fishery; however, it was not contemplated by *Sparrow* that the recognition and affirmation of Aboriginal rights should result in the common law right of public access in the fishery ceasing to exist with respect to all those fisheries in respect of which exist an Aboriginal right to sell fish commercially. As a common law, not constitutional, right, the right of public access to the fishery must clearly be second in priority to Aboriginal rights; however, the recognition of Aboriginal rights should not be interpreted as extinguishing the right of public access to the fishery.

68.   That this should not be the case becomes particularly clear when it is remembered that, as was noted above, the existence of Aboriginal rights varies amongst different Aboriginal peoples, with the result that the notion of priority applies not only between Aboriginals and other Canadians, but also between those Aboriginal peoples who have an Aboriginal right to use the fishery and those who do not. For Aboriginal peoples like the Sheshaht, Opetchesaht and the Sto:lo, the fact that they were unable to demonstrate that their Aboriginal rights include the right to sell fish on a commercial basis should not mean, if another Aboriginal group is able to establish such a right, that the rights they hold in common with other Canadians— to participate in the commercial fishery—are eliminated. This could not have been intended by the enactment of s. 35(1).

69.   I now turn to the second significant difference between this case and *Sparrow.* In *Sparrow,* while the Court recognized at p. 1113 that, beyond conservation, there could be other "compelling and substantial" objectives pursuant to which the government could act in accordance with the first branch of the justification test, the Court was not required to delineate what those objectives might be. Further, in delineating the priority requirement, and the relationship between Aboriginal rights-holders and other users of the fishery, the only objective considered by the Court was conservation. This limited focus made sense in *Sparrow* because the net-length restriction at issue in that case was argued by the Crown to have been necessary as a conservation measure (whether it was necessary as such was not actually decided in that case); in this case, however, while some aspects of the government's regulatory scheme arguably relate to conservation—setting the total allowable catch at 20% of the estimated herring stock, requiring the herring roe fishery to bear the brunt of variations in the herring stock because it is more environmentally destructive—other aspects of the government's regulatory scheme bear little or no relation to issues of conservation. Once the overall level of the herring catch has been established, and allocated to the different herring fisheries, *it makes no difference in terms of conservation who is allowed to catch the fish.* Conservation of the fishery is simply not affected once, after the herring spawn on kelp fishery is set at 2,275 tons, 224 tons or 2,275 tons is allocated to the commercial fishery or to some other use. This is not to suggest that these decisions are unimportant or made pursuant to unimportant objectives, but simply that, whatever objectives the government is pursuing in making such decisions, conservation is not (or is only marginally) one of them. As such, it is necessary in this case to consider what, if any, objectives the government may pursue, other than conservation, which will be sufficient to satisfy the first branch of the *Sparrow* justification standard.

70.   Considering this question is made more difficult in this case because, as will be discussed below, almost no evidence has been provided to this Court about the objectives the government was pursuing in allocating the herring resource as it did. Absent some concrete objectives to assess, it is difficult to identify the objectives other than conservation that will meet the "compelling and substantial" standard laid out in *Sparrow.* That being said, however, it is possible to make some general observations about the nature of the objectives that the government can pursue under the first branch of the *Sparrow* justification test.

71.   In *Oakes, supra,* Dickson C.J. observed at p. 136 that it is not only the case that the rights and freedoms protected by the *Charter* must be understood through the purposes underlying the protection of those rights, but that the limitations on rights allowed under s. 1 of the *Charter* must, similarly, be understood through the purposes underlying the *Charter:*

> A second contextual element of interpretation of s. 1 is provided by the words "free and democratic society". Inclusion of these words as the final standard of justification for limits on rights and freedoms refers the Court to the very purpose for which the *Charter* was originally entrenched in the Constitution. . . . The underlying values and principles of a free and democratic society are the genesis of the rights and freedoms

guaranteed by the *Charter* and the ultimate standard against which a limit on a right or freedom must be shown, despite its effect, to be reasonable and demonstrably justified.

Although the Aboriginal rights recognized by s. 35(1) are, as was noted in *Van der Peet,* fundamentally different from the rights in the *Charter,* the same basic principle—that the purposes underlying the rights must inform not only the definition of the rights but also the identification of those limits on the rights which are justifiable—applies equally to the justification analysis under s. 35(1).

72.   In *Van der Peet* the purposes underlying s. 35(1)'s recognition and affirmation of Aboriginal rights were identified, at para. 39, as

> first, the means by which the constitution recognizes the fact that prior to the arrival of Europeans in North America the land was already occupied by distinctive aboriginal societies, and as, second, the means by which that prior occupation is reconciled with the assertion of Crown sovereignty over Canadian territory.

In the context of the objectives which can be said to be compelling and substantial under the first branch of the *Sparrow* justification test, the import of these purposes is that the objectives which can be said to be compelling and substantial will be those directed at either the recognition of the prior occupation of North America by Aboriginal peoples or—and at the level of justification it is this purpose which may well be most relevant—at the reconciliation of Aboriginal prior occupation with the assertion of the sovereignty of the Crown.

73.   Aboriginal rights are recognized and affirmed by s. 35(1) in order to reconcile the existence of distinctive Aboriginal societies prior to the arrival of Europeans in North America with the assertion of Crown sovereignty over that territory; they are the means by which the critical and integral aspects of those societies are maintained. Because, however, distinctive Aboriginal societies exist within, and are a part of, a broader social, political and economic community, over which the Crown is sovereign, there are circumstances in which, in order to pursue objectives of compelling and substantial importance to that community as a whole (taking into account the fact that Aboriginal societies are a part of that community), some limitation of those rights will be justifiable. Aboriginal rights are a necessary part of the reconciliation of Aboriginal societies with the broader political community of which they are part; limits placed on those rights are, where the objectives furthered by those limits are of sufficient importance to the broader community as a whole, equally a necessary part of that reconciliation.

74.   The recognition of conservation as a compelling and substantial goal demonstrates this point. Given the integral role the fishery has played in the distinctive cultures of many Aboriginal peoples, conservation can be said to be something the pursuit of which can be linked to the recognition of the existence of such distinctive cultures. Moreover, because conservation is of such overwhelming importance to Canadian society as a whole, including Aboriginal members of that society, it is a goal the pursuit of which is consistent with the reconciliation of Aboriginal

societies with the larger Canadian society of which they are a part. In this way, conservation can be said to be a compelling and substantial objective which, provided the rest of the *Sparrow* justification standard is met, will justify governmental infringement of Aboriginal rights.

75.   Although by no means making a definitive statement on this issue, I would suggest that with regards to the distribution of the fisheries resource after conservation goals have been met, objectives such as the pursuit of economic and regional fairness, and the recognition of the historical reliance upon, and participation in, the fishery by non-Aboriginal groups, are the type of objectives which can (at least in the right circumstances) satisfy this standard. *In the right circumstances, such objectives are in the interest of all Canadians and, more importantly, the reconciliation of Aboriginal societies with the rest of Canadian society may well depend on their successful attainment.*

76.   I now turn to the application of the *Sparrow* justification test to the government regulatory scheme challenged in this case. As has already been noted, the government's regulatory scheme has four constituent parts, which, for ease of reference, I will reiterate here: (1) the government determines the amount of the herring stock that will be harvested in a given year; (2) the government allots the herring stock to the different herring fisheries (herring roe, herring spawn on kelp and other herring fisheries); (3) the government allots the herring spawn on kelp fishery to various user groups (commercial users and the Indian food fishery); and, (4) the government allots the commercial herring spawn on kelp licences.

77.   Other than with regards to the first aspect of the government's regulatory scheme, the evidence and testimony presented in this case is insufficient for this Court to make a determination as to whether the government's regulatory scheme is justified. The trial in this case concluded on May 7, 1990, several weeks prior to the release of this Court's judgment in *Sparrow*. Perhaps as a result of this fact, the testimony, evidence and argument presented at the trial simply do not contain the information that is necessary for this Court to assess whether, in allocating the 40,000 tons of herring allotted to the herring fishery, the government has either acted pursuant to a compelling and substantial objective or has acted in a manner consistent with the fiduciary obligation it owes to Aboriginal peoples. It is not that the Crown has failed to discharge its burden of demonstrating that the scheme for allocating the 20% of the herring stock was justified; it is simply that the question of whether or not that scheme of allocation was justified was not addressed at trial, at least in the sense necessary for this Court to decide the question of whether, under the *Sparrow* test, it was justified.

78.   The lack of evidence is problematic with regards to both aspects of the *Sparrow* analysis. First, in so far as an evaluation of the government's objective is concerned, no witnesses testified, and no documents were submitted as evidence, with regards to the objectives pursued by the government in allocating the herring, and the herring spawn on kelp, amongst different user groups. As was noted above,

there was evidence presented about the selection criteria used by the Department of Fisheries and Oceans in allocating herring spawn on kelp licences in 1975; however, no evidence was presented as to how or why those selection criteria were chosen or applied. Also, the evidence does not indicate whether those selection criteria changed over time (not all licences were allocated in 1975) or whether the emphasis placed on the different criteria varied. Clear evidence was presented at trial demonstrating that setting the total herring catch at 20% was directed at conservation, but no evidence was presented regarding the objectives sought to be attained in allocating that 20% amongst different user groups.

79.   Second, with regards to priority, there is no evidence as to how much (if any) Aboriginal participation there is in the herring roe fishery or as to whether there are any existing Aboriginal rights to participate in the herring roe fishery, whether for food or commercial purposes. Whether the allocation of herring between the herring roe and herring spawn on kelp fishery meets the *Sparrow* test for priority will depend in part on the existence (or non-existence) of such rights. There is, similarly, no evidence as to whether other Aboriginal rights in the herring spawn on kelp fishery exist—whether for food or commercial purposes—and as to the number of such rights holders there might be.

80.   Other evidentiary problems exist with regards to the priority analysis. There is no evidence as to how, between the different Aboriginal bands holding Category J licences, allocation decisions are made. There is no evidence as to how, or to whom, the remaining 2,051 tons of herring spawn on kelp is allocated after the 224 tons of herring spawn on kelp is allocated to Category J licences. There is also no evidence as to how many Aboriginal groups live in the region of the herring spawn on kelp fishery, what percentage Aboriginal peoples are of the population in that region, and the size of the Heiltsuk Band relative to other Aboriginal groups and the general population in the region.

81.   In the courts below, the judges considering the justification issue avoided the difficulties created by the inadequacy of the evidentiary record in two ways: they either held that the nature of the appellants' actions rendered the government's actions justifiable (the approach of the trial judge) or they held that the allocation of 60% of Category J licences to Aboriginal groups demonstrated that the government's regulatory scheme was justifiable. The problem with the first of these approaches is that the nature of the appellants' actions is not relevant to the inquiry into the constitutionality of the regulation under which they were charged. The problem with the second approach is that the fact that 60% of the Category J licences were held by Aboriginal people does not demonstrate, in itself, that the licences were allocated in a manner which took into account the existence of Aboriginal rights. It is, perhaps, consistent with that having taken place, but absent some further evidence as to how or why this result was reached, about the percentage of Aboriginal people in relation to the population of the British Columbia coast as a whole, and about the other allocation issues in the herring roe and herring spawn on kelp fisheries, the fact that 60% of the Category J licences are held

by Aboriginal peoples does not, on its own, serve to justify the government's actions.

82.   Obviously a new trial will not necessarily provide complete and definitive answers to all of these questions; however, given that the parties simply did not address the justifiability of the government scheme, other than the setting of the herring catch at 20% of the total herring stock, a new trial will almost certainly provide the court with better information than currently exists. Prior to *Sparrow* it was not clear what the government, or parties challenging government action, had to demonstrate in order to succeed in s. 35(1) cases; this lack of clarity undoubtedly contributed to the deficiency of the evidentiary record in this case. A new trial on the question of justification will remedy this deficiency.

83.   A new trial is not, however, necessary with regards to the first aspect of the government's scheme; the evidentiary record clearly demonstrates that this aspect of the government's scheme was justified. Witnesses testified as to the conservation objectives of setting the stock at 20% and as to the difficulties encountered by the herring fishery when the catch was set at much higher levels, as was the case in the 1960s. Moreover, the defence witness Dr. Gary Vigers testified that "fisheries management is full of uncertainty"; in the context of such uncertainty this Court must grant a certain level of deference to the government's approach to fisheries management.

84.   Although the evidence regarding consultation is somewhat scanty, and more will hopefully be presented at a new trial on the justification issue, there is some evidence to suggest that the government was cognizant of the views of Aboriginal groups with regards to the herring fishery. The correspondence between the Native Brotherhood and the Department is indicative of the existence of such consultation. Finally, the setting of the herring catch at 20% of the fishable herring stock, because aimed at conservation, and not affecting the priority of Aboriginal *versus* non-Aboriginal users of the fishery, is consistent with the priority scheme as laid out in *Sparrow* and as elaborated in this judgment.

V.   DISPOSITION
85.   In the result, the appeal is allowed and a new trial directed on the issue of guilt or innocence and, with regards to the constitutionality of s. 20(3), on the issue of the justifiability of the government's allocation of herring.

86.   For the reasons given above, the constitutional question must be answered as follows:

Question:
Is s. 20(3) of the *Pacific Herring Fishery Regulations,* SOR/84-324, as it read on April 28, 1988, of no force or effect with respect to the appellants in the circumstances of these proceedings, in virtue of s. 52 of the *Constitution Act, 1982,* by

reason of the Aboriginal rights within the meaning of s. 35 of the *Constitution Act, 1982,* invoked by the appellants?

Answer:
This question will have to be sent back to trial to be answered in accordance with the analysis set out in these reasons. . . .
LA FOREST J. (dissenting) . . .
L'HEUREUX-DUBÉ J. (concurring with result of Lamer C.J.) . . .

7. **R. v. *Adams,* [1996] 4 C.N.L.R. 1 (S.C.C.). Lamer C.J., La Forest, L'Heureux-Dubé, Sopinka, Gonthier, Cory, McLachlin, Iacobucci, and Major JJ., October 3, 1996**

> In *R. v. Adams,* the Supreme Court of Canada determined that regulations that do not have, as their purpose, conservation, but rather sport fishing, are not justifiable using the *Sparrow* analysis. The Supreme Court also applied the *Van der Peet* test. Here, a Mohawk Indian was charged with fishing without a licence in Quebec. The court held that the licence requirement infringed the appellant's Aboriginal right to fish for food and that the regulatory scheme was dependent upon ministerial discretion that had no criteria attached to its application. Using the *Van der Peet* criteria, the court determined that although the Mohawk's claim to occupancy over the area was weak, their claim with respect to their use of the lands and waters in question, that is their distinct practices in the area, was strong. Thus, although a link to land may be critical to support Aboriginal rights, a link to a particular piece of land is not necessary.

LAMER C.J. (LA FOREST, SOPINKA, GONTHIER, CORY, MCLACHLIN, IACOBUCCI and MAJOR JJ., concurring):— . . .

1.   This appeal and the appeal of *R. v. Côté,* [1996] 3 S.C.R. 139, have been released simultaneously and should be read together in light of the closely related issues raised by both cases.

2.   The appellant, a Mohawk, was charged with the regulatory offence of fishing without a licence in Lake St. Francis in the St. Régis region of Quebec. He challenges his conviction on the basis that he was exercising an Aboriginal right to fish as recognized and affirmed by s. 35(1) of the *Constitution Act, 1982.*

3.   In resolving this appeal and the appeal in *Côté,* this Court must answer the question of whether Aboriginal rights are necessarily based in Aboriginal title to land, so that the fundamental claim that must be made in any Aboriginal rights case is to Aboriginal title, or whether Aboriginal title is instead one subset of the larger category of Aboriginal rights, so that fishing and other Aboriginal rights can exist independently of a claim to Aboriginal title.

4.   In the trilogy of *R. v. Van der Peet,* [1996] 2 S.C.R. 507, *R. v. N.T.C. Smokehouse Ltd.,* [1996] 2 S.C.R. 672, and *R. v. Gladstone,* [1996] 2 S.C.R. 723, this Court had opportunity to consider the question of the scope of the Aboriginal

rights recognized and affirmed by s. 35(1). This case and *Côté* will require the application of the principles articulated in those cases to the question of the relationship between Aboriginal title and the other Aboriginal rights, particularly fishing rights, recognized and affirmed by s. 35(1). Furthermore, these two related appeals involve the claim of an Aboriginal right to fish within the historical boundaries of New France. As such, this Court must answer the question of whether, under the principles of the *Van der Peet* trilogy, the constitutional protection of s. 35(1) extends to Aboriginal practices, customs, and traditions which may not have achieved legal recognition under the colonial regime of New France prior to the transition to British sovereignty in 1763. . . .

5.   The appellant, George Weldon Adams, is a Mohawk who lives on the St. Regis (Akwesasne) Reserve. He was charged with fishing for perch without a licence contrary to s. 4(1) of the *Quebec Fishery Regulations,* C.R.C., c. 852. . . .

24.   Leave to appeal to this Court was granted on December 9, 1993 ([1993] 4 S.C.R. v). On June 22, 1994 the following constitutional question was stated:

> Is s. 4(1) of the *Quebec Fishery Regulations,* as they read on May 7, 1982, of no force or effect with respect to appellant in the circumstances of these proceedings in virtue of s. 52 of the *Constitution Act, 1982* by reason of the Aboriginal rights within the meaning of s. 35 of the *Constitution Act, 1982* invoked by appellant?

The appellant appealed on the basis that the Court of Appeal erred in holding that Aboriginal fishing rights could not exist where there was no Aboriginal title; moreover, the appellant argued that on the facts of this case such a fishing right had been shown to exist. The appellant appealed on the further basis that the Court of Appeal erred in holding that the Mohawks did not have Aboriginal title to the fishing area; the appellant argued that such title did exist and that an Aboriginal right to fish arose as an incident to that title.

V. ANALYSIS

Aboriginal Title and Aboriginal Rights
25.   As was noted at the outset, the fundamental question to be answered in this case is as to whether a claim to an Aboriginal right to fish must rest in a claim to Aboriginal title to the area in which the fishing took place. In other words, this Court must determine whether Aboriginal rights are inherently based in Aboriginal title to the land, or whether claims to title to the land are simply one manifestation of a broader-based conception of Aboriginal rights. The reasons of this Court in *Van der Peet* demonstrate that it is the latter characterization of the relationship between Aboriginal rights and Aboriginal title that is correct.

26.   In *Van der Peet,* at para. 43, Aboriginal rights were said to be best understood as:

> . . . first, the means by which the Constitution recognizes the fact that prior to the arrival of Europeans in North America the land was already occupied by distinctive

aboriginal societies, and as, second, the means by which that prior occupation is reconciled with the assertion of Crown sovereignty over Canadian territory.

From this basis the Court went on to hold, at para. 46, that Aboriginal rights are identified through the following test:

> . . . in order to be an Aboriginal right an activity must be an element of a practice, custom or tradition integral to the distinctive culture of the Aboriginal group claiming the right.

What this test, along with the conceptual basis which underlies it, indicates, is that while claims to Aboriginal title fall within the conceptual framework of Aboriginal rights, Aboriginal rights do not exist solely where a claim to Aboriginal title has been made out. Where an Aboriginal group has shown that a particular practice, custom or tradition taking place on the land was integral to the distinctive culture of that group then, *even if they have not shown that their occupation and use of the land was sufficient to support a claim of title to the land,* they will have demonstrated that they have an Aboriginal right to engage in that practice, custom or tradition. The *Van der Peet* test protects activities which were integral to the distinctive culture of the Aboriginal group claiming the right; it does not require that that group satisfy the further hurdle of demonstrating that their connection with the piece of land on which the activity was taking place was of a central significance to their distinctive culture sufficient to make out a claim to Aboriginal title to the land. *Van der Peet* establishes that s. 35 recognizes and affirms the rights of those peoples who occupied North America prior to the arrival of the Europeans; that recognition and affirmation is not limited to those circumstances where an Aboriginal group's relationship with the land is of a kind sufficient to establish title to the land.

27.   To understand why Aboriginal rights cannot be inexorably linked to Aboriginal title it is only necessary to recall that some Aboriginal peoples were nomadic, varying the location of their settlements with the season and changing circumstances. That this was the case does not alter the fact that nomadic peoples survived through reliance on the land prior to contact with Europeans and, further, that many of the practices, customs and traditions of nomadic peoples that took place on the land were integral to their distinctive cultures. The Aboriginal rights recognized and affirmed by s. 35(1) should not be understood or defined in a manner which excludes some of those the provision was intended to protect.

28.   Moreover, some Aboriginal peoples varied the location of their settlements both before and after contact. The Mohawks are one such people; the facts accepted by the trial judge in this case demonstrate that the Mohawks did not settle exclusively in one location either before or after contact with Europeans. That this is the case may (although I take no position on this point) preclude the establishment of Aboriginal title to the lands on which they settled; however, it in no way subtracts from the fact that, wherever they were settled before or after contact, *prior to contact the Mohawks engaged in practices, customs or traditions on the land which were integral to their distinctive culture.*

29.   Finally, I would note that the Court in *Van der Peet* did address itself to this question, holding at para. 74 that:

> Aboriginal rights arise from the prior occupation of land, but they also arise from the prior social organization and distinctive cultures of Aboriginal peoples on that land. In considering whether a claim to an Aboriginal right has been made out, courts must look at both the relationship of an Aboriginal claimant to the land and at the practices, customs and traditions arising from the claimant's distinctive culture and society. Courts must not focus so entirely on the relationship of Aboriginal peoples with the land that they lose sight of the other factors relevant to the identification and definition of Aboriginal rights. [Emphasis in original.]

This analysis supports the position adopted here.

30.   The recognition that Aboriginal title is simply one manifestation of the doctrine of Aboriginal rights should not, however, create the impression that the fact that some Aboriginal rights are linked to land use or occupation is unimportant. Even where an Aboriginal right exists on a tract of land to which the Aboriginal people in question do not have title, that right may well be site specific, with the result that it can be exercised only upon that specific tract of land. For example, if an Aboriginal people demonstrates that hunting on a specific tract of land was an integral part of their distinctive culture then, even if the right exists apart from title to that tract of land, the Aboriginal right to hunt is nonetheless defined as, and limited to, the right to hunt on the specific tract of land. A site-specific hunting or fishing right does not, simply because it is independent of Aboriginal title to the land on which it took place, become an abstract fishing or hunting right exercisable anywhere; it continues to be a right to hunt or fish on the tract of land in question.

Aboriginal Rights and The Colony of New France

31.   The respondent raises another important question concerning the doctrine of Aboriginal rights under s. 35(1). The Aboriginal right to fish claimed in this instance relates to a tract of territory, specifically Lake St. Francis, which falls within the boundaries of New France prior to 1763. The respondent argues that this claimed right should be rejected as the French colonial regime never legally recognized the existence of Aboriginal title or any incident Aboriginal right to fish prior to the commencement of British sovereignty.

32.   Under the British law governing colonization, the Crown assumed ownership of newly discovered territories subject to an underlying interest of Indigenous peoples in the occupation and use of such territories. By contrast, it is argued that under the French regime of colonization, the French monarch assumed full and complete ownership of all newly discovered territories upon discovery and symbolic possession. In the absence of a specific concession, colonists and Aboriginal peoples were only entitled to enjoy the use of the land through the grace and charity of the French monarch, but not by any recognized legal right. As the respondent explained its position:

> [TRANSLATION] In establishing its sovereignty over the New World, France estab-

lished a legal regime in which the ownership of land and fishing rights belonged to the Crown from the point of departure. This translated into a general presumption of non-concession from the public domain, a presumption which went against the recognition of any right outside the terms of the specific concession. . . . [In this instance, it] was only through the tolerance of the French Crown and the absence of a specific concession that the Mohawks were able to establish themselves in Saint-Régis in 1754. One therefore cannot contend that the Mohawks were conceded a right to fish in Lake St. Francis. . . .

33.   For the reasons developed in *Côté, supra,* this argument must be rejected. The respondent's characterization of the status of Aboriginal rights under French colonial law is open to question, although, as in *Côté,* I need not decide the point here. What is important is that, as explained in *Van Der Peet, supra,* the purpose of the entrenchment of s. 35(1) was to extend constitutional protection to the practices, customs and traditions central to the distinctive culture of Aboriginal societies prior to contact with Europeans. If the exercise of such practices, customs and traditions effectively continued following contact in the absence of specific extinguishment, such practices, customs and traditions are entitled to constitutional recognition subject to the infringement and justification test outlined in *Sparrow, supra,* and more recently, in *Gladstone, supra.* The fact that a particular practice, custom or tradition continued following the arrival of Europeans, but in the absence of the formal gloss of legal recognition from the European colonizers, should not undermine the protection accorded to Aboriginal peoples. Section 35(1) would fail to achieve its noble purpose of preserving the integral and defining features of distinctive Aboriginal societies if it only protected those defining features which were fortunate enough to have received the legal approval of British and French colonizers.

The Van der Peet Test
34.   I now turn to the claim made by the appellant in this case. The appellant argues that the Mohawks have an Aboriginal right to fish in Lake St. Francis. In order to succeed in this argument the appellant must demonstrate that, pursuant to the test laid out by this Court in *Van der Peet,* fishing in Lake St. Francis was "an element of a practice, custom or tradition integral to the distinctive culture" of the Mohawks. For the reasons given below, I am of the view that the appellant has satisfied this test. Given that this is so, it will be unnecessary to address the appellant's argument that the Mohawks have Aboriginal title to the lands in the fishing area that gives rise to an incidental right to fish there. The appellant himself rests his claim primarily on the existence of a free-standing Aboriginal right to fish in Lake St. Francis; since I accept this argument it is unnecessary to consider any subsidiary arguments the appellant makes.

35.   The first stage in the application of the *Van der Peet* test requires the Court to determine the precise nature of the claim being made, taking into account such factors as the nature of the action said to have been done pursuant to an Aboriginal right, the government regulation argued to infringe the right, and the practice, custom

or tradition relied upon to establish the right.

36.   In this case, the appellant's claim is best characterized as a claim for the right to fish for food in Lake St. Francis. First, Francis Lickers, a biologist working for the St. Regis band, testified at trial that the "Indians used perch *for food* in the winter and caught the fish during summer in order to store it for the winter" (emphasis added). There was no suggestion that the perch caught by the appellant was to be used for any purpose other than to meet the food requirements of the appellant and his band. Second, the regulation under which the appellant was charged prohibits all fishing without a licence, whether for food or any other purpose; the only manner in which an Indian food fishing licence can be issued is by an act of ministerial discretion under s. 5(9) of the Regulations, a provision which the appellant challenges the constitutional validity of. The breadth of this scheme, and the limits it places on the Aboriginal food fishery, support the characterization of the appellant's essential challenge as to the prohibition of food fishing. Finally, all the evidence presented at trial to support the appellant's claim was directed at demonstrating that it was a custom of the Mohawks to rely on the perch in Lake St. Francis for food. The evidence was not directed towards demonstrating any other use of the fish, for example use for ceremonial or commercial purposes.

37.   The second stage of the *Van der Peet* analysis requires the Court to determine whether the activity claimed to be an Aboriginal right is part of a practice, custom or tradition which was, prior to contact with Europeans, an integral part of the distinctive Aboriginal society of the Aboriginal people in question. The Court must determine in this case, therefore, whether fishing for food in Lake St. Francis was a central, significant or defining feature of the distinctive culture of the Mohawks.

38.   In making this determination the normal approach of this Court—and that followed in *Van der Peet, N.T.C. Smokehouse Ltd.* and *Gladstone*—is to rely on the findings of fact made by the trial judge and to assess whether those findings of fact (if not made as a result of a clear and palpable error) support the claim that an activity is an aspect of a practice, custom or tradition integral to the distinctive culture of the Aboriginal people in question. In this case, however, in deciding that the appellant had an Aboriginal right to fish in Lake St. Francis, the trial judge did not explicitly articulate the findings of fact on which this decision was based. With regards to this question the trial judge said at pp. 139–40:

> [TRANSLATION] In addition to their rights over their lands, the Mohawks have always had and have always exercised a right of hunting and fishing on the St. Lawrence River and in particular on Lake St. Francis in this part situated in the southwest area of this lake and where there are numerous islands and very vast marshes.
>
>   This right of hunting and fishing is distinct from the right of use of their lands. This right can be exercised over vast territories and even over lands belonging to the Crown.
>   . . .
>   This was a hunting and fishing territory situated in the immediate neighbourhood of their village and which is part of an easily identifiable whole.

The trial judge thus came to a clear legal conclusion on the issue of whether the Mohawks have an Aboriginal right to fish in the area but did not articulate the facts on which this legal conclusion is based. In his consideration of the Aboriginal title issue Barrette Ct. S.P.J. did articulate his findings of fact regarding the Mohawks' historical presence on the lands of the fishing area; however, these findings do not relate specifically to, and nor are they determinative of, the question of whether the reliance on fish in the St. Lawrence River and Lake St. Francis as a source of food was a significant part of the life of the Mohawks prior to contact.

39.   That the trial judge did not make explicit findings of fact on this question is not surprising given that he was writing entirely without any guidance from this Court on the factual basis necessary for determining whether an Aboriginal right under s. 35(1) has been demonstrated; however, that he did not do so means that in this appeal the Court cannot rely entirely on his reasons to determine whether the Mohawks have demonstrated the existence of an Aboriginal right to fish for food in Lake St. Francis. That the Court cannot do so is not, however, fatal to the appeal. At trial testimony was received from two expert witnesses: Dr. Bruce Trigger for the appellant and Dr. Rénald Parent for the respondent. The testimony of these two witnesses, despite being contradictory in some respects, provides a sufficient basis for this Court to review, and to uphold, the trial judge's conclusion that the Mohawks have a right to fish for food in Lake St. Francis. . . .

44.   The general picture presented by the testimony of Parent and Trigger, when considered together, is that prior to 1603 it is unclear which Aboriginal peoples made use of the St. Lawrence Valley, although there is evidence to suggest that at that time the lands were occupied in part by a group of Iroquois unrelated to the Mohawks. From 1603 to the 1650s the area was the subject of conflict between various Aboriginal peoples, including the Mohawks. During this period the Mohawks clearly fished for food in the St. Lawrence River, either because the Mohawks exercised military control over the region and adopted the territory as fishing and hunting grounds, or because the Mohawks conducted military campaigns in the region during which they were required to rely on the fish in the St. Lawrence River and Lake St. Francis for sustenance.

45.   This general picture, regardless of the uncertainty which arises because of the witnesses' conflicting characterizations of the Mohawks' control and use over this area from 1603 to 1632, supports the trial judge's conclusion that the Mohawks have an Aboriginal right to fish for food in Lake St. Francis. Either because reliance on the fish in the St. Lawrence River for food was a necessary part of their campaigns of war, or because the lands of this area constituted Mohawk hunting and fishing grounds, the evidence presented at trial demonstrates that *fishing for food in the St. Lawrence River and, in particular, in Lake St. Francis, was a significant part of the life of the Mohawks from a time dating from at least 1603 and the arrival of Samuel de Champlain into the area.* The fish were not significant to the Mohawks for social or ceremonial reasons; however, they were an important and significant source of subsistence for the Mohawks.

46.   This conclusion is sufficient to satisfy the *Van der Peet* test. The arrival of Samuel de Champlain in 1603, and the consequent establishment of effective control by the French over what would become New France, is the time which can most accurately be identified as "contact" for the purposes of the *Van der Peet* test. The evidence presented clearly demonstrates that from that time fishing for food in the fishing area was a significant part of the Mohawks' life. Further, where there is evidence that *at the point of contact* a practice was a significant part of a group's culture (in this case fishing for food in the fishing area) then the Aboriginal group will have demonstrated that the practice was a significant part of the Aboriginal group's culture prior to contact. No Aboriginal group will ever be able to provide conclusive evidence of what took place prior to contact (and here the witnesses agree that it is unclear which Aboriginal peoples were fishing in the fishing area prior to 1603); evidence that *at contact* a custom was a significant part of their distinctive culture should be sufficient to demonstrate that *prior to contact* that custom was also a significant part of their distinctive culture. The appellant here has clearly demonstrated that at the time of contact fishing in the St. Lawrence River and Lake St. Francis for food was a significant part of the life of the Mohawks. This is sufficient to demonstrate that it was so prior to contact.

47.   As part of the second stage of the *Van der Peet* analysis, there must be "continuity" between Aboriginal practices, customs and traditions that existed prior to contact and a particular practice, custom or tradition that is integral to Aboriginal communities today: *Van der Peet, supra,* at para. 63; *Gladstone, supra,* at para. 28. This part of the *Van der Peet* test has been met as well. The evidence of numerous witnesses at the trial proves the existence of continuity. Francis Henry Lickers, a biologist, testified that according to the Mohawk, the practice of fishing had been going on for years and years. Reverend Thomas Eagan, a Jesuit Pastor at St. Regis, testified that before the establishment of the village of Akwesasne and while living at Akwesasne, the Mohawks used the area for hunting and fishing. This was the way of life of their ancestors, and these practices continued into the present. Chief Lawrence Francis testified that hunting and fishing have been practised by the Mohawks since time immemorial, and that the practice of fishing has not been interrupted. It was no doubt this testimony which led Barrette Ct. S.P.J. to make the finding of fact at trial that the Mohawks had and had always exercised a right to fish on the St. Lawrence River and in particular on Lake St. Francis.

Extinguishment

48.   Having accepted the appellant's claim that he was exercising an Aboriginal right to fish in the fishing area, the Court must now consider whether, prior to 1982, that right was extinguished. In *Sparrow, supra,* the Court held that in order for an Aboriginal right to be extinguished the Crown must demonstrate a "clear and plain intention" for such extinguishment. In this case, the Crown rests its argument that such an intention has been demonstrated on two events: the submersion of the lands constituting the fishing area in 1845 as part of the construction of the Beauharnois canal and the 1888 surrender agreement entered into between the Mohawks and the Crown in which the lands around the fishing area were surren-

dered to the Crown, in exchange for $50,000 in compensation.

49.   While these events may be adequate to demonstrate a clear and plain intention in the Crown to extinguish any Aboriginal *title to the lands* of the fishing area, neither is sufficient to demonstrate that the Crown had the clear and plain intention of extinguishing the appellant's Aboriginal *right to fish for food* in the fishing area. The enlargement of the body of water on which the appellant has the Aboriginal right to fish for food does not relate to the existence of that right, let alone demonstrate a clear and plain intention to extinguish it. The surrender of lands, because of the fact that title to land is distinct from the right to fish in the waters adjacent to those lands, equally does not demonstrate a clear and plain intention to extinguish a right. The surrender agreement dealt only with the Mohawks proprietary interest to the lands in question; it did not deal with the free-standing aboriginal right to fish for food which existed in the waters adjacent to those lands. There is no evidence to suggest what the parties to the surrender agreement, including the Crown, intended with regards to the right of the Mohawks to fish in the area; absent such evidence the *Sparrow* test for extinguishment cannot be said to have been met.

Infringement and Justification

50.   Given that the appellant was exercising an existing Aboriginal right to fish for food when he was fishing in Lake St. Francis, the next question this Court must address is whether s. 4(1) of the *Quebec Fishery Regulations* constituted an infringement of the appellant's Aboriginal rights and, if it did so, whether that infringement was justified. In order to answer this question the nature of the impact on the appellant's rights from the operation of the provision must be determined, taking into account the broader regulatory scheme of which the provision is a part.

51.   The basic structure of the government's regulatory scheme, in terms of its application to the appellant, is as follows: under s. 4(1) of the *Regulations* fishing is prohibited absent a licence of the type described in Schedule III. Under Schedule III licences are available for sport and commercial fishing only; the Schedule does not allow for the issuance of licences for Aboriginal food fishing. Under s. 5(9) of the *Regulations* the Minister may, at his discretion, issue a special permit to an Indian or Inuk authorizing them to fish for their own subsistence. In essence, under the regulatory scheme as it currently exists, the appellant's exercise of his Aboriginal right to fish for food is exercisable only at the discretion of the Minister.

52.   This scheme infringes the Aboriginal rights of the appellant under the test for infringement laid out in *Sparrow*. In *Sparrow* the Court held at p. 1112 that to determine whether an Aboriginal right has been infringed the Court must consider the following questions:

> First, is the limitation unreasonable? Second, does the regulation impose undue hardship? Third, does the regulation deny to the holders of the right their preferred means of exercising that right?

In this instance, the regulatory scheme subjects the exercise of the appellant's

Aboriginal rights to a pure act of Ministerial discretion, and sets out no criteria regarding how that discretion is to be exercised. For this reason, I find that the scheme both imposes undue hardship on the appellant and interferes with his preferred means of exercising his rights.

53.   In a normal setting under the *Canadian Charter of Rights and Freedoms,* where a statute confers a broad, unstructured administrative discretion which may be exercised in a manner which encroaches upon a constitutional right, the court should not find that the delegated discretion infringes the *Charter* and then proceed to a consideration of the potential justifications of the infringement under s. 1. Rather, the proper judicial course is to find that the discretion must subsequently be exercised in a manner which accommodates the guarantees of the *Charter.* See *Slaight Communications Inc.* v. *Davidson,* [1989] 1 S.C.R. 1038, at pp. 1078–79; *R.* v. *Swain,* [1991] 1 S.C.R. 933, at pp. 1010–11; and *Schachter* v. *Canada,* [1992] 2 S.C.R. 679, at p. 720.

54.   I am of the view that the same approach should not be adopted in identifying infringements under s. 35(1) of the *Constitution Act, 1982.* In light of the Crown's unique fiduciary obligations towards Aboriginal peoples, Parliament may not simply adopt an unstructured discretionary administrative regime which risks infringing Aboriginal rights in a substantial number of applications in the absence of some explicit guidance. If a statute confers an administrative discretion which may carry significant consequences for the exercise of an Aboriginal right, the statute or its delegate regulations must outline specific criteria for the granting or refusal of that discretion which seek to accommodate the existence of Aboriginal rights. In the absence of such specific guidance, the statute will fail to provide representatives of the Crown with sufficient directives to fulfil their fiduciary duties, and the statute will be found to represent an infringement of Aboriginal rights under the *Sparrow* test. . . .

56.   Moreover, the Crown has failed to adduce evidence sufficient to demonstrate that this infringement was justified. Under *Sparrow,* in order to demonstrate that an infringement of an Aboriginal right is justified the Crown must demonstrate, first, that the infringement took place pursuant to a compelling and substantial objective and that, second, the infringement is consistent with the Crown's fiduciary obligation to Aboriginal peoples. On the evidence presented in this case the Crown has satisfied neither of these criteria. I would note here, and adopt, the description of the Crown's evidence regarding the regulatory scheme given by Proulx J.A. at the Court of Appeal at pp. 127–28:

> [TRANLSATION] Far from proving that perch fishing for food would have harmful ecological effects (the witness did not even know the incidence of sport fishing on conservation), the evidence tends instead to prove *the existence of a policy that essentially favours sport fishing, to the detriment of those wanting to fish for food.*
>
>   . . . [I]t appears to me that what has been shown instead in the case at bar is that *sport fishing is the major concern, after conservation* [emphasis added].

What counts as a compelling and substantial objective for the purposes of limiting s. 35(1) rights was recently discussed by this Court in *Gladstone*. The lack of evidence in that case precluded us from determining whether the government's regulatory scheme was justified. We therefore did not have to definitively determine what particular objectives, beyond conservation, do or do not meet the test of justification set out in *Sparrow*. Nevertheless, we made some general observations about the kinds of objectives which might be compelling and substantial enough to justify governmental infringements on Aboriginal rights.

57.   As with limitations of the rights enshrined in the *Charter,* limits on the Aboriginal rights protected by s. 35(1) must be informed by the same purposes which underlie the decision to entrench those rights in the Constitution to be justifiable: *Gladstone, supra,* at para. 71. Those purposes are the recognition of the prior occupation of North America by Aboriginal peoples, and the reconciliation of prior occupation by Aboriginal peoples with the assertion of Crown sovereignty: *Van der Peet,* at para. 39, *Gladstone,* at para. 72. Measures which are aimed at conservation clearly accord with both these purposes, and can therefore serve to limit Aboriginal rights, as occurred in *Sparrow.*

58.   I have some difficulty in accepting, in the circumstances of this case, that the enhancement of sports fishing *per se* is a compelling and substantial objective for the purposes of s. 35(1). While sports fishing is an important economic activity in some parts of the country, in this instance, there is no evidence that the sports fishing that this scheme sought to promote had a meaningful economic dimension to it. On its own, without this sort of evidence, the enhancement of sports fishing accords with neither of the purposes underlying the protection of Aboriginal rights, and cannot justify the infringement of those rights. It is not aimed at the recognition of distinct Aboriginal cultures. Nor is it aimed at the reconciliation of Aboriginal societies with the rest of Canadian society, since sports fishing, without evidence of a meaningful economic dimension, is not "of such overwhelming importance to Canadian society as a whole" (*Gladstone,* at para. 74) to warrant the limitation of Aboriginal rights.

59.   Furthermore, the scheme does not meet the second leg of the test for justification, because it fails to provide the requisite priority to the Aboriginal right to fish for food, a requirement laid down by this Court in *Sparrow*. As we explained in *Gladstone,* the precise meaning of priority for Aboriginal fishing rights is in part a function of the nature of the right claimed. The right to fish for food, as opposed to the right to fish commercially, is a right which should be given first priority after conservation concerns are met. . . .

60.   In the result the appeal is allowed and the appellant's conviction is set aside.

61.   For the reasons given above, the constitutional question must be answered as follows:

Question:

Is s. 4(1) of the *Quebec Fishery Regulations,* as they read on May 7, 1982, of no force or effect with respect to appellant in the circumstances of these proceedings in virtue of s. 52 of the *Constitution Act, 1982* by reason of the Aboriginal rights within the meaning of s. 35 of the *Constitution Act, 1982* invoked by appellant?

Answer:
Yes. . . .

62.   L'HEUREUX-DUBÉ J. (concurring) . . .

8.   *Thomas v. Norris,* [1992] 2 C.N.L.R. 139 (B.C.S.C.). Hood J., February 5, 1992

> *Thomas v. Norris* provides an interesting example of the conflict between the individual and collective rights of Aboriginal peoples. This case concerns an Indian who was taken, imprisoned, and assaulted and battered against his will for four days. The defendants, also Indians, defended their actions by claiming that they were exercising their Aboriginal right of "spirit dancing" and were attempting to help the individual. Hood J. held that the evidentiary burden of proving the existence of an Aboriginal right was not met and that, even if it had been met, Aboriginal rights do not include "civil immunity from coercion, force, assault, [and] unlawful confinement." In addition, if the Aboriginal right had existed, it would not have survived the introduction of English law in the colonies.

HOOD J.:— . . . [The plaintiff and defendants are "Indians" within the meaning of the *Indian Act.*] In this action the plaintiff claims against the defendants for nonpecuniary, aggravated, punitive and special damages, for assault, battery and false imprisonment during the period February 14 to 18, 1988. . . .

The events giving rise to the action began late on the afternoon of February 14, 1988 in the home of David Louie, a friend of the plaintiff, whose residence is located in Duncan, British Columbia. The plaintiff alleges that at that time he was forcibly seized and taken from his friend's home by the defendants, and then transported to the Somenos Long House of the Cowichan Indian Band No. 642. The House is a community House located on Allenby Road, on the Cowichan Indian Band No. 642 Reserve, near Duncan, British Columbia. The plaintiff says that he was falsely imprisoned in the House for four days. During this time he was forced to go through the initiation ceremonies, or tradition, required in order to become a spirit dancer of the House. He was assaulted, battered and wrongfully confined, and as a result he suffered injuries and required hospitalization. . . .

The issues are (1) whether the defendants assaulted, battered or falsely imprisoned the plaintiff, and this includes the defenses asserted, lack of intent, and consent or acquiescence on the part of the plaintiff; (2) is spirit dancing a protected Aboriginal right under ss. 35 and 52 of the *Constitution Act, 1982* thus rendering inoperative, as against the defendants, infringing common law of assault, battery and false imprisonment; (3) if successful, what damages is the plaintiff entitled to?

Issue No. 1

I do not propose to deal at length with issue No. l, the tort issues. I am fully satis-fied on the evidence that the plaintiff was seized or "grabbed" by the defendants, carried to the van and confined to it, carried into the long House and there detained for four or five days, all forcibly and without his consent or acquiescence. He was assaulted immediately he left the bathroom and continually thereafter, because the threat or menace of violence or restraint, and the ability to make it stick, was al-ways present; as, no doubt, was the plaintiffs fear which he subsequently expressed to Dr. Griffin. A battery was committed when he was grabbed and thereafter when-ever he was touched or beaten. He was falsely or unlawfully imprisoned from the moment he was grabbed until his departure for the hospital. He would not have been permitted to leave the long House, even had he made a strenuous attempt to do so. The threat of force and restraint, as well as the actual confinement, consti-tuted the imprisonment. . . .

The plaintiff has proven, beyond any question, almost continuous assault, battery and wrongful or false imprisonment during his ordeal, in which each of the defendants participated.

He is entitled to recover damages from each of the defendants, unless the con-stitutional defense succeeds.

Issue No. 2 . . .

The plaintiff says that ever since English law was proclaimed to be the law on Vancouver Island in the mid-1800s, the defendants have been subject to the com-mon law of the Province like any other citizens; that when participating in any Aboriginal tradition or religious practise, the defendants must abide by the com-mon law, and in this case, the law of assault, battery and false imprisonment. On the other hand, the defendants say that their right to traditional practises is an Abo-riginal right protected by s. 35(l) of the *Constitution Act, 1982* and that accordingly they enjoy a form of civil immunity. In performing the Spirit Dance Tradition they are not bound by the common law, and the plaintiff's civil rights against assault, battery and false imprisonment are subordinate, and must give way, to the collec-tive right of the Aboriginal nation to which he belongs, and which is protected by s. 35(l). . . .

In conclusion counsel said that the rights of the defendants to exercise their Aboriginal religious practises are not protected by the Charter, or by any other provision of the *Constitution Act, 1982*, so as to permit the defendants to interfere with the common law rights and freedoms of another member of society. The ac-tions of all citizens, including these defendants, are subject to the general laws of Canada and to the scrutiny of the courts, acting as independent arbiters. In the area of tort liability there is no system of justice for Aboriginal peoples, which is sepa-rated from the system that applies to all Canadians. He concludes:

> The fundamental rights and freedoms enjoyed by any citizen may not be abrogated or denied by any other group of citizens claiming the protection of a system of tradition or beliefs that predates the entry of British law to this jurisdiction.

I turn now to the submissions of counsel for the defendants. I will first deal with the Aboriginal right claimed by the defendants, that is, the right to carry on and exercise what their counsel described as "their ancient and sacred tradition called the Coast Salish Spirit Dance." I think it is common ground, and the evidence suggests, that spirit dancing has been performed or practised by Coast Salish people, including the Cowichan Indians, for some time; that it is considered to be a tradition as well as a religion.

The initiation process is commenced by the initiate being "grabbed," by his or her initiators, and taken to a Long House and there detained for a number of days, presumably the time it takes to complete the initiation. It is completed when the initiate has his or her vision experience, which is evidenced by the initiate dancing and singing his or her song. While in the Long House, the initiate undergoes a process which includes being lifted horizontally to shoulder or head height, by eight or so initiators who, among other things, blow on the body of the initiate to help the initiate "bring out" or sing his or her song. This ritual is repeated daily, four times each morning and four times each afternoon. The initiation is done under the guidance of elders who are in charge of the process, which takes a number of days. During the process the initiate participates in rituals including a ceremonial bath, dressing in clean clothes, fasting and sleeping in a blanket tent set up in the House. The initiate is always accompanied by an attendant who is called his or her "babysitter."

The initiate is captured or grabbed either with or without his or her consent. The only consent required is that of a senior member of the initiate's family. Apparently, it is not uncommon for a wife to ask the elders to have her husband initiated by the house dancers. It is said that in the end the initiate sings his or her song while dancing, and the song is said to be proof of supernatural vision experience. . . .

In the case at bar the evidence is insufficient to prove that Spirit dancing is an Aboriginal right, or that it was in existence and practised at all the material times, even applying what I would call the "tempered onus" referred to by Selbie J. in *R. v. Vanderpeet*, [1991] 3 C.N.L.R. 161 (B.C.S.C.). . . .

Counsel relies on an indexed collection of Indian Acts and Amendments [Sharon Venne, *Indian Acts and Amendments 1868–1975, An Indexed Collection* (Saskatoon, Sask.: Native Law Centre, 1981)] prepared in 1981, commencing in 1884, when the *Indian Act* of 1880 was amended to prohibit Indians from engaging or celebrating,in "the Indian Festival known as the 'Potlach' or in the Indian dance known as the 'Tamanawas'." She traced the relevant sections of the Act to 1951 when they were repealed. A description of the conduct prohibited, contained in the 1886 Act, is as follows:

> 114. . . . any Indian festival, dance or other ceremony of which the giving away or paying or giving back of money, goods or articles of any sort forms a part, or is a feature . . . or . . . who engages or assists in any celebration or dance of which the wounding or mutilation of the dead of living body of any human being or animal forms a part or is a feature, . . .

Counsel submits that the repeal of the Act in 1951 requires me "to conclude by necessary inference that Indian dancing again became lawful" and that spirit dancing was in existence in April of 1982 when the Constitution Act came into force. Counsel did not address the effect of the fact that the specified dancing had been prohibited for some 67 years, or the effect of the repeal of the Act, other than to suggest that at that point they became lawful again. I am not satisfied that that is the case.

It seems to me that the very prohibition of the specified dancing is some evidence of the early existence of those dances. However, even assuming that the specified dances fall within the definition of "Aboriginal rights" (and I am not satisfied that they do) I am not satisfied that I can lump spirit dancing with them, and then conclude that spirit dancing is an Aboriginal right and that it existed and was practised at the material times, particularly in the mid-1800s when British sovereignty was asserted, and the law of England proclaimed to be in force, in the Colonies of Vancouver Island and British Columbia. It is a question of proof, and as I have already said, I am not satisfied on the evidence before me, or perhaps I should say the lack of it, that such has been proven by the defendants.

Further, I am not satisfied that even an ancient tradition or activity carried on by the defendants and their ancestors, which involves force, assault, injury and confinement, all against the will of the initiate, can be said to be a continuing Aboriginal right. If spirit dancing includes criminal conduct as an integral part of it, it could not be said to be an Aboriginal right which survived the introduction of English law into the colonies. In this regard I note that under the *Criminal Code* both assault and confinement of a person are criminal offenses in certain circumstances. I will assume, for the purposes of this case, that the conduct of the defendants, the acts complained of, are not criminal. However, the question remains whether conduct amounting to civil wrongs or "crimes" should be considered in the same light.

Civil rights against such torts as assault and false imprisonment protect the freedoms and rights of Aboriginal and non-Aboriginal citizens of this country, from infringement, and punish offenders just as the criminal law does. They protect citizens from the wrongful conduct of others, including those who engage in such conduct while purporting to be exercising their religious practises or other freedoms or rights. In my opinion, conduct amounting to civil wrongs (rights from the point of view of the person wronged) should stand on the same footing as criminal conduct. If such conduct cannot be separated from the spirit dancing, and thus is an integral part of it, then in my opinion spirit dancing is not an Aboriginal right recognized or protected by the law.

Notwithstanding having reached these conclusions, I have decided that in the circumstances of this case I should still deal with all of the submissions of counsel for the defendants but, of course, on an alternative basis. For the sole purposes of such task, that is, when dealing with defendants' counsel's submissions, I will assume that spirit dancing is an Aboriginal right which somehow survived the introduction of English law in the mid-1800s, was continuously practised, and was in existence in 1982 when the *Constitution Act* came into force. . . .

I agree generally with the submissions of counsel for the plaintiff. In my opinion s. 35(1) is not applicable in the case at bar. Assuming that spirit dancing was an Aboriginal right, and that it existed and was practised prior to the assertion of

British sovereignty over Vancouver Island, and the imposition of English law, in my opinion those aspects of it which were contrary to English common law, such as the use of force, assault, battery and wrongful imprisonment, did not survive the coming into force of that law, which occurred on Vancouver Island in 1846 or, at the latest, in 1866, when the two colonies of Vancouver Island and British Columbia were merged.

While I appreciate that in *Delgamuukw* Chief Justice McEachern was dealing in the main with Aboriginal rights as they relate to land, in my opinion, what he had to say with regard to the extinguishment of those rights, and the supremacy of English law to the exclusion of all other, applies to all Aboriginal rights. If spirit dancing generally was in existence in April of 1982 when the *Constitution Act, 1982*, came into force, the impugned aspects of it, to which I have referred, had been expressly extinguished. If those aspects were practised as of April 1982, which appears to be the case, they were maintained contrary to the law. It has never been the law of this Province that any person, or group of persons, Indians or non-Indians, had the right to subject another person to assault, battery or false imprisonment, and violate that person's original rights, with impunity. This is so whether or not it is done under the umbrella of religion or some other tradition of long-standing or an Aboriginal right. The assumed Aboriginal right, which I perceive to be more a freedom than a right, is not absolute and the Supreme Court of Canada reaffirmed this in *Sparrow*. Like most freedoms or rights it is, and must be, limited by laws, both civil and criminal, which protect those who may be injured by the exercise of that practise.

I find it most difficult to accept counsel's submissions as to the applicability of the principles laid down in *Sparrow* to the case at bar; that in the contest between them the individual rights of the plaintiff must automatically give way to the communal rights of the defendants. The honour of the Crown is not involved and no fiduciary relationship exists between the parties. I see no reason why there should be any onus on the plaintiff to justify the paramountcy of the common law to the alleged Aboriginal right, or to justify his enjoyment of his civil rights to be free from assault and wrongful imprisonment. Further, if some justification inquiry or reconciling process were necessary, the protection of the rights of the individual plaintiff from these wrongs would prevail, and for obvious reasons.

In *Sparrow* the court made it clear that even in the context of state versus citizen, just as rights guaranteed under the Charter are not absolute, those guaranteed under s. 35 are not absolute. The court specifically stated that because s. 35(1) is not subject to s. 1 of the Charter, it does not follow that any law or regulation affecting Aboriginal rights would automatically be of no force or effect. A law that affects the exercise of Aboriginal rights will nonetheless be valid "if it meets the test for justifying an interference with a right recognized and affirmed under s. 35(1)."

In my opinion the Aboriginal right guaranteed by s. 35(1) is not absolute as well from another perspective. It seems to me that in determining the nature and scope of the right protected, reference must be made to both the criminal and civil laws which govern the relationships between Canadian citizens in a peaceful society in order to protect the freedoms and rights of all. Freedoms or rights, including constitutionally protected rights under s. 35(1), if any, are not absolute and may be limited by criminal and civil law. They can only be exercised in accordance with those laws, which prohibit certain kinds of conduct and, on the civil side, create civil rights in persons who may be injured by their exercise. Whatever the freedoms or rights guaranteed under s. 35(l) are, they do not include freedom from compliance with the *Criminal Code* or provide civil immunity for these lands of tortious conduct. In terms of civil rights, the guaranteed Aboriginal right, instead of being absolute, is the residue of the right remaining after the civil rights of the persons who may be injured by its exercise are recognized. . . .

In summary, making all the necessary assumptions with regard to the Aboriginal right claimed, it is my opinion that the defendants still cannot succeed. Placing the Aboriginal right at its highest level it does not include civil immunity for coercion, force, assault, unlawful confinement, or any other unlawful tortious conduct on the part of the defendants, in forcing the plaintiff to participate in their tradition. While the plaintiff may have special rights and status in Canada as an Indian, the "original" rights and freedoms he enjoys can be no less than those enjoyed by fellow citizens, Indian and non-Indian alike. He lives in a free society and his rights are inviolable. He is free to believe in, and to practise, any religion or tradition, if he chooses to do so. He cannot be coerced or forced to participate in one by any group purporting to exercise their collective rights in doing so. His freedoms and rights are not "subject to the collective rights of the Aboriginal nation to which he belongs.". . .

SECTION 25

9.   Section 25, *Canadian Charter of Rights and Freedoms*

GENERAL

25. The guarantee in this Charter of certain rights and freedoms shall not be construed so as to abrogate or derogate from any aboriginal, treaty or other rights or freedoms that pertain to the aboriginal peoples of Canada including

   (a) any rights or freedoms that have been recognized by the Royal Proclamation of October 7, 1763; and

   (b) any rights or freedoms that now exist by way of land claims agreements or may be so acquired. . . .

10. *Attorney-General of Ontario* v. *Bear Island Foundation*, [1985] 1 C.N.L.R. 1 (Ont. S.C.). Steele J., December 11, 1984

In this decision regarding the nature of Aboriginal title, Steele J. provides a succinct discussion on the effects of s. 25 of the *Charter*. A larger excerpt from this decision, including the Supreme Court of Canada's judgment, can be found in chapter 1.

Section 25 of the *Constitution Act, 1982* provides that no guarantee of rights and freedoms set out in the Charter shall be construed so as to abrogate or derogate from any aboriginal, treaty or other rights that pertain to the aboriginal peoples of Canada, including any rights or freedoms that have been recognized by the Royal

Proclamation and any rights or freedoms that may have been acquired by way of land claims settlements. Obviously, this section means that the rights and freedoms given generally to the people of Canada shall not be construed so as to override aboriginal rights. It has nothing to do with the question of what aboriginal and treaty rights are protected by the *Constitution Act, 1982*, that question being specifically dealt with in section 35. I cannot interpret section 25 to be a limitation upon what was dealt with in section 35. The Parliaments of the United Kingdom and Canada knew full well that many aboriginal rights that existed in 1763 had been interfered with over the centuries by the statutes and actions of the United Kingdom, and Canada Ontario. If the Parliaments had intended to reverse all of those encroachments and reinstate aboriginal rights to the state they were in when enjoyed in 1763, the Parliaments would have clearly said so, rather than inserting the word "existing" in the *Constitution Act, 1982*. The reference in section 25 cannot, by inference, move the clock back over 200 years, nor was it intended so to do.

11. *R. v. Nicholas and Bear,* [1989] 2 C.N.L.R. 131 (N.B.Q.B.). Dickson J., March 16, 1988

> *Nicholas* results from an appeal by four members of the Maliseet Indian Band who were convicted of obstructing a fisheries officer and for using illegal fishing nets. They appealed their conviction using ss. 25 and 35 of the *Constitution Act, 1982* as the basis of their argument. The court held that s. 25 does not confer any new substantive rights on Aboriginal peoples. The convictions were upheld.

DICKSON J.:—. . . I do point out that s. 25 of the *Constitution Act, 1982* confers no new substantive rights or freedoms other than the right not to have aboriginal rights or freedoms derived from a treaty or otherwise abrogated or derogated from by any other guarantee, of general application, contained in the Charter. In my view what Parliament was saying in enacting s. 25 was that, even though aboriginal and treaty rights then existing and recognized under s. 35 might offend against, say, s. 15(1) of the Charter, which provides for equality before and under the law, s. 15(1) cannot serve to abrogate or derogate from such rights. The possible application of s. 25 to other sections of the Charter is not readily apparent to me although it may be to others. In one sense the purpose of s. 25 was to supplement and extend explicitly to the aboriginal people of Canada s. 15(2) of the Charter. . . .

■ SELECTED BIBLIOGRAPHY

Asch, M., and P. Macklem, "Aboriginal Rights and Canadian Sovereignty: An Essay on *R. v. Sparrow*" (1991) 26:2 *Alta. L. Rev.* 502.

Binnie, W.I.C., "The Sparrow Doctrine: Beginning of the End or End of the Beginning?" (1991) 15 *Queen's L.J.* 217.

Elliot, D.W., "In the Wake of *Sparrow*" (1991) 40 *U.N.B.L.J.* 23.

———, "Fifty Dollars of Fish: A Comment of *R. v. Van der Peet*" (1997) 35:3 *Alta. L.R.*

Gaffney, R.E., G.P. Gould, and A.J. Semple. *Broken Promises: The Aboriginal Constitutional Conferences.* Fredericton, N.B.: Association of Metis and Non-Status Indians, 1984.

Isaac, T., "Individual Versus Collective Rights: Aboriginal People and the Significance of *Thomas* v. *Norris*" (1992) 21:3 *Man. L.J.* 618.

―――, "The Honour of the Crown: Aboriginal Rights and the *Constitution Act, 1982*; The Significance of *R.* v. *Sparrow*" (1992) 13:1 *Policy Options/Politiques* 22.

―――, "The *Constitution Act, 1982* and the Constitutionalization of Aboriginal Self-Government in Canada: The *Cree-Naskapi (of Quebec) Act*" [1991] 1 C.N.L.R. 1.

Pentney, W., "The Rights of the Aboriginal Peoples of Canada and the *Constitution Act, 1982*; Part I: The Interpretive Prism of Section 25" (1988) 22:1 *U.B.C. L. Rev.* 21.

Scwartz, B. *First Principles, Second Thoughts: Aboriginal Peoples, Constitutional Reform and Canadian Statecraft.* Kingston, Ont.: Institute for Intergovernmental Relations, Queen's University, 1985.

Slattery, B., "The Constitutional Guarantee of Aboriginal and Treaty Rights" (1983) 8 *Queen's L.J.* 232.

―――, "First Nations and the Constitution: A Question of Trust" (1992) 71 *Can. Bar Rev.* 261.

Zlotkin, N. *Unfinished Business: Aboriginal Peoples and the 1983 Constitutional Conference.* Kingston, Ont.: Institute of Intergovernmental Relations, Queen's University, 1983.

―――, "The 1983 and 1984 Constitutional Conferences: Only the Beginning" [1984] 3 C.N.L.R. 3.

CHAPTER 8
SELF-GOVERNMENT

■ INTRODUCTION

Since the early 1980s, self-government has been a pressing national issue for Aboriginal peoples that has seized the attention of the Canadian political and legal community. Aboriginal people have argued that they possess an "inherent right of self-government" and that this right best expresses their self-governing objectives and aspirations. The debate surrounding the "inherent right of self-government" has recently become a focal point for self-government discussions. Politically, it was not until the 1992 round of constitutional (Charlottetown) negotiations that the inherent right of self-government took a central place in the constitutional process. The 1992 Charlottetown Accord proposed the constitutional entrenchment of the inherent Aboriginal right of self-government and the recognition that Aboriginal governments comprise a distinct and separate order of government, alongside the federal and provincial governments, within Canada. Finally, the Royal Commission on Aboriginal Peoples, both with its specific report of self-government and in its general report, focused a great deal of its energy on the questions surrounding Aboriginal self-government.[1]

The definition of self-government presents legal and political difficulties. On the one hand, federal and provincial governments fear its meaning is too broad while, on the other hand, Aboriginal peoples fear a restrictive interpretation. Nevertheless, both parties agree that the term "self-government" expresses the desire of Aboriginal peoples to control their destiny. It expresses their desire for self-reliance and for the accountability of their leadership to their own people and not to the federal Parliament, provincial or territorial legislatures, or federal bureaucrats.

Part of the problem has been that the debate has been focused at an either/or level and on legal presuppositions and jargon. In reality, most would agree that the issue of governance generally is not one easily confined to what a constitutional document may or may not lay out. Rather, in many instances, although the constitutional reality is present, the issue of governance is one that should have its focus on the day-to-day realities of managing public society in a highly complex and interdependent world. Thus, although municipal governments in Canada are, strictly speaking, creatures of provincial statutes, they are for most Canadians an important element in their daily lives. Similarly, many of the management boards that exist in northern Canada as a result of several important land claims agreements are not simply administrative structures. They most likely have the force of constitutionally protected modern treaties behind them and they make decisions about

---

1   For a brief summary of general issues inherent in the self-government debate, see A. Doerr, "Building New Orders of Government—The Future of Aboriginal Self-Government" (1977) 40:2 *Can. Pub. Admin.* 274.

such issues as renewable resources and water that affect the lives of many people. Governance is a broad concept, and governments cannot be looked upon as either possessing jurisdictional authority or not. Governance may mean exclusive constitutionally protected legislative authority, or it may simply mean being consulted regarding decisions that affect a group. In between are an array of mechanisms that can achieve many governance aspirations, including the ability of a group of people to effect change and have control over their lives. The debate, if it continues to focus on only one end of the spectrum, will not deal with broader issues of governance. If the debate is broadened, this will mean an increased responsibility not only for Aboriginal governments to examine other options but also on public governments in Canada to facilitate a fruitful exchange and implementation of ideas.

Although some Aboriginal leaders argue for total sovereignty outside the Canadian state, most Aboriginal leaders and their peoples want to stay within the existing federal structure of Canada. Self-government is primarily concerned with sovereignty within the Canadian state, such as that exercised by the provincial legislatures and the federal Parliament.

Although the concept of self-government is not easily defined and the right of self-government is a topic of considerable debate, there exists widespread agreement that the right of self-government consists of two distinguishing factors. They are (1) the source of the right of self-government and (2) the implementation of the right of self-government.

The on-going debate about the source of the right of self-government centres around two questions: where does the right of self-government originate and has it been extinguished? The Supreme Court of Canada appears to support the view that Aboriginal governments historically were self-governing. In *R.* v. *Sioui*[2] the Supreme Court cites with approval the following passage from the United States Supreme Court decision of *Worcester* v. *Georgia*.[3]

> Such was the policy of Great Britain towards the Indian nations inhabiting the territory from which she excluded all other Europeans; such her claims, and such her practical exposition of the charters she had granted: *she considered them as nations capable of maintaining the relations of peace and war; of governing themselves, under her protection; and she made treaties with them, the obligation of which she acknowledged.* [Emphasis by Lamer J.][4]

This passage affirms the view that Aboriginal governments were historically seen as, at the least, semi-sovereign entities capable of governing their internal affairs. The Supreme Court also offered favourable comments regarding Aboriginal autonomy in *Sioui*:

> The British Crown recognized that the Indians had certain ownership rights over their land. . . . It also allowed them autonomy in their internal affairs, intervening as little as possible.[5]

2   *R.* v. *Sioui*, [1990] 3 C.N.L.R. 127 (S.C.C.).

3   *Worcester* v. *Georgia* (1832), 6 Peters 515 at 548–49.

4   *R.* v. *Sioui*, [1990] 3 C.N.L.R. 127 at 146 (S.C.C.).

5   Ibid., 147.

Some argue that an inherent right of self-government exists at common law and has been constitutionalized in s. 35(1).[6] However, at the other end of the spectrum are those who maintain that the inherent right of self-government, strictly defined, has been extinguished, although it existed at one time. Notwithstanding the issue of the origins of the right of self-government, and even though the courts have acknowledged some historical degree of sovereignty enjoyed by Aboriginal peoples, the Supreme Court of Canada seems clear on its views of Aboriginal self-government and Canadian sovereignty. In *R.* v. *Sparrow*[7] the Supreme Court of Canada stated:

> [T]here was from the outset never any doubt that sovereignty and legislative power, and indeed the underlying title, to such lands vested in the Crown.[8]

In *Sparrow*, the Supreme Court of Canada wrote, in relation to federal legislative authority and s. 35(1):

> Rights that are recognized and affirmed are not absolute. Federal legislative powers continue, including, of course, the right to legislate with respect to Indians pursuant to s. 91(24) of the *Constitution Act, 1867*. . . . [T]here was from the outset never any doubt that sovereignty and legislative power, and indeed the underlying title, to such lands vested in the Crown.[9]

In *Mitchell* v. *Peguis Indian Band*, La Forest J. of the Supreme Court of Canada stated:

> The historical record leaves no doubt that native peoples acknowledged the ultimate sovereignty of the British Crown, and agreed to cede their traditional homelands on the understanding that the Crown would thereafter protect them in the possession and use of such lands as were reserved for their use.[10]

Thus, self-government, at least within the existing constitutional framework, means something other than possession of the underlying title of Aboriginal lands in Canada and means something other than the sovereignty now exercised by the federal Parliament and provincial, and to a lesser degree territorial, legislatures.

---

6   Bruce Clark, *Native Liberty, Crown Sovereignty* (Montreal & Kingston: McGill-Queen's University Press, 1990). Also see Michael Asch, "Aboriginal Self-Government and the Construction of Canadian Constitutional Identity" (1992) 30:2 *Alta. L. Rev.* 465; Patrick Macklem, "First Nations, Self-Government and the Borders of the Canadian Legal Imagination" (1991) 36 *McGill L.J.* 382; S. Nakatsuru, "A Constitutional Right of Indian Self-Government" (1985) 43 *U.T. Fac.L. Rev.* 72; the Royal Commission on Aboriginal Peoples, *Partners in Confederation: Aboriginal Peoples, Self-Government and the Constitution* (Ottawa: RCAP, 1993); and Thomas Isaac, "The Storm Over Aboriginal Self-Government: Section 35 of the *Constitution Act, 1982* and the Redefinition of the Inherent Right of Aboriginal Self-Government" [1992] 2 C.N.L.R. 6.

7   *R.* v. *Sparrow*, [1990] 3 C.N.L.R. 160 (S.C.C.).

8   Ibid., 177.

9   Ibid., 181.

10   *Mitchell* v. *Peguis Indian Band*, [1990] 3 C.N.L.R. 46 at 56 (S.C.C.).

The debate over the source of the Aboriginal right of self-government is important because it ignores political compromise and goes to the heart of the Canadian legal system. On the one hand, if the right of self-government is inherent, a constitutional deal—such as the Charlottetown Accord—may be unnecessary, to the extent that the right of self-government is already recognized and, more importantly, not contingent upon federal, provincial, or territorial recognition. On the other hand, if the right of self-government is contingent, that is, if it depends upon some sort of recognition by the federal, provincial, and territorial governments or the courts for its existence, then the right is not based upon the historical use and occupation of Aboriginal peoples over the lands now known as Canada. The distinction between the two approaches signifies a fundamental element in the debate over self-government.

The *Sparrow* decision contains several important principles in understanding Aboriginal rights and therefore assists in understanding the relationship between Aboriginal rights and an inherent right of self-government. For example, the court speaks of a "flexible interpretation" of Aboriginal rights so as to permit their "evolution." Certainly, because of recent judicial and political events, the judicial recognition of a limited right of self-government is possible. This is further supported by the purposive approach adopted by the court, which calls for a liberal and generous interpretation of Aboriginal rights. The affirmation of the principles in *Nowegijick*[11] that treaties and statutes relating to Indians be construed in favour of Indians also supports the position that Aboriginal peoples possess some degree of internal sovereignty. Specifically, the treaties did not extinguish their internal sovereignty but rather strengthened their claim of independence.

The Supreme Court noted that sovereignty and underlying title to the land vests in the Crown. However, the issue of underlying title may not necessarily rule out a favourable interpretation on internal Aboriginal sovereignty in the future from the Supreme Court.

Although there are now a number of Supreme Court decisions dealing directly with s. 35(1), such as *Sparrow, Van der Peet, Adams, Pamajewon,* and *Delgamuukw,* they provide little substantive guidance with respect to self-government. These decisions speak only to the regulation of rights and the means of dealing with s. 35 generally. In particular, these decisions do not deal with ongoing relationships between Aboriginal governments and the federal, provincial, and territorial governments; however, both *Sparrow* and *Delgamuukw* clearly state that negotiations are the best way of resolving the broader issue of Aboriginal rights generally, including the right of self-government.

In *R.* v. *Delgamuukw*[12] the British Columbia Court of Appeal considered the application of Gitksan and Wet'suwet'en hereditary chiefs for a declaration affirming their "ownership" of approximately 57,000 square kilometres of British Columbian land, including their right to govern their traditional territory and to receive compensation for the loss of land and resources. An excerpt from the 1993 Court of Appeal decision is provided in this chapter. The Supreme Court did not

---

11   *R.* v. *Nowegijick*, [1983] 2 C.N.L.R. 89 (S.C.C.).

12   *Delgamuukw* v. *British Columbia*, [1993] 5 C.N.L.R. (B.C.C.A.).

deal with the self-government issue when it ruled on *Delgamuukw* in 1998; its decision is provided for in chapter 1. In 1993, the Court of Appeal overturned a considerable portion of the earlier lower court decision and held that the Gitksan and Wet'suwet'en peoples possess unextinguished non-exclusive Aboriginal rights, other than a right of ownership, over much of their traditional territory. On the issue of self-government, Macfarlane J.A. held:

> [T]here is no question the Gitksan and Wet'suwet'en people had an organized society. It is pointless to argue that such a society was without traditions, rules and regulations. Insofar as those continue to exist there is no reason why those traditions may not continue so long as members of the Indian community agree to adhere to them. But those traditions, rules, and regulations cannot operate if they are in conflict with the laws of the Province or of Canada. In 1871, when British Columbia joined Confederation, legislative power was divided between Canada and the provinces. The division exhausted the source of such power. Any form of Indian self-government, then existing, was superseded by the *Constitution Act, 1867*, as adopted by the Province in 1871.[13]

Lambert J.A. in his dissenting judgment concluded:

> I would declare that the present Aboriginal rights of self-government and self-regulation of the Gitksan and Wet'suwet'en peoples, would include rights of self-government and self-regulation exercisable through their own institutions to preserve and enhance their social, political, cultural, linguistic and spiritual identity.[14]

Clearly, Macfarlane J.A.'s majority judgment represents the most prevalent position taken by courts, including the Supreme Court of Canada, on the issue of whether or not Aboriginal peoples retain a right of self-government. Only a decision by the Supreme Court of Canada on the self-government issue specifically will settle the ambiguity. Lambert J.A.'s judgment can be read restrictively in that self-government and self-regulation are exercisable only to "preserve and enhance" the identity of Aboriginal peoples. It remains to be seen whether self-government and self-regulation could include legislative authority akin to that held by the provinces or the federal Parliament. To date the courts have not dealt substantively, or convincingly, with whether, and to what extent, the right of self-government is extinguished. However, in *R. v. Williams,*[15] the British Columbia Court of Appeal agreed with the Trial Court decision that any possibility that Aboriginal self-government authority remained unextinguished was terminated by British Columbia's *Terms of Union 1871* and by the *Constitution Act, 1867,* wherein all legislative powers were divided between the federal and provincial governments. The fact that Indians are subjects of the Crown either by treaty,[16] or otherwise[17] sets a limit-

---

13   Ibid., 76.
14   Ibid., 250.
15   *R. v. Williams,* [1995] 2 C.N.L.R. 229 (B.C.C.A.).
16   See *Logan* v. *Styres,* 5 C.N.L.C. 261 (Ont. H.C.).
17   See *R. v. Pawis,* [1979] 2 C.N.L.R. 52 (F.C.T.D.).

ing context within which self-government could exist, by means other than negotiated agreements, in Canada.

In *R.* v. *Pamajewon*[18] the Supreme Court of Canada affirmed the Ontario Court of Appeal's convictions of a number of Aboriginal peoples under the *Criminal Code* concerning charges related to illegal gaming activities. The court affirmed a number of principles that are useful in exploring how courts may interpret an Aboriginal right of self-government. First, assuming that s. 35(1) may encompass a right of self-government, the claim of such a right is no different from any other claim for an Aboriginal right under s. 35(1) and must therefore be held to the same legal standard (such as that laid out in *Van der Peet* and presumably other relevant tests such as *Sparrow*). The appellants claimed the right to operate casinos and regulate high-stakes gambling on reserve, describing this as a "broad right to manage the use of their reserve lands."[19] The court noted that this right is not specific enough for the *Van der Peet* test, which requires that the asserted right must be examined in light of the specific history and culture of the Aboriginal group claiming the right and in light of the specific circumstances of the case. This position was reaffirmed by the court in its decision in *Delgamuukw* v. *British Columbia,*[20] wherein Lamer C.J. noted that "rights to self-government, if they existed, cannot be framed in excessively general terms."[21] Second, the court held that based on the evidence presented, high-stakes gambling was not an activity that formed an integral part of the distinctive cultures of the Shawanaga and Eagle Lake First Nations. Of particular importance is the fact that court focuses on the need for specificity in analyzing any Aboriginal right to self-government, if such a right exists within the rubric of s. 35(1). The onus to demonstrate this level of specificity is placed on the Aboriginal group claiming such a right.

Based on the jurisprudence to date, it seems clear that there will not be legal recognition of a general overriding right of self-government. Rather, if the right exists at all, the Supreme Court seems focused on limiting that right to specific activities of governance, as it has done with other Aboriginal rights. This approach, combined with the fact that Canadian sovereignty generally is not being questioned by the courts with respect to its overarching supremacy, seems to impose a high standard on demonstrating in the legal system the substantive right of self-government envisioned by many First Nations and Aboriginal peoples in Canada. Like treaty-making discussed in chapter 2, negotiation appears to be the best means for Aboriginal people to reach accommodation on their claims of self-government.

In August 1993, the Royal Commission on Aboriginal Peoples (RCAP) released a report entitled *Partnerships in Confederation: Aboriginal Peoples, Self-Government, and the Constitution,*[22] which examined the argument that s. 35(1) contains

---

18   *R.* v. *Pamajewon,* [1996] 4 C.N.L.R. 164 (S.C.C.).

19   Ibid., para. 27.

20   *Delgamuukw* v. *British Columbia*, [1998] 1 C.N.L.R. 14 (S.C.C.).

21   Ibid., para. 170.

22   For commentary, see C. Bell, "Comments on Partners in Confederation: A Report on Self-Government by the Royal Commission on Aboriginal Peoples" (1993) 27:2 *U.B.C. Law Rev.* 361.

an existing right of self-government and that therefore the right of self-govern-ment does not require any explicit constitutional recognition. RCAP argued that the inherent right of self-government is recognized by both federal constitutional com-mon law and by s. 35. RCAP stated that although the right is inherent in its origin, it is, nevertheless, a right held under Canadian law. This means that it can be exer-cised only within the "framework of Confederation." RCAP proposed that the in-herent right could be implemented immediately (in certain core areas) by Aborigi-nal governments without either court action or self-government agreements. Ne-gotiation, however, was singled out as probably being the best means of imple-menting the right. RCAP suggested that a "middle path" would be more appropri-ate, whereby the right of self-government would be viewed "organically." It used the term "organic" to mean something that is not static but is, rather, flexible and capable of growing in clarity and substance.

The "organic" model of self-government affirms that Aboriginal governments retain the right to exercise jurisdiction over certain "core subject areas" on a de-fined land base. Such "core subject areas" would include matters vital to the life and welfare of a community and that do not have a major effect on adjacent juris-dictions or communities. The "outer limits" of Aboriginal jurisdiction within the inherent right would be governed by three guiding principles:

- that Aboriginal governments would hold the same jurisdiction now held by the federal Parliament under s. 91(24);
- that where conflict arises between federal and Aboriginal laws, Aboriginal laws would prevail, except where the federal laws meet the justificatory analysis addressed in *R.* v. *Sparrow;* and
- that the interaction between Aboriginal and provincial laws would be regu-lated by the rules that govern the relationship between federal and provincial legislation.

RCAP's argument is not perfect, especially considering that it could be inter-preted that Aboriginal governments possess the better part of federal and provin-cial jurisdiction. Taken this way, RCAP's argument fundamentally alters the exist-ing division of powers in Canada between the federal and provincial governments. The scope of the "outer limits" of Aboriginal jurisdiction would require the estab-lishment of a dispute-resolution mechanism that ensures the principles of negotia-tion are maintained. Even if that were done, based on numerous Supreme Court of Canada and Court of Appeal decisions, the likelihood that s. 35 contains the type of "inherent right of self-government" envisioned by RCAP remains unlikely.

In late 1996, the RCAP released its comprehensive report, which provides a great deal of focus to the issue of self-government.[23] The recommendations made by RCAP are many and readers are encouraged to examine the contents of the re-port. Of particular interest is the summary of recommendations found in volume 5.

Some of the more notable recommendations in the report include the sugges-

---

23 *Report of the Royal Commission on Aboriginal Peoples* (Ottawa: RCAP, 1996); the report comprises more than 3,000 pages in five volumes with focus on land, govern-ance, treaties, history generally, women's issues, elders and youth, Métis, and off-reserve Indians.

tions that the federal government acknowledges its past mistakes, an acknowledgment of the need for the federal government to have a nation-to-nation relationship with Aboriginal peoples, and a recognition that the inherent right of self-government is protected by s. 35(1). RCAP discusses the establishment of an Aboriginal house in Parliament, which would complement the existing House of Commons and Senate, and proposes dual citizenship for Aboriginal peoples (to be implemented by having Aboriginal and Canadian passports for Aboriginal peoples). The recommendations are wide ranging, and the report is a useful tool for researchers, students and scholars alike in analyzing the wide array of issues affecting Aboriginal peoples today.

With respect to self-government, the RCAP focused on the legal aspects of the inherent right of self-government as opposed to the practical mechanisms that are required to implement it. Although RCAP's thoughts and recommendations are interesting and at times thought provoking, they are nevertheless simply recommendations. It might have been more useful for RCAP to focus its energies on the practical issues facing present and future self-government negotiations, instead of placing so much emphasis on strictly legal and constitutional considerations.

In 1995, the federal government released its policy guide and approach to implementing the inherent right of self-government in Canada.[24] The guide is a direct response to the Liberals' 1993 election platform outlined in *Creating Opportunity: The Liberal Plan for Canada* (The Liberal Red Book) and it articulates the government's commitment to dealing with the implementation of self-government. From a broad policy perspective, it is notable that the Government of Canada "recognizes the inherent right of self-government as an existing right within section 35 of the *Constitution Act, 1982*."[25]

The government policy guide emphasizes that litigation should be the last resort in sorting out the issue of self-government and that negotiation is, by far, the best road to follow. The guide states that any Aboriginal governments or institutions exercising the inherent right of self-government will do so within the framework of the Constitution of Canada, and that Aboriginal laws, jurisdictions, and authorities should work harmoniously with the powers exercised by other governments in Canada. The *Canadian Charter of Rights and Freedoms* will apply to Aboriginal governments and their institutions. The guide also affirms that a "cookie-cutter" approach or a "one-size-fits-all" approach to self-government will not work in Canada. Rather, negotiations must proceed within a generally agreed upon framework but must allow for case-by-case analyses and negotiations to occur.

The federal government believes that Aboriginal governments could negotiate to handle matters such as internal constitutions and governing structures, membership, marriage, adoption and child welfare, education, health, social services, enforcement of Aboriginal laws and policing, property rights, natural resources management, agriculture, hunting, fishing and trapping on Aboriginal lands, direct taxation and property taxes of Aboriginal governments' members, housing, local

---

24 *Federal Policy Guide: Aboriginal Self-Government* (Ottawa: Minister of Public Works and Government Services Canada, 1995).

25 *Creating Opportunity: The Liberal Plan for Canada,* 1.

transportation and the licensing of businesses. This position is based on the premise that Aboriginal jurisdiction extends to matters that are "internal to the group, integral to its distinct Aboriginal culture, and essential to its operation as a government or institution."[26] The degree of authority to be held by Aboriginal governments over these areas is unclear. This is especially true since most of the areas of jurisdiction "on the table" are provincial or territorial in nature and are not within the exclusive realm of the federal government. Primary law-making authority would remain with the federal and provincial governments with respect to matters such as divorce, labour and training, administration of justice, penitentiaries and parole, environmental protection and assessment, fisheries and migratory birds co-management, gaming, and emergency preparedness. The federal government would be willing to negotiate only some degree of Aboriginal involvement (where it has the authority to do so) in these areas because these areas of jurisdiction may go beyond matters that are integral to an Aboriginal culture. Finally, there are matters that are not on the table for negotiation with Aboriginal governments. These include areas related to Canadian sovereignty, defense and external relations, currency, criminal law, aeronautics, the postal service, and navigation and shipping. Although formal federal acknowledgment of the right of Aboriginal peoples to govern themselves was a watershed, by itself the policy has little weight. The real test will come at the negotiating table. To date, there have been no substantive achievements under this policy.

The federal policy is only one portion of the equation. The vast majority of the issues that the federal government has put on the table are provincial and territorial in nature—most of the core federal powers are not up for negotiation—and the provincial and territorial governments may well be unwilling to discuss these areas of jurisdiction. This underscores how important it is for the federal, provincial, and territorial governments to work in harmony, on a table-by-table basis, if the issue of Aboriginal governance is to be settled. Without cooperation between the public governments in Canada, many Aboriginal governments will continue to find themselves squeezed out by the respective interests being brought to the table by non-Aboriginal governments.

Politics aside, the real test for the policy will be a financial one. Although the federal government stresses that provincial and territorial governments must share the financial burden of making the policy work, it is the federal government that will be responsible for establishing financing mechanisms for Aboriginal peoples that serve the country as a whole. As provincial and territorial transfer payments continue to be reduced by Ottawa, the pressure on Ottawa by the territorial and provincial governments to deal with the Aboriginal financing issue will mount. Without federal leadership on the financing issue, the expectation that self-government will be achieved in the near future, in any real sense, will not materialize.

An example of how the lack of appropriate fiscal resources directly affects the ability of Aboriginal governments to exercise their authority, at whatever level or in whatever form, can be found in the Naskapi Band's presentation to the Cree-Naskapi Commission regarding the implementation of the *Cree-Naskapi Act* in

---

26   Ibid., p. 5.

northern Quebec. The Naskapi Band stated that it was "reluctant to adopt certain by-laws in the knowledge that the Band has no funds budgeted for the costs of prosecuting offenders under those by-laws."[27] The Mistassini Band noted, in the same process:

> A related problem to this incredible lack of the basic elements of a viable justice system is our inability to properly and fully enforce our by-laws. Without the ability to enforce our by-laws, the powers and rights granted under the Act are rendered nugatory.[28]

Models of self-government exist in Canada today. In 1999, the new northern territory of Nunavut comes into existence. It will give the eastern Arctic a public government that will be largely dominated by Inuit. The Metis Settlements of Alberta have their own legislative base and have been governing themselves successfully for many years. Although riddled with problems, the *Indian Act* provides for a system of Indian band governance, including governance by custom. The Sechelt Band of British Columbia, the Cree and Naskapi Bands of northern Quebec, and four Yukon First Nations have federal legislation that guides their government structures. Finally, the *Nisga'a Final Agreement,* initialed on August 4, 1998, and in the final steps of ratification, provides for a form of self-government, with a land base, that forms part of a constitutionally protected treaty.

The precise legal nature of an Indian band remains unclear. Whereas some cases suggest that a band is neither a legal person nor a corporation, other cases suggest a more liberal approach.[29] Indian band councils, which are the legal delegated governing bodies constituted under the *Indian Act,* carry out four basic functions as acknowledged in *Whitebear Indian Council* v. *Carpenter's Provincial Council of Saskatchewan.*[30] These functions are (1) municipal government, (2) acting as an agent of the minister of Indian Affairs, (3) acting as an instrument of communication between the band members and other governments, and (4) acting in an advisory capacity to the minister.[31] Sections 81, 83, and 85.1 of the *Indian Act* constitute the bylaw-making authority of Indian band councils. Section 81 states that a band council may make bylaws for a variety of purposes so long as the bylaws are not inconsistent with the *Indian Act* or any regulation made by the minister or by the governor in council.

---

27   Cree-Naskapi Commission, Special Hearing on Implementation of the *Cree-Naskapi (of Quebec) Act* (Hull, Que.: October 28, 1986), 218.

28   Ibid., October 29, 1986, p. 31.

29   *R.* v. *Cochrane,* 9 C.N.L.C. 485 (Man. Co. Ct.), and *R.* v. *Peter Ballantyne Band,* [1987] 1 C.N.L.R. 67 (Sask. Q.B.), held that a band is neither a natural nor a legal person and is not a corporation. However, some recent cases have held that a band can sue and be sued and is a legal entity with legal rights and obligations, notwithstanding that it may not be a "legal person." See *Springhill Lumber Ltd.* v. *Lake St. Martin Indian Band,* [1986] 2 C.N.L.R. 179 (Man. Q.B.), and *Clow Darling Ltd.* v. *Big Trout Lake Band of Indians,* [1990] 4 C.N.L.R. 7 (Dist. Ct.).

30   *Whitebear Indian Council* v. *Carpenter's Provincial Council of Saskatchewan,* [1982] 3 C.N.L.R. 181 (Sask. C.A.).

31   Ibid., 186.

The courts have interpreted s. 81 to mean that band bylaws have no effect outside of the reserve,[32] just as municipal bylaws have no effect outside of a municipality. In many ways, the powers conferred under s. 81 resemble those of a municipality. In *Re Stacey and Montour*[33] the Quebec Court of Appeal stated:

> [Section 81 powers are] powers to regulate, and to regulate only "administrative statutes". In other words, a band council has, in this area, the same sort of legislative powers as those possessed by the council of a municipal corporation.

Section 82(2) allows the minister to disallow any bylaw made pursuant to s. 81. The minister is not required to give reasons for the disallowance and is not required to give notice to the band that a bylaw is disallowed.[34] Section 83 confers, subject to the approval of the minister, the power to make bylaws relating to taxation for local purposes, licensing of businesses, appointment of officials to conduct business, remunerating chief and council in such amounts as are approved by the minister, enforcement of payment of amounts duly raised, raising of money from band members to support band projects, and any ancillary matters arising out of this section. Section 85.1 permits band councils to make bylaws relating to the prohibition of the sale, barter, supply, or manufacturing of intoxicants on the reserve.

Regardless of the limited authority that the *Indian Act* confers on band councils, the legislation is still essentially paternalistic in that the minister of Indian Affairs can disallow any bylaw and the fundamental purpose of the act remains to control Indians. Only recently has Indian Affairs begun to relinquish its full control and even these

> delegated federal powers under the *Indian Act* are not a path to full Indian government as much as they are a path leading towards bands and tribal councils increasing their capacity to implement INAC programs, which are designed and funded in a centralized fashion and are based on principles that deny the essential spirit of Indian government.[35]

For most Aboriginal governments, control over service delivery is not enough to meet their aspirations for self-government. In addition, they want the authority to determine the substance of the programs they deliver to their people. They want autonomous legislative and jurisdictional authority.

Possession and allocation of reserve lands involve a large degree of ministerial authority. The band council must seek ministerial approval in order to allocate land and the minister has the final authority to secure possession of reserve land. Moreover, the band council's power to manage reserves and surrendered or designated lands under ss. 53–60 are delegated by the minister to the band council. The

---

32   *R. v. Sam*, [1986] 1 C.N.L.R. 129 (B.C. Prov. Ct.).

33   *Re Stacey and Montour*, [1982] 3 C.N.L.R. 158 at 166 (Que. C.A.).

34   See *Twinn* v. *Canada (Minister of Indian Affairs and Northern Development)*, [1988] 1 C.N.L.R. 159 (F.C.T.D.).

35   Frank Cassidy and Robert Bish, *Indian Government: Its Meaning In Practice* (Montreal: The Institute for Research on Public Policy, 1989), 50.

same is true for the authority of band councils to manage Indian moneys.

In addition to the ministerial powers, the *Indian Act* provides for a wide range of regulatory powers held by the governor in council. Section 73 of the act contains a lengthy list of regulations that can be enacted by the governor in council. Note that these regulations supersede a band bylaw passed by a band council pursuant to s. 81.

The *Indian Act* severely restricts the ability of Indians to manage their own affairs and to determine their destiny. The act is paternalistic, and it seeks to assimilate Aboriginal peoples. It remains the single largest impediment to Aboriginal self-government and Aboriginal social and economic development within Canada today. Some Indian bands have been excluded from application of the act. These bands include the Sechelt Band, the Cree and Naskapi Bands of northern Quebec, and the Nisga'a of British Columbia.

The *Cree-Naskapi Act*[36] resulted from the 1975 *James Bay and Northern Quebec Agreement* (*JBNQA*),[37] which permitted the Quebec government to proceed with the James Bay hydroelectric project. In return for ceding most of their land, the Cree, Inuit, and subsequently the Naskapi, received certain environmental, land use, and government rights. For the purposes of this chapter, the most notable provision of the *JBNQA* is outlined in s. 9.0.1 of the *JBNQA*. It imposed an obligation on the federal Parliament to enact legislation providing for local government for the Cree, and subsequently the Naskapi.[38] In 1984, the federal Parliament enacted the *Cree-Naskapi Act* pursuant to its obligation under the *JBNQA*. The act provides the Cree and Naskapi Bands with bylaw-making authority similar to that held by most municipalities. These powers, outlined in s. 45 of the act, include, in addition to the matters outlined in the *Indian Act*, the authority to make bylaws relating to the administration of band affairs and internal management, public order, taxation for local purposes, and local services, including fire protection.

A major weakness of the *Cree-Naskapi Act* is that it does not confer independent legislative authority on the Cree and Naskapi Bands; however, they possess local government–type powers that are inextricably tied to a constitutionally protected treaty. Notably, these bands do not have the power to create their own constitutions. Although the minister does not have a general disallowance power for bylaws made under the act, the minister may disallow or create bylaws relating to local taxation, hunting and trapping, elections, special band meetings, land registry system, long-term borrowing, band expropriation, and fines and penalties for breaking band bylaws. The Cree and Naskapi Bands are subservient to the federal

---

36   *Cree-Naskapi (of Quebec) Act*, S.C. 1984, c. 46.

37   *James Bay and Northern Quebec Agreement* (Quebec: Editeur official du Québec, 1976).

38   Section 9.0.1 of the JBNQA provides: "Subject to all other provisions of the Agreement, there shall be recommended to Parliament special legislation concerning local government for the James Bay Crees on Category IA lands allocated to them." The corresponding text and section for the Naskapi Band is s. 7.1 of the *Northeastern Quebec Agreement* (Ottawa: DIAND, 1984).

Parliament and to the Quebec National Assembly, as the case may be.[39]

The Cree and Naskapi do not retain their traditional rights and title to the land. The *JBNQA* states that the Cree "cede, release, surrender and convey all their Native claims, rights, title and interest"[40] in the land. All the bands are separate corporate entities under their umbrella regional organization, the Cree Regional Authority. The act outlines permissible forms of government. Each community must have a band council that follows a prescribed set of rules and orders.[41] Band bylaws and resolutions must be enacted according to the procedures set out in the act and elections must be carried out in the prescribed manner (with election bylaws being subject to ministerial approval).[42]

In *Eastmain Band* v. *Gilpin*,[43] Lavergne P.C.J. of the Quebec Provincial Court noted that the *Cree-Naskapi (of Quebec) Act*, by way of s. 35(3) of the *Constitution Act, 1982*, maintains the "proposition that the Crees hold some sort of residual sovereignty as regards their local governments." Indeed, in the Court of Quebec decision of *Tawich Development Corp.* v. *Dep. Min. of Revenue of Que.*,[44] the court found that the Cree Nation of Wemindji (a band under the auspices of the *JBNQA* and an incorporated local government under the *Cree-Naskapi (of Quebec) Act*) was not a "municipality" for the purposes of the *Taxation Act*.[45] The band did not exercise delegated authority. Rather its authority comes from a treaty (the *JBNQA*) and the band thus has a *sui generis* form of government.

The *Sechelt Indian Band Self-Government Act*[46] came into force in October 1986 and provides a form of Aboriginal government for the Sechelt Band of British Columbia. The act establishes a municipal form of government and delegates legislative authority to the band council in areas similar to those provided to the Cree and Naskapi Bands. Although the band is no longer under the auspices of the *Indian Act*, except where a void in legislation has not yet been filled by the Sechelt band council, it still possesses only delegated authority. The act can be amended or repealed by Parliament since it remains federal legislation. The band also possesses the authority to enact its own constitution. Sechelt is also involved in the

---

39   This conclusion is not absolute. For example, in *Chisasibi Band* v. *Barbara Chewanish* (Que. Prov. Ct., No: 640–27–000099–842), 27 Ouellet J. held the following: "[I]t would seem to me that the Band Council constitutes an autonomous level of government when it exercises the powers conferred upon it by the *Cree-Naskapi (of Quebec) Act*. As long as it remains within the powers so conferred, the Band Council represents a level of government independent from the Canadian Parliament and the Quebec legislature."

40   *James Bay and Northern Quebec Agreement* (Quebec: Editeur official du Québec, 1976), s. 21.

41   *Cree-Naskapi (of Quebec) Act*, S.C. 1984, c. 46 at ss. 25–39.

42   Ibid., ss. 49–57, 63–78.

43   *Eastmain Band* v.*Gilpin*, [1987] 3 C.N.L.R. 54 at 67 (Que. Prov.Ct.).

44   *Tawich Development Corp.* v. *Dep. Min. of Revenue of Que.*, [1997] 2 C.N.L.R. 189 (C.Q.).

45   *Taxation Act*, R.S.Q., c. I–3.

46   *Sechelt Indian Band Self-Government Act*, S.C. 1986, c. 27.

British Columbia treaty process, which, if successful, can only increase the band's authority and governance stature.

In terms of natural resources, Indian bands do not own the natural resources on their land and are still subject to the *Indian Oil and Gas Act,*[47] which provides for little band involvement. As well, the *British Columbia Indian Reserves Mineral Resources Act*[48] and the *Indian Reserves Minerals Resources Act,*[49] both provincial laws, apply to the Sechelt Band. These examples are particularly important considering the dependence of many governments on the exploitation of natural resources. Ownership and control of natural resources are significant for many Indian nations that have either vast mineral deposits, timber reserves, or oil and gas reserves.

The Sechelt legislation replaces, for the most part, the *Indian Act,* as it applies to Sechelt lands and members. The purpose of the act is to

> enable the Sechelt Indian Band to exercise and maintain self-government on Sechelt lands and to obtain control over and the administration of the resources and services available to its members.[50]

The Sechelt legislation also raises questions about the nature of land tenure and government. The act provides that Sechelt lands shall be held in fee simple.[51] Usually the Crown holds the lands in trust for the use and benefit of Indians. The issue of fee simple title is noteworthy in that it signifies what title does not vest in the band; namely radical or sovereign title.[52] Ultimate title still resides with the federal or provincial Crown. Nevertheless, fee simple title enables the Sechelt Band to engage in a much broader economic development strategy by offering security for investors.

The Cree and Naskapi Bands and the Sechelt Band are not autonomous governments that exercise jurisdiction and authority at the same level as the federal and provincial governments. They are improvements over the *Indian Act* system, but they do not represent autonomous orders of government in Canada because they are subject to the ultimate legislative authority of either one of the other two orders of government. For the Cree, Naskapi, and Sechelt Bands, the federal and their respective provincial governments continue to play a major role in the allocation and level of funding, in the establishment of spending priorities, and in the ability of the band governments to operate on a day-to-day level. At the same time,

---

47 *Indian Oil and Gas Act,* R.S.C. 1985, c. I–7.

48 *British Columbia Indian Reserves Mineral Resources Act,* S.C. 1943–1944, c. 9.

49 *Indian Reserves Minerals Resources Act,* R.S.B.C. 1979, c. 192.

50 *Sechelt Indian Band Self-Government Act,* S.C. 1986, c. 27, s. 4.

51 Ibid., s. 23(1) reads: "The title to all lands that were, . . . reserves, . . . of the *Indian Act* Sechelt band is hereby transferred in fee simple to the Band."

52 Professor Sinclair writes: "The Crown at the top owns the land. At the base is O who owns a fee simple (a "bundle" of rights) in relation to that land. He then may easily dispose of some of these rights. This leaves totally undisturbed the ownership of the land; that's up above." A.M. Sinclair, *Introduction to Real Property Law,* 3d ed. (Toronto: Butterworths, 1987), 9.

it is unclear exactly what realm these band governments do occupy. In the case of the Cree and Naskapi, their forms of government are tied directly to constitutionally protected land claims agreements and they have been described by some courts as being *sui generis* in nature.

On August 4, 1998, the governments of British Columbia and Canada and the Nisga'a initialed the *Nisga'a Final Agreement*. Discussed in the introduction to chapter 2 on treaty rights, at pp. 130–32, the *Nisga'a Final Agreement* outlines an extensive array of land, economic, and governance provisions. The excerpt from the *Agreement* contained in this chapter focuses on chapter 11, "Nisga'a Government." What is notable is that the *Nisga'a Agreement,* including all of the governance powers, is a treaty and a land claims agreement within the meaning of ss. 25 and 35 of the *Constitution Act, 1982.*[53] Although the *Agreement* does not specify what is, and what is not, to be constitutionally protected, s. 1, chapter 11, of the *Agreement* provides that the Nisga'a Nation has a "right to self-government, and the authority to make laws, as set out in this Agreement." Thus, for the first time in Canada, a treaty has been constitutionally protected and has constitutionally "recognized and affirmed" an Aboriginal right of self-government.

The British Columbia treaty process, the Dogrib comprehensive claims and self-government negotiations in the Northwest Territories, and the Metis Settlements legislation enacted by the province of Alberta[54] all represent the many changes that have occurred and that will continue to occur on the self-government front.

Although Aboriginal governments rightly focus on jurisdiction, jurisdiction is only part of the equation. Without adequate fiscal resources, jurisdiction may be meaningless. With jurisdiction comes a serious responsibility to ensure that the necessary democratic systems of governance are in place, and that the necessary checks and balances on power are easily identified and accessible. These systems and the corresponding checks and balances require many fiscal resources and much infrastructure, and the majority of Aboriginal groups in Canada may not have the population base to support them. This fiscal reality needs to be recognized by Aboriginal groups. By focusing on jurisdiction, they are increasing the need for financial resources, and they may end up requiring more resources than are available or than can be sustained by a community or group of communities. In some instances, Aboriginal governments may be better served by focusing on practical arrangements, with all the necessary safeguards, so that their interests and objectives are met, as opposed to focusing on more abstract mechanisms such as jurisdictional authority.

The excerpts provided in this chapter regarding the Yukon self-government process are from the *Teslin Tlingit Council Self-Government Agreement.*[55] On May 29, 1993, the Yukon government, the federal government, and the Council for Yukon Indians signed an *Umbrella Final Agreement* and the final agreements for

---

53   *Nisga'a Final Agreement,* chap. 2, s. 1.

54   See chap. 5.

55   Signed on May 29, 1993, the *Teslin Tlingit Agreement* is similar to the other three self-government agreements signed to date in the Yukon Territory with the Nacho Nyak Dun, Vuntut Gwich'in, and Champagne and Aishihik First Nations.

four Yukon First Nations: the Vuntut Gwitchin First Nation, the Champagne and Aishihik First Nations, the Teslin Tlingit Council, and the First Nation of Nacho Nyak Dun. These four First Nations also signed separate self-government agreements negotiated under the framework of the *Umbrella Agreement.* The *Umbrella Agreement* provides for a total of more than 41,000 square kilometres of land with a portion of it holding surface and subsurface rights. The *Umbrella Agreement* also provides for a cash envelope of approximately $242 million (1989 dollars) to be divided between the 14 beneficiary First Nations under the *Umbrella Agreement* (with a total population of approximately 8,000). Since 1993, the Little Salmon/Carmacks First Nation and the Selkirk First Nation signed self-government agreements in 1997. The *Yukon First Nations Self-Government Act*[56] was proclaimed into force on February 14, 1995, and is the federal implementing legislation.

The Yukon agreements replace the *Indian Act,* with the exception of determining who is an "Indian." Although they are forms of delegated government, the Yukon models provide for a wide range of legislative authority. The Yukon self-government agreements offer a new approach to self-government within a comprehensive claims framework, particularly with respect to powers of taxation. The real test for the Yukon First Nations will be their success in implementing what they have negotiated.[57]

To date the courts have offered a restrictive interpretation of s. 35 and the right of self-government. Negotiation may be the only forum for Aboriginal peoples to address the issue of broad forms of self-government unless the courts take a more liberal view of whether self-government has been extinguished. However, history has shown that Aboriginal peoples are well advised to pursue the route of negotiation with caution.

■ CASES AND MATERIALS

SOVEREIGNTY

1. ***R. v. Sioui,*** **[1990] 3 C.N.L.R. 127 (S.C.C.)**

   The following excerpt from the *Sioui* decision illustrates a more liberal approach to self-government from the Supreme Court of Canada in examining the historical relationship between First Nations and the Crown. This is contrasted with the Supreme Court of Canada's statements in *Sparrow,* which, in terms of self-government, are restrictive in that the pre-eminent sovereignty of the Crown is clearly recognized.

---

56 *Yukon First Nations Self-Government Act,* S.C. 1994, c. 35.

57 The *Umbrella Agreement* makes it clear that self-government agreements are not accorded constitutional protection. Section 24.12.1 reads: "Agreements entered into pursuant to this chapter and any legislation enacted to implement such agreements shall not be construed to be treaty rights within the meaning of section 35 of the Constitution Act, 1982." This clause is mirrored in the individual First Nations' final agreements (see s. 24.12.1 of the *Teslin Tlingit Council Final Agreement*).

LAMER J.:— . . . I consider that, instead, we can conclude from the historical documents that both Great Britain and France felt that the Indian nations had sufficient independence and played a large enough role in North America for it to be a good policy to maintain relations with them very close to those maintained between sovereign nations.

The mother countries did everything in their power to secure the alliance of each Indian nation and to encourage nations allied with the enemy to change sides. When these efforts met with success, they were incorporated in treaties of alliance or neutrality. This clearly indicates that the Indian nations were regarded in their relations with the European nations which occupied North America as independent nations. The papers of Sir William Johnson (*The Papers of Sir William Johnson,* 14 vol.), who was in charge of Indian affairs in British North America, demonstrate the recognition by Great Britain that nation-to-nation relations had to be conducted with the North American Indians. As an example, I cite an extract from a speech by Sir Johnson at the Onondaga Conference held in April 1748, attended by the Five nations:

> Brethren of the five Nations I will begin upon a thing of a long standing, our first Brothership. My Reason for it is, I think there are several among you who seem to forget it; It may seem strange to you how I a Foreigner should know this, But I tell you I found out some of the old Writings of our Forefathers which was thought to have been lost and in this old valuable Record I find, that our first Friendship Commenced at the Arrival of the first great Canoe or Vessel at Albany . . . [Emphasis added.](*The Papers of Sir William Johnson,* vol. 1, 1921, at p. 157)

As the Chief Justice of the United States Supreme Court said in 1832 in *Worcester* v. *State of Georgia*, 31 U.S. (6 Pet.) 515 (1832), at pp. 548–49, about British policy towards the Indians in the mid-eighteenth century:

> Such was the policy of Great Britain towards the Indian nations inhabiting the territory from which she excluded all other Europeans; such her claims, and such her practical exposition of the charters she had granted: *she considered them as nations capable of maintaining the relations of peace and war: of governing themselves, under her protection: and she made treaties with them, the obligation of which she acknowledged.* [Emphasis added.]

Further, both the French and the English recognized the critical importance of alliances with the Indians, or at least their neutrality, in determining the outcome of the war between them and the security of the North American colonies.

2.   *R.* v. *Sparrow*, [1990] 3 C.N.L.R. 160 (S.C.C.)

. . . It is worth recalling that while British policy towards the native population was based on respect for their right to occupy their traditional lands, a proposition to which the *Royal Proclamation of 1763* bears witness, there was from the outset never any doubt that sovereignty and legislative power, and indeed the underlying title, to such lands vested in the Crown: see *Johnson* v. *M'Intosh* (1823); . . . see also the Royal Proclamation . . . [and] *Calder* . . . . And there can be no doubt that over the years the rights of the Indians were often honoured in the breach (for one instance in a recent case in this Court, see *Canadian Pacific Ltd* v. *Paul*, [1989] 1

C.N.L.R. 47). As MacDonald J. stated in *Pasco* v. *Canadian National Railway Co.*, [1986] 1 C.N.L.R. 35 at 37, (B.C.S.C.): "We cannot recount with much pride the treatment accorded to the native people of this country." . . .

There is no explicit language in the provision that authorizes this Court or any court to assess the legitimacy of any government legislation that restricts aboriginal rights. Yet, we find that the words "recognition and affirmation" incorporate the fiduciary relationship referred to earlier and so import some restraint on the exercise of sovereign power. Rights that are recognized and affirmed are not absolute. Federal legislative powers continue, including, of course, the right to legislate with respect to Indians pursuant to s. 91(24) of the *Constitution Act, 1867.* These powers must, however, now be read together with s. 35(1). In other words, federal power must be reconciled with federal duty and the best way to achieve that reconciliation is to demand the justification of any government regulation that infringes upon or denies aboriginal rights. . . .

3. **_Delgamuukw_ v. _British Columbia_, [1993] 5 C.N.L.R. (B.C.C.A.). Taggart, Lambert, Hutcheon, Macfarlane, and Wallace JJ.A., June 25, 1993**

> This decision affirms that the Gitksan and Wet'suwet'en peoples of British Columbia retained "unextinguished non-exclusive aboriginal rights" that do not include ownership over their traditional territory. Although the Court of Appeal decision was later affirmed in part by the Supreme Court of Canada (see chapter 1), an excerpt is included here because of the reference to self-government. The Supreme Court did not deal with the self-government issue because of an error in the pleadings.
>
> Two excerpts are provided: the judgment of Macfarlane J.A. and the dissenting judgment of Lambert J.A. Lambert's judgment is most interesting since it represents an appeal court judge affirming the Aboriginal right of self-government and self-regulation. Although the Supreme Court of Canada agreed to hear a further appeal from the Gitksan and Wet'suwet'en, the province and the Gitksan and Wet'suwet'en chiefs signed an "Accord of Recognition and Respect" on June 13, 1994. This accord allowed one year to proceed with treaty negotiations. Since the 1997 Supreme Court decision in *Delgamuukw,* the Gitksan and Wet'suwet'en have resumed discussions with the federal government and the government of British Columbia.

MACFARLANE J.A. (TAGGART J.A., concurring):— . . . The plaintiffs' claim to jurisdiction (a right of self-government) is stated in paragraph 73 of the statement of claim, and is mentioned in several paragraphs of the relief claimed.

> 73. The laws of the Province of British Columbia are subject to the reservation of aboriginal title, ownership and jurisdiction by the Gitksan Chiefs and the Wet'suwet'en Chiefs and do not confer any jurisdiction over the Territory and resources thereon and therein claimed by the Plaintiffs.

The extent of the plaintiffs' claim to jurisdiction is better understood by reference to the relief claimed under the heading, "The Content of Aboriginal Rights", set out in Part II. The claim involves an unextinguished right to control the lands and natural resources of the Territory, and to govern the Territory and the plaintiffs' people by Gitksan and Wet'suwet'en laws. The claim seeks to exclude the operation of the British Columbia laws in the Territory.

At p. 13 C.N.L.R. the trial judge discussed the claim:

(a) *Jurisdiction over land.*

The plaintiffs say that their ownership interest in the territory entitles them, or their Houses or members, at their option, to govern the territory free of provincial control in all matters where their aboriginal laws conflict with the general law. I understand the position taken by their counsel to be that, upon a judgment granting them ownership and jurisdiction over these lands, they, and not the government of British Columbia, may control all land-related activities in the territory.

(b) *Jurisdiction over people.*

As an examination of the transcript of my various exchanges with counsel during argument will disclose, I have encountered some difficulty understanding this claim. I shall discuss it in greater detail later but I now understand this claim relates not just to land but rather to partial self-government limited to those areas where traditional Gitksan or Wet'suwet'en "laws" conflict with laws enacted by British Columbia pursuant to s. 92 of the *Constitution* of Canada.

I do not understand the plaintiffs are seeking a judgment striking down or declaring inoperative against them any present British Columbia enactment or regulation. Instead, they wish the court to make a declaration that some agency of the Gitksan and Wet'suwet'en people, presumably their chiefs or some other aboriginal body (although its identity was not made clear), are entitled to govern Gitksan and Wet'suwet'en people in the territory.

Then, their argument goes, they may decide which of the general laws of the province, such as laws relating to education, health, family matters and land use, etc., conflict with their own laws.

They wish such a declaration so that, if they decide not to obey any general laws of the province and proceedings are brought to force compliance, they may plead their own laws and the declaration of this court in their defence.

The plaintiffs argue that this right to jurisdiction over people is confined to Gitksan and Wet'suwet'en persons within the territory, and they say this is a right conferred upon them by the law. It appears, however, that the plaintiffs intend to require non-Gitksan or Wet'suwet'en persons within the territory to comply with aboriginal law relating to land.

Members of this court also had some difficulty in understanding the claim. Finally, counsel for the plaintiffs submitted a draft of the new remedies they were claiming in this court. They withdrew it when members of the court questioned them. Later, they made further argument and submitted a final draft in which they asserted, in connection with a claim to ownership, a right to manage the lands and resources. They claimed that in order to determine their development and safeguard their integrity as Aboriginal peoples they must have:

- a right to maintain and develop their own institutions for the regulation of the ownership, harvesting, management and conservation of those lands and resources;
- an inherent right of self-government exercisable through their own institutions, to preserve and enhance their social, political, cultural, linguistic and spiritual identity;

They were asked whether they were now challenging the validity of any particular federal or provincial law, and said they were not. Nevertheless, their position is that their jurisdiction would take priority over provincial laws, and thus this claim does have important implications for the validity or operation of provincial laws in the future.

The claim to control and manage the use of lands and resources in the territory is linked to the claim of ownership. It questions the right of the Province to legislate with respect to such things as forestry, mining, lands, and water resources within the territory.

They also claim a general right to govern the people within the territory, and to decide whether the general laws of the Province apply to those people. Furthermore, they seek to govern people who are not parties to this litigation.

There may be a third possible interpretation of the claim, which Mr. Justice Hutcheon describes in his reasons as a right of "self-regulation", a right to practice certain traditions. It would involve the consent of members of the Indian community to live by certain internal rules and to continue traditions which are not in conflict with the general laws of the Province or of Canada. Mr. Justice Hutcheon describes the area of self-regulation this way [para. 1164]:

> The traditions of the Gitksan and Wet'suwet'en societies existed long before 1846 and continued thereafter. They included the right to names and titles, the use of masks and symbols in rituals, the use of ceremonial robes and the right to occupy or control places of economic importance. The traditions, in these kinship societies, also included the institution of the clans and of the Houses in which membership descended through the mother and of course the feast system. They regulated marriage and the relations with neighbouring societies.

However, what specific system of laws and customs have continued was not made clear.

If there is no conflict between certain traditions, and provincial or federal laws, then I see no reason why the Indian people cannot agree to continue or revive such traditions. I understand, however, that they seek to extend their regulatory power to other matters. In an addendum to their factum the plaintiffs stated it was beyond the scope of this litigation to determine whether there exists a developed body of laws which can be placed alongside provincial laws.

The addendum concluded with these paragraphs:

> 64. The Appellants have, in fact, begun the process, which in some cases is quite developed, of articulating a contemporary legal framework for the management, harvesting and conservation of the resources. Particular examples of this are the fishery bylaws and the blanket trapline proposal which are both referred to in the evidence.
>
> 65. This is an ongoing process, and one likely to be spurred by the opening of real negotiations with the Provincial and Federal Respondents and, even more importantly, by this Court, through its declarations, providing the legal and constitutional space for the Appellants' laws.

I think it was this ongoing process which the trial judge had in mind when he said, at p. 204 C.N.L.R.:

It is apparent that on this issue the plaintiffs' thrust is directed not to historical practices and customs, but rather to undefined, unspecific forms of government which
some of the chiefs are just beginning to think about.

No declaration by this court is required to permit internal self-regulation in
accordance with Aboriginal traditions, if the people affected are in agreement. But
if any conflict between the exercise of such Aboriginal traditions and any law of
the Province or Canada should arise the question can be litigated. No such specific
issue is presented on this appeal.

In any event, the declaration of jurisdiction/self-government sought by the
plaintiffs is of a sort quite different from the self-regulation I have described above.
In my view, the plaintiffs' claim for jurisdiction, relating to both people and to the
territory, is for broader powers of government.

Rights of self-government encompassing a power to make general laws governing the land and resources in the territory, and the people in that territory, can
only be described as legislative powers. They serve to limit provincial legislative
jurisdiction in the territory and to allow the plaintiffs to establish a third order of
government in Canada. Putting the proposition another way: The jurisdiction of
the plaintiffs would diminish the provincial and federal share of the total distribution of legislative power in Canada.

The trial judge concluded that Aboriginal jurisdiction did not survive the assertion of British sovereignty. In particular, he said at p. 226 C.N.L.R.:

> It is inconceivable, in my view, that another form of government could exist in the
> colony after the Crown imposed English law, appointed a Governor with power to
> legislate, took title to all the land of the colony and set up procedures to govern it by a
> Governor and Legislative Council under the authority of the Crown.

In addition, in my view, the enactment of the British North America Act, 1867,
and adherence to it by the colony of British Columbia in 1871, which was accomplished by Imperial, Canadian and colonial legislation, confirmed the establishment of a federal nation with all legislative powers divided only between Canada
and the province. This also clearly and plainly extinguished any residual aboriginal
legislative or other jurisdiction, if any, which might have existed in the colonial
period.

Thus, he tied the extinguishment of any Aboriginal law-making power to the
imposition of English law in the colony of British Columbia in 1858.

It was on the date that the legislative power of the Sovereign was imposed that
any vestige of Aboriginal law-making competence was superseded. This likely
occurred when the mainland colony was founded and became a territory under the
jurisdiction of the Imperial Parliament in 1858.

Even if this view is inaccurate, a continuing Aboriginal legislative power is
inconsistent with the division of powers found in the *Constitution Act, 1867* and
introduced into British Columbia in 1871. Sections 91 and 92 of that Act exhaus-
tively distribute legislative power in Canada.

Sections 91 and 92 were interpreted in *Bank of Toronto* v. *Lambe* (1887), 12
App. Cas. 575 at 588, 4 Cart. B.N.A. 7 (P.C.) as exhausting the whole range of
legislative power in Canada. A more compelling and explicit interpretation is pro-

vided in *Ontario (Attorney General)* v. *Canada (Attorney General)* (the *References* Case) [1912] A.C. 571 at 581, 584, 3 D.L.R. 509 (P.C.):

> Now, there can be no doubt that under this organic instrument the powers distributed between the Dominion on one hand and the provinces on the other hand *cover the whole area of self-government within the whole area of Canada.* It would be subversive of the entire scheme and policy of the Act to assume that any point of internal self-government was withheld from Canada. . . .

For whatever belongs to *self-government* in Canada belongs either to the Dominion or to the provinces, within the limits of the British North America Act. [My emphasis] . . .

Any doubt that Aboriginal people are subject to this distribution is eliminated by s. 91(24), which awards legislative competence in relation to Indians to Parliament.

With respect, I think that the trial judge was correct in his view that when the Crown imposed English law on all the inhabitants of the colony and, in particular, when British Columbia entered Confederation, the Indians became subject to the legislative authorities in Canada and their laws. In 1871, two levels of government were established in British Columbia. The division of governmental powers between Canada and the Provinces left no room for a third order of government.

Such a view is in accord with the definition of Parliamentary sovereignty provided by Professor Dicey in his *Law of the Constitution*, 10th ed. (London: MacMillan & Co., 1959) at 40, quoted by the trial judge at p. 385, the key part of which is in these words:

> There is no person or body of persons who can, under the English constitution, make rules which override or derogate from an Act of Parliament, or which (to express the same thing in other words) will be enforced by the courts in contravention of an Act of Parliament.

It is also in accord with the view expressed in *Sparrow* at p.177 C.N.L.R.:

> . . . there was from the outset never any doubt that sovereignty and legislative power, and indeed the underlying title, to such lands vested in the Crown. . . .

For these reasons, the claim to jurisdiction as pleaded, in both its aspects, must fail. Furthermore, the claim to the right to control and manage the use of lands and resources in the Territory cannot succeed because the plaintiffs failed to establish the necessary ownership needed to support such a jurisdiction.

The establishment of some form of Indian self-government beyond the regulatory powers delegated by the *Indian Act* is ripe for negotiation and reconciliation. Undoubtedly, at the heart of all discussions will be the extent to which Indian self-regulation and other levels of government can co-exist. However, for the purposes of this litigation it is sufficient to repeat the views of the trial judge expressed at p. 211 C.N.L.R.:

> No court has authority to make grants of constitutional jurisdiction in the face of clear and comprehensive statutory and constitutional provisions. . . .

LAMBERT J.A. (dissenting): . . . It is important to understand that if the plaintiffs' claim to jurisdiction could ever have been considered a claim to govern the territory, and everything within it, as a form of Sovereign Government, that was certainly not the position of the plaintiffs on this appeal.

On this appeal, one aspect of the claim to self-government and self-regulation was put in two alternative ways, one relating to self-government under a concept of ownership of land and one relating to self-government resting on a proprietary interest in land. I have decided that the plaintiffs' interest need not be regarded as an ownership interest in the full sense of the common law derived from England, and I have decided that the question of whether it is a proprietary or a personal interest is a fruitless question. The interests of the plaintiffs in the lands and resources of the claimed territory are best described as Aboriginal title and as Aboriginal sustenance rights. The former I have dealt with in Division 1 of this Part and the latter I will deal with in Division 3.

If the plaintiffs' statement of their claim in this appeal had the words "aboriginal title" substituted for the words "ownership" or "proprietary interest", and if the necessary grammatical changes were made, then the plaintiffs' statement of their claim would read like this:

(a) aboriginal title to exclusive possession and occupation of lands and the use and enjoyment of the resources of those lands within the claimed territory;

(b) a right to harvest, manage and conserve those lands and resources, having regard to:

    (i) the preservation and enhancement of the quality and productivity of the natural environment;

    (ii) the immediate and long term economic, social and cultural benefits that may accrue to the Plaintiffs and their future generations; and

    (iii) consultation and cooperation with ministries and agencies of the Crown and with the private sector who may be affected by the exercise of the Plaintiffs' rights;

(c) a right to maintain and develop their institutions for the regulation of their aboriginal title and for the harvesting, management and conservation of the lands and resources;

(d) an inherent right of self-government exercisable through their own institutions to preserve and enhance their social, political, cultural, linguistic and spiritual identity;

I do not regard those claims as claims to govern the territory. I regard them as a claim to govern themselves, consisting of a claim to govern the exercise of their own rights in relation to their own Aboriginal title, and a claim to govern themselves through their own institutions in relation to the preservation of the integral parts of their distinctive cultures.

I repeat, I regard the claim to self-government and self-regulation, as it was ultimately advanced in the appeal, as a claim by the Gitksan and Wet'suwet'en peoples, first, to manage and control the exercise of their rights in relation to the use of land and resources encompassed within their collective Aboriginal title and within their other collective Aboriginal rights, and, second, to regulate the internal relationships within their own society and culture in accordance with their own customs, traditions and practices. I do not regard the claim that was ultimately advanced as a claim to sovereignty over the territory; or as a claim to control by law all legal aspects of whatever happens within the territory; or as a claim to ultimate legislative power in relation to the laws applicable within the territory; or as a claim to exclude the operation of all British Columbia law in the territory; or as a claim that in all circumstances Gitksan and Wet'suwet'en customary law must prevail over any contrary British Columbia law. Accordingly, in my opinion, arguments dealing with the division of legislative powers in Canada under the *Constitution Act, 1867*, to which British Columbia adhered in 1871, including whatever may be thought to flow from the decision of the Privy Council in *Ontario (Attorney General)* v. *Canada (Attorney General)*, [1912] A.C. 571 (P.C.), have no relevance to the claim which was ultimately advanced in this appeal. Plenary and overriding law-making power is not a part of the claim.

Without seeking to limit the claims in any way, it may be helpful to compare Aboriginal self-government and self-regulation to the self-government and self-regulation practised by a forest company or a ranching company or a Hutterite community in relation to their own land and the resources on their land, and to the ordering of their internal affairs. Such self-government and self-regulation is not in opposition to the Sovereign Power, it is an aid to the Sovereign Power and a necessary adjunct to the realization and exercise of communal rights.

So that is the claim that I will address in this Division of these reasons.

I think Aboriginal rights of self-government and self-regulation are, in their origin and nature, the same as other Aboriginal rights. They rest on the customs, traditions, and practices which formed an integral part of the distinctive culture of the Aboriginal people in question as an organized society at the time of Sovereignty. At that time those customs, traditions and practices became not only protected and nurtured by the Aboriginal society, but they also became recognized, adopted and protected by the common law and, on the assertion of Sovereignty, came to be a part of the common law.

In my opinion the rights of self-government and self-regulation of the Gitksan and Wet'suwet'en peoples in 1846 were the rights of self-government and self-regulation that their customs, traditions, and practices recognized as being an integral part of their distinctive culture at that time. I would certainly consider that the rights of self-government and self-regulation in their organized society in 1846 and earlier would have included all the rights of self-government and self-regulation set out in the claim as presented in this appeal as I have amended it above.

Whatever the self-government and self-regulation rights of the Gitksan and Wet'suwet'en peoples were in 1846, a number of events have occurred since then which might serve to diminish those rights:

(a) The assertion of British Sovereignty over the whole geographic extent of British Columbia (taken in this appeal to have occurred in 1846) would have had the following potential diminishing consequences quite apart from the enlarging consequence of protecting all Aboriginal rights by absorbing them as part of the common law.

    (i)   Those rights which should properly be considered to be inconsistent with British Sovereignty would have been implicity extinguished by the assertion of British Sovereignty. That would include the right to make war and the right to impose their own customs on the settlers who were themselves protected by British Sovereignty and by the common law.

    (ii)   Those rights which were so entirely repugnant to natural justice, equity, and good conscience that they could not, without modification, ever be a part of the common law would never have been absorbed by the common law or have been recognized and protected by it, at least not until such a modification occurred. (See *Mabo* v. *Queensland* at p. 51 C.N.L.R.] and *Inasa* v. *Oshodi* at [1934] A.C. 99 at 105 (J.C.P.C.))

(iii)   The common law, to the extent that it was not from local circumstances inapplicable, would apply throughout the territory and if it was inconsistent with specific Aboriginal rights of self-government and self-regulation, and if the common law, in those parts of it that were inconsistent with the Gitksan and Wet'suwet'en rights of self-government and self-regulation, was not from local circumstances inapplicable, then the common law might have brought about an implicit extinguishment of those aspects of the Gitksan and Wet'suwet'en rights of self-government and self-regulation on which the inconsistency occurred. In my opinion there would have been very little of the civil side of the common law, which, in its potential application to the Gitksan and Wet'suwet'en peoples in their area of the Province (where no settlers or administrators had arrived in 1846), would not have been "from local circumstances inapplicable". This view is the view adopted by Blackstone in relation to the American colonies, as quoted in *Mabo* v. *Queensland* at pp. 22–23 [A.L.R.; pp. 28–29 C.N.L.R.].

(b)   Those aspects of the common law which were from local circumstances inapplicable to the Gitksan and Wet'suwet'en peoples in 1846 might have become applicable to them by 18 November, 1858 when the common law of England was proclaimed to apply throughout British Columbia, though after that, in its application in British Columbia, it became British Columbia common law and no longer English common law. I do not think it likely that such a change occurred, though it is possible.

(c)   Between 1858 and 1871, there may have been Proclamations or Ordinances of the Sovereign Power, acting legislatively, which might have extinguished, by clear and plain intention, aspects of the rights of self-government or self-regulation of the Gitksan or Wet'suwet'en peoples. We were not referred in the course of this appeal to any such Proclamation or Ordinance.

(d)   Between 1871 and 1982 there may have been enacted by the Sovereign Power acting legislatively in the Parliament of Canada an enactment which might have extinguished, by clear and plain intention, aspects of the rights of self-government or self-regulation of the Gitksan and Wet'suwet'en peoples. We were not referred in this appeal to any such enactments.

Apart from the diminution of rights brought about by extinguishment in one of the four ways I have described in paragraphs (a), (b), (c) and (d) above, it is my opinion that the Aboriginal rights of self-government and self-regulation of the Gitksan and Wet'suwet'en peoples based on their customs, traditions, and practices in 1846 and earlier, to the extent that those customs, traditions and practices formed an integral part of their distinctive culture, became rights recognized, affirmed, and protected by the common law in 1846 and have been carried forward to 1982 when they received constitutional protection under s. 35 of the *Constitution Act, 1982*. Those rights now exist in modern form, based on their 1846 form, but expressed in modern terms and with modern usages.

I propose to summarize. The Gitksan and Wet'suwet'en peoples had rights of self-government and self-regulation in 1846, at the time of sovereignty. Those rights rested on the customs, traditions and practices of those peoples to the extent that they formed an integral part of their distinctive cultures. The assertion of British Sovereignty only took away such rights as were inconsistent with the concept of British Sovereignty. The introduction of English Law into British Columbia was only an introduction of such laws as were not from local circumstances inapplicable. The existence of a body of Gitksan and Wet'suwet'en customary law would be expected to render much of the newly introduced English Law inapplicable to the Gitksan and Wet'suwet'en peoples, particularly since none of the institutions of English Law were available to them in their territory, so that their local circumstances would tend to have required the continuation of their own laws. The division of powers brought about when British Columbia entered confederation in 1871 would not, in my opinion, have made any difference to Gitksan and Wet'suwet'en customary laws. Since 1871, Provincial laws of general application would apply to the Gitksan and Wet'suwet'en people, and Federal laws, particularly the *Indian Act*, would also have applied to them. But to the extent that Gitksan and Wet'suwet'en customary law lay at the core of their Indianness, that law would not be abrogated by Provincial laws of general application nor by Federal laws, unless those Federal laws demonstrated a clear and plain intention of the Sovereign power in Parliament to abrogate the Gitksan or Wet'suwet'en customary laws. Subject to those over-riding considerations, Gitksan and Wet'suwet'en customary laws of self-government and self-regulation have continued to the present day and are now constitutionally protected by s. 35 of the *Constitution Act, 1982.* . . .

The trial judge treated the claim to "jurisdiction" as a claim to complete sovereignty. He then disallowed that claim as being inconsistent with the sovereignty of the Crown over the whole of British Columbia. I do not think that the claim to "jurisdiction" was ever intended to be a claim to sovereignty. Rather, it was a claim to a measure of self-government and self-regulation. It was a claim resting, like all the claims, on Aboriginal rights. As such, it should have been considered by the trial judge who had decided to consider the plaintiffs' claims to all the rights to which they were entitled. But what happened was that again the trial judge put the claim on the most extreme basis possible, relied on the authorities to disallow it on that basis, and failed to consider the included claim to simple rights of self-government and self-regulation at all. By treating this claim as a claim to sovereignty and as a claim to govern the territory and everyone and everything within it, the trial judge misconceived the law applicable to questions of Aboriginal self-government and self-regulation. When he applied the incorrect law to the basic evidence, he reached the wrong conclusions on the subject. Those conclusions cannot stand and do not bind this Court.

In my opinion the Gitksan and Wet'suwet'en peoples have Aboriginal rights of self-government and self-regulation which they may employ to control the exercise of their Aboriginal title to the possession, occupation, use and enjoyment of land within the territory and to the resources of that land. Further, in my opinion, the Gitksan and Wet'suwet'en peoples have rights of self-government and self-regulation, exercisable through their own institutions, to preserve and enhance their social, political, cultural, linguistic and spiritual identity. These Aboriginal rights of self-government and self-regulation will in large measure be supplementary to and entirely consistent with the overall government functions carried out by Canada and British Columbia, just like the rights of self-government and self-regulation of a forest company over itself and its forests, a cattle company over itself and its grazing land, or a Hutterite community over the social and religious life of its members. However, there may be other functions of self-government and self-regulation, resting on Aboriginal practices, traditions and customs which form a part of the distinctive culture of the Gitksan and Wet'suwet'en peoples, which supplant and prevail over general laws which are inconsistent with those practices, traditions and customs and which were brought into effect without any clear and plain intention to extinguish those practices, traditions and customs. Consideration of such questions must await the time when they are specifically raised.

4.   *R. v. Pamajewon,* **[1996] 4 C.N.L.R. 164 (S.C.C.). Lamer C.J., La Forest, L'Heureux-Dubé, Sopinka, Gonthier, Cory, McLachlin, Iacobucci, and Major JJ., August 22, 1996**

> The Supreme Court of Canada affirmed the Ontario Court of Appeal's decision in *Pamajewon* by upholding the convictions under the *Criminal Code* dealing with gaming. The court affirmed a number of principles that are useful in exploring how courts may interpret an Aboriginal right of self-government. First, assuming that s. 35(1) may encompass a right of self-government, the claim of such a right is no different from any other claim for an Aboriginal right under s. 35(1) and must therefore be held to the same legal standard (such as that laid out in *Van der Peet* and presumably other relevant tests such as *Sparrow*). The appellants claimed the right to operate casinos and regulate high-stakes gambling on reserve, describing this as a "broad right to manage the use of their reserve lands." The court noted that this right is not specific enough for the *Van der Peet* test, which requires that the asserted right must be examined in light of the specific history and culture of the Aboriginal group claiming the right and in light of the specific circumstances of the case. Second, the court held that based on the evidence presented, high-stakes gambling was not an activity that formed an integral part of the distinctive cultures of the Shawanaga and Eagle Lake First Nations. Of particular importance is the fact that court focuses on the need for specificity in analyzing any Aboriginal right to self-government, if such a right exists within the rubric of s. 35(1). The onus to demonstrate this level of specificity is placed on the Aboriginal claiming such a right.

LAMER C.J. (LA FOREST, SOPINKA, GONTHIER, CORY, MCLACHLIN, IACOBUCCI and MAJOR JJ., concurring)— . . .

1.   This appeal raises the question of whether the conduct of high stakes gambling by the Shawanaga and Eagle Lake First Nations falls within the scope of the Aboriginal rights recognized and affirmed by s. 35(1) of the *Constitution Act, 1982.* . . .

3.   The appellants Pamajewon and Jones are members of the Shawanaga First Nation. On March 29, 1993, both were found guilty of the offence of keeping a common gaming house contrary to s. 201(1) of the *Criminal Code,* R.S.C., 1985, c. C–46. Section 201(1) of the *Criminal Code* reads:

> 201. (1) Every one who keeps a common gaming house or common betting house is guilty of an indictable offence and liable to imprisonment for a term not exceeding two years.

4.   The charges arose out of the high stakes bingo and other gambling activities which took place on the Shawanaga First Nation Reservation between September 11, 1987 and October 6, 1990. Throughout this period Jones was Chief of the Shawanaga First Nation and Pamajewon was a member of the Shawanaga Band Council.

5.   Gambling on the reservation took place pursuant to the authority of the Shawanaga First Nation lottery law. This lottery law, enacted by the Band Council in August 1987, was not a by-law passed pursuant to s. 81 of the *Indian Act*, R.S.C., 1985, c. I–5.

6.   The Shawanaga First Nation did not have a provincial licence authorizing its gambling activities. The band had met with the Ontario Lottery Corporation but had refused the Corporation's offer of a gambling licence on the basis that such a licence was unnecessary because the band had an inherent right of self-government.

7.   At trial the appellants Pamajewon and Jones were convicted. Their convictions were upheld by the Ontario Court of Appeal.

Gardner, Pitchenese and Gardner

8.   The appellants Arnold Gardner, Jack Pitchenese and Allan Gardner are all members of the Eagle Lake First Nation. On November 19, 1993 they were found guilty of conducting a scheme for the purpose of determining the winners of property, contrary to s. 206(1)(*d*) of the Code. Section 206(1)(*d*) of the Code reads:

> 206. (1) Every one is guilty of an indictable offence and liable to imprisonment for a term not exceeding two years who . . .
>
> (*d*) conducts or manages any scheme, contrivance or operation of any kind for the purpose of determining who, or the holders of what lots, tickets, numbers or chances, are the winners of any property so proposed to be advanced, lent, given, sold or disposed of. . . .

9.   At the time they were charged Arnold Gardner was Chief of the Eagle Lake Band and chairman of the bingo committee. Jack Pitchenese managed the bingo operations. Allan Gardner was the chief bingo caller.

10.   The gambling activities on the Eagle Lake Reserve were conducted pursuant to the Eagle Lake First Nation Band Council's lottery law, enacted in March 1985. This lottery law was not a by-law passed pursuant to s. 81 of the *Indian Act*.

11.   The Eagle Lake First Nation did not have a provincial licence authorizing its

gambling operations; the band had refused to negotiate with the Ontario Lottery Commission, even though it was approached for this purpose by the Ministry of Consumer and Commercial Relations. The band would not negotiate because it asserted the right to be self-regulating in its economic activities.

12.   The appellants Gardner, Pitchenese and Gardner were convicted at trial. Their convictions were upheld by the Ontario Court of Appeal. . . .

20.   Leave to appeal to this Court was granted on June 1, 1995, [1995] 2 S.C.R. viii. On July 6, 1995 the following constitutional question was stated:

> Are s. 201, s. 206 or s. 207 of the *Criminal Code,* separately or in combination, of no force or effect with respect to the appellants, by virtue of s. 52 of the *Constitution Act, 1982* in the circumstances of these proceedings, by reason of the aboriginal or treaty rights within the meaning of s. 35 of the *Constitution Act, 1982* invoked by the appellants?

21.   The appellants appealed on the basis that the Court of Appeal erred in restricting Aboriginal title to rights that are activity and site specific and in concluding that self-government only extends to those matters which were governed by ancient laws or customs. The appellant argued further that the Court of Appeal erred in concluding that the Code extinguished self-government regarding gaming and in not addressing whether the Code's gaming provisions unjustifiably interfered with the rights recognized and affirmed by s. 35(1) of the *Constitution Act, 1982.* . . .

23.   The resolution of the appellants' claim in this case rests on the application of the test, laid out by this Court in *R. v. Van der Peet,* [1996] 2 S.C.R. 507, for determining the Aboriginal rights recognized and affirmed by s. 35(1) of the *Constitution Act, 1982.* The appellants in this case are claiming that the gambling activities in which they took part, and their respective bands' regulation of those gambling activities, fell within the scope of the Aboriginal rights recognized and affirmed by s. 35(1). *Van der Peet, supra,* lays out the test for determining the practices, customs and traditions which fall within s. 35(1) and, as such, provides the legal standard against which the appellants' claim must be measured.

24.   The appellants' claim involves the assertion that s. 35(1) encompasses the right of self-government, and that this right includes the right to regulate gambling activities on the reservation. Assuming without deciding that s. 35(1) includes self-government claims, the applicable legal standard is nonetheless that laid out in *Van der Peet, supra.* Assuming s. 35(1) encompasses claims to Aboriginal self-government, such claims must be considered in light of the purposes underlying that provision and must, therefore, be considered against the test derived from consideration of those purposes. This is the test laid out in *Van der Peet, supra.* In so far as they can be made under s. 35(1), claims to self-government are no different from other claims to the enjoyment of Aboriginal rights and must, as such, be measured against the same standard.

25.   In *Van der Peet, supra,* the test for identifying Aboriginal rights was said to be as follows, at para. 46:

> in order to be an aboriginal right an activity must be an element of a practice, custom or tradition integral to the distinctive culture of the aboriginal group claiming the right.

In applying this test the Court must first identify the exact nature of the activity claimed to be a right and must then go on to determine whether, on the evidence presented to the trial judge, and on the facts as found by the trial judge, that activity could be said to be (*Van der Peet,* at para. 59) "a defining feature of the culture in question" prior to contact with Europeans.

26.   I now turn to the first part of the *Van der Peet* test, the characterization of the appellants' claim. In *Van der Peet, supra,* the Court held at para. 53 that:

> To characterize an applicant's claim correctly, a court should consider such factors as the nature of the action which the applicant is claiming was done pursuant to an Aboriginal right, the nature of the governmental regulation, statute or action being impugned, and the practice, custom or tradition being relied upon to establish the right.

When these factors are considered in this case it can be seen that the correct characterization of the appellants' claim is that they are claiming the right to participate in, and to regulate, high stakes gambling activities on the reservation. The activity which the appellants organized, and which their bands regulated, was high stakes gambling. The statute which they argue violates those rights prohibits gambling subject only to a few very limited exceptions (laid out in s. 207 of the Code). Finally, the applicants rely in support of their claim on the fact that the "Ojibwa people . . . had a long tradition of public games and sporting events, which predated the arrival of Europeans". Thus, the activity in which the appellants were engaged and which their bands regulated, the statute they are impugning, and the historical evidence on which they rely, all relate to the conduct and regulation of gambling. As such, the most accurate characterization of the appellants' claim is that they are asserting that s. 35(1) recognizes and affirms the rights of the Shawanaga and Eagle Lake First Nations to participate in, and to regulate, gambling activities on their respective reserve lands.

27.   The appellants themselves would have this Court characterize their claim as to "a broad right to manage the use of their reserve lands". To so characterize the appellants' claim would be to cast the Court's inquiry at a level of excessive generality. Aboriginal rights, including any asserted right to self-government, must be looked at in light of the specific circumstances of each case and, in particular, in light of the specific history and culture of the Aboriginal group claiming the right. The factors laid out in *Van der Peet,* and applied, *supra,* allow the Court to consider the appellants' claim at the appropriate level of specificity; the characterization put forward by the appellants would not allow the Court to do so.

28.   I now turn to the second branch of the *Van der Peet* test, the consideration of whether the participation in, and regulation of, gambling on the reserve lands was an integral part of the distinctive cultures of the Shawanaga or Eagle Lake First

Nations. The evidence presented at both the Pamajewon and Gardner trials does not demonstrate that gambling, or that the regulation of gambling, was an integral part of the distinctive cultures of the Shawanaga or Eagle Lake First Nations. In fact, the only evidence presented at either trial dealing with the question of the importance of gambling was that of James Morrison, who testified at the Pamajewon trial with regards to the importance and prevalence of gaming in Ojibwa culture. While Mr. Morrison's evidence does demonstrate that the Ojibwa gambled, it does not demonstrate that gambling was of central significance to the Ojibwa people. Moreover, his evidence in no way addresses the extent to which this gambling was the subject of regulation by the Ojibwa community. His account is of informal gambling activities taking place on a small-scale; he does not describe large-scale activities, subject to community regulation, of the sort at issue in this appeal.

29.   I would note that neither of the trial judges in these cases relied upon findings of fact regarding the importance of gambling to the Ojibwa; however, upon review of the evidence I find myself in agreement with the conclusion arrived at by Osborne J.A. when he said first, at p. 400, that there "is no evidence to support a conclusion that gambling generally or high stakes gambling of the sort in issue here, were part of the First Nations' historic cultures and traditions, or an aspect of their use of their land" and, second, at p. 400, that "there is no evidence that gambling on the reserve lands generally was ever the subject matter of Aboriginal regulation". . . .

30.   Given this evidentiary record, it is clear that the appellants have failed to demonstrate that the gambling activities in which they were engaged, and their respective bands' regulation of those activities, took place pursuant to an Aboriginal right recognized and affirmed by s. 35(1) of the *Constitution Act, 1982.* . . .

31.   These are my reasons for dismissing the appeal and for affirming the decision of the Court of Appeal upholding the trial judge's conviction of the various appellants for violating ss. 201 and 206 of the Code. . . .

32.   For the reasons given above, the constitutional question must be answered as follows: . . . No. . . .

EXAMPLES

5.   *Indian Act*, **R.S.C. 1985, c. I–5**

Selected provisions of ss. 81–83 of the *Indian Act* relating to powers of a band council.

POWERS OF THE COUNCIL . . .

81.(1) The council of a band may make by-laws not inconsistent with this Act or with any regulation made by the Governor in Council or the Minister, for any or all of the following purposes, namely:

(a)   to provide for the health of residents on the reserve and to prevent the spreading of contagious and infectious diseases;

(b)   the regulation of traffic;

(c)   the observance of law and order;

(d)   the prevention of disorderly conduct and nuisances;

(e)   the protection against and prevention of trespass by cattle and other domestic animals, the establishment of pounds, the appointment of pound-keepers, the regulation of their duties and the provision for fees and charges for their services;

(f)   the construction and maintenance of water courses, roads, bridges, ditches, fences and other local works;

(g)   the dividing of the reserve or a portion thereof into zones and the prohibition of the construction or maintenance of any class of buildings or the carrying on of any class of business, trade or calling in any such zone;

(h)   the regulation of the construction, repair and use of buildings, whether owned by the band or by individual members of the band;

(i)   the survey and allotment of reserve lands among the members of the band and the establishment of a register of Certificates of Possession and Certificates of Occupation relating to allotments and the setting apart of reserve lands for common use, if authority therefor has been granted under section 60;

(j)   the destruction and control of noxious weeds;

(k)   the regulation of bee-keeping and poultry raising;

(l)   the construction and regulation of the use of public wells, cisterns, reservoirs and other water supplies;

(m)   the control and prohibition of public games, sports, races, athletic contests and other amusements;

(n)   the regulation of the conduct and activities of hawkers, peddlers or others who enter the reserve to buy, sell or otherwise deal in wares or merchandise;

(o)   the preservation, protection and management of fur-bearing animals, fish and other game on the reserve;

(p)   the removal and punishment of persons trespassing upon the reserve or frequenting the reserve for prohibited purposes;

(p.1) the residence of band members and other persons on the reserve;

(p.2) to provide for the rights of spouses and children who reside with members of the band on the reserve with respect to any matter in relation to which the council may make by-laws in respect of members of the band;

(p.3) to authorize the Minister to make payments out of capital or revenue moneys to persons whose names were deleted from the Band List of the band;

(p.4) to bring subsection 10(3) or 64.1(2) into effect in respect of the band;

(q)   with respect to any matter arising out of or ancillary to the exercise of powers under this section; and

(r)   the imposition on summary conviction of a fine not exceeding one thousand dollars or imprisonment for a term not exceeding thirty days, or both, for violation of a by-law made under this section.

(2) Where any by-law of a band is contravened and a conviction entered, in addition to any other remedy and to any penalty imposed by the by-law, the court in which the conviction has been entered, and any court of competent jurisdiction thereafter, may make an order prohibiting the continuation or repetition of the offence by the person convicted.

(3) Where any by-law of a band passed is contravened, in addition to any other remedy and to any penalty imposed by the by-law, such contravention may be restrained by court action at the instance of the band council. R.S. 1970. c. I–6. s. 81; 1980–81–82–83, c. 47, s. 53; R.S. 1985 (lst Supp.). c. 32. s. 15.

82.(1) A copy of every by-law made under the authority of section 81 shall be forwarded by mail by the chief or a member of the council of the band to the Minister within four days after it is made.

(2) A by-law made under section 81 comes into force forty days after a copy thereof is forwarded to the Minister pursuant to subsection (l), unless it is disallowed by the Minister within that period, but the Minister may declare the by-law to be in force at any time before the expiration of that period. R.S. 1970, c. I–6. . . .

83.(1) Without prejudice to the powers conferred by section 81, the council of a band may, subject to the approval of the Minister, make by-laws for any or all of the following purposes, namely,

(a) subject to subsections (2) and (3), taxation for local purposes of land, or interests in land, in the reserve, including rights to occupy, possess or use land in the reserve;

(a.1) the licensing of businesses, callings, trades and occupations;

(b) the appropriation and expenditure of moneys of the band to defray band expenses;

(c) the appointment of officials to conduct the business of the council, prescribing their duties and providing for their remuneration out of any moneys raised pursuant to paragraph (a);

(d) the payment of remuneration, in such amount as may be approved by the Minister, to chiefs and councillors, out of any moneys raised pursuant to paragraph (a);

(e) the enforcement of payment of amounts that are payable pursuant to this section, including arrears and interest;

(e.1) the imposition and recovery of interest on amounts that are payable pursuant to this section, where those amounts are not paid before they are due, and the calculation of that interest;

(f) the raising of money from band members to support band projects; and

(g) with respect to any matter arising out of or ancillary to the exercise of powers under this section.

(2) An expenditure made out of moneys raised pursuant to subsection (l) must be so made under the authority of a by-law of the council of the band.

(3) A by-law made under paragraph (1)(a) must provide an appeal procedure in respect of assessments made for the purposes of taxation under that paragraph.

(4) The Minister may approve the whole or a part only of a by-law made under subsection (1).

(5) The Governor in Council may make regulations not inconsistent with this section respecting the exercise of the by-law making powers of bands under this section.

(6) A by-law made under this section remains in force only to the extent that it is consistent with the regulations made under subsection (5). R.S. 1970. c. I–6. s. 83; R.S. 1985 (4th Supp.), c. 17. s. 10. . . .

6. ***Whitebear Band Council* v. *Carpenters Provincial Council of Saskatchewan*, [1982] 3 C.N.L.R. 181 (Sask. C.A.). Bayda C.J.S., MacDonald and Cameron JJ.A., April 6, 1982**

> This decision concerned whether labour relations between Indians and individuals hired to build on a reserve are a matter of federal jurisdiction. In so deciding, the Saskatchewan Court of Appeal provided a widely accepted discussion on the nature of Indian band councils. Jack Woodward, in *Native Law*, states (p. 166, n. 76) that the generalized nature of the court's comments are flawed and points out that not all band councils are elected, some are governed by band custom, not all powers exercised by band councils relate to the reserve, and not all adults resident on reserve are necessarily electors, only band members are electors.

CAMERON J.A.:— . . . As municipal councils are the "creatures" of the legislatures of the provinces, so Indian band councils are the "creatures" of the Parliament of Canada. Parliament, in exercising the exclusive jurisdiction conferred upon it by s. 91(24) of the *B.N.A. Act* to legislate in relation to "Indians, and Lands reserved for the Indians", enacted the *Indian Act*, R.S.C. 1970, c. I–6, which provides—among its extensive provisions for Indian status, civil rights, assistance, and so on, and the use and management of Indian reserves—for the election of a chief and 12 councillors by and from among the members of an Indian band resident on an Indian reserve. These elected officials constitute Indian band councils, who in general terms are intended by Parliament to provide some measure—even if rather rudimentary—of local government in relation to life on Indian reserves and to act as something of an intermediary between the band and the Minister of Indian Affairs.

More specifically, s. 8l of the Act clothes Indian band councils with such powers and duties in relation to an Indian reserve and its inhabitants are usually associated with a rural municipality and its council: a band council may enact by-laws for the regulation of traffic, the construction and maintenance of public works, zoning, the control of public games and amusements and of hawkers and peddlers, the regulation of the construction, repair and use of buildings, and so on. Hence a band council exercises—by way of delegation from Parliament—these and other municipal and governmental powers in relation to the reserve whose inhabitants have elected it.

I think it worth noting that the *Indian Act* contemplates a measured maturing of self-government on Indian reserves. Section 69 of the Act empowers the Governor in Council to "permit" a band to manage and spend its revenue moneys—pursuant to regulation by the Governor in Council—and by s. 83 the Governor in Council may declare that a band "has reached an advance stage of development", in which event the band council may, with the approval of the minister, raise money by way of assessment and taxation of reserve lands and the licensing of reserve businesses. Until then, the band council derives its funds principally from the government of Canada.

The Governor in Council has made no declaration under s. 83 of the Act declaring the Whitebear Band Council to have reached an advanced stage of development; however, the Whitebear Band Council is the subject of an order of the Governor in Council made pursuant to s. 69 of the Act, and has been empowered to control, manage and expend in whole or in part its revenue moneys in accordance with the regulations made pursuant to this section, which require it to establish, as it has done, an account with a recognized financial institution, under the authority of three persons, two of whom are members of the band. The chief and Mr. Paul, both members of the council, were given this authority.

In addition to their municipal and governmental function, band councils are also empowered by the *Indian Act* to perform an advisory role, and in some cases to exercise a power of veto with respect to certain activities of the minister in relation to the reserve, including the spending of Indian moneys, both capital and revenue, and the use and possession of reserve lands.

Moreover, in light of the provisions of the single contribution agreement and some of the terms of the consolidated contribution agreement, it appears that in practice Indian band councils from time to-time act as agents of the Minister of Indian Affairs and representatives of the members of the reserve with respect to the implementation of certain federal government programs designed for Indian reserves and their residents—a complementary role consistent with their function.

In summary, an Indian band council is an elected public authority, dependent on Parliament for its existence, powers and responsibilities, whose essential function it is to exercise municipal and government power—delegated to it by Parliament—in relation to the Indian reserve whose inhabitants have elected it; as such, it is to act from time to time as the agent of the minister and the representative of the band with respect to the administration and delivery of certain federal programs for the benefit of Indians on Indian reserves, and to perform an advisory, and in some cases a decisive, role in relation to the exercise by the minister of certain of his statutory authority relative to the reserve. . . .

As I have observed, the primary function of an Indian band council is to provide a measure of self-government by Indians on Indian reserves. In enacting by-laws pursuant to their power to do so, and in performing generally their local government function, an Indian band council is doing that which Parliament is exclusively empowered to do pursuant to s. 92(24) of the *B.N.A. Act* but which Parliament, through the *Indian Act,* has delegated band councils to do. In this sense, the function of an Indian band council is very much federal. So too, in my opinion, are their associated functions—acting at once as the representative body of the inhabitants of the reserve and the agent of the minister with regard to federal programs for reserves and their residents—and participating in certain of the decisions of the minister in relation to the reserve. Given this, the provisions of the *Indian Act* to which I have referred and the origin and nature, purpose and function of an Indian band council, I am satisfied that the power generally to regulate the labour relations of a band council and its employees, engaged in those activities contemplated by the *Indian Act*, forms an integral part of primary federal jurisdiction in relation to "Indians, and Lands reserved for the Indians" pursuant to s. 91(24) of the *B.N.A. Act. . . .*

7.   *Sechelt Indian Band Self-Government Act,* S.C. **1986, c. 27**

An act relating to self-government for the Sechelt Indian Band. . . .

3.   For greater certainty, nothing in this Act shall be construed so as to abrogate or derogate from any existing aboriginal or treaty rights of the members of the Sechelt Indian Band, or any other aboriginal peoples of Canada, under section 35 of the Constitution Act, 1982.

PURPOSES OF ACT

4.   The purposes of this Act are to enable the Sechelt Indian Band to exercise and maintain self-government on Sechelt lands and to obtain control over and the administration of the resources and services available to its members.

SECHELT INDIAN BAND

5.(1)   The Sechelt Indian Band is hereby established to replace the Indian Act Sechelt band.

(2)   The Indian Act Sechelt Band ceases to exist, and all its rights, titles, interests, assets, obligations and liabilities, including those of its band council, vest in the Sechelt Indian Band established under subsection (1).

Capacity and Powers of Band

6.   The Band is a legal entity and has, subject to this Act, the capacity, rights, powers and privileges of a natural person and, without restricting the generality of the foregoing, may

      (a)   enter into contracts or agreement;

      (b)   acquire and hold property or any interest therein, and sell or otherwise dispose of that property or interest;

      (c)   expend or invest moneys;

      (d)   borrow money;

      (e)   sue or be sued; and

      (f)   do such other things as are conducive to the exercise of its rights, powers and privileges.

7.   The powers and duties of the Band shall be carried out in accordance with its constitution.

SECHELT INDIAN BAND COUNCIL

8.   The Sechelt Indian Band Council shall be the governing body of the Band, and its members shall be elected in accordance with the constitution of the Band.

9.   The Band shall act through the Council in exercising its powers and carrying out its duties and functions.

BAND CONSTITUTION

10.(1) The constitution of the Band shall be in writing and may

      (a)   establish the composition of council, the terms of office and tenure of its members and procedures relating to the election of council members

    (b)   establish the procedures or processes to be followed by Council in exercising the Band's powers and carrying out its duties

    (c)   provide for a system of financial accountability of the council to the members of the Band, including audit arrangments and the publication of financial reports

    (d)   include a membership code for the Band;

    (e)   establish rules and procedures relating to the holding of referenda referred to in section 12 or subsection 21(3) or provided for in the constitution of the Band;

    (f)   establish rules and procedures to be followed in respect of the disposition of rights and interests in the Sechelt lands;

    (g)   set out specific legislative powers of the Council selected from among the general class of matters set out in section 14; and

    (h)   provide for any other matters relating to the government of the Band, its members or Sechelt lands.

(2) A membership code established in the constitution of the Band shall respect rights to membership in the *Indian Act* Sechelt band acquired under the *Indian Act* immediately prior to the establishment of that code. . . .

Legislative Powers of Council

14.(1) The Council has, to the extent that it is authorized by the constitution of the Band to do so, the power to make laws in relation to matters coming within any of the following classes of matters:

    (a)   access to and residence on Sechelt lands;

    (b)   zoning and land use planning in respect of Sechelt lands;

    (c)   expropriation, for community purposes, of interests in Sechelt lands by the Band;

    (d)   the use, construction, maintenance, repair and demolition of buildings and structures on Sechelt lands;

    (e)   taxation, for local purposes, of interests in Sechelt lands, and of occupants and tenants of Sechelt land in respect of their interests in those lands, including assessment, collection and enforcement procedures and appeals relating thereto;

    (f)   the administration and management of property belonging to the Band;

    (g)   education of Band members on Sechelt lands;

    (h)   social and welfare services with respect to Band members, including, without restricting the generality of the foregoing, the custody and placement of children of Band members;

    (i)   health services on Sechelt lands;

    (j)   the preservation and management of natural resources on Sechelt lands;

    (k)   the preservation, protection and management of fur-bearing animals, fish and game on Sechelt lands;

    (l)   public order and safety on Sechelt lands;

    (m)   the construction, maintenance and management of roads and the regulation of traffic on Sechelt lands;

(n)　the operation of businesses, professions and trades on Sechelt lands;

(o)　the prohibition of the sale, barter, supply, manufacture or possession of intoxications on Sechelt lands and any exceptions to a prohibition of possession;

(p)　subject to subsection (2), the imposition on summary conviction of fines or imprisonment for the contravention of any law made by the Band government;

(q)　the devolution, by testate or intestate succession, of real property of Band members on Sechelt lands and personal property of Band members ordinarily resident on Sechelt lands;

(r)　financial administration of the Band;

(s)　the conduct of Band elections and referenda;

(t)　the creation of administrative bodies and agencies to assist in the administrative of the affairs of the Band; and

(u)　matters related to the good government of the Band, its members or Sechelt lands.

(2) A law made in respect of the class of matters set out in paragraph (1)(p) may specify a maximum fine or a maximum term of imprisonment or both, but the maximum fine may not exceed two thousand dollars and the maximum term of imprisonment may not exceed six months.

(3) For greater certainty, the Council has the power to adopt any laws of British Columbia as its own law if it is authorized by the constitution to make laws in relation to the subject-matter of those laws.

(4) A law made by the Council may require the holding of a licence or permit and may provide for the issuance thereof and fees therefor. . . .

15.　　The Council may exercise any legislative power granted to it by or pursuant to an Act of the legislature of British Columbia. . . .

TRANSFER OF LANDS

23(1)　The title to all lands that were, immediately prior to the coming into force of this section, reserves, within the meaning of the *Indian Act*, of the Indian Act Sechelt band is hereby transferred in fee simple to the Band, subject to the rights, interests and conditions referred to in section 24.

(2) In subsection (1), "reserves" includes surrendered lands, within the meaning of the *Indian Act*, that have not been sold or the title to which has not been otherwise transferred.

(3) All rights and interests of the Indian Act Sechelt band in respect of the lands referred to in subsection (1) cease to exist on the coming into force of this section. . . .

SECHELT LANDS

31.　　For greater certainty, Sechelt lands are lands reserved for the Indians within the meaning of Class 24 of section 91 of the *Constitution Act, 1867.*

APPLICATION OF THE INDIAN ACT

35.(1) Subject to section 36, the *Indian Act* applies, with such modifications as the circumstances require, in respect of the Band, its members, the Council and

Sechelt lands except to the extent that the *Indian Act* is inconsistent with this Act, the constitution of the Band or a law of the Band.

(2) For greater certainty, the *Indian Act* applies for the purpose of determining which members of the Band are "Indians" within the meaning of the Act.

(3) For greater certainty, section 87 of the *Indian Act* applies, with such modifications as the circumstances require, in respect of the Band and its members who are Indians within the meaning of that Act, subject to any laws made by the Council in relation to the class of matters set out in paragraph 14(1)(e).

36.   The Governor in Council may, on the advice of the Minister, by order declare that the *Indian Act* or any provision thereof does not apply to

(a)   the Band or its members, or

(b)   any portion of Sechelt lands,

and may, on the advice of the Minister, by order revoke any such order.

APPLICATION OF LAWS OF CANADA

37.   All federal laws of general application in force in Canada are applicable to and in respect of the Band, its members and Sechelt lands, except to the extent that those laws are inconsistent with this Act.

APPLICATION OF LAWS OF BRITISH COLUMBIA

38.   Laws of general application of British Columbia apply to or in respect of the members of the Band except to the extent that those laws are inconsistent with the terms of any treaty, this or any other Act of Parliament, the constitution of the Band or a law of the Band. . . .

8.   *Cree-Naskapi (of Quebec) Act,* S.C. 1984, c. 18

APPLICATION OF INDIAN ACT

5.   Except for the purpose of determining which of the Cree beneficiaries and Naskapi beneficiaries are "Indians" within the meaning of the *Indian Act,* the *Indian Act* does not apply to Cree bands or the Naskapi band, nor does it apply on or in respect of Category IA or IA-N land.

BAND BY-LAWS AND RESOLUTIONS

6.   A by-law of a band made under this Act may have application within the following territorial limits:

(a)   that band's Category IA or IA-N; and

(b)   Category III land situated within the perimeter of that band's Category IA or IA-N land and the ownership of which was ceded by letters patent or by any other method

(i)   prior to November 11, 1975, in the case of Category III land within the perimeter of Category IA land, or

(ii)   prior to January 31, 1978, in the case of Category III land within the perimeter of Category IA-N land. . . .

REGULATIONS

10.   The Governor in Council may make regulations.

(a)   prescribing anything that by this Act is to be prescribed; and

(b)   generally for carrying out the purposes and provisions of this Act.

INCORPORATION BY REFERENCE OF PROVINCIAL LAWS

11.(1)   For the purpose of applying the portion of paragraph 5.1.13 of the *James Bay and Northern Quebec Agreement* and of paragraph 5.1.13 of the Northeastern Quebec Agreement dealing with the leasing of lands and the granting of real rights to non-Natives, the Governor in Council may make regulations for the purpose of making provincial law in force in the Province applicable to leasehold interests or other real rights in Category IA or IA-N land granted to non-beneficiaries for periods exceeding five years, including any renewal thereof.

(2)   For the purposes of subsection (1), a non beneficiary is a person who is not

(a)   a Cree beneficiary, Naskapi beneficiary or Inuk of Fort George;

(b)   a corporation or other body established pursuant to either of the Agreements;

(c)   a corporation or other body the majority of whose shareholders or members are Cree beneficiaries, Naskapi beneficiaries or Inuit of Fort George; or

(d)   a corporation or other body in which Cree beneficiaries, Naskapi beneficiaries or Inuit of Fort George participate, as shareholders or members or otherwise, and that is prescribed.

PART I
LOCAL GOVERNMENT
Incorporation of Bands

12.(1)   Pursuant to subparagraph 9.0.1a) of the *James Bay and Northern Quebec Agreement,* the Indian Act Cree bands of

(a)   Great Whale River,

(b)   Chisasibi,

(c)   Old Factory,

(d)   Eastmain,

(e)   Rupert House,

(f)   Nemaska,

(g)   Waswanipi, and

(h)   Mistassini are hereby separately constituted as corporations bearing the names set out in paragraphs (2)(a) to (h), respectively, subject to section 16.

(2)   The bands incorporated by subsection (1) may, respectively, be legally designated by any of their English, French or Cree names, as follows:

(a)   Great Whale River Band, Bande de Poste-de-la-Balaine, Whapmagoostoo Aeyouch;

(b)   Chisasibi Band, Bande de Chisasibi, Chisasibi Eeyouch;

(c)   Wemindji Band, Bande de Wemindji, Wemindji Eeyou;

(d)   Eastmain Band, Bande de Eastmain, Wapanoutauw Eeyou;

(e)   Waskaganish Band, Bande de Waskaganish, Waskaganish Eeyou;

(f)   Nemaska Band, Bande de Nemiscau, Nemaskauw Eenouch;

(g)   Waswanipi Band, Bande de Waswanipi, Waswanipi Eenouch; and

(h)   Mistassini Band, Bande de Mistassini, Mistasini Eenouch. . . .

Objects and Powers of Bands

21.   The objects of a band are

(a)   to act as the local government authority on its Category IA or IA-N land;

(b)   to use, manage, administer and regulate its Category IA or IA-N land and the natural resources thereof;

(c)   to control the disposition of rights and interests in its Category IA or IA-N land and in the natural resources thereof;

(d)   to regulate the use of buildings on its Category IA-N land;

(e)   to use, manage and administer its moneys and other assets;

(f)   to promote the general welfare of its members of the band;

(g)   to promote and carry out community development and charitable works in the community;

(h)   to establish and administer services, programs and projects for members of the band, other residents of Category IA and IA-N land and residents of the Category III land referred to in paragraph 6(b);

(i)   to promote and preserve the culture, values and traditions of the Crees or Naskapis, as the case may be; and

(j)   to exercise the powers and carry out the duties conferred or imposed on the band or on its predecessor *Indian Act* band by any Act of Parliament or regulations made thereunder, and by the Agreements.

22.(1) A band has, subject to this Act and the regulations, the capacity, rights, powers and privileges of a natural person.

(2) A band shall not engage, directly or indirectly, in any commercial activity, except in so far as it is related to

(a)   the management or administration of

(i)   its Category IA or IA-N land or the natural resources thereof, or

(ii)   its buildings or other immovable assets on its Category IA or IA-N land; or

(b)   the provision of public services to or in respect of its Category IA or IA-N land or residents thereof.

(3) Notwithstanding subsection (2), a band may own shares in corporations that carry on commercial activities. . . .

By-Laws Respecting Local Government

45.(1) Subject to this section, a band may make by-laws of a local nature for the good government of its Category IA or IA-N land and of the inhabitants of such land, and for the general welfare of the members of the band, and, without limiting the generality of the foregoing, may make by-laws respecting

(a)   the administration of band affairs and the internal management of the band;

(b)   the regulation of buildings for the protection of public health and safety, including the construction, maintenance, repair and demolition of buildings;

(c) health and hygiene, including
  (i) the prevention of overcrowding of residences,
  (ii) the sanitary condition of public and private property,
  (iii) the control or prohibition of activities or undertakings that constitute a danger to public health,
  (iv) the construction, operation and regulation of waste disposal systems and the collection, removal and disposal of waste generally, and
  (v) subject to the laws of the Province, the establishment, maintenance and operation of cemeteries;

(d) public order and safety, including
  (i) the establishment, maintenance and operation of fire departments;
  (ii) the discharge of firearms or of arms discharged by compressed air or any other means,
  (iii) the keeping of animals,
  (iv) curfews,
  (v) the prohibition of the sale or exchange of alcoholic beverages,
  (vi) the possession or consumption of alcoholic beverages in public places, and
  (vii) the control of public games, sports, races, athletic contests and other amusements;

(e) the protection of the environment, including natural resources;

(f) the prevention of pollution;

(g) the definition of nuisances and the control and prohibition of nuisances;

(h) the taxation for local purposes, otherwise than by means of an income tax,
  (i) of interests in its Category IA or IA-N land, except those of Canada and Quebec and, and
  (ii) of occupants and tenants of its Category IA or IA-N land, except Canada and Quebec,
  subject to subsections (2) and (3) and subject to and in accordance with regulations made under subsection (4);

(i) subject to subsection (5), the establishment, maintenance and operation of local services relating to water, sewers, fire protection, recreation, cultural activities, roads, garbage removal and disposal, lighting, heating, power, transportation, communications or snow removal, and respecting user charges for any such service;

(j) roads, traffic and transportation, including
  (i) the operation and speed of vehicles,
  (ii) the maintenance, construction and operation of roads,
  (iii) the regulation of traffic of all kinds,
  (iv) the transportation of dangerous substances, and

      (v)   the establishment, maintenance and operation of wharves, harbours, drydocks and other landing places;

  (k)   the operation of businesses and the carrying on of trades; and

  (l)   parks and recreation.

(2) A band

  (a)   may not make taxation by-laws other than those described in paragraph (1)(h); and (b)may not make by-laws under paragraph (1)(h) until there are in force regulations made under (4).

(3) A by-law made under paragraph (1)(h) must be approved by the electors of the band at a special band meeting or referendum at which at least ten per cent of the electors of the band voted on the matter.

(4) The Governor in Council may make regulations respecting the exercise, pursuant to paragraph (1)(h), of a band's power of taxation, including, without restricting the generality of the foregoing, regulations respecting

  (a)   assessments and the determination of tax rates;

  (b)   contestation of assessments;

  (c)   collection of taxes;

  (d)   contestation of taxation; and

  (e)   enforcement procedures.

(5) A by-law described in paragraph (1)(i) respecting a user charge for a service may differentiate on an equitable basis between different categories of users and different categories of land that benefit from the service, but

  (a)   may not delegate to anyone the power to prescribe user charges or user charge rates but must itself prescribe the user charges or the user charge rates; and

  (b)   may not prescribe user charges or user charge rates that exceed the total actual or anticipated cost of providing the service.

(6) A band may accept payment of a tax referred to in paragraph (1)(h)or a user charge referred to in paragraph (1)(i) in a form other than money.

46.(1) A band may make by-laws respecting land and resource use and planning, including, without limiting the generality of the foregoing, by-laws respecting

  (a)   the inventory, use and management of its Category IA or IA-N land and the natural resources thereof;

  (b)   the adoption of land use plans and resource use plans in relation to its Category IA or IA-N land; and

  (c)   use permits relating to its Category IA or IA-N land and buildings located thereon, and the conditions relating to the issuance, suspension or revocation of such permits. . . .

47.(1) A band may make by-laws respecting zoning, including, without limiting the generality of the foregoing, by-laws respecting

  (a)   the division of all or part of its Category IA or IA-N land into zones for the purpose of regulating the use of the land, natural resources thereof and buildings; and

  (b)   the implementation of a land use plan or resource use plan referred to in subsection 46(1) that was approved by the electors of the band under subsection 46(2). . . .

48.(1) Subject to this section, a band may make by-laws respecting hunting, fishing and trapping and the protection of wildlife, including, without limiting the generality of the foregoing, by-laws respecting

     (a)   the exercise of the right to harvest referred to in section 24 of the *James Bay and Northern Quebec Agreement* and in An Act respecting hunting and fishing rights in the James Bay and New Quebec territories (Quebec);

     (b)   matters described in section 85 and 86 of that Act;

     (c)   residence requirements relating to sport hunting and sport fishing by persons other than Cree or Naskapi beneficiaries, as contemplated by section 37 of that Act; and

     (d)   the right of persons of Cree or Naskapi ancestry to harvest for personal use, as contemplated by sections 38 and 38.1 of that Act. . . .

RESIDENCE RIGHTS

103.(1) The following persons have the right to reside on the Category IA or IA-N land of a band:

     (a)   a member of that band;

     (b)   the member's consort, within the meaning of section 174; and

     (c)   the family to the first degree of a person described in paragraph (a) or (b). . . .

RIGHTS OF BANDS, QUEBEC AND OTHERS IN RELATION TO CATEGORY IA AND IA-N LAND

109.(1) Quebec retains the bare ownership of Category IA and IA-N land.

(2) Subject to this Act, a band has the exclusive use and benefit of its Category IA or IA-N land and the natural resources thereof, and may administer, manage, control, use and enjoy that land and the natural resources thereof for community, commercial, industrial, residential or other purposes, as if it were the owner thereof. . . .

Mineral, Subsurface and Mining Rights

113.(1) Subject to this Act, Quebec retains the ownership of all mineral rights and subsurface rights on Category IA and IA-N land.

(2) Subject to subsection (3), after November 11, 1975 (in the case of Category IA land) or January 31, 1978 (in the case of Category IA-N land) no mineral right or subsurface right on Category IA or IA-N land of a band may be granted or exercised and no mineral or other subsurface material or substance may be mined or extracted from such land without the consent of the band and payment to the band of compensation agreed to by the band. . . .

PART XIV
TAX EXEMPTIONS

187.(1) In this Part, "Indian" means

     (a)   in subsection (2), a Cree beneficiary or Naskapi beneficiary who is an Indian as defined in the *Indian Act*; and

(b)   in section 188, an Indian as defined in the *Indian Act.*

(2)   For the purposes of this Part, personal property

(a)   that became the property of a band by virtue of section 13 or 15 and had been purchased by Canada with money appropriated by Parliament,

(b)   that is purchased by Canada after the coming into force of this Part with money appropriated by parliament for the use and benefit of Indians or bands, or

(c)   that is given, after the coming into force of this Part, to Indians or to a band under a treaty or agreement between a band and Canada shall be deemed always to be situated on Category IA or IA-N land.

188.(1) Notwithstanding any other Act of Parliament or of the legislature of any province, but subject to any by-laws of a band made pursuant to paragraph 45(1)(h), the following property is exempt from taxation:

(a)   the interest of an Indian or a band in Category IA or IA-N land; and

(b)   the personal property of an Indian or a band on Category IA or IA-N land. . . .

9.   *Eastmain Band* v. *Gilpin,* [1987] 3 C.N.L.R. 54 (Que. Prov. Ct.). Lavergne P.C.J., April 1, 1987

> The Quebec Provincial Court affirmed that a form of self-government, as enacted in the *Cree-Naskapi Act*, has been constitutionalized. This may prove to be an interesting case study as the Quebec sovereignty issue proceeds.

[Gilpin was charged for allowing his child to be in breach of a curfew, contrary to a band by-law enacted under the *Cree-Naskapi (of Quebec) Act,* S.C. 1983–84, c. 18, s. 45(1)(d)(iv). This decision deals with the accused's motion challenging the validity of the band council to adopt the by-law.]. . .

LAVERGNE P.C.J.:— . . . The *Cree-Naskapi (of Quebec) Act,* assented to on June 14, 1984, gave substance to Canada' s pledge under article 9.0.1 of the Agreement. In fact, the Act emanates from this pledge. The preamble to the Act stresses the wishes already formulated in the Agreement and the approving legislation, and confirms the will to give the Crees and Naskapis an organized and efficient local government regime, the management and control of Category IA lands, and the power to ensure the safeguard of their individual and collective rights. Without a doubt, the Act includes a wide range of powers similar to those given the municipalities governed by the *Cities and Towns Act* (R. S. Q. , c. C–19) and the *Municipal Code of Quebec* (R.S.Q., c.C–27.1). The *Cree-Naskapi (of Quebec) Act* includes provisions reflecting the legislator's will to ensure the right for the Crees to set their own standards of behaviour according to their social needs.

Under ss. 7 and 8 of this Act, the band councils may require the holding of a licence permit, and prohibit an activity. According to s. 9, the *Statutory Instruments Act* (S.C. 1970–71–72, c. 38) does not apply to resolutions or by-laws of bands made under the *Cree-Naskapi (of Quebec) Act.* Section 3 provides that where there is any inconsistency between the *Cree-Naskapi (of Quebec) Act* and any other federal act, the former Act will prevail. Section 4 stipulates that provincial laws do not apply where they are inconsistent with by-laws made by band councils. Finally, under s. 5, the *Indian Act* does not apply to Cree and Naskapi bands, except for the purpose of determining Indian status within the meaning of the *Indian Act.*

The subjects and powers of bands are described at ss. 21(a) to 21(j). Section 21(f) reads:

> 21.The objects of a band are
> (f) to promote the general welfare of the members of the band;

When interpreting the validity of a by-law, the objective of the organization described in the law should be taken into account. This method of interpretation was recognized by a majority of Supreme Court justices in *CKOY Ltd.* v. *R.* ((1979) 1 S.C.R. 2). In the case at bar, s. 45(l)(d)(iv) authorizes the bands to make by-laws respecting curfew. There is good reason to wonder whether the Eastmain Council, for the good of its members' general welfare, could avail itself of s. 2l(f) to introduce discrimination in its curfew by-law. There is room for doubt in the light of the reasons given by Beetz J. in the *Arcade Amusements* case.

Nevertheless, the Court believes that this case does not concern statutory instruments within the meaning generally accepted in public law, because of the spirit reflected by the Agreement and the ensuing legislation.

Native rights have been given constitutional recognition. Section 35(1) of the *Constitution Act, 1982* stipulates:

> The existing aboriginal and treaty rights of the aboriginal peoples of Canada are hereby recognized and affirmed.

And as though to remove all ambiguity as to whether or not the James Bay Agreement was a treaty, the proclamation of 1983 amending the Constitution (O.G. part. III, August 10, 1984, p.1581) added a third paragraph to s. 35:

> (3) For greater certainty, in subsection (1) "treaty rights" includes rights that now exist by way of land claims agreements or may be so acquired.

Similarly, s-s. 1 of s. 52 of the *Constitution Act, 1982* states:

> The Constitution of Canada is the supreme law of Canada, and any law that is inconsistent with the provisions of the Constitution is, to the extent of the inconsistency, of no force or effect.

Since patriation of the Constitution had raised some bad feelings among the Natives because they were not consulted, s. 35.1 was added by the proclamation of 1983. This section provided for an agreement to invite the Native peoples of Canada to be present when amendments were to be made to s. 91(24) of the *Constitution Act, 1867* giving the federal Parliament jurisdiction over the Indians and lands set aside for Indians, as well as to ss. 35 and 35.1 of the *Constitution Act, 1982.*

Therefore, the Crees' rights conferred and recognised by the James Bay agreement as regards Category IA lands, have been made constitutional. These rights were given legislative approval by the *Cree Naskapi (of Quebec) Act* as promised in the Agreement. That being the case, it seems that the federal Parliament cannot adopt laws encroaching upon the rights conferred upon the Crees and the Naskapis under the *Cree Naskapi (of Quebec) Act,* without violating the Constitution. Such laws would be inoperative as they would be inconsistent with the rights guaranteed the Natives by s. 35(3) of the *Constitution Act, 1982* (s. 52). Any change to the Natives' existing rights would be legal only if brought about by a constitutional amendment.

Consequently, subordination, which is one of the essential characteristics of regulatory power in our juridical system, does not apply to the case at bar. Band councils' regulatory power is not subjected to the will of the federal Parliament, because this power is included in the rights guaranteed by the Constitution. In the Court's opinion the right of a local administration to make by-laws is part of those guaranteed rights. The federal Parliament could not adopt a law taking away from the band councils the power to regulate curfews, for instance. This situation is unique in Canada. The constitutional amendment proclaims the permanence and stability of the James Bay Cree population and, therefore, undoubtedly confers upon it a particular status. Since the Constitution prevents Parliament from adopting laws encroaching upon the guaranteed rights regarding Category IA lands, it would be rather strange were this same Parliament to retain the right to delegate to Cree bands the power to make discriminatory by-laws. It would be illogical and inconsistent to transfer a power irrevocably, subject only to a constitutional amendment, and retain a right to supervise the manner in which this power is exercised.

Respect for those fundamental freedoms which mainly motivated the principle of non-discrimination in matters of regulatory power, except when expressly stipulated in the enabling law, is safeguarded by s. 15 of the *Charter of Human Rights and Freedoms.*

The Court concludes that the principle of non-discrimination in the exercise of regulatory power does not apply to this case. The above-mentioned texts must be interpreted, by necessary implication, as conferring the Cree bands full power to legislate within specified fields, according to community needs identified by themselves.

In this perspective, the Court agrees with the proposition that the Crees hold some sort of residual sovereignty as regards their local governments.

Therefore, the Court: Declares the Eastmain Band Curfew By-Law legal, and dismissed the preliminary motion submitted by the accused.

10. *Waskaganish Band* v. *Blackned*, [1986] 3 C.N.L.R. 168. (Que. Prov. Ct.). Ouellet J., March 18, 1986

Like the *Gilpin* decision, *Waskaganish* deals with the *Cree-Naskapi Act* and illustrates the effect that s. 35(3) has had on the potential for land claims agreements to be vehicles for self-government. In the case of the *Cree-Naskapi Act*, the argument is that since it flows directly from the 1975 *James Bay and Northern Quebec Agreement,* which is constitutionalized by virtue of s. 35(3), so too is the act.

OUELLET J.:— . . . Under these circumstances, it would seem to me that the band council constitutes an autonomous level of government when it exercises the powers conferred upon it by the *Cree-Naskapi (of Quebec) Act.* As long as it remains within the powers so conferred, the band council represents a level of government independent from the Canadian Parliament and the Quebec legislature. Its members are the elected representatives of the community who, in giving them their mandate, invest them with the powers granted to the band under the Treaty Convention and especially the *Cree-Naskapi (of Quebec) Act.* It is to the band members that the council is accountable for its administration and the exercise of its powers, and not to Parliament, of which it is not an agent. . . .

It is therefore obvious to me that Parliament's intention was to create a level of local government for the Cree communities. Such local government would be invested with the powers of local administration generally conferred upon municipalities as well as certain other powers coming under the provincial legislatures, in the case of non-Indians, and of the federal parliament itself, in the case of Indians. . . .

11. Excerpts from the 1992 Charlottetown Accord

. . . Inherent right of self-government

35.1(1) The Aboriginal peoples of Canada have the inherent right of self-government within Canada.

Three orders of government

(2) The right referred to in subsection (1) shall be interpreted in a manner consistent with the recognition of the governments of the Aboriginal peoples of Canada as constituting one of three orders of government in Canada.

Contextual statement

(3) The exercise of the right referred to in subsection (1) includes the authority of duly constituted legislative bodies of the Aboriginal peoples, each within its own jurisdiction,

> (a) to safeguard and develop their languages, cultures, economies, identities, institutions and traditions, and
> (b) to develop, maintain and strengthen their relationship with their lands, waters and environment, so as to determine and control their development as peoples according to their own values and priorities and to ensure the integrity of their societies. . . .

Commitment to negotiate

35.2(1) The government of Canada, the provincial and territorial governments and the Aboriginal peoples of Canada, including the Indian, Inuit and Métis peoples of Canada, in the various regions and communities of Canada shall negotiate in good faith the implementation of the right of self-government, including issues of

> (a) jurisdiction,
> (b) lands and resources, and
> (c) economic and fiscal arrangements, with the objective of concluding agreements elaborating relationships between governments of Aboriginal peoples and the government of Canada and provincial or territorial governments.

Process of negotiation

(2) Negotiations referred to in subsection (1) may be initiated only by the representatives or governments of the Aboriginal peoples concerned, and shall,

unless otherwise agreed by the parties to the negotiations, be conducted in accordance with the process for negotiations outlined in an accord entered into by the government of Canada, the provincial and territorial governments and representatives of the Aboriginal peoples. . . .

Delay of justiciability

35.3(1) Except in relation to self-government agreements concluded after the coming into force of this section, section 35.1 shall not be made the subject of judicial notice, interpretation or enforcement for five years after that section comes into force.

For greater certainty

(2) For greater certainty, nothing in subsection (1) prevents the justiciability of disputes in relation to

    (a)   any existing rights that are recognized and affirmed in subsection 35(1), including any rights relating to self-government, when raised in any court; or

    (b)   the process of negotiation under section 35.2.

Idem

(3) Nothing in subsection (1) abrogates or derogates from section 35.1 or renders section 35.1 contingent on the happening of any future event, and subsection (1) merely delays for five years judicial notice, interpretation or enforcement of that section.

Application of laws

35.4(1) Except as otherwise provided by the Constitution of Canada, the laws of Canada and the laws of the provinces and territories continue to apply to the Aboriginal peoples of Canada, subject nevertheless to being displaced by laws enacted by legislative bodies of the Aboriginal peoples according to their authority.

Peace, order and good government in Canada

(2) No aboriginal law or any other exercise of the inherent right of self-government under section 35.1 may be inconsistent with federal or provincial laws that are essential to the preservation of peace, order and good government in Canada.

Legislative authority not extended

(3) For greater certainty, nothing in this section extends the legislative authority of the Parliament of Canada or the legislatures of the provinces or territories.

Affirmative action

35.5(1) Subsections 6(2) and (3) of the *Canadian Charter of Rights and Freedoms* do not preclude a legislative body or government of the Aboriginal peoples of Canada from exercising authority pursuant to this Part through affirmative action measures that have as their object the amelioration of conditions of individuals or groups who are socially or economically disadvantaged or the protection and advancement of aboriginal languages and cultures.

For greater certainty

(2) For greater certainty, nothing in this section abrogates or derogates from section 15, 25 or 28 of the *Canadian Charter of Rights and Freedoms* or from section 35.7 of this Part.

Interpretation of treaty rights

35.6(1) The treaty rights referred to in subsection 35(1) shall be interpreted in a just, broad and liberal manner taking into account their spirit and intent and the context of the specific treaty negotiations relating thereto.

Commitment to processes to clarify, implement or rectify treaties

(2) The government of Canada is committed to establishing treaty processes to clarify or implement treaty rights and, where the parties agree, to rectify terms of the treaties, and is committed, where requested by the Aboriginal peoples of Canada concerned, to participating in good faith in the process that relates to them.

Participation of provinces and territories

(3) The governments of the provinces and territories are committed, to the extent that they have jurisdiction, to participating in good faith in the processes referred to in subsection (2), where jointly invited by the government of Canada and the Aboriginal peoples of Canada concerned or where it is specified that they will do so under the terms of the treaty concerned.

Spirit and intent

(4) The participants in the processes referred to in subsection (2) shall have regard to, among other things and where appropriate, the spirit and intent of the treaties, as understood by the Aboriginal peoples concerned. . . .

Rights of the Aboriginal peoples of Canada guaranteed equally to both sexes

35.7   Notwithstanding any other provision of this Act, the rights of the Aboriginal peoples of Canada referred to in this Part are guaranteed equally to male and female persons.

12. *Teslin Tlingit Council Self-Government Agreement,* May 29, 1993

This is one of six self-government agreements reached in the Yukon resulting directly from the *Yukon Final Agreement.*

Teslin Tlingit Council Final Agreement, May 29, 1993

. . . 24.1.1 Government shall enter into negotiations with each Yukon First Nation which so requests with a view to concluding self-government agreements appropriate to the circumstances of the affected Yukon First Nation. . . .

Teslin-Tlingit Council Self-Government Agreement, May 29, 1993

An agreement among the Teslin-Tlingit Council, the Government of the Yukon Territory and Canada. . . .

3.0   GENERAL PROVISIONS

      3.1   This agreement shall not affect any aboriginal claim, right, title or interest of the Teslin Tlingit Council or if its Citizens.

      3.2   This Agreement shall not affect the identity of Citizens as aboriginal people of Canada.

      3.3   This Agreement shall not affect the ability of the aboriginal people of the Teslin Tlingit Council to exercise, or benefit from, any existing or future constitutional rights for aboriginal people that may be applicable to them.

      3.4.   Unless otherwise provided pursuant to this Agreement or in a law enacted by the Teslin Tlingit Council, this Agreement shall not affect the ability of citizens to participate in and benefit from Government programs for status Indians, non-status Indians or native people, as the case may be. Benefits under such programs shall be determined by the general criteria for such programs established from time to time.

      3.5   Except for the purpose of determining which Citizens are "Indians" within the meaning of the *Indian Act*, R.S.C. 1985, c. I–5, the *Indian Act*, R.S.C. 1985, c. I–5, does not apply to Citizens, the Teslin Tlingit Council or Settlement Land. . . .

8.0   INTERPRETATION AND APPLICATION OF LAW

      8.1   Subject to 8.1.1, where there is any inconsistency or conflict between the provisions of federal Self-Government Legislation and any other federal Legislation, the federal Self-Government Legislation shall prevail to the extent of the inconsistency or conflict.

           8.1.1.   Where there is any inconsistency or conflict between the provisions of federal Self-Government Legislation and the Final Agreement or Settlement Legislation shall prevail to the extent of the inconsistency of conflict.

      8.2   Subject to 8.2.1, where there is any inconsistency or conflict between the provisions of Yukon Self-Government Legislation and any other Yukon Legislation, the Yukon Self-Government Legislation shall prevail to the extent of the inconsistency or conflict.

           8.2.1   Where there is any inconsistency or conflict between the provisions of Yukon Self-Government Legislation, the Final Agreement or Settlement Legislation shall prevail to the extent of the inconsistency or conflict.

      8.3   This Agreement is subject to the Final Agreement, and in the event of any inconsistency or conflict, the Final Agreement shall prevail to the extent of the inconsistency or conflict. . . .

      8.7   The preamble and the principles in this Agreement are statements of the intentions of the Parties and shall only be used to assist in the interpretation of doubtful or ambiguous expressions in this Agreement. . . .

9.0   LEGAL STATUS OF THE TESLIN TLINGIT COUNCIL

      9.1   Upon the Effective Date, the *Indian Act*, R.S.C. 1985, c. I–5, Teslin Tlingit Council Indian Band shall cease to exist and its rights, titles, interests, assets, obligations and liabilities, including those of its band council, shall vest in the Teslin Tlingit Council.

9.2 The Teslin Tlingit Council is a legal entity and has the capacity, rights, powers and privileges of a natural person and, without restricting the generality of the foregoing, may:

    9.2.1 enter into contracts or agreements;

    9.2.2 acquire and hold property or any interest therein, sell or otherwise dispose of property or any interest therein;

    9.2.3 raise, invest, expend and borrow money;

    9.2.4 sue or be sued;

    9.2.5 form corporations or other legal entities; and

    9.2.6 do such other things as may be conducive to the exercise of its rights, powers and privileges.

9.3 The act of acquiring or the holding of any rights, liabilities or obligations by the Teslin Tlingit Council or by any entity described in 9.2.5, shall not be construed to affect any aboriginal right, title or interest of the Teslin Tlingit Council, its Citizens or their heirs, descendants or successors.

10.0 TESLIN TLINGIT COUNCIL CONSTITUTION

10.1 The Teslin Tlingit Council Constitution shall:

    10.1.1 contain the Teslin Tlingit Council citizenship code;

    10.1.2 establish governing bodies and provide for their powers, duties, composition, membership and procedures;

    10.1.3 provide for a system of reporting, which may include audits, through which the Teslin Tlingit Council government shall be financially accountable to its Citizens;

    10.1.4 recognize and protect the rights and freedoms of Citizens;

    10.1.5 provide for the challenging of the validity of laws enacted by the Teslin Tlingit Council and for the quashing of invalid laws;

    10.1.6 provide for amending the Constitution by the Citizens; and

    10.1.7 be consistent with this Agreement.

10.2 The Constitution may provide for any other matters relating to the Teslin Tlingit Council government or to the governing of Settlement Land, or of persons on Settlement Land. . . .

12.0 DELEGATION

12.1 The Teslin Tlingit Council may delegate any of its powers, including legislative powers, to:

    12.1.1 a public body or official established by a law of the Teslin Tlingit Council;

    12.1.2 Government, including a department, agency or official of Government;

    12.1.3 a public body performing a function of government in Canada, including another Yukon First Nation;

    12.1.4 a municipality, school board, local body, or legal entity established by Yukon Law;

    12.1.5   a tribal council;

    12.1.6   the Council for Yukon Indians; or

    12.1.7   any legal entity in Canada.

12.2   Any delegation under 12.1.2 to 12.1.7 shall be made by written agreement with the delegate.

12.3   The Teslin Tlingit Council has the capacity to enter into agreements to receive powers, including legislative powers, by delegation. . . .

13.0   LEGISLATIVE POWERS

13.1   The Teslin Tlingit Council shall have the exclusive power to enact laws in relation to the following matters:

    13.1.1   administration of Teslin Tlingit Council affairs and operation and internal management of the Teslin Tlingit Council;

    13.1.2   management and administration of rights or benefits which are realized pursuant to the Final Agreement by persons enrolled under the Final Agreement, and which are to be controlled by the Teslin Tlingit Council; and

    13.1.3   matters ancillary to the foregoing.

13.2   The Teslin Tlingit Council shall have the power to enact laws in relation to the following matters in the Yukon;

    13.2.1   provision of programs and services for Citizens in relation to their spiritual and cultural beliefs and practices;

    13.2.2   provision of programs and services for Citizens in relation to their aboriginal languages;

    13.2.3   provision of health care and services to Citizens, except licensing and regulation of facility-based services off Settlement Land;

    13.2.4   provision of social and welfare services to Citizens, except licensing and regulation of facility-based services off Settlement Land;

    13.2.5   provision of training programs for Citizens, subject to Government certification requirements where applicable;

    13.2.6   adoption by and of Citizens;

    13.2.7   guardianship, custody, care and placement of Teslin Tlingit children, except licensing and regulation of facility-based services off Settlement Land;

    13.2.8   provision of education programs and services for Citizens choosing to participate, except licensing and regulation of facility-based services off Settlement Land;

    13.2.9   inheritance, wills, intestacy and administration of estates of Citizens, including rights and interests in Settlement Land;

    13.2.10   procedures consistent with the principles of natural justice for determining the mental competency or ability of Citizens, including administration of the rights and interests of those found incapable of responsibility for their own affairs;

13.2.11 provision of services to Citizens for resolution of disputes outside the courts;

13.2.12 solemnization of marriage of Citizens;

13.2.13 licences in respect of matters enumerated in 13.1, 13.2 and 13.3 in order to raise revenue for Teslin Tlingit Council purposes;

13.2.14 matters necessary to enable the Teslin Tlingit Council to fulfill its responsibilities under the Final Agreement or this Agreement; and

13.2.15 matters ancillary to the foregoing.

13.3 The Teslin Tlingit Council shall have the power to enact laws of a local or private nature on Settlement Land in relation to the following matters:

13.3.1 use, management, administration, control and protection of Settlement Land;

13.3.2 allocation or disposition of rights and interests in and to Settlement Land, including expropriation by the Teslin Tlingit Council for Teslin Tlingit Council purposes;

13.3.3 use, management, administration and protection of natural resources under the ownership, control or jurisdiction of the Teslin Tlingit Council;

13.3.4 gathering, hunting, trapping or fishing and the protection of fish, wildlife and habitat;

13.3.5 control or prohibition of the erection and placement of powers, advertising signs, and billboards;

13.3.6 licensing and regulation of any person or entity carrying on any business, trade, profession, or other occupation;

13.3.7 control or prohibition of public games, sports, races, athletic contests and other amusements;

13.3.8 control or prohibition of public games, sports, races, athletic contests and other amusements;

13.3.9 prevention of overcrowding of residences or other buildings or structures;

13.3.10 control of the sanitary condition of buildings or property;

13.3.11 planning, zoning and land development;

13.3.12 curfews, prevention of disorderly conduct and control or prohibition of nuisances;

13.3.13 control or prohibition of the operation and use of vehicles;

13.3.14 control or prohibition of the transport, sale, exchange, manufacture, supply, possession or consumption of intoxicants;

13.3.15 establishment, maintenance, provision, operation or regulation of local services and facilities;

13.3.16   caring and keeping of livestock, poultry, pets and other birds and animals, and impoundment and disposal of any bird or animal maltreated or improperly at-large, but the caring and keeping of livestock does not include game farming or game ranching;

13.3.17   administration of justice;

13.3.18   control or prohibition of any actions, activities or undertakings that constitute, or may constitute, a threat to public order, peace or safety;

13.3.19   control or prohibition of any activities, conditions or undertakings that constitute, or may constitute, a danger to public health;

13.3.20   control or prevention of pollution and protection of the environment;

13.3.21   control or prohibition of the possession or use of firearms, other weapons and explosives;

13.3.22   control or prohibition of the transport of dangerous substances; and

13.3.23   matters coming within the good government of Citizens on Settlement Land. . . .

13.5.0   *Laws of General Application*

13.5.1   Unless otherwise provided in this Agreement, all laws of General Application shall continue to apply to the Teslin Tlingit Council, its Citizens and Settlement Land.

13.5.2   Canada and the Teslin Tlingit Council shall enter into negotiations with a view to concluding, as soon as practicable, a separate agreement or an amendment of this Agreement which will identify the areas in which laws of the Teslin Tlingit Council shall prevail over federal Laws of General Application to the extent of any inconsistency or conflict.

13.5.2.1   Canada shall Consult with the Yukon prior to concluding the negotiations described in 13.5.2.

13.5.2.2   Clause 13.5.2 shall not affect the status of the Yukon as a party to the negotiations or agreements referred to in 13.6.0 or 17.0.

13.5.3   Except as provided in 14.0, a Yukon Law of General Application shall be inoperative to the extent that it provides for any matter for which provision is made in a law enacted by the Teslin Tlingit Council.

13.5.4   Where the Yukon reasonable foresees that a Yukon Law of General Application which it intends to enact may have an impact on a law enacted by the Teslin Tlingit Council, the Yukon shall Consult with the Teslin Tlingit Council before introducing the Legislation in the Legislative Assembly.

13.5.5   Where the Teslin Tlingit Council reasonably foresees that a law which it intends to enact may have an impact on a Yukon Law of

General Application, the Teslin Tlingit Council shall Consult with the Yukon before enacting the law.

13.5.6 Where the Commissioner in Executive Council is of the opinion that a law enacted by the Teslin Tlingit Council has rendered a Yukon Law of General Application partially inoperative and that it would unreasonably alter the character of a Yukon Law of General Application or that it would make it unduly difficult to administer that Yukon Law of General Application in relation to the Teslin Tlingit Council, Citizens or Settlement Land, the Commissioner in Executive Council may declare that the Yukon Law of General Application ceases to apply in whole or in part to the Teslin Tlingit Council, Citizens or Settlement Land.

13.5.7 Prior to making a declaration pursuant to 13.5.6, the Yukon shall:

13.5.7.1 Consult with the Teslin Tlingit Council and identify solutions, including any amendments to Yukon Legislation, that the Yukon considers would meet the objectives of the Teslin Tlingit Council; and

13.5.7.2 after Consultation pursuant to 13.5.7.1, where the Yukon and the Teslin Tlingit Council agree that the Yukon Law of General Application should be amended, the Yukon shall propose such amendment to the Legislative Assembly within a reasonable period of time. . . .

14.0 TAXATION

14.1 The Teslin Tlingit Council shall have the power to enact laws in relation to:

14.1.1 taxation, for local purposes, of interests in Settlement Land and of occupants and tenants of Settlement Land in respect of their interests in those lands, including assessment, collection and enforcement procedures and appeals relating thereto;

14.1.2 other modes of direct taxation of Citizens (and, if agreed under 14.5.2, other persons and entities) within Settlement Land to raise revenue for Teslin Tlingit Council purposes; and

14.1.3 the implementation of measures made pursuant to any taxation agreement entered into pursuant to 14.8.

14.2 The Teslin Tlingit Council powers provided for in 14.1 shall not limit Government's powers to levy tax or make taxation laws. . . .

14.6 When the Teslin Tlingit Council exercises its jurisdiction, or assumes responsibility, for the management, administration and delivery of local services and, as a consequence, exercises property taxation powers under 14.1.1, the Yukon shall undertake to ensure a sharing of tax room in respect of property taxes consistent with equitable and comparable taxation levels.

14.6.1 To the extent that the Teslin Tlingit Council imposes property taxation for local purposes, the Yukon shall ensure that Yukon municipalities do not incur any consequential net loss.

14.6.2 The Teslin Tlingit Council and the Yukon shall enter into negotiations as necessary to provide for the efficient delivery of local services and programs. . . .

16.0 SELF-GOVERNMENT FINANCIAL TRANSFER AGREEMENT

16.1 Canada and the Teslin Tlingit Council shall negotiate a self-government financial transfer agreement in accordance with 16.3, with the objective of providing the Teslin Tlingit Council with resources to enable the Teslin Tlingit Council to provide public services at levels reasonably comparable to those generally prevailing in Yukon, at reasonably comparable levels of taxation.

16.2 Subject to such terms and conditions as may be agreed, the self-government financial transfer agreement shall set out:

16.2.1 the amounts of funding to be provided by Canada towards the cost of public services, where the Teslin Tlingit Council has assumed responsibility;

16.2.2 the amounts of funding to be provided by Canada towards the cost of operation of Teslin Tlingit Council government institutions; and

16.2.3 such other matters as Canada and the Teslin Tlingit Council may agree.

16.3 In negotiating the self-government financial transfer agreement, Canada and the Teslin Tlingit Council shall take into account the following:

16.3.1 the ability and capacity of the Teslin Tlingit Council to generate revenues from its own sources;

16.3.2 diseconomies of scale which impose higher operating or administrative costs on the Teslin Tlingit Council, in relation to costs prevailing prior to conclusion of this Agreement;

16.3.3 due regard to economy and efficiency, including the possibilities for co-operative or joint arrangements among Yukon First Nations for the management, administration and delivery of programs or services;

16.3.4 any funding provided to the Teslin Tlingit Council through other Government transfer programs;

16.3.5 demographic features of the Teslin Tlingit Council;

16.3.6 results of reviews pursuant to 6.6;

16.3.7 existing levels of Government expenditure for services to Yukon First Nations and Yukon Indian People;

16.3.8 the prevailing fiscal policies of Canada;

16.3.9 other federal Legislation respecting the financing of aboriginal governments; and

16.3.10 such other matters as Canada and the Teslin Tlingit Council may agree. . . .

13. *Nisga'a Final Agreement;* **Intialed August 4, 1998, Between the Governments of British Columbia and Canada and the Nisga'a Nation**

The following excerpt is from the *Nisga'a Final Agreement*—British Columbia's first modern treaty. The excerpted chapter deals with governance. Broader discussion of the *Final Agreement* can be found in the introduction to chapter 2 at pp. 130–32.

CHAPTER 11—NISGA'A GOVERNMENT
SELF-GOVERNMENT

1. The Nisga'a Nation has the right to self-government, and the authority to make laws, as set out in this Agreement.

RECOGNITION OF NISGA'A LISIMS GOVERNMENT AND NISGA'A VILLAGE GOVERNMENTS

2. Nisga'a Lisims Government and Nisga'a Village Governments, as provided for under the Nisga'a Constitution, are the governments of the Nisga'a Nation and the Nisga'a Villages, respectively.

3. Except as may otherwise be agreed to by the relevant Parties in respect of particular matters, Nisga'a Lisims Government is responsible for intergovernmental relations between the Nisga'a Nation on the one hand, and Canada or British Columbia, or both, on the other hand.

4. The exercise of Nisga'a Government jurisdiction and authority set out in this Agreement will evolve over time.

LEGAL STATUS AND CAPACITY

5. The Nisga'a Nation, and each Nisga'a Village, is a separate and distinct legal entity, with the capacity, rights, powers, and privileges of a natural person, including to:
   a. enter into contracts and agreements;
   b. acquire and hold property or an interest in property, and sell or otherwise dispose of that property or interest;
   c. raise, spend, invest, or borrow money;
   d. sue and be sued; and e.do other things ancillary to the exercise of its rights, powers and privileges.

6. The rights, powers, and privileges of the Nisga'a Nation, and of each Nisga'a Village, will be exercised in accordance with:
   a. this Agreement;
   b. the Nisga'a Constitution; and
   c. Nisga'a laws.

7. The Nisga'a Nation will act through Nisga'a Lisims Government in exercising its rights, powers, and privileges and in carrying out its duties, functions, and obligations.

8. Each Nisga'a Village will act through its Nisga'a Village Government in exercising its rights, powers, and privileges and in carrying out its duties, functions, and obligations.

NISGA'A CONSTITUTION

9.   The Nisga'a Nation will have a Nisga'a Constitution, consistent with this Agreement, which will:

   a. provide for Nisga'a Lisims Government and Nisga'a Village Governments, including their duties, composition, and membership;

   b. provide that this Agreement sets out the authority of Nisga'a Government to make laws;

   c. assign to Nisga'a Lisims Government and Nisga'a Village Governments the rights, powers, privileges, and responsibilities under this Agreement that are not specifically assigned to Nisga'a Lisims Government;

   d. provide for the enactment of laws by Nisga'a Government;

   e. provide for challenging the validity of Nisga'a laws;

   f. provide for the creation, continuation, amalgamation, dissolution, naming, or renaming of:

      i. Nisga'a Villages on Nisga'a Lands, and

      ii. Nisga'a Urban Locals;

   g. provide for Nisga'a Urban Locals, or other means by which Nisga'a citizens residing outside of the Nass Area may participate in Nisga'a Lisims Government;

   h. provide for the establishment of Nisga'a Public Institutions;

   i. provide for the role of the Nisga'a elders, Simgigat and Sigidimhaanak, in providing guidance and interpretation of the Ayuuk to Nisga'a Government;

   j. provide that in the event of an inconsistency or conflict between the Nisga'a Constitution and the provisions of any Nisga'a law, the Nisga'a law is, to the extent of the inconsistency or conflict, of no force or effect;

   k. require that Nisga'a Government be democratically accountable to Nisga'a citizens, and, in particular:

      i. that elections for Nisga'a Lisims Government and each Nisga'a Village Government be held at least every five years, and

      ii. that, subject to residency, age, and other requirements set out in the Nisga'a Constitution or Nisga'a law, all Nisga'a citizens are eligible to vote in Nisga'a elections and to hold office in Nisga'a Government;

   l. require a system of financial administration comparable to standards generally accepted for governments in Canada, through which Nisga'a Lisims Government will be financially accountable to Nisga'a citizens, and Nisga'a Village Governments will be financially accountable to Nisga'a citizens of those Nisga'a Villages;

   m. require conflict of interest rules that are comparable to standards generally accepted for governments in Canada;

   n. provide conditions under which the Nisga'a Nation or a Nisga'a Village may:

      i. dispose of the whole of its estate or interest in any parcel of Nisga'a Lands or Nisga'a Fee Simple Lands, and

      ii. from the whole of its estate or interest, create or dispose of any lesser estate or interest in any parcel of Nisga'a Lands or Nisga'a Fee Simple Lands;

o. recognize and protect rights and freedoms of Nisga'a citizens;

p. provide that every Nisga'a participant who is a Canadian citizen or permanent resident of Canada is entitled to be a Nisga'a citizen;

q. provide for Nisga'a Government during the period from the effective date until the date on which the office holders elected in the first Nisga'a elections take office;

r. provide for amendment of the Nisga'a Constitution; and

s. include other provisions, as determined by the Nisga'a Nation.

10. The Nisga'a Constitution, as approved in accordance with the Ratification Chapter, comes into force on the effective date.

11. The Nisga'a Constitution will initially include an amending procedure requiring that an amendment be approved by at least 70% of Nisga'a citizens voting in a referendum.

NISGA'A GOVERNMENT STRUCTURE

12. Each Nisga'a Village Government consists of elected members as set out in the Nisga'a Constitution.

13. On the effective date, there are three Nisga'a Urban Locals, as set out in the Nisga'a Constitution, known as:

a. Greater Vancouver Urban Local;

b. Terrace Urban Local; and

c. Prince Rupert/Port Edward Urban Local.

14. Nisga'a Lisims Government consists of the following members, as set out in the Nisga'a Constitution:

a. at least three officers elected by the Nisga'a Nation in a general election;

b. the elected members of the Nisga'a Village Governments; and

c. at least one representative elected by the Nisga'a citizens of each Nisga'a Urban Local. . . .

APPEAL AND REVIEW OF ADMINISTRATIVE DECISIONS

16. Nisga'a Government will provide appropriate procedures for the appeal or review of administrative decisions of Nisga'a Public Institutions.

17. The Supreme Court of British Columbia has jurisdiction in respect of applications for judicial review of administrative decisions of Nisga'a Institutions exercising a statutory power of decision under Nisga'a law, but no application for judicial review of those decisions may be brought until all procedures for appeal or review provided by Nisga'a Government and applicable to that decision have been exhausted.

REGISTER OF LAWS

18. Nisga'a Lisims Government will:

a. maintain a public registry of Nisga'a laws in the English language and, at the discretion of Nisga'a Lisims Government, in the Nisga'a language;

b. provide Canada and British Columbia with a copy of a Nisga'a law as soon as practicable after that law is enacted; and

c. establish procedures for the coming into force and publication of Nisga'a laws.

RELATIONS WITH INDIVIDUALS WHO ARE NOT NISGA'A CITIZENS

19. Nisga'a Government will consult with individuals who are ordinarily resident within Nisga'a Lands and who are not Nisga'a citizens about Nisga'a Government decisions that directly and significantly affect them.

20. Nisga'a Government will provide that individuals who are ordinarily resident within Nisga'a Lands and who are not Nisga'a citizens may participate in a Nisga'a Public Institution, if the activities of that Nisga'a Public Institution directly and significantly affect them.

21. The means of participation under paragraph 20 will be:
    a. a reasonable opportunity to make representations to the Nisga'a Public Institution in respect of activities that significantly and directly affect them;
    b. if the members of a Nisga'a Public Institution are elected:
        i. the ability to vote for or become members of the Nisga'a Public Institution, or
        ii. a guaranteed number of members, with the right to vote, on the Nisga'a Public Institution; or
    c. other comparable measures.

22. Nisga'a Government will provide that individuals who are ordinarily resident within Nisga'a Lands and who are not Nisga'a citizens may avail themselves of the appeal or review procedures referred to in paragraph 16.

23. Nisga'a Government may appoint individuals who are not Nisga'a citizens as members of Nisga'a Public Institutions. . . .

LEGISLATIVE JURISDICTION AND AUTHORITY

General

32. In the event of an inconsistency or conflict between this Agreement and the provisions of any Nisga'a law, this Agreement prevails to the extent of the inconsistency or conflict.

33. Nisga'a Lisims Government and Nisga'a Village Governments, respectively, have the principal authority, as set out in, and in accordance with, this Agreement, in respect of Nisga'a Government, Nisga'a citizenship, Nisga'a culture, Nisga'a language, Nisga'a Lands, and Nisga'a assets.

Nisga'a Government

34. Nisga'a Lisims Government may make laws in respect of the administration, management and operation of Nisga'a Government, including:
    a. the establishment of Nisga'a Public Institutions, including their respective powers, duties, composition, and membership;
    b. powers, duties, responsibilities, remuneration, and indemnification of members, officials, employees, and appointees of Nisga'a Institutions;
    c. the establishment of Nisga'a Corporations, but the registration or incorporation of the Nisga'a Corporations must be under federal or provincial laws;
    d. the delegation of Nisga'a Government authority, but the authority to make laws may be delegated only to a Nisga'a Institution;
    e. financial administration of the Nisga'a Nation, Nisga'a Villages, and Nisga'a Institutions; and

f. elections, by-elections, and referenda.

35. Each Nisga'a Village Government may make laws in respect of the administration, management, and operation of that Nisga'a Village Government, including:

   a. the establishment of Nisga'a Public Institutions of that Nisga'a Village Government, including their respective powers, duties, composition, and membership;

   b. powers, duties, responsibilities, remuneration, and indemnification of members, officials, employees, and appointees of Nisga'a Public Institutions referred to in subparagraph (a); and

   c. the delegation of the Nisga'a Village Government's authority, but the authority to make laws may be delegated only to a Nisga'a Institution.

36. In the event of an inconsistency or conflict between a Nisga'a law under paragraphs 34 or 35 and a federal or provincial law, the Nisga'a law prevails to the extent of the inconsistency or conflict.

37. Nisga'a Lisims Government may make laws in respect of the creation, continuation, amalgamation, dissolution, naming, or renaming of:

   a. Nisga'a Villages on Nisga'a Lands; and

   b. Nisga'a Urban Locals.

38. In the event of an inconsistency or conflict between a Nisga'a law under paragraph 37 and a federal or provincial law, the Nisga'a law prevails to the extent of the inconsistency or conflict.

Nisga'a Citizenship

39. Nisga'a Lisims Government may make laws in respect of Nisga'a citizenship. The conferring of Nisga'a citizenship does not:

   a. confer or deny rights of entry into Canada, Canadian citizenship, the right to be registered as an Indian under the Indian Act, or any of the rights or benefits under the Indian Act; or

   b. except as set out in this Agreement or in any federal or provincial law, impose any obligation on Canada or British Columbia to provide rights or benefits.

40. In the event of an inconsistency or conflict between a Nisga'a law under paragraph 39 and a federal or provincial law, the Nisga'a law prevails to the extent of the inconsistency or conflict.

Culture and Language

41. Nisga'a Lisims Government may make laws to preserve, promote, and develop Nisga'a culture and Nisga'a language, including laws to authorize or accredit the use, reproduction, and representation of Nisga'a cultural symbols and practices, and the teaching of Nisga'a language.

42. Except as provided for by federal or provincial law, Nisga'a Lisims Government jurisdiction under paragraph 41 to make laws in respect of Nisga'a culture and Nisga'a language does not include jurisdiction to make laws in respect of intellectual property, the official languages of Canada or the prohibition of activities outside of Nisga'a Lands. . . .

Nisga'a Property in Nisga'a Lands

44.   Nisga'a Lisims Government may make laws in respect of:

 a. the use and management of Nisga'a Lands owned by the Nisga'a Nation, a Nisga'a Village, or a Nisga'a Corporation;

 b. the possession of Nisga'a Lands owned by the Nisga'a Nation, a Nisga'a Village, or a Nisga'a Corporation, including the granting of rights of possession in Nisga'a Lands and any conditions or restrictions on those rights;

 c. the disposition of an estate or interest of the Nisga'a Nation, a Nisga'a Village or a Nisga'a Corporation, in any parcel of Nisga'a Lands, including: . . .

 d. the conditions on, and restrictions subject to which, the Nisga'a Nation, a Nisga'a Village or a Nisga'a Corporation may create or dispose of its estates or interests in any parcel of Nisga'a Lands;

 e. the conditions or restrictions, to be established at the time of the creation or disposition of an estate or interest of the Nisga'a Nation, a Nisga'a Village or a Nisga'a Corporation in any parcel of Nisga'a Lands, in respect of that and any subsequent disposition;

 f. the reservation or exception of interests, rights, privileges, and titles from any creation or disposition of an estate or interest of the Nisga'a Nation, a Nisga'a Village, or Nisga'a Corporation in Nisga'a Lands; and

 g. other similar matters relating to the property interests of the Nisga'a Nation, Nisga'a Villages, and Nisga'a Corporations in Nisga'a Lands.

45.   In the event of an inconsistency or conflict between a Nisga'a law under paragraph 44 and a federal or provincial law, the Nisga'a law prevails to the extent of the inconsistency or conflict.

46.   Nisga'a laws under paragraph 44(c) in respect of estates or interests that are recognized and permitted by federal or provincial laws of general application will be consistent with federal and provincial laws of general application in respect of those estates or interests, other than the provincial Torrens system and any federal land title or land registry laws.

Regulation, Administration and Expropriation of Nisga'a Lands

47.   Nisga'a Lisims Government may make laws in respect of:

 a. the use, management, planning, zoning, and development of Nisga'a Lands;

 b. regulation, licensing, and prohibition of the operation on Nisga'a Lands of businesses, professions, and trades, including the imposition of licence fees or other fees, other than laws in respect of the accreditation, certification, or professional conduct of professions and trades; and

 c. other similar matters related to the regulation and administration of Nisga'a Lands.

48.   Each Nisga'a Village Government may make laws in respect of the matters referred to in paragraph 47, to apply on their respective Nisga'a Village Lands.

49.   In the event of an inconsistency or conflict between a Nisga'a law under paragraph 47 or 48 and a federal or provincial law, the Nisga'a law prevails to the extent of the inconsistency or conflict.

50.   Nisga'a Lisims Government may make laws in respect of:

a. subject to paragraphs 2, 3, and 4 of the Land Title Chapter, the establishment and operation of a land title or land registry system, in respect of estates, interests, charges, encumbrances, conditions, provisos, restrictions, exceptions, and reservations on or in Nisga'a Lands, including the establishment of a requirement similar to subsection 20(1) of the Land Title Act;

b. designation of any parcel of Nisga'a Lands as Nisga'a Private Lands or Nisga'a Village Lands;

c. expropriation by Nisga'a Government for public purposes and public works, of estates, or interests in Nisga'a Lands other than:

   i. interests referred to in paragraphs 30 and 41 of the Lands Chapter to which Nisga'a Lands are subject on the effective date,

   ii. subject to paragraphs 35 and 36 of the Lands Chapter, interests referred to in paragraphs 33 and 34 of the Lands Chapter to which Nisga'a Lands are subject on the effective date,

   iii. estates or interests expropriated by Canada in accordance with the Lands Chapter, and

   iv. rights of way acquired by British Columbia or a public utility in accordance with the Roads and Rights of Way Chapter; and

d. other similar matters related to the regulation and administration of Nisga'a Lands.

51. In the event of an inconsistency or conflict between a Nisga'a law under paragraph 50 and a federal or provincial law, the Nisga'a law prevails to the extent of the inconsistency or conflict.

52. Notwithstanding paragraph 51, in the event of a conflict between a Nisga'a law and a federal law of general application in respect of prospecting for, production of, refining, and handling of uranium or other products capable of releasing atomic energy, the federal law prevails to the extent of the conflict. Nothing in this paragraph is intended to require the production of uranium or other products capable of releasing atomic energy. . . .

Public Order, Peace, and Safety

59. Nisga'a Lisims Government may make laws in respect of the regulation, control, or prohibition of any actions, activities, or undertakings on Nisga'a Lands, or on submerged lands within Nisga'a Lands, other than actions, activities, or undertakings on submerged lands that are authorized by the Crown, that constitute, or may constitute, a nuisance, a trespass, a danger to public health, or a threat to public order, peace, or safety.

60. A Nisga'a Village Government may make laws in respect of the regulation, control, or prohibition of any actions, activities, or undertakings on the Nisga'a Village Lands of that Nisga'a Village, or on submerged lands within those Nisga'a Village Lands, other than actions, activities, or undertakings on those submerged lands that are authorized by the Crown, that constitute, or may constitute, a nuisance, a trespass, a danger to public health, or a threat to public order, peace, or safety.

61. For greater certainty, Nisga'a Government authority does not include authority in respect of criminal law. 62. In the event of a conflict between a Nisga'a law

under paragraph 59 or 60 and a federal or provincial law of general application, the federal or provincial law prevails to the extent of the conflict. . . .

Buildings, Structures, and Public Works

69. Subject to the Roads and Rights of Way Chapter, Nisga'a Lisims Government may make laws in respect of the design, construction, maintenance, repair, and demolition of buildings, structures, and public works on Nisga'a Lands.

70. Subject to the Roads and Rights of Way Chapter, a Nisga'a Village Government may make laws in respect of the matters referred to in paragraph 69, to apply on the Nisga'a Village Lands of that Nisga'a Village.

71. In the event of a conflict between a Nisga'a law under paragraph 69 or 70 and a federal or provincial law of general application, the federal or provincial law prevails to the extent of the conflict.

Traffic and Transportation

72. A Nisga'a Village Government may make laws in respect of the regulation of traffic and transportation on Nisga'a Roads within its village, to the same extent as municipal governments have authority in respect of the regulation of traffic and transportation in municipalities in British Columbia.

73. Nisga'a Lisims Government may make laws in respect of the regulation of traffic and transportation on Nisga'a Roads, other than Nisga'a Roads within Nisga'a villages, to the same extent as municipal governments have authority in respect of the regulation of traffic and transportation in municipalities in British Columbia.

74. In the event of a conflict between a Nisga'a law under paragraphs 72 or 73 and a federal or provincial law of general application, the federal or provincial law prevails to the extent of the conflict.

Solemnization of Marriages

75. Nisga'a Lisims Government may make laws in respect of solemnization of marriages within British Columbia, including prescribing conditions under which individuals appointed by Nisga'a Lisims Government may solemnize marriages.

76. In the event of a conflict between a Nisga'a law under paragraph 75 and a federal or provincial law of general application, the federal or provincial law prevails to the extent of the conflict.

77. Individuals appointed by Nisga'a Lisims Government to solemnize marriages:
    a. will be registered by British Columbia as persons authorized to solemnize marriages; and
    b. have the authority to solemnize marriages under British Columbia law and Nisga'a law, and have all the associated rights, duties and responsibilities of a marriage commissioner under the provincial Marriage Act.

Social Services

78. Nisga'a Lisims Government may make laws in respect of the provision of social services by Nisga'a Government to Nisga'a citizens, other than the licensing and regulation of facility-based services off Nisga'a Lands.

79. In the event of a conflict between a Nisga'a law under paragraph 78 and a federal or provincial law of general application, the federal or provincial law prevails to the extent of the conflict.

80. If Nisga'a Lisims Government makes laws under paragraph 78, at the request of any Party, the Parties will negotiate and attempt to reach agreements in respect of exchange of information, avoidance of double payments, and related matters.

81. At the request of any Party, the Parties will negotiate and attempt to reach agreements for administration and delivery by Nisga'a Government of federal and provincial social services and programs for all individuals residing within Nisga'a Lands. Those agreements will include a requirement that Nisga'a citizens and individuals who are not Nisga'a citizens be treated equally in the provision of those social services and programs.

Health Services

82. Nisga'a Lisims Government may make laws in respect of health services on Nisga'a Lands.

83. In the event of a conflict between a Nisga'a law under paragraph 82 and a federal or provincial law of general application, the federal or provincial law prevails to the extent of the conflict.

84. Notwithstanding paragraph 83, in the event of an inconsistency or conflict between a Nisga'a law determining the organization and structure for the delivery of health services on Nisga'a Lands, and a federal or provincial law, the Nisga'a law prevails to the extent of the inconsistency or conflict.

85. At the request of any Party, the Parties will negotiate and attempt to reach agreements for Nisga'a Lisims Government delivery and administration of federal and provincial health services and programs for all individuals residing within Nisga'a Lands. Those agreements will include a requirement that Nisga'a citizens and individuals who are not Nisga'a citizens be treated equally in the provision of those health services and programs.

Aboriginal Healers

86. Nisga'a Lisims Government may make laws in respect of the authorization or licensing of individuals who practice as aboriginal healers on Nisga'a Lands, but, this authority to make laws does not include the authority to regulate products or substances that are regulated under federal or provincial laws of general application.

87. In the event of an inconsistency or conflict between a Nisga'a law under paragraph 86 and a federal or provincial law, the Nisga'a law prevails to the extent of the inconsistency or conflict.

88. Any Nisga'a law under paragraph 86 will include measures in respect of competence, ethics and quality of practice that are reasonably required to protect the public.

Child and Family Services

89. Nisga'a Lisims Government may make laws in respect of child and family services on Nisga'a Lands, provided that those laws include standards

comparable to provincial standards intended to ensure the safety and well-being of children and families.

90. Notwithstanding any laws made under paragraph 89, if there is an emergency in which a child on Nisga'a Lands is at risk, British Columbia may act to protect the child and, in those circumstances, unless British Columbia and Nisga'a Lisims Government otherwise agree, British Columbia will refer the matter back to Nisga'a Lisims Government after the emergency.

91. In the event of an inconsistency or conflict between a Nisga'a law under paragraph 89 and a federal or provincial law, the Nisga'a law prevails to the extent of the inconsistency or conflict.

92. At the request of Nisga'a Lisims Government, Nisga'a Lisims Government and British Columbia will negotiate and attempt to reach agreements in respect of child and family services for Nisga'a children who do not reside on Nisga'a Lands.

93. Laws of general application in respect of reporting of child abuse apply on Nisga'a Lands.

Child Custody

94. Nisga'a Government has standing in any judicial proceedings in which custody of a Nisga'a child is in dispute, and the court will consider any evidence and representations in respect of Nisga'a laws and customs in addition to any other matters it is required by law to consider.

95. The participation of Nisga'a Government in proceedings referred to in paragraph 94 will be in accordance with the applicable rules of court and will not affect the court's ability to control its process.

Adoption

96. Nisga'a Lisims Government may make laws in respect of the adoption of Nisga'a children, provided that those laws:
    a. expressly provide that the best interests of the child be the paramount consideration in determining whether an adoption will take place; and
    b. require Nisga'a Lisims Government to provide British Columbia and Canada with records of all adoptions occurring under Nisga'a laws.

97. Nisga'a law applies to the adoption of a Nisga'a child residing off Nisga'a Lands if:
    a. the parent, parents, or guardian of the child consent to the application of Nisga'a law to the adoption; or
    b. a court dispenses with the requirement for the consent referred to in subparagraph (a), in accordance with the criteria that would be used by that court in an application to dispense with the requirement for a parent or guardian's consent to an adoption.

98. If the Director of Child Protection, or a successor to that position, becomes the guardian of a Nisga'a child, the Director will:
    a. provide notice to Nisga'a Lisims Government that the Director is the guardian of the Nisga'a child;
    b. provide notice to Nisga'a Lisims Government of any plan for the Nisga'a child's care that could result in an application to adopt the Nisga'a child; and

c. consent to the application of Nisga'a law to the adoption of that child, unless it is determined under provincial law that there are good reasons to believe it is in the best interests of the child to withhold consent.

99. In the event of an inconsistency or conflict between a Nisga'a law under paragraph 96 and a federal or provincial law, the Nisga'a law prevails to the extent of the inconsistency or conflict.

Pre-school to Grade 12 Education

100. Nisga'a Lisims Government may make laws in respect of pre-school to grade 12 education on Nisga'a Lands of Nisga'a citizens, including the teaching of Nisga'a language and culture, provided that those laws include provisions for:

a. curriculum, examination, and other standards that permit transfers of students between school systems at a similar level of achievement and permit admission of students to the provincial post-secondary education systems;

b. certification of teachers, other than for the teaching of Nisga'a language and culture, by:

i. a Nisga'a Institution, in accordance with standards comparable to standards applicable to individuals who teach in public or independent schools in British Columbia, or

ii. a provincial body having the responsibility to certify individuals who teach in public or independent schools in British Columbia; and

c. certification of teachers, for the teaching of Nisga'a language and culture, by a Nisga'a Institution, in accordance with standards established under Nisga'a law.

101. In the event of an inconsistency or conflict between a Nisga'a law under paragraph 100 and a federal or provincial law, the Nisga'a law prevails to the extent of the inconsistency or conflict.

102. If Nisga'a Lisims Government makes laws under paragraph 100, at the request of Nisga'a Lisims Government or British Columbia, those Parties will negotiate and attempt to reach agreements concerning the provision of Kindergarten to Grade 12 education to:

a. persons other than Nisga'a citizens residing within Nisga'a Lands; and

b. Nisga'a citizens residing off Nisga'a Lands.

Post-Secondary Education

103. Nisga'a Lisims Government may make laws in respect of post-secondary education within Nisga'a Lands, including:

a. the establishment of post-secondary institutions that have the ability to grant degrees, diplomas or certificates;

b. the determination of the curriculum for post-secondary institutions established under Nisga'a law;

c. the accreditation and certification of individuals who teach or research Nisga'a language and culture; and

d. the provision for and coordination of all adult education programs.

104. Nisga'a laws in respect of post-secondary education will include standards

comparable to provincial standards in respect of:

a. institutional organizational structure and accountability;
b. admission standards and policies;
c. instructors' qualifications and certification;
d. curriculum standards sufficient to permit transfers of students between provincial post-secondary institutions; and
e. requirements for degrees, diplomas, or certificates.

105. In the event of an inconsistency or conflict between a Nisga'a law under paragraph 103 and a federal or provincial law, the Nisga'a law prevails to the extent of the inconsistency or conflict.

106. Nisga'a Lisims Government may operate and provide post-secondary education services outside Nisga'a Lands in accordance with federal and provincial laws.

107. Nisga'a Lisims Government may prescribe the terms and conditions under which Nisga'a post-secondary institutions may enter into arrangements with other institutions or British Columbia to provide post-secondary education outside Nisga'a Lands.

Gambling and Gaming

108. British Columbia will not licence or approve gambling or gaming facilities on Nisga'a Lands other than in accordance with any terms and conditions established by Nisga'a Government that are not inconsistent with federal and provincial laws of general application.

109. Any change in federal or provincial legislation or policy that permits the involvement of aboriginal peoples in the regulation of gambling and gaming will, with the consent of Nisga'a Lisims Government, apply to Nisga'a Government.

Intoxicants

110. Nisga'a Government may make laws in respect of the prohibition of, and the terms and conditions for, the sale, exchange, possession, or consumption of intoxicants on Nisga'a Lands.

111. In the event of a conflict between a Nisga'a law under paragraph 110 and a federal or provincial law of general application, the federal or provincial law prevails to the extent of the conflict.

112. The Nisga'a Nation, its agents and assignees have:

a. the exclusive right to sell liquor on Nisga'a Lands in accordance with laws of general application; and
b. the right to purchase liquor from the British Columbia Liquor Distribution Branch, or its successors, in accordance with federal and provincial laws of general application. . . .

Devolution of Cultural Property

115. In paragraphs 116 to 119, "cultural property" means:

a. ceremonial regalia and similar personal property associated with a Nisga'a chief or clan; and
b. other personal property that has cultural significance to the Nisga'a Nation.

116. Nisga'a Lisims Government may make laws in respect of devolution of the cultural property of a Nisga'a citizen who dies intestate. In the event of an inconsistency or conflict between a Nisga'a law under this paragraph and a federal or provincial law, the Nisga'a law prevails to the extent of the inconsistency or conflict.

117. Nisga'a Lisims Government has standing in any judicial proceeding in which:
    a. the validity of the will of a Nisga'a citizen; or
    b. the devolution of the cultural property of a Nisga'a citizen is at issue, including any proceedings under wills variation legislation.

118. Nisga'a Lisims Government may commence an action under wills variation legislation in British Columbia in respect of the will of a Nisga'a citizen that provides for a devolution of cultural property. . . .

Other Areas of Legislative Jurisdiction

121. In addition to the laws that Nisga'a Government may make under this Chapter, Nisga'a Government may make laws in respect of matters within Nisga'a Government jurisdiction as set out in, and in accordance with, this Agreement.

EMERGENCY PREPAREDNESS

122. Nisga'a Lisims Government, with respect to Nisga'a Lands, has the rights, powers, duties, and obligations of a local authority under federal and provincial legislation in respect of emergency preparedness and emergency measures.

123. Nisga'a Lisims Government may make laws in respect of its rights, powers, duties, and obligations under paragraph 122. In the event of a conflict between a Nisga'a law under this paragraph and a federal or provincial law of general application, the federal or provincial law prevails to the extent of the conflict.

124. For greater certainty, Nisga'a Lisims Government may declare a state of local emergency, and exercise the powers of a local authority in respect of local emergencies in accordance with federal and provincial laws in respect of emergency measures, but any declaration and any exercise of those powers is subject to the authority of Canada and British Columbia set out in those federal and provincial laws.

125. Nothing in this Agreement affects the authority of:
    a. Canada to declare a national emergency; or
    b. British Columbia to declare a provincial emergency in accordance with federal and provincial laws of general application.

OTHER MATTERS

126. For greater certainty, the authority of Nisga'a Government to make laws in respect of a subject matter as set out in this Agreement includes the authority to make laws and to do other things as may be necessarily incidental to exercising its authority.

127. Nisga'a Government may make laws and do other things that may be necessary to enable each of the Nisga'a Nation, a Nisga'a Village, and Nisga'a Government to exercise its rights, or to carry out its responsibilities, under this Agreement.

128. Nisga'a Government may provide for the imposition of penalties, including

fines, restitution, and imprisonment for the violation of Nisga'a laws, within the limits set out for summary conviction offences in the Criminal Code of Canada or the British Columbia Offence Act.

129. Nisga'a Government may adopt federal or provincial laws in respect of matters within Nisga'a Government jurisdiction as set out in this Agreement. . . .

■ SELECTED BIBLIOGRAPHY

Asch, M., "Aboriginal Self-Government and the Construction of Canadian Constitutional Identity" (1992) 30:2 *Alta. L. Rev.* 465.

Borrows, J., "A Genealogy of Law: Inherent Sovereignty and First Nations Self-Government" (1992) 30 *Osgoode Hall L.J.* 2.

Cassidy F., and R. Bish, *Indian Government: Its Meaning in Practice*. Montreal: The Institute for Research on Public Policy, 1989.

Clark, B., *Native Liberty, Crown Sovereignty*. Montreal: McGill-Queen's University Press, 1990.

Doerr, A., "Building New Orders of Government—The Future of Aboriginal Self-Government" (1997) 40:2 *Can. Pub. Admin.* 274.

Isaac, T., "The Storm Over Aboriginal Self-Government: Section 35 of the *Constitution Act, 1982* and the Redefinition of the Inherent Right of Aboriginal Self-Government" [1992] 2 C.N.L.R. 6.

Macklem, P. ,"First Nations, Self-Government and the Borders of the Canadian Legal Imagination" (1991) 36 *McGill L.J.* 382.

Morse, B.W., "Permafrost Rights: Aboriginal Self-Government and the Supreme Court in *R.* v. *Pamajewon*" (September 1997) 42 *McGill L.J.* 1011.

Nakatsuru, S., "A Constitutional Right of Indian Self-Government" (1985) 43 *U.T. Fac. L. Rev.* 72.

Olynyk, J., "Approaches to Sorting Out Jurisdiction in a Self-Government Context" (1995) 53 *U.T. Fac. L. Rev.* 235.

Royal Commission on Aboriginal Peoples, *Partners in Confederation: Aboriginal Peoples, Self-Government and the Constitution*. Ottawa: RCAP, 1993.

CHAPTER 9
ABORIGINAL WOMEN

INTRODUCTION[1]

Aboriginal women deserve special attention in an examination of Aboriginal law because of the profound effect the law, particularly the *Indian Act* and its governmental regimes, has had on the lives of many Aboriginal women. The issue of sexual equality is a major issue in Aboriginal law. Subsection 35(4) of the *Constitution Act, 1982* provides:

> Notwithstanding any other provision of this Act, the Aboriginal and treaty rights referred to in subsection (1) are guaranteed equally to male and female persons.

This section is significant because it ensures constitutionalized equal treatment for Aboriginal women in the application of Aboriginal and treaty rights. This special protection is necessary because, in part, of the negative and disruptive effects that the *Indian Act* system of government has on the traditional checks and balances on government in traditional Aboriginal societies. For example, members of the Iroquois Confederacy, which occupied parts of what is now the state of New York, southern Quebec, and Ontario, were governed by a matriarchal system (which continues to this day).

> [Iroquois women] played a profound role in Iroquois political life. . . . The basic unit of government was the "hearth", which consisted of a mother and her children. Each hearth was part of a wider group called an otiianer, and two or more otiianers constituted a clan. The word otiianer specifically referred to the female heirs to the chieftainship titles of the League. The otiianer women selected one of the males within the group to fill any of the fifty seats in the League. . . . Iroquois political philosophy was rooted in the concept that all life was spiritually unified with the natural environment and other forces surrounding people. . . . Iroquois youth were trained to enter a society that was egalitarian, with power more evenly distributed between male and female, young and old.[2]

Aboriginal women are not only members of a minority group (Aboriginal people) that has been subject to adverse discrimination, but are also disadvantaged because of the adverse discrimination they receive as a result of being female. On this point, Gerber writes:

---

1 Parts of this introduction come from T. Isaac and M.S. Maloughney, "Dually Disadvantaged and Historically Forgotten?: Aboriginal Women and the Inherent Right of Aboriginal Self-Government" (1992) 21:3 *Man. L.J.* 453. Readers are encouraged to reference vol. 4, chap. 2 of the *Report of the Royal Commission on Aboriginal Peoples* (Ottawa, RCAP: 1996), entitled "Women's Perspectives," and J. Silman, ed., *Enough Is Enough* (Toronto: Women's Press, 1987).
2 D. Grinde and B. Johansen, *Exemplar of Liberty: Native America and the Evolution of Democracy* (Los Angeles: University of California Press, 1991), 27–28.

[N]ative females suffer multiple jeopardy on the basis of a number of objective indicators of social and economic well-being. The fact that Indians as a group are and Indian females in particular suffer the greatest disadvantage suggests that Indian status, with its historical trappings of colonial dependency, does indeed create additional barriers to economic and social health. The position of Indian women with respect to labour-force participation and income, suggests that they are the most severely handicapped in their exchange relations with employers.[3]

The first comprehensive legislation concerning Indians was enacted by the federal Parliament in 1869.[4] The 1869 act imposed European ideals and practices. For example, prior to European contact, many Aboriginal women possessed what could be compared to the right to vote, which it took European women hundreds of years to attain. This traditional system was restricted with the imposition of the act. The "imposition of the *Indian Act* in Canada actively destroyed traditional government."[5] Jamieson summarizes the three main functions of the *Indian Act* legislation as follows:

> (1) "civilizing" the Indians—that is, assimilating them (and their lands) into Eurocanadian citizenry;
> (2) while accomplishing this, the ever more efficient "better management" of Indians and their lands was a always a goal to be pursued and, following on this, an important element in better management was controlling expenditure and resources;
> (3) to accomplish this efficiency it became important to define who was an Indian and who was not.[6]

The 1869 act imposed many changes on the traditional ways in which Indian women were treated. Upon the death of an Indian male, his goods and possessions passed to his children and not to his spouse. She was excluded because her care was seen as being the responsibility of the children. Band councils were to be elected, which is non-traditional to many Indian tribes, and the group entitled to elect councillors was restricted to adult males. Females and children had no substantive role in elections and government. Section 6 of the 1869 act provided that any Indian women who married a non-Indian lost her status as an "Indian" under the act. Her children also lost their status. This provision eventually became s. 12(1)(b). Finally, an Indian woman who married an Indian man from another band lost her status (and so did her children) to her own band and automatically became a member of the male's band.

---

3   G.M. Gerber, "Multiple Jeopardy: A Socio-Economic Comparison of Men and Women Among the Indian, Metis and Inuit Peoples of Canada" (1990) 22:3 *Canadian Ethnic Studies* 80.

4   *An Act for the gradual enfranchisement of Indians, the better management of Indian affairs, and to extend the provisions of the Act 31st Victoria, Chapter 42*, S.C. 1869, c. 6.

5   V. Kirkness, "Emerging Native Women" (1987–88) 2:2 *C.J.W.L.*, 411.

6   K. Jamieson, "Sex Discrimination and the Indian Act." In *Arduous Journey: Canadian Indians and Decolonization*, J.R. Ponting, ed. (Toronto: McClelland & Stewart, 1986), 117.

The 1869 act promoted assimilation. In addition, the act affirmed the principle that, like European women, Indian women should be subject to their husbands and that by law, the children belonged to him. The first act to bear the name "Indian Act" was enacted in 1876 and embodied all of the above-mentioned provisions. This new act also expanded the definition of "Indian" by promoting the legitimacy of descent through the male line. Although some of the above provisions vanished with time, the requirement that Indian women lost their status upon marrying non-Indian men was not abolished until 1985.

What eventually became s. 12(1)(b) of the *Indian Act*,[7] provided that Indian women who married non-Indian men lost their "Indian" status. As such, they could not receive the benefits accorded to registered Indians. The same did not hold true for Indian men. The *Indian Act* institutionalised discrimination in many ways. Douglas Sanders reported the following to the Standing Committee on Indian Affairs and Northern Development:

> Section 12(1)(b) is not an aberration; it reflects the main thesis in the membership system of the Indian Act which is determining membership on the basis of kinship and not on the basis of race. . . . The Indian Act focused on nuclear family units, and to ensure that all members of the nuclear family unit could reside on the reserve or not reside on the reserve, it was determined that the units should be single status units. To achieve that, the male was used as the head of the household to determine status for all members of the nuclear family unit. This of course did not coincide with traditional Indian kinship systems, which were not always patrilineal, nor did it align itself with another characteristic of Indian kinship systems which is that they did not focus on nuclear family units but on extended family units.[8]

The 1969 Supreme Court of Canada decision of *R. v. Drybones*[9] considered s. 94(b) of the *Indian Act,* which provided that it was an offence for an Indian to be intoxicated off a reserve. Drybones was convicted under s. 94(b) and ultimately appealed the decision to the Supreme Court of Canada. The Supreme Court held that the use of the racial classification of "Indian" in s. 94 violated the equality guarantee set out in the *Canadian Bill of Rights.*[10] The *Bill of Rights* had the effect of limiting the extent to which the *Indian Act* could discriminate against Indians. The *Drybones* decision was the first and only decision by the Supreme Court to hold that a federal statute was inconsistent with the *Bill of Rights*. This decision set the stage for a bright future for the *Bill of Rights*. However, the Supreme Court's 1973 decision of *Attorney-General of Canada* v. *Lavell and Bedard*[11] quickly dampened such hopes.

In *Lavell and Bedard*, the issue was whether s. 12(1)(b) of the *Indian Act* violated the *Bill of Rights'* "equality before the law" provision. *Lavell and Bedard*

---

7   *Indian Act*, R.S.C. 1985, c. I–5.
8   Canada, House of Commons, Standing Committee on Indian Affairs and Northern Development, *Minutes of Proceedings and Evidence of the Sub-Committee on Indian Women and the Indian Act* (September 14, 1982, 5:13).
9   *R. v. Drybones*, 6 C.N.L.C. 273 (S.C.C.).
10 *Canadian Bill of Rights*, S.C. 1960, c. 44; R.S.C. 1985, App. III.
11 *A.-G. of Canada* v. *Lavell and Bedard*, 7 C.N.L.C. 236 (S.C.C.).

is similar to *Drybones* in that they both deal with the definition of "equality" under the *Bill of Rights*. Section 12(1)(b) denied an Indian woman who married a non-Indian her Indian status, including her right to hold property and live on an Indian reserve. A male Indian who married a non-Indian retained his Indian status.

The Supreme Court held, five to four, that s. 12(1)(b) did not constitute a violation of equality before the law. Justice Ritchie, writing for the majority, wrote that the *Indian Act* might discriminate against women, but so long as the provision applied equally to all women affected, there was no violation of equality before the law. It is difficult to reconcile this decision with that of *Drybones*, which Ritchie J. also wrote.

The issue surrounding s. 12(1)(b) took on an international stature when Sandra Lovelace, an Indian woman divorced from her non-Indian male spouse, tried unsuccessfully for three years to obtain housing for herself and for her son on her home reserve in New Brunswick. Lovelace petitioned the United Nations' Human Rights Committee to examine s. 12(1)(b) in light of its discriminatory effects on Indian women. In July 1981, the Human Rights Committee issued its final decision on the matter and declared that s. 12(1)(b) was inconsistent with the United Nations' *International Covenant on Civil and Political Rights*.[12] However, because the Human Rights Committee's decision had no direct domestic legal impact, it took until 1985 before the provisions were amended.

After much public pressure, including the negative decision by the United Nations' Human Rights Committee, in 1985, Parliament passed Bill C–31, an *Act to Amend the Indian Act*,[13] to bring the *Indian Act* into accord with the *Canadian Charter of Rights and Freedoms* to ensure equality of treatment to Indian men and women. Changes were made to the act to recognize the right of Aboriginal governments to control their own membership. The amendments also abolished the concept of "enfranchisement," which permitted Indians to give up their Indian status and band membership for a number of reasons.

Under Bill C–31 Indian women who lost their Indian status and band membership because of sexual discrimination under s. 12 of the act were once again eligible to have their Indian status and band membership restored. As well, children of reinstated women were accorded the right to have their status and band membership restored.

The positive effects of Bill C–31 are obvious. Bands received increased control over membership and the *Indian Act* was brought into accord with the equality provisions of the *Charter*. Women and their children regained their status as Indians.[14] However, there are some not so apparent impacts. One example is found in s. 6(2). Wendy Moss writes:

> Section 6(2), the so-called "second-generation cut-off" or "half-descent" rule, terminates Indian status for persons with fewer than two "Indian" grandparents—Indian

---

12 Adopted and opened for signature, ratification and accession by General Assembly resolution 2200 A (XXI) of December 16, 1966. Entered into force on March 23, 1976.

13 *An Act to Amend the Indian Act*, S.C. 1985, c. 31 (June 28, 1985).

14 Canada, Indian and Northern Affairs, *Impacts of the 1985 Amendments to the Indian Act (Bill C–31): Summary Report* (Ottawa: 1990).

meaning with legal status as an "Indian" under the *Indian Act*. This rule applies to children born after, and children of women, *but not men*, who married out prior to 17 April 1985. In the case of descendants of Indian men who married out before 1985, a quarter-descent rule applies. . . . The new by-law powers of band councils over residency on reserves have been exercised by some in a restrictive manner, effectively excluding reinstated women and their children from band membership and access to services. . . . These problems are by no means universal.[15]

A Canadian Human Rights Tribunal decision underscores some of the problems that women reinstated by Bill C–31 have encountered upon returning to their home reserves. In *Courtois* v. *Canada*,[16] Louise Courtois and Marie-Jeanne Raphael, Indian women reinstated under Bill C–31, complained to the Canadian Human Rights Commission that they and their children were being discriminated against by the Department of Indian Affairs in that the department was not permitting their children to have access to the Pointe-Bleue Band–controlled school. The discrimination related to a moratorium declared by the band council pursuant to s. 11(2) of the *Indian Act*, which suspended for two years the provision of services to reinstated Indian women. The Department of Indian Affairs agreed with the band council's decision. Both women filed complaints of discrimination against the department on the grounds of sex and marital status under the *Canadian Human Rights Act*.[17]

The Human Rights Tribunal concluded that the department's proposal to educate the children of reinstated Indian women off-reserve had the effect of creating distinctions between band and non-band members on the basis of sex and marital status. The tribunal held that the "moratorium was clearly aimed at women reinstated by Bill C–31."[18] The department should have "taken action to ensure school service was provided to children of reinstated women at Pointe-Bleue."[19]

The Federal Court of Canada, Trial Division, decision of *Corbiere* v. *Canada*[20] provides an example of the discrimination faced by off-reserve band members, especially reinstated Indian women. The decision concerns the right of off-reserve band members to vote in band elections. The issue of off-reserve voting rights strikes at the heart of democratic government and the fundamental rights of, in this case, many reinstated Indian women living off-reserve to participate in their government. The court held that the provisions denying non-resident band members

---

15 Wendy Moss, "Indigenous Self-Government in Canada and Sexual Equality under the Indian Act: Resolving Conflicts Between Collective and Individual Rights" (1990) 15:2 *Queen's L.J.* 281.

16 *Courtois* v. *Canada*, [1991] 1 C.N.L.R. 40 (Can. H.R.T.). In *Jacobs* v. *Mohawk Council of Kahnawake*, [1998] 3 C.N.L.R. 68 (Can. H.R.T.), a Canadian human rights tribunal held that the Mohawk Council of Kahnawake discriminated against a number of individuals and their children on the basis that they were registrants under Bill C-31.

17 *Canadian Human Rights Act*, R.S.C. 1985, c. H–6.

18 *Courtois* v. *Canada*, [1991] 1 C.N.L.R. 40 at 41 (Can. H.R.T.).

19 Ibid.

20 *Corbiere* v. *Canada*, [1994] 1 C.N.L.R. 71 (F.C.T.D.); for commentary see T. Isaac, "Case Commentary: *Corbiere* v. *Canada*" [1994] 1 C.N.L.R. 55.

the right to vote (in matters relating to communal property) violated s. 15 of the *Charter* and could not be justified by s. 1.

The Federal Court of Appeal affirmed the Trial Court judgment but altered the remedy.[21] The court applied the *Van der Peet* analysis (see chapter 7) and concluded that there was not enough evidence to establish that the exclusion of non-resident band members from voting is an Aboriginal right protected by s. 35 nor is it one of the "other rights or freedoms" referenced by s. 25 of the *Charter*. Instead of affirming the invalidity of s. 77(1) in its entirety as the Trial Court did, the Court of Appeal severed the words "and is ordinarily resident on the reserve" from s. 77(1) as it applies to the Batchewana Band and ordered a constitutional exemption. Section 77(1) now reads for the band: "A member of a band who has attained the age of eighteen years is qualified to vote for a person nominated to be chief of the band and, where the reserve for voting purposes consists of one section, to vote for persons nominated as councillors." The Trial Court decision is provided because it was affirmed on appeal and it provides greater analysis of the circumstances.

Menno Boldt underscores the significance of the rights of reinstated Indian women in the following passage:

> Bill C–31, which restored Indian status to approximately 100,000 Indians . . . , thus making them eligible for band/tribal membership. Many band/tribal councils opposed Bill C–31 on grounds that their ancestral heritage (i.e. reserve lands and treaty benefits, etc.) is inadequate to provide their present membership with an acceptable standard of living. Therefore, they could not accommodate additional members. This resulted in a squabble among blood heirs over their ancestral heritage. The squabble over this heritage is complicated by "privatization," that is, the Indian Act provision under which communal benefits (assets and entitlements) are being transferred into individual benefits. The Indian elite class, which benefits disproportionately from privatization, is motivated by a powerful class-based interest to protect their bloated share of band/tribal assets from potential diminishment by claims from any additional "heirs."[22]

On April 4, 1995, federal minister of Indian Affairs and Northern Development, Ron Irwin, wrote to all chiefs, councillors, and leaders of First Nations organizations asking for their views on possible amendments to the *Indian Act*. This may provide the necessary impetus to make the shift from "non-Indian" to "reinstated Indian" easier and less contentious.

The issue in the 1994 Supreme Court of Canada decision *Native Women's Assn. of Canada* v. *Canada*[23] was whether or not the Native Women's Association of Canada (NWAC) was entitled to funding similar to that provided to the other

---

21 *Batchewana Indian Band* v. *Canada* (sub nom. *Corbiere* v. *Canada*), [1997] 3 C.N.L.R. 21 (F.C.A.); application for leave to appeal to S.C.C. granted April 24, 1997.

22 M. Boldt, *Surviving as Indians: The Challenge of Self-Government* (Toronto: University of Toronto Press, 1993), 212–13.

23 *Native Women's Assn. of Canada* v. *Canada*, [1995] 1 C.N.L.R. 47 (S.C.C.).

national Aboriginal organizations to participate in the 1992 constitutional discussions (that is to say, the Inuit Tapirisat of Canada, the Metis National Council, the Assembly of First Nations, and the Native Council of Canada). The court held that the federal government's decision not to provide equal funding and participation to NWAC in the constitutional review discussions which lead to the 1992 Charlottetown Accord did not violate their rights under ss. 2(b) and 28 of the *Charter.* The freedom of expression under s. 2(b) of the *Charter* does not guarantee any particular means of expression or place a positive obligation upon the federal government to consult anyone. The Supreme Court also held that s. 35 of the *Constitution Act, 1982* was inapplicable because the right of Aboriginal people to participate in constitutional discussions does not derive from any existing Aboriginal or treaty right under s. 35. NWAC's primary argument was that the decision to fund these primarily "male-dominated" groups had the effect of leaving out the voices of Aboriginal women in the constitutional process. The court rejected this claim due to a lack of evidence.

On May 26, 1997, the residents of the eastern Northwest Territories, to become Nunavut on April 1, 1999, voted by plebiscite on whether or not the first Nunavut Legislative Assembly would have equal numbers of men and women, one man and one woman for each electoral district. The purpose of the proposal, put forward by the advisory Nunavut Implementation Commission, was to provide for equality of representation between men and women in the Nunavut legislature and to deal with the historical pattern of fewer women than men participating in public office. The people of Nunavut rejected the proposal by a vote of 57 percent against and 43 percent in favour.

■ CASES AND MATERIALS

1. Relevant Legislative and Constitutional Provisions

1a. Section 12(1) and (2) of the *Indian Act*, R.S.C. 1970, c. I–6

Section 12 was repealed by S.C. 1985, c. 27, s. 4.

12.(1) The following persons are not entitled to be registered, namely,
  (a)   a person who
     (i)   has received or has been allotted half-breed lands or money scrip,
     (ii) is a descendant of a person described in subparagraph (i),
     (iii) is enfranchised, or
     (iv) is a person born of a marriage entered into after the 4th day of September 1951 and has attained the age of twenty-one years, whose mother and whose father's mother are not persons described in paragraph 11(1)(a), (b) or (d) or entitled to be registered by virtue of paragraph 11(1)(e),
     unless, being a woman, that person is the wife or widow of a person described in section 11, and
  (b)   a woman who married a person who is not an Indian, unless that

woman is subsequently the wife or widow of a person described in section 11.

(2) The addition to a Band List of the name of an illegitimate child . . . may be protested at any time within twelve months after the addition, and if upon the protest it is decided that the father of the child was not an Indian, the child is not entitled to be registered under that paragraph.

1b. Selected provisions of the *Indian Act*, R.S.C. 1985, c. I–5, relating to membership criteria and Bill C–31 amendments

. . . INDIAN REGISTER . . .

5. (1) There shall be maintained in the Department an Indian Register in which shall be recorded the name of every person who is entitled to be registered as an Indian under this Act.

(2) The names in the Indian Register immediately prior to April 17, 1985 shall constitute the Indian Register on April 17, 1985.

(3) The Registrar may at any time add to or delete from the Indian Register the name of any person who, in accordance with this Act, is entitled or not entitled, as the case may be, to have his name included in the Indian Register.

(4) The Indian Register shall indicate the date on which each name was added thereto or deleted therefrom.

(5) The name of a person who is entitled to be registered is not required to be recorded in the Indian Register unless an application for registration is made to the Registrar. R.S. 1970, c. I–6, s. 5: R.S. 1985 (1st Supp.), c. 32, s. 4. . . .

6. (1) Subject to section 7, a person is entitled to be registered if

(a)　that person was registered or entitled to be registered immediately prior to April 17, 1985;

(b)　that person is a member of a body of persons that has been declared by the Governor in Council on or after April 17, 1985 to be a band for the purposes of this Act;

(c)　the name of that person was omitted or deleted from the Indian Register, or from a Band List prior to September 4, 1951, under subparagraph 12(1)(a)(iv), paragraph 12(1)(b) or subsection 12(2) or under subparagraph 12(1)(a)(iii) pursuant to an order made under subsection 109(2), as each provision read immediately prior to April 17,1985, or under any former provision of this Act relating to the same subject-matter as any of those provisions;

(d)　the name of that person was omitted or deleted from the Indian Register, or from a Band List prior to September 4, 1951, under subparagraph 12(1)(a)(iii) pursuant to an order made under subsection 109(1), as each provision read immediately prior to April 17, 1985, or under any former provision of this Act relating to the same subject-matter as any of those provisions;

(e)　the name of that person was omitted or deleted from the Indian Register, or from a Band List prior to September 4, 1951,

(i)　under section 13, as it read immediately prior to September 4,

1951, or under any former provision of this Act relating to the same subject-matter as that section, or

 (ii) under section 111, as it read immediately prior to July 1, 1920, or under any former provision of this Act relating to the same subject-matter as that section; or

 (f) that person is a person both of whose parents are or, if no longer living, were at the time of death entitled to be registered under this section.

(2) Subject to section 7, a person is entitled to be registered if that person is a person one of whose parents is or, if no longer living, was at the time of death entitled to be registered under subsection (1).

(3) For the purposes of paragraph (1)(f) and subsection (2),

 (a) a person who was no longer living immediately prior to April 17, 1985 but who was at the time of death entitled to be registered shall be deemed to be entitled to be registered under paragraph (1)(a); and

 (b) a person described in paragraph (1)(c), (d), (e), or (f) or subsection (2) who was no longer living on April 17, 1985 shall be deemed to be entitled to be registered under that provision. R.S. 1970, c. I–6, s. 6; R.S. 1985 (1st Supp.), c. 32, s. 4; R.S. 1985 (4th Supp.), c. 43, s. 1.

7. (1) The following persons are not entitled to be registered:

 (a) a person who was registered under paragraph 11(1)(f), as it read immediately prior to April 17,1985, or under any former provision of this Act relating to the same subject-matter as that paragraph, and whose name was subsequently omitted or deleted from the Indian Register under this Act or

 (b) a person who is the child of a person who was registered or entitled to be registered under paragraph 11(1)(f), as it read immediately prior to April 17, 1985, or under any former provision of this Act relating to the same subject-matter as that paragraph, and is also the child of a person who is not entitled to be registered.

(2) Paragraph (1)(a) does not apply in respect of a female person who was, at any time prior to being registered under paragraph 11(1)(f) entitled to be registered under any other provision of this Act.

(3) Paragraph (1)(f) does not apply in respect of the child of a female person who was, at any time prior to being registered under paragraph 11(1)(f), entitled to be registered under any other provision of this Act. R.S. 1970, c. I–6, s. 7; R.S. 1985, (1st Supp.), c. 32, s. 4.

BAND LISTS . . .

8. There shall be maintained in accordance with this Act for each band a Band List in which shall be entered the name of every person who is a member of that band. R.S. 1970, c. I–6:, s. 8; R.S. 1985 (1st Supp.), c. 32, s. 4. . . .

9. (1) Until such time as a band assumes control of its Band List, the Band

List of that band shall be maintained in the Department by the Registrar.

(2) The names in a Band List of a band immediately prior to April 17,1985 shall constitute the Band List of that band on April 17, 1985.

(3) The Registrar may at any time add to or delete from a Band List maintained in the Department the name of any person who, in accordance with this Act, is entitled or not entitled, as the case may be, to have his name included in that List.

(4) A Band List maintained in the Department shall indicate the date on which each name was added thereto or deleted therefrom.

(5) The name of a person who is entitled to have his name entered in a Band List maintained in the Department is not required to be entered therein unless an application for entry therein is made to the Registrar. R.S. 1970, c. I–6, s. 9; 1974–75–76, c. 48, s. 25; 1978–79, c. 11, s. 10; 1984, c. 41, s. 2; R.S. 1985 (1st Supp.), c. 32. s. 4. . . .

10.(1) A band may assume control of its own membership if it establishes membership rules for itself in writing in accordance with this section and if, after the band has given appropriate notice of its intention to assume control of its own membership, a majority of the electors of the band gives its consent to the band's control of its own membership.

(2) A Band may, pursuant to the consent of a majority of the electors of the band,

    (a)   after it has given appropriate notice of its intention to do so establish membership rules for itself; and

    (b)   provide for a mechanism for reviewing decisions on membership.

(3) Where the council of a band makes a by-law under paragraph 81(p. 4) bringing this subsection into effect in respect of the band, the consents required under subsection: (1) and (2) shall be given by a majority of the members of the band who are of the full age of eighteen years.

(4) Membership rules established by a band under this section may not deprive any person who had the right to have his name entered in the Band List for that band, immediately prior to the time the rules were established, of the right to have his name so entered by reason only of a situation that existed or an action that was taken before the rules came into force.

(5) For greater certainty, subsection (4) applies in respect of a person who was entitled to have his name entered in the Band List under paragraph 11(1)(c) immediately before the band assumed control of the Band List if that person does not subsequently cease to be entitled to have his name entered in the Band List.

(6) Where the conditions set out in subsection (1) have been met with respect to a band, the council of the band shall forthwith give notice to the Minister in writing that the band is assuming control of its own membership and shall provide the Minister with a copy of the membership rules for the band.

(7) On receipt of a notice from the council of a band under subsection (6), the Minister shall, if the conditions set out in subsection (1) have been complied with, forthwith

    (a)   give notice to the band that it has control of its own membership; and

    (b)   direct the Registrar to provide the band with a copy of the Band List maintained in the Department.

    (8) Where a band assumes control of its membership under this section, the membership rules established by the band shall have effect from the day on which notice is given to the Minister under subsection (6), and any additions to or deletions from the Band List of the band by the Registrar on or after that day are of no effect unless they are in accordance with the membership rules established by the band.

    (9) A band shall maintain its own Band List from the date on which a copy of the Band List is received by the band under paragraph (7)(b), and, subject to section 13.2, the Department shall have no further responsibility with respect to that Band List from that date.

    (10) A band may at any time add to or delete from a Band List maintained by it the name of any person who, in accordance with the membership rules of the band, is entitled or not entitled, as the case may be, to have his name included in that list.

    (11) A Band List maintained by a band shall indicate the date on which each name was added thereto or deleted therefrom. R.S. 1970, c. I–6. s. 10; R.S. 1985 (1st Supp.), c. 32. s. 4.

    11.(1) Commencing on April 17,1985, a person is entitled to have his name entered in a Band List maintained in the Department for a band if

        (a)   the name of that person was entered in the Band List for that band, or that person was entitled to have his name entered in the Band List for that band, immediately prior to April 17, 1985;

        (b)   that person is entitled to be registered under paragraph 6(1)(b) as a member of that band;

        (c)   that person is entitled to be registered under paragraph 6(1)(c) and ceased to be a member of that band by reason of the circumstances set out in that paragraph; or

        (d)   that person was born on or after April 17,1985 and is entitled to he registered under paragraph 6(1)(f) and both parents of that person are entitled to have their names entered in the Band List or, if no longer living, were at the time of death entitled to have their names entered In the Band List.

    (2) Commencing on the day that is two years after the day that an Act entitled An Act to amend the Indian Act, introduced in the House of Commons on February 28, 1985, is assented to, or on such earlier day as may be agreed to under section 13.1, where a band does not have control of its Band List under this Act, a person is entitled to have his name entered in a Band List maintained in the Department for the band

        (a)   if that person is entitled to be registered under paragraph 6(1)(d) or (e) and ceased to be a member of that band by reason of the circumstances set out in that paragraph; or

        (b)   if that person is entitled to be registered under paragraph 6(1)(f) or subsection 6(2) and a parent referred to in that provision is entitled to have his name entered in the Band List or, if no longer living, was at the time of death entitled to have his name entered in the Band List.

(3) For the purposes of paragraph (1)(d) and subsection (2),

   (a) a person whose name was omitted or deleted from the Indian Register or a band list in the circumstances set out in paragraph 6(1)(c), (d) or (e) who was no longer living on the first day on which the person would otherwise be entitled to have the person's name entered in the Band List of the band of which the person ceased to be a member shall be deemed to be entitled to have the person's name so entered; and

   (b) a person described in paragraph 2(b) shall be deemed to be entitled to have the person's name entered in the Band List in which the parent referred to in that paragraph is or was, or is deemed by this section to be, entitled to have the parent's name entered.

(4) Where a band amalgamates with another band or is divided so as to constitute new bands, any person who would otherwise have been entitled to have his name entered in the Band List of that band under this section is entitled to have his name entered in the Band List of the amalgamated band or the new band to which he has the closest family ties, as the case may be. R.S. 1970, c. I–6, s. 11; R.S. 1985 (1st Supp.), c. 32, s. 4; R.S. 1985 (4th Supp.). c. 43, s. 2.

12. Commencing on the day that is two years after the day that an Act entitled An Act to amend the Indian Act, introduced in the House of Commons on February 28, 1985, is assented to, or on such earlier day as may be agreed to under section 13.1, any person who

   (a) is entitled to be registered under section 6, but is not entitled to have his name entered in the Band List maintained in the Department under section 11, or

   (b) is a member of another band, is entitled to have his name entered in the Band List maintained in the Department for a band if the council of the admitting band consents. R.S. 1970, c. I–6, s.12; R.S. 1985 (1st Supp.), c. 32, s. 4.

13. Notwithstanding sections 11 and 12, no person is entitled to have his name entered at the same time in more than one Band List maintained in the Department. R.S. 1970, c. I–6, s. 13; R.S. 1985 (1st Supp.). c. 32, s. 4.

13.1(1)A band may, at any time prior to the day that is two years after the day that an Act entitled An Act to amend the Indian Act, introduced in the House of Commons on February 28,1985, is assented to, decide to leave the control of its Band List with the Department if a majority of the electors of the band gives its consent to that decision.

(2) Where a band decides to leave the control of its Band List with the Department under subsection (1) the council of the band shall forthwith give notice to the Minister in writing to that effect.

(3) Notwithstanding a decision under subsection (1), a band may, at any time after that decision is taken, assume control of its Band List under section 10. R.S. 1985(1st Supp.), c. 32, s. 4.

13.2(1)A band may, at any time after assuming control of its Band List under section 10, decide to return control of the Band List to the Department if a majority of the electors of the band gives its consent to that decision.

(2)   Where a band decides to return control of its Band List to the Department under subsection (1), the council of the band shall forthwith give notice to the Minister in writing to that effect and shall provide the Minister with a copy of the Band List and a copy of all the membership rules that were established by the band under subsection 10(2) while the band maintained its own Band List.

(3)   Where a notice is given under subsection (2) in respect of a Band List, the maintenance of that Band List shall be the responsibility of the Department from the date on which the notice is received and from that time the Band List shall be maintained in accordance with the membership rules set out in section 11. R.S. 1985 (1st Supp.), c. 32, s. 4.

13.3   A person is entitled to have his name entered in a Band List maintained in the Department pursuant to section 13.2 if that person was entitled to have his name entered, and his name was entered, in the Band List immediately before a copy of it was provided to the Minister under subsection 13.2(2), whether or not that person is also entitled to have his name entered in the Band List under section 11. R.S. 1985 (1st Supp.), c. 32, s. 4.

1c.   *Canadian Charter of Rights and Freedoms*

EQUALITY RIGHTS

15.(l)   Every individual is equal before and under the law and has the right to the equal protection and equal benefit of the law without discrimination and, in particular, without discrimination based on race, national or ethnic origin, colour, religion, sex, age or mental or physical disability. . . .

General

25.   The guarantee in this Charter of certain rights and freedoms shall not be construed so as to abrogate or derogate from any aboriginal, treaty or other rights or freedoms that pertain to the aboriginal peoples of Canada including

   (a)   any rights or freedoms that have been recognized by the Royal Proclamation of October 7, 1763; and

   (b)   any rights or freedoms that now exist by way of land claims agreements or may be so acquired. . . .

28.   Notwithstanding anything in this Charter, the rights and freedoms referred to in it are guaranteed equally to male and female persons. . . .

1d.   *Constitution Act, 1982*

PART II
RIGHTS OF THE ABORIGINAL PEOPLES OF CANADA

35.(l)   The existing aboriginal and treaty rights of the aboriginal peoples of Canada are hereby recognized and affirmed. . . .

(4)   Notwithstanding any other provision of this Act, the aboriginal and treaty rights referred to in subsection (1) are guaranteed equally to male and female persons. . . .

2.   *R. v. Drybones,* 6 C.N.L.C. 273 (S.C.C.). Cartwright C.J.C., Pigeon and Abbott JJ. (dissenting), Fauteux, Hall, Spence, Martland, and Judson JJ. concur with Ritchie, November 20, 1969

In *Drybones*, the Supreme Court of Canada held that the use of the racial classification of "Indian" violated the equality provisions of the *Canadian Bill of Rights*. Ironically, the Supreme Court of Canada held in *Lavell and Bedard*, just a few years later, that the "equality before the law" provision of the *Bill of Rights* meant equality among Indian women and not equality between Indian men and women when applied to s. 12(1)(b) of the *Indian Act*.

RITCHIE J.:—This is an appeal brought with leave of this Court from a judgment of the Court of Appeal for the Northwest Territories dismissing an appeal by the Crown from a judgment of Morrow, J., of the Territorial Court of the Northwest Territories by which he had acquitted Joseph Drybones of being "unlawfully intoxicated off a reserve" contrary to s. 94(b) of the *Indian Act,* R.S.C. 1952, c. 149, . . .

The important question raised by this appeal has its origin in the fact that in the Northwest Territories it is not an offence for anyone except an Indian to be intoxicated otherwise than in a public place. The *Liquor Ordinance,* R.O.N.W.T. 1956, c. 60, s. 19(1)(a) which is of general application in the Territories, provides that: "No person shall be in an intoxicated condition in a public place . . ." but unlike s. 94 of the *Indian Act*, there is no provision for a minimum fine and the maximum term of imprisonment is only 30 days as opposed to three months under the *Indian Act.*

The result is that an Indian who is intoxicated in his own home "off a reserve" is guilty of an offence and subject to a minimum fine of not less than $10 or a term of imprisonment not exceeding three months or both, whereas all other citizens in the Territories may, if they see fit, become intoxicated otherwise than in a public place without committing any offence at all. And even if such other citizen is convicted of being intoxicated in a public place, the only penalty provided by the Ordinance is "a fine not exceeding $50 or . . . imprisonment for a term not exceeding 30 days or . . . both fine and imprisonment". . . .

I think that the word "law" as used in s. 1(b) of the Bill of Rights is to be construed as meaning "the law of Canada" as defined in s. 5(2) (i.e., Acts of the Parliament of Canada and any orders, rules or regulations thereunder) and without attempting any exhaustive definition of "equality before the law" I think that s. 1(b) means at least that no individual or group of individuals is to be treated more harshly than another under that law, and I am therefore of opinion that an individual is denied equality before the law if it is made an offence punishable at law, on account of his race, for him to do something which his fellow Canadians are free to do without having committed any offence or having been made subject to any penalty.

It is only necessary for the purpose of deciding this case for me to say that in my opinion s. 94(b) of the *Indian Act* is a law of Canada which creates such an offence and that it can only be construed in such manner that its application would operate so as to abrogate, abridge or infringe one of the rights declared and recognized by the Bill of Rights. For the reasons which I have indicated, I am therefore of opinion that s. 94(b) is inoperative.

For the purpose of determining the issue raised by this appeal it is unnecessary to express any opinion respecting the operation of any other section of the *Indian Act.*

For all the above reasons I would dismiss this appeal.

Since writing the above I have had the advantage of reading the reasons for judgment prepared by the Chief Justice and by Mr. Justice Pigeon which, when read together, appear to me to lead to the conclusion that, even on the assumption that the application of the provisions of prior federal legislation has the effect of denying equality before the law, and thus discriminating against, a sector of the population "by reason of race", they must nevertheless be given full effect notwithstanding the provisions of the Bill of Rights. In view of this conclusion, I find it necessary to restate the position which I take in the matter. . . .

It may well be that the implementation of the Canadian Bill of Rights by the Courts can give rise to great difficulties, but in my view full effect must be given to the terms of s. 2 thereof.

The present case discloses laws of Canada which abrogate, abridge and infringe the right of an individual Indian to equality before the law and in my opinion if those laws are to be applied in accordance with the express language used by Parliament in s. 2 of the Bill of Rights, then s. 94(b) of the *Indian Act* must be declared to be inoperative.

It appears to me to be desirable to make it plain that these reasons for judgment are limited to a situation in which, under the laws of Canada, it is made an offence punishable at law on account of race, for a person to do something which all Canadians who are not members of that race may do with impunity; in my opinion the same considerations do not by any means apply to all the provisions of the *Indian Act.* . . .

3. *Attorney-General of Canada* v. *Lavell and Bedard; Isaac et al.* v. *Bedard,* 7 C.N.L.C. 236 (S.C.C.). Fauteux C.J.C., Abbott, Martland, Judson, Ritchie, Hall, Spence, Pigeon, and Laskin JJ., August 27, 1973

> In *Lavell and Bedard* the Supreme Court of Canada considered whether s. 12(1)(b) of the *Indian Act* violated the *Canadian Bill of Rights'* "equality before the law" provision. *Lavell and Bedard* is similar to *Drybones* in that both cases concern the definition of "equality" under the *Bill of Rights.* The court held that s. 12(1)(b) did not constitute a violation of equality before the law. Although the *Indian Act* might discriminate against Indian women, as long as the provision applied equally to all women affected, there was no violation of equality before the law. It is difficult to reconcile this decision with that of *Drybones,* both of which were written by Ritchie J.

[FAUTEUX, MARTLAND, JUDSON JJ. concur with RITCHIE J.]

ABBOTT (dissenting) . . .

RITCHIE, J.:—I have had the advantage of reading the reasons for judgment prepared for delivery by my brother Laskin.

These appeals, which were heard together, are from two judgments holding that the provisions of s. 12(1)(b) of the *Indian Act,* R.S.C. 1970, c. 1–6, are rendered inoperative by s. 1(b) of the *Canadian Bill of Rights,* R.S.C. 1970, App. III, as denying equality before the law to the two respondents.

Both respondents were registered Indians and "Band" members within the meaning of s. 11(b) of the *Indian Act* when they elected to marry non-Indians and thereby relinquished their status as Indians in conformity with the said s. 12(1)(b) which reads as follows:

> 12(1) The following persons are not entitled to be registered, namely,
>
> (b) a woman who married a person who is not an Indian, unless that woman is subsequently the wife or widow of a person described in section 11.

It is contended on behalf of both respondents that s. 12(1)(b) of the Act should be held to be inoperative as discriminating between Indian men and women and as being in conflict with the provisions of the *Canadian Bill of Rights* and particularly s. 1 thereof which provides:

> 1. It is hereby recognized and declared that in Canada there have existed and shall continue to exist without discrimination by reason of race, national origin, colour, religion or sex, the following human rights and fundamental freedoms, namely,
>
> (b) the right of the individual to equality before the law and the protection of the law; . . .

In my opinion the exclusive legislative authority vested in Parliament under s. 91(24) could not have been effectively exercised without enacting laws establishing the qualifications required to entitle persons to status as Indians and to the use and benefit of Crown "lands reserved for Indians". The legislation enacted to this end was, in my view, necessary for the implementation of the authority so vested in Parliament under the Constitution.

To suggest that the provisions of the Bill of Rights have the effect of making the whole *Indian Act* inoperative as discriminatory is to assert that the Bill has rendered Parliament powerless to exercise the authority entrusted to it under the Constitution of enacting legislation which treats Indians living on reserves differently from other Canadians in relation to their property and civil rights. The proposition that such a wide effect is to be given to the Bill of Rights was expressly reserved by the majority of this Court in the case of *R. v. Drybones* (1969), 9 D.L.R. (3d) 473 at pp. 485–6, to which reference will hereafter be made, and I do not think that it can be sustained.

What is at issue here is whether the Bill of Rights is to be construed as rendering inoperative one of the conditions imposed by Parliament for the use and occupation of Crown lands reserved for Indians. These conditions were imposed as a necessary part of the structure created by Parliament for the internal administration of the life of Indians on reserves and their entitlement to the use and benefit of Crown lands situate thereon, they were thus imposed in discharge of Parliament's constitutional function under s. 91(24) and in my view can only be changed by plain statutory language expressly enacted for the purpose. It does not appear to me that Parliament can be taken to have made or intended to make such a change by the use of broad general language directed at the statutory proclamation of the fundamental rights and freedoms enjoyed by all Canadians, and I am therefore of opinion that the Bill of Rights had no such effect. . . .

The contention that the Bill of Rights is to be construed as overriding all of the special legislation imposed by Parliament under the *Indian Act* is, in my view, fully answered by Pigeon, J., in his dissenting opinion in the *Drybones* case where he said, at pp. 489–90:

If one of the effects of the *Canadian Bill of Rights* is to render inoperative all legal provisions whereby Indians as such are not dealt with in the same way as the general public, the conclusion is inescapable that parliament, by the enactment of the Bill, has not only fundamentally altered the status of the Indians in that indirect fashion but has also made any future use of federal legislative authority over them subject to the requirement of expressly declaring every time "that the law shall operate notwithstanding the *Canadian Bill of Rights*". I find it very difficult to believe that Parliament so intended when enacting the Bill. If a virtual suppression of federal legislation over Indians as such was meant, one would have expected this important change to be made explicitly, not surreptitiously, so to speak.

That it is membership in the band which entitles an Indian to the use and benefit of lands on the reserve is made plain by the provisions of ss. 2 and 18 of the *Indian Act,* Section 2(1)(a) reads as follows:

> 2(1)   In this Act
> "band" means a body of Indians
> (a) for whose use and benefit in common, lands, the legal title to which is vested in Her Majesty, have been set apart before, on or after the 4th day of September 1951.

Section 18 reads as follows:

> 18(1) Subject to this Act, reserves are held by Her Majesty for the use and benefit of the respective bands for which they were set apart; and subject to this Act and to the terms of any treaty or surrender, the Governor in Council may determine whether any purpose for which lands in a reserve are used or are to be used is for the use and benefit of the band. . . .

In my view the meaning to be given to the language employed in the Bill of Rights is the meaning which it bore in Canada at the time when the Bill was enacted, and it follows that the phrase "equality before the law" is to be construed in light of the law existing in Canada at that time. In considering the meaning to be attached to "equality before the law" as those words occur in s. 1(b) of the Bill, I think it important to point out that in my opinion this phrase is not effective to invoke the egalitarian concept exemplified by the 14th Amendment of the U.S. Constitution as interpreted by the Courts of that country: see *R.* v. *Smythe* (1971), 19 D.L.R. (3d) 480, 3 C.C.C. (2d) 366, [1971] S.C.R. 680, per Fauteux, C.J.C., at pp. 482 and 484–5. I think rather that, having regard to the language employed in the second paragraph of the preamble to the Bill of Rights, the phrase "equality before the law" as used in s. 1 is to be read in its context as a part of "the rule of law" to which overriding authority is accorded by the terms of that paragraph.

In this connection I refer to Stephen's *Commentaries on the Laws of England,* 21st ed., vol. 111 (1950), where it is said at p. 337:

> Now the great constitutional lawyer Dicey, writing in 1885 was so deeply impressed by the absence of arbitrary . . . governments present and past, that he coined the phrase "the rule of law" to express the regime under which Englishmen lived; and he tried to give precision to it in the following words which have exercised a profound influence on all subsequent thought and conduct.

> That the rule of law, which forms a fundamental principle of the constitution has three meanings, or may be regarded from three different points of view.

The second meaning proposed by Dicey is the one with which we are here concerned and it was stated in the following terms:

> It means again equality before the law or the equal subjection of all classes to the ordinary law of the land administered by the ordinary courts; the "rule of law" in this sense excludes the idea of any exemption of officials or others from the duty of obedience to the law which governs other citizens or from the jurisdiction of the ordinary courts.

"Equality before the law" in this sense is frequently invoked to demonstrate that the same law applies to the highest official of Government as to any other ordinary citizen, and in this regard Professor F. R. Scott, in delivering the Plaunt Memorial Lectures on Civil Liberties and Canadian Federalism (1959), speaking of the case of *Roncarelli* v. *Duplessis* (1959), 16 D.L.R. (2d) 689, [1959] S.C.R. 121, had occasion to say:

> . . . it is always a triumph for the law to show that it is applied equally to all without fear or favour. This is what we mean when we say that all are equal before the law.

The relevance of these quotations to the present circumstances is that "equality before the law" as recognized by Dicey as a segment of the rule of law, carries the meaning of equal subjection of all classes to the ordinary law of the land as administered by the ordinary Courts, and in my opinion the phrase "equality before the law" as employed in s. 1(b) of the Bill of Rights is to be treated as meaning equality in the administration or application of the law by the law enforcement authorities and the ordinary Courts of the land. This construction is, in my view, supported by the provisions of paras. (a) to (g) of s. 2 of the Bill which clearly indicate to me that it was equality in the administration and enforcement of the law with which Parliament was concerned when it guaranteed the continued existence of "equality before the law".

Turning to the *Indian Act* itself, it should first be observed that by far the greater part of that Act is concerned with the internal regulation of the lives of Indians on reserves and that the exceptional provisions dealing with the conduct of Indians off reserves and their contracts with other Canadian citizens fall into an entirely different category.

It was, of course necessary for Parliament, in the exercise of s. 91(24) authority, to first define what Indian meant, and in this regard s. 2(1) of the Act provides that: "Indian" means a person who pursuant to this Act is registered as an Indian or is entitled to be registered as an Indian. It is therefore clear that registration is a necessary prerequisite to Indian status. . . .

The *Drybones* case can, in my opinion, have no application to the present appeals as it was in no way concerned with the internal regulation of the lives of Indians on reserves or their right to the use and benefit of Crown lands thereon, but rather deals exclusively with the effect of the Bill of Rights on a section of the *Indian Act* creating a crime with attendant penalties for the conduct by Indians off a reserve in an area where non-Indians, who were also governed by federal law, were not subject to any such restriction.

The fundamental distinction between the present case and that of *Drybones,* however, appears to me to be that the impugned section in the latter case could not be enforced without denying equality of treatment in the administration and enforcement of the law before the ordinary Courts of the land to a racial group, whereas no such inequality of treatment between Indian men and women flows as a necessary result of the application of s. 12(1)(b) of the *Indian Act.*

To summarize the above, I am of opinion:

1. that the Bill of Rights is not effective to render inoperative legislation, such as s. 12(1)(b) of the *Indian Act,* passed by the Parliament of Canada in discharge of its constitutional function under s. 91(24) of the *British North America Act, 1867,* to specify how and by whom Crown lands reserved for Indians are to be used;

2. that the Bill of Rights does not require federal legislation to be declared inoperative unless it offends against one of the rights specifically guaranteed by s. 1, but where legislation is found to be discriminatory, this affords an added reason for rendering it ineffective;

3. that equality before the law under the Bill of Rights means equality of treatment in the enforcement and application of the laws of Canada before the law enforcement authorities and the ordinary Courts of the land, and no such inequality is necessarily entailed in the construction and application of s. 12(1)(b).

I would allow the appeal of the *Attorney-General of Canada* v. *Lavell,* reverse the judgment of the Federal Court of Appeal and restore the decision of judge B.W. Grossberg. In accordance with the terms of the order of the Federal Court of Appeal granting leave to appeal to this Court, the appellant will pay to the respondent her solicitor-and-client costs of the appeal and the application for leave. There should be no further order as to costs.

On the appeal of *Isaac et al.* v. *Bedard,* a question was raised in this Court as to the jurisdiction of the trial Court. In view of the conclusion reached on the merits, no decision is now necessary on that question. The appeal to this Court should be allowed, the judgment at trial should be reversed and the action dismissed. Under the circumstances, there should be no order as to costs in that case in any Court . . . .

HALL and SPENCE, JJ., concur with LASKIN, J. . . . .

PIGEON, J.: I agree in the result with Ritchie, J. I certainly cannot disagree with the view I did express in *R.* v. *Drybones* (1969), 9 D.L.R. (3d) 473 at pp. 489–90, [1970] 3 C.C.C. 355, [1970] S.C.R. 282, that the enactment of the *Canadian Bill of Rights* was not intended to effect a virtual suppression of federal legislation over Indians. My difficulty is Laskin, J.'s strongly reasoned opinion that, unless we are to depart from what was said by the majority in *Drybones,* these appeals should be dismissed because, if discrimination by reason of race makes certain statutory provisions inoperative, the same result must follow as to statutory provisions which exhibit discrimination by reason of sex. In the end, it appears to me that, in the circumstances, I need not reach a firm conclusion on that point. Assuming the situation is such as Laskin, J., says, it cannot be improper for me to adhere to what was my dissenting view, when a majority of those who did not agree with it in respect of a particular section of the *Indian Act,* R.S.C. 1970, c. I–6, now adopt it for the main body of this important statute.

I would observe that this result does not conflict with any of our decisions subsequent to *Drybones.* In no case was the *Canadian Bill of Rights* given an invalidating effect over prior legislation. . . .

LASKIN, J. (dissenting): . . . In my opinion, unless we are to depart from what was said in *Drybones,* both appeals now before us must be dismissed. I had no disposition to reject what was decided in *Drybones*; and on the central issue of prohibited discrimination as catalogued in s. 1 of the *Canadian Bill of Rights*, it is, in my opinion, impossible to distinguish *Drybones* from the two cases in appeal. If, as in *Drybones*, discrimination by reason of race makes certain statutory provisions inoperative, the same result must follow as to statutory provisions which exhibit discrimination by reason of sex.

I would dismiss both appeals. . . .

4.   Human Rights Committee Decision; re: Sandra Lovelace. *Lovelace* v. *Canada*, [1981] 2 H.R.L.J. 158 (U.N.H.R.C.)

The following excerpt is from the United Nations Human Rights Committee decision of *Lovelace* v. *Canada.* The committee held that Canada violated art. 27 of the *International Covenant on Civil and Political Rights* by way of the old s. 12(1) (b) of the *Indian Act.* That section provided that Indian women who married non-Indian men lost their Indian status and accordingly lost their rights to live on their home reserves. Note that because the discrimination (the actual loss of status), which was based on sex, took place before the *Covenant* applied to Canada (Sandra Lovelace's marriage was before 1976, when the *Covenant* became applicable), the committee relied on art. 27, which provided for discrimination on a continuing basis (right to enjoy culture with community, etc.). This decision led the way for the 1985 Bill C–31 amendments to the *Indian Act.*

. . .The Human Rights Committee, in the examination of the communication before it, has to proceed from the basic fact that Sandra Lovelace married a non-Indian on 23 May 1970 and consequently lost her status as a Maliseet Indian under Section 12(1)(b) of the *Indian Act.* This provision was—and still is—based on a distinction de jure on the ground of sex. However, neither its application to her marriage as the cause of her loss of Indian status nor its effects could at that time amount to a violation of the Covenant, because this instrument did not come into force for Canada until 19 August 1976. Moreover, the Committee is not competent, as a rule, to examine allegations relating to events having taken place before the entry into force of the Covenant and the Optional Protocol. Therefore, as regards Canada it can only consider alleged violations of human rights occurring on or after 19 August 1976. In the case of a particular individual claiming to be a victim of a violation, it cannot express its view on the law in the abstract, without regard to the date on which this law was applied to the alleged victim. In the case of Sandra Lovelace it follows that the Committee is not competent to express any view on the original cause of her loss of Indian status, i.e. the *Indian Act* as applied to her at the time of her marriage in 1970.

11.   The Committee recognizes, however, that the situation may be different if the alleged violations, although relating to events occurring before 19 August 1976, continue, or have effects which themselves constitute violations,

after that date. In examining the situation of Sandra Lovelace in this respect, the Committee must have regard to all relevant provisions of the Covenant. It has considered, in particular, the extent to which the general provisions in articles 2 and 3 as well as the rights in articles 12(1), 17(1), 23(1), 24, 26 and 27, may be applicable to the facts of her present situation.

12. The Committee first observes that from 19 August 1976 Canada had undertaken under article 2(1) and (2) of the Covenant to respect and ensure to all individuals within its territory and subject to its jurisdiction, the rights recognized in the Covenant without distinction of any kind such as sex, and to adopt the necessary measures to give effect to these rights. Further, under article 3, Canada undertook to ensure the equal right of men and women to the enjoyment of these rights. These undertakings apply also to the position of Sandra Lovelace. The Committee considers, however, that it is not necessary for the purposes of her communication to decide their extent in all respects. The full scope of the obligation of Canada to remove the effects or inequalities caused by the application of existing laws to past events, in particular as regards such matters as civil or personal status, does not have to be examined in the present case, for the reasons set out below.

13.1 The Committee considers that the essence of the present complaint concerns the continuing effect of the *Indian Act,* in denying Sandra Lovelace legal status as an Indian, in particular because she cannot for this reason claim a legal right to reside where she wishes to, on the Tobique Reserve. This fact persists after the entry into force of the Covenant, and its effects have to be examined, without regard to their original cause. Among the effects referred to on behalf of the author (quoted in paragraph 9.9, above, and listed (1) to (9)), the greater number, ((1) to (8)), relate to the *Indian Act* and other Canadian rules in fields which do not necessarily adversely affect the enjoyment of rights protected by the Covenant. In this respect the significant matter is her last claim, that "the major loss to a person ceasing to be an Indian is the loss of the cultural benefits of living in an Indian community, the emotional ties to home, family, friends and neighbours, and the loss of identity".

13.2 Although a number of provisions of the Covenant have been invoked by Sandra Lovelace, the Committee considers that the one which is most directly applicable to the complaint is article 27, which reads as follows:

> In those States in which ethnic, religious or linguistic minorities exist, persons belonging to such minorities shall not be denied the right, in community with the other members of their group, to enjoy their own culture, to profess and practise their own religion, or to use their own language.

It has to be considered whether Sandra Lovelace, because she is denied the legal right to reside on the Tobique Reserve, has by that fact been denied the right guaranteed by article 27 to persons belonging to minorities, to enjoy their own culture and to use their own language in community with other members of their group.

14. The rights under article 27 of the Covenant have to be secured to "persons belonging" to the minority. At present Sandra Lovelace does not qualify as

an Indian under Canadian legislation. However, the *Indian Act* deals primarily with a number of privileges which, as stated above, do not as such come
within the scope of the Covenant therefore have to be distinguished. Persons
who are born and brought up on a reserve, who have kept ties with their
community and wish to maintain these ties must normally be considered as
belonging to that minority within the meaning of the Covenant. Since Sandra
Lovelace is ethnically a Maliseet Indian and has only been absent from her
home reserve for a few years during the existence of her marriage, she is, in
the opinion of the Committee, entitled to be regarded as "belonging" to this
minority and to claim the benefits of article 27 of the Covenant. The question
whether these benefits have been denied to her, depends on how far they
extend.

15.   The right to live on a reserve is not as such guaranteed by article 27 of the
Covenant. Moreover, the *Indian Act* does not interfere directly with the functions which are expressly mentioned in that article. However, in the opinion
of the Committee the right of Sandra Lovelace to access to her native culture
and language "in community with the other members" of her group, has in
fact been, and continues to be interfered with, because there is no place outside the Tobique Reserve where such a community exists. On the other hand,
not every interference can be regarded as a denial of rights within the meaning of article 27. Restrictions on the right to residence, by way of national
legislation, cannot be ruled out under article 27 of the Covenant. This also
follows from the restrictions to article 12(1) of the Covenant set out in article
12(3). The Committee recognizes the need to define the category of persons
entitled to live on a reserve, for such purposes as those explained by the
Government regarding protection of its resources and preservation of the
identity of its people. However, the obligations which the Government has
since undertaken under the Covenant must also be taken into account.

16.   In this respect, the Committee is of the view that statutory restrictions affecting the right to residence on a reserve of a person belonging to the minority
concerned, must have both a reasonable and objective justification and be
consistent with the other provisions of the Covenant, read as a whole. Article
27 must be construed and applied in the light of the other provisions mentioned above, such as articles 12, 17 and 23 in so far as they may be relevant
to the particular case, and also the provisions against discrimination, such as
articles 2, 3 and 26, as the case may be. It is not necessary, however, to
determine in any general manner which restrictions may be justified under
the Covenant, in particular as a result of marriage, because the circumstances
are special in the present case.

17.   The case of Sandra Lovelace should be considered in the light of the fact that
her marriage to a non-Indian has broken up. It is natural that in such a situation she wishes to return to the environment in which she was born, particularly as after the dissolution of her marriage her main cultural attachment
again was to the Maliseet band. Whatever may be the merits of the *Indian
Act* in other respects, it does not seem to the Committee that to deny Sandra
Lovelace the right to reside on the reserve is reasonable, or necessary to
preserve the identity of the tribe. The Committee therefore concludes that to

prevent her recognition as belonging to the band is an unjustifiable denial of her rights under article 27 of the Covenant, read in the context of the other provisions referred to.

18. In view of this finding, the Committee does not consider it necessary to examine whether the same facts also show separate breaches of the other rights invoked. The specific rights most directly applicable to her situation are those under article 27 of the Covenant. The rights to choose one's residence (article 12), and the rights aimed at protecting family life and children (articles 17, 23 and 24) are only indirectly at stake in the present case. The facts of the case do not seem to require further examination under those articles. The Committee's finding of a lack of a reasonable justification for the interference with Sandra Lovelace's rights under article 27 of the Covenant also makes it unnecessary, as suggested above (paragraph 12), to examine the general provisions against discrimination (articles 2, 3 and 26) in the context of the present case, and in particular to determine their bearing under inequalities predating the coming into force of the Covenant for Canada.

19. Accordingly, the Human Rights Committee, acting under article 5(4) of the Optional Protocol to the International Covenant on Civil and Political Rights, is of the view that the facts of the present case, which establish that Sandra Lovelace has been denied the legal right to reside on the Tobique Reserve, disclose a breach by Canada of article 27 of the Covenant.

5. ***Courtois v. Canada (Department of Indian Affairs and Northern Development)*, [1991] 1 C.N.L.R. 40 (C.H.R.T.). Maurice Bernatchez, February 12, 1990**

> In *Courtois* a Canadian Human Rights Tribunal concluded that the Department of Indian Affairs and Northern Development's proposal to educate the children of reinstated Indian women off-reserve had the effect of creating distinctions between band and non-band members on the basis of sex and marital status. The tribunal held that the "moratorium was clearly aimed at women reinstated by Bill C–31." The department has a responsibility to ensure that on-reserve services are provided to children of reinstated women of the Pointe-Bleue Band.

. . . First, the two complaints filed by Ms. Louise Courtois were introduced as Exhibits HRC 1 and HRC 2. The complaint filed as Exhibit No. 1 reads as follows:

> The Department of Indian Affairs and Northern Development discriminated against me and my underage daughter, Julie Girard, by not taking measures to fund on-reserve education for the children of female Indians who are Band members and who, prior to April 17, 1985, married persons who are not Band members—in contravention of section 5 of the *Canadian Human Rights Act*. Moreover, the Department of Indian Affairs and Northern Development funds on-reserve education for the children of male band members who, prior to April 17, 1985, married non-members; this is the reason for my complaint of discrimination on the grounds of sex and martial status.

The complaint filed as Exhibit HRC 2 reads as follows:

> The Department of Indian Affairs and Northern Development discriminated against

me and my underage daughter, Julie Girard, by not taking measures to fund on-reserve education for the children of female Indians who are Band members and who, prior to April 17, 1985, married persons who are not Band members—in contravention of section 5 of the *Canadian Human Rights Act.* I sent a letter to the Minister of Indian Affairs and Northern Development on September 3, 1986, but obtained no concrete results. Moreover, the Department of Indian Affairs and Northern Development funds on-reserve education for the children of male Band members who prior to April 17, 1985, married non-members; this is the reason for my complaint of discrimination on the grounds of sex and martial status.

These two complaints were subsequently the object of an amendment application by counsel for the Commission. This amendment was authorized with the consent of counsel for the respondent, and hence the beginning of these two complaints is to be read as follows:

> The Department of Indian Affairs and Northern Development discriminated against me and my underage daughter, Julie Girard, *by denying her access to the Pointe-Bleue school* . . . (There are no further changes to the text of the two complaints). . . .

It is evident from the testimony of Ms. Louise Courtois that she was born on the Pointe-Bleue Reserve to Indian parents and that she has always lived there; she has worked on the reserve for more than fourteen years. In 1979, she married a non-Indian but continued to live on the reserve. Her marriage produced two children, Julie Girard born in 1980 and another child born in 1983.

The events leading to the filing of these complaints (Exhibits HRC 1 and HRC 2) can be summarized as follows. In the spring of 1985 Ms. Courtois took steps to enrol her little girl Julie in the reserve's nursery school at the Amishk School for the 1985–86 school year. Exhibit HRC 3, dated April 24, 1985, is a list of the nursery school pupils for 1985–86. The name of Julie Girard, the complainant's daughter, appears on the list, but unlike most of the other children listed, there is no band number indicated beside Julie Girard's name. Ms. Courtois testified that during April 1985 she took steps to ensure that her daughter Julie was enrolled for the 1985–86 school year at the band school located on the reserve. She also participated during the month of May 1985 in information sessions for the parents of children who would be attending nursery school during the 1985–86 school year, and particularly, in information sessions regarding the "Amerindianization" program. In May 1985 Julie Girard and her mother Louis Courtois met with the nursery school teacher for the class of children who names appeared on the list of pupils (Exhibit HRC 3). From then on, according to the testimony of Ms. Courtois, both she and her daughter were satisfied and confident that Julie Girard would enter the Amishk School in the fall of 1985.

The 1985 autumn term was delayed until October because of work on an addition to the reserve school. On September 13, 1985 the Girards received a letter (Exhibit HRC 4) from the Amishk School notifying them that Julie Girard was not eligible to attend the school "by virtue of a status quo impose by Council." From that date on, the complainant Louise Courtois took countless steps to have this Council decision reversed so that her daughter Julie Girard could gain access to the band school. In fact the evidence shows that she had letters sent and sent letters herself to anyone who might be able to help her cause. She wrote letters to the Minister of Indian Affairs, Exhibits HRC 5, HRC 6, and HRC 9, informing him of her situation and requesting that her daughter Julie be admitted to the band school. In spite of the efforts of Ms. Courtois, Julie Girard was not permitted to attend the band school in 1985–86.

In February 1986 the complainant again applied (Exhibit HRC 13) to the Pointe-Bleue Band Council, which administered the Amishk School, to have her daughter Julie admitted for the 1986–87 school year. On February 24, 1986 the Director of Education for the Montagnais due Lac Saint-Jean Council notified Ms. Courtois that Julie had not been accepted for the 1986–87 school year because of a moratorium passed by the Pointe-Bleue Band Council (Exhibit HRC 14).

On February 25, 1986 the complainant again wrote to the respondent Minister of Indian Affairs (Exhibit HRC 15) to complain about this second refusal of admission to the band school, a refusal that she considered discriminatory.

In any event, in spite of the efforts of Ms. Courtois, Julie Girard was unable to attend the Amishk School during the 1986–87 school year. Finally, the evidence revealed that Julie Girard has been attending the band school, Amishk School, since September 1987 (Exhibit HRC 21). . . .

At p. 1025 of the stenographic notes, the respondent's counsel argues the following:

> Here the prohibited ground of discrimination is sex or marital status. This is rather troublesome, however, because cases of discrimination on the basis of sex or marital status have ordinarily been interpreted in a very restrictive manner by the courts. The discrimination must truly pertain to sex or marital status.

In support of these claims, he made reference to *Air Canada* v. *Bain*, [1982] 2 F.C. 341, particularly at p. 346 [F.C.] where the Federal Court states:

> Miss Bain's complaint, which the Tribunal found substantiated, was that Air Canada had, in the provision of services available to the general public, been guilty of discrimination on the ground of marital status. In my view, it cannot be said, in the circumstances, that Miss Bain was the victim of discrimination by reason of her marital status or, *to put it more generally, that the Air Canada Family Fare Plan discriminated between travellers on the basis of their marital status.* Miss Bain was single and intended to travel with a friend. The reason why she could not take advantage of the family fare was that she was not related to her travel companion so that the two of them could be said to form a family; that reason was not that she was single. Married or not, a person who travels with a friend is not entitled to the family fare. *The denial of an advantage to a single person cannot constitute discrimination based on marital status if that same benefit is equally denied in identical circumstances to married persons.* [Emphasis added].

The respondent also introduced the case of *Blanchette* v. *Canada Life Assurance Co.*, [1984] C.S. 1240 to illustrate the same point.

The respondent's counsel states the following at pp. 1028–29 of the stenographic notes:

> We reply madame that, even women who, even Indian men who may have wanted to

send their children to the school in 1985 . . . no excuse me, even Indian women, even non-Indian women and white women who may have wanted to send their children to the reserve school in 1985, were not entitled to do so, because the discrimination was by reason of membership. Band membership, and not whether or not someone was reinstated or not; and once again, that is why I again quoted Denis Gill a few minutes ago, once again even Africans, white children and Haitian children had no more right than Julie Girard in 1985.

The true discrimination—if there was discrimination—related not the fact that Ms. Girard was reinstated, but to the fact that her daughter was not a Band member.

I cannot share this opinion. And I am supported in this by Denis Gill's previously cited testimony, in which he acknowledges that the only effect of the 1985 moratorium was to victimize women reinstated by the 1985 legislation, Bill C–31. Furthermore, former s. 12(1)(b) of the *Indian Act* resulted in a loss of Indian status for Indian women who married non-Indians. The purpose of Bill C–31 was to restore their status and correct this discrimination. Section 114 and following of the Act deal with the Minister's responsibility regarding education for *Indians*. Thus, it is not at all relevant to say that "even Africans, which children and Haitian children had not more right than Julie Girard in 1985."

In other words, *non-Indians* have no right to the education that must be provided by the Minister, and the latter has no obligation to *non-Indian*. However, the Minister does have obligations to the children of the complainants, who, through the coming into force of Bill C–31, automatically obtained *Indian status.*

Furthermore, the restrictive interpretation of marital status, as raised in *Air Canada* v. *Bain,* supra, was set aside in *Brossard (Town)* v. *Quebec (Comm. des drotis de la personne)*, [1988] 2 S.C.R. 279, in which the Supreme Court adopted a more broad and liberal interpretation of what is meant by marital status. Moreover, in this judgment confirming the principle put forward in *Cashin* v. *Canadian Broadcasting Corp.*, [1989] 3 F.C. 495, Beetz J. writes in the following at p. 286 [S.C.R.]

> The town of Brossard, in good faith effort to combat nepotism within the local public service, has adopted a hiring policy which disqualifies members of the immediate families of full-time employees and town councillors from taking up employment with the Town . . .

And at p. 294 [S.C.R.], Beetz J. writes:

> What about marital status in relative terms? Is the identity of a person's spouse relevant to discrimination under s. 10?
>
> The respondent argues that a narrow interpretation should be given to "civil status" in this respect. But as I have observed, to understand the civil status of one person one must often refer to the civil status of another. Being a widow or a widower is just one such example. Filiation, fraternity and sorority, of course, are others. It is difficult to imagine a hiring policy which excludes "*all sons and daughters*" *without specifying whose sons and daughters.* [Emphasis added].

At p. 298 [S.C.R.], Beetz J. cites the following passage by MacGuigan J. in the *Cashin* case:

In fine, what the Act discourages is a discrimination against an individual, not in his/her individuality, but as a group cypher, identified by a group characteristic.

And later, at p. 293 [S.C.R.], Beetz J. writes the following:

To paraphrase MacGuigan J. for the purposes of the case at bar, a general no-relative, no-spouse employment rule, precisely because in its generality it may have the effect of imposing a general or group category, does fall into civil status.

And finally, Beetz J., concludes at p. 300 [S.C.R.]:

While in some circumstances the mother-daughter relationship can be viewed separately from the position occupied by the mother, for the purposes of determining the cause of Line Lauren's exclusion these two factors operate together to form a single, indivisible cause. It is the civil status of Line Laurin, an appreciation of which requires an examination of the situation of her mother, which is the cause of her exclusion.

Application of these principles to the present case clearly shows that the moratorium was aimed at women reinstated by Bill C–31. These reinstated women are women who married non-Indians, producing children, such as Julie Girard and the Raphaël children, who were denied access to the Amishk School, unlike all the other young Indians on the reserve, even though these women and children had become Indians pursuant to Bill C–31.

Consequently, given the passages of testimony already cited, and in light of the law, as well as the case law on interpretation and scope of ss. 3 and 5 of the *Canadian Human Rights Act*, I have reached the conclusion that the complainants were, *prima facie*, victims of discrimination, as stated in complaints HRC 1, HRC 2, and HRC 23. . . .

Before examining the defence put forward by the respondent, we should keep in mind the decision rendered by the Supreme Court in *Robichaud* v. *Canada (Treasury Board)*, [1987] 2 S.C.R. 84, already cited at the beginning of the present decision, in which the "almost constitutional" nature of the *Canadian Human Rights Act* was recognized and it was asserted that the Act must be given such large and liberal interpretation as will best ensure the attainment of its objects. We must also remember that, under the *Indian Act*, *only* the Department of Indian Affairs has responsibilities and obligations regarding the education of Indians.

Defence Put Forward by the Respondent

Except for the preliminary objection to the jurisdiction of the present Tribunal, under s. 67 of the *Canadian Human Rights Act*, the respondent's defence is fundamentally and mainly drawn from s. 11(2) of the *Indian Act*, which reads as follows:

(2)   Commencing on the day that is two years after the day after an Act entitled *An Act to amend the Indian Act*, introduced in the House of Commons on February 29, 1985, is assented to, or on such earlier day as may be agreed to under section 13.1, where a band does not have control of its Band List under the Act, a person is entitled to have his name entered in a Band List maintained in the Department for the band

(a)   if that person is entitled to be registered under paragraph 6(1)(d) of (e) and ceased to be a member of that band by reason of the circumstance set out in that paragraph; or

(b)   if that person is entitled to be registered under paragraph 6(1)(f) or subsection 6(2) and a parent referred to in that provision is entitled to have his name entered in the Band List or, if no longer living, was at the time of death entitled to have his name entered in the Band List.

This brings us to the moratorium that has been at issue throughout the proceedings. A moratorium described as "a phantom" by counsel for the Commission and the complainants, given the lack of any official document attesting its existence. What is more, according to Ms. Soroka for the complainants, this moratorium cannot and could not exist in view of the provisions of s. 82(2) of the *Indian Act*, which stipulates the following:

(2)   A by-law made under section 81 comes into force forty days after a copy thereof is forwarded to the Minister pursuant to subsection (1) . . .

According to Exhibit HRC 32, the Minister stated that he had not received any moratorium, and I quote an excerpt from this letter:

I believe that the Band moratorium to which you are referring is regulation 35–85 passed by the Band Council in February 1986. To date, my department has not received this regulation from the Montagnais du Lac Saint-Jean Council.

And later in this letter, the Minister adds that this regulation, which could be seen as a kind of by-law, must conform to the *provisions of s. 81* of the *Indian Act*, and that, after it is forwarded to the Department of Indian Affairs, it is subject to a forty-day period during which it may be disallowed. It is true that there is actually no "*written*" moratorium. This said, ss. 10 and 11 of the *Indian Act* deal with a band's power to establish its own membership rules, and the procedures to be followed in order to do this. Section 11(2) serves notice that, unless the Band Council has established its own membership code in accordance with the Act during the two years following assent to the Act, the children of women reinstated under Bill C–31 are automatically entitled to have their names entered in the band list.

There is reason to reproduce s. 114 of the *Indian Act*, which reads as follows:

114.(1)   The Governor in Council may authorize the Minister, in accordance with this Act, to enter into agreements on behalf of Her Majesty for the education in accordance with this Act of Indian children, with

(a)   the government of a province;
(b)   the Commissioner of the Northwest Territories;
(c)   the Commissioner of the Yukon Territories;
(d)   a public or separate school board; and
(e)   a religious or charitable organization.

(2)   The Minister may, in accordance with this Act, establish, operate and maintain schools for Indian children.

Section 116(1) and (2) stipulates that:

116.(1)   Subject to section 117, every Indian child who has attained the age of seven years *shall* attend school.

(2)   The Minister *may*

(a) require an Indian who has attained the age of six years to attend school; . . . [Emphasis added.]

It emerges from ss. 114 and 116 that the Minister has obligations and the responsibility to assume the education of "*Indian*" children. There is no provision in Bill C–31, now c. 27 of the 1985 statutes, giving the band council any power whatsoever over education. It cannot be maintained that there was no discrimination against the complainants and their children because they were treated in the same manner as any children who are not band members. Whether or not non-Indian children were admitted before 1985 does not change the rights and obligations of the respondent with regard to Indian children. The Minister has no obligation to non-Indians and, consequently, these non-Indians are not entitled to education funded by the Minister. With respect to "Indians," however, in spite of the existence of ss. 10 and 11 of the Act, enabling the band council to assume control of its membership, the fact remains that only the children of women who were re-registered and reinstated became entitled to Indian status, pursuant to s. 6(2), which stipulates:

(2) Subject to section 7, a person is entitled to be registered if that person is a person one of whose parents is or, if no longer living, was at the time of death entitled to be registered under subsection (1).

Let us recall the testimony of Mr. Denis Gill, witness for the respondent, who states the following at p. 392:

. . . the Department cannot give in two places: it transfers funds to the Band and asks the Band to administer these funds for a very specific clientele. *In principle, this clientele is the Indian students of Pointe-Bleue.* [Emphasis added].

We should also keep in mind Mr. Denis Gill's previously cited testimony that, in fact, only reinstated women had been affected by the moratorium declared by the band council.

Although the Band has no statutory power in the area of education, the respondent Department maintains that there are three types of schools, as stated by witness Cumberland at p. 598 of the stenographic notes.

There are three types of schools. It is the one that you just mentioned. There are Indian students who attend provincial schools, school boards that are part of the Quebec Department of Education (MEQ) system. There are schools administered by the Department. There are still some of these left, there will still be three next September. The employees of these schools are my employees; they are public servants, government employees. The third category is made up of Band schools, schools that have been turned over to local authorities, to elected governments on reserves.

Because of the growing desire of various band councils to obtain autonomy, in particular by taking charge of their education, the Minister has reached the conclusion that the cannot intervene and so does not, in order to avoid being accused by the band councils of *interference*. Certainly, this a politically commendable motive.

But I cannot subscribe to such reasoning, since the *Indian Act* does not confer any responsibilities or power relating to education on the band council. Therefore, the privilege of attending the so-called band school can in no way be legally connected to the fact of being a band member. The education that must be provided by the Department in accordance with the *Indian Act* is fundamentally related to Indian status and the rights and privileges of *Indians*, regardless of whether or not they have membership in a band council. In my opinion, band councils are creatures of the *Indian Act* and have only the powers expressly vested in them by this Act. The Tribunal does, however, share the opinion of the respondent's counsel when he states the following at p. 1146 of the stenographic notes:

> From the moment in the Act that the notion of Band Council member is accepted and the Band Council is given the right to establish its own membership code, by this very fact, it is accepted that the Band Council will limit its services to those who are Band members.

Even if it is true that the band council can limit its services to its members, this band council must still be empowered to provide those services. For example, the band council has power and authority relating to the allotment of reserve lands (s. 20), roads and bridges on the reserve (s. 34), and the adjustment of contracts (s. 59). In fact, the band council has only those powers vested in it by the Act; and nothing in the *Indian Act* gives the band council power over education.

The respondent's counsel also maintained that the Minister's sole obligation in the area of Indian education was to provide this educational service, whether off or on the reserve; he said that it was not important where, as long as it was provided. I cannot share this opinion, since the educational services sought by the complainants—that is, admission to the Amishk School—was available on the Pointe-Bleue Reserve and, because of their Indian status, the children of the complainants were entitled to this service. On-reserve education should be offered and provided to them, since to do otherwise would be to use a double standard, which would constitute discrimination. In this regard, I concur with the remarks made in *Druken* v. *Canada (Employment and Immigration Comm.)* [8 C.H.R.R. D/ 4379], [D/4384 C.H.R.R.]:

> Where a service otherwise available to the general public is being denied, the justification for such denial must be based on the strongest possible evidence. The justification must be a question of fact in each situation and not merely a *blanket application to a particular group of individuals.* [Emphasis added].

In the complaints under consideration, it emerges from the evidence given that only the children of reinstated women were denied access to the band school, that is, the Amishk School. In addition, these were the only children whom the respondent offered school services, but *off* the reserve.

Finally, I believe that in the specific case of Louise Courtois and her child Julie Girard, the Department of Indian Affairs, because of the obligations and responsibilities vested in it by ss. 114 and following of the *Indian Act*, should have been intervened when the contribution agreement for the 1986–87 school year was made (Exhibit HRC 39), particularly under the terms of para. 8 of this agreement, which reads as follows:

If the Band Council fails in its obligation to provide the agreed services, the Minister may terminate the agreement . . .

Since the Minister was aware of the situation of Louise Courtois and her daughter Julie during the 1985–86 school year, the Minister, in accordance with his obligations, should have taken action in 1986–87 to ensure that the Pointe-Bleue Band Council provided this school service to the children of reinstated women, and in particular to Julie Girard.

Objection based on Section 67 of the Canadian Human Rights Act
As previously mentioned the preliminary objection to the jurisdiction of this Tribunal could not be allowed, since before determining whether s. 67 of the *Canadian Human Rights Act* was applicable, it was necessary to first establish whether the acts and practices alleged against the Minister were in accordance with the *Indian Act*. Counsel for the respondent asserted on several occasions that the "text" for the Act could not be dissociated from "its application" and/or its effect. At p. 650 of the stenographic notes, counsel makes the following statement:

> Because one cannot say to someone, your practice is legal, your practice is legal [*sic*]. I cannot do anything against the section under which you carried it out, but your practice is discriminatory and must be curbed.

I am unable to agree with this argument after reading the *Druken* case, supra, particularly the following passage [D/4384, C.H.R.R.]:

> Where a service otherwise available to the general public is being denied, the justification for such denial must be based on the strongest possible evidence. The justification must be a question of fact in each situation and not merely a *blanket application to a particular group of individuals*. [Emphasis added].

The service sought by the complainants was offered and available on the Pointe-Bleue Reserve. But the complainants alone, as reinstated women, were denied this service. It is not "dissociating the text from its application" to note that a similar group (of Indians) with the same rights (school) received different treatment and service, depending upon whether or not it was composed of band members, even though the law does not permit any distinction.

We should keep in mind that the Federal Court of Appeal in *Desjarlais* v. *Piapot Band (No. 75)*, [1990] 1 C.N.L.R. 39 (Fed. Ct. A.D.), wrote in its May 8, 1989 decision, at p. 6 [p. 42 C.N.L.R.]:

> In the case at bar, the motion of the band council of Piapot dated June 11, 1984, and described as "a vote of non-confidence for . . . Rose Desjarlais," is nowhere, expressly or by implication, provided for by the *Indian Act*; accordingly, it is not a "provision made under or pursuant to that Act," so as to bring it within the exempting provisions of s. 63(2) of the *Canadian Human Rights Act*.

Applying this principle to the case under study leads us to the conclusion that the moratorium declared in June 1985 and aimed at denying the children of reinstated women admission to the Pointe-Bleue Band school is in no way authorized by the *Indian Act*, since the band council has no rights regarding education.

Whereas the complainant, Ms. Louise Courtois, is an Indian woman reinstated under Bill C–31, c. 27 of the 1985 statutes;

Whereas Julie Girard is the child of Louis Courtois, and whereas Julie Girard obtained Indian status through the application of s. 6(2) of the same Act;

Whereas, in addition, according to the evidence, Louise Courtois and Julie Girard ordinarily resided on the Pointe-Bleue Reserve between 1985 and 1987, in accordance with s. 4(3) of this same Act;

Considering the obligations of the Minister of Indian Affairs with regard to education, ensuing from the provisions of ss. 114 and following of the *Indian Act*;

Whereas the existence of a school on the Pointe-Bleue Reserve is the result of the Minister's obligations regarding education, and its existence is made possible only through funding from the Department of Indian Affairs;

And, whereas the Minister acted in a discriminatory manner by refusing access to the service of the Pointe-Bleue Reserve school, a service to which the complainant Louise Courtois and her daughter Julie Girard were entitled, I conclude that the complaints HRC 1 and HRC 2, as initially filed and subsequently amended during the hearing, are substantiated in fact and in law, pursuant to the provisions of the *Canadian Human Rights Act*. . . .

6. ***Corbiere* v. *Canada*, [1994] 1 C.N.L.R. 71 (F.C.T.D.); *sub nom. Batchewana Indian Band* v. *Canada*. Strayer J., September 9, 1993**

> This decision concerns the right of off-reserve band members to vote in band elections. As such, the decision could have a major impact on reinstated Indian women, many of whom live off-reserve. The issue of off-reserve voting rights strikes at the heart of democratic government and the fundamental rights of, in this case, many reinstated Indian women living off-reserve to participate in their government. The court held that the provisions denying non-resident band members the right to vote (in matters relating to communal property, which includes chief and council) violated s. 15 of the *Charter* and could not be justified by s. 1. The Federal Court of Appeal upheld the decision ([1997] 3 C.N.L.R. 21 (F.C.A.)) but altered the remedy so that s. 77(1) continued to apply but the words "and is ordinarily resident on the reserve" are dropped from the section when applied to the Batchewana Band. This approach is more consistent with the purposive approach to statutory interpretation confirmed by the *Sparrow* decision. The Trial Court decision is provided because of its more detailed analysis of the circumstances.

STRAYER J.: —. . .The plaintiffs are all members of the Batchewana Indian Band. The plaintiff Corbiere resides on Rankin Indian Reserve 15D, a reserve of the Batchewana Band. The other plaintiffs reside off the reserve. In their statement of claim they seek: a declaration that "in the circumstances of this case" certain sections of the *Indian Act*, R.S.C. 1985, c. I–5, the Indian Band Election Regulations, C.R.C. 1978, c. 952, and certain bylaws of the Batchewana Indian Band contravene ss. 15, 2(d) and 7 of the Canadian Charter of Rights and Freedoms; a declaration that these provisions, providing as they do that a band member must be ordinarily resident on the reserve to be eligible to vote in band elections, do not apply to elections held under the *Indian Act* for the Batchewana Band of Indians; orders which would in effect grant or restore to all adult members of the band, wherever resident, the right to vote; an order to set aside the result of any election held after the issuance of the statement of claim filed on November 19, 1990; and costs. . . .

ISSUES

The following appear to be the relevant issues:

1. Does the denial of the vote in band elections or the status of "elector" to members of the Batchewana Band not ordinarily resident on its reserves infringe s. 15 of the Charter?
2. If so, can such limitations be justified under s. 1 of the Charter?
3. Is the "freedom of association" of band members not ordinarily resident on the reserve, as guaranteed by para. 2(d) of the Charter, infringed by such restrictions?
4. If so, are such limitations justified under s. 1 of the Charter?

CONCLUSIONS

Is Subsection 15(1) of the Charter Infringed?
Subsection 15(1) provides as follows:

> 15.(1) Every individual is equal before and under the law and has the right to the equal protection and equal benefit of the law without discrimination and, in particular without discrimination based on race, national or ethnic origin, colour, religion, sex, age or mental or physical-disability.

It must first be observed that the alleged ground of discrimination here is based on the place of residence of band members. Place of residence is not one of the grounds enumerated in subsection 15(1). In accordance with the decision of the Supreme Court of Canada in *Andrews et al.* v. *Law Society of British Columbia,* [1989] 1 S.C.R. 143, I must first determine whether there is discrimination within the meaning of s-s. 15(1). For there to be discrimination, there must be a law with some negative impact on those who allege discrimination. I am satisfied that the denial of the vote in band council elections, or for other purposes such as the approval of the surrender of any interest in the reserve, has a significant negative impact on those not ordinarily resident on the reserve. I must then, however, determine whether the ground upon which that denial occurs is one which is analogous to the grounds listed in s-s. 15(1). There have been several cases where province of residence has not been considered to be an analogous ground (see, e.g., *Turpin* v. *Her Majesty the Queen,* [1989] 1 S.C.R. 1296; *Her Majesty the Queen* v. *Sheldon S.,* [1990] 2 S.C.R. 254). This conclusion was reached in part because the non-residents in question did not have the characteristics of a "discrete and insular minority," that is they did not constitute a group which in the "entire social, political and legal fabric of our society" constituted a group which was inherently or historically disadvantaged. There was also a recognition in those cases of the impact of federalism which legitimizes differences of treatment of individuals from one province to another.

I am of the view that band members not resident on a reserve may well constitute such a traditionally disadvantaged group, at least such members of the Batchewana Band who make up the group that is relevant for the declarations I have been asked to make. I make no observation or findings with respect to the situation of other bands. But in respect of the Batchewana Band, historically ever since 1850 there has been a substantial portion of the band which has not been able to reside on reserve lands. While the evidence is insubstantial as to the reasons for this at various times throughout their history, I believe I can conclude that for a substantial part of that period the lands were either inadequate in scope (being almost nonexistent for a certain period) or unsuitable to sustain large numbers of people. It is apparent from the rate of settlement of the Rankin Reserve after its creation in 1952 that there had been many members who wished to live on a reserve. Between 1953 and 1985 the proportion of band members living on reserves had more than doubled from approximately 34 percent to some 69 percent. This demonstrates the impact which the creation of an appropriate reserve and a vigorous housing programme had on the ability of non-residents to exercise a choice of residence. With the amendments to the *Indian Act* in 1985, however, the proportions were again reversed so that by 1991 some 68 percent were living off the reserve. By far the largest cause of this phenomenon was the sudden large increase in membership of the band brought about by Bill C–31 in 1985 (See Exhibit D–16, Table 2–2; see also note 6, supra, and accompanying text). It is important to keep in mind why the new members added pursuant to Bill C–31 had previously been denied even membership in the band and thus any possibility of residence on the reserve. For the most part they were women, or the children of such women, who had lost their Indian status through marriage to a non-Indian, a result which was dictated by the former para. 12(1)(b) of the *Indian Act*. (Indian men did not, however, lose status by marrying non-Indians.) This provision was successfully attacked before the United Nations Human Rights Committee (*Lovelace* v. *Canada,* [1983] *Can. Human Rights Yearbook* 305. While the U.N. Human Rights Committee found that para. 12(1)(b) discriminated on grounds of sex in depriving Mrs. Lovelace of Indian status, the Covenant had not been in force when that happened. The Committee found other ongoing violations of the International Covenant). It is no coincidence that it was repealed by Parliament in Bill C–31 effective the day s. 15 of the Charter came into force. Some others who retrieved their status pursuant to Bill C–31 had been denied such status because of their own, or (such as in the case of the plaintiff Frank Nolan) their parents' actions in choosing to be "enfranchised" and to exercise the rights of a Canadian citizen, this having caused them to lose their Indian status. It may fairly be said, therefore, that those regaining status through Bill C–31 were historically denied membership in their band (and thus the right to live on a reserve) because of sex or race, their mother having married outside the Indian race or their parents having been obliged to give up Indian status in order to enjoy the same rights and undertake the same obligations as Canadians of other races. Having been restored to the band membership they had lost under gender or racially based laws, they now find that their ability to reside on a reserve is limited. Further, their right to have a say directly or indirectly in the use or disposition of lands and revenues held by the Crown on behalf of all members of the band is nonexistent because they do not live on the reserve. Having no electoral voice in the election of the band council they have no say in the pace at which the band council makes land available on the reserve for newcomers nor in the allocation of housing funds which the band council obtains from the Government of Canada for the provision of housing on the reserve. I believe it is therefore possible to characterize those persons not ordinarily resident on any of the Batchewana Band's reserves as, in general, forming a group which historically has suffered disadvantages because of their inability to move onto the reserves. This is not to say, of course, that there are not some members of the group who have no desire to move onto reserves and who are by any normal measurement better off by not being on the reserves. But as demonstrated earlier, there must be many among those on whose behalf this action is brought who cannot change their place of residence to the reserve, any more readily than a person can change his citizenship—a characteristic found in *Andrews* to be analogous to those specifically mentioned in s-s. 15(1). Although it was described there as "immutable" ([1989] 1 S.C.R. at 195), citizenship like residence on or off a reserve is sometimes capable of change, but with considerable difficulty and is subject to the decisions of others.

Also, according to *Andrews,* in determining whether such a group is the victim of "discrimination" it is proper to look at the purpose of the law which allegedly denies them certain advantages. The Court in that case emphasized that discrimination involves distinctions based on irrelevant personal differences (ibid at 165, 193). To determine whether a characteristic is "irrelevant" one must look at the nature and purpose of the legislation. Here it appears to me that the conclusions one may draw will differ with the provision of the *Indian Act* in question. I am persuaded by the expert evidence and argument submitted on behalf of the defendant Ministers that in part it is the object of the *Indian Act* to provide for a form of local government on reserves which is analogous to municipal government. It is apparent, for example, that most of the by-law making powers which the band council has under s-s. 81(l) relate purely to the administration of the reserve. Further, the evidence indicates that most of the operational funding provided by the federal government to Indian bands (which does not, as I understand it, consist of "Indian moneys" as defined by the Act) and whose expenditure is controlled by the latter subject to certain government guidelines, relates to purely local purposes such as the provision of education on the reserve, social assistance, land management, and recreation. It is true that some of these funds can be spent in ways which will have a direct impact on non-resident members, such as the provision by the band council out of government funds of bursaries to band members for post-secondary education or the allocation of housing funds for non-residents such as the new members brought in by Bill C–31. With respect to such local government functions of the band council, I do not think it is possible to say that a requirement of residence on a reserve as a condition for voting for such a local government can be described as an irrelevant personal characteristic. It is of course true, according to the evidence, that in at least four provinces in Canada non-resident property owners may vote in municipal elections. In the remaining provinces provincial law requires that a person reside in the municipality in order to vote there. While no doubt arguments can be made for the merits of both approaches, a strong rationalization can be developed for requiring that in order to vote in a municipality a person should have a very direct connection with it by residing in the municipality: it is the residents who must bear the consequences of decisions by the municipal council as to the allocation of resources or the imposition of laws and it is those persons who arguably should have the exclusive right to vote for the municipal council. To the extent that the

Indian Act similarly requires that band members reside on the reserve in order to be able to chose a band council which is primarily involved in the governance of the territory making up the reserve, I do not think it can be regarded as for a discriminatory purpose.

It appears to me, however, that the restriction of the franchise to those band members ordinarily resident on the reserve is based on an irrelevant personal characteristic when that franchise has to do with the disposition of lands and Indian moneys held by Her Majesty "for the use and benefit of the band" (see *Indian Act,* s-ss. 18.(1), 61(1)), the "band" including all members and not simply those resident on the reserve. The impact of decisions concerning these dispositions is not, like that of ordinary band council decisions, confined primarily to residents of the reserve. Such decisions relate instead to the use and disposition of communal property in which every band member has a share wherever he or she may live. Therefore to impose as a condition of voting on such matters the requirement of ordinary residence on the reserve is to deny rights because of a personal characteristic which is irrelevant to the scope and existence of those rights.

I must therefore conclude that the combination of provisions of the *Indian Act* denying those members of the Batchewana Band not ordinarily resident on any of its reserves the right to vote, directly at a meeting or in a referendum, or indirectly through voting for the band council, on the use or disposition of lands or moneys held by Her Majesty for the use and benefit of the band, contravene s-s. 15(1) of the Charter. The only relevant provision of the Act which the plaintiffs have specifically attacked in their pleadings is s-s. 77(1) which requires ordinary residence on a band reserve to vote in band elections. This provision when used by reference to define "electors" creates the infringing result which is complained of, inter alia, in paras. 65–68 of the statement of claim quoted earlier. It will suffice to hold s-s. 77(1) an infringement of s-s. 15(1) for the purposes I have identified, although the unconstitutional consequences flow from its impact on such provisions as para. 39(1)(b), s-ss. 64(1) and 66(1). The latter two are included because they require the consent only of the band council which under the present dispensation is elected only by those members of the band resident on the reserve.

On the other hand, I do not include in my finding of invalidity arrangements whereby the band council has the sole authority to make decisions on the spending of grants from the government of Canada from sources other than "Indian moneys" as referred to in s. 62 of the Act. As I understand it, there are many funds provided by the government to Indian bands for various programmes which do not come within the regime of ss. 61 to 69. Such parliamentary appropriations are for the most part for purely on-reserve purposes and reflect the judgment of Parliament as to how its funds should be spent. It appears to me that in respect of such funds non-resident band members can assert no communal rights.

If subsection 15(1) rights are infringed, is such limitation justifiable under section 1?

This question must be answered in two parts: first in respect of the application of s-s. 77(1) to band council elections for the purpose of electing a council to carry on the ordinary governance of the reserve itself; and secondly, with respect to the effect of s-s. 7(1) on entitlement to vote directly or indirectly (by electing members of the band council) on the disposition of reserve lands or Indian moneys held by Her Majesty for the use and benefit of the band as a whole.

With respect to the first application of s-s. 77(l), I have already concluded that this does not infringe s-s. 15(1) of the Charter. If however I should be wrong in this, I would still find for essentially the same reasons that the limitation of the vote for the band council, in respect of the functions of the band council in ordinary governance of the reserve, to those ordinarily resident on that reserve, is a reasonable limit prescribed by law which is demonstrably justified in a free and democratic society. While this is not the only conceivable way of qualifying the right to vote it is clearly within a permissible range of legitimate options for Parliament.

With respect to the application of s-s. 77(l) in a way to preclude members of the band not ordinarily resident on a reserve from having any political say in decisions concerning the disposition of the reserve itself or of "Indian moneys", I find no justification within the requirements of s. l of the Charter. No rationale has been seriously advanced as to why members not resident on a reserve should have no input into such decisions when these decisions involve property held for the use and benefit of the entire band and in which each member of the band has a communal interest. In the present case it is clear that band membership has always exceeded by a substantial proportion the number of members resident on the reserves of the Batchewana band. A fundamental concept of the *Indian Act* is that a person may have Indian status, band membership, and enjoy communal rights in property, both land and moneys, held by Her Majesty for the use and benefit of the band, without living on a reserve. How then can a law be justified which denies those who do not live on a reserve—some willingly, some unwillingly—any control over the disposition of that property when the consent of those who happen to live on the reserve must be obtained by Her Majesty for any such disposition? Counsel for the defendants suggested that it would be most unfair if a majority of members not resident on the reserve could outvote those resident on the reserve and approve the surrender of part or all of a reserve. He suggested that the limitation of the vote in such matters to reserve residents was therefore reasonable. I do not accept this rationale. In my view it is instead reasonable that both the resident and non-resident members of the band should have a vote directly or indirectly in such matters. It will be noted that in s-ss. 39(l), 64(l), and 66(1) involving respectively the surrender of reserve lands, and the expenditure of capital and revenue moneys, the approval of the Governor in Council or of the Minister of Indian Affairs is required in addition to band approval. Thus the government can prevent unfair treatment of either the resident or non-resident members: but to do so it is important that the government first know the views of each category of members. At the moment there is at least no formal machinery for the government to know the views of non-resident members so that these may be taken into account. For these reasons I conclude that s-s. 77(l) insofar as it precludes any participation by non-resident members in such decisions is not a reasonable limitation on the rights of those members under s-s. 15(1) of the Charter . . . .

DISPOSITION

I have therefore concluded that a declaration should issue, to the effect that the restriction on the right to vote in s-s. 77(1) of the Act to those ordinarily resident on the reserve infringes in certain respects the rights under s-s. 15(1) of the Charter of such of the plaintiffs and those on whose behalf they sue who are not resident on any reserve of the Batchewana Band. Such rights are infringed by the effects of s-s. 77(1) in preventing such persons any vote in respect of any potential surrender of all or part of a reserve under s-s. 39(1) of the Act, or in respect of any use of Indian moneys under s-ss. 64(l) and 66(l) which provide for consent being given on behalf of the band by the band council for which such persons cannot vote.

Such a declaration is based, inter alia, on the allegations in paras. 65 to 68 of the statement of claim, as quoted above. The declaration being made is a portion of the relief sought in para. 74(a) of the statement of claim. It is confined to voting rights of members of the Batchewana Band because as a trial judge I must confine myself to the actual case I have before me, its pleadings and its evidence. The declaration must be for invalidity of s-s. 77(1) in its entirety, even though I have endeavoured to describe the particular effects of it which are impermissible. It is not possible to sever the invalid parts as s-s. 77(1) conforms with or violates the Charter depending on the other sections governed by it. Nor is it possible to "read in" some saving interpretation: to attempt to apply the criteria laid down by the Supreme Court in Schachter (*Schachter* v. *Her Majesty the Queen,* [1992] 2 S.C.R. 701 at 705–15) for reading in would in the circumstances of this case be completely speculative as to Parliament's intentions.

I believe that this is a case where the operation of such a declaration should be suspended to allow time for parliamentary consideration of the modifications in the *Indian Act* which might be appropriate. There is no simple deletion or addition which will readily correct this situation and Parliament must have the opportunity to consider its options to make the Act conform to the constitution. Any declaration with immediate effect could bring into doubt the ability of the Batchewana Band council as presently elected to carry on the ordinary governance of the reserve. This is therefore an appropriate case in which to postpone the effect of the declaration.

7. ***Native Women's Association of Canada* v. *Canada,* [1995] 1 C.N.L.R. 47 (S.C.C.). Lamer C.J., La Forest, L'Heureux-Dubé, Sopinka, Gonthier, Cory, McLachlin, Iacobucci, and Major JJ., October 27, 1994**

> This decision concerns whether or not the Native Women's Association of Canada (NWAC) should have been entitled to funding similar to that provided to the other national Aboriginal organizations to participate in the 1992 constitutional discussions. The Supreme Court of Canada held that the federal government's decision not to provide equal funding and participation in the constitutional review discussions to NWAC did not violate their rights under ss. 2(b) and 28 of the *Charter.* The freedom of expression under s. 2(b) of the *Charter* does not guarantee any particular means of expression or place a positive obligation upon the federal government to consult anyone. The Supreme Court also held that s. 35 of the *Constitution Act, 1982* is inapplicable because the right of Aboriginal people to participate in constitutional discussions does not derive from any existing Aboriginal or treaty right under s. 35.

SOPINKA J.:—This case raises the issue of the extent to which the freedom of expression and equality provisions of the *Canadian Charter of Rights and Freedoms* require that government funding be provided to various groups in order to promote the representation of certain interests at constitutional reform discussions. Specifically, where the Government of Canada provides funding to certain Aboriginal groups, alleged to be male-dominated, does s. 2(b) in combination with s. 28 of the Charter oblige the Government of Canada to provide equal funding to an association claiming to represent the interests of female Aboriginal persons so that they may also express their views at the constitutional discussions? Alternatively, is this result mandated by s. 15 of the Charter or s. 35 of the *Constitution Act, 1982*? This case also invites consideration of whether there is any violation of the Charter if the Government of Canada refuses to extend an invitation to a group representing the interests of Aboriginal women to come to the table to discuss possible constitutional reform.

Subsidiary issues are also raised concerning the justiciability of the Charter matters as well as the jurisdiction of the Federal Court of Appeal to grant the remedy of a declaration when it was not specifically requested at the Trial Division.

Following a review of the facts, I will briefly analyze the issue of the jurisdiction of the Federal Court of Appeal. I will next embark on a discussion of the main focus of this appeal regarding the alleged violations of the Charter. In light of my conclusion that there was no Charter violation in this case, it will be unnecessary to address the issue concerning justiciability. Therefore, for the purposes of this appeal, I will assume that the matters raised herein are justiciable. . . .

The substance of the complaint is that by financing the four recipient Aboriginal groups with respect to the constitutional renewal discussions, the Government of Canada assisted the propagation of the view that the Charter should not apply to Aboriginal self-government. The respondents allege that by funding male-dominated groups and failing to provide equal funding to NWAC, the Government of Canada violated their freedom of expression and right to equality. The respondents' application was dismissed by the Federal Court, Trial Division . . . [and] [T]he Federal Court of Appeal. . . .

CANADIAN CHARTER OF RIGHTS AND FREEDOMS

    2.   Everyone has the following fundamental freedoms: . . .
        (b)   freedom of thought, belief, opinion and expression, including freedom of the press and other media of communication;
    15.(1) Every individual is equal before and under the law and has the right to the equal protection and equal benefit of the law without discrimination and, in particular, without discrimination based on race, national or ethnic origin, colour, religion, sex, age or mental or physical disability.
    28.   Notwithstanding anything in this Charter, the rights and freedoms referred to in it are guaranteed equally to male and female persons. . . .

The conclusions reached in *Haig* v. *Canada,* [1993] 2 S.C.R. 995 have application to the case at bar. Similar to a referendum, the Government of Canada was engaging in a consultative process to secure the public opinion with respect to potential constitutional amendments. To further this goal, a parallel process of consultation was established within the Aboriginal community. It cannot be claimed that NWAC has a constitutional right to receive government funding aimed at promoting participation in the constitutional conferences. The respondents conceded as much in paragraph 91 of their factum as well as in oral argument. Furthermore, the provision of funding and the invitation to participate in constitutional discussions facilitated and enhanced the expression of Aboriginal groups. It did not stifle expression.

However, the respondents rely on *Haig* for the proposition that the Government cannot provide a platform of expression in a discriminatory fashion or in a way which otherwise violates the Charter. They state that this result is clearly mandated by s. 28 of the Charter. The following passage from the reasons of L'Heureux-Dubé J., at pp. 1041–42, is relied on:

> In my view, though a referendum is undoubtedly a platform for expression, s. 2(b) of the Charter does not impose upon a government, whether provincial or federal, any positive obligation to consult its citizens through the particular mechanism of a referendum. Nor does it confer upon all its citizens the right to express their opinions in a referendum. A government is under no constitutional obligation to extend this platform of expression to *anyone,* let alone to *everyone.* A referendum as a platform of expression is, in my view, a matter of legislative policy and not of constitutional law.
>
> The following caveat is, however, in order here. *While s. 2(b) of the Charter does not include the right to any particular means of expression, where a government chooses to provide one, it must do so in a fashion that is consistent with the Constitution. The traditional rules of Charter scrutiny continue to apply. Thus, while the government may extend such a benefit to a limited number of persons, it may not do so in a discriminatory fashion, and particularly not on ground prohibited under s. 15 of the Charter.*
>
> I would add that issues of expression may on occasion be strongly linked to issues of equality. In *Schachter* v. *Canada,* [1992] 2 S.C.R. 679, the Court said that s. 15 of the Charter is indeed a hybrid of positive and negative protection, and that a government may be required to take positive steps to ensure the equality of people or groups who come within the scope of s. 15. It might well be that, in the context of a particular equality claim, those positive steps may involve the provision of means of expression to certain groups or individuals. However, despite obvious links between various provisions of the Charter, I believe that, should such situations arise, it would be preferable to address them within the boundaries of s. 15, without unduly blurring the distinctions between different Charter guarantees. [Underlining in original; emphasis in italics added.]

Therefore, *Haig* establishes the principle that generally the government is under no obligation to fund or provide a specific platform of expression to an individual or a group. However, the decision in *Haig* leaves open the possibility that, in certain circumstances, positive governmental action may be required in order to make the freedom of expression meaningful. Furthermore, in some circumstances where the government does provide such a platform, it must not do so in a discriminatory fashion contrary to the Charter. It is this last proposition upon which the respondents rely in conjunction with s. 28 of the Charter to support their position that their rights under s. 2(b) of the Charter were violated in that they did not receive an equal platform to express their views.

At this point, I should add that it cannot be said that every time the Government of Canada chooses to fund or consult a certain group, thereby providing a platform upon which to convey certain views, that the Government is also required to fund a group purporting to represent the opposite point of view. Otherwise, the implications of this proposition would be untenable. For example, if the Government chooses to fund a women's organization to study the issue of abortion to assist in drafting proposed legislation, can it be argued that the Government is bound by the Constitution to provide equal funding to a group purporting to represent the rights of fathers? If this was the intended scope of s. 2(b) of the Charter, the ramifications on government spending would be far reaching indeed. . . .

Therefore, while it may be true that the Government cannot provide a particular means of expression that has the effect of discriminating against a group, it cannot be said that merely by consulting an organization, or organizations, purportedly representing a male or female point of view, the Government must automatically consult groups representing the opposite perspective. It will be rare indeed that the provision of a platform or funding to one or several organizations will have the effect of suppressing another's freedom of speech.

Although it appears that the respondents' arguments relate more closely to an equality argument under s. 15 of the Charter, the respondents devoted much of their energy addressing s. 2(b). In either case, regardless of how the arguments are framed, it will be seen that the evidence does not support the conclusions urged by the respondents. . . .

I am in complete agreement with the intervener AFN's submissions that there was no evidence before the Federal Court of Appeal, nor before this Court, that AFN or the other funded groups advocated "male-dominated Aboriginal self-governments". Nor was there any evidence to suggest that AFN, NCC, ITC or MNC were less representative of the viewpoint of women with respect to the Constitution. The main argument of NWAC in this regard is that only they were advocating the inclusion of the Charter in any negotiated form of Aboriginal self-government. The evidence clearly discloses that of the four funded groups at least MNC also supported its inclusion. Furthermore, NCC did not oppose application of the Charter, rather it desired that each Aboriginal self government be free to determine the issue for itself. ITC was also willing to consider application of the Charter. Thus, it was not exclusively the position of NWAC that the Charter be maintained.

Furthermore, in a letter dated March 2, 1992 (exhibit A to the supplementary affidavit of Gail Stacey-Moore), the Minister Responsible for Constitutional Affairs wrote the following:

> The national Aboriginal associations do represent both men and women from their communities. I encourage you to work within your communities to ensure your views are heard and represented through those associations.

Thus, in the opinion of the Government of Canada as well, the funded organizations were not perpetuating only a male-dominated point of view. Although this is certainly not determinative, it is indicative that a minister of the Crown who was familiar with the position and views advanced by them regarded the four national organizations as bona fide representatives of Aboriginal persons. . . .

The evidence is also indicative of the fact that Aboriginal women, including members of NWAC, did have a direct voice regarding the position of the funded groups with respect to the constitutional discussions. NWAC participated in the parallel process set up by the four national Aboriginal organizations to discuss consti-

tutional reform. For example, the respondent Stacey-Moore and other women secured positions on the Constitutional Working Group of the AFN. The respondent
McIvor was the NWAC representative to the AFN Constitutional Commission, while
Jane Gottfriedson, President of the British Columbia Native "Women's Society
(affiliated with NWAC) was appointed to the NCC Constitutional Commission. As
well, on March 13, 14 and 15, 1992, an Aboriginal Conference on the Constitution
was held in Ottawa. After a sustained effort, NWAC secured eight official seats and
four observers out of a total of 184 delegates.

Furthermore, NWAC also received some of the Government funding under the
Contribution Agreements, as all four groups were required to direct a portion of
the funds received specifically to address women's issues. AFN and NCC each supplied $130,000 to NWAC. ITC contributed $170,000 to its women's organization,
Pauktuutit, for research and other work related to constitutional affairs and more
funding was expected. Pauktuutit, as the representative of Inuit women, was actively involved in the constitutional process.

Rather than illustrate that the funded groups advocated male-dominated Aboriginal self-government, the evidence discloses that the four funded groups made
efforts to include the viewpoint of women. As well, there was no evidence to suggest that NWAC enjoyed any higher level of support amongst Aboriginal women as
compared to the funded Aboriginal groups.

(c) *Conclusions on Sections 2(b) and 28 of the Charter*
The freedom of expression guaranteed by s. 2(b) of the Charter does not guarantee
any particular means of expression or place a positive obligation upon the Government to consult anyone. The right to a particular platform or means of expression
was clearly rejected by this Court in *Haig.* The respondents had many opportunities to express their views through the four Aboriginal groups as well as directly to
the Government, for example, through the Beaudoin-Dobbie Commission. NWAC
even took the opportunity to express its concerns directly to the Minister Responsible for Constitutional Affairs and received a response, albeit one that did not
satisfy NWAC.

Even assuming that in certain extreme circumstances, the provision of a platform of expression to one group may infringe the expression of another and thereby
require the Government to provide an equal opportunity for the expression of that
group, there was no evidence in this case to suggest that the funding or consultation
of the four Aboriginal groups infringed the respondents' equal right of freedom of
expression. The four Aboriginal groups invited to discuss possible constitutional
amendments are all *bona fide* national representatives of Aboriginal people in
Canada and, based on the facts in this case, there was no requirement under s. 2(b)
of the Charter to also extend an invitation and funding directly to the respondents.

Although I would hope that it is evident from these reasons, I wish to stress
that nothing stated in them is intended to detract in any way from any contention
by or on behalf of Aboriginal women that they face racial arid sexual discrimination which impose serious hurdles to their equality.

(3) SECTION 15(1) OF THE CHARTER: EQUALITY RIGHTS
It seems that the respondents' contentions regarding ss. 2(b) and 28 of the Charter

are better characterized as a s. 15 Charter argument. As L'Heureux-Dubé J. stated in *Haig,* supra, the allegations that a platform of expression has been provided on a discriminatory basis are preferably dealt with under s. 15.

The respondents contend that the refusal to fund NWAC and invite them to be equal participants at the round of constitutional discussions violated their rights under s. 15(1) of the Charter due to the under-inclusive nature of the Government's decision. Again relying on *Haig* in their factum, the respondents submit that an equality claim may involve the provision of means of expression to certain groups or individuals.

I have concluded that the arguments of the respondents with respect to s. 15 must also fail. The lack of an evidentiary basis for the arguments with respect to ss. 2(b) and 28 is equally applicable to any arguments advanced under s. 15(1) of the Charter in this case. I agree with the Court of Appeal that s. 15(1) is of no assistance to the respondents.

(4) SECTION 35 OF THE CHARTER: EXISTING ABORIGINAL AND TREATY RIGHTS

I also agree with the conclusions of the Court of Appeal with respect to the inapplicability of s. 35 of the *Constitution Act, 1982* to the present case. The right of the Aboriginal people of Canada to participate in constitutional discussions does not derive from any existing Aboriginal or treaty right protected under s. 35. Therefore, s. 35(4) of the *Constitution Act, 1982,* which guarantees Aboriginal and treaty rights referred to in s. 35(1) equally to male and female persons, is of no assistance to the respondents. . . .

I respectfully disagree with the conclusion of the Federal Court of Appeal that the failure to provide funding to the respondents and invite them as equal participants in the constitutional discussions violated their rights under ss. 2(b) and 28 of the Charter.

I am, however, in agreement with the Federal Court of Appeal that s. 15(1) of the Charter and s. 35 of the *Constitution Act, 1982* have no application in this case.

Therefore, I would allow the appeal, set aside the declaration made by the Federal Court of Appeal and restore the judgment of Walsh D.J. with costs to the appellant both here and in the Court of Appeal if demanded. . . .

L'HEUREUX-DUBÉ J.: . . . I cannot agree with my colleague when be states that *Haig* "establishes the principle that generally the government is under no obligation to fund or provide a specific platform of expression to an individual or a group". In my view, *Haig* rather stands for the proposition that the government *in that particular case* was under no constitutional obligation to provide for the right to a referendum under 9. 2(b) of the Charter, but that if and when the government does decide to provide a specific platform of expression, it must do so in a manner consistent with the Charter.

This Court has always fostered a broad approach to the interpretation of 2(b) of the Charter, freedom of expression being a important aspect of the healthy functioning of the democratic process (see, *Inter alia: Irwin Toy Ltd.* v. *Québec* (Attorney General), [1989] 1 S.C.R. 927). *Haig* is consistent with this approach in that it underlines the possible consequences of disparate financing of viewpoints and the importance of promoting a variety of views. It is also recognised in *Haig*, at p. 1037, "that a philosophy of non-interference may not *in all circumstances* guarantee the optimal functioning of the marketplace of ideas". (Emphasis added.)

The approach in *Haig* is one that in fact affords significant relevance to circumstances, and this is why I am of the view that in certain ones, funding or consultation may be mandated by the Constitution by virtue of the fact that when the government does decide to facilitate the expression of views, it must do so in a manner that is mindful of the Charter. In this respect, one must note that the circumstances in which the government may be held to a positive obligation in terms of providing a specific platform of expression invariably depend on the nature of the evidence presented by the parties.

In the present case, the evidence demonstrates that the complainant organization was not prevented from expressing its views, albeit not in the way it would have desired. I would therefore agree that on its facts, this case does not give rise to a positive obligation analogous to the type referred to in *Haig* since not providing the complainant organization with the funding and constitutional voice requested did not amount to a breach of its freedom of expression. However, I cannot resist reiterating that pursuant to *Haig*, had the government extended such a platform of expression to other organizations in a manner that had the effect of violating the complainant organization's freedom of expression, this would most definitely have amounted to a breach of 2(b) of the Charter. In other words, the outcome of the present case should in no way be interpreted as limiting the proposition for which *Haig* stands for.

In the result, I would allow the appeal. . . .

MCLACHLIN J.: [concurs with judgment of SOPINKA J.]

■ SELECTED BIBLIOGRAPHY

Bayefsky, A., "The Human Rights Committee and the Case of Sandra Lovelace" (1982) 20 *Can. Y.B. Int'l L.* 244.

Boldt, M. *Surviving as Indians: The Challenge of Self-Government.* Toronto: University of Toronto Press, 1993.

Gilbert, L. *Entitlement to Indian Status and Membership Codes in Canada,* Toronto: Caswell, 1996.

Greschner, D., "Aboriginal Women, the Constitution and Criminal Justice" (1992) *U.B.C. Law Rev.* 338.

Isaac, T., and M.S. Maloughney, "Dually Disadvantaged and Historically Forgotten?: Aboriginal Women and the Inherent Right of Aboriginal Self-Government" (1992) 21:3 *Man. L.J.* 453.

Isaac, T., "Case Commentary: *Corbiere* v. *Canada*" [1994] 1 C.N.L.R. 55.

Montour, M. , "Iroquois Women's Rights with Respect to Matrimonial Property on Indian Reserves" [1987] 4 C.N.L.R. 1.

Monture, P., "Reflecting on Flint Women." In *Canadian Perspectives on Legal Theory,* R. Devlin, ed. Toronto: Edmond Montgomery, 1991.

Moss, W., "Indigenous Self-Government and Sexual Equality under the *Indian Act*: Resolving Conflicts Between Collective and Individual Rights" (1990) 15 *Queen's L.J.* 279.

Sanders, D., "Indian Status: A Women's Issue or an Indian Issue" [1984] 3 C.N.L.R. 30.

Silman, J., ed. *Enough Is Enough: Aboriginal Women Speak Out.* Toronto: Women's Press, 1987.